The **Rough Guide** to

Poland

written and researched by

Jonathan Bousfield and Mark Salter

with additional contributions by

Jeroen van Marle

D1550534

www.roughguides.com

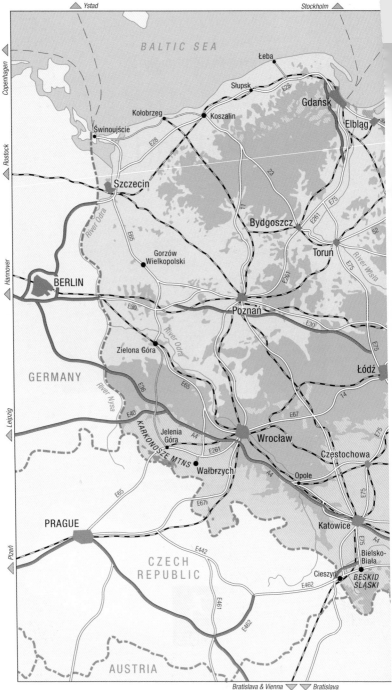

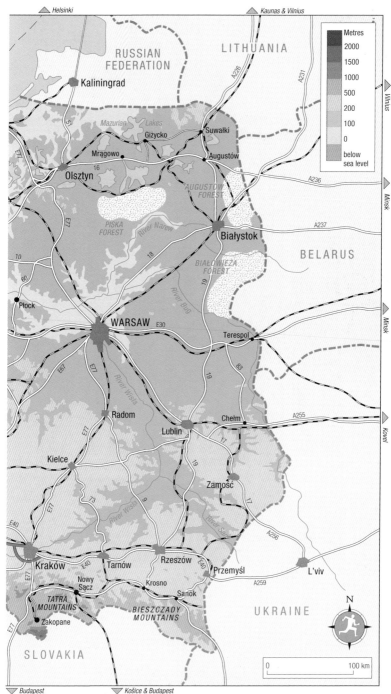

△ Helsinki △ Kaunas & Vilnius

RUSSIAN
FEDERATION
Kaliningrad

LITHUANIA

▷ Vilnius

Metres
2000
1500
1000
500
200
100
0
below
sea level

Mazurian Lakes
Giżycko
Suwałki
Mrągowo
Augustów
Olsztyn 16
A236

▷ Minsk

AUGUSTÓW
FOREST

PISKA
FOREST
River Narew
Białystok
A237

BELARUS

18
BIAŁOWIEŻA
FOREST
19
River Bug
Płock

WARSAW E30
Terespol

▷ Minsk

83
19
Radom
Chełm
A255
Lublin
17
Kielce
19

▷ Kovel

Zamość
73
9
17
River Wisła
River San
A256

E40
Kraków E40 Tarnów Rzeszów
Nowy Przemyśl L'viv
Sącz Krosno A259
Sanok
TATRA
MOUNTAINS
BIESZCZADY
MOUNTAINS
UKRAINE
Zakopane

N

SLOVAKIA

0 100 km

3

▽ Budapest ▽ Košice & Budapest

Contents

◄◄ Tatra mountains ◄ Long Market, Gdańsk

Introduction to
Poland

In many ways, Poland is one of the success stories of new Europe, transforming itself from communist-bloc one-party state to parliamentary democracy and European Union member in a remarkably short period of time. Two decades of non-communist governments have wrought profound changes on the country, unleashing entrepreneurial energies and widening cultural horizons in a way that pre-1989 generations would have scarcely thought possible. Gleaming corporate skyscrapers have taken root in Warsaw, and private shops and cafés have established themselves in even the most provincial of rural towns. The country has a radically different look about it, having exchanged the greyish tinge of a state-regulated society for the anything-goes attitude of private enterprise – and all the billboards and window displays that go with it.

All this may come as a shock to those who recall the Poland of the 1980s, when images of industrial unrest and anti-communist protest were beamed around the world. Strikes at the Lenin shipyards of Gdańsk and other industrial centres were the harbingers of the disintegration of communism in Eastern Europe, and, throughout the years of martial law and beyond, Poland retained a near-mythical status among outside observers as the country that had done most to retain its dignity in the face of communist oppression.

▲ Wrocław architecture

For many Poles, the most important events in the movement towards a post-communist society were the visits in 1979 and 1983 of Pope John Paul II, the former archbishop of Krakow, for whose funeral in April 2005, televised live on huge video screens, crowds of almost a million massed in the city. Poland was never a typical communist state: Stalin's verdict was that imposing communism on the nation was like trying to saddle a cow. Polish society in the postwar decades remained fundamentally traditional, maintaining beliefs, peasant life and a sense of nationhood to which the **Catholic Church** was integral. During periods of foreign oppression – oppression so severe that Poland as a political entity has sometimes vanished altogether from the maps of Europe – the Church was always the principal defender of the nation's identity, so that the Catholic faith and the struggle for independence have become fused in the Polish consciousness. The physical presence of the Church is inescapable – in Baroque buildings, roadside shrines and images of the national icon, the **Black Madonna of Częstochowa** – and the determination to preserve the memories of an often traumatic past finds expression in religious rituals that can both attract and repel onlookers.

World War II and its aftermath profoundly influenced the character of Poland: the country suffered at the hands of the **Nazis** as no other in Europe, losing nearly twenty percent of its population and virtually its entire **Jewish** community. In 1945 the **Soviet**-dominated nation was once again given new borders, losing its eastern lands to the USSR and

> The sense of social fluidity, of a country still in the throes of major transitions, remains a primary source of Poland's fascination

gaining tracts of formerly German territory in the west. The resulting make-up of the population is far more uniformly "Polish" than at any time in the past,

7

Fact file

• **Poland** occupies a vast swathe of territory in north-central Europe, bordered by Germany to the west, the Czech Republic and Slovakia to the south, and Ukraine, Belarus, Lithuania and Russia to the east.

• Much of northern and central Poland is made up of **agricultural plainland** and gently rolling country-side, although the Tatra and Carpathian **mountains** in the south provide a dramatic contrast.

• Its **population** of 38.5 million is predominantly both Polish and devoutly Catholic, although, unsurprisingly for a country which has changed its borders many times in the past, significant pockets of Ukrainians, Belarusians, Bojks and Łemks exist in the east of the country.

• Traditionally, Poland is known for its ship-building, coal and steel **industries**, although these days cosmetics, medicines and textile products – often made under licence for Western conglomerates – are increasingly important sources of foreign income.

• The vast bulk of foreign visitors head for splendid old **cities** like Kraków, or the ski resorts of the Tatras, although Baltic **beaches** and inland **lake resorts** – both much patronized by the Poles themselves – help to complete a varied tourist picture.

in terms of both language and religion, though there are still **ethnic minorities** of Belarusians, Germans, Lithuanians, Slovaks, Ukrainians and even Muslim Tatars.

To a great extent, the sense of social fluidity, of a country still in the throes of major transitions, remains a primary source of Poland's fascination. A decisive attempt to break with the communist past as well as tenacious adherence to the path of radical market **economic reforms** adopted in the late 1980s, have remained the guiding tenets of Poland's new political leadership – a course seemingly unaltered by the changing political complexion of successive governments. Few would question the economic and human cost of Poland's attempt to reach the El Dorado of capitalist prosperity – not least among the most vulnerable sectors of society: public sector employees, farmers, pensioners and the semi- or unemployed. Paradoxically, many of those who made the country's democratic revolution possible – militant

▲ Stary Kleparz market, Kraków

Folk music in Poland

Polish **folk music** may hold a significant position in the general national consciousness, but it's especially vibrant in the folk cultures found chiefly among the country's minorities and in its southern and eastern parts. Thanks to Chopin, whose inspiration came in large part from his native **Mazovia**, music from here is probably the best known, but there are other equally worthwhile traditions in **Silesia**, the **Tatras** and the **Beskid Niski**. The festivals in **Zakopane** and **Kazimierz Dolny** offer excellent opportunities for getting to grips with many of these rootsy rural styles, while along the **Baltic coast** the popularity of sea shanties is demonstrated in many an annual festival. For a more detailed look at Polish music see p.643.

industrial workers and anti-communist intellectuals – have found themselves marginalized in a society in which street-smart businessmen and computer-literate youth are far better poised to take advantage of the brave new Poland's burgeoning opportunities.

Dramatically changed geopolitical circumstances have seen Poland join **NATO**, the US-led military alliance of which it was – officially at least – a sworn enemy only ten years previously. Perhaps even more significantly, Poland, along with neighbours the Czech Republic and Hungary, is now a fully-fledged member of the **EU,** a status which promises to transform the country more profoundly than anything since the advent of communism.

Tourism is proving no exception to Poland's general "all change" rule, but despite the continuing state of flux in the country's tourist infrastructure, it is now easier to explore the country than anyone could have imagined only

▲ A café in Kazimierz, Kraków

a few years back. This sea change is reflected in continuing and significant increases in the numbers of people visiting the country.

Encounters with the **people** are at the core of any experience of Poland. On trains and buses, on the streets or in the village bar, you'll never be stuck for opportunities for contact: Polish hospitality is legendary, and there's a natural progression from a chance meeting to an introduction to the extended family.

Where to go

Poles delineate their country's attractions as "the mountains, the sea and the lakes", their emphasis firmly slanted to the traditional, **rural heartlands**. To get the most out of your time, it's perhaps best to follow their preferences. The mountains – above all the Carpathian range of the Tatras – are a delight, with a well-established network of hiking trails; the lakes provide opportunities for canoeing and a host of other outdoor pursuits; and the dozen or so national parks contain areas of Europe's last primeval forests, still inhabited by bison, elks, wolves, bears and eagles. Yet you will not want to miss the best of the cities – Kraków, especially – nor a ramble down rivers like the Wisła for visits to Teutonic castles, ancient waterside towns and grand, country mansions, redolent of a vanished aristocratic order. Regions inhabited by ethnic minorities offer insights into cultures quite distinct from the Catholicism of the majority, while the former centres of the **Jewish community**, and the concentration camps in which the Nazis carried out their extermination, are the most moving testimony to the complexity and tragedy of the nation's past.

Polish vodka

The tipple most associated with Poland, **vodka** is actually in danger of being eclipsed in popularity by beer among young Poles, so it's well worth seeking out the varieties you can't find abroad before they disappear from Polish shops and bars completely. Traditionally served chilled and neat – although increasingly mixed with fruit juice – vodka can be **clear** or **flavoured** with anything from bison grass to mountain herbs to juniper berries or honey. There's even been a revival of **kosher** vodkas, although whether their rabbinic stamps of approval are kosher themselves or just a marketing gimmick isn't always obvious.

Unless you're driving to Poland, you're likely to begin your travels in one of the three major cities: Warsaw, Kraków or Gdańsk. Each provides an immediate immersion in the fast-paced changes of the last decade or so and a backdrop of monuments which reveal the twists and turns of the nation's history. **Warsaw**, the capital, had to be rebuilt from scratch after World War II, and much of the city conforms to the stereotype of Eastern European greyness. However, the reconstructed Baroque palaces, churches and public buildings of the historic centre, the burgeoning street markets and the bright shopfronts of Poland's new enterprise culture are diverting enough. **Kraków**, the ancient royal capital, is the real crowd-puller for Poles and foreign visitors alike, rivalling the central European elegance of Prague and Vienna. This is the city where history hits you most powerfully, in the royal Wawel complex, in the fabulous open space of the Rynek, in the one-time Jewish quarter of Kazimierz, and in the chilling necropolis of nearby Auschwitz-Birkenau, the bloodiest killing field of the Third Reich. **Gdańsk**, formerly Danzig, the largest of the Baltic ports and home of the legendary shipyards, presents a dynamic brew of politics and commerce against a townscape reminiscent of mercantile towns in the Netherlands.

German and Prussian influences abound in the **north** of the country, most notably in the austere castles and fortified settlements constructed by the Teutonic Knights at **Malbork**, **Chełmno** and other strategic points along the **River Wisła** – as the Vistula is known in Poland. **Toruń** is one of the most atmospheric and beautiful of the old Hanseatic towns here.

◄ Rural landscape near Haluszowa

◄ Gasienicowa Valley, Tatras

Over in the **east**, numerous minority communities embody the complexities of national boundaries in central Europe. The one-time Jewish centre of **Białystok**, with its Belarusian minority, is a springboard for the eastern borderlands, where onion-domed Orthodox churches stand close to Tatar mosques. Further south, beyond **Lublin**, a famous centre of Hassidic Jewry, and **Zamość**, with its magnificent Renaissance centre, lie the homelands of Ukrainians, Łemks and Boyks – and a chance to see some of Poland's extraordinary wooden churches.

In the **west**, ethnic Germans populate regions of the divided province of **Silesia**, where **Wrocław** sustains the dual cultures of the former German city of Breslau and the Ukrainian city of L'viv (formerly Lwów), whose displaced citizens were moved here at the end of World War II. The other main city in western Poland is the quintessentially Polish **Poznań**, a vibrant and increasingly prosperous university town.

Despite its much-publicized pollution problems – something it is now finally making a serious attempt to address – Poland has many regions of unspoilt natural beauty, of which none is more pristine than the **Białowieźa Forest**, straddling the Belarusian border. The last virgin forest of the European mainland, it is the habitat of the largest surviving herd of European bison. Along the southern borders of the country lie the wild **Bieszczady** mountains and the alpine **Tatras** and, further west, the bleak **Karkonosze** mountains – all of them excellent walking country – interspersed with less demanding terrain. North of the central Polish plain, the wooded lakelands of **Mazury** and **Pomerania** are as tranquil as any lowland region on the continent, while the Baltic coast can boast not just the domesticated pleasures of its beach resorts, but also the extraordinary desert-like dunes of the **Słowiński national park**.

When to go

Spring is arguably the ideal season for some serious hiking in Poland's mountainous border regions, as the days tend to be bright – if showery – and the distinctive flowers are at their most profuse. **Summer**, the tourist high season, sees plenty of sun, particularly on the Baltic coast, where the resorts are crowded from June to August and temperatures are consistently around 24°C (75°F).

Autumn is the best time to come if you're planning to sample the whole spread of the country's attractions: in the cities the cultural seasons are

Seeing Poland's Jewish heritage

The history of Poland is inexorably linked to that of its **Jewish** population which, before World War II, comprised roughly ten percent (three million) of the country's total; Europe's largest Jewish community and the world's second largest. Of the current world population of fifteen million, over half are thought to be related to Polish Jewry, but up until the late 1980s those travelling to their ancestral home remained few in number due largely to fear of anti-Semitism and apprehension about travelling in communist Eastern Europe.

Nowadays, **organized tours**, particularly from Israel and the US, are common, visiting the traditional focal points of Polish-Jewish life and culture. Every effort has been made in the Guide to cover sites of interest to Jews, and many of the organizations on p.000 can provide further information. For more sources of information on Jewish heritage, see the "Books" section of Contexts, p.633.

beginning at this time, and the pressure on hotel rooms is lifting. In the countryside, the golden Polish October is especially memorable, the rich colours of the forests heightened by brilliantly crisp sunshine, and it's often warm enough for t-shirts.

In **winter** the temperature drops rapidly, icy Siberian winds blanketing many parts of the country with snow for anything from one to three months. Though the central Polish plain is bleak and unappealing at the end of the year, in the south of the country skiers and other wintersports enthusiasts will find themselves in their element. By mid-December the slopes of the Tatras and the other border ranges are thronged with holidaymakers, straining the established facilities to the limit.

◀ Mariacka Church, Floriańska Street, Kraków

Average temperatures and rainfall

	Jan	March	May	July	Sept	Dec
Kraków						
max (°F)	32	45	67	76	67	38
max (°C)	0	7.2	19.4	24.4	19.4	3.3
Rainfall (mm)	28	35	46	111	62	36
Gdynia						
max (°F)	35	40	59	70	64	38
max (°C)	1.7	4.4	15	21.1	17.8	3.3
Rainfall (mm)	33	27	42	84	59	46
Poznań						
max (°F)	33	45	67	76	67	38
max (°C)	0.6	7.2	19.4	24.4	19.4	3.3
Rainfall (mm)	24	26	47	82	45	39
Przemyśl						
max (°F)	32	43	67	76	67	38
max (°C)	0	6.1	19.4	24.4	19.4	3.3
Rainfall (mm)	27	25	57	105	58	43
Warsaw						
max (°F)	32	41	67	76	67	36
max (°C)	0	5	19.4	24.4	19.4	2.2
Rainfall (mm)	27	27	46	96	43	44

27

things not to miss

It's not possible to see everything that Poland has to offer in one trip – and we don't suggest you try. What follows is a selective taste of the country's highlights: outstanding buildings, historic sites and natural wonders. They're arranged in five colour-coded categories, which you can browse through to find the very best things to see and experience. All highlights have a page reference to take you straight into the Guide, where you can find out more.

01 Zamość Page **284** • A model Renaissance town located deep in the countryside of eastern Poland, and stuffed with the palaces and churches built by the Zamoyskis, one of the country's leading aristocratic families.

02 **Rynek Główny, Kraków** Page **354** • A spectacular medieval market square, packed with fine architecture, in a country that's famous for them. Settle down in one of the numerous pavement cafés and soak up the atmosphere.

03 **The Tatras** Page **450** • Poland's prime highland playground is a paradise for hikers of all abilities, with relaxing rambles in sub-alpine meadows for the easy-going and hair-raising mountain ridge walks for the more experienced.

04 **Vodka** Pages **11** & **44** • The essential accompaniment to any social occasion. It has to be drunk neat and downed in one go if you want to do things properly.

06 Młoda Polska Page **363** • Get to grips with the Belle Époque art movement that transformed Polish culture by visiting the Wyspiański Museum in Kraków.

05 Wooden churches Page **447** • An age-old form of folk architecture still preserved in rural corners of the country. Visit some of the best examples in Jaszczurówka near Zakopane, or in the remote villages of the Bieszczady.

07 Baltic beaches Page **579** • Experience the bracing sea breezes and mile upon mile of unspoilt sands in laid-back, old-fashioned seaside resorts like Międzyzdroje (shown above, p.591), Hel (p.170) and Mielno (p.599).

08 **Zalipie** Page **433** • For an insight into the riches of Polish folk culture, visit the village whose householders are famous for their distinctive taste in interior design.

09 **The Mazurian Lakes** Page **208** • The central Mazurian Lakes are a hugely popular destination for Polish tourists in summer, but the further east you head into the lakeland, the closer you get to the lakes' essence as discovered by the first visitors here – beauty and solitude.

10 **Hiking in the Bieszczady** Page **316** • The grassy summits and bald ridges of the Bieszczady mountains provide Poland with some of its most alluring and accessible walking terrain.

11 **Lublin** Page **255** • A jewel of an old town and a large student population make Lublin the liveliest and most rewarding of Poland's eastern cities – and one that's relatively undiscovered by tourists.

12 Kazimierz Dolny Page **273** • One of the best-preserved small towns of Poland's rural heartland, and an age-old centre of Jewish culture, now popular with the Warsaw arts-and-media set, who descend on Kazimierz en masse on summer weekends.

13 Słowiński national park Page **604** • Trek across Sahara-like dunes just outside the seaside town of Łeba, pausing to sunbathe, birdwatch or explore World War II rocket installations along the way.

14 **Gdańsk's ulica Długa** Page 150 • A stroll down one of Poland's most beautiful set-piece streets will take you past a string of wonderfully restored town houses, recalling the mercantile dynasties that made Gdańsk one of the great trading centres of northern Europe.

15 **Wieliczka Salt Mine** Page 397 • One of Poland's most unexpected man-made marvels, featuring fabulously decorated subterranean galleries carved from rock salt.

17 **Rafting on the Dunajec** Page 455 • Drift down the river Dunajec as it winds its way between the craggy peaks of the Pieniny mountains.

16 **Poznań** Page 535 • Recharge your urban batteries in the down-to-earth, work-hard-and-play-hard city that epitomizes the invigorating mercantile bustle of the new Poland.

18 **Toruń** Page **188** • Birthplace of the astronomer Copernicus, and famous for the local gingerbread, Toruń is a medieval university town with a satisfying jumble of historical monuments, and a laid-back, easy-going charm.

19 **The Great Escape** Page **561** • Investigate the real story behind the Hollywood movie by paying a visit to Żagań, site of the notorious Stalag Luft III POW camp.

20 **Wrocław** Page **487** • Wrocław's historic core is an exhilarating mixture of architectural influences, from Flemish-style Renaissance mansions to the late Gothic monstrosity of its town hall. At its heart stands a typically vibrant, café-splashed Rynek.

21 **Palace of Culture, Warsaw** Page **87** • Love it or hate it, this soaring Art Deco monument to Stalinist ideology is still the outstanding feature of the downtown skyline.

22 **Białowieża national park** Page **246** • One of the most extensive areas of primeval forest in Europe, which you can explore on foot or by horse-drawn cart. Also famous for being home to a beast indigenous to Poland: the European bison.

24 Auschwitz-Birkenau
Page **411** • The most notorious extermination camp of them all, Auschwitz-Birkenau offers the profoundest of insights into the nature of human evil, and demands to be visited – few who come here will be unchanged by the experience.

23 Malbork Castle Page **179** •
The Teutonic Knights lorded it over northern Poland for more than 200 years, and this – a rambling complex of fortifications on the banks of the Wisła – is their most imposing monument.

25 Industrial Architecture in Łódź Page **129** • Iconic nineteenth-century manufacturing city filled with mills, chimneys and other monuments to the industrial revolution.

26 **Warsaw's Old Town** Page **73** • Lively pavement cafés, fine restaurants and exuberant street life in a historic town centre that was faithfully reconstructed after its almost total destruction by the Nazis. As strong a symbol as any of Poland's struggle to rebuild in the aftermath of World War II.

27 **Wawel** Page **369** • One of the most striking royal residences in Europe and a potent source of national and spiritual pride.

Basics

Basics

Getting there

The easiest way to reach Poland is by air, with direct flights from the UK, Ireland and North America, and indirect flights from Australasia. Travelling overland from Britain is a relatively long haul, and you'll save little, if anything, going by train; although with an Inter-Rail pass you can take in Poland as part of a wider European trip. Approaching Poland by car or bus from the UK involves a journey of at least 1000km and takes the best part of two days.

Airfares always depend on the **season**. Peak times for flights to Poland are May to September, and around the Easter and Christmas holidays; at these times be prepared to book well in advance. Fares drop during the "shoulder" seasons (April and Oct); and you'll usually get the best prices during the low season (Nov–March, excluding Easter and Christmas). The skiing season in southern Poland (Dec–March) ensures that in some regional airports (notably Kraków) there never really is a low season.

The best deals are usually to be found by booking through discount travel websites or the websites of the airlines themselves.

Flights from the UK and Ireland

With a flying time of 2 hour 30 minutes and plenty of airlines to choose from, getting to Poland **from the UK** by air is relatively problem-free. The cheapest way of flying from the UK is with one of the **budget airlines** such as **easyJet**, **Ryanair** or **Wizzair**. The sheer number of routes on offer ensures that there are plenty of potential entry points to Poland: most major airports in the UK have direct links with Warsaw and Kraków, while several airports also serve Gdańsk, Wrocław, Poznań, Łódź, Katowice, Rzeszów, Szczecin and Bydgoszcz.

For full details of which routes are offered by which airlines see p.30 – although be aware that the cheap-flight market is in a state of constant fluidity and there may be changes in operators and routes in the future.

Above all, beware that budget airline tickets booked at the last minute may work out just as expensive as their major airline counterparts. Bear in mind too that prices advertised on budget airline websites often fail to include **airport tax** – which may well amount to an additional £40/€50 in each direction.

Most useful of the mainstream airlines is **British Airways**, who fly daily from London Heathrow to Kraków and Warsaw; and Poland's national carrier **LOT**, who operate daily flights from London Heathrow to Warsaw, with connecting flights to Polish regional cities.

From Ireland, the budget airlines are the cheapest and most convenient option. **Ryanair** fly direct from Dublin to almost every major Polish city – although, curiously, not to Warsaw – while **Wizzair** fly from Cork to Gdańsk, Warsaw, Poznań and Katowice/Kraków. From **Northern Ireland easyJet** offer flights from Belfast to Kraków.

Flights from the US and Canada

From the US, **LOT (Polish Airlines)** offers daily flights to Warsaw from New York and Chicago. It also flies several times a week from Chicago to Kraków. Approximate fares in high season are: New York–Warsaw US$1300; Chicago–Warsaw and Chicago–Kraków US$1350. If you're coming from another part of the USA, LOT will connect you with a domestic carrier, **United Airlines** being their favoured partner. Typical fares from LA to Warsaw, flying with United and LOT, are roughly US$1550. Several other carriers, including **British Airways**, **Austrian Airlines**, **Swiss Airlines**, **Northwest/KLM** and **Lufthansa** have daily flights from the US to Warsaw via their European hub cities. **Delta** has flights connecting via Paris.

Six steps to a better kind of travel

At Rough Guides we are passionately committed to travel. We feel strongly that only through travelling do we truly come to understand the world we live in and the people we share it with – plus tourism has brought a great deal of benefit to developing economies around the world over the last few decades. But the extraordinary growth in tourism has also damaged some places irreparably, and of course climate change is exacerbated by most forms of transport, especially flying. This means that now more than ever it's important to travel thoughtfully and responsibly, with respect for the cultures you're visiting – not only to derive the most benefit from your trip but also in order to preserve the best bits of the planet for everyone to enjoy. At Rough Guides we feel there are six main areas in which you can make a difference:

- Consider what you're contributing to the local economy, and indeed how much the services you use do the same, whether it's through employing local workers and guides or sourcing locally grown produce and local services.
- Consider the environment on holiday as well as at home. Water is scarce in many developing destinations, and the biodiversity of local flora and fauna can be adversely affected by tourism. Patronise businesses that take account of this rather than those that trash the local environment for short-term gain.
- Give thought to how often you fly and what you can do to redress any harm that your trips create. Reduce the amount you travel by air; avoid short hops by air and more harmful night flights.
- Consider alternatives to flying, travelling instead by bus, train, boat and even by bike or on foot where possible. Take time to enjoy the journey itself as well as your final destination.
- Think about making all the trips you take "climate neutral" via a reputable carbon offset scheme. All Rough Guide flights are offset, and every year we donate money to a variety of charities devoted to combating the effects of climate change.
- Travel with a purpose, not just to tick off experiences. Consider spending longer in a place, and really getting to know it and its people – you'll find it much more rewarding than dashing from place to place.

From Canada, LOT operates a direct service to Warsaw from Toronto (twice a week in the winter months, five flights a week in the summer). Fares cost at around CAN$1400. Starting from another Canadian airport, **Air Canada** will connect you with LOT's Toronto flight for a reasonable add-on fare.

Discount agents sometimes come up with cheaper deals involving other major airlines which fly daily to Warsaw, but require a change of plane in Western Europe – **British Airways** flies to Warsaw via London, **Lufthansa** via Frankfurt, **Northwest/KLM** via Amsterdam and **Swiss** via Zürich. The cost of these occasionally turns out slightly cheaper than LOT, depending on the route.

A cheaper option is to book a flight to London on a major airline and then connect to Warsaw or Kraków using Ryanair, easyJet or one of the other **budget carriers**. Return flights with Virgin Atlantic cost US$720 (New York to London Heathrow) and US$1280 (Los Angeles to London Heathrow). This will give you the option of a stop in London, but as the budget flights leave from smaller airports, you'll need to cross the city to catch your second flight: plan carefully. National Express (⊛www.nationalexpress.com) is a British bus company that runs inter-airport shuttles.

Flights from Australia and New Zealand

Although there are no direct flights to Poland from Australia or New Zealand, there are plenty of one- or two-stop alternatives. **From Australia**, typical one-stop routings involving European hubs such as London, Frankfurt or Vienna tend to be expensive, with the average return fare from Sydney, Melbourne or Perth to Warsaw or Kraków hovering around the AUS$3000 mark. Cheaper deals involve a **combination** of airlines and two stops en route: Sydney–Kuala Lumpur–Vienna–Warsaw or Sydney–Bangkok–Frankfurt–Warsaw are typical examples. Fares on these routes are around AUS$2600.

From New Zealand, Air New Zealand operates daily flights from Auckland to London and Frankfurt, where you can pick up connecting flights to Warsaw and other Polish cities. All other flights from New Zealand involve at least two stops. Return fares start at around NZ$3400 in high season.

By rail

Travelling by train to Poland is a relaxing and leisurely way to travel for those who don't like flying, although it can't compare price-wise with taking the plane. The fastest option from London involves taking the Eurostar from St Pancras to Brussels, and then continuing across Belgium and Germany, either with a direct Brussels–Warsaw train or with a change in Berlin (where you can pick up expresses to Warsaw, Wrocław or Kraków). None of these options take longer than 24 hours. A return ticket for the whole journey will set you back around £220, more if you book a couchette or sleeper for the overnight part of the journey.

Rail passes

If you're planning to visit Poland as part of a more extensive trip around Europe, it may be worth buying a **rail pass**. Poland is covered in the Inter-Rail pass scheme, which is available to European residents. Non-European residents can make use of the Eurail pass.

Inter-Rail passes can be bought at Rail Europe in the UK and come in over-26 and (cheaper) under-26 versions. They cover most European countries, including Poland and all the countries you need to travel through in order to get there. A pass for five days' travel

in a ten-day period (£212 for adults, £135 for those under 26) will just about suffice to get you to Poland and back; although a more leisurely approach would require a pass for ten days' travel within a 22-day period (£305 and £203 respectively) or a pass for one month's continuous travel (£508 and £339). Inter-Rail passes do not include travel between Britain and the continent, although pass-holders are eligible for discounts on rail travel in the UK and on cross-Channel ferries.

Non-European residents qualify for the **Eurail Global** pass, which must be purchased before arrival in Europe from selected agents in North America, Australia and New Zealand or from Rail Europe in London. The pass allows unlimited free first-class train travel in twenty European countries, including Belgium and Germany, but not Poland itself or neighbouring Czech Republic and Slovakia, so you're effectively limited to certain cross-European routes. The pass is available in increments of fifteen days ($503), 21 days ($653) and one month ($810). A **Eurail Global Flexi pass** will give you ten days' first-class travel in a two-month period for $798. If you're under 26, you can save money with a **Eurail Global Youthpass** (second-class travel only; $327 for fifteen days, $530 for one month, or $390 for ten days' travel in a two-month period). Further details of these passes can be found on Ⓦwww.raileurope.com.

By bus

Bus travel is an attractively cheap way of getting to Poland although the journey itself is relatively dull unless you have a penchant for northern European motorway landscapes. Virtually all Polish towns of any size are covered from a wide range of UK departure

Useful publications

The *Thomas Cook European Timetables* details schedules of over fifty thousand trains in Europe, as well as timings of over two hundred ferry routes and rail-connecting bus services. It's updated and issued every month; the main changes are in the June edition (published end of May), which has details of the summer European schedules, and the October edition, (published end of Sept), which includes winter schedules; some also have advance summer/winter timings. The book can be purchased online (which gets you a ten percent discount) at Ⓦwww.thomascooktimetables.com or from branches of Thomas Cook (see Ⓦwww.thomascook.co.uk for your nearest branch) and costs £15.99. Their *Rail Map of Europe* (regular price £8.99) is also useful.

points, with the most reliable services being operated by **Eurolines**, a division of the National Express bus company. They run regular services from London to Warsaw and Kraków (either direct or with a change somewhere en route) and a whole host of other Polish cities. Return tickets for Warsaw start at around £100 (with minimal reductions for under 26s, senior citizens and children). Tickets can be bought at any **National Express** office in the UK, and will include connecting fares from anywhere outside London.

Better deals might be available from Polish-run companies, especially if you're travelling from outside London, with tickets handled by a number of UK-based travel agents (see below). Prices hover around the £100 mark for a northern England–Poland return.

By car

Driving to Poland means a long haul of 1000km from Calais or Ostend to the Polish border – and another 450–500km from there to Warsaw or Kraków. Flat out, and using the Channel Tunnel, you could do the journey to the border in eighteen hours, but it makes more sense to allow longer, breaking the journey in central Germany.

The most convenient Channel crossings are on the **P&O Stena** services from Dover or Folkestone to Calais, **Hoverspeed** to Ostend, or the **Eurotunnel** from Folkestone to Calais. From any of these ports, the most popular and direct route is on toll-free motorways all the way, bypassing Brussels, Düsseldorf, Hannover and Berlin.

A more relaxing alternative, which halves the driving distance, is to catch the thrice-weekly **DFDS Seaways** ferry from Harwich to Esbjerg in Denmark (19hr) and then drive south and east through Germany. The most convenient ferry routes from the north of England are the **P&O North Sea Ferries** service from Hull to Rotterdam and DFDS's Newcastle–Amsterdam service.

Airlines, agents and operators

Online booking

A selection of good online booking websites is listed below.

Ⓦ **www.ebookers.com** (UK), Ⓦ **www.ebookers .ie** (Ireland)

Ⓦ **www.expedia.co.uk** (UK), Ⓦ **www.expedia .com** (US), Ⓦ **www.expedia.ca** (Canada)

Ⓦ **www.lastminute.com** (UK),

Ⓦ **www.opodo.co.uk** (UK),

Ⓦ **www.orbitz.com** (US),

Ⓦ **www.travelocity.co.uk** (UK), Ⓦ **www .travelocity.com** (US), Ⓦ **www.travelocity .ca** (Canada), Ⓦ **www.travelocity.co.nz** (New Zealand)

Ⓦ **www.travelonline.co.za** (South Africa),

Ⓦ **www.zuji.com.au** (Australia).

Airlines

Aer Lingus Ⓦ www.aerlingus.com. Direct flights from Dublin to Warsaw and Kraków.

Air Canada Ⓦ www.aircanada.com. Flights from most Canadian airports to Warsaw, with a change of plane and airline in Toronto.

Air New Zealand Ⓦ www.airnz.co.nz. Daily flights from Auckland to London via Los Angeles, then onward connections to Warsaw or Kraków.

Austrian Airlines Ⓦ www.aua.com. Flights from North America and Australasia to Warsaw and Kraków via Vienna.

British Airways Ⓦ www.ba.com. Daily flights from London Heathrow to Warsaw, and London Gatwick to Kraków with connections from other worldwide cities.

Cathay Pacific Ⓦ www.cathaypacific.com. Flights from Australia and New Zealand to Hong Kong, with onward connections to major European hubs, then Poland.

CSA (Czech Airlines) Ⓦ www.czechairlines.co.uk. Flights to Warsaw from New York, Washington and Toronto, changing planes in Prague.

Delta Ⓦ www.delta.com. Flights to Warsaw via Paris and other European hubs.

easyJet Ⓦ www.easyjet.com. Flights from Bristol and London Luton to Warsaw; and from Belfast, Bristol, Edinburgh, Newcastle, Liverpool, London, London Gatwick and Luton and to Kraków.

LOT (Polish Airlines) Ⓦ www.lot.com. Direct flights from London Heathrow, Toronto, Chicago and New York to Warsaw, with connecting flights from Warsaw to most other Polish cities. Also direct flights from London Gatwick and Chicago to Kraków. LOT also handle one- or two-stop flights to Poland from Australia involving at least one other airline.

Lufthansa Ⓦ www.lufthansa.com. Flights from Australia, Canada and the USA to Frankfurt, with onward connections to Warsaw and other Polish cities.

Northwest/KLM Ⓦ www.nwa.com. Flights from several North American cities to Poland, with a stop-off in Amsterdam.

Qantas Airways ⊛ www.qantas.com. Flights from Sydney to a European hub with onward connections to Warsaw.

Ryanair ⊛ www.ryanair.com. Flights from Birmingham, Bournemouth, Bristol, Dublin, East Midlands, Edinburgh, Glasgow, Liverpool, London Luton, London Stansted and Shannon to Bydgość, Gdańsk, Katowice, Kraków, Łódź, Poznań, Rzeszów, Szczecin, Wrocław.

United Airlines ⊛ www.united.com. Flights from most American cities to Poland via New York or Chicago.

Virgin Atlantic Airways ⊛ www.virgin-atlantic.com. Flights from North America to London.

Wizzair ⊛ www.wizzair.com. Flights from Cork, Doncaster, Glasgow, Liverpool and London Luton to Gdańsk, Poznań, Katowice/Kraków, Warsaw and Wrocław.

Agents

Gosia UK ☎ 020/7828 5550, ⊛ www.gosia24.com.

Orbis Express Travel Australia ☎ 02/9891 6133, ⊛ www.orbisexpress.com.au.

Polish Regency Tours UK ☎ 020/8992 6001, ⊛ www.polish-travel.co.uk. Poland specialist dealing in flights, bus tickets and packages.

Polish Travel Center US ☎ 215/533-1294 or 1-800/247 5710, ⊛ www.polishtravel.com. Flights, tailor-made itineraries and escorted tours.

Poltours UK ☎ 020/8810 5625, ⊛ www.poltours.co.uk. Flights to Poland, package tours and city breaks.

STA Travel US ☎ 1-800/781-4040, UK ☎ 0871/230 0040, Australia ☎ 134 782, New Zealand ☎ 0800/474 400, South Africa ☎ 0861/781 781, ⊛ www.statravel.com. Worldwide specialists in independent travel; also student IDs, travel insurance, car rental, rail passes, and more. Good discounts for students and under-26s.

Trailfinders UK ☎ 0845/058 5858, Republic of Ireland ☎ 01/677 7888, Australia ☎ 1300/780 212, ⊛ www.trailfinders.com. One of the best-informed and most efficient agents for independent travellers.

Rail contacts

CIT World Travel Australia ☎ 1300/361 500, ⊛ www.cittravel.com.au. Eurail passes.

Deutsche Bahn UK ☎ 0871/880 8066, ⊛ www.bahn.co.uk. Timetable information and through ticketing on European routes.

Europrail International Canada ☎ 1-888/667-9734, ⊛ www.europrail.net. Eurail, Europass and individual country passes.

Eurostar UK ☎ 0870/518 6186, ⊛ www.eurostar.com. Passenger train from London St Pancras to Paris (2hr 15min) and Brussels (1hr 51min), and from Ebbsfleet International station, off Junction 2 of the M25 (journey times 10min shorter).

Rail Europe UK ☎ 0870/584 8848, ⊛ www.raileurope.co.uk; US ☎ 1-877/257-2887, Canada ☎ 1-800/361-RAIL, ⊛ www.raileurope.com. Agents for Eurail, Inter-Rail and Eurostar.

Rail Plus Australia ☎ 1300/555 003 or 03/9642 8644, ⊛ www.railplus.com.au. Sells Eurail and Eurostar passes.

The Man in Seat 61 ⊛ www.seat61.com. Enthusiast-run site packed with information on all aspects of international rail travel, including tips on the best way to reach Poland by train. Far more reliable than many official sites.

Trainseurope UK ☎ 0871/700 7722, ⊛ www.trainseurope.co.uk. Tickets from the UK to European destinations, Inter-Rail and other individual country passes.

Bus contacts

Eurolines UK ☎ 0871/781 8181, Republic of Ireland ☎ 01/836 6111; ⊛ www.eurolines.co.uk.

Gosia UK ☎ 020/7828 5550, ⊛ www.gosia24.com.

Orbis Express Group UK ☎ 020/7730 6872, ⊛ www.orbisexpress.com.

Polish Regency Tours UK ☎ 020/8992 6001, ⊛ www.polish-travel.co.uk.

Ferry contacts

DFDS Seaways UK ☎ 0871/522 9955, ⊛ www.dfdsseaways.com. Harwich to Esbjerg; Newcastle to Amsterdam.

Irish Ferries UK ☎ 0870/517 1717, Northern Ireland ☎ 0818/300 400; ⊛ www.irishferries.com. Dublin to Holyhead; Rosslare to Pembroke.

Norfolkline UK ☎ 0870/164 2114, ⊛ www.norfolkline.com. Dover to Dunkerque.

P&O Ferries UK ☎ 0870/598 0303, ⊛ www.poferries.com. Dover to Calais; Hull to Rotterdam; Hull to Zeebrugge; Dublin to Liverpool.

Sea Cat UK ☎ 0870/552 3523, Republic of Ireland ☎ 1800/805 055; ⊛ www.seacat.co.uk. Belfast to Stranraer, Heysham and Troon; Dublin to Liverpool.

Sea France UK ☎ 0870/443 1653, ⊛ www.seafrance.com. Dover to Calais.

Stena Line UK ☎ 0870/570 7070, Northern Ireland ☎ 0870/520 4204, Republic of Ireland ☎ 1/204 7777; ⊛ www.stenaline.co.uk. Harwich to the Hook of Holland.

Channel tunnel

Eurotunnel UK ☎ 0870/535 3535, ⊛ www.eurotunnel.com. Runs continuously between

Folkestone and Coquelles, near Calais, with up
to four departures per hour (only one per hour
midnight–6am) and takes 35min (45min for some
night departure times), though you must arrive at least
30min before departure.

Tour operators

Adventures Abroad UK ☎0114/247 3400, USA
and Canada ☎1-800/665-3998, ⊛www
.adventures-abroad.com. Exclusive Poland tours plus
Poland/Baltics/Russia combinations.
American Travel Abroad US ☎1-800/228-0877,
⊛www.amta.com. Poland specialists offering flights,
hotels, car rental and escorted tours.
Bridge Travel UK ☎0870/727 5855, ⊛www
.bridgetravel.co.uk. City breaks in Kraków.
Canadian Travel Abroad Canada ☎416/364-
2738 or 1-800/387-1876, ⊛www.cantrav.ca.
General interest tours of Poland's historic cities.
Chopin Express Tours Canada ☎416/537-9202
or 1-800/533-0369. City breaks and a big choice of
escorted tours covering folklore, history and culture.
Contal Tours Australia ☎02/9212 5077, ⊛www
.contaltours.com.au. Eastern European specialist
offering flights, hotel bookings and packages.
Eastern Eurotours Australia ☎07/5526 2855 or
1800/242 353, ⊛www.easterneurotours.com.au.
Flights, accommodation, city breaks and guided tours.
Explore Holidays ☎1300/731 000, ⊛www
.exploreholidays.com.au. City breaks in Warsaw and
Kraków.
Elderhostel US ☎1-800/454-5768, ⊛www
.elderhostel.org. Specialists in educational and
activity programmes for senior travellers, offering
general Central European art-and-culture tours and
Polish heritage tours.
Exodus UK ☎0870/240 5550, ⊛www.exodus
.co.uk. Nine-day treks in the Tatras, and two-week
tours mixing culture and nature.
Explore UK ☎0845/013 1537, ⊛www
.exploreworldwide.com. Hiking tours in the Tatra
mountains and the eastern borderlands, and two-
week tours of Poland's natural beauty spots.
Fregata UK ☎020/7420 7305, ⊛www
.fregatatravel.co.uk. Tailor-made city breaks, tours
and activity holidays.
Gateway Travel Australia ☎02/9745 3333 or
1800/700 333, ⊛www.russian-gateway
.com.au. Eastern European specialists offering flights
and packages.
General Tours US ☎1-800/221-2216, ⊛www
.generaltours.com. Warsaw and Kraków city
packages.

GoPoland UK ☎0870/991 7380, ⊛www
.gopoland.co.uk. Specialist operator who can organize
tailor-made holidays, tours, car hire and city breaks.
Isram US ☎1-800/223-7460, ⊛www.isram.com.
City breaks in Warsaw and Kraków.
Kirker Holidays UK ☎020/7593 1899, ⊛www
.kirkerholidays.com. City breaks in Kraków and
Warsaw.
Naturetrek UK ☎01962/733 051, ⊛www
.naturetrek.co.uk. Expertly led wildlife treks
concentrating on seasonal fauna (there's one tour
each in winter, spring and autumn).
Orbis US ☎212/867-5011 or 1-800/TO POLAND,
⊛www.orbistravel.com. The biggest of the Polish
travel companies, Orbis has an extensive selection of
city breaks and escorted tours, ranging from eight to
fifteen days, including flights, accommodation and two
daily meals. They also handle flight bookings, car hire
and tailor-made arrangements for individual travellers.
Page & Moy UK ☎0870/833 4012, ⊛www
.pageandmoy.com. City breaks in Kraków, plus
Kraków-and-Tatras tours.
PAT (Polish American Tours) US ☎413/747-
7702 or 1-800/388-0988, ⊛www.polandtours
.com. Hotel bookings, car rental, and a range of
escorted tours with historical or folklore themes.
Polish Regency Tours UK ☎020/8992 6001,
⊛www.polish-travel.co.uk. Poland specialist dealing
in flights, bus tickets and packages.
Polish Travel Center US ☎215/533-1294 or
1-800/247-5710, ⊛www.polishtravel.com. Flights,
tailor-made itineraries and escorted tours.
Polorbis UK ☎020/7636 4701, ⊛www.polorbis
.co.uk. Weekend breaks in Warsaw, Kraków and
Gdańsk, and seven- and fourteen-day tours of the
country's top sights.
Regent Holidays UK ☎0845/277 3317, ⊛www
.regent-holidays.co.uk. City breaks and tailor-made
itineraries in Poland and neighbouring countries from
a long-standing specialist.
Stay Poland Poland ☎022/351 2222, ⊛www
.staypoland.com. Warsaw-based firm with a series
of airfare-exclusive guided trips, including "Jewish
Heritage" and "Off the Beaten Path", as well as
custom-designed tours.
Tradesco Tours US ☎1-800/448-4321, ⊛www
.tradescotours.com. Tailor-made arrangements and
upmarket city breaks in Warsaw and Kraków.
Travelsphere UK ☎0870/240 2426, ⊛www
.travelsphere.co.uk. Kraków city breaks and eight-
day Kraków-plus-mountains combinations.
Travellers' Cities UK ☎01959/540 700, ⊛www
.travellerscities.com. City breaks in Warsaw and
Kraków.

Getting around

Poland has comprehensive and cheap public transport services, though they can often be overcrowded and excruciatingly slow. As a general rule, trains are the best means of moving across the country, as all but the most rural areas are still crisscrossed by passenger lines. Buses come into their own in the more remote regions of the country, where you'll find that even the smallest of villages are served by at least one bus a day. For information on major train and bus connections, consult the "Travel details" section at the end of each chapter. Car rental prices are fairly reasonable, and taxis are cheap enough to be considered for the occasional inter-town journey, especially if you can split costs three or four ways.

By plane

The domestic network of **LOT**, the Polish national airline, operates regular flights from Warsaw to Gdańsk, Katowice, Kraków, Poznań, Rzeszów, Szczecin and Wrocław – each of which take about an hour. Some routes are covered several times a day, but services are reduced during the **winter** months (end Oct to mid-April).

Tickets can be purchased at the airport itself or from LOT agents in city centres, where you can also pick up free **timetables** (ask for *rozkład lotów*). Prices vary according to how far in advance you book and which day you choose to travel – expect anything between 180zł and 400zł each way. Children up to the age of 2 travel free, provided they do not occupy a separate seat.

By rail

Polish State Railways (PKP) is a reasonably efficient organization, though its services, particularly on rural routes, have been heavily cut since the fall of communism and continue to be reduced at frequent intervals.

PKP runs four main types of train (*pociąg*). **Intercity** services (IC; marked in red on timetables) run on premium routes (such as Warsaw–Kraków or Kraków–Berlin) and only stop at major cities. They're by far the fastest and most comfortable means of getting around, but are more expensive than other trains and **reservations** (*miejscówka*; 5zł) are obligatory. **Express** services (*ekspresowy*; marked in red as "Ex") link Poland's main cities, are only slightly slower than IC trains, and often operate long cross-country routes which allow you to traverse Poland from north to south or east to west without changing trains. Again, reservations are compulsory. **Fast** trains (*pospieszny*; marked in red as "posp.") have far more stops than express trains, are correspondingly slower, and come much cheaper than expresses – which is why they're often overcrowded. Cheapest of all are the **normal** services (*osobowy*; marked in black), which travel at snail-like speeds stopping at every wayside halt, and often feature outdated carriages with uncomfortable seats.

Fares shouldn't burn too big a hole in your pocket: using *pospieszny* trains, cross-country journeys such as Warsaw to Wrocław, Kraków or Gdańsk shouldn't set you back much more than 50zł. Travelling with an express or intercity train will be fifty to a hundred percent more expensive. It's sometimes worth paying the thirty percent extra to travel **first class** (*pierwsza klasa*), in order to avoid the sardine-like conditions that sometimes occur in second-class (*druga klasa*) coaches – especially at weekends or during holidays.

Many long intercity journeys can be made overnight, with trains conveniently timed to leave around 10 or 11pm and arrive between 6 and 9am. For these, it's advisable to book either a **sleeper** (*sypialny*) or **couchette** (*kuszetka*) in advance; the total cost will probably be less than a room in a cheap hotel. Sleepers cost about 120zł per head in a three-bunk compartment (though it's rare that all three beds are used), complete with washbasin, towels, sheets, blankets and a snack. At about 90zł, couchettes have six bunks and also come with sheets, a blanket and a pillow.

Overnight sleepers on the principal lines are prime targets for **robberies**. One major hazard to watch out for is nighttime stops at Warsaw's Central station en route to elsewhere – thieves regularly hop on, steal what they can, and hop off again. The best advice is to keep your compartment locked and your valuables well hidden at all times.

Tickets and passes

Buying **tickets** in the main city train stations can be a time-consuming process, with a bewildering array of counters and long queues. Make sure you join the line at least 45 minutes before your train is due to leave, though usually the absolute maximum you'll have to wait is half an hour. Booking a sleeper or couchette is often done at a separate counter (look for the bed logo). Since most officials don't speak any English, a good way to get the precise ticket you want is to write all the details down and show them at the counter.

Discounted tickets (*ulgowy*) are available for pensioners and for children aged between 4 and 10 years; those under 4 travel free, though they're not supposed to occupy a seat. For students, ISIC cards no longer entitle you to discounted travel within Poland.

Inter-Rail **passes** are valid in Poland but Eurail passes are not (see p.29).

Station practicalities

In train stations, the **departures** are normally listed on yellow posters marked *odjazdy*, with **arrivals** on white posters headed *przyjazdy*. Fast trains are marked in red and normal services in black. An "R" in a square means that seat reservations are obligatory. Additionally, there may be figures at the bottom indicating the dates between which a particular train does (*kursuje*) or doesn't (*nie kursuje*) run – the latter usually under-lined by a warning wiggly line. The platform (*peron*) is also indicated.

Information counters, if they exist, are usually heralded by long queues and manned by non-English-speaking staff. Train times can be looked up on the internet (in Polish and English) on Ⓦrozklad-pkp.pl.

Polish stations have a rather confusing platform numbering system, in which one set of numbers refers to the platforms themselves and another set of numbers refers to the tracks on either side – so take care that you board the right train. Electronic departure boards are yet to be installed in many Polish stations, and trains don't always display boards stating their route, so it pays to ask before boarding.

The main station in a city is identified by the name Główny or Centralny. These are open round the clock and usually have such **facilities** as waiting rooms, toilets, kiosks, restaurants, snack bars, cafés, and a left-luggage office (*przechowalnia bagażu*) or, in the largest cities, lockers.

Facilities on the trains are much poorer, though IC and express trains have a buffet car, and light **refreshments** are available on all overnight journeys. Ticket control is rather haphazard, particularly on crowded services, but it does happen more often than not. If you've boarded a train without the proper ticket, you should seek out the **conductor**, who will issue the right one on payment of a small supplement.

By bus

Poland's bus network (often referred to as "PKS" after the state-run company that used to operate it) consists of a multitude of **regional** and **national** companies, and is extraordinarily comprehensive. Some intercity routes are just as quick as the train, although it's in **rural districts** not touched by the railway network that buses come into their own.

Routes linking major towns and cities are usually operated by comfortable modern vehicles. Out in the provinces, **vehicles** are more likely to be old, smelly and uncomfort-able. Rural journeys can be time-consuming because of poor road quality – in some areas buses rarely exceed an average of 30km per hour.

Noticeboards show departures (*odjazdy*) and arrivals (*przyjazdy*) not only in the bus stations, but on all official stopping places along the route. "Fast" (*pospieszny*) buses (which carry a small supplement) are marked in red; slow in black. As at the train stations, departures and arrivals are marked on different boards, so make sure you're looking at the right one. It's very rare to find an English speaker in the average Polish bus station, so it's best to write your destination down to avoid any confusion.

Tickets

In towns and cities, the main bus station (*dworzec autobusowy* or *dworzec PKS*) is usually alongside the train station. **Tickets** can be bought in the terminal building; in larger places there are several **counters**, each dealing with clearly displayed destinations. In a few places the terminal is shared with the train station, so make sure you go to the right counter.

Booking in the departure terminal ensures a **seat**, as a number will be allocated to you on your ticket. However, the lack of computerized systems means that many stations cannot allocate seats for services starting out from another town. In such cases, you have to wait until the bus arrives and buy a ticket – which may be for standing room only – from the **driver**. The same procedure can also be followed (provided the bus isn't already full to overflowing) if you arrive too late to buy a ticket at the counter. Some of the bigger bus companies offer **student discounts**, so it always pays to ask.

By car

Although access to a car will save you a lot of time in exploring the country, **traffic** is heavy on Poland's main roads. There's a dearth of multi-lane highways on the trunk routes, ensuring that you'll spend much of your time trailing behind a stream of slow-moving cars and lorries. Poland's rural **backroads** are quiet and hassle-free by comparison, and – providing you have a decent map – present the perfect terrain for unhurried touring.

Motorways are still confined to a couple of stretches in the south (between Katowice and Kraków, for example), and major new projects remain the subject of much discussion.

If you're bringing your own car, you'll need to carry your vehicle's **registration** document. If the car is not in your name, you must have a letter of permission signed by the owner and authorized by your national motoring organization. You'll also need your driving **licence** (international driving licences aren't officially required, though they can be a help in tricky situations), and you may need an international insurance green card to extend your insurance cover – check with your insurers to see whether you're covered or not.

Car rental

Car rental in Poland works out at about 200zł a day and 1000zł a week for a Fiat Punto or equivalent with unlimited mileage. An Opel Vectra, Nissan Primera or equivalent will cost fifty percent more. Cars can be booked through the usual **agents** (see below) or in Poland itself: all the four major operators now have their own agents in all or most of the big Polish cities.

Cars will only be rented to people **over 21** (or for some types of vehicle, over 25) who have held a full licence for more than a year.

Car-rental agencies

Avis ⓦ www.avis.com.
Budget ⓦ www.budget.com.
Europcar ⓦ www.europcar.com.
Hertz ⓦ www.hertz.com.
Irish Car Rentals ⓦ www.irishcarrentals.ie.
Joka ⓦ www.joka.com.pl.
SIXT ⓦ www.sixt.com.

Rules of the road

The main **rules** of the road are pretty clear, though there are some particularly Polish twists liable to catch out the unwary. The basic rules are: traffic drives on the right; it is compulsory to wear seat belts outside built-up areas; children under 12 years of age must sit in the back; seat belts must be worn in the back if fitted; and right of way must be given to public transport vehicles (including trams). Driving with more than 0.2 promile (parts per thousand) of alcohol in the bloodstream (about equivalent to one glass of beer or wine) is strictly prohibited – anyone with a foreign numberplate driving around after 11pm, however innocently, has a strong chance of being stopped and **breathalyzed**. Talking on hand-held mobile phones while driving is also against the law and headlights must be switched on at all times.

You're also required to carry a red warning triangle, a first-aid kit and a set of replacement bulbs, and display a national identification sticker. Note that rear-wheel **mud flaps** are obligatory in Poland.

Speed limits are 60kph in built-up areas (white signs with the place name mark the start of a built-up area; the same sign with a diagonal red line through it marks the end), 90kph on country roads, 110kph on main highways, 120kph on dual carriageways, 130kph on motorways, and 80kph if you're pulling a caravan or trailer. **Speed traps** are common, particularly on major trunk roads such as the Gdańsk–Warsaw route, so caution is strongly advised, especially on the approach to, and when travelling through, small towns and villages. Fines for transgressors are administered on the spot.

Other problems occur chiefly at **night**, especially on country roads, where potential disasters include horses and carts, mopeds without lights and staggering inebriated peasants. In cities, beware of a casual attitude towards traffic lights and road signs by local drivers and pedestrians.

Fuel

Poland's roads are pretty well served with filling stations. Many stations in cities and along the main routes are open 24 hours a day, others from around 6am to 10pm; almost all out-of-town stations close on Sundays. **Unleaded** fuel (*benzyna bezołowiowa)* and **diesel** are available at most stations. Carrying at least one fuel can permanently topped up will help to offset worries in rural areas.

Car crime

With car-related **crime** – both simple break-ins and outright theft – one of the biggest criminal growth areas in Poland today, and foreign-registered vehicles one of the major targets, it pays to take note of some simple **precautions**. In big towns especially, always park your vehicle in a guarded parking lot

(*parking strzeżony*), never in an open street – even daylight break-ins occur with depressing frequency. Never leave anything of importance, including vehicle documents, in the car. **Guarded lots** are not too expensive (about 20zł a day, more in major city centres) and in most towns and cities you can usually find one located centrally – the major hotels almost always have their own nearby. If you have a break-in, report it to the **police** immediately. They'll probably shrug their shoulders over the prospects of getting anything back, but you'll need their signed report for insurance claim purposes back home.

Breakdowns and spares

The national breakdown emergency number is ☏9637. If you have insurance against breakdowns, the tow will be free.

The wide range of cars now available in Poland means that you will not have problems finding **spares** for major Western makes. If it's simply a case of a flat tyre, head for the nearest sizeable garage.

Cycling

Cycling is often regarded as an ideal way to see a predominantly rural country like Poland. Particularly on the backroads, surfaces are generally in good shape, and there isn't much traffic around – anyone used to cycling in Western traffic is in for a treat. An additional plus is the mercifully **flat** nature of much of the terrain, which allows you to cycle quite long distances without great effort. You'll need to bring your own bike and a supply of spare parts: except in a few major cities like Warsaw and Kraków and a number of southern mountain areas like the Bieszczady, bike rental and spare part facilities are still a comparative rarity. In rural areas, though, bikes are fairly common, and with a bit of ingenuity you can pick up basic **spares** like inner tubes and puncture repair kits.

Taking your bike on **trains** isn't a problem as long as there's a luggage van on board: if there isn't you usually have to sit with it in the last carriage of the train where, if you're lucky, there'll be fewer passengers; either way there's a nominal fee. **Hotels** will usually put your bike either in a locked luggage room or a guarded parking lot. You need to exercise at least as much caution concerning security as you would in any city at home: strong **locks** and chaining your bike to immobile objects are the order of the day, and you should always try to take your bike indoors at night.

City transport

Trams are the basis of the public transport system in nearly all Polish cities. They usually run from about 5am to 11pm, and departure times are clearly posted at the stops. **Tickets** can be bought from newspaper kiosks and can only be used in the city where they were bought. On boarding, you should immediately validate your ticket in one of the machines; checks by inspectors are rare, but they do happen from time to time. Note that some tickets have to be **validated** at both ends (arrows will indicate if this is so); this is for the benefit of children and pensioners, who travel half-price and thus have to cancel only one end per journey. In some cities (like Gdańsk) each ticket is valid for a particular time-span so if you have a 30-minute ticket you won't need a new ticket each time you change from one tram to another providing the 30 minutes aren't up. In other cities (including Warsaw) you pay a flat fare for each single journey – and if you **transfer** from one tram to another you'll need a second ticket.

Tram tickets are valid on **municipal buses**, and the same system for validating them applies. The routes of the municipal buses go beyond the city boundaries into the outlying countryside, so many nearby villages have several connections during peak times of the day. Note that on both buses and trams, **night services** are often priced differently to daytime services and require different tickets.

The price of **taxis** is cheap enough to make them a viable proposition for regular use during your visit. Taxi ranks are usually easy to find outside stations and in town centres. Make sure you choose a taxi with an illuminated sign on its roof bearing the company name and phone number.

If you pick up a taxi in the street, you're more likely to pay above-average prices; the safest and cheapest option is to ring a quoted taxi number and order one. Generally speaking, you should pay 15-25zł for a cross-city journey, depending on your time of travel (prices are fifty percent higher after 11pm). Prices are also raised by fifty percent for journeys outside the city limits. However, costs are always **negotiable** for longer journeys – between towns, for example – and can work out very reasonable if split among a group. For more advice on travelling by taxi, see the Warsaw account (p.68).

Accommodation

Accommodation will probably account for most of your essential expenditure in Poland. The hotel market has witnessed a considerable shake-up in recent years, with the construction of new business-oriented international franchises and the privatization and refurbishment of old state-run establishments.

The overall effect of these developments has been to force prices upwards, although accommodation **bargains** are still easy to come by in Poland – especially in the rural resort areas favoured by the Poles themselves. Listings in the Guide have been made as wide-ranging as possible to reflect the immense diversity on offer: privately run hotels, pensions, hostels, youth hostels, upmarket B&Bs, rooms in private houses and a good range of campsites.

Hotels

There's a growing range and diversity of **hotel accommodation** in Poland, although standards of service and value for money vary widely from place to place. The international five-star grading system is in use but is yet to be applied universally – and even in those cases where star ratings are in use, they aren't always an accurate guide to quality. As a general rule however, **one-star** hotels provide rooms with a bed and not much else; **two-star** hotels offer rooms with at least an en-suite shower; and **three-star** hotels are likely to provide you with a telephone and a TV. Anything **four-star** or **five-star** is in the international business league.

Most Polish towns and cities still retain one or two (often unclassified) **budget hotels**, often run by organizations such as the PTTK (see p.57) or local sports clubs. These usually offer sparsely furnished rooms (sometimes with shared bathroom facilities located in the hallway), and maybe some multi-bed **dormitories** too. These places are usually clean and well run, and shouldn't be discounted if all you need is a bed for the night. They rarely cost more than 60zł per person per night, although they're decreasing in number – largely because of the temptation to refurbish and upgrade

these establishments as soon as investment becomes available.

There are plenty of competitively priced **mid-range hotels** which would fit comfortably into the international two- and three-star brackets. Prices and quality vary considerably in this category (see box below), but for a standard medium-range double room expect to pay anything from 160zł to 220zł a night – significantly more in Warsaw and Kraków. **Breakfast** is usually included in the room price. The oldest of these mid-range hotels often have a few cheap rooms with shared facilities as well as the standard en suites which are invariably offered to new arrivals – there will be a substantial difference in price, so always ask.

Five-star hotels are still something of a rarity outside Warsaw and Kraków, but four-star establishments are mushrooming all over the place, largely thanks to the booming numbers of business travellers roaming around Poland post-EU membership. Double-room prices at this level start at about 360zł, although you may well find significant reductions at weekends.

Hostels

Cities like Kraków and Warsaw are increasingly well-served by small, privately run backpacker-oriented **hostels** providing

---

Accommodation price codes

All accommodation listed in the Guide (apart from youth hostels) is price graded according to the scale below. Unless specified otherwise, prices given are for the cheapest double room.

In the cheapest places (categories ❶–❷), rooms generally come without their own private bath/shower, breakfast is often not included, and in some instances (specified in the text) beds are in dorms only. In categories ❸–❺ you can normally expect breakfast and an en-suite shower/bath.

Overall, room quality in the middle ranges is affected by the age of the building (generally speaking, the newer the place, especially post-1990, the better) and its geographical location – the more popular tourist centres are improving room quality faster than the rest, and the east of the country still lags noticeably behind western regions.

Into the top bracket hotels (categories ❽–❾), it's another story: high prices are generally matched by consistently high standards.

The majority of places will expect you to pay in złoty, though prices are often quoted in euros.

❶ 60zł and under	❹ 121–160zł	❼ 301–400zł
❷ 61–90zł	❺ 161–220zł	❽ 401–600zł
❸ 91–120zł	❻ 221–300zł	❾ 601zł and over

neat and tidy dormitory accommodation and a friendly atmosphere. They're invariably equipped with kitchen, washing machine and common room, and aren't subject to curfews. Most backpacker hostels also offer a handful of **self-contained doubles** – they're not always cheap, but are perfect if you want to enjoy the hostel atmosphere but require privacy at the same time. Prices for **dorm beds** are around the 50–60zł mark; while doubles start at around 160zł.

If you are in a city which doesn't have any backpacker hostels, bear in mind that many of Poland's budget hotels (see p.39) have rooms sleeping three or four people – ideal for groups travelling together.

Elsewhere in Poland there is a network of rather old-fashioned hostels (*schroniska młodzieżowe*) run by the Polish Youth Hostel Federation (PTSM; ⓦ www.ptsm.org.pl). Accommodation often consists of rickety beds in sparsely furnished dorms, and many hostels are permanently full with Polish school groups. There may also be curfews. Prices, however, are cheap, at around 25zł a bed.

Apartments

An increasing number of establishments in Warsaw (and to a lesser extent, Kraków) are offering **serviced apartments** in modern blocks. These usually offer the same comforts as a three-star hotel or above, but come with the added advantage of a small **kitchenette** (breakfast won't be provided) and – depending on what size of apartment is available – the chance to spread yourself out a bit more than you would do in a hotel room.

A range of apartments from simple studios to one- and two-bedroom affairs are on offer from outfits such as **Old Town Apartments** in Warsaw and Kraków (see the accommodation sections of the relevant chapters for details). Prices depend on how many of you are sharing, but are usually slightly cheaper than the equivalent level of accommodation in a hotel. Always enquire about the **dimensions** of an apartment before committing yourself: some are generously proportioned, others are little more than glorified cupboards.

Pensions and rural homestays

Some of Poland's best accommodation deals can be found in the growing stock of **pensions** (*pensjonaty*) situated in major holiday areas – especially in the mountains, the Mazurian lake district, and along the coast. There's no hard and fast rule governing what constitutes a pension in Poland: some are actually full-size hotels that use the *pensjonat* title to convey a sense of cosiness and informality; others are private houses transformed into family-run B&Bs.

In addition, an increasing number of Polish **farmers** are offering B&B-style accommodation (known as *agroturystyka*) in order to augment their income. As well as being ideal for those seeking rural tranquillity, they also offer the chance to observe a working farm and sample locally produced food and drink.

All of the above tend to offer simple en-suite rooms, often equipped with the additional comforts of a fridge and an electric kettle. **Rates** are usally between 90zł and 120zł per double. Breakfast is sometimes available at an extra cost.

The local tourist information office (if there is one) will have lists of local pensions and rural homestays.

Private rooms

You can get a room in a **private house** (*kwatera prywatna*) in many parts of the country. In urban areas these tend to be located in shabby flats, which may be situated some way from the centre of town. You will be sharing your hosts' bathroom, and breakfast will not be included. In lake, mountain and seaside resorts, however, hosts are often more attuned to the needs of tourists and may provide rooms with an en-suite bathroom, electric kettle, and even TV. Staying in private rooms doesn't necessarily constitute a great way of meeting the **locals**: some hosts will brew you a welcome glass of tea and show a willingness to talk; most will simply give you a set of house keys and leave you to get on with it.

Local travel agencies undertake the job of **allocating rooms** – otherwise the local tourist information centre will hand out a list of addresses. Expect to pay around 40zł per person per night, slightly more in Warsaw.

In case you don't like the place you're sent to, it makes sense not to **register** for too many nights ahead, as it's easy enough to extend your stay by going back to the agency, or paying your host directly.

At the unofficial level, many houses in the main holiday areas hang out signs saying *Noclegi* (lodging) or *Pokoje* (rooms). It's up to you to **bargain** over the price. In the cities, you won't see any signs advertising rooms, but you may well be approached outside stations and other obvious places. Before accepting, establish the price and check that the location is suitable.

Mountain huts

In mountain areas, a reasonably generous number of **mountain huts** (*schroniska*), many of them PTTK-run (see p.57), enable you to make long-distance treks without having to make detours down into the villages for the night; they are clearly marked on hiking maps. Accommodation is in very basic **dormitories** but costs are nominal and you can often get cheap and filling hot meals; in summer the huts can be very crowded indeed, as they are obliged to accept all comers. As a rule, the refuges are open all year round but it's always worth checking for closures or renovations in progress before setting out.

Campsites

There are some five hundred **campsites** throughout the country, classified in three categories: **category 1** sites usually have amenities such as a restaurant and showers, while **category 3** sites amount to little more than poorly lit, run-down expanses of grass; **category 2** sites could be anywhere in between.

The most useful are listed in the Guide; for a complete list, get hold of the *Camping w Polsce* map, available from bookshops (particularly EMPiK stores) and some tourist offices. Apart from a predictably dense concentration in the main holiday areas, sites can also be found in most **cities**: the ones on the outskirts are almost invariably linked by bus to the centre and often have the benefits of a peaceful location and a swimming pool. The major drawback is that most are open between May and September only, though a few do operate all year round. Charges usually work out at a little under 16zł per tent or caravan space plus 16zł per person, and 10zł per vehicle.

One specifically Polish feature is that you don't necessarily have to bring a tent to stay at many campsites, as there are often **bungalows** or **chalets** for rent, generally complete with toilet and shower. Though decidedly spartan in appearance, these are good value at around 40zł per head. In summer, however, they are invariably booked long in advance.

Eating and drinking

Poland has a distinctive national cuisine, with trademark dishes like *pierogi*, potato pancakes, pork chops and roast joints of poultry ensuring that there's plenty to work your way through while you're here (see *Food and Drink* colour section). As in much of northern Europe, traditional Polish cooking is strong on calories, although fresh vegetables and salads are making serious in-roads into the culinary scene.

Poland's cities are increasingly cosmopolitan places, and – whether you're aiming for fast food or fine dining – international food is never hard to find. In particular, inexpensive

Chinese restaurants are everywhere in Poland, serving the standard range of Oriental dishes found in Chinese places across Europe.

Restaurants and cafés

There's a high concentration of **restaurants** (*restauracja*) in tourist-trodden areas of Warsaw, Kraków and other major cities, ranging in style from upmarket eateries with French-flavoured menus to unpretentious, informal places serving Polish staples at moderate prices. Out in the provinces, the choice is more limited, with most restaurant menus sticking to the simpler Polish dishes.

One type of eatery you'll find throughout Poland is the **cafeteria** (usually called *bar mleczny* or "milk bar", although in Kraków and the south they're more commonly labelled *jadłodajnia*), where customers order their food at the counter and then await a shout from the kitchen indicating that their chosen dish is ready. These cafeterias are often the best places to find the full repertoire of traditional Polish food, and prices are reassuringly cheap.

Cafés (*kawiarnia*) usually concentrate on food of the ice cream and cakes variety, although several also offer salads, sandwiches and other light meals.

Tips aren't usually given in a cafeteria, but in restaurants and cafés with table service it's polite to leave ten percent or round up the bill to the nearest convenient figure.

Local dishes

Most restaurants and canteens will offer a broadly similar menu of **Polish standards**, kicking off with a solid repertoire of soups, of which the beetroot-flavoured borsht (*barszcz*) is the most common.

One undoubted Polish culinary classic is the *pieróg* (plural *pierogi*), a small parcel of boiled **dough** stuffed with a variety of savoury or sweet fillings. Other ubiquitous national specialities include *bigos* (a filling **stew** comprising a mixture of meats, cabbage, mushrooms and spices), *gołąbki* (cabbage leaves stuffed with rice and meat) and *placki* (potato pancakes), either served on their own with sour cream or covered in goulash (*gulasz*).

Otherwise, the basis of most main courses is a fried or grilled cut of **meat** in a thick sauce, most common of which is the *kotlet schabowy*, a pork cutlet which is often fried in batter. Other favourites include

flaczki (tripe cooked in a spiced bouillon stock with vegetables – usually very spicy), and *golonka* (pig's leg with horseradish). Roast duck with apples is the standout **poultry** dish; while Baltic Sea halibut and freshwater trout (*pstrąg*) feature most frequently among the **fish**. Main meals usually come with a side order of **salad** (*surówka*), which in Poland usually means grated carrot, beetroot and cabbage.

As far as **desserts** are concerned, cheesecake (*sernik*) and apple pie (*szarlotka*) both have the status of national culinary institutions, while pancakes (*naleśniki*) filled with a variety of sweet fillings also crop up on pretty much every menu.

Vegetarians

A meal without meat is a contradiction in terms for most Poles, and **vegetarians** will often be forced to find solace in customary stand-bys like omelettes, cheese-based dishes and salads. Thankfully, Kraków and a handful of other cities now boast a sprinkling of dedicated vegetarian cafeterias, and most mainstream restaurants have a (albeit limited) vegetarian section in the menu. Crucially, Poland's main centres have a growing number of good-quality Italian restaurants, where Mediterranean salads and meat-free pastas are the order of the day.

Vegetarian dishes are listed on menus as *potrawy jarskie*; other useful phrases are *bez mięsa* ("without meat") and *bez ryby* ("without fish").

Street food and snacks

Despite the onward march of the **kebab stall** (there's hardly a single high street in Poland without one), indigenous snack food has proved surprisingly resilient to globalization. The **fried fish** stall (*smażalnia ryb*) is a ubiquitous sight in seaside, lake and mountain resorts. In the towns and cities, best bet for a substantial post-pub bite is the *zapiekanka*, a baguette-like piece of toasted bread topped with cheese, mushrooms and a choice of other toppings. Stalls selling grilled chicken (*kurczak z rożna*) have long been a local favourite, and no self-respecting high street is likely to be without one.

Drinking

Most **daytime** drinking takes place in a café or *kaviarnia*, which range in style from functional spaces with plastic furniture to grand nineteenth-century establishments with apron-wearing staff and a full menu of patisserie-style goodies. From here onwards however distinctions become rather blurred, with places that call themselves pubs or bars catering for coffee-drinkers during the daytime and serious beer- and spirit-guzzlers come the evening. There's certainly no shortage of characterful **night-time** drinking holes in the major cities, with candle-lit bohemian haunts, flashy disco-pubs and swanky cocktail bars all vying for custom.

Tea and coffee

Tea (*herbata*), is usually served black, so you will need to specify if you want it with milk (*z mlekiem*). The quality of **coffee** (*kawa*) varies considerably from place to place, with international-style coffee bars in city centres serving up espresso, cappuccino and other Italian-inspired brews; while provincial cafés and train station snack bars offer a dispiriting brown liquid made by dumping grounds (or instant powder) in a cup and pouring water over them. If you're anything of a coffee connoisseur it's best to stick to the classier-looking places. In the cheaper cafés, coffee is served black unless you ask otherwise, in which case specify with milk (*z mlekiem*) or with cream (*ze śmietanką*).

Alcoholic drinks

Night-time drinking venues all offer a broad range of international drinks, although traditional Polish spirits frequently occupy pride of place. **Vodka** (*wódka*) is very much the national drink, and most self-respecting bars will have a broad selection in stock (see *Food and drink* colour section).

Most Polish **beer** is of the palatable but unexciting lager variety, and there's little to distinguish between the stuff churned out by mass-market brewers Żywiec, Tyskie and Lech. Tastiest of the lagers is Żubr ("Bison"), produced by the Doilidy brewery in Białystok, while the distintive local beers made in Leżajsk (see p.304) and Zwierzyniec (p.290) are well worth seeking out. Beer is usually sold on draught – ask for *jedno duże* ("a big one") if you want the full half-litre; *jedno małe* ("a small one") will get you a 33cl glass.

The media

The Polish *media* scene has long been one of the liveliest in Eastern Europe, not least because of the popularity enjoyed by semi-official and dissident publications during the communist period.

Newspapers and magazines

Among Polish-language daily **newspapers**, most popular is the tabloid-sized *Gazeta Wyborcza* (Ⓦwww.gazeta.pl), Eastern Europe's first independent daily. *Gazeta* is strong on investigative journalism, has a liberal political stance and, even if you don't read Polish, is worth getting for its cultural listings – especially on Fridays, when the week's attractions are previewed in the *Co jest Grane?* supplement.

Other national daily papers include *Rzeczpospolita*, originally the official voice of the communist government, now a highbrow independent paper with a following among business people and government officials because of its good economic coverage.

Glossy **monthly magazines** are devoured as eagerly in Poland as anywhere else in the developed world. Home-grown women's magazines like *Ewa* and *Twój Styl* have been joined by Polish-language versions of *Cosmopolitan*, *Marie Claire* and others; the worldwide explosion in men's lifestyle magazines has been mirrored here too.

English-language publications

There are a number of **English-language publications**. Longest established is the *Warsaw Voice* (🌐 www.warsawvoice.com.pl), a Warsaw-based weekly that's widely available throughout the country. It's readable and informative, with good listings, though noticeably slanted towards the business community.

Western newspapers and magazines are now available on the day of publication in the big cities. Most common are the *Guardian* international edition, the *Financial Times*, *The Times* and the *Herald Tribune*, plus magazines like *Newsweek*, *Time* and *The Economist*.

Ruch and other **kiosks** are the main outlets for papers and magazines, with a wide selection also available in EMPiK stores.

TV and radio

Poland's **TV network** has improved by leaps and bounds in recent years, with the previously rather staid state-run channels now competing for viewers with private stations. The regular shows, soap operas and A doesn't differ that much from in Europe, although Polish TV to preserve a few quirks of its the tendency for foreign imports to be dubbed by a single *lektor*, who reads all the parts in the same voice. For increasing numbers of Poles, **satellite** and, in the big cities, cable TV, are popular additions to the range of viewing options. Most hotels now carry a selection of international cable/satellite channels, although German-language stations tend to be more common than English.

The most popular Polish **radio stations** are Warsaw-based Zet, and Kraków's RMF FM (both of which now broadcast to other cities on a variety of different frequencies), offering a varied and often rather imaginative diet of pop, rock and other contemporary musical styles. A number of local stations broadcast occasional English-language news bulletins, although for a full English-language service you'll have to track down **BBC World Service**, for which you'll need a shortwave radio; 🌐 www.bbc.co.uk/world-service lists all the World Service frequencies around the globe.

Festivals

One manifestation of Poland's intense commitment to Roman Catholicism is that all the great feast days of the Church calendar are celebrated with wholehearted devotion, many of the participants donning the colourful traditional costumes for which the country is known.

This is most notable in the mountain areas in the south of the country, where the annual festivities play a key role in maintaining a vital sense of **community**. As a supplement to these, Poland has a calendar bursting with cultural festivals, particularly in the fields of film, music and drama. As well as a strong ethnic/folk music scene, there are an increasing number of open-air pop/rock festivals in summer.

Religious and traditional festivals

The highlight of the Catholic year is **Easter** (*Wielkanoc*), which is heralded by a glut of spring fairs, offering the best of the early livestock and agricultural produce. **Holy Week** (*Wielki Tydzień*) kicks off in earnest on **Palm Sunday** (*Niedziela Palmowa*), when palms are brought to church and paraded in processions. Often the painted and decorated "palms" are handmade, sometimes with competitions for the largest or most beautiful. The most famous procession takes place at Kalwaria Zebrzydowska near Kraków (see p.415), inaugurating a spectacular week-long series of mystery plays, re-enacting Christ's Passion.

Good Friday (*Wielki Piątek*) sees visits to mock-ups of the Holy Sepulchre – whether permanent structures such as at Kalwaria Zebrzydowska and Wambierzyce in Silesia, or ad hoc creations, as is traditional in Warsaw. **Easter Saturday** (*Wielka Sobota*) is when baskets of painted eggs are taken along to church to be blessed and sprinkled with holy water. The consecrated food is eaten at breakfast on **Easter Day** (*Niedziela Wielkanocna*), when the most solemn Masses of the year are celebrated. On **Easter Monday** (*Lany Poniedziałek*) girls are doused with water by boys to "make them fertile" (a marginally better procedure than in the neighbouring Czech Republic where they're beaten with sticks). Even in the cosmopolitan cities you'll see gangs of boys waiting in the streets or leaning out of first-floor windows waiting to throw water bombs at passing girls.

Corpus Christi (*Boże Ciało*) is another important date in the Catholic calendar, marked by colourful processions everywhere and elaborate floral displays, notably in Łowicz.

The first of two major Marian festivals on consecutive weeks comes with the **Feast of the Holy Virgin of Sowing** on August 8 in farming areas, particularly in the southeast of the country. By then, many of the great pilgrimages to the Jasna Góra shrine in Częstochowa (see p.472) have already set out, arriving for the **Feast of the Assumption** (*Święto Wniebowzięcia NMP*) on August 15. This is also the occasion for the enactment of a mystery play at Kalwaria Pacławska near Przemyśl (see p.306).

All Saints' Day (*Dzień Wszystkich Świętych*), November 1, is the day of national remembrance, with flowers, wreaths and candles laid on tombstones. **St Barbara's Day**, December 4, is the traditional holiday of the miners, with special Masses held for their safety as a counterweight to the jollity of their galas.

During **Advent** (*Adwent*), the nation's handicraft tradition comes to the fore, with the making of cribs to adorn every church. In Kraków, a competition is held on a Sunday between December 3 and 10, the winning entries being displayed in the city's Historical Museum. On **Christmas Eve** (*Wigilia*) families gather for an evening banquet, traditionally of twelve courses to symbolize the number of the Apostles. This is also the time when children receive their gifts. **Christmas Day** (*Boże Narodzenie*) begins with the midnight Mass; later, small round breads decorated with the silhouettes of domestic animals are consumed. **New Year's Eve** (*Sylwester*) is the time for magnificent formal balls, particularly in Warsaw, while in country areas of southern Poland it's the day for practical jokes – which must go unpunished. The Christmas period winds up with **Epiphany** (*Dzień Trzech Króli*) on January 6, when groups of carol singers move from house to house, chalking the letters K, M and B (symbolizing the three Kings, Kaspar, Melchior and Balthazar) on each doorway as a record of their visit. The chalk marks are usually left untouched throughout the coming year, thereby ensuring good fortune for the household.

Events calendar

Poland offers a substantial menu of serious arts and culture festivals throughout the year, with outdoor rock, pop and folk events fleshing out the festival calendar in spring and summer. Precise dates can change from one year to the next, so check websites or local tourist information offices before travelling.

February

Musica Polonica Nova ⓦwww .musicapolonicanova.pl. Chamber music festival premiering new works by contemporary classical composers. Mid Feb. Wrocław.

All-Polish Festival of Artistic Song (Ogólnopolski festiwal piosenki artystycznej) ⓦ www.ofpa.pl, ⓦ www.ppa .art.pl. Singer-songwriters, experimental musical theatre and intellectual cabaret, with a fair smattering of international guests. Mid Feb. Wrocław.

March

Jazz on the Oder (Jazz nad Odrą) ⓦ www .jnofestival.pl. Five days of top-quality international jazz ranging from big bands to freeform improvisation. Early to mid March. Wrocław.

KRT (Krakowskie reminiscencje teatralne) ⓦ www.reminiscencje.pl. International theatre festival with a strong alternative edge. Mid March. Kraków.

Misteria Paschalia ⓦ www.misteriapaschalia.pl. Festival of religious music through the ages. Easter week. Kraków.

April

Gdańsk Spring (Gdańska wiosna) ⓦ www .gedanensis.pl/gdanskawiosna. Chamber concerts featuring promising young violinists from around the globe. Throughout April. Gdańsk.

May

Probaltica ⓦ www.probaltica.art.pl. Orchestral and chamber music featuring musicians from the Baltic region. Early May. Toruń.

Night of the Museums (Noc muzeów) Museums and galleries open up in the evening for free, generating an atmosphere of cultural carnival. Mid to late May. Venues all over Poland.

International Festival of Orthodox Church Music (Miedzynarodowy festiwal muzyki cerkiewnej) ⓦ www.festiwal-hajnowka.pl. Haunting choral music from Orthodox choirs, with guest ensembles from all over Eastern Europe. Late May. Hajnówka.

Contact Theatre Festival (Kontakt) One of Europe's foremost theatrical events, featuring outstanding drama from all over the continent. Late May. Toruń.

Łańcut Music Festival (Muzyczny festiwal w Łańcucie) ⓦ www.filharmonia.rzeszow .pl. Chamber music from some top international performers, with concerts taking place in southeast Poland's most sumptuous palace. Late May. Łańcut.

International Puppet Festival (Międzynarodowy festiwal sztuki lalkarskiej) ⓦ www.banialuka.pl. Prestigious gathering of Europe's best puppet theatres, held every even-numbered year. Late May. Bielsko Biała.

Kraków Film Festival (Krakowski festiwal filmowy) ⓦ www.kff.com.pl. International festival of documentaries, animated films and shorts. Late May to early June. Kraków.

Jazz on the Borderlands (Jazz na kresach) ⓦ www.kosz.zam.pl. A weekend of open-air jazz on Poland's finest Renaissance Rynek. Late May to early June. Zamość.

Corpus Christi The mother of all Corpus Christi processions, producing a colourful folkloric pageant. Late May or early June. Łowicz.

June

Dragon Parade (Parada smoków) ⓦ www .groteska.pl. A fantastic parade of dragons on Kraków's main square followed by a son et lumière show by the river. First or second Sat in June. Kraków.

Hetman's Fair (Jarmark Hetmański) Folk and crafts fair with market stalls and live music. Second weekend in June. Zamość.

Midsummer's Eve (Wianki) Traditionally celebrated by virgins throwing wreaths into rivers while bonfires are lit on the water's edge, Wianki is nowadays celebrated with outdoor pop concerts and fireworks. June 23 or nearest weekend. Venues across Poland.

Malta Theatre Festival ⓦ www.malta-festival .pl. Outstanding modern drama with performances making full use of the city's outdoor spaces. Late May. Poznań.

Łowicz Fair (Jarmark Łowicki) Market stalls, crafts for sale, and live folk music. Late June. Łowicz.

Festival of Folk Bands and Singers (Festiwal kapel i śpiewaków ludowych) ⓦ www .kazimierzdolny.pl. Traditional musicians from all over Poland ripping it up on an outdoor stage. Late June. Kazimierz Dolny.

Festival of Jewish Culture (Festiwal kultury żydowskiej) ⓦ www.jewishfestival.pl. Ten days of music, theatre, film and discussion. Late June to early July. Kraków.

Zamość Theatre Summer (Zamojskie lato teatralnie) Drama groups from around Poland performing in the open air to big crowds. Late June to early July. Zamość.

July

Warsaw Summer Jazz Days ⓦ www .adamiakjazz.pl. Jazz, jazz-rock and fusion from around the world in venues across town and outdoors on the pl. Zamkowy square. Throughout July. Warsaw.

Open'er ⓦ www.opener.pl. Poland's biggest commercial pop rock festival, with international acts entertaining a 100,000-strong crowd on an airfield outside Gdynia. Early July.

Jarocin ⓦwww.jarocinfestiwal.pl. Poland's longest-standing alternative rock gathering, with punk music ancient and modern figuring heavily. Open-air, with tent site provided. Early to mid July. Jarocin (east of Poznań).

Przystanek Woodstock ⓦwosp.org. Open-air festival of rock, reggae and world music with anti-globalization, peace-and-solidarity theme. Mid July. Kostrzyn (south of Szczecin).

Lemko Vatra (Łemkowska Watra) Open-air folklore festival celebrating the culture of the Lemkos, pastoral inhabitants of the Polish Carpathians. Second-to-last weekend of July. Zdynia (south of Gorlice).

Crossroads (Rozstaje) ⓦwww.biurofestiwalowe.pl. A weekend of world music from Poland and abroad. Late July. Kraków.

Globaltika ⓦwww.globaltika.pl. Impressive world music weekender in a seaside park. Late July. Gdynia.

New Horizons (Nowe Horizonty) ⓦwww.eranowehorizonty.pl. Big international film festival featuring many of the best new movies from around Europe. Accompanying concerts and clubbing events round out the programme. Late July to early Aug. Wrocław.

Mrągowo Country Picnic Guitar-twanging country singers from Poland, Europe and the USA descend on this Mazurian Lake resort for a weekend-long hoedown. Late July to early Aug. Mrągowo.

St Dominic's Fair (Jarmark św. Dominika) Three weeks of markets, craft stalls and outdoor concerts. Late July to early Aug. Gdańsk.

August

Audio River ⓦwww.audioriver.pl. Cutting-edge dance music with trance and techno acts from all over Europe. Early Aug. Płock.

Beskidy Culture Week (Tydzień Kultury Beskidzkiej) ⓦwww.rok.bielsko.pl. Two festivals in one, with a three-day meeting of Polish highland folk groups (Festiwal Górali Polskich) swiftly followed by an international folklore festival (Międzynarodowe Spotkania Folklorystyczne). Early Aug. Żywiec, just east of Bielsko-Biała.

Two Rivers (Dwa Brzegi) ⓦwww.dwabrzegi.pl. Independent film, world music and art exhibitions take over towns on opposite banks of the Wisła river. Early Aug. Kazimierz Dolny and Janowiec nad Wisłą.

Shakespeare Festival (Festiwal Szekspirowski) ⓦwww.festiwalszekspirowski.pl. Highly regarded drama fest featuring groundbreaking interpretations of the bard from around the world. Early Aug. Gdańsk.

Chopin Festival (Festiwal Chopinowski) ⓦwww.chopin-festival.pl. Top international piano-playing talents pay tribute to Chopin in a charmingly

old-fashioned spa resort once patronized by the maestro himself. Early Aug. Duszniki-Zdrój.

Off Festival ⓦwww.ofc.off-festival.pl. Top-notch alternative rock with an international line-up. On the train line from Katowice to Kraków, and easily accessible from both. Early to mid Aug. Mysłowice.

International Festival of Highland Folklore (Międzynarodowy festiwal folkloru ziem górskich) ⓦwww.festiwal.ezakopane.pl. Folk groups from the mountain regions of the world, with a strong Polish presence. Mid to late Aug. Zakopane.

September

Wratislavia Cantans ⓦwww.wratislavia.art.pl. Choral music over the centuries, performed by outstanding choirs and soloists from around the globe. Early to mid Sept. Wrocław.

Dialogue of Four Cultures (Festiwal dialogu 4 kultur) ⓦwww.4kultury.pl. Art, theatre and music representing Polish, Jewish, German and Russian cultural traditions. Early to mid Sept. Łódź.

March of the Dachshunds (Marsz Jamników) Sausage dogs wearing fancy dress are paraded through town. First or second Sun in Sept. Kraków.

Sacrum Profanum ⓦwww.sacrumprofanum.pl. Modern music from contemporary classical to the avant garde. Mid to late Sept. Kraków.

Warsaw Spring (Warszawska jesień) ⓦwww.warszawska-jesien.art.pl. One of Europe's most formidable festivals of contemporary music, inaugurated in the early Sixties and still going strong. Mid to late Sept. Warsaw.

Festival of Polish Feature Films (Festiwal polskich filmów fabularnich) ⓦwww.festiwalfimow.pl. Poland's answer to the Oscars, with the best domestic features of the year competing for top prizes. Mid to late Sept. Gdynia.

October

Opowiadania Short Story Festival ⓦwww.opowiadanie.info. Literary readings featuring Polish and international authors (so there will be some events in English). Early Oct. Wrocław.

Warsaw Film Festival (Warszawski festiwal filmowy) ⓦwww.wff.pl. Ten-day celebration of independent filmmaking with a sizeable international contingent. Early to mid Oct. Warsaw.

Jazz Jamboree ⓦwww.jazz-jamboree.pl. Mainstream jazz festival featuring big international names. Late Oct to early Nov. Warsaw.

November

Jazz Autumn (Jazzowa Jesień) ⓦwww.jazzowajesien.pl. Founded by top trumpeter Tomasz

Stańko, this two- to three-week series of concerts features the giants of European jazz together with major Polish names. Mid Nov to early Dec. Bielsko-Biała.
Camerimage ⓦ www.pluscamerimage.pl. Film festival with the accent on cinematography, featuring screenings and lectures by the world's great camera operators. Late Nov to early Dec. Łódź.

December

Advent market (Targi Bożonarodzeniowe)
Craft stalls selling jewellery, accessories, woodcarving, speciality foodstuffs and mulled wine fill the main square. Throughout Dec. Kraków.
Divine Comedy (Boska Komedia) ⓦ www .boskakomedia.pl. Review of the best new theatre productions from Poland and abroad. Early Dec. Kraków.
St Nicholas Folk Festival (Mikołajki Folkowe) ⓦ www.mikolaiki.folk.pl. Traditional music from Poland and beyond. Early to mid Dec. Lublin.

Outdoor activities and spectator sports

For a growing number of visitors, it's the wide range of outdoor pursuits Poland has to offer, as well as its better-known cultural and architectural attractions, that constitute the country's chief lure. Most obvious of these are the hiking opportunities provided by the extensive national (and regional) parks, several of which incorporate authentic wilderness areas of great beauty.

Equally attractive for **skiers** are the slopes of the Tatra mountains – long the country's most developed (but by no means its only) ski resort area. Lakes and rivers offer generous opportunities for **water-based activities**. Anglers can sample Poland's significant collection of pristine fishing areas, notably in the outlying eastern regions of the country.

Hiking

Poland has some of the best **hiking** country in Europe, especially in the mountainous regions on the country's southern and western borders. There's a full network of marked trails, the best of which are detailed in the Guide. Many of these take several days, passing through remote areas served by mountain huts (*schroniska*; see p.42). However, much of the best scenery can be seen by covering sections of these routes on one-day walks.

Unless you're in the High Tatras (see p.450), few of the one-day trails are especially strenuous and although specialist **footwear** is recommended, well-worn-in sturdy shoes are usually enough.

Skiing

Poland's mountainous southern rim provides some good **skiing** opportunities, seized on, in season, by what can often seem like the country's entire population. The best and, not surprisingly, most popular ski slopes are in the Tatras, the highest section of the Polish Carpathians, where the skiing season runs from December through to March.

Although still in the shadow of the Alps and other well-known European resorts, **Zakopane**, the resort centre of the Tatras, has acquired a strong and growing international following, not least in the UK, where a variety of travel operators specialize in cheap, popular **skiing packages**. Though the skiing facilities in and around Zakopane may still leave a little to be desired, both in quantity and quality, they have improved considerably over the last few years, not least in the provision of ski lifts. Certainly, you shouldn't have any problems renting skiing gear in Zakopane itself.

Less dramatic alternatives to the Tatras include the Beskid Sudety, notably the resorts at Karpacz and Szklarska Poręba;

the Beskid Śląski resort of Szczyrk; and the Bieszczady (a favourite with **cross-country** skiers). One great advantage with all these is that they are relatively unknown outside Poland, although, consequently, facilities are fairly undeveloped – usually involving a single ski lift and a limited range of descents. As yet relatively free from package hotels, these smaller resorts are perhaps better suited to individual tourists than Zakopane, which can be jam-packed with groups throughout the season.

Kayaking, sailing and windsurfing

Large stretches of lowland Poland are dotted with **lakes**, especially Mazuria (see p.208) in the northeast of the country, and it is relatively easy for travellers to rent a variety of watercraft – from simple kayaks to luxury yachts – once they arrive. Most people content themselves with a day or two on the water, although the number of navigable waterways in Mazuria ensures there's a host of lengthy **canoeing** and **kayaking** itineraries to choose from, often involving overnight stops at campsites or hostels en route. The most popular of these are the nine-day traverse of the Mazurian lakes (see p.209), and the three-day journey down the Czarna Hańcza river (see p.225). Well-equipped **marinas** at Mikołajki (see p.219), Giżycko (p.215) and Ruciane-Nida (p.220) are packed with **sailing** folk in the summer months. Simple sailing boats are easy enough to rent at these places; although at least one member of your party will have to have sailing experience if you want to rent out a bigger craft.

Given the short duration of the Baltic summer, Poland's northern coast doesn't offer the kind of watersports opportunities that you'll find in the Mediterranean. However there's an established **windsurfing** scene in Łeba (see p.602), and in the resorts on the southern side of the Hel peninsula (p.170).

Fishing

Especially in the outlying regions of the country – where the rivers are generally less polluted – **fishing** is a popular pastime. The season effectively runs all year in one form or another, with winter fishing through holes in the ice and on the major Mazurian lakes, and fishing for lavaret with artificial spinners in summer.

The best fishing areas include the Mazurian lakes (pike and perch), the Bieszczady, notably the River San and its tributaries (trout), and the southeast in general. For details on how to buy compulsory fishing **licences**, contact the National Tourist Office (see p.56).

Spectator sports

The Polish media devote a vast amount of coverage to team games as diverse as **basketball** (*koszykówka*), **handball** (*piłka ręczna*) and **volleyball** (*siatkówka*). One sport that enjoys enormous popularity in Poland is **speedway** (*żużel*). Most enormous cities boast a team and a stadium, although it's in the industrial conurbations of the southwest that the sport arouses the greatest passions. Events usually take place on Saturdays; street posters advertise times and venues.

Football (*piłka nożna*) remains the only sport that commands a genuine mass following nationwide. Franz Beckenbauer described the Polish national side as "the best team in the world" in 1974's World Cup, when they were unlucky to finish only in third place. The Poles remained a significant force in the world game for the next decade, with players such as Grzegorz Lato, Kazimierz Deyna and Zbigniew Boniek becoming household names. Polish teams of the nineties and the noughties have been fairly anonymous, frequently qualifying for major competitions only to perform disappointingly once they get there.

Despite receiving blanket coverage from the country's private TV stations, Polish **league football** is currently in the doldrums: few clubs are rich enough to pay the wages of top players, and the country's best talents ply their trade in Germany, Italy or elsewhere. Kraków club Wisła currently enjoys the biggest countrywide following, with Warsaw's Legia running them a close second. Other teams with proud historical pedigrees are the Silesian trio of GKS Katowice, Ruch Chorzów and Górnik Zabrze; and the two Łódź sides, LKS and Widzew. The **season** lasts from August to

November, then resumes in March until June. Some of the top teams have equipped their stadia with plastic seating; elsewhere wooden benches, or uncovered concrete terraces, remain the rule. Inside, grilled sausages and beer are the order of the day. Regular league **fixtures** suffer from pitifully low attendance figures, not least because the emergence of a serious hooligan problem has scared many stadium-goers away. Unsurprisingly, you shouldn't have trouble buying tickets (20–30zł) on the gate for most games, although you may be asked to show ID before being subjected to a spot of vigorous security frisking. For details of results and fixtures, check out the Polish Football Federation's website ⓦwww.pzpn.pl.

Travel essentials

Addresses

In Poland the **street name** is always written before the number. The word for street (*ulica*, abbreviated to ul.) or avenue (*aleja*, abbreviated al.) is often missed out – for example ulica Senatorska is simply known as Senatorska. The other frequent abbreviation is pl., short for *plac* (square). See p.664 for details on the most common street names.

Costs

Although **costs** are on the rise in Poland, it's still a reasonably inexpensive destination compared to Western Europe. Hotel and restaurant prices are at their highest in Warsaw, Kraków and other major cities, although outside these areas a little money can go a long way.

Accommodation is likely to prove your biggest expense. Hostel beds in the main cities cost around 50–60zł; while simple double rooms in pensions and rural B&Bs start at around 90zł. Good 3-star hotels cost around 150zł for a double room in the provinces; at least double that in Warsaw, Kraków and Gdańsk.

Prices for **public transport** are relatively low – even travelling across half the length of the country by train or bus only costs around 100zł. Similarly, you are unlikely to fork out much more than 12zł to visit the more popular tourist sights, with half that the normal asking price.

If you are shopping in markets for picnic ingredients during the daytime and sticking to the cheaper cafés and bars in the evening, then 45zł per person per day will suffice for **food and drink**. In order to cover a sit-down lunch and a decent dinner followed by a couple of nighttime drinks, then a daily outlay of 100zł per person seems more realistic. Pushing the boat out in fine restaurants and fancy cocktail bars will set you back even further.

ISIC cardholders can pick up all kinds of discounts, with some hostels offering ten percent reductions, and most museums offering significant savings on entrance charges. A handful of bus companies, several theatres, and even some high-street pizzerias are among the other organizations offering a small discount.

Crime and personal safety

The biggest potential hassle for visitors to Poland comes from **petty crime** – notably hotel-room thefts and pickpocketing in crowded places such as train stations (especially in Warsaw) and markets. A few common-sense precautions should help you avoid trouble: display cameras, fancy mobile phones and other signs of affluence as little as possible; never leave valuables in your room; and keep large sums of cash in a (well-hidden) money-belt. Guard against opportunistic thefts on overnight trains by booking a couchette or sleeper and keeping it well locked. If you're travelling in the regular carriages, try not to fall asleep. **Theft** of Western cars and/or their contents is something of a national sport in Poland (see p.36).

Your best protection against crime is to take out **travel insurance** before you go (see p.52). If you do have anything stolen, report the loss to the police as soon as possible, and be patient – the Polish police rarely speak English, and filling out a report can take ages. The chances of getting your gear back are virtually zero.

Poles are obliged to carry some form of ID with them at all times. You should always keep your **passport** with you, even though you're unlikely to get stopped unless you're in a car; Western numberplates provide the excuse for occasional unprovoked spot checks. It's also a good idea to make a photocopy of the final, information-bearing page of your passport. This will help your consulate to issue a replacement document if you're unlucky enough to have it stolen.

Electricity

Poland uses the standard Continental 220 volts. Round two-pin plugs are used.

Entry requirements

Citizens of EU countries, the USA, Canada, Australia and New Zealand can stay in Poland for up to ninety days without a **visa**. Once the ninety days are up, you have to leave the country or apply for a residence permit. Nationals of other countries should check current visa regulations with the nearest Polish consulate before setting out.

Polish embassies abroad

Australia 7 Turrana St, Yarralumla, Canberra, ACT
℡02/6272 1000, ⊛www.canberra.polemb.net.
Canada 443 Daly Ave, Ottawa, Ontario K1N 6H3
℡613/789-0468, ⊛www.ottawa.polemb.net.
Ireland 5 Ailesbury Rd, Ballsbridge, Dublin 4
℡01/283 0855, ⊛www.dublin.polemb.net.
New Zealand 17 Upland Rd, Kelburn, Wellington
℡04/475 9453, ⊛www.wellington.polemb.net.

UK 47 Portland Place, London W1B 1JH
℡0870/774 2700, ⊛www.london.polemb.net.
US 2640 16th Street NW, Washington, DC 20009
℡202/234-3800, ⊛www.washington.polemb.net.

Gay and lesbian travellers

Although homosexuality is **legal** in Poland, it remains something of an underground phenomenon, and public displays of affection between members of the same sex may provoke outrage and hostility, especially outside the big cities. Warsaw has a small gay scene, and Kraków and Gdańsk are beginning to develop one.

Health

Citizens of the EU are entitled to free emergency **healthcare** in Poland providing they have an EHIC card, obtainable in the UK from most post offices or online at ⊛www.ehic.org; and in Ireland at local health offices or online at ⊛www.ehic.ie. Lengthy courses of treatment (as well as any prescribed drugs) must be paid for, however, so it's sensible to take out adequate **health insurance**. North Americans, Canadians, Australians and New Zealanders must arrange full insurance before leaving home.

Inoculations are not required for a trip to Poland. Drinking tap water is perfectly safe.

Pharmacies and hospitals

Simple complaints can normally be dealt with at a regular **pharmacy** (*apteka*), where basic medicines are dispensed by qualified pharmacists. In the cities, many of the staff will speak at least some English or German. Even in places where the staff speak only Polish, it should be easy enough to obtain repeat **prescriptions** if you bring along the empty container or remaining pills. In every town there's always at least one *apteka* open 24 hours; addresses are printed in local newspapers and guides.

For more serious problems, or anything the pharmacist can't work out, you'll be directed to a public **hospital** (*szpital*), where conditions will probably be cramped, with more patients than beds, a lack of resources and occasionally insanitary conditions. Health service staff are heavily overworked and

Rough Guides travel insurance

Rough Guides has teamed up with Columbus Direct to offer you tailor-made **travel insurance**. Products include a low-cost **backpacker** option for long stays; a **short break** option for city getaways; a typical **holiday package** option; and others. There are also annual **multi-trip** policies for those who travel regularly. Different sports and activities (trekking, skiing, etc) can usually be included.

See our website (ⓦwww.roughguides.com/shop) or call UK ☎0870/033 9988, Australia ☎1300/669 999, New Zealand ☎0800/559 911, or worldwide ☎+44 870/890 2843.

scandalously underpaid. Hospital patients may be required to pay for the better-quality medicines, and will probably need friends to bring food in for them. If you are required to pay for any medical treatment or medication, remember to keep the receipts for your insurance claim when you get home.

In the larger cities you can opt for **private healthcare**. Kraków and Warsaw now have a considerable Western expatriate population, with health centres run on Western lines. In a crisis, it may even be best to ring the 24-hour emergency service of one of these clinics rather than an ambulance; the ethics of private versus public healthcare aside, there are advantages to being able to talk to someone in English. See the relevant city listings – or check the local press – for details.

Insurance

Even though EU health care privileges apply in Poland, you'd do well to take out an insurance policy before travelling to cover against theft, loss and illness or injury.

Internet

Internet cafés are fairly ubiquitous in Poland, and are listed in the Guide where relevant. Usage rarely costs more than 4zł/hr.

Laundry

Self-service facilities are virtually non-existent in Poland – although most towns do boast a **laundry** (*pralnia*), these tend to concentrate exclusively on dry-cleaning. Some of them offer service washes, too, although this might take up to three days. You can get things service-washed in the more upmarket hotels within 24 hours, but at a cost.

Left luggage

Most train and bus stations of any size have a **left-luggage office** (*przechowalnia bagażu*). In big-city train stations these are often open 24 hours; elsewhere, take note of opening and closing times.

Mail

Big-city **post offices** (*Poczta*) are usually open Monday to Friday from 7/8am until 8pm, with some open on Saturday mornings. Smaller branches usually close at 6pm, often earlier in rural areas. A restricted range of services is available 24 hours a day, seven days a week, from post offices in or outside the main train stations of major cities.

Each post office bears a number, with the head office in each city being no. 1. Theoretically, each head office has a **poste restante** (general delivery) facility: make sure, therefore, that anyone addressing mail to you includes the no. 1 after the city's name. This service works reasonably well, but don't expect complete reliability.

Mail to the UK takes four days, a week to the US, and is a day or so quicker in the other direction. It costs 2.60zł to send a card or letter to the UK, 3.20zł to the USA, Australia or New Zealand. Always mark your **letters** "*Par avion*", or better still "*Lotnicza*", or pick up the blue stickers with both on from post offices; if you don't, they may take longer. Postboxes are red.

Maps

Best of the **general maps** available outside the country are Freytag & Berndt's 1:750,000 map; and the 1:800,000 GeoCenter Euro map. GeoCenter Euro also produces a useful set of 1:300,000 regional maps, covering northeast, northwest, southeast and southwest Poland separately.

More easily available once you're inside the country are the series of **national and regional maps** produced by local publishers Demart and Copernicus. Demart's spiral-bound 1:250 000 road atlas (*atlas samochodowy*) is particularly useful if you're touring the country by car.

Both companies produce detailed and up-to-date **city maps** (*plan miasta*) of almost every urban area in Poland, invariably with public transport routes clearly marked and an A–Z street index on the back.

Hiking maps (*mapa turystyczna*) of the national parks and other rural areas are produced by an array of small companies. They're universally clear and simple to use, although it's wise to choose a larger-scale map – 1:25,000 or greater – if you want to walk a particular route.

The best places to buy maps are the EMPiK multimedia stores found in big city centres – although most other bookshops and newspaper kiosks will carry a small selection.

Money

The Polish unit of currency is the **złoty** (abbreviated to zł). It comes in notes of 10zł, 20zł, 50zł, 100zł and 200zł; and coins in 1, 2 and 5zł denominations, subdivided into *groszy* (1, 2, 5, 10, 20 and 50). Currently the **exchange rate** is around 4.30zł to the pound sterling, 4.15zł to the euro and 3.00zł to the US dollar, but future fluctuations are always possible.

Prices of hotels and other tourist services are often quoted in euros, although payment is made in złoty.

Exchange

The easiest place to change money is at an **exchange bureau** (*kantor*). Very often little more than a simple booth with a single cashier sitting behind a thick plate of glass, these can be found on the main streets of virtually every Polish town. They tend to work longer hours than regular banks (in big cities some *kantors* are open 24 hours a day), usually offer competitive exchange **rates** and rarely charge any commission. Be

aware, however, that it pays to shop around in well-touristed parts of Warsaw and Kraków, where a *kantor* on the main street will offer a substantially less advantageous rate than a similar establishment in a side alley nearby.

Exchange rates at Polish **banks** (usually Mon–Fri 7.30am–5pm, Sat 7.30am–2pm) tend to be the same from one establishment to the next, although banks are much more subject to long queues and usually deduct a commission. It's wise to avoid changing money in hotels: they tend to offer poor rates and charge commissions.

Traveller's cheques, credit cards and ATMs

Although **traveller's cheques** are the safest way of carrying your money, they're also the least convenient way of getting local currency, with only main banks, Orbis offices and hotels accepting them. American Express, which now has offices in Warsaw, is a useful alternative and will cash most brands of traveller's cheques, in addition to their own. Cashing a traveller's cheque can often be a lengthy process, with cashiers so unfamiliar with the procedure that you can be kept waiting for hours. Hotels usually charge a **commission** of five percent, banks around one percent, while American Express will cash cheques free of charge (into local currency only).

Major **credit and debit cards** are accepted by an increasing number of travel agents, hotels, restaurants and shops. You can also arrange a cash advance on most of these cards in big banks. **ATMs** are now ubiquitous in urban areas: you'll find them dotted around the main squares, outside banks and in hotel lobbies. It is now perfectly viable to arrive in the country with a plastic card and a PIN number and pull out złotys wherever you go.

Opening hours and public holidays

Most shops are open on weekdays from approximately 10am to 6pm. Exceptions are grocers and food stores, which may open as early as 6am and close by mid-afternoon – something to watch out for in rural areas in particular. On Saturdays, most shops will have shut by 2 or 3pm, while there's a minority trade on Sunday afternoons.

Street **kiosks**, where you can buy newspapers and municipal transport tickets, are generally open from about 6am to 5pm, although many remain open for several hours longer. Increasing numbers of street traders and makeshift kiosks also do business well into the evening, while you can usually find one or two **food shops** in most towns offering late-night opening throughout the week.

As a rule, **tourist information** offices are open from 9 or 10am until 5pm (later in major cities) during the week; hours are shorter on Saturdays and Sundays.

Tourist sites

Visiting **churches** seldom presents any problems: the ones you're most likely to want to see are open from early morning until mid-evening without interruption. However, a large number of less famous churches are fenced off beyond the entrance porch by a grille or glass window for much of the day; to see them properly, you'll need to turn up around the times for **Mass** – first thing in the morning and between 6 and 8pm. Otherwise it's a case of seeking out the local priest (*ksiądz*) and persuading him to let you in.

Visiting times for **museums** and historic monuments are listed in the text of the Guide. They are almost invariably closed one day per week (usually Mon) and many are closed two days. The rest of the week some open for only about five hours, often closing at 3pm, though 4pm or later is more normal.

Public holidays

The following are **national public holidays**, on which you can expect some shops, restaurants and most sights to be **closed**. It's well worth checking if your visit is going to coincide with one of these to avoid frustrations and disappointments. It's particularly worth noting that because Labour Day and Constitution Day are so close together, most **businesses** (including the majority of banks and shops) give their employees a full four days of holiday.

January 1 New Year's Day
March/April Easter Monday
May 1 Labour Day
May 3 Constitution Day
May/June Corpus Christi
August 15 Feast of the Assumption
November 1 All Saints' Day
November 11 Independence Day
December 25 & 26 Christmas

Phones

Travellers with GSM **mobile phones** will find that almost all of Poland enjoys coverage – apart from the odd remote mountain valley. Local operators like Era, Idea and Simplus sell pre-paid SIM cards and top-up vouchers so you can use the **local network** while

Phone codes

Phoning Poland from abroad
Dial the international access code (given below) + 48 (country code) + area code (minus initial 0) + number.
UK ☎00
Ireland ☎010
US & Canada ☎011
Australia ☎0011
New Zealand ☎00

Phoning abroad from Poland
Dial the country code (given below) + area code (minus initial 0) + number.
UK ☎0044
Ireland ☎00353
US & Canada ☎001
Australia ☎0061
New Zealand ☎0064

you're here. Some mobile phones automatically block if you insert a new SIM card into them, however, so check with your operator before trying this out.

Public payphones are operated by a card (*karta telefoniczna*), bought at post offices and Ruch kiosks, the latter usually marginally more expensive. Cards come in denominations of 25, 50 or 100 units, and cost 10, 18 and 37zł respectively. Trim off the top corner of the card before you insert it into the machine. You can also make long-distance calls from the main post offices in large cities, phoning from a booth with the time monitored and paying the cashier after you've made your call. **Emergency calls** (police ☎997, fire ☎998, ambulance ☎999) are free.

To make a **collect call**, go to a post office, write down the number you want and "*Rozmówa R*" and show it to the clerk. Remember, too, that calls from hotels are usually far more expensive than calls from a payphone.

Polish cultural organizations abroad

All the major English-speaking countries have **Polish cultural organizations** that are worth contacting if you want to learn more about the country or if you have Polish heritage yourself. Some of the more active groups around the globe include the Polish Cultural Institute in London (@www.polishculture .org.uk), the Polish Cultural Institute in New York (@www.polishculture-nyc.org) and the Polish Community of Australia (@www .polish.org.au).

Jewish tourism

Cities such as Warsaw, Łódź and Lublin had particularly large pre-Holocaust Jewish populations, and are increasingly receptive to the needs of organized **heritage tours** and individuals seeking out family roots. Kraków – site of the thriving Jewish suburb of Kazimierz and within visiting distance of **Holocaust memorials** such as Auschwitz-Birkenau – is particularly well organized in this regard. If you find yourself hunting around the back streets of a town in search of Jewish buildings and monuments – a

common experience in the further flung reaches of the country – the basic words and phrases to know when asking for directions are synagogue (*bóżnica* or *synagoga*) and Jewish cemetery (*cmentarz żydowski*). Many of the Polish-Jewish **organizations** listed below can be extremely helpful in providing further information and contacts.

Polish-Jewish organizations

Jewish Communities Federation (Związek Religijny Wyznania Mojzeszowego) ul. Twarda 6, Warsaw ☎ 022/620 4324, @www.jewish.org.pl. Headquarters of religious congregations throughout Poland.
Jewish Historical Institute ul. Tlomackie 3/5, Warsaw ☎ 022/827 9221, @www.jewishinstitute .org.pl. Archives, exhibitions, library and bookshop.
Judaica Cultural Centre ul. Meiselsa 17, Kraków ☎012/430 6449, @www.judaica.pl. Cultural centre in the heart of the Kazimierz district, with a library, reading room, gallery, café and bookshop.
Our Roots ul. Twarda 6, Warsaw ☎022/620 0556, @our-roots.jewish.org.pl. Jewish travel agency that provides general information and local guides, produces guidebooks, and helps with tracing family ancestry in Poland.

Time

Poland is one hour ahead of GMT and six hours ahead of EST. Polish Summer Time lasts from the beginning of April to the end of October.

Toilets

Public toilets (*toalety*, *ubikacja* or WC) can be found at most bus and train stations, and usually cost 1–2zł. The days when you had to buy toilet paper by the sheet are numbered, but there may be a rural toilet somewhere in Poland where it still happens. Gents are marked ▼, ladies ● or ▲.

Tourist information

Poland has a National Tourist Office with branches in a number of European countries and the US (see below for addresses). Within the country, however, tourist information centres of the Western European kind are a relatively new phenomenon, and the level of help you will get from them remains unpredictable.

Most towns and cities now have a **tourist information centre** (often known as *informator turystyczny* or "it") run by the local municipality, offering full hotel listings, accommodation bookings and a range of brochures and maps (which are usually for sale rather than given away free). Sometimes the tourist information centre shares space with a privately run travel agency, and is rather more geared to selling tours and travel tickets than handing out unbiased **information**. Many provincial towns, especially those that see few tourists, have yet to establish tourist information centres of any kind.

In some rural areas tourist information responsibilities are handled by the **PTTK** (ⓦ www.pttk.com.pl) – which translates literally as "The Polish Country Lovers' Association" – an organization responsible for maintaining hiking routes and administering mountain huts, hostels and hotels. PTTK offices can often book basic accommodation and provide a wealth of local advice, although staff might not speak any language other than Polish.

Tourist offices abroad

UK Level 3, Westgate House, West Gate, London W5 1YY ☎ 08700 675 010, ⓦ www.poland .travel/en-gb.
US 5 Marine View Plaza, Hoboken, NJ 07030 ☎ 201/420-9910, ⓦ www.poland.travel/en-us.

Travellers with disabilities

In the past, very little attention was paid to the needs of the **disabled** (*niepełnosprawni*) in Poland. Attitudes are slowly changing – the 1997 Constitution included provision banning discrimination against people with disabilities – but there is still a long way to go and there is not a lot of money available for improvements.

The State Fund for the Rehabilitation of the Disabled, established in 1991, now sponsors a number of programmes designed to make buildings and other public facilities wheelchair-accessible. **Lifts** and **escalators** are gradually becoming more common in public places, although the majority of set-piece museums in Warsaw and Kraków remain difficult to get in and out

Emergencies

Police ☎ 997; Fire ☎ 998; Ambulance ☎ 999.

of. An increasing number of hotels in big cities, especially those of four stars and above, have access and rooms designed for the disabled. The downside is that the majority of these places are expensive, meaning that such provision is still, by and large, a luxury. Outside the cities, traditional spa resorts such as Krynica and Ustroń have a reasonable stock of hotels offering wheelchair-accessible rooms.

Public **transport** remains a major problem. The newer buses in Warsaw and Kraków are equipped with hydraulic platforms to ease wheelchair access, although only a couple of these run on each route and English-language timetable information is difficult to come by. The **Warsaw metro** boasts lifts at each station, although they're badly signed from the surface. Polish Railways claims that seats in each carriage are designated for disabled passengers, but this can't be relied on. Taxi drivers in Eastern Europe in general are also very reluctant to lift passengers to and from their wheelchairs.

For those who can read Polish, the ⓦ www .niepelnosprawni.info website is an invaluable source of news, views and links. Otherwise contact the State Fund for the Rehabilitation of the Disabled (Państwowy Fundusz Rehabilitacji Osób Niepełnosprawnych) ul. Jana Pawła II 13, Warsaw ☎ 022/505 5500, ⓦ www.pfron.org.pl.

Work and study

Despite the booming international business scene in cities like Warsaw, Gdańsk and Poznań, it's extremely unlikely that you'll want to pick up **casual work** in Poland, given that the average monthly wage is still below €700.

The popularity of **learning English** has mushroomed in recent years, leading to a constant demand for native-language English teachers both in the state education system and in the private language schools that seem to have sprung up all over the country. However, you'll probably need a **TEFL certificate** or equivalent in order to secure a job at any but the most fly-by-night organizations. Some of the bigger English-teaching organizations actually organize TEFL courses in Polish cities, and may well help you get a job there once you've qualified. **Vacancies** are sometimes adver-tised in the education supplements of Western newspapers; otherwise it's a question of touting your CV around the language schools and making use of local contacts once you arrive.

Polish **language courses** are run by most universities in Poland, covering all levels from beginners to advanced. Some universities limit themselves to long-term courses lasting a semester or an academic year, while others offer two- or three-week summer courses. A typical two-week course will cost something in the region of €800 for **tuition** and basic accommodation. Information on courses can be obtained from the Polish Cultural Institute in London (see p.56) or Polish consulates abroad.

In addition, many private language schools in Poland are beginning to offer language courses to the growing army of expatriate Westerners keen to learn Polish. A two-week course (without accommodation) will cost around €480.

Useful contacts

Silesia University Katowice ⓦ sjikp us.edu.pl. Summer schools and long-term courses.

Łódź University Łódź ⓦ www.uni.lodz.pl/ulan/ sjpdc.htm. Long-term courses.

Catholic University Lublin ⓦ www.kul.lublin .pl/school/. Summer school.

Marie Curie-Skłodowska University Lublin ⓦ www.cjkp.umcs.lublin.pl. Summer school.

Jagiellonian University Kraków ⓦ www.uj .edu.pl/Polonia/. Long-term courses and summer schools.

Glossa Language School Kraków ⓦ www.glossa .edu.pl. Short or long courses with regular start dates throughout the year.

Mały Rynek Kraków ⓦ www.malyrynek.krakow.pl. A variety of long- and short-term courses.

Prolog Language School Kraków ⓦ www.prolog .ed.pl. Short or long courses with regular start dates throughout the year.

Nicholas Copernicus University Toruń ⓦ www .umk.pl. Long-term courses and summer schools.

IKO Institute of Polish for Foreigners Warsaw. ⓦ www.iko.com.pl. Short courses and tailor-made tuition.

Warsaw

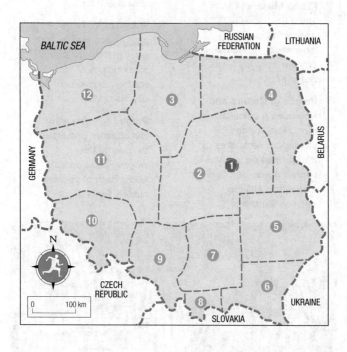

CHAPTER 1 # Highlights

✳ **Warsaw's Old Town** A testament to Poland's postwar efforts to reconstruct itself after World War II, this historic town centre was re-created from almost nothing after being razed by the Nazis. See p.73

✳ **Rising Museum** Learn about the daring but doomed attempt to independently liberate Warsaw from the Nazis. See p.86

✳ **Palace of Culture and Sciences** A colossal monument to the ideological certainties of the Stalinist period, this imposing neo-Baroque monolith is still the defining feature of downtown Warsaw's skyline. See p.92

✳ **Łazienkowski Park** The most elegant of Poland's urban parks, crisscrossed with oak-lined promenades and a favourite with strollers whatever the time of year. See p.95

✳ **Wilanów** Warsaw's grandest palace, tucked away in the almost rural surroundings of the southern outskirts of the city. See p.97

✳ **Praga** Leave the safe tourist zones and cross the river to this working-class district with a dash of counter-culture. See p.99

▲ Royal Palace, Wilanów

Warsaw

WARSAW (**WARSZAWA**) has two enduring points of definition: the Wisła River, running south to north across the Mazovian plains, and the Berlin–Moscow road, stretching across this terrain – and through the city – east to west. Such a location, and four hundred years of capital status, have ensured a history writ large with occupations and uprisings, intrigues and heroism. Warsaw's sufferings, above all the World War II uprising which led to the city's near-total obliteration, have lodged it in the national consciousness, although in the most recent era of political struggle Warsaw was at times overshadowed by events in Gdańsk and the industrial centres of the south. Its role has always been a key one nonetheless, as a focus of popular and intellectual opposition and the site of past and future power, and today, as memories of communist Poland recede into the distance, the city is again pre-eminent economically, politically and culturally.

The extensive renovation and development that has come in tandem with Poland's 2004 accession to the European Union have left Warsaw looking better than at any time in the last sixty years – though all the same no one is likely to confuse it with Prague or Vienna: austere postwar planning left the city awash with concrete, and there's sometimes a hollowness to the faithful reconstructions of what was destroyed in the war. But a knowledge of Warsaw's rich and often tragic history can transform the city in the eye of the beholder, revealing voices from the past in even the plainest quarters: a pockmarked wall becomes a precious prewar relic, a housing estate the one-time centre of Europe's largest ghetto, the whole city a living book of modern history. The pace of social change is tangible and fascinating, and, in the city centre, you'll find a new generation of museums, restaurants and nightspots with genuine style.

Wending its way north towards Gdańsk and the Baltic Sea, the **Wisła** river divides Warsaw neatly in half: the main sights are located on the western bank, while the eastern consists predominantly of residential and industrial districts. Marking the northern end of the city centre, the busy Old Town (**Stare Miasto**) and the quietly atmospheric New Town (**Nowe Miasto**) provide the historic focal point. Rebuilt from scratch after World War II, the districts are home to the most striking examples of the capital's reconstruction.

West of the Old Town, in the **Muranów** and **Mirów** districts, is the former **ghetto** area, where the Nożyk Synagogue and the Jewish cemetery bear poignant testimony to the lost Jewish population. South from the Old Town lies **Śródmieście**, the city's commercial centre, which was rebuilt in a haphazard manner following World War II and has recently seen major investments. Despite a glut of new high-rise constructions, the city skyline is still dominated by the

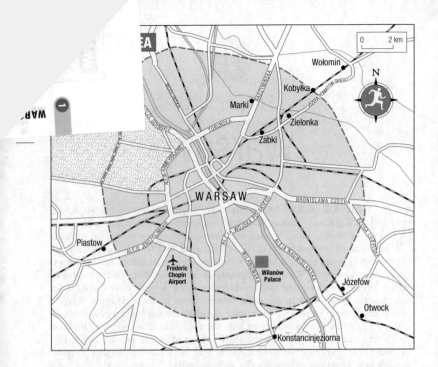

Palace of Culture and Science (Pałac Kultury i Nauki), Stalin's enduring legacy to the citizens of Warsaw. Linking the Old Town and Śródmieście, **Krakowskie Przedmieście** street is dotted with palaces and Baroque spires, and forms the first leg of the **Royal Way** (Trakt Królewski), a procession of open boulevards leading to the stately king's residence at **Wilanów** on the southern outskirts of the city. Along the way is **Park Łazienkowski**, the most delightful of Warsaw's many green spaces, with its charming palace. Further out, the city becomes a welter of high-rise developments, but historic suburbs like **Praga** across the river give an authentic flavour of contemporary Warsaw life.

Warsaw is much livelier and more cosmopolitan than it's often given credit for, and a constantly growing range of inviting bars, restaurants and clubs has appeared to cater for the new consumer classes and the thousands of resident expatriates. If prices are high by Polish standards they still compare favourably to those in Western Europe. If you're arriving without personal connections or contacts, the city can seem forbidding, with much of the place still shutting down within a few hours of darkness, but Varsovians are generous and highly hospitable people. If you strike up a friendship here (and friendships in Warsaw are quickly formed) you'll find much to enrich your experience of the city.

Some history

For a European capital city, Warsaw entered history late. Although there are records of a settlement here from the tenth century, the first references to anything resembling a town at this point on the Wisła date from around the mid-fourteenth century. It owes its initial rise to power to the Mazovian ruler **Janusz**

the Elder, who made Warsaw his main residence in 1413 and developed it as the capital of the Duchy of Mazovia. Following the death of the last Mazovian prince in 1526, Mazovia and its greatly enlarged capital were incorporated into **Polish** royal territory and the city's fortunes improved rapidly. Following the Act of Union with Lithuania, the Sejm – the Polish parliament – voted to transfer to Warsaw in 1569. The first election of a Polish king took place here four years later, and then in 1596 came the crowning glory, when **King Sigismund III** moved his capital two hundred miles from Kraków to its current location – a decision chiefly compelled by the shift in Poland's geographical centre after the union with Lithuania.

Capital status inevitably brought prosperity, but along with new wealth came new perils. The city was badly damaged by the **Swedes** during the invasion of 1655 – the first of several assaults – and was then extensively reconstructed by the **Saxon** kings in the late seventeenth century. The lovely Saxon Gardens (Ogród Saski), in the centre of Warsaw, date from this period. Poles tend to regard the **eighteenth century** as the golden age of Warsaw, when its concert halls, theatres and salons were prominent in European cultural life.

The **Partitions** abruptly terminated this era, as Warsaw was absorbed into Prussia in 1795. Napoleon's arrival in 1806 gave Varsovians brief hopes of liberation, but the collapse of his Moscow campaign spelled the end of those hopes, and, following the 1815 Congress of Vienna, Warsaw was integrated into the Russian-controlled **Congress Kingdom of Poland**. The failure of the **1830 uprising** brought severe reprisals: Warsaw was relegated to the status of "provincial town" and all Polish institutes and places of learning were closed. Its position as the westernmost major city in the Tsar's domain brought commercial prosperity towards the turn of the century, but it was only with the outbreak of **World War I** that Russian control began to crumble, and late in 1914 the **Germans** occupied the city, remaining until the end of the war.

Following the return of Polish independence, Warsaw reverted to its position as capital; but then, with the outbreak of **World War II**, came the progressive annihilation of the city. The Nazi assault in September 1939 was followed by round-ups, executions and deportations – savagery directed above all at the Jewish community, who were crammed into a ghetto area and forced to live on a near-starvation diet. It was the Jews who instigated the first open revolt, the **Ghetto Uprising** of April 1943, which resulted in the wholesale destruction of Warsaw's six-centuries-old Jewish community.

As the war progressed and the wave of German defeats on the Eastern Front provoked a tightening of the Nazi grip on Warsaw, **resistance** stiffened in the city. In August 1944, virtually the whole civilian population participated in the **Warsaw Uprising**, an attempt both to liberate the city and to ensure the emergence of an independent Poland. It failed on both counts. Hitler, infuriated by the resistance, ordered the total elimination of Warsaw and, with the surviving populace driven out of the city, the SS systematically destroyed the remaining buildings. In one of his final speeches to the Reichstag, Hitler was able to claim with satisfaction that Warsaw was now no more than a name on the map of Europe. By the end of the war, 850,000 Varsovians – two-thirds of the city's 1939 population – were dead or missing. Photographs taken immediately after the **liberation** in January 1945 show a scene not unlike Hiroshima: General Eisenhower described Warsaw as the most tragic thing he'd ever seen.

The momentous task of **rebuilding** the city took ten years. Aesthetically the results were mixed, with acres of socialist functionalism spread between the Baroque palaces, but it was a tremendous feat of national reconstruction nonetheless. The recovery that has brought the population up to 1.7 million, exceeding its prewar level, is, however, marred by a silence: that of the exterminated Jewish community.

Arrival and orientation

The wide, open expanse of the Wisła River is the most obvious aid to **orientation**. Almost everything you will want to see lies on the western bank, with the **Old Town** (Stare Miasto) squatting on high ground to the north, and the modern commercial heart of Warsaw, the **Śródmieście** district, stretching out to the south. Linking the two is the grand, two-kilometre-long **Krakowskie Przedmieście** street (which changes name to **Nowy Świat** in its lower reaches), the city's main artery of tourist traffic, which cuts through the centre from north to south. The main points of arrival are all within easy reach of the city centre.

By plane

Frederic Chopin airport (flight information ☎022/650 4220, ⓦwww .lotnisko-chopina.pl; locally still known as Okęcie), handling both international and domestic flights, is 8km southwest of the city. Budget carriers arrive at the Etiuda terminal, a short walk south of the two main terminals. From either, **bus** #175 runs every ten to fifteen minutes and takes you to the old town in about half an hour, passing Warszawa Centralna train station (see below) and Krakowskie Przedmieście on the way. Twice an hour from about 11pm to 5am, night bus #N32 heads from the airport to Warszawa Centralna. Buy your tickets (2.80zł) from the Ruch kiosk inside the terminal building, or from the driver and remember to stamp the ticket in the bus; watch out for **pickpockets** on all buses. Ignore all drivers waiting in the building and only go with the official taxi companies (MPT, Sawa and Merc) to avoid overcharging; the trip to the centre will cost 30 to 40zł, and fifty percent more at night.

By train

Warszawa Centralna, the main train station (information ☎022/9436) is just west of the central shopping area, a ten-minute bus ride (#175; wait opposite the station, in front of the Marriott hotel) or a thirty-minute walk from the Old Town. There are always reliable taxis waiting outside on **ulica Emilii Plater**, east of the station.

A confusing, cacophonous hive serving all international routes and the major national ones, the station is much cleaner than it used to be but is still definitely not a place in which to hang around: keep a close eye on your luggage. To get your bearings, head for the tourist office inside the main ticket hall. Just downstairs from here you'll find **lockers** of varying sizes, where you can store luggage.

Most trains also stop at **Warszawa Wschodnia** (East) station, out in the Praga suburb, or **Warszawa Zachodnia** (West), in the Ochota district – the latter is also the site of the main bus station (see below). Both stations have regular connections to Centralna. **Warszawa Śródmieście** station, just east of Warszawa Centralna, handles local traffic to regional destinations.

By bus

Warsaw's **main bus station** (information ☎022/9433), 3km west of the centre on aleja Jerozolimskie, handles all international services from Western Europe and the Baltic States, as well as those from major domestic destinations in the south and west. Although officially known as Dworzec Centralny PKS, this bus station is usually referred to as **Warszawa Zachodnia** (Warsaw West), because it's housed in the same building as the Warszawa Zachodnia train station (see opposite). From here, a short train ride will take you in to Warszawa Centralna – virtually every eastbound municipal bus will take you there too; #127 continues on to plac Bankowy on the fringes of the Stare Miasto. Some buses from eastern Poland terminate at the **Stadion** station on the east bank of the Wisła; from here a suburban train will take you to Warszawa Centralna. Intercity buses run by private companies like Polski Express drop off on **aleja Jana Pawła II**, next to Warszawa Centralna train station.

Information

Warsaw's municipal **tourist office** (☎022/9431, ⓦwww.warsawtour.pl) operates several **tourist information centres** (Informacja Turystyczna, or IT) in the city, with English-speaking staff who can provide information on accommodation throughout Warsaw, handle hotel bookings, have plenty of brochures to give away and sell maps and guidebooks. There are branches at ul. Krakowskie Przedmieście 36 near the Old Town (daily: May–Sept 9am–8pm; Oct–April 9am–6pm) and at Warszawa Centralna train station (in the main ticket hall) and at the airport's Terminal 2 hall (both open daily: May–Sept 8am–8pm; Oct–April 8am–6pm).

The growing influx of tourists and the large number of expatriates has resulted in a number of English-language publications in the city. Most useful of these is *Warsaw in Your Pocket* (5zł; ⓦwww.inyourpocket.com), a **listings** magazine that's updated every two months and has critical reviews of all the latest bars and restaurants as well as the addresses of all kinds of useful services. It's available at the IT office, from bookshops and many hotels. Less info-packed but with more feature-based content is the booklet-sized monthly *Warsaw Insider* (10zł; ⓦwww .warsawinsider.pl), available from the IT offices and bigger bookshops around town. The weekly **newspaper** *Warsaw Voice* (ⓦwww.warsawvoice.pl) is good on local politics and business news but not so strong on listings. Even if you can't read Polish, it's worth buying the Warsaw edition of the national daily *Gazeta Wyborcza* for news of what's on in town, especially on Fridays, when the *Co jest grane* entertainment supplement covers cinema, concerts and clubs – the listings are fairly straightforward, and you'll just need to translate the days of the week and some film titles. The monthly *Aktivist*, also is Polish a given away in bars and restaurants, is a more youth-oriented source of listings.

Depending on what you want to see and how you want to get around, it might be good idea to invest in a Warsaw Tourist Card (24hrs 35zł, 3 days 65zł; ⓦwww.warsawtour.pl), which gives discounted or free access to several museums (though students with ISIC may get similar deals) and includes public transport; buy the card at the IT offices or from hotels and hostels.

The tourist office gives away an excellent **map** of the central area with sights and hotels marked; good plans of the whole city cost under 10zł and are widely available.

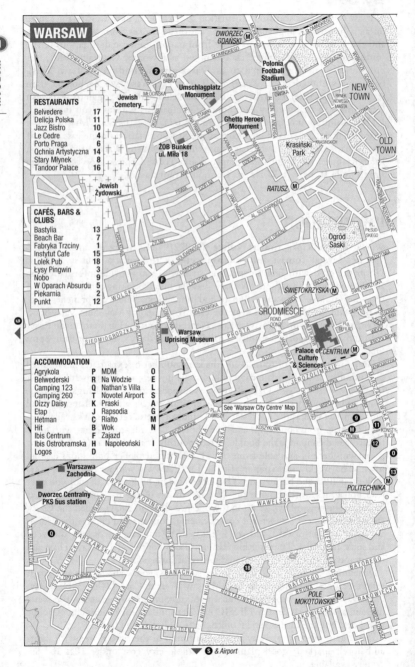

WARSAW

RESTAURANTS

Belvedere	17
Delicja Polska	11
Jazz Bistro	10
Le Cedre	4
Porto Praga	6
Qchnia Artystyczna	14
Stary Młynek	8
Tandoor Palace	16

CAFÉS, BARS & CLUBS

Bastylia	13
Beach Bar	7
Fabryka Trzciny	1
Instytut Cafe	15
Lolek Pub	18
Łysy Pingwin	3
Nobo	9
W Oparach Absurdu	5
Piekarnia	2
Punkt	12

ACCOMMODATION

Agrykola	P	MDM	O
Belwederski	R	Na Wodzie	E
Camping 123	Q	Nathan's Villa	L
Camping 260	T	Novotel Airport	S
Dizzy Daisy	K	Praski	A
Etap	J	Rapsodia	G
Hetman	C	Rialto	M
Hit	B	Wok	N
Ibis Centrum	F	Zajazd	
Ibis Ostrobramska	H	Napoleoński	I
Logos	D		

DWORZEC GDAŃSKI

Polonia Football Stadium

NEW TOWN

OLD TOWN

Jewish Cemetery

Umschlagplatz Monument

Ghetto Heroes Monument

ŻOB Bunker ul. Miła 18

Krasiński Park

Jewish Żydowski

RATUSZ

Ogród Saski

ŚWIĘTOKRZYSKA

SRÓDMIEŚCIE

Warsaw Uprising Museum

Palace of Culture & Sciences CENTRUM

See 'Warsaw City Centre' Map

Warszawa Zachodnia

Dworzec Centralny PKS bus station

POLITECHNIKA

POLE MOKOTOWSKIE

S & Airport

Many drivers, however, do not, and it helps if you write down the name of the street you want and the place you're going to.

Bicycle

Cycling is an efficient and pleasant way to get around a city as big and flat as Warsaw, as long as you avoid the busy boulevards and use the quieter backstreets. An increasing number of hostels offer bicycle rental (*Oki Doki* is one that rents to non-guests). Wygodny Rower (☎888 498 498, ⓦwww.wygodnyrower.pl) at al. Jerozolimskie 49 (opposite the Palace of Culture) and ul. Niowiniarska 10 (near the Old Town; weekends only) rents out new and second-hand bikes, and also does bicycle tours of the city. Costs are around 30zł per day, and you'll need to leave a 200zł deposit and bring ID.

Accommodation

There's an ever-growing number of accommodation options in Warsaw, but the city's newfound importance as a European commercial centre has ensured that many of the new places are aimed squarely at expense-account visitors rather than budget-minded tourists. These **upmarket** establishments are on a par with anything in Western Europe in both price and quality. Although the number – and quality – of hostels has increased dramatically in recent years, the number of good-value places is limited for **low-** and **mid-range** travellers, and booking ahead will pay off.

For those who haven't booked in advance, the IT offices at the airport, train and bus stations (see p.65) can help find hotel and hostel rooms, although they're beset by queues in summer and may not be well informed about the places they're recommending.

There's also a choice of **private accommodation and apartments** in Warsaw, often excellent value for much less than the price of a hotel room. **Camping** in Warsaw's suburbs is a reasonable option if you don't mind being a lengthy public-transport ride away from the centre.

Hotels

Warsaw's **hotel** scene has been through several boom years, with no shortage of new, Western-financed high-rise hotels charging high prices. It's difficult – though not impossible – to find a double room in central Warsaw for anything below the 200zł mark, and most establishments charge considerably more than this, regardless of whether their rooms are up to scratch. Bargains are still to be had: many hotels offer **weekend reductions** of twenty percent or more – be sure to ask when you phone – and shopping around on online booking websites may also get you substantial discounts.

The cheapest options in the **centre** require advance bookings in order to secure a bed – a task made all the more difficult by the fact that reception staff in these places don't always speak English. Otherwise finding a budget place to stay involves settling for something in **Praga**, just east over the Wisła, or the **southern** and **western suburbs**.

The Old Town and around

🏃 **Castle Inn** ul. Świętojańska 2 ☎022/425 0100, ⓦwww.castleinn.pl. Oddly, this is the only hotel in the Old Town, and it's a pleasantly strange place with some extravagantly decorated en suite rooms, with themes including pop art, oriental and trees. ⑥

Harenda Krakowskie Przedmieście 4/6 ☎022/826 0071, ⓦwww.hotelharenda.com. pl. International-standard rooms furnished in a pleasing, beige colour-scheme. Friendly staff and a great location. At weekends your second night is free, and guests in the suites get a free rental car. ❼

Ibis Stare Miasto ul. Muranowska 2 ☎022/310 1000, ⓦwww.ibishotel.com. The most central of the three Ibis hotels, 500m northwest of the Stare Miasto, offers quality, if anonymous, modern rooms and facilities at a decent price (breakfast 29zł extra); big reductions on weekends. Bus #175 from the train station. ❺

Le Meridien Bristol Krakowskie Przedmieście 42/44 ☎022/551 1000, ⓦwww.lemeridien.com. The legendary prewar *Bristol* has been completely modernized and is right in the centre – this is also the finest Art Nouveau building in the city. The rooms have more character than those in the modern high-rise hotels, and are tasteful and superbly comfortable. ❾

Le Regina ul. Kościelna 12 ☎022/531 6000, ⓦwww.leregina.com. Boutique hotel in a restored eighteenth-century palace in the New Town, with individually designed rooms, crisp service and a lovely courtyard. ❾

Mazowiecki ul. Mazowiecka 10 ☎022/827 2365, ⓦwww.mazowiecki.com.pl. Mid-range hotel on a quiet side street in the centre. A dozen of the adequately comfortable rooms are en suite, a larger number have shared bathrooms. ❺–❻

Metalowcy ul. Długa 29 ☎022/831 4021, ⓦwww .federacja-metalowcy.org.pl. Spartan and shabby but more or less clean former workers' hostel, with en-suite and shared-facility rooms, mainly monoglot staff and a brilliant location just a few steps west of the Old Town. For availability and reservations, click on *Pokoje* on the website for the English booking form. ❹

Sofitel Victoria ul. Królewska 11 ☎022/657 8011, ⓦwww.orbisonline.pl. International-class business hotel on pl. Piłsudskiego, in a sleek block that has been furnished to meet contemporary standards. Quite comfortable, with spacious, attractive rooms and good views of the Ogród Saski. Just a few minutes' walk from the Old Town. ❼

Śródmieście

Campanile ul. Towarowa 2 ☎022/582 7200, ⓦwww.campanile.com.pl. Similar to but more expensive than the attached *Premiere Classe* (see opposite), but still excellent value. Rooms at the *Campanile* have a/c and are slightly larger and better furnished. The third hotel at the same address, the

Kyriad Prestige (☎022/582 7500; ❼), is a fairly good, but not especially interesting, luxury option. ❻

Etap ul. Zagórna 1 ☎022/625 4400, ⓦwww .orbisonline.pl. A basic chain hotel with simple but adequately furnished rooms and a good location just east of Śródmieście by the river. ❺

Gromada pl. Powstanców Warszawy 2 ☎022/582 9900, ⓦwww.gromada.pl. Comfortable mid-range hotel with pretty standard rooms in a large modern building; fair value, though, if you're looking for something central and not too pricey. ❻–❼

Hilton ul. Grzybowska 63 ☎022/356 5555 ⓦwww.hilton.com. Warsaw's most luxurious hotel, in a new skyscraper in the business district. Rooms are as good as you'd expect, and many – especially the suites – have stunning views. ❽–❾

Ibis Centrum al. Solidarności 165 ☎022/520 3000, ⓦwww.ibishotel.com. Warsaw's second Ibis hotel, though not as central as the name would indicate, has the same trustworthy standards as the other branches. Located three trams stops west of the Old Town. From Warszawa Centralna take trams #22 or #24 to Okopowa. ❺

Intercontinental ul. Emili Plater 49 ☎022/328 8888, ⓦwww.intercontinental.com. The most imposing of the high-rise five-stars has deluxe rooms that meet all expectations; the best aspect is the 43rd floor swimming pool, offering marvellous views as you splash around. ❽–❾

Logos Wybrzeże Kościuszkowskie 31/33 ☎022/625 5185, ⓦwww.hotellogos.pl. By the river, downhill from the centre. Basic place with small but modern rooms, both en suites and rooms with clean, shared facilities. Take any tram from the train station east, and get off at the fourth stop, on the bridge. ❺–❻

Marriott al. Jerozolimskie 65/79 ☎022/630 6306, ⓦwww.marriott.com/wawpl. This looming glass landmark, right opposite Warszawa Centralna station in the heart of the business district, was the first skyscraper hotel in town. Blandly luxurious rooms, many with outstanding views of the Palace of Culture. ❼–❾

MDM Pl. Konstytucji 1 ☎022/339 1600, ⓦwww .hotelmdm.com.pl. Pleasant and quiet rooms overlooking the socialist-realist expanse of pl. Konstytucji – the next best thing to staying in the Palace of Culture. Popular with tour groups but not especially good value for independent travellers. Students, however, can stay for half-price at weekends. ❻–❽

Mercure Grand ul. Krucza 28 ☎022/583 2100, ⓦwww.orbisonline.pl. Startlingly pretty concrete 1950s hotel that's been completely overhauled inside and now has sparkling modern rooms.

Within walking distance of the train station and handy for the Śródmieście shopping and nightlife options. ❼–❽

Na Wodzie Wybrzeże Kościuszkowskie ☎022/628 5883, ⓦwww.hostel-warsaw.pl. A central "boatel" with small but clean cabins with shared facilities, and the option to fish from the nice café on the deck. Moored just north of Poniatowski bridge; same directions as for the *Logos* hotel (see above). Closed Nov–April. ❸

Premiere Classe ul. Towarowa 2 ☎022/624 0800, ⓦwww.premiereclasse.com.pl. The cheapest of three high-quality hotels (the others are *Campanile* and *Kyriad*) in the same building on pl. Zawiszy, two tram stops west of the train station; the small but pleasant en-suite doubles here are the best bargain in town. ❺

Rialto ul. Wilcza 73 ☎022/584 8700, ⓦwww.rialto.pl. A delightful boutique hotel in Art Deco style, in a pleasant corner of Śródmieście. Rooms are large and luxurious, many with a unique theme, and furnished with antiques, right down to the original 1920s light switches. ❾

Sheraton ul. Prusa 2 ☎022/450 6100, ⓦwww.sheraton.pl. The best located of the Western chain hotels, on the east side of the attractive and fashionable pl. Trzech Krzyży. Standards are impeccable, and there are good restaurants and bars on site. ❼–❾

Praga and the other suburbs

Belwederski ul. Sulkiewicza 11 ☎022/840 4011, ⓦwww.hotelbelwederski.pl. Boxy mid-range hotel right by the southern reaches of Park Łazienkowski. Rooms are clean and well lit, but drab, and the beds are rather small. Buses #131 from Centrum and #180 from Nowy Świat pass right by. ❻

Hetman ul. Kłopotowskiego 36 ☎022/511 9800, ⓦwww.hotelhetman.pl. Friendly, modern place down a quiet side street in the Praga quarter, with attractive, very well-furnished cream-coloured rooms. Tram #26 from Warszawa Centralna to Ząbkowska or any tram two stops east from below the Old Town. ❼

Hit ul. Kłopotowskiego 33 ☎022/618 9470, ⓦwww.hithotel.pl. Directly opposite the *Hetman* in Praga, this excellent new budget hotel has simple, spacious rooms; the apartments have kitchens, jacuzzis and washing machines. ❺–❻

Ibis Ostrobramska al. Ostrobramska 36 ☎022/515 7800, ⓦwww.ibishotel.com. Rooms and service identical to the other *Ibis* hotels but cheaper because it's in the far fringes of the Praga district. From Warszawa Centralna trams #24 or #44 to the last stop. ❹

Novotel Airport ul. 1 Sierpnia 1 ☎022/575 6000, ⓦwww.orbisonline.pl. Smart, modern, business-oriented place with a swimming pool, 6km southwest of the centre, and 1km short of the airport. Bus #175 stops right by it. ❼

Praski al. Solidarności 61 ☎022/201 6300, ⓦwww.praski.pl. Decent two-star hotel in the Praga district, only one tram stop from the heart of the Old Town. Pleasantly situated opposite the Praski park, with a great Lebanese restaurant next door (see p.104). Rooms are fairly comfortable, and good value for the price and location. Shared and en-suite facilities. Tram #4 from Centrum. ❺–❻

Zajazd Napoleoński ul. Płowiecka 83 ☎022/815 3068, ⓦwww.napoleon.waw.pl. 8km east of the centre, a small luxury inn dating from the sixteenth century and reputedly visited by Napoleon on his way to Moscow. Genuinely elegant, understated rooms with furnishings of a superior quality, and a good restaurant. Bus #525 from Warszawa Centralna. ❼

Hostels

Warsaw has a decent choice of central **hostels**, many of them offering cheap double rooms with shared facilities, and it's no longer necessary to endure the old-fashioned state hostels with their lockouts and curfews – though it's still a good idea to book, especially in summer. Free internet access (PCs and/or wi-fi) is standard in most hostels; breakfast is usually charged extra (10–15zł).

Agrykola ul. Myśliwiecka 9 ☎022/622 9110, ⓦwww.agrykola-noclegi.pl. Bright, modern rooms in a youth athletic facility. Just east of Łazienkowski park; bus #151 from the station to the "Rozbrat" stop before the bridge. Dorms 25–56zł; rooms ❺

Dizzy Daisy ul. Górnośląska 14 ☎022/205 0042, ⓦwww.dizzydaisy.pl. Clean and friendly summer hostel in a student residence north of Łazienkowski park. Take bus #171 from Centrum to the Śniegockiej stop, or call (before 10pm) for a free pick-up. Open early July to late Aug.

Two- and three-bed dorms (50–60zł) and en suites ❸.

Helvetia ul. Kopernika 36/40 (entrance on ul. Sewerynów) ☎022/826 7108, ⓦwww .hostel-helvetia.pl. Dead central yet in a quiet street, this nicely furnished hostel has plenty of showers, a women's dorm and a separate apartment. Bus #175 to the Uniwersytet stop. Rooms with bath ❺ and without ❹; dorms 45–70zł.

Kanonia ul. Jezuicka 2 ☎022/635 0676, ⓦwww .kanonia.pl. The only hostel in the Old Town, in a charming reconstructed building, with small private and dorm rooms, but loads of atmosphere. Doubles ❺, dorms 50–60zł.

Nathan's Villa ul. Piękna 24/26 ☎022/622 2946, ⓦwww.nathansvilla.com. Excellent hostel with perks like a nice garden and free breakfast and laundry service, but it's away from the centre and there's no bar. Off Marszałkowska, two tram stops south of Centrum. A few doubles ❺; dorms 45–65zł.

Oki Doki pl. Dąbrowskiego 3 ☎022/826 5112, ⓦwww.okidoki.pl. Warsaw's best hostel, with its individually designed rooms, is on the top floors of an office building, halfway between the train station (10min walk) and the Old Town. There's a female dorm, a café/bar, bike rental and well-informed staff. Rooms with bath ❺ and without ❹; dorms 42–75zł.

Dom Przy Rynku Rynek Nowego Miasta 4 ☎022/831 5033, ⓦwww.cityhostel.net. The best of the summer hostels, in a school residence right on the New Town Square, with friendly and helpful staff. July–Aug only. Bus #175 to the Francisz-kanska stop. No curfew; lockout 11am–4pm. Two doubles ❸; otherwise dorms 55zł.

Tamka ul. Tamka 30 ☎022/826 3095, ⓦwww .tamkahostel.com. A lively hostel in a great location just downhill from the city centre and near a clutch of bars, albeit with cramped dorms and traffic noise. Bus #102 to the Topiel stop or #175 to Ordynacka (weekends: Nowy Świat). A few doubles ❺, dorms 50–55zł.

Apartments, private rooms and B&Bs

Well-furnished, inexpensive apartments in the Old Town and other good locations are available via Old Town Apartments, at Rynek Starego Miasta 12/14 (☎022/**351 2260**, ⓦwww.warsawshotel.com), starting at around 250zł for up to four people which is very good value, especially if you're travelling in a small group. **Private rooms** as well as apartments can be booked via the Syrena travel agency at ul. Krucza 17, a fifteen-minute walk east from Warszawa Centralna (☎022/629 4978, ⓦwww .kwatery-prywatne.pl). Single (❶) and double (❷) rooms with host families have shared bathrooms.

The excellent ⚜Boutique Bed & Breakfast at ul. Smolna 14/7 (☎022/829 48, ⓦwww.bedandbreakfast.pl), has impeccably furnished apartments and en-suite rooms (❻–❼), with a communal dining room and office for guests. There's also a very central **gay**-run guesthouse, *Friends* (☎601 243 444, ⓦwww.gay .pl/friendswarsaw), with three comfortable rooms (❺) on ul. Sienkiewicza that come with complementary mobile phone rental.

Campsites

Even in Warsaw, **camping** is extremely cheap and popular with Poles and foreigners alike. On the whole, facilities are reasonable and several offer bungalows. In all cases expect small extra charges for linen and parking.

Camping 123 ul. Bitwy Warszawskiej 1920, nr 15/17 ☎022/823 3748, ⓦwww.astur.waw.pl. Closest campsite to the centre, about 600m south of the Warszawa Zachodnia bus and train station, with some bungalows (❷). May–Sept.

Camping 260 ul. Inspektowa 1 ☎022/842 2768, ⓦwww.camping260.pl. Camping in the middle of a sports complex, with clean but very basic facilities. May–Sept.

Rapsodia ul. Fort Wola 22. ☎022/634 4165, ⓦwww.rapsodia.com.pl. Campsite with simple but decent amenities and some bungalows (❷); popular with Polish families.

Wok ul. Odrębna 16 ☎022/612 7951, ⓦwww .campingwok.warszawa.pl. Small family camping with sites and cabins (❶) between the trees, 10km southeast of the city.

The Old Town

The term **Old Town** (Stare Miasto) is in some respects a misnomer for the historic nucleus of Warsaw. Sixty years ago, this compact network of streets and alleyways lay in rubble – even the cobblestones are replacements. Yet surveying the tiered houses of the main square, for example, it's hard to believe they've been here only decades. Some older residents even claim that the restored version is in some respects an improvement, perhaps because the postwar builders worked from Baroque-era drawings by Bellotto, nephew of Canaletto, rather than prewar photographs showing nineteenth- and early twentieth-century alterations. Today, although the streets of the Stare Miasto are thronged with tourists, Varsovians themselves can be in short supply here; with the shift of Warsaw's centre of gravity south to Śródmieście, the small streets and market square of the Stare Miasto are now more historical cul-de-sac than heart of the modern city.

Castle Square (Pl. Zamkowy), on the south side of the Old Town, is the obvious place to start a tour. Here the first thing to catch your eye is the bronze **statue of Sigismund III**, the king who made Warsaw his capital. Installed on his column in 1640, Sigismund suffered a direct hit from a tank in September 1944, but has now been replaced on his lookout; the base is a popular and convenient rendezvous point.

The Royal Castle

On the east side of the square is the **Royal Castle** (Zamek Królewski), once home of the royal family and seat of the Polish parliament, much of which is now occupied by a **museum** with two separate sections (May–Sept Mon 11am–6pm, Tues–Sat 10am–6pm, Sun 11am–6pm, June–Aug Mon 11am–4pm; Oct–April Tues–Sat 10am–4pm, Sun 11am–4pm; ⓦ www.zamek-krolewski .pl). What you can see in the castle is divided into two separate "routes" with

▲ Warsaw Old Town

WARSAW CITY CENTRE

ACCOMMODATION

Boutique Bed & Breakfast	R
Campanile	X
Castle Inn	F
Dom Przy Rynku	C
Friends	P
Gromada	Q
Harenda	J
Helvetia	K
Hilton	O
Ibis Stare Miastro	A
Intercontinental	S
Kanonia	E
Kyriad Prestige	Z
Le Meridien Bristol	H
Le Regina	B
Marriott	T
Mazowiecki	M
Mercure Grand	U
Metalowcy	G
Oki Doki	N
Old Town Apartments (booking office)	D
Premiere Classe	Y
Sheraton	V
Sofitel Victoria	I
Syrena (booking office)	W
Tamka	L

RESTAURANTS

Bar Mleczny Pod Barbakan	4
Biblioteka	17
Bierhalle	29
Browarmia	21
Chianti	42
Chlopskie Jadlo	15
Co Tu	46
Concept	J
Freta 33	1
Gar	P
Green Way	44
Jazz Bistro Gwiazdeczka	10
Kom	33
Le Jardin Foksal	36
Marak	31
Na Prowincji	6
Namaste India	8
Nowa La Boheme	14

(Map of Warsaw City Centre showing the following labelled locations:)

Polonia Football Stadium · Trauguta Park · Church of the Virgin Mary · Marie Skłodowska Curie Museum · NEW TOWN · Asian Gallery · St Jacek's Church · Barbakan · Historical Museum · Union of Warsaw Insurgents Museum · Little Insurgent Statue · Mickiewicz Museum · Jesuit Church · St John's Cathedral · OLD TOWN · Royal Castle · Garrison Church · Uprising Monument · Krasiński Palace · Borchtów Palace · Paca-Radziwiłłów Palace · Archeological Museum · Krasiński Park · Ghetto Heroes Monument · Pawiak Prison Museum · Capuchin Church · St Martin's Church · Warsaw Heroes Monument · St Anne's Church · Carmelite Church · Namiestnikowski Palace · Church of the Nuns of the Visitation · Mickiewicz Monument · Jabłoński Palace · Muzeum Żydowskiego Instytutu Historycznego (Jewish Historical Institute) · Blue Palace · Franciscan Church · Grand Theatre · John Paul II Museum · River Wisła · Park Praski

0 — 300 m

N

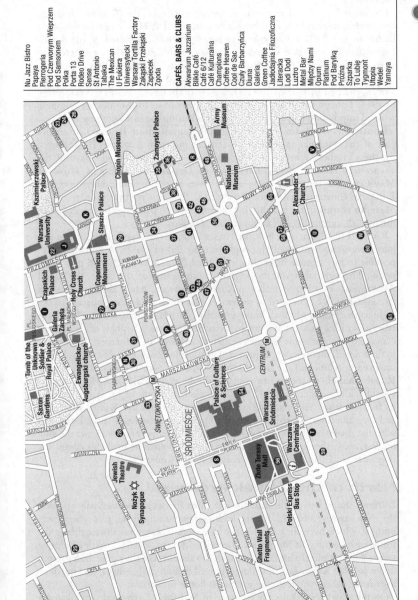

Nu Jazz Bistro	58
Papaya	39
Pierrogeria	5
Pod Czerwonym Wieprzem	32
Pod Samsonem	3
Polka	11
Porta 13	49
Rodeo Drive	41
Sense	50
St Antonio	18
Tabaka	30
The Mexican	38
U Fukiera	9
Uniwersytecki	22
Warsaw Tortilla Factory	61
Zakąski Przekąski	20
Zapiecek	53
Zgoda	47

CAFÉS, BARS & CLUBS

Akwarium Jazzarium	56
Blikle Café	37
Café 6/12	57
Café Kulturalna	54
Champions	59
Coffee Heaven	34
Cool de Sac	35
Czuły Barbarzyńca	26
Diuna	24
Galeria	25
Green Coffee	52
Jadłodajnia Filozoficzna	23
Literacka	12
Lodi Dodi	60
Luztro	48
Metal Bar	7
Między Nami	51
Opium	16
Platinum	19
Pod Barylką	13
Próżna	28
Szparka	55
To Lubię	2
Tygmont	27
Utopia	40
Wedel	43
Yamaya	45

different ticket prices; admission is free on Sundays in May and September and on Mondays from June to August, when there's one route past the highlights of the castle.

Dynamited by German troops in the aftermath of the Warsaw Uprising, the seventeenth-century castle stood in ruins until 1971, when reconstruction began. In July 1974 a huge crowd gathered to witness the clock of the domed Sigismund Tower being started up again – the hands set exactly where they were stopped by the first Luftwaffe attack. A crucial symbol of independent nationhood, the project was funded by personal donations from home and abroad, and hundreds of volunteers helped with the labour, which was completed in 1984. Though the structure is a replica, many of its furnishings are originals, scooted into hiding by percipient employees during the first bombing raids.

Route I (14zł) takes you through the **Jagiellonian Rooms**, originally part of the residence of eighteenth-century monarch Augustus III, followed by the chambers where the Sejm (parliament) used to meet. Beyond the chancellery comes the **Old Chamber of Deputies**; the famous **Third of May Constitution**, passed here in 1791, was one of the radical highpoints of European constitutional history (see p.615). The first route culminates in the **Matejko rooms** in the north wing, crammed with paintings by the doyen of nineteenth-century Polish painters, Jan Matejko.

Route II (22zł) can only be visited in the company of an official guide, so you may have to wait for enough people (usually 25) to gather. Alternatively, it's possible to hire a guide in English (call ahead ☏022/355 5170; 95zł plus ticket price). This part takes you to the most lavish section of the castle, the **Royal Apartments** of King Stanisław August Poniatowski. Amid all the pomp and circumstance, it can be hard to remember that this is all a reconstruction of the eighteenth-century original. You eventually come to the magnificent **Canaletto Room**, with its views of Warsaw by Bernardo Bellotto, a nephew of the famous Canaletto – whose name he appropriated to enhance his reputation. Marvellous in their detail, these cityscapes provided invaluable information for the architects involved in rebuilding the city after the war. Next door is the richly decorated **Royal Chapel**, where an urn contains the heart of Tadeusz Kościuszko, the swashbuckling leader of the 1794 insurrection, and hero of the American War of Independence (see box, p.82). After walking through the **King's Bedroom** and the sumptuous **Marble Room**, the highlight of the castle is the **Ballroom** with the *Apotheosis of the Genius of Poland* ceiling allegory. Napoleon met the elite of Warsaw society here in 1806, the occasion on which he made his comments (legendary in Poland) about the beauty of Polish women.

North of the Zamek Królewski

Souvenir shops, bars and restaurants line **ulica Piwna** and **ulica Świętojańska**, the two narrow cobbled streets leading northwards from plac Zamkowy, both of which have churches worthy of a stopoff. On ulica Piwna there's the fourteenth-century **St Martin's Church** (Kościół św. Martina), with a Baroque facade and completely modern interior. You should take the opportunity to nip down to **plac Kanonia** at this point (lodged behind ul. Jezuitska, just north of the castle), where you'll see the narrowest house in Warsaw.

On ulica Świętojańska is the entrance to **St John's Cathedral** (Archikatedra św. Jana), the main city church, an early fourteenth-century structure built in the Mazovian Gothic style. Some of the most bitter fighting of the 1944 Warsaw Uprising took place around here. German tanks entered the church after destroying its southern side, and you can see sections of their caterpillar tracks built into the wall along **ulica Dziekania**. Next to the cathedral is the **Jesuit Church** (Kościół Jezuitski), a popular shrine dedicated to Our Lady of Charity, the city's patron saint. Its high belfry is the tallest in the Stare Miasto area, standing out for miles around.

Old Town Square and around

The compact **Old Town Square**, **Rynek Starego Miasta**, is one of the most remarkable bits of postwar reconstruction anywhere in Europe. Flattened during the Warsaw Uprising, the three-storey merchants' houses surrounding the square have been scrupulously rebuilt to their seventeenth- and eighteenth-century designs, multicoloured facades included. By day the buzzing Rynek teems with visitors, who are catered for by buskers, artists, cafés, moneychangers and *doroski*, horse-drawn carts that clatter tourists around for a sizeable fee. Plumb in the centre is a gurgling fountain with a statue of the Warsaw mermaid (Syrena), the city's symbol.

The **Warsaw Historical Museum** (Muzeum Historyczne Starej Warszawy; Tues & Thurs 11am–6pm, Wed & Fri 10am–6pm, Sat & Sun 10.30am–4.30pm; 6zł, free on Sun; ⓦwww.mhw.pl) takes up a large part of the north side of the square; entrance is through a house called the Pod Murzynkiem ("Under the Negro"), a reference to the inn sign that used to hang above the doorway. Exhibitions here cover every aspect of Warsaw's life from its beginnings to the present day, crammed tightly into a warren of rooms on three floors. There's an evocative display of old photographs, theatre posters and fashion magazines, and a particularly moving chronicle of everyday resistance to the Nazis – an uplifting complement to the wartime horrors documented in the film shown in the cinema at the entrance (English version plays Tues–Sat at noon; 6zł).

On the square's east side, the **Mickiewicz Museum** (Muzeum Mickiewicza; Mon, Tues & Fri 10am–3pm, Wed & Thurs 11am–6pm, Sun 11am–5pm, closed one varying Sun every month; 6zł; ⓦwww.muzeumliteratury.pl) is a temple to the national Romantic poet, with a stack of first editions, contemporary newspapers, and family memorabilia, as well as temporary exhibitions devoted to other Polish authors.

The west side of the square features a number of fine reconstructed residences, notably the Fukier House (Dom Fukiera) and the Klucznikowska mansion at no. 21, which has a reconstructed Gothic doorway.

West of the square, the narrow cobbled streets and alleyways bring you out to a long section of the old **city walls**, split-level fortifications with ramparts, rebuilt watchtowers and apple trees lining their grassy approaches. Along Podwale, the open path surrounding the walls and a favourite with evening strollers, an array of plaques commemorates foreigners who supported the Polish cause. Here, as in many places around the city, the fresh flowers laid on the ground mark places where the Nazis carried out wartime executions. The most poignant of the memorials, however, is the **Little Insurgent** (Mały Powstaniec), a bronze figure of a small boy with an oversized helmet carrying an automatic rifle – a solitary figure commemorating the children and young people killed fighting in the Warsaw Uprising (see box, p.82). The most impressive part of the old fortifications is the sixteenth-century **Barbakan,** which formerly guarded the Nowomiejska Gate, the northern entrance to the city. In summer, the Barbakan attracts street artists, buskers and hawkers of kitsch souvenirs. Walk east along the walls to the Marshal's Tower, and you have a good view over the river to the Praga district.

Adam Mickiewicz (1789–1855)

If one person can be said to personify the Polish literary Romantic tradition it is **Adam Mickiewicz**. A passionate, mystically inclined writer, Mickiewicz's unabashedly patriotic writings have served as a central literary (and, in times of crisis, political) reference point for generations of Poles. Quotations from and references to Mickiewicz's considerable volume of writings litter subsequent Polish literature and politics – even the avowedly unacademic Lech Wałęsa has been known to quote the national epic poem, *Pan Tadeusz* – and performances of his plays are still among the most popular in the country. More controversially, there's a muted discussion of the man's "ethnic" origins, with several scholars now claiming that at least one of Mickiewicz's parents was Jewish, a view that might go some way, it is argued, to accounting for the sympathetic portrayal of Jews – notably the musical innkeeper, Jankiel – in a work like *Pan Tadeusz*. Despite the fact that the best of Mickiewicz's writings rank among the finest outpourings of Romanticism, he's still relatively unknown in the West, a situation not helped by the general lack of decent, readily available translations of his works.

Born in Lithuania of an impoverished Polish *szlachta* (gentry) family, Mickiewicz studied at Vilnius University where, like many of his generation, he was drawn into conspiratorial anti-Russian plotting. Already a budding writer (*Poezje*, his first collection of ballads and romances based on Lithuanian folklore, appeared in 1822), Mickiewicz was arrested along with fellow members of a secret student organization on suspicion of "spreading Polish nationalism" and was deported to Russia in 1823, where he remained, mostly in Moscow, for the rest of the decade, befriending – and sometimes quarrelling with – Russian writers such as Pushkin. Notable works of this period include *Dziady* ("Forefather's Eve"), the innovative patriotic drama whose Warsaw performance in spring 1968 sparked student protests, and *Konrad Wallenrod*, an epic poem depicting the medieval struggle between Teutonic Knights and Lithuanians, in reality an allegory of the age-old Polish–German conflict.

Following the failure of the **November 1830 uprising**, Mickiewicz moved in exile to Paris, like many Polish intellectuals, and quickly immersed himself in émigré politics. It was here too that he wrote *Pan Tadeusz* (1834), his greatest work. Modelled on the novels of Walter Scott, it is a masterful, richly lyrical depiction of traditional gentry life in his native Polish–Lithuanian homeland, a region dear to many Polish writers – Miłosz and Konwicki are two contemporary examples – both for its outstanding natural beauty and powerful historical associations.

The remaining years of Mickiewicz's life read like a litany of personal and political disappointments. Appointed to a professorship in Lausanne in 1839, he resigned the following year to teach Slavonic literature at the Collège de France. With the outbreak of the **1848 revolutions** in central Europe, the "Springtime of the Nations" that briefly appeared to herald a new dawn for the oppressed nations of the region, Mickiewicz travelled to Rome to try to persuade the new pope, Pius IX, to come out in support of the cause of Polish independence. Later the impassioned Mickiewicz also organized a small Polish military unit to fight with Garibaldi's forces – the nucleus, he hoped, of a future Polish national liberation army – and assumed editorship of the radical agitprop newspaper *Tribune des Peuples* ("Tribune of the Peoples"), a move which led to dismissal from his tenure at the Collège de France by Napoleon III.

The writer's life came abruptly to an end in 1855 when Prince Adam Czartoryski, a leader of the Paris exile community, sent Mickiewicz on a mission to Turkey to try to resolve the factional quarrels bedevilling the Polish military forces that had volunteered to fight against Russia in the approaching Crimean War; having contracted typhus soon after his arrival, Mickiewicz died in November 1855 in Istanbul, and is commemorated in a museum there. He was already a national hero of almost mythic proportions, and his remains were eventually brought back to Poland and placed in the crypt of Kraków's cathedral on Wawel Hill.

The New Town

Across the ramparts from the Barbakan is the **New Town** (Nowe Miasto) district, which, despite its name, dates from the early fifteenth century, although it wasn't formally joined to Warsaw until the end of the eighteenth. At that time, the wooden buildings of the artisan settlement were replaced by brick houses, and it's in this style that the area has been rebuilt.

Along ulica Freta to the New Town Square

From the Barbakan, **ulica Freta** runs north through the heart of the New Town. On the right is **St Jacek's Church** (Kościół św. Jacka), a Dominican foundation, which is an effective blend of Renaissance and early Baroque. The adjoining monastery, the largest in Warsaw, was a field hospital and was heavily bombed as a consequence; hundreds died here when the Nazis regained control in October 1944. Today there's a pleasant café in the church bell tower, while the **Asian Gallery**, across the street at no. 5 (Galeria Aziatycka: Tues–Sun noon–6pm; 5zł; Ⓦ www.muzeumazji .pl) holds changing exhibitions of Asian and Pacific art. For a time, the German Romantic writer E.T.A. Hoffmann lived at ul. Freta no. 5, and no. 16 was the birthplace of one of Poland's most famous women, **Marie Skłodowska-Curie**, the double Nobel Prize-winning discoverer of radium (see box, p.80). Inside there's a small, interesting **museum** (Tues–Sat 10am–4pm, Sun 10am–3pm; 8zł) dedicated to her life and work, where photographs of her with other scientists are reminders of the male preserve she managed to break into.

Ulica Freta leads to the **New Town Square** (Rynek Nowego Miasta) – once the commercial hub of the district. Surrounded by elegantly reconstructed eighteenth-century facades, this pleasant square makes a soothing change from the bustle of the Old Town. Tucked into the eastern corner is the **Church of the Holy Sacrament** (Kościół Sakramente), commissioned by Queen Maria Sobieska in memory of her husband Jan's victory over the Turks at Vienna in 1683 (see p.614); the highlight of the calm, white interior is the Sobieski funeral chapel. Photographs of the church in its ruined postwar state hang in a side chapel.

Just off the northern edge of the square, the early fifteenth-century **Church of the Virgin Mary** (Kościół Mariacki or NMP), one of the oldest churches in Warsaw and once the New Town parish church, has retained something of its Gothic character despite later remodellings. Staggered rows of benches outside provide a wonderful viewing point across the river.

Plac Krasińskich

The streets west of the square lead past ulica Bonifraterska toward the Muranów district (see p.81). Heading south on ulica Bonifraterska brings you to **plac Krasińskich**, augmented by one of Warsaw's several **Uprising monuments**, this one a controversial piece commissioned by the communist authorities. Now dwarfed by the green National Court building, the monument was built on the spot where AK (Home Army) battalions launched their assault on the Nazis on August 1, 1944. The large metal sculpture depicts AK insurgents surfacing from manholes on to the street to begin their attack on the Germans, as well as their final forlorn retreat into the sewers of the city. Just beyond the monument, on the corner of ulica Długa, is the **Union of Warsaw Insurgents Museum** (Mon–Thurs 10am–4pm; free), a one-room display arranged by surviving combatants from the Uprising, with black-and-white photos and a scale model of the main battleground.

Marie Curie (1867–1934)

One of many Poles to rise to fame abroad rather than at home, the Nobel Prize-winning scientist Marie Curie (née Maria Skłodowska) was born during the Partition era into a scientifically oriented Warsaw family. The young Maria showed academic promise from the start, and after completing her secondary education at the city's Russian lyceum, Curie travelled to Paris in early 1890 to follow the lectures of the prominent French physicists of the day at the Sorbonne.

The intellectually voracious Curie threw herself into the Parisian scientific milieu, landing a job in the laboratory of the noted physicist Gabriel Lipmann and meeting fellow researcher Pierre Curie, whom she married in 1895. Thus began a partnership that was to result in a number of spectacular scientific achievements, first the discovery of polonium – so named in honour of her native country – in summer 1898, and soon afterwards, radium. Following her colleague Henri Becquerel's discovery of the phenomenon she eventually dubbed "radioactivity", Curie set to work on systematic research into the revolutionary new wonder, which eventually gained worldwide recognition in the Nobel Prize for Physics which she, Pierre Curie and Becquerel were awarded jointly in 1903. Pierre's sudden death in 1906 was a heavy emotional blow, but led to Curie's appointment to his professorship, making her the first woman ever to teach at the Sorbonne. A second Nobel Prize, this time in chemistry, came in 1911 for the isolation of pure radium.

Despite the upheavals of World War I, with the assistance of one of her two daughters Curie worked on developing the use of X-rays and was a prime mover in the founding of the famous Institut de Radium in 1918, which rapidly developed into a worldwide centre for chemistry and nuclear physics. By now known internationally, and deeply committed to developing the medical applications of the new radiological science, Curie and her daughters visited the US in 1921, receiving a symbolic gram of prized radium from the president, Warren G. Harding, in the course of the visit. During the rest of the 1920s Curie travelled and lectured widely, founding her own Curie Foundation in Paris and eventually realizing a long-standing ambition, the setting up of a Radium Institute in her native Warsaw in 1932, to which her sister Bronia was appointed director. Constant exposure to radiation began to have its effect, however, and in early 1934 it was discovered that Curie had leukaemia, of which she died later that year. The scientific community in particular mourned the loss of one of its outstanding figures, a woman whose research into the effects of radioactivity pioneered both its medical and research-oriented applications, simultaneously paving the way for subsequent developments in nuclear physics.

Immediately opposite the monument is the **Garrison Church** (Kościół Garnizonowy), the soldiers' main place of worship, with the key Uprising symbol, a large anchor, and a tablet on the facade with a roll call of World War II battles in which Polish units participated. Overlooking the west side of the square is the majestic **Krasiński Palace** (Pałac Krasińskich), built for regional governor Jan Krasiński, its facade bearing fine sculptures by Andreas Schlüter. As a branch of the National Library, most of the palace's documents – forty thousand in all – were destroyed in the war, so today's collection comes from a whole host of sources. Theoretically, the building is only open to official visitors, but enquiries at the door should get you in to see the splendid Neoclassical library. Behind the palace are **gardens**, now a public park, and beyond that the ghetto area.

Ulica Długa and around

Back on plac Krasińskich, at the corner of **ulica Długa** and ulica Miodowa, is a small streetside **plaque**, one of the least conspicuous yet most poignant memorials in the city. It commemorates the thousands of half-starved Varsovians who attempted to escape from the besieged Old Town through the sewer network during the Warsaw Uprising. Many drowned in the filthy passageways, were killed by grenades thrown into the tunnels, or were shot upon emerging, but a hundred or so did make it to freedom.

A number of old patrician residences can be seen west along ulica Długa, which leads to the **Archeological Museum** (Muzeum Archeologiczne: Mon–Thurs 9am–4pm, Fri 11am–6pm, Sun 10am–4pm; 8zł, Sun free; ⓦwww.pma.pl), housed in the seventeenth-century arsenal. Starting with Neolithic, Paleolithic and Bronze Age sites, the museum continues through to early medieval Polish settlements, the highlight being a reconstruction of the early Slav settlements in Wielkopolska and records of other excavations from around the country, notably the Jacwingian cemetery site at Jegleniec near Suwałki (see p.228).

Ulica Miodowa and around

South from plac Krasińskich, along **ulica Miodowa**, you find yourself in the heart of aristocratic old Warsaw. The palaces lining Miodowa date mainly from the prosperous pre-Partition era, when this section of the city hummed with the life of European high society. Next door to the **Borchów Palace** (Pałac Borchów) – now the residence of the Catholic Primate – stands the **Radziwiłłów Palace** (Pałac Radziwiłłów), adjoined by the later **Paca Palace** (Pałac Paca), with its distinctive frieze-topped entrance. Across the street is the Basilan church and monastery, the city's only Greek Catholic (Uniate) church, designed with an octagonal interior in the 1780s. A few steps down ulica Miodowa to the southwest is the late seventeenth-century **Capuchin Church**, (Kościół Kapucyński) repository of the heart of Jan Sobieski.

Muranów and Mirów

Like Lublin, Białystok and Kraków, Warsaw was for centuries one of the great Jewish centres of Poland. In 1939 there were an estimated 380,000 Jews living here, one-third of the city's total population. By May 1945, only around three hundred were left. Most of **Jewish** Warsaw was destroyed after the Ghetto Uprising (see box, p.85), to be replaced by the sprawling housing estates and tree-lined avenues of the **Muranów** and **Mirów** districts, a little to the west of the city centre. However, a few traces of the Jewish presence in Warsaw do remain, along with a growing number of monuments to the notable personalities of the city's historic Jewish community. Just as importantly, there's a small but increasingly visible Jewish community here – well supported by its exiled diaspora. Today, Mirów is also the home to the new **Warsaw Uprising Museum**.

Virtually all the Jewish monuments and memorials you will find here are enclosed within the confines of the wartime ghetto area, sealed off from the city's "Aryan" population by the Nazis in November 1940. Warsaw Jews actually lived in a considerably larger part of the city before World War II. Following the wholesale obliteration of the area both during and after the 1943 Ghetto Uprising, streets like ulica Grzybowska, the centre of Jewish life in Isaac Bashevis Singer's panoramic Warsaw novel *The Family Moskat* (see "Books", p.640), lack even the slightest resemblance to their former selves. Other streets changed their name or course, or simply disappeared altogether after the war, making it difficult to gain an impression of what the ghetto area looked like.

The 1944 Warsaw Uprising

Of the many acts of resistance to the savage Nazi occupation of Poland, the 1944 Warsaw Uprising was the biggest. Over 65 years on, the heroic, yet ultimately tragic, events of the autumn of 1944 remain firmly lodged in the national memory, at once a piece of history whose interpretation remains controversial, and a potent source of national self-definition.

The immediate circumstances of the Uprising were dramatic. With Nazi forces reeling under the impact of the determined push west launched by the Red Army in mid-1944, a German withdrawal from Warsaw began to seem a possibility. The **Polish Home Army** (Armia Krajowa) or AK as they were commonly known, the largest of the Polish resistance forces (indeed, with more than 400,000 soldiers, the largest resistance force anywhere in Europe) were thereby confronted by an agonizing dilemma. On one side, they were being strongly urged by the Allies to cooperate actively with advancing Soviet forces in driving back the Nazis. On the other, news of the treatment being meted out to AK units in areas of eastern Poland already liberated by the Red Army served to confirm the long-held suspicion that there was little, if any, room for the AK or its political backing – the Polish government-in-exile in London – in the Soviet scheme of things to come, a fact chillingly symbolized in news of the Soviet detention of AK units in the ex-Nazi concentration camp at Majdanek.

Throughout the second half of July, AK Commander **Tadeusz Komorowski**, known as Bór, hesitated over which course of action to take. With the arrival of the first Soviet tanks across the Wisła in the Praga district, the decision to launch a single-handed attack on the Germans was taken and, on August 1, the main Warsaw AK corps of around fifty thousand poorly armed troops sprang an assault on the city centre. For the first few days the element of surprise meant AK forces were able to capture large tracts of the city centre. By August 5, however, the tide was already beginning to turn against them. Supported by dive bombers and hastily drafted reinforcements, Nazi troops under the command of ruthless General von dem Bach-Zelewski began the task of clearing out the insurgents. Partisans and civilians alike were treated as legitimate targets for reprisals by the fearsome collection of SS and Wehrmacht units – including three battalions of half-starved Soviet POWs, an "anti-partisan" brigade made up of pardoned criminals and the notorious RONA Red Army deserters brigade – assembled for the task. The Nazi recapture of the Wola district, the first to be retaken on August 11, was followed by the massacre of more than eight thousand civilians. Even worse followed in Ochota, where more than forty thousand more civilians were murdered. Hospitals were burned to the ground with all their staff and patients; during the initial attack, women and children were tied to the front of German tanks to deter ambushes, and rows of civilians were marched in front of infantry units to ward off AK snipers.

With German troops and tanks systematically driving the beleaguered partisans into an ever diminishing pocket of the city centre, the decision was made to abandon the by now devastated Stare Miasto. On September 2, around 1500 of the surviving AK troops, along with more than five hundred other wounded, headed down into the city sewers through a single manhole near plac Krasiński – an event imprinted firmly on the national consciousness as much thanks to Wajda's legendary film *Kanał*, a stirring 1950s rendition of the Uprising, as to its symbolic depiction in the contemporary Warsaw Uprising monument. Fighting continued for another month in the suburbs

The Nożyk Synagogue and the ghetto wall

First stop on any itinerary of Jewish Warsaw is the **Nożyk Synagogue**, a stately ochre structure hidden behind a white office block at ul. Twarda 6, the only one of the ghetto's three synagogues still standing. The majestic Great Synagogue on ulica Tłomackie – which held up to three thousand people – was blown up by the Nazis and is now the site of a skyscraper.

and pockets of the city centre until October 2, when General Bór and his troops finally surrendered to the Germans, 63 days after fighting had begun. Heavy AK casualties – around twenty thousand dead – were overshadowed by the huge losses sustained by the city's civilian population, with more than 225,000 killed during the fighting.

With the AK and eventually almost the entire population of Warsaw out of the way, Nazi demolition squads set about the task of fulfilling an enraged Hitler's order to wipe the city off the map, dynamiting and razing building after building until the city centre had to all intents and purposes ceased to exist, as confirmed in the photos taken when the Soviets arrived in January 1945.

Of the many controversial aspects of the Uprising, the most explosive, in Polish eyes at least, remains that of the **Soviet role**. Could the Red Army have intervened decisively to assist or save the Uprising from defeat? Throughout the postwar years, the official Soviet line combined the arguable claim that the Uprising was a mistimed and strategically flawed diversion from the goal of driving the Germans west in 1944 with absurd ideological denigrations of the AK as reactionary, anti-Soviet nationalists whose actions were a betrayal of the anti-Nazi cause. Certainly the lack of Soviet action during August 1944 was fertile ground for subsequent Polish misgivings about Stalin's real intentions. The Soviet tanks that had reached Praga, for example, sat idly by throughout September 1944 as the Germans pounded the city across the river. Equally significantly, on several occasions the Soviet authorities refused Allied access to Soviet airbases for airlifts of supplies to the beleaguered insurgents, and the secret telegram correspondence between Stalin, Roosevelt and Churchill at the time reveals a Stalin contemptuous of the whole operation, arguing on one occasion that sooner or later "the truth about the handful of criminals who started the Warsaw disturbance to take over power will become known to all".

The essence of the Polish interpretation of all this was that Stalin had simply allowed the Germans to do what his future plans for Poland would have anyway necessitated – systematically to annihilate those sections of Polish society that formed the core of the AK forces, with their uncompromising commitment to a free, independent postwar Poland. With sentiments like these around, it's not surprising that the Warsaw Uprising has remained a controversial subject in the context of Polish–Russian relations.

Tensions surfaced visibly during the solemn **fiftieth anniversary commemorations** of the start of the Uprising, held in the city throughout August 1994. In a move widely criticized in Poland, particularly among older sections of Polish society, President Wałęsa invited his Russian and German counterparts to participate at the opening ceremony held in Warsaw on August 1. While the German President Roman Herzog accepted the invitation and made a speech asking Polish forgiveness for the country's treatment at the hands of the Nazis, Russian President Boris Yeltsin declined the invitation, sending a lower-level aide instead, giving rise to the wry popular quip that the Russians had accepted the invitation but decided to stay in Praga instead. The **sixtieth anniversary** in 2004 was celebrated with less controversy but even more avidity, and saw the release of the new history of the Uprising by Norman Davies (see "Books", p.634) and the opening of the new Uprising Museum (see p.85).

The Nożyk, a more modest affair built in the early 1900s, was used as a stable, a food store and then gutted during the war, reopening in 1983 after a complete restoration. To see the refined interior you have to ring the buzzer on the opposite side of the building from the main door (Mon–Fri 11am–7pm; 6zł; ⓦwww .warszawa.jewish.org.pl). The **Jewish Theatre**, just east of the synagogue on plac Grzybowski, continues the theatrical and musical traditions of the ghetto.

Before you leave the area, walk across plac Grzybowski to **ulica Próżna**. This street has somehow survived the ravages of war and reconstruction, and is the only place where you can get an idea of the old ghetto area. It stands scaffolded but surviving as a testimony to prewar Warsaw.

Ten minutes' walk south of the synagogue at the southern edge of the wartime ghetto area are two of the few surviving fragments of the three-metre-high wartime **ghetto wall**, wedged between ul. Sienna 55 and ul. Złota 62 (to reach it enter the courtyard from ul. Złota 62; if the gate is locked ring the buzzer of apartment #24 or #38 and say you're a tourist). The two short sections of brick wall stand as a poignant testimony to the rude separation of the ghetto – so close, and yet so far from life (and death) on the other side. The isolation was never absolute – post and phone communication with the "Aryan" sector continued long into the Nazi occupation, and food was continually smuggled into the starving ghetto, despite the threat of instant execution for anyone, Pole or Jew, caught doing so. In the first section a small commemorative plaque records former Israeli president Chaim Herzog's official unveiling of the monument in 1992, along with a map showing you just how much of Warsaw the ghetto covered. At the second section, another plaque records the removal of two bricks from the wall to the Holocaust Museum in Washington, DC.

The Jewish Historical Institute and Pawiak Prison

The **Jewish Historical Institute** (Żydowski Instytut Historyczny) , near the site of the former Great Synagogue at ul. Tłomackie 3/5, stands on the site of the prewar Judaic Library ten minutes' walk north of the Nozyk Synagogue, and is part museum (Mon–Wed & Fri 9am–4pm, Thurs 11am–6pm; 10zł; ⓦ www.jhi .pl), part library and research archive. The first section of the museum details life in the wartime ghetto, a fascinating and moving corrective to the familiar images of passive victims; the rest is devoted to ritual objects, folk art and secular paintings. The library includes a large collection of books rescued from Lublin at the outset of World War II, and documents of Jewish life in Poland going back to the seventeenth century, along with an extensive collection of more than thirty thousand photos.

The sobering **Pawiak Prison Museum** (Muzeum Pawiaka: Wed 9am–5pm, Thurs & Sat 9am–4pm, Fri 10am–5pm, Sun 10am–4pm; free), ten minutes' walk west at ul. Dzielna 24/26, tells the grim story of Warsaw's most notorious prison from tsarist times to the Nazi occupation.

Plac Bohaterów Getta and the Path of Remembrance

A few minutes' walk north is the **Ghetto Heroes Monument** (Pomnik Bohaterów Getta), actually built from blocks ordered from Sweden by Hitler in 1942 to construct a monument to the Third Reich's anticipated victory. Unveiled in 1948 on the fifth anniversary of the Ghetto Uprising, the stark monument recalls both the immense courage of the Jewish resistance, and the helplessness of the deportees, to moving effect. Once at the heart of the ghetto area, the plac Bohaterów Getta itself is a wide-open green expanse surrounded by drab apartment buildings, with only the occasional rubble-filled bump disturbing the surface to remind you of the ghetto that used to be there. The new **Museum of the History of Polish Jews** (ⓦ www.jewishmuseum.org.pl) is scheduled to open on this square in 2011.

84

The decline of communism enabled local Jewish groups to commemorate their history actively in a way that had been officially discouraged before, and, beginning in the late 1980s, a series of memorial plaques known as the **Path of Remembrance** was laid out, starting from plac Bohaterów Getta, then north along ulica Zamenhofa and up to the Umschlagplatz on ulica Stawki. The plaques, nineteen simple granite blocks engraved in Polish and Hebrew, honour important individuals and events of the ghetto. Along the way the route takes you past the grass-covered memorial mound covering the site of the **ŻOB Bunker** at ul. Miła 18 (see box below) – the mound's height representing the level of rubble left after the area's destruction. In many of the surrounding streets you'll find houses built on a similar level, as the postwar communist authorities simply went ahead and constructed new housing blocks on the flattened remains of the ghetto.

A short walk north on the edge of a housing estate is the **Umschlagplatz**, where Jews were loaded onto cattle wagons bound for Treblinka and the other death camps. The simple white marble monument standing here, raised in the late 1980s and designed to resemble the cattle trucks used in the transportations, is covered inside with a list of four hundred Jewish first names, the method chosen to symbolize the estimated 300,000 Jews deported from here to the death

The Warsaw Ghetto and the Ghetto Uprising

In 1940, on the order of Ludwig Fisher, the governor of the Warsaw district, 450,000 Jews from Warsaw and the surrounding area were sealed behind the walls of the Nazi-designated ghetto area, creating the largest **ghetto** in Nazi-occupied Europe. By 1941, nearly one and a half million Jews from all over Poland had been crammed into this unsanitary zone, with starvation and epidemics the predictable and intended consequence. By mid-1942, nearly a quarter of the ghetto population had died, a plight communicated to the Allied command by a series of searingly forthright reports from the budding Polish underground.

Deportations to the death camps from Umschlagplatz began in summer 1942, with 250,000 or more taken to Treblinka by mid-September. After further mass round-ups, the Nazis moved in to "clean out" the ghetto in January 1943, by which time there were only sixty thousand people left. Sporadic resistance forced them to retreat, but only until April, when a full-scale Nazi assault provoked the **Ghetto Uprising** under the leadership of the Jewish Combat Organization (ŻOB). For nearly a month, Jewish partisans battled against overwhelming Nazi firepower, before the ŻOB's bunker headquarters, on the corner of ulica Miła and ulica Zamenhofa, was finally surrounded and breached on May 9, following the suicide of the legendary Mordechai Anieliewicz and his entire ŻOB staff. A few combatants survived and escaped to join up with the Polish resistance in the "Aryan" sector of the city, as did the musician Władysław Szpilman, subject of Roman Polański's Oscar-winning movie The Pianist. Of those remaining in the ghetto, seven thousand were shot immediately, the rest dispatched to the camps. On May 15, Jürgen Stroop, commander-in-chief of the German forces, reported to Himmler, "The Jewish quarter in Warsaw no longer exists."

The Ghetto Uprising has remained a potent symbol both of the plight of Jews under Nazi tyranny and – contrary to the dominant received images – of the absolute will to resist under conditions of systematic terror manifested by a small but significant minority of the Jewish community. The dual nature of the Uprising's legacy was amply attested to in the fiftieth anniversary commemorations held in Warsaw in May 1993, attended by a broad assembly of Jewish and Gentile dignitaries from around the world and a handful of survivors of the Uprising, notably Marek Edelman, the only ŻOB commander still alive today.

camps. A stone stands at the exact point from which the trains departed, while across the road, one of the few surviving prewar buildings (no. 5/7) was the house of the SS commander supervising operations at the Umschlagplatz.

The Jewish Cemetery and the Korczak orphanage

West along ulica Stawki and down ulica Okopowa (about fifteen minutes' walk in all, or take tram #22 west from Warszawa Centralna, or bus #175 north along Krakowskie Przedmieście), the large **Jewish Cemetery** (**Cmentarz Żydowski**: Mon–Thurs 10am–5pm, Fri 9am–1pm, Sun 9am–4pm; 4zł; ⓦwww.beisolam .jewish.org.pl; men should cover their heads – skullcaps are provided) established in 1806, contains the graves of more than 250,000 people, and is one of the very few Jewish cemeteries still in use in Poland today. This site was left almost untouched during the war, due to the fact that, unlike in smaller Polish towns, the Nazis didn't need the materials for building new roads. The tombs range from colossal Gothic follies to simple engraved stones.

Scattered among the plots are the graves of eminent Polish Jews including **Ludwig Zamenhof**, the inventor of Esperanto (see p.236), early socialist activist **Stanisław Mendelson**, and writer **D.H. Nomberg**. Also worth seeking out is a powerful sculpted monument to Janusz Korczak (see p.639), erected in his honour in the 1980s. The caretaker at the entrance lodge has detailed guidebooks to the tombstones for anyone wanting to know more (information is also available from the Jewish Historical Institute and the Our Roots offices; see box, p.56).

The Warsaw Rising Museum

In the southern reaches of Mirów, a century-old former tramway power station has been converted into the **Warsaw Rising Museum** (Wed & Fri-Mon 10am–6pm, Thurs 10am–8pm; 4zł; ⓦwww.1944.pl). Coming from the train station, take tram #12, #22 or #24 west to "Grzybowska". An Uprising museum, for decades a political impossibility due to the negative role that the Soviet Union played, had been in planning stages since 1981, but only opened for the sixtieth anniversary of the Uprising in August 2004.

The centrepiece of the collection is a series of **photographs** by former PE teacher, Olympic javelin thrower and Polish officer **Eugeniusz Lokajski**, who after being taken prisoner in 1939 by the Soviet army escaped to Nazi-occupied Warsaw and opened a photography studio. He remained in the city throughout the occupation, commanded a platoon in the Uprising and died in a house on Marszałkowska in September 1944, leaving a legacy of more than one thousand photos depicting everyday life both before and during the Uprising. Other exhibits focus on the role – or lack of one – played by Soviet and Allied forces at the time, while there's also a reconstruction of part of the sewer system through which combatants fled the destroyed city. Outside is a park with a 156-metre wall inscribed with the names of several thousand soldiers who died in the struggle.

Śródmieście

Śródmieście, the large area that stretches from the Old Town down towards Łazienkowski Park, is the increasingly fast-paced heart of Warsaw. However, in keeping with the Polish spirit of reverence for the past, the sector immediately below the Old Town contains an impressive number of reconstructed palaces, parks, churches and museums, all contributing to the distinctive atmosphere of faded grandeur spruced up. The broad boulevard known as **Krakowskie Przedmieście** (which becomes **Nowy Świat** in its southerly reaches) is the main artery of the Śródmieście, a popular promenading route lined with cafés, boutiques and private galleries. To the west, the brash shopfronts, office blocks and fast-food stands around **ulica Marszałkowska** are overshadowed by the looming form of the **Palace of Culture and Sciences**, an architectural monument to Stalinist megalomania. Further west still, around the Warszawa Centralna train station, a growing collection of **skyscrapers** epitomizes the changing face of Warsaw city life. The broad expanse of **aleja Jerozolimskie**, a chaotic strip of trams and traffic, cuts a wide swath through the centre of this area, running west to east just below the Palace of Culture and providing access to the impressive collections of the **National Museum**.

Plac Teatralny and around

Running west from plac Zamkowy is ulica Senatorska, once one of Warsaw's smartest shopping streets, now studded with wall plaques recording the civilian victims of Nazi street executions. The pseudo-classical giant dominating the nearby **plac Teatralny** is the **Grand Theatre** (Teatr Wielki), Warsaw's main venue for drama, opera and ballet. Dating from the 1820s, it boasts a fine classicist facade decorated with Greek sculptures. Rebuilt and enlarged after wartime destruction, the main theatre now holds almost two thousand people. Inside, the elegant entrance hall has a sumptuous rotunda overhead and an intricate parquet floor – worth a look even if you're not planning to attend one of the lavish productions staged here (see p.108).

On the north side of plac Teatralny, Citibank hides its business concerns behind the facade of the Neoclassical **Jabłońskich Palace** (Pałac Jabłońskich), the city hall from 1817 until World War II. The building was torn down after being damaged in the war; what you see today was built from scratch in 1997.

The redoubtable sword-waving goddess who once rose from the stone plinth on the other side of the square, Nike, otherwise known as the **Warsaw Heroes Monument** (Pomnik Bohaterów Warszawy), a state tribute to the war dead, has been moved a few blocks north and now stands directing traffic on the highway under the Old Town – walk down Nowy Przejazd from plac Teatralny and she's on the right. At the west end of plac Teatralny, just north along ulica Bielańska stands the ruins of the **Bank of Poland**. Originally built as the Russian Imperial Bank in 1911, the building was used as a fortress by Polish soldiers during the 1944 Uprising and then bombed by the Nazis, one of the only such buildings in the city centre that was neither restored nor demolished. Continuing west along Senatorska, the **Baroque Franciscan Church** (Kościół Franciszkański) – a quiet place with restful cloisters – is followed by the **Blue Palace** (Pałac Błękitny), where Chopin gave one of his earliest concerts at the age of six. Tragically, the palace's destruction in 1944 engulfed the fabulous Zamoyski library of more than 250,000 books and manuscripts.

Plac Bankowy

Senatorska ends at **plac Bankowy**, formerly plac Dzierżyńskiego; the giant statue of its former namesake Felix Dzierżyński, the unloved Polish Bolshevik and founder of the NKVD, was removed in 1990 to public rejoicing, and his place has been taken by the Romantic poet **Juliusz Słowacki**. On the northeast corner of the square is a tower known locally as the Blue Skyscraper, or **Błękitny Wieżowiec**, that's long been a talking point: built on the site of the Great Synagogue (see p.82) – and cursed, according to local legend, as a consequence – from its inception in the early 1970s it took over twenty years to complete this lumbering Yugoslav-financed giant of a project. The west edge of the busy square is taken up by a palatial early nineteenth-century complex originally housing government offices. This grand building has been the seat of the city's administrative authorities since the destruction of the original town hall in 1944.

The John Paul II Museum

On the southwest corner of Plac Bankowy is the old **National Bank** building, long the official Museum of the Workers' Movement but now taken over by the **John Paul II Museum** (Muzeum Kolekcji im. Jana Pawła II: Tues–Sun May–Sept 10am–5pm, Oct–April 10am–4pm; 12zł; ⓦwww.muzeummalarstwa.pl), entered from ulica Elektoralna. It comprises a large art collection assembled by the wealthy émigré Carroll-Porczyński family in the early 1980s and donated to the Polish Catholic church a few years later. The museum has proved controversial: sections of the academic world are dubious about the authenticity of some works, the galleries are musty and poorly lit, and the whole collection is a hit-and-miss affair. Ask for a sheet with English explanations to the exhibits at the entrance.

Highlights include **Impressionist** works like the early and typically brooding *Farm in Hoogeveen* by Van Gogh, and *Still Life with Cauliflower* by Renoir. The Rotunda, a large, domed auditorium once occupied by the Warsaw Bourse and now doubling as a concert recital hall is hung with more than eighty **portraits** including some by Velázquez, Rembrandt, Titian and Tintoretto (or, more often, their workshops). Upstairs, beyond the **Still Life and Landscape** hallway and the **Mother and Child** room, the **Gerson** room features a monumental *Baptism of Lithuania* painted in 1889 by nineteenth-century Polish artist Wojciech Gerson, in which Władysław Jagiełło leads the Lithuanian knights to the cross while a crowd of awestruck peasants look on.

Plac Piłsudskiego, the Saxon Gardens and around

Returning to plac Teatralny, the way south leads onto an even larger square, **plac Piłsudskiego**. This was the site of Warsaw's largest Russian Orthodox church in the time of the Partitions, a beautiful building, but one seen as a symbol of oppression and torn down once Poland regained independence in the 1920s. Following the imposition of martial law in the 1980s, a huge flower cross was laid here by Varsovians in protest. After the authorities had cleared the cross away, the whole area was closed off for public works for years, presumably to prevent embarrassing demonstrations happening in full view of the tourists staying in the adjacent hotels. The north end of the square is the site of Sir Norman Foster's love-it-or-hate-it **Metropolitan Building**.

The focus of the square used to be the massive colonnaded **Royal Palace** (Pałac Saski), built by August II; this was blown up by the Nazis in 1944. The prewar Tomb of the Unknown Soldier, beneath the few remaining palace arches, has an eternal flame, military guard and, chiselled into the pillars the names of all battlegrounds that saw Poles in action. In 2007, work started on the rebuilding of the palace, a huge project that will take a few years to complete.

Beyond the tomb stretch the handsome and well-used promenades of the **Saxon Gardens** (Ogród Saski), laid out for August II by Tylman van Gameren in the early 1700s and landscaped as a public garden in the following century. Some elements of the original park survived, notably the scattering of Baroque sculptures symbolizing the Virtues, Sciences and Elements, an elegant nineteenth-century fountain pool above the main pathway, the old **water tower** (Warsaw's first) built by Marconi in the 1850s and the park's fine crop of **trees**, more than a hundred species in all.

Immediately south of the gardens on plac Małachowskiego, to the west of the plush *Victoria* hotel, is the **Galeria Zachęta** (Tues–Sun noon–8pm; 10zł, Thurs free; ⓦwww.zacheta.art.pl), built at the turn of the twentieth century as the headquarters of the Warsaw Fine Arts Society, and one of the few large buildings in central Warsaw left standing at the end of World War II. The stucco decoration in the entrance gives a taste of the building's original qualities. The gallery's considerable original art collection (Matejko's *Battle of Grunwald* included) was packed off into hiding in the National Museum (see p.93) at the start of the war, subsequently forming part of that museum's permanent collection. The Zachęta is now a leading contemporary art gallery, hosting a wealth of high-quality exhibitions by international artists.

Krakowskie Przedmieście

Of all the long thoroughfares bisecting central Warsaw from north to south, the most important is the one often known as the **Royal Way** (Trakt Królewski), which runs almost uninterrupted from plac Zamkowy to the palace of Wilanów. **Krakowskie Przedmieście**, the first part of the Royal Way, is lined with historic buildings and was recently renovated, giving more space to pedestrians. **St Anne's Church** (Kościół św. Anny), directly below plac Zamkowy, is where Polish princes used to swear homage to the king; founded in 1454, the church was destroyed in 1656 by the besieging Swedes, then rebuilt in Baroque style in the following century. By 1983, the second year of martial law, resourceful oppositionists had assembled a new flower cross on this courtyard after the authorities removed the huge one from plac Piłsudskiego (see opposite). For good views of the Old Town and river, you can climb the **belfry** on the northern side of the courtyard (May–Sept daily 10am–5pm; 5zł).

Behind the belfry a pedestrian path leads through a sloping park to the quiet district of **Mariensztat**. An important market area before World War II, the quarter was redesigned in the 1950s as a neo-Baroque housing project, and the interceding decades have given its streets something close to an eighteenth-century feel; Rynek Mariensztacki square is a pleasant place for a drink on a terrace.

South of St Anne's the street broadens to incorporate a small green. The **Mickiewicz Monument** (Pomnik Mickiewicza: see box, p.78) stuck in the middle of it is one of many you'll see if you travel round the country. It was unveiled on the centenary of the poet's birth in 1889, before a twelve-thousand-strong crowd, despite a ban on rallies and speeches.

Just south of the statue stands the seventeenth-century **Carmelite Church** (Kościół Karmelitów) whose finely wrought facade, capped by a distinctive globe, is one of the first examples of genuine classicism in Poland. Next door is the **Namiestnikowski Palace** (Pałac Namiestnikowski), a Neoclassical pile dating from 1819, built on the site of the seventeenth-century palace where the Constitution of 3 May 1791 was passed. The present building was witness to the signing of the Warsaw Pact in 1955, at the height of the Cold War, and 34 years later, in spring 1989, it hosted the "Round Table" talks between the country's communist authorities and the Solidarity-led opposition. In 1995 the palace became the official presidential residence, following Lech Wałęsa's decision to move here from the Belvedere (see p.96). In front of the large courtyard is a statue of another favourite son, Józef Poniatowski (see p.616).

Back on Krakowskie Przedmieście, two grand old hotels face each other a little further down the street: the **Bristol** and the **Europejski**, Warsaw's oldest hotel, undergoing renovations at time of writing. Begun in the 1850s, the *Europejski* was badly hit in World War II, and the current restoration should bring all the *fin de siècle* grandeur back to life. After years out of action, the *Bristol*, a neo-Renaissance pile that was one of Europe's top hotels when completed in 1901, is now part of the *Meridien* chain. Originally owned by musician-premier Ignacy Paderewski, and a legendary prewar journalist's hangout, the building somehow survived World War II but was then neglected by the authorities, leading to its present sorry state. The spectacled figure in the park opposite the hotel is **Bolesław Prus**, author of the nineteenth-century Warsaw saga *The Doll* (see p.639), whose works covered extensively the social life of the *fin de siècle* period.

Even in a city not lacking in Baroque churches, the triple-naved **Nuns of the Visitation** (Kościół Sióstr Wizytek) stands out, with its columned, statue-topped facade; it's also one of the very few buildings in central Warsaw to have come through World War II unscathed. The most curious feature of the richly decorated interior is a boat-shaped pulpit dating from the nineteenth century. The church's main claim to fame is that Chopin used to play the church organ here, mainly during services for schoolchildren.

The university

Most of the rest of Krakowskie Przedmieście is taken up by Warsaw's **university**. Established in 1818, it was closed by the tsar in 1832 as part of the punishment for the 1831 Insurrection, and remained closed till 1915. During the Nazi occupation, educational activity of any sort was made a capital offence, and thousands of academics and students were murdered. However, clandestine university courses continued throughout the war – a tradition revived in the 1970s with the "Flying University", when opposition figures travelled around the city giving open lectures on politically controversial issues. On the main campus courtyard, the old **library** stands in front of the seventeenth-century **Kazimierzowski Palace** (Pałac Kazimierzowski), once a royal summer residence and now home to the rector and associated bureaucrats.

Across the street from the university gates is the **Czapskich Palace** (Pałac Czapskich), which now houses the Academy of Fine Arts. Just south is the twin-towered **Baroque Holy Cross Church** (Kościół św. Krzyża), which was ruined by a two-week battle inside the building during the Warsaw Uprising. Photographs of the distinctive stone figure of Christ left standing among the ruins became poignant emblems of Warsaw's suffering and now hang in the first chapel to the right of the altar. The church is also known for containing **Chopin's heart** – it's in an urn standing within a column on the left side of the nave.

Biggest among Warsaw's consistently large palaces is the early nineteenth-century **Staszica Palace** (Pałac Staszica), which virtually blocks the end of Krakowskie Przedmieście. Once a Russian boys' grammar school, it's now the headquarters of the Polish Academy of Sciences. In front of the palace is the august **Copernicus Monument** (Pomnik Mikołaja Kopernika), showing the great astronomer holding his revolutionary heliocentric model.

Ulica Marszałkowska, the Palace of Culture and around

The area below the Saxon Gardens and west of Krakowskie Przedmieście is the city's busiest commercial zone. **Ulica Marszałkowska**, the main road running south from the western tip of the gardens, is lined with department stores and clothes shops while just east, smaller streets like ulica **Zgoda** and the pedestrianized

▲ The Palace of Culture

ulica Chmielna are good for shopping, despite recent competition from the large new malls outside the city centre.

North of ulica Świętokrzyska, on ulica Kreditowa, the eighteenth-century **Lutheran church** (Kościół Ewangelicko-Augsburski) is topped with Warsaw's largest dome. The building's excellent acoustics have long made it popular with musicians – Chopin played a concert here at the age of fourteen, and the church still holds regular choral and chamber concerts (see p.106).

Towering over everything in this part of the city is the **Palace of Culture and Sciences** (Pałac Kultury i Nauki or PKiN for short: Ⓦwww.pkin.pl), a gift from Stalin to the Polish people, and not one that could be refused. Officially dubbed "an unshakeable monument to Polish-Soviet friendship" and in fact representing a kind of Soviet-style Marshall Plan, the palace was completed in 1955 after three years of work by 3500 construction workers brought specially from Russia for the job. Popularly known as "the Russian cake", this neo-Baroque leviathan provokes intense feelings from Varsovians. Some residents maintain that the best **views** of Warsaw are from the palace's top floor – the only viewpoint from which one can't see the building itself – while others are willing to grant it a sinister kind of elegance, especially when compared to the glass skyscrapers that have sprouted up nearby. Few dispute, however, that the building's sheer size and breadth creates a vacuum at the centre of the Warsaw. Plans to build up the massive, messy **plac Defilad** square around it are only slowly being realized – the Złote Tarasy mall may give an idea of things to come.

The entrance to the palace is on the eastern side of the building, up the steps from **plac Defilad**. Inside, a lift whisks visitors 114 metres up to the thirtieth-floor platform (daily 9am–8pm, Fri & Sat till 11pm; 20zł), from which, on a good day, you can see out into the plains of Mazovia. The cavernous interior, which is all marble and chandeliers, can be visited on a guided tour (July & Aug, by appointment only; 45zł per person, minimum 4 people; ☎022/656 6345), which takes in, among other sights, Brezhnev's favourite lounge, the opulent Gagarin Hall and the famous **Congress Hall** (Sala Kongresowa), today used for concerts. One truly epoch-defining gig to take place here was the appearance of the Rolling Stones in 1967 (a time when Western groups hardly ever made the trip to Eastern Europe), an event that kick-started the Polish beat boom of the Sixties. Three-dozen cats keep the basement rodent-free, while the rest of the building contains offices, a multiplex cinema, a swimming pool, a youth centre and a lively bar (see p.106). The complete story is told in Agata Passent's wry account, *Long Live the Palace!* (see p.633).

South and west of the palace lie the areas of Warsaw that have experienced the most intense development in the years following the introduction of the free market. The high-rise office and hotel towers along the main westbound highway **Aleja Jerozolimskie** and in the streets surrounding Warszawa Centralna train station now define Warsaw's skyline.

South of the Palace of Culture, ulica Marszałkowska leads south towards **plac Konstitucji**, another massive Stalinist ensemble, where buildings are decorated with outsized workers and other proletarian heroes. The surrounding residential cross-streets such as Wilcza and Piękna are home to a number of bars and restaurants that are worth seeking out.

Nowy Świat and around

South of the university, Krakowskie Przedmieście becomes **Nowy Świat** ("New World"), an area first settled in the mid-seventeenth century. The southern end of this wide boulevard, closed to traffic at weekends, has Warsaw's biggest concentration of quality restaurants, bars, and cafés, and may be the best place to start or end an evening out.

This street has been home to several cultural luminaries, including Joseph Conrad, who once lived at no. 45. A left turn down ulica Ordynacka brings you to the late seventeenth-century Ostrogskich Palace on ulica Okólnik, which houses the **Chopin Museum** (Muzeum Fryderyka Chopina: Tues–Sun 10am–6pm; ⓦwww.nifc.pl), closed for renovations until March 2010. Memorabilia that will be back on display now include the last piano Chopin played, now used for occasional concerts, as well as sheet music, personal letters and a few sketches by the pianist. The museum also puts on summertime Sunday concerts in Park Łazienkowski (see p.96) and at Żelazowa Wola (see p.122). In the same building, the Chopin Society (Towarzystwo im. Fryderyka Chopina: ⓦwww.tifc.chopin.pl) organizes the International Chopin Piano Competition, held every five years.

The neo-Renaissance **Zamoyski Palace**, off to the left of Nowy Świat at the end of ulica Foksal (a Polonization of "Vauxhall"), is one of the few Warsaw palaces you can see inside. In 1863, an abortive attempt to assassinate the tsarist governor was made here; as a consequence the palace was confiscated and ransacked by Cossacks, who hurled a grand piano used by Chopin out of the window of his sister's flat here. These days it's a suitably elegant setting for an upmarket restaurant (see p.103). Round one side of the palace, an outwardly unassuming building houses the **Galeria Foksal** (Mon–Fri noon–5pm, Thurs till 7pm; ⓦwww.galeriafoksal.pl; free), one of the better contemporary galleries in the city, with a regular programme of temporary exhibitions by artists both Polish and foreign.

Further down Nowy Świat, wander though the passageway at number 22 and you'll find yourself in something called the "secret garden", a collection of motley concrete "pavilions" housing dozens of offbeat bars, cafés, restaurants and galleries, with a friendly anarchist mood that couldn't be further removed from the polished capitalism on display on the main street. The concrete monster on the southern side of the junction with aleja Jerozolimskie was for decades the headquarters of the now defunct Polish **communist party**. After a pleasingly ironic stint as the new Warsaw Stock Exchange, today it houses offices.

The National Museum

Immediately east along aleja Jerozolimskie from the old communist HQ is the **National Museum** (Muzeum Narodowe: Tues–Fri 10am–4pm, Sat & Sun 10am–6pm; 12zł or 17zł with temporary exhibitions, permanent collection free Sat; ⓦwww.mnw.art.pl), a daunting grey-brown building that was considered a masterpiece of modern functionalism when first built in the 1930s, and which managed to survive World War II intact.

The displays of **Egyptian**, **Greek** and **Roman** finds in the first section are overshadowed by the stunning collection of art from Faras, a town in **Nubia** (present-day Sudan), excavated by Polish archaeologists in the early 1960s. There are capitals, friezes, columns and other architectural fragments, together with 69 murals dating from between the eighth and thirteenth centuries. The earliest paintings – notably *St Anne*, *The Archangels Michael and Gabriel and Sts Peter and John Enthroned* – are direct and powerful images comparable in quality with later European Romanesque works, and prove the vibrancy of African culture at this period.

The **medieval art collection** is another highlight, with a kaleidoscopic array of carved and painted altarpieces. Note in particular the lovely late fourteenth-century polyptych from Grudziądz castle; a monumental fifteenth-century canopied altar from St Mary's in Gdańsk; and the altar from Pławno depicting the life of St Stanisław, painted by Hans Süss von Kulmbach, a pupil of Dürer.

Much of the first floor is given over to **Polish painting**. Important works here include the sixteenth-century portrait of Queen Anna Jagiellońka, wife of Stefan Batory, the famed king of Poland and Transylvania; and the *Battle of Orsza*, painted in the 1520s by a follower of Lucas Cranach the Elder and depicting the Polish-Lithuanian rout of the Muscovite army on the banks of the River Dnieper in 1514. The centrepiece of the eighteenth-century gallery is Jan Matejko's huge *Battle of Grunwald*, showing one of the momentous clashes of the Middle Ages, the defeat of the Teutonic Knights by Polish-Lithuanian forces in 1410. The Polish section continues with late nineteenth-century artists, especially those from the turn-of-the-twentieth-century Młoda Polska school (see p.364). Stanisław Wyspiański's intense self-portraits stand out, as do his 1905 views of the Kościuszko Mound in Kraków.

The rest of the museum is given over to the extensive but patchy department of foreign paintings, many "inherited" from museums in Wrocław and other formerly German cities following World War II. In the **Italian section**, look for some lovely Florentine primitives and *A Venetian Admiral* by Tintoretto. Among the **French paintings** in the following rooms is Jean-Marc Nattier's portrait of Queen Maria Leszczyńska, Louis XV's Polish wife. The **German Renaissance** is represented by a fine group of works by Cranach, including a gruesome *Massacre of the Innocents*. The most noteworthy piece from the **Low Countries** is the sculpted altarpiece commissioned in Antwerp in 1516 for the Church of Our Lady in Gdańsk. Regular temporary exhibitions are held; visit the museums' English-language website for the programme.

The Army Museum

The **Army Museum** (Muzeum Wojska Polskiego: Wed 10am–5pm, Thurs–Sun 10am–4pm; 8zł, free on Wed), next door to the National Museum, was established in the 1920s and is devoted to an institution that has long played a pivotal role in the national consciousness, as much for its role in preserving national identity during periods of foreign occupation as for militaristic self-glorification. Parked outside is an intimidating collection of heavy combat equipment, from sixteenth-century cannons through to modern tanks and planes. A unique item is Kubuś (Little Jakob), as it's affectionately known, an improvised truck-cum-armoured car cobbled together by Home Army forces and used to notable effect during the Warsaw Uprising. Inside, there's a wide array of guns, swords and armour from over the centuries. Exhibits include an eleventh-century Piast-era helmet; early cannon prototypes produced by the Teutonic Knights; and fearsome Hussar "whistling" feather headgear.

Plac Trzech Krzyży, the Parliament, the Senate and around

South of the museum, the fashionable **plac Trzech Krzyży** (Three Crosses square), with the Pantheon-style **St Alexander's Church** (Kościół św. Aleksandra) in the centre, leads to the tree-lined pavements and magisterial embassy buildings of aleja Ujazdowskie. Past the US embassy and off to the left, down ulica Jana Matejki, is the squat 1920s **Parliament** (Sejm) and **Senate** (Senat) building; a feeble institution stuffed with government-approved yes-men until it regained its former status with the epoch-making democratic elections of July 1989.

Many of the streets in this area are lined with dull postwar frontages plastered over the pockmarks of World War II gunfire. However, these unprepossessing edifices often mask red-brick or stone buildings a century or more old, some also featuring elaborate shrines to the Virgin Mary; step through the archways ul. Mokotowska nos. 65 or 73, just south of plac Trzech Krzyży, for good examples.

Ujazdowski and Łazienkowski parks

The old royal parks south of the city centre are one of Warsaw's most attractive features. The most popular and well-kept stretch of greenery begins with Ujazdowski Park, a half-kilometre south of the National Museum, and continues beyond a highway overpass to the grounds of the **Ujazdowski Castle** (Zamek Ujazdowski) and then the **Botanical Gardens** (Ogród Botaniczny), before arriving at the most luxuriant public space of them all, **Łazienkowski Park**. If you haven't got the time to walk the whole distance, the numerous buses running along aleja Ujazdowskie on the parks' western fringes provide a good way of getting around.

Ujazdowski Park

Aleja Ujazdowskie itself is one of the city's more elegant thoroughfares, with opulent nineteenth-century villas (many occupied by embassies) lining its western side, and the regimented flower beds and duck pond of **Ujazdowski Park** on the other. Lurking on the far side of the highway overpass at Park Ujazdowski's southern edge is the **Ujazdowski Castle** (Zamek Ujazdowski), a rebuilt Renaissance structure with its own grounds separate from the park proper. Once inhabited by King Sigismund August's Italian-born mother Bona Sforza, it's now home to the **Contemporary Art Centre** (Centrum Sztuki Współczesnej: Tues–Thurs, Sat & Sun 11am–7pm, Fri 11am–9pm; 12zł, free on Thurs; ⓦ www.csw.art.pl), the city's leading venue for modern art shows along with the Galeria Zachęta (see p.89). As well as organizing themed exhibitions, the centre mounts innovative theatre, film and video events. The building also contains an excellent café-restaurant overlooking the park (see p.105).

South of the castle across ulica Agrykola, the **Botanical Gardens** (Ogród Botaniczny: April–Aug Mon–Fri 9am–8pm, Sat–Sun 10am–8pm; Sept daily 10am–6pm; Oct daily 10am–5pm; 5zł, on Sun 7zł; ⓦ www.ogrod.uw.edu .pl) has an impressive collection of carefully landscaped shrubs and trees, with a sizeable rose garden, a knot garden crammed full of fragrant medicinal herbs and greenhouses that are open on Sundays.

Łazienkowski Park

South and east of here lie several entrances to the main body of **Łazienkowski Park** (open daily 8am–sunset). Once a hunting ground on the periphery of town, the area was bought by King Stanisław August in the 1760s and turned into an English-style park with formal gardens. A few years later the slender Neoclassical **Łazienkowski Palace** was built across the park lake. Designed for the king by the Italian architect Domenico Merlini, in collaboration with teams of sculptors and other architects, it's the best memorial to the country's last and most cultured monarch. Before this summer residence was commissioned, a **bathhouse** built by Tylman van Gameren for Prince Stanisław Lubomirski stood here – hence the name, "Łazienki" meaning simply "baths".

The oak-lined promenades and pathways leading from the park entrance to the palace are a favourite with tourists and Varsovians, many of the latter coming prepared to feed the park's resident fauna, which include peacocks, squirrels and mandarin ducks. On summer Sundays, **concerts** and other events take place under the watchful eye of the ponderous Chopin Monument, just beyond the entrance, as well as in the Great Outbuilding (see below). On the way down to the lake you'll pass a couple of the many buildings designed for King Stanisław by Merlini; the **New Guardhouse** (Nowa Kordegarda), just before the palace, is now a pleasant terrace **café**.

Łazienkowski Palace

Often referred to as the Island Palace (Pałac na Wyspie) due to its location, the **Łazienkowski Palace** (Pałac Łazienkowski: Tues–Sun 9am–4pm; 12zł; ⓦ www .lazienki-krolewskie.pl) is the smallest of Warsaw's royal palaces and the only one that can be visited without a guided tour. Nazi damage to the building itself was fairly severe, with all but three of the rooms destroyed, but many of the lavish furnishings, paintings and sculptures survived, having been hidden during the occupation.

The rest of the park

The buildings scattered round the park are all in some way connected with King Stanisław. Across the lake from the palace, and north along the water's edge, is the **Old Guardhouse** (Stara Kordegarda: Tues–Sun 9am–4pm; free), built in the 1780s in a style matching the north facade of the main palace, which features regular exhibitions of contemporary art. Immediately next to it is the **Great Outbuilding** (Wielka Oficyna), the former officers' training school where young cadets hatched the anti-tsarist conspiracy that resulted in the November 1830 Uprising. The building now houses the **Polish Expatriates Museum** (Muzeum Wychodźstwa Polskiego: Tues–Sun 10am–3pm; 6zł), inaugurated during the summer 1992 celebrations surrounding the return of composer Ignacy Jan Paderewski's body to Warsaw from the US. Much of what's here was bequeathed to the country by the exiled Paderewski in his will, with pride of place going to the grand piano he used at his longtime home on the shores of Lake Geneva. There's also a section devoted to mementoes of the Polish *emigracja*, detailing the Polish experience of America.

Immediately next to the museum is the **Myślewicki Palace** (Pałac Myślewicki: Sun–Tues 9am–4pm; 3zł), a present from the king to his nephew Prince Józef Poniatowski. Back up towards the main park entrance, past the Nowa Kordegarda, is the **White House** (Biały Dom; May–Sept Tues–Sun 9am–4pm; 5zł) built in the 1770s by Merlini for King Stanisław August's favourite mistress. It retains the majority of its original eighteenth-century interiors, including a dining room decorated with a wealth of grotesque animal frescoes, and an octagonal-shaped study which features enjoyable trompe l'oeil floral decoration.

Just beyond it, the **Old Orangerie** (Stara Pomarańczarnia: closed for renovation until 2010) contains a well-preserved wooden theatre (one of the few in Europe to retain its original eighteenth-century decor) with royal boxes and seating for more than two hundred.

The path leading south up the hill from here ends back at aleja Ujazdowskie, next to the **Belvedere** (Belweder), another eighteenth-century royal residence redesigned in the 1820s for the governor of Warsaw, the tsar's brother Konstantine. It was the official residence of Polish heads of state since the end of World War I until 1995, when Wałęsa moved it to the Namiestnikowski Palace

AGRYKOLA

Ujazdowski Castle
(Contemporary Art Centre)

MYŚLIWIECKA

Ogród Botaniczny

SZWOLEŻERÓW

Astronomical
Observatory

Old Orangerie

Old
Guardhouse

AL. UJAZDOWSKIE

White House

New
Guardhouse

Great
Outbuilding

Łazienkowski
Palace

Myślewicki
Palace

Chopin
Monument

N

P a r k

Amphitheatre

KLONOWA

Belvedere

BELWEDERSKA

Łazienkowski

**RESTAURANTS,
CAFÉS & BARS**
Instytut Café   1
Qchinia Artystyczna 2
Belvedere   3

0   100 m

ŁAZIENKOWSKI PARK

▼ Wilanów   ▼ ❸(100m) & New Orangerie

on Krakowskie Przedmieście (see p.89). Back down the hill, a path through one of the wilder sections of the park leads to the **New Orangerie** (Nowa Pomarańczarnia), where you'll find the *Belvedere* restaurant (see p.103), among the finest in Warsaw.

The Royal Way (Trakt Królewski) slopes gently down from here towards the Mokotów district, continuing a few kilometres south to Wilanów, its ultimate destination.

Wilanów

The grandest of Warsaw's palaces, **Wilanów** (May to mid-Sept: Mon, Wed & Sat 9.30am–6.30pm; Tues, Thurs & Fri 9.30am–4.30pm, Sun 9.30am–6.30pm; mid-Sept to April: Mon & Wed–Sat 9.30am–4.30pm, Sun 10.30am–4.30pm; last entry ninety minutes before closing; 23zł with guide or audioguide, 16zł without, free on Sun, no guided tours on Sun; ☎022/842 0795, ⓦwww .wilanow-palac.art.pl) is tucked away in almost rural surroundings on the outskirts of Warsaw, and makes an easy excursion from the city centre: it's the final stop of several bus routes, including #116 and #180 from plac Zamkowy, and #130 and #522 from the Centralna station. Nicknamed the Polish Versailles, it was originally the brainchild of King Jan Sobieski, who purchased the existing manor house and estate in 1677. He spent nearly twenty years turning it into his ideal country residence, and it was later extended by a succession of monarchs and aristocratic families. Wilanów was badly damaged during World War II, when the Nazis stole the cream of the art collection and tore up the park and surrounding buildings. In 1945 the palace became state property and for

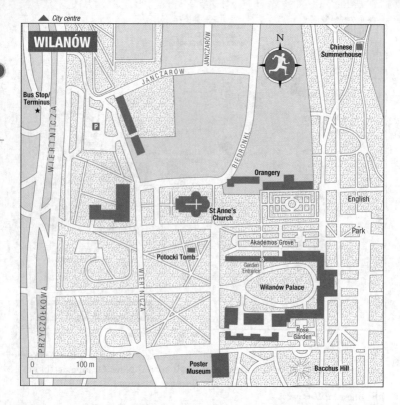

City centre

WILANÓW

JANCZARÓW

N

Chinese
Summerhouse

JANCZARÓW

Bus Stop/
Terminus
★

WIERNICZA

P

BIEDRONKI

Orangery

St Anne's
Church

English

Park

Akademos Grove

WIERNICZA

Potocki Tomb

Garden
Entrance

PRZYCZÓŁKOWA

Wilanów Palace

Rose
Garden

0   100 m

Poster
Museum

Bacchus Hill

eleven years was extensively renovated. It's now a tourist favourite, visitable by **guided tour** or audioguide (both available in various languages, book ahead for non-Polish tours).

The approach to the palace takes you past former outhouses, including the smithy, the butcher's and an inn. Also close at hand are some decent cafés, welcome refuges after the palace tour. The **entrance gates**, where you buy your tickets, are just beyond the domed eighteenth-century **St Anne's Church** (Kościół św. Anny) and the ornate neo-Gothic Potocki mausoleum across the road.

The palace

Laid out in a horseshoe plan with a central core flanked by a pair of projecting wings, the classical grandeur of the **facade**, complete with Corinthian columns, Roman statuary and intermingled Latin inscriptions, reflects Sobieski's original conception. The centrepiece, a golden sun with rays reflecting from decorated shields bearing the Sobieski coat of arms, clarifies the fundamental idea: the glorification of Sobieski himself.

Despite extensive wartime damage, the essentials of the interior design have remained largely unchanged. Among the sixty or so rooms of Wilanów's **interior** you'll find styles ranging from the lavish early Baroque of the apartments of Jan Sobieski and John III, to the classical grace of the nineteenth-century Potocki museum rooms.

The tour starts with a basement exhibit on the palace's **history**, ending with photos of objects taken by the Nazis and never recovered. Several flights of stairs lead to the **portrait galleries.** One of the undoubted highlights of the collection is the great masterpiece of Neoclassical portraiture, *Stanisław Kostka Potocki on Horseback* by Jacques-Louis David.

After Sobieski's **Library**, with its beautiful marble-tiled floor and allegorical ceiling paintings, you come to the **Faience Room**, clad in blue with white Delft tiles and topped by an elegant copper-domed cupola surrounded by delicate period stucco mouldings, the centrepiece an eagle raising aloft the ubiquitous Sobieski coat of arms. The **Etruscan Study** and **Lower North Gallery** are filled with antiquities such as the third- and fourth-century BC vases collected in Naples by nineteenth-century palace owner Stanisław Potocki. Converted into a mini-museum in 1805 to show off his archeological finds, it's now been restored to its original early eighteenth-century state. The inscription on the floor, *Cuncti Patet Ingressus* ("Admittance free to all"), attests to the democratic ideals of the time.

The end of the gallery brings you into the **Queen's Apartments**, originally used by Maria Kazimierza, Sobieski's wife. The most impressive rooms are the **Antechamber** and the **Great Vestibule**, a three-storeyed affair of marble pillars and classicist mouldings. Past the simple **Chapel**, you pass through further galleries before ending at the **Grand Hall of August II**, also known as the White Hall. Designed in the 1730s for King August II, the mirrors on the walls combine to create a feeling of immense space.

The palace gardens

The gate on the left side beyond the main entrance opens onto the stately **palace gardens** (daily 9am–dusk; 5zł, Thurs free). Overlooking the garden terrace, the palace's graceful rear facade is topped by statuary featuring a golden sundial, designed by Gdańsk astronomer Jan Hevelius, on the southern side. The fresco sequence punctuating the facade shows scenes from classical literature, notably the *Aeneid* and the *Odyssey*. Strolling along the back terrace, it's easy to appreciate the fine synthesis between regal residence and country mansion achieved by the palace.

The Baroque gardens reach down to the waterside, continuing rather less tidily along the lakeside to the north and south. Beyond the **Orangery** is the romantic **English Landscape Park,** modelled on eighteenth-century gardens in Britain. Back outside and just below the main gates, the **Poster Museum** (Muzeum Plakatu; Mon noon–4pm, Tues–Sun 10am–4pm; 9zł, Mon free; ⓦwww .postermuseum.pl) is a mishmash of the inspired and the bizarre and is well worth a visit. The poster as an art form is highly regarded in Poland although there's no permanent collection of classics on display; the changing exhibitions generally display posters from around the world.

Praga

Across the river from the Old Town is the large **Praga** suburb; so named not after the Czech capital but after the fires set here long ago: the Polish verb prażyć means "to roast". This was the main residential area for the legions of tsarist bureaucrats throughout the nineteenth century; particularly the Saska Kępa district, south of aleja Waszyngtona. Out of range of the main

World War II battles and destruction, Praga still has some of its prewar architecture and atmosphere, and an increasingly bohemian reputation. The impoverished parts of the district are best avoided at night, but during the day there's no need to worry. For information, visit the excellent English-language website about the district at Ⓦwww.warszawskapraga.pl, also available as a book, which has detailed information on Praga's history, sights and cultural activities.

Immediately across from the Old Town is **Warsaw Zoo** (Ogród Zoologiczny: daily April–Sept 9am–7pm, Oct–March 9am–4pm; 7zł; Ⓦwww.zoo.waw.pl), whose attractive park-like expanse houses, among others, elephants, hippos and bears, the latter kept in an enclosure visible from the road. The **Orthodox Church of Sts Cyril and Methodius** (Cerkiew św. Cyryla i Metodego: Mon–Sat 11am–4pm, Sun 1–4pm; services daily at 9am & 5pm) just beyond on aleja Solidarności, is one remaining sign of the former Russian presence. A large neo-Byzantine structure topped by a succession of onion domes, its original mid-nineteenth-century interior decoration remains intact. If you visit during services you might hear the excellent **choir** in action. Continuing one block east you'll come to the heart of modern Praga, the multi-level shopping centre built above the Warszawa Wileńska train station.

Praga's most notorious connection with the Soviet Union stems from the time of the Warsaw Uprising (see box, p.82). At the beginning of September 1944, Soviet forces reached the outer reaches of Praga. Insurrectionists from the besieged city centre used radio to plead with them to intervene against the Nazis, to no avail, though a group of Polish soldiers fighting in the Red Army did make an attempt to cross the river, ending in bloodshed. Throughout the Uprising, the Soviet tanks waited, moving in to flush out the Nazis only when the city had been virtually eradicated. For the next forty years, the official account gave "insufficient Soviet forces" as the reason for the nonintervention; as with the Katyń massacre, every Pole knew otherwise. A **monument** to the Soviet arrival, alongside the highway behind the Orthodox church, features four somnolent-looking Red Army soldiers known locally as the "four sleeping soldiers".

Warsaw's best-known and longest-running flea and black market – the **Bazar Różyckiego** – is five minutes' walk south from the Orthodox church on ulica Ząbkowska (Mon–Fri 6am–5pm, Sat 6am–3pm), though it's little more than another place to buy cheap clothes and fake leather bags. If you do go, watch out for pickpockets. The infamous outdoor market at the **Dziesięciolecia** stadium close to the Poniatowski bridge was recently closed, as it's now the building site for the city's new football stadium.

Praga was once home to a significant proportion of the city's Jewish population. Directly over the Śląsko–Dąbrowski bridge, south of the leafy Park Praski, there are a number of streets, notably **ulica Kłopotowskiego** and **ulica Sierakowskiego** where you can still see some typical old Jewish residences; the building at **ul. Kłopotowskiego 31** used to house the Jewish baths. Also worth exploring are the streets north of the Wileńska station, such as **ulica Środkowa**. A number of artists have moved their studios to the nearby **ulica Inżynierska**, and it was here and on the badly beaten **ulica Mała** that Roman Polański shot street scenes for his movie *The Pianist*.

A little further out, in the Brodno district, is the **Jewish Cemetery** (Cmentarz Żydowski; entrance at the corner of ulica Odrowąża and ulica Wincentego; take tram #3 or #25 north from the Wileńska station), founded in the 1780s but badly damaged by the Nazis, who used many of the stones for paving.

Eating and drinking

Warsaw is one of the best places to eat in central Europe. Alongside **restaurants** specializing in traditional Polish cuisine, which range from homely to sumptuous, there's a welcome range of culinary variety; modern European, Italian and Japanese are some of the more widespread choices, but you'll find many others. With a few exceptions, the restaurants in the Old Town are geared towards tourists, offering a conventional range of Polish staples, often at inflated prices. More adventurous and fashionable places can be found further south.

Cafés range from upscale and old-fashioned to modern minimalist, while there are also plenty of down-to-earth student hangouts. Cakes and pastries worthy of the best of Central Europe are easy to come by.

There's a good variety of **bars** of all sorts. Besides the grotty corner bars where the locals have their first beer or two in the morning, there's a range of upmarket places, from flashy bars aimed at expats and Warsaw's upwardly mobile to well-hidden Bohemian clubs. There are also "ethnic" pubs, bars in wooden ranch-type shacks in the city's parkland, theme bars and unpretentious local haunts: in short, everything you need.

The distinction between Warsaw's eating and drinking venues is inevitably blurred, with many of the latter offering both snacks and full meals as well as booze – so bear in mind that many of the places listed below under "Cafés and bars" are also good places for a bite to eat.

Restaurants

All the central areas are packed with restaurants, many of which invitingly offer outdoor chairs and tables during the summer months. English-language **menus** are available in better restaurants and even some low-end places; if you need help refer to p.660.

Warsaw is the most expensive city in Poland, and restaurant prices are slowly edging towards those charged in Western Europe. A number of the famously cheap **milk bars** – canteen-style places doling out filling Polish staples for well under 10zł a head – still survive, but there's also a new generation of places, some excellent, where it's easy to eat well for 15 to 20zł. Otherwise, the price of a main course and drink at a proper restaurant can range in price from as little as 25 to 35zł in casual establishments to 100zł or more at the most upmarket ones. Wherever you choose to eat, however, traditional Polish dishes like *barszcz* (beetroot soup), *placki* (potato pancakes) and *kotlet schabowy* (pork chop) invariably work out cheaper than the fancier items on the menu. In late summer and autumn you'll find *kurki* (chanterelles) and other forest mushrooms on the menus at most upscale restaurants and also a few of the cheaper ones. We've included telephone numbers for those restaurants where making a **reservation** – especially at weekends – is advisable.

Fast-food joints are firmly established. As well as burgers and hot dogs you'll find pizza, both genuinely Italian and the Polish pickled vegetable variety, *zapiekanka*. Numerous kiosks dish out sandwiches and salads, while kebab stands and Vietnamese/Chinese outlets are also widespread.

The Old Town and New Town

Bar Mleczny Pod Barbakan ul. Mostowa 27/29. Milk bar on the edge of the old town serving the standard range of *pierogi*, soups and potato pancakes; convenient for cash-strapped tourists, and with an English-language menu. Open 8am–5pm, Sat & Sun from 9am.

Chłopskie Jadło ul. Wierzbowa 9/11. A fantastic chain restaurant serving Polish food, peasant style.

Think tubs of lard, slabs of meat, big sausages, wooden forks and a farmhouse setting. Open noon–midnight.

Freta 33 ul. Freta 33/35. Fresh and moderately priced Mediterranean food on the New Town Square, with a popular terrace and small, stylish dining room. Try the penne with mixed seeds, tomato and spinach (28zł) for a treat; salads and appetizers are also recommended. Open noon–11pm.

Jazz Bistro Gwiazdeczka ul. Piwna 40. The most elegant of the *Jazz Bistro* branches (see also opposite), and, with its ensemble of whitewash, steel and glass, the only modern restaurant interior in the Old Town. The *Jazz* pork pasta (29zł) is superb, and the salads (28zł) and meat dishes (35–45zł) are good, too. Open 10am–midnight.

Namaste India ul. Piwna 46/1 ☏ 022/635 7766. Some of the best Indian food in Poland, with curries under 25zł, served in a tiny four-table Old Town restaurant – book ahead if you want to be sure of a seat. Open 11am–10pm, Sun from noon.

Na Prowincji ul. Nowomiejska 10. Classic and well-prepared range of pizza (17–33zł) and pasta (21–29zł) in simple surroundings; a very nice change from the nearby tourist-only venues stuffed with fake antiques. Open noon–11pm.

Pierrogeria ul. Krzywe Koło 30 (entrance on ul. Nowomiejska). Pricey but good *pierogi*, soups, *krokiety* and other Polish favourites, in a tourist-friendly restaurant near the Barbakan. Open 11am–11pm.

Pod Samsonem ul. Freta 3/5. A popular tourist-oriented restaurant with good-quality Polish dishes and a variety of non-kosher Jewish choices. Main courses are priced moderately at 15–30zł. Open 10am–10pm.

Polka ul. Świętojańska 2. Traditional and upmarket Polish food at fair prices; Warsaw pork chop for 32zł, crispy duck in honey at 39zł and salads between 21–28zł. The setting is rustic with a dash of Laura Ashley; plenty of flowery patterns. Open noon–11pm.

U Fukiera Rynek Starego Miasta 27 ☏ 022/831 1013. Top-notch, lavishly decorated and suitably pricey restaurant (main courses up to 100zł) with a strong line in imaginatively reinterpreted traditional Polish cuisine, and candlelight after dark. Open noon till midnight.

Krakowskie Przedmieście and around

Browarmia ul. Królewska 1. Four types of beer, plus three seasonal varieties, are brewed on the premises at this excellent restaurant. Use them to wash down a grilled chicken sandwich (24zł), the

pork knuckle (42zł) or a steak (62zł). On weekdays there's 20 percent reduction on beer before 4pm. Open noon–midnight.

Nowa La Boheme pl. Teatralny 1 ☏ 022/692 0681. Excellent modern European food in the cellars below the Teatr Wielki, popular, with a well-dressed and prosperous crowd, for inventive dishes such as halibut with hibiscus sauce and quail with chicken livers and fruit jam. Main courses around 50zł. Open noon–11pm.

St Antonio ul. Senatorska 37 ☏ 022/826 3008. Upmarket but moderately priced Italian/Polish restaurant with a perfect location in the northwest corner of Ogród Saski park. The menu nicely balances homemade pastas like ravioli with goats' cheese and spinach (21zł) with traditional Polish dishes like pork cutlets stuffed with ham and cheese (49zł), fresh mussels and oysters. Open noon–11pm.

Uniwersytecki Krakowskie Przedmieście 20/22. Classic, typically cheap milk bar by the university with an English menu; convenient for a quick break from sightseeing. Much frequented by students. Open 7am–8pm, Sat & Sun 9am–5pm.

Zakąski Przekąski ul. Ossolińskich 7. All six dishes are priced 8zł at this tongue twister of a stand-up snackbar; simply point at the sausages, herring, pork knuckle, pie, steak tartare or "surprise" painted on the wall, pay, and wait for your plate to arrive. Drinks are all 4zł, vodka too. Open 24hr.

Nowy Świat and around

Bierhalle ul. Nowy Świat 64. A chain of beer restaurants, serving good portions of hearty Polish food – plus tortilla – though it's best to focus on the six varieties of Warsaw's best beer, available by the glass, jug or barrel. Open noon–11pm, Sat & Sun 11am–11.30pm. There's also an outlet at Pole Mokotowskie park in summer.

Chianti ul. Foksal 17 ☏ 022/828 0222. Candlelit cellar restaurant with intimate feel and great Italian food. The fresh pasta dishes, such as red tagliatelle with truffles and prosciutto (34zł), are recommended. Open noon–11pm.

Co Tu Nowy Świat 22 pavilion 21. A hip Vietnamese-run Chinese restaurant with cheap fresh food, with meals from 10zł, and a tiny terrace area. Entrance through the passageway. Open 10am–9pm, Sat & Sun 11am–7pm.

Green Way ul. Szpitalna 6. Crowded Warsaw branch of the national chain vegetarian restaurant, with a range of Polonized international dishes such as Mexican goulash, lasagne, and samosas (10–15zł), as well as dark wheat pancakes with fruit toppings and fresh fruit drinks. Take out service available. Daily 10am–9pm.

Le Jardin Foksal ul. Foksal 2. ☎022/827 8707. French cuisine in the unimpeachably formal surroundings of the Zamoyski Palace. A high standard of cooking, with mains priced around 50–70zł; try the roast catfish with bacon or stewed rabbit legs in cream and white wine. In summer, there's a great garden terrace. Open 11am–midnight.

Papaya ul. Foksal 16 ☎022/826 1199. Thai, Japanese and Chinese fusion dishes served in a modern white interior, with mains costing 30–50zł, up to 190zł for the lobster. A great place for Sunday brunch with the kids – they have a supervised play area. Open noon–midnight.

Rodeo Drive ul. Chmielna 2. A formulaic steak-house with plenty of cowboy attributes, burgers from 25zł, and some of Warsaw's best steaks – in cowboy and cowgirl sizes – from 35zł. Open noon–11pm, Fri–Sun till midnight.

Sense ul. Nowy Świat 19 ☎022/826 6570. A sensation when it first opened a few years ago, *Sense* is no longer the only designer restaurant, but it does consistently serve excellent fusion food like Thai shrimp soup (19zł), chicken tikka with honey (35zł) and stir-fried rice dishes (45zł).

The Mexican ul. Foksal 10. Good-looking chain restaurant with a gurgling fountain in an adobe courtyard. The Tex-Mex cuisine is good (try swallowing the 700 gram burrito), but the fun really starts when the cocktail menus come out for the night. Open 11am–11.30pm, Sat & Sun till 1am.

Zapiecek al. Jerozolimskie 28. Dainty girls in traditional dress serve big portions of granny-style *pierogi* and other Polish delights, in rustic settings with plenty of wood – one of three such outlets in Warsaw. Open 10am–11pm.

Zgoda ul. Zgoda 4. Classy and comfortable grill bar, with country-style decor that's not overbearing. Good Polish dishes at low prices – grilled meats, all under 25zł, are a speciality. Open 9am–11pm, Sun from noon.

The rest of Śródmieście

Belvedere New Orangerie in Łazienkowski Park ☎022/841 4806. One of Warsaw's best and most expensive eateries, with fresh oysters and other seafood a speciality, in an old orangery at the southern end of the park. Tasteful, understated decor, and popular with politicians. Open noon–11pm.

Biblioteka University of Warsaw Library, ul. Dobra 56/66 ☎022/552 7195. Imaginative, modern European menu in swish, modernist surround-ings, with such specialities as grilled swordfish with lime sauce (75zł) and, for dessert, orange pie with strawberries and wine (29zł). Open Mon–Sat noon–11pm; also closed Sat in July & Aug.

Concept ul. Krakowskie Przedmieście 16/18 ☎022/492 7409. The elegant old Central Bathhouse, which survived the war unscathed, is now the upmarket Likus Concept Store, with a fantastic haute cuisine restaurant beneath a high skylight. The refined main dishes (75–150zł) include filet steak with foie gras and deer osso buco with corn cakes. Open noon–11pm, Sun till 5pm.

Delicja Polska ul. Koszykowa 54 ☎022/630 8850. An outstanding and very traditional Polish restaurant, with sumptuous decor, polished service and prices to match. Specialities include lamb, duck and goose dishes, with main courses priced around 50zł, and desserts to die for. Open noon–midnight.

Gar ul. Jasna 10 ☎022/828 2605. Fabulous-looking restaurant with upmarket interpretations of Polish classics – like cabbage veal parcels and sirloin steak marinated in rosemary and garlic. Quality is high, as are the prices, at 70–90zł for a main course. Open noon–11pm.

Jazz Bistro/Nu Jazz Bistro ul. Piękna 20, ul. Żurawia 6/12. Café-restaurant chain with several addresses. The one on ul. Piękna is less formal, with a reliable, good-value menu (sandwiches 14zł; pasta 20–25zł), and is the only branch with regular live piano jazz. The artfully sparse ul. Żurawia "Nu" branch has an adventurous fusion menu, with emphasis on wholewheat pasta (35zł), coconut curry and fresh vegetables. Open 11am–1am, Fri & Sat noon–2am, Sun noon–1am.

Kom ul. Zielna 37 ☎ 022/338 6353. Wonder-fully designed restaurant in the prewar telegraph building, with original elements such as the cables through which Churchill chatted to Stalin. The menu has film-themed fusion dishes like Great Escape lobster, Titanic scallops, Hobbit duck breast and Forrest Gump chocolate truffles (mains from 45–80zł). Open Mon–Sat noon–11pm.

Marak ul. Świętokrzyska 18, ul. Piękna 20, Nowy Świat 22 and in the train station. Smart soup kitchen chain serving up a range of Polish soups such as *ogórkowa* (pickle soup) and more exotic flavours like *tajska* (Thai chicken curry), as well as seasonal choices, including an outstanding *chłodnik* (chilled summer borscht). Large bowls 8–19zł.

Pod Czerwonym Wieprzem ul. Żelazna 68. A little out of the way but worth dropping by, the "red hog inn" is Warsaw's only communist-themed restau-rant, with posters, paintings and other memorabilia and dishes like the First of May beetroot soup (7zł), Mao chicken (24zł) and Fidel's cigars pork chops (24zł) – which taste much better than they did back in the bad old days. Open noon–11pm.

Porta 13 ul. Chmielna 13. Only certified "bio food" is served at this light and pleasant courtyard restaurant, starting with buffet breakfast, well-priced lunch deals (12–23zł) and dinners like sander fillet with crayfish sauce (68zł) and wild boar chops (66zł). Open 6.30am–10am & noon–11pm, Sun till 10pm.

Qchnia Artystyczna al. Ujazdowski 6. Wonderful location in the Ujazdowski Castle, quirky decor and a great outdoor terrace with excellent views down towards the river. Well-chosen menu, with a handful of meat (50–60zł), pasta (35–45zł) and potato pancake (35zł) dishes, some of which are vegetarian. Open noon–midnight.

Stary Młynek al. Ujazdowskie 6a. Modest and pleasant little Polish cellar restaurant with a selection of conventional meat-and-potatoes dishes (15–25zł), good salads and a relaxing terrace. Convenient for Łazienkowski Park. Open 11am–11pm.

Tabaka ul. Szkolna 2/4. Rambling cellar restaurant serving excellent dishes from the Balkans; the mixed starters are a must at 38zł, perhaps followed by Bulgarian salad (7zł), grilled meat or seafood (35–40zł). There's Turkish ayran yoghurt to wash it all down, as well as wines from Moldova, Croatia and Slovenia. Open 11am–midnight, Sat & Sun from noon.

Tandoor Palace ul. Marszałkowska 21/25. Award-winning Indian cuisine, with curries from 30zł, some interesting Balti dishes from Kashmir and even Singaporean food. Open noon–10.30pm.

Warsaw Tortilla Factory ul. Wilcza 46. An expat institution, lively Tex-Mex place serving large, well-spiced burritos (29zł) and plenty of less expensive bar snacks. On Wed, Thurs and Sat, visit for the great live music; DJs play on Fri. Open noon–11pm, Fri & Sat till 1am.

Praga
Le Cedre al. Solidarności 61 ☏ 022/670 1166. Great Lebanese restaurant next to the *Hotel Praski*, with belly dancing in the evening and grilled meats at around 35zł. The hot and cold mezze plates (12–20zł each) are especially recommended. Open 11am–11pm.

Porto Praga ul. Stefana Okrzei 23 ☏ 022/698 50 01. Fantastic upmarket designer restaurant with imaginatively prepared international dishes in the 40–80zł range. The wine and cocktail list are worth a visit alone. Open noon–11pm, Fri & Sat till 1am.

Cafés and bars

Warsaw can boast a vivacious **café** life, though interest is as much social as gastronomic. Establishments vary between cosy haunts serving cakes and ice cream to trendier modern places offering a range of fancy coffees and an international menu of snacks. Many of the latter stay open well into the night, competing for custom with **bars**, which range in style from hip designer joints to raucous beer halls with live bands and dancing. With a few exceptions, **pubs** are bland affairs that have little in common with their British or Irish namesakes. The cost of drinks in Warsaw are significantly higher than elsewhere in Poland, but still compare favourably with Western Europe.

Most cafés and bars are concentrated in the Old Town and the modern centre to the south, but there are few obvious strolling areas where you'll find one establishment after another – it's best to plan your evening's itinerary before setting out or else have the numbers of the main taxi companies handy. In summer, head for the fair-weather al fresco bars along Wybrzeże Gdańskie, just below the Old Town on the western bank of the Wisła; or in Pole Mokotowskie, an area of parkland southwest of the centre (easily reached from the Pole Mokotowskie metro station), which is bustling with Varsovians on balmy evenings.

Cafés

The Old Town and around
Literacka ul. Krakowskie Przedmieście 87/89. Atmospheric, romantic place with quiet jazz at weekends. Serves toothsome snacks too. Open Mon–Sat 9am–11pm, Sun 10am–11pm.
To Lubię ul. Freta 10. Coffee, wine and tasty desserts in a church bell tower. Open 10am–10pm.

Śródmieście and beyond
Blikle Café ul. Nowy Świat 33. Open since 1869, this is the oldest cake shop in the city and an elegant place in which to enjoy coffee and desserts. Famous for its doughnuts (*pączki*), it also does excellent but pricey breakfasts (27–58zł). Open 10am–10pm.
Café 6/12 ul. Żurawia 6/12. A café, bar and restaurant in one, with an eclectic menu; the

emphasis is on Asian and Mediterranean dishes (30–45zł), but homely Polish choices are just as good. There's also a long list of fruit and vegetable shakes, and foreign newspapers to read. Open Mon–Fri 8am–11pm, Sat & Sun 10am–11pm.

Coffee Heaven ul. Nowy Świat 46; also Warszawa Centralna and other locations. Western-style coffee chain with drinks and snacks. Open Mon–Fri 7am–10pm, Sat 8am–11pm, Sun 8am–10pm.

Czuły Barbarzyńca ul. Dobra 31. Interesting bookstore/café buzzing with students; serves excellent cappuccino and has a swing in the middle of the room. Open Mon–Sat 10am–10pm, Sun from noon.

Green Coffee ul. Bracka 16 and several other places. Fresh and bright modern chain café with coffee, tea, sandwiches, quiche and tasty cakes – try the Charleston chocolate cake. Open 7am–11pm.

Instytut Cafe al. Ujazdowskie 6. The designer café in the new theatre institute building in front of Ujazdowski Castle – handy for coffee, quiche or cakes on your way to or from Łazienkowski Park. There's a gallery, theatre and bookshop too. Open 9am–10pm.

Między Nami ul. Bracka 20. Hip but relaxed place with two levels of seating, hosting an easy-going gay and straight crowd. Full food menu includes breakfasts, curry chicken and excellent salads, while DJs spin discs some evenings. Open Mon–Sat 10am–11pm, Sun from 4pm.

Próżna ul. Próżna 12. Charming, modern café in a crumbling tenement building on Warsaw's last intact street. Photos of Warsaw decorate the walls; *pierogi*, salads, soups and fresh juice feature on the menu. Open Mon–Sat 10am–11pm, Sun & Mon till 10pm.

Wedel ul. Szpitalna 8. Poland's top chocolaterie, with a stunning range of cocoa products. Try the hot chocolate *ekstra gorskie* (extra bitter). Open Mon–Sat 8am–10pm, Sun 11am–8pm.

Bars

The Old Town and around

Diuna ul. Dobra 33/35. Relaxed, student-oriented bar down towards the river, with cheap beer, artificial fur on the walls and live music almost every evening. Open 4pm–1am.

Jadłodajnia Filozoficzna ul. Dobra 33/35. Next to *Diuna* and a bit more artsy and pretentious, with frequent DJs. Open 4pm–1am.

Metal Bar Rynek Starego Miasta 8. One of the few establishments to bring nightlife to the Old Town, a cosy small bar with photo and art exhibitions, cocktails and bar snacks. Open 10am–midnight, Fri & Sat till 2am.

Pod Barylką ul. Garbarska 5/7. Down from pl. Zamkowy on the Rynek Mariensztacki, with outdoor seating in a pleasantly shady arcade. For those who go to a pub to savour beer, with six draught varieties on offer. Open 10am–1am.

▲ Warsaw bar

śnieście

fé Kulturalna pl. Defilad 1. An airy student hangout in the southeast wing of the Palace of Culture, with bizarre plastic chandeliers and DJs at weekends. Open 2pm–1am, Fri & Sat till 3am.

Champions al. Jerozolimskie 65/79. Large and garish sports bar and restaurant, on the ground floor of the Marriott hotel (see p.70). Best place in town to catch football and other sporting events on TV, but beer is expensive. Open 11am–midnight.

Nobo ul. Wilcza 58a. A cut above other bars, with first-rate cocktails, professional staff and a small but truly excellent selection of European and Asian food (mains 29–50zł). Open noon–11pm, Sat & Sun 6pm–midnight.

Szparka pl. Trzech Krzyży 16a. Unspectacular but buzzing café on Warsaw's most fashionable square; pricey, posey and hard to leave. Open 7am–4am.

Yamaya Nowy Świat 22. Tiny, alternative reggae bar in a maze of hip dive bars in the "pavilions"

just behind the polished facades of Nowy Świat. This is the place to come for the cheapest beer in the city centre. Open 6pm–2am.

Praga and the other suburbs

Lolek Pub ul. Rokitnicka 20. The best of several watering holes in the middle of Pole Mokotowskie. Barbecue-style food, beer and daily live music at 8pm in and around a log cabin. Pole Mokotowskie metro station. Open 11am–3am.

Łysy Pingwin ul. Ząbkowska 11. A popular Seventies-style lounge with beer, snacks and good music. The "bald penguin" is a good starting point for a Praga bar crawl. Open 3pm–1am, Fri & Sat till 2am.

W Oparach Absurdu ul. Ząbkowska 6. The giant spider marking this bar gives away its defining characteristic – utter madness. Inside it's several creaky levels of second-hand furniture, nooks, crannies and misplaced antiques – and there's still space for live music on Wed and Sat. Unmissable. Open noon–3am.

Nightlife and entertainment

There's a quality **club** scene in Warsaw, with a fair spread that should cater for most tastes. If a Chopin **concert** or avant-garde **drama** (sometimes in English) is your idea of a good night out, you're unlikely to be disappointed. In summer, especially, high-quality theatre productions, operas and recitals abound, many of them as popular with tourists as with Varsovians themselves. They are also affordable, particularly if you buy tickets that entail taking whatever seats are available after the third and final call (it sounds risky, but there are always places).

For up-to-date information about what's on, check the current **listings** sections of the *Warsaw In Your Pocket*, *Warsaw Insider* or *Gazeta Wyborcza* (see p.65), ask at the tourist office or look for posters around the city. The main **jazz festivals** are the excellent Warsaw Summer Jazz Days, a summer-long event featuring big western names with many of the concerts free; the related Jazz na Starówce (Jazz in the Old Town), with high-quality free concerts on the Rynek Starego Miasta at 7pm every Saturday in July and August; and the October Jazz Jamboree, a long-standing bash which has over the years attracted luminaries such as Duke Ellington and Miles Davis. The most important **film festivals** are the Warsaw Film Festival (Ⓦwww.wff.pl), held in mid-October; and in May the Warsaw International Jewish Film Festival (Ⓦwww.warsawjff .ant.pl). **Classical music festivals** include the Chopin Piano Competition, always a launch pad for a major international career and held every five years – the next is in September 2010; the Festival of Contemporary Music (Ⓦwww .warsaw-autumn.art.pl) held every September; the Easter week Beethoven Festival (Ⓦwww.beethoven.org.pl); and the prestigious Mozart Festival, held in early summer. The tourist office (see p.65) will have details of these and other upcoming events.

The best place to find listings is the "Kino" page of the *Gazeta Wyborcza* (see p.44), in the paper every day but most extensive on Fridays. Cinema tickets cost about 10–20zł, usually with reductions on Mondays.

Theatres

Contemporary Art Centre ul. Jazdów 2 ☎022/628 1271, ⓦwww.csw.art.pl. Plays host to many international theatre and dance performances.

Syrena ul. Litewska 3 ☎022/628 5093, ⓦwww .teatrsyrena.pl. Modern drama in Polish.

Teatr Buffo ul. Konopnickiej 6 ☎022/625 4709, ⓦwww.studiobuffo.com.pl. Concerts, musicals, avant-garde plays. Has performances in English at times.

Teatr Dramatyczny Palace of Culture ☎022/656 6844, ⓦwww.teatrdramatyczny.pl. A huge complex with two venues – one for big productions, another for intimate studio performances – both staging plays in Polish.

Teatr Żydowski pl. Grzybowski 12/16 ☎022/620 6281, ⓦwww.teatr-zydowski.art.pl. Warsaw's Jewish theatre, with most performances in Polish or Yiddish.

Cinemas

Iluzjon ul. Narbutta 50a ☎022/646 1260, ⓦwww .fn.org.pl. National Film Archives venue, screening cinema classics from all over the world.

Kino Lab u. Jazdów 2 ☎022/628 1271, ⓦwww .kinolab.independent.pl. Art movies and assorted cinematic weirdness in the Contemporary Art Centre.

Kinoteka Palace of Culture ☎022/511 7070, ⓦwww.kinoteka.pl. Multiple screens showing commercial films in this extraordinary Stalinist building (see p.92).

Kultura/Rejs Krakowskie Przedmieście 21/3 ☎022/826 3335. Mostly specialist films. Late-night screenings at weekends and good Dolby sound system.

Shopping

The old sparsely stocked state-run establishments are a distant memory in Warsaw, and **shopping** here today is not very different from shopping in any other major European city, with a variety of department and specialist stores catering to most consumer whims. Biggest of the central department stores is the **Galeria Centrum** on Marszałkowska, opposite the Palace of Culture, while the new **Złote Tarasy** complex beside the main train station is the most central shopping mall. The pedestrianized **ulica Chmielna**, running east from here, is still somewhat dowdy but has its fair share of clothes shops and boutiques.

Bookshops, newsagents and music stores

Thanks to the sizeable English-speaking community you won't find yourself lost for a newspaper or book in English. As well as the bookshops listed below, **antykwariats** (second-hand booksellers) invariably have a few curiosities in English, sometimes including out-of-print works on Poland, and are always good for cut-rate, communist-era art albums. Try Troszkiewiczów at ul. Wspólna 51 and ul. Piękna 54, or Zaścianek, ul. Wilcza 5. Atticus, ul. Krakowskie Przedmieście 20/22, and Kosmos, al. Ujazdowskie 16, also sell prints and old maps.

American Bookstore Nowy Świat 61, ul. Koszykowa 55 and others ⓦwww .americanbookstore.pl. Chain of excellent bookshops with fiction, guidebooks and Poland-related titles. Stocks *Warsaw In Your Pocket* and *Warsaw Insider*.

EMPiK ul. Nowy Świat 15/17 (corner of al. Jerozolimskie) and ul. Marszałkowska 116/122 ⓦwww.empik.com. Chain store with lots of books, DVDs and CDs and a good selection of foreign press. Both stores open Mon–Sat 9am–10pm, Sun 11am–7pm.

Traffic Club ul. Bracka 25 ⓦwww.traffic-club .pl. Warsaw's largest bookstore, with a good music section, a fair number of English titles and major newspapers. Nice on-site café, free wi-fi and plenty of armchairs.

Art, crafts and antiques

Ambra ul. Piwna 15. One of the better Polish amber jewellery stores on a street that's stuffed full with them.

Bolesławiec ul. Prosta 2/14, ⓦwww .ceramicboleslawiec.com.pl. Poland's favourite stoneware: bowls, mugs and the like with distinctive blue-and-white patterns.

Cepelia Nowy Świat 35, Krucza 23/31, Marszałkowska 99/101 and other branches. Chain of handicraft shops specializing in Polish ceramics, textiles and woodcarving – as well as more tacky souvenirs.

Galeria Zapiecek Rynek Starego Miasta 8. Cutting-edge jewellery, with an emphasis on minimalist silver pieces.

Food

Shopping for food in Warsaw has improved dramatically in recent years. For a wide range of imported food and wines try the Piotr i Paweł **supermarket in** the Blue City shopping centre, 3km west of the centre at al. Jerozolimskie 179 (bus #517 from the main station); or Carrefour, one tram stop across the river from the Old Town, in the Wileński shopping centre.

Blikle ul. Nowy Świat 33 The famous café/sweet shop has an adjacent delicatessen, serving luxury meats, cheeses, breads and wines.

Hala Mirowska pl. Mirowski, west of the Ogród Saski. The two Art Nouveau market halls contain grim supermarkets, but the surrounding outdoor stalls are excellent for fresh produce, meats and flowers.

Marcpol In one of the "temporary" pavilions in the shadow of the Palace of Culture, this is a handy central supermarket. Open 7am–9pm, Sun 9am–6pm.

Sezam ul. Marszałkowska 140. An old-fashioned but good supermarket in the Centrum area, just down from the intersection with Świętokrzyska. Mon–Fri 8am–8pm, Sat 9am–5pm, Sun 10am–4pm.

Markets and bazaars

Shopping centres have all but killed the outdoor markets in recent years; the infamous Dziesięciolecia stadium "Russian" market was recently closed so that a new stadium could be built there for the 2012 European Championships.

The Sunday Koło Bazaar, ulica Obozowa, in the Wola district (tram #12, #13 or #24 to Koło), is the main antiques and bric-a-brac market, with everything from sofas and old Russian samovars to genuine Iron Crosses on offer. On Monday mornings, there's a pets market selling hamsters, carnivorous turtles and more.

Activities and sports

Ice-skating is possible on the ice rink in front of the Palace of Culture in winter months (daily 8am–8pm; free). You can rent skates for a nominal fee.

The best of the city's **swimming** centres is the Wodny Park Warszawianka, ul. Merliniego 4, where there's an Olympic-sized pool as well as water slides and children's areas, and squash, archery and a fitness club (Mon–Fri 6.30am–10pm, Sat & Sun 8am–10pm; 18-24zł/hr; ⓦwww.wodnypark .com.pl; from the centre take tram #4, #18 or #36 4km south to Malczewskiego). In summer, there's an open-air pool at WOW Wisła, in the Praga suburb at Namysłowska 8 (July & Aug daily 9am–7pm; tram #32 from pl. Zamkowy). You can also use the pools at the better hotels, but this is expensive (80zł and up).

As for spectator sports, your best bet is **football**. Legia Warszawa, the army club with a nationwide following, plays at Stadion Wojska Polskiego, just southeast of the centre at ulica Łazienkowska (buses #155, #159 and #166). Their biggest rivals, Polonia, play at ul. Konwiktorska 6, a ten-minute walk north of Stare Miasto (or tram #2 from Centrum).

Listings

Airlines Air France, Nowy Świat 64 ☎022/556 6400, ⓦwww.airfrance.com; American Airlines, al. Ujazdowskie 20 ☎022/625 3002, ⓦwww .aa.com; British Airways, ul. Marszałkowska 76 ☎022/529 9000, ⓦwww.ba.com; LOT, al. Jerozolimskie 65/79 (*Marriott hotel*) ☎022/9572, ⓦwww.lot.pl; Lufthansa, airport ☎022/338 1300, ⓦwww.lufthansa.pl; Wizzair ⓦwww.wizzair.com.

American Express ul. Chłodna 51 ☎022/581 5100, ⓦwww.americanexpress.pl. Mon–Fri 9am–5pm.

Banks and exchange There are ATMs and exchange *kantors* all over the city. Shop around for the best rates; the attractive rate posted in the window is often for large amounts.

Car rental Avis (ⓦwww.avis.pl), at the airport (☎022/650 4872), and at the *Marriott* (al. Jerozolimskie 65/79; ☎022/630 7316); Budget (ⓦwww.budget.pl), at the airport (☎022/650 4062) and the *Marriott* (☎022/630 7280); Hertz (ⓦwww.hertz.com.pl), at the airport (☎022/650 2896) and ul. Nowogrodzka 27 (☎022/621 1360); Joka (ⓦwww.joka.com.pl), a slightly cheaper local firm, ul. Okopowa 47 ☎022/636 6393.

Embassies Australia, ul. Nowogrodzka 11 ☎022/521 3444, ⓦwww.australia.pl; Belarus, ul. Wiertnicza 58 ☎022/742 0990 ⓦwww .belembassy.org; Canada, ul. Matejki 1/5 ☎022/584 3100, ⓦwww.canada.pl; Czech Republic, ul. Koszykowa 18 ☎022/525 1850 ⓦwww.mzv .cz/warsaw; Germany, ul. Jazdów 12 ☎022/584 1700, ⓦwww.ambasadaniemiec.pl; Ireland, ul. Mysia 5 ☎022/849 6633, ⓦwww.irlandia. pl; Lithuania, al. Ujazdowskie 12 ☎022/635 9794 ⓦwww.consulate-warsaw.mfa.lt; New Zealand, al. Ujazdowskie 51 ☎022/521 0500 ⓦwww .nzembassy.com/poland; UK, al. Róż 1 ☎022/311 0000, ⓦwww.britishembassy.pl; Ukraine, al. Szucha 7 ☎022/622 4797, ⓦwww.ukraine-emb .pl; USA, al. Ujazdowskie 29/31 ☎022/625 1401, ⓦpoland.usembassy.gov.

Hospitals and emergencies The private Damian hospital at ul. Wałbrzyska 46 (☎022/566 2222, ⓦwww.damian.pl) has English-speaking staff, 24hr service and a clinic in the centre at ul. Foksal 3/5; Medicover at ul. Bitwy Warszawskiej 1920 r. 18 (☎0804/22 9596, ⓦwww.medicover.pl) offers

Moving on

Warszawa Zachodnia (see p.65) handles all **international bus departures** to Western Europe and the Baltic States, as well as major domestic destinations to the south and west. Dworzec Stadion (see p.65) is the departure point for buses to eastern Poland, Belarus and Ukraine. International tickets can be purchased through Orbis offices (see "Travel agents", p.112) and international counters at bus stations. **Domestic intercity buses** run by the private Polski Express (☎022/620 0326, ⓦwww.polskiexpress.pl) are fast and comfortable, though slightly more expensive than state-run PKS buses (☎022/9433, ⓦwww.pksbilety .pl); they operate from a stop beside the Złote Tarasy mall on aleja Jana Pawła II, west of Warszawa Centralna station. From the same stop you can catch HaloBus (☎0602/66 4419, ⓦwww.halobus.pl) services to Kazimierz Dolny, which stop at Puławy.

Warszawa Centralna (see p.64) **train station** serves all international routes and the major national ones. For Sochaczew, Łowicz, Arkadia and Nieborów you'll need to use the adjacent Śródmieście station, while trains to Małkinia, near the site of the Treblinka concentration camp monument, leave from the Wileńska station in the Praga district. Train tickets can also be bought at Orbis offices (see p.112), or online as e-tickets (ⓦwww.pkp.pl for domestic trains, ⓦwww.polrail.com for both domestic and international routes). For train information call ☎022/9436, or visit ⓦwww .rozklad-pkp.pl.

a similar 24hr service. Most central of the main hospitals is the University Hospital, ul. Marszałkowska 24 (☎022/522 7333). The emergency ambulance number is ☎022/999, but the private Falck ambulance service (☎022/9675) will also respond, and you've more chance of being understood in English.

Internet cafés Good, central places include *Casablanca*, ul. Krakowskie Przedmieście 4/6 (Mon–Fri 9am–1am, Sat 10am–2am, Sun 10am–midnight) and *Eccoms*, Nowy Świat 53 (daily 9am–11pm). Expect to pay about 5zł per hr.

Laundry Pralnia Wodnik, ul. Złotopolska 1 (entrance on ul. Handlowa. Mon–Fri 8am–6pm, Sat 9am–2pm.

Left luggage There are left-luggage facilities at Warszawa Centralna train station (see p.64).

Lost property If you've lost something on city transport, ul. Włościańska 52 ☎022/663 3297.

Pharmacies There are 24hr *aptekas* on the top floor of Warszawa Centralna train station and at al. Solidarności 149. In the New Town there's a pharmacy at ul. Freta 13/15 (Mon–Sat 8am–8pm, Sun 10am–8pm).

Police Report crimes at the police office at ul. Wilcza 21.

Post offices The main office is at ul. Świętokrzyska 31/33. It handles fax, poste restante (postcode 00-001) and is open 24hr. Also at Rynek Starego Miasta 15 (Mon–Fri 8am–8pm, Sat 11am–8pm); and Warszawa Centralna station main hall (Mon–Fri 8am–8pm, Sat 8am–2pm; phones 24hr). For mail rates see ⓦwww .poczta-polska.pl.

Telephone and fax facilities In main post offices; some internet cafés have fax facilities and cheap international calling (see "Internet cafés", above).

Travel agents STA Travel, ul. Krucza 41/43 (☎022/626 0080, ⓦwww.statravel.pl). Orbis (ⓦwww.orbistravel.pl) at ul. Bracka 16 (☎022/827 7140; Mon–Fri 9am–6pm, Sat 9am–3pm) sells all train tickets and international bus tickets. Intourist, ul. Nowogrodzka 10 (☎022/625 0852, ⓦwww .intourist.ru), can help arrange visas to Russia, Ukraine, Belarus and the CIS.

Western Union ul. Nowogrodzka 11 ☎022/652 9600, ⓦwww.westernunion.com.pl.

Travel details

Trains

Warsaw to: Białystok (10 daily; 2hr 30min); Bydgoszcz (9 daily; 3hr 45min); Częstochowa (9 daily; 2hr 30min–3hr); Gdańsk/Sopot/Gdynia (11 daily; 4hr 30min–5hr 30min); Jelenia Góra (1 overnight; 10hr 30min); Katowice (17 daily; 2hr 30min–4hr); Kraków (19 daily; 2hr 45min–5hr); Lublin (11 daily; 2hr 30min); Łódź (Mon–Fri hourly; Sat & Sun every 2hr; 1hr 20min); Olsztyn (4 daily; 4hr); Poznań (hourly; 2hr 45min–4hr); Przemyśl (4 daily; 7hr); Rzeszów (2 daily; 5hr); Suwałki (2 daily; 5hr); Świnoujście (1 overnight; 11hr); Szczecin (7 daily; 5–8hr); Toruń (10 daily; 2hr 45min); Wrocław (12 daily; 5hr–6hr 30min); Zamość (2 daily; 5hr); Zakopane (2 daily of which 1 overnight; 6hr–10hr).

Buses

Warsaw Polski Express/HaloBus stop on al. Jana Pawła II to: Kazimierz Dolny via Puławy (9–12 daily; 3hr).
Warsaw Zachodnia to: Żelazowa Wola (3 daily; 1hr 15min).

Flights

Warsaw to: Gdańsk (5–6 daily; 1hr); Katowice (2 daily; 1hr); Kraków (4–5 daily; 1hr); Poznań (4 daily; 1hr); Rzeszów (5–6 daily; 1hr); Szczecin (3–4 daily; 1hr 20min); Wrocław (4-5 daily; 1hr).

International trains

Warsaw to: Amsterdam (1 overnight; 16hr 30min); Berlin (5 daily; 6hr); Bratislava (1 overnight; 9hr); Budapest (2 daily of which 1 overnight; 11hr 30min); Cologne (1 overnight; 12hr); Kiev (2 daily; 16–17hr); Lviv (1 daily; 22hr); Minsk (2 daily; 9–10hr); Moscow (3 daily; 18–21hr); Prague (2 daily of which 1 overnight; 8hr 30min–10hr); Vienna (3 daily of which 1 overnight; 7hr 30min–9hr 30min).

International buses

Warsaw Zachodnia to: Frankfurt (2–3 daily; 18hr); London (2–6 daily; 27hr); Paris (2–6 daily; 24hr); Riga (1–2 daily; 13hr); Tallinn (1–2 daily; 17hr); Vilnius (2 daily; 8–10hr).

Mazovia and Łódź

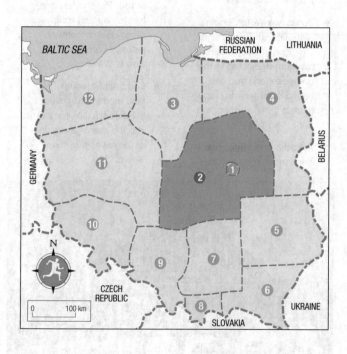

CHAPTER 2 # Highlights

* **Kampinoski National Park** A patchwork of virgin forest and squelchy bog, this former hunting ground of Poland's kings is covered in well-marked trails and is easily accessible from central Warsaw. See p.119

* **Żelazowa Wola** Chopin's birthplace and nowadays a national shrine; there's a museum dedicated to the composer and you can attend summertime piano recitals in the surrounding park. See 122

* **Arkadia and Nieborów** The landscaped gardens laid out for the Radziwiłł family are among the best-preserved aristocratic parks in the country. See p.128

* **Industrial architecture in Łódź** The red-brick factories and warehouses of the "Polish Manchester" are a must for lovers of nineteenth-century industrial architecture. See p.129

* **Łódź Art Museum** The best modern art collection in Poland, full of insights into the avant-garde side of the nation's culture. See p.133

▲ Manufaktura, Łódź

2

Mazovia and Łódź

Mazovia – the sandy plain surrounding Warsaw – contains a sprinkling of sights that make good trips out from the Polish capital. Passing through the northern stretches of Mazovia, there are worthy detours to the market town of **Pułtusk** and the castle at **Ciechanów**, while the solemn monument to the vanished concentration camp at **Treblinka** lies to the east. West of Warsaw, the beautiful forest of the **Kampinoski National Park** is an easily accessible area of natural wilderness; while the village of **Żelazowa Wola** just beyond is home to the delightful country house where composer Chopin was born. Other likely day-trip destinations include the market town of **Łowicz**, an important centre of folk crafts and a convenient jumping-off point for the nearby aristocratic estates of **Arkadia** and **Nieborów**; and **Płock** on the banks of the Wisła, where a historic old town harbours a couple of worthwhile museums.

Southwest of the capital, the great manufacturing city of **Łódź** offers a rich cultural scene and, unusually for Poland, a wealth of nineteenth-century architecture. With a generous handful of museums and a burgeoning nightlife, Łódź is the one place in this chapter that merits a stay of several days.

Just about everywhere covered in the following section can be reached by **bus** and **train** from Warsaw; although Łódź serves equally well as a base if you're primarily interested in the western half of the chapter.

Northeastern Mazovia

North of Warsaw, the main routes whisk you through the suburbs and out into the flat Mazovian countryside, its windswept farmland divided by the Wisła from the west and by the smaller and less polluted rivers Narew and Bug to the east. The old centres of **Pułtusk** and **Ciechanów** retain the rustic feel of a traditional Mazovian market town, while to the east the monument on the site of the **Treblinka** concentration camp is a more sober destination. **Transport** from Warsaw to Pułtusk and Ciechanów, by bus and train respectively, is straightforward, but getting to Treblinka is more difficult without your own transport.

Pułtusk

Sixty kilometres north of Warsaw along the west bank of the River Narew stands **PUŁTUSK**, a lively Mazovian market town that was long a grain-trading centre on the river route to Gdańsk. Pułtusk twice hit the headlines in the nineteenth century, first in 1806 when Napoleonic and Russian forces fought

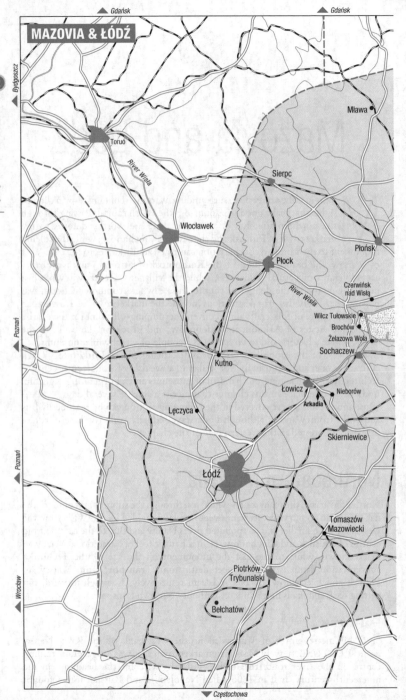

MAZOVIA & ŁÓDŹ

▲ Gdańsk

▲ Gdańsk

◄ Bydgoszcz

Toruń

River Wisła

Mława

Sierpc

Włocławek

Płońsk

Płock

River Wisła

Czerwińsk nad Wisłą

Wilcz Tułowskie

Brochów

Żelazowa Wola

Sochaczew

◄ Poznań

Kutno

Łowicz

Nieborów

Arkadia

Lęczyca

Skierniewice

◄ Poznań

Łódź

Tomaszów Mazowiecki

◄ Wrocław

Piotrków Trybunalski

Bełchatów

▼ Częstochowa

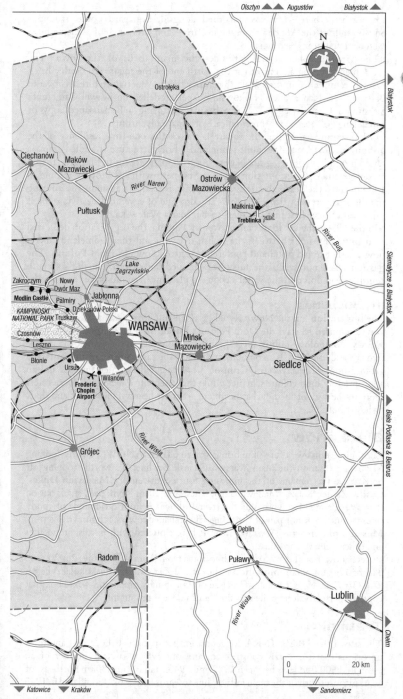

N

Ostrołęka

Białystok

Ciechanów   Maków
Mazowiecki

River Narew

Ostrów
Mazowiecka

Pułtusk

Małkinia
Treblinka

River Bug

Siemiatycze & Białystok

Lake
Zegrzyńskie

Zakroczym   Nowy
Dwór Maz

Modlin Castle   Palmiry   Jabłonna
Dziekanów Polski
KAMPINOSKI   Truskaw
NATIONAL PARK

WARSAW

Mińsk
Mazowiecki

Siedlce

Czosnów
Leszno

Błonie   Ursus   Wilanów
Frederic
Chopin
Airport

Biała Podlaska & Belarus

Grójec

River Wisła

Dęblin

Puławy

Radom

Lublin

River Wisła

Chełm

0   20 km

117

a major battle here – a victory recorded alongside Bonaparte's other triumphs on the walls of the Arc de Triomphe in Paris – and later, in 1868, when a huge meteorite fell near the town.

The large cobbled **Rynek** provides the main focus of the town. The monumental collegiate **church** at the north end of the square is a Gothic brick basilica, remodelled in the sixteenth century by the Venetian architect Giovanni Battista. The Renaissance Noskowski chapel modelled on Wawel Cathedral's Sigismund Chapel (see p.372) is a beauty, featuring a Renaissance copy of Michelangelo's *Pietà*, and some delicate original polychromy.

Off the southern end of the square is the **castle**, one-time residence of the bishops of Płock, an oft-rebuilt semicircular brick structure straddled across a raised mound overlooking the Narew. As with many towns in Mazovia, there's a Napoleonic connection: Bonaparte stayed here with his brother Jérôme in 1806 prior to the nearby battle against Russian forces, and again in 1812 during the disastrous retreat from Moscow. It's also one of several places where he is supposed to have first met his lover-to-be, Maria Walewska.

In the 1970s, the castle was taken over by Polonia, the organization dedicated to maintaining links between the Polish diaspora and their homeland, and is now a rather grand hotel and conference centre known as **Dom Polonii**. The **gardens**, laid out when the moat was drained and covered in the sixteenth century, lead down to the water's edge – a pleasant, tranquil place for a stroll.

Practicalities

The **bus station**, on the Nowy Rynek, is a ten-minute walk from the Rynek. If you're tempted to stay, the Dom Polonii's **hotel**, the *Zamek* (☎023/692 9000, ⓦ www.dompolonii.pultusk.pl; ❺), with rooms either in the castle or in one of two riverside annexes, is an obvious option. Of the castle's three **restaurants**, the ground-floor *Karmazynowa* ("Crimson") has chandeliers, huge mirrors and an appropriately loud colour scheme; while the basement *Piwnica pod Wieżą* offers more in the way of medieval atmosphere – expect hearty Polish pork and duck dishes at both places.

Ciechanów

Continuing northwest for 40km brings you to **CIECHANÓW**, a dowdy-looking Mazovian town on the main Warsaw–Gdańsk rail line. It's worth stopping off here to see the remains of the imposing fourteenth-century **Mazovian Dukes' Castle** (Zamek Książąt Mazowieckich; Tues–Sun 10am–4pm; 5zł), stuck out on the eastern edge of town beside the river Łydynia. A stout quadrangle of ruddy bricks framed by a fine pair of thrusting, barrel shaped towers, it houses a diverting **Museum of Firearms** (Wystawa Broń Palna), cluttered with pistols, arquebuses and other military hardware.

Ciechanów is on the main railway line north from Warsaw (10 daily; 2hr 20min). The best bet for **accommodation** is the central *Zacisze* hotel, ul. Mikołaczyka 8A (☎023/672 2046, ⓦ www.hotelzacisze.pl; ❹), an ugly green-and-white box that conceals perfectly acceptable en suites, and a decent restaurant.

Treblinka

The site of the **TREBLINKA** concentration camp, one of the largest and most notorious that the Nazis constructed, and one which saw the murder of an estimated 800,000 Jews between 1942 and 1943, stands some 80km northeast of Warsaw, just south of the main railway line towards Białystok. Liquidated in 1943

Treblinka

The **Treblinka I** labour camp, opened in an isolated tract of forest in 1941, held up to two thousand prisoners at a time, mostly Poles and Jews from Warsaw. More than half of the 20,000 held here between 1941 and 1944 were either shot or worked to death in the adjacent gravel pit. In April 1942, construction on the larger **Treblinka II** was started two kilometres to the east, a death camp nearly identical to the one in the Lublin suburb of Majdanek (see p.265), but without crematoria, and with the addition of an artificial train station, used to convince victims they were merely in transit. By July it was complete, and by mid-September 300,000 Jews from the evacuated Warsaw ghetto had already been gassed. The vast majority of those killed at Treblinka during the next year were Polish Jews, but thousands of Jews from Greece, Slovakia and elsewhere were also sent here, as well as two thousand Gypsies. The camp was run by two to three dozen Germans and Austrians, as well as around one hundred Ukrainian guards, including the infamously sadistic Ivan the Terrible, who wielded a sword at the camp and was responsible for the torture and murder of thousands. In 1943, following an uprising in which two hundred inmates escaped (sixty of whom survived the war), the Nazis, fearing a Soviet advance, liquidated the camp and transferred the remaining Jews to Sobibór (see p.269). Every trace of the camp's existence was erased – an enormous task which involved the exhumation and incineration of over three-quarters of a million bodies – at the conclusion of which one of the guards was settled on the site to pose as a farmer.

by the Nazis, fearing a Soviet advance, nothing of the camp itself remains and the site today is a **museum** (daily 9am–7pm; 2zł), comprising a series of **stone memorials.** Placed here under the auspices of the Polish authorities in 1959–63, these trace the outline and principal features of the camp: one set represents railway tracks, leading to a platform and cremation pit; another series marks the camp boundaries and gates; and a third, a symbolic graveyard, is dedicated to the victims and the countries they came from. The main monuments are on the site of Treblinka II, from which a path leads to Treblinka I, where there are more symbolic tombs. Little has changed at the museum since it was set up forty years ago, and information in English is scant: in spite of the gravity of the memorial it can be hard to get a feeling for what took place here, especially in good weather, when the surrounding forest is as pleasantly serene as any other.

The only way to get to Treblinka without your own transportation or on a **guided tour** (which can be arranged by the Our Roots agency in Warsaw; see p.56) is by taking a **train** to Małkinia (there are frequent connections from Dworzec Wileński in Warsaw's Praga district and a few daily services from Warszawa Centralna), 8km north of the camp. There are usually **taxis** waiting outside the Małkinia station, and hiring one to take you to Treblinka and back shouldn't cost more than 40zł. The drive takes you across a creaking, old-fashioned bridge over the River Bug, and through several pretty villages, including Treblinka village itself, halfway to the camp, where there's a small grocery store. No buses run along this route, but hitching is a possibility.

The Kampinoski National Park

With its boundaries touching the edge of Warsaw's Żoliborz suburb, the **Kampinoski National Park** (Kampinoski Park Narodowy; ⑩ www.kampinoska .waw.pl) stretches some 30km west of the capital, a rare example of an extensive woodland coexisting with a major city. Originally submerged under the waters of the Wisła, which now flows north of the forest, the picturesque landscape intersperses dense tracts of woodland – pine, hornbeam, birch and oak are the most common trees – with a patchwork terrain of swamp-like marshes and belts of sand dune. Protected as a national park, this open forest harbours the summer houses of numerous Varsovians, and in autumn draws legions of mushroom-pickers. Elk, wild boar, beaver and lynx (the latter two recently reintroduced) are sighted from time to time, and the park is rich in bird life – watch out for storks, cranes and buzzards. Access for walkers and cross-country skiers is pretty much unrestricted, though it's all too easy to get lost in the woods: stick to marked routes (good maps are available in the major Warsaw bookstores). There aren't many shops or snack bars at the entrance points to the park, so it's best to bring your own supplies.

Truskaw and around

Buses from plac Wilson in the Warsaw suburb of Żoliborz (#708 or #714; to get to plac Wilson from the centre, take tram #4 or #36 north) take you 10km out to **TRUSKAW**, a rapidly developing village on the eastern edge of

Frédéric Chopin (1810–49)

Of all the major Polish artists, **Frédéric Chopin** – Fryderyk Szopen as he was baptized in Polish – is the one whose work has achieved the greatest international recognition. He is, to all intents and purposes, the national composer, a fact attested to in the wealth of festivals, concerts and, most importantly, the famous international piano competition held in his name. Like other Polish creative spirits of the nineteenth century, the life of this brilliantly talented composer and performer reflects the political upheavals of Partition-era Poland. Born of mixed Polish–French parentage in the Mazovian village of Żelazowa Wola, where his French father was a tutor to a local aristocratic family, Frédéric spent his early years in and around Warsaw, holidays in the surrounding countryside giving him an early introduction to the Mazovian folk tunes that permeate his compositions. Musical talent began to show from an early age: at six Chopin was already making up tunes; a year later he started to play the piano, and his first concert performance came at the age of eight. After a couple of years' schooling in Warsaw, the budding composer – his first polonaises and mazurkas had already been written and performed – was enrolled at the newly created Warsaw Music Conservatory.

Chopin's first journey abroad was in August 1829, to Vienna, where he gave a couple of concert performances to finance the publication of some recent compositions, a set of Mozart variations. Returning to Warsaw soon afterwards, Chopin made his official **public debut**, performing the virtuoso Second Piano Concerto (F Minor), its melancholic slow movement inspired by an (unrequited) love affair with a fellow Conservatory student and aspiring opera singer. In the autumn of 1830 he travelled again to Vienna, only to hear news of the **November uprising** against the Russians at home. Already set upon moving to Paris, the heartbroken Chopin was inspired by the stirring yet tragic events in Poland to write the famous *Revolutionary Étude*, among a string of other works. As it turned out, he was never to return to Poland, a fate shared by many of the fellow exiles whose Parisian enclave he entered in 1831. He rapidly befriended them and the host of other young composers (including Berlioz, Bellini, Liszt and Mendelssohn) who lived in the city. The elegantly dressed, artistically sensitive Chopin soon became a high society favourite, earning his living teaching and giving the occasional recital. Some relatively problem-free years followed, during which he produced a welter of new compositions, notably the rhapsodic *Fantaisie-Impromptu*, a book of études and a string of nationalistically inspired polonaises and mazurkas.

the forest. Following ulica Skibińskiego from the bus stop into the forest will bring you after 5km to the **Palmiry memorial site**, where a small museum (Tues–Sun 9am–3pm; free) honours victims of the Nazis, who used the forest as a killing ground in World War II. The adjacent cemetery contains the bodies of about two thousand prisoners and civilians, who were herded out to the forest, shot and hurled into pits. From the museum there's a second path leading back to Truskaw, or you could press on a further 5km to the quiet hamlet of **PALMIRY**, though be warned that the path runs alongside a mosquito-ridden swamp. From the highway, one kilometre north of Palmiry, there are hourly buses back to the capital, though it's not an especially pleasant place to wait.

A few kilometres northeast of here, on the banks of the Wisła, the area around the village of **DZIEKANÓW POLSKI** is a noted birdwatchers' haunt. Among species regularly sighted is the **white stork**, whose nests can be seen on special platforms atop telegraph poles around the village. You're also likely to find **lapwings** and several kinds of **raptors** in the surrounding fields, while closer to the water you can spot brilliantly coloured **kingfishers** and **bluethroats** as well as a variety of gulls, terns and ducks.

Chopin's life changed dramatically in 1836 following his encounter with the radical novelist **George Sand**, who promptly fell in love with him and suggested she become his mistress. After over a year spent hesitating over the proposal in the winter of 1838, Chopin – by now ill – travelled with her and her two children to Majorca. Though musically productive – the B Flat Minor Sonata and its famous funeral march date from this period – the stay was not a success, Chopin's rapidly deteriorating health forcing a return to France to seek the help of a doctor in Marseille. Thereafter Chopin was forced to give up composing for a while, earning his living giving piano lessons to rich Parisians and spending the summers with an increasingly maternal Sand at her country house at **Nohant**, south of Paris. The rural environment temporarily did wonders for Chopin's health, and it was in Nohant that he produced some of his most powerful music, including the sublime *Polonaise Fantasie*, the Third Sonata and several of the major ballades. Increasingly strained relations with Sand, however, finally snapped when she broke with him in 1847. Miserable and almost penniless, Chopin accepted an invitation from an admiring Scottish pupil Jane Stirling to visit **Britain**. Despite mounting illness, Chopin gave numerous concerts and recitals in London, making friends with Carlyle, Dickens and other luminaries of English artistic life. Increasingly weak, and unable either to compose or return Stirling's devoted affections, a depressed Chopin returned to Paris in November 1848.

Just a few months later he finally succumbed to the tuberculosis that had dogged him for years, dying in his apartment on place de Vendôme in central Paris; in accordance with his deathbed wish, Mozart's *Requiem* was sung at the funeral, and his body was buried in the **Père-Lachaise Cemetery**, the grave topped, a year later, with a monument of a weeping muse sprinkled with earth from his native Mazovia. Admired by his friends, yet also criticized by many of his peers, the music Chopin created during his short life achieved a synthesis few other Polish artists have matched – a distinctive Polishness combined with a universality of emotional and aesthetic appeal. For fellow Poles, as for many foreigners, the emotive Polish content is particularly significant: many, indeed, feel his music expresses the essence of the national psyche, alternating wistful romanticism with storms of turbulent, restless protest – "guns hidden in flower-beds", in fellow composer Schumann's memorable description.

121

Żelazowa Wola

Fifty kilometres west of Warsaw, just beyond the western edge of the Park Narodowy Puszcza Kampinoska, is the little village of **ŻELAZOWA WOLA**, the birthplace of composer and national hero, **Frédéric Chopin**. The journey through the rolling Mazovian countryside makes an enjoyable day out from the city; unless you've got a car, you'll need to take a **train** from Warszawa Zachodnia to the town of Sochaczew, from where bus #6 from the train station forecourt trundles (roughly hourly; 20min) to Żelazowa Wola.

The house where Chopin was born is now a **museum** (Tues–Sun: mid-April to mid-Oct 9am–5.30pm; mid-Oct to mid-April 9.30am–4pm; 12zł; park only 4zł) surrounded by a large, tranquil garden. The Chopin family lived here for only a year after their son's birth in 1810, but young Frédéric returned frequently to what became his favourite place – not least because of the musical inspiration he drew from the folk traditions of Mazovia. Bought by public subscription in 1929, the Chopin family residence was subsequently restored and turned into a museum to the composer run by the Warsaw-based Chopin Society. The Society also organizes **piano recitals** here throughout the summer (May–Sept 11am & 3pm; free with museum ticket) – check Warsaw listings sources (see p.108) or with the Chopin Society (based at Warsaw's Chopin Museum; see p.93) for the current programme details. Concerts take place in the museum's music room, although on fine days the audience sits outside, the music wafting through the open windows.

The house itself is a typical nineteenth-century *dwór* or country mansion, mixing rustic architecture with mock-palatial features – notably the coyly aristocratic colonnaded entrance porch. Restored to period perfection, the building contains a collection of family portraits and other Chopin memorabilia (though none of it was actually here during his own lifetime). Exhibits are small in number but powerfully evocative: a few framed pages of an original score, a nineteenth-century grand piano that the composer is believed to have played in Paris, and a fine example of a so-called "giraffe" – an upright grand piano with a sensually curvy frame.

Back outside, the surrounding garden was transformed into a magnificent **botanical park** during the 1930s, the colour-charged floral arrangements supposedly inspired by Chopin's music. Planted with a shrewd sprinkling of evergreen shrubs, it's a colourful place whatever the season.

The Sochaczew–Wilcz Tułowskie railway

Ten kilometres southwest of Żelazowa Wola, the unremarkable town of **Sochaczew** (reached by local train from Warszawa Zachodnia station) is the starting point for steam-hauled narrow-gauge railway excursions to the tiny village of **Wilcz Tułowskie**, a scenic, eighteen-kilometre journey which takes you through the forests on the western fringes of Kampinoski National Park. Services run every Saturday from June to September, departing at 9.40am and arriving just over an hour later, giving you time for a short walk in the forest before the train leaves for Sochaczew at noon. The narrow-gauge train station in Sochaczew has a museum (May–Oct Tues–Sun 10am–3pm; 6zł), featuring an impressive line-up of narrow-gauge rolling stock from all over Poland. Further details about train running times are available from the Narrow-Gauge Railway Museum (Muzeum Kolej Wąskotorowy: ☏046/862 5976) inside Sochaczew station, ul. Towarowa 7, 95-500 Sochaczew.

Warsaw-based chocolatier *Wedels* operate an al fresco **café** in the gardens during summer – a great place to sip hot chocolate or simply sink one's face into ice creams and fancy cakes. The moderately priced *Pod Wierzbami* **restaurant**, on the corner of the main road, will fix you up with anything from simple soups to roast duck.

Along the Wisła

Northwest of Warsaw, the Mazovian countryside is dominated by the meandering expanse of the **Wisła** as it continues its trek towards the Baltic Sea. Many of the towns along its banks still bear the imprint of the river-bound trade they once thrived on. Of these, the most important is **Płock**, one-time capital of Mazovia, and a thriving industrial centre. With a major museum and an enjoyable historic complex, it makes an eminently worthwhile outing from Warsaw. Closer to the capital is the ancient church complex at **Czerwińsk nad Wisłą**.

Modlin Castle

Some 36km northwest of Warsaw, at the intersection of the Wisła and the Narew rivers, stand the eerie ruins of **Modlin Castle** – you can see them from the northbound E81 road to Gdańsk. A huge earth and brick fortress raised in the early nineteenth century on Napoleon's orders, the already large complex was restored and extended by Russian forces in the 1830s and 1840s; at its height it accommodated a garrison of some 26,000 people. It was devastated during the early part of World War II, but you can still wander through the atmospheric remains (daily 9am–4pm; 5zł), which offer a pleasant view over the river below.

Czerwińsk nad Wisłą

CZERWIŃSK NAD WISŁĄ, around 70km from Warsaw along the Płock road, is a placid village on the north bank of the Wisła. What pulls the crowds (and there can be plenty of them in summer) is the Romanesque **Church of St Leonard** (Kościół Św Leonarda), which sits on a hilltop above the village, together with an adjoining monastery complex. The twin-towered church is entered through a twelfth-century **portal** (the surrounding brickwork was added in the seventeenth century), its original ceiling decorated with geometric frescoes featuring plant motifs and representations of the Virgin Mary. Inside the building, a couple of fine Romanesque stone columns have survived, as has a remarkable selection of early polychromy, notably in the **chapel** off the east aisle – its luminous Romanesque frescoes were uncovered during renovation in the 1950s. It's worth taking a stroll down the hill into the tumbledown **village** on the riverbank, which has a notable predominance of wooden houses. Non-express **buses** to Płock from Warszawa Zachodnia call at Czerwińsk (8 daily), a ninety-minute journey. The selection of food in the village **shop** is adequate for a picnic.

Płock

The fact that **PŁOCK** is an oil-industry town is immediately apparent, with refinery pipes and gantries dominating the horizon west of the centre. However Płock is also a former royal capital, and retains a charming **Old Town** perched on a bluff above the Wisła river.

2

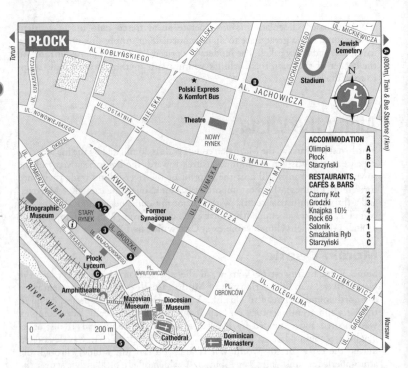

The oldest urban settlement in Mazovia, Płock became the seat of the Piast dynasty in the eleventh century, and remained so for nearly a hundred years. An important bishopric, and one of a number of riverside towns that grew fat on the medieval Wisła-bound commercial boom, Płock felt the full weight of mid-seventeenth-century Swedish invasions – much of the Płock bishopric's valuable library was purloined and taken to Uppsala, where it remains.

Arrival, information and accommodation

The **bus and train stations** are next to each other on the northeastern side of town, a twenty-minute walk (or a short ride on bus #20) from the centre. With trains only running to the middle-of-nowhere junctions of Kutno and Sierpc, the most convenient way of getting to Płock by public transport is by bus: the roughly hourly Warsaw–Bydgoszcz services run by Polski Express (which use the main bus station) and Komfort Bus (which pick up and drop off on al. Jachowicza 40 near the Nowy Rynek). The **tourist office** at Stary Rynek 8 (Mon–Fri 9am–5pm, Sat 10am–4pm; ☎024/367 1944, ⒲www.itplock.pl) is a fine source of maps and accommodation information.

Although Płock makes an easy day trip from Łódź or Warsaw, there is a good choice of **accommodation** in town, beginning with the well-placed *Starzyński*, overlooking the river at ul. Piekarska 1 (☎024/366 0200, ⒲www.starzynski .com.pl; ⓪), a functional block, not much to look at from outside, but with very comfortable, fairly tastefully furnished rooms, including some with outstanding views. Other options include the basic but friendly *Płock* (☎024/262 9393, ⒲www.hotelplock.pl; ⑤), just north of the centre at al. Jachowicza 38 and quite good for the price but a step down from the *Starzyński*; and, northeast of the centre towards the stations at ul. Dworcowa 26, *Olimpia* (☎024/262 0407, Ⓦwww.motelik-olimpia.eu; ❷–❸), a pension with passable, decent value rooms with or without bath.

The Old Town

Spread along a ridge overlooking the north bank of the Wisła, Płock's **Old Town** is a compact and easy-to-explore area. Occupying the ridge's highest point is the Romanesque **cathedral** (Mon–Sat 10am–5.30pm, Sun 2–5.30pm), begun after the installation of the Płock bishopric in 1075 and completed in the following century. Successive rebuildings have left few traces of the building's original character; what you see today reflects the Classicist remodelling of the Italian architect Merlini in the mid-eighteenth century.

Inside, the **royal chapel** contains the nineteenth-century sarcophagi of Polish princes **Władysław Herman** (1040–1102) and his son, **Bolesław the Wrymouth** (1086–1138), while Art Nouveau-influenced frescoes decorate the nave. The cathedral's most famous feature is the pair of **bronze doors** sculpted by Magdeburg artist Riquin in the mid-twelfth century, and featuring two dozen **panels** filled with a magnificent series of **reliefs** depicting scenes from the Old Testament and the Gospels. Unfortunately they're a replica of the originals, presented by Polish King Władysław Jagiełło to the Princes of Novgorod – where they have been ever since. Back from the building, the skyline is dominated by the twin brick Gothic **Zegarowa** and **Szlachecka towers** beside the cathedral, the best-preserved fragments of the fourteenth-century castle that once stood here. The former tower is the cathedral belfry.

The Diocesan Museum

Directly across from the cathedral entrance is the **Diocesan Museum** (Muzeum Diecezjalne; May–Sept Tues–Sat 10am–3pm, Sun 11am–4pm; Oct–April Wed–Sat 10am–1pm, Sun 11am–2pm; 6zł), in its own way just as interesting as the main museum. The highlight is the extraordinary collection of antiquarian books, starting with the Biblia Płocka (Płock Bible), an enormous twelfth-century tome that sits beside an even larger thirteenth-century choir book. There's also a gorgeous, Renaissance-era edition of St Augustine's *City of God*; a first edition of Mickiewicz's *Pan Tadeusz* (very much a treasure in Poland); and, most unusual of all, an Arabic translation of the works of Thomas à Kempis, printed in Rome in 1653. In addition there's a good collection of Gothic sculpture, taken from churches around the region; a case of mammoth tusks, trilobites and other fossils; some attractive nineteenth-century folk art; and, upstairs, what must be one of the world's worst displays of old master-era paintings, with one ghastly still life or allegorical landscape following another.

The Mazovian Museum

Occupying a former ducal castle right opposite the Diocesian Museum, the **Mazovian Museum** (Muzeum Mazowieckie; May–Sept: Tues–Sat 10am–3pm, Sun 10am–4pm; Oct–April: Wed–Sat 10am–1pm, Sun 10am–2pm; 8zł), is renowned for its collection of **Art Nouveau** in all its forms. The museum starts with **period rooms**, showing how the style was applied to the ordinary everyday business of living (much of the furniture and decorative art is Austrian or Belgian) while in the last room there's a shaving set from Japan and a lovely desk from Kraków. Młoda Polska-school paintings are hung in the next rooms, with desolate landscapes by Julian Fałat and memorable portraits by Stanisław

Wyspiański and Alfons Karpiński. The rest of the floor displays stained glass and a bewildering array of silverware, while upstairs there's a section on local military history and some older period rooms with Biedermeier-type furniture.

The waterfront, the Rynek and around

Running west from the cathedral is a ridge-top path overlooking the Wisła waterfront. An open, blustery spot, on a fine day it offers huge panoramas over the wide expanse of the river below, at its widest around Płock. If you're here in summer, you'll see townsfolk stretched out on the expansive sandy **beach** just down the hill from here. Working your way north via ulica Piekarska brings you shortly to a rather charming **Rynek**, lined with eighteenth- and nineteenth-century houses, including several decent outdoor cafés. One block further west, on ulica Kazimierza Wielkiego, is the **Ethnographic Museum** (Muzeum Etnograficzne; same hours as the Mazovian Museum; 5zł), in an attractive nineteenth-century granary, housing temporary exhibitions related to Mazovian folk culture.

There are reminders of the city's vanished Jewish population in the former **synagogue**, north of the Rynek at ul. Kwiatka 7, built in 1810 but now boarded up and left to go to ruin, and the untended, overgrown **Jewish cemetery** on ulica Mickiewicza, fifteen minutes' walk northeast of the centre, where there's a monument honouring local Jews who perished in the concentration camps.

Eating and drinking

The *Starzyński* hotel (see p.124) has a luxury **restaurant** with outstanding views over the Wisła, while if you descend to the riverfront you'll be rewarded with excellent fish and chips at *Smażalnia Ryb* (April–Oct only). On the Rynek, the antique-stuffed *Czarny Kot* at no. 21 is an atmospheric place in which to relax over coffee and apple pie, and has a reasonable menu of main meals to boot. The next-door-but-one *Salonik*, Stary Rynek 19, serves up a satisfying meat-and-potatoes repertoire in charmingly chintzy surroundings; while *Knajpka 10 ½*, pl. Narutowicza 2, offers passable pizzas in a wooden-bench-filled courtyard. *Blikle*, Tumska 14, is the place for cakes, ice cream and coffee.

Drinking venues include *Rock 69*, in the same courtyard as *Knajpka 10 ½* (see above), a friendly bar that has regular live music; and *Grodzki*, an appealingly seedy local at the eastern edge of the Rynek. There are also beer-oriented outdoor bars on the banks of the Wisła.

Łowicz and around

At first sight **ŁOWICZ**, 80km southwest of Warsaw, looks just like any other small, concrete-ridden central Polish town, but this apparently drab place is, in fact, a well-established centre of folk art and crafts. Locally produced handwoven materials, carved wood ornaments and *wycinanki* (coloured paper cutouts) are popular throughout the country, the brilliantly coloured, broad-skirted Mazovian costumes (*pasiaki*) being the town's best-known product. A former royal hunting ground (indeed the name Łowicz is derived from the verb "to catch"), the town was for several centuries the main residence of the archbishops of Gniezno, who endowed the town with its historic **churches**.

The ideal time to come here is at **Corpus Christi** (late May/early June), when the town's womenfolk turn out in beautiful handmade traditional costumes for the two-hour procession to the collegiate church. Wearing full skirts, embroidered

▲ Folk costumes in Łowicz

cotton blouses and colourful headscarves, they are followed by neat lines of young girls preparing for first Communion. Another date for the diary is the **Jarmark Łowicki** (last or second-to-last weekend in June), a seven-century-old fair featuring handicraft stalls, folk music and dancing.

The Town

Łowicz is based around two market squares, with the broad, square-shaped Stary Rynek and the even broader, triangular Nowy Rynek linked together by the lively shopping street of ulica Zduńska. It's on the Stary Rynek that you'll find the vast **collegiate church**, a brick fifteenth-century construction, remodelled to its present form in the mid-seventeenth century. Size apart, its most striking features are the richly decorated tombstones of the archbishops of Gniezno and former Polish primates, and the ornate series of Baroque chapels.

The other attraction is the local **museum** across the square (Tues–Sun 10am–4pm; 7zł), housed in a Baroque missionary college designed by Tylman van Gameren and rebuilt following wartime destruction. On the ground floor is the former seminary **chapel**, adorned with frescoes by Michelangelo Palloni, court painter to King Jan Sobieski. Upstairs lies an extensive collection of folk artefacts, including furniture, pottery, tools and costumes resembling those still worn on feast days. Round the back of the museum is a mini-*skansen*, containing two old cottages complete with their original furnishings.

For a more in-depth look at local folk traditions, head for the open-air **Museum of the Łowicz Village** (Skansen wsi łowickiej: daily April & Oct 9am–4pm; May–Sept 10am–7pm; 5zł) in Mauzryce, 7km northwest of town on the Kutno road. It's an impressive ensemble of thatched-hut farmstead buildings, many decorated with *pasiaki* paper cut-outs hanging from ceiling beams. Cut-out artists – along with other local craftspeople – are usually on hand to demonstrate their skills.

Practicalities

Łowicz is an easy day trip from either Warsaw or Łodź, with direct trains from Warszawa Centralna, or from Łódź Fabryczna with a change of trains at Skierniewice – if taking the latter route, check out the well-preserved socialist-realist murals in the Skierniewice train station building. In town itself there are a couple of **cafés** on the Stary Rynek, with *Bordo* at no. 8 offering the best in terms of coffees and cakes. There's a dearth of good **restaurants** in Łowicz, although *Pizza House*, just of Stary Rynek at ul. 3-go Maja 8, should at least stave off any serious pangs of hunger.

Arkadia and Nieborów

A short distance southeast of Łowicz, the main Łowicz-Skierniewice road passes two sights redolent of the bygone Polish aristocracy: the landscaped park of **Arkadia**, and seventeenth-century palace at **Nieborów**. They combine for an easy and enjoyable day trip from Warsaw or Łódź – if you're relying on public transport, head for Łowicz first and then use the regular Łowicz-Skierniewice **buses** to shuttle between Nieborów, Arkadia and back.

Arkadia

Eight kilometres out of Łowicz, the eighteenth-century **Arkadia** park (daily 10am–dusk; 6zł) is as wistfully romantic a spot as you could wish for an afternoon stroll. Conceived by Princess Helen Radziwiłł as an "ancient monument to beautiful Greece", the classical park is dotted with lakes and walkways, a jumble of reproduction classical temples and pavilions, a sphinx and a mock-Gothic building that wouldn't look out of place in a Hammer House film production. Many of the pieces were collected by the princess on her exhaustive foreign travels, and the air of decay – the place hasn't been touched since World War II – only adds to the evocation of times long past consciously created by the princess, who was caught up in the cult of the Classical that swept through the Polish aristocracy in the latter half of the eighteenth century.

Nieborów

Five kilometres further southeast lies the village of **NIEBORÓW**, whose country **palace** was designed for Cardinal Michał Radziejowski by the ever-present Tylman van Gameren in the 1690s. In 1766 the palace was acquired by Grand Hetman of Lithuania Michał Ogiński, who set about redecorating the interior in Rococo style before selling the place to another Lithuanian magnate, Michał Radziwiłł, who filled Nieborów with his fine collection of European paintings. Now a branch of Warsaw's Muzeum Narodowe, the Pałac Nieborów (Ⓦwww .nieborow.art.pl) is one of the handsomest and best maintained in the country, surrounded by landscaped grounds.

The **palace** interior (May–June daily 10am–6pm; July–September Mon–Fri 10am–4pm, Sat & Sun 10am–6pm; Oct, March & April Tues–Sun 10am–4pm; 15zł; gardens only 10am–dusk; 6zł) is a lavish recreation of Nieborów's eighteenth-and nineteenth-century heyday. Roman tombstones and sculptural fragments fill a lot of space downstairs, gathered about the palace's prize exhibit, a classical-era sculpture known as the **Nieborów Niobe**. The grandest apartments (including a library with a fine collection of globes) are on the first floor, reached by a staircase clad in finely decorated Delft tiles. Outside, the palace gardens mix formal flowerbeds and tree-lined avenues with extensive sections of landscaped park – including two lakes linked by embankment-lined canal.

The *Biała Dama* **restaurant**, opposite the palace entrance at al. Legionów Polskich 2, serves up a sizeable repertoire of Polish pork and poultry dishes, and rents out cosy en-suite **rooms** on the floor above (☎0602/574 891; ❸). Signed off the road at the northern end of the village, *Pod Złotym Prosiakiem*, Nieborów 175 (☎0698/342 811, ⓦwww.zlotyprosiak.pl), serves up local food in a traditional-style partly, timbered building, and also offers **accommodation** in one double room (❸) and a four-person apartment (200zł).

Łódź

Mention **ŁÓDŹ** (pronounced "Woodge") to many Poles and all you'll get is a grimace, but Poland's second city, 110km southwest of Warsaw, is fascinating in its own way, with a significant place in the country's development and a unique and authentic atmosphere that grows on you the longer you stay. Essentially a creation of the Industrial Revolution and appropriately nicknamed the Polish Manchester, the nineteenth-century core has largely survived – you'll find tall chimneys (no longer smoking) atop castellated red-brick factories; grand historicist and Secessionist villas; dark slum quarters; and theatres, art galleries and philanthropic societies. With much of the whole ensemble still caked in a century and a half of soot and grime, the city served as the ready-made location for Andrzej Wajda's film *The Promised Land*, based on the novel depicting life in Industrial Revolution-era Poland by Nobel laureate Władysław Reymont.

Today Łódź is in the process of reinventing itself as a cultural destination. The pedestrianized **ulica Piotrkowska** is at the heart of things, lined with restaurants and bars and teeming with life night and day. One of the old factories is being converted into a major entertainment complex, and the city now plays host to several important **festivals**. Łódź also boasts one of the best **orchestras** in the country, as well as an impressive array of galleries, theatres and museums. The **film school** here is also internationally renowned, attracting aspiring movie-makers aiming to follow in the footsteps of alumni such as Wajda, Polański, Kieślowski and Zanussi.

Some history

Łódź was an obscure village until the 1820s, when an imperial Russian **edict** earmarked the area for industrial development, encouraging foreign weavers and manufacturers to come and settle. The city, on the westernmost edge of the Tsar's domain, was uniquely poised to use European skills and technology to supply the vast Russian and Chinese markets with cheap fabrics. People poured in by the thousand each year, and within twenty years Łódź had become the nation's second largest city. It was also a multicultural city, comprising Russian civil servants, German factory owners and a largely Polish urban proletariat. The **Jews** were another highly significant community. They were mostly artisans and traders, but several rose to become great industrial magnates – notably the Poznańskis, whose luxurious homes now house many of the city's institutions. Łódź's Jewish community produced a host of prominent cultural figures, pianist Artur Rubinstein, poet Julian Tuwim and cosmetics pioneer Max Factor among them.

Łódź's prosperity declined following World War I when, no longer part of the Russian Empire, the city lost its privileged access to eastern markets; but it remained a melting-pot of peoples and religions until **World War II**. Under the

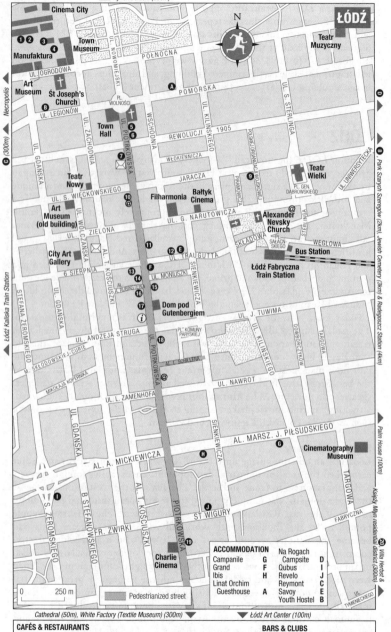

CAFÉS & RESTAURANTS

A. Blikle	17	Ciągoty Tesknoty	8	Restauracja Polska	6
Anatewka	13	Costa del Mar	1	Revelo	J
Anatewka (Manufaktura)	2	Greenway	15	U Chocoła	19
Bar Kawowy	F	Klub Spadkobierców	16	U Szwajcara	20
Café Tuwim	A	Presto	14	Varoska	12

BARS & CLUBS

Bagdad Café	9	Łódź Kaliska	18
Elektrownia	3	Paparazzi	4
Irish Pub	16	Peron 6	5
JazzGa	7	Port West	18
Lizard King	11	Zapiecek	10

Germans, Łódź was incorporated into the Reich and renamed "Litzmannstadt" in honour of a somewhat obscure German general. The Nazis established the first and longest-lasting of their notorious Jewish ghettos here in Łódź (see box, p.135), and almost all of the city's Jews were murdered in the ensuing Holocaust.

After the war, Łódź remained a textile-producing powerhouse right up until the economic changes of the 1990s, when most of the city's mills were driven towards bankruptcy. However derelict factories are slowly being transformed into shopping centres, art galleries and apartment blocks, turning twenty-first century Łódź into a leading example of post-communist, post-industrial regeneration.

Arrival and information

Łódź's **airport** (℡042/683 5255, ⓦwww.airport.lodz.pl) is 6km southwest of the centre. From here bus #65 goes to Łódź Kaliska train station, while bus #L passes Łódź Kaliska before terminating at Łódź Fabryczna; a taxi into the centre will set you back 25–30zł. The main **train station**, Łódź Fabryczna, on the eastern fringes of the town centre, handles services to and from Warsaw and a number of other east-bound destinations. Trains passing through Łódź en route to other destinations stop at Łódź Kaliska, 2km west of the city centre and connected by tram #12. The main **bus station** is right next to Łódź Fabryczna.

The English-speaking **tourist information** office at ul. Piotrkowska 87 (May–Sept Mon–Fri 9am–7pm, Sat & Sun 10am–4pm; Oct–April Mon–Fri 9am–6pm, Sat 10am–4pm; ℡042/638 5955, ⓦwww.cityoflodz.pl) has an excellent range of free maps and publications. There are **internet cafés** on ul. Piotrkowska no. 53 (daily 10am–midnight) and at Spadochronowa, ul. Narutowicza 41 (24hr).

The best way to **get around** the ulica Piotrkowska area is by rickshaw (see p.132), but for less central destinations there's a good **tram** network (tickets 1.70/2.40/3.60/4.80zł for 10/30/60/120min, or 9.60zł for a day pass). **Taxis** are also widely available.

You can buy local maps and English-language magazines from EMPiK Piotrkowska 87 Mon–Sat 9am–9pm, Sun 11am–9pm. There are **internet cafés** on ul. Piotrkowska no. 53 (daily 10am–midnight) and at Spadochronowa, ul. Narutowicza 41 (24hr).

Accommodation

Łódź has a reasonable range of hotels (though too many fall into the bland communist-era category), and the only time it will be difficult to find a room is during the film festival (see p.137). Most of the places listed below offer substantial weekend reductions.

Hostel and campsite

Na Rogach ul. Łupkowa 10/16, 5km northeast of the centre ℡042/659 7013. Camping and decent-quality bungalows, including some with television and bath (❹). Take bus #60 from ul. Narutowicza.

Youth Hostel ul. Legionów 27 ℡042/630 6680, ⓦwww.yhlodz.pl. One of the better of the old-style "youth" hostels, with functional but comfortable dorms (from 30zł), triples (120zł) and doubles (❷) – WC/shower facilities are for the most part shared

between every two rooms although there are some en suites. No breakfast, but there are a couple of simple kitchens and a handful of internet terminals. Tends to fill up with groups so ring ahead.

Hotels

Campanile al. Pilsudskiego 27 ℡042/664 2600, ⓦwww.campanile.com.pl. Relatively new business-class hotel offering neat en suites decorated in inoffensive colours, each featuring desk space and wireless internet. ❻–❼

Grand ul. Piotrkowska 72 ☎042/633 9920, ⓦwww
.orbis.pl. A *belle époque* establishment that doesn't
quite live up to its name, although the en-suite rooms
are comfortable enough and the main-street location
can't be bettered. There's a small gym, and wi-fi
internet throughout. ⑥–⑦
Ibis al. Piłsudskiego 11 ☎042/638 6700, ⓦwww
.ibishotel.com. Large, centrally located hotel that
follows the international Ibis recipe, with slightly
cramped but crisply decorated en suites, and
businesslike service. ⑤
Linat Orchim Guesthouse ul. Pomorska 18
☎042/632 4699, ⓦwww.linatorchim-lodz.inter-
netdsl.pl. Guesthouse in the Jewish community
centre featuring small but cosy en suites with bunk
beds – which can serve as anything from singles
to quads depending on requirements. Wi-fi or cable
internet access. ④
Qubus al. Mickiewicza 7 ☎042/275 5100,
ⓦwww.qubushotel.com. Modern business
hotel with suave-looking en suites, situated a
10min walk west of the main downtown area.

Fancier rooms come with desk-top computers, all
others have wi-fi coverage. ⑦
Revelo ul. Wigury 4/6 ☎042/636 8686, ⓦwww
.revelo.pl. Totally different in atmosphere to the
mainstream business-oriented hotels, this is an
intimate upmarket pension in a bay-windowed
1920s villa. Each of the six rooms is decorated
in historical style, with Art Nouveau and Art Deco
design features predominating. ⑦
Reymont ul. Legionów 81 ☎042/633 8023, ⓦwww
.hotele21.pl. A good mid-range choice a short walk
west of the Manufaktura complex, offering mildly
chintzy rooms with small TV and adequate desk
space. Wi-fi coverage and a small gym complete the
picture. Ask about weekend reductions. ⑥
Savoy ul. Traugutta 6 ☎042/632 93 60, ⓦwww
.hotelspt.com.pl. Centrally located nineteenth-
century building immortalized in Joseph Roth's
eponymous novel of post-World War I paranoia (see
"Books" p.642). The en-suite rooms are comfortable
if slightly dowdy; there are also a couple of "retro"
rooms with faux antiques. Wi-fi in the lobby. ⑥

The City

Running through the centre of Łódź on a north–south axis is the largely pedestrianized **ulica Piotrkowska**, a three-kilometre-long boulevard that bustles with activity day and night. **Rickshaws** will whisk you from one end of Piotrkowska to the other for a few złotys, although there's plenty here to render a more lengthy stroll worthwhile. The street is lined with the mansions of the city's former *haute bourgeoisie*, many peeling with age, others restored to their former splendour. A scattered collection of modern statues recall famous Łódź folk of the past – you'll see locals and tourists alike pausing for photo opportunities at **Rubenstein's Piano**, near the junction with ulica Moniuszki, or the **Three Industrialists** (portraying mill owners Poznański, Grohmann and Scheiber lolling around a dinner table), at the crossroads of Piotrkowska and Jaracza. Near the *Hotel Grand* (see above), hall-of-fame-style plaques embedded in the pavement honour luminaries of the Łódź Film School – Roman Polański, Andrzej Wajda and Krzystow Kieślówski among them.

There are some fine examples of nineteenth-century architecture among the tenement-lined streets on either side of Piotrkowska. A couple of blocks west at Więckowskiego 36, a mock-Renaissance palace once belonging to the Poznański clan now holds a branch of the **Łódź Art Museum** (Muzeum Sztuki: Tues 10am–5pm, Wed & Fri 11am–5pm, Thurs noon–7pm, Sat & Sun 10am–4pm; 8zł; ⓦwww.muzeumsztuki.lodz.pl) which hosts high-profile temporary exhibitions – worth visiting simply to admire the original stained glass and stuccoed ceilings. Just south of here at ul. Wólczańska 31 is Łódź's finest Secessionist building, the **Leopold Kindermann Villa** (Willa Leopolda Kindermanna). An eclectic palace with a floral-motif facade and fine chandeliers and woodwork inside, it was completed in 1903 for the industrialist whose name it bears and today houses the **City Art Gallery**, which displays temporary exhibitions (Tues, Wed & Fri noon–5pm, Thurs noon–6pm, Sat & Sun noon–4pm; 4zł, Thurs free) by contemporary artists from Poland and abroad.

Marking the northern end of Piotrkowska, the circular **plac Wolności** boasts a flamboyant statue of eighteenth-century Polish patriot Tadeusz Kościuszko, and the attractively plump dome of the **Church of the Holy Spirit** (Zesłania ducha świętego), a nineteenth-century Uniate foundation.

The Manufaktura

Nothing symbolizes Łódź's post-industrial transformation more spectacularly than the **Manufaktura** (Ⓦwww.manufaktura.lodz.pl), a vast shopping and leisure complex one block northwest of plac Wolności. Comprising malls, museums and a multiplex cinema, Manufaktura occupies a huge ensemble of red-brick factory halls and warehouses that once belonged to Izrael Poznański, the nineteenth-century Jewish shopkeeper who rose to become one of the biggest textile magnates in the Russian Empire. Nationalized and re-named Pol-tex after 1945, the Poznański factory finally ceased production in 1997 since when this stark monument to the industrial revolution has been turned into a major visitor attraction.

Unlike most other Polish cities Łódź never had a proper Rynek, and the fountain-splashed plazas of the Manufaktura – thronging with shoppers and fun-seekers seven days a week – already look like making up for this deficiency. As well as shops and cafés, daytime attractions also include the **Eksperymentarium** (daily 10am–9pm; 10zł), a hands-on science museum where children can learn some basic scientific principles by playing with plasma balls, gyroscopes, mirrors, magnets and so forth. On the north side of the complex, beside the entrance to the Cinema City multiplex, the **Factory Museum** (Muzeum Fabryki: Tues–Fri 9am–1pm & 3–7pm; Sat 11am–7pm, Sun 10am–6pm; 4zł) tells the history of the Poznański factory in accessible audio-visual style – staff are on hand to switch on some of the antiquated cloth-weaving machines if you show an interest.

The Art Museum

Recently re-housed in a part of the Poznański factory on the south side of the Manufaktura, Łódź's **Art Museum** (Muzeum Sztuki: Tues 10am–5pm, Wed & Fri 11am–5pm, Thurs noon–7pm, Sat & Sun 10am–4pm; 8zł; Ⓦwww.muzeumsztuki.lodz.pl) is the best collection of modern art in Poland, having been initiated in the 1920s by well-connected local artists who had a pretty good idea which paintings were worth investing in. Artists represented include Chagall, Mondrian, Max Ernst and Fernand Léger, and there's also an excellent selection of work by Polish abstract painters of the inter-war years such as Władysław Strzemiński, Henryk Stażewski and Katarzyna Kobro – quite a revelation if you've not come upon their work before. Further displays move on to the 1960s and 1970s, revealing how Polish art remained close to the cutting edge throughout the communist period.

The City Historical Museum

Next door to the Manufaktura, on the corner of Ogrodowa and Zachodnia, the family home built by Izrael Poznański is an ostentatiously palatial building that now serves as the **City Historical Museum** (Muzeum Historii Miasta Łodzi: Mon 10am–2pm, Tues & Thurs 10am–4pm, Wed 2–6pm, Sat & Sun 10am–6pm; 7zł, free on Sun). The building features a lavish mixture of styles both inside and out: it is said that Poznański didn't understand what terms like neo-Gothic, neo-Renaissance or neo-Baroque actually meant, so simply ordered all of them from his architects. Downstairs are temporary exhibitions of modern art and photography, while up the heavily grand staircase are the showpiece chambers, the dining room and the ballroom, filled with elaborately carved doorframes, stained glass and stucco nymphs. The more modest-sized rooms contain displays relating to the city's history, with archive photographs of prewar Łódź including the – now-demolished synagogues. There's an extensive collection of memorabilia of **Artur Rubinstein**, one of the greatest pianists of the last century, and a quintessential hedonist. He was particularly celebrated for his performances of Chopin, and his recordings remain the interpretive touchstone for the composer.

Lower Ulica Piotrkowska and Księży Młyn

There's a lot more of Łódź's industrial heritage to be seen around the southern end of ulica Piotrkowska, beginning with the huge **Biała Fabryka** ("White Factory') at no. 282, the oldest mechanically operated mill in the city. Part of it is now given over to the **Textile Museum** (Muzeum Włókiennictwa: Tues, Wed & Fri 9am–5pm, Thurs 11am–7pm, Sat & Sun 11am–4pm; 8zł, Sat free), which features a large number of historic looms, documentary material on the history of the industry in Łódź and an impressive exhibition of contemporary examples of the weaver's art.

Walking east from the museum for fifteen minutes along ulica Tymienieckiego, you'll come to the **Księży Młyn** district, an extensive complex of manufacturing and residential buildings developed by German magnate Karl Scheiber. On the way you'll pass a group of former factory halls now occupied by the **Łódź Art Center** at ul. Tymienieckiego 3 (opening times depend on what's on, enquire at the tourist office; Ⓦ www.lodzartcenter.com), which mounts major contemporary art shows as well as housing the *Fabryka Sztuki* gig and theatre venue (see p.138). A little way further east is the handsome red-brick former **fire station** where Scheiber's private fire-fighting force was based – Scheiber himself used to dress up in uniform and parade with his firemen on ceremonial occasions.

The heart of Księży Młyn lies at the eastern end of ulica Tymienieckiego. The mills have long since shut down, but the area remains a fascinating place to explore: most of the gorgeous red-brick buildings survive, including rows of terraced houses built for the workers. Standing in stark contrast to the dwellings of Księży Młyn's proletarians is the **Villa Herbst** (sometimes referred to as "Rezydencja Księży Młyn": Tues 10am–5pm, Wed & Fri noon–5pm, Thurs noon–7pm, Sat & Sun 11am–4pm; 7zł, Thurs free) on the corner of Tymienieckiego and Przędzialnia, built for Scheiber's son-in-law Edward Herbst in 1875 on the model of a Palladian villa. Its interiors – with the grand public rooms downstairs, the intimate family ones above – betray influences ranging from ancient Rome via the Orient to Art Nouveau.

The Palm House and the Film Museum

North of Księży Młyn, past the workers' houses, lies the green expanse of Park Źródliska and the **Palm House** (Palmiarnia: Tues–Sun 9am–6pm; 5zł), a swish-looking modern glasshouse packed with palms, cacti and subtropical shrubs. The Palm House's mezzanine café offers great views of the treetops.

Immediately west of the Park lies the fortress-like Pałac Scheibera, former home of Karl Scheiber and now the **Film Museum** (Muzeum Kinematografii: Tues noon–5pm, Wed & Fri–Sun 9am–4pm; 4zł, free on Tues), which celebrates Łódź's status as one of Europe's major film schools. There's a disappointing lack of substance to the permanent display, but temporary exhibitions devoted to particular directors are usually worth a visit. The building is also an attraction in itself, with its wood-panelled rooms, stuccoed ceilings and huge ceramic-tiled ovens.

North of the centre: Jewish Łódź

Until World War II Łódź was home to an estimated quarter of a million Jews. The bulk of them lived in the area around **Rynek Bałucki**, 1km north of plac Wolności (and it was here that the wartime ghetto was situated), although Jewish heritage sites and Holocaust memorials are scattered throughout the city's northern suburbs. The "Trail of Litzmannstadt Ghetto" **map**, available from the tourist office (see p.131), is a thorough guide to the area.

Although Rynek Bałucki was at the heart of the ghetto, there are few reminders of that period now, and you're more likely to visit the square on account of its

The Łódź Ghetto

The fate of the **Jews** of Łódź is undoubtedly one of the most poignant and tragic episodes of World War II, particularly as a pivotal role was played by one of their own number, **Chaim Rumkowski**. One of the most controversial figures in modern Jewish history, he has been widely denounced as the worst sort of collaborator, yet seen by others as a man who worked heroically to save at least some vestiges of the doomed community to which he belonged.

Within two days of the Nazi occupation of the city on September 8 1939, the first definite anti-Semitic measures were taken, with Jews hauled at random off the streets and forced to undertake pointless manual tasks. The following month, Rumkowski, a former velvet manufacturer who had made and lost fortunes in both Łódź and Russia before turning his attentions towards charitable activities, was selected by the Nazis as the "Ältesten der Juden" (Eldest of the Jews), giving him absolute power over the internal affairs of his community and the sole right to be their spokesman. The Nazis laid plans to turn the entire Jewish community into a vast pool of slave labour for the war machine, and the run-down suburb of **Bałuty** to the north of the centre was earmarked for this **ghetto**.

Rumkowski soon made the ghetto a self-sufficient and highly profitable enterprise, which pleased his Nazi masters no end. He ruled his domain as a ruthless **despot**, attended by a court of sycophants and protected by his own police force. Those who crossed him did so at their peril, as his omnipotence extended to the distribution of the meagre food supplies and to selecting those who had to make up the regular quotas demanded by the Nazis for deportation to the concentration camps. He cultivated a variation on the oratorical style of Hitler for his frequent addresses to the community. The most notorious and shocking of these was his "Give me your children" speech of 1942, in which he made an emotional appeal to his subjects to send their children off to the camps, in order that able-bodied adults could be spared.

Whether or not Rumkowski knew that he was sending people to their deaths is unclear. He certainly believed that the Nazis would establish a Jewish protectorate in central Europe once they had won the war, with himself as its head.

The Łódź ghetto was **liquidated** in the autumn of 1944, following a virulent dispute at the top of the Nazi hierarchy between Speer, who was keen to preserve it as a valuable contributor to the war effort, and Himmler, who was determined to enforce the "Final Solution". Although one thousand Jews remained in Łódź to dismantle valuable machinery, Rumkowski voluntarily chose to go with the others to Auschwitz, albeit armed with an official letter confirming his special status. He died there soon afterwards, though there are three versions of how he met his end: that he was lynched by incensed fellow Jews; that he was immediately selected for the gas chambers on account of his age; and that he was taken on a tour of the camp as a supposedly honoured guest, and thrown into the ovens without being gassed first. Had he remained in Łódź, he would have been among those who were **liberated** by the Red Army soon afterwards. Perhaps not surprisingly, the staunchest apologists for Rumkowski's policies have come from this group of survivors.

chaotic outdoor **market** rather than any sense of historical resonance. Just over a kilometre northeast, **Park Szarych Szeregów** (if coming from the centre take tram #1 from Kilińskiego or tram #6 from Zachodnia; get off at ul. Glowackiego) is centred on a monument honouring the 1600 Polish children who passed through a nearby children's work camp, few of whom emerged alive. Consisting of a concrete heart with a child-size human silhouette cut out of the middle, it's not the most subtle of memorials, but does at least provide a focus for remembrance. From here it's a ten-minute walk east along ulica Bracka, followed by a left turn up ulica Zmienna, to Łódź's **Jewish Cemetery** (Cmentarz żydowski: tram #6 to the Strykowska terminus; May–Sept Sun–Thurs 9am–5pm, Fri 9am–3pm; Oct–April Sun–Fri 8am–3pm; 4zł; skullcaps provided). Although it dates from only 1892, this is the largest Jewish cemetery in Europe, with some 180,000 tombstones (and twice as many graves), including the spectacular domed mausoleum of Izrael Poznański (died 1900), with fine Art Nouveau mosaics inside. At the south end of the cemetery is the so-called "ghetto field", full of small plaques remembering Łódź residents who passed through the ghetto before being murdered in camps elsewhere.

Going back outside the cemetery walls, and following ulica Inflancka west before turning north into ulica Stalowa, you'll come to **Radegoszcz Station**, which under its German-language name of Radegast was where ghetto Inhabitations – over 140,000 Jews all told, as well as five thousand Gypsies – boarded trains to the Chełmno and Auschwitz death camps. The restored station building now holds a small museum display (Mon & Tues 10am–6pm, Wed 9am–5pm, Thurs 8am–4pm, Sat & Sun 10am–5pm), while examples of the kind of cattle trucks in which victims were transported stand beside the platform.

Eating and drinking

Łódź's **restaurant**, **bar** and **café** scene can compete with almost any city in Poland. By night, ulica Piotrkowska in the centre of town is the heart of the action, although there's a scattering of dining and drinking venues around the Manufaktura area too.

Cafés

A. Blikle ul. Piotrkowska 89. Not up to the Warsaw original (see p.104), but fine for coffee, doughnuts and cakes. Mon–Sat 10am–7pm, Sun 10am–6pm.
Bar Kawowy Inside the *Grand*, see p.132. Unpretentious coffee bar (not to be confused with the hotel's posh *kawiarnia* on the other side) offering up good, cheap brews and excellent cakes and ice cream. Mon–Sat 9am–7pm, Sun 10am–7pm.

Restaurants

Anatewka ul. 6 Sierpna 2/4 ☎042/630 3635. High-quality Jewish-themed restaurant featuring crocheted tablecloths, candles, old clocks and sideboards, popular with local elite and well-heeled tourists. Daily 11am–11pm. Also at Manufaktura (same times).
Café Tuwim ul. Pomorska 18. Occupying the same courtyard as the Jewish Community Centre this is the only genuinely kosher restaurant in town, although the menu is relatively short. Always good for fish, or *blintzes* (pancakes) stuffed with

cheese or spinach. Mon–Thurs 10am–10pm, Fri 10am–3pm, Sat 8–11pm, Sun noon–10pm.
Ciągoty Tęsknoty ul. Wojska Polskiego 144. Café-restaurant close to the Jewish cemetery, with good and affordable French-influenced food and occasional live music. Popular with students from the Fine Arts Academy in the park opposite. Tram #1 or #6 to "Sporna". Daily noon–10pm.
Costa del Mar Manufaktura. Spanish-themed restaurant with a terrace looking out on Manufaktura's main plaza with a broad-based Mediterranean menu and a good wine list. Probably your best bet in Łódź for fish and seafood. Mon–Sat 11am–11pm, Sun 11am–10pm.
Greenway ul. Piotrkowska 80. Branch of the affordable vegetarian chain, offering order-at-the-counter stews, salads, pancakes and more. Daily 9am–9pm. Also at Manufaktura (daily 11am–10pm).
Klub Spadkobierców ul. Piotrkowska 77 ☎042/633 7670. Behind the stained-glass windows,

a Wall Street atmosphere prevails in the impeccably furnished former banking house of *fin-de-siècle* tycoon Maximilian Goldfeder. The name means "Inheritors' Club". Strong on fresh fish and steaks. Mon–Fri noon–11pm, Sat & Sun 1–11pm.

Presto ul. Piotrkowska 67. The best choice for inexpensive Italian food, with a fairly extensive menu and good-quality pizza and pasta in a comfortable, unpretentious setting. Sun–Thurs noon–11pm, Fri & Sat noon–midnight.

Restauracja Polska ul. Piotrkowska 12. Upscale traditional Polish restaurant serving everything from *golonka* (boiled pork knuckle) to rabbit. Fine decor and polished service. Daily noon–10pm.

Revelo ul. Wigury 4/6 ☎042/636 8686. Atmospheric Art Deco restaurant attached to the upmarket pension of the same name. Serving a mix of Polish, German and Jewish-themed dishes, including an excellent lamb *czulent* (barley stew). Reservations recommended. Daily noon–11pm.

U Chochoła ul. Piotrkowska 200. Folklore-themed restaurant with wooden-bench seating, bunches of dried herbs hanging from the rafters and traditional, reasonably priced Polish dishes, including fish and game. Sun–Thurs noon–11pm, Fri & Sat noon–midnight.

U Szwajcara ul. Tymienieckiego 22. Smart but not over-formal bistro squeezed into the former guard-house of one of Scheiber's factories. Perfect for lunch if you've been looking round the Księży Młyn area: the strawberry dumplings served with fried cabbage is fast becoming a cult dish among Łódź foodies. Mon–Fri noon–6pm, Sat noon–4pm.

Varoska ul. Traugutta 4. Pleasant, mid-priced Hungarian place with a nice line in *bigos*, goulash and potato pancakes and a good selection of Hungarian wines and spirits. Daily noon–11pm.

Bars and clubs

Bagdad Café ul. Jaracza 45. Legendary home of Łódź bohemians, hidden away beneath the *Da Antonio* pizzeria. Four rooms furnished in different styles give the place the feel of a house party. At weekends DJs spin anything from reggae to techno. Mon–Wed 10am–midnight, Thurs–Sat 10am–4am.

Elektrownia Manufaktura ⓦwww .elektrownia1912.pl. State-of-the-art disco on three floors, concentrating on dancefloor-filling commercial and retro styles. Fri & Sat 9pm–5am.

Irish Pub ul. Piotrkowska 77. Attractive upscale drinking spot with occasional live jazz and blues. Daily noon–1am.

JazzGa ul. Piotrkowska 17. Mildly offbeat music bar reached via a cast-iron stairway in an off-street courtyard. Expect gigs and club nights (with an admission fee) at weekends; otherwise background music ranging from funk to things you couldn't tap your foot to if you tried. Daily 3pm–1am.

Lizard King ul. Piotrkowska 62. Main-street rock-music pub with a bar in the shape of a guitar, post-modern toilets, and local cover bands at weekends. Sun–Thurs 4pm–2am, Fri & Sat 4pm–4am.

Łódź Kaliska ul. Piotrkowska 102. Hidden down an alley, a wonderful and very popular pub full of mirrors, curios, and artworks by the Łódź Kaliska art collective, with a rooftop section that's open in good weather. Mon–Thurs noon–2am, Fri & Sat noon–3am, Sun 4pm–3am.

Paparazzi Manufaktura. Łódź branch of a pan-Polish bar chain known for decent cocktails and snazzy lounge-bar ambience. The interior retains the rough red-brick look of the original factory. Also serves breakfasts and light meals. Daily 10am–1am.

Peron 6 Pietrkowska 6. Beer connoisseurs favourite, with a sizeable menu of bottled beers from around the world, and a reasonable range on tap, too. Mon–Thurs noon–1am, Fri & Sat noon–3am, Sun 4–11pm.

Port West ul. Piotrkowska 102 ⓦwww .portwestklub.pl. Mainstream club with commercial techno and themed party nights, right next to the *Łódź Kaliska* bar (see above). Fri & Sat 9pm–4am.

Zapiecek Piotrkowska 43. Laid-back and welcoming studenty bar with candles on the tables, cheap beer, sausage-and-chips-type snacks and occasional live music or spoken-word events in the downstairs bar. Sun–Thurs noon–11pm, Fri & Sat noon–midnight.

Entertainment

Łódź can hold its own when it comes to culture. Most important of the **festivals** is **Camerimage** in late November and early December (ⓦwww.camerimage .pl), attracting cinema luminaries from around the world. No less interesting is the annual **Festiwal Dialogu Czterech Kultur** (Four Cultures Festival: ⓦwww.4kultury.pl), held in September and featuring films, concerts and discussions of and between the city's traditional residents – Poles, Jews, Germans and Russians. Other regular events are the **Meeting of Styles** graffiti festival, held in July, which features hip-hop concerts as well as the redecoration of a section of the Kaliska train station (Ⓦwww.meetingofstyles.pl); and the **ballet festival** (Łódzkie Spotkania Baletowe: Ⓦwww.teatr-wielki.lodz.pl) in May and June every odd-numbered year.

For **theatre** there's the highly rated Teatr Nowy at ul. Więckowskiego 15 (Ⓣ042/633 4494, Ⓦwww.nowy.pl) and the Teatr Wielki on pl. Dąbrowskiego 1 (Ⓣ042/633 9960, Ⓦwww.teatr-wielki.lodz.pl), which also presents **opera**; visiting foreign companies regularly perform at both venues. The **concert** programmes of the Arthur Rubenstein Philharmonic Orchestra at ul. Narutowicza 20-22 (Ⓣ042/664 7997, Ⓦwww.filharmonia.lodz.pl) feature soloists of international renown, while the Teatr Muzyczny, ul. Połnocna 47/51 (Ⓣ042/678 3511, Ⓦwww.teatr-muzyczny.lodz.pl), is the main venue for operetta and musicals. Fabryka Sztuki, Tymienieckiego 3 (Ⓦwww .fabrykasztuki.org), is the place to go for alternative gigs, fringe theatre and performance art.

Of numerous **cinemas**, Cinema City in the Manufaktura (Ⓦwww.cinema-city .pl) has a big choice of current commercial films; while Charlie, ul. Piotrkowska 203 (Ⓦwww.charlie.pl) has more of an art-house repertoire.

Travel details

Trains

Łódź Fabryczna to: Łowicz (Mon–Fri hourly, Sat & Sun every 2hr; 2hr; change at Skierniewice); Warsaw (Mon–Fri hourly, Sat & Sun every 2hr; 1hr 30min–2hr 30min).

Łódź Kaliska to: Gdańsk (2 daily; 7hr); Kraków (1 daily; 4hr 30min); Poznań (4 daily; 3hr 45min–5hr); Warsaw (3 daily; 2hr); Wrocław (2 daily; 4hr 20min).

Warsaw to: Ciechanów (10 daily; 2hr 20min); Łódź (Mon–Fri hourly; Sat & Sun every 2hrs; 2hr); Łowicz (10 daily; 1hr–1hr 30min); Sochaczew (hourly; 40min–1hr).

Buses

Łódź to: Bydgoszcz (3 daily; 4hr); Ciechocinek (5 daily; 3hr); Częstochowa (10 daily; 2hr 30min–3hr);

Gdańsk (1 daily; 6hr 15min); Kraków (7 daily; 5hr); Płock (10 daily; 2hr 30min); Toruń (3 daily; 3hr–4hr); Warsaw (21 daily; 2–3hr).

łowicz to: Arkadia (hourly; 20min); Nieborów (hourly; 30min).

Płock to: Bydgoszcz (7 daily; 2hr 30min); Łódź (17 daily; 2hr 30min); Toruń (10 daily; 1hr 45min); Warszawa Zachodnia (hourly; 2–3hr).

Sochaczew to: Żelazowa Wola (hourly; 20min).

Warsaw Polski Express/HaloBus stop on al. Jana Pawła II to: Łódź (7 daily; 2hr); Płock (hourly; 1hr 45min).

Warsaw Zachodnia to: Żelazowa Wola (5 daily; 1hr 40min).

3

The Bay of Gdańsk and the Wisła delta

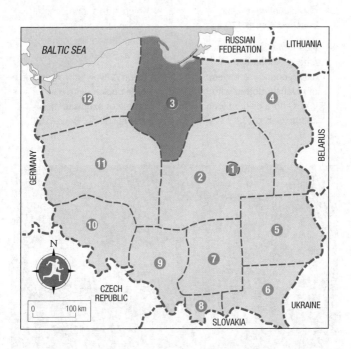

CHAPTER 3 # Highlights

✳ **Gdańsk** An archetypal north European maritime city, full of Gothic architecture, fog-bound quays and buzzing nightlife. See p.142

✳ **Hel** This quaint fishing village provides easy access to mile upon mile of pristine white-sand beaches. See p.170

✳ **Kashubia** Spend some time exploring the rolling countryside west of Gdańsk, dotted with lakes and a distinct local culture.See p.172

✳ **Elbląg–Ostróda Canal** Go on a boat trip with a difference – you're hauled uphill on an intricate railway system. See p.177

✳ **Malbork Castle** For centuries the headquarters of the Teutonic Knights, this monumental medieval castle sprawls along the banks of the Wisła. See p.181

✳ **Toruń** A lively university town packed with a jumble of exquisite medieval buildings. See p.188

▲ Gdańsk

3

The Bay of Gdańsk and the Wisła delta

E ven by Polish standards, the northern **Tri-City** (Trójmiasto) – the dominant conurbation in northern Poland, consisting of Gdańsk, Sopot and Gdynia – is a heavyweight in the history department, as the place where World War II started with a bang and where the communist dictatorship ended with a whimper fifty years later. But rather than lingering on the past, the region is thundering forward, and a new generation has made its mark in the twenty years since democracy arrived. A decade of economic boom has ensured a rising standard of life, noticeable in the number of quality hotels and restaurants that have recently opened up, in the improved transportation links, as well as in the large number of Polish tourists visiting the area. It's only really in the last sixty years that the region has become Polish – traditionally the domain of the Teutonic Knights, Hansa merchants and, for parts of the region right up until the end of World War II, the Prussians, the area's Germanic and other international influences have left their marks in both architecture and demography.

Historic **Gdańsk** was obliterated in World War II but the carefully reconstructed parts of the city centre are now full of life. Nearby **Sopot**, with its golden beach, is the lively summertime party capital of Poland, but is pleasant to visit in any season. The industrial port city of **Gdynia** only appeared on the map in the 1920s, but now has seen much investment and is attracting tourism and business.

The Tri-City is a good base for exploring neighbouring **Kashubia**, to the west, with its rolling hills, lakeside forests and distinctive communities of Prussianized Slavs. While waters around the Trójmiasto are a dubious (if ever-improving) proposition, the **Hel Peninsula** and the coast further west make a pleasant seaside alternative. On the other side of the Trójmiasto, **Frombork**, chief of many towns in the region associated with the astronomer Nicolaus Copernicus, is an attractive and historic lagoon-side town across the water from the **Wiślana Peninsula**, a beachside holiday-makers' favourite. South from Gdańsk, a collection of Teutonic castles and Hanseatic centres dot the banks of the Wisła and its tributaries. Highlights include the huge medieval fortress at **Malbork**, once the headquarters of the Teutonic Knights, and **Toruń**, with its spectacular medieval ensemble. In the south of the region is, **Bydgoszcz** a city still in the throes of change, its historical district currently being restored.

The area is well served by **public transport** from the hubs of Gdańsk, Gdynia and Bydgoszcz, though visiting out-of-the-way destinations like Kashubia and some Wisła towns requires careful planning.

Gdańsk and around

To outsiders, **GDAŃSK** was until recently perhaps the most familiar city in Poland. The home of Lech Wałęsa, Solidarity and the former Lenin Shipyards, its images flashed across a decade of news bulletins during the 1980s, and the harbour area fulfills expectations formed from the newsreels, with its harsh industrial landscape. By contrast, the streets of the town centre are lined with tall, narrow merchants' houses dating back to Gdańsk's days as a key member of the Hanseatic League. As the economy grows – with a helping hand from the ever-increasing numbers of tourists visiting the city – many of these historic buildings are being restored and new shops, restaurants and businesses are opening, giving the city a confident, lively feel.

What is surprising is the cultural complexity of the place. Prewar Gdańsk – or **Danzig** as it then was – was forged by years of Prussian and Hanseatic domination, and the reconstructed city centre looks not unlike Amsterdam, making an elegant backdrop. What has changed entirely, however, is the city's demography. At the outbreak of the last war, nearly all of the 400,000 citizens were German-speaking, with fewer than 16,000 Poles. The postwar years marked a radical shift from all that went before, as the ethnic Germans were expelled and Gdańsk became Polish for the first time since 1308. Germans are returning in numbers now, chiefly as tourists and business people, making an important contribution to the city's rapid emergence as one of Poland's economic powerhouses.

With a population of more than 950,000, the **Trójmiasto** conurbation, comprising **Gdańsk** (itself with 456,000 residents), **Gdynia** and **Sopot**, ranks as one of the largest in the country. It's an enjoyable area to explore, with ferries, buses and trains tripping between the three centres and up to the **Hel Peninsula**, and offering a good mix of Poland's northern attractions: politics and monuments in Gdańsk, seaside chic in Sopot, gritty port life in Gdynia and sandy beaches and clean water up at the Hel Peninsula. The lakes and forests of **Kashubia** are just an hour or two from Gdańsk by bus, as are the castles of **Malbork** and **Frombork** and the beaches of the **Wiślana Peninsula**. As you'd expect, Gdańsk also has excellent **transport connections**, with a host of buses, trains and flights.

Some history

The city's position near the meeting point of the Wisła and the Baltic has long made Danzig/Gdańsk an immense strategic asset: in the words of Frederick the Great, whoever controlled it could be considered "more master of Poland than any king ruling there". First settled in the **tenth century**, the city assumed prominence when the Teutonic Knights arrived in 1308. The knights established themselves in their accustomed style, massacring the locals and installing a colony of German settlers in their place.

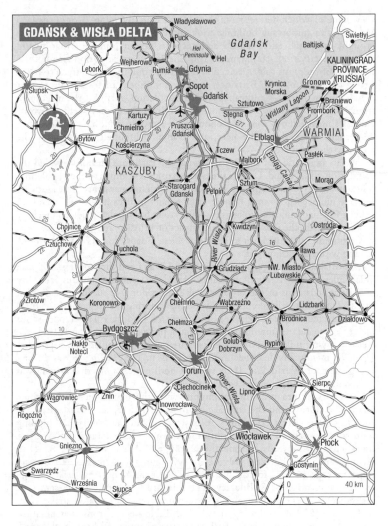

GDAŃSK & WISŁA DELTA

The city's economy flourished, and with the end of the knights' rule in the **mid-fifteenth century** – accompanied by the brick-by-brick dismantling of their castle by the city's inhabitants – Danzig, by now an established member of the mercantile Hanseatic League, became to all intents and purposes an independent city-state. It had its own legislature, judiciary and monopolies on the Wisła trade routes, restricted only by the necessity of paying homage, and an annual tax, to the Polish monarch.

Gdańsk's main period of development occurred between the **sixteenth century** and the Partitions of the **late eighteenth century**. The scale of its trading empire at this time is illustrated by the fact that the Danzig Eastland Company had a bigger turnover than even London's mighty East India Company. (One of their major exports was wood, specifically spruce, the very name of which derives from the Polish *z Prus*, meaning "from Prussia".) Most of the important building took place at this time, as the burghers brought in Dutch and Flemish architects to design buildings that would express the city's self-confidence. From the Renaissance period also dates a tradition of religious tolerance, a pluralism that combined with trade to forge strong connections with Britain: a sizeable contingent of foreign Protestant merchants included a significant Scottish population, many of them refugees from religious persecution at home. The following century yielded two of Gdańsk's most famous sons – astonomer Jan Heweliusz (Johannes Hevelius), who spent most of his life here, and Daniel Fahrenheit, inventor of the mercury thermometer.

Prussian annexation of the city following the Partitions abruptly severed the connection with Poland. Despite the German origins of much of the population, resistance to Prussianization and support for Polish independence were as strong in early nineteenth-century Danzig as elsewhere in Prussian-ruled Poland. In 1807, a Prussian campaign to recruit soldiers to fight Napoleon yielded precisely 47 volunteers in the city. The biggest impact of Prussian annexation, however, was economic: with its links to Poland severed, Gdańsk lost its main source of trading wealth, Polish wheat.

Territorial status changed again after **World War I** and the recovery of Polish independence. The Treaty of Versailles created the semi-autonomous Free City of Danzig, terminus of the so-called Polish Corridor that sliced through West Prussia (an area heavily dominated by Germans during the nineteenth century) and connected Poland to the sea. This strip of land gave Hitler one of his major propaganda themes in the 1930s and a pretext for attacking Poland: the German assault unleashed on the Polish garrison at Westerplatte on September 1, 1939 – memorably described by Günter Grass in *The Tin Drum* – was the first engagement of **World War II**. It was not until March 1945 that Danzig was liberated, after massive Soviet bombardment.

The **postwar era** brought communist rule, the expulsion of the ethnic German majority, and the formal renaming of the city as Gdańsk. Parts of the old centre were meticulously reconstructed and the traditional shipping industries revitalized. As the **communist era** began to crack at the edges, however, the shipyards became the harbingers of a new reality. Riots in Gdańsk and neighbouring Gdynia in 1970 and the strikes of 1976 were important precursors to the historic 1980 Lenin Shipyards strike, which led to the creation of **Solidarity**. The shipyards remained at the centre of resistance to General Jaruzelski's government, the last major strike wave in January 1989 precipitating the Round Table negotiations that heralded the end of communist rule. Following the traumas of "shock therapy", the reform programme pursued with vigour in the **early 1990s**, Gdańsk blossomed economically, profiting especially from the boom in tourism in the first decade of the twenty-first century. Such new-found economic optimism didn't extend to the famous shipyards, however, which were on the verge of bankruptcy in 1997, when a wave of workers' protests prevented the government from closing down the yards altogether. The EU may yet force the Polish government to take action – in 2008 the Competition Commissioner ruled that the billions of euros that were paid to the shipyards of Gdańsk since Poland joined the EU represent illegal state aid and must be paid back, and recommended that the shipyards refocus their activities. Despite their diminishing economical role, the shipyards remain a powerful emotional symbol of today's Poland.

Arrival and information

Gdańsk's **airport** (Gdańsk Lech Wałęsa; information ☎058/348 1111, ⓦwww
.airport.gdansk.pl) is about 15km west of the city. Bus #B runs to the main train
station between 5am and 10pm twice hourly on weekdays, and hourly at weekends;
buy tickets (2.80zł; valid for 45min from validation) from the news kiosk or from
the driver (exact change required) and punch it when you get on the bus. A taxi
into town from the rank outside the airport will set you back around 45zł.

The main **train station** (Gdańsk Główny) is a ten-minute walk west of the core
of the old city – take the pedestrian underpass to get to the tram stops in the
middle of Wały Jagiellońskie and to the city centre. The **bus station** (Dworzec
PKS) is located behind the train station across ulica 3 Maja.

For those coming in **by car**, signposting into the city centre is reasonably clear;
note that parking in the Main Town is reserved for residents only. If you're
arriving **by boat** from Scandinavia, you'll find yourself disembarking at the
Nowy Port ferry terminal, 6km north of the city centre. Ignore the unscrupu-
lous taxi drivers congregating outside and walk 500m to Brzeźno train station
where you can take one of the regular local trains into town.

Information

The helpful **tourist information** centre at ul. Heweliusza 27 (Mon–Fri
9am–4pm; ☎058/301 4355, ⓦwww.got.gdansk.pl), a five-minute walk from
the train station, has a good supply of maps and brochures and can make hotel
reservations. The **PTTK office** at ul. Długa 45, bang in the centre of the Main
Town (8am–6pm; ☎058/301 6096, ⓦwww.pttk-gdansk.pl), is very helpful,
with internet access, brochures, and transport timetables posted both in and
outside. **Online information** is available at ⓦwww.en.gdansk.gda.pl.

The small-format English-language **listings** guide *Gdańsk In Your Pocket* (6zł
or downloadable for free from ⓦwww.inyourpocket.com) is available from
newsstands and offers good up-to-the-minute information on hotels, restaurants and bars throughout the Trójmiasto area. More detailed entertainment
and clubbing listings appear in Polish-language publications such as the Friday
edition of the daily newspaper, *Gazeta Wyborcza*.

Orientation and getting around

Orientation is fairly straightforward, the main sights of interest being located
in three historic districts. The **Main Town** (Główne Miasto), the central area,
is within easy walking distance of the main station. The main pedestrianized
avenues, ulica Długa and its continuation Długi Targ, form the heart of the
district, which backs east onto the attractive and, in summer, very lively waterfront of the Motława Canal and the island of Spichlerze. To the north is the **Old
Town** (Stare Miasto), bounded by the towering cranes of the shipyards, beyond
which the suburbs of Wrzeszcz, Zaspa and Oliwa sprawl towards Sopot. South
of the centre stands the quieter **Old Suburb** (Stare Przedmieście).

Trains

Travelling within the urban area is also pretty straightforward. A regular commuter
train service, Szybka Kolej Miejska (SKM; colloquially known as the Kolejka),

runs between Gdańsk Główny (the SKM platforms are immediately north of the mainline platforms), Sopot and Gdynia, with plenty of stops in between, leaving roughly every ten minutes in the middle of the day, with services thinning out to once every hour or so in the early hours. **Tickets**, which must be validated before you get on the train, can be bought in the passage beneath the main station or at any local station. Total journey time from Gdańsk to Gdynia is 35 minutes.

Trams, trolleybuses and buses

Trams run within all districts of Gdańsk, and **trolleybuses** in Sopot and Gdynia. **Buses** operate right across the conurbation – #117, #122 and #143 connect Gdańsk with Sopot, #171 connects Oliwa with Gdynia, while #181 connects Gdynia with Sopot. Maps of Gdańsk available from kiosks and bookshops give all bus and tram **routes**. **Tickets** for both trams and buses can be bought from any kiosk, public transport board (ZTM) sales points or from the driver (for exact change only) and must be validated upon entry. A full-fare ticket, valid for fifteen minutes, costs 2zł: punch a 2.80zł ticket for a ride up to 45 minutes and a 4.20zł ticket for one hour of travel (timetables at bus and tram stops tell you how long your journey should take). ISIC Card holders under 26 can get half-price tickets. You can change between buses and trams during the life of your ticket. Alternatively, a 24-hour ticket costs 9.10zł.

Ferries

From May to mid-September, **ferry services** (*tramwaj wodne* or "water trams", part of the ZTM public transport system) operate between Gdańsk, Sopot (20zł return) and Hel (32zł return), as well as between Gdynia and Hel (20zł return). From April to November, Żegluga Gdańska additionally has boat tours of the harbour (30zł) and ferries between Gdańsk and Westerplatte (45zł return). The Gdańsk landing stage is on the main waterfront (Długie Pobrzeże), close to the Green Gate; in Sopot and Gdynia, it's on the pier. Current timetables (adjusted seasonally) are posted at all landing stages. **Tickets** are sold at the landing stages or, occasionally on the boats themselves; children under seven travel half-price and those under four for free. In summer, ferries are frequently full and it's a good idea to arrive very early or to buy a ticket in advance. Further **information** on the boats is available on ☎058/498 0874 and at ⓦwww.mzkzg.org (click to *tramwaje wodne* and then select English). For Żegluga Gdańska, call ☎058/301 7426 or check ⓦwww.zegluga.pl.

Accommodation

As in the other big tourist cities, **accommodation** in Gdańsk ranges from the ultra-plush to the ultra-basic, and rooms in the centre are at a premium in summer. A number of new five-star **hotels** are set to open in years to come, though there's already a decent choice in and around the city centre. The number of centrally located low-budget options has increased considerably in recent years, though for a little more comfort you'll still have more choice if you're prepared to stay a little further out; the Wrzeszcz suburb, which is undergoing regeneration, is a good choice for its lively, studenty atmosphere. All hotels are marked on the main Gdańsk map on p.149, except where indicated.

Private rooms and apartments (❶–❷) are a cheap alternative to hotels, and often offer much more space for less money; they can be booked through Grand-Tourist

THE TRÓJMIASTO

ACCOMMODATION
Abak	D
Camping Orlina	G
Camping Stogi	E
Dom Nauczyciela	C
Pension	F
Posejdon	A
Villa Eva	B

RESTAURANTS, CAFÉS & BARS
Margherita	1
Scruffy O'Brien	2

Szczecin

Hel   Hel

see 'Gdynia' map for detail

Gdynia Główna
Station

Pier

GDYNIA

Wzgórze Św.
Maksymiliana
Station

Redłowo Station

Orłowo
Station

ORŁOWO

Kamienny
Potok Station

see 'Sopot' map for detail

Gdańsk Bay

SOPOT

Pier

Opera
Leśna

Sopot
Station

Oliwa
Park

Wyścigi
Station

Zoo

Żabianka
Station

Oliwa Cathedral

A

Abbots' Palace &
Contemporary Art
Museum

Oliwa Station

JELITKOWO

BRZEŹNO

OLIWA

Schopenhauer
House

Przymorze
Uniwersytet
Station

ZASPA

Westerplatte
Museum

Ferry
Terminal

Westerplatte Monument

Mosque

Brzeźno Station

WESTERPLATTE

Lech Wałęsa Airport

Zaspa
Station

NOWY
PORT

Port
Station

Wisła Fortress

B

2

Shipyards

Wrzeszcz Station

Politechnika Station

WRZESZCZ

C

Opera House

Miniatura Puppet
Theatre

Stocznia Station

Kartuzy

D

F

BKS Lechia
Stadium

E

STOGI

Main Station

GDAŃSK

Akademia
Muzyczna

River Wisła

Sztutowo & Krynica Morska

STARE SZKOTY

see 'Gdańsk' map for detail

N

0   2 km

Tczew

Elbląg, Frombork, Olsztyn & Warsaw

in the mall at the end of the underpass leading from the station (Podwale Grodzkie 8; Mon–Fri 9am–6pm, Sat 10am–2pm; ☎058/301 2634, ⓦwww.gt.com.pl) or through Gdańsk Apartments (☎022/351 2260, ⓦwww.apartmentsapart.com). All of the **hostels** listed below are open year-round; if they are full between mid-June and mid-September you can turn to the seven **student dormitories** in Gdańsk and Sopot, which can booked via ⓦwww.akademikigdansk.pl. The city's **campsites** are open from May to September.

Hotels and pensions

Abak ul. Beethovena 8 ☎058/322 0440, ⓦwww .abak.gda.pl. Friendly pension with comfortable rooms, with or without bathroom, in a quiet suburb 2km west of the centre. Easily reached on buses #130 and #184. See map, p.147. ④–⑥

Dom Aktora ul. Straganiarska 55/56 ☎058/301 5901, ⓦwww.domaktora.pl. Simple but cosy pension in good central location. Rooms are en suite and come with TV. Apartments, kitted out with kitchens, sleep two (400zł), three (410–460zł) four (540zł) and five (610zł) people. ⑦

Dom Harcerza ul. Za Murami 2-10 ☎058/301 3621, ⓦwww.domharcerza.pl. Simple but clean place just a few minutes' walk from Długa. Dormitory-style accommodation (from 22zł), frugal doubles with shared bathrooms (90zł) and a small number of en-suite doubles and triples with kitchenettes (220zł). ④

Dom Nauczyciela ul. Upenhaga 28 ☎058/341 9116, ⓦwww.gdansknp.tp1.pl. Overlooking a park out in Wrzeszcz in a quiet side street ten minutes' walk northwest of Gdańsk-Politechnika station. Basic singles and three- to four-person rooms, as well as en-suite doubles and doubles with shared facilities. There's a car park next door. See map, p.147. ③–④

Dom Schumannów ul. Długa 45 ☎058/301 5272, ⓦwww.domschumannow.pl. Rooms with Empire-style furniture offering unbeatable views of the town hall and Długi Targ. In the same Renaissance building as the PTTK office. ⑥

Hanza ul. Tokarska 6 ☎058/305 3427, ⓦwww .hanza-hotel.pl. Luxury hotel with lots of atmosphere right by the Motława Canal. Some rooms come with dockside views. ⑧

Holiday Inn Podwale Grodzkie 9 ☎058/300 6000, ⓦwww.gdansk.azurehotel.pl. Bang opposite the station and as comfortable and well run as you would expect from the international chain. ⑨

🏃 **Kamienica Goldwasser** ul. Długie Pobrzeże 22 ☎058/301 8878, ⓦwww.goldwasser.pl. Lovely, antique-furnished apartments near the crane and overlooking the Motława, some equipped with balconies, kitchenettes and/or fireplaces. ⑥

Mercure Hevelius ul. Heweliusza 22 ☎058/321 0000, ⓦwww.orbis.pl. Big, modern business hotel 5min from the central station with tastefully decorated rooms. Some have great views of the Old Town. ⑧

Novotel Centrum ul. Pszenna 1 ☎058/300 2750, ⓦwww.orbis.pl. Business hotel beside a busy road but within easy walking distance of the Old Town. ⑧

Pension ul. Beethovena 69 ☎058/301 5901, ⓦwww.rena.org.pl. No-frills guesthouse with clean and good-value rooms. See *Abak* (above) for directions and map, p.147. ③–④

Posejdon ul. Kapliczna 30 ☎058/511 3000, ⓦwww.orbis.pl. Eight kilometres northwest of the centre in the seaside suburb of Jelitkowo, this is arguably the nicest Orbis hotel in town. Rooms have balconies and some have a sea view; others look onto the woods. There's also an indoor swimming pool and fitness centre. It's near a pleasant stretch of beach, along which you can walk to Sopot. Take tram #2, #6 or #8 from the train station to the Jelitkowo terminus (a 40min ride). See map, p.147. ⑦

Villa Eva ul. Batorego 28 ☎058/341 6785, ⓦwww.villaeva.pl. Upmarket bed and breakfast in a quiet suburban street, just ten minutes' walk southwest from Gdańsk Wrzeszcz station. ⑦

Hostels

Baltic Hostel ul. 3 Maja 25 ☎058/721 9657, ⓦwww.baltichostel.com.pl. Just northwest of the train station, the friendly but rather cramped *Baltic Hostel* has small but colourful private rooms (④) and dorms (beds from 40zł). Prices include breakfast, internet and coffee.

Pepperland ul. Wartka ☎793 376 667, ⓦwww .pepperlandhostel.com. Simple rooms (④) and dorms (from 40zł) on a boat moored on the Motława, just east of Targ Rybny.

Przy Targu Rybnym ul. Grodzka 21 ☎058/301 5627, ⓦwww.gdanskhostel.com.pl. Relaxed place, close to waterfront, offering free bike and canoe rental and a laundry service. Some doubles (⑤–⑥) as well as dorm beds at 55zł, including breakfast.

Campsites

Camping Orlina ul. Lazurowa 5 ☎058/307 3915. In a lovely location on a lonely beach by the woods, though some way out of town (about 15km east).

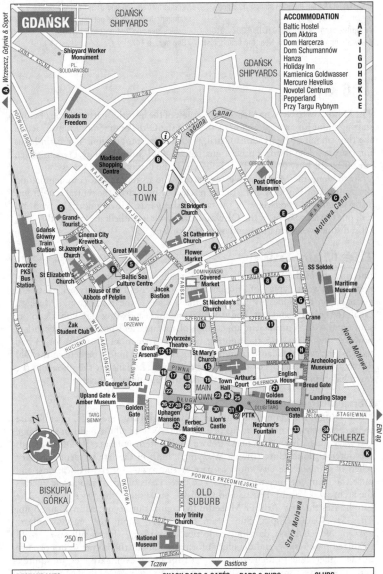

GDAŃSK

GDAŃSK SHIPYARDS

◄ Wrzeszcz, Gdynia & Sopot

ACCOMMODATION

Baltic Hostel	A
Dom Aktora	F
Dom Harcerza	J
Dom Schumannów	I
Hanza	G
Holiday Inn	D
Kamienica Goldwasser	H
Mercure Hevelius	B
Novotel Centrum	K
Pepperland	C
Przy Targu Rybnym	E

Shipyard Worker Monument

PL. SOLIDARNOŚCI

GDAŃSK SHIPYARDS

Roads to Freedom

Canal

Raduna

PL. OBROŃCÓW

Madison Shopping Centre

OLD TOWN

Post Office Museum

St Bridget's Church

Grand-Tourist

St Catherine's Church

Mottawa Canal

Gdańsk Główny Train Station

Cinema City Krewetka

St Joseph's Church

Great Mill

Flower Market

Dworzec PKS Bus Station

St Elizabeth's Church

Baltic Sea Culture Centre

PL. DOMINIKAŃSKI

Covered Market

SS Sołdek

Maritime Museum

House of the Abbots of Pelplin

Jacek Bastion

ŚWIĘTOJAŃSKA

St Nicholas's Church

Crane

Żak Student Club

TARG DRZEWNY

SZEROKA

SZEROKA

Wybrzeże Theatre

Great Arsenal

St Mary's Church

Archeological Museum

St George's Court

Town Hall

Arthur's Court

English House

Bread Gate

Upland Gate & Amber Museum

Golden Gate

MAIN TOWN

Golden House

Landing Stage

Uphagen Mansion

Ferber Mansion

Lion's Castle

PTTK

Green Gate

STAGIEWNA

TARG SIENNY

Neptune's Fountain

SPICHLERZE

Elbląg ►

N

OLD SUBURB

PODWALE PRZEDMIEJSKIE

0   250 m

BISKUPIA GÓRKA

Holy Trinity Church

National Museum

Stara Mottawa

▼ Tczew   ▼ Bastions

RESTAURANTS				SNACK BARS & CAFÉS		BARS & PUBS		CLUBS	
Czerwone Drzwi	19	Scampi	7	Bar Mleczny		Blue Café	34	Gazeta Rock	
Euro	22	Swojski Smak	1	Neptun	30	Celtic Pub	20	Café	16
Green Way	27	Tawerna	33	Capri	24	Gospoda pod		Intro	8
Kansai	32	Turbot	6	Kamienica	14	Wielkim Młynem	5	Parlament	13
Kresowa	35			Maraska	25	Irish Pub	6	Piękni, Młodzi i	
Mestwin	9			Pellowski	4 & 31	La Dolce Vita	21	Bogaci	12
Metamorfoza	10			Pi Kawa	17	Rabarbar	28	Yesterday	15
Napoli	23			Tawerna Baszta		Winifera	2		
Pierogarnia u Dzika	18			Łabędź	3				
Pod Łososiem	11			W Biegu Café	26				
Salonik	29								

Take bus #112 from the train station. 12zł per person. See map, p.147.
Camping Stogi ul. Wydmy 9 ☎058/307 3915, ⓦwww.kemping-gdansk.pl. Near the beach, just

20min by tram (#8 and #13) from the centre. Camping from 12zł per person, plus simple cabins sleeping 2–4 people 60–110zł. See map, p.147.

The City

The **Main Town** (Główne Miasto), the largest of the historic quarters, is the obvious starting point for an exploration of the city; the **Old Town** (Stare Miasto), across the thin ribbon of the Raduna Canal, is the natural progression. The main focus for visitors to the third, southern quarter, the **Old Suburb** (Stare Przedmieście), cut off by the busy Podwale Przedmiejskie, is the National Museum.

North along the Motława, **Westerplatte** – and its monument commemorating the outbreak of World War II – can be reached by **boat** from the central waterfront, a trip that allows good views of the famous **shipyards**. Moving north by road and rail, out towards Sopot, is the **Oliwa** suburb, with its cathedral – one of the city's most distinctive landmarks – and botanical gardens.

The Main Town

Entering the **Main Town** is like walking straight into a Hansa merchants' settlement. The layout, typical of a medieval port, comprises a tight network of streets, bounded on four sides by water and main roads – the Raduna and Motława canals to the north and east, Podwale Przedmiejskie and Wały Jagiellońskie to the south and west. The ancient appearance of this quarter's buildings is deceptive, however: by May 1945 the fighting between German and Russian forces had reduced the core of Gdańsk to smouldering ruins, with ninety percent of the Old Town and sixty percent of the suburbs destroyed. A glance at the photos in the town hall brings home the scale of the destruction and of its reversal.

Ulica Długa and Długi Targ

Ulica Długa, the main thoroughfare, and **Długi Targ**, the wide, open square to its east, form the natural focus of attention. As with all the main streets, huge gateways guard both entrances. Before the western entrance to Długa stands the outer **Upland Gate** (Brama Wyżynna), built in the late sixteenth century when it spanned the city moat as part of the town's outer fortifications, and once the main entrance to Gdańsk. The three coats of arms emblazoned across the archway – Poland, Prussia and Gdańsk – encapsulate the city's history. The gate houses the new **Amber Museum** (Muzeum Bursztynu: Mon 11am–3pm, Tues–Sat 10am–5.30pm, Sun 11am–6pm; 10zł, Mon free; ⓦwww.mhmg .gda.pl), which has a dazzling collection of amber – forty-million-year-old fossilized pine resin – and detailed information about the immense importance of the amber trade to the region. Some of the pieces even have flies, mosquitos, and in one case a small lizard, trapped inside. Exiting the Amber Museum you walk through the Gothic **prison tower** that's attached to the gate and which housed the city's torture chambers.

The Upland Gate gate was the starting point of the "royal route" used by Polish monarchs on their annual state visits. They would pass from here through the richly decorated **Golden Gate** (Brama Złota) alongside **St George's Court** (Dwór św. Jerzego), a fine Gothic mansion (nowadays home to the architects' society) with a statuette of St George and the Dragon on its roof; a copy of the original is now housed in the National Museum in the Old Suburb (see p.156). From here, ulica Długa leads down to the town hall (see below), past several gabled facades worth studying in detail, including the sixteenth-century **Ferber Mansion** (Dom Ferberów; no. 28) and the imposing **Lion's Castle** (Lwi Zamek; no. 35), where King Władysław IV entertained local dignitaries.

One of the few houses open to the public along this stretch is the **Uphagen Mansion** at ul. Długa 12 (Dom Uphagena; Mon 11am–3pm, Tues–Sun 10am–6pm, Sun 11am–4pm; 10zł, Mon free; ⓦ www.mhmg.gda.pl), former home of a leading Gdańsk merchant dynasty, which was turned into a museum in 1911 and was rebuilt and refurnished in late eighteenth-century style after World War II. The reception rooms on the first floor are particularly elegant, each boasting original carved wooden panels on a different theme.

The town hall

Topped by a golden statue of King Sigismund August that dominates the central skyline, the huge and well-proportioned tower of the **town hall** (Ratusz Głównego Miasta) makes a powerful impact. Originally constructed in the late fourteenth century, with the tower and spire added later, the building was badly damaged during the last war, but the restoration was so skilful you'd hardly believe it. It now houses the **Historical Museum** (Muzeum Historyczne; Mon 10am–3pm, Tues–Sat 10am–6pm; 8zł; ⓦ www.mhmg.gda.pl) but the lavish decoration almost upstages the exhibits on display. The highlight of the **Red Room** (Sala Czerwona), the main council chamber, is the central oval ceiling painting by Dutchman Isaac van den Block depicting *The Glorification of the Unity of Gdańsk with Poland*. Renovation work recently uncovered Gothic wall paintings behind the red wallpaper that will be on display in future. Other rooms have haunting **photographs** of the city in 1945 after it had been almost completely flattened by Allied and Soviet bombing. The **upper floor** has reconstructions of shops and homes in the Free City of Danzig in the 1920s and 1930s, and allows access to the **tower** (same times; closed Mon; 4zł), from where there are excellent views across the rooftops to the harbour and beyond.

Długi Targ

Immediately east of the town hall, overlooking Długi Targ, is **Arthur's Court** (Dwór Artusa: Tues–Sat 10am–4pm, Sun 11am–4pm; 10zł, Tues free; ⓦ www .mhmg.gda.pl): even in a street lined with many fine mansions, this one is impressive. The origins of the building date back to the early fourteenth century, a period marked by a widespread awakening of interest in British Arthurian legends among the European mercantile class. Attracted by the ideals of King Arthur's fabled court at Camelot, merchants began establishing their own latter-day courts, where they could entertain in the chivalrous and egalitarian spirit of their knightly forebears. Founded in 1350, the Gdańsk court grew rapidly to become one of the most fabulous and wealthy in Europe. Initially occupied by the Brotherhood of St George, it became a focal point of the city, with a growing array of guild- and trade-based brotherhoods establishing their own meeting benches in the main hall. The court's development was encouraged (and financed) by the city authorities, creating what was effectively northern Europe's first non-sectarian, non-political meeting place, combining the functions of guild house, civic hall, judicial court and reception centre for foreign guests. Rebuilt in the 1480s, with the main facade reworked by Abraham van den Block in the early seventeenth century, the building was almost completely destroyed in 1945. Mercifully, much of the court's rich interior was removed at the beginning of the war and thus saved. Original features in the cavernous, reconstructed main hall and adjoining chamber include sections of the original ceiling, including the starred vaulting, supported on graceful columns, and the "Great Stove", a huge Renaissance ceramic heating oven. Arthur's Court is flanked by two elegant sixteenth-century patricians' houses, incorporated into the museum and used for exhibitions.

Immediately outside Arthur's Court is the wonderful **Neptune Fountain** (Fontanna Neptuna), with water trickling from the very tips of the god's trident. Continuing just to the south, you'll come to the **Golden House** (Złota Kamieniczka), an impressive Renaissance mansion named after the luminous gilding that covers its elegant four-storeyed facade.

The waterfront and the Maritime Museum

The archways of the **Green Gate** (Brama Zielona), a former royal residence for the annual visit, open directly onto the **waterfront**. From the bridge over the Motława River you get a good view to the right of the old granaries on **Spichlerze** island (there used to be over three hundred of them), and to the left of the old harbour quay, now a tourist hangout and local promenade.

Halfway down the waterfront is the massive and partly original fifteenth-century **crane** (Żuraw; May–Sept Mon–Fri 10am–6pm, Sat & Sun from 10.30am; Oct–April Tues–Sun 10am–4pm), the biggest in medieval Europe. It's part of the **Maritime Museum** (Muzeum Morskie: 8zł per section or 18zł for all; ⓦwww .cmm.pl), which sprawls across both sides of the Motława and will be extended with the new Maritime Cultural Centre beside the crane in 2011. Inside the crane, as well as the massive lifting gear used to unload goods at the harbourside, is an exhibition describing port life in the prosperous sixteenth to eighteenth centuries. Just across the Motława – the 1zł ferry ride is included in the all-in ticket – the main section of the museum is housed in three Renaissance **granaries** (May–Sept daily 10am–6pm; Oct–April Tues–Sun 10am–3pm), known as the "Panna" (Virgin), "Miedź" (Copper) and "Oliwski" (Oliwa). Here there are extensive displays on Poland's history as a seafaring nation, sweeping right through from the earliest Slav settlements along the Wisła to the late twentieth century, taking in the seventeenth-century power struggles around the Baltic, an exhibit on underwater archeology and numerous astonishingly detailed models of ships along the way. On the ground floor you'll also find a haul of Swedish cannons recovered by museum divers. Back out on the quayside you can explore the sturdy-looking **Sołdek** (same times), the first steamship built in Gdańsk after World War II.

All the streets back into the town from the waterfront are worth exploring. Next up from Brama Zielona is **ulica Chlebnicka**, reached through the fifteenth-century **Bread Gate** (Brama Chlebnicka). The **English House** (Dom Angielski), built in 1569 and the largest house in the city at the time, is a reminder of the strong Reformation-era trading connections with Britain. It's the ornate grey building on the left, a few houses down as you walk away from the waterfront, and now converted into student halls.

St Mary's Church and around

Running parallel to ulica Chlebnicka to the north is **ulica Mariacka**, a charmingly atmospheric and meticulously reconstructed street of spindly iron railings and dragon-faced gutter spouts, its gabled terraced houses now occupied by expensive amber jewellery shops and stylish cafés. Near the waterfront, the **Archeological Museum** (Muzeum Archeologiczne: May–Sept Tues–Sun 10am–5pm; Oct–April Tues, Thurs & Fri 8am–4pm Wed 9am–5pm Sat & Sun 10am–4pm; 6zł, Sat free) describes the prehistory of Gdańsk and the surrounding areas. Though it's rather

Food and drink

**Polish cuisine contains much that is distinctive, but little
that is truly unique, most of it representing a blend of
culinary styles that run across neighbouring countries such
as Ukraine, Belarus and Lithuania. A combination of cold
winters and a peasant lifestyle have ensured that solid
helpings of meat and potatoes play an important role in the
national diet. North European vegetables such as carrots,
cabbage and beetroot provide the main accompaniment.
The predominance of unspoiled forest ensures a wealth of
wild fungi and berries – mushroom-picking in particular is a
much-loved national pastime.**

Soups

Mainstay of any Polish menu is the rundown of soups, which can serve as the introduction to a multi-course meal or a mid-day stomach-filler in their own right. Most famous of these is **borscht** (*barszcz*), a reddish beetroot-flavoured broth with a mildly sweet-and-sour taste. A refreshing summer variation on this theme is *chłodnik* – cold borscht served with lashings of sour cream and a side order of boiled potatoes. Three more **soup** staples are the deliciously tangy *żurek*, a grey-green concoction made from fermented rye and with slices of boiled egg floating on top; *krupnik*, a thick barley and potato soup with chunks of meat and carrots; and *fasolka*, a solid, almost stew-like combination of beans and smoked sausage.

Polish soup ▲

Alfresco grill bar, Plac nary Krata ▼

Pork

Although poultry plays an important role in Polish cooking, especially on festive occasions, it's pork that takes top billing as far as main courses are concerned. One hearty dish that crops up in restaurants from the functional to the fancy is the *kotlet schabowy*, a seasoned slab of pork fried either in breadcrumbs or batter. Equally representative of the Polish pork repertoire is *golonka*, deliciously tender roast pork knuckle traditionally served with horseradish sauce (*chrzan*).

However it's at the delicatessen counter that the true importance of the pig to Polish society is revealed, through the sheer array of sausages and smoked cuts (collectively known as *wędlina*). The generic name for sausage is *kiełbasa*, although there are plenty of varieties to chose from: the thin, smoked *kabanos*, the stocky, garlic-rich *wiejska*, and the pinkish and mildly spicy *krakowska* are all well worth trying.

Pierogi

If Polish cuisine had one single trademark then it would be the *pierog* (plural *pierogi*), a scallop shell-sized pocket of boiled dough with a savoury or sweet filling. Most common varieties are *pierogi z mięsem* (stuffed with minced meat), *z kopustą* (with cabbage), *z grzybami* (with mushroom) and *pierogi ruskie* (with cottage cheese and potato), although the specialist *pierogi* bars you'll find in Warsaw and Kraków are constantly experimenting with other ingredients including lentils, buckwheat and spinach.

Savoury *pierogi* are served either piled up on a plate (and in the best cafés and restaurants they'll come with a garnish of fried onion, sour cream and bacon bits); or swimming in a bowl of broth or borscht. In some places you can also get sweet *pierogi* which are stuffed with strawberries, cherries or other fruit, and dusted with icing sugar.

Spirits

Social life in Poland would be unimaginable without vodka, the liquid that lubricates family celebrations, folk holidays and business deals as well as dedicated nights on the town. Most of the vodka manufactured in Poland is made from pure grain spirit – in contrast to the blend of various vegetables employed by many western distillers. Alongside vodka pure-and-simple there are innumerable flavoured varieties, most famous of which is the yellowish-looking *Żubrówka*, flavoured with extract of bison grass from the Białowieża forest. Local wags will tell you that the grass has to be urinated on by a bison first, although this part of the recipe is probably optional. Other **spirits** frequently consumed as

▲ Polish staple, pierogi

▼ Joint of pork with salad

▼ Traditional Polish borscht

A shot of wsciekly pies ▲

A Kazimierz café ▼

down-in-one shots include *Wiśniówka*, or cherry vodka; the amber-coloured, herb-infused *Żolądkowa*, and the honey-flavoured liqueur, *krupnik*. Occupying a category all of its own is *Żoládkowa gorzka* (literally "a bitter drink for the stomach"), an amber-coloured, herb-infused concoction that works wonders for the digestion and soothes a whole host of minor ailments besides, chesty coughs included. Polish plum brandy (*śliwowica*) frequently contains more than fifty percent alcohol and should be treated with extreme caution. Among the **mixed drinks,** the incendiary *wsciekly pies* ("crazy dog", containing vodka, raspberry syrup and tabasco sauce) is guaranteed to get your evening going. For something more restrained, try *szarlotka* (also known as *tatanka*), a longer drink combining *Żubrówka* vodka with apple juice.

Desserts

Wherever you are in Poland you're never too far away from a tray of cakes, with establishments from high-street bakeries to high-class restaurants offering plenty to tempt the sweet-toothed. One classic Polish confection that you'll find everywhere is *sernik*, a dense, spongy cheesecake that makes the ideal accompaniment to afternoon tea or coffee. Another trademark Polish dessert that won't do your waistline any favours is *szarlotka*, a succulent apple pie which often features a crumble or meringue topping, and is frequently consumed with a side-order of ice cream. Alongside the above, restaurant menus frequently feature a choice of *naleśniki*, deliciously light pancakes filled with fruit, jam or honey.

academic in tone there are some interesting exhibits, like the display of ancient skulls and bones showing evidence of battle scars, injury and disease.

At the western end of Mariacka stands the gigantic **St Mary's Church** (Kościół Mariacki), reputedly the biggest brick church in the world. Estimates that it could fit 20,000 people inside were substantiated during the early days of martial law, when huge crowds crammed the cold, whitewashed interior. The south aisle is dominated by a copy of the miraculous **Madonna of the Gates of Dawn** from Wilno (now Vilnius in Lithuania), a city whose Polish inhabitants were encouraged to emigrate in 1945 – many of them ending up in Gdańsk, where they replaced the departing German population. The **high altar**, reconstructed after the war, is a powerful sixteenth-century triptych featuring a *Coronation of the Virgin*. Of the chapels scattered round the church, two of the most striking are the **Chapel of 11,000 Virgins**, with a tortured Gothic crucifix – the artist was said to have nailed his son-in-law to a cross as a model – and **St Anne's Chapel**, containing the wooden *Beautiful Madonna of Gdańsk* from around 1415. A curiosity is the reconstructed fifteenth-century **astronomical clock**, which tells not only the day, month and year but the whole saints' calendar and the phases of the moon; when completed in 1470 it was the world's tallest clock. If you're feeling fit, make sure you climb the 402 steps up to the rickety viewing platform on top of the church **tower** (Mon–Sat 9am–5pm, Sun 9am–1pm; 4zł).

From the Great Arsenal to the market

West of the church entrance, **ulica Piwna**, another street of high terraced houses, ends at the monumental **Great Arsenal** (Wielka Zbrojownia), an early seventeenth-century armoury built in Flemish Renaissance style. It backs on to **Targ Węglowy** (Coal Market), now a busy shopping centre, which leads north to Targ Drzewny (Wood Market), and on to the Old Town over the other side of the canal. **Ulica Szeroka**, first off to the right, is another charming old street with a nice view of St Mary's from the corner with ulica Grobla.

The Dominican-run **St Nicholas' Church** (Kościół św. Mikołaja) on ulica Świętojańska is another fourteenth-century brick structure, the only city centre church to come through the war relatively unscathed. The interior houses a rich array of furnishings, in particular some panelled early Baroque choir stalls, a massive high altar and a fine Gothic pietà in one of the nave bays.

The terraced houses and shops tail off as you approach the outer limits of the main town, marked by several towers and other remnants of the **city wall**. **Baszta Jacek** (Jacek Bastion), the tower nearest the canal, stands guard over ulica Podmłyńska, the main route over the canal into the Old Town. The area around the tower provides the focus of the annual Dominican fair (Jarmark) in August (see p.160). The **market hall** opposite sells flowers and a fine selection of fruits and vegetables. As well as the regular traders at the stalls, along the pavement you'll see old ladies in from the countryside to sell a few mushrooms or bunches of herbs.

The old post office

Continuing northeast, at the edge of plac Obrońców Poczty Polskiej stands the **old post office** building immortalized by Günter Grass in *The Tin Drum*. Rebuilt after the war, it's here that a small contingent of employees of the Free City's Poczta Polska (Polish Post Office) battled it out with German forces in September 1939. As at Westerplatte (see p.156), the Germans clearly weren't anticipating such spirited resistance; despite the overwhelmingly superior firepower ranged against them the Poles held out for nine hours, finally surrendering when the Nazis sent in flame-throwers. The spiky **monument** on the square in front of the building commemorates the event that has played an important role in the city's postwar communist mythology, the Poles' heroic resistance presented as a further vindication of the claimed "Polishness" of the city. Inside the post office there's a small **museum** (closed for renovations at time of writing, but expected to reopen in 2009; Ⓦwww.mhmg.gda.pl), mainly devoted to the events of 1939.

③ The Old Town

Crossing the canal bridge brings you into the **Old Town** (Stare Miasto), altogether a patchier and less reconstructed part of town, characterized by a jumbled mix of old and new buildings. Dominating the waterside is the seven-storey **Great Mill** (Wielki Młyn), built in the mid-fourteenth century by the Teutonic Knights and the biggest mill in medieval Europe. Its eighteen races milled corn for six hundred years; even in the 1930s it was still grinding out two hundred tons of flour a day. The building has been converted into a modest shopping centre, but traces of the original building are still in evidence, notably the old foundations.

Immediately opposite is the fourteenth-century brick **Church of St Catherine** (Kościół św. Katarzyny), the former parish church of the Old Town, and one of the nicest in the city, though it's currently being restored after a large part of the roof was destroyed by fire in 2006. The astronomer Jan Hevelius and his family are buried here in a tomb in the choir. Nearby **St Bridget's Church** (Kościół św. Brygidy) became a local Solidarity stronghold in the 1980s, and was the local church of Lech Wałęsa, the Solidarity leader. An amber statue of Mary indicates the spot where a huge six- by eleven-metre amber altarpiece will commemorate the 28 workers killed during strikes in 1970.

As you move further into the Old Town, the merchants' mansions give way to postwar housing. The most interesting part of the district is just west along the canal from the mill, centred on the Old Town Hall (Ratusz Staromiejski), on the corner of ulica Bielańska and ulica Korzenna. Built by the architect of the main town hall, this delicate Renaissance construction has been converted into the **Baltic Sea Culture Centre** (Nadbałtyckie Centrum Kultury: daily 10am–6pm), a venue for performances, festivals and exhibitions. The bronze figure in the entrance hall is of Jan Hevelius.

Continuing west from the town hall, the Gothic churches of **St Joseph's Church** (Kościół św. Józefa) and **St Elizabeth's Church** (Kościół św. Elżbiety) – facing each other across ulica Elżbietańska – and the Renaissance **House of the Abbots of Pelplin** (Dom Opatów Pelplińskich) make a fine historic assemblage. From here you're only a short walk through the tunnels under the main road (Podwale Grodzkie) from the train station.

The shipyards

Looming over the city from most angles you'll see the cranes of the famous **Gdańsk Shipyards** (Stocznia Gdańska), once known as the Lenin Shipyards. With the Nowa Huta steelworks outside Kraków, this was the crucible of the political struggles of the 1980s.

Ten minutes' walk or one tram stop north from the railway station brings you to the shipyard gates on plac Solidarności. In front of them stands a set of towering steel crosses, a **monument** to workers killed during the 1970 shipyard riots; it was inaugurated in 1980 in the presence of Party, Church and opposition leaders. A precursor to the organized strikes of the 1980s, the 1970 riots erupted when workers took to the streets in protest at price rises, setting fire to the Party headquarters after police opened fire. Riots erupted again in 1976, once more

▲ The Gdańsk Shipyards

in protest at price rises on basic foodstuffs, and in August 1980 Gdańsk came to the forefront of world attention when a protest at the sacking of workers rapidly developed into a national strike.

The formation of **Solidarity**, the first independent trade union in the Soviet bloc, was a direct result of the Gdańsk strike, instigated by the Lenin Shipyards workers and their charismatic leader **Lech Wałęsa**. Throughout the 1980s the Gdańsk workers remained in the vanguard of political protest. Strikes here in 1988 and 1989 led to the Round Table Talks that forced the Communist Party into power-sharing and, ultimately, democratic elections.

Standing at the gates today, you may find it hard to experience this as the place where, in a sense, contemporary Poland began to take shape. Yet the shipyards remain in the news: unlike those at nearby Gdynia, the sprawling Gdańsk yards have always been unprofitable, and it was a post-communist government that attempted to modernize them, bitterly opposed by President Wałęsa (as he had by then become). Attempts to interest foreign investors collapsed because of the insistence that the full local workforce must be retained by any buyer. Successive Polish governments have faced a quandary: they cannot appear hostile to Solidarity, yet they are left supporting a shipyard that requires millions of euros in subsidies, seen as illegal state support by the EU, to stay in business.

The story of Solidarity's pivotal role in Poland's recent history is told nearby in the **Roads to Freedom** exhibition (Drogi do wolności: Tues–Sun 10am–4pm; 5zł, Wed free), temporarily housed at ul. Wały Piastowskie 24 but expected to move back to the shipyard in 2010. The exhibition is an impressionistic but moving multimedia portrayal of the events of the Solidarity era, illustrated using news clips, black and white stills and crackly recordings of strikers' songs. If you want to get a look at the working end of the yards, the best way is to take a cruise to Westerplatte (see p.156).

Old Suburb

Old Suburb – the lower part of old Gdańsk – was the limit of the original town, as testified by the ring of seventeenth-century bastions running east from plac

Wałowy over the Motława. The main attraction today is the **National Museum** (Muzeum Narodowe: Tues–Sun 10am–5pm; 15zł; ⓦwww.muzeum.narodowe .gda.pl), housed in a former Franciscan monastery at ul. Toruńska 1. There's a wealth of Gothic art and sculpture here, all redolent of the town's former wealth. The range of Dutch and Flemish art – Memling, the younger Brueghel, Cuyp and van Dyck are the best-known names – attests to the city's strong links with the Netherlands.

The museum's most famous work is Hans Memling's colossal *Last Judgement* triptych (1471), the painter's earliest known work – though by then he was already in his thirties and a mature artist. It depicts Jesus overseeing St Michael weighing souls, with the saved entering a Gothic portal of heaven and the damned being dragged to hell by black demons, each representing a particular sin. Look closely at St Michael's belt and you'll see the reflection of people viewing the painting – involving you in the scene too. The work has something of a chequered past – it was commissioned by the Medici family banker in Florence, then diverted to Gdańsk by pirates, looted by Napoleon, moved to Berlin, returned to Gdańsk, stolen by the Nazis and finally, after being discovered by the Red Army, hidden in the Thuringian hills, to be returned to Gdańsk by the Russians in 1956.

Adjoining the museum is the **Holy Trinity Church** (Kościół św. Trójcy: May–Sept Sun 10am–6pm; Oct–April Sun 1–6pm), a towering brick Gothic structure with characteristic period net vaulting. The recently restored interior features a fine high altar, an assemblage of triptych pieces cobbled together following the wartime destruction of Isaac van Blocke's original, a delicately carved pulpit (the only Gothic original left in the city) and the elegant fifteenth-century St Anna's Chapel.

Westerplatte

It was at **Westerplatte**, the promontory guarding the harbour entrance, that the German battleship *Schleswig-Holstein* fired the first salvo of World War II on September 1, 1939. For a full week the garrison of 170 badly equipped Poles held off the combined assault of aircraft, heavy guns and over 3000 German troops, setting the tone for the Poles' response to the subsequent Nazi–Soviet invasion. The ruined army guardhouse and barracks are still there, one of the surviving buildings housing a small **museum** (May–Oct daily 9am–4pm; 3zł) chronicling the momentous events of September 1939. Beyond the museum it's a fifteen-minute walk to the main **Westerplatte Monument**, a grim, ugly-looking 1960s slab in the best Socialist Realist traditions, whose symbolism conveys a tangible sense of history. The green surroundings of the exposed peninsula make a enjoyable, if generally blustery, walk to the coast, with good views out onto the Baltic.

There are a number of ways of getting to Westerplatte. You can take bus #106 from outside the train station all the way, but more fun is a trip on one of the tour boats (see p.146; late June–Sept hourly 9am–7pm; Oct–late June three times daily) from near the Green Gate. Taking about thirty minutes each way, the trip provides an excellent view of the **shipyards** and the array of international vessels anchored there. If you have children in tow, consider taking a cruise to Wester-platte on the *Lew* or *Regina* galleons (5–6 sailings per day June–Sept; 35zł return). Alternatively, tram #10 will take you to the Nowy Port harbour district from where you can cross the Wisła by ferry (every 30min). While in Nowy Port, another short hop on tram #15 will bring you to the elegant nineteenth-century red-brick **lighthouse** at ul. Przemysłowa 6a (May–Sept daily 10am–6pm; 5zł).

It's topped by a time ball that was dropped at noon every day to allow captains to reset their chronometers. From the top there's a great view over Westerplatte and the Baltic and back over the shipyards to the city.

If you take the boat out to Westerplatte, you'll pass the sturdy brick walls of the fifteenth-century **Wisła Fortress** (Twierdza Wisłoujście), designed by Dutch architects using the octagonal zigzag defence plan popular at the time. It was enlarged to its current size in the mid-eighteenth century, and reinforced by Napoleon's forces in the early nineteenth.

Oliwa

The modern **Oliwa** suburb, the northernmost area of Gdańsk, has one of the best-known buildings in the city – its cathedral. To get here, take the local train to Gdańsk-Oliwa station, walk west across the main Sopot road and carry on through the park.

The cathedral

Originally part of the monastery founded by the Danish Cistercians who settled here in the mid-twelfth century at the invitation of a local Pomeranian prince, the **cathedral** (Katedra Oliwska: Mon–Fri 9am–5pm, Sat 9am–3pm, Sun 2pm–5pm) has seen its fair share of action over the years. First in a long line of plunderers were the Teutonic Knights, who repeatedly ransacked the place in the 1240s and 1250s. A fire in the 1350s led to a major Gothic-style overhaul, the structural essence of which remains to this day. The wars of the seventeenth century had a marked impact on Oliwa, the Swedish army carrying off much of the cathedral's sumptuous collection of furnishings as booty in 1626, the church bells and main altarpiece included. The second major Swedish assault of 1655–60 eventually led to the Oliwa Peace Treaty (1660), signed in the abbey hall: the following century brought lavish refurbishment of the building (notably the organ, begun in 1755), most of which you can still see today. The Prussian Partition-era takeover of Gdańsk spelled the end of the fabulously wealthy abbey's glory days, the monastery finally being officially abolished in 1831. Unlike most of its surroundings, the cathedral miraculously came through the end of World War II largely unscathed, though the retreating Nazis torched the abbey complex. Today the complex, having been restored is a remarkable sight.

Approached from the square in front of the building, the towering main **facade** combines twin Gothic brick towers peaked with Renaissance spires and dazzling white Rococo stuccowork to unusually striking effect. The fine late seventeenth-century portal brings you into the lofty central **nave**, an exuberant structure topped by a star-spangled vaulted ceiling supported on arched pillars. Past the side chapels filling the two side aisles, the eye is drawn to the **high altar**, a sumptuous Baroque piece from the 1680s containing several pictures from the Gdańsk workshops of the period. Above the altar rises a deliciously over-the-top decorative ensemble, a swirling mass of beatific-looking cherubs being sucked into a heavenly whirlpool, surrounded by angels, with gilded sun rays breaking out in all directions – the whole thing leading towards a central stained-glass window.

Apart from some fine Baroque choir stalls and the old Renaissance high altarpiece, now in the northern transept, the building's finest feature is the exuberantly decorated eighteenth-century **organ**, which in its day was the largest instrument in Europe – seven men were needed to operate the bellows. The dark heavy oak of the organ is ornamented with a mass of sumptuous Rococo woodcarving, the whole instrument framing a stained-glass window of Mary and Child. With its rich, sonorous tone and a wealth of moving parts, trumpet-blowing angels included, it's a beautiful instrument. Its 110 registers allow for an extraordinary range of pitch – there are frequent ribcage-rippling recitals to show it off (Mon–Sat 10am, 11am, noon & 1pm; free).

The Abbot's Palace and Contemporary Art Museum

Passing through the gateway down the lane running alongside the cathedral brings you to the stately **Abbots' Palace**, which now houses the **Contemporary Art Museum** (Wystawa Sztuki Współczesnej; May–Sept Tues–Sun 10am–5pm; Oct–April Tues–Fri 9am–4pm, Sat & Sun 10am–5pm; 10zł, free Tues). Upstairs is an enjoyable gallery of twentieth-century Polish art – the centrepiece being a large selection of 1960s Pop Art and conceptual sculptures – all going to show how postwar Polish art successfully escaped the ideological fetters of communist cultural policy. The museum also hosts temporary exhibitions, mainly retrospectives of contemporary Polish artists. Across the courtyard from the palace, an old granary contains an **ethnographic museum** (same hours; 7zł), a collection of furniture, handicrafts and fishing and farmyard tools from across the region. Surrounding the complex is the old palace **park**, an appealing, shaded spot with an enjoyable collection of exotic trees, hanging willows and a stream meandering through the middle – a pleasant place for an afternoon stroll.

Around the cathedral

Like several Polish cities, Gdańsk has a small, low-profile **Tatar** community (see p.243), who use the new **mosque** south of the cathedral on the corner of ulica Polanki and ulica Abrahama (Gdańsk-Zaspa station; trams #6, #12 and #15 also run nearby). Further up the same road, the attractive, late eighteenth-century mansion at no. 122 is where **Arthur Schopenhauer** (1788–1860), the Danzig/Gdańsk-born philosopher, grew up. North of the cathedral is the **Trójmiejskie Park Krajobrazowy**, a hilly patch of forest behind the city, with trails and, when there's a break in the trees, refreshing views.

Eating, drinking and nightlife

Finding a place to eat in Gdańsk is relatively straightforward, and there's a good range of **cafés** and **snack bars** and some genuinely recommendable **restaurants**; making reservations is advised at those listed with phone numbers. For a quick lunch in summer you could do a lot worse than visit the cluster of fried-fish stalls at the northern end of Rybackie Pobrzeże. Fish dishes are a local speciality and are well worth sampling.

Drinking in the city tends to centre on a number of bars and cafés on ulica Długa and parallel streets to the north. In summer the attractive terrace cafés of ulica Chlebnicka and ulica Mariacka make the ideal place to sit out and enjoy the sun. The waterfront is the centre of activity, however, with a few good spots (and plenty of tackier ones) to sit.

The **clubbing** scene in Gdańsk is very active, thanks in large part to the Trójmiasto's large student population. Several of the places listed as bars below also offer live music and/or dancing at weekends; while official closing times for clubs are given below, in practice they tend to stay open till the last person leaves. Dedicated clubbers should note that there's also a good range of nightlife opportunities in **Sopot** (see p.166).

All places are marked on the main Gdańsk map on p.149, except where noted.

Snack bars and cafés

Bar Mleczny Neptun ul. Długa 33. Reliable milk bar with a wide range of cheap Polish meals on the menu. Mon–Fri 7.30am–6pm, Sat & Sun 10am–6pm.

Capri ul. Długa 59/61. Outdoor seating in summer, good coffee and cakes, and the best place in town for ice cream. Daily 10am–10pm.

Kamienica ul. Mariacka 37/39. Cosy intimate café on two floors in an old town house with quiet nooks and a terrace overlooking Mariacka. Good for a daytime coffee break or evening drinks. Daily 10am–midnight.

Maraska ul. Długa 31/32. Cosy café with a wide range of delicious teas, coffees and desserts. Daily 9am–9pm.

Pellowski ul. Długa 44 and Podwale Staromiejskie 82. Bright, modern self-service café with excellent coffee, cakes and pastries. Several branches around town. Daily 9am–7pm.

Pi Kawa ul. Piwna 5/6. Delightfully bohemian café with coffee, tea, cakes and a cool crowd. Daily 10am–10pm.

Tawerna Baszta Łabędź Targ Rybny. Set in an atmospheric old tower, this simple fish and pizza restaurant also has a buzzing terrace in summer. Daily noon–11pm.

W Biegu Café ul. Długa 6/8. A popular modern café with good coffee, cakes, breakfasts (11–13zł) and snacks. Mon–Sat 8am–10pm, Sun 10am–10pm.

Restaurants

Czerwone Drzwi ul. Piwna 52/53. Imaginative Polish and Western European dishes, all beautifully presented in very romantic surroundings. Daily noon–10pm.

Euro ul. Długa 79/80 ☎058/305 2383. Vaguely Rococo-style place serving upmarket, traditional European classics, including a tasty smoked eel in honey sauce. Worth splashing out on. Daily noon–11pm.

Green Way ul. Długa 11. Reputable low-budget vegetarian chain with big portions of healthy food. Daily 10am–9pm.

Kansai ul. Ogarna 124/125. The best of several new Japanese restaurants, serving quality sushi meals for 23–100zł. Daily noon–9pm.

Kresowa ul. Ogarna 12. Waitresses in period dress scurry around serving fabulous traditional food from Lithuania, Ukraine and Russia, including *pelmeni*, shashlik and *kwas*, a fermented grain drink. Daily 10am–10pm.

Margherita ul. Cysterstów 11, Oliwa. Fine pizzas from a brick oven, near to Oliwa Cathedral. Daily noon–10pm. See map, p.147.

Mestwin ul. Straganiarska 20. Delicious traditional Kashubian peasant food – mainly variations on meat, cabbage and potatoes – served in a restaurant crammed with artefacts and artworks from the region. Daily 11am–10pm.

Metamorfoza ul. Szeroka 22/23. The bright, modern white interior here, decorated with huge flowers, is a relief after so many rustic places. The international dishes like chicken in spinach (25zł) can be enjoyed on the sunny terrace in summer. Daily noon–11pm.

Napoli ul. Długa 62/63. Central pizzeria with plenty of room and fast service. Daily 11am–10pm.

Pierogarnia u Dzika ul. Piwna 59/60. Perfect *pierogi* of every conceivable variety, from mushroom to cherry, in comfortable surroundings. Daily 11am–10pm.

Pod Łososiem ul. Szeroka 52/54 ☎058/301 7652. One of the most luxurious restaurants in town, so you may have to book, though it's not as pricey as you might think. Specializing in game and seafood, it's also known locally as the home of Goldwasser vodka liqueur, a thick yellow concoction with flakes of real gold. Daily noon–11pm.

Salonik ul. Długa 18. The best choice on the main drag – excellent Polish food, including halibut fillet (54zł) or *pierogi* with salmon, spinach and chilli sauce (28zł), in classy surroundings. Daily 11am–11pm.

Scampi Targ Rybny 10c. An elegant fish restaurant serving a surprising variety of fresh scampi dishes as well as other fish meals. Daily noon–10pm.

Swojski Smak ul. Heweliusza 25/27. Delicious, good-value Polish food in peasant-style surroundings, right next to the tourist information office. Daily noon–10pm.

Tawerna ul. Powroźnicza 19/20. Widely trumpeted as Gdańsk's best seafood restaurant, with an imaginative and luxurious menu including smoked eel, caviar and fish soufflé. The ship marking the entrance to the restaurant leaves no doubt about the theme of the interior. Daily 11am–11pm.

Turbot ul. Korzenna 33/35. Every meal mentioned in Gunther Grass's books is available here in the formal-looking basement of the Old Town Hall, along with other well-prepared European dishes. Daily noon–10pm.

Bars and pubs

Blue Café ul. Chmielna 103/104. Spacious modern café-bar featuring live jazz and blues, and DJ nights at weekends (anything from acid jazz to golden oldies). Daily noon–midnight.

Celtic Pub ul. Lektykarska (off ul. Długa) ⓦwww .celticpub.pl. Big, fun basement pub with homely wooden benches, giant screen for music videos, and live music and dancing at weekends. Daily 7am–1am, till 4am at weekends.

Gospoda pod Wielkim Młynem ul. Na Piaskach 1. Outdoor summer pub behind the Great Mill, on an island between two canals. Good on warm nights. Daily 10am–11pm.

Irish Pub ul. Korzenna 33/35 ℗ www.irish.pl. It's as Irish as a plate of curry, but this cavernous venue underneath the Old Town Hall, often full of students, guarantees a good night out. Frequent live music and dancing at weekends. Daily 3pm–midnight, till 4am at weekends.

La Dolce Vita ul. Chlebnicka 2. A trendy modern bar with normal and XL-sized drinks and a great atmosphere. Daily 2pm–2am.

Rabarbar ul. Długa 18. The best bar on Długa, with a cool vibe, covered summer terrace, a dark interior that's perfect for bumping into complete strangers, decent cocktails and also top-notch food from the *Salonik* kitchen next door. Daily noon–2am.

Scruffy O'Brien al. Grunwaldzka 76/78, Wrzeszcz. Decent pub grub, decent beer and a bit more authenticity than other Irish pubs. A good place to head if you're in the area. Daily 11am–midnight. See map, p.147.

Winifera ul. Wodopój 7. A quirky bar-cum-café serving cheap Polish food in a tiny canal-side house (this is the little doll's house referred to in Günter Grass's *The Call of the Toad*). Daily 2–11pm.

Clubs

Gazeta Rock Café ul. Tkacka 7/8 ℗ www .alternatywy775.pl/rock-cafe. Friendly and fashionable basement bar decked out with pop memorabilia – it styles itself as the "Museum of Polish Rock" – with regular DJs and parties. Open 6pm–2am, Fri & Sat till 4am.

Intro ul. Straganiarska 18/19 ℗ www.klubintro .pl. A small but funky club with a tiny dancefloor in a dimly lit arched basement. Open 6pm–midnight, Thurs–Sat till 5am.

Parlament ul. św. Ducha 2 (entrance on ul. Kołodziejska) ℗ www.parlament.com.pl. Popular and unpretentious place for mainstream dance music and a lot of beer. Open Wed–Sat 8pm–4am.

Piękni, Młodzi i Bogaci ul. Teatralna 1 ℗ www .pieknimlodziibogaci.pl. Posey place – the name means "young, rich and beautiful" – with a lively dance floor. Open 8pm–1am, till 5am Fri & Sat.

Yesterday ul. Piwna 50 ℗ www.yesterday-klub .pl. A large club with 1960s-style decor and current dance music. Open 7pm–2am, Fri & Sat till 4am.

Entertainment

The National Philharmonic and Opera House, al. Zwycięstwa 15 (nearest station Gdańsk-Politechnika) is one of the best **classical venues** in the country, with a varied programme of classical performances and occasional ballet productions. Information and ticket reservations are available from the box office (℗ 058/320 6262, ℗ www.operabaltycka.pl). In addition, there are frequent chamber music recitals at the Music Academy (Akademia Muzyczna), ul. Łąkowa 1/2 (℗ 058/300 9200, ℗ www.amuz.gda.pl), and in the Baltic Sea Culture Centre, ul. Korzenna 33/35 (℗ 058/301 1051, ℗ www.nck.org.pl), which is also the venue for small-scale drama productions. The main city-centre **theatre** is the Wybrzeże, just behind the Great Arsenal at ul. św. Ducha 2 (℗ 058/301 1328, ℗ www.teatrwybrzeze.pl).

The **cinema**'s a valid option as foreign films are shown with subtitles, not dubbed. None of the old city-centre cinemas have survived the onslaught of multiplexes and DVD, and the only central choice is the Cinema City Krewetka (℗ 058/769 3102, ℗ www.cinema-city.pl), opposite the main train station at ul. Karmelicka 1. Other options include the Multikino Wrzeszcz (℗ 058/732 1010, ℗ www.multikino.pl/gdansk) and the Kinoplex Alfacentrum (℗ 058/767 9999, ℗ www.alfacentrum.pl) along the main road to Sopot.

The Trójmiasto boasts a variety of **festivals** and other major cultural get-togethers; the tourist office and the *Gdansk In Your Pocket* city guide (see p.145) offer an up-to-date overview of events. The three-week Dominican Fair (Jarmark Dominikański), held annually between the end of July and

Moving on from the Trójmiasto

Gdańsk's modern Lech Wałęsa **airport** (☎058/348 1111, ⓦwww.airport.gdansk.pl) can be reached from Gdańsk's main station by bus #B, departing about every 30 minutes; additionally, bus #110 runs from Gdynia to the airport five times per day. Snacks are available at the airport and there are a limited number of shops.

The Gdynia, Sopot and Gdańsk Główny **train stations** are all well connected to the rest of Poland, with express services stopping at all three stations; consider using night trains to cover longer distances, such as to Wrocław, Kraków or Zakopane, while saving on daytime travel and a hotel night. There are also daily trains to Berlin (overnight 10hr 30min) and Kaliningrad (daytime; 5hr 30min).

Gdańsk's **bus station** (dworzec autobusowy: ☎058/301 2515, ⓦwww.pks.gdansk.pl) is right behind the station, reached through the underpass, and serves destinations throughout the region as well as dozens of cities outside Poland, including to Kaliningrad (2 buses daily, 5hr 30min) and Vilnius (one overnight bus daily, 9hr).

Buy train and bus tickets in advance at Orbis offices to avoid queues at the stations.

mid-August is an important local occasion, with artists and craftspeople setting up shop in the centre of town, accompanied by street theatre and a wealth of other cultural events. St Nicholas's Fair (Jarmark Mikołaja), in the first three weeks of December, is a pre-Christmas variation on the same theme. Musically, there's the annual international Chamber Music Festival, timed to coincide with the Jarmark Dominikański; an International Choral Festival, held in the town hall (June–Aug); and the Festival of Organ Music in Oliwa Cathedral during July and August (ⓦwww.filharmonia.gda.pl). For Polish-speaking film buffs, the Gdynia Film Festival takes place in late September (ⓦwww.fpff.pl).

There are some worthwhile diversions and entertainments for **children** in town. The Miniatura **puppet theatre**, ul. Grunwaldzka 16 (☎058/341 1209, ⓦwww.teatrminiatura.pl), is excellent, and performances are held nearly every day. There's a nice theatre interior, and children love the performances. The **zoo** in Oliwa at Karwieńska 3 is set in enjoyably forested, hilly surroundings and can be reached by bus #122 (Aug 9am–7pm; Sept–July 9am–3pm).

Listings

Airline offices LOT, ul. Wały Jagiellońskie 2/4 ☎0801/703 703.

Ambulance For emergency medical help call ☎999.

Banks and exchange ATMs and *kantors* for cash exchange are everywhere. Regular banks, such as the Bank Pekao at ul. Wały Piastowskie 1, will handle major credit cards and travellers' cheques.

Books For maps, guidebooks and English-language papers and periodicals visit EMPiK on ul. Podwale Grodzkie 8 (opposite the central station).

Car rental All international agencies have offices at the airport: Avis ☎058/348 1289, ⓦwww.avis.pl; Budget ☎058/348 1298, ⓦwww.budget.pl; Hertz ☎058/301 4045, ⓦwww.hertz.com.pl; Joka, ul. Wały Piastowskie 1/1502 (400m north of the station) ☎609/235 424, ⓦwww.joka.com.pl.

Consulates UK, al. Grunwaldzka 102 ☎058/341 4365. All other nationalities need to contact their embassy in Warsaw (see p.111).

Football The main city football team, Lechia Gdańsk, play at the BKS Lechia stadium at ul. Traugutta 29; nearest station is Gdańsk-Politechnika. Tickets can be bought at the stadium before the game.

Internet There are six free wi-fi hotspots across the city centre. The Jazz 'n Java internet café is at ul. Tkacka 17/18 (daily 10am–10pm).

Left luggage At the train station (24hr).

Parking Guarded parking is available at the main Orbis hotels (*Hevelius; Novotel*) and is available to non-guests for a fee.

Pharmacy There's a 24hr pharmacy at the main train station.

Police City headquarters are at ul. Okopowa 15. In an emergency call 997, or (in summer) ☎0800/200 300, a special number for tourists.

Post office The main office is at ul. Długa 23/28 (Mon–Fri 8am–8pm, Sat 9am–3pm).

Shopping If you want to browse round a market, then try the covered market (Hala Targowa) on ul. Pańska, which has vegetables and fruit, brought in fresh each day from the countryside, and stalls inside and outside. Madison on ul. Rajska near the train station, is the best of the modern shopping

malls. Ul. Długa is the place to browse for antiques and souvenirs; and ul. Mariacka is good for amber and other jewellery.

Taxi Only take taxis with metres showing company names and phone numbers, or order your cab by phone. Reliable firms include MTP (☎058/9633) and City Plus (☎058/9686).

Train tickets International train tickets are available from the main stations in Gdańsk and Gdynia and from Orbis, ul. Podwale Staromiejskie 96/97 (☎058/301 4544).

Sopot

One-time stamping ground for the rich and famous, who came from all over the world to sample its casinos and high life in the 1920s and 1930s, the beach resort at **SOPOT** is very popular with Poles, and is increasingly attractive to Westerners. It has an altogether different atmosphere from its neighbour: the fashionable clothes shops and bars scattered round ulica Bohaterów Monte Cassino, the main street, seem light years away from both historic central Gdańsk and the industrial grimness of the shipyards. Sopot has always enjoyed a special position in Polish popular culture, as the birthplace of Polish beat music and as the place where media personalities traditionally come to see and be seen. Today, Sopot's position slap in the middle of the Trójmiasto ensures that it's more than just a summertime seaside resort: it's a year-round nightlife centre servicing the big-city populations of both Gdynia and Gdańsk, as well as a growing business centre and an enduringly fashionable place in which to live. In terms of local affluence and outside invest-ment, it's the fastest growing town in Poland, and the current multi-million-złoty project to redevelop the seafront area will do much to improve its appeal.

Arrival, information and accommodation

The simplest way to get to Sopot is by SKM **train** from Gdańsk, a twenty-minute journey; mainline trains from Warsaw to Gdynia also stop here. **Buses** drop passengers off where aleja Niepodleglosci, the main road, meets ulica Bohaterów Monte Cassino. **Ferries** from Gdańsk and Hel moor along the pier. The **tourist office**, in the booth diagonally opposite the train station at ul. Dworcowa 4 (daily: June to mid-Sept 9am–8pm; mid-Sept to May 10am–6pm; ☎058/550 3783, ⓦwww.sopot.pl) has free maps and can help book private rooms (❶), pensions and hotels; in 2009, it may relocate to the newly developed area at the bottom of ulica Bohaterów Monte Cassino. There's an **internet** café, the Net Cave, in a courtyard off ulica Bohaterów Monte Cassino at ul. Pułaskiego 7a (daily 10am–9pm).

Sopot's holiday popularity means that rooms can be scarce, and in July and August prices can rocket. Three good, cheap **student dorm** buildings are open to travellers in July and August, two in the forest west of town and one along the beach, half an hour's walk south of the pier at ul. Bitwy pod Płowcami 64 (all bookable via ⓦwww.akademikigdansk.pl). Note that some hotels in Gdańsk's northern suburbs (see p.167) are very close to Sopot too. Best of the **campsites** are *Kamienny Potok*, at the northern end of the resort near the Kamienny Potok SKM station (☎058/550 0445, ⓦwww.kampotok.maxmedia.pl), and *Przy Plaży* (☎058/551 6523, ⓦwww.camping67.sopot.pl), close to the beach at Bitwy pod Płowcami 73, about a kilometre south of the pier.

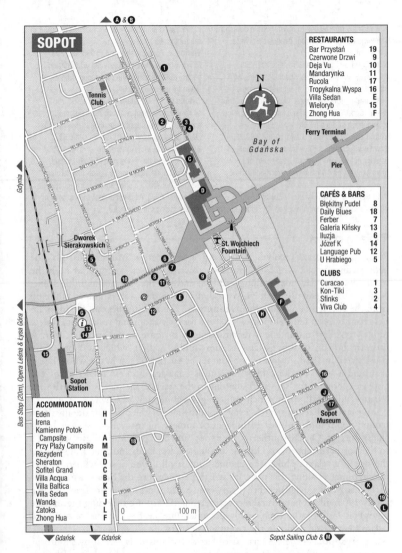

SOPOT

RESTAURANTS

Bar Przystań	19
Czerwone Drzwi	9
Deja Vu	10
Mandarynka	11
Rucola	17
Tropykalna Wyspa	16
Villa Sedan	E
Wieloryb	15
Zhong Hua	F

N

Bay of Gdańska

Ferry Terminal

Pier

St. Wojchiech Fountain

CAFÉS & BARS

Błekitny Pudel	8
Daily Blues	18
Ferber	7
Galeria Kiński	13
Iluzja	6
Józef K	14
Language Pub	12
U Hrabiego	5

CLUBS

Curacao	1
Kon-Tiki	3
Sfinks	2
Viva Club	4

Tennis Club

Dworek Sierakowskich

Sopot Station

Sopot Museum

ACCOMMODATION

Eden	H
Irena	I
Kamienny Potok Campsite	A
Przy Plaży Campsite	M
Rezydent	G
Sheraton	D
Sofitel Grand	C
Villa Acqua	B
Villa Baltica	K
Villa Sedan	E
Wanda	J
Zatoka	L
Zhong Hua	F

0   100 m

Gdynia

Bus Stop (20m), Opera Leśna & Łysa Góra

Gdańsk   Gdańsk   Sopot Sailing Club & M

Hotels

Eden ul. Kordeckiego 4/6 ☎058/551 1503, ⓦwww.hotel-eden.com.pl. Nicely located in a park just south of the pier, this pension's rooms are not exceptional but many have balconies and original parquet floors. ⑥

Irena ul. Chopina 36 ☎058/551 2073, ⓦwww.pensjonat-irena.gda.pl. Small, reasonably priced and well-kept *pensjonat* a short way down the hill from Sopot station. All rooms are en suite. ⑥

Rezydent pl. Konstytucji 3 Maja 3 ☎058/555 5800, ⓦwww.hotelrezydent.com.pl. Bang opposite

the train station and along the main drag. The plush "retro-designed" rooms are comfy, and there's a small spa. ⑨

Sheraton ul. Powstańców Warszawy 10 ☎058/767 1000, ⓦwww.sheraton.com. The brand-new and best hotel in town overlooks the pier and beach, and has large rooms, a club floor, spa and excellent marine-themed bar and restaurants. ⑨

Sofitel Grand ul. Powstańców Warszawy 12/14 ☎058/551 0041, ⓦwww.orbis.pl. Built in the 1920s in regal period style, the beachside *Grand* was recently refurbished to meet modern demands. The large rooms at the front overlook a private section of beach. ❾

Villa Aqua ul. Zamkowa Góra 35 ☎058/522 4400, ⓦ www.villaaqua.pl. Spacious rooms with elegant wooden furniture, in a quiet spot on a hill just minutes from the beach. Two hundred metres east of Sopot's Kamienny Potok station, and about 1.5km north of the pier. ❻

Villa Baltica ul. Emilii Plater 1 ☎058/555 2800, ⓦ www.villabaltica.com. A lovely early twentieth-century hotel near the beach, just south of the town centre. The stylish rooms are modern, and there's an in-house spa too. ❽

Villa Sedan ul. Puławskiego 18/20 ☎058/551 0617, ⓦ www.sedan.pl. A wooden Art Nouveau villa

in the town centre with elegant wooden furniture in the rooms. ❼

Wanda ul. Poniatowskiego 7 ☎058/550 3037, ⓦ www.bws-hotele.pl. Lovely old villa right on the beach, 800m south of the pier, though slightly let down by the basic decor inside. ❻

Zatoka ul. Emilii Plater 7/11 ☎058/551 2367, ⓦ www.zatokasopot.pl. Basic rooms, some tiny, in a rambling hotel near the seaside walkway 1km south of the pier. All rooms are en suite. ❺

Zhong Hua al. Wojska Polskiego 1 ☎058/550 2020, ⓦ www.zhonghua.com.pl. Well-located, upmarket hotel, right on the beach just south of the pier, housed in a spectacular Norwegian-style wooden building. All ground-floor rooms have a terrace facing the beach. ❽

The Town

Most life in Sopot revolves around **ulica Bohaterów Monte Cassino**, the pedestrianized road which slopes down towards the sea, and acts as both the main venue for daytime strolling and the centre of the summer nightlife scene. Near the lower end of the street, you can drink the salty water pumped 800m up from the covered St Wojchiech spa **fountain**. The area just beyond the fountain has recently been redeveloped, with space for new shops and restaurants, a new tunnel to divert traffic and a reconstructed spa house set to open in 2009. A little further on is Sopot's famous **pier** (molo; 3.80zł), which was originally constructed in 1928. At just over 500m it's by far the longest in the whole Baltic area, and a walk to the café at the end is considered an essential part of the Sopot experience for visitors. Adjacent to the start of the pier is a **lighthouse** (10am–10pm; 3zł), from which you can get a good view of town.

Long sandy **beaches** stretch away on both sides of the pier. On the northern section you'll find ranks of bathing huts, some with marvellous wicker beach chairs for rent. On the southern side, a foot- and bike path leads all the way back to the northern suburbs of Gdańsk, passing endless sands and fried fish stalls on the way – a relaxing bike ride or one-hour stroll if you're so inclined. A few hundred metres along this path, it's worth popping into the **Sopot Museum** at ul. Poniatowskiego 8 (Tues–Fri 10am–4pm, Sat & Sun 11am–5pm; free). Set in a lovely 1903 villa, it has several reconstructed period rooms reflecting the affluent bourgeois taste of the time, while documenting the bad fortune of a typical Gdańsk merchant family in the twentieth century.

Upper Sopot, as the western part of town is known, is a wealthy suburb of entrepreneurs, architects and artists with many turreted wooden houses. Its **park** offers lovely walks in the wooded hills around Łysa Góra, where there's a ski track in winter.

For **sailing and windsurfing** go to the Sopot Sailing Club at ul. Hestii 3, down the seaside bike path about 2km south of the pier. Rental operations alongside the bike path in Sopot will provide **cycles** (and Segways) for a deposit. Back in town there are **tennis** courts at the Klub Tenisowy, ul. Haffnera 57.

Eating, drinking and entertainment

There's a pleasing spread of **restaurants** in Sopot, both Polish and international. Most of the **bars and cafés** are conveniently concentrated on ulica Bohaterów

▲ Sopot pier

Monte Cassino; in summer especially, those in the pier area are buzzing all day long. The best **clubs** are in the park just to the north of the *Sofitel Grand* hotel. With the student halls not far away in the Oliwa district, Sopot scores over Gdańsk and Gdynia for a buzzing nightlife.

The open-air **Opera Leśna**, in the peaceful hilly park in the west of Sopot, hosts large-scale productions throughout the summer, including an **International Song Festival** in August which includes big names from the Western rock scene alongside homegrown performers; for tickets and current details of what's on, check with the tourist office. The "Friends of Sopot" hold **chamber music** concerts every Thursday at 6pm in the Dworek Sierakowskich café/gallery, ul. Czyżewskiego 12 (off ul. Bohaterów Monte Cassino), in a room where Chopin is said to have played.

Restaurants

Bar Przystań al. Wojska Polskiego 11. Sopot's finest seafood café in a lovely spot about 1.5km along the beach path to Gdańsk. The self-service fish dishes are very good value, though expect queues of hungry Poles at the weekend. Daily 11am–11pm.

Czerwone Drzwi ul. Ogrodowa 8. Great Polish food with a few international dishes priced around 30zł, in a small house near the pier. Daily 1pm–11pm.

Deja Vu ul. Bohaterów Monte Cassino 43. A small basement restaurant offering tasty Mediterranean dishes, such as duck in ginger sauce (42zł) and pancakes with spinach (15zł). Daily 1pm–11pm.

Mandarynka ul. Bema 6. A bright, modern, three-storey café-bar-restaurant with varied snacks, meals priced between 17–25zł, and a relaxed atmosphere. Just off the main drag. Daily noon–10pm.

Rucola ul. Poniatowskiego 8 ☏ 058/551 5046. Italian and Polish dishes served in the romantic restaurant of the Sopot Museum villa. Daily 1pm–10pm.

Tropykalna Wyspa ul. Traugutta. A popular summertime restaurant right on the beach, south of the pier, serving affordable, delicious seafood as well as other dishes. After dinner the place turns into a bar. Daily 10am–11pm.

Villa Sedan ul. Puławskiego 18/20. In the hotel's conservatory, this place is traditional with a twist (witness the old erotica photos in the toilets), and serves good French cooking – try the frogs' legs ragout (36zł) or halibut (45zł), or the Sunday brunch. Daily noon–11pm.

Wieloryb ul. Podjazd 2. Experimental French-style cooking served in surreal underwater grotto-style surroundings. Have a veal steak (48zł) or grilled squid (39zł). Daily 1pm–midnight.

Zhong Hua al. Wojska Polskiego 1. Skip the overrated Chinese section and go for the authentic sushi bar. Daily 1pm–11pm.

Cafés and bars

Błękitny Pudel ul. Bohaterów Monte Cassino 44. Kitsch but cosy café-pub which also does fusion dishes, *pierogi* and a tasty herring in cream. Daily 10am–midnight.

Daily Blues ul. Władysława IV 1a ⓦ www .dailyblues.com.pl. Atmospheric little bar with gigs or jam sessions most nights. Daily 5pm–2am.

Ferber ul. Bohaterów Monte Cassino 48. Central café with a cool crowd, good coffee and killer cakes. Daily 8am–2am, Fri & Sat till 4am.

Galeria Kiński ul. Kościuszki 10. Bar with antique clutter, an intimate atmosphere and good coffee. Something of a shrine to crazed German actor Klaus Kinski, who was born on the premises. Daily 1pm–2am.

Iluzja ul. Bohaterów Monte Cassino 57/59. Set in the weird Crooked House, this small but popular jazz bar has great atmosphere in the evenings, but no live music. Daily 10am–midnight.

Józef K ul. Kościuszki 4-1b. Charming Kafkaesque café near the station stuffed with typewriters, megaphones, birdcages and books. Daily 10am–midnight, Fri & Sat till 1am.

Language Pub ul. Puławskiego 8. The Tri-City's best expat pub is just south of ul. Bohaterów Monte Cassino. Decent selection of beers, Sky Sports and always someone to chat to. Daily 4pm–1am, Fri & Sat till 4am.

U Hrabiego ul. Czyżewskiego 12. Refined daytime café housed in the Dworek Sierakowskich gallery. The best place in town for tea and cakes. Daily 10am–10pm.

Clubs

Curacao al. Mamuszki 14. A bouncing student club with two dancefloors and a good party atmosphere. Open Fri & Sat 9pm–4am.

Kon-Tiki al. Mamuszki 21 ⓦ www.kon-tiki.pl. Large state-of-the-art beachside club featuring visiting DJs and house parties. Open noon–1am, Fri & Sat till 4am.

Sfinks ul. Powstańców Warszawy 18 ⓦ www .myspace.com/sfinks_sopot. Art gallery-cum-club located in a pavilion. Superbly atmospheric bar that's a magnet for bohemians and arty types. Live gigs and top DJ nights feature regularly. Open Thurs–Sat 4pm–4am.

Viva Club al. Mamuszki 2 ⓦ www.vivaclub.pl. Big, brash and popular place on the beach, with several bars and dancefloors. Hosts innovative live shows as well as the usual rave-style club nights. Open Thurs–Sat till 6am.

Gdynia

The endearingly run-down atmosphere of the port city of **GDYNIA** makes an interesting contrast to the more cultured Gdańsk. The northernmost section of the Trójmiasto, Gdynia was originally a small Kashubian village, and from the fourteenth to the eighteenth century the property of the Cistercian monks of Oliwa. Boom time came after World War I when Gdynia, unlike Gdańsk, returned to Polish jurisdiction. The limited coastline ceded to the new Poland – a thirty-two-kilometre strip of land stretching north from Gdynia and known as the "Polish Corridor" – left the country strapped for coastal outlets, so the Polish authorities embarked on a massive port-building programme. By the mid-1930s Gdynia had been transformed from a small village into a bustling harbour city, which by 1937 boasted the largest volume of naval traffic in the Baltic region. Hitler's propaganda portrayed the very existence of the corridor as an injustice, and after Gdynia was captured in 1939 the Germans deported most of the Polish population, established a naval base and, to add insult to injury, renamed the town Gotenhafen. Their retreat in 1945 was accompanied by wholesale destruction of the harbour installations, which were subsequently rebuilt from scratch by the postwar authorities. In the 1990s the city centre saw major changes as the state-owned shops and buildings were privatized; thanks to Gdynia's historical position within Polish territory it was a much easier business than in the old Free City, where establishing retroactive property rights is still proving a tricky business. In the centre of town shopping streets like ulica Starowiejska have received a facelift, and the building of the futuristic 140-metre-high Sea Towers in 2008 helped develop Gdynia's position at the forefront of the country's burgeoning economic transformation and development.

Arrival, information and accommodation

Gdynia Główna station is a thirty-minute journey from central Gdańsk by SKM **train** (every 10min). Trains from Warsaw and other major cities terminate here too – the bus station is right next door. Stena Line **ferries** from Karlskrona in Sweden dock to the north of the centre – take bus #119, #137 or #147 to get to the centre. Boats and hydrofoils from Hel arrive at the city's main pier, where there's a ticket office too. There are two **tourist offices**: one in the main train station (May–Sept Mon–Fri 8am–6pm, Sat 9am–4pm, Sun 9am–3pm; Oct–April Mon–Fri 10am–5pm, Sat 10am–3pm; ☎058/721 2466, ⓦwww .gdynia.pl), the other beside the aquarium at the end of the pier (May–Oct Mon–Fri 9am–6pm, Sat 10am–4pm, Sun 9am–3pm; ☎058/620 7711). Both hand out free maps for walking and cycling trips in and around town. There's free wireless **internet** along the pier and an internet café inside the Gemini Centre mall on Skwer Kościuszki.

Accommodation

There's a fair spread of beds in town, most of them acceptable if not outstanding. The tourist offices have lists of **private rooms** (❶–❹) and can help with bookings. The main **youth hostel**, open all year, is near the Stena Line terminal at ul. Energetykow 13a (☎058/627 1005, ⓦwww.ssm-gdynia.neostrada.pl; 25–35zł); from Gdynia Główna take any bus going away from town (that's left as you come out of the station) along ulica Wiśniewskiego and get off at the second stop.

Hotels

Blick ul. Jana z Kolna 6 ☎058/783 0300, ⓦwww.hotelblick.pl. Modern, central hotel with well-designed rooms, a restaurant and gym. ❻

Gdynia ul. Armii Krajowej 22 ☎058/666 3040, ⓦwww.orbis.pl. Big grey lump of concrete on the outside but quite comfortable inside, with an excellent swimming pool and a good central location. ❼

Nadmorski ul. Ejsmonda 2 ☎058/622 1542, ⓦwww.nadmorski.pl. The best place to stay in Gdynia: smart rooms, tennis courts, spa and a terrace café overlooking the sea. ❽

Villa Admiral ul. 10 Lutego 29a ☎058/661 2038, ⓦwww.admiralvilla.com. pl. Lovely villa bang in the centre of town with small but modern, well-furnished rooms. ❻

The City

Betraying its 1930s origins, sections of the **city centre** are pure Bauhaus, with curved balconies and huge window fronts: the contrast with the faceless postwar concrete jungle that envelops much of the rest of the centre couldn't be more striking. The place to head for is the **port area**, directly east across town from the main station. From the train and bus stations walk down bustling ulica 10 Lutego and through the park, and you'll find yourself at the foot of the main, southernmost **pier**. Moored on the northern side is the **Błyskawica**, a World War II destroyer (Tues–Sun 10am–5pm; 8zł). The sailors manning the ship are quick to point out to British visitors the desktop plaque commemorating the vessel's year-long wartime sojourn in Cowes on the Isle of Wight, where it helped to defend the port against a major German attack in May 1942. Further along is another proudly Polish vessel, the three-masted frigate **Dar Pomorza** (May–Sept daily 9am–6pm; Oct & Nov Tues–Sun

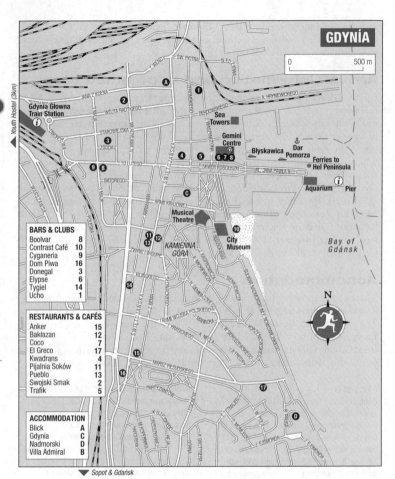

▼ Sopot & Gdańsk

10am–4pm; 8zł), built in Hamburg in 1909 and used as a Polish Navy training ship during the 1930s and again after World War II. At the very end of the pier, a lumpy monument to Polish seafarer and novelist Joseph Conrad stands near the **aquarium** (Tues–Sun: May–Sept 9am–8pm; Oct–April 10am–5pm; 12zł), where you can see a model of the whole Baltic Sea region, and sealife including piranhas, lungfish and turtles.

The brand-new **City Museum** at ul. Zawiszy Czarnego 1 (Museum Miasta Gdyni: Tues–Sun 10am–5pm; 7zł, Fri free), a short walk through the park south of the pier, documents the amazing development of Gdynia from a humble farming village and holiday resort to a booming city, with imaginative use of photos, postcards and period items to illustrate the rate of progress. The adjacent **Maritime Museum** was still under construction at the time of writing, but you can already view its impressive collection of cannons, boats and planes in the museum garden. To complete the tour, join the locals on a stroll along the Bulwar Nadmorski or climb the hill, **Kamienna Góra**, for a great view over the harbour.

Eating, drinking and entertainment

Gdynia is the least affluent part of the Trójmiasto, with a more run-down air than its neighbours. As a consequence it lacks the range of **eating and drinking** venues enjoyed by Sopot and Gdańsk, though there are a few places worth seeking out.

The **Musical Theatre**, pl. Grunwaldzki 1 (Teatr Muzyczny: ☎058/621 6024, ⓦ www.teatrmuzyczny.gdynia.pl), near the *Gdynia Hotel*, is a popular venue featuring quality Polish-language musical productions. Every July, Gdynia hosts the annual four-day **Open'er Festival** (ⓦ www.opener.pl), Poland's biggest music festival, featuring both local and big-name international acts. Silver Screen, inside the Gemini Centre on ul. Waszyngtona 21 (☎058/628 1800, ⓦ www.silverscreen.com.pl), is the main multiplex **cinema**.

Restaurants

Anker al. Piłsudskiego 50. Busy budget restaurant, usually packed at lunchtime, serving up simple but satisfying dishes like pizza, crêpes and fried chicken. Mon–Fri 7.30am–10pm, Sat & Sun 10am–10pm.

Bakłazan ul. Świętojańska 49. Simple but excellent Balkan restaurant serving spicy grilled sausages, stuffed vegetables and more. Daily noon–11pm.

Coco ul. Waszyngtona 21. A swanky café, bar and restaurant inside the Gemini Centre. The food selection includes well-prepared Thai and Mexican dishes. Daily noon–midnight.

El Greco al. Piłsudskiego 1. Top-notch Greek food served by an affable chef who likes to chat to guests from his open kitchen. Daily noon–11pm.

Kwadrans Skwer Kościuszki 20. Simple restaurant serving filling breakfasts and a straightforward selection of pizzas, salads and toasted sandwiches the rest of the day. Mon–Fri 9am–10pm, Sat & Sun 10am–10pm.

Pueblo ul. Abrahama 56 (entrance on ul. Władysława IV). Genuine Tex-Mex food, much better than average in Poland, at reasonable prices. Later at night, drop by for the cocktails. Daily noon–11pm.

Swojski Smak ul. Władysława IV 1-5. Delicious, traditional Polish favourites including *pierogi*, pork ribs in honey, meatballs and pancakes, served in rustic surroundings. Mercifully, small portions are available too. Mon–Fri 11.30am–8pm, Sat & Sun 1–8pm.

Cafés

Pijalnia Soków ul. Abrahama 39. Make your own healthy fruit juice or cocktail, combining items from the pile of fruit and vegetables available. Mon–Fri 10am–6pm.

Trafik Skwer Kościuszki 10. Relaxed and stylish café serving coffee, cakes, breakfast and light meals. Great for reading a book on a rainy day. Daily 9am–10pm.

Bars and clubs

Boolvar Inside the Gemini Centre, ul. Waszyngtona 21 ⓦ www.boolvar.pl. Immensely popular club with Italian food served till 11pm, after which a friendly local crowd and loud DJ music take over the place. Open 9am–midnight, weekends till 5am.

Contrast Café Bulwar Nadmorski. On the beach by the City Museum, this boisterous ship-themed shack really comes alive in the early evening with revellers singing along to live shanty concerts. Daily 9am–2am.

Cyganeria ul. 3 Maja 27. Large wooden tables and deep, relaxing sofas make this a great place for daytime coffee or evening beers. Open 10am–midnight, weekends till 1am.

Dom Piwa ul. Świętojańska 130 (entrance on ul. Władysława IV). The aptly named "house of beer" has hundreds of brews on offer and a fitting interior with beer memorabilia and funky furniture. Open Tues–Thurs & Sun 3pm–10pm, Fri & Sat 3pm–midnight.

Donegal ul. Zgoda 10. The most authentic-feeling Irish pub in the Tri-City, based around a cosy suite of dark, woody rooms. Packed at weekends. Open 2pm–midnight, weekends till 3am.

Elypse inside the Gemini Centre, ul. Waszyngtona 21 ⓦ www.elypse-club.pl. The hottest club in town, serving good food till evening, and afterwards attracting pretty, student-aged people and international DJs. Open 2pm–midnight, weekends till 5am.

Tygiel ul. Abrahama 86 (entrance on ul. Władysława IV). Absinthe helps wash down the eccentric decoration, including a life-sized winged horse. Daily 2pm–midnight.

Ucho ul. św. Piotra 2 ⓦ www.ucho.com.pl. Big warehouse on the edge of the docklands with special events, live acts and regular Indie club nights.

North of the Trójmiasto

If the prospect of escaping from the rigours of the city appeals, head for the **Hel Peninsula**, a long thin strip of woods and sand dunes sticking out into the Baltic Sea. The tip of the peninsula is just 25km north of Gdańsk by boat, but over 100km by road. The sandy beaches dotted along the north side have cool but clean water, are easily accessible and, away from the main resorts, never overcrowded. Of all the settlements along the peninsula, the most rewarding is the fishing village of **Hel** itself. A convenient place to stop off en route to Hel and well worth a visit in its own right, is the quiet fishing town of **Puck**, home to a fine medieval church.

Puck

Sheltered by the Hel Peninsula, **PUCK** is a small Kashubian fishing port with a smattering of elegant merchants' homes and a tremendous Gothic church. Back in the sixteenth century this was the base for Gdańsk's mercenary navy, and the sailing tradition continues with yacht and dinghy racing most weekends. Unlike many of the smaller resort towns along the Baltic coast, where the only business is the summer tourist trade, Puck is a bustling local centre worth visiting all year round.

Trains and buses from Gdynia stop at ulica Dworcowa. From there, a right turn down ulica Wejherowska and a left onto ulica 1 Armii Wojska Polskiego bring you to the old town square, **plac Wolności**. Here, there's a pleasant variety of houses, some plastered and painted in pastel colours, some in the local warm red brick. The **town hall**, set into the east side of the square has a relatively plain brick facade and dates back to the fourteenth century. On the north side at pl. Wolności 28 is a small town **museum** (July & Aug Tues–Fri 9am–5pm, Sat & Sun 10am–2pm; Sept–June Mon–Fri 9am–5pm, Sat 10am–2pm; 5zł), displaying a varied collection of archeological, ethnographic and historical items from across Kashubia. One street to the north of the square stands Puck's Gothic parish **church**, Sts Peter and Paul. It's a magnificent building, small compared to the enormous edifices to be seen in Gdańsk, but beautifully proportioned, and enjoys a superb setting on a hillock above the **fishing harbour**. From the harbour there's a pleasant walk east along the sea front, past the sailing school and beach volleyball courts, to two wooden **piers**, the second of which serves the bustling marina. Beyond the piers lies a small sandy **beach**.

You can easily look round Puck in an hour or so and continue to Hel (by bus or train). For a quick coffee try *Café Mistral* down by the yacht club but the best place to **eat** is back in town at the Kashubian fish restaurant *U Budzisza* at ul. Morska 13, with outdoor seating overlooking the harbour where the fish is landed.

Hel

HEL, the small fishing port at the tip of the peninsula, is a day-tripper's favourite. Despite heavy wartime fighting – a German army of 100,000 men was rounded up on the peninsula in 1945 – the town preserves some nineteenth-century fishermen's cottages, sturdy one-storey brick-built affairs which add character to the resort's compact centre. It's a fast-developing place, with souvenir shops and amber jewellery stores aplenty, but preserves enough old-world appeal to distinguish it from the majority of Baltic holiday spots, and access to miles of beach is a definite plus.

Arrival, information and accommodation

In summer, direct **trains** run to Hel from Gdańsk, but there's a wider range of year-round train and **bus** services from Gdynia, as well as faster minibuses (departing when full), which leave from the northern side of Gdynia bus station. Tourist **boats** run to Hel several times a day in summer from both Gdynia and Gdańsk. It's wise to book tickets in advance or queue up early as boats sell out on busy days; for times and fares contact MZK (☏058/342 2500 ⓦwww.mzkzg.org). Ferries dock right beside ulica Morska in the village centre; trains and buses stop at ulica Dworska, a few minutes' walk from ulica Wiejska, the pedestrianized main street. **Bicycles** can be rented for 8zł per hour from Andrzej Buller at ul. Leśna 10c (☏608/581 970), amongst other places.

There are numerous **private rooms** (❷–❹) in Hel, and you may well be propositioned by prospective landladies upon arrival. If not, the area around ulica Sikorskiego (at the northwestern end of ul. Wiejska) is the place to look for *wolne pokoje* signs. The nearest decent **hotel** is the luxury *Bryza Spa Resort* at ul. Międzymorze 2 in Jurata, one stop by train towards the mainland (☏058/675 5100, ⓦwww.bryza.pl; ❼–❽). In town, make for *Willa Helios*, ul. Lipowa 2 (☏058/675 0996; ❸) or *Captain Morgan*, ul. Wiejska 21 (☏058/675 0091, ⓦwww.captainmorgan.cypel.pl; ❸), both family-run establishments offering cosy en suites. Alternatively, there are **campsites** tucked away under the trees all along the peninsula, many of them offering bungalows for 40–120zł per person.

The Town

A good place to start your exploration is Hel's **Fishing Museum** (Muzeum Rybołówstwa: Tues–Sun 10am–3pm; 6zł), housed in the Gothic fifteenth-century St Peter's Church (Kościół św. Piotra) on ulica Wiejska. Inside are model ships and plenty of fishing tackle, as well as some local folk art. As on the adjoining mainland, the people of the peninsula are predominantly Kashubian, as evidenced in the local dialect and the distinctive **embroidery** styles on show in the museum.

A firm favourite with younger visitors is the **Fokarium** (Seal Enclosure: daily 9.30am–7pm; 2zł), about 50m west of the Fishing Museum along the seashore. Here five or six seals spend their days eating (feeding times 11am & 2pm), swimming and lazing about – much like the average human visitor to Hel. There's a strong emphasis on conservation with lots of information on sea life posted alongside the tanks.

At the southern end of ulica Wiejska, walk along ulica Leśna eastwards for fifteen-minutes through the woods to reach Hel's biggest attraction, the **beach** – a luxurious, semolina-coloured ribbon of sand that extends as far as the eye can see.

Eating and drinking

Dozens of snack-food joints along ulica Wiejska dole out fried fish at reasonable prices: the local halibut is particularly good. There are also a number of more formal **eating** places, often filled with chunky wooden furniture and ceilings hung with fishing nets. *Maszoperia*, at ul. Wiejska 110, offers a full menu of fish and meat dishes in an intimate candle-lit interior, and you can enjoy similar offerings on the covered terrace or in the dainty rooms of *Norda* at ul. Wiejska 123. The most convivial place for **drinking** is the *Captain Morgan*, a popular pub-style meeting place crammed with antique maritime junk.

Kashubia

The area of lakes and hills stretching west of Gdańsk – **Kashubia** (Kaszuby) – is the homeland of one of Poland's lesser-known ethnic minorities, the **Kashubians**. "Not German enough for the Germans, nor Polish enough for the Poles" – Grandma Koljaiczek's wry observation in *The Tin Drum* – sums up the historic predicament of this group.

Originally a western Slav people linked ethnically to Poles, and historically spared the ravages of invasion and war thanks to their relative geographical isolation, the Kashubians were subjected to a German cultural onslaught during the Partition period, when the area was incorporated into Prussia. The process was resisted fiercely: in the 1910 regional census, only six out of the 455 inhabitants of one typical village gave their nationality as German, a pattern of resistance that continued during World War II.

However, the Kashubians' treatment by the Poles has not always been better, and it's often argued that Gdańsk's domination of the region has kept the development of a Kashubian national identity in check. You can hear the distinctive Kashubian language (supposedly derived from the original Pomeranian tongue) spoken all over the region, particularly by older people, and many villages still produce Kashubian handicrafts such as embroidered cloths and tapestries.

The heartland of Kashubia is easily explored from the regional capital **Kartuzy** and the lake resort of **Chmielno**. The surrounding countryside of low hills and tranquil woodland dotted with villages is perfect for hiking and cycling, while the open-air museum at **Wdzydze Kiszewskie** is the place to aim for if you're interested in Kashubian folk culture. With your own **transport** you can do a round-trip from Gdańsk, taking in Chmielno and Wdzydze. Travelling by bus, a day each for both destinations seems more reasonable.

Kartuzy

The old capital of the region, the quiet market town of **KARTUZY**, is tucked away among the lakes and woods 30km west of Gdańsk, and despite some recent efforts to spruce it up, feels a long way from the city. The **Kashubian Museum** at ul. Kościerska 1 (Muzeum Kaszubskie: Tues–Fri 8am–4pm, Sat 8am–3pm, plus Sun 10am–2pm May–Sept; 7.50zł) has some nice examples of Kashubian arts and crafts. The Gothic **church**, part of a group of buildings erected in 1380 on the western edge of town by Carthusian monks from Bohemia, is a sombre sort of place. The building itself is coffin-shaped – the original monks actually used to sleep in coffins – while the pendulum of the clock hanging below the organ sports a skull-like angel swinging the Grim Reaper's scythe and bears the cheery inscription, "Each passing second brings you closer to death." Apart from the church, nothing much remains of the original monastery. More appealing are the paths leading through the beech groves which surround nearby **Klasztorne Lake**, a nice place to cool off on a hot summer's day.

The **train and bus stations** are 300m east of the main square on ulica Dworcowa. The **tourist office**, Rynek 2 (July & Aug Mon–Fri 9am–5pm, Sat 9am–3pm, Sun 10am–2pm; Sept–June Mon–Fri 9am–4pm, Sat 9am–3pm; ☏058/684 0201), can help booking **private rooms** (❶–❷) at the *U Gosi* pension, ul. Reja 16 (☏609 797 464), and in the surrounding countryside. The *Korman*, ul. 3 Maja 36 (☏058/685 3400; ❹), is the only **hotel** in town, with basic but comfortable rooms, while *Kaszubska* at ul. Parkowa 4 is the best **restaurant** in town with hearty local food (try the *gburski* potato dish) and dancing on

Saturday. *Be Mol*, just off the Rynek at ul. Kościuszki 19, offers cheap pasta and pizza dishes named after different styles of music (a dub reggae pizza comes with tuna and peas, if you were wondering).

Chmielno and around

CHMIELNO is the most idyllic of several holiday centres around the area, and also the easiest to get to, lying some 12km west of Kartuzy and easily reachable by bus. Set in tranquil, beautiful surroundings overlooking the shores of three lakes – Białe, Rekowo and Kłodno – the waterside nearest the village is dotted with holiday homes and *pensjonaty*. Chmielno is a centre of traditional Kashubian ceramics, and the **Museum of Kashubian Ceramics** on ulica Gryfa Pomorskiego (Muzeum Ceramiki Kaszubskiej: April–Nov Mon–Sat 9am–6pm; Dec–March Mon–Sat 9am–3pm; 4zł) is in fact a working pottery workshop, run by the English-speaking Necel brothers.

The **tourist office**, right by the **bus** stop in the village cultural centre (Mon–Fri 9am–5pm; ☎058/684 2205), can fix you up with a **private room** (❷). Beside the museum at ul. Gryfa Pomorskiego 68, *U Czorlińściego* (☎058/684 2278, ⓦwww.czorlinski.maxmedia.pl; ❹) is a homely **hotel** with lake views and a restaurant serving local food, while of the **pensions** the modern *Krystian* at ul. Grzędzickiego 20 (☎058/684 2135; ❶) has en suites with balconies. Walking east from the village centre, between lakes Białe and Rekowo, will bring you round to the far shore of Lake Kłodno, where the *Krefta* **campsite** (☎058/684 2234, ⓦwww.krefta.pl) has bungalows from 45zł per person and rents out boats and kayaks. **Bicycles** can be rented at Świt, ul. Grodziska 1. Back in the centre, the lakeside *Chëcz u Kaszëbë* **restaurant** is housed in a cute thatched building, serves good-value grilled trout and meat dishes, and doubles as the local **bar**.

Moving west, the town of **SIERAKOWICE**, 15km further on, borders on a large expanse of rolling forestland, some of the prettiest in the region, and deservedly popular hiking country. **MIRACHOWO**, a ten-kilometre bus journey northeast across the forest, is a good base for walkers. The village has several traditional half-timbered Kashubian houses similar to those featured at the *skansen* at Wdzydze Kiszewskie (see below). The same holds for **ŁEBNO**, some 15km north, and many of the surrounding villages.

Wdzydze Kiszewskie

Continuing south through the region, **WDZYDZE KISZEWSKIE** lies 56 kilometres south of Kartuzy. Feasible as a day-trip from Gdańsk (77km) – in summer **buses** travel direct, at other times you have to change in Kościerzyna – the **skansen** here (Kaszubski Park Etnograficzny; April & Sept Tues–Sun 9am–4pm; May & June Tues–Fri 9am–4pm, Sat & Sun 10am–6pm; July & Aug Tues–Sun 10am–6pm; Oct Tues–Sun 10am–3pm; Nov–March Mon–Fri 10am–3pm; 8zł; ⓦwww.muzeum-wdzydze.gda.pl) is one of the best of its kind, bringing together a large and carefully preserved set of traditional Kashubian wooden buildings. Spread out in a field overlooking the nearby Lake Goluń, the *skansen's* location couldn't be more peaceful. Most people join the hourly **guided tours** round the site (English- and German-speaking guides are available in summer) since most of the buildings are kept locked when a guide's not present. The panoply of buildings, taken from villages across the region and reconstructed here, range from old windmills and peasant cottages to barns, wells, furnaces, a pigsty and a working sawmill. The early eighteenth-century **wooden church** is a treat: topped by a traditional wood-shingled roof, the interior is covered with regional folk-baroque designs and biblical motifs. The thatched cottage interiors are immaculately restored with original beds and furniture to reflect the typical domestic setup of the mostly extremely poor Kashubian peasantry of a century ago.

East of Gdańsk

East from Gdańsk a short stretch of Baltic coastline leads up to the Russian border and beyond to the city of Kaliningrad. An attractive and largely unspoilt region, the beaches of the **Wiślana Peninsula** and its approaches are deservedly popular seaside holiday country with Poles and returnee Germans – **Krynica Morska** is the resort to aim for if the idea of a few days on the beach appeals. Inland, the lush rural terrain, well watered by countless little tributaries of the Wisła, boasts a host of quiet, sturdy-looking old Prussian villages and, more chillingly, the Nazi concentration camp at **Sztutowo (Stutthof)**. This is the region most closely associated with astronomer **Nicolaus Copernicus**, and several towns, notably the medieval coastal centre of **Frombork**, bear his imprint. Of the other urban sites, **Elbląg** is a major former Prussian centre which has lost much of its old character, but remains an important transport hub.

As for **transport**, cross-country bus links are generally good in this part of the country, with the additional option of a scenic coastal train route along the southern shore of the Wiślany Lagoon and short-hop ferry services between several places.

Stutthof (Sztutowo) concentration camp

May our fate be a warning to you – not a legend. Should man grow silent, the very stones will scream.

Franciszek Fenikowski, *Requiem Mass*, quoted in camp guidebook

The Wiślana Peninsula begins at **Sztutowo** but 2km before the main road reaches the village a monument marks the entrance to the Nazi concentration camp site at **Stutthof** – a rude awakening after passing through so much idyllic countryside. The first camp to be built inside what is now Poland (construction began in Aug 1939, before the German invasion), it started as an internment camp for Poles from the Free City of Danzig area but eventually became a Nazi extermination centre for the whole of northern Europe. The first Polish prisoners arrived at Stutthof early in September 1939, their numbers rapidly swelled by legions of other locals deemed "undesirables" by the Nazis. The decision to transform Stutthof into an international camp came in 1942, and eventually, in June 1944, the camp was incorporated into the Nazi scheme for the "Final Solution", the whole place being considerably enlarged and gas ovens installed. Although not on the same scale as other death camps, the toll in human lives speaks for itself: by the time the Red Army liberated the camp less than a year later in May 1945, an estimated 65,000–85,000 people had disappeared here.

Regular Gdańsk–Krynica Morska and Elbląg–Krynica Morska **buses** pass by the short access road to the camp.

The camp

In a large forest clearing surrounded by a wire fence and watchtowers, the peaceful, isolated setting of the **camp** (May–Oct 8am–6pm; Oct–April 8am–3pm; free, audioguides 15zł, cinema 3zł; no guides or films Mon; children under 13 not allowed) makes the whole idea of what went on here seem unreal at first. Once through the entrance gate, however, like all the Nazi concentration camps it's a shocking place to visit. Rows of stark wooden barrack blocks are interspersed with empty sites with nothing but the bare foundations left – much of the camp was torn down in 1945 and used as firewood.

A **museum** – housed in the barracks – with most text in Polish only details life and death in the camp, the crude wooden bunks and threadbare mats indicating the living conditions the inmates had to endure. A harrowing gallery of photographs of gaunt-looking inmates brings home the human reality of what happened here: name, date of birth, country of origin and "offence" are listed below each of the faces staring down from the walls, the victims, of 25 different nationalities, including political prisoners, communists and gays. Over in the far corner of the camp stand the gas ovens and crematoria. During the summer, the museum cinema provides further evidence of the atrocities.

Krynica Morska and the Wiślana Peninsula

East from Sztutowo, the coast road leads onto the **Wiślana Peninsula** (Mierzeja Wiślana), a long, thin promontory dividing the sea from the Wiślana Lagoon (Zalew Wiślany), which continues some 60km up towards Kaliningrad. On the northern side of the peninsula a dense covering of mixed beech and birch forest suddenly gives way to a luxuriant strip of sandy shore, while to the south the marshy shore beyond the road looks out over the tranquil lagoon. A naturalist's paradise, the peninsula forest is idyllic walking country, while the northern coastline offers some of the best and most unspoilt beaches on the Baltic coast.

Twenty kilometres beyond Sztutowo and just a few kilometres short of the Russian border, **KRYNICA MORSKA** is the main holiday resort on the peninsula, patronized by Poles and a smattering of Germans. Relatively small in scale and uncommercialized, it straggles along a single main street, ulica Gdańska. Just above here, on the wooded spine of the peninsula, sits a cluster of factory-owned rest homes, beyond which (a fifteen-minute walk from the village centre) lies an alluring white-sand beach. Krynica Morska is full of hotels and pensions, while camping sites dotted along the peninsula provide an alternative source of local accommodation.

Practicalities

Regular **buses** from Gdańsk come to a halt at the eastern end of Krynica Morska's ulica Gdańska, just below the agglomeration of cafés and knick-knack shops on ulica Portowa that pass for the village centre. The **tourist office**, at ul. Żeromskiego 6 (Mon–Sat 8am–2pm; ☎055/247 6444, ⓦwww.mierzeja.pl), can help find a place to stay both in town and in other villages along the peninsula.

Numerous houses in town offer **private rooms** (❸–❻). Of the many **pensjonaty** in town, the *Polonia*, ul. Świerczewskiego 19 (☎055/247 6097, ⓦwww.polonia .mierzeja.pl; ❻ including a superb breakfast and dinner), is friendly and comfortable, while the *Pod Lwem*, at the eastern end of the village at ul. Wodna 10 (☎055/247 6141; ❺), is plusher but still intimate in feel. The *Kahlberg*, at ul. Bosmańska 1 (☎055/247 6017, ⓦwww.kahlberg.mierzeja.pl; ❼), is probably the town's most comfortable **hotel** and has its own tennis court.

As in most Polish seaside resorts, **eating** out in Krynica revolves around unpretentious snack-food outlets. There's a knot of fish-and-chip stalls on the beach and around the central streets of Portowa and Świerczewskiego, although for quality fish from the Wiślany Lagoon try the *Karczma Rybna* inside the

Polonia pension or the homely *Tawerna Yachtowa*, by the yachting harbour on the lagoon side of town. Cheap meals are also available from *Koga*, a bar on ulica Gdańska built in the shape of a sailing ship, which is also one of the best places in town to **drink**.

Elbląg

The ancient settlement of **ELBLĄG**, after Gdańsk the region's most important town, was severely damaged at the end of World War II: its pretty old town was totally flattened in the bitter fighting that followed the Nazi retreat in 1945. After languishing for decades in a postwar architectural limbo, at the beginning of the 1990s work finally started on filling in the gaps in Elbląg's Old Town. It's now being rebuilt on the principle that investors copy the feel though not necessarily the precise architectural details of the city's prewar architecture.

The Town

The **Old Town** is a small section at the heart of modern Elbląg. Some parts of the old city walls remain, most notably around the recently renovated **Market Gate** tower (Brama Targowa: April–Sept daily 10am–6pm; Oct–March Mon–Fri 8am–4pm; free) at the northern entrance to the area. Rising dramatically out of the old market place, the **cathedral**, rebuilt after the war, is another massive brick Gothic structure, its huge tower the biggest in the region. A couple of fine original Gothic triptychs and statues and some traces of the original ornamentation aside, the interior is mostly rather vapid postwar decoration, leaving the place with a sad, empty feel to it. The area immediately surrounding the cathedral combines old Prussian-style mansions with new restaurants, bars and cafés, mostly catering for the busloads of (principally German) day-trippers piling in throughout the summer season.

Not far from the cathedral is the Gothic St Mary's Church: no longer consecrated, the building houses a small **modern art gallery** (Mon–Fri 10am–5pm, Sat & Sun 10am–4pm; 4zł). The art on display is not desperately exciting but makes for an interesting contrast with the crumbling red-brick surroundings. The English merchant Samuel Butler was buried here – one of many English traders who settled in Elbląg, headquarters for the Eastland Company, in the Reformation era.

South along the river, the local **museum** is located at ul. Bulwar Zygmunta Augusta 11 (mid-May to Oct Tues–Sun 9am–5pm, Nov to mid-May Tues–Sun 8am–4pm; 5zł), featuring the usual displays dedicated to local history and archeology, as well as an absorbing collection of photos of the German city from the prewar era and earlier.

Practicalities

Elbląg's **bus** and **train stations** are a fifteen-minute walk east of the Old Town or a short ride on trams #1 or #2. Decent onward bus connections ensure that you're unlikely to need to stay in town, though if you do get stuck here there's a fair range of accommodation – the friendly **tourist information centre** inside the Market Gate (☎055/611 0820, ⊛www.ielblag.pl; same opening hours) can help. The contemporary *Vivaldi*, Stary Rynek 16 (☎055/236 2542, ⊛www.viwaldi.m.walentynowicz.pl; ⑥), is the best **place to stay** in the Old Town, while on the other side of the cathedral the new *Pensjonat MF* at ul. św. Ducha 26 (☎055/642 3144, ⊛www.pensjonatmf.pl; ⑥), is a good alternative.

The Ostródzko–Elblaski Canal

Part of the network of canals stretching east to Augustów (see p.224) and over the Belarus border, the 81-kilometre-long **Elbląg–Ostróda Canal** (Kanał Ostródzko–Elblaski) was constructed in the mid-nineteenth century as part of the Prussian scheme to improve the region's economic infrastructure. Building the canal presented significant technical difficulties, in particular the large difference in water level (over 100m) between the beginning and end points. To deal with this problem, Prussian engineers devised an intricate and often ingenious system of locks, chokepoints and **slipways**. These slipways, the canal's best-known feature, are serviced by large rail-bound carriages that haul the boats overland. Five of these amazing constructions operate over a ten-kilometre stretch of the northern section of the canal, located roughly halfway between Elbląg and Małdyty.

    Day-trips along the whole stretch of the canal route operate daily from mid-May to the end of September, although you'll need to call Zegluga Ostródzko-Elblągska (℡055/232 4307) at least a week in advance to reserve tickets (70–85zł). Boats start at 8am from Elbląg, arriving in **Ostróda**, at the southern tip of the canal, at 7pm. You can also get off at 2.30pm in **Małdyty**, where trains back to Elbląg depart at 3pm and 3.30pm. If you're travelling by car and want to view the slipways, turn west off the main road at **Marzewo**, a few kilometres north of Małdyty, and you'll meet the canal 5km down the road.

A few minutes northeast of the Old Town, the cheap, clean student rooms of the *Dom Studencki PWSZ* (℡055/239 8861, 🖳www.pwsz.elblag.pl; ❸) at ul. Zacisze 12 are available to travellers from July to September.

    Plenty of good **eating** options are now available around the cathedral. *Wędrowiec* at ul. Wigilijna 12 serves dishes from Poland and around the world – think burgers, tortillas and "Shanghai pizza" – in stylish surroundings; the lively *Jedynka Pub*, right next door, has regular events. The *Kardamon Café*, ul. Stary Rynek 49, is good for coffee and light snacks.

Frombork

A little seaside town 90km east along the Baltic coast from Gdańsk, **FROMBORK** was the home of **Nicolaus Copernicus** (see box, p.178), the Renaissance astronomer whose ideas overturned church-approved scientific notions, specifically the earth-centred model of the universe. Most of the research for his famous *De Revolutionibus* was carried out around this town, and it was here that he died and was buried in 1543. Just over a century later, Frombork was badly mauled by marauding Swedes, who carted off most of Copernicus's belongings, including his library.

The Town

The only part of Frombork to escape unscathed from the last war was the **Cathedral Hill** (Wzgórze Katedralne), up from the old market square in the centre of town. A compact unit surrounded by high defensive walls, its main element is the dramatic fourteenth-century Gothic **cathedral** (Mon–Sat: May–Aug 9.30am–5pm; Sept–April 9am–3.30pm; 4zł), with its huge red-tiled and turreted roof. Inside, lofty expanses of brick rise above a series of lavish Baroque altars. The seventeenth-century Baroque **organ** towering over the nave is one of the best in the country, and the Sunday afternoon and occasional weekday recitals in summer are an established feature.

To the west of the cathedral, the **Copernicus Tower** (Wieża Kopernika: May–Aug Tues–Sat 9.30am–5pm; 4zł), the oldest part of the complex, was possibly the great man's workshop and observatory. The **Belfry Tower** (daily: May–Aug 9.30am–5pm; Sept–April 9am–3.30pm; 5zł), in the southwest corner of the walls, has a Foucault pendulum swinging to and fro, proving conclusively that the Earth rotates. There's an excellent view from the top of the tower of Wiślana Lagoon stretching 70km north towards Kaliningrad. Across the tree-lined cathedral courtyard in the Warmia Bishops' Palace is the **Copernicus Museum** (Muzeum Kopernika: Tues–Sun: May–Aug 9.30am–4.30pm; Sept–April 9am–3.30pm; 4zł, Sun free). Exhibits include early editions of Copernicus's astronomical treatises, along with a number of his lesser-known works on medical, political and economic questions, a collection of astrolabes, sextants and other instruments, plus pictures and portraits.

Back on the town square, you can climb up the fourteenth-century **water tower** (daily: May, June & Sept 10am–6pm, July & Aug 9.30am–7pm, Oct 10am–4pm; 4zł) for great views of the Cathedral Hill and town. There's not much else to do but stroll around town – in the park look for the monument, still unusual for Poland, commemorating the 450,000 forgotten German refugees from the region who died during and immediately after World War II.

Practicalities

Frombork's **bus** and **train stations** are located next to each other near the seafront, while in summer there are also daily **boats** from Elbląg and Krynica Morska. The Elbląg–Frombork train service runs just two trains a day, but plenty of Elbląg–Braniewo buses pass through here. It's perfectly feasible to treat Frombork as a day-trip from Gdańsk.

The Globus **information office** in the souvenir shop beside the water tower can help with public transport information and direct you towards the town's stock of **private rooms** (❷) – otherwise look out for signs advertising *pokoje*. The *Rheticus* at ul. Kopernika 10 (☎055/243 7800; ❸) is a charming **pension** boasting neat modern en suites, while the *Kopernik* **hotel**, ul. Kościelna 2 (☎055/243 7285; ❺), has spic-and-span en-suite doubles with views up to the cathedral. On the road in from Elbląg there's the summer-only *Copernicus* **youth hostel** at ul. Elbląska 11 (☎055/243 7193), which also has a modern double

Nicolaus Copernicus

Nicolaus Copernicus – Mikołaj Kopernik as he's known to Poles – was born in **Toruń** in 1473. The son of a wealthy merchant family with strong Church connections, he entered Kraków's Jagiellonian University in 1491 and subsequently joined the priesthood. Like most educated Poles of his time, he travelled abroad to continue his studies, spending time at the famous Renaissance universities of Bologna and Padua.

On his return home in 1497 he became administrator for the northern bishopric of Warmia, developing a wide field of interests, working as a doctor, lawyer, architect and soldier (he supervised the defence of nearby Olsztyn against the Teutonic Knights) – the archetypal Renaissance man. He spent some fifteen years as canon of the **Frombork** chapterhouse and constructed an observatory here, where he undertook the research that provided the empirical substance for the *De Revolutionibus Orbium Caelestium*, whose revolutionary contention was that the sun, not the earth, was at the centre of the planetary system. The work was published by the church authorities in Nuremberg in the year of Copernicus's death in 1543; it was later banned by the papacy.

room (❶); the PTTK **campsite** (mid-May to mid-Sept), meanwhile, is some way from the centre on the Braniewo road. Apart from some summer takeaway bars and hotel restaurants, the best **place to eat** is *Akcent*, ul. Rybecka 4, which serves up traditional treats like *żurek*.

The Wisła delta

Following the **Wisła** south from Gdańsk takes you into the heart of the territory once ruled by the **Teutonic Knights**. Physically, the river delta is a flat plain of isolated villages, narrow roads and drained farmland, while the river itself is wide, slow-moving and dirty, the landscape all open vistas. The religio-militaristic Teutonic order controlled the lucrative medieval grain trade from a string of fortress towns along the river – it was under their protection that merchant colonists from the northern Hanseatic League cities established themselves down the Wisła as far south as Toruń. The knights' architectural legacies are distinctive red-brick constructions: tower-churches, sturdy granaries and solid burghers' mansions surrounded by rings of defensive walls and protected by castles. **Malbork**, the knights' headquarters, is the prime example – a town settled within and below one of the largest fortresses of medieval Europe. Continuing downriver a number of lesser-fortified towns – **Gniew**, **Kwidzyn** and **Chełmno** – lead to the ancient city of **Toruń**, near the lively regional centre of **Bydgoszcz**.

During the Partition era – from the late eighteenth century up until World War I – this upper stretch of the Wisła was **Prussian** territory, an ownership that has left its own mark on the neat towns and cities. After 1918, part of the territory returned to Poland, while part remained in East Prussia. During World War II, as throughout this region, much was destroyed during the German retreat.

Travel connections aren't too bad in the area, with buses and trains between the main towns, all of which are within reasonable striking distance of Gdańsk.

Malbork

For Poles brought up on the novels of Henryk Sienkiewicz, the massive riverside fortress of **MALBORK** conjures up the epic medieval struggles between Poles and Germans that he so vividly described in *The Teutonic Knights*. The intimidating stronghold dominates the town, imparting the threatening atmosphere of an ancient military headquarters to an otherwise quiet, modern town.

The history of the town and castle is intimately connected with that of the **Teutonic Knights** (see box, p.180), who established themselves here in the late thirteenth century and proceeded to turn a modest fortress into the labyrinthine monster you can see today. After two centuries of Teutonic domination, the town returned to Polish control in 1457, and the Knights, in dire financial difficulties, were forced to sell the castle. For the next three hundred years the castle was a royal residence, used by Polish monarchs as a stopover en route between Warsaw and Gdańsk. Following the Partitions, the **Prussians** turned it into a barracks and set about dismantling large sections of the masonry – a process halted only by public outcry in Berlin. The eastern wings of the castle, including the main church, were badly damaged by the Soviet assault at the end of World War II; most of the Old Town was destroyed in the process. The damaged sections have in the main been restored to their original state and Malbork is now on the UNESCO World Heritage list. If you can, visit during the lively **Siege Days** (Oblężenie Malborka: Ⓦ www.oblezenie.malbork.pl), held in June or July, when locals in period dress re-enact the siege of the fortress, and there are jousting tournaments, crafts fairs and concerts – booking a room well in advance is essential if you plan to stay the night.

Other than the castle, there is little to say about Malbork. Evidence of the intense fighting which took place in these parts during the war can be seen in the **Commonwealth War Graves** on the edge of the town.

The Teutonic Knights

The Templars, the Hospitallers and the **Teutonic Knights** were the three major military-religious orders to emerge from the Crusades. Founded in 1190 as a fraternity serving the sick, the order combined the ascetic ideals of monasticism with the military training of a knight. Eclipsed by their rivals in the Holy Land, the Knights – the **Teutonic Order of the Hospital of St Mary**, to give them their full title – established their first base in Poland at Chełmno in 1225, following an appeal from Duke Konrad of Mazovia for protection against the pagan Lithuanians, Jacwingians and Prussians. The Knights proceeded to annihilate the Prussian population, establishing German colonies in their place.

With the loss of their last base in Palestine in 1271, the Teutonic Knights started looking around for a European site for their headquarters. Three years later they began the construction of Malbork Castle – **Marienburg**, "the fortress of Mary", as they named it – and in 1309 the Grand Master transferred here from Venice.

Economically, the Knights' chief targets were control of the Hanseatic cities and of the trade in Baltic amber, over which they gained a virtual monopoly. Politically, their main aim was territorial conquest, especially to the east – which, with their religious zealotry established in Palestine, they saw as a crusade to set up a theocratic political order. The Polish kings soon began to realize the mistake of inviting the Knights in.

The showdown with Poland came in 1410 at the **Battle of Grunwald**, one of the most momentous clashes of medieval Europe. Recognizing a common enemy, an allied force of Poles and Lithuanians inflicted the first really decisive defeat on the Knights, yet failed to follow up the victory and allowed them to retreat to Malbork unchallenged. It wasn't until 1457 that they were driven out of their Malbork stronghold by King Kazimierz Jagiełło. The Grand Master of the Order fled eastward to Königsberg.

In 1525, the Grand Master, Albrecht von Hohenzollern, having converted to Lutheranism, decided to dissolve the Order and transform its holdings into a **secular duchy**, with himself as its head. Initially, political considerations meant he was obliged to accept the Polish king as his overlord, and thus he paid homage before King Sigismund at Kraków. But the duchy had full jurisdiction over its internal affairs, which allowed for the adoption of Protestantism as its religion. This turned out to be a crucially important step in the history of Europe, as it gave the ambitious Hohenzollern family a power base outside the structures of the Holy Roman Empire, an autonomy that was later to be of vital importance to them in their ultimately successful drive to weld the German nation into a united state.

Arrival, information and accommodation

The **train station** and **bus station** are sited next to each other about ten minutes' walk east of the castle. Malbork is on the main Gdańsk–Warsaw line and all trains stop here; there are also regular bus services from Gdańsk. On the main street in town, the **tourist office** (daily: May–Sept 10am–7pm; Oct–April 8am–4pm; ℡055/647 4747, ⓦwww.malbork.pl), ul. Kościuszki 54, offers free **internet** access and can direct you towards **private rooms** (❶). There's a basic **youth hostel** 500m south of the castle at ul. Żeromskiego 45 (℡055/272 2408).

Hotels and pensions

Grot ul. Kościuszki 22d ℡055/646 9660, ⓦwww.grothotel.pl. Newly built hotel with two-dozen decent non-smoking rooms in a central location. ❻

Parkowy ul. Portowa 3 ℡055/272 2413, ⓦwww .osirmalbork.pl. Neat and cosy en suites in a riverside hotel, 1.5km north of the castle. There's also a campsite (April to mid-Oct). ❷–❸

Szarotka ul. Dworcowa 1 ℡055/612 1444. Careworn but clean rooms with shared facilities in Malbork's best budget option. Near the bus and train stations. ❶

Zamek ul. Starościńska 14 ℡055/272 2738. The best positioned of the hotels, right at the castle gates in the Knights' hospital. The decor is brown and heavy but the en-suite rooms are very comfortable. ❼

The fortress

The approach to the main **fortress** (grounds open daily 9am–8pm; exhibitions Tues–Sun: early April & late Sept 10am–5pm; mid-April to mid-Sept 9am–7pm; Oct–March 10am–3pm; 35zł; ⓦwww.zamek.malbork.pl) is through the old outer castle, a zone of utility buildings that weren't rebuilt after the war. Entrance is by guided tour only (regular Polish tours; English-language tours at 11am, 1.30pm & 3.30pm; ℡055/647 0978), and it's worth calling ahead to confirm the times of the excellent three-hour English-language tours that take you through all parts of the huge fortress, and allow you to wander around at your own pace afterwards.

Passing over the moat and through the daunting main gate, you come to the **Middle Castle**. The right-hand side of the spacious **courtyard** is taken up by the **Grand Master's Palace**. The fourteenth-century chambers are wonderfully elegant, especially the recently renovated **Grand Refectory** with its slender pillars leading up to delicately traced vaulting, and its ingenious central heating system, using long channels to pipe hot air from cellar fireplaces, and allowing the knights to use even large halls in winter. Leading off from the courtyard are a host of cavernous chambers, many of which house exhibitions on the history of the castle and the Teutonic Knights. In summer, the main courtyard provides the spectacular backdrop for the castle's son et lumière shows.

From the Middle Castle a drawbridge leads under a portcullis into the smaller courtyard of the **High Castle**, the oldest part of the fortress. At the centre of the courtyard is the castle well and all along one side are the kitchens, with an enormous chimney over the stove running straight through five storeys to the roof. The stairs just to the right as you enter the smaller courtyard lead to a first-floor balcony that runs its perimeter. From here you can enter the beautiful **Chapter House** with palm-leaf vaulting and wall paintings of Grand Masters of the Order. The balcony also gives access to the knights' and monks' dormitories and to the **Church of Our Lady**, damaged during the Soviet siege in 1945, but currently undergoing restoration.

A long, narrow corridor leads away from the courtyard to the **dansker**, positioned over the old moat. This tower had a dual purpose – the knights' final refuge in times of war, in peacetime it functioned as the castle lavatory. From the second floor above the courtyard you can climb the castle's central tower (6zł) for fantastic views over the plains. Back down at the drawbridge, a path leads round the outer walls of the High Castle to the **Chapel of St Anne**, where eleven former Grand Masters were buried, and the castle mill, which has been reconstructed on the east wall.

When you've finished looking around inside, head over the wooden **footbridge** leading from the castle to the other side of the Nogat River, where the view allows you to appreciate what a Babylonian project the fortress must have seemed to medieval visitors.

Eating and drinking

For a quick meal there are several **snack stalls** around the castle entrance, including the *Tawerna Karaoke* and *Bos* floating bar-restaurants moored on the riverbank. The *Piwniczka* **restaurant** inside the castle wall opposite the Nogat bridge is the most atmospheric place for traditional Polish fare; the *Zamkowa*, inside the *Zamek* hotel, is a more upmarket choice. Finally, *Pizzeria Euro*, ul. Kościuszki 23c, offers simple and filling pizzas, pasta dishes and *pierogi*.

South of Malbork

The former Teutonic towns of **Kwidzyn** and **Grudziądz**, along the eastern banks of the Wisła, and **Gniew**, on the western bank, are easily reached by bus or train from Malbork, and make for pleasant places to stop off for a short while. Further west, **Pelplin**, with its fantastic cathedral, is an easy day-trip from Gdańsk. Public transport connections can be scarce and even with a car seeing all towns efficiently is difficult due to a lack of bridges on this stretch of the river, but the tourist offices will be happy to help you plan your trip. Pelplin and Gniew both have good places to stay the night.

Pelplin

Seventy kilometres south of Gdańsk, the small town of **PELPLIN** is worth a short stop for its impressive **cathedral** (Mon–Sat 9am–5pm; 4zł; English-language tours on request). Built over a period of three hundred years after the arrival of the Cistercian Order in 1276, the massive brick building was used as a monastery church until it was turned into a cathedral for the bishops of Chełm in 1823. The main eye-catcher in the richly decorated interior is the Renaissance altar, at 25m the second highest in Europe – guides point out that it would be number one if they counted the flag on top – though there are plenty of other highlights, including a carved seventeenth-century pulpit with a statue of Samson ripping a lion apart, a winged Baroque organ and a large fourteenth-century fresco of St Christopher carrying Christ. The fifteenth-century wooden stalls in the choir abound with carved figures, the abbot's stall uniquely depicting the Holy Spirit as a morose chap holding a dove. Looking up, the elegant ceilings boast no fewer than three types (net, stellar and crystal) of Gothic rib vaulting.

Pelplin is an easy day-trip by direct **train** from Gdańsk (1hr) or by **bus** from Gniew (see opposite), 20km to the southeast. The *Nad Wierzycą* **hotel and**

restaurant opposite the cathedral at pl. Tumski 1 ☎058/536 1949, Ⓦwww
.hotel.pelplin.com; ❷) occupies the former abbey watermill, with heavy
wooden beams in its simple en-suite rooms.

Gniew

Eighty kilometres south of Gdańsk, the little town of **GNIEW** is one of the
most attractive and least known of the former Teutonic strongholds studding
the northern shores of the Wisła. Gniew's strategic location overlooking the
river led the Teutonic Knights to set themselves up here in the 1280s, taking the
place over from the Cistercian Order and completing the requisite castle within
a few years. Untouched by wars, it's a quiet and, by Polish standards, remarkably
well-preserved country town.

At the centre of the Old Town the solid-looking brick 1920s **town hall**
is surrounded by many original sixteenth- to eighteenth-century dwellings.
Overlooking the square is the towering Gothic red-brick St Nicholas **parish
church**, while a short walk east of the square brings you to the bulky square
castle (May–Oct: Tues–Sun 9am–5pm; 8zł; Ⓦwww.zamek-gniew.pl), which
has hourly tours in Polish but is mainly used for parties and events, including
regular jousting tournaments in summer.

Buses to and from Gdańsk stop off along the main road, on the western edge
of the town centre. Just behind the castle, perched on the spur overlooking
the river, the Marysieńki Palace (Pałac Marysieńki) holds a reasonably
priced **hotel** (☎058/535 3880; ❹) with an excellent **restaurant**. There's
also a summer-only **hostel**, the *Dormitorium*, occupying a wing of the castle
(☎058/535 2162).

Kwidzyn

Eighty-two kilometres from Gniew (though just 29km when using the car
ferry across the Wisła, often closed in summer due to low water levels),
KWIDZYN is a smallish fortified town ringed by a sprawling, dirty industrial
belt and set in the loop of a tributary a few kilometres east of the Wisła. The
first stronghold established by the Teutonic Knights – in the 1230s, some forty
years before the move to Malbork – its original fortress was rapidly joined
by a bishop's residence and cathedral. Three hundred years on, the castle was
pulled down and rebuilt but the cathedral and bishop's chapterhouse were left
untouched. Unlike the rest of the Old Town area, the entire complex survived
1945 unscathed.

Most of the **castle** is poised on a hilltop over the River Liwa, but
the immediately striking feature is the *dansker* toilet and defense tower,
stranded out in what used to be the riverbed and connected to the main
building by means of a precarious roofed walkway. Ranged around a
large open courtyard, the castle houses a modest local **museum** (Tues–Sun
9am–5pm; 6zł). Despite later reconstructions, the large, moody **cathedral**
adjoining the castle retains several original Gothic features, the most
noteworthy being a beautiful late fourteenth-century mosaic in the southern
vestibule.

The town is best reached by regular trains and buses from Malbork or
Grudziądz; the **train and bus stations** are an easy ten-minute walk east of the
castle. The *Kaskada* **restaurant** beside the train station at ul. Chopin 42 is a good
place to eat.

Grudziądz

The garrison town of **GRUDZIĄDZ**, 35km upriver of Kwidzyn, was an early Teutonic stronghold that retains some of its charm despite the damage of World War II – the forests near town have plenty of memorials for the human victims of the war, however, including some 10,000 local Poles murdered by the Nazis. A bustling provincial centre with an impressive riverside position, Grudziądz is convenient for a short stopover en route to Toruń and Bydgoszcz.

The Old Town is surrounded by a massive **fortress**, one of the largest in Poland, the bricks used to construct it coming from the now ruined hilltop Teutonic **castle** north of the centre. Though very little remains of the castle the views of the river make it worth the slog uphill. Descending the hill along ulica Spichrzowa, you'll find the **town hall**, attached to the Baroque **Jesuit Church and College** on ulica Ratuszowa, and the brick Gothic **St Nicholas's Church** with its elegant Baroque interior along side it. At the lower end of ulica Spichrzowa on ul. Wodna 3 stands the **Grudziądz Museum** (Tues 10am–4pm, Wed–Sat 10am–3pm, Sun 10am–2pm; 2zł, Sun free), with an interesting display of historical and modern art. The adjacent medieval **River Gate** (Brama Wodna) gives access to the riverside and a massive wall of six-storey **granaries**, a reminder of the importance once attached to the grain trade.

Grudziądz is easy to reach by **train** from Malbork and Toruń, or by **bus** from Kwidzyn and Bydgoszcz. Bus and train terminals are fifteen minutes' walk southeast of the city centre. As for **food**, eclectically furnished *Kameleon* at ul. Długa 22/5 is a good place for Polish dinner, while *Kontynenty* at ul. Starorynkowa 12/14, on the corner with ulica Długa, serves excellent pancakes and other light meals, and dozens of different coffees and teas.

Chełmno

The hilltop town of **CHEŁMNO**, another important old Prussian centre, escaped World War II undamaged and has remained untouched by postwar industrial development. Named the "city of lovers" because of the relics of St Valentine that are kept in the parish church, and with a thirteenth-century street pattern, nearly 3000m of town walls and a dozen Gothic monuments, this archetypal rural town is perhaps most memorable for its atmosphere – steeped in the powerful mixture of the Polish and Prussian that characterizes the whole region.

Although a Polish stronghold is known to have existed here as early as the eleventh century, Chełmno really came to life in 1225 with the arrival of the Teutonic Knights. They made the town their first political and administrative centre, which led to rapid and impressive development. An academy was founded in 1386 on the model of the famed University of Bologna and, despite the damage inflicted by the Swedes in the 1650s, the town continued to thrive right up to the time of the Partitions, when it lapsed into provincial Prussian obscurity.

The Old Town

On foot, the best way to enter the Old Town is via the **Grudziądz Gate**, a well-proportioned fourteenth-century Gothic construction topped by fine Renaissance gables. This leads to the pedestrianized ulica Grudziądzka, which

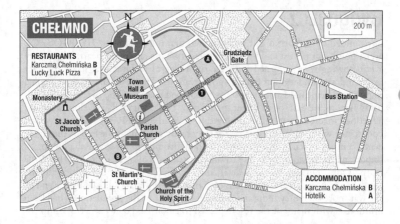

continues to the Prussian ensemble of the **Rynek**, a grand open space at the heart of the town. Gracing the centre of the square is the brilliant-white **town hall**, with an exuberantly decorated facade. Rebuilt in the 1560s on the basis of an earlier Gothic hall, its elegant exterior, decorated attic and soaring tower are one of the great examples of Polish Renaissance architecture. Inside there's a fine old courtroom and an appealing local **museum** (Tues–Fri 10am–4pm, Sat 10am–3pm, Sun 11am–2pm; 3zł), which illustrates life in town under Prussian and Polish rule. At the back of the town hall hangs the 4.35-metre "Chełmno rod", a measure employed for the original planning of the town and used up until the nineteenth century.

Most of Chełmno's seven churches are Gothic, their red-brick towers and facades punctuating the streets of the Old Town at regular intervals. Best of the lot is the **parish church** standing just west of the Rynek, an imposing thirteenth-century building with a fine carved doorway. The interior retains sculpted pillars, a Romanesque stone font and fragmentary frescoes; climb the tower (4zł) for grand views of town and the surrounding countryside. Further west, past the recently renovated **St Jacob's Church** (Św. Jakuba) with its worryingly crooked pillars, is an early fourteenth-century **monastery** (9–11.40am, 1–2.10pm & 3.10–5pm), former home to a succession of Cistercian and Benedictine orders, and now to nuns who run a hostel here for disabled children. Its church, whose Baroque altar is reputed to be the tallest in the country, features some original Gothic painting and a curious twin-level nave. A door in the town wall gives access to the monastery gardens along the former defences.

Practicalities

The **bus station** is on ulica Dworcowa, a fifteen-minute walk from the Old Town. The **tourist office** is inside the town hall (Tues–Fri 8am–4pm, Sat 8am–3pm, July & Aug also Mon 8am–5pm; ☎056/686 2104, ⓦwww .chelmno.pl). **Accommodation** options include the cosy en-suite rooms at the family-run *Hotelik*, just inside the Grudziądz Gate at Podmurna 3 (☎056/676 2030, ⓦwww.hotelik.info; ❹), or the modern-rustic rooms at the *Karczma Chełmińska*, ul. 22 Stycznia 1b (☎056/679 0605, ⓦwww.karczmachelminska .pl; ❺). *Karczma Chełmińska* also has the best **restaurant** in town, serving hearty Polish dishes; otherwise try *Lucky Luck Pizza* at ulica Grudziądzka 2.

Bydgoszcz

Surrounded by industrial and retail sprawl, first impressions of **BYDGOSZCZ** aren't good, but persist and you'll find the city has a charming heart, bisected by a fast-flowing river, adorned with the full range of architectural styles on offer in Poland and undergoing extensive renovations. Throw in the student-fuelled nightlife and cultural scene and you've got a good reason to hop over from Toruń, just 45km to the east, or to linger for a day or two. Originally developed around a fortified medieval settlement strategically located on the River Brda, close to its confluence with the Wisła, Bydgoszcz only really took off at the end of the eighteenth century when, as the Prussian town of Bromberg, it became the hub of an important waterway system due to the construction of a canal linking the Wisła to the Odra. During World War II, the city suffered particularly badly at the hands of the Nazis: mass executions of civilians followed its fall, and by the end of the war more than fifty thousand people – a quarter of the population – had been murdered, with many of the rest deported to labour and concentration camps.

Arrival, information and accommodation

The **train station** is located to the northwest of the city centre: a fifteen-minute walk straight down ulica Dworcowa (or take bus #67) brings you to ulica Gdańska, from where it's a short hop over the river to the Rynek. Bydgoszcz's **bus station** is 1km east of the centre along Jagiellońska (trams #1, #3, #5, #8 and #10 all head for the centre).

The **tourist office** on ul. Grodzka 7 (mid-May to Sept Mon–Fri 10am–9pm, Sat & Sun noon–6pm; Oct to mid-May Mon–Fri 10am–6pm, Sat & Sun noon–4pm; ⊤052/348 2373, ⊛www.bydgoszcz.pl) can help with booking **private rooms** (❷–❹). Free wi-fi **internet** is available in the area around the town hall on the main square, and there's an internet café on ul. Jezuicka 2. There's a good range of mid-range to upmarket accommodation in town, though proper private hostels have yet to arrive on the scene. The **youth hostel** is a couple of minutes' walk from the train station at ul. Sowińskiego 5 (⊤052/322 7570, ⊛www.ssm.bydgoszcz.pl).

Hotels

Agat ul Ludwikowo 1 ⊤052/327 5020, ⊛www
.agat.bydgoszcz.pl. Basic but perfectly respectable
en suites just behind the train station. ❷

Bohema ul. Konarskiego 9 ⊤052/560
0600, ⊛www.hotelbohema.pl. This newly
opened hotel in an elegant town house is the best
in town, with large Art Nouveau-inspired rooms
and smiling staff. In a quiet area just east of ul.
Gdańska. ❽–❾

Centralny ul. Dworcowa 85 ⊤052/322 8876. A

modest hotel between the station and city centre
with rooms in various styles – from basic to
glamorous. ❹–❺

Pod Orłem ul. Gdańska 14 ⊤052/583 0530,
⊛www.orbis.pl. An opulent Orbis-run hotel,
dripping with *fin de siècle* elegance. Rooms are of
a decent size and very comfortable. ❽

Ratuszowy ul. Długa 37 ⊤052/322 8861,
⊛www.hotelratuszowy.com.pl. Small but
comfortable rooms in a superbly located hotel in
the heart of town. ❻

The City

Bydgoszcz's small Old Town area lies to the south of the Brda, with the Mill Island immediately to the west. Across the river to the north lies the commercial centre, with its shops, hotels and parks.

The Old Market Square and Mill Island

As ever, the focal point of the old centre is the **Old Market Square** (Stary Rynek) on the south bank of the Brda, a pleasant space with a clutch of

Baroque and Neoclassical mansions. A communist-era n.
victims of Nazism marks the spot where Nazi planners a
side of the square to make space for parades – plans are afoot to
monument and rebuild the houses and church that once stood here.
the monument, the vast bulk of the **Jesuit college** currently closes the
side of the square.

In a secluded corner on ulica Farna, just to the north, is the red-brick fifteenth-
century **cathedral**, its exterior graced by a fine Gothic gable, while inside the
highlight is the sixteenth-century high altar of *The Madonna with the Rose*.
The church overlooks **Mill Island** (Wyspa Mlynska), a small island situated
at the point where the Brda separates into several little channels. Crossed by
dainty bridges and overlooked by old half-timbered granaries and red-brick
warehouses, these fast-flowing waterways make up an area that has been fancifully styled as the "Bydgoszcz Venice". One of the warehouses, tucked away at
the northern end of Mill Island at ul. Mennica 8a, holds the newly renovated
Red Granary (Czerwony Spichrz) branch of the town's **district museum**
(Muzeum Okręgowe; all branches Tues–Fri 10am–6pm, Sat & Sun noon–4pm;
5zł each, Sat free), which has six branches in total, some of which were closed
for renovation at time of writing. The Red Granary has displays on the history
of the town, including archive material on the Nazi atrocities.

East of the main square at ul. Grodzka 7–11 stand three quaint half-
timbered riverside granaries dating from 1793–1800; these house the new
Brda Granaries (Spichrza nad Brdą) district museum branch, worth visiting
for the eclectic collection of artefacts relating to the history of the city as well
as changing exhibitions of modern art. A couple of blocks south lies ulica
Długa, the pedestrianized main shopping street, with a couple of interesting
craft shops amongst the more ordinary stores.

Across the river

Following ulica Mostowa across the bridge from the main square to the northern
bank, you'll come to the *Crossing the river* statue, suspended over the river on a
tightrope, which symbolizes Poland's accession to the EU in 2004. The first
church along ulica Gdańska, the main road leading away from the river, is the
former **Convent Church of the Poor Clares** (Kościół Klarysek), a curious
amalgam of late Gothic and Renaissance. The convent buildings next door
house another branch of the **district museum**, this time displaying a varied
collection of twentieth-century Polish art. Six hundred metres further north,
ulica Cieszkowskiego on the left is Bydgoszcz's prettiest street, despite the city
buses roaring through, lined with dozens of Secession-style apartment buildings
showing off elegant architectural details.

Eight hundred metres southeast of here, the basilica of **St Vincent de Paul**
(Bazylika św. Wincentego a Paulo) on Rondo Ossolińskich is a vast circular
church modelled on the Pantheon in Rome and capable of accommodating twelve
thousand worshippers. Its construction was a direct result of the town's change
in ownership from Protestant Prussia to Catholic Poland, which necessitated the
creation of a much larger space for celebrating the main feast days.

Eating and drinking

Bydgoszcz's eating and drinking scene has long been modest, though the
opening of several new restaurants and cafés have brought more life to the Old
Market Square area.

afés

...xcellent
...otel. Mains
...ushroom ragout
...hes. Daily

...Overlooking the
...for coffee and
...walk by. Open

...Tasty self-service
vegetarian me...   ...rices. Open 10am–
8pm, Sat 10am–6pm, Sun noon–6pm.

Karczma Młyńska ul. Mennica 1. A friendly, rustic restaurant on Mill Island – good for Polish meals with river views. Open noon–11pm, Fri & Sat till midnight.

Naleśniki jak Smok ul. Kręta. Specializes in tasty pancakes, with a chameleon called Smok ogling at diners from his terrarium. Open 11am–10pm, Fri & Sat till midnight.

Stary Port ul. Stary Port 13, opposite the Brda Granaries. Excellent Polish food served in an over-the-top rustic interior complete with ponds and clattering watermills. Daily noon–11pm.

Weranda ul. Konarskiego 9 ☎052/560 0600. Eclectically furnished café and restaurant overlooking the park at the rear of the Bohema hotel. Great service and a wide range of food. Booking recommended. Daily 9am–11pm.

Bars and clubs

Jack ul. Długa 65. Cosy pub-style bar south of the Rynek that welcomes groups too. Open noon–2am, weekends till 4am.

Smak ul. Mostowa 4. Lively bar with a mixed crowd enjoying the terrace, ideal for afternoon people-watching. Daily 9am–11pm.

Vanila Club ul. Zygmunta Augusta 20 ⓦwww .vanilaclub.pl. The best party place in town, near the station, crams in the students on weekends. Fri & Sat 9pm–4am.

Mózg ul. Gdańska 10 ⓦwww.mozg.art.pl. Hangout for the alternative crowd, this is a rambling café-cum-music club with regular jazz and rock gigs. Entrance down ul. Parkowa. Open 6pm–2am; July–Sept Thurs–Sat only.

Eljazz ul. Kręta 3 ⓦwww.eljazz.com.pl. A funky small jazz bar with weekly live gigs. Open 4pm–1am, Fri & Sat till 4am.

Entertainment

The Filharmonia Pomorska, just east of ulica Gdańska at ul. Szwalbego 6 (box office daily 11am–6pm; ☎052/321 0234, ⓦwww.filharmonia.bydgoszcz.pl), is the main **musical** venue: as well as regular concerts, it features a fortnight-long classical festival each September. The main **theatre** is the nearby Teatr Polski, al. Mickiewicza 2 (box office Tues–Fri noon–6pm; ☎052/339 7818, ⓦwww .teatrpolski.pl). Opera Nova at ul. Marszałka Focha 5 (box office Tues–Thurs & Sat 3–6.30pm, Sun 4–6.30pm; ☎052/325 1555, ⓦwww.opera.bydgoszcz.pl) is the venue for **opera**.

Toruń and around

Poles are apt to wax lyrical on the glories of their historical cities, and with **TORUŃ** – the biggest and most important of the Hanseatic trading centres along the Wisła – it's more than justified; only Kraków has more medieval buildings. Miraculously surviving the recurrent wars afflicting the region, the historic centre remains one of the country's most evocative, bringing together a rich assembly of architectural styles. The city's main claim to fame is as the birthplace of **Nicolaus Copernicus** (see box, p.178), whose house still stands. Today, Toruń is a university city: large, reasonably prosperous and – once you're through the standard postwar suburbs – one with a definitely cultured air.

Some history

The pattern of Toruń's early history is similar to that of other towns along the northern Wisła. Starting out as a Polish settlement, it was overrun by Prussian tribes from the east towards the end of the twelfth century, and soon afterwards the Teutonic Knights moved in. The Knights rapidly developed the town, thanks to its access to the burgeoning river-borne grain trade, a position further consolidated with its entry to the **Hanseatic League**. As in rival Gdańsk, economic prosperity was expressed in a mass of building projects through the thirteenth century; together these make up the majority of the historic sites in the city.

Growing disenchantment with the Teutonic Knights' rule and heavy taxation in the fifteenth century, especially among the merchants, led to the formation of the **Prussian Union** in 1440, based in Toruń. In 1454, as war broke out between the Knights and Poland, the townspeople destroyed the castle in Toruń and chased the order out of town. The 1466 **Treaty of Toruń** finally terminated the Knights' control of the area.

The sixteenth and seventeenth centuries brought even greater wealth as the town thrived on extensive royal privileges and increased access to goods from all over Poland. The Swedish invasion of the 1650s was the first significant setback, but the really decisive blow to the city's fortunes came a century later with the Partitions, when Toruń was annexed to Prussia and thus severed from its hinterlands, which by now were under Russian control. Like much of the region, Toruń was subjected to systematic Germanization, but as in many other cities a strongly Polish identity remained, clearly manifested in the cultural associations that flourished in the latter part of the nineteenth century. The twentieth century saw Toruń returned to Poland (under

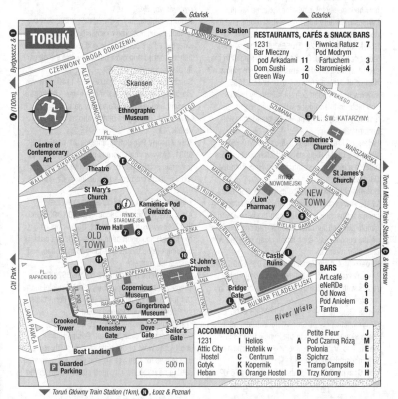

RESTAURANTS, CAFÉS & SNACK BARS

1231		Piwnica Ratusz	7
Bar Mleczny	I	Pod Modrym	
pod Arkadami	11	Fartuchem	3
Dom Sushi	2	Staromiejski	4
Green Way	10		

BARS

Art.café	9
eNeRDe	6
Od Nowa	1
Pod Aniołem	8
Tantra	5

ACCOMMODATION

1231	I	Petite Fleur	J
Attic City		Helios	A	Pod Czarną Różą	M
Hostel	C	Hotelik w		Polonia	E
Gotyk	K	Centrum	B	Spichrz	L
Heban	G	Kopernik	F	Tramp Campsite	N
		Orange Hostel	D	Trzy Korony	H

the terms of the 1919 Versailles Treaty as part of the "Polish Corridor" that so enraged Hitler), captured by the Nazis during World War II and liberated in 1945.

Arrival, information and accommodation

The main stations are on opposite sides of the Old Town. Toruń Główny, the main **train station**, is south of the river. It's a one-kilometre walk to the city centre over a busy road bridge – a better option is to take bus #22 or #27 (every 20min) from the stop outside the main station entrance and get off at plac Rapackiego, just to the west of the Old Town. Some trains stop at Toruń Miasto station, about 1km east of the centre. The **bus station** is on ulica Dąbrowskiego, a short walk north of the centre.

The **tourist office** at Rynek Staromiejski 25 (Mon & Sat 9am–4pm, Tues–Fri 9am–6pm, plus Sun 9am–1pm in July & Aug; ☏056/621 0931, ⓦwww .it.torun.pl) doles out free brochures and maps and can help book good-value **private accommodation** and apartments (❶–❹). From July to late September, **student rooms** (❷) are available near the centre at ul. Słówackiego 1/3, building 6 (☏056/612 1548, ⓦwww.umk.pl/studenci/ds).

Hotels

1231 ul. Przedzamcze 6 ☏056/619 0910, ⓦwww.hotelesolaris.pl. Fantastic new boutique hotel inside the Teutonic Knights' thirteenth-century mill, with stylish rooms and an excellent restaurant downstairs (see p.194). ❼

Gotyk ul. Piekary 20 ☏056/658 4000, ⓦwww .hotel-gotyk.com.pl. Comfortable small hotel in the centre with classically furnished en-suite rooms. ❻

Heban ul. Małe Garbary 7 ☏056/652 1555, ⓦwww.hotel-heban.com.pl. Centrally located and historic town house with plush rooms in a variety of styles, from 1900s bland to lavish Empire. ❻

Helios ul. Kraszewskiego 1/3 ☏056/619 6550, ⓦwww.orbis.pl. High-standard *Mercure* business hotel in a modern building a short walk from the Old Town. ❼

Hotelik w Centrum ul. Szumana 2 ☏056/652 2246, ⓦwww.hotelikwcentrum.pl. Good budget choice a few minutes' walk from the centre with simple but well-furnished rooms. The cheaper ones on the second floor each share clean facilities with one other room. ❹

Kopernik ul. Wola Zamkowa 16 ☏056/659 7333, ⓦwww.kopernik.torun.pl. Modern, comfortable rooms with TV and shower in an ugly building in the New Town. ❺

Petite Fleur ul. Piekary 25 ☏056/663 4400, ⓦwww.petitefleur.pl. Small hotel with an intimate feel a stone's throw from the Rynek. Rooms are simple and bright with pine floors and furnishings and modern bathrooms. ❺–❻

Pod Czarną Różą ul. Rabiańska 11 ☏056/621 9637, ⓦwww.hotelczarnaroza.pl. Cosy and good-value rooms with TV and shower in an old town house on a quiet city-centre street. Rooms in the new rear section have river views. ❺

Polonia pl. Teatralny 5 ☏056/622 3028, ⓦwww .polonia.torun.pl. Some rooms are on the small side, but all are comfortable and reasonably taste-fully decorated and most have views of the elegant theatre across the road. ❺

Spichrz ul. Mostowa 1 ☏056/657 1140, ⓦwww .spichrz.pl. New hotel in a monumental city-centre granary beside the Mostowa city gate. Rooms have plenty of wooden beams and other original details. ❻

Trzy Korony Rynek Staromiejski 21 ☏056/622 6031, ⓦwww.hotel3korony.pl. The only hotel on the main square has cheap but musty-smelling rooms, some with en-suite facilities. ❹–❺

Hostels and campsite

Attic City Hostel ul. Chłopickiego 4B ☏056/659 8517, ⓦwww.atticcityhostel.pl. Decent double rooms (❸) and dorm beds (from 40zł) in a brick building beside the Toruń Miasto train station, just east of the centre.

Orange Hostel ul. Prosta 19 ☏056/652 0033, ⓦwww.hostelorange.pl. Lively, simple hostel in the Old Town with double rooms (❶) and dorm beds for 35zł; free breakfast and internet.

Tramp ul. Kujawska 14 ☏056/654 7187, ⓦwww.tramp.mosir.torun.pl. Campsite a short walk west of the train station, with some bungalows for rent year-round (❶). Nice wooded setting near the river, though suffers from traffic noise.

The City

The historic core of Toruń is divided into old and new town areas, both established in the early years of Teutonic rule. Traditional economic divisions are apparent here, the **Old Town** (Stare Miasto) quarter being home for the merchants, the **New Town** (Nowe Miasto) for the artisans; each had its own square, market area and town hall.

Overlooking the river from a gentle rise, the medieval centre constitutes a relatively small section of the modern city and is clearly separated from it by a ring of parks. Motorists are advised to use the guarded parking below the road bridge and continue on foot.

The Rynek and around

The **Old Town** area is the obvious place to start looking around – and as usual it's the **Rynek**, in particular the **town hall** that provides the focal point. Town halls don't come much bigger or more striking than this: converted in the late fourteenth century from an older cloth hall, it's a tremendous, if rather austere, statement of civic pride. A three-storey brick structure topped by a sturdy tower, its outer walls are punctuated by indented windows, framed by a rhythmic succession of high arches peaking just beneath the roof, and complemented by graceful Renaissance turrets and high gables.

The south side entrance, beside a noble bronze statue of Copernicus, leads to an inner courtyard surrounded by fine brick doorways, the main one leading to the **town museum** (Tues–Sun: May–Sept 10am–6pm; Oct–April 10am–4pm; 10zł), which now occupies much of the building. Over the centuries Toruń's wealth attracted artists and craftsmen of every type, and it's their work that features strongest here. Most of the ground floor – once the wine cellar – is devoted to medieval artefacts, with a gorgeous collection of the **stained glass** for which the city was famed and some fine **sculptures**, especially the celebrated "Beautiful Madonnas" in which the Virgin is portrayed swooning in an S-shaped posture of grace. Also housed on this floor is a collection of material relating to the guilds founded by the city's craftsmen, including locks, inlaid wooden furniture and wrought-iron street signs. On the first floor, **paintings** take over, with rooms covered in portraits of Polish kings and wealthy Toruń citizens. A small portrait of the most famous city burgher, Copernicus, basks in the limelight of a Baroque gallery. It's worth the additional 10zł to climb the **tower** (April 10am–6pm; May–Sept 10am–8pm; Oct–March 10am–4pm) for the view of the city.

Lining the square itself are the stately mansions of the Hansa merchants, many of whose high parapets and decorated facades are preserved intact. The finest houses flank the east side of the square. No. 35, next to one of the Copernicus family houses, is the fifteenth-century **Kamienica Pod Gwiazdą**, with a finely modelled late Baroque facade: inside, a superbly carved wooden staircase ends with a statue of Minerva, spear in hand. The house is now the small **Museum of Far Eastern Art** (Muzeum Sztuki Dalekiego Wschodu; Tues–Sun: May–Sept 11am–6pm; Oct–April 10am–4pm; 7zł, Wed free), based on a private collection of art and weapons from China, India and other Asian countries.

Off to the west of the square stands **St Mary's Church** (Kościół Mariacki), a large fourteenth-century building with elements of its early decoration retained in the sombre interior. There's no tower to the building, apparently because the church's Franciscan founders didn't permit such things.

South of the Rynek

South of the main square, on the narrow and atmospheric ulica Żeglarska, is **St John's Church** (Kościół św. Jana: April–Oct 9am–5.30pm, Sun 2–5.30pm; 3zł), another large, magnificent Gothic structure, where Copernicus was baptized in 1473. The presbytery, the oldest part of the building, dates from the 1260s, but the main nave and aisles were not completed till the mid-fifteenth century. The tower, closed for renovations at time of writing, houses amagnificent fifteenth-century *Tuba Dei*, the largest bell in Poland outside Kraków, which can be heard all over town.

▲ Monastery Gate, Toruń

West from the church runs ulica Kopernika, halfway down which you'll find the **Copernicus Museum** (Muzeum Kopernika; Tues–Sun: May–Sept 10am–6pm; Oct–April 10am–4pm; 10zł), installed in the high brick house where the great man was most probably born. Restored to something resembling its original layout, this Gothic mansion contains a studiously assembled collection of Copernicus artefacts: facsimiles of the momentous *De Revolutionibus*, models of astronomical instruments, original household furniture and early portraits.

You smell the **Gingerbread Museum** (Muzeum Piernika), nearby on ul. Rabiańska 9, before you see it. A delightful place to take children, visitors get a hands-on cooking class as staff in period dress teach how gingerbread was made five hundred years ago – and you can eat the biscuits you make (daily 9am–6pm, sessions start hourly; 10zł).

Further down towards the river, the high, narrow streets meet the old defensive **walls**, now separating the Old Town from the main road. These fortifications survived virtually intact right up to the late nineteenth century, only for some enterprising Prussian town planners to knock them down, sparing only a small section interspersed by old gates and towers near the river's edge.

To the west, at the bottom of ulica Pod Krzywą Wieżą, stands the mid-fourteenth-century **Crooked Tower** (Krzywa Wieża), followed in quick succession by the **Monastery Gate** (Brama Klasztorna), **Dove Gate** (Brama Gołębnik) and **Sailors' Gate** (Brama Żeglarska), all from the same period, the last originally leading to the main harbour. Head through the Monastery Gate down to the riverbank to find a landing stage, from which in summer you can take forty-minute **boat trips**, departing on the hour between 9am and 7pm. Heading east, past the large **Bridge Gate** (Brama Mostowa), brings you to the ruins of the Teutonic Knights' **castle**, sandwiched between the two halves of the medieval city (March–Oct daily 10am–6pm; 5zł, Mon free). The impressive Gdanisko outer tower and several basement rooms can be visited, and while the castle here was nowhere near as massive as the later Malbork fortress, the scale of what's left is enough to leave you impressed by the Toruń citizenry's efforts in laying waste to it.

The New Town

Following ulica Przedzamcze north from the castle brings you onto ulica Szeroka, the main thoroughfare linking the old and new town districts. Less grand than its mercantile neighbour, the **New Town** still boasts a number of illustrious commercial residences, most of them grouped around the **Rynek Nowomiejski**. On the west side of this square, the fifteenth-century Pod Modrym Fartuchem inn (no. 8) and at no. 13 the Gothic Pod Lwem ("Lion") pharmacy with a golden lion as its shop sign are particularly striking. The fourteenth-century **St James's Church** (Kościół św. Jakuba), east of the market area of the Rynek, completes the city's collection of Gothic churches. Inside, mainly Baroque decoration is relieved by occasional Gothic frescoes, panel paintings and sculpture – most notably a large fourteenth-century crucifix.

North of the centre

The green belt to the north and west of the Old Town houses several worth-while sights. The old city arsenal houses the **Ethnographic Museum** (Muzeum Etnograficzne: mid-April to June Tues & Thurs 9am–5pm, Wed & Fri 9am–4pm, Sat & Sun 10am–6pm; July–Sept Tues, Thurs, Sat & Sun 10am–6pm, Wed & Fri 9am–4pm; Oct to mid-June Tues–Fri 9am–4pm, Sat & Sun 10am–4pm; 14zł, Wed free; ⓦwww.etnomuseum.pl), which deal with the customs and crafts of northern Poland. It's surrounded by a park with an enchanting *skansen* containing an enjoyable collection of traditional wooden buildings. Just to the west, the imposing new **Centre of Contemporary Art** (Centrum Sztuki Współczesnej: ⓦwww.csw.torun.pl) on Wały Sikorskiego 13 hosts changing exhibitions of local and foreign modern art, and an excellent museum shop with art books and quirky Toruń souvenirs (Tues–Thurs & Sun 10am–6pm, Fri & Sat 10am–8pm; 10zł). The pleasant **city park** is further west along the riverside, reached by tram #1 from plac Rapackiego.

Eating, drinking and entertainment

There's an excellent choice of **places to eat** in Toruń, with some more exotic cuisines popping up in recent years. **Cafés** and **bars** are in plentiful supply, with daytime pavement-café places on streets such as ulica Szeroka providing an opportunity to enjoy the atmosphere of the Old Town. The riverbank also provides good outdoor café spots on warm summer nights. For **events information** ask the tourist office or check the listings in the *IKAR* cultural magazine, for sale at kiosks and bookshops.

Restaurants and snack bars

1231 ul. Przedzamcze 6. Upmarket eatery inside the old millhouse, with well-prepared Mediterranean dishes washed down with fresh beer from the on-site brewery. Open noon–midnight.

Bar Mleczny pod Arkadami ul. Różana 1. Traditional fast food, including filling *barszcz*, bean soups, pancakes and takeaway waffles (*gofry*). April–Sept Mon–Fri 9am–10pm, Sat 9am–6pm, Sun 10am–6pm; Oct–March Mon–Fri 9am–7pm, Sat & Sun 9am–4pm.

Dom Sushi ul. Franciszkańska 8. Freshly made sushi and other Japanese dishes, delivered to diners in sushi boats that float around the bar. Daily noon–10pm.

Green Way ul. Łazienna 13. Cheap and tasty vegetarian self-service food below a stunning ceiling. Mon–Sat 10am–9pm, Sun noon–7pm.

Piwnica Ratusz Rynek Staromiejski. The town hall's medieval beer cellar, on the west side of the building, is a good place for solid Polish meat-and-potatoes meals. Daily noon–11pm.

Pod Modrym Fartuchem Rynek Nowomiejski 8. Authentic Indian food including masala chicken and veg kormas served by the Indian owner, who has kept the Polish look and menu of this ancient restaurant (in business since 1489) intact for the old regulars. Mon–Thurs 10am–10pm, Fri & Sat 10am–11pm, Sun 11am–9pm.

Staromiejski ul. Szczytna 2/4. A popular Italian restaurant with big pizzas and a good range of pasta dishes. Daily noon–10pm.

Bars and clubs

Art.café ul. Szeroka 35. Club playing electro, house and hip-hop, with frequent visits by foreign DJs. Open 5pm–2am, Fri & Sat till 4am.

eNeRDe ul. Browarna 6. A run-down but friendly centre of alternative culture, with regular art events, DJs and concerts. Open 6pm–4am.

Od Nowa ul. Gagarina 37a ☏058/611 4593, ⓦwww.odnowa.umk.pl. One of the best venues in town, a theatre, student club and rock/jazz venue in the university district northwest of the centre.

Pod Aniołem Rynek Staromiejski 1. Best of the evening haunts, a wonderfully atmospheric vaulted cellar under the town hall. Often features live music, cabaret performances or DJs at weekends. Open 10am–1am, weekends till 4am.

Tantra ul. Ślusarska 5. Mad, sensually decorated bar that specializes in hot wines, special teas and coffees, and drinks that can burn. Open 6pm–midnight, Fri & Sat till 2am.

Entertainment

The grand old Toruń **theatre**, pl. Teatralny 1 (☏056/622 5597, ⓦwww.teatr .torun.pl), is home to one of the country's most highly regarded repertory companies. Classical **concerts** take place in the town hall and in the Dwór Artusa at Rynek Staromiejski 6 (☏056/655 4929, ⓦwww.artus.torun.pl).

The city has a number of regular **festivals**, notably the International Theatre Festival (May; ⓦwww.teatr.torun.pl), the most prestigious theatrical event in

Poland; an organ festival (May/June); the Toruń Day on June 24; the Gotyk na Dotyk Goth festival (June); a folk festival (June); and the Artus Jazz festival (July/Aug; Ⓦ www.artus.torun.pl).

Golub-Dobrzyń

About 35km east of Toruń, the elegant facades of the castle at **GOLUB-DOBRZYŃ** are a traditional tourist poster favourite. While the town itself is nothing to write home about, the castle, located high up on a hill overlooking the town, is certainly an impressive sight.

A Teutonic stronghold, **Golub Castle** (Zamek Golubski: Ⓦ www.zamekgolub .pl) was originally built in the early 1300s, and fell into Polish hands in 1466. Anna Waza, sister of King Sigismund III, had the whole place remodelled in Polish Renaissance style in the early 1600s, adding the elegantly sculptured facades and Italianate courtyard you see today. After taking a severe battering during the Swedish wars of the 1650s, several storms and two world wars, the abandoned castle was left to crumble away, restoration work only beginning in the 1960s. The result is a rather prettified castle that's nicer from the outside than within. Entrance to the castle **museum** (Tues–Sun: June–Sept 9am–7pm; Oct–May 9am–4pm; 10zł) is by Polish-language guided tour (every 30min in summer), which take in the banqueting hall (*refektarz*), chapel (*kaplica*) and several rooms with an impressive collection of cannons and other weapons. The field beside the castle hosts a major international **chivalry tournament** in early July.

The regular **bus** service between Toruń and Golub-Dobrzyń makes this an easy day-trip, but should you want to stay overnight, note that the castle also houses a fairly basic **hotel** (☎056/683 2466; ❷) as well as a **restaurant**.

Ciechocinek

Twenty kilometres southeast of Toruń, and reached by frequent trains and buses, **CIECHOCINEK** has rather more life about it than the normal run of Polish spas. The **Spa Park** (Park Zdrojowy), just down from the bus and train stations, is pleasant for a stroll but the main attraction is the **Tężniówy Park** (dawn–dusk; 4zł) immediately to the west. Here, in three separate sections stretching for 1700m, is the massive wall of wooden beams and twigs that makes up the **saltworks** (*tężnie*), begun in 1824 but not completed until several decades later. The saltworks still functions as intended today, as the simple technology is very effective: water from the town's saline springs is pumped to the top of the structure – originally using windmills – from where it trickles down through the twigs. The evaporating water not only concentrates the salt, it also creates a reputedly recuperative atmosphere around the structures which is gratefully inhaled by spa visitors. You can climb onto the top of the first stretch of saltworks for 4zł, where you can view the channel systems distributing the brine along the walls.

East of the spa park, 1km out along ul. Wojska Polskiego, lies a dainty, turquoise-painted wooden **Orthodox church** erected by carpenters from the Urals in the nineteenth century. The interior is usually only accessible at service times (Wed 4pm; Sun 8.45am).

The **tourist information office** at ul. Zdrojowa 2b (April–Oct Mon–Sat 10am–6pm, Sun 11am–4pm, Nov–March Mon–Fri 7.30am–3.30pm; ☎054/416 1005) can help find **rooms** if necessary and also provides free **internet**. The glam **restaurant** of the *Willa Nowa* hotel by the saltworks on ul. Tężniówa 1 is good for Polish dishes, while the *Zdrojowa Café* right beside the tourist information office is perfect for coffee and cakes.

Travel details

Trains

Bydgoszcz to: Częstochowa (4 daily; 6hr); Gdańsk (hourly; 3hr); Kraków (1 daily; 8hr); Łódź Kaliska (5 daily; 4–5hr); Poznań (7 daily; 2hr); Toruń (hourly; 1hr); Warsaw (8 daily; 4hr); Wrocław (3 daily; 5hr).
Gdańsk to: Białystok (2 daily; 7hr 30min); Bydgoszcz (hourly; 3hr); Częstochowa (5 daily; 8–9hr); Elbląg (hourly; 1hr 20min); Hel (July & Aug only: 3 daily; 2–3hr); Katowice (4 daily; 8–10hr); Kraków (8 daily; 8–12hr); Łódź (5 daily; 5hr 30min–6hr); Malbork (every 30 min; 45–55min); Olsztyn (6 daily; 3hr); Pelplin (19 daily: 1hr); Poznań (6 daily; 4hr 30min); Przemyśl (1 daily; 12hr); Szczecin (3 daily; 5hr 20min); Toruń (5 daily; 3hr 30min); Warsaw (13 daily; 4–5hr); Wrocław (3 daily; 7hr).
Gdynia to: Hel (via Puck; 9 daily; 1hr 45min).
Toruń to: Bydgoszcz (hourly; 1hr); Gdańsk (5 daily; 3hr 30min); Kraków (1 daily; 7hr); Łódź Kaliska (6 daily; 2hr 30min–3hr 30min); Olsztyn (5 daily; 2hr 30min–3hr); Poznań (7 daily; 2hr 30min); Warsaw (8 daily; 2hr 30min); Wrocław (3 daily; 5hr).

Buses

Bydgoszcz to: Chełmno (1 daily; 1hr); Toruń (hourly; 1hr).
Chełmno to: Toruń (4 daily; 1hr).
Elbląg to: Frombork (every 30min; 45min); Krynica Morska (every 30min; 1hr 30min).

Gdańsk to: Chmielno (6 daily; 1hr 30min); Elbląg (every 30min; 1hr 30min); Frombork (6 daily; 2hr 30min); Gniew (9 daily; 1hr 20min); Hel (June–Sept only: 2 daily; 2hr 30min); Kartuzy (every 15–30min; 1hr); Krynica Morska (hourly; 1hr 45min); Malbork (6 daily; 1hr 30min); Olsztyn (6 daily; 3hr 20min); Sztutowo (hourly; 1hr 15min); Toruń (2 daily; 3hr).
Gniew to: Pelplin (9 daily, 20–50min).
Gdynia to: Hel (via Puck; 15 daily; 2hr); Łeba (1 daily; 2hr 30min).
Kartuzy to: Chmielno (hourly; 15min).
Toruń to: Bydgoszcz (hourly; 1hr); Ciechocinek (10 daily; 40min); Łódź (7 daily; 3hr 20min); Warsaw (3 daily; 4hr).

Ferries

Gdańsk to: Hel (May–Sept 1–3 daily); Sopot (late June to Aug 3 daily).
Gdynia to: Hel (late June to Aug 4 daily).
Sopot to: Gdańsk (late June to Aug 3 daily); Hel (late June to Aug 3 daily).

International Trains

Gdańsk to: Berlin-Lichtenberg (1 daily; 8hr); Kaliningrad (1 daily; 8hr)

International Buses

Gdańsk to: Kaliningrad (2 daily; 5hr 30min); Vilnius (daily; 9hr).

Mazuria and Podlasie

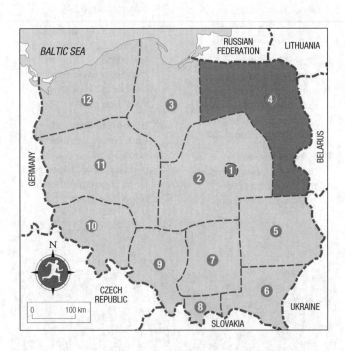

CHAPTER 4 # Highlights

* **The Wolf's Lair** Grimly compelling site of Hitler's secret command bunker, once the nerve centre of German military power. **See p.214**

* **Mikołajki** Poland's prime venue for yachting, kayaking and generally messing about in boats, situated in the heart of the Mazurian lake district. **See p.218**

* **Suwałki Landscape Park** Bewitching area of gently rolling farmland and forest, sprinkled with deep lakes and the odd rustic village. **See p.231**

* **Supraśl** Traditional, timber-built village beside the Belarusian border, boasting a sumptuous museum collection of Orthodox icons. **See p.238**

* **Tykocin** Riverside town of cobbled alleys and one-storey houses, site of one of the most beautifully preserved synagogues in the country. **See p.240**

* **Biebrża National Park** Captivating lowland landscape of reeds and marshes, criss-crossed by accessible walking trails. **See p.241**

* **Białowieża National Park** Europe's largest surviving area of primeval forest, famous for its large population of bison. **See p.246**

▲ Mamry Lake, Wegezewo

Mazuria and Podlasie

A sk Poles to list the natural wonders of their country and they will automatically answer "lakes and forests" – things that the northeastern territories of Mazuria and Podlasie offer in rich abundance. These predominantly agricultural and largely **unspoilt areas** offer everything necessary for a country-based holiday, with walking trails, canoeing routes, wildlife reserves and characterful B&Bs enticing an increasing number of tourists. Although there aren't any great historical cities in this part of Poland there is plenty in the way of **history** – much of this area was in German hands for many centuries and their fortresses and churches still scatter the area. Religious and **ethnic diversity** become increasingly evident the further east you go, with Polish communities rubbing shoulders with Lithuanians, Belarusians and even Tatars in the bucolic villages on Poland's eastern rim.

The so-called "land of a thousand lakes", **Mazuria** (Mazury) was formed by the last Ice Age, when retreating glaciers carved out the hollows now filled with water. A sparsely populated area of thick forests and innumerable lakes and rivers, Mazuria is one of the country's main holiday districts – and rightfully so. It's a wonderful haunt for walkers, campers, watersports enthusiasts or just for those who want to take it easy. The western fringes of Mazuria rub up against **Warmia**, a rich agricultural plain dotted with historic towns. The main entry point to the region is **Olsztyn**, a pleasant small-scale city which is worth a short stay in itself. From here bus and train links fan out towards the main lakeside resorts, with **Mrągowo**, **Mikołajki** and **Wilkasy** offering most in terms of active opportunities and natural beauty.

East of Mazuria, **Podlasie** literally means "Under the Trees" – a name that only hints at the landscape of wide, open plains, and tracts of primeval forest. The northern corner of Podlasie, named Suwalszczyzna after its main town **Suwałki**, offers an extraordinary wealth of rolling farmland, dense woods and reed-fringed lakes, providing the perfect opportunity to explore a uniquely unspoiled and relatively little-visited corner of Europe. The large tracts of forest for which Podlasie is famous lie further south around **Augustów**, **Supraśl**, and most importantly, **Białowieża**. It's in the **Białowieża National Park** that you can explore continental Europe's last belt of virgin forest – the haunt of bison, elk and hundreds of varieties of flora and fauna, and home, too, of the wondrous Żubrówka "bison grass" vodka.

Standing in total contrast to the forests of Białowieża are the compelling marshlands of the **Biebrza National Park**, north of Białystok; while the nearby village of **Tykocin** is a beautifully preserved monument to the region's now-disappeared Jewish community. **Białystok** is the one large

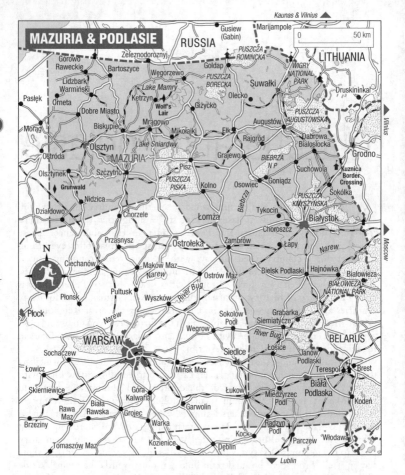

city in this part of Poland, and is the main hub for public transport to Podlasie's far-flung rural communities.

Olsztyn

Of several possible stepping-off points for the lakes, **OLSZTYN** is the biggest and the easiest to reach, and owing to the summertime tourist influx, it's well kitted out to deal with visitors, most of whom stop here en route to points further east. The town is surrounded by pleasant woodland, but as a result of wartime destruction – Soviet troops burnt the place down in 1945 after the fighting had ceased – much of the old centre has the usual residential postwar greyness. Among the concrete blocks and dusty main thoroughfares, however, quiet streets of neat brick houses built by the city's former German inhabitants remain, and there are relaxing tree-lined riverside walks around the Old Town.

Prussia and the Prussians

Present-day Warmia and Mazuria make up the heartlands of what, until sixty years ago, was known as **East Prussia** (Ostpreussen), the territory carved out by the **Teutonic Knights** (a semi-monastic crusading order) in the Middle Ages and subjected to various forms of German-speaking rule right up until 1945.

Despite competing German and Polish claims to the area, however, it was originally populated by neither: the indigenous inhabitants were Baltic tribes, most numerous of whom were the Borussians (later shortened to "**Prussians**"), a people closely related in language and culture to the Lithuanians and Latvians of today. The Prussians were among the last of Europe's **pagans**, venerating sun, moon, trees and rivers. Polish chronicler Jan Długosz wrote that they were extremely hospitable people who considered themselves bad hosts if they didn't drink their guests under the table, and who used the social ritual of the sauna to recover from such binges.

The job of **Christianizing** the Prussians was begun by Polish rulers as early as the tenth century, when Bolesław the Brave dispatched Bishop (and future Saint) **Adalbert** to the Baltic shores – the Prussians expressed their gratitude by having him chopped to pieces. In the 1220s **Duke Konrad of Mazovia** invited the Teutonic Knights to help him convert the Prussians, believing that he could use the knights to expand his own territories. The plan backfired, with the Knights receiving the backing of the pope to carve out their own crusader state in Prussia, keeping the Poles out.

The Prussian tribes were too disunited to offer adequate resistance to the crusaders, who set about forcibly converting the locals to Christianity and massacring any that resisted. A major Prussian revolt under **Herkus Mantas** put the Teutonic Knights on the back foot in the 1260s, but the final defeat of Mantas in 1274 presaged the eclipse of Prussian culture. The remaining Prussians were gradually assimilated by German-speaking colonizers, or fled east where they were absorbed into the Lithuanian nation.

Although the Prussians disappeared, their name lived on as a geographical label, and was ultimately adopted by the very people who had wiped them out. Following the secularization of the Teutonic Knights' lands in 1525, much of what is now northern Poland became the **Duchy of Prussia**, with the Brandenberg Hohenzollern family as its hereditary rulers and Kónigsberg (now Kaliningrad in Russia) as its capital. The Prussian Dukes swore fealty to the Polish crown in 1525, but were able to shake off the connection a century later. The centre of power in Prussia gradually shifted westwards, and it was Berlin that emerged as the capital of a newly established **Kingdom of Prussia** in 1701. Prussia subsequently became the nucleus of the modern German state, which came into being in 1871.

The disintegration of German-ruled Prussia began in the wake of World War I, when Poland was granted a strip of land on the Baltic coast, thereby separating East Prussia from the rest of the country. With Germany's total defeat in World War II, East Prussia ceased to exist, with its southern half going to Poland and its northern half becoming the Kaliningrad province of the USSR. Everybody of German origin was ordered to leave, with most ending up in West Germany, where their descendants still live today.

Much of Warmia and Mazuria still has a Germanic flavour, as evidenced by the many Protestant churches and German-looking towns dotted around. Today the most obvious sign of German influence is the influx of German tourists (many of whom have family roots here) who flock to the major lakeside holiday resorts in the summer.

Olsztyn was something of a latecomer, gaining municipal status in 1353, twenty years after its castle was begun. Following the 1466 Toruń Treaty, the town was reintegrated into Polish territory, finally escaping the clutches of the Teutonic Knights. Half a century later, Nicolaus Copernicus took up residence as an administrator of the province of Warmia, and in 1521 helped organize the defence of the town against the Knights.

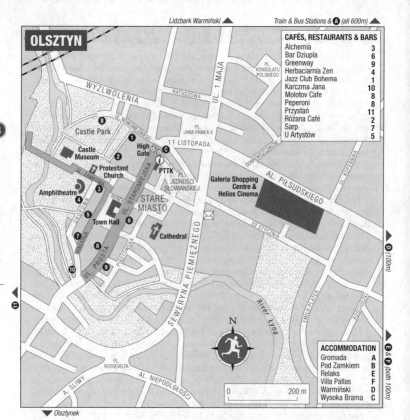

OLSZTYN

Lidzbark Warmiński ▲   Train & Bus Stations & **A** (all 600m) ▲

CAFÉS, RESTAURANTS & BARS	
Alchemia	3
Bar Dziupla	6
Greenway	9
Herbaciarnia Zen	4
Jazz Club Bohema	1
Karczma Jana	10
Molotov Cafe	8
Peperoni	8
Przystań	11
Różana Café	2
Sarp	7
U Artystów	5

ACCOMMODATION	
Gromada	A
Pod Zamkiem	B
Relaks	E
Villa Pallas	F
Warmiński	D
Wysoka Brama	C

▼ Olsztynek

Coming under Prussian control after the First Partition, it remained part of East Prussia until 1945. Resistance to Germanization during this period was symbolized by the establishment here, in 1921, of the Association of Poles in Germany, an organization dedicated to keeping Polish culture alive. With Hitler's accession, the Association became a target for Nazi terror, and most of its members perished in the concentration camps. The town also suffered, roughly forty percent being demolished by 1945.

The majority of the German-speaking population were expelled after World War II, to be replaced by Polish settlers from the eastern provinces annexed by the Soviet Union. Postwar development soon established Olsztyn as the region's major administrative and industrial centre, and it is now a prosperous and animated city of some 180,000 people.

Arrival, information and accommodation

The Stare Miasto is fifteen minutes' walk west of the **bus** and **train stations**; as an alternative to walking, just about any bus heading down aleja Partyzantów will drop you at plac Jana Pawła II. The **tourist information centre**, beside the High Gate at Staromiejska 1 (July & Aug Mon–Fri 8am–6pm, Sat & Sun 10am–3pm; June & Sept Mon–Fri 8am–5pm, Sat & Sun 10am–3pm; Oct–May Mon–Fri 8am–4pm; ☎089/535 3566, ⓔwcit@warmia.mazury.pl), will fill you

4

MAZURIA AND PODLASIE | Olsztyn

in on most aspects of tourism in the region. In the same building, PTTK/Mazury (Mon–Fri 8am–4pm, Sat 10am–2pm; ℡089/523 5320) organizes boat rental and accommodation for the Krutynia kayaking route (see box, p.209). There's a reasonable choice of cheap to moderate **hotels**, while the all-year **youth hostel** is about ten minutes' walk from the town centre in a pleasant red-brick house at ul. Kosciuszki 72/74 (℡089/527 6650; 25zł per person).

Hotels

Gromada pl. Konstytucji 3 Maja 4 ℡089/534 5864, ⓦwww.gromada.pl. Right opposite the train and bus stations, this ungainly concrete lump offers comfortable if unexciting rooms and guarded parking. Weekend discounts. ❺

Pod Zamkiem ul. Nowowiejskiego 10 ℡089/535 1287, ⓦhotel-olsztyn.com.pl. Right under the castle walls, this is a small and welcoming place in a carefully renovated Art Nouveau villa. Cute en suites with TV and wi-fi access. ❺

Relaks ul. Żołnierska 13A ℡089/527 7336, ⓦwww.osir.olsztyn.pl, ⓦwww.relaks.olsztyn.pl. A slightly tatty medium-rise block 1km south of the train and bus stations, with a choice of clean and comfortable doubles with shared bathroom (❷) or en suite (❺).

Villa Pallas ul. Żołnierska 4 ℡089/535 0115, ⓦwww.villapallas.pl. Early twentieth-century villa set in leafy grounds, within walking distance of the centre. Tasteful rooms with modern bathrooms, and a highly regarded restaurant. Ask about weekend discounts. ❻

Warmiński Kołobrzeska 1 ℡089/522 1400, ⓦwww.hotel-warminski.com.pl. Large, recently refurbished modern hotel aimed at the business market with correspondingly efficient service. Free internet access. ❻

Wysoka Brama ul. Staromiejska 1 ℡089/527 3675, ⓦwww.hotelwysokabrama.olsztyn.pl. Simply decorated, no-frills doubles right next to the High Gate at the entrance to Olsztyn's Old Town, and a cheap pizzeria on the ground floor. Rooms with shared facilities ❷; en suites ❸.

The Town

The main places to see are concentrated in the **Old Town**, and you won't need more than a couple of hours to take in the main sights. **Plac Jana Pawła II** is the modern town's central square, with the Gothic **High Gate** (Brama Wysoka) – the entrance to the Old Town – a short walk away at the end of ulica 11 Listopada. Once through the gate, ulica Staromiejska brings you to the **Rynek**. At the centre stands the former town hall, the older half of which is red-brick; the more recent eighteenth-century part is lemon yellow. Surrounding the square are houses with an extraordinary variety of gables, taking the form of pediments, peaks and coronets.

Over to the west is the **castle**, fourteenth-century but extensively rebuilt, surveying the steep little valley of the River Łyna. Its **museum** (Tues–Sun: June–Sept 9am–5pm; Oct–May 10am–4pm; 9zł) is an institution with an ideological mission: defining the region's historical record from an unashamedly Polish perspective. The ethnography section contains a good selection of folk costumes, art and furniture, while the historical section stresses the Warmians' general resistance to all things German. **Copernicus'** living quarters, on the first floor of the southwest wing, are the castle's other main feature; along with a wistful portrait by Matejko and several of the astronomer's instruments, the rooms contain a sundial supposed to have been designed by Copernicus himself. It's also worth making the climb up the **castle tower** (same ticket, June–Sept only) for the view over the town and surroundings. Directly below the castle is a large open-air **amphitheatre**, used for theatre and concert performances in summertime, nestled on the leafy banks of the River Łyna. Coming out of the back of the castle you can stroll across the bridge over the gently coursing river to the park on the other side – an atmospheric spot, particularly at sunset.

Back towards the centre, up from the castle entrance, there's a stern neo-Gothic Protestant **church**, formerly used by the predominantly non-Catholic German population. To get to the early fifteenth-century Catholic **cathedral**, whose high brick tower dominates the surroundings, walk back across the Rynek. Originally a grand parish church, it retains some of its original Gothic features, including an intricately patterned brick ceiling – among the most beautiful in the region – and a powerful Crucifixion triptych hanging over the high altar. Despite extensive renovations it's still a moodily atmospheric place.

Eating and drinking

Most eating and drinking venues are concentrated in the Old Town where there's a bar or pub every fifty metres or so, and a fair sprinkling of good restaurants, too.

Restaurants

Bar Dziupla Stare Miasto 9/10. Order-at-the-counter snack bar with a tasty selection of soups, potato pancakes, pork chops and *pierogi*, all cheaply priced. Daily 8.30am–8.30pm.

Greenway Prosta 11. Branch of a Poland-wide chain serving up inexpensive and filling vegetarian food. Tortilla wraps, tofu-filled stews, savoury and sweet pancakes and a good choice of salads. Mon–Sat 11am–8pm, Sun noon–8pm.

Karczma Jana ul. Kołłątaja 11. Traditional Polish restaurant near the bridge at the south end of the Old Town, serving good *pierogi* (16zł) and excellent steak, duck, lamb and venison dishes (40–50zł). Folksy pine furnishings, dried herbs and farm implements provide the requisite down-on-the-farm tone. Daily 11am–11pm.

Peperoni Prosta 38. Bright businesslike pizzeria that does good thin-crust pies in the 20–25zł range, alongside a handful of more substantial fish and veal dishes. Noon–10pm.

Przystań ul. Żeglarska 3. The one restaurant that is worth venturing beyond the Old Town to find, Przystań is a modern timber and glass pavilion on the shores of Lake Ukiel, 20min walk northwest of the centre. The menu covers everything in the Polish culinary repertoire but it's the fresh fish that stands out, with fillets of halibut, pike-perch or salmon clocking in at around 40zł. Daily noon–11pm.

Różana Café Targ Rybny 14. Mildly posh restaurant with plush furnishings, oil paintings on the walls and attentive service. High-quality Polish pork dishes plus duck, goose, rabbit and game. Mains in the 30–50zł bracket. Daily noon–11pm.

U Artystów Kołłątaja 20. Pitched midway between restaurant and lounge bar, U Artystów offers a bit more in the way of salads and pasta dishes than the other places in town. Good for fish also. Mains 25–35zł. Daily 11am–midnight.

Cafés and bars

Alchemia corner of Zamkowa & Okopowa. Soothingly atmospheric pub with paintings of ethereal-looking women on the walls, candles on the tables, and jazz, funk, blues or world music in the background. Sun–Thurs noon–midnight; Fri & Sat noon–3am.

Herbaciarnia Zen ul. Okopowa 23. Speciality teahouse serving brews from around the world, decent coffee and good ice cream. Sun–Thurs 11am–10pm, Fri & Sat 11am–11pm.

Jazz Club Bohema Targ Rybny 15. Roomy, popular pub with a long cocktail list and a small stage for occasional bands and DJs – although weekends usually feature dance music and chart hits rather than jazz pure and simple. Daily noon–2am.

Molotov Café Prosta 38. In the yard behind Peperoni (see above) and up the stairs, this friendly two-tier bar offers a regular menu of live indie bands, film screenings and jazz-to-reggae DJ nights (when there may be a 5-10zł cover charge). The big choice of bottled beers from around Europe provides a welcome alternative to the customary Polish lager swill. Mon–Sat 2pm–3am, Sun 6pm–3am.

Sarp ul. Kołłątaja 14. Smart café-bar housed in a restored granary with comfy deep chairs strewn around a wonderful half-timbered attic. Good list of cocktails, and outdoor riverside seating in summer. Daily noon–2am.

North of Olsztyn

If you're not eager to press straight on to the lakes, it's worth considering a day-trip to one of the old towns in the attractive countryside north of Olsztyn, much of which old belongs to the agriculturally rich province of

Warmia. Highlights are the churches and castles of **Orneta** and **Lidzbark Warmiński**, both of which lie an easy bus ride away from Olsztyn.

The forty-kilometre journey to Lidzbark Warmiński takes you through the open woodlands and undulating farmland characteristic of western Mazuria and if you've caught an early bus there should be time for a stopoff en route at **DOBRE MIASTO**, a small town with a vast Gothic **church** – the largest in the region after Frombork cathedral – rising majestically from the edge of the main road. Baroque ornamentation overlays much of the interior, and there's a florid late Gothic replica of Kraków's Mariacki altar.

Lidzbark Warmiński

Set amid open pastureland watered by the River Łyna, **LIDZBARK WARMIŃSKI** was an important outpost of the Teutonic Knights and subsequently served as the residence of the bishops of Warmia. Lidzbark was a significant centre of culture and learning in the sixteenth century – **Copernicus** lived here, just one member of a community of artists and scientists. Sadly, much of the old town centre was wiped out in 1945, with only the parish church, town gate and a few sections of the fortifications managing to survive the fighting. Lidzbark's impressive Teutonic **castle**, however, came through unscathed, a stylish, well-preserved, riverside fortress which ranks as one of the architectural gems of the region. Used as a fortified residence for the Warmian bishops, it echoes Frombork cathedral in its tiled roof; Malbork fortress in the turreted towers rising from the corners. Much of the building is now occupied by the **regional museum** (Tues–Sun: mid-May to Aug 9am–5pm; Sept to mid-May 9am–4pm; 8zł), which begins with portraits of Copernicus and other local luminaries before moving on to a display of **Gothic sculpture** in the Great Refectory. On the second floor is a collection of modern Polish art (not very riveting) as well as an exquisite exhibition of **icons**. These come from the convent at Wojnowo (see p.221), where the nuns are members of the strongly traditionalist **Old Believers** (*Starowiercy*) sect, a grouping which broke away from official Orthodoxy in protest at the religious reforms instigated by Peter the Great (see box, p.221).

The east wing of the castle was demolished in the mid eighteenth century to make way for a bishop's palace and gardens. The **winter garden** opposite the approach to the castle is the most attractive bit left, with a Neoclassical orangery that wouldn't be out of place in a royal residence. The tall **parish church** in the town centre is another Gothic brick hall structure, similar in style to Dobre Miasto: the aisles off the vaulted nave reveal some fine Renaissance side altars and old tombstones. The old Protestant church in town is now an **Orthodox church** used by the Eastern settlers who moved here following the postwar border shifts.

Orneta

Just under 50km northwest of Olsztyn lies **ORNETA**, a small market town that boasts one of the finest and most satisfying of Warmia's Gothic churches. It's well worth the detour to get here, and the journey itself is a real pleasure, passing through numerous attractive villages. Arriving in town by bus brings you almost immediately into the attractive old market square, at the centre of which stands the Gothic brick **town hall**, with a *kawiarnia* tucked away in its dimly lit medieval cellars.

Set slightly back from the square in one corner stands the magnificent, robust-looking Gothic **St John's Church** (Kościół św Jana). Here, for once, the austere brick facade customary in the Gothic churches of northern Poland is transformed by exuberant decoration. A welter of tall slender parapets rises up on all sides of the building, while close inspection of the carved walls reveals sequences of grotesquely contorted faces leering out at the world – the masons obviously retained their sense of humour. Above them, a set of five menacing-looking dragon heads jut out from the roof edge, spitting fire down on the onlooker. Surmounting the church is a

▲ St John's church, Orneta

characteristic high brick tower, thicker and stockier than usual, lending solidity to the ensemble. Inside, an unusually ornate high altarpiece and pulpit are matched by the large, solid-looking Baroque **organ** astride the entrance portal. A fine Gothic triptych stands in the right-hand aisle and Gothic and Renaissance murals decorate several of the side chapels, one sporting a colourful portrait of Renaissance-era Warmian cardinal Stanislaus Hosius.

By **bus**, Orneta is a one-and-a-half-hour journey from Olsztyn with departures every thirty to forty minutes, making it a feasible day-trip. Like Dobre Miasto, it's also on the Olsztyn–Braniewo rail line, with services running three times a day in each direction and taking one hour.

South of Olsztyn

Heading south from Olsztyn takes you into more of the attractive rolling countryside for which Warmia is known. The main reason for heading this way is the well-kept *skansen* at **Olsztynek**, with the nearby battlefield at **Grunwald** providing an additional worthwhile stopoff.

Olsztynek and around

OLSZTYNEK, 26km south of Olsztyn, is home to an excellent **skansen** (Tues–Sun: April & Oct 9am–3pm; May–Aug 9am–5.30pm; Sept 9am–4.30pm; 9zł). Located on the northern edge of the small town, the park is devoted to eighteenth- and nineteenth-century **folk architecture** from Warmia, Mazuria and Lithuania. Many fine examples of sturdy regional architecture have been gathered here: take a close look at the joints on some of the **half-timbered cottages** and you'll appreciate the superb workmanship that went into these buildings. Alongside the assorted farm buildings, barns, workshops and a water mill, there's a fine early- eighteenth-century wooden Protestant **church** with a thatched roof. The highlight of the lot, though, is undoubtedly the group of old windmills, two of them over two hundred years old. With its huge coloured blades and sturdy plank frame, the **Lithuanian mill** at the edge of the park, known as Paltrak, is a picture-postcard favourite.

Minibuses run to Olsztynek every thirty minutes from ulica Partyzantów, just outside Olsztyn train station. The *Karczma* at the *skansen* gates (mid-April to late Sept only) is a good spot for an inexpensive Polish lunch.

The Tannenberg Memorial

About a kilometre west of the *skansen*, close to the village of Sudwa, lie the ruins of the notorious **Tannenberg Memorial**. The original monument, consisting of eight towers surrounding a central enclosure for ritualistic parades, was built by the Germans in 1925 to commemorate Field Marshal Hindenburg's victory over the Russians at the battle of Tannenberg in August 1914. After Hindenburg's death in 1934, Hitler ordered the monument's transformation into a mausoleum for this much-loved military figure but, in 1945, with defeat in sight, the retreating Nazis moved Hindenburg's remains to Worms Cathedral in Germany. The mausoleum was subsequently blown up by the Germans and some of the stones were salvaged to help build the communist party headquarters in Warsaw. Though not marked on the road, you'll find it behind the village surrounded by oak trees, a large enclosure marking the site of what was once a massive structure.

Grunwald

If there's one historical event every Polish schoolchild can give you a date for it's the **Battle of Grunwald** (1410). One of the biggest and bloodiest battles of the medieval era, it saw the crushing defeat of the Teutonic Knights by a combined Polish-Lithuanian army commanded by King Władysław Jagiełło and his cousin Grand Duke Vytautas – the latter bringing a cosmopolitan contingent including Russians, Ukrainians and Tatars. Involving more than 30,000 men on each side, the battle left Grand Master Ulrich von Jungingen and an estimated 11,000 of his Knights dead, with another 14,000 taken prisoner. Victory at Grunwald removed the threat of Teutonic expansion, leaving both Poland and Lithuania free to concentrate on their eastern territories.

The battlefield

The **battle site** lies 20km southwest of Olsztynek. It's not easy to get here without your own vehicle – local buses run from Olsztynek and, less frequently, Olsztyn. The odd modern farmhouse apart, the battlefield probably doesn't look that different today from the site that greeted the opposing armies nearly six hundred years ago. Walking up from the bus stop past the souvenir kiosk brings you to the centrepiece of the site, an imposing thirty-metre-high **steel monument**) that looks uncannily like the Gdańsk Shipyard Memorial (set on a hilltop overlooking the battlefield. Just beyond the monument there's a large stone diagram set out on the ground illustrating the battle positions of the two armies and their movements throughout the fighting.

Back behind the monument, the Grunwald **museum** (May to mid-Oct daily 8am–6pm; 6zł) contains a few bits and pieces of armour and weaponry, some original, most later, copies. Unless you're able to read the Polish wall displays there's little of interest on show; much more interesting is the extraordinary 1960s building housing the museum which looks like a granite spaceship half-buried in the battlefield.

The Mazurian lakes

East of Olsztyn, the central Mazurian lakeland opens out amid thickening forests. In summer the biggest lakes – **Mamry** and **Śniardwy** – are real crowd-pullers, with all the advantages and disadvantages that brings. On the plus side, tourist facilities are well developed in many places, and you can rent sailing and canoeing equipment in all the major resorts. If the weather's good, Mazuria can get pretty busy on summer weekends, and accommodation can be hard to find in the main centres. If solitude and clean water are what you're after, the best advice is to get a detailed map and head for the smaller lakes: as a general principle, tranquillity increases as you travel east. In almost every village you'll find a house or two offering private rooms.

Among the highlights, **Mikołajki**, commanding the approaches to Lake Śniardwy in the centre of the region, is arguably the most pleasant and most attractively located of the major-league lakeside resorts; while **Giżycko** and **Węgorzewo**, both perched on the rim of Lake Mamry to the north, attract yachters and canoeists and are useful bases for exploring the lakes. **Ruciane-Nida** provides access to the lakes and waterways of southern Mazuria, and has a pleasantly laid-back, forest-shrouded feel. **Mrągowo**, the most westerly of the major towns and a useful transport hub, is nowadays best known

Canoeing in the lakes

If you like messing about in boats, one of the best and most exciting ways of exploring the region is from the water. The vast complex of **lakes**, **rivers** and **waterways** means there are literally thousands of options to choose from. For those who haven't lugged their canoes, kayaks and yachts on trailers all the way across Poland – and increasing numbers of Scandinavians and Germans are joining Poles in doing so every summer – the key issue is getting hold of the necessary equipment. It's becoming easier to turn up and rent yourself a canoe on the spot but demand is increasingly high in season, so it would definitely pay to try to organize yourself a boat in advance.

A good resource is the PTTK office in Olsztyn, ul. Staromiejska 1 (℡089/527 5156), which arranges kayak hire and advance accommodation bookings on some of the more popular routes. There are plenty of detailed maps of the region appropriate for canoeists: the most useful ones are the 1:120,000 *Wielkie Jezioro Mazurskie* and the new Polish–English language 1:300,000 *Warmia and Mazuria*.

Sorkwity and the Krutynia route

SORKWITY, 12km west of Mrągowo, is the starting point for a beautiful and popular canoeing run which ends 90km downstream at Lake Bełdany. As well as the PTTK in Olsztyn, the Orbis hotel in **Mrągowo** can help sort out canoe rental for the trip, but in summer advance notice is virtually essential. **Accommodation** along the route is provided by PTTK-run river stations (*stanice wodne*; usually open from mid-April to Sept); basically, these are kayak and canoe depots which also have bungalows and camping space.

Canoeists generally start from the *stanica wodna* at the edge of Sorkwity village. Known as the **Krutynia route**, after the narrow, winding river that makes up the last part of the journey, the route takes you through a succession of eighteen lakes, connected by narrow stretches of river, the banks often covered with dense forest. The journey takes anything from nine days upwards, with Ruciane-Nida or Mikołajki the final destination, though you can also shorten the route to a five-day trip ending at Krutyń. The Krutynia route is very popular in high summer, so the best time to make the trip is either in spring or late summer. Overnight stops are generally in the following places (in *stanice wodne* unless specified):

day one BIEŃKI (15km)

day two BABIĘTA (12km); there's also a youth hostel here (July–Aug)

day three SPYCHOWO (12.5km)

day four ZGON (10.5km)

day five KRUTYŃ (14km)

day six UTKA (18.5km), the first stop on the Krutynia river itself

day seven NOWY MOST (6.5km)

day eight KAMIEŃ (10.5km) on the beautiful Lake Bełdany

day nine ending up at RUCIANE-NIDA (13.5km; see p.220)

Olsztyn PTTK offers ten-day kayak trips along the route including overnight stops for around 850zł. You will need to provide your own gear, including a sleeping bag. For **advance booking** (strongly recommended in summer) write to or call the office.

---

for its country and western festival. As well as lakeside pursuits, Mazuria also has a wealth of historic churches and castles, including the famous monastery complex at **Święta Lipka** and the Gothic ensemble at **Reszel**. A detour into the region's complex ethnic history is provided by the Orthodox nunnery at **Wojnowo**. In addition, Mazuria hides one of the strangest and most chilling of

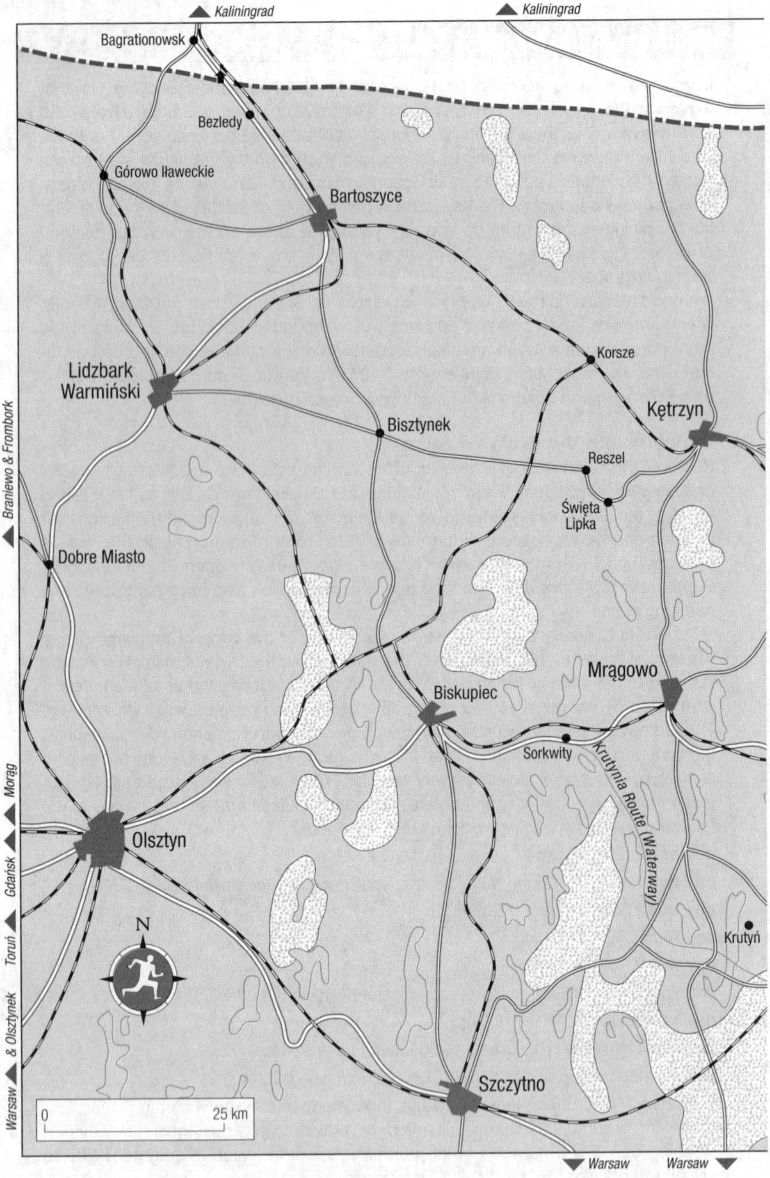
Kaliningrad
Kaliningrad
Bagrationowsk
Bezledy
Górowo Iławeckie
Bartoszyce
Lidzbark Warmiński
Bisztynek
Korsze
Kętrzyn
Reszel
Święta Lipka
Braniewo & Frombork
Dobre Miasto
Mrągowo
Biskupiec
Sorkwity
Krutynia Route (Waterway)
Olsztyn
Morąg
Gdańsk
Toruń
Warsaw & Olsztynek
N
Krutyń
Szczytno
0
25 km
Warsaw
Warsaw

all World War II relics, Hitler's wartime base at **Gierłoz** – a short bus ride away from the pleasant small town of **Kętrzyn**.

On the whole, **transport** around the lakes isn't too problematic. While a car is a definite advantage for venturing into the further-flung reaches, **bus** connections between the main centres are more than adequate. **Olsztyn** is the usual jumping-off point if you're heading this way, while

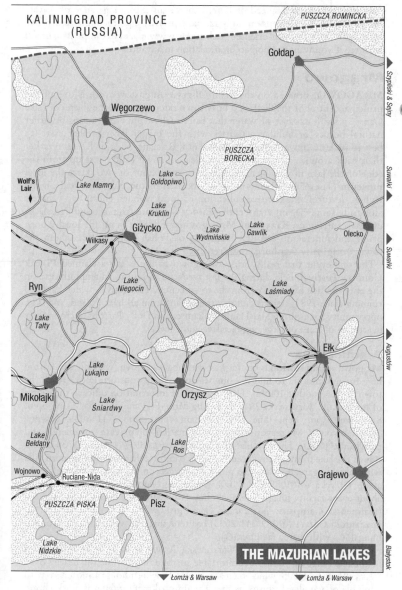

KALININGRAD PROVINCE
(RUSSIA)

PUSZCZA ROMINCKA

Gołdap

Węgorzewo

PUSZCZA
BORECKA

Lake
Gołdopiwo

Wolf's
Lair

Lake Mamry

Lake
Kruklin

Giżycko

Lake
Wydmińskie

Lake
Gawlik

Olecko

Wilkasy

Ryn

Lake
Niegocin

Lake
Laśmiady

Lake
Tałty

Ełk

Lake
Łukajno

Mikołajki

Lake
Śniardwy

Orzysz

Lake
Bełdany

Lake
Ros

Wojnowo

Ruciane-Nida

Grajewo

PUSZCZA PISKA

Pisz

Lake
Nidzkie

THE MAZURIAN LAKES

Szypliński & Sejny

Suwałki

Suwałki

Augustów

Białystok

Łomża & Warsaw

Łomża & Warsaw

Mrągowo and **Giżycko** offer most in the way of onward connections to smaller resorts once you arrive. In addition, a number of **railway lines** run east from Olsztyn towards the lakes: one goes through Kętrzyn and Giżycko, another through Mrągowo and Mikołajki, and a third through Ruciane-Nida – though services on these lines tend to be less frequent than buses.

As well as the usual spread of hotels, there's an expanding range of private rooms and B&B-style pensions in Mazuria, especially in burgeoning resorts like Mikołajki. The tourism-oriented website Ⓦwww.mazury.com.pl is a useful resource if you want to book accommodation in advance.

Mrągowo

MRĄGOWO, situated on the main Olsztyn–Augustów road, is one of the principal centres of the district, a busy town ranged around the shores of Lake Czos – a small expanse of water that can't really compete in terms of either natural beauty or holiday activities with the bigger lakes further east. It's best to pick up onward **buses** to Mikołajki, Ruciane-Nida or Kętrzyn rather than stick around, although there's a pleasant town centre just up from the edge of the lake in which to while away a spare hour or two. Here the local **museum** (Tues–Sun 10am–4pm; 6zł), housed in the old town hall on the Rynek, features an extensive collection of local wooden chests and cabinets alongside some elegant eighteenth-century furniture from around Prussia. A display centring on **Krzysztof Mrongoviusz** fills you in on the locally born priest and nineteenth-century champion of Polish culture after whom the town – originally Sensburg – was renamed in 1945.

The one event that really brings Mrągowo to life is the acclaimed **Piknik Country Festival**, held during the last weekend in July in an amphitheatre on the opposite side of the lake from the town centre. The festival, which has been running since 1983, attracts country music fans from all over Poland, and is an opportunity for aspiring Slav Hank Williamses and Dolly Partons to croon their hearts out in front of large, appreciative audiences.

Practicalities

Mrągowo's **train station** is on the western fringes of town: walk downhill from here for ten minutes to find the **bus station**, where you turn left to reach the town centre (another 10min). There's a **tourist information** office in the centre of town at ul. Warszawska 26 (July & Aug Mon–Fri 9am–5pm, Sat 10am–5pm, Sun 10am–4pm; Sept–June Mon–Fri 8am–4pm; ℡089/741 8039, Ⓦwww.it.mragowo.pl), where you can get information on **private rooms** (❷) and **pensjonats** (❹–❺). The *Edyta*, at ul. Laskowa 10 (℡089/741 4366; ❻) on the far side of the lake from the town centre, offers comfortable rooms in a modern villa with lakeside garden, while the plush *Mrongovia*, on the eastern edge of town at ul. Giżycka 6 (℡089/743 3100, Ⓦwww.mrongovia.hotel.pl; ❽), has just about every facility imaginable, including two swimming pools, tennis and spa treatments. **Campsite** *Jaszczurcza Góra*, just below the *Mrongovia* at ul. Jaszczurcza Góra 1 (℡089/741 2533) has tent space as well as simple wooden bungalows with shared facilities (❷).

For **eating**, try *Lasagne* at ul. Warszawska 7c which offers pasta dishes and a reasonable range of pizzas in comfortable surroundings, while the nearby *Stara Chata*, Warszawska 9b, which recreates an old-time farmhouse atmosphere with a jumble of wooden furnishings, has a traditional menu taking in pork chops, fried fish and *kołduny* (meat-filled *pierogi* from Lithuania).

Święta Lipka

Some 20km north and a forty-minute bus ride from Mrągowo is the church at **ŚWIĘTA LIPKA**, probably the country's most famous Baroque shrine. Lodged on a thin strip of land in between two lakes, this magnificent **church** is stuck out in the middle of nowhere but – as an approach area stuffed with souvenir stalls suggests – the out-of-the-way location doesn't stop the tourists turning up in droves. As an important Marian shrine the church is jammed with pilgrims during religious festivals, creating an intense atmosphere of fervent Catholic devotion.

The name Święta Lipka – literally "holy lime tree" – derives from a local medieval legend according to which a Prussian tribal leader, released from imprisonment by the Teutonic Knights, is supposed to have placed a statue of the Virgin in a lime tree as a token of thanks. Within a few years healing **miracles** were being reported at the place, and a chapel was built on the site by the Knights in 1320. Following their conversion to Lutheranism, the Knights destroyed the chapel in 1526. The ruins were purchased for the Polish Crown in 1620, and Jesuits brought in from neighbouring Lithuania to run the site. The present basilica was begun in 1687 under the direction of Vilnius architect Jerzy Ertly – so to anyone familiar with the churches of the Lithuanian capital, the "Eastern" Baroque of Święta Lipka will come as no surprise.

The church

In a country with a major predilection for Baroque richness, Święta Lipka is unquestionably one of the most exuberant of them all. Approached from a country road, the tapering twin towers of the church **facade** and plain yellow and white stucco covering the exterior are quintessential eastern Polish Baroque. **Entrance** to the complex (Mon–Sat 8am–6pm; Sun in between Masses) is through a magnificent early eighteenth-century wrought-iron gate designed by Johann Schwartz, a local from Reszel.

Inside, much of the ceiling is covered by superb **frescoes** by local painter Maciej Meyer, depicting themes ranging from the lives of Christ and Mary to the Marian cult of Święta Lipka itself. The lofty main **altarpiece**, imposing wooden structure completed in 1714, has three levels: the upper two contain pictures on biblical themes; the lowest a seventeenth-century icon of the Madonna and Child based on an original kept at Santa Maria Maggiore in Rome. Imitating the original medieval shrine, a rather grubby-looking eighteenth-century lime tree stands to the left of the altar, topped by a silver statue of the Virgin and Child, the base smothered in pennants pinned there by devout pilgrims.

Filling virtually the entire west end of the building is the church's famous Baroque **organ** – a huge, fantastically ornate creation, decked with two layers of blue gilded turrets topped by figures of the saints, built in 1720 by Johann Mozengel, a Jew from Königsberg. During the regular organ performances (May–Sept: hourly 9.30–11.30am & 1.30–5.30pm; April & Oct: at 10am, noon and 2pm) the whole instrument appears to come alive, with gyrating angels playing mandolins, cherubs blowing horns, stars jingling and cymbals crashing – an extraordinary sight and sound. Additionally, there are special evening organ **concerts** every second and fourth Friday of the month in July and August.

Practicalities

Święta Lipka is easy to do as a **day trip**, with hourly buses from Kętrzyn, which is on the main Olsztyn–Giżycko rail route. Otherwise, there are a couple of daily direct services from Mrągowo. The *Hotel 500* (℡089/755 3737, ⓦwww .hotel500.com.pl; ⓺) over the road from the church offers smart en suites and a **restaurant** with a terrace overlooking the church.

Reszel

Some 6km northwest of Święta Lipka is the historic Warmian centre of **RESZEL**. Seat of the bishops of Warmia for over five centuries, from the establishment of Christianity in the region (1254) until the First Partition (1772), Reszel is another of Copernicus' many old regional haunts. These days the town is another quiet end-of-the-world provincial hangout, the main attraction being the fourteenth-century bishop's **castle**, just uphill from the small Old Town.

An impressive red-brick hulk surrounded by the ruins of the old town walls, the castle now houses a contemporary **art gallery** (Tues–Sun: mid-May to mid-Sept 10am–5pm; mid-Sept to mid-May 10am–4pm; 5zł) featuring regular exhibitions by artists from Poland and abroad. Painters and sculptors are regularly invited to live and work in the castle for a few months, so in summer in particular the place is a mine of creative activity. To enjoy the views over the surrounding countryside you can climb the castle tower (same hours and same ticket as the gallery).

Practicalities

Reszel is served by numerous daily buses from Kętrzyn; it's also easily accessible by bus from Mrągowo or Olsztyn. There's a rather stylish **hotel** in the castle, the *Zamek Reszel*, whose rooms feature plenty of exposed brickwork and rustic-looking wooden furniture (☎089/755 0109, ⓦwww.zamek-reszel.com; ❻, ask about student reductions). Down in the town a cheaper option is the neat and cosy *Pensjionat U Renaty* at ul. Wyspiańskiego 3 (☎089/755 2160, ⓦwww.u-renaty.reszel.pl; ❸). The castle **restaurant** is a good place to try fish from the local lakes; while the chic **café** inside the castle courtyard is exactly what you'd expect of an artists' centre – more *quartier Latin* than back-of-the-woods Warmia.

Kętrzyn

Known as Rastenburg until its return to Polish rule in 1945, **KĘTRZYN**, 15km east of Święta Lipka, is a quiet, unexceptional town whose main interest lies in its proximity to Gierłoz – Hitler's **Wolf's Lair** (*Wilczy Szaniec*). It does at least boast a well-restored Teutonic Knights' castle which is home to a regional **museum** (mid-June to mid-Sept: Mon–Fri 9am–6pm, Sat & Sun 9am–5pm; mid-Sept to mid-May: Mon, Sat & Sun 9am–3pm, Tues–Fri 9am–4pm; 6zł) housing an exhibition combining local archeology and wildlife. If you don't get to see boars, beavers or badgers in the Mazurian wild you'll find plenty of stuffed ones here, alongside a selection of similarly preserved eagles, owls, cormorants and other birds. The second floor is largely devoted to **Wojciech Kętrzyński**, a nineteenth-century local historian and patriot, the epitome of the sort of character after whom the postwar Polish authorities renamed Mazurian towns.

Practicalities

Kętrzyn is easily accessible from either Olsztyn or Giżycko (by train) or Mikołajki (by bus). The **tourist information office**, sharing premises with Orbis at pl. Piłsudskiego 1 (Mon–Fri 8.30am–4pm; ☎089/751 2040, ⓦwww.ketrzyn.com.pl), will fill you in on **private room** possibilities (❷–❹), although most of these are in outlying farms. The *Zajazd Pod Zamkiem* **hotel**, ul. Struga 3a (☎089/752 3117; ❺), offers comfortable en-suite rooms in a pretty old house at the castle gates, and has a good **restaurant** with an outdoor terrace.

The Wolf's Lair

It's among the forests just north of **GIERŁOZ**, 8km east of Kętrzyn, that Hitler established the **Wolf's Lair** (Wilczy Szaniec in Polish, Wolfss-chanze in German: daily 8am–dusk; 10zł plus 8zł for parking; 50zł for an English-speaking guide; ⓦwww.wolfsschanze.pl), a huge underground command centre responsible for the entire Eastern Front. Private bunkers encased in several metres of concrete were built for Nazi bigwigs Bormann, Göring, Himmler and **Hitler** himself, alongside offices, SS quarters and operation rooms. The 27-acre site was camouflaged by a suspended screen of vegetation that was altered to match the changing seasons. In 1945 the retreating **Germans** attempted to blow the whole place up but succeeded in only cracking the bunkers, ensuring the Wolf's Lair's survival as one of Mazuria's most popular – and most sobering – tourist attractions. The site can be reached from Kętrzyn by a regular municipal bus service (#1; June–Sept only), or by Kętrzyn–Węgorzewo buses, some (but not all) of which pass the site. Be careful to check return times, and allow two hours to look around.

Peering into the cavernous underground bunkers today is an eerie experi-ence. You can see the place, for example, where the assassination attempt on Hitler failed in July 1944 (see box, pp.216–217), the SS living quarters, the staff cinema and other ancillaries of domestic Nazi life. Gruesome photographs and films remind visitors of the scale of German atrocities but, as so often with such material, there's a tendency to resort to horrifying images at the expense of information and critical explanation.

The **airstrip** from which von Stauffenberg departed after his abortive assas-sination attempt is a couple of kilometres east from the main site, a lone runway in the middle of some heathland – you'll need a guide to show you the way.

There's a simple **hotel** at the bunker site, *Wilcze Gniazdo* (☏089/752 4429; ❸), and you can pitch a tent or park a trailer in the grounds. There's also a reasonable **restaurant** at the hotel, although it may only be open during the day.

Giżycko

Squeezed between Lake Niegocin and the marshy backwaters of Lake Mamry, **GIŻYCKO** is one of the main lakeland centres. It was flattened in 1945, however, and the rebuilding didn't create a lot of character: if greyish holiday-resort architecture lowers your spirits, don't plan to stay for long before heading out for the lakes. **Wilkasy** (see p.218) is a much more pleasant base.

The Town

The liveliest part of town is the attractive waterside area south of the centre on the shores of Lake Niegocin, characterized by grassy open spaces and occasional stands of trees. Here you'll find the passenger jetty for **boat trips** (see box, p.219), and a swanky yachting marina. Carry on westwards for about a kilometre and you'll reach Giżycko's principal historical sight, **Boyen Fortress** (Twierdza Boyen), an enormous star-shaped affair built by the Prussians in the mid-nineteenth century to shore up their defences against the tsarist empire. A walking trail takes you all the way around the ramparts (allow at least thirty minutes for the full circuit), allowing excellent views of red-brick barrack blocks, gun emplacements and defensive ditches. There's a small museum near the entrance to the fortress, run by volunteers and open in the summer season.

The July Bomb Plot

In the summer of 1944, the Wolf's Lair was the scene of the assassination attempt on Adolf Hitler that came closest to success – the **July Bomb Plot**. Its leader, **Count Claus Schenk von Stauffenberg**, an aristocratic officer and member of the General Staff, had gained the support of several high-ranking members of the German army. Sickened by atrocities on the Eastern Front, and rapidly realizing that the Wehrmacht was fighting a war that could not possibly be won, von Stauffenberg and his fellow conspirators decided to kill the Führer, seize control of army headquarters in Berlin and sue for peace with the Allies. Germany was on the precipice of total destruction by the Allies and the Soviet Army: only such a desperate act, reasoned the plotters, could save the Fatherland.

On July 20, Stauffenberg was summoned to the Wolf's Lair to brief **Hitler** on troop movements on the Eastern Front. In his briefcase was a small bomb, packed with high explosive: once triggered, it would explode in under ten minutes. As Stauffenberg approached the specially built conference hut, he triggered the device. Taking his place a few feet from Hitler, Stauffenberg positioned the **briefcase** under the table, leaning it against one of the table's stout legs no more than six feet away from the Führer. Five minutes before the bomb exploded, Stauffenberg slipped from the room unnoticed by the generals and advisers, who were listening to a report on the central Russian front. One of the officers moved closer to the table to get a better look at the campaign maps and, finding the briefcase in the way of his feet, picked it up and moved it to the other side of the table leg. Now, the very solid support of the table leg lay between the briefcase and Hitler.

At 12.42 the bomb went off. Stauffenberg, watching from a few hundred yards away, was shocked by the force of the **explosion**. It was, he said, as if the hut had been hit by a 155mm shell; there was no doubt that the Führer, along with everyone else in the room, was dead.

Stauffenberg hurried off to a waiting plane and made his way to **Berlin** to join the other conspirators. Meanwhile, Hitler and the survivors staggered out into the daylight: four people had been killed, including Colonel Brandt, who had moved Stauffenberg's briefcase and thus unwittingly saved the Führer's life. Hitler himself, despite being badly shaken, suffered no more than a **perforated eardrum** and minor injuries.

It did not take long to work out what had happened and the **hunt** for Stauffenberg was on. Hitler issued orders to the SS in Berlin to summarily execute anyone who was slightly suspect, and dispatched Himmler to the city to quell the rebellion.

West of here is the modern town centre around plac Grunwaldzki. Head uphill to reach the **Pressure Tower** (Wieża Ciśnień; May–Oct daily 9am–10pm; 10zł), a sturdy red-brick water tower with a panoramic viewing deck complete with café at its summit.

Practicalities

The adjacent **train and bus stations** are at the eastern end of the Niegocin lakefront, ten minutes' walk downhill from the town centre. The **tourist office**, plac Grunwaldzki (Mon–Fri 9am–4pm; ☎087/428 5265, ⓦwww.gizycko.turystyka.pl), will point you in the direction of private rooms (❷); otherwise the cheapest option is the **youth hostel** near the bus and train stations at ul. Kolejowa 10 (☎087/428 2224; dorm beds from 22zł per person). The *Zamek*, between the centre and the fortress at ul. Moniuszki 1 (☎087/428 2419; ⓦwww.cmazur.pl; ❺) offers tidy little rooms in an attractive wooded area near the lake. The same company operates the *Wodnik*, ul. 3 Maja 2 (☎087/428 3872, ⓦwww.cmazur.pl; ❻) a big concrete affair just off ulica

Back in the military Supreme Command headquarters in Berlin, the conspiracy was in chaos. Word reached Stauffenberg and the two main **army conspirators**, generals Beck and Witzleben, that the Führer was still alive; they had already lost hours of essential time by failing to issue the carefully planned order to mobilize their sympathizers in the city and elsewhere, and had even failed to carry out the obvious precaution of severing all communications out of the city. After a few hours of tragicomic scenes as the conspirators tried to persuade high-ranking officials to join them, the Supreme Command HQ was surrounded by SS troops. The coup was over.

The conspirators were gathered together, taken to the courtyard of the HQ and, under the orders of General Fromm, shot by firing squad. Stauffenberg's last words were "Long live our sacred Germany!" Fromm had known about the plot almost from the beginning, but had refused to join it. By executing the leaders he hoped to save his own skin – and, it must be added, knowingly saved them from the torturers of the SS.

Hitler's **ruthless revenge** on the conspirators was without parallel even in the bloody annals of the Third Reich. All the colleagues, friends and immediate relatives of Stauffenberg and the other conspirators were rounded up, tortured and taken before the "People's Court", where they were humiliated and given more-or-less automatic **death sentences**. Many of those executed knew nothing of the plot and were found guilty merely by association. As the bloodlust grew, the Nazi Party used the plot as a pretext for settling old scores, and eradicated anyone who had the slightest hint of anything less than total dedication to the Führer. General Fromm, who had ordered the execution of the conspirators, was among those tried, found guilty of cowardice and shot by firing squad. Those whose names were blurted out under torture were quickly arrested, the most notable being Field Marshal Rommel, who, because of his popularity, was given the choice of a trial in the People's Court or suicide and a state funeral. He opted for the state funeral.

The July Bomb Plot caused the deaths of at least **five thousand people**, including some of Germany's most brilliant military thinkers and almost all of those who would have been best qualified to run the postwar German government. Within six months the country lay in **ruins** as the Allies and Soviet Army advanced; had events been only a little different, the entire course of the war – and European history – would have been altered incalculably.

Warszawska that offers fully equipped but rather bland rooms. There's also a **campsite** next to the *Hotel Zamek* (May–Sept; ☏087/428 2419).

The best **restaurant** in town is the *Siwa Czapla*, occupying a half-timbered building at the western end of the lakefront at ul. Nadbrzeżna 11; fish, but also Polish staples like *pierogi* and potato pancakes with imaginative fillings, are on offer here. There's also a big range of fish dishes at *Pod Złotą Rybką*, ul. Olsztyńska 15. There are several **bars** along the lakefront in summer, while *Pub Jazz Club*, in the town centre at ul. Warszawska 17 is an unpretentious but lively place for a night out.

Giżycko is one of the main bases for **yacht charter** companies, with craft being rented out between May and September – bear in mind that in peak periods (July & Aug), yachts often cannot be chartered for anything less than a seven-day period. Places at which to make enquiries include *Marina Bełbot*, ul. Smętka 20a (☏087/428 0385, ⓦwww.marina.com.pl), and *Wiking*, ul. Królowej Jadwigi 10/9 (☏087/428 9602, ⓦwww.wiking.mazury.info.pl). Depending on whether you're looking for a four- or six-person craft, you'll be paying 250–450zł per day in high season, 100zł less in May and September.

Wilkasy

Some 5km west of Giżycko, and served by Giżycko–Mikołajki buses, **WILKASY** is a pleasingly laid-back holiday resort squeezed onto a neck of land separating Lake Niegocin from the smaller Lake Tajty to the west. If you want to experience how Poles (who flood the place in summer) take their Mazurian holidays, this is the place to head for, with its assortment of lakeside peaceful homes, holiday cabins and hostels – and may make for a more peaceful base than Giżycko itself. Apart from some nice enclosed swimming areas by the lakes, the other attraction of Wilkasy is that it's easy to **rent canoes** or **kayaks** here. Before they are allowed to set oar to water, Poles have to produce an official card proving they can swim, but you should be able to persuade the attendants to let you aboard. It makes for a pleasant day, paddling round the lake, hiving off into reed beds or canals as the fancy takes you.

Best place to **stay** for an activity-based holiday is the *Osródek AZS*, ul. Niegocińska 5 (☏087/428 0700, ⓦwww.azs-wilkasy.com.pl), a sizeable settlement of simple chalets (❸) and a well-appointed hotel (❻), complete with tennis courts and boat-rental. Other alternatives include the *Tajty*, ul. Przemysłowa 17 (☏087/428 0194, ⓦwww.hoteltajty.pl; ❺), a medium-sized, family-oriented hotel with respectable en suites; and the *Fregata*, a cosy pension in the southwestern part of the resort beside the Mrągowo road at Olsztyńska 86 (☏087/428 0202, ⓔpensjonat.fregata@poczta.onet.pl; ❹). Plenty of fish-and-chip stalls sprout up during the summer, and both the *AZS* and the *Tajty* have solid **restaurants**.

Mikołajki

Hyped in the brochures as the Mazurian Venice, **MIKOŁAJKI** is unquestionably the most attractive of the top Mazurian resorts. Straddled across the meeting point of two attractive small lakes – the Tałty and Mikołajskie – the small town has long provided a base for yachting enthusiasts on popular nearby Lake Śniardwy. Legend associates the town's name with a **monster** creature, known as the King of the Whitefish, that terrorized the local fishermen and destroyed their nets. The beast finally met its match in a young local boy called Mikołaj who caught the huge fish in a steel fishing net.

Despite being the most popular resort in Mazuria among well-heeled Varsovians, present-day Mikołajki has succeeded in retaining its low-rise, **fishing village** appearance. There's been a rash of new construction work in recent years – mostly in the form of luxury flats and shops – but new buildings have by and large blended in with their surroundings, aping the half-timbered styles of the past. Although there's an abundance of decent **accommodation**, it can be hard work finding a place to stay on summer weekends.

Arrival, information and accommodation

The **train station** is twenty minutes' walk northeast of the centre, while the **bus station** lies just west of the centre next door to the Protestant church. From here, a five-minute walk down ulica 3 Maja will bring you to the main square, plac Wolności. At no. 3, you'll find the **tourist office** (May–Sept Mon–Fri 9am–6pm; ☏087/421 6852, ⓦwww.mikolajki.pl), where you can enquire about **kayak** and **boat rental**. Most of the lakeside hotels also have their own stock of canoes and watersports equipment for use by guests, some also extending to bicycles.

The tourist office will direct you towards private rooms (❸) and **pensjonaty** (❹–❻). Otherwise it's a question of looking for the numerous *wolne pokoje* signs

Boat trips on the main lakes

From mid-April to October the Żegluga Mazurska boat company (Ⓦ www.zeglugama-
zurska.pl) runs regular **ferry services** on the main lakes. Numerous itineraries are on
offer, ranging from short circuits around a particular lake, to longer trips linking Mazuria's
main towns. They're intended as tourist excursions rather than as a means of public
transport, but they represent a scenic and leisurely way of getting around. Prices are
about 30zł per person for the shorter trips, rising to about 75zł per person for a long trip
through the whole lake system. Some of the more important routes are as follows:

Giżycko–Mikołajki (3hr–4hr 30min)
Węgorzewo–Giżycko–Mikołajki (7hr 30min)
Mikołajki–Ruciane (2hr 30min)
Giżycko–Węgorzewo (2hr 30min)

During peak season (June–Aug) boats depart daily; otherwise, depending on
demand, it's likely to be weekends and national holidays only. Often packed, the
boats are mostly large, open-deck steamers with a basic snack bar on board for
refreshments. **Tickets** are purchased at the passenger jetties at each stop, or on the
boats themselves. **Timetables** (*rozkłady*) for departures are posted by the jetties at
all the major lakeside stopoff points, and should also be available from the tourist
offices in both Mikołajki and Giżycko. Otherwise contact Żegluga Mazurska's main
office in Giżycko at al. Wojska Polskiego 8 (℡ 087/428 5332).

hanging outside private houses: ulica Kajki, the main street running east from
the square, is a good place to start looking.

There are plenty of **hotels** and **pensions** to choose from. The main
campsite is the *Wagabunda*, perched on a hill above town at ul. Leśna 2
(℡ 087/421 6018), a large tree-shaded site with bungalows and plenty of
space for tents and caravans. In addition, numerous private gardens across the
footbridge from the town centre accept tent-campers in summer (look for
pole namiotowe signs).

Hotels and pensions

Gołębiewski ul. Mrągowska 34 ℡ 087/429 0700,
Ⓦ www.golebiewski.pl. This 600-room mammoth
northwest of town is a resort in itself, fully equipped
for family holidays, with indoor pools, ice rink, riding
stables, golf course and tennis courts. **❽**

Król Sielaw ul. Kajki 5 ℡ 087/421 6323, Ⓦ www
.krolsielaw.mazury.info. Small and intimate hotel
with neat en suites, including some cosy mansard-
roofed rooms on the top floor. Also one triple room
and a four-person apartment. **❹**

Mazur pl. Wolności 6 ℡ 087/421 6941, Ⓦ www
.hotelmazur.pl. Nineteenth-century villa on the main
square, with stylish if petite en suites. **❻**

Mikołajki ul. Kajki 18 ℡ 087/421 6437, Ⓦ www
.pensjonatmikolajki.pl. Attractive pension in a
creaky but comfortable house that backs right onto
the lakeside promenade. **❺**

Na Skarpie ul. Kajki 96 ℡ 087/421 9950,
Ⓦ mazury.info.pl/naskarpie. Large, modern pension
with comfortable if characterless en suites and an
attractive lakeside position. **❺**

The Town

Most activity centres on the waterfront, just downhill from the main Rynek.
Here you'll find an extensive **marina**, thronging with yachting types over
the summer, and a generous collection of outdoor **cafés** and **bars**. Working
your way west along the waterfront towards the three bridges (foot, road and
rail) brings you to the passenger jetty used by the excursion boats operated by
Żegluga Mazurska (see box, above). There's also a **beach** of sorts on the other
side of the lake (basically a grassy area with a couple of wooden piers), reached
by crossing the footbridge and bearing left.

Unusually for modern Poland, the main church in town is the Protestant **Holy Trinity Church** (Kościół św. Trójcy), overlooking the shores of Lake Tałty. Designed by German architect Franz Schinkel, this solid-looking early nineteenth-century structure is the centre of worship for the region's Protestant community. Portraits of two early pastors apart, it's a fairly spartan place, light years away in feel from the usual Catholic churches.

Lake Łukajno

Prime out-of-town attraction is the nature reserve round **Lake Łukajno**, 4km east of town and home to one of Europe's largest remaining colonies of wild swans. It's an easy walk across rolling countryside, following the signed road which heads eastwards just uphill from Mikołajki bus station. The best viewing point is the **look-out tower** (*wieża widokowa*), signposted off the road and located at the lake's edge, though whether you get to see the birds is a matter of luck and timing. The best months are July and August, when the birds change their feathers – from a distance, the surface of the lake can look like a downy bed.

Eating and drinking

The *Cukiernia* at ulica 3 Maja 4 is the best place to stock up on **bread and pastries**, and it also does a roaring trade in waffles (*gofry*) piled high with fruit and cream. *Café Mocca*, between plac Wolności and the lakefront at Kowalska 4, does a decent **set- breakfast**, alongside cheap **lunches** and good ice cream. There are any number of stalls along the lakefront offering cheap **fried fish**: *Okoń*, just beneath the main road bridge into town, is one of the more stylish of the fry-up joints. Slightly inland, *Cinema Malajkino*, pl. Wolności 10, serves up a good-quality meat and fish menu in a movie-themed interior, and has a terrace from which you can observe goings-on on the square, while *Pizzeria Królewska* in the *Hotel Sielaw* (see p.219) is a good spot for pizza. For **drinking**, *Prohibicja*, plac Handlowy 13, is part-pub, part-piano bar, and has a decent choice of cocktails as well as a menu of full meals.

Ruciane-Nida

Some 25km south of Mikołajki along a scenic forest road is the lakeside resort of **RUCIANE-NIDA**. Actually two towns connected by a short stretch of road, it's an understandably popular holiday centre, offering a combination of forest and lakeland. Ruciane, the resort end of town, provides the main focus of interest; Nida is home to some postwar concrete housing blocks, a deserted factory and little else.

Travelling south from the town you're soon into the depths of the **Pisz Forest** (Puszcza Piska), a characteristic Mazurian mix of woodlands and water. A huge tangle of crystal-clear lakes, lazy winding rivers and dense forest thickets, it's the largest *puszcza* in the region, one of the surviving remnants of the primeval forest that once covered much of northeastern Europe. The forest is mainly pine – many of the trees reaching thirty to forty metres in height – with some magnificent pockets of mixed oak, beech and spruce in between. A favourite with both canoers – the Krutynia River (see box, p.209) runs south through the middle of the forest – and walkers, who use the area's developed network of hiking trails, the Puszcza Piska is a delightful area well worth exploring.

Practicalities

Despite its forest location, Ruciane-Nida is fairly accessible, with regular **trains** from Olsztyn, and **buses** from Mrągowo and (less frequently) Mikołajki. Arriving by train from the Olsztyn direction, Ruciane is the first stopoff point – although

The Old Believers

The origins of the Old Believers – or *Staroviertsii* as they are known in Russian – lie in the liturgical reforms introduced into the Russian Orthodox Church by Nikon, the mid-seventeenth-century patriarch of Moscow. Faced with the task of systematizing the divergent liturgical texts and practices then in use in the national church, Nikon opted to comply with the dominant Greek practices of the time, such as the use of three fingers instead of two when making the sign of the cross, and the use of Greek ecclesiastical dress. Priests who opposed the reforms were removed from office, but many of their congregations persisted with the old practices and were dubbed "Old Believers" by a church hierarchy eager to see them marginalized. Peter the Great was particularly keen to get rid of them and it was under his rule that groups of Old Believers moved to Lake Peipsi in modern-day Estonia – and other areas on the western fringes of the empire – in the hope that here at least they would be left alone to practise their religion as they wished. In liturgical matters, the Old Believers are egalitarian, rejecting the ecclesiastical hierarchy of conventional Orthodoxy, choosing clergy from among the local community rather than relying on a priesthood. Services are conducted in Old Church Slavonic – the medieval tongue into which the scriptures were originally translated – rather than in modern Russian.

There are only about 500 active Old Believers left in Poland, although the number of people claiming descent from or kinship with these people is far larger – ensuring the survival of several Old Believer churches in rural pockets of the northeast.

buses sometimes drop off at Nida first before terminating at Ruciane train station. Walk just south of the station and you're at the water's edge, in this case the narrow canal connecting the two lakes nearest the town: the jetty with the sign marked *Żegluga Mazurska* is the boarding point for excursion boats on the Giżycko–Mikołajki–Ruciane line, the boats travelling through the connecting series of lakes culminating in Lake Nidzkie running south from the town. If you're staying in town, there are also daily summertime excursions round the lake itself.

The **tourist information centre**, in Ruciane at ul. Dworcowa 14 (June–Sept: Mon–Fri 7am–7pm, Sat & Sun 9am–6pm; Oct–May: Mon–Fri 7am–3pm; ⓣ087/423 1989, ⓦwww.rucianenida.pl) can help find private rooms (❷). At the other end of the scale, *Hotel Nidzki* ul. Nadbrzeżna (ⓣ087/423 6401, ⓦwww.hotel.nidzki.oit.pl; ❻), offers comfortable rooms with lovely lake views from the terrace.

The Wojnowo Nunnery

Some 6km west of Ruciane-Nida, **WOJNOWO** is an attractively bucolic village of low wooden houses set among lush meadows. It was founded in the nineteenth century by **Old Believers** (*staroobrzędowcy*), a traditionalist Orthodox Russian sect that had rebelled against the reforms of 1651 and been forced into exile as a result. Old Believers are still found in rural areas of Estonia, Latvia and eastern Poland, although their numbers are dwindling (see box above).

At the centre of Wojnowo stands the former Old-Believer **nunnery** (June–Sept daily 9am–6pm; other times ring in advance ⓣ087/425 7030), a simple whitewashed building that began life as a monastery in 1847, was refounded as a nunnery in 1885, and is now a private house. The interior is not particularly grand but does have a very impressive collection of old **icons** – unfortunately mounted in an iconostasis made of cheap laminate. These are just some of the convent's collection, the remainder of which is displayed at Lidzbark Warmiński's castle museum (see p.205).

Clearly visible on the other side of the village is the charming **Orthodox parish church** made of white-painted wood and crowned with a blue onion dome (Mon–Sat 9am–noon & 1–6pm); if the church is locked, go down the path past the cemetery and through the flower garden to the house and ask for the key. There's no entry fee as such but you should certainly make a donation of a few złoty.

Ełk

Straddling the road and rail routes from Giżycko and Olsztyn eastwards to Augustów (see p.224) and Białystok (p.232), the medium-sized lakeside town of **EŁK** is worth a brief stopoff on account of its **narrow-gauge railway** (Ełcka kolej wąskotorowa: ℡087/610 0000, ⓦwww.mosir.elk.com.pl), remnant of a once busy network of logging lines which has recently been adapted for tourist needs. Located on the far side of Ełk's main **train** and **bus stations** (and accessible by pedestrian underpass), the narrow-gauge station is the site of a small **skansen** of locomotives and rolling stock, a **museum display** (daily; 8am–3pm; 2zł) of railway paraphernalia – including a bafflingly uninteresting collection of train-station telephones – and, rather oddly, an outdoor collection of historic **beehives** that includes wood-carved hives in the form of owls and bears.

The narrow-gauge station is also the starting point for **train excursions** to the village of Sypitki (June: Sat; July & Aug: Wed and Sat; 20zł) some 30km distant, departing from Ełk at about 10am and returning around 2pm. The journey takes passengers through rolling countryside of mixed farmland and forest, and allows plenty of time for exploring woodland trails around Sypitki once you get there. The services are usually hauled by diesel, although an immaculately well-kept steam locomotive is sometimes laid on for festive occasions – and groups can always hire their own steam-pulled train (prices range from 1200–3000zł depending on the length of the trip) providing they book well in advance.

If you've still got time to kill in Ełk, follow ulica Armii Krajowej west from the train and bus stations to find the shores of **Lake Ełk** (Jezioro Ełckie) 1km away, site of some attractive waterside paths. Just above the lakefront on the corner of ulica Armii Krajowej and ulica Wojska Polskiego is a helpful **tourist information office** (℡087/621 7010, ⓦwww.elk.pl). *Café No Name*, in a nearby courtyard just behind Wojska Polskiego 53, serves up excellent **coffee** and a good apple pie (*szarlotka*).

The Suwalszczyzna

Named after the market town and administrative centre of **Suwałki**, the Suwalszczyzna is one of the least visited parts of Poland; even for Poles, anything beyond Mazuria is still pretty much *terra incognita*. Visually the area isn't that different from Mazuria: a pleasing landscape of rolling hills and fields interspersed with crystal-clear lakes – often small, but extremely deep – the end product of the final retreat of the Scandinavian glacier that once covered the area. The main centre of the southeast is the lake resort of **Augustów**, east of which stretches the **Puszcza Augustowska** forest – what remains of a vast primeval forest that once extended well into Lithuania. In the north around Suwałki itself, the spectacular forest and lakescape of the **Wigry National Park** and the picture-postcard lakes and hillocks of the **Suwałki Landscape Park** provide the main natural highlights. Slightly off the main roads but well worth visiting are some interesting oddities, notably the rustic market town of **Sejny**, the Lithuanian-inhabited village of **Puńsk** and the eerie, railway-less viaducts at **Stańczyki**. Wandering through the fields and woodland thickets you'll find storks, swallows, brilliantly coloured butterflies and wild flowers in abundance, while in the villages modern life often seems to have made only modest incursions, leaving plenty of time to sit on the porch and talk.

Historically this part of Poland was inhabited by the **Jacwingians**, (a Baltic tribe closely related to the Lithuanians and Latvians of today) who disappeared in the early middle ages, gradually squeezed out by migrating Lithuanians and Poles. Many of the place names in the Suwalszczyzna have Jacwingian or Lithuanian roots, and a small population of **Lithuanians** still

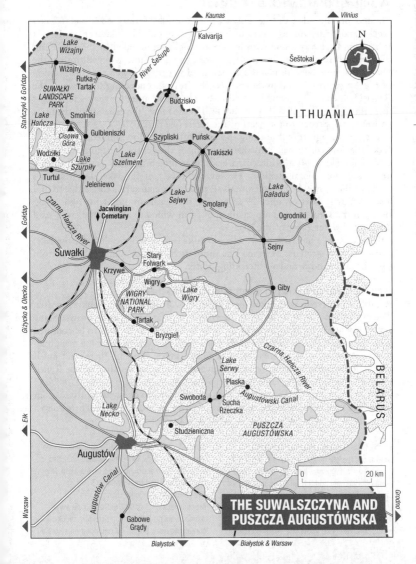

THE SUWALSZCZYNA AND PUSZCZA AUGUSTÓWSKA

remains, concentrated around the village of **Puńsk**. **Jews** also figured as a major element of the region's fluid ethnic mix, although the only surviving sign of this today are the **cemeteries** crumbling away at the edge of numerous towns and villages.

Getting around is reasonably straightforward: Augustów and Suwałki are the main transport hubs for bus services to the region's smaller towns and villages; and both have good train and bus connections with Warsaw and Białystok (see p.232). Most bus and train links to and from neighbouring Mazuria go through **Ełk** (see p.222).

Augustów and around

Located on the edge of the Puszcza Augustowska forest and close to lakes Necko and Białe, Augustów is an increasingly popular holiday centre. In fact it has long been associated with leisure, having been founded in 1557 by **King Sigismund August** to serve as his base for extended hunting expeditions in the woods that now bear his name. Further development followed the construction of the **Augustów Canal** in the nineteenth century, connecting the town to the River Niemen in the east and providing a convenient outlet for the region's most important natural commodity, wood. Still in use today, the canal offers the most convenient approach to the heart of the forest (see p.226).

As a town Augustów is nothing special, but it does allow immediate access to **Lake Necko**, which lies immediately north of the centre. Heading west from the Rynek along ulica Nadrzeczna leads after fifteen minutes or so to a small beach and boat rental facilities. However, the best of the lakeside terrain lies north of the centre: head east from the Rynek and north across the bridge to find a small tourist **port** on ulica 29 Listopada, the departure point for sightseeing **boats** in the summer, and a pleasant spot from which to admire the swan- and duck-filled waterscapes of the lake.

Beyond here, a network of woodland **walks** lead round the shore of the lake, passing several stretches of beach (the shore itself is grassy, but the lake bottom itself is quite sandy), and a waterskiing centre.

Arrival, information and accommodation

Augustów's **bus** station is right in the middle of town on Rynek Zygmunta Augusta. The main **train** station is 3km to the northeast; regular buses run into town. Some slower *osobowy* (local train) services also stop at Augustów Port (not to be confused with the tourist port as mentioned above), a small halt 1km west of the main train station. Augustów Port is slightly closer to the centre, although there's not much in it. The tourist information centre, in an angular modern building on the Rynek (July & Aug Mon–Sat 9am–5pm; Sept–June Mon–Fri 9am–3pm; ℡087/643 2883), is reasonably well organized, and can help sort you out with a private room (❷), many of which are in the nicest part of town towards the lake. There's also a **campsite** at ul. Sportowa 1, next to the *Hetman* (see below).

Hotels and pensions

Dom Nauczyciela ul. 29 Listopada 9 ℡087/643 2021, ⓦwww.augustow-dn.pl. A medium-sized place offering neat and tidy en suites next to the tourist port. ❹

Hetman ul. Sportowa 1 ℡087/643 4289, ⓦwww.hetman.augustow.pl. A rather functional hotel right by the lake, designed in the late 1930s by Maciej Nowicki, one of the architects responsible for the UN building in New York. Unassuming en suites, leafy woodland surrounds, and wi-fi access. Near the Augustów Port train station. ❹

Krechowiak ul. I Pułku Ułanów Krechowieckich 2 ℡087/643 2033, ⓦwww.krechowiak.pl) Grim-looking modern block containing neat, bright, TV-equipped en suites a

short walk east of the lake, near Augustów Port train station. ❹
Warszawa ul. Zdrojowa 1 ☎087/643 8500, ⓦwww.hotelwarszawa.pl. Snazzy en suites in a prime location, with the lake on one side and dense woodland on the other. Spa and gym facilities on site. Near the Augustów Port train station. ❼

Eating and drinking

Eating out in Augustów revolves around the kind of **fish-fry stalls** common to all of Poland's lake resorts. You'll find a couple next to the tourist port, as well as several along ulica Mostowa, which heads north from the main Rynek. For something more upscale than fish and chips, try *Maska*, Rynek 9, which serves up poultry, fish, and steak dishes in a basement room decorated with Venetian carnival masks and Egyptian hieroglyphics; while *Karczma Kaktusik*, diagonally opposite the tourist port at ul. 29 Listopada 2, offers traditional Polish food in faux-farmstead surroundings, plus ponds and play-area outside. Flashiest of the restaurants is the *Kolumnowa*, inside the *Hotel Warszawa*, where you'll find a mixture of Polish and modern European cuisine, a few vegetarian choices, and bearable prices.

You can also get **snacks** at the al fresco cafés that sprout up around the Rynek in summer, and serve as handy daytime **drinking** venues. *Pub Bab*, Rynek 7, is an animated, brick-vaulted cellar pub which also does substantial food.

There are numerous agencies in Augustów renting out **kayaks** and **canoes** by the day, which can also arrange longer trips down the Czarna Hańcza river (see box, p.225).

Canoeing along the Czarna Hańcza River

Along with the Krutynia (see box, p.209) the **Czarna Hańcza River** is one of the most beautiful – and popular – **canoeing routes** in the northeast Polish lakelands. If you've ever had a hankering for a backwater canoeing expedition this is as good a chance as any to satisfy it.

Rising in Belarus, the 140-kilometre-long river, a tributary of the Niemen, flows into the Puszcza Augustówska, winding its way through the Wigry National Park up to **Lake Hańcza**, 15km northwest of **Suwałki**. On the usual canoe route, the first leg of the journey starts from **Augustów**, following the Augustów Canal (see opposite) east to the point where it meets the Czarna Hańcza, a few kilometres short of the Belarusian border; from there the route continues on up the river to Suwałki and, stamina allowing, beyond to Lake Hańcza.

An alternative route involves exploring **Lake Wigry** and the surrounding national park. This trip heads east from Augustów along the canal, turning north at **Swoboda** and continuing 12km into **Lake Serwy**, an attractive forest-bound tributary. From here the canoes are transported across land to the village of **Bryzgiel**, on the southern shores of Lake Wigry. Three days are given over to exploring the peaceful and unspoilt lake and its protected surroundings. Overnight camps are on the island of **Kamien**, one of several on the lake, and by the lakeside at **Stary Folwark** (see p.228), with a trip up to the monastery included. Leaving Wigry near the **Klasztorny peninsula**, canoeists re-enter the Czarna Hańcza, heading south through a spectacular forest-bound section of the river before rejoining the Augustów Canal and making their way back to Augustów.

Both the above trips can be organized through agencies in Augustów and take ten or eleven days, with accommodation – mostly in *stanice wodne* (waterside hostels) – and meals provided throughout: you'll need to provide your own sleeping bag and appropriate clothing, ideally including rubber boots. The current cost for either trip is around 900zł – a bargain. Contact the **PTTK** office, ul. Nadrzeczna 70a (☎087/644 3850); the **Sirocco** agency, ul. Zarzecze 5a (☎087/643 0084, ⓦhttp://.siroccokajaki .pl); or **Solarsky**, ul. Nadrzeczna 70a (☎087/643 6727, ⓦwww.solarsky.com.pl).

The forest and the canal

The combination of wild forest, lakes and narrow winding rivers around Augustów has made the Puszcza Augustowska a favourite with canoeists, walkers, cyclists and naturalists alike. The least strenuous way to explore the area is to take a **day-trip** from Augustów along the **canal system**. Boats leave from the tourist port on ulica 29 Listopada (see p.224) – *żegluga* (meaning, very loosely, "boats") is the key word when asking the way. There are usually about seven different excursions per day in the height of the season (July & Aug), falling to a couple per day in May, June and September. First departure is at 9.30am, and you should get there early to queue for tickets (25zł). It's also a good idea to take some food: most boats don't carry any, and restaurant stops on the way are unpredictable.

The shortest trips – a couple of hours – go east through the **Necko**, **Białe** and **Studzieniczne** lakes to **Swoboda** or **Sucha Rzeczka**, giving at least a taste of the beauty of the forest. Other boats go onward to **Plaska** and the lock at **Perkuc**, returning in the evening. Beyond this point, the canal is for canoeists only, and even they can only go another twenty or so kilometres to the Belarusian border.

The **forest** is mainly coniferous, but with impressive sections of elm, larch, hornbeam and ancient oak creating a slightly sombre atmosphere, particularly along the alley-like section of the canal between Swoboda and Sucha Rzeczka where the tallest trees blot out the sun, billowing reeds brush the boat, and the silence is suddenly broken by echoing bird calls. Among the varied wildlife of the forest, cranes, grey herons and even the occasional beaver can be spotted on the banks of the canal, while deeper into the *puszcza* you might glimpse wild boar or elk.

If exploring the highways and byways on wheels appeals, the Puszcza Augustowska makes for some enticing **cycling** territory. There are plenty of decent paths and roads, although they're not always particularly clearly marked. The *Puszcza Augustowska* **map** (1:70,000) shows all the main routes through the forest, right up to the Belarusian border. Several places in town rent out bikes – ask the tourist office (see p.224) for details.

▲ Czarna Hańcza River

Gabowe Grądy

Some 8km south of Augustów down a track through the woods (the nearest bus stop is a kilometre east), is the village of **GABOWE GRĄDY** which is populated by a sizeable number of Russian Orthodox **Old Believer** (*Starowierców*) families (see box, p.221). The wizened old characters with flowing white beards sitting by their front gates indicate you've arrived in the right place. People apart, the main interest here is the church (*molenna*) at the north end of the village, one of three remaining places of Orthodox worship in the region. The Gabowe Grądy *molenna* boasts a superb all-women **choir**, the only such group in the country: you can usually hear them at the Sunday morning service, the only time you're guaranteed to be able to get into the place anyway. For anyone interested in Orthodox music this is a must, the sonorous harmonies of the old liturgical chants intermeshing with the full-throated exuberance of the melodizing.

Suwałki

The main market centre of Poland's rural northeast, **SUWAŁKI** is a rather formless place, consisting of a long central street and a scattering of grey suburbs. Although the main roads through town are choked with Poland-to-the-Baltics through traffic, few people actually stop off here, ensuring that Suwałki retains a modicum of provincial middle-of-nowhere charm. It's certainly a good place from which to explore the surrounding Suwalszczyzna, although **accommodation** in town is limited, and B&Bs in the nearby Wigry National Park (see p.228) may offer more in the way of rural seclusion.

Arrival, information and accommodation

The **train station** lies an easy 15-minute walk east of the centre, while the **bus station**, on ulica Utrata, is closer to the centre in the same direction. The helpful **tourist office** on the main road through town at ul. Kościuszki 45 (June–Aug Mon–Fri 8am–6pm, Sat & Sun 9am–2pm; Sept–May Mon–Fri 8am–4pm; ☎087/566 5494, ⓦwww.suwalki-turystyka.info.pl), is keen on promoting eco-tourism in the region and can book you into **farmhouse B&Bs** (❷–❸) in the surrounding countryside – you'll need your own transport to get there, though. Best of the **hotels** are the *Dom Nauczyciela* (ZNP), ul. Kościuszki 120 (☎087/566 6900, ⓦwww.domnauczyciela.suwalki.pl; ❺); and the *Suwalszczyzna*, ul. Noniewicza 71a (☎087/565 1929, ⓦwww.hotelsuwalszczyzna.pl; ❺), both of which are central and offer comfy en suites with TV. There's a basic summer-only (June–Aug) **youth hostel** at ul. Klonowa 51 (☎087/566 5878), 2km northeast of the town centre.

The Town

Suwałki's only real focal point is ulica Kościuszki, which runs straight through town on a north–south axis. Nearer its southern end is the stately Neoclassical Parish Church of St Alexandra on plac Piłsudskiego, while 400m further north is a small **museum** at no. 81 (Tues–Fri 8am–4pm, Sat & Sun 9am–5pm; 5zł) containing a number of archeological finds relating to the Jacwingians, and paintings by local artist Alfred Wierusz-Kowalski.

Just over a kilometre east of plac Piłsudskiego is Suwałki's **molenna**, a small wooden building serving the town's Old Believer population and retaining some fine original icons. It is tucked away on a side street off aleja Sejneńska close to the train station; the only reliable time to gain entry is during the Sunday morning service.

The jumbled ethnic mix that characterized Suwałki up until the outbreak of World War II is clearly illustrated in the town **cemetery** on the west side of town on the corner of ulica Bakałarzewska and ulica Zarzecze, overlooking the Czarna Hańcza River. The cemetery is divided up into religious sections – Catholic, Orthodox, Protestant, Tatar and Jewish, the Orthodox section housing a special part for Old Believers. The Jewish cemetery was devastated by the Nazis – a lone memorial tablet now stands in the middle of the area.

Continuing along Zarzecze south of the cemetery brings you to the **Arkadia Lake**, site of a beach and a string of waterside cafés in summertime.

Eating and drinking

Good places to **eat** and **drink** include *Karczma Polska*, Kościuszki 101a (the far northern end of the street), which features wooden furnishings, archaic farmyard implements hanging from the ceiling and a traditional Polish menu of pork chop, *golonka* (boiled pork knuckle) and chicken dishes. *Rozmarino*, further south at Kościuszki 75, is a pleasant pizzeria which also does a good range of pastas and salads; there's a separate bar and winter garden in the courtyard at the back. Best of a brace of **pubs** along ulica Chłodna (just off pl. Piłsudskiego) is *Piwiarnia*, a lively pub dominated by a long, narrow, stool-lined bar.

Lake Wigry and the Wigry National Park

Lake Wigry, the district's largest, lies 11km southeast of Suwałki. The lake and a large part of the surrounding area were designated as the **Wigry National Park** (Wigiersky Park Narodowy: ⓦwww.wigry.win.pl) in 1989, an unspoilt area of nearly 15,000 hectares comprising a mixture of lake, river, forest and agricultural territory. The lake in particular is a stunningly beautiful spot, a peaceful haven of creeks, marshes and woods, with the occasional village in between. A wealth of wildlife shelters largely undisturbed in and around its waters, the lake itself harbouring more than twenty species of fish – lavaret, whitefish, smelt and river trout included – while in the shoreland woods you can find stag, wild boar, elk, martens and badgers. Wigry's most characteristic animal, however, is the **beaver**, and particularly round the lake's southern and western shores you'll find plenty of evidence of their presence in the reservations set aside for them. The park is also a rambler's paradise, with a good network of **marked trails** running through much of the area. For anyone tempted by the idea of exploring the region on foot, the *Wigierski Park Narodowy* **map** (1:46,000), which shows all the main trails, is a must. The longest route, marked green, takes you round the entire lake – nearly 50km in total – but there are also plenty of good shorter routes. **Cycling** is another more challenging option: the trails take in narrow forest paths and sandy roads, which can make the going hard. Bike rental is theoretically possible from the PTTK (see p.225) or via the tourist office in Suwałki. Finally, the lake itself is a magnet for anglers. To cast your rod you'll need a local **fishing licence**; the Suwałki tourist office will put you onto the local branch of the Polish Angling Association – Polski Związek Wędkarski (PZW) – which issues the requisite papers.

The park is easy to access, with **buses** on the Suwałki–Sejny route passing through main entry points Krzywe and Stary Folwark roughly every hour until about 5–6pm.

Krzywe and Stary Folwark

The park's headquarters (May–Sept daily 7am–7pm; Oct–April Mon–Fri 7am–3pm) at the village of **KRZYWE**, 5km from Suwałki on the border of the park, is the best source of detailed information and has a small natural history **museum**.

A few kilometres further down the road, **STARY FOLWARK** is a quiet spot on the lakeshore and the main base for **accommodation** in the park. Good places to stay include the pension *Nad Wigrami* (℡087/563 77752; ❸), a family house right in the village offering doubles, family rooms sleeping three or four, and bike hire; the *Holiday Hotel* (℡087/563 7120, ⓦwww.hotel-holiday.pl; ❻), which looks like a bland motel from the road but has comfortable rooms and friendly staff; and a **campsite** near the water. For a bite to **eat** you can choose between the restaurant of the *Holiday Hotel* and the *Pod Sieją*, both of which serve freshwater fish from the lake. You can **rent canoes** from a couple of outlets down by the water.

Wigry

A short drive or walk round the lake – or a quick paddle across it – is the tiny village of **WIGRY**, dwarfed by a former **Camadolese Monastery** (Klasztor Kamedułów), founded here by King Władysław Waza in the 1660s. Originally the monastery stood on an island but this is now linked to the shore. The monks were thrown out by the Prussians following the Third Partition and their sizeable possessions – three hundred square kilometres of land and several dozen villages – sequestered. The church is a typical piece of Polish Baroque, with exuberant frescoes in the main church and monks' skeletons in the catacombs (guided visits only), standard practice for the death-fixated Camadolese. The monastery itself has been turned into a popular conference centre and **hotel**, the *Dom Pracy Twórczej* (℡087/563 7000, ⓦwww.wigry.org; ❺), with homely doubles – either en suite or with one bathroom shared between two rooms – set in bungalow-sized buildings where monks once lived. The *Dom* has a good **restaurant** and modern art gallery. You can also find **private rooms** and **boat hire** in the village.

Sejny

Continuing east from Stary Folwark the main road (and regular buses) arrives at **SEJNY**, a quiet market town dominated by a creamy-coloured **basilica** at the top of town. The twin-towered church was originally built in the late Renaissance as part of a Dominican monastery and refurbished in Rococo style in the mid-eighteenth century. The fourteenth-century Madonna carved from limewood, located in the main side chapel on the right, is a long-standing object of popular veneration: on feast days the body of the statue is opened to reveal an intricately carved Crucifixion scene inside. The crown on the Madonna's head was put in place by the then bishop of Kraków, **Karol Wojtyła**, in 1975.

At the other end of the short main street, ulica Piłsudskiego, is the **former synagogue**, dwarfed by the basilica but nonetheless a substantial building – indicating the importance of the former Jewish population here. Built in the 1860s and devastated by the Nazis (who turned it into a fire station), it has since been carefully restored and turned into a **museum** and cultural centre (Mon–Fri 9am–5pm; free) run by the Borderland Foundation (Fundacja Pogranicze: ⓦwww.pogranicze.sejny.pl), dedicated to promoting the culture, music and art of "the borderland nations". Started in the early 1990s, the Foundation organizes cultural events aimed at bringing together the peoples of the region (Poles, Lithuanians, Belarusians, Ukrainians and Russians), publishes books relating to intercultural tolerance and understanding, and also runs a Klezmer band in honour of Sejny's Jewish heritage.

The main **hotel** in town is the slightly grotty *Skarpa* at ul. Piłsudskiego 13 (☎087/516 2187, ◉www.skarpa.sejny.pl; ④), which has neat en suites with TV and also has a restaurant serving up tasty Lithuanian *blynai* (potato pancakes). You can also stay at the Lithuanian cultural centre, the *Lietuviu Namai* (or *Dom Litewski* in Polish), ul. 22 Lipca 9 (☎087/516 2908,

Poles and Lithuanians

In Poland's relations with its eastern neighbours, none are as fraught with paradox and misunderstanding as those with **Lithuania**. This is almost entirely due to the fact that the two countries have large chunks of history and culture in common, but can rarely agree on which bits of the Polish-Lithuanian heritage belong to whom.

Dynastically linked by the marriage of Polish Queen Jadwiga to the Lithuanian Grand Duke Jogaila (or Władysław II Jagiełło, as he is known in Polish) in 1386, the two countries coexisted in curious tandem, and embarked on mutual conquests, until the **Union of Lublin** finally bound them together in a single state – the so-called **Commonwealth** – in 1569. They were to stay together until the **Partitions** of Poland brought the Commonwealth to an end at the close of the eighteenth century. However, the precise nature of the Polish-Lithuanian state has always been a source of disagreement to both sides: the Lithuanians tend to regard it as a mutual enterprise undertaken by equal partners, while the Poles reserve for themselves the leading role.

One of the reasons why the Poles traditionally looked upon the Grand Duchy of Lithuania as a constituent part of a Polish-dominated state was that the Lithuanian aristocracy had become almost wholly Polish-speaking by the sixteenth century, and increasingly identified with the courtly culture of Warsaw and Kraków rather than their own native ways. Lithuanian language and culture was reduced to the status of quaint folklore, spoken of rapturously by nineteenth-century romantic poets like Adam Mickiewicz (see p.78), but hardly ever taken seriously by the educated elite. This left Lithuanians with an inferiority complex vis-à-vis their overbearing Polish neighbours, an outlook that was transformed into outright hostility by the national struggles of the twentieth century.

When the end of **World War I** put the resurrection of the Polish state back on the political agenda, Polish leaders including Marshal Piłsudski, himself a Polish-Lithuanian aristocrat) were consumed by dreams of resuscitating the Polish-Lithuanian Commonwealth of old. However the Lithuanians, eager to escape from Polish tutelage, rushed to declare an independent state of their own. The two sides came to blows over the status of **Vilnius** which, as the medieval capital of Lithuania, was regarded by the Lithuanians as a natural part of their heritage. The Poles pointed to the city's large Polish-speaking population, and annexed it by force in 1920. The Lithuanians got it back in 1939.

With both Poland and Lithuania now members of both the EU and NATO, relations between the two countries are as good, if not better, than at any point since the sixteenth century. Polish culture is still characterized by nostalgia for the Grand Duchy of Lithuania, frequently portraying it as a slightly wilder, more authentic version of Poland itself. This feeling is not reciprocated by the Lithuanians, however, who tend to regard the Poles as overbearing former imperialists who are claiming the heritage of the Grand Duchy for themselves.

On an individual level Poles and Lithuanians remain staggeringly indifferent towards each others' cultures, and yet frequently travel to visit each others' countries to sightsee or shop – proof, of a sort, that they are well on the way to becoming normal European neighbours.

@ www.ltnamai.sejny.pl; ❸), which has well-appointed en suites, and a café-bar serving Lithuanian snacks.

Puńsk

Set in lovely countryside 30km northwest of Sejny, the village of **PUŃSK** is the main centre of the Suwalszczyzna's Lithuanian population, possessing Lithuanian-language church, schools, cultural centre and weekly newspaper that together add up to a strong sense of community. A handful of daily buses run from both Suwałki and Sejny; otherwise catch the one daily **train** to **Trakiszki** and walk the last three kilometres.

It's in the cultural centre on ulica Szklona that you'll find the **Ethnographical Museum**, packed with wonderful decorative fabrics, bizarre-looking farm implements, and prewar Lithuanian books and magazines. A kilometre out on the Sejny road is a small **skansen**, its single timber-built farmstead set in a colourful cottage garden. As well as Lithuanians, Puńsk was for centuries home to another minority – Jews. Almost every Jew from this region was either slaughtered or uprooted, but a few signs of the past are still left. The Dom Handlowy on the main street in Puńsk used to be the rabbi's house, and the older locals can point you in the direction of the abandoned **Jewish cemetery**, on the northern edge of the village, where a few Hebrew inscriptions are still visible among the grass and trees.

The *Sodas* **café**, at ul. Mickiewicza 17, handles food and drink duties, including the refreshing summer soup *saltibarsciai* (cold borscht with boiled potatoes), alongside more calorific fare like *blynai* (Lithuanian potato pancakes).

The Suwałki Landscape Park

The Suwalszczyzna's trademark landscape of low green hills and glittering lakes is arguably at its best in the **Suwałki Landscape Park** (Suwalski Park Krajobra-zowy; @ www.spk.org.pl), a nature conservation area located just northwest of **Jeleniewo**, 10km out on the main road north from Suwalki. The best way to get there from Suwałki by public transport is to take a bus to Wiżajny (three to four daily) and get off at either **Gulbieniszki** on the eastern side of the park, or **Smolniki**, the main entrance point on the northern side of the park.

If you're driving then it's well worth aiming for **TURTUL**, 7km west of Jeleniowo, where the park's **tourist information point** (June–Sept Mon–Fri 8am–7pm, Sat 9am–5pm; Sept–May Mon–Fri 8am–3pm; ☎569 1801) hands out maps of local walking trails. It's from here that a **red-marked trail** proceeds north through the heart of the park, entering after 2km the off-the-beaten-track settlement of **WODZIŁKI**, tucked away in a quiet wooded valley. The hamlet is home to a small community of Orthodox **Old Believers** (see box p.221) whose original wooden *molenna* is still in use, along with a nearby sauna (*bania*). Life in this rural settlement seems to have changed little since the first settlers moved here in the 1750s: the houses are simple, earth-floored buildings with few concessions to modernity, the old men grow long white beards, and the women don't appear to cut their hair. If you're lucky enough to get invited into one of their homes, you'll see amazing collections of icons, rosaries, Bibles and other precious relics.

North of Jeleniewo along the main road is **GULBIENISZKI**, the point of access for **Cisowa Góra** (258m), the hill known as the Polish Fujiyama. It was the site of pre-Christian religious rituals, and it's rumoured that rites connected with Perkunas, the Lithuanian fire god, are still observed here; bear in mind that the

Lithuanians, who still make up a small percentage of the population of this region, were the last Europeans to be converted to Christianity, in the late fourteenth century. Whatever the historical reality of the hill, it's a powerful place.

North of Gulbieniski the road divides: Wiźajny to the left, Rutka-Tartak to the right. Continuing along the Wiźajny route, the next village is **SMOLNIKI**, just before which there's a wonderful **panorama** of the surrounding lakes; if you're on the bus ask the driver to let you off at the viewpoint (*punkt wyściowy*). If you happen to have a compass with you, don't be surprised if it starts to go haywire around here – the area has large deposits of iron-rich ore, as discovered by disorientated German pilots based at Luftwaffe installations here during World War II. Despite the obvious commercial potential, the seams haven't been exploited to date owing to the high levels of uranium in the ore and the risk from direct exposure to it.

A couple of kilometres west of Smolniki, along a bumpy track through woods, is **Lake Hańcza**, the deepest in Poland at 108 metres; it's quiet, clean and unspoilt. The Czarna Hańcza River (see box, p.225) joins the lake on its southern shore. There's a **youth hostel** at the southeastern edge at Błaskowizna (June–Aug; ☎087/566 1769; dorm beds 25zł) and several houses offer **private rooms**. To get to the village take the Wiźajny bus from Suwałki and get off at Bachanowo, a kilometre past Turtul Rutka; it's a short walk from here.

Stańczyki

STAŃCZYKI, west of Lake Hańcza close up by the Russian border on the edge of the Puszcza Romincka, bit over-stated can be reached by car if you follow the main route west of Wiźajny, turning left off the road about 4km past Żytkiejmy. The reason for coming is to admire the huge deserted twin **viaduct** straddling the Błędzianka River valley, seemingly lost out in the middle of nowhere. Before World War II this hamlet was right on the East Prussian–Polish border: in 1910 the Germans built a mammoth double viaduct here as part of a new rail line, one side scheduled to carry timber trains leaving Prussia; the other, trains entering the country from Poland. The viaduct was duly completed, the only problem being that the promised rail track never materialized. The viaducts have stood ever since, a towering monument to an architect and engineer's folly, no one apparently having the heart – or cash – to pull them down. These days a stroll on and around the viaducts is a favourite Sunday outing for local people. You could also take a more adventurous walk into the forests of the Romincka nature reserve – signs in the car park detail possible routes.

Camping is possible here as the viaducts lie just outside the reserve. In summer there's also the *Biały Dwór* pension (☎087/615 8172; ❹), which has comfortable en suites with TV and a small restaurant.

Białystok

Even the habitually enthusiastic official Polish guidebooks are mute on the glories of **BIAŁYSTOK**, industrial centre of northeast Poland; it's not a beautiful place and its main development occurred during the industrialization of the nineteenth century. Uniquely among major Polish cities today, however, it has kept the healthy ethnic and religious mix – Poles, Belarusians and Ukrainians, Catholic and Orthodox – characteristic of the country before the war; though the Jews, of course, are absent. The city contains a modest

On to Vilnius

With **Poland and Lithuania** both members of the EU, a trip over the border to the Lithuanian capital, Vilnius, is a straightforward option. Both countries belong to the EU's Schengen group of states, which means that border controls are minimal and any passports and visas valid for travel in Poland are valid for Lithuania too.

Situated around 160km east of Suwałki, Vilnius (in Polish, Wilno) is unmistakeably central European in feel, a jumbled mix of cobbled alleyways, high spires, Catholic shrines and Orthodox churches. Originating as the medieval capital of the Lithuanian grand dukes, Vilnius was for centuries a multinational city which served as an important cultural centre for many different peoples – Lithuanians, Poles and Belarusians included. On the eve of World War II, the Jews made up the biggest ethnic group in the city – a fact that is skated over by present-day Lithuanian and Polish historians.

Vilnius is very tourist-friendly, and recent years have witnessed an explosion in the number of cafés, bars, restaurants and hotels. There are tourist information centres at the train station and in the town hall, bang in the middle of the old town at Didžioji 31 (℡+370 5-262/9660, ☞www.vilnius-touism.lt).

Practicalities

There are several options for overland **travel** to Vilnius. There are border crossings at Budzisko (for Kaunas) and Ogrodniki (for Vilnius) if you're travelling **by car.** There is one **train** a day from Warsaw to Vilnius, calling at Białystok, Augustów and Suwalki on the way – with a change of carriages at Šeštokai, where the west-European rail network ends and the wider (formerly imperial Russian) gauge begins. Finally, going **by bus** is also a reasonable option, with direct services from Warsaw (daily; 12hr), Gdańsk (5 weekly; 12hr) and Białystok (daily; 9hr) – although most of these services are overnight.

collection of historic sights, and good transport links make it an ideal base for exploring the border region to the east.

Some history

According to legend, Białystok was founded in 1320 by the Lithuanian Grand Duke Gediminas (or **Gedymin** as he's known in Polish), but its emergence really began in the 1740s when local aristocrat Jan Branicki built a palace in the town centre. Partitioned off to Prussia and then to Russia, Białystok rapidly developed as a textile city, in competition with Łódź further west. In both cities, industrialization fostered the growth of a sizeable urban proletariat and a large and influential **Jewish community**. Factory strikes in 1905 provided Russian nationalists with the perfect excuse to mount a pogrom, in which many Białystok Jews lost their lives. Fifteen years later, invading Bolshevik troops installed a provisional government in Białystok led by **Felix Dzierżyński**, notorious Polish-born revolutionary and creator of the first ever Soviet secret police force – forerunner of the KGB. Dzierżyński's Soviet regime was soon driven out.

World War II brought destruction and slaughter to Białystok. Hitler seized the town in 1939, then handed it over to Stalin before reoccupying it in 1941 – which is when the Jewish population was herded into a ghetto area and deported to the death camps. The heroic Białystok **Ghetto Uprising** of August 1943 (the first within the Reich) presaged the extinction of the city's Jewry. The killing was not confined to Jews: by 1945 more than half the city's population was dead, with three-quarters of the town centre destroyed.

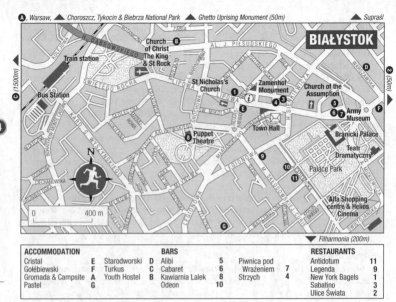

BIAŁYSTOK

▼ Filharmonia (200m)

ACCOMMODATION				BARS				RESTAURANTS	
Cristal	E	Starodworski	D	Alibi	5	Piwnica pod		Antidotum	11
Gołębiewski	F	Turkus	C	Cabaret	6	Wrażeniem	7	Legenda	9
Gromada & Campsite	A	Youth Hostel	B	Kawiarnia Lalek	8	Strzych	4	New York Bagels	1
Pastel	G			Odeon	10			Sabatino	3
								Ulice Świata	2

Following the end of the war, the authorities set about rebuilding the town and its industrial base. From a strictly utilitarian point of view they succeeded: today Białystok is a developed economic centre for textiles, metals and timber, with a population of more than 250,000.

Arrival and information

The main **train station** is a five-minute bus ride (#2, #4 or #21) west of the city centre – supposedly it was built outside the centre as a punishment for anti-tsarist protests in the city. Somewhat confusingly the main exit also faces away from the town centre. On foot turn left out of the front door then left again over the footbridge and you'll be heading in the right direction. Close by, on ulica Bohaterów Monte Cassino, is the large, modern **bus station**.

Białystok's **tourist information centre**, just off the main ulica Lipowa at ul. Malmeda 6 (Mon–Fri 9am–5pm; ☎085/732 6831, ⓦ www.podlaskieit .pl), doles out information on Białystok and can advise on exploring the Podlasie region as a whole. The *Obieżyświat* **map shop** on the upstairs floor of Białystok train station (Mon–Fri 8.30am–8pm, Sat 10am–6pm) sells local maps and guidebooks and is a good all-round source of travel advice.

Accommodation

Białystok's supply of hotels is fairly modest for a city of its size and it's always worth ringing in advance if you want to be sure of a bed. There are dorm beds (25zł per person) in the all-year **youth hostel**, al. Piłsudskiego 7b (reception 8am–8pm; ☎085/652 4250), a quaint wooden house squeezed between apartment blocks a fifteen-minute walk east of the train station – buses #1, #9, #12, #18 and #20 pass by. **Campers** have only one real option – the site next to the *Hotel Gromada* on ulica Jana Pawła II – bus #4 will take you there.

Hotels

Cristal ul. Lipowa 3 ☎085/749 6100, ⓦwww .cristal.com.pl. Slick and efficient upmarket hotel in a central location. The pricey restaurant is open till late. ❻

Gołębiewski ul. Pałacowa 7 ☎085/743 5435, ⓦwww.golebiewski.pl. Big, well-run place aimed at business travellers and upmarket tourists. Located close to the Branicki Palace. Big weekend discounts. ❼

Gromada ul. Jana Pawła II 77 ☎085/651 1641, ⓦwww.gromada.pl. Motel-like concrete building right next to a main highway on the edge of town (bus #4 from the station). Worth considering if all central choices are full. ❹

Pastel ul. Waszyngtona 24a ☎085/748 6060, ⓦwww.kasol.com.pl. Smallish modern hotel offering all the creature comforts, including a restaurant which does excellent game dishes. Surrounded by somewhat severe university and hospital buildings but within easy walking distance of the centre. ❺

Starodworski ul. Warszawska 7 ☎085/653 7418. Old-fashioned but friendly overnighter in a fine Neoclassical building 10min walk east of the Rynek. Rooms with showers and TV or shared facilities. No breakfast. ❹

Turkus ul. Jana Pawła II 54 ☎085/662 8100, ⓦwww.jard.pl. Simple en suites with TV, 1.5km west of the train station. Nothing special but perfectly adequate for the price. ❹

The Town

Białystok's main sights are situated on and around **ulica Lipowa**, the long thoroughfare cutting east–west across the city centre. Hovering above the street's western end is the **Church of Christ the King and St Rock** (Kościół Khrystysa Króla i św. Rocha) built in the 1920s and sporting a skyline-hogging belfry of spectacular ugliness.

Moving east along Lipowa you'll reach **St Nicholas's Church** (Cerkiew św. Mikołaja) built in the 1840s to serve the swelling ranks of Russian settlers. A typically dark, icon-filled place of Orthodox devotion, its ornate frescoes are careful copies of those in the Orthodox cathedral in Kiev. It is filled to capacity for the Sunday services – worth coinciding with to hear the choir. A kiosk inside the entrance sells replica icons while the one outside sells books and CDs of Orthodox music.

The Podlasie Museum and the cathedral

Midway down ulica Lipowa the street opens out to form the triangular **Rynek Kościuszki**, at the centre of which sits the **town hall**. A small, squat, eighteenth-century building, it was reconstructed from scratch after the war; these days it houses the **Podlasie Museum** (Muzeum Podlaskie: Tues–Sun 10am–5pm; 6zł). A good selection of works by some of Poland's better-known nineteenth- and twentieth-century artists – Malczewski, Witkiewicz, Krzyzanowski – is complemented by an enjoyable collection of local art, the portraits and landscapes displaying a strong feeling for the distinctive character of the region. In addition, the museum has an imaginative programme of temporary shows.

A short distance east of the square is the **Cathedral of the Assumption** (Katedra Wniebowzięcia), a vast 1900 neo-Gothic building with spaceship-like towers. According to local legend the tsarist authorities only permitted construction of such a huge edifice because it was billed as an "extension" of a small seventeenth-century church that still stands – totally overshadowed – on its western flanks.

The former ghetto area

The streets south of ulica Lipowa comprise part of the old **ghetto area**. A tablet in Polish and Hebrew on the side of a building opposite the local courthouse on ulica Suraska commemorates the one thousand Jews burned to death in June 1941 when the Nazis set fire to the Great Synagogue, reputedly one of the finest in Poland, which used to stand on this site.

For a town whose population was roughly seventy percent Jewish at the turn of the twentieth century there are precious few other Jewish monuments left. Though you'd hardly guess so from today's uniform housing blocks, the streets leading north of ulica Lipowa were all mainly Jewish-inhabited before the war. Across the road from the town hall, in the leafy little park on the edge of ulica Malmeda, a **statue** commemorates the town's most famous Jewish citizen, **Ludwik Zamenhof**, the creator of Esperanto (see box below), as does a plaque at the southern end of the same street. Continuing northwest over busy ulica Piłsudskiego and through streets of high concrete buildings brings you to another small park, off ulica Żabia. Tucked among the housing blocks, the monument to the **Białystok Ghetto Uprising** (August 16, 1943) recalls an important moment in the wartime history of the town.

The Branicki Palace and around

The most striking building in the town centre is the **Branicki Palace** (Pałac Branickich), destroyed by the Nazis in 1944 but rebuilt on the lines of the eighteenth-century building commissioned by Jan Branicki – itself a reconstruction of an earlier palace. The main building is now a medical academy, whose classical

Ludwik Zamenhof and the Esperanto movement

Białystok's most famous son is **Ludwik Zamenhof** (1859–1917), the creator of **Esperanto**, the artificial language invented as an instrument of international communication. Born in what was then a colonial outpost of the tsarist empire, Zamenhof grew up in an environment coloured by the continuing struggle between the indigenous Polish population and its Russian rulers – both of whom were apt to turn on the Jews as and when the occasion suited them.

Perhaps because of this experience, from an early stage Zamenhof, an eye doctor by training, dedicated himself to the cause of racial tolerance and understanding. Zamenhof's attention focused on the fruits of the mythical Tower of Babel, the profusion of human languages: if a new, easily learnable **international language** could be devised it would, he believed, remove a key obstacle not only to people's ability to communicate directly with each other, but also to their ability to live together peaceably. On the basis of extensive studies of the major Western classical and modern languages, Zamenhof – Doktoro Esperanto or "Doctor Hopeful" as he came to be known – set himself the task of inventing just such a language, the key source being root words common to European, and in particular Romance, languages.

The first primer, *Dr Esperanto's International Language*, was published in 1887, but Zamenhof continued to develop his language by translating a whole range of major literary works; Hamlet, Goethe's and Molière's plays and the entire Old Testament included. The new language rapidly gained international attention, and the world's first **Esperanto congress** was held in France in 1905. In the same year Zamenhof completed *Fundamento de Esperanto*, his main work, which soon became the basic Esperanto textbook and the one still most commonly in use today.

Even if it has never quite realized Zamenhof's dreams of universal acceptance, Esperanto – **Linguo Internacia** as it calls itself – has proved considerably more successful than any other "invented" language. With a worldwide membership of over 100,000 and national associations in around fifty countries, the Universala Esperanto Associo represents a significant international movement of people attracted to the universalist ideals as much as the linguistic practice of Esperanto. In Białystok itself there's a thriving **Esperanto-speaking community**, with an office just southwest of the Rynek at ul. Piękna 3 and a website – naturally enough – in Polish and Esperanto: ⓦ www.espero.bialystok.pl.

grandeur you can wander in and admire without much trouble if you look the student part. The main front balcony, the so-called **Dzierżyński balcony**, is where Felix Dzierżyński and associates proclaimed the creation of the Polish Soviet Socialist Republic in 1920. There's a pleasant outdoor café in the inner courtyard. The **park** and formal gardens surrounding the palace are very pleasant and popular with the locals for Sunday promenading.

East of the palace across the busy main road is the **Army Museum** (Muzeum Wojska) at Kilińskiego 7 (Tues–Sun 9.30am–5pm; 4zł). Among the usual collection of military items there's an interesting set of photos, newspapers and other documents from the wartime era of Soviet occupation (1939–41) and the original proclamation of the 1943 Białystok Ghetto Uprising. You can also see a Nazi **"Enigma" code machine** – it was Polish military intelligence who first discovered how these machines worked, passing on their knowledge to Allied codebreakers after the fall of Poland in 1939. Opposite the museum is a **monument** to the AK (Home Army) – one of a number you can find spread around the city now – this time to the AK forces in the former Eastern Polish borderlands, now within Lithuania and Belarus.

The Jewish Cemetery

Perhaps the saddest reminder of the city's one-time Jewish population is the **Jewish cemetery**, off ulica Wschodnia on the northeast edge of the city. Starting from Rynek Kościuszki in the centre of town, bus #3 stops right by the cemetery, just after the junction of ulica Władysława Wysockiego and ulica Władysława Raginisa, a ten-to-fifteen-minute journey. The Jewish section of the cemetery makes for a sad contrast with the Catholic sections on either side – while the Catholic graves are without exception pristine and immaculately cared for, graves in the Jewish section have had no one to look after them since the war. The few surviving **gravestones** are scattered around in the undergrowth, some of them still legible, but if things carry on this way there may not be anything left in the not-too-distant future.

The Church of the Holy Spirit

Largest Orthodox building in the country and testament to the importance of the local Belarusian community is the massive new **Orthodox Church of the Holy Spirit** (Cerkiew św Ducha) on ulica Antoniuk Fabryczny, 3km out of the centre in the northwest outskirts of the city (bus #5 will take you there). The exterior attempts a blend of tradition and innovation and is impressive for size alone but it's the interior that's really worth seeing. Every available surface is decorated with murals and mosaic tiling, and icons hang everywhere from ground level to the base of the lofty dome. Sunday Mass is the best time to get inside; otherwise the priest living behind the church may unlock the doors for you.

Eating, drinking and entertainment

Białystok doesn't have a huge number of **restaurants** but given its size it does offer some fairly imaginative options. Not surprisingly, most of the best places to eat are in the centre, on or around ulica Lipowa.

Restaurants and snack-bars

Antidotum ul. Akademicka 26. Trendy cellar bar with a mixed menu of grilled meats and tortilla wraps, a big screen for sports, and wi-fi. Daily noon–1am.

Legenda ul. Skłodowskiej Curie 3. Unconvincing but enjoyable recreation of a traditional farmstead, with a menu of moderately priced and filling Polish staples. Also a popular place to drink. Daily noon–midnight.

New York Bagels ul. Lipowa 12. A good option for something quick, with a range of breakfast menus, bagels, sandwiches and soups. Mon–Thurs 9am–9pm, Fri & Sat 9am–10pm, Sun 11am–9pm.

Sabatino ul. Sienkiewicza 3. Specializes in Mediterranean cuisine, including scrumptious seafood, served attentively in an interior that looks like something out of a design magazine. Mains in the 30–40zł range. Daily noon–midnight.

Ulice Świata ul. Warszawska 30b. Located round the corner from the *Gołębiewski* hotel, this place has an odd mixture of Polish, Italian, Mexican and Chinese food. None of the food's exceptional but it's a relaxed and friendly place. Daily noon–1am.

Bars

Alibi Kilińskiego 8. A relaxed and cosy cocktail bar which livens up considerably on weekend evenings. Noon–midnight; later at weekends.

Cabaret Kilińskiego 15 Ⓦ www.cabaret.com.pl. A classy bar-restaurant, serving up modern European food. Live jazz, blues, cabaret or DJ performances

at weekends. Sun–Thurs noon–midnight, Fri & Sat noon–3am.

Kawiarnia Lalek ul. Kalinowskiego 1. Inside the puppet theatre (see below), this is a lively place for an evening drink and has an outdoor patio in summer.

Odeon ul. Akademicka 10. Comfortable two-level bar in an octagonal glass pavilion, with occasional live jazz or blues, and weekly karaoke. Popular with students and thirtysomethings alike. Sun–Mon noon–11pm, Tues–Thurs noon–1am, Fri & Sat noon–3am.

Piwnica pod Wrażeniem ul. Kilińskiego 13 (entrance from pl. Jana Pawła II). Minimalist bare-brick cellar pub with low-key lighting and rocky but unobtrusive background music. Daily 4pm–midnight; later at weekends.

Strych Rynek Kościuszki.22. Atmospheric beer bar located in the timber-beamed attic of a downtown apartment building. Good choice of bottled beers from around eastern Europe, a pool table, alternative rock music on the sound system and wi-fi. Daily 4pm until the bar staff get bored.

Nightlife and entertainment

Central **nightlife** options revolve around *Fama*, ul. Legionowa 5, a teen disco-bar which hosts occasional live gigs; and *Metro*, ul. Białówny 9A, which offers mainstream dance music at the weekends, and more specialized styles (reggae, jungle) on weeknights. For **classical music**, the *Filharmonia*, ul. Podleśna 2 (box office Mon–Fri 8am–3.30pm; ☎085/732 0066, Ⓦ www.filharmonia .bialystok.pl), runs concerts usually at least once a week. Most outstanding of the local **drama** groups is the *Wierszalin* workshop theatre (Ⓦ www.wierszalin.pl), performing hypnotic, ritualistic pieces in the village of Supraśl (see below). The *Teatr Lalek* at ul. Kalinowksiego 1 (☎058/742 5033, Ⓦ www.btl.bialystok.pl) is an acclaimed puppet theatre, while the city theatre, *Teatr Dramatyczny*, is at ul. Elektryczna 12 (☎058/749 9175, Ⓦ www.dramatyczny.pl).

Around Białystok

A handful of trips into the city's immediate surroundings are worth considering, notably the Orthodox monastery at **Supraśl**, north of the city, the Branicki Summer Palace at **Choroszcz** and the synagogue of **Tykocin**. The terrain offers some decent walking, too, chiefly the tranquil **Puszcza Knyszyńska** stretching east of the town, a popular weekend haunt with city folk. All of these are accessible using local bus connections. Further afield is the **Biebrza National Park**, a rural idyll that's particularly popular with bird-watchers.

Supraśl and the Puszcza Knyszyńska

A sixteen-kilometre bus journey northeast of Białystok is **SUPRAŚL**, a sleepy place made up largely of single-storey timber houses surrounded by neat gardens. The village grew up around the **Basilian Monastery**, a walled complex of buildings surrounding an impressive Orthodox church. An eye-catching structure featuring four corner towers and zestful zig-zagging **brickwork**, the church was built in the sixteenth century by the Grand Hetman of Lithuania, Aleksander Chodkiewicz, for the Orthodox order of St Basil. Destroyed by German shelling in 1944, it was painstakingly reconstructed in the 1980s, although the famed Byzantine-style frescoes of the interior are still being repainted. The monastery buildings surrounding the church spent most of the communist period as a local school. Now renovated, they are once again occupied by bearded, black-robed Orthodox monks.

Fragments of the church's original frescoes can be seen in the extensive **Icon Museum** (Muzeum Ikon: Tues–Sun: May–Sept noon–7pm; Oct–April 10am–5pm; 10zł) at the back of the monastery courtyard. The main aim of the museum is to explain the importance of the icon in Orthodox art, with reproductions of historical icons, English-language texts, and a sumptuous collection of church art from eastern Poland – all atmospherically lit and accompanied by ethereal background music. The works gathered here encompass a range of themes and images: scenes from the lives of Mary and Jesus, benign-looking early church fathers and saints, ethereal archangels and cherubim. Particularly interesting are the locally produced brass icons, sufficiently durable to fit into someone's luggage – thus ensuring saintly protection while on one's travels.

There's no better place to **eat** in Supraśl than *Bar Jarzębinka* at ul. 3 Maja 22 (Tues–Sun 11am–6pm), a simple order-at-the-counter eatery that's famous for its *babka* – a delicious Belarusian-Lithuanian potato mush which is baked in square tins and then covered in (usually mushroom) sauce.

Supraśl's other main claim to fame is the **Wierszalin theatre** (℡085/710 8845, ⓦwww.wierszalin.pl), based in a semi-timbered building behind the parish church at ul. Kościelna 4. Famous for reinterpreting classical drama through folklore and rural ritual, they perform on Saturdays throughout the year (except in summer), with events usually starting at 6pm.

The Puszcza Knyszyńska

Stretching either side of Supraśl is the **Puszcza Knyszyńska**, a popular walking area with Białystok residents. The sandy local terrain is pretty easy-going underfoot, but the lack of signs once you get into the forest makes a local map, such as *Okolice Białegostoku* 1:150,000, readily available in Białystok, essential.

This is attractive and enjoyable walking country, the silence of the forest broken at intervals by cackling crows overhead or startled deer breaking for cover. Starting from the southern edge of Supraśl, a marked path takes you south through the lofty expanses of forest to the village of **Ciasne**, ending up by the bus stop near **Grabówka** at the edge of the main road back into Białystok – a twelve-kilometre hike in total.

Branicki Summer Palace

The highways and byways of eastern Poland hide a wealth of neglected old aristocratic piles, most of them relics of a not-so-distant period when a small group of fabulously wealthy families owned most of the eastern part of the country. The eighteenth-century **Branicki Summer Palace** (Lietna Rezydencja Branickiego) at **Choroszcz**, located 10km west of Białystok off the main Warsaw road, is a fine example of this phenomenon, the key difference being that the palace here has been completely renovated and converted into a **museum** (Tues–Sun 10am–3pm; 8zł, free on Sun). To get here, catch a local **bus** from Białystok bus station; the palace is on the west side of town, just a short walk from the main stop.

The elegant statue-topped **Summer Palace** makes for quite a contrast with the architectural rigours of Bialystok, with its tranquil country location on the edge of the grounds of the local hospital another agreeable feature. Few of the building's original furnishings remain; instead the house is arranged as a **museum** of furniture and interior decoration from the time of the Branickis. The main ground-floor room is the **salon**, its sedate parquet floor complemented by a choice collection of period furniture. A portrait of the original master of the house, Jan Branicki, along with a number of other family portraits, hangs in the hallway, the finely wrought iron balustrades of the staircase illuminated by a lamp held aloft by a rather tortured-looking classical figure. The **second floor** is equally ornate, featuring a number of meticulously decorated apartment rooms, a dining room with a fine set of mid-eighteenth-century Meissen porcelain and a **Chippendale room**.

Back outside, it's worth taking a stroll along the canal running from beneath the salon windows at the back of the palace, its overgrown **grounds** stretching out in all directions. From the bridge over the canal you have a good view of the house along with the old lodge and manor farm.

Tykocin

Some 40km west of Białystok, north of the main Warsaw road (the E18), is the quaint, sleepy little town of **TYKOCIN**, set in the open vistas of the Podlasie countryside. Tykocin's size belies its historical significance: as well as the former site of the national arsenal, it also has one of the best-restored **synagogues** in Poland today, much visited by Jewish tourist groups, and a reminder that this was once home to an important Jewish community. It's a forty-minute journey from the main bus station in Białystok; services depart roughly hourly throughout the day.

The bus deposits you just beyond the enchanting **town square**, bordered by well-preserved nineteenth-century wooden houses. The **statue** of Stefan Czarnecki in the centre of the square was put up by his grandson Jan Branicki in 1770, while he was busy rebuilding the town and his adopted home of Białystok.

The Baroque **parish church**, commissioned by the energetic Branicki in 1741 and recently restored, has a beautiful polychrome ceiling, a finely ornamented side chapel of the Virgin and a functioning Baroque organ. The portraits of Branicki and his wife, Izabella Poniatowska, are by Silvester de Mirys, a Scot who became the resident artist at the Branicki palace in Białystok. Also founded by Branicki was the nearby Bernardine convent, now a Catholic seminary. Next to the church looking onto the river bridge is the **Alumnat**, a hospice for war veterans founded in 1633 – a world first. Continue out of town over the River Narew and you'll come to the sixteenth-century **Radziwiłł Palace** (Pałac Radziwiłłów), where the national arsenal was once kept. Destroyed by the Swedes in 1657, the palace is currently the site of a huge rebuilding project that will ultimately see several of its towers rise again.

The synagogue and museum

Jews first came to Tykocin in 1522, and by the early nineteenth century seventy percent of the population was Jewish, the figure declining to around fifty percent by 1900. The original wooden **synagogue** in the town centre was replaced in 1642 by the Baroque building still standing today. Carefully restored in the 1970s following the usual severe wartime damage by the Nazis, it now houses an excellent **museum** (Tues–Sun 10am–5pm; 5zł, free on Sun), where background recordings of Jewish music and prayers add to an evocative atmosphere. Information sheets in English and German give detailed background on both the building and the history of Tykocin Jewry. Beautifully illustrated Hebrew inscriptions, mostly prayers, adorn sections of the interior walls, as do some lively colourful **frescoes**. Most striking of all is the large Baroque bimah, and there's a fine, ornate Aron Kodesh in the east wall. Valuable religious artefacts are on display, as well as historical documents relating to the now-lost community.

Over the square in the old Talmud house there's a well-kept local history **museum** (same hours and ticket), featuring an intact apothecary's shop and photos of Tykocin folk past and present. The **Jewish cemetery** on the edge of town is gradually blending into the surrounding meadow – as so often, there's no one able or willing to take care of it. Among the eroded, weather-beaten gravestones, however, a few preserve their fine original carvings.

Practicalities

There's not a lot going on in Tykocin and it's consequently an extremely restful place to **stay**. *Pensjonat Austeria*, pl. Czarneckiego 11 (☎085/718 7582, ☯www .austeria.tiu.pl; ❷) offers appealing en-suite rooms with attic ceilings above the main-square pizzeria of the same name, while *Pod Czarnym Bocianem*, ul. Poświętna 16 (☎085/718 7408 & 515 668 583; ❷) is a homely B&B on a cobbled street behind the parish church. There's a courtyard restaurant inside the Alumnat building serving up moderately priced Polish staples. The *Tejsza*, behind the museum at ul. Kozia 2, is pretty unexceptional, despite admirable attempts to reproduce some traditional Jewish dishes.

Biebrza National Park

North and west of Tykocin lies one of Poland's unique natural paradises, a large area of low-lying marshland encompassed within the **Biebrza National Park** (Biebrzański Park Narodowy: ☯www.biebrza.org.pl), added to the country's stock of officially protected areas in 1993, and, at around 600 square kilometres, its largest. Running through the area is the Biebrza River, which has its source southeast of Augustów close to the Belarusian border. The river feeds a sizeable network of bogs and marshes that constitutes one of Europe's most extensive and unspoilt **wetlands**. The scenic river basin landscape is home to richly varied flora and fauna. Important animal residents include otters, a large beaver population, wild boar, wolves and several hundred elk. The plant community includes just about every kind of marshland and forest species to be found in the country, including a rich assortment of rare mosses. The park's bird life – of which more than 260 species have been recorded to date, many of them with local breeding habitats – is proving a major attraction with bird-watchers from all over Europe. **Spring** is the time to come, when floodwaters extend for miles along the river valley, making an ideal habitat for a large number of **waterfowl**, including the pintail, shoveler and teal, as well as such rarities as the black tern and, most prized of all, the aquatic warbler.

The park is divided into three sections, corresponding to portions of the river. The **Northern Basin**, the smallest and least easily accessible, lies in the upper part of the river, and is not much visited. The **Middle Basin** encompasses a scenic section of marshland and river forest, notably the **Red Marsh** (*Czerwone Bagno*) area, a stretch of strictly protected peat bog located some distance from the river valley floodlands which is home to a large group of elk as well as smaller populations of golden and white-tailed eagles. The area is off-limits to anyone not accompanied by an official guide (see below). The **Southern Basin**, coursed by the broad, lower stretches of the river, consists of a combination of peat bogs and marshland, and is the most popular bird-watching territory on account of the large number of species to be found here. It's relatively easy to spot elk browsing among the shrubs from the viewing towers in this area.

Osowiec-Twierdza and around

The main entry point to the park is **OSOWIEC-TWIERDZA** (served by several daily trains on the Białystok–Ełk line), a drab village built to serve a massive tsarist-era fortress (*twierdza*) whose imposing grey walls can be seen stretching beside the railway tracks as you approach. A short walk north of the train station, the **National Park Information Centre** (May–Sept daily 8am–7pm; Oct–April Mon–Fri 7.30am–3.30pm; ☏086/738 3035, ✉it@biebrza .org.pl) sells entrance tickets to the park (5zł), offers advice on walking routes, and has a small photographic display of the Biebrza region's wildlife. The centre also arranges **guides** (150zł flat fee per group) for those eager to visit the restricted Red Marsh zone (see above).

The central part of the park is within easy walking distance of Osowiec. After about 2km, the road north from the information centre will bring you to a bridge over the Biebrza River. Beyond here a pair of well-marked boardwalk trails take you across the soggy surface of the Biebrza's flood plain, providing access to a captivating landscape of tufted grasses and sedge. After another 2km the trail meets the main Białystok–Ełk road, where a **viewing tower** provides a wonderful panorama of the hypnotically desolate landscape of rush-filled swamp. Along the way you'll pass several remnants of the tsarist-era fortification system, as well as half-destroyed concrete bunkers built by the Germans in World War II. Many of these relics are used as nesting platforms by the park's bird population.

Alternatively, and more adventurously, you can explore the park **by boat**, especially worthwhile if you want to head beyond the immediate vicinity of Osowiec. The most ambitious locally organized **excursion** takes you along the Biebrza and Narew rivers all the way from Rajgród in the north down as far as Łomza – a five- to seven-day trip involving stopovers at campsites and forester's lodges along the river route. Check with the BPN office for current details or contact any of the Augustów agencies (see box, p.225).

Practicalities

A village shop near Osowiec's information centre sells basic food and drink, and there's a folksy restaurant at the northern end of Osowiec (open daily in spring and summer, but much more erratic in autumn and winter) serving inexpensive Polish staples.

The information centre in Osowiec can help find **accommodation** in **private rooms** (❷), although these are mostly in the village of **Goniądz**, 5km to the east. Goniądz is also the site of two fair-sized **hotels**; the *Zbysko*, ul. Rozali 1 (☏085/738 0074, ⓦwww.zbysko.com; ❸), a plain but comfortable place with a simple restaurant; while the *Bartlowizna* at the edge of the village at ul. Nadbrzeżańska 32 (☏085/738 0630, ⓦwww.biebrza.com.pl; ❻) is almost a self-contained resort in its own right, offering a folk-style restaurant, landscaped garden, tennis courts and stables.

To pitch a tent, there's the *Bóbr* **campsite** (☏085/738 0620) at the northern end of Osowiec.

Kruszyniany and Bohoniki

Hard up against the Belarusian frontier, the old Tatar villages of **Kruszyniany** and **Bohoniki** are an intriguing ethnic component of Poland's eastern border-lands, with their wooden mosques and Muslim graveyards. The story of how these people came to be here is fascinating in itself (see box, below), and a visit to the villages is an instructive and impressive experience.

Getting to them is no mean feat. Direct **buses to Kruszyniany** from Białystok are scarce: the alternative is to take the bus to **Krynki** (about 40km) and wait for a connection to Kruszyniamy. If there aren't any of these, the only thing left to do is hitch. The only **buses to Bohoniki** are from **Sokółka**, an hour's train journey north of Białystok. If you're trying to visit both villages in the same day, the best advice is to go to Kruszyniamy first, return to Krynki (probably by hitching) then take a bus towards Sokółka. Ask the driver to let you off at **Stara Kamionka**, and walk the remaining 4km east along the final stretch of the Tatar Way (Szlak Tartarski), which runs between the two villages. To get back to Białystok, take the

The Tatars

Early in the thirteenth century, the nomadic Mongol people of Central Asia were welded into a confederation of tribes under the rule of Genghis Khan. In 1241 the most ferocious of these tribes, the **Tatars**, came charging out of the steppes and divided into two armies, one of which swept towards Poland, the other through Hungary. Lightly armoured, these superlative horsemen moved with a speed that no European soldiery could match, and fought with cruel and brutal efficiency, fuelled by a diet of raw meat and horse's milk thickened with blood. On Easter Sunday they destroyed **Kraków**, and in April came up against the forces of the Silesian ruler, Duke Henryk the Pious, at Legnica. Henryk's troops were annihilated, and a contemporary journal records that "terror and doubt took hold of every mind" throughout the Christian West. Before the eventual withdrawal of the Tatar hordes, all of southern Poland was ravaged repeatedly – Kraków, for example, was devastated in 1259 and again in 1287.

Within a generation, however, the Tatars had withdrawn into central Russia and the Crimea, ceasing to pose a threat to the powers of central Europe. By the late fourteenth century the Tatars of the Crimea had come under the sway of the **Grand Duchy of Lithuania** – a vast east-European empire which became dynastically linked to Poland after 1386. Lithuanian ruler Vytautas the Great drafted Tatar units into his armies, and a contingent of Tatars helped the Polish-Lithuanian army defeat the Teutonic Knights at the **Battle of Grunwald** in 1410 (see box, p.180 & p.208). Over the next few centuries communities of Tatars continued to migrate into the Grand Duchy of Lithuania (which at the time covered most of Belarus and parts of present-day eastern Poland). In time, Poland effectively absorbed Lithuania and its peoples (see box, p.230). In the late seventeenth century, **King Jan Sobieski** granted additional lands in eastern Poland to Tatars who had taken part in his military campaigns, creating further pockets of Tatar settlement in the region, many of which – Kruszyniamy and Bohoniki included – have remained up to this day.

Today some six thousand descendants of these **first Muslim citizens** of Poland are spread all over the country, particularly in the Szczecin, Gdańsk and Białystok areas. Though thoroughly integrated into Polish society, they are distinctive both for their Asiatic appearance and for their faith – the Tatars of Gdańsk, for example, have recently completed a **mosque**. Apart from the mosques and graveyards at Bohoniki and Kruszyniamy, little is left of the old settlements in the region east of Białystok, but there are a number of mosques still standing over the border in Belarus.

late afternoon bus to Sokołka, then a train back to the city – they depart regularly up until around 10pm. When visiting, bear in mind that to visit the mosques men and women should be appropriately dressed, with arms and legs covered.

The villages

Walking through **KRUSZYNIAMY** is like moving back a century or two: the painted wooden houses, cobbled road and wizened old peasants on their front porches are like something out of Tolstoy. Surrounded by trees and set back from the road is the eighteenth-century **mosque**, recognizable by the Islamic crescent hanging over the entrance gate, though the architecture is strongly reminiscent of the wooden churches of eastern Poland. A notice on the door of the mosque will tell you who the current keyholder is and where you can find them. You'll be expected to leave a few złoty as an offering.

Though the Tatar population is dwindling – currently the village musters only a handful of people for the monthly services conducted by the visiting imam from Białystok – the mosque's predominantly wooden interior is well maintained. A glance at the list of Arab diplomats in the visitor's book explains where the money comes from. The building is divided into two sections, the smaller one for women, the larger carpeted one for men, containing the *mihrab*, the customary recess pointing in the direction of Mecca, and a *mimber* (pulpit) from which the prayers are directed by the imam.

The **Muslim cemetery**, five minutes' walk beyond the mosque, contains a mixture of well-tended modern gravestones and, in the wood behind, old stones from the tsarist era. Despite the Tatar presence, the population of the village is predominantly Belarusian, a fact reflected in the presence of an Orthodox church, an uninspiring concrete structure that replaced the wooden original, which was destroyed by fire. In summer you'll find moderately priced traditional Tatar **food** such as skewer-grilled lamb kebabs and meat-filled kolduny (Lithuanian-Tatar ravioli) at the *Tatarska Jurta* across the road from the mosque or at *Pod Lipami*, a comfortable pension at no. 51 (☎085/722 7554, Ⓦwww.dworekpodlipami.pl; ❹), with en-suite doubles as well as three- to four-person family rooms.

The mosque in more remote **BOHONIKI** is a similar, though smaller, building, colour-washed in bright green on the outside, and stuffed with cosy-looking carpets within. Again, you'll need to find the keyholder to let you in – the noticeboard will tell you where to go – and you should donate a few złoty for your visit.

In the **Tatar cemetery**, hidden in a copse half a kilometre south of the village, gravestones are inscribed in both Polish and Arabic with characteristic Tatar names like Ibrahimowicz – in other words, Muslim names with a Polish ending tacked on. Search through the undergrowth right at the back of the cemetery and you'll find older, tumbledown gravestones inscribed in Russian from the days when Bohoniki was an outpost of the tsarist empire. Tatars from all over Poland are still buried here, as they have been since Sobieski's time (see box, p.243).

South from Białystok

Moving south of Białystok you're soon into the villages and fields of southern Podlasie, the heartland of the country's Belarusian population – you'll see the Cyrillic lettering of their language on posters (though not as yet on street signs) throughout the area. It's a poor, predominantly rural region that retains a distinctively Eastern feel. For visitors, the best-known attraction is the ancient **Białowieża Forest** straddling the border with neighbouring Belarus. **Hajnówka**, a regional focus of Orthodox worship, provides an intriguing gateway to the area. The extraordinary convent at **Grabarka**, the focal point of Orthodox pilgrimage in Poland, is also worth investigating.

Buses represent the best way of getting around the region. A plentitude of services trundle south from Białystok to Hajnówka and Siemiatycze: change in Hajnówka for the Białowieża Forest and in Siemiatycze for Grabarka. On the way through the flat, wooded greenery of the Podlasie countryside you'll see more Orthodox onion domes than Catholic spires, a sure indication of the strength of the Belarusian population in the surrounding region.

Hajnówka

Some 70km southeast of Białystok, the sleepy settlement of **HAJNÓWKA** is the obvious entry point to the Białowieża forest, which stretches east of the town as far as the Belarusian border. Hajnówka itself is an important centre for Poland's Belarusian minority, a position symbolized by the magnificent Orthodox **Holy Trinity Church** (Cerkiew Świętej Trójcy), an uncompromisingly modern structure consecrated in 1992 which guards the northern approaches to the town. With a curving roof punctured by a pair of onion-domed towers topped by Orthodox crucifixes, the interior boasts a glittering iconostasis, a spectacular series of luminous frescoes, and a fine set of stained-glass windows.

Hidden in a courtyard just off the main street, ulica 3 Maja, Hajnówka's House of Culture (Dom Kultury) contains a small **museum** (Tues–Sun: June–Sept 9am–4pm; Oct–May 10am–3pm; 4zł), with a modest collection of agricultural implements and traditional textiles.

There are two international festivals of **Orthodox church music** associated with Hajnówka, both of which take place in May. The International Festival of Orthodox Choral Music (Ⓦwww.festival-hajnowka.pl) involves concerts in both Hajnówka and Białystok; while the other one (Ⓦwww.festiwal.cerkiew.pl) takes place in Hajnówka's Holy Trinity Church. Featuring **choirs** from Poland and its eastern neighbours, both offer a rare chance to hear haunting liturgical music of the highest quality.

The forest railway

The easiest way to access the gorgeously thick woodland around Hajnówka is to take a trip on the **forest railway** (*kolejka leśna*), the remainder of a dense network of narrow-gauge lines built by German occupying forces in 1916. The network was used by local logging companies right up until 1992, when it became more economical to transport the wood by truck. Departing from a tiny **station** on ulica Celna, twenty minutes' walk east of the centre, the line runs to the village of Topiło, 8km south of town, three times a week between June 1 and the last weekend in September (currently Tues, Thurs & Sat at 10am; 22zł return). The trip takes you through hauntingly dense forest, and halts for about 45 minutes in Topiło itself (where there's a small café) before the return journey to Hajnówka.

Practicalities

Hajnówka's bus station is fifteen minutes' walk southwest of the town centre – although most services also pick up and drop off on the main ulica 3 Maja. Note that the Oktobus and Lob-Trans services to and from Białowieża only use the stops on ul 3 Maja. The helpful **tourist information** office at ul. 3 Maja 45 (Mon–Fri 9am–5pm, Sat 9am–1pm; ℗085/682 5141) sells maps of the Białowieża forest and has bus timetable information on how to get there. If you need a **place to stay**, try the *Zajazd Orzechowski*, ul. Piłsudskiego 14 (℗085/682 2758; ❺), which has cramped but acceptable en suites and a breakfast room-cum-restaurant that only functions when large groups arrive; while *Dom Nauczyciela*, ul. Piłsudskiego 6 (℗085/682 2585; ❹), has a mixture of en suites and spartan rooms with shared facilities – there's no breakfast, but you might get an electric kettle in the room. The main **eating** options are *Leśny Dworek*, in the same building as the museum, offering Belarusian dishes (such as pork chops stuffed with ham and peas), and the order-at-the-counter *Lokal Gastronomiczny* just off the eastern end of ulica 3 Maja, which serves up soups, stodgy Polish staples and *żubr* beer.

The Białowieża Forest

Twenty kilometres east of Hajnówka, **Białowieża** stands at the centre of the **Białowieża Forest** (Puszcza Białowieska), the last major tract of primeval forest left in Europe. Covering 1260 square kilometres and spreading way over the border into Belarus, most of the forest falls within the **Białowieża National Park** (Białowieski Park Narodowy), the first national park to be established in Poland and the only one currently numbered among UNESCO's World Natural Heritage sites. As well as being an area of inestimable beauty, the forest is also famous for harbouring a large population of **European bison**. Captive specimens can be seen in a special reserve.

For centuries Białowieża was a **private hunting ground** for a succession of Lithuanian and Belarusian princes, Polish kings, Russian tsars and other potentates – patronage which ensured the forest survived largely intact. Recognizing its environmental importance, the Polish government turned large sections of the *puszcza* into a national park in 1921, not least to protect its **bison herds**, which had been hunted and eaten to extinction by famished soldiers during World War I. Like most *puszcza*, Białowieża has hidden its fair share of partisan armies, most notably during the 1863 uprising and World War II; monuments scatter the area, as, no doubt, do the bones of countless unknown dead.

Nearly forty percent of the forest located on the Polish side of the border belongs to a so-called **strict reserve** (*rezervat ścisły*), a tightly controlled area clearly marked on the maps that can only be visited accompanied by a guide. The rest of the national park is open to unaccompanied individuals, and there are plenty of marked paths and biking routes to enjoy – especially around the **Bison Reserve** west of Białowieża village and the **Royal Oaks Way** to the northwest. If you're planning on spending any time in this part of the country, the extraordinary, primeval feel of the forest makes even a day-trip an experience not to be missed.

Getting to Białowieża is straightforward. There are three daily **buses** from Białystok to the village; if you miss one of these, take one of the (roughly hourly) buses to Hajnówka, where you can pick up one of the frequent buses to Białowieża from the main street (see p.245). If you start early in the day, you can treat the forest as a day-trip and be back in Białystok by nightfall. However there's plenty of **accommodation** in Białowieża, and the idea of a reposeful night or two in this beautiful landscape has undoubted appeal.

Białowieża

BIAŁOWIEŻA, a mere 2km from the Belarusian border, is a sleepy agricultural village full of the single-storey wooden farmhouses that characterize Poland's eastern borderlands. Colour-washed in a variety of ochres, maroons and greens, with neatly stacked woodpiles in every yard, they're a picture of domestic tidiness. As the sprinkling of satellite dishes and gleaming new red roofs shows, tourism has made the village relatively prosperous compared with other parts of Podlasie.

Buses terminate at the eastern end of the village, opposite a red-brick Catholic church, although you'll save time by getting off earlier – either at the southern gate of the **Palace Park** (Park Pałacowy), near the disused train station, or at the eastern entrance to the Park, opposite the typical late nineteenth-century Orthodox **Church of St Nicholas** (Cerkiew św. Mikołaja), which boasts a unique and very attractive tiled iconostasis.

The Palace Park was laid out in the 1890s to accompany a neo-Gothic palace built to serve as the hunting lodge of the Russian tsars. The palace itself was damaged in World War II and demolished totally in the 1960s, but there's still much to enjoy, including a brace of ornamental lakes and a strollable collection of tree-lined avenues. At its centre rises the gleaming new National Park Centre, which contains hotel, restaurant and the state-of-the-art **Natural History Museum** (Muzeum Przyrodniczo-Leśne: June–Sept Mon–Fri 9am–4.30pm, Sat & Sun 9am–5pm; Oct–May Tues–Sun 9am–4pm; 22zł). The hefty entrance fee (which includes an English-speaking guide) is justified by an impressively detailed and well-presented introduction to the forest, including examples of the amazingly diverse flora and fauna. The tour lasts about an hour and includes a climb up the viewing tower to look out over the park and forest. Just downhill from the museum to the west is the deep blue-green **Governor's House** (Dworek: Mon–Fri 8am–4pm; 6zł), a charming former hunting lodge in which the Russian tsars stayed while awaiting the construction of their much bigger palace. The house now hosts art and photography exhibitions, usually with an ecological theme.

One kilometre northwest of the village, a small **skansen** displays the picturesque timber houses typical of farmsteads in the Polish-Belarusian borderlands, with a pair of wooden windmills adding to the spectacle. The *skansen* doesn't have regular opening times and isn't always staffed, although the gate is usually open during daylight hours.

The strict reserve

The most dramatic stretches of deep forest lie within the "strict reserve" to the north of the village, which can only be visited in the company of an **official guide**. To arrange a guide, ask at the National Park Centre (same times as museum; ℡085/681 2360, Ⓦwww.bpn.com.pl), or at the PTTK office at the southern entrance to the Palace Park (Mon–Fri 8am–4pm, Sat & Sun 8am–3pm; ℡085/681 2295, Ⓦwww.pttk.bialowieza.pl). Either place will fix you up with a three-hour guided walking tour costing 165zł per group plus an additional 6zł per person for the National Park entrance ticket.

The PTTK office can also arrange a three-hour **horse-drawn cart tour** of the strict reserve (160zł for a four-person cart) although there are limits on the numbers of carts allowed into the reserve on any given day, and booking a day or two ahead is sound policy in summer. A Polish-speaking guide is included in the price; an English-speaking guide will cost an additional 100zł.

However you decide to enter the strict reserve, it's likely to be a magical experience. At times the serenity of the forest's seemingly endless depths is exhilarating, the trunks of oak, spruce and hornbeam swell threateningly to a dense canopy,

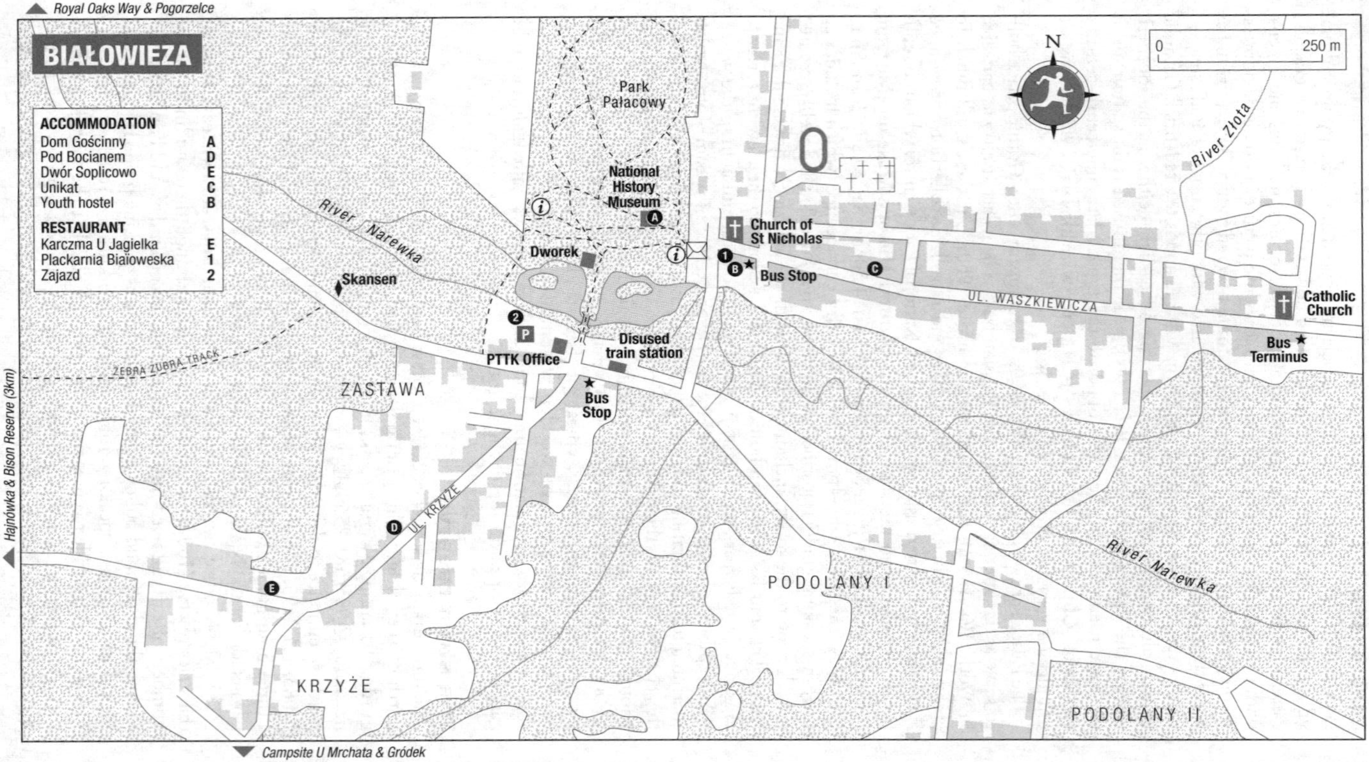

◀ Royal Oaks Way & Pogorzelce

BIAŁOWIEZA

ACCOMMODATION
Dom Gościnny   A
Pod Bocianem   D
Dwór Soplicowo   E
Unikat   C
Youth hostel   B

RESTAURANT
Karczma U Jagiełka   E
Piackarnia Białowieska   1
Zajazd   2

River Złota

River Narewka

PODOLANY II

Catholic Church

Bus Terminus

UL. WASZKIEWICZA

Church of St Nicholas

Bus Stop

C

Park Pałacowy

National History Museum

A

Disused train station

Dworek

PTTK Office

P

Bus Stop

PODOLANY I

ZASTAWA

River Narewka

Skansen

D

UL. KRZYŻE

KRZYŻE

E

ŻEBRA ŻUBRA TRACK

N

0   250 m

▼ Hajnówka & Bison Reserve (3km)

Campsite U Mrchata & Gródek ▶

momentarily pierced by shafts of sunlight that sparkle briefly before subsiding into gloom. Along with the larger animals, such as wolves, elk and beavers, the forest supports an astounding profusion of **flora and fauna**: over twenty species of tree, twenty of rodents, thirteen varieties of bat, 228 of birds and around 8000 different insect species.

The Bison Reserve

Situated some 4km west of the village on the road to Hajnówka, the **Bison Reserve** (Rezervat Pokazowy Zwierząt: Tues–Sun 9am–5pm; 6zł) is a large fenced area where some of the most impressive species living in the forest are on display. You can walk to the reserve in fifty minutes by following the **Żebra Żubra path**, a fascinating forest trail which leaves the Białowieża–Budy road just beyond the *skansen* (see p.247). A raised boardwalk takes you above the squelchy, fern-and-moss-covered forest floor, with a bewildering diversity of deciduous trees crowding in on either side – information boards along the way will help you to tell your Ash from your Alder.

The reserve itself contains several representatives of the forest's 250-strong population of bison. Don't be fooled by their docile demeanour: when threatened, the bison – *żubr* in Polish – can charge at over 50km an hour, which makes for a force to be reckoned with when you bear in mind that the largest weigh in excess of 1000kg. The stout, sandy-coloured horses with a dark stripe on their backs that are also on show are **tarpans**, relations of the original steppe horses that died out in the last century. The tarpans are gradually being bred back to their original genetic stock after centuries of interbreeding with village horses. In other enclosures round the reserve you can see wolves, elk, wild boar and lynx.

The Royal Oaks Way

One of the most memorable parts of the forest lying outside the strict reserve is the **Royal Oaks Way** (Szlak Dębów Królewskich: 6zł) located 4km north of the bison reserve along a yellow marked trail. It consists of a group of forty-metre-high oaks, the oldest of which are over four hundred years old. The brooding, venerable specimens ranged along the path are all named after Polish kings and Lithuanian grand dukes – a reminder that the forest lies along the historical boundary between these two realms.

Park practicalities

The park **information centre**, just inside the eastern entrance to the Park Pałacowy (June–Sept 9am–4pm; ℡085/681 2901), gives away English-language leaflets detailing the attractions of the forest, sells local maps, and keeps a list of **private rooms** (reckon on 40–50zł per person) in the village. There are several family-run **B&Bs** around the village's main street, of which *Pod Bocianem* (The Stork House), ul. Olgi Gabiec 14 (℡085/681 2681; ❷–❸) is one of the most charming, with snug rooms – some en suite, some not – located in three traditional farmhouse buildings, grouped around a lawn.

Altogether different in style is the *Dom Gościnny* (Guesthouse) in the National Park building (℡085/682 9729, ⓦwww.bpn.com.pl; ❸) offering smart en-suite doubles (❸) and triples (120zł) in a sleek ultra-modern building right in the Palace Park. Moving more upmarket, the *Dwór Soplicowo*, ul. Krzyże 2a (℡085/681 2840, ⓦwww.dworsoplicowo.pl; ❻), offers plush carpets, smart furniture, an indoor pool and a beauty spa, all set in an enjoyably kitsch building that looks like a nineteenth-century rural manor house. *U Michala* at ul. Krzyże

11 (☎085/681 2703) is the best-organized **campsite** but many villagers also allow more informal camping in their gardens in summer – look for *pole namiotowe* signs.

For **eating**, the *Zajazd* in the car park south of the Palace Park looks on the hum-drum side but serves superbly succulent locally made *pierogi*: try the *bialowieskie* (stuffed with cabbage and mushrooms) or *dziskie* (featuring tasty bits of wild boar). For a top-quality meal you should visit the *Karczma u Janielka* at the *Dwór Soplicowo*, where you can dine on duck, boar, deer and other classics of the Polish country kitchen, in a dining room strewn with hunting trophies and animal skins.

Grabarka

Hidden away in the woods 60km southwest of Hajnówka, the **convent** near the village of **GRABARKA** is for Orthodox Poles the most important pilgrimage site in the country. Although the site of a chapel since medieval times, Grabarka didn't become a convent until 1947, when several groups of Orthodox nuns (some from eastern territories recently occupied by the Soviet Union) chose this isolated rural spot as the site of a new community. It quickly became the country's most venerated Orthodox spiritual centre, and the site of major pilgrimages on the main Orthodox holy days. By far the biggest takes place during the **Feast of the Transfiguration** (Przemienienia Panskiego) on August 19, when thousands of faithful from around the country flock to Grabarka, many by foot.

Approached by a quiet forest road, the convent **church** stands at the top of a small wooded hill. Burnt to the ground in 1990 and rebuilt over the next eight years, the dainty timber structure is crowded with brightly painted saintly icons. Outside the church is a striking thicket of **wooden crosses**, the oldest dating back to the early eighteenth century, when pilgrims drawn by stories of miracles said to have occurred during a local epidemic of cholera first began coming here, packing the slopes below the church. A traditional gesture of piety carried by pilgrims and placed here on completing their journey, the thousands of characteristic Orthodox crucifixes clustered together in all shapes and sizes are an extraordinarily powerful sight.

Practicalities

Buses run to Grabarka village (roughly half a kilometre from the convent) two or three times a day from the drab market town of Siemiatycze, which in turn can be reached by regular bus from Białystok or Lublin. Alternatively, you can take a **train** to the village of Sycze from Białystok (three daily; changing at Czeremcha) or Hajnówka (three daily; one of which involves changing at Czeremcha), and walk the approximately one-kilometre distance remaining though the woods up to the convent. However you get here it's likely to be a long if leisurely day out, with few snack-buying opportunities en route – so pack a **sandwich** and something to **drink**.

Biała Podlaska

BIAŁA PODLASKA is a sleepy market town commanding the approaches to the Belarusian border at Terespol, forty-odd kilometres east. The town's one real attraction is the **Radziwiłł Castle** (Zamek Radziwiłłów), west of the main square, a seventeenth-century structure built by the Radziwiłłs, a powerful family of Polish-Lithuanian magnates who held estates all over Poland. Today

Some 20km north of Biała Podlaska, close up by the Belarus border, **JANÓW PODLASKI** is home to the country's most famous **stud farm**, specializing in the rearing of thoroughbred Arab horses. Located 2km east of the town centre (clearly signposted from the Rynek and served by local bus), the stables are regularly visited by luminaries of the international equestrian scene, principally during the Polish National Arabian Horse Show and Auction, held annually in mid-August.

Established by Tsar Alexander I in 1817 in order to replace horses killed during the Napoleonic wars, the farm has gone through its ups and downs: the stock was decimated by German soldiers late in World War I, and taken over by the Nazis during World War II, when the horses were transported to Germany, many dying in the Allied bombing of Dresden in February 1944. The elegant stable complex you see today is essentially that designed by the Warsaw architect Marconi in the 1830s and 1840s.

Visiting the stables is by guided tour with prior appointment only (☎083/341 3009, ⓦ www.janow.arabians.pl). Janów is easy to reach from Biała Podlaska, with frequent **buses** making the thirty-minute journey. The best option for **accommodation** is the *Wygoda* guesthouse on the territory of the farm (☎083/341 3060, ⓦ www.wygoda .bt.pl; ❷) at ul. Wygoda 2.

the main building is a music academy, while the old Tower House contains the well-organized regional **museum** (Tues–Sun 9/10am–3/4pm; 4zł). Exhibitions on the upper floor feature an interesting display of local ethnography, including folk tapestries and examples of the pagan-influenced "sun" crucifixes typical of the Lithuanian part of the old Commonwealth. There's also an excellent collection of eighteenth- and nineteenth-century Orthodox **icons** from the Brest (formerly Brześć) area, now in Belarus. Of a number of churches in town, the basilica-shaped **St Anne's Church** (Kościół św. Anny), just up from the palace, is the most striking, an exuberant sixteenth-century structure with twin cupolas and a richly decorated side chapel devoted to the Radziwiłłs.

The **train station** is on the southern side of the town, a five-minute bus ride from the centre, with the **bus station** on plac Wojska Polskiego, a little to the east of the main Rynek along ulica Brzeska. For **accommodation**, the *Capitol* in residential streets immediately west of the Rynek at ul. Reymonta 3 (☎083/344 2358, ⓦ www.hotelcapitol.com.pl; ❺) is a privately run venture with a good selection of rooms and one of the town's better **restaurants**.

Kodeń

Some 40km southeast of Biała Podlaska along the border with Belarus lies the pilgrimage town of **KODEŃ**, home to a graceful seventeenth-century **parish church** combining Renaissance and Baroque elements, and built to house an icon thought to represent Our Lady of Guadeloupe. The town's owner, powerful nobleman Mikołaj Sapieha, miraculously recovered from a serious illness after praying before the icon in Rome in 1631. Determined to possess the painting, after Pope Urban VIII refused to sell it to him, Sapieha bribed a sacristan, who helped him to steal it. Sapieha was excommunicated when the crime was discovered, but, having fled with the treasure, he held his ground, building the church for the painting, and was eventually received back into the fold. Today the **icon**, which remains one of the most venerated in Poland, is the centrepiece of a splendid gilt altar, while the church interior is adorned with fine Renaissance stucco. The building's Baroque facade was added early in the eighteenth century.

Behind the church is a small **museum** (daily 8am–4pm; 2zł) displaying kitschy souvenirs brought from around the world by returning missionaries, and a very complete collection of birds' eggs and nests, gathered by a local priest in boyhood and left here when he was sent to Canada. Down the dirt road leading east from the church you'll find a park containing the scant remains of a sixteenth-century **fortress** that belonged to the Sapieha family, and a brick church from the same period, originally Orthodox (Mikołaj himself was a convert to Catholicism).

Although only easily accessible if you're driving, Kodeń is served by two daily **buses** from Włodawa (see p.269) and a half-dozen from Biała Podlaska.

Travel details

Trains

Augustów to: Białystok (5 daily; 2hr); Suwałki (5 daily; 30min).

Białystok to: Ełk (7 daily; 1hr 20min–1hr 45min); Gdańsk (2 daily; 7hr); Kraków (1 daily; 7hr); Olsztyn (3 daily; 4hr 30min); Suwałki (5 daily; 3hr); Warsaw (8 daily; 2hr 30min–3hr).

Ełk to: Giżycko (6 daily; 50min); Mikołajki (2 daily; 1hr 30min); Mrągowo (2 daily; 2hr 10min); Olsztyn (6 daily; 2hr 50min–3hr 30min).

Mikołajki to: Mrągowo (2 daily; 50min); Olsztyn (2 daily; 2hr 15min).

Mrągowo to: Olsztyn (2 daily; 1hr 20min).

Olsztyn to: Elbląg (8 daily; 1hr 30min–2hr); Gdańsk (6 daily; 2hr 50min); Giżycko (4 daily; 2hr); Kraków (1 daily; 8hr 30min); Ruciane-Nida (1 daily; 1hr 50min); Warsaw (4 daily; 3hr 30min).

Suwałki to: Ełk (1 daily; 1hr 50min); Kraków (June–Sept only: 1 daily; 12hr); Warsaw (3–5 daily; 5hr).

Buses

Augustów to: Białystok (7 daily; 1hr 40min); Ełk (8 daily; 1hr 20min); Giżycko (1 daily; 2hr 40min); Sejny (4 daily; 1hr); Suwałki (20 daily; 45min); Warsaw (4 daily; 4hr 20min).

Biała Podlaska to: Białystok (2 daily; 4hr); Janów Podlaski (6 daily; 30min); Kodeń (6 daily; 1hr); Lublin (8 daily; 2hr).

Białystok to: Białowieża (3 daily; 2hr 30min); Choroszcz (hourly; 30min); Hajnówka (hourly; 1hr 25min); Lublin (2 daily; 6hr); Olsztyn (2 daily; 5hr); Suwałki (6 daily; 2hr 20min); Tykocin (8 daily; 40min); Warsaw (1 daily; 6hr).

Ełk to: Suwałki (6 daily; 2hr).

Giżycko to: Gdańsk (4 daily; 5hr 20min); Kętrzyn (9 daily; 50min); Mikołajki (4 daily; 50min); Mrągowo (every 20min; 1hr 20min).

Hajnówka to: Białowieża (10 daily; 45min).

Kętrzyn to: Gdańsk (4 daily; 5hr 30min); Mrągowo (20 daily; 40min); Olsztyn (2 daily; 2hr 20min); Reszel (20 daily; 25min); Węgorzewo (18 daily; 1hr 5min).

Mikołajki to: Mrągowo (2 daily; 30min); Olsztyn (1 daily; 2hr 15min); Warsaw (4 daily in summer; 5hr 40min).

Mrągowo to: Białystok (2 daily; 4hr); Gdańsk (1 daily; 5hr 30min); Olsztyn (24 daily; 1hr 30min); Pisz (8 daily; 1hr); Ruciane-Nida (8 daily; 40min); Suwałki (4 daily; 3hr) Warsaw (1 daily; 5hr).

Olsztyn to: Gdańsk (3 daily; 4hr); Kętrzyn (2 daily; 1hr 30min); Lidzbark Warmiński (8 daily; 1hr 10min); Warsaw (3 daily; 5hr).

Sejny to: Puńsk (5 daily; 45min).

Suwałki to: Puńsk (5 daily; 50min); Sejny (hourly; 50min); Warsaw (4 daily; 5hr).

International trains

Augustów to: Vilnius (1 daily; change at Šeštokai; 5hr 30min).

Białystok to: Vilnius (1 daily; change at Šeštokai; 7hr).

Suwałki to: Vilnius (1 daily; change at Šeštokai; 5hr).

International buses

Białystok to: Minsk (1 daily; 7hr), Vilnius (1 daily; 9hr).

Mrągowo to: Vilnius (5 weekly; 9hr).

Olsztyn to: Vilnius (5 weekly; 8hr).

Suwałki to: Vilnius (1 daily; 6hr).

5

Lublin and the east

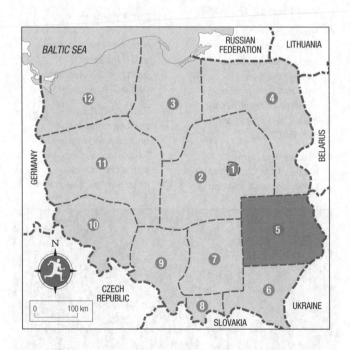

CHAPTER 5

Highlights

* **Lublin** Youthful and vibrant city with a wonderfully atmospheric old centre. See p.255

* **Majdanek** Former Nazi extermination camp, preserved as a stark warning to future generations. Harrowing but necessary. See p.265

* **Kozłówka** A stunning Baroque palace with lavish interiors, some of which have been given over to a mesmerizing museum of communist-era art and propaganda. See p.267

* **Puławy** The former estate of the Czartoryski family boasts a relaxing park sprinkled with follies. See p.272

* **Kazimierz Dolny** The best-preserved medieval town in this part of Poland, long the favoured weekend destination for arty Warsaw folk. See p.273

* **Sandomierz** Historic Wisła valley trading town with many of its medieval and Renaissance buildings still standing. See p.279

* **Zamość** Sixteenth-century model town, built as a showcase for Renaissance ideals and with a pronounced Italianate feel. See p.284

▲ Medieval frescoes, Chapel of the Holy Trinity, Lublin

Lublin and the east

S tretching from the Wisła River to the Belarusian and Ukrainian borders, the Lublin region is one of agricultural plains punctuated by backwoods villages and sleepy towns. This is historically one of Europe's main grain-producing areas, with local aristocrats amassing huge riches by shipping their produce down the river to the markets of Gdańsk. The palaces of these feudal landowners still dot the countryside, alongside market towns endowed by the magnates with fine public buildings and churches.

The main city of the region is bustling, self-confident **Lublin**, an economic and intellectual centre that also boasts one of Poland's most magical old towns. The smaller towns, particularly the old trading centres of **Kazimierz Dolny** and **Sandomierz** along the Wisła River, are among the country's most beautiful, long favoured by artists and retaining fine historic centres. A cherished weekend retreat of the Warsaw artistic set, Kazimierz in particular is one of the liveliest summertime destinations that Poland has to offer. Over to the east, **Zamość** has a superb Renaissance centre, miraculously preserved through wars and well worth a detour.

All of these places had significant **Jewish populations** before World War II, and the well-preserved synagogue at **Włodawa** provides some insight into what the whole of eastern Poland must have looked like before 1939. Lublin in particular was one of the most important Jewish centres in Poland, which probably explains why its suburb **Majdanek** was chosen by the Nazis as the site of one of their most notorious death camps – a chilling place that demands to be visited.

Public transport in the region is straightforward, with buses and minibuses fanning out from Lublin to all the outlying towns. Lublin itself is less than three hours away from Warsaw by express train.

Lublin

The city of **LUBLIN**, the largest in eastern Poland, is one of the most alluring urban centres in the whole country, thanks in large part to the evocative hive of alleys that constitute its magnificent Old Town. New arrivals are sometimes put off by the sprawling high-rise buildings and smokestacks of the suburbs, but once you're in the heart of the place, it's all cobbled streets and dilapidated mansions – a wistful reminder of past glories. The fabric of this old quarter came through World War II relatively undamaged, and recent restoration has made the city centre ripe for tourism, though Lublin sees nothing like the crowds

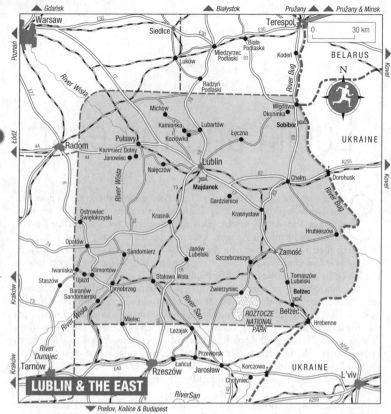

flowing into Kraków, Warsaw or Gdańsk. In among the numerous churches you'll find reminders that for centuries Lublin was home to a large and vibrant **Jewish community**, a population exterminated in the Nazi concentration camp at **Majdanek**, 6km from the city centre.

Some history

Like many eastern towns, Lublin started as a **medieval** trade settlement and guard post, in this case on the trade route linking the Baltic ports with Kiev and the Black Sea. With the informal union of Lithuania and Poland that followed the marriage of Grand Duke Jogaila to Queen Jadwiga in 1386, Lublin became an important centre of economic and political contact between the two countries. It was no surprise that the city was chosen to host the signing of the **Union of Lublin** in 1569, when the nobility of both nations agreed to establish the **Polish-Lithuanian Commonwealth** – at the time the largest mainland state in Europe. Over a century of prosperity followed, during which the arts flourished and many fine buildings were added to the city. The **Partitions** rudely interrupted this process, leaving Lublin to languish on the edge of the Russian-ruled Duchy of Warsaw for the next hundred years or so.

Following **World War I** and the regaining of national independence in 1918, a Catholic university – the only one in Eastern Europe – was established, which grew to become a cradle of the Polish Catholic intelligentsia, most notably during the communist era. It was to Lublin, too, that a group of Polish communists known as the **Committee of National Liberation** (PKWN) returned in 1944 from their wartime refuge in the Soviet Union to set up a new communist-dominated government. After the war, the city's industrial and commercial importance grew considerably, with a belt of factories mushrooming around the town centre.

Arrival and information

The **train station** is 2km to the south of the centre: from here bus #1 will take you to the edge of the Old Town, while bus #13 and trolleybus #150 both run to Krakowskie Przedmieście, just west of the centre. The **bus station** is much more conveniently located, lying just beyond the castle at the northern end of the Old Town. A separate **minibus station** (where minibuses from Kazimierz Dolny, Puławy and other local towns arrive) is sited one block north of the bus station.

Lublin's **tourist information centre**, in the Old Town on the corner of Bramowa and ulica Jezuicka (Mon–Fri 9am–7pm, Sat 10am–5pm, Sun 10am–4pm; ☎081/532 4412, ⓦwww.loit.lublin.pl), has helpful staff, comprehensive accommodation listings, and a big choice of maps for sale.

Accommodation

The city's supply of **hotels and pensions** has improved over the last few years, but the selection of good, central budget places is still inadequate. The **youth hostel**, al. Długosza 6 (☎081/533 0628; bus #13 or trolleybus #150 from the train station), an old-style place with a 10pm curfew, offers space in dorms or in triples (25–38zł per person) and is 1.5km west of the city centre, off the street behind a high school. The all-year **student hostel**, the *Hotel Studenta Zaocznego*, ul. Sowińskiego 17 (☎081/525 1081; ❷), in the university area, is another cheap alternative, with en-suite doubles and triples. Lublin's best **campsite** is the *Graf Marina*, at the edge of Lake Zemborzycki, 7km south of the centre at ul. Kręźnicka 6 (☎081/744 1070, ⓦwww.graf-marina.pl; May–Sept; bus #8 from ul. Narutowicza).

Hotels and pensions

The establishments under "Old Town and around" are marked on the Lublin Old Town map on p.260; those under "Outside the Old Town" are marked on the main Lublin map on p.258.

Old Town and around

Bramma Café ul. Grodzka 23 ☎081/532 1397, ⓦwww.bramma.pl. Four cosy en suites with TV, above the café of the same name, right next to the Grodzka Gate. No breakfast, no credit cards. ❹

Vanilla ul. Krakowskie Przedmieście 12 ☎081/536 6720, ⓦwww.vanilla-hotel.pl. Design-conscious hotel featuring orange corridors, rooms decked out in purples, reds and creams. Ask about weekend reductions. ❼

Waksman ul. Grodzka 19 ☎081/532 5454, ⓦwww.waksman.pl. Upmarket but good-value retro pension in the heart of the Old Town, with four doubles and two suites furnished with faux

antiques in styles ranging from Louis XVI to Victorian-era. Comfortable and generally tasteful, although one room does have a water bed. Wi-fi throughout. ❻

Outside the Old Town

Campanile ul. Lubomelska 14 ☎081/531 8400, ⓦwww.campanile.com.pl. Recently opened branch of the French chain, offering reliable standards and neat rooms. Just over a kilometre northeast of the Old Town. ❻

Dom Nauczyciela (ZNP) ul. Akademiczka 4 ☎081/533 8285, ⓦwww.hotelsinpoland.com/ domn-lub.htm. A basic but not especially cheap teachers' hotel near the university; often full, so

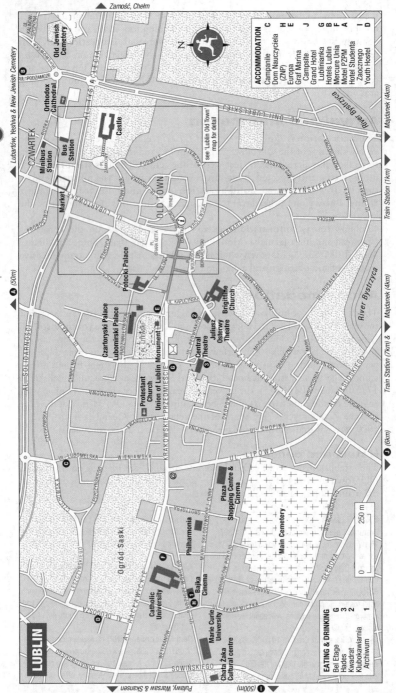

LUBLIN

▲ *Zamość, Chełm*

◀ *Lubartów, Yeshiva & New Jewish Cemetery*

◀ Ⓐ (50m)   ◀ Ⓘ (500m)   ▲ *Puławy, Warsaw & Skansen*

▶ Ⓙ (6km)   ▼ *Train Station (7km) &*   ▼ *Majdanek (4km)*

▶ *Train Station (1km)*   ▼ *Majdanek (4km)*

Old Jewish Cemetery
Orthodox Cathedral Ⓑ
Castle
Bus Station
Minibus Station
Market
OLD TOWN
RYNEK
ⓘ
see 'Lublin Old Town' map for detail
Potocki Palace
Czartoryski Palace
Lubomirski Palace Ⓔ
Brigittine Church
Juliusz Osterwy Theatre ②
Central Theatre ③
Ⓖ
Union of Lublin Monument
Protestant Church
Catholic University
Philharmonia
Plaza Shopping Centre & Cinema
Main Cemetery
Bajka Cinema
Marie Curie University
Chata Żaka Cultural centre
Ogród Saski
River Bystrzyca
Ⓒ
Ⓓ
Ⓕ ①
Ⓗ

0 ___ 250 m

ACCOMMODATION

Campanile	C
Dom Nauczyciela (ZNP)	H
Europa	E
Graf Marina	J
Campsite	
Grand Hotel	G
Hotels Lublin	B
Lublinianka	F
Mercure Unia	A
Motel PZPM	
Hotel Studenta Zaocznego	I
Youth Hostel	D

EATING & DRINKING

Bel Etage	G
Hades	3
Kwadrat	2
Klubokawiarnia	
Archiwum	1

try to ring in advance. Trolleybus #150 or bus #13 from the train station. En suites and rooms with shared facilities, plus dorm beds for 40zł per person. ❸–❹

Europa Krakowskie Przedmieście 29 ☎081/535 0303, ☺www.hoteleuropa.pl. Historic hotel (see p.264) that's nowadays aimed squarely at business travellers, with plush-carpeted rooms with desk space and big TVs. Ask about weekend discounts. ❼

Grand Hotel Lublinianka Krakowskie Przedmieście 56 ☎081/446 6100, ☺www .lublinianka.com. Recently renovated luxury hotel in a stately *belle époque* pile, with polished service, Turkish bath and a rooftop café. Rooms are discounted heavily at weekends and even more so during July and Aug. ❻

Hotels Lublin ul. Podzamcze 7 ☎081/747 4407, ☺www.hotels-lublin.pl. Tall concrete block north of the castle, with basic but clean en-suite rooms, with or without TV. No breakfast. ❸

Mercure Unia al. Racławickie 12 ☎081/533 2061, ☺www.orbis.pl. Respectable and modern Orbis hotel, with a reliable but unexceptional restaurant. Popular with well-heeled tour groups. ❻

Motel PZM ul. Prusa 8 ☎081/533 4232. Though unattractively set on a main highway, this is within walking distance of the city centre and bus station and is a good base for sightseeing in or around Lublin. Neat and fairly modern en suites, breakfast included. ❺

The City

Most of Lublin's medieval splendours are located in the **Old Town**, a compact and easily explored web of cobbled alleys connected by footbridge to the adjacent **castle hill**. The administrative centre of the city lies along **Krakowskie Przedmieście**, west of the Old Town, a strip which still retains many of its *belle époque* facades. Reminders of Lublin's once-thriving **Jewish community** are mostly found in the inner-city areas of Podzamcze and Czwartek, immediately north of the Old Town.

The Old Town

Marking the eastern end of Krakowskie Przedmieście, the busy plac Łokietka forms the main approach to the **Old Town** (Stare Miasto), with the imposing nineteenth-century **New Town Hall** (Nowy Ratusz) on one side. Straight across the square is the fourteenth-century **Kraków Gate** (Brama Krakowska), one of three gateways to the Old Town. Originally a key part of the city's defences against Tatar invaders, this now houses the **Historical Museum** (Muzeum Historyczne; Wed–Sat 9am–4pm, Sun 9am–5pm; 5zł); the contents aren't greatly inspiring, but the view of the new town from the top floor makes it worth a visit to orient yourself. A short walk round to the right along ulica Królewska brings you to the **Trinity Tower** (Wieża Trinitarska: Tues–Sun 10am–5pm; 7zł), home to a modest Diocesan Museum (Muzeum Diecezjalne), although it's the tower's top-floor view that's the main attraction. There's a cleverly arranged collection of Baroque sculpture to divert you on the way up.

The cathedral

Opposite the Trinity Tower is the **cathedral**, a large sixteenth-century basilica with an entrance framed by ornate Neoclassical pillars. A doorway at the rear of the nave leads to the Treasury (Tues–Sun 10am–4pm; 3zł), whose display cabinets are filled with lavishly embroidered vestments, chalices and crosiers. Adjoining the treasury is the **Whispering Room**, so called because its acoustic properties allow you to hear even the quietest voices perfectly from the other side of the chamber. Its ceiling is covered with ebullient frescoes by Joseph Meyer depicting the "triumph of faith over heresy". Steps descend to the recently restored crypt (same times; 4zł) where several seventeenth- and eighteenth-century bishops, nobles and townsfolk are buried. An open coffin holds one Bishop Jan Michał de la Mars (died 1725), his fine boots and gloves hanging surreally from the ends of his withered limbs.

The Rynek and Dominican Church

Both Trinity Tower and Kraków Gate lead into the Rynek, dominated by the outsized **Old Town Hall** (Stary Ratusz). Built in 1389, it was given a Neoclassical remodelling in 1781 by Merlini, the man who designed Warsaw's Łazienki Palace. The well-restored cellars underneath the building now house the **Lublin Underground Trail** (Lubelski podzemia: tours on the hour; 45min; 6zł), where the history of the city is told with the aid of scale models at various stages of its development, and a cupboard-sized tableau (aided by lights and music) tells the story of the fire of Lublin of 1719 – when friars from the Dominican monastery allegedly saved the Old Town from the flames by parading through the streets holding holy images aloft.

Of the surrounding burghers' houses, the **Konopnica House** (no. 12) – where Charles XII of Sweden and Peter the Great were both guests – has Renaissance sculptures and medallions of the original owners decorating its facade, currently being restored, while the **Lubomelski House** (no. 8) – now housing the *Piwnica Pod Fortuną* restaurant – hides some racy fourteenth-century frescoes in its large triple-tiered wine cellars. The **Cholewiński House** (no. 9), on the northeast

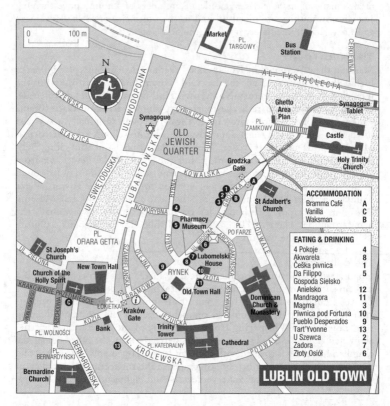

LUBLIN OLD TOWN

ACCOMMODATION

Bramma Café	A
Vanilla	C
Waksman	B

EATING & DRINKING

4 Pokoje	4
Akwarela	8
Češka pivnica	1
Da Filippo	5
Gospoda Sielsko Anielsko	12
Mandragora	11
Magma	3
Piwnica pod Fortuna	10
Pueblo Desperados	9
Tart'Yvonne	13
U Szewca	2
Zadora	7
Złoty Osioł	6

corner of the square, features further lively Renaissance decoration on the facade, with a faded but fierce-looking pair of lions.

East of the Rynek, at the end of ulica Złota, stands the fine **Dominican Church and Monastery**, founded in the fourteenth century and reconstructed in the seventeenth. The church suffers from the familiar Baroque additions, but don't let that deflect you from the Renaissance Firlej family **chapel** at the end of the southern aisle, built for one of Lublin's leading aristocratic families.

Towards the Grodzka Gate

North of the Rynek, ulica Grodzka slants downhill, passing a small **Pharmacy Museum** at no. 5 (Muzeum Aptekarstwa: Wed–Fri 10am–4pm; 5zł), with a fine nineteenth-century interior packed with strange-shaped bottles and ceramic containers. Further on, **plac Po Farze** is a square created early in the nineteenth century when the Gothic St Michael's Church was demolished – its foundations have been restored to give the square a bit of historical character. From here, ulica Grodzka continues its descent towards the **Grodzka Gate** (Brama Grodzka), traditionally the main northern entrance to the Old Town and for centuries the symbolic divide between Christian and Jewish Lublin. The gate has been restored by Teatr NN, an independent cultural organization which hopes to install a multimedia exhibition about Lublin's multicultural past in the rooms above the gate itself. On the far side of the gate a brick bridge leads across to the castle (see below). Until World War II, there was another brick bridge adjacent to Brama Grodzka known as Brama Zasrana ("Shit Gate") – it was here that the Old Town's waste was taken out every night before the advent of modern plumbing.

The castle

On a hill just east of the Old Town is the **castle**, an offbeat 1820s neo-Gothic edifice built on the site of Kazimierz the Great's fourteenth-century fortress. One of the highlights of any trip to Lublin is a visit to the frescoes at its **Holy Trinity Chapel**.

The museum

The castle houses a sizeable **museum** (Wed, Thurs & Sun 9am–5pm, Fri 9am–2pm, Sat 10am–5pm; 6.50zł; ⓦwww.zamek.lublin.pl), the high points of which are the **ethnography** section, including a delightful collection of contemporary folk art and woodcarving, and the **art gallery**, where Jan Matejko's monumental *Union of Lublin* occupies a whole wall. Showing King Sigismund II August presiding over Polish–Lithuanian unification talks in 1569, it's actually quite a restrained picture by the painter's customarily florid standards, although the strange gestures of Cardinal Hozjusz (seated on the left) seem to confirm that Matejko was incapable of painting anything without turning it into a melodrama. Elsewhere, the Mausers, Webleys and Walthers on display in the **militaria** section will send a frisson of excitement through firearms fans, while the gallery of **applied art** includes a disturbing pair of nineteenth-century nodding dolls that bear an uncanny resemblance to a grinning Tony Blair.

The Holy Trinity Chapel

An elegant two-storey Gothic structure, the **Holy Trinity Chapel** (Kaplica św. Trójcy: Tues & Thurs–Sat 9am–4pm, Wed & Sun 9am–5pm; tickets from the museum, 6.50zł) is located at the back of the castle complex behind one of its two remaining towers. The reason for its status as one of Lublin's finest draws is its stunning set of **medieval frescoes**, painted in Byzantine style by Orthodox artists commissioned by King Władysław II Jagiełło – who as Grand Duke of Lithuania (and son of an Orthodox Russian princess) had been surrounded by Eastern art since birth. Accidentally uncovered by builders at the end of the nineteenth century, they were subject to sporadic bursts of restoration over the next hundred years, but it wasn't until 1995 that the project was finally completed. The chapel has to be climate-controlled to preserve the frescoes: entrance is limited to 25 viewers at a time, and the chapel is closed for ten minutes in every hour to ensure that the ventilation system does its job.

The frescoes are composed of panels, each painted in a single day. These, in keeping with the principles of Byzantine iconography, form sections illustrating a progression of themes, beginning with depictions of God the Father and moving on through the cosmic hierarchy to scenes from the life of Jesus and the saints, images of the archangels and other spiritual entities and ending with the risen Christ. There's an engrossing wealth of detail to take in here, which the well-produced English-language guide sheet available at the museum entrance will help you through. Highlights include the vivid sequence of scenes from the life of Christ and the Virgin Mary covering the upper section of the nave and choir, in particular a powerful Passion cycle, along with an intriguing pair of frescoes involving Jagiełło himself, the first depicting him kneeling in humble supplication before the Virgin, the second showing the king mounted on a galloping horse while receiving a crown and crucifix from an angel – a reference to Jagiello'srole in converting the pagan Lithuanians to Christianity.

North of the castle: Podzamcze and Jewish Lublin

A stairway descends from the castle to the oval-shaped **plac Zamkowy**, where a plaque on a raised pedestal shows a detailed plan of the surrounding **Podzamcze** district, the main Jewish quarter destroyed by the Nazis in 1942 (see box opposite). Nowadays Podzamcze is cut through by a noisy main road (al. Tysiąclecia), on the opposite side of which lie the bus station and the **Orthodox cathedral**, the latter a dark, icon-filled structure built in 1633 on the site of an older wooden building and containing a late Renaissance iconostasis. Originally a Uniate building, it is the sole active place of Orthodox worship in town, and is open only on Sundays. Occupying the high ground above the cathedral is the part of town known as **Czwartek** ("Thursday"), in honour of the huge Thursday market that used to be held here from the late Middle Ages onwards.

The old Jewish cemetery

Heading east along aleja Tysiąclecia, turning up ulica Podzamcze, then bearing right onto ulica Lwowska brings you to the cobbled ulica Kalinowszczyzna and the **old Jewish cemetery** (Stary cmentarz żydowski), a small walled area which covers a ramshackle, overgrown hill. Unless a group happens to be there at the time, you'll have to contact the **caretaker**, Pani (Mrs) Honig, at ul. Dembowsk-iego 4, apt. #17 (☎081/747 8676), across from the main cemetery entrance. She speaks no English but is usually happy, at least on weekdays, to show visitors around, and while there's no set fee contributions are welcome.

Despite the Nazis' best efforts to destroy the oldest-known Jewish cemetery in the country – literally thousands of the gravestones were used for wartime building purposes – the small groups of surviving tombstones display the full stylistic variety of Jewish monumental art. The oldest section of the cemetery, with tombstones from as early as 1541, houses the graves of many famous Jews, among them the legendary Hassidic leader **Yaakov Yitzchak Horovitz**, one of several here regularly covered with pilgrims' candles, and **Shalom Shachna**, the renowned sixteenth-century master of the Lublin *yeshiva*. Climbing to the top of the cemetery hill gives you a fine view back over the Old Town.

The Jews of Lublin

Along with Kraków and Warsaw, Lublin ranked as one of the major Jewish centres in Poland: at its peak in the sixteenth century the Lublin Jewry exerted a Europe-wide influence, dispatching locally trained rabbis to serve communities as far away as Spain and Portugal.

The first recorded account of Jews in Lublin dates from 1316, though it's quite possible that merchants established themselves here considerably earlier. King Kazimierz's extension of the **Statute of Privilege** for Jews to the whole territory of Poland in the mid-fourteenth century paved the way for the development of the first major Jewish settlement in the **Podzamcze** district, located below the castle walls. Originally a marshy river delta, the area was bought up by Jewish merchants, who drained the waters and established a community there. The first brick **synagogue** and **yeshiva** (Talmudic school) were built in the mid-sixteenth century: from then on synagogues and other religious buildings proliferated – by the 1930s there were more than a hundred synagogues in operation inside the city area. Lublin's increasingly important position on trade routes resulted in its choice as one of two locations (Jarosław was the other) for meetings of the **Council of the Four Lands**, traditionally the main consultative body of Polish Jewry, a position it retained up to the 1760s.

In the 1790s Lublin emerged as an important centre of **Hassidism**, the ecstatic revivalist movement that swept through Eastern Jewry in the latter part of the eighteenth century. The charismatic Hassidic leader **Yaakov Yitzchak Horovitz** settled in town during this period, drawing crowds of followers from all over Poland to his "court" in the Podzamcze district. Always a controversial figure – contemporary opponents, for example, claimed that Horovitz died of excessive alcohol consumption – Jews from all over the world continue to make the pilgrimage to his grave in the old Jewish cemetery. From 1862 onwards Jews were permitted to settle in the Old Town and the neighbouring streets around ulica Lubartowska, which became the centre of their community. At the close of the century they numbered around 24,000, a little over half of the town's population. Following the trials of **World War I**, during which many Lublin Jews died fighting in both the Russian and Austro-Hungarian armies, Lublin Jewry flourished in the interwar years, developing an active web of religious and cultural associations, publishing houses, newspapers (notably the Yiddish-language daily *Lubliner Sztyme* – "Lublin Voice"), trade unions and political organizations. Following their capture of the town in September 1939, the **Nazis** quickly set about the business of confining and eventually murdering the nearly 40,000-strong Lublin Jewry. In early 1940 Lublin was chosen as the coordinating centre for the Nazis' efforts to liquidate the Jewish population of the Générale Gouvernement – those portions of Poland that were under German administration (but not directly incorporated into the German Reich). An official **ghetto area** was established, west of the castle, in March 1941, and the construction of **Majdanek concentration camp** (initially a work camp, subsequently an extermination camp) commenced four months later. The ghetto was cleared in spring 1942, its inhabitants either shot in nearby forests or sent to **Bełżec camp** (see p.291).

The city was liberated by Soviet troops in July 1944, after which **Jewish partisan groups** began using Lublin as their operational base. At the end of the war several thousand Jewish refugees resettled in Lublin. Many of these emigrated, however, in the wake of **anti-Semitic outbreaks** in Poland in 1945–46 and again in 1968. A tiny and largely elderly Jewish community remains in Lublin today.

The new Jewish cemetery and the yeshiva

Leaving the cemetery and heading north along ulica Lwowska and into ulica Walecznych brings you to the entrance of the **new Jewish cemetery** (Nowy cmentarz żydowski). Established in 1829 in what was then the outskirts of the city, the cemetery was plundered by the Nazis, who also used it for mass executions. What you see today covers a fragment of the original plot, the northern section having been cleared and levelled in the 1970s to make way for a trunk road. Most of the few remaining graves date from the late nineteenth century and the postwar years, and there are also a number of collective graves for Nazi wartime victims. The whole cemetery has been renovated in the past few years with financial support from the Frenkel family, whose relatives died in Majdanek. The domed **mausoleum** (unpredictable hours, so check at the tourist office; donation), recently erected behind the cemetery entrance, houses a small but engrossing exhibition detailing the history of the Lublin Jewry.

Out of the cemetery and west along ulica Unicka brings you to the corner of ulica Lubartowska, a long, straight thoroughfare running through the heart of the prewar Jewish quarter. The large, palatial-looking yellow building at the top corner of Lubartowska is the **yeshiva** – the School of the Sages of Lublin as it was once known. Built in the late 1920s using funds collected from Jewish communities around the world, the Lublin *yeshiva* was set up as an international school to train rabbis and other community functionaries. It functioned for just over nine years until 1939, when the Nazis closed it down and publicly burned the contents of its huge library. Occupied by a university medical faculty after World War II, the *yeshiva* is once more in the hands of the Jewish community, and is earmarked as the site of a future **museum of Hassidism**.

Along Krakowskie Przedmieście

West of the Old Town stretches **Krakowskie Przedmieście**, a busy, shop-lined thoroughfare pedestrianized for several blocks. After about five minutes' walk it links up with **plac Litewski**, a large open square dominated by the cast-iron 1826 **Monument to the Union of Lublin** (Pomnik Unii Lubelskiej), commemorating the agreement which created the Polish–Lithuanian Commonwealth in 1569. Celebrated by Poles as a defining moment in their rise to mastery in north-central Europe, the Union was always regarded as a sell-out by the Lithuanians, whose aristocracy found itself bound ever closer to the Polish crown. Occupying the southeastern corner of the square is the grand ochre bulk of the **Europa**, Lublin's oldest hotel. It was here that Nazi and Soviet officers held a celebratory dinner that Russian historians would prefer to forget, toasting the success of their joint invasion of Poland in September 1939. The north side of the square features two old aristocratic palaces: the former **Czartoryski Palace** (Pałac Czartoryskich) in the northeast corner, and to its west the fading seventeenth-century **Lubomirski Palace** (Pałac Lubomirskich), with a Neoclassicist facade dating from the 1830s. The imperial-looking building to its left is the old tsarist-era city governor's residence, built in the 1850s.

Continuing west, Krakowskie Przedmieście becomes aleja Racławickie and runs past the Catholic University (Katolicki Uniwersytet) or **KUL**, a compact campus housed on the site of an old Dominican monastery. The KUL's most famous professor was **Karol Wojtyła**, who taught part-time here from the 1950s up until his election as pope in 1978. He is commemorated in a bronze statue in the main courtyard, accompanied by his predecessor as primate of Poland, Cardinal Wyszyński.

Directly opposite the university building lie the **Ogród Saski** ("Saxon Gardens"), so named because they were inspired by August III of Saxony's gardens in Warsaw. They make up Lublin's principal open space, with fastidiously tended flowerbeds sloping down towards wilder, densely wooded sections in the park's northern reaches.

The skansen

Three kilometres northwest of the Ogród Saski, out along aleja Warszawska (bus #5, #18 or #20 from al. Racławickie), Lublin's extensive **skansen** (April & Oct daily 9am–5pm; May–Sept daily 10am–6pm; Nov to mid-Dec Mon, Sat & Sun 9am–3pm; Jan–March by appointment ⓣ081/533 8513, ⓦwww.skansen.lublin.pl; 6zł) presents an attractive jumble of rural buildings from surrounding villages. You can only visit the interiors of the buildings if you pay for the hour-long guided tour (25zł in Polish, 35zł in English, though there's not always an English-speaker on duty), but a visit here will be rewarding either way. The entrance is marked by a massive, 1939 windmill from the village of Zygmuntów, while other highlights include a gate from Łańcuchów, carved in the Zakopane style by Stanisław Witkiewicz; a manor house from the village of Zyrzyna, crouching beneath an organic-looking mansard roof covered in wooden shingles; and a *cerkiew* from Tarnoszyna, which sports an exotic trio of bulbous domes.

Majdanek

The proximity of **Majdanek concentration camp** (grounds 8am–dusk; free; ⓦwww.majdanek.pl), just 4km southeast of the city centre, is something of a shock. Established on Himmler's orders in October 1941, this was no semi-hidden location that local people could long be ignorant of – a plea more debatable at Auschwitz and Treblinka.

The first view of the camp is a large monument, erected in 1969 on the twenty-fifth anniversary of its liberation by the Red Army, which stands beside the main entrance on the main road, Droga Męcienników Majdanka (bus #23 and trolleybus #156 from ulica Królewska or trolleybuses #153 and #158 from ul. Lipowa). To the left of the monument, a modern pavilion has a cinema showing a short documentary about Majdanek (3zł; minimum five viewers) as well as a bookshop selling maps, brochures and other publications in several languages. Guided tours are available in Polish (60zł) and English (120zł).

To the right of the monument, a path slants across the fields to the main **museum** part of the site (Tues–Sun 8am–4pm; free), where barracks and watchtowers have been reconstructed to give visitors some idea of what the camp looked like. Wandering among the rows of wooden huts crammed with three-level plank beds, it's hard to take in the fact that an estimated 230,000 people, of which 40 percent were Jewish and 35 percent Polish, were murdered here – more than half through hunger, disease or exhaustion and the rest by execution or in gas chambers. Between November 3 and 5, 1943, the Nazis concluded their extermination of local Jewry by machine-gunning over 43,000 inhabitants of the nearby ghetto district, 18,000 of whom, were killed in a single day. Immediately following the war, Majdanek was used by the Soviet NKVD (secret police) to hold captured Polish resistance fighters before they were shipped to Siberian gulags.

At the end of the main path through the site, a domed mausoleum contains the ashes of many of those murdered here. Below the mausoleum are the gas chambers and crematoria, blown up by the Nazis as they retreated but reconstructed afterwards to serve as a chilling lesson to future generations.

Eating and drinking

In Lublin as elsewhere in Poland, there's a blurring of distinctions between **cafés**, **restaurants** and **bars** – a place which looks like a good venue for an intimate meal on a weekday may well be buzzing with drinkers come the weekend. The main concentration of eating and drinking establishments is in the Old Town, although there's a string of places along the eastern, pedestrianized portion of Krakowskie Przedmieście too. The establishments listed under "Old Town" are marked on the Lublin Old Town map on p.260; those under "Outside the Old Town" are shown on the main Lublin map on p.258.

Old Town

4 Pokoje ul. Rybna 13. Relaxed, student-oriented pub with an uncoordinated jumble of furniture, vinyl record covers on the walls and a pool table. Small food menu. Tues–Sun noon–midnight.

Akwarela Rynek 6. Arty café with photo exhibitions and jazz music (usually on CD but occasionally live). A great place for a pot of tea, hot chocolate and slice of apple pie. Daily 10am–10pm.

Čéská Pivnica ul. Grodzka 28. Cellar bar with several chambers. Also has Czech beers on tap and a hearty meat-and-dumplings food menu. Daily noon–midnight.

Da Filippo Rybna 9. Excellent pizzas and pastas in relaxing surroundings, with mains clocking in at 12–25zł. Daily 1–10.30pm.

Gospoda Sielsko Anielsko Rynek 17. Rustic-themed place offering hearty traditional food in a dining room stuffed with rural implements. Lighter dishes like *pierogi* and omelettes at around 12zł, and main courses 18–35zł. An imitation of (but not quite matching in quality) the *Chłopskie Jadło* chain. Daily 11am–11pm.

Magma ul. Grodzka 18. Smallish bar in the Old Town whose arty-industrial decor blends rather nicely with the barrel-vaulted Baroque ceiling. An amenable place to sink a few pints. Sun–Thurs 11am–11pm, Fri & Sat till 1am.

Mandragora Rynek 9. Middle European and Middle Eastern dishes with a Jewish theme, and live klezmer music at the weekends. Daily 11am–11pm.

Piwnica pod Fortuną Rynek 8. Elegant restaurant occupying a series of subterranean chambers decorated with medieval-style frescoes. The usual range of Polish meat dishes is augmented by a few duck and goose recipes. Slightly more expensive than the other places in the Old Town, with mains in the 40–60zł range. Daily 11am–11pm.

Pueblo Desperados Rynek 5. Tiny, three-table Mexican restaurant with surprisingly tasty burritos, enchiladas and chilli con carne. Prices are cheap and there's a big square-side beer garden in summer. Sun–Thurs 11am–10pm, Fri & Sat till midnight.

Tart'Yvonne ul. Królewska 3. Quaint and cosy café in an off-street courtyard serving up delicious slices of quiche, irresistible fruit flans and decent coffee. Mon–Fri 10am–6pm, Sat 10am–2pm.

U Szewca ul. Grodzka 20. Relaxing pub with a range of Polish, English and Irish beers, comfy settees and a varied, mid-price menu of bar food. Sun–Thurs 1am–midnight, Fri & Sat till 2am.

Zadora Rynek 8. Small and excellent *creperie*, good for a quick and cheap meal in the Old Town. Daily 10am–11pm.

Złoty Osioł ul. Grodzka 5a. Multi-purpose café, bar, restaurant and art gallery housed in a suite of medieval rooms. Lots of wicker furniture to lounge around in, and a laid-back atmosphere. Serves mid-price Polish dishes. Daily noon–11pm.

Outside the Old Town

Bel Etage Krakowskie Przedmieście 56 ☎081/466 100. Lublin's most formal and expensive restaurant, situated within the *Grand Hotel Lublinianka,* serving fine international cuisine (mains in the 40–60zł range) and an enchanting rooftop café in summer. Daily noon–10.30pm.

Hades ul. Peowiaków 12 ☎081/532 8761. In the basement of the Central Theatre but decked out to look like a rustic bistro, *Hades* offers the best across-the-board range of Polish and European cuisine in the city. Famous for its variants on the steak tartare theme, which take up a whole page of the menu. Live gigs and club nights in the adjoining disco space (see opposite). Daily noon–10pm.

Kvadrat ul. Pieowiaków 7. Relaxing two-tier pub with understated decor, low-key lighting and rocky (but not over-loud) music on the sound system. The kind of place you can happily sink into and not emerge from until several beers later. Daily noon–midnight.

Klubokawiarnia Archiwum ul. Radziszewskiego 8. Spacious disco pub behind the Bajka cinema. Right behind KUL, so liable to be full of young bodies at weekends. Daily 9am–1am.

Entertainment

Drama is Lublin's strong point, with the internationally reputed experimental theatre group Gardzienice, ul. Grodzka 5a (☎081/532 9840, ⓦwww.gardzienice .art.pl), performing occasionally in various venues in the city itself but more often in the village of Gardzienice, 30km south – an experience not to be missed if you have the chance. Elsewhere, the Juliusz Osterwa Theatre, ul. Narutowicza 17 (Teatr im. Juliusz Osterwy: ☎081/532 2935, ⓦwww.teatrosterwy.pl), offers an imaginative and varied programme of modern and classical Polish drama; while the Teatr Centralny, ul. Peowiaków 12 (ⓦwww.ck.lublin.pl) has a more contemporary repertoire of theatre and dance. The Lublin Philharmonia, ul. Skłodowskiej 5 (☎081/743 7821, ⓦwww.filharmonia.lublin.pl), has a regular programme of high-quality **classical concerts**. For **film**, Plaza, ulica Lipowa, is a modern multi-screen in the Plaza shopping centre, while the Bajka cinema, next to the *Dom Nauczyciela* at ul. Radziszewskiego 8, shows independent films.

There's a string of bars along Krakowskie Przedmeście which have **DJs and dancing** at weekends. *Hades* (see opposite) has a large cellar bar hosting club nights and gigs (Thurs–Sun only); while the *Chata Żaka* student club, ul. Radziszewskiego 16, has a cinema, concert venue, and a smoky student bar to boot. The Chata Żaka's resident **folk band**, Orkiestra św Mikołaja (ⓦwww.mikolaje.lublin.pl), is one of the top roots-music acts in this part of Poland – they organize the hugely enjoyable Mikołajki Folkowe festival in mid-December.

Listings

Banks and exchange ATMs and exchange *kantors* are widespread. Note that the rate posted in the window is often for $100 or €100; you may get a lower rate if changing smaller notes.

Books and maps Biggest selection is at EMPiK, with branches at Krakowskie Przedmeście 6, and the Plaza shopping centre, ul. Lipowa.

Internet access @storia, corner of Krakowskie Przedmeście and ul. Lipowa (Mon–Fri 10am–10pm, Sat 10–9pm, Sun noon–9pm).

Markets al. Tysiąclecia, next to the bus station. Foodstuffs, flowers, cheap clothes and more.

Pharmacy Apteka, ul. Bramowa 8 (24hr; ring the bell 8pm–8am).

Post office Krakowskie Przedmeście 50 (24hr); ul. Grodzka 7 (Mon–Fri 8.30am–4.30pm).

Travel agents Orbis, ul. Narutowicza 31/33 (☎081/532 2256) is useful for air and rail tickets.

North and east of Lublin

North and east of Lublin lie broad expanses of open farmland interspersed with belts of thick forest. The Zamoyski Palace at **Kozłówka**, with its museum of socialist art, is the one unmissable sight in the region, and makes an entertaining day-trip from Lublin. Elsewhere there's plenty of evidence of eastern Poland's multicultural past, with an ornate synagogue at **Włodawa** and the Uniate (Greek-Catholic) cathedral at **Chełm** providing the main points of interest.

Kozłówka

Thirty-five kilometres northwest of Lublin, the **Zamoyski Palace** (Pałac Zamojskich) at **KOZŁÓWKA** is among the grandest in the region. Fully restored in the 1990s, the palace is the recipient of a good deal of tourist hype – hence the processions of day-tripper buses lined up outside the entrance gates. Kozłówka is served by about eight **buses** a day from Lublin, most bound for the village of Michów. Bear in mind that as an intermediate destination Kozłówka won't be listed on the departure board at Lublin bus station; ask at the information counter for details.

The palace

Built in the 1740s by the Bieliński family after they inherited the local estate, the original two-storey Baroque **palace complex**, flanked by a courtyard to the front and gardens at the back, was reconstructed and expanded in the early 1900s by its longtime owner, Count Konstanty Zamoyski, whose family took over the property in 1799 and kept it up to the beginning of World War II. Zamoyski's remodelling retained the essentials of the original Baroque design, adding a number of fine outbuildings, the iron gateway, chapel and elegant porticoed terrace leading up to the entrance to the building.

The interior

The palace **interior** (mid-March to Oct Tues–Fri 10am–4pm, Sat & Sun 10am–5pm; Nov to mid–Dec Tues–Sun 10am–3pm; 16zł; Ⓦwww .muzeumkozlowka.lublin.pl) can only be visited as part of a **guided tour**, usually starting on the hour. English-language guides can be booked in advance for an extra 50zł (Ⓣ081/852 8310).

Once inside, you're immediately enveloped in a riot of artistic decor: the whole place is positively dripping in pictures, mostly family portraits and copies of Rubens, Canaletto and the like, along with a profusion of sculptures and mostly nineteenth-century furniture. First port of call is the **hallway**, the gloom partially lightened by sumptuous lamps and the delicate stuccowork of the ceiling. Past the huge Meissner stoves and up the portrait-lined marble staircase brings you to the main palace rooms. Upstairs in **Count Konstanty's private rooms** the procession of family portraits and genre painting continues relentlessly, the elaborate Czech porcelain toilet set in the bedroom suggesting a man of fastidious personal hygiene. After the countess's bedroom and its handsome selection of nineteenth-century French furniture, the tour takes you into the voluminous **Red Salon**, with embroidered canopies enveloping the doors and a mass of heavy velvet curtains. The portraits are at their thickest here, with emphasis on royalty, hetmans and other national figures collected by Count Konstanty during the Partition. The **Exotic Room** houses a fine selection of chinoiserie, while the **dining room** is sumptuous, heavy Baroque with a mixture of Gdańsk and Venetian furniture and enough period trinkets to keep a horde of collectors happy. The **chapel**, out round the side of the palace, is a fine though rather cold place partly modelled on the royal chapel in Versailles and built in the early 1900s.

Outside, the elegantly contoured **palace gardens** stretch out behind the back of the building. Refreshments are available at the **café** near the entrance gate, while the nearby **Coach House** (same hours; 4zł) holds a display of carriages, old bicycles, saddlery and vintage travel equipment.

The museum

After overdosing on opulence, the **Gallery of Socialist Art** (Galeria sztuki realizmu socjalistycznego: same hours; 6zł) housed in the one-time palace theatre makes for a real surprise. The exhibition brings together a large collection of postwar Polish Socialist Realist art and sculpture, much of which was on display in the palace itself during the 1960s. Alongside busts of Bolesław Bierut, Mao Zedong, Ho Chi Minh and others, there's a gallery of sturdy proletarian heroes building factories and joyously implementing Five-Year Plans, while playing in the background are important speeches by Stalin and others. More traditional themes are also given a Socialist-Realist twist, as in such paintings as Zygmunt Radricki's *Still Life with Party Journal* and *Chopin's Polonaise in A-flat Major Performed in the Kościuszko Ironworks* by Mieczysław Oracki-Serwin. There's also a selection of buttons, postcards and propagandistic matchboxes.

Włodawa and around

Hard up by the Belarusian border, 70km northeast of Lublin, the sleepy little town of **WŁODAWA** sits on a low hill overlooking the River Bug. What makes the place worth visiting is its wonderfully well-preserved synagogue, which serves as a graceful memorial to a Jewish community that formed a clear majority of the town population until World War II. Virtually all of Włodawa's Jews perished in the concentration camp at Sobibór, 10km southeast of town.

Built in the 1760s on the site of an earlier wooden structure, the **synagogue** is a typically solid-looking late Baroque construction with a palatial main facade topped by some typically Polish mansard roofing. Despite severe damage by the Nazis, and postwar conversion into a warehouse, the synagogue was thoroughly and well restored in the 1960s and has since functioned as a **museum** (Mon–Fri 9am–3pm, Sat & Sun 10am–2pm; 5zł). In the main interior room, the prayer hall, four pillars supporting the barrel-cross vaulting indicate the spot where the bema once stood. The major surviving original feature is the restored **Aron ha Kodesh**, a colourful, triple-tiered neo-Gothic structure raised in the 1930s and covered with elaborate stucco decoration. Upstairs there's a re-creation of the room where local rabbi, Melamed Menachem, lived and taught, complete with tattered prayer books, worn furniture and his children's toys. Across the courtyard from the main synagogue is another smaller house of worship from the mid-nineteenth century (same opening hours), which has preserved sections of polychromy as well as its Aron ha Kodesh. The upper floor here holds the local **ethnographic collection**, arranged as a *chłopskie pielgrzymowanie* ("peasant's pilgrimage"). After a captivating display featuring the contents of an old Jewish shop, handmade canoes and various traditional implements, the peasant's ultimate destination is revealed: the bleak concrete landscape of a proletarian Warsaw suburb.

Włodawa's **bus station** is a couple of blocks west of the town centre. The **tourist information centre**, just east of the synagogue at ul. Rynek 4 (Mon–Fri 8am–5pm, Sat 8am–noon) is well stocked with leaflets. For refreshments, *Kawiarnia Centrum*, 100m west of the synagogue, serves up tea, coffee and basic Polish **snacks**. *Astur*, at Okuninka 5km south on the Chełm road (T 081/532 9864 and 082/571 7037), has **camping**, bungalows and **hotel** rooms on the edge of the forest-shrouded Lake Biały.

Sobibór

Ten kilometres southeast of Włodawa (and well-signed from the main Włodawa–Chełm road), the tranquil, village of **SOBIBÓR** was the site of a brutally efficient Nazi extermination camp, which – despite only being operational from May to October 1942 – accounted for the murder of an estimated 250,000 Jews from Poland, Ukraine and Holland. The camp was hurriedly dismantled following a revolt led by a Soviet Jewish POW officer in which an estimated 300 inmates escaped – 47 of whom survived the war. Today the site (May to mid-Oct 9am–2pm) contains a modest **museum** with a words-and-pictures display, and a memorial mound made from the ashes of the victims.

Chełm

First impressions of **CHEŁM**, 70km east of Lublin, are of emerald-green church domes poking above the treetops of the city's central hill. This is an attractive reminder of Chełm's historical role as a stronghold of the **Uniate** (Greek Catholic) church, formed in 1596 when many of the Polish–Lithuanian Commonwealth's Orthodox subjects agreed to accept the primacy of the pope. The Uniates have long since departed from Chełm, although their magnificent cathedral (now a Catholic church) is still the town's principal landmark. Chełm's other main claim to fame is the chalk it is built on, and the underground passages linking the Old Town's **chalk cellars** are a major tourist attraction.

Chełm's Jewish community (which constituted roughly half of the population until 1939) enjoyed an unenviable reputation in Yiddish folklore as the most stupid and accident-prone people in Eastern Europe. The "**fools of Chełm**", as they were popularly known, were the butt of many a joke.

The Old Town

Everything worth seeing is concentrated within the relatively tight confines of the Old Town, centred on the lively plac Łuczowskiego. From here it's a brisk climb along the path up **Góra Zamkowa**, the hill overlooking the town from the east and the site of the original fortified settlement, to the cathedral complex.

The cathedral

The grandiose set of whitewashed buildings that make up the **Uniate cathedral** includes the Uniate bishop's former residence and a seventeenth-century monastery, as well as the cathedral itself, an imposing twin-towered Baroque structure with a fine high facade dating from the 1740s. The interior is comparatively bare, focusing attention on the gilded image of the Madonna that presides over the high altar. Outside, the freestanding nineteenth-century **bell tower** (Mon–Sat 9.30am–6pm, Sun 2–4pm; 3zł) is well worth scaling for a grandstand view over the town.

The parish church and chalk cellars

West of the main square down ulica Lubelska stands the extravagantly Baroque **parish church**, built by the Piarist educational order in the 1750s and designed by Italian architect Paolo Antonio Fontana. The walls and vaults of the interior boast a fine series of trompe l'oeil paintings and frescoes by Joseph Meyer, similar in style to the ones in Lublin's cathedral.

Immediately west of the parish church at ul. Lubelska 55a is the entrance to the town's major curiosity, a labyrinthine network of **underground tunnels** hewn out of the chalk bedrock – the only such system of chalk tunnels in Europe. Entrance is by torch-lit **guided tour** only (tours daily at 11am, 1pm and 4pm; 9zł; ☎082/565 2530), and in English by advance appointment, though there's often an English speaker on duty. Chełm's chalk was never mined on an industrial basis, but ad hoc excavations by the locals created a warren of passageways underneath the Old Town. Activity was wound down in the nineteenth century due to the danger of subsidence but since the 1960s a two-kilometre section of tunnels twelve metres deep has been accessible to tourists. The forty-minute trip takes in a stock of historical anecdotes as well as legends of spirits and demons.

The temperature of the tunnels remains at 9°C regardless of the season, so bring a jacket or sweater.

Practicalities

Served by frequent trains and buses from Lublin, and accessible by bus from Zamość, Chełm is an easy day-trip destination from either. Of the town's two **train stations**, Chełm is a good 2km northeast of the centre (regular buses shuttle into town), while Chełm Miasto is a fifteen-minute walk west of plac Łuczowskiego, the main square; all trains stop at both. The **bus** and **minibus station** are near to each other on ulica Lwowska, a five-minute walk south of the centre. The helpful **tourist office**, centrally located at ul. Lubelska 63 (Mon–Fri 8am–5pm, Sat & Sun 9am–2pm; ⓦwww.chelm.pl), is well stocked with maps and other information, including a number of English-language brochures, and there's **internet access** at ul. Popiełuszki 11, opposite the bus station.

With Lublin only 75 minutes away, there's little need to stay overnight in Chełm. The pedestrianized ulica Lwowska, running off the main square to the south, is the place to seek out **cafés**, snack bars and summertime beer gardens. The top **restaurant** is *Gęsia Szyja* (noon–midnight), just east of the main square at ul. Lubelska 27, which has good meat dishes, a wonderful cellar setting, and one of the only jukeboxes in Poland.

West to Kazimierz

The Lublin–Warsaw route has a major attraction in the town of **Kazimierz Dolny**, an ancient and highly picturesque grain-shipping centre set above the Wisła. Of all the small towns in rural Poland this is – by a long stretch – the best preserved, and continues to swallow up ever-growing numbers of tourists as a result. To reach it on public transport, the easiest approach from Warsaw is to go by train to **Puławy**, home to the wonderful Czartoryski Palace, and catch a connecting bus from there; from Lublin there are direct buses via the old spa town of **Nałęczów**, itself a pleasant excursion.

Nałęczów

Twenty-five kilometres west of Lublin, the small town of **NAŁĘCZÓW** saw its heyday at the turn of the twentieth century, when it was the favoured resort of Warsaw's cultural elite – notably writers Bolesław Prus and Stefan Żeromski, and pianist Ignacy Paderewski. The town retains much of its old-time atmosphere, and a leisurely stroll through the spa park makes for an attractive day out from either Lublin or Kazimierz Dolny – regular buses and minibuses run here from both.

Centrepiece of the **spa park** is an oval swan-filled lake, around which spa buildings from various epochs are grouped. Nearest at hand is a small pavilion holding the **tap room** (*pijalnia*), whre you can sample a cup of Nałęczów's iron-rich spa water for a few *groszy*. A short walk southeast is the **Małachowski Palace** (Pałac Małachowskiego), a Neoclassical structure featuring an elegantly stuccoed ballroom and a small **museum** devoted to nineteenth-century novelist Bolesław Prus (Wed–Sun 9.30am–3pm; 3.50zł). With sepia photographs and a typewriter that Prus once bashed away at, it's a place of pilgrimage for fans rather than a general-interest tourist attraction. Far more interesting is the **Żeromski Villa**, a short way north of the park at ulica Żeromskiego (Tues–Sun

10am–3pm; 3.50zł), a pointy-roofed wooden hut built by the Warsaw-based novelist in 1905 to serve as a writing studio. Both a patriot and a progressive man of the left, Żeromski wrote decade-spanning sagas that were both emotionally involving and politically committed, earning him huge popularity in pre-World War I Poland – and enabling him to pay for this studio with the royalties. Designed in the style of a Tatra mountain cottage by Zakopane-based architect Jan Witkiewicz (cousin of Stanisław; see p.265), the villa houses an attractive little museum with the author's original furnishings. At the bottom of the garden a cone-shaped brick **mausoleum** (also by Witkiewicz) holds the tomb of Żeromski's son Adam, who died of tuberculosis here in 1918.

The **tourist information centre** at the western end of the spa park (☎081/501 6101, ⓦwww.naleczow.org.pl) will tell you everything you need to know about the town and give you a free map into the bargain. For a bite **to eat** before moving on, the *Atrium* restaurant just west of the spa park's lake serves Polish food with a few pizzas and pastas thrown in, and also grills freshwater fish in the garden during the summer.

Puławy

Sprawling over the eastern bank of the Wisła 20km northwest from Nałęczów, **PUŁAWY** is a largely featureless sprawl grouped around its one great monument, the palace and park built by the Czartoryski family – the aristocratic dynasty who made Puławy their base in the 1730s. From 1775 onwards **Prince Adam Czartoryski** (1734–1823) and his wife **Izabela** (1746–1835) transformed their palace here into Poland's leading cultural and intellectual centre, Izabela establishing the nucleus of a national museum. In 1830, however, the estate was confiscated and the family exiled after the failure of the November Uprising (see p.616), in which Adam and Izabela's son **Adam Jerzy Czartoryski** was a leading participant. Adam Jerzy had been a childhood friend of Tsar Nicholas I, who took the Czartoryskis' perceived treason particularly hard. Renaming the town "New Alexandria", he turned the Czartoryski Palace into a finishing school for Russian ladies. The estate is currently an agricultural school, although the palace retains a handful of showpiece interiors, and the surrounding park provides fascinating insights into aristocratic tastes of the period.

The palace

Approached from a wide courtyard just south of what passes for a town centre, the **Czartoryski Palace** (Pałac Czartoryskich: daily tours in Polish on the hour; May–Sept 9am–3pm; Oct–April 9am–2pm; 5zł) was built in the 1670s by indefatigable Dutch-Polish architect Tylman van Gameren, although the current Neoclassical exterior owes a great deal to subsequent rebuildings. Through the main entrance and up the grand cast-iron staircase, the **Music Hall** and arcaded **Gothic Hall** offer hints of former grandeur. The latter was originally the palace ballroom, lined with floor-to-ceiling mirrors – the mirrors were sold off during the tsarist period, Nicholas I declaring that such splendour would demoralize the young ladies attending the institute he established here.

Designed and developed by the industrious Izabela over a twenty-year period (1790–1810), the meandering palace **park** (daily: April–Sept 6am–10pm; Oct–March 7am–6pm; free) is quintessentially Romantic in feel and conception. Noted for their variety of trees, the grounds are also dotted with a hotchpotch of "historical" buildings and monuments in the manner popular with the Polish aristocracy of the period (as at, for example, Arkadia; see p.128). Southeast of the palace is the **Gothic House** (Dom Gotycki: Tues–Sun 9am–5pm; 5zł), a square, two-storey building with a graceful portico, now housing a display of period furnishings. The same ticket is valid for the **Temple of Sibyl** (Świątynia Sybilli; same times) just opposite, consciously echoing the temple of the same name in Tivoli, near Rome. The rest of the park contains other follies, including grottoes, a Chinese pavilion, the marble family sarcophagus and assorted imitation classical statuary.

Practicalities

Puławy is on the major train line from Warsaw (2hr) to Lublin (45min), with frequent connections in both directions. The main **train station** (Puławy Miasto) is 2km northeast of the centre on ulica Żyrzyńska, from where local bus #12 runs into town. The main **bus station** is 500m northwest of the centre at the junction of ulica Lubelska and ulica Wojska Polskiego. **Minibuses** operating the Warsaw–Kazimierz Dolny and Lublin–Kazimierz Dolny routes pick up and drop off on ulica Lubelska, near the bus station. The *Sybilla* **restaurant**, near the palace at al. Królewska 17, serves inexpensive Polish standards and is also a decent place to take a coffee-and-cake break.

Kazimierz Dolny and around

Tiny, riverside **KAZIMIERZ DOLNY** ("Lower Kazimierz"), picturesquely set between two hills and possessing one of Poland's finest architectural ensembles as well as quiet, rustic backstreets, is unquestionably established as a major tourist venue, a fact reflected in its wealth of pensions, restaurants and galleries. Artists have been drawn here since the nineteenth century, attracted by the effervescent light and ancient buildings, while in more recent decades Kazimierz has been used by film directors as a backdrop for historical thrillers and romances.

The town is closely associated with its royal namesake, **Kazimierz the Great** (1333–70), who rescued Poland from dynastic and economic chaos and transformed the country's landscape in the process. It is said of him that he "found a wooden Poland and left a Poland of stone", and Kazimierz Dolny is perhaps the best remaining example of his ambitious town-building programme. Thanks to the king's promotion of the Wisła grain and timber trade, a minor village was transformed into a prosperous mercantile town by the end of the fourteenth century, gaining the nickname "little Danzig" in the process, on account of the goods' ultimate destination. Much of the money that poured in was used to build the ornate burghers' houses that still line the main square.

It was during this period, too, that **Jews** began to settle in Kazimierz, grateful for the legal protection proclaimed for them throughout Poland by King Kazimierz, and for the next five centuries Jewish traders and shopkeepers were integral to the character of towns like this. Jews accounted for up to fifty percent of Kazimierz's population when World War II began, but only a handful survived the war, with the result that Kazimierz entered the postwar era as a half-empty shell. However, Warsaw's elite soon rediscovered its rural charm and nowadays it is thronging with tourists over the summer and at weekends throughout the year. It still manages to retain a relaxed, bohemian feel, however, and despite overcrowding during its cultural festivals (see p.277), the town never has the feel of being oppressively over-touristed.

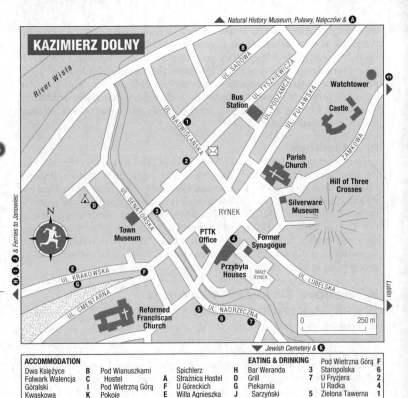

▲ Natural History Museum, Puławy, Nałęczów & Ⓐ

KAZIMIERZ DOLNY

River Wisła

UL. NADWIŚLAŃSKA

UL. SADOWA

UL. TYSZKIEWICZA

UL. PODZAMCZE

UL. PUŁAWSKA

Bus Station

Watchtower

Castle

ZAMKOWA

Parish Church

Hill of Three Crosses

Silverware Museum

RYNEK

UL. SENATORSKA

N

Town Museum

PTTK Office

Former Synagogue

Przybyła Houses

MAŁY RYNEK

UL. LUBELSKA

UL. KRAKOWSKA

UL. CMENTARNA

Reformed Franciscan Church

UL. NADRZECZNA

0   250 m

Lublin

⑤ LUBLIN AND THE EAST | West to Kazimierz

Ⓗ, Ⓘ, Ⓙ & Ferries to Janowiec

▼ Jewish Cemetery & Ⓚ

ACCOMMODATION						EATING & DRINKING		Pod Wietrzna Górą	F
Dwa Księżyce	B	Pod Wianuszkami		Spichlerz	H	Bar Weranda	3	Staropolska	6
Folwark Walencja	C	Hostel	A	Strażnica Hostel	D	Grill	7	U Fryzjera	2
Góralski	I	Pod Wietrzną Górą	F	U Góreckich	G	Piekarnia		U Radka	4
Kwaskowa	K	Pokoje	E	Willa Agnieszka	J	Sarzyński	5	Zielona Tawerna	1

Arrival and information

Although it lies some way off the main intercity road routes, Kazimierz Dolny is easy to reach by **bus**, with several daily departures from Warsaw, including minibus services run by HaloBus and TransBus – both leaving from aleja Jana Pawła next to the *Holiday Inn* – and up to fourteen PKS services from Lublin, which arrive at the bus station between ulica Tyszkiewicza and ulica Podzamcze. Alternatively you can catch a **train** to Puławy (on the Warsaw–Lublin line) and pick up a Kazimierz-bound suburban bus #12 from the train station.

There's a helpful **PTTK office** at no. 27 on the Rynek (May–Sept Mon–Fri 8am–5.30pm, Sat & Sun 10am–5.30pm; Oct–April Mon–Fri 8am–4pm, Sat & Sun 10am–4.30pm; ☎081/881 0046), with good maps and a list of **private rooms** (❶–❷). Two competing **websites**, ⓦwww.kazimierzdolny.pl and ⓦwww.kazimierz-news.com.pl have more information. If you're taken by the idea of exploring the charming surrounding countryside, **bike rental** is widely available. The stall at ul. Nadrzeczna 48 (4zł per hr) is a good choice, and they also have scooters (30zł per hr). There's a small **internet** café (daily 10am–9pm) at ul. Lubelska 4a. A **produce market** is held on the Rynek on Tuesday and Friday mornings.

Accommodation

There's a wide range of accommodation in Kazimierz, and outside festival times (see box, p.277) you should be able to find a cheap private rooms: for all of the places listed below, however, it's advisable to book ahead, especially at weekends. The main **youth hostel**, *Pod Wianuszkami*, ul. Puławska 64 (℡081/881 0327, ✉wianuszki@poczta.onet.pl), 2km north of town in an old riverside granary, has dorms (30zł) as well as a few doubles (**❷**). It's open year-round but is often full with school groups. The alternative is the newer *Strażnica Hostel*, in the fire station building at ul. Senatorska 23 (℡081/881 0427), which has doubles (**❷**) and dorms (28zł) but also fills up quickly. The main **campsite** is behind the *Spichlerz*, 1.5km west of the centre, at Krakowska 59/61 (May–Aug; ℡081/881 0401), but the *Strażnica Hostel* also has space, and plenty of locals rent out their lawns – try along ulica Krakowska or ulica Tyszkiewicza.

Hotels and pensions

Dwa Księżyce ul. Sadowa 15 ℡081/881 0833, ✉dwa_ksiezyce@interia.pl. Medium-sized hotel in a posh-looking house on a quiet street in the town centre, offering stylish en suites. Breakfast included. **❺**

Folwark Walencja ul. Góry 16 ℡081/882 1165, ⓦwww.folwarkwalencja.pl. In an eighteenth-century manor on the hill overlooking the town 2km to the east, this is a quiet pension with good rooms and an adjacent horse-riding school. **❹–❻**

Góralski ul. Krakowska 47 ℡081/881 0263. Reasonable-quality *górale* chalet-style *pensjonat* overlooking the river 1km west of the town centre. Some rooms are en suite, others use a bathroom in the hallway. **❷**

Kwaskowa ul. Czerniawy 3D ℡042/882 1330, ⓦwww.kwaskowa.pl. A 10min walk southeast of town on the way to the Jewish cemetery. Friendly, English-speaking pension with clean rooms and Ikea-style furnishings. En suites and rooms with shared bath **❷–❹**

Pod Wietrzną Górą ul. Krakowska 1 ℡042/881 0543, ⓦwww.wietrznagora.pl. Smallish, centrally located *pensjonat* with cosy en suites and a good restaurant (see p.278). **❹**

Pokoje ul. Krakowska 14 ℡081/881 0871. One of the better pensions in town, with small but modern and comfortable rooms, attractive surroundings and friendly (though not English-speaking) management. **❸**

Spichlerz ul. Krakowska 59/61 ℡081/881 0036. PTTK-run hotel 1.5km west of town in a large, refurbished granary with simple but decent rooms. Restaurant, tennis courts and weight room on site. **❹**

U Góreckich ul. Krakowska 23 ℡081/881 0190. Smart pension with a lovely garden and well-furnished rooms. The best choice in its price range. **❸**

Willa Agnieszka ul. Krakowska 41a ℡081/882 0411, ✉willa_agnieszka@wp.pl. High-quality pension in a new building west of the centre, with a nice terrace and some of the best rooms in town. **❹**

The Rynek

The **Rynek**, with its solid-looking wooden well at the centre, is ringed by an engaging mixture of original buildings, the opulent town houses of rich Kazimierz merchants rubbing shoulders with more folksy structures, many boasting first-floor verandas which jut out from underneath plunging, shingle-covered roofs. Most striking of the merchants' residences around the square – all of which were restored after the war – are the **Houses of the Przybyła Brothers** (Kamienice Przybyłów), both on the southern edge. Built in 1615, they bear some striking Renaissance sculpture: the guidebooks will tell you that the largest one shows St Christopher, but his tree trunk of a staff and zodiacal entourage suggest something more like a Polish version of the Green Giant. Next door is the former **Lustig House** (Kamienica Lustigowska), once home to a notable local Jewish mercantile dynasty. Inside, its beams display the only surviving original Hebrew inscription in town, a quotation from the Psalms. On the western side of the square stands the late eighteenth-century **Gdańsk House** (Kamienica Gdańska), a sumptuous Baroque mansion originally owned by grain merchants.

▲ Rynek, Kazimierz Dolny

West of the Rynek

Other houses still carrying their Renaissance decorations can be seen on ulica Senatorska, which runs alongside the stream west of the square. Of these, the **Celejowski House** (Kamienica Celejowska no. 17) has a fabulous high attic storey, a balustrade filled with the carved figures of saints and an assortment of imaginary creatures, richly ornamented windows and a fine entrance portal and hallway. It houses the **Town Museum** (Muzeum Kazimierza Dolnego: May–Sept Tues–Thurs & Sun 10am–5pm, Fri & Sat 10am–7pm; Oct–April Tues–Sun 10am–5pm; 5zł), which has a small exhibition on town history and a larger gallery of paintings of Kazimierz and its surroundings. Some of the paintings, which date from the nineteenth century, focus on the Jews, whose exotic looks and costumes were a source of endless fascination to the predominantly Gentile painters who descended on the town in summer. The ground floor also houses temporary exhibitions.

Heading southwest up the hill from ulica Senatorska brings you to the late sixteenth-century **Reformed Franciscan Church** (Kościół Reformatów), from where there's a nice view back down over the winding streets and tiled rooftops.

South of the Rynek

Southeast of the main square, the **Mały Rynek** was the Jewish marketplace, and on its northern side you'll find the old **synagogue**. Dating from King Kazimierz's reign, the building you see today was reconstructed in the 1950s, following wartime damage by the Nazis, and converted into a cinema. The interior's rich polychromy didn't survive, but the octagonal wooden dome, characteristic of many Polish synagogues, was repaired, as was the women's gallery. In the centre of the square stand the former **kosher butchers' stalls**, a rough-looking wooden building from the nineteenth century. Continuing east along ulica Lubelska takes you further into the old **Jewish quarter**, where there are a number of fine old wooden houses.

Walking one kilometre out of town, first east along ulica Nadreczna and then south on ulica Czerniawa, brings you to the Czerniawa Gorge, the site of the main **Jewish cemetery**. Dating from at least the sixteenth century, the cemetery was destroyed by the Nazis, who ripped up the tombstones and used them to pave the courtyard of their headquarters in town. In the 1980s the tombstones were salvaged and re-assembled into a Wailing Wall-like monument – six hundred fragments in all – to moving and dramatic effect. A jagged split down the middle symbolizes the dismemberment of the local Jewish population, making this one of the most powerful Jewish memorials in the country. Wander up the hill behind the monument and you'll find decaying remnants of the former cemetery among the trees.

East of the Rynek

Back in the centre, just east of Rynek is the **Silverware Museum** (Muzeum Sztuki Złotniczej: Tues–Sun: May–Sept 10am–5pm; Oct–April 10am–3pm; 6zł, Thurs free), containing a highly impressive collection of ornamental silverwork and other decorative pieces dating back to the seventeenth century. A notable feature is the collection of Jewish ritual objects and vessels, many from the town itself. The **parish church** stands opposite the museum, a fourteenth-century building that was remodelled impressively in the early seventeenth century. The interior boasts a magnificent organ, a Renaissance font and fine stuccoed vaulting.

Further up stand the ruins of the fourteenth-century **castle** (daily: May–Sept 10am–5.30pm; Oct–May 10am–dusk; 3zł), built by King Kazimierz and largely destroyed by the Swedes in the 1650s; the remaining parapets provide good views of the town below. The panorama from the top of the **watchtower** above the castle is even better, taking in the Wisła and the full sweep of the countryside. Built in the thirteenth century, during the age of the grain trade it was used as a lighthouse, with bonfires set inside. Another popular alternative is the vantage point from the top of **Three Crosses Hill** (Góra Trzech Krzyży: same hours as castle; 1zł), a steepish climb fifteen minutes' east of the square (there's also a path leading directly here from the castle). The crosses were raised in memory of the early eighteenth-century plague that wiped out a large part of the local population.

Northeast of town

Spread out alongside the main road to Puławy northeast of town lie several of Kazimierz's sixteenth- and seventeenth-century **granaries** (*spichlerze*) – sturdy affairs with Baroque gables that attest to the erstwhile prosperity of town merchants. One of these, a ten-minute walk from the centre, now houses the **Natural History Museum** (Muzeum Przyrodnicze: Tues–Sun: May–Sept 10am–5pm; Oct–April 10am–3pm; 5zł), a didactic collection of stuffed

The Festival of Folk Bands and Singers

Kazimierz's longest-running annual event is the **Festival of Folk Bands and Singers** (Festiwal kapiel i spiewaków ludowych; ℗ www.kazimierzdolny.pl), a wildly popular event that takes place in late June. Now over forty years old, the festival is undoubtedly the country's premier folk music event, and has spearheaded something of a revival of interest in Polish roots music, particularly in regional styles that not much more than a decade ago seemed on the verge of extinction. You'll find plenty of CDs on sale, and there's an accompanying **Handicraft Fair**, on the Mały Rynek.

animals from the region, while in front of the building stands the massive trunk of one of many poplar trees planted along the river around 1800 by Princess Izabela Czartoryski.

Eating and drinking

There are some excellent places to eat in Kazimierz, and your choices are not limited to Polish food. In addition to what's listed below there are open-air **bars** by the river offering fried fish and beer. Most **drinking** takes place in the restaurants or in the café-bars grouped around the Rynek.

Bar Weranda opposite the museum on ul. Senatorska. Simple Polish milk-bar dishes like *pierogi* and *placki* on a shady terrace corralled with pot plants.

Grill ul. Nadrzeczna 24. Despite the unassuming title and rather plain outdoor courtyard, this is a wonderful place for grilled trout, with the added attractions of a salad bar and an extensive wine list.

Piekarnia Sarzyński ul. Nadrzeczna 4. Smart patisserie selling excellent cakes, gingerbread and ice cream to eat in or takeaway. Also the best place to pick up *koguty* (bread buns baked in the form of a cockerel).

Pod Wietrzną Górą ul. Krakowska 1. Restaurant belonging to the pension of the same name (see p.275), offering traditional meat dishes, fresh fish and a decent range of omelettes. Blaring pop music detracts from an otherwise attractive back patio.

Staropolska ul. Nadrzeczna 14. Long-established restaurant with a good line in mid-price traditional Polish cuisine and a few serviceable pizzas on the side.

U Fryzjera ul. Witkiewicza 2. One of Poland's best Jewish-themed restaurants, with wooden floorboards, distressed furniture and sepia photos of the Kazimierz of yore. Very good traditional dishes like *kugel* (a slab of baked potato mush) and *czulent* (barley stew), though out of season they won't have everything on the menu.

U Radka Rynek. Relaxing café-bar with great jumble-shop decor and artworks on the walls. It also hosts occasional literary readings and live music events.

Zielona Tawerna ul. Nadwiślańska 4. Excellent but not overpriced restaurant with a relaxing country-house interior, a delightful garden, and a wider range of vegetarian choices than anywhere else in this part of Poland.

Around Kazimierz

There's some good **walking** territory around Kazimierz. If you really want to get the feel of the town's gentle surroundings, follow one of the marked paths from the town centre: either the five-kilometre green path that takes you southwest past the *Strażnica Hostel* and along the banks of the Wisła to the sleepy riverside settlement of **Mecmierz**; or the four-kilometre red path that heads northeast to the ruined castle of **Bochotnica**. King Kazimierz is said to have built the castle here for one of his favourite mistresses, a Jewess called Esterka, with a secret tunnel connecting it with the fortress in Kazimierz.

Walking two kilometres west of the centre to the end of ulica Krakowska, you'll come to a **ferry** (every 30min: May–Sept 9am–7pm; 5zł) to the village of **JANOWIEC**, known for the ruins of the Firlej family **castle**, perched on a hill a half-hour walk from the landing point. In its heyday this imposing early sixteenth-century fortress is reputed to have been one of the grandest in the country, with no fewer than eight ballrooms. Today, apart from the fine views it affords, the castle's most striking feature is its zany exterior decoration, which consists of alternating red-and-white-painted stripes and occasional contorted human figures. Also of interest is the freshly cleared well in the castle courtyard, allegedly the ancient entrance to a secret passage joining this fortress to that of Kazimierz. The castle **interior** (May–Aug Mon 10am–2pm, Tues–Fri 10am–5pm, Sat–Sun 10am–7pm; Sept Tues–Fri 10am–4pm, Sat 10am–5pm; Oct–April Tues–Fri 10am–3pm, Sat & Sun 10am–4pm; 8zł) holds a small exhibit on the building's history, including a nice series of photographs. To one side of the castle is a small **skansen** (same hours and ticket) devoted to regional folk architecture. The highlight is a wooden manor house dating from the 1770s and with period furniture inside; other displays include wooden cottages from around the region, a collection of horse carts and a nineteenth-century wooden granary. Back down in the village there's a fine Gothic **parish church** that contains the Firlej family tomb, designed by Italian Renaissance architect Santi Gucci, the man behind the grotesque heads of Kraków's Sukiennice (see p.355). If the ferry isn't running, you can also get to Janowiec by taking **bus** #17 from Puławy.

Sandomierz and around

Eighty kilometres south from Kazimierz Dolny along the Wisła, **SANDOMIERZ** is another fascinating old town with a well-preserved hilltop centre and a wealth of worthy monuments. Like other places in the southeast, Sandomierz rose to prominence through its position on the medieval trade route running from the Middle East, through southern Russia and the Ukraine, into central Europe. Following repeated sackings by Tatars and Lithuanians, the town was completely rebuilt by **Kazimierz the Great** in the mid-fourteenth century, gaining defensive walls and a cathedral which can still be seen today. Sandomierz subsequently flourished by shipping local timber and corn down the Wisła to Gdańsk, but suffered badly at the hands of the Swedes, who blew up the castle in 1656 – after which Sandomierz went into a long period of decline. Stranded away from today's growth centres (and thus economically moribund), Sandomierz is nonetheless easy to reach, with two daily train services from Warsaw and frequent buses from Lublin. Tourist facilities have improved in the last few years, and you'll find plenty of places to stay and eat.

Arrival, information and accommodation

The **train station** is 3km south on the far side of the river (local bus #8 to the centre), while the **bus station** is 1.5km northwest of town (to get into town walk west to the end of ul. 11 Listopada and turn left onto ul. Mickiewicza); buses arriving from the south drop off by the Opatów Gate, however. The staff at the **PTTK office** at Rynek 12 (May–Oct daily 8am–6pm; Nov–April Mon–Fri 8am–4.30pm; ℡015/832 2305, www.pttk-sandomierz.pl) don't speak English but have a list of all **accommodation** options, including several private rooms (❶–❷). Near the main square, the homes at ul. Forteczna 2 (℡015/832 3751; ❷) and 6 (℡015/832 2814; ❷) rent modest **private rooms** with shared facilities, as does the restaurant *Winnica*, ul. Mały Rynek 2 (℡015/832 3130; ❷).

Hotels and pensions

Hotel Basztowy pl. Poniatowskiego 2 ℡015/833 3450, www.hotelbasztowy.pl. Large, business-oriented hotel that's an architectural mess from the outside but is all smoothness and comfort within. Rooms come with desk space, TV and internet access. ❻

Królowej Jadwigi ul. Krakowska 24 ℡015/832 2988, www.motel.go3.pl. Family-run place down the hill past the castle, with cosy and well-appointed rooms. ❹

Pod Ciżemką Rynek 27 ℡015/832 0550, www.sandomierz-hotel.com.pl. Intimate main-square hotel offering plush en suites in a burgher's mansion. ❻

Sandomiria ul. Podwale Górne 10 ℡015/644 5244, www.sandomiria.pl. Spotless pension on the north edge of the centre, with en-suite rooms, kitchen facilities and a café. ❹

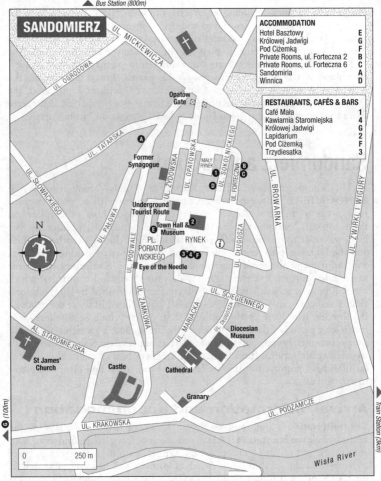

SANDOMIERZ

ACCOMMODATION

Hotel Basztowy	E
Królowej Jadwigi	G
Pod Ciżemką	F
Private Rooms, ul. Forteczna 2	B
Private Rooms, ul. Forteczna 6	C
Sandomiria	A
Winnica	D

RESTAURANTS, CAFÉS & BARS

Café Mała	1
Kawiarnia Staromiejska	4
Królowej Jadwigi	G
Lapidarium	2
Pod Ciżemką	F
Trzydziesatka	3

The Town

The entrance to the Old Town (Stare Miasto) is the fourteenth-century **Opatów Gate** (Brama Opatowska), a surviving part of King Kazimierz's fortifications. Climbing to the top (daily 10am–6.30pm; 3zł) will get you a view over the town and surrounding area.

The Rynek and around

From here on it's alleyways and cobblestones, as ulica Opatowska leads to the delightful, sloping **Rynek**. At its heart is the fourteenth-century **town hall**, a Gothic building which had its decorative attic, hexagonal tower and belfry added in the seventeenth and eighteenth centuries. The ground floor section contains a small **museum** (Tues–Fri 9am–4pm, Sat 9am–3pm, Sun 10am–3pm; 4zł) devoted to the history of the town. There's not much here other than pieces from an artful twelfth-century chess set – one of the oldest in Europe – dug up near the Church of St James (see p.282) some years back. Many of the well-preserved **burghers' houses** positively shout their prosperity: nos. 5 and 10 are particularly fine Renaissance examples.

Just off the square on ulica Oleśnickich is the entrance to the **Underground Tourist Route** (Podziemna trasa; Polish only; daily 10am–5pm; 6.50zł), a trip through the honeycomb of chambers beneath the Rynek where medieval merchants stored their food and wine. The forty-minute guided tour takes you through thirty or so chilly Renaissance-era cellars, reaching a depth of 12m at one point. Back at ground level, the registrar's office on nearby ulica Żydowska was an eighteenth-century **synagogue**, though there is little to indicate its origins.

The cathedral and Diocesan Museum

Continuing down either of the streets leading off the southern edge of the Rynek will bring you to the murky **cathedral** (Tues–Sat 10am–2pm & 3–5pm, Sun 3–5pm), constructed around 1360 on the site of an earlier Romanesque church but with substantial Baroque additions. Notable features include the set of early fifteenth-century Russo-Byzantine **murals** in the presbytery, probably by the same artist who painted the Holy Trinity Chapel in Lublin (see p.261). Unfortunately they're kept roped off and unlit most of the time, so you'll probably have to crane your neck for a glimpse of them. There are no such problems with the gruesome series of eighteenth-century paintings surrounding the nave, charmingly entitled *The Torture Calendar* and depicting early church martyrs being skewered, decapitated and otherwise maimed in every conceivable way. As if this weren't enough, there's also a group of murals underneath the organ depicting violent scenes from the town's past, including Tatars enjoying a massacre of the local populace in 1259, Swedes blowing up the castle four centuries later and, far more disturbing, an incident of supposed Jewish child sacrifice at Passover – a standard theme of anti-Semitic discourse.

Set back from the cathedral, the **Diocesan Museum** (Muzeum Diecezjalne; April–Oct Tues–Sat 9am–4pm, Sun 1.30–4pm; Nov–March Tues–Sat 9am–3pm, Sun 1.30–3pm; 5zł) and its peaceful, well-tended garden was the home of **Jan Długosz** (1415–80), author of one of the earliest Polish chronicles. The building is filled to bursting with an absorbing, well-presented collection of religious art, ceramics, glass and other curios; the latter include an early seventeenth-century portable organ that still works, a collection of Renaissance locks and keys, and a wonderful old pipe supposed to have belonged to Mickiewicz. Also look for the piece of bread left over from the Swedish invasion of 1656 and the set of seventeenth-century French playing cards illustrating the nations of the world. Among the artistic works there's a fine set of fifteenth- and sixteenth-century altarpieces, including the delicate *Three Saints* triptych from Kraków, as well as a Romanesque *Madonna and Child* stone carving and a *John the Baptist* dubiously attributed to Caravaggio.

The castle

Downhill from the cathedral is the **castle**, the west wing of which was rebuilt by the Austrians in the nineteenth century after its destruction by the Swedes three hundred years earlier. The large open terrace, also used for open-air concerts and theatre performances in summer, affords good views back over the Old Town. The **museum** that occupies part of the building (May–Sept Tues–Sun 10am–5pm; Oct–April Tues–Fri 9am–4pm, Sat 9am–3pm, Sun 10am–3pm; 5zł) holds an undistinguished permanent collection of silver, numismatics and regional folk art, although its temporary exhibitions are often more interesting. Towards the river stands a medieval **granary**; others are to be found north of town.

St James's Church and around

Aleja Staromiejska runs from in front of the castle to **St James's Church** (Kościół św. Jakuba), a lime-shaded late Romanesque building that's thought to be the first brick basilica in Poland – its restored entrance portal is particularly striking. Inside, the **Martyrs' Chapel** (Mon–Sat 10am–5pm, Sun 10.30–11.30am & 1.30–3.30pm) has a vivid painting of the martyrdom of local Dominicans by the Tatars in 1260, while in the northern nave there are glass cases said to contain the bones of the murdered monks.

The area around the church was the site of the original town, destroyed by the Tatars. Archeological digs have uncovered finds such as the twelfth-century chess set now on display in the town museum (see p.280). Since the 1960s, this whole southern district has had to be shored up: the network of tunnels and cellars dug for grain storage that runs for hundreds of metres through the soft undersoil has caused significant subsidence.

Head back down the path in front of St James's and you re-enter the town walls through the **Eye of the Needle** (Ucho Igielne), a narrow entrance whose name refers to the Biblical proverb.

Eating, drinking and entertainment

There are plenty of **places to eat** and **drink** around the Rynek, many of which have attractive outdoor terraces for people-watching. The best place for coffee is *Café Mała*, just off the Rynek at ulica Sokolnickiego, while *Kawiarnia Staromiejska* on the southern side off the square doles out light Polish meals as well as coffee and cakes. Next door, *Trzydziesatka* at Rynek 30 has tasty dishes like grilled chicken with kasha (pornage). The upstairs restaurant of the *Pod Ciżemką* is the most formal in town (see p.279); the Italian place below, also part of the hotel, fares better with pasta than pizza. Slightly further afield, the restaurant of the *Królowej Jadwigi* offers traditional home cooking in endearingly chintzy surroundings (see p.279).

For **entertainment** the *Lapidarium*, a cellar club beneath the town hall, has occasional live gigs. The town puts on an annual week-long **music festival** from late June to early July, featuring a variety of classical, folk and jazz concerts; check with the tourist office for details.

Opatów

Some 25km west of Sandomierz on the Kielce road, the somnolent town of **OPATÓW** is worth a brief stop if you're heading towards the Świętokrzyskie region (see p.425), and is also the obvious jumping-off point for the magnificent ruins of Krzyżtopór Castle (see p.283). A medieval market town straddling a major east–west trade route, Opatów was badly mauled during the Tatar raids (1500–1502), and owes much of its current appearance to Chancellor Krzysztof Szydłowiecki, who purchased the town soon afterwards and had the central Rynek area rebuilt along Renaissance lines.

The Town

The Rynek's most notable building, **St Martin's Church** (Kościół św. Marcina), is a towering three-aisled Romanesque basilica raised in the mid-twelfth century and remodelled in later centuries. A few features of the original Romanesque decoration survive, notably the main doorway and some frieze decoration on the facade. These aside, the thing to look out for is the group of Szydłowiecki family **tombs**, especially that of Chancellor Krzysztof. Executed in the 1530s by Italian architects from the court in Kraków, the tomb has a powerful bronze bas-relief of the citizens of Opatów mourning the chancellor's death – a moving tribute to a man whose family name had died out by the end of the century owing to a persistent failure to produce male heirs.

Ten minutes' walk away, back down the hill, through the **Warsaw Gate** (Brama Warszawska) and across the River Opatówka, is the **Bernardine church**, an ornate late Baroque structure with a fine high altarpiece that replaced the earlier fifteenth-century church destroyed by Swedish troops during the invasions of the mid-1650s.

Practicalities

The **bus station**, in the centre of town, has good connections to Sandomierz. The **PTTK office** at Obrońców Pokoju 18 (Mon–Sat 10am–6pm, Sun 11am–5pm; ☎015/868 2778) sells maps and provides local information, and there's a seasonal tourist information point in the Warsaw Gate (May–Sept daily 10am–4pm). With little in the way of accommodation save for a spartan seasonal hostel and an out-of-town motel, however, it's best to press on.

Krzyżtopór

Despite its dilapidated state, the **Krzyżtopór Castle**, near the village of Ujazd, 15km southwest of Opatów, is one of the most spectacular ruins in Poland. Nothing in the surrounding landscape prepares you for the mammoth building that suddenly rears up over the skyline. Even then, it's not until you actually enter the castle compound (Tues–Sun sunrise–sunset; 4zł) that you really begin to get a handle on the scale of the place, a magnificent ruin still bearing many hallmarks of the considerable architectural ingenuity that went into designing and constructing the complex.

The **history** of the castle is a textbook case of grand aristocratic folly. Built at enormous expense for Krzysztof Ossoliński, the governor of Sandomierz province, by Italian architect Lorenzo Muretto, and completed in 1644, only a year before Ossoliński's death, the castle was thoroughly ransacked by the Swedes only a decade later, a blow from which it never really recovered, despite being inhabited by the Ossoliński family up until the 1770s.

The basic **layout** of the castle comprises a star-shaped set of fortifications surrounding a large inner courtyard and, within this, a smaller elliptical inner area. The original architectural conception mimicked the calendar at every level: thus there were four towers, representing the seasons, twelve main walls for the months, 52 rooms for the weeks, 365 windows for the days, and even an additional window for leap years, kept bricked up when out of sync with the calendar. Ossoliński's passion for horses was accommodated by the network of **stables**, some 370 in all, built underneath the castle, each equipped with its own mirror and marble manger. While remnants of the stables survive, the same can't be said for the fabled dining hall in the octagonal entrance tower, originally dominated by a crystal aquarium built into the ceiling.

Carved on the **entrance tower** before the black marble portal are a large cross (*krzyż*) and an axe (*topór*), a reference to the castle's name, the former a symbol of the Catholic Church's Counter-Reformation, of which Ossoliński was a firm supporter, the latter part of the family coat of arms. Inside the complex, you're inevitably drawn to wandering around the castle's rather unstable nooks and crannies. The longer you stay, the more the sheer audacity and expanse of the place hits home – in particular, the murky ruins of the cellars, which seem to go on for ever.

Practicalities

The site is fairly easy to get to if you're **driving**: follow the Staszów road out of Opatów and turn east at the village of Iwaniska. By **bus**, there are five daily services to Ujazd from Opatów (fewer at weekends). If you're coming from the Sandomierz direction you could just as easily catch a bus to Klimontów, 10km southeast of Krzyżtopór (10 daily), where you can change to an Ujazd service (7 daily).

Baranów Sandomierski

South of Sandomierz along the Wisła basin, fifteen kilometres beyond the sulphur mining centre of Tarnobrzeg, the castle at **BARANÓW SANDOMIERSKI** is one of the most impressive in Poland and as fine a period piece as you'll come across anywhere. Erected on the site of a fortified medieval structure owned by the Baranów family, the exquisitely formed and well-preserved Renaissance **castle** (Tues–Sat 9am–3pm, Sun 9am–4pm; 6zł) is thought to have been designed by Santi Gucci (see p.355). The epithet "castle" is a bit of a misnomer – the building is really an elegant palace, with fortifications added for appearance's sake. Built in the 1590s for the Leszczyński family, it is constructed on a rectangular plan with a cool Italianate courtyard surrounded by two tiers of arcaded passageways. An entertaining collection of grotesques, many of them animal figures, decorate the bases of the courtyard pillars. Inside the building, you can view a section of the ground floor that has retained its ornate period furnishings, while down in the castle basement there's a small **museum** (same hours and ticket) with temporary exhibitions. On the south side of the building the well-tended gardens are a pleasant strolling ground.

Practicalities

By **bus**, local services run fairly regularly from Tarnobrzeg and Mielec, accessible from Sandomierz and Rzeszów respectively. Ask the driver to drop you off at the castle (*zamek*); otherwise it's a ten-minute walk south of the bus stop at the Rynek. The lavishly decorated rooms of the upper floors of the castle are occupied by a luxury **hotel**, the *Zamkowy* (⊕015/811 8039, ⓦwww.zamekbaranow.maxmedia .pl) with rooms in the castle itself (❼) and an adjacent building (❺), and there's a high-quality restaurant on the castle's south side. The whole place is often reserved for banquets, so particularly in summer it's best to book ahead. A cheaper and perfectly acceptable alternative is the *Zajazd Wisła*, about 1km out of town, on ulica Dąbrowskiego (⊕015/811 0380; ❸), which also has its own restaurant.

Zamość

Many of the old towns and palaces of southeast Poland have an Italian feel to them, and for none is this more the case than **ZAMOŚĆ**, 96km southeast of Lublin. The brainchild of the dynamic sixteenth-century chancellor Jan Zamoyski, the town is a remarkable demonstration of the way the Polish ruling class looked towards Italy for ideas. Zamoyski, in many ways the archetypal Renaissance man, built this model town close to his childhood village to his own ideological specifications, commissioning the design from Bernardo Morando of Padua – the city where he had earlier studied. Morando produced a beautiful Italianate period piece, with a wide piazza, grid-plan streets, an academy and defensive bastions. These fortifications were obviously well thought out, as Zamość was one of the few places to withstand the seventeenth-century "Swedish Deluge" that flattened so many other Polish towns. Strategically located on the major medieval trading routes linking Kraków and Kiev from west to east, Lublin and Lwów from north to south, the town attracted an international array of merchants from early on, notably Jews, Armenians, Greeks, Scots, Hungarians and Italians, whose presence remained embedded in the diverse architecture of the city even after political changes during the Partition era brought economic decline: early in the nineteenth century Zamość had sunk so far that even the Zamoyskis themselves had moved on.

Somehow, Zamość managed to get through World War II unscathed, so what you see today is one of Europe's best-preserved Renaissance town centres, classified by UNESCO as an outstanding historical monument. Chiefly due to its

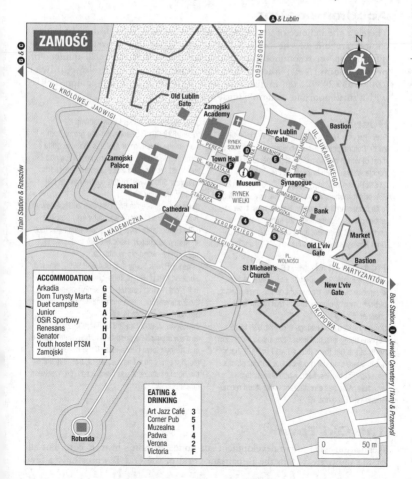

off-the-beaten-track location, the town has neither assumed the prominence it deserves on the tourist trail, nor seen the sort of economic success that has revitalized Lublin and Rzeszów.

Arrival and information

There are only a handful of daily services to the **train station**, located 1km southwest of the centre off ulica Akademiczka (take any bus two stops from the station side of the street), so you're more likely to arrive at the main **bus station**, 2km east of the town centre (local buses #10, #22, #44, #47 or #59 will drop you off in the centre). Zamość's **tourist office**, in the town hall at Rynek 13 (May–Sept Mon–Fri 8am–6pm, Sat 10am–4pm, Sun 10am–3pm; Oct–April Mon–Fri 8am–4pm; ☎084/639 2292, ✉zoit@osir.zamosc.pl), is helpful for accommodation. The official town website (Ⓦwww.zamosc.pl) is more helpful, while the best English-language background on the web is maintained by a local high school (Ⓦwww.cf2004.zamosc.pl). There's **Internet** access at Rynek 10.

Accommodation

There's a good choice of **accommodation** in Zamość, though the best budget choices are out of the centre. The tourist office (see above) will provide information on accommodation possibilities as well as the small number of **private rooms** (❶–❷) in town. The *Duet* **campsite** on ulica Królowej Jadwigi (☎084/639 2499), a ten-minute walk west of the centre, is a well-equipped place with a small pool and modern bungalows (❷).

Hostels

Dom Turysty Marta ul. Zamenhofa 11 ☎084/639 2639. Central pension-cum-hostel with nine rooms, most of which are dorms (45zł per person). One double without bath or breakfast (❶).

PTSM Hostel ul. Zamoyskiego 4 ☎084/627 9125. Sparsely furnished school hostel that opens its doors to all comers in the summer. Not the most convenient of places, located some 25 minutes' walk northeast of the centre, but a useful standby if the *Dom Turysty* is full. July & Aug only; 30zł per person.

Hotels and pensions

Arkadia Rynek 9 ☎084/638 6507, ✉arkadia @zamosc.pl. Small place right on the main square, but with musty, gloomy rooms that ought to be cheaper. ❸–❹

Junior ul. Gen. Sikorskiego 6 ☎084/638 6615, Ⓦwww.hoteljunior.pl. Pleasant roadside hotel 2km north of the Old Town (bus #3, #11 or #19) that's better value than the more central budget places, especially at the weekend when discounts are available. Also has a restaurant and billiard room. Breakfast 10zł extra. ❸

OSiR Sportowy ul. Królowej Jadwigi 8 ☎084/638 6011. Despite looking grotty from the outside, this former athletes' hotel is quite comfortable within, with roomy en suites, and breakfast for an extra 20zł. Located in a sports complex, 500m west of the centre next to the football stadium. ❸

Renesans ul. Grecka 6 ☎084/639 2001, Ⓦwww .hotelrenesans.pl. Bland and outwardly ugly but quite comfortable hotel built where long ago stood an Armenian church. Handily close to the Rynek, and with weekend discounts. ❹

Senator Rynek Solny 4 ☎084/638 9990, Ⓦwww .senatorhotel.pl. Small, high-quality newish hotel in the old Jewish quarter, of a similar standard to the *Zamojski* but much more intimate. Ask about discounts at weekends. ❺

Zamojski ul. Kołłątaja 2/6 ☎084/639 2516, Ⓦwww.orbis.pl. Polished Orbis-chain hotel located in a historic town house just off the Rynek. With plush rooms and a fine restaurant, this is definitely the hotel of choice if you fancy a splurge. Weekend discounts. ❻

The Old Town

Regulation-issue urban development surrounds Zamość's historic core, but all of the sights are within the Renaissance grid of the Old Town or only a few minutes' walk beyond it. Coming from the bus station you'll arrive at **plac Wolności** on the eastern edge of the centre, from where the main Rynek is a two-minute walk further west.

The Rynek

Ringed by a low arcade and the decorative former homes of the Zamość mercantile bourgeoisie, the geometrically designed **Rynek Wielki** – exactly 100m in both width and length – is a superb example of Renaissance town architecture. Dominating the ensemble from the north side of the square is the **town hall**, among the most photographed buildings in the country. A solid, three-storey structure topped by a soaring clock tower and spire, the original, lower construction designed by Morando acquired its present Mannerist modelling in the 1640s, with the sweeping, fan-shaped double stairway not added until the eighteenth century. Occupied by local government offices, it offers little to see inside.

Wilczek House and the town museum

From the town hall the vaulted arcade stretching east along ulica Ormiańska features several of the finest houses on the square. Once inhabited by the Armenian merchants who moved here under special privilege in 1585, the house facades are a whirl of rich, decorative ornamentation, with a noticeable intermesh of oriental motifs. First along is the splendid **Wilczek House** (Dom Wilczeka), built by an early professor at the Zamość Academy, with some fine decorated bas-reliefs of Christ, Mary and the Apostles gracing the upper storey of the facade. Number 26 sports similarly exuberant decoration, this time with zoological themes. It and the adjoining mansions house the town **museum** (Tues–Sun 9am–4pm; 5zł), focusing on the Zamoyskis and local history. There are copies of portraits of the town's founder, Jan, though these are outshone by a beautiful series of full-sized paintings, dating from the 1630s, of his son Tomasz Zamoyski and daughter-in-law Katarzyna. Elsewhere, the archeological section contains ornate jewellery worn by the Goths who settled hereabouts, together with a display of mannequins wearing replica Goth robes and dresses – anyone seriously into hippy chic will find a wealth of inspiration here. Finally, there's a colourful assemblage of Polish folk costumes, and a roomful of locally made, brightly decorated ceramics.

The cathedral

Southwest of the square, first port of call is the towering collegiate church, recently restored and upgraded to the status of **cathedral**, a magnificent Mannerist basilica designed by Morando to Zamoyski's exacting instructions and completed in 1600. It's a three-aisled structure with numerous side chapels and delicate pillars reaching up to the ceiling's well-proportioned Renaissance stuccowork – the whole interior is marked by a strong sense of visual and architectural harmony, a powerful expression of the self-confidence of the Polish Counter-Reformation. The **presbytery** houses a finely wrought eighteenth-century Rococo silver tabernacle, as well as a series of paintings of scenes from the life of St Thomas attributed to Tintoretto. The grandest of the **chapels** is that of the Zamoyski family, which contains the marble tomb of Chancellor Jan and is topped with elegant Baroque stucco by the Italian architect Giovanni Battista Falconi. Adjoining the main building is a high **bell tower** (May–Sept Mon–Fri 10am–4pm; 3zł); the biggest of its bells, known as Jan, is over three centuries old.

The military museum and Zamoyski Palace

West across the main road, ulica Akademiczka, are two buildings that played a key role in the historic life of the town. As its name implies the **Arsenal**, built by Morando in the 1580s, is where the town's ample stock of weaponry used to be kept alongside Zamoyski spoils of war. These days it houses a small **military museum** (Tues–Sun 9am–4pm; 4zł) where, among the pictures of Polish soldiers through the ages, you can view a scale model of the seventeenth-century town, surrounded by defensive bastions arranged in the shape of a seven-pointed star. Southwest along ulica Akademiczka it's a five-minute walk to the **Wystawa Plenarna**, the military museum's outdoor branch (same hours; 4zł), where a helicopter and several post-World War II artillery pieces sit on a tiny scrap of parkland.

Back by the Arsenal, the massive **Zamoyski Palace** (Pałac Zamojskich) is a shadow of its former self, Morando's original building having undergone substantial modification early in the nineteenth century, after the Zamoyskis sold it to the Russian government for use as an army hospital. Currently occupied by the town court, the palace is a rather mournful, run-down place, with only the courtyard at the back hinting at its former grandeur.

Old Lublin Gate and Zamoyski Academy

Continuing north along ulica Akademiczka, west of the main street is the **Old Lublin Gate** (Stara Brama Lubelska), oldest of the entranceways dotted around the Old Town fortifications, and long since bricked up. Now stranded on the edge of school playing fields, it's worth seeking out for the bas-relief uncovered during renovation earlier this century.

The impressive-looking former **Zamoyski Academy** (Akademia Zamojska) across the street, built in the 1630s and an important centre of learning until it was closed by the Austrian government shortly after the First Partition, is now a school, albeit on a humbler scale than it was originally.

The former Jewish quarter

Much of the northern section of the Old Town belongs to the former **Jewish quarter**, centred around ulica Zamenhofa and Rynek Solny. As in so many other eastern towns, Jews made up a significant portion of the population of Zamość – some 45 percent on the eve of World War II. The first Sephardic Jews from L'viv arrived here in the 1580s, their numbers subsequently swelled by kindred settlers from Turkey, Italy and Holland, to be displaced subsequently by the powerful local Askenazi community. With much of eastern Polish Jewry in the grip of the mystical Hassidic revival, Zamość developed as a centre for the progressive Haskalah, an Enlightenment-inspired movement originating in Germany that advocated social emancipation, the acceptance of "European" culture and scientific and educational progress within the Jewish community. Among its products were **Itzak Peretz** (1851–1915), a notable nineteenth-century Yiddish novelist born here, and **Rosa Luxemburg** (1871–1919), though it's as a radical communist rather than Jewish progressive that she's primarily known.

A few of the old Jewish merchants' houses ranged around the small square have been renovated, one of which is the smart *Senator* hotel, and more restoration is in the works. The most impressive Jewish monument, however, is the **former synagogue** on ulica Pereca, a fine early seventeenth-century structure built as part of Zamoyski's original town scheme. It is currently closed pending long-term renovation by the Foundation for the Preservation of Jewish Culture (@www.fodz.pl), after which it will become a municipal cultural centre containing a multimedia museum on Jewish Zamość.

The town fortifications

East across ulica Łukasińskiego takes you over onto the former town fortifications. Designed by Morando and Italian-inspired, they originally consisted of a set of seven **bastions** with three main gates. Wide moats and artificial lakes blocked the approaches to the town on every side. After holding out so impressively against the Cossacks and the Swedes, the whole defensive system went under in 1866, when the Russians ordered the upper set of battlements to be blown up and the town fortress liquidated. The interior of the bastion on the eastern edge of the Old Town has been renovated and now houses a **market**, while park area covers much of the rest of the battlements, leaving you free to wander along the tops and see for yourself why the marauding Swedes were checked. The ornamental **Old L'viv Gate** (Stara Brama Lwowska), another Morando construction, bricked up in the 1820s, and the **New L'viv Gate** (Nowa Brama Lwowska), added at the same time, complete the surviving elements of the fortifications.

The Rotunda

The Nazis spared the buildings of Zamość, but not its residents. In the **Rotunda**, a nineteenth-century arsenal ten minutes' walk south of the Old Town on ulica Wyspiańskiego, more than eight thousand local people were executed by the Germans; a simple **museum** housed in its tiny cells (May–Sept Tues–Sun 9am–8pm; free) tells the harrowing story of the town's wartime trauma. In fact, Zamość (preposterously renamed "Himmlerstadt") and the surrounding area were the target of a brutal "relocation" scheme of the kind already carried out by the Nazis in Western Prussia. From 1942 to 1943 nearly three hundred villages were cleared of their Polish inhabitants and their houses taken by German settlers – all part of Hitler's plan to create an Aryan eastern bulwark of the Third Reich. The remaining villages were left alone only because the SS lacked the manpower to clear them out. Three cells in the museum are dedicated to the Soviet wartime massacre of Polish army officers at Katyń (see p.620), and there's a sombre chapel in memory of local people deported to Siberia following the Soviet occupation of eastern Poland in 1939.

The Jewish cemetery

A fifteen-minute walk east of the Old Town, there's a tiny **Jewish cemetery** at the north end of ulica Prosta. A monument made out of gravestones uprooted by the Nazis commemorates the many thousands of the town's Jewish population that the nazis murdered. Interestingly, the monument was erected in 1950, a good deal earlier than most others in Poland.

Eating, drinking and entertainment

Restaurant and bar life in the Old Town is flourishing, especially around the Rynek itself, where most places combine the roles of **café** and **restaurant** in a single establishment. However, outside the summer season you may be hard-pressed to find a meal after 8pm. For drinking, most people opt for the alfresco **bars** on the Rynek in summer.

If you happen to be in town at the right time there are several annual cultural happenings worth checking out. The **Jazz Na Kresach** ("Jazz on the Borderlands"; late May/early June) festival, usually held in the last week of May or early June, is popular with Polish and other Slav jazzers. For the **Jarmark Hetmański** (second weekend in June) you'll find Polish and Ukrainian traditional music and a handmade-crafts market on the Rynek. **Theatre Summer** (Zamojskie Lato Teatralnie), a drama festival held in the latter part of June and early July, features some excellent theatre groups from all over the country, many of whom perform on the stairway in front of the town hall. The tourist office (see p.286) will have details on all the above.

Restaurants and bars

Art Jazz Café Rynek 2. Basement beer hall with musical instruments hanging from the walls and occasional live gigs.

Corner Pub Żeromskiego 6. Upmarket pub with reproduction posters and adverts on the walls, and a food menu ranging from *pierogi* (12zł) to tortilla wraps (18zł).

Muzealna Rynek 30. Cosy brick cellar with warm burgundy textiles, offering a good choice of traditional food from Poland's eastern borderlands, including *gołąbki* with buckwheat and mushrooms and *chłodnik litewski* (Lithuanian cold *barszcz* with boiled potatoes), a refreshing summer dish. Mains fall within the 12–17zł range.

Padwa Rynek 23 Multi-purpose café-restaurant, occupying a historic building with original ceilings. Good range of pastries and cakes and a straightforward selection of Polish pork-chop and potato-pancake main courses.

Verona Rynek 5. Chic Italian-themed café serving reasonably authentic pizzas, pasta dishes and Mediterranean salads, with prices hovering around the 20zł mark. Also popular for coffee and cake.

Viktoria in the *Zamojski Hotel*, ul. Kołłątaja 2/6. Though lacking the atmosphere of those in the main square, this hotel restaurant is good for quality Polish cuisine, with fish and game dishes adding variety to the usual pork-and-poultry fare. Mains 25–45zł.

South from Zamość

South of Zamość lies more of the open, sparsely populated countryside characteristic of much of the country's eastern borderlands. The agricultural monotony is broken by occasional forests, the few surviving swaths of the *puszcza* that once covered the whole area. The biggest of these, now protected by the bounds of the **Roztoczański National Park**, offers a glimpse of the original untamed wilderness. **Zwierzyniec**, the gateway to the park, is an uneventful little place with good tourist facilities and a locally famous brewery. Heading southeast from Zamość, the road to the Ukrainian border at Hrebenne passes through **Bełżec**, site of an infamous Nazi death camp whose victims are commemorated by a moving modern memorial.

Zwierzyniec and Roztocze National Park

Thirty-two kilometres southwest from Zamość is **Zwierzyniec**, principal gateway to the **Roztocze National Park**. Frequent local bus connections and two daily trains to and from Zamość make a day-trip a feasible option, although the air of peaceful rusticity ensures that a stay of a night or two is well worth considering.

Zwierzyniec

Zwierzyniec owes its existence to chancellor Jan Zamoyski, who purchased the surrounding forests in 1589 and commissioned Bernando Morando (of Zamość fame) to build him a country palace here. Most of the palace complex was demolished in the 1830s, but a few important elements were spared, most notably the Zamoyski **chapel**, a delicate Baroque construction scenically located on one of a series of islands in the willow-fringed palace lake.

The **bus station** is five minutes' north of the palace lake, on the far side of an unkempt town park. There is a wealth of **pensions** (②) in the countryside around the town, though many are only accessible if you're driving. One central choice is the clean and new *Anna*, just off the main road at ul. Dębowa 1 (☎084/687 2590, ⓦwww.annazwierzyniec.pl; ❸); there's also bicycle rental here. The *Karczma Młyn*, facing the lake on ulica Aleksandry Wachniewskiej, is a homely timber restaurant (see below) with a few small but decent rooms above (☎084/687 2527, ⓦwww.karczma-mlyn.pl; ❸). Of places further out, the *Zacisze*, north of the centre at ul. Rudka 5B (☎084/687 2306, ⓦwww.zacisze.zwierzyniec.com; ❷), is a tranquil and attractive pension with comfortable rooms and a good restaurant and bar.

For **eating**, *Karczma Młyn* serves a reasonable selection of pizzas and meaty Polish favourites, while further along the lake there's a takeaway stand with great ice cream in season. The local beer, a smooth, lager-style brew that's extremely difficult to find outside the region, is ideally savoured at the **café-bar** of the brewery itself, a grand nineteenth-century building on ulica Browara.

Roztocze National Park

The wild expanses of the **Roztocze National Park** (Roztoczański Park Narodowy: ⓦwww.roztoczanskipn.pl), adjacent to Zwierzyniec, are a must for both walkers and naturalists. Created in 1974 and covering an area of almost eighty square kilometres, the park is a picturesque region of forested hills rising to 390m at their highest point. Cutting across its heart is the beautiful and uncontaminated **River Wieprz**, which has its source just to the east. Most of the park is forested, with flora including pine, fir, and pockets of towering beeches up to 50m high. Fauna includes tarpans – wild ponies that virtually died out in the nineteenth century but were brought back from the brink of extinction through a controlled breeding programme – as well as storks, cranes and beavers.

Maps and detailed information about **walking routes**, as well as entrance tickets (2.50zł), are available from the **National Park Museum** (Ośrodek Muzealny RPN: Tues–Sun: May–Oct 9am–5pm; Nov–April 9am–4pm; 3.50zł), a short walk south of central Zwierzyniec along ulica Browara, which also contains a display on the park's flora and fauna. The park is easily navigable with the help of a map, with several short walks branching off from the museum itself. The easiest of these leads southeast through pine forest to the reed-shrouded **Echo Lake** (15min), the northern banks of which boast a wonderful, sloping sandy beach. From here, continue 200m along the road passing the lake and you'll come to an **observation deck**, from which you're likely to see grazing tarpans. Another popular trail traces the old palace path southwest to Bukowa Góra (20min), an upland area of dense woodland where daylight is almost blotted out by the thick canopy of beech and firs. On the far side of Bukowa Góra lies an area of sandy-soiled heath with some fine views southwards: from here you can work your way eastwards towards Echo Lake in about twenty minutes.

Bełżec

Forty kilometres southeast of Zamość, the unassuming village of **BEŁŻEC** is the site of one of Nazi Germany's most notorious extermination camps (ⓦwww.belzec.org.pl). Established on the southeastern fringes of the village in early 1942, the Bełżec camp was a key component of Operation Reinhard – the methodical annihilation of eastern Poland's entire Jewish population. Using six gas ovens to dispose of its victims at a rate of 4500 a time, the camp only accommodated a small number of long-term inmates, whose job it was to dispose of the bodies and process the victims' belongings. Only a handful of prisoners survived Bełżec, and with the Nazis razing the entire facility in spring 1943, the camp has remained one of the least known, least documented of Poland's Holocaust sites. The site was largely abandoned to the weeds until 2004, when a new memorial was erected incorporating a huge open-air abstract sculpture comprising stark lumps of grey rubble. There's a state-of-the-art **museum** (Tues–Sun: April–Oct 9am–6pm, Nov–March 8am–4pm; free) containing photos, films and English-language texts.

A single daily train runs from Zamość to Bełżec – departing in the morning and returning in late afternoon, making a day-trip feasible.

Travel details

Trains

Chełm to: Lublin (10 daily; 1hr 15min).
Lublin to: Chełm (10 daily; 1hr 15min); Kielce (3 daily; 3–4hr); Kraków (2 daily; 5hr 30min); Przemyśl (1 daily; 5hr); Puławy (15 daily; 40–55min); Warsaw (8 daily; 2hr 30min–3hr).
Zamość to: Bełżec (1 daily; 1hr 30min); Kraków (2 daily; 7hr 30min); Rzeszów (1 daily; 5hr); Zwierzyniec (2 daily; 1hr).

Buses

Chełm to: Lublin (10 daily; 2hr); Włodowa (13 daily; 1hr 30min); Zamość (8 daily; 1hr 20min).
Kazimierz Dolny to: Lublin (14 daily; 1hr 40min); Rzeszów (1 daily; 4hr); Sandomierz (1 daily; 2hr); Warsaw Stadion (1 daily; 3hr); Warsaw Zachodnia (2 daily; 3hr 30min).
Lublin to: Biała Podlaska (hourly; 3hr); Białystok (2 daily; 4hr); Chełm (10 daily; 1hr 40min); Kazimierz Dolny (14 daily; 1hr 40min); Kielce (3 daily; 4hr); Kozłówka (8 daily; 1hr); Nałęczów (24 daily; 50min); Puławy (every 30min; 1hr 30min–2hr); Przemyśl (1 daily; 5hr); Sandomierz (5 daily; 2hr 15min); Siemiatycze (hourly; 1hr 30min); Włodawa (20 daily; 1hr 20min); Zamość (every 30min; 2hr).
Sandomierz to: Kazimierz Dolny (1 daily; 2hr); Kielce (8 daily; 2hr); Lublin (5 daily; 2hr 15min); Opatów (hourly; 45min); Rzeszów (4 daily; 2hr); Tarnobrzeg (10 daily; 30min); Warsaw Zachodnia (8 daily; 5hr 45min).
Zamość to Chełm (8 daily; 1hr 20min); Lublin (every 30min; 2hr); Rzeszów (2 daily; 4hr 15min); Zwierzyniec (Mon–Fri 10 daily, Sat & Sun 6 daily; 45min).

International trains

Lublin to: Kiev (1 daily; 12hr).

International buses

Lublin to: Kiev (2 daily; 12hr).

The Polish Carpathians

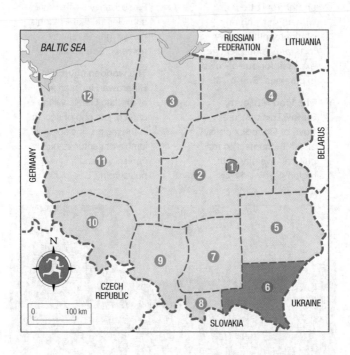

CHAPTER 6 # Highlights

* **Łańcut Palace** Sumptuous period rooms and well-kept gardens make this the most worthwhile of Poland's aristocratic seats outside Warsaw to visit. See p.302

* **Przemyśl** A quaint city of historic churches and narrow streets, with an outlying ring of nineteenth-century forts providing plenty of excuses for out-of-town excursions. See p.306

* **The Icon Museum, Sanok** This treasure-trove of Orthodox art is also a monument to the cultural diversity of the region. See p.312

* **The Bieszczady** The bare-topped Bieszczady are among the most starkly beautiful mountains in Poland. See p.316

* **The forest railway** Trundle at a leisurely pace through the western Bieszczady on this rare surviving relic of Poland's narrow-gauge railway network. See p.322

* **The wooden church in Binarowa** The interior of this late Gothic village church, just one of scores in the region, is a splendid jumble of centuries-old furnishings and polychromy. See p.330

▲ The Bieszczady forest railway

The Polish Carpathians

R
ising in the Czech Republic, then running east along the Polish–Slovak border before arcing through Ukraine and Romania, the **Carpathians** form one of the continent's major mountain chains. The highest range of the Polish Carpathians is the Tatras, whose rugged alpine character is so distinctive that we've given them a chapter all to themselves (see p.435–458). Running east from the Tatras, Poland's remaining share of the Carpathians is relatively low in altitude and smooth in shape, but the deeply forested, sparsely populated valleys still exude a palpable sense of mystery. The main ranges – the **Beskid Sądecki**, the **Beskid Niski** and the **Bieszczady** – make ideal hiking territory, and with few peaks over 1200m they're easily baggable by the moderately fit walker. Although tourism is on the increase (and B&B culture is taking hold of the highland villages), this corner of Poland is rarely swamped with visitors, ensuring perfect conditions for communing with nature.

Traditionally, Carpathian Poland was one of the most culturally mixed areas in the country, and remains rich in contrasting folklores. Poles mingled with **Jews** in the market towns, while villages were inhabited by **Boyks** and **Lemkos** – highlanders who spoke dialects closer to Ukrainian than Polish. The majority of Boyks and Lemkos were deported following a bitter civil war in 1947 (see box, p.314), seriously depopulating the highland areas and lending the region a half-abandoned aura that still pervades today. Many of the amazing **wooden churches** built by them do, however, remain, their pagoda-like domes and painted interiors making up some of the most spectacular folk architecture in Europe.

The main point of entry to the region is **Rzeszów**, an engaging, modestly sized city which has good transport links with the hills to the south. Just northeast of Rzeszów the stately **Łańcut Palace** is one of Poland's most visited attractions, an extraordinary reminder of prewar, aristocratic Poland, while the churches and museums of **Przemyśl** and **Sanok** shed light on the region's multicultural history. Southeast of Sanok, the **Bieszczady** are the most appealing Polish range after the Tatras, their stark bare summits rising above dark forests of pine and beech. To the west, nestling beneath the **Beskid Niski** range, the towns of **Gorlice** and **Krosno** were unlikely centres of a major oil-drilling boom in the mid-nineteenth century: local museums are full of oil memorabilia, including a skansen in the village of **Bóbrka** devoted to oil-drilling. Further west still, the

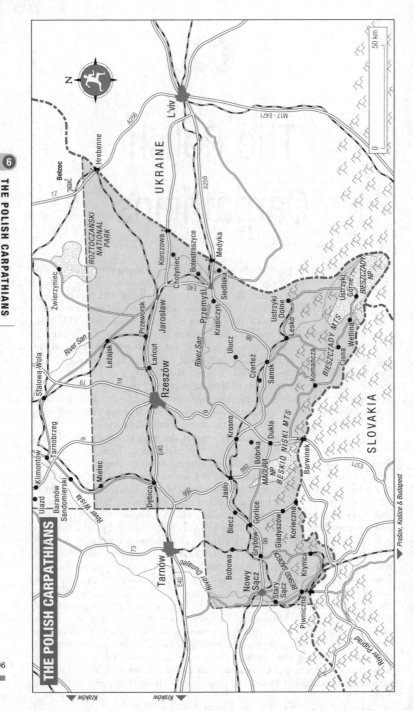

THE POLISH CARPATHIANS

green **Beskid Sądecki** wrap themselves around the quaint spa resort of **Krynica** and the bustling regional centre of **Nowy Sącz**.

The main eastbound railway line from Kraków provides easy access to Rzeszów and Przemyśl, although elsewhere in the region **trains** are either painfully slow or non-existent. **Buses** between the main towns are plentiful, and most of the outlying villages receive some sort of service, even if it's restricted to one or two buses a day. Extra services for the hiking centres of the Bieszczady are laid on in July and August.

Rzeszów

The largest city in southeastern Poland and administrative capital of "Subcarpathia" (Podkarpackie), predominantly modern **RZESZÓW** may lack the kind of historical punch delivered by some of Poland's other regional centres but it still offers plenty to enjoy. Its handsome Rynek bears witness to the city's long history as a local market centre, and is as lively as any central square in the country when cafés and bars spill out onto its paving stones in summer. The area's best museums are nevertheless a bus ride away in Łańcut or Sanok, and southeastern Poland's main attraction – the mountains – lie well to the south. As a place to arrive, however, Rzeszów is perfectly pleasant. There's an acceptable choice of hotels and restaurants, some characterful places to drink, and onward transport is problem-free.

One event that might have you making a beeline for the city is the **Festival of Polonia Music and Dance Ensembles**, which takes place in Rzeszów in June and July every third year (next one is in 2011; contact the tourist information office below for details). It's a riotous assembly of groups from Polish émigré communities all over the world, including Britain, France, the USA, Argentina and Australia.

Arrival and accommodation

Rzeszów's **airport** (☎017/852 0081, ⊛www.lotnisko-rzeszow.pl) is at Jasionka, 10km north of the city. It is currently no more than a hut with a runway, although there are plans to build a proper terminal building in future. Bus L (6zł; pay the driver) runs from here to the **train** and **bus stations**, which stand next door to each other on the northern fringes of the centre, a short walk north of the Rynek. There's a **tourist information office** (Mon–Fri 9am–6pm, Sat 10am–4pm; ☎017/875 4774, ⊛www.rcit.res.pl) on the Rynek, inside the entrance to the Underground Tourist Route (see p.298); the staff have accommodation listings and there's a good selection of books and maps. For **internet** access, make for the *Hard Drive Café* off the Rynek at ul. Kościuszki 13.

Rzeszów's **hotels** are creeping up in price, and the only genuinely budget choice is the PTSM **youth hostel** (☎017/853 4430), Rynek 25, which has timeworn and somewhat gloomy doubles (❶), triples (25zł per person) and quads (from 18zł per person), plus a basic kitchen.

Hotels

Ambassador Rynek 13 ☎017/250 2444, ⊛www .hotel-ambassador.pl. Swish business-oriented hotel with deep-carpeted en suites, uniformed reception staff, and gym and sauna facilities on site. ❼

Forum ul. Lisa Kuli 19 ☎017/859 4038, ⊛www .hotelforum.pl. Functional concrete block some 10min walk from the centre, offering bland but fully equipped rooms in neutral colours, and the Galeria Graffica shopping mall just outside. ❻

Grand Hotel ul. Kościuszki 9 ☎017/250 0000, ⓦwww.grand-hotel.pl. Ranged around a galleried courtyard with a glass roof, this is a swish, design-conscious hotel with smart en suites – some with bathtub, some with state-of-the-art shower. Wi-fi coverage throughout. ❼

Hubertus ul. Mickiewicza 5 ☎017/852 6007, ⓦwww.hubertus.rzeszow.pl. Highly polished but intimate thirteen-room hotel offering en-suite rooms with a/c and minibar, and a good restaurant ❻

Pod Ratuszem ul. Matejki 8 ☎017/852 9780, ⓦwww.hotelpodratuszem.rzeszow.pl. Just off the Rynek, and with views of the town hall from some of the upper-storey rooms, this tall, narrow town house is an informal place with cosy en-suite rooms. Breakfast is delivered to your room on a tray. ❺

Polonia ul. Grottgera 16 ☎017/852 0312, ⓦwww.hotel-polonia.com. Right across the street from the bus and train stations, this is a utilitarian but adequate mid-priced place offering 1970s furnishings and en-suite facilities. ❹

The City

The star turn of Rzeszów's bustling **Rynek** is the endearingly eccentric-looking **town hall**. Remodelled just over a hundred years ago, it's a squat, sixteenth-century edifice, part Disney castle and part Baroque church. Just behind it, steps descend towards the entrance of the **Underground Tourist Route** (Podziemna Trasa Turystyczna: Tues–Fri 10am–6pm, Sat & Sun 11am–5pm; tours last 50min and depart roughly hourly; 7zł), a series of passageways linking over twenty cellars where the city's merchants once stored their wares. Along the way you'll pass exhibits linked to the city's history, alongside costumed mannequins representing Rzeszów citizens of centuries past. Occupying a town house on the south side of the square, the **Ethnographic Museum** (Muzeum Etnograficzne: Tues–Fri 9am–3.30pm, Sun noon–6pm; 5.50zł) contains a modest but beautifully presented collection of local costumes and folk art, including a fine display of the painted wooden statuettes traditionally used to decorate wayside shrines.

West of the Rynek

Directly west of the Rynek an attractively pedestrianized street lined with cast-iron street lamps leads to the main **parish church**. A Gothic structure, it was given a dull Baroque overlay in the eighteenth century, though there are some notable features, including some fine Renaissance decoration in the vaulted nave ceiling, and the early tombstone tablets up by the altar. Heading south down ul. 3 Maja, the main shopping thoroughfare, brings you to a former Piarist monastery complex, where the **town museum** (Tues–Fri 9am–3.30pm, Sat & Sun noon–6pm; 6.50zł) is ranged around the monastery courtyard. Aside from some undistinguished Polish and European paintings, the collection contains the biblical frescoes that once decorated the former cloister arcade and has changing exhibitions focused on local history. The **monastery church** next door has an elegant Baroque facade fashioned by Tylman van Gameren in the early 1700s, and a small but well-proportioned interior.

At the bottom of ul. 3 Maja, past the post office, is the **Lubomirski Palace** (Pałac Lubomirskich), another early eighteenth-century Tylman van Gameren creation; originally owned by one of the country's most powerful aristocratic clans, it's now occupied by the local music academy. From here it's a short walk to the walls of Rzeszów's **castle**, a huge seventeenth-century edifice also once owned by the Lubomirskis. The castle was converted into a prison in Austrian times and is now occupied by the law courts.

Northwest off ulica 3. Maja is Rzeszów's most interesting church, the **Bernardine Church** (Kościół Bernardynów), a sumptuous early seventeenth-century structure founded by the Ligęza family. Inside you'll find late Renaissance statues of eight family members praying solemnly from niches above the choir. Also

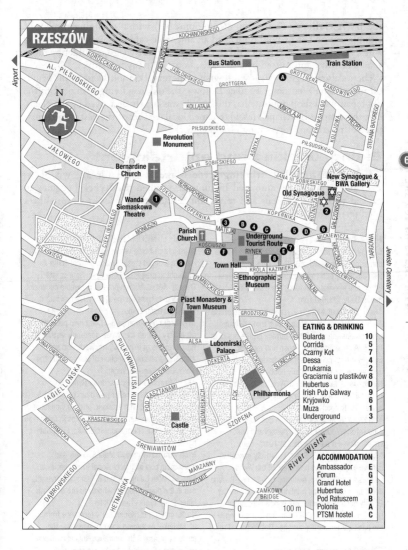

RZESZÓW

KOCHANOWSKIEGO

Airport ◄

AL. PIŁSUDSKIEGO

KORDECKIEGO

Bus Station

Train Station

GROTTGERA

BARDOWSKIEGO

JABŁOŃSKIEGO

GROTTGERA

Ⓐ

MIKOŁAJA

LEROMSKIEGO

KOLLĄTAJA

KOLEJOWA

PIŁSUDSKIEGO

FREDRY

STEFANA BATOREGO

JAŁOWEGO

PIŁSUDSKIEGO

JANA III SOBIESKIEGO

ASNYKA

Revolution Monument

BERNARDYŃSKA

JANA III SOBIESKIEGO

OKRZEI

New Synagogue & BWA Gallery

Bernardine Church ✝

GRUNWALDZKA

Old Synagogue ✡

BOŻNICZA

GAŁĘZOWSKIEGO

Wanda Siemaskowa Theatre

SOKOŁA

Ⓞ①

KOPERNIKA

KOPERNIKA

②

SOŁA

MONIUSZKI

AL. CIEPLIŃSKIEGO

③ Ⓞ Ⓐ Ⓞ

MATEJKI

⑤ Ⓞ

MICKIEWICZA

⑥

KRACHMAR

TARGOWA

PUŁASKIEGO

Parish Church ✝

KOŚCIUSZKI

Underground Tourist Route

Ⓐ Ⓕ

RYNEK

Ⓔ ⑦

⑨

Town Hall

⑧

NARUSZEWICZA

SPYTALNA

DYMNICKIEGO

KRÓLA KAZIMIERZA

SOBACKIEGO

BALDACHÓWKA

Ethnographic Museum

SŁOWACKIEGO

PONIATOWSKIEGO

MOCHNACKIEGO

Ⓖ

⑩

Piast Monastery & Town Museum

ZYGMUNTOWSKA

GRODZISKO

LESZCZYŃSKA

JAGIELLOŃSKA

PUŁKOWNIKA LISA KULI

ALSA

Lubomirski Palace

DEKERTA

SŁONECZNA

EATING & DRINKING

Bularda **10**
Corrida **5**
Czarny Kot **7**
Dessa **4**
Drukarnia **2**
Graciarnia u plastików **8**
Hubertus **D**
Irish Pub Galway **9**
Kryjowko **6**
Muza **1**
Underground **3**

UNI LUBELSKIEJ

KASZTANAMI

ZAMKOWA

POD

KRASZEWSKIEGO

REFORMACKA

LUBOMIRSKICH

PCK

SZOPENA

Philharmonia

ACCOMMODATION

Ambassador **E**
Forum **F**
Grand Hotel **G**
Hubertus **D**
Pod Ratuszem **B**
Polonia **A**
PTSM hostel **C**

DĄBROWSKIEGO

HETMAŃSKA

ŚRENIAWITÓW

Castle

MARZANNY

PODPROMIE

MICKIEWICZA

ZAMKOWY BRIDGE

River Wisłok

0   100 m

note the eighteenth-century organ and, in a chapel to the right of the transept, a late Gothic sculpted Madonna considered to be miraculous. Rather less attractive is the nearby **monument** to the Revolutionary Movement, a communist-era monstrosity that has, thankfully, been removed from the front of local tourist brochures.

East of the Rynek: Jewish Rzeszów

Immediately east of the Rynek, ulica Boźnicza runs past a fine pair of former synagogues, all that remains of what was once the city's lively Jewish quarter. The so-called **New Synagogue** (Nowa Synagoga), a large seventeenth-century brick building designed by Italian architect Giovanni Bellotti, is now the **BWA Gallery** (Thurs–Sun 10am–5pm; 5zł) with a changing display of exhibitions on the ground floor, and an amenable café upstairs (closed July & Aug). Next door, the rebuilt **Old Synagogue** (Stara Synagoga), older by more than a century and gutted by the Nazis, houses the town archives.

There's also a large, overgrown **Jewish cemetery** 1km southeast of the centre off ulica Rejtana (entrance on ulica Dołowa; the old man living next door to the car-repair workshop opposite has the key). It was largely destroyed by the Nazis. The three memorial chapels (*ohels*) to famed local *tzaddiks* of the past are a regular place of pilgrimage for visiting Hassidic Jews.

Eating, drinking and entertainment

Rzeszów's **eating** and **drinking** scene is pretty good for a town of its size, and is especially animated in summer – when the Rynek becomes so packed with beer gardens and restaurant terraces that it looks almost like a Mediterranean resort.

Restaurants

Czarny Kot ul. Mickiewicza 4 (entrance round the corner on ul. Joselewicza). Plush café-restaurant with adjoining pub (see opposite), serving up fine Polish and international food. There's an English menu. Daily 11am–11pm.

Dessa ul. Matejki 2. A combined restaurant/gallery/antique shop with a trinket-stuffed dining room and an outdoor terrace on the adjacent Rynek. A mixed menu of Polish and modern European fare includes some substantial salads and delicious desserts. Daily noon–11pm.

Hubertus ul. Mickiewicza 5. A respectable menu of traditional Polish food, including some fine game dishes. Daily noon–11pm.

Kryjówka ul. Mickiewicza 19. A good bet for order-at-the-counter soups, *pierogi* and pork chops. Mon–Fri 9am–9pm, Sat 10am–8pm.

Muza ul. M. Sokoła 7. Smart but mildly eccentric café-restaurant in the basement of the Wanda Siemaszkowa Theatre, featuring twiddly neo-Rococo decor in one room and hunting trophies in another. Equally good for a coffee break or a substantial pork-and-potatoes Polish meal. Outdoor seating in the back garden during summer. Daily 11am–11pm.

Cafés and bars

Bularda ul. 3 Maja 20. Probably the best cakes and coffee in town. Mon–Sat 9am–9pm, Sun 10am–9pm.

Corrida ul. Mickiewicza 13. Spacious pub cum late-night clubbing venue on two levels, which fills up with a broad cross-section of local youth as midnight approaches. Daily 6pm–3am or later.

Czarny Kot ul. Mickiewicza 4. Enjoyable cellar club in the vaults beneath the *Czarny Kot* restaurant. Wed–Sun 8pm–2am.

Drukarnia ul. Boźnicza 6a. Combined pub and art gallery just off the Rynek, featuring distressed furniture, lots of exposed brickwork, and an attention-grabbing collection of paintings on the walls. Daily 6pm–midnight.

Graciarnia u plastików Rynek 10. Labyrinthine cellar pub deep below the Rynek, crammed with artwork, posters, household junk and (in one corner at least) tables in the shape of coffins. Sun–Thurs noon–midnight; Fri & Sat noon–3am.

Irish Pub Galway ul. 3 Maja 8. Lively and welcoming pub with occasional live music and karaoke. With Guinness and Kilkenny on draught, this is the place to come when you tire of Polish lager. Daily 11am–1am or later.

Underground ul. Kopernika 4 (entrance from ul. Matejki). Assuming you can negotiate the spiral staircase at the entrance, this is a relaxing cellar pub attracting a broad social mix. The music policy steers clear of top-40 pop, and there are occasional gigs by local bands. Daily 4pm–midnight or later.

East from Rzeszów

From Rzeszów the main road and rail line heads east towards the Ukrainian borderlands. A characteristically eastern mix of villages, farmsteads and wayside shrines is the region's main feature, along with a smattering of historic towns, notably **Łańcut**, **Leżajsk** and **Jarosław**. All are within easy travelling distance of Rzeszów, a mix of local bus and train services providing **transport** around the area.

Łańcut

Surrounded by immaculately kept gardens, the palace complex that dominates the centre of **ŁAŃCUT** (pronounced "Winesoot"), 17km east of Rzeszów, is one of the most visited attractions in the country. The palace itself is a treasure-trove of fine art and even finer interior decor, while the surrounding park offers a compelling menu of attractions both historical and horticultural – all of which add up to a great day out.

The first building on the site, constructed by the Pilecki family in the second half of the fourteenth century, was burnt down in 1608 when royal troops ambushed its robber-baron owner Stanisław Stadnicki, known by his contemporaries as "The Devil of Łańcut" (see box below). The estate was then bought by Stanisław Lubomirski, who set about building the sturdier construction that forms the basis of today's palace. Completed in 1641, the four-sided palace was surrounded by a pentagonal outer defence of moat and ramparts, the outlines of which remain.

The fortifications were dismantled in 1760 by Izabela Czartoryska (see p.272), wife of the last Lubomirski owner, who turned Łańcut into one of her artistic salons, laid out the surrounding park and built a theatre in the

The Devil of Łańcut

In an era replete with tales of rapacious brigands and unruly aristocrats, the figure of **Stanisław Stadnicki** (c.1551–1610) stands out from the crowd. Brought up in a remote Carpathian outpost by independent-minded parents, Stadnicki quickly made his name as a valiant but unruly military officer, distinguishing himself in King Stefan Batory's Muscovy campaigns but switching allegiances to Habsburg Austria when slighted by lack of recognition from the Polish crown. Returning to Poland, he seized the estate at **Łańcut** in lieu of unpaid debts, and brutally set about establishing his control over the local area. Nothing was spared his vicious attentions: passing travellers were attacked, properties inexplicably razed to the ground, and local traders and markets systematically terrorized and eventually forced to operate to his benefit through the unlicensed fair he started at nearby Rzeszów. With the help of a motley assortment of spies, torturers, thugs and mercenaries, he extended his grip on the terrorized local populace. Inevitably, Stadnicki's illicit activities eventually caught the attention of the authorities and in 1600 he was sued at the Crown Tribunal in Lublin by another magnate over his illegal Rzeszów fair, to which Stadnicki responded by leading an armed raid on his opponent's nearby estate. The conflicts surrounding Stadnicki multiplied. An active participant in the nobles' *rakosz* (rebellion) against Zygmunt III in 1605, his public denunciations of the king as a "perjurer, sodomite and card-sharper" can hardly have endeared him to the authorities. Stadnicki's penchant for goading opponents with libellous verses, however, eventually led to his downfall. In 1608 the nobleman **Łukasz Opaliński**, the subject of a withering Stadnicki broadside entitled "A Gallows for my Guest", retaliated by storming the castle at Łańcut, where prodigious quantities of loot were discovered in the cellars, and massacring everyone there – except Stadnicki, who in characteristic fashion just managed to escape in time. Bloodied, but unbowed, Stadnicki eventually returned to the area in a bid to pick up his malevolent career once more. Things were never the same again, however: pursued relentlessly by Opaliński's Cossack guard and finally given away in the hills by his personal servant, a mortally wounded Stadnicki was at last beheaded with his own sword.

palace. Louis XVIII of France was among those entertained at Łańcut during this period, and the next owners, the Potocki family, carried on in the same manner, Kaiser Franz Joseph being one of their guests. Oxford graduate Count Alfred Potocki, the last private owner, abandoned the place in the summer of 1944 as Soviet troops advanced across Poland. Having dispatched six hundred crates of the palace's most precious objects to liberated Vienna, Potocki himself then departed, ordering a Russian sign reading "Polish National Museum" to be posted on the gates. The Red Army left the place untouched, and it was opened as a museum later the same year.

The palace

Forty or so of the **palace**'s hundreds of rooms are open to the public (June–Sept: Mon 11.30am–4pm, Tues–Fri 9am–4pm, Sat & Sun 10am–6pm; Feb–May, Oct & Nov: Mon noon–3.30pm, Tues–Sat 9am–4pm, Sun 9am–5pm; Ⓦ www .zamek-lancut.pl), and in summer they are crammed with visitors. The **ticket office** is in the gate at the western entrance to the park: an 18zł ticket allows you to wander round the palace on your own; a 21zł ticket gets you a Polish-speaking guided **tour**, which includes the palace as well as the carriage museum and orangery. Separate tickets are needed for the icon museum and Orchid House; consider visiting one or both of these before exhausting yourself at the palace. The minimum fee for an English-speaking **guide** is 180zł (by appointment; Ⓣ017/225 2008, Ⓔmuzeum@zamek-lancut.pl).

Most of the interesting rooms are on the **first floor**, reached by a staircase close to the entrance hall which is large enough to allow horse-drawn carriages to drop off their passengers. The **corridors** are an art show in themselves: family portraits and busts, paintings by seventeenth-century Italian, Dutch and Flemish artists and eighteenth-century classical copies commissioned by Izabela. Some of the bedrooms have beautiful inlaid wooden floors, while the bathrooms have giant old-fashioned bathtubs and enormous taps. Adjacent to an opulent **ballroom** is the extraordinary eighty-seater **Łańcut theatre** commissioned by Izabela; as well as the ornate gallery and stalls, the romantic scenic backdrops are still there, as is the stage machinery to crank them up and down. Beyond lie the **dining room**, its floor laid out in a curious braid pattern, and the **old study**, decorated in frilliest Rococo style – all mirrors and gilding – with a fine set of eighteenth-century French furniture. The domed ceiling of the **Zodiac Room** still has its seventeenth-century Italian stucco, while the **Pompeii Hall** houses genuine Roman antiquities set in an amusing mock-ruin.

The palace park

South and east of the palace lie large stretches of ornamental gardens and open parkland (daily 8am–dusk), dotted with various outbuildings – some of which house a further clutch of museums. Most prominent of these is the **Carriage Museum** (Wozownia: Mon 1–4.30pm, Tues–Sat 10am–5pm, Sun 10am–6pm; free if on a tour of the palace, otherwise 15zł), set in the coach house, built in 1902, and including over fifty horse-drawn vehicles for every conceivable purpose, from state ceremonies to mail delivery. There are also drivers' uniforms, sepia photos from a Potocki expedition to the Sahara and a variety of hunting trophies from similar jaunts.

Next door, the old stables contain the **Orthodox Religious Art Museum** (Sztuka cerkiewna: May–Sept Tues–Sat 10am–4pm, Sun 10am–5pm; Oct–April Tues–Sun 10am–4pm; 6zł), housing a large and fabulous collection of icons and

▲ Łańcut Palace

decorative art from Poland's Ukrainian, Boyk and Lemko communities, the best in Poland after the museum in Sanok (see p.313). The bulk of the collection was removed from the Uniate and Orthodox churches of the surrounding region in the years following the notorious Operation Vistula of 1947 (see box, p.314). Only a fraction of what's here is displayed for viewing, with the rest of the icons hanging from the walls in huge, densely packed racks. Among the choice items on show there's a complete eighteenth-century iconostasis, a superb, meditative fifteenth-century *Mandilion* and a poignant, suffering *Christus Pantocrator*, reflecting the humanizing influences of Roman Catholic art on later Uniate and Orthodox iconography. In addition there's a rich collection of vestments and Old Slavonic Bibles, and a display of colour photos of some of the wooden churches from which the icons were taken.

Due east of the palace is the **Orchid House** (Storczykarnia; May–Sept Tues–Fri 10am–6pm, Sat & Sun 11am–7pm; Oct–April Tues–Sun 10am–4pm; 5zł), established under the Potockis in the nineteenth century, and reopened in a state-of-the-art glasshouse in summer 2008. With jets of mist zapping the orchids every few seconds from pipes in the ceiling, it's a bit like going to the horticultural equivalent of a rock concert.

The synagogue and the Jewish cemetery

Łańcut town has one other main point of interest: the old **synagogue**, just southwest of the palace ticket office on ulica Zamkowa, which now houses a newly renovated **Jewish Museum** (recently handed over to the Foundation for the Preservation of Jewish Heritage in Poland; visiting arrangements yet to be decided; ⓦwww.fodz.pl). It's a simple cream-coloured structure built in the 1760s on the site of an earlier wooden synagogue, the interior of which survived the Nazi era relatively intact, preserving an authentic and virtually unique taste of what scores of similar such synagogues throughout Poland would have looked like before the war. The walls and ceiling are a mass of rich, colourful decoration including stucco bas-reliefs, frescoes, illustrated Hebrew prayers, zodiacal signs and false marble ornamentation. In the centre of the building stands the bimah, its cupola decorated with some striking frescoes of biblical tales and a memorable depiction of a leviathan consuming its own tail – a symbol for the coming of the Messiah – adorning the inner canopy.

The Hassidic movement that swept through Eastern Europe in the nineteenth century took strong hold among the Jews of Łańcut. The **old Jewish cemetery**, fifteen minutes' walk north of the palace complex off ulica Moniuszki, houses the recently rebuilt *ohel* (tomb) of **Reb Horovitz**, a noted nineteenth-century *tzaddik* whose grave remains a much-visited place of Hassidic pilgrimage. The key to the cemetery is kept by the family living at ul. Jagiellońska 17, round the corner from the entrance.

Practicalities

Łańcut's **train station** is a short taxi ride or a two-kilometre walk north of the centre; the **bus station**, however, is on the north edge of the palace park, just a few minutes' walk from the main entrance. The best **hotel** is the *Pałacyk*, ul. Paderewskiego 18 (☏017/225 2043, ⓦwww.palacyk-lancut.pl; ❸), offering comfortable en suites in a grand early twentieth-century mansion. Occupying a wing of the palace, the *Zamkowy* (☏017/225 2805, ⓦwww.zamkowy.rze.pl) is a pleasantly old-fashioned affair featuring creaky floors and colour-clash carpets – the en-suite doubles with TV (❹) and triples with shared facilities (140zł) are perfectly comfortable. The **restaurant** of the *Zamkowy* has a decent but pricey selection of traditional Polish dishes, while the one in the *Pałacyk* offers similar fare but is a bit cheaper. There are also al fresco **cafés** just west of the castle on Łańcut's main Rynek – *Caffe Antico* at no. 3 serves up decent coffee as well as a selection of Greek and Italian dishes.

Every May, the palace hosts the prestigious **Łańcut Music Festival** (ⓦwww .filharmonia.rzeszow.pl) an increasingly popular event on the international circuit, now into its fourth decade, with a focus on chamber music – expect hotels to be booked solid at this time. Festival **tickets** are sold by the Philharmonia in Rzeszów in late April (☏017/862 8408), though some are available an hour before each concert, either from the office in the palace vestibule or outside the concert venue itself. In the summer international master classes for aspiring young instrumentalists are also held at the palace.

Leżajsk

Thirty kilometres northeast of Rzeszów, the sleepy rural town of **LEŻAJSK** is an important pilgrimage site for Polish Catholics and Hassidic Jews alike. The former are drawn to the monumental **Bernardine church and monastery**, (a 20min walk north of the train and bus stations) that was built in the late 1670s to commemorate a celebrated series of miraculous appearances by the Virgin a century earlier. The cavernous church interior is a mass of Baroque decoration, with a huge gilded main altarpiece and a side altar (to the right) containing a miracle-working icon of the Madonna and Child. Pride of place, however, goes to the monster Baroque **organ** filling the back of the nave, one of the finest – and most famous – in Poland. With nearly six thousand pipes, and an organ case simply dripping with sculpted saints, angels and other fanciful creatures, the exquisitely decorated instrument produces a stunning sound more than capable of filling the building. Services apart, you can hear the organ at the concerts held during the summer-long **International Organ Festival** (concerts roughly weekly from mid-June to mid-Aug; Ⓦwww.mck.lezajsk.pl), a major musical event well worth trying to catch.

Walking south from the stations takes you past the ochre **Staroszyński Palace**, where a small **regional museum** (Muzeum Ziemi Leżajskiej; Mon–Fri noon–4pm, Sun 11am–9pm; 6zł; Ⓦwww.muzeum-lezajsk.pl) displays colourful wooden toys and memorablia relating to the local brewing industry – the locally-made Leżajsk is one of Poland's tastiest beers, and it's well worth stocking up with a few bottles of the stuff at local shops before leaving.

Beyond the museum lies the **Rynek**, bordered by narrow streets which were once home to a sizeable Jewish population. Leżajsk was a major centre of the Hassidic movement, thanks in large part to local seventeenth-century teacher **Tzaddik Elimelech**, one of Hassidism's leading intellectual figures. The *tzaddik*'s tomb, enclosed by a cast-iron grille, lies in a whitewashed pavilion inside the Jewish cemetery (daily except Sat 8am–4pm; ring ☎604 536 914 if the gatekeeper isn't around), which spreads across a hillock just behind the Rynek. The tomb is regularly visited by Orthodox Jewish pilgrims, never more so than on Tzaddik Elimelech's anniversary which, according to the traditional Hebrew calendar, is on Adar 21 – a shifting date which usually falls in March.

Practicalities

It's easy enough to get here from Łańcut, with **buses** running every hour or so; otherwise there are several daily train connections from Rzeszów (change at Przeworsk). The **tourist information centre**, Rynek 1 (☎017/240 1818), is well stocked with brochures and can help organize accommodation. Most convenient **place to stay** in Leżajsk is the small but quite comfortable *U Braci Zygmuntów*, by the monastery at ul. Klasztorna 2e (☎017/242 0469, Ⓦwww .hotel-lezajsk.pl; ❹), which also has a good **restaurant** serving everything from fried fish to shashlik-style skewer-kebabs.

Jarosław

Fifty kilometres east of Rzeszów on the main road and rail line to the Ukrainian border, **JAROSŁAW** is one of the oldest towns in the country. Yaroslav the Wise, prince of Kiev, established a stronghold here some time in the eleventh century, and the town's position on major east–west trade routes led to its rapid development. Such was the importance of Jarosław's **Jewish population** that the Council of the Four Lands (Polish Jewry's main consultative body) met regularly here during the seventeenth and eighteenth centuries. Today Jarosław is smaller and less prosperous than other old towns in the region, but what remains of the historic centre makes a short visit more than worthwhile.

The Town

Jarosław's focal point is the breezy, open central square where medieval fairs used to be held. Filling the centre is the **town hall**, a handsome-looking building topped by a tall spire that was burnt down by a fire in 1625 and subsequently remodelled in neo-Renaissance style. The square is lined with the arcaded merchants' houses, most impressive of which is the **Orsetti Mansion** (Kamienica Orsettich) on the south side, built in the 1670s and featuring a beautifully decorated upper attic and a typically open, airy arcade. It's also the home of the **town museum** (Wed–Sun 10am–2pm; 5zł), which contains a substantial collection of Sarmatian portraits (see box, p.430), as well as weapons and period furniture.

Ten minutes' walk uphill to the north, the **Benedictine Convent** (Klasztor Sióstr Benedyktynek) is a fine early seventeenth-century complex surrounded by its own set of fortified walls. Jarosław's sole surviving **synagogue**, northwest off the main square on the corner of ulica Opolska, dates from 1810 and is now a school building.

Practicalities

The combined **bus** and **train station**, at the bottom of ulica Słowackiego, is a fifteen-minute walk southwest of the main square. You should be able to see Jarosław as a day-trip from Rzeszów or Przemyśl; if not, your best accommodation option is the *Asticus* **hotel**, Rynek 25 (℡016/623 1344, Ⓦwww.hotelasticus.pl; ❹), which offers a limited number of comfortable en suites, and also serves good Polish food in its restaurant.

Przemyśl and around

Huddled on a hill above the River San, **PRZEMYŚL** is one of the most beguiling cities in eastern Poland. It served as both a key garrison town and an important spiritual centre in Habsburg times, and strolling through the church-filled old quarter can still feel like walking back through history to some far-flung corner of the Austro-Hungarian empire. Boasting an absorbing clutch of churches, museums and former military installations, the city is an ideal stop-off if you're heading towards Ukraine: the border is only 10km away, and transport connections to L'viv and Kiev are good.

Founded in the eighth century on the site of a prehistoric settlement, Przemyśl is the oldest city in southern Poland after Kraków, although its location on the borders between Poland and Kievan Rus made it a constant bone of contention. Only under Kazimierz the Great did Poles establish firm control of the town, developing it as a link in the trade routes across the Ukraine. Much of the town's character derives from the period after the First Partition, when Przemyśl became part of the Austrian-ruled Galicia; as the province's third biggest centre after Kraków and L'viv, Przemyśl was a multi-faith city which was home to Catholic, Uniate and Orthodox bishops. In 1873 the Habsburgs turned Przemyśl into a major military strongpoint, building a huge ring of fortifications around the town – the crumbling remnants of which are increasingly popular as an offbeat tourist destination.

Arrival, information and accommodation

Przemyśl's elegant Habsburg-era **train station** is ten minutes' walk northeast of the centre; the **bus station** is on the far side of the tracks from the train station, to which it is linked by pedestrian underpass. There are left-luggage lockers at the train station. The PTTK office at ul. Grodzka 1 serves as a **tourist information** point (Mon–Fri 9am–4pm, Sat & Sun 10am–2pm) and has a good selection of local maps. **Internet** access is available at the café at ul. Ratuszowa 8.

There's a modest range of **hotels** in Przemyśl but rooms are snapped up quickly in summer – always try to ring in advance. The *Zamek* **campsite**, ul. Sanocka 8a (℡016/675 0265), about half a mile west of the Old Town just behind the *Gromada* hotel, has simply furnished two-person en-suite bungalows (❷).

Europejski ul. Sowińskiego 4 ☎016/675 7100, ⓦwww.hotel-europejski.pl. Small but comfortable and clean en-suite rooms in a completely refurbished nineteenth-century building by the train station. **③**

Gromada Wybrzeże J. Piłsudskiego 4 ☎016/676 1111, ⓦwww.gromada.pl. Large, concrete lump on the riverbank just west of the centre, with bland but comfortable en suites and wi-fi access in the lobby. Small discount at weekends. **⑤**

Hala ul. Mickiewicza 30 ☎016/678 3849, ⓦwww.posir.pl. Basic sports hotel 500m east of the train station. Looks run-down from the outside, but the rooms (with and without bath) have been thoroughly renovated. Breakfast not included but there is a café-restaurant on site. **①–②**

Pod Białym Orłem ul. Sanocka 13 ☎016/678 6107, ⓦwww.podbialymorlem.com.pl. Medium-sized place occupying a futuristic (in a 1980s sort of way) villa, in a peaceful location 1.5km west along the river from the centre (bus #10 or #40). Dated but tolerable en suites, and the restaurant serves good home-cooked specialities. **③**

Podzamcze PTTK ul. Waygarta 3 ☎016/678 5374, ⓦprzemysl.pttk.pl. Very basic place close to the cathedral, offering dorms (from 23zł per person) and sparsely furnished doubles. **②**

The City

Appropriately enough for a city stuffed full of church spires and domes, the late Baroque bell tower on ulica Władycze is the first thing you see when entering the Old Town from the east. All that remains of an eighteenth-century Uniate cathedral project that was abandoned when the money ran out, the bell tower is today home to the well-organized **Museum of Bells and Pipes** (Muzeum Dzwonów i Fajek: Tues & Fri 10.30am–5.30pm, Wed & Thurs 10am–3pm, Sat 10am–2pm, Sun noon–2pm; 5zł), harbouring roomfuls of locally made

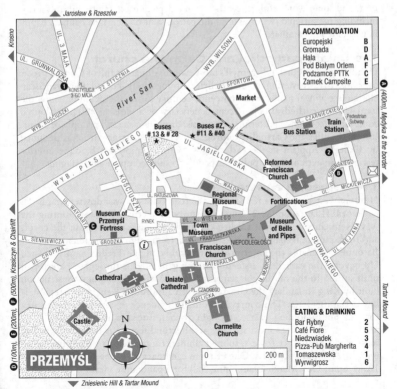

pipes and bells. The climb to the top of the tower is rewarded with a fine view of the city. From here ulica Franciszkańska leads west to the busy, sloping **Rynek**, where the mid-eighteenth-century **Franciscan church** offers a florid demonstration of unbridled Baroque, including a wealth of sumptuous interior decoration and a fine columned facade.

Occupying a sturdy town house at Rynek 9, the **town museum** (Muzeum Historii Miasta Przemyśla: Tues & Fri 9.30am–4pm, Wed, Thurs & Sat 10am–3pm, Sun 10am–2pm; 6zł) is something of a nostalgic tribute to nineteenth-century Przemyśl, with period interiors (complete with laboriously hand-painted Art Nouveau wall decorations), and a nice collection of Habsburg-era photographs.

The regional museum

North of the Rynek and slightly downhill, an impressive modern building on plac Berka Joselewicza provides a sleek new home to the **Regional Museum** (Muzeum Narodowe Ziemi Przemyskiej: Tues & Fri 10.30am–6pm, Wed, Thurs, Sat & Sun 10am–2pm; 6zł). Its main attraction is the excellent collection of fifteenth- to seventeenth-century icons removed from the Uniate and Orthodox churches of the surrounding region after World War II. The influence of Catholic art and theology on icon painters working in the Byzantine tradition is evident in the later works: many of the eighteenth-century Madonnas and *Christus Pantocrator* figures are decidedly Roman in feel. Other highlights include a mystical early eighteenth-century *Assumption of Elijah*, a fabulously earthy *Day of Judgement* from the same era, which has a team of prancing black devils facing off against a beatific angelic host, and some wonderful sixteenth-century depictions of saints and holy men, including the intrepid św. Paraskeva, the patron saint of "engaged couples, happy households and commerce".

The Uniate cathedral and Carmelite church

Uphill from the Rynek is Przemyśl's most evocative quarter, full of slanting streets overlooked by towering church belfries. Immediately behind the Franciscan church (see above) stands the seventeenth-century former Jesuit church, now the local **Uniate cathedral**. The recent beneficiary of a pleasing custard-coloured paint job, it contains a glittering iconostasis, displaying the full panoply of saints. Just up the hill is the **Carmelite church**, a fine late Renaissance structure designed by Gelleazo Appiani in the early 1600s, with a sumptuous Baroque interior featuring an extraordinary pulpit shaped like a ship, complete with rigging.

The cathedral and castle

Heading west along ulica Katedralna, the road twists its way down towards the **cathedral** (10am–noon & 2–4pm), its sturdy 71-metre bell tower pointing the way. Remnants of the first twelfth-century rotunda can be seen in the crypt, and there's a fine Renaissance alabaster pietà to the right of the main altar, but Baroque dominates the interior, most notably in the Fredro family chapel. Up beyond the cathedral, a steeply climbing path leads through a park (open until sunset) to the **castle**, the remains of the fourteenth-century construction built by King Kazimierz the Great and given a thorough Renaissance remodelling a century later. The courtyard contains evidence of an eleventh-century rotunda and adjoining palace, thought to be associated with Poland's Piast monarchs. The castle's most striking architectural feature is the pair of newly renovated Renaissance towers, tubby cylinders topped with a ring of decidedly unmilitary-looking baubles. One of them can be scaled (Tues–Sun: April–Sept 10am–6pm; Oct–March 10am–4pm; 3zł) for a panoramic view.

Przemyśl Fortress

Beginning in the 1870s the Austrians set about turning Przemyśl into a major military strongpoint, constructing an inner ring of defensive positions in the immediate vicinity of the city (including the one at the Tatar Mound; see below), and an outer ring of fourteen full-sized forts and twenty-three artillery bastions, pushing far out into the countryside. Accommodating a 150,000-strong garrison, the resulting **Przemyśl Fortress** (Twierdza Przemyśl) was intended to render Habsburg-ruled Galicia impregnable from Russian attack. With the outbreak of World War I, however, a relatively small Russian army simply surrounded Przemyśl and cut it off from supplies. Having eaten their way through their own cavalry horses, the fortress's defenders finally surrendered on March 22, 1915 due to lack of further food. The Austrians blew the forts up as they left, but enough of the system remains to make it a fascinating target for excursions. The *Twierdza Przemyśl* **map**, available from the PTTK office (see p.306), is a useful aid to exploration; otherwise pick up the 1:75,000 *Pogórze Przemyskie* map from local bookshops.

One of the best-preserved installations is the **Salis Soglio** fort just outside the village of **Siedliska** (bus #13 from ul. Jagiellońska in Przemyśl), 10km southeast of Przemyśl right by the Ukrainian border. A short walk east of the village, the fort's barrack blocks, powder magazines and ramparts are in good shape and are open to walkers. From Salis Soglio, you can follow a black-marked trail through rolling, partly wooded countryside to the remains of **Fort Borek**, 2km northeast, or **Fort Jaksmanice**, 4km west.

Another easily visited stretch of the fortress is near the village of **Bolestraszyce** (bus #Z from ul. Jagiellońska), 7km to Premyśl's northwest, which is also the site of a major horticultural attraction. Buses drop off at **Bolestraszyce Arboretum** (May–Oct 10am–6pm; 5zł; ⊛www.bolestraszyce.com), an extensive botanical garden filled with trees and shrubs from around the world. Immediately to the east of the gardens, the ruins of **Fort San Rideau** provide ample opportunity to scramble around long-abandoned gun positions.

Zniesienie Hill and Tatar Mound

Behind the castle to the southwest, paths ascend through the leafy **castle park** towards **Zniesienie Hill**, where a 1600-metre-long ski slope (*stok narciarski*) descends westward to ulica Sanocka, just west of the *Gromada* hotel. A two-stage **chairlift** from ulica Sanocka operates in the winter season (daily 9am–9pm), and gear can be rented from a hut near the terminal.

In summer you can simply enjoy the view from Zniesienie then move on to **Tatar Mound** (Kopiec Tatarski) fifteen minutes' to the east, a roughly pyramidal hillock constructed (according to legend) to mark the burial place of a sixteenth-century Tatar khan – a not unreasonable hypothesis, given the number of times the Crimean Tatars sent raiding parties into eastern Poland. From the summit there's an excellent view of the distant Carpathians, and adjacent pathways lead around the overgrown remains of **Fort XIV**, part of the nineteenth-century Habsburg defensive system. Bus #28 from ulica Jagiellońska runs by the mound if you don't fancy walking.

Eating and drinking

There's a modest collection of **restaurants** in Przemyśl, and plenty of **bars** which also serve food on the side.

Bar Rybny pl. Legionów. Unassuming fish bar opposite the train station entrance serving up battered fillets of fresh- and saltwater fish. Culinary standards are pretty basic (fillets are fried in batches then microwaved at the individual customer's convenience), but this is still one of the best sources of fish and chips in the east. Mon–Fri 10am–8pm, Sat 11am–7pm.

Café Fiore ul. Kazimierza Wielkiego 176. Fantastic ice cream, superb cakes and easily the best coffee in town in an ersatz Venetian-garden interior complete with plastic fig plants. Mon–Fri 9am–9pm, Sat & Sun 10am–6pm.

Niedźwiadek Rynek 1. Jazz-pub with moderately priced food, located in a suite of Baroque rooms in one wing of the town hall. Daily noon–midnight.

Pizza-Pub Margherita Rynek 4. Functional pizza and pasta dishes in plain surroundings but in a near-perfect location on the main square. Daily 10am–10pm.

Tomaszewska pl. Konstytucji 3-go Maja. Bare-breasted caryatids hold up a ceiling decorated with stucco dragonflies, while portraits of Emperor Franz Jozeph observe the scene calmly from the sidelines at this elegant first-floor restaurant. Food is of the hearty pork or poultry variety, but is prepared and presented with a bit more class than elsewhere in town. Café and pizzeria on the ground floor. Daily 11am–11pm.

Wyrwigrosz Rynek 20. Bar-restaurant with a good selection of Polish and Chinese dishes and a large terrace overlooking the main square. Daily 11am–11pm.

Krasiczyn

Apart from the ring of forts (see box, p.306), the other obvious destination for a day-trip from Przemyśl is the **castle** at **Krasiczyn**, a ten-kilometre ride west of town by bus #40, which leaves every seventy minutes or so from the Jagiellońska bus stop, north of the Rynek. Built in the late sixteenth century for the Krasicki family by Italian architect Gallazzo Appiani, the castle has flamboyant exterior sgraffito decorations, notably in the frieze of frolicking beasts and huntsmen that runs above the eastern gate. The interior can only be visited by **guided tour** (daily April–Oct: tours on the hour 10am–4pm; 5.50zł), which takes in the impressive central courtyard and three of the four cone-shaped corner towers, which are named after the pillars of the contemporary order – the pope, the king, the nobility and the Almighty. There is also a tapestry collection and small portrait gallery. The surrounding **park** (daily 9am–sunset; 1zł) makes a cool, relaxing spot for a stroll.

On to L'viv

There's no better illustration of the current revival of cross-border ties in Poland than the growing tourist influx to **L'viv** (Lwów to Poles) 70km across the Ukrainian border. As well as being one of the main eastern centres of Polish culture, L'viv has long been characterized by a **multicultural population**, and three cathedrals – Armenian, Orthodox and Catholic – remain today. The city served as the capital of the Habsburg province of Galicia until 1918, when it became part of the reborn Polish state. Its subsequent loss after World War II to the Soviet Republic of the Ukraine led to an exodus of Poles, although Polish nostalgia for the city remains strong, as evidenced by the scores of photo albums and guidebooks you can find in Polish bookshops these days. Now a predominantly Ukrainian-speaking city, L'viv is an important centre of Ukrainian culture and in many ways represents a counterbalance to the Russian-speaking regions of central and eastern Ukraine.

Central L'viv remains stacked full of Habsburg-era architecture, and is well worth a trip from Przemyśl to see. With at least one daily train and six daily buses, it's also easily accessible. Services are on the slow side and often involve long delays at the border, so treating L'viv as a day trip from Przemyśl can be pretty exhausting. Far better to stay a night or two – consider reserving a room at the city's grand if fading *Hotel George* (pl. Mitskevicha 1 ☏+38/(0)32 272 5952, ⊛ www.georgehotel.com.ua; doubles from 300 hryvnia/€40), an atmospheric throwback to L'viv's Habsburg past.

Citizens of EU countries and the USA do not require a visa to enter the Ukraine, though those of other countries should check current visa regulations with their local Ukrainian embassy or consulate before setting out.

Parts of the castle provided holiday **accommodation** for factory managers until the mid-nineties, when the *Zamkowy* hotel (☎016/671 8316, ⓦ www.krasiczyn .com.pl; ⓪) opened its doors to allcomers; it now offers fully equipped en suites, housed either in the park gatehouse or in a creaky-floored wing of the castle itself. Nearby, the *Juvena* **campsite** (☎603 864 745, ⓦ www.juvena.luck.pl), occupying a wooded hillside beside the River San, has simple two- to four-person wooden chalets (from 10zł per person). The **restaurant** of the *Zamkowa* offers solid pork-and-cabbage Polish cuisine with a few game dishes thrown in for good measure.

Chotyniec

Some thirty kilometres northeast of Przemyśl, and only easy to get to if you're driving (though a few buses do head this way; ask at the station), is the Uniate *cerkiew* in **Chotyniec**. A two-domed structure dating from around 1600, this is one of the finest, and oldest, wooden churches in the region, with an interior that includes a complete seventeenth-century iconostasis and, on the southern wall, a Baroque, Western-influenced *Last Judgement* painted in 1735.

Sanok and around

The main routes south from Przemyśl and Rzeszów towards the **Bieszczady** head through a rustic landscape of wooded foothills to the provincial town of **Sanok**, a sleepy sort of place perched on a hilltop above the San River. Best known within Poland for its rubber and bus factories – the latter's Autosan vehicles can be seen all over the country – it's also figuring ever larger as a tourist destination, not least because of its extraordinary icon collection and spectacular *skansen*. Extensive transport links make it a good forward base from which to explore Poland's far southeast, especially the extraordinary wooden church at **Ulucz** and the Jewish-heritage sites at nearby **Lesko**.

Arrival, information and accommodation

The **bus station** is close to the **train station**, about fifteen minutes' walk southeast of the town centre; most buses from here will take you up to the main square. The **tourist office**, Rynek 14 (☎013/463 6060, ⓦ www.sanok.pl), can help find **accommodation** throughout the area and has a good stock of local **maps** for sale. You can pitch a tent or park a caravan at the *Biała Góra* **campsite** (☎013/463 2818), on a hilltop overlooking the river just next to the *skansen*, where there are also A-frame bungalows (30zł per person).

Hotels

Bona ul. Białogórska 47 ☎013/464 1520, ⓦ www .bona.sanok.pl. Recently built hotel on the northern fringes of town, right opposite the *skansen*, that looks a bit like an oversized alpine chalet. Neat en suites with TV, some of which have balconies overlooking the San River. ④

Dom Turysty PTTK ul. Mickiewicza 29 ☎013/463 1439. Budget option just downhill from the town centre, offering frumpish but tolerable en suites (price varies depending on bathroom facilities), and some hostel-style triples (25zł per person). ①–②

Jagielloński ul. Jagiellońska 49 ☎013/463 1208, ⓦ www.hoteljagiellonski.pl. Comfortable, intimate hotel midway between the town centre and the train and bus stations with knowledgeable, English-speaking management and spacious en suites with TV. ④

Pod Trzema Różami ul. Jagiellońska 13 ☎013/463 0922, ⓦ www.trzyroze.bieszczady24 .pl. Plain but scrupulously clean in a good central position; a useful mid-priced fallback if the *Jagielloński* is full. ③

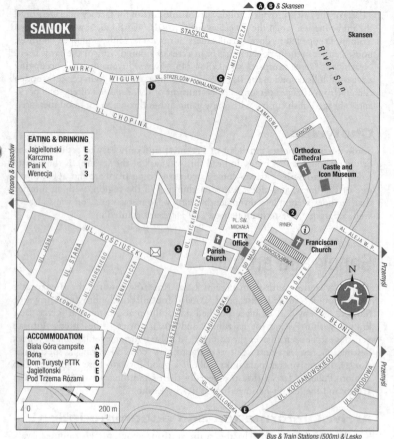

EATING & DRINKING

Jagiellonski	E
Karczma	2
Pani K	1
Wenecja	3

ACCOMMODATION

Biala Góra campsite	A
Bona	B
Dom Turysty PTTK	C
Jagiellonski	D
Pod Trzema Rózami	E

0   200 m

▲ **Ⓐ, Ⓑ & Skansen**

Skansen

River San

Przemyśl ►

Przemyśl ►

▼ Bus & Train Stations (500m) & Lesko

The Town

Once beyond the industrial suburbs, Sanok's historic centre is pleasant
enough, with commercial life focused on the pedestrianized section of ulica
3-go Maja leading to the Rynek and castle. There are several fine chapels in
the seventeenth-century **Franciscan Church** (Kościół Franciszkanów), on the
edge of the Rynek, while just to the west on plac św. Michała is the original
fourteenth-century **parish church**, and which destroyed in a fire in 1782
and rebuilt a century later, hosted the wedding in 1417 of King Władysław
Jagiełło and Elźbieta Granowska (his third, her fourth). A short way down the
hill is the **Orthodox cathedral**, an imposing late eighteenth-century edifice
with a fine iconostasis (open for Sunday services at 10.30am and 5pm, but at
other times you can peer in through the vestibule).

The castle and Sanok Icon Museum

Perched on a low hill north of the Rynek is the **castle**, a sixteenth-century
construction built on the site of the original twelfth-century fortress, which
guarded the main highway linking the southern Carpathians to the Baltic. Today

the castle houses the fabulous **Sanok Icon Museum** (April to mid-June & Oct Mon 8–10am, Tues & Wed 9am–5pm, Thurs–Sun 9am–3pm; mid-June to Sept Mon 8–10am, Tues–Sun 9am–5pm; Nov–March Mon, Thurs & Fri 8am–3pm, Tues & Wed 9am–5pm, Sat & Sun 9am–3pm; 8zł), Poland's largest collection of Ukrainian, Boyk and Lemko icons. As with those in Łańcut, Przemyśl and Nowy Sącz, the existence of this collection is related to postwar "resettlements". With many local villages deserted in the aftermath of Operation Vistula (see box, p.314), their wooden churches neglected and falling apart, the oldest and most important icons were removed to museums.

Though most of the pieces date from the sixteenth and seventeenth centuries, the oldest come from the mid-1300s. Later icons manifest the increasing influence of Western Catholicism – which culminated in the formation of the Uniate Church in 1595 (see box, pp.318–319) – both in their style and subject matter. After the expected Madonnas, the most common subject is St Nicholas, always clad in luxuriant robes. Look out for a large *Icon of Hell*, a type traditionally housed in the women's section of Orthodox churches, and a three-metre-long depiction of the twelve feast days of the Orthodox church.

On the top floor of the castle is the **Beksiński Gallery** (same hours and ticket), displaying a selection of the imaginative canvases – part Dali-surrealist, part *Lord of the Rings* stage set – of the noted local artist, Zdzisław Beksiński (1929–2005).

The skansen

Sanok's other draw is its **skansen**, well signposted 2km north of the centre in the Biała Góra district (daily: April 9am–4pm; May–Sept 8am–6pm; Oct 8am–4pm; Nov–March 9am–2pm; 9zł; ☎013/463 1672); if you don't want to walk, take a bus north along ulica Mickiewicza to the bridge – the *skansen* is on the other side of the river, spread along the bank. This open-air museum, the largest and best in Poland, brings together examples of the different styles of all the region's main ethnic groups – Boyks, Lemkos, Dolinianie ("Inhabitants of the Valley") and Pogórzanie ("Uplanders"); for a detailed ethnography, an excellent English guidebook is available at the entrance (10zł). Many of the buildings are open only when there's a guide on hand: your options are to tag along with a larger group or hire a **guide** (50zł for a two-hour tour in Polish or English, but call ahead for the latter).

Specimens of every kind of country building have been (and still are being) carefully moved and reassembled here: smithies, inns, granaries, windmills, pigsties and churches, and for added verisimilitude you'll find storks, goats and other animals wandering about. A huge area just beyond the *skansen* entrance has been earmarked as the site of a re-created nineteenth-century **market square**, featuring Jewish merchants' houses rescued from formerly bustling market towns like Ustrzyki Dolne and Jaćmierz. Up on the hillside in the **Boyk section** a couple of typical eighteenth-century *cerkwie*, one with a complete iconostasis, nestle peacefully in the shade of the trees. The neighbouring **Lemko section** has a good set of farmhouses, while the **Dolinianie area** features a quaint old fire station, complete with nineteenth-century fire engines, a church and a fine range of rural dwellings from stately *dwór* right down to the humblest and poorest cottage. In the **Pogórzanie section** there's a nineteenth-century school building holding some amazing old textbooks and report cards; note too the carefully preserved maps of pre-1914 Poland, showing this area as a region of the Austro-Hungarian province of Galicia – hence the portrait of Kaiser Franz Joseph behind the teacher's desk. Nearby you'll find an apiary with nineteenth-century figural beehives, carved from tree trunks into likenesses of St Francis, St Ambrose (patron of beekeepers) and others.

As if all this weren't enough, a building in the Dolinianie section displays the *skansen*'s own **icon collection** (9am–4pm; 4zł), which, if not as large as that of the Sanok Museum, is still one of the country's finest. Especially noteworthy is the seventeenth-century *Last Judgement* from the church in the village of Paszowa, in which the damned are swallowed whole by animals and pierced by spear-wielding devils. A nearby pavilion houses excellent temporary exhibitions focusing on past and present village life.

Eating and drinking

The cellar **restaurant** in the *Jagielloński* hotel serves up good Polish cuisine in comfortable surroundings. A more interesting choice is *Karczma*, on the northern side of the Rynek, which offers regional treats such as *hreczanyki* (pork-and-buckwheat burgers) and delicious *fuczki* (pancakes made from grated potato, sauerkraut and carrot), washed down with draught Leżajsk beer. For

Boyks, Lemkos and Operation Vistula

The Carpathian valleys of southeastern Poland form the traditional heartland of the **Boyks** (Boykowie) and **Lemkos** (Łemkowie), both groups descended from nomadic shepherds who settled in the **Bieszczady** and **Beskid Niski** regions between the thirteenth and fifteenth centuries. Geographically speaking, the Boyks populated the eastern Bieszczady, while the Lemkos inhabited the western Bieszczady, the Beskid Niski and part of the Beskid Sądecki. Speaking dialects similar to modern Ukrainian, the Boyks and Lemkos led a life separate from that of the lowland Poles. Both groups belonged initially to the Orthodox faith, but many converted to the Uniate (or "Greek Catholic") Church, created in 1595 in order to place the non-Catholic communities of the southeast under firmer Polish control.

For centuries, these farming communities lived more or less peacefully. Despite their linguistic and cultural affinities with the Ukrainians, neither Boyks nor Lemkos showed any real interest in the Ukrainian nationalist movements that emerged in the early twentieth century. Their real troubles began towards the end of World War II, when units of the **Ukrainian Resistance Army** (**UPA**) were forced out of western Ukraine by the Red Army and took refuge in the hills of southeastern Poland. Like many anti-communist groups of the period, the UPA assumed that worsening relations between the Soviet Union and the West would ultimately lead to some kind of American–British invasion. Sustained by this forlorn hope, UPA guerrillas held out against Soviet-supported Polish forces for two years, famously assassinating the regional commander, General Karol Świerczewski, at Jabłonki in March 1947.

Suspecting that the UPA was sustained by Boyk and Lemko support, the Polish authorities decided to have the entire population of the Bieszczady and Beskid Niski deported. In a notorious operation codenamed **Operation Vistula** (Akcja Wisła), whole villages were emptied and their inhabitants resettled – either (in the case of many Lemkos) to the former German territories of the north and west, or (for most of the Boyks) to the Soviet Union. As a result, the Polish Carpathians have remained seriously depopulated to this day. Many villages evacuated in 1947 have simply disappeared, their crumbling buildings swallowed up by grass and shrubs.

Nowadays Boyks and Lemkos are free to settle where they wish, but the sense of uprooted community still remains. Nowhere is this more evident than in the religious field: over 250 Uniate churches were taken away from the Lemkos in the wake of 1947, and given to the Catholic or Orthodox communities instead. Only a handful have since been returned.

pizza or pasta, try *Wenecja*, ul. Mickiewicza 3. There are plenty of **cafés** and **bars** along ulica 3-go Maja; but for something with a bit more character head for *Pani K*, just west of the *Dom Turysty PTTK* on ulica Strzelców Podhalańskich, a mildly arty cellar bar which organizes occasional gigs.

Ulucz and Czerteż

If you have your own transport, the *cerkiew* in **ULUCZ**, a tiny village 20km north of Sanok on the River San, is worth seeking out. Built in 1510, it's the oldest, and among the finest, of the Boyk *cerkwie* located within Polish territory (others of similar vintage are all in Ukraine). A graceful, well-proportioned building poised on a hilltop, it has a large bulbous dome, fine Baroque iconostasis (though sadly several icons were stolen a few years back) and mural paintings of the Passion and Crucifixion. The key is kept in a house marked by a sign at the village entrance.

At **CZERTEŻ**, immediately north of the main Krosno road, 6km west of Sanok, there's another beautiful Boyk *cerkiew* from 1742, hidden in a clump of trees up above the village. It houses another fine iconostasis, although the church is now a Catholic place of worship. The freestanding belfry was added in 1887.

Lesko

East of Sanok the southbound road continues to **LESKO**, a tranquil town in the foothills with enough sights to merit a quick stop and, for those wishing to stay, a sixteenth-century **castle** that's now a good and affordable hotel (see p.316).

As in other towns in the area, Lesko's **Jewish community** made up more than half of the prewar population. Just north of the Rynek, on ulica Moniuszko, stands the **former synagogue**, a solid-looking Renaissance structure that was originally part of the town's defensive system. The vivacious, finely sculptured facade is emblazoned with a quotation from the Torah. Damaged in wartime, the building was reconstructed in the early 1960s, and is now an **art gallery** (Tues–Sun 10am–5pm; 3zł). Alongside the temporary art exhibitions you can view the converted synagogue interior, including the few elements of the original decoration. A small display in the entrance hall has some prewar photos of the synagogue, records of local families murdered by the Nazis and a detailed list of the location and size of Jewish communities throughout southeastern Poland.

Head past the building and bear right at the bottom of the hill to reach the **Jewish cemetery**, one of the most beautiful and evocative in the whole country. Hidden from a distance by the trees, the steps up from the roadside – the Star of David on the rust-coloured gate tells you you're at the right entrance – take you up through a tangled knot of twisted tree trunks and sprawling undergrowth to the peaceful hilltop cemetery site, around which are scattered about two thousand gravestones, the oldest dating back to the early 1500s. As in other major surviving cemeteries there's a wealth of architectural styles in evidence: note particularly the numerous ornately decorated Baroque tablets, featuring seven-branched candelabra, animal motifs and often a pair of hands reaching up in prayer towards the heavens from the top of the stone. It's the setting as much as the stones that makes this cemetery so memorable, a powerful testimony to centuries of rural Jewish presence.

Practicalities

Lesko's **bus station** is on the Sanok road, about 1km downhill from the main Rynek. Occupying a low concrete pavilion beside the Rynek's town hall, the **tourist information office** (Mon–Sat 8am–5pm) has a wealth of leaflets on the region and details of **private rooms** in farmhouses (*agroturystyka*) in nearby villages – although you'll need your own transport to get to these. The *Zamek* **hotel** (℡013/469 6268, ⓦwww.gat.pl/30.php; ❹), in the castle, is the best place to stay, with simple but pleasant rooms as well as a terrace restaurant, fitness club and a pool table. Reservations may be necessary: conferences regularly occupy the whole place. The *Ratuszowa*, at Rynek 12 (℡013/469 8632; ❷) is serviceable as a second choice, and has the best **restaurant** after the one in the castle.

The Bieszczady

Of all the ranges that make up the Polish Carpathians, the **Bieszczady** are undeniably the most beautiful. Tucked into the far southeastern corner of the country, they are characterized by the mountaintop meadows known as **połoniny**, where grasses can grow beyond waist height. The *połoniny* often take the form of long undulating ridges, with exhilarating views opening up on either side. Seriously depopulated as a result of Operation Vistula in 1947 (see p.314), the Bieszczady have retained their unspoilt nature, with the diverse fauna including **black storks**, far rarer than their ubiquitous white relatives, and fifty-odd **brown bears**, as well as numerous **raptors**, **wolves**, **lynx** and even **bison**, which were reintroduced here in the 1960s. Much of the area falls under the **Bieszczady National Park** (Bieszczadzki Park Narodowy or BdPN: ⓦwww.bdpn.pl), which has information offices at Usztryki Dolne (see below) and Lutowiska (p.318).

The highest peaks in the region, at around 1300m, won't present many **hiking** problems as long as you're well equipped. Like all mountain regions, however, **weather** changes quickly, particularly on the exposed *połoniny*, where terrific storms can come at a moment's notice throughout the year. The best **map** for hikers is the green *Bieszczady Mapa Turystczyna* (1:65,000), published by *euromapa* and available throughout the region.

The best bases to aim for are the valley-bottom settlements of **Uztrzyki Górne** and **Wetlina**, both of which have a variety of accommodation and offer access to Połonina Caryńska and Połonina Wetlińska, two of the most starkly beautiful summits in the region. In the more densely wooded western Bieszczady, the village of **Cisna** is known for both its cosy B&Bs and the chance to ride on the Bieszczady **forest railway**.

Getting around the Bieszczady is easy enough in July and August, with several buses a day plying a circuit that takes in Sanok, Ustrzyki Dolne, Ustrzyki Górne, Wetlina and Cisna. Outside this period there may be only one or two buses linking the Ustrzyki Górne–Wetlina–Cisna parts of the route, and you'll have to plan your itinerary carefully as a result.

Ustrzyki Dolne and Krościenko

Twenty-five kilometes east of Lesko, **USTRZYKI DOLNE** is the last sizeable town before the mountains, but really serves as an information-gathering point rather than as a destination in its own right. There's a **Bieszczady National Park Museum** just off the Rynek on ul. Bełska 7 (Muzeum Przyrodnicze BdPN: Tues–Sat 9am–5pm, plus Sun July & Aug 9am–2pm; 6zł); with a display of flora and fauna and a helpful information desk (same times; ℡013/461 1091), and an enthusiastic **tourist office** at Rynek 16 (Mon–Fri 8am–4pm; ℡013/471 1130, ⓦcit.ustrzyki-dolne.pl), which can advise on accommodation in local villages.

6

Nine kilometres northeast of Ustrzyki Dolne the village of **KROŚCIENKO** is a renowned regional curiosity on account of its small community of Greeks – part of a little-known diaspora of **Greek communists** who fled their country following the outbreak of civil war in 1946. Only a few remain these days, the younger generation having mostly elected to return. The chief reminder of their presence is the village **cemetery**, a tranquil, wooded spot 1km east off the road to the Ukrainian border. Back in the village, there's a fine late eighteenth-century **cerkiew** over the river, while just north of Krościenko on the edge of the Przemyśl road is a **Protestant cemetery**, all that remains of an earlier generation of local German settlers, who named the area Obersdorf.

South to Ustrzyki Górne

The main road south out of Ustrzyki Dolne – a section of the Bieszczady loop route built in the 1970s to open up this hitherto untouched area to tourism – winds south through the mountain valleys towards Ustrzyki Górne, an eighty-minute (50km) journey by bus. The countryside here is rich in wooden churches, and if you have time to spare and your own transport, consider a detour a few kilometres off the main road to the villages of **Jałowe**, **Równia** and **Moczary** (the first two are also reachable by bus or hiking from Ustrzyki Dolne) to see fine examples of Boyk architecture. Back on the road to Ustrzyki Górne you'll also find Boyk churches at **Hoszów**, **Czarna Górna**, **Smolnik** (one of the few remaining places of Orthodox worship in the region), and – on a road off to the east – at **Bystre** (now disused) and **Michniowiec**, the latter accessible by bus from Czarna Górna.

Wooden churches in southeastern Poland

Despite a modern history characterized by destruction and neglect, both the Bieszczady and neighbouring Beskid Niski retain a significant number of the wooden churches – known as *cerkwie* if they are Uniate or Orthodox, *kościoły drewniane* if Catholic) – traditional to this part of Europe.

Uniate or Orthodox churches (cerkwie)

The oldest surviving **cerkwie** date from the sixteenth century: there are two in Poland from this period – graceful, intricately crafted structures in the isolated villages of **Ulucz** (see p.315), **Czerteż** (p.315) and **Chotyniec** (p.311). Later ones are more numerous and just as remarkable, especially those from the eighteenth century, when Baroque influences spread to the Carpathians. The simpler churches with shingled onion domes typical of the Bieszczady region have their origin in later, **Boyk**-derived architectural styles, while in the **Lemko**-inhabited districts of the Beskid Niski you'll often encounter grander, showier structures with a marked Ukrainian influence, built in the 1920s and 1930s at the height of Lemko self-assertion within Poland.

Both Uniate and Orthodox *cerkwie* share similar interior features, with the **iconostasis**, where the holy images are kept, commanding attention at the end of the nave. Doors in the centre of the iconostasis (through which the priest emerges to conduct the service) bear an image of the Annunciation, while icons on either side of the door are positioned according to a strict hierarchy. The Virgin Mary is always on the left side as you face it, flanked by the saint to whom the church is dedicated, while Christ is always on the right, flanked by John the Baptist.

Many *cerkwie* were handed over to the Catholic church or simply abandoned after 1947, when their original congregations were deported during Operation Vistula (see p.314). The icons from these churches frequently ended up in museums like those in Sanok (p.313) and Łańcut (p.302).

Catholic churches (kościoły drewniane)

The architecture of wooden, Catholic **kościoły drewniane** displays more in the way of Western influences than their Orthodox and Uniate counterparts, often adapting

Coming over the hill into the old market town of **LUTOWISKA** you'll see makeshift barracks and drilling rigs, signs of the oil industry that has developed here sporadically since the last century. Up until 1939, more than half the residents of this remote area were Jews, and the abandoned Jewish cemetery east of the main road contains several hundred tombstones from the nineteenth and twentieth centuries. Near the village church a **monument** commemorates the more than six hundred local Jews shot here by the Nazis in June 1942. The **Bieszczady National Park Information and Education Centre** (Ośrodek Informacji I Edukacji BdPN: July–Aug Mon–Fri 7am–7pm, Sat 8am–3pm; Sept–June Mon–Fri 7.30am–3.30pm, Sat 9am–2pm; ☎013/461 0350, ⓦwww.bdpn.pl) is a good place to pick up advice on exploring the region before pressing on. In the centre of town the roadside café and gallery *U Biesa i Czada* has great snacks and coffee.

A further 15km south, in the village of **PSZCZELINY**, you can stay at the *Magura* (☎013/461 0238, ⓦwww.bieszczady.net.pl/magura; ❷), a fresh-smelling timber-built **pension** with deer and ostriches residing out front.

Ustrzyki Górne and around

Spread out along the bottom of a peaceful river valley and surrounded by the peaks of the Bieszczady, **USTRZYKI GÓRNE** has an end-of-the-world the styles used in lowland stone churches – complete with sloping shingle roofs, high bell towers and protective surrounding verandas. Six of the oldest and best preserved have been added to UNESCO's World Heritage list (fairly or not, Polish Catholics are better poised to sponsor their monuments than the minority Uniates). Undoubtedly the most stunning are those in **Dębno** (see p.453), east of Zakopane, and **Binarowa** (p.330), north of Biecz, both with rich polychromy and an extraordinary variety of original furnishings. East of Krosno, the fifteenth-century church in **Haczów** (p.326) is the oldest wooden church in Poland and has another fine interior, while the one in nearby **Blizne** (p.326) is nearly as old and has a grand *Last Judgement* painted on its northern wall. The other two listed by UNESCO are the elegant, fifteenth-century church of St Leonard in **Lipnica Murowana** (p.434) and the picturesque sixteenth-century church in **Sękowa** (p.331).

Visiting the churches

The possibility of reaching many of the churches by public transport is limited, though a few are within striking distance of several of the larger towns. If you're driving, finding the churches won't be a problem: all are clearly signposted from the road as part of the nationwide **Trail of Wooden Architecture** (Szlak Architektury Drewnianej); the Małopolska route can be viewed at ⓦszlak.wrotamalopolski.pl/en, while the Bieszczady section is posted at ⓦwww.sanok.pl, under The Trail of Icons). Alternatively, the easiest way of having a close look is to visit the **skansens** at Sanok or Nowy Sącz, both of which contain complete churches.Nearly all churches, whether Uniate, Orthodox or Roman Catholic, are kept **locked**. If you can, try to arrive thirty minutes before or after mass, held daily or at least weekly during the summer in most cases. Otherwise you'll have to find the key (*klucz*), generally in the hands of the local priest (*ksiądz*). Ask politely if you can see the church – "Dzień dobry, można/możemy (may I/may we) zobaczyć kościoł?" Many village priests teach school mornings, and it's bad form to come at lunch time, so your best bet is after 2pm. The process can be frustrating, and don't be surprised if you only get to see inside every third church you visit. When you do get into one, though, it's more than worth the trouble.

feel to it. The final destination for most buses heading into the Bieszczady, it's little more than a bus stop girdled by snack bars and holiday villas, and there's nothing to do here but **hike**: luckily, well-marked trails start right next to the bus stop, getting you up onto the forest-carpeted hillsides within a matter of minutes.

Accommodation choices in Ustrzyki Górne are limited, and there's a better range of places to stay on the far side of the park in Wetlina and Cisna. Highest on the comfort list, but overpriced, is the PTTK-run *Hotel Górski* (☎013/461 0604, ⓦwww.hotel.ustrzyki.biz; ❺), in a good riverside location at the north end of the village, with sparsely furnished en suites and amenities such as a sauna and a swimming pool but a gloomy restaurant. One budget option is the *Hotelik Biały* (☎013/461 0641, ⓦwww.hotelik-bialy.bieszczady.info .pl), signposted to the southeast of the bus stop, with careworn but adequate four- and five-bed dorms (25zł per person) and no breakfast. The best of several **campsites** is attached to the *Hotel Górski* (same contact details) offering two- and four-person chalets (32–40zl per person) as well as tent space. There's a huddle of **restaurants** near the bus stop, all basically similar setups with outdoor seating and specializing in the local trout. The main village **shop** has a basic range of food but attracts a devoted band of idlers with its plentiful supplies of Leżajsk beer.

Połonina Caryńska and Połonina Wetlińska

Usztryki Górne is the perfect point from which to launch yourself onto the Bieszczady's famous *połoniny*, with the **Połonina Carynska**, a two-hour climb to the west, offering an immediate taste of the Bieszczady's unique landscape. Once above the treeline and onto the grassy shoulders of the *połonina*, marvellous views open up on either side. From the summit of Caryńska you can follow the ridge west, descending to meet the Ustrzyki–Wetlina road before ascending again onto the **Połonina Wetlińska**, another long ridge offering great views. On the eastern shoulder of the *połonina* is the *Chatka Puchatka* **mountain hut** (☎502 472 893, ⓦwww.bieszczady.net.pl/chatkapuchatka; beds from 16zł), a twenty-bed hostel with no electricity, no running water but a wonderful ambience and great home-cooked food. From *Chatka Puchatka*, the ridge-top walk heads westward to the summit of the Połonina Wetlińska, the 1256-metre Roh. Here you can savour yet more amazing vistas before descending to Wetlina village (see opposite), where you can book yourself into a hotel or catch a bus back to Ustrzyki Górne.

Another exhilarating hike from Ustrzyki Górne involves walking or catching a bus to **Przełecz Wyźniański**, 6km west on the Wetlina road, before picking up a southbound path to Mała Rawka (1267m), which then rises again towards **Wielka Rawka** (1307m), right on the Slovak border (2hr 30min).

Wołostate and around

Seven kilometres south of Ustrzyki Górne, **WOŁOSTATE** is an important trail-head for hikes to the east. It's also home to the **Bieszczady National Park Hucul Horse Centre** (Zachowawcza Hodowla Konia Huculskiego BdPN: ☎013/461 0650, ⓦwww.bdpn.pl), a major breeding centre for the *hucul*, a stocky thick-necked horse hailing from the eastern Carpathians. There's a full menu of *hucul*-riding excursions: book in advance to enjoy anything from a 45-minute ride on a *hucul* in the paddock (25zł) to a day-long excursion in the surrounding hills (minimum of 4 people required; 150zł each). The nearby *Stacja Badawcza* **guesthouse** (☎013/461 0634; ❷) is primarily intended for visiting biologists, but tourists can stay there if rooms are available.

Wołostate is the starting point for ascents of **Tarnica** (1346m), a typically grass-topped *połonina* standing a two-hour walk to the east. From here there's a mouth-watering range of up-and-down *połonina*-top hikes, with **Krzemien** (1335m) and the long ridge of the **Bukowe Berdo** (1213) lying to the northeast; and **Halicz** (1333m) and **Rozsypaniec** (1280m) to the southeast. Either would make a feasible day's hike from Wołosate; the really fit could do an outing from Ustrzyki to Krzemien and back in a day.

Muczne

Heading for Bukowo Berdo and carrying on down its eastern side would bring you to **MUCZNE** (also accessible by road via a turn-off on the Ustrzyki Górne–Lutowiska route), formerly site of a secret hunting hotel used by the Communist Party leadership and international guests including French president Giscard d'Estaing and Romanian leader Nicolae Ceauşescu. Now dilapidated, it is flanked on either side by a high-quality new **pension**: *Wilcza Jama* (☎013/461 0269, ⓦwww.muczne.pl) has doubles with bath and five-person bungalows (all ❹ with mandatory full board June–Aug; otherwise ❷, board optional), and an excellent bar and **restaurant**, serving game and trout.

The nearby *Siedlisko Carpathia* (☎013/461 0122, Ⓦwww.muczne.com.pl; ❸) is more family-oriented, with a relaxed restaurant and a children's playground.

Wetlina

Down in the valley floor directly below Połonina Wetlińska, **WETLINA** is a long, roadside-hugging village offering a growing choice of **accommodation**. The *Leśny Dwór* (☎013/468 4654, Ⓦlesnydwor.bieszczady.pl/wetlina; ❺), a family-run *pensjonat* on the north side of the main road, is one of the best places to stay in the Bieszczady, with carefully furnished rooms, concerts in its fine restaurant and even a library. Another good choice is the *Chata Wędrowca* (☎500 225 533, Ⓦwww.chatawedrowca.pl), with one double (❸) and two triples (150zł) in cosy attic rooms above a restaurant (see below). Plenty of other houses in town offer private accommodation (❶) – there's a full list on the Cisna municipal internet site (see p.322). There are also a year-round PTTK **hostel** (☎013/468 4615 and 694 431 611, Ⓦwww.wetlinapttk.pl; dorms from 20zł) and **campsite** run by a friendly local family, and the BdNP-run *Górna Wetlińska* campsite, right at the eastern end of Wetlina at the bottom end of the trail to the *Chatka Puchatka* mountain hut (see p.320) and the Połonina Wetlińska.

Wetlina is also the culinary capital of the Bieszczady, with two adjacent **restaurants** vying with the countryside for your attention. The larger of them, *Chata Wędrowa*, is known for its *naleśnik gigant z jagodami* (gigantic blueberry pancake) and grilled marinated meats. Next door, the small and affordable *W Starym Siole* has good Polish dishes like *pierogi z soczewicą* (*pierogi* with lentils) as well as meaty grills, great desserts and what must be the best wine list east of Kraków. Thirsty hikers tend to congregate in the *Baza Ludzi z Mgły* ("Basecamp for the People of the Fog"), an enjoyably offbeat **bar** at the eastern end of the village run by the same people as the *Chatka Puchatka*.

The western Bieszczady

West of Wetlina the main road winds its way over the Przysłup pass before descending to **Cisna**, another engagingly rustic village with a burgeoning B&B industry. The densely forested hills above Cisna don't quite have the charisma of the eastern Bieszczady's *połoniny*, but there are plenty of fine local walks and the narrow-gauge **forest railway** provides extra reason to linger. Beyond Cisna there is a choice of routes looping through the western Bieszczady and back towards Sanok. The main one winds its way north towards **Jabłonki** and **Baligród**, starting points for some rewarding hiking routes, while a less travelled road runs through **Nowy Łupków**, **Komańcza** and a series of tiny Uniate villages such as **Rzepedź**, famous for their wooden churches. Public transport is meagre except in July and August, when extra Cisna–Sanok buses are laid on.

Cisna

Nesting in a bowl of green hills, **CISNA** is a typical example of a village largely emptied by the deportations of 1947, only to re-emerge fifty years later as a major beneficiary of the Bieszczady tourist boom. A large graffiti-covered monument near the village's main T-junction commemorates Cisna's role in the 1945–47 civil war, when the UPA (see box, p.314) had one of their main bases nearby. Cisna is the starting point for several easy-going hikes: the three-hour southbound ascent to the border-hugging **Okrąglik** (1101m) is the pick of the bunch, offering fine views of the rippling Slovak Carpathians as you approach the summit.

Practicalities

The **tourist information centre**, in the centre of town (Tues–Fri 10am–6pm, Sat 7.30am–3.30pm; ☎013/468 6465), has information on B&B options, as does the town **website** (Ⓦwww.cisna.pl; under "Noclegi"). There's a summer-only **bike-hire** hut (40zł per day) near the main T-junction.

Eating options include a string of café-cum-snack bars near Cisna's main T-junction, and a marginally higher-quality **restaurant**, the *Karczma Lemkowyna*, occupying a log-built house set back slightly from the road. The nearby *Siekierezada*, decorated with wood-carved demons and iron chains, is something of a cult **bar** hereabouts and is a fine place to sink a few beers after a hard day in the hills.

As for accommodation, there's a **campsite**, *Tramp* (☎013/468 6419), right in the centre of the village.

Hotels and pensions

Bacówka pod Honem ☎503 137 279, Ⓦwww.podhonem.home.pl. PTTK-run place 15min walk to the northwest of the village centre, with a handful of simple doubles and dorms (from 20zł per person) in a traditional timber building that looks like a huge wooden shed. ❷

Przystanek Cisna Cisna 59 ☎013/468 6396 & 691 845 492, Ⓦwww.przystanek.bieszczady .info.pl. Cosy pension a short distance uphill from the tourist office serving good vegetarian-only meals and run by an English-speaking family. Half-board only. ❺

Troll Cisna 86 ☎792 015 254, Ⓦwww.bieszcza-dytroll.pl. Timber-built twelve-room pension in the centre of the village, owned by a Polish family who lived in Norway and brought back a Scandinavian taste for bright, clean rooms with lots of wood. ❹

Ostoja Cisna 55 ☎013/468 4792 & 691 892 657, Ⓦwww.bieszczady.net.pl/cisna55. Family-run pension in a timber building but with all mod cons. ❹

Wołosan Cisna 87 ☎013/468 6373, Ⓦwww .wolosan.pl. Hotel and congress centre at the northern end of the village with bland but comfortable en suites. ❹

The forest railway

Three kilometres west of Cisna, **MAJDAN** is the main boarding point for the **Bieszczady forest railway** (*kolejka leśna*), a narrow-gauge line originally built for the local logging industry and nowadays one of the most popular tourist attractions in the region. The diesel-powered train, accompanied by a string of open-sided carriages, operates two short stretches of track: one running 20km east of Majdan to the mountain pass of Przysłup, calling at Cisna on the way; the other running about 30km west to Wola Michowa (see opposite). Much of the route is through hillside forests filled with a gloriously rich and diverse flora, the beautiful views over the valleys adding a touch of mountain thrill to the experience.

Trains for Przysłup leave Majdan at 10am (May, June & Sept Sat, Sun & public hols; July & Aug daily), arriving in Przysłup at around 11.10am and setting off on the return leg twenty minutes later. Trains for Wola Michowa only run at weekends and on public holidays in July and August, departing from Majdan at 1pm and reaching Wola Michowa at 2.25pm. The **timetables** have been set for several years, but it's still worth checking beforehand either at Cisna tourist information centre or on the Cisna website (see above). Antiquated steam engines occasionally pull trains in summer, but advance information on running times is hard to come by – again, the tourist information centre might help.

Jabłonki and Baligród

From Cisna, buses head north to Lesko and Sanok, through a region that was the scene of some of the heaviest fighting between the Polish Army and the Ukrainian resistance. At **JABŁONKI** there's a large monument to **General**

Karol Świerczewski, the veteran Spanish Civil War commander whose assassination in March 1947 goaded Poland's newly established communist authorities into a decisive all-out assault on the UPA, culminating in Operation Vistula (see box, p.314). The monument is the starting point for hikes into the wooded ridges to the east, including the green-marked path to Berdo (890m) and the black route which heads southeast via the peaks of Kiczera (725m) and Łopiennik (1069m), before descending to the village of Dołżyca just east of Cisna (4hr in all).

Further north is the larger village of **BALIGRÓD**, the headquarters of the Polish Army during the Polish–Ukrainian conflict. Evidence of its prewar ethnic population group lies in the **Jewish cemetery**, a short walk northwest of the square; around a hundred tombstones remain, the oldest dating back to 1718. Sticking to the main road north out of Baligród brings you to Lesko after about 20km, where you join the main road back to Sanok.

Wola Michowa and Nowy Łupków

Heading west from Cisna, the road winds over a wooded pass before decending towards the village of **WOLA MICHOWA** and the *Latarnia Wagabundy* holiday centre, which has a restaurant, en-suite rooms (☎502 472 112, ⓦlatarnia.pl; ❷) and offers horse-riding lessons in a rural setting. Seven kilometres further on is **NOWY ŁUPKÓW**, a tiny place whose name is familiar to Poles for the nearby internment camp, to which many prominent Solidarity leaders were consigned during martial law. There's an interesting Uniate **cerkiew**, now a Roman Catholic church, which is worth a visit at the village of Smolnik, just to the east if you have access to transport.

Komańcza

North from Nowy Łupków, the main Sanok road runs through the village of **KOMAŃCZA**, whose churches illustrate graphically the religious divisions of the region. West of the main road is a modern church with an attractive iconostasis constructed in the 1980s by the majority local Lemko **Uniate** population – curiously, the ethnic cleansing effected by Operation Vistula on the surrounding region seems not to have touched Komańcza itself. Round the back of the church is a **museum** of Lemko culture (open when the family who own it are around) housed in a traditionally decorated farm building and with a small but enjoyable collection of traditional costumes, religious artefacts and farming implements. Further up the same road, hidden away in the woods on the edge of the hill, is a beautiful early nineteenth-century *cerkiew*, used by the tiny local **Orthodox** community, while back on the main road, opposite the disused railway station, is the **Roman Catholic** church, (a rarity around here up until World War II), that was built in the 1950s for the village's Polish settlers. Roughly 1km further north, on a track leading uphill to the left under the railway bridge, is the **Nazarene Sisters' Convent**, something of a shrine for Polish tourists: it was here that Cardinal Wyszyński, the redoubtable ex-primate of Poland, was kept under house arrest in the mid-1950s during the Stalinist campaign to destroy the independence of the Catholic church. Plenty of locals offer private accommodation (❶). At the northern end of the village, the *Schronisko PTTK* (☎013/467 7013) offers basic doubles (❶) and five-person dorms (25zł per person), while the adjacent seasonal **campsite** has chalets. The best place for a bite to **eat** is *Kawiarenka Eden*, back in the centre on the main road.

Rzepedź and Turzańsk

There's a particularly fine and typically Lemko-style **Uniate church** from the 1820s at **RZEPEDŹ**, just 5km north of Komańcza. Nestled away on a hillside surrounded by tranquil clusters of trees, the church merges into the landscape – a common quality in *cerkwie* that may explain how they escaped the destruction of Bieszczady villages in the wake of Operation Vistula. Surprisingly, this one only closed down for ten years after World War II, reopening in 1956. The interior of the church gives a sense of the twin strands of Uniate worship: on the one hand Western Madonnas and oil paintings; on the other the Eastern iconostasis, the absence of an organ (in the Orthodox tradition the choir provides all the music), the pale blue Ukrainian saints, and Ukrainian-script wall inscriptions. If you're planning on **staying** here, the best option is the *Willa Grażyna* (☎013/467 8200 and 601 158 967; ❷), an amenable little place right in the town centre. **Turzańsk**, 1.5km east of the village along the Baligród road, has another fine *cerkiew* in the most peaceful location imaginable; built in the 1830s, its interior decoration is preserved almost intact, a fine Rococo iconostasis included.

The Beskid Niski

West from Sanok the main road, closely tracked by the slow rail line, heads towards the provincial capital of **Gorlice** through the Wisłok valley, a pleasant pastoral route, with a succession of wooden villages in the hills of the **Beskid Niski** to the south. The main stops on the way to Gorlice are the medieval centres of **Krosno** and **Biecz**, while back roads in this area are full of surprises, with plenty of *cerkwie* and other wooden churches, as well as specialized *skansens*: south of Krosno there's one in **Bóbrka**, devoted to the local oil industry's history and, closer to the Slovak border, another in **Zyndranowa**, focusing on Lemko architecture. Krosno is the main public transport hub, with buses and minibuses serving most of the outlying towns and villages.

▲ Wooden church, Turzańsk

Krosno

At the heart of the country's richest oil reserves, **KROSNO** is the **petroleum centre** of Poland and also a major glassware producer. Prior to the discovery of oil, which helped the town grow wealthy in the late 1800s, Krosno had quite a record of mercantile prosperity: a favourable position on medieval trade routes meant it rapidly became one of the wealthiest Renaissance-era towns in the country, as evidenced by the sturdy burghers' mansions lining the Rynek. Despite a brace of worthwhile museums and the café-lined main square, modern-day Krosno is a pretty uneventful place, its convenience as a touring base being the only reason to stick around.

The Town

From the adjacent train and bus stations, head downhill and turn right onto the main road, which leads to the hilltop Old Town after about ten minutes. Ranged around the compact-looking **Rynek** are the Italianate merchants' houses fronted by arcaded passages – reconstructed in the nineteenth century in this case – characteristic of several towns in the southeast.

The Franciscan church

South of the Rynek on ulica Franciszkanska is the brick-facaded late Gothic **Franciscan church** (Kościół Franciszkanów), where there are a few Renaissance tombstones as well as, in the north aisle, Krosno's most famous monument, the Baroque **Oświęcim family chapel**. A sumptuously ornate piece – the ceiling is especially impressive – the chapel was designed by Italian architect Falconi in 1647–48 following the death of Anna of Oświęcim, whose full-sized portrait hangs on the wall, next to that of her half-brother Stanisław. As guides will point out, the placement is more befitting husband and wife than half-siblings, which helped fuel the tale of incestuous love for which the pair is known. According to legend, Stanisław's boyish affection for Anna grew into a mature passion, leading him to abandon his position as courtier in Warsaw to petition the pope for a dispensation. When he returned, his request granted, Anna, overwhelmed with joy, expired, and Stanisław soon followed, dying of sorrow. In fact, according to Stanisław's diary, there was no trip to Rome, and he returned to court soon after his beautiful half-sister succumbed to fever, from where he made arrangements for the raising of the chapel, "for worship and glory of God and, along with that, my beloved sister".

The parish church and around

North from the Rynek along ulica Sienkiewicza, the main shopping street, a statue on plac Konstytucji 3 Maja commemorates **Ignacy Łukasiewicz**, the local man who sank what's claimed to be the world's first oil well in 1854 in the village of Bóbrka, 10km south of town (see p.328). North of the square on ulica Piłsudskiego is the large Gothic **parish church**, featuring an interior that almost overflows with treasures and curiosities. Note especially the fine, late Gothic crucifix above the spirited Baroque altar; the ceiling polychromy; the richly carved choir stalls; the massive incense burner; and, to the right of the altar, an exquisite fifteenth-century *Coronation of Our Lady* from Kraków. Hanging on the walls, above the Baroque side chapels – the grandest was endowed by the Scot Portius – you'll find a series of large-scale seventeenth-century paintings by the Venetian Thomas Dolabella and his workshop, mostly after Dutch and German engravings: highlights include St George battling a many-headed dragon and a gruesome *Last Judgement*.

The Subcarpathian Museum and the Handicraft Museum

Further down ulica Piłsudskiego you'll come to Krosno's two museums. Housed in the sixteenth-century former bishops' palace, the highlight of the **Subcarpathian Museum** (Muzeum Podkarpacie: Tues–Sun: May–Oct 10am– 4pm; Nov–April 10am–2pm; 6.50zł) is a large and lovingly polished display of early kerosene lamps, the revolutionary device of which Łukasiewicz was the inventor, including an elegant set of Secessionist lamps culled from around Europe. There's also a collection of paintings, with a series of attractive studies of Krosno by Matejko pupil Seweryn Bieszczad (1852–1923), and a series of objects found in recent excavations of the Rynek, including a thirteenth-century sword and fragments of medieval-era shoes. Across the street from the main museum, the excellent **Handicraft Museum** (Muzeum Rzemiosła: Mon–Fri 8am–3pm, Sat 10am–2pm; 4zł) is full of surprises, including an intact barber shop from the 1920s, still in use until a few years ago. Also here is a seventeenth-century iron chest that the staff will let you open, and a wealth of old lathes, looms and other tools.

The Jewish cemetery

Most of the town's thriving prewar **Jewish community** (Jews arrived here in the fifteenth century) perished in the Bełżec concentration camp during 1942. The Jewish cemetery, northwest of the Old Town, across the River Wisłok on ulica Okerzej, still contains a hundred or so gravestones and a monument to those murdered by the Nazis.

Practicalities

Krosno's helpful **tourist information** office at Rynek 5 (Mon–Fri 9am–5pm, Sat 9am–4pm; June–Aug also Sun 9am–3pm; ☎013/432 7707, ⊛www.krosno .pl) publishes a detailed English-language booklet on the town (6zł) and also has maps and can help you find a place to stay. Your best bet for **accommodation** is the *Śnieżka*, ul. Lewakowskiego 22 (☎013/432 3449, ⊛www.hotel.sniezka .webpark.pl; ❹), a clean and professionally run five-room hotel in a characterful nineteenth-century old villa two blocks north of the train station. The *Elenai* on ul. Łukasiewicza 3 (☎013/436 4334) is more basic, and has a choice between rooms with TV and bathroom (❺) or sparsely furnished affairs with shared facilities (❸). The concrete-and-glass palace that is *Krosno-Nafta*, southwest of town on ul. Lwowska 21 (☎013/436 6212, ⊛www.hotel.nafta.pl; ❻), caters to visitors from the oil industry and offers big discounts at weekends.

The main square is lined with places to **eat** and **drink**; *Piwnica Wojtowska*, Rynek 7, serves up some elaborate and filling Polish recipes in an atmospheric cellar or on a square-side terrace; while *Ambrozia*, Rynek 5, offers excellent pasta and pizza on an off-square patio.

Around Krosno

The area around Krosno holds a number of worthy diversions, most of which are linked to Krosno by **bus**, even if there may only be the odd service a day and none at all at weekends.

Odrzykoń, Haczów and Blizne

Eight kilometres to the north of Krosno, the ruins of the fourteenth-century **Kamieniec**, one of the oldest fortresses in the Carpathian Mountains, can be seen at **ODRZYKOŃ**. Kamieniec was the subject of a notorious ownership dispute between the Skotnicki and Firlej familes, which culminated both

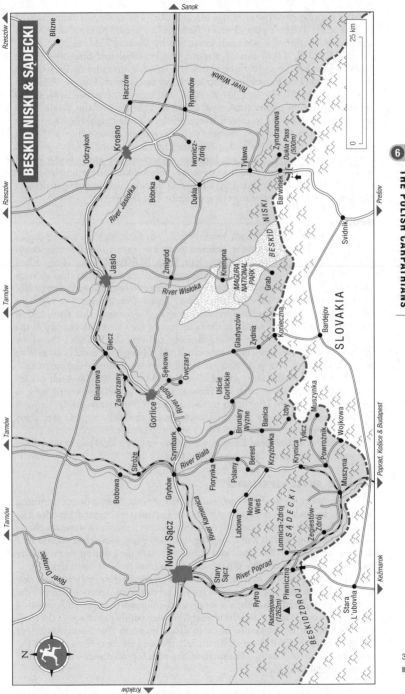

BESKID NISKI & SĄDECKI

0   25 km

N

Sanok

Rzeszów

Blizne

Haczów

Rymanów

River Wisłok

Krosno

Odrzykoń

Iwonicz-
Zdrój

Żyndranowa

Dukla Pass
(500m)

Tylawa

Barwinek

Dukla

Bóbrka

River Jasiołka

Prešov

Jasło

Żmigród

Krempna

MAGURA
NATIONAL
PARK

Grab

BESKID
NISKI

Svidník

River Wisłoka

Gładyszów

Żydnia

Konieczna

Bardejov

SLOVAKIA

Biecz

Sękowa

Owczary

Uście
Gorlickie

Binarowa

Zagórzany

Gorlice

River Ropa

Brunary
Wyżne

Izby

Muszynka

Poprad, Košice & Budapest

Str’że

Szymbark

River Biała

Banica

Wojkowa

Bobowa

Gryboów

Florynka

Polany

Berest

Krzyżówka

Krynica

Tylicz

Powroźnik

Muszyna

River Kamienica

Labowa

Nowa
Wieś

Łomnica-Zdrój

Żegiestów-
Zdrój

SĄDECKI

Tarnów

Nowy Sącz

Stary
Sącz

River Poprad

Piwniczna

Stara
L'ubovňa

Kežmarok

River Dunajec

Rytro

Radziejowa
(1262m)

BESKID ZDRÓJ

Kraków

families occupying different wings of the castle. The story was immortalized in Aleksander Fredro's play *Zemsta* ("Revenge"), a classic piece of nineteenth-century social satire that was made into a film by Andrzej Wajda in 2002.

At **HACZÓW**, 12km east of Krosno, the beautiful mid-fifteenth-century Gothic **church** is thought to be the oldest wooden structure in Poland, and the largest wooden framed building left from its era in all Europe. Added to UNESCO's World Heritage list in 2003, the nave is decorated with a fine sequence of scenes of the Passion of Christ and the lives of the Virgin Mary and the saints, arranged in several layers, while in a side chapel there's an early fifteenth-century wood pietà thought to be miraculous. Unusually – and a sign of things to come, it is to be hoped – the church is generally kept open and charges admission (2zł). There are, however, no set hours; if you do find it locked look for the local priest, who lives opposite. Some 25km further northeast, the church in **BLIZNE**, also listed by UNESCO, is only slightly younger than its Haczów counterpart and features a spectacular *Last Judgement*.

Bóbrka

Historic sites of the petroleum industry may not rank high on most people's must-see lists, but the intriguing **skansen** (Muzeum przemysłu naftowego: daily: May–Sept 9am–5pm; Oct–April 7am–3pm; 5zł) at **BÓBRKA**, a tiny village 10km south of Krosno, makes a strong bid at the non-specialist's interest. Its chief claim to fame rests on the presence of what's widely reckoned to be the world's first proper oil well, sunk here in 1854 by local pioneer Ignacy Łukasiewicz. The highlight of the *skansen*, devoted to the development of the oil industry that flourished in the eastern Carpathian foothills in the latter part of the nineteenth century, is the enjoyable collection of early drilling derricks and rigs. At "Franek", the oldest specimen, built in 1860, you can see the crude oil bubbling away at the bottom of its well, while "Janina", ten years younger, is still in low-level commercial operation.

At the far end of the area, which takes a good hour to walk around, is a set of old workshops along with Łukasiewicz's former offices, converted into an informative **museum**. Highlights include a chart of the first oil field, complete with the locations of the first drill shafts, and a fine collection of Art Deco kerosene lamps, including Łukasiewicz's prototype, made in 1853.

To get to the *skansen* from Krosno, you'll have to take a local bus to the village and walk the remaining 2km through the forest.

Dukla and around

DUKLA, 24km south of Krosno, was for centuries the main mountain crossing point on the trade route from the Baltic to Hungary and central Europe. The location has also ensured an often bloody history, the most savage episode occurring during World War II, in August 1944, when more than 60,000 Red Army soldiers and 6500 Czech and Slovak partisans died during an eventually successful attempt to capture the mountain pass from its Nazi defenders.

Today Dukla is windy, quiet and bleak, with an eerie, whitewashed square that wouldn't be out of place in Spain or Italy. There are two sights of interest: the reconstructed **parish church**, a warm, pastel-coloured Baroque edifice with a pleasing Rococo interior; and the former Mniszech family palace across the road, badly battered in 1944 and now home to a local **museum** (Tues–Sun: May–Sept 10am–5pm; Oct–April 10am–3.30pm; 5zł), focusing on the chilling story of the wartime "Valley of Death." The surrounding park is graced with a collection of Soviet and Polish artillery.

For an **overnight stay**, the *PTTK Dom Wycieczkowy*, Rynek 18 (☎013/433 0046) offers plain en suites (❷) and even plainer dorms (from 20zł per person), along with a simple café-restaurant; while the *Zajazd Galicja* (☎013/433 1455, ⓦzajazd-galicja.prv.pl; ❸) is an eight-room pension on the main road heading south out of town, where there's also a modest **restaurant**. The *Tawerna pod Piratem* on the square is a good place to go for a **drink**.

Around Dukla

Twenty-five kilometres south of Dukla, off the road to Barwinek and the Slovak border, the village of **ZYNDRANOWA**, really no more than a collection of farmhouses, is the location of another of the region's diverse collection of **skansens** (Tues–Sun: May–Sept 9am–4pm; Oct–April 10.30am–3.30pm; 5zł). Devoted to local **Lemko culture**, it was established in 1966 by Teodor Gocz, an energetic local Lemko, and occupies a set of wooden farm buildings themselves typical of Lemko rural architecture. The *skansen* houses a vivid collection of folk religious art, traditional costumes and venerable old agricultural implements; a display detailing the results of Operation Vistula (see box, p.314); and, equally poignantly, a set of Soviet uniforms and other military leftovers from the 1944 Battle of Dukla Pass, picked up in the surrounding woods over the past few decades. Interestingly, two hundred metres down the road a recently renovated **Jewish village house** (*chata*) has now been added to the *skansen*'s collection of buildings, containing a small but informative and well-presented exhibition about rural Jewish life and culture. Getting here without your own transport isn't easy. The only option is to take a local **bus** from Dukla to the signposted turnoff from the main road, just south of Tylawa, and walk or thumb a lift the remaining 5km.

Biecz and around

BIECZ is one of the oldest towns in Poland and, thanks to a royal charter, was the conduit for nearly all the wine exported north from Hungary in medieval times. This trade thrived until the middle of the seventeenth century, when the Swedish invasion flattened the economy. Much of the town, fortunately, survived, and these days it's a placid and little-known rural backwater living amidst past architectural glories. A visit to Biecz and nearby **Binarowa** is feasible on a day trip by bus from Kraków (changing at Gorlice), but only if you start early.

The Town

Biecz's **Rynek** is dominated by the fifty-metre tower of the late Renaissance **town hall**, smartly renovated over the last few years. West along ulica Węgierka is the **parish church**, a massive Gothic brick structure complete with a forty-metre fortified bell tower, containing Renaissance and Gothic pews, a fine seventeenth-century high altar and, from the same era, a noteworthy pulpit decorated with musicians. The church is open on weekdays (Mon–Fri 10am–1pm; 4zł) and for Sunday masses, though at other times you can peer in through the vestibule. Over the road, the wide-ranging and eccentric town **museum** (May–Sept Tues–Fri 8am–5pm, Sat 8am–4pm, Sun 9am–4pm; Oct–April Mon–Sat 8am–3pm, Sun 9am–2pm; 6zł), housed in an early sixteenth-century burgher's mansion once part of the town fortifications, is a real treat. Among the exhibits are the entire contents of an old pharmacy – sixteenth-century medical books, herbs and prescriptions included – and an extraordinary collection of musical instruments and early phonographs, notably a sixteenth-century *dudy* (Carpathian bagpipe), several old hurdy-gurdys, and a colourful organ handmade in 1902 by "illiterate peasant" Andrzej Wojtanowski. For the record, a Polish-only leaflet on town history informs you that Biecz once had a school of public executioners. They were kept busy: in 1614, for example, 120 public executions took place in the square. A second section of the museum, on the other side of the church at ul. Kromera 1 (Tues–Sat 8am–3pm; also Sun 9am–3pm May–Aug; 4zł), houses temporary exhibitions, a small display of old weapons and a roomful of early editions of the works of Polish historian Marcin Kromer, born in this building in 1512. There's also a 1558 map of Poland, said to be the first accurate one of the country.

Practicalities

Trains stop near the centre, with the Old Town a short walk up on the top of the hill, while the frequent **buses and minivans** from Gorlice drop you off right on the Rynek. For an overnight stay there are two **hotel** options: the shabby *Grodzka*, ul. Kazimierza Wielkiego 35 (T 013/447 1121; ❷), a former synagogue just east of town on the main Krosno road; and the upmarket but excellent-value *Centennial*, a haven of luxury at Rynek 6 (T 013/447 1576, W www.centennial.com.pl) with apartments in the main building (❻), smaller rooms at ul. Węgierska 13 (❺) and twenty percent discounts at weekends. **Places to eat** include the *U Becza*, a lively restaurant and bar in a fine old beamed mansion on the Rynek, or one of the *Centennial's* three restaurants: the two within the hotel feature French and Mediterranean cuisine at high prices, while the *Ogród*, next door at Rynek 6, is an excellent and cheap pizzeria.

Binarowa

Several villages in this area have beautiful wooden churches but the finest is at **BINAROWA**, 5km northwest of Biecz and reached by (infrequent) local buses or by taxi (25–30zł return with 30min at the church). Constructed around 1500, the timber **church** here, which was added to the UNESCO World Heritage list in 2003, rivals the better-known one at Dębno in the Podhale (see p.453). The polychromy is only partly original but it all merits close attention. The marvellous *Passion* series near the altar dates from the seventeenth century; note the devils with huge eyes and long noses cowering in the background at the Resurrection. The harrowing *Last Judgement* scenes on the north wall date from the same period, while the exquisite floral motifs on the ceiling are older, painted soon after the church was built. Just as interesting is the furniture, mostly Baroque, including ornamented pews and painted confessionals from the 1600s. The church is usually open during the day, and for mass at 6pm.

Gorlice and around

Just 12km southwest of Biecz along the main road, the smallish industrial city of **GORLICE** has, like Krosno, been for a century associated with the oil industry, Ignacy Łukasiewicz having set up the world's first refinery here in 1853. There's no real reason to stay, but the town's decent facilities means that is a good base for excursions to the surrounding countryside.

The Town

The local **museum**, just south of the battered hilltop Rynek on ulica Wąska (Tues–Fri 9am–4pm, Sat & Sun 10am–2pm; 3zł), is devoted to Łukasiewicz and the petroleum industry, with some interesting paintings of early oil wells.

The town's other points of interest relate to the bloody World War I battle of spring 1915, when the Russians were routed by a combined German and Austro-Hungarian force. The legacy of the combat, which caused over 20,000 casualties, is the series of **war cemeteries** dotted around the town. Examples can be found west of the Rynek, near ulica Krakowska; 3km south of town, off ulica Łokietka; and, largest of all, in the Korczak district, 2km northwest of the centre. In all cases you'll find tombs of soldiers – Russians, Poles, Hungarians, Czechs and others – from around the region. A short walk south of the centre is the **Jewish cemetery**. A monument commemorates local Jews murdered by the Nazis in the nearby forests or in the death camp at Bełżec.

Practicalities

The **bus station** is close to the centre on the northern side of town; the main **train station** is Gorlice Zagórzany, 4km east and serviced by frequent local buses. The **tourist office**, just downhill from the Rynek at ul. Legionów 3 (Mon–Fri 8am–6pm; ℡018/353 7720, ⓦwww.dolinaropy.gorlice.pl), has accommodation information, books, maps and also a nice selection of local handicrafts and art.

Places to stay include *Dwór Karwacjanów*, ul. Wróblewskiego 10A (℡018/353 5601, ⓦwww.gorlice.art.pl; ❷), a reconstructed fifteenth-century mansion with three basic but clean doubles and one triple above an art gallery/café; the *Hotelik*, ul. Wąska 11 (℡018/352 0238, ⓦwww.hotelik.gorlice.pl; ❹) a pension just off the Rynek that does a good breakfast; and *Margot*, just across the river from the centre at ul. Sportowa 11 (℡018/355 1500, ⓦwww .hotelmargot.pl; ❺) offering contemporary en suites next to a sports ground and a large indoor swimming pool.

To **eat**, try the *Dark Pub*, below the *Hotelik*, which has good meat dishes and an attractive back terrace; otherwise there are a handful of bars and pizzerias around the Rynek. *Lamus*, beneath the *Dwór Karwacjanów*, is an atmospheric and popular cellar **bar**.

South of Gorlice

Seven kilometres south of Gorlice, the UNESCO-listed Roman Catholic church at **SĘKOWA** straddles the historic borderline between the ethnic Polish and Lemko populations. A graceful structure with an extraordinary, two-tiered sloping roof that forms a rounded arcade, the church was a favourite subject of Polish artists from the Młoda Polska movement (see box, p.364). What you see today dates from the 1520s but was added on to – and in the case of World War I Austro-Hungarian soldiers who pillaged it for firewood, taken away from – several times in subsequent centuries. The building is usually locked outside of mass times (4pm Sun), but the nuns who live opposite are likely to open it for you. It's no great loss, however, if you don't get in: most of the furnishings have either been lost or removed to the Diocesan Museum in Tarnów (see p.431) and what remains is unspectacular. Local **buses** (#6, #7 & #17) run here from the ulica Biecka stop outside the Gorlice bus station, dropping you a half-kilometre from the church. The oldest Lemko *cerkiew* in the area is in the village of **OWCZARY**, a further 5km south of Sękowa (bus #7 from Gorlice). Now used by Roman Catholics, the triple-domed church dates from the 1653 and preserves a rich, seventeenth-century iconostasis.

Horse-riding enthusiasts will want to consider visiting the **stables** at **GŁADYSZÓW**, 20km or so southeast of Gorlice. A group of Carpathian *hucul* horses is bred and maintained in Regietów just west of the village, and

Zdynia Vatra

Twenty-five kilometres southeast of Gorlice on the road to Konieczna, the straggling hamlet of **Zdynia** hosts the annual **Lemko Vatra** ("Lemko Bonfire"), a three-day celebration of traditional culture that attracts Lemkos – and fans of Carpathian culture in general – from all over Poland and beyond. Taking place on the second-to-last weekend in July, the *Vatra* provides a showcase for music from all over the Carpathian region, with village musicians and folklore societies from southern Poland, Slovakia and Ukraine among the guests. Bearing in mind that Zdynia lies at the heart of the Lemko territories forcibly depopulated by the Polish government in 1947, it is a highly symbolic occasion.

As one of the friendliest, and most musically varied festivals you're likely to come across in Poland, the *Vatra* is emphatically well worth visiting. Plentiful food and drink is available from stallholders, and camping is possible on the hillsides overlooking the site. With buses from Gorlice only running to Zdynia on weekdays, it's a good idea to arrive with a tent on the Friday and stay until Monday if you can. Otherwise, try hitching a lift with other festival-goers, or pick up a taxi from Gorlice bus station (100zł each way).

the stables (☎018/351 0018, ⓦwww.huculy.com.pl) organize horse-riding excursions in the surrounding hills, starting at around 25zł/hr. Winter sleigh rides (*kuligi*) cost about 250zł for a party of four, grilled sausage and mulled wine thrown in. Basic **accommodation** is available at the stables (❶–❷), and there's a rustic restaurant.

Stróże and Bobowa

West of Gorlice, the road to Nowy Sącz (see opposite) passes through **GRYBÓW**, jumping-off point for an intriguing pair of rustic destinations. Six kilometres north of the town on the Tarnów road, just beyond the village of **STRÓŻE**, the **Museum of Apiculture** (Muzeum Pszczelarstwa; Mon–Fri 9am–4pm, Sat & Sun 11am–4pm; 3zł) is devoted to the long-standing beekeeping traditions of the Carpathians. Of the more than one hundred whimsically carved former hives on display, many date from the nineteenth century or earlier; and there's also a simple, hollow log that was used to keep bees as early as the thirteenth century. Uphill from the main exhibition are hundreds of real beehives, source of various honey products you'll find on sale at the entrance. Stróże is served by a handful of buses from Gorlice (Mon–Fri only).

A further 8km north lies the small town of **BOBOWA** (Bobover in Yiddish), an important centre of Hassidism in the nineteenth century, when the Nowy Sącz *tzaddik* Shlomo Halberstam moved his yeshiva here. His son Ben Zion carried on the tradition, establishing schools throughout Małopolska and also earning fame as a musician. During World War II he helped other Jews, including his son Solomon, flee the Nazis before being murdered in L'viv in 1942. After the war Solomon refounded the yeshiva in Brooklyn, and by his death in 2000 the Bobover community had spread to London, Toronto and elsewhere. Today, old photos of the Halberstam-dynasty rabbis hang in the entrance of the Bobowa **synagogue**, off the northeast side of the tree-lined Rynek. Built in 1756 and one of the best preserved in Poland, the building was damaged by the Nazis, then restored and used as a vocational school from 1955 to 1994, when it was given to the Kraków Jewish community. Ask the barber (*fryzjer*) next-door to unlock the building for you (Mon–Fri 10am–5pm; 10zł per individual or group). The interior, whitewashed during communist times, was originally decorated with frescoes, including a large-scale depiction of Jerusalem: a few segments have been uncovered by the current restoration project, and more may come to light. Like many synagogues, this is a "nine fields" building, with four pillars dividing the main room into nine equal sections, at the front of which stands the vivid blue **Aron ha Kodesh**, a triumph of folk Baroque. There's also a fifteenth-century **parish church** north of the Rynek, with a wooden roof, a rough stone floor and interesting primitive paintings on the walls. Frequent **buses** from Gorlice will drop you off right on the Rynek; coming by **train** (services run from Kraków, Tarnów and Nowy Sącz), alight at the Bobowa Miasto station and walk uphill to the square. There are no hotels or restaurants here, but you'll find excellent, locally made ice cream in a café on the west side of the Rynek.

The Beskid Sądecki

Southwest of Gorlice the hills continue with a range known as the **Beskid Sądecki**, another picturesque stretch of low-lying slopes. In addition to small market towns, scattered villages and traditional peasant farms, there's a sizeable Lemko population here and – enticingly – a wealth of old wooden churches. **Nowy Sącz**, the regional capital, has a handful of attractions and makes for an agreeable base, although you may find a better choice of tourist facilities in **Krynica**, a well-known spa town further south. The *Beskid Sądecki: Mapa Turystyczna* (1:75,000) is widely available and particularly helpful when searching out the numerous *cerkwie* scattered in and around the hills and valleys.

Nowy Sącz

Perched above the confluence of the Dunajec and Kamienica rivers, **NOWY SĄCZ** was one of Poland's principal market towns in the Middle Ages, when it was the site of a royal residence and home to an important school of painters. The town is nowadays a rather workaday service centre and transport hub, although a couple of worthwhile **museums** and the fine **skansen** out in the suburbs ensure that there's plenty here to see. With the hills of the Beskid Sądecki a short bus or train ride to the south, it's an ideal base for exploration.

Arrival, accommodation and information

There are two **train stations**: the more central Miasto station handles only a few local trains, while all others use the Główny station, 2km south of town. Local buses shuttle from here to the town centre, via the **bus station**, located between aleja Wolności and ulica Jana Długosza. The main **tourist office**, located at ul. Piotr Skargi 2 (Mon–Fri 8am–6pm, Sat 9am–2pm; ℡018/443 5597, ⓦwww .nowy-sacz.info), has a decent supply of maps and brochures and information about **private rooms** (❶) and **pensions** (❷) further up the Poprad valley (see p.337). At the top of the **accommodation** range in town is the smart but somewhat bland *Beskid Hotel*, a seven-storey, Orbis-run, concrete affair near the train station at Limanowskiego 1 (℡018/443 5770, ⓦwww.orbis.pl; ❺). More central is the *Panorama*, offering recently renovated rooms at ul. Romanowskiego 4a (℡018/443 7110, ⓦwww.htpanorama.emeteor.pl; ❹). A good budget choice, very clean, but 3km south of the centre in the Osiedle Studentskie ("Student Suburb") on ulica Jana Pawla II, is the *Akademiki* (℡018/449 9900, ⓦwww .osiedlecampus.pl; ❷), a brand new hotel catering to students of the local business school but open to all; it's reached on bus #11 from the bus and train

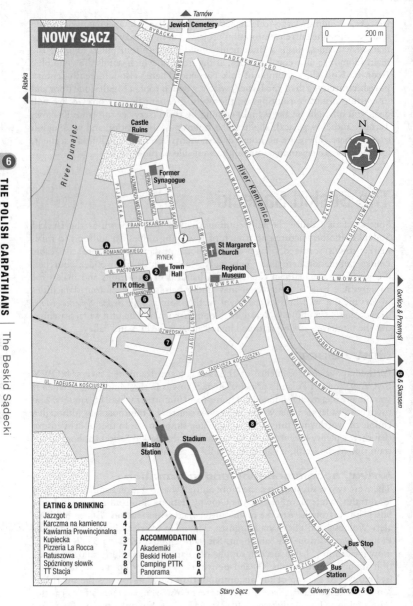

NOWY SĄCZ

Tarnów
Jewish Cemetery

UL. RYBACKA

PADEREWSKIEGO

Rabka

LEGIONÓW

River Dunajec

Castle
Ruins

Former
Synagogue

FRANCISKAŃSKA

KRASZEWSKIEGO

BULWAR NARWIKU

River Kamienica

N

SKOLNA

KOCHANOWSKIEGO

UL. ROMANOWSKIEGO

A

RYNEK

UL. PIASTOWSKA

1

2

3

Town
Hall

St Margaret's
Church

Regional
Museum

UL. LWOWSKA

Gorlice & Przemyśl

PTTK Office

UL. HOFFMANOWEJ

6

5

4

UL. LWOWSKA

4

ŚW. DUCHA

WAŁOWA

B & Skansen

SZWEDZKA

7

UL. JAGIELLOŃSKA

NADBRZEŻNA

BULWARY NARWIKU

UL. TADEUSZA KOŚCIUSZKI

8

UL. TADEUSZA KOŚCIUSZKI

JANA DŁUGOSZA

JANA MATEJKI

Miasto
Station

Stadium

JAGIELLOŃSKA

MICKIEWICZA

JANA DŁUGOSZA

Bus Stop

AL. WOLNOŚCI

KUNEGUNDY

STASZICA

Bus
Station

EATING & DRINKING

Jazzgot	5
Karczma na kamiencu	4
Kawiarnia Prowincjonalna	1
Kupiecka	3
Pizzeria La Rocca	7
Ratuszowa	2
Spózniony słowik	8
TT Stacja	6

ACCOMMODATION

Akademiki	D
Beskid Hotel	C
Camping PTTK	B
Panorama	A

Stary Sącz ▼

▼ Główny Station, C & D

0   200 m

stations. *Camping PTTK*, Nadbrzeżna 40 (☎018/441 5012; buses #5, 6, 7) is a
clean and grassy site 2km east of the centre.

The Town

Nowy Sącz's spacious **Rynek** is dominated by its incongruous neo-Gothic
town hall, ringed in summer by a collection of open-air cafés and beer gardens.

Just off the square to the east, the Gothic **St Margaret's Church** (Kościół św. Małgorzata) has been fully modernized inside, but you'll find fragments of Renaissance-era polychromy to the left of the altar.

The Regional Museum

Over the road from the church on ulica Lwowska, the sixteenth-century Canonical House contains the **Regional Museum** (Muzeum Okręgowe: Mon, Wed & Thurs 10am–5pm, Fri 10am–5.30pm, Sat–Sun 9am–2.30pm; 6zł, free Sun), a first-rate display of icons gathered from village churches throughout the region. The collection is not as extensive as that in Sanok (see p.312) but amply demonstrates the distinctive regional style of icon painting, and includes some wonderful examples of the *Hodigitria* (Holy Virgin and Child) theme popular in Uniate iconography, as well as a seventeenth-century composite iconostasis assembled from different village churches. There's plenty of folk art on show, too, including some *Christus Frasobliwy* sculptures, showing a seated Christ propping his mournful face on one hand.

The former synagogue and around

The seventeenth-century **former synagogue** (Wed & Thurs 10am–2.30pm, Fri 10am–5.30pm, Sat & Sun 9am–2.30pm; 5zł), where the popular nineteenth-century *tzaddik* Chaim Ben Halbertsam had his base (before his better-known son moved to Bobowa; see p.332) is located on ulica Berka Joselewicza in the former Jewish quarter north of the Rynek. It houses a contemporary art gallery and a small photo exhibition of local Jewish life. An English-language brochure available here provides details of the layout of the former Jewish quarter; the north section of ulica Kazimierza Wielkiego (the parallel street) alone used to have no fewer than four synagogues. The surrounding area was also the location of a Nazi wartime ghetto, eventually liquidated in August 1942, when its residents were either shot or transported to Bełżec concentration camp. The *ohel* of Ben Halberstam rests in the predictably overgrown **Jewish cemetery** on ulica Rybacka, north of the centre over the River Kamienica; a monument here commemorates the place where mass executions of local Jews were carried out by the Nazis. Overlooking the confluence of the two rivers, the ruins of the **castle**, built during Kazimierz the Great's reign, give a good view over the valley below. After being used for mass executions of local civilians, the castle was blown up by the Germans in 1945.

The skansen

About 3.5km east of town (bus #14 from the train station, bus station or ulica Lwowska; a brisk 40-minute walk from the centre or a 15zł taxi ride), the extensive **skansen** on ulica Wienawy-Długoszewskiego (Sądecki Park Etnograficzny: May–Sept Tues–Sun 10am–6pm; Oct–April Mon–Fri 10am–2pm; 10zł, free Sat; Ⓦwww.muzeum.sacz.pl) provides a fantastic introduction to Carpathian culture. If you've already visited the *skansen* at Sanok (see p.313), the buildings in the Lemko and Pogórzanie sections here will be familiar, a couple of recently erected wooden churches included. What you won't have seen before, however, are buildings like the fragments of a Carpathian Roma hamlet – realistically situated some distance from the main village – and the assortment of manor houses, including a graceful seventeenth-century specimen from Małopolska, complete with its original interior wall paintings. Other highlights include a comfortable farmstead from nearby Zagorzyn, formerly the property of wealthy peasant Wincenty Myjak, an MP in Vienna from 1911 to 1918; and a nineteenth-century brick granary from Kicznia, featuring extravagantly carved wooden gables. The building interiors are opened only on the guided tours, which leave the entrance on the hour from 11am to 4pm; for an English tour call in advance (☎013/441 4412; no extra charge).

Eating and drinking

There are plenty of eating, drinking and snacking options on the Rynek, and along the pedestrianized ulica Jagiellońska which runs off to the south.

Restaurants

Karczma na Kamieńcu ul. Rzeczna 5. Farmstead-style timber building on the opposite side of the river from the Old Town, offering two floors of wooden-bench seating and a tasty menu of chops, steaks and fried freshwater fish. Daily 10am–10pm.

Kupiecka Rynek 10. Classy cellar restaurant with a solid menu of Polish favourites alongside decent steaks, game dishes and – something of a rarity in southern Poland – home-made *kołduny* (Lithuanian ravioli). Daily 11am–10pm.

Pizzeria La Rocca ul. Szwedska 3. Atmospheric underground pizzeria featuring stone-lined walls and tables made out of barrels. Becomes a youth-oriented drinking den on weekend nights. Daily 11am–11pm.

Ratuszowa Rynek 1. Occupying pleasant rooms underneath the town hall, this is *Kupiecka*'s main rival for the title of best restaurant in town. Pretty much everything in the Polish culinary repertoire is on the menu, but it's the various varieties of *pierogi* (including a local lamb-stuffed version) that stand out. Daily 10am–11pm.

Cafés and bars

Jazzgot Rynek 2. Jazz-themed pub with distressed brick walls, cosy, sofa-furnished corners and a secluded beer garden out back. Discos and karaoke nights at weekends, when there's a small admission charge. Daily noon–1am or later.

Kawiarnia Prowincjonalna corner of ul. Pijarska and ul. Piastowska. A piece of bohemian Kraków plonked down in the Beskids, this homely candle-lit hangout features a winningly eccentric mix of lived-in furniture, ancient radiograms, piles of old magazines and a funky collection of paintings and graphic art on the walls. Mon–Fri 9am–midnight; Sat & Sun 5pm–midnight.

Spóźniony Słowik ul. J. Długosza 10. Occupying a pavilion in the town park, the "Late Nightingale" (the title of a poem by Julian Tuwin) is a characterful café strewn with 1950s furniture, sundry *objets d'art* and the odd antique. Good for tea, coffee and cakes, plus a small menu of main meals. Outdoor terrace in summer. Daily 10am–10pm.

TT Stacja ul. Hoffmanowej 5. Brash modern café-bar with cocktails, wi-fi access, and DJ-driven weekend party nights. Daily 11am–2am.

Into the Poprad Valley

The **Poprad River** – which feeds the Dunajec just south of Nowy Sącz – creates the broadest and most beautiful of the **Beskid Sądecki valleys**. A minor road runs its length to the Slovak border, which it then proceeds to trail for the best part of 25km. Meandering along this route is as good an experience of rural Poland as you could hope for, with forests covering the hills above fields where farmers still scythe the grass. Tracks lead off to remote hamlets, ripe for church-hunting, while along the main body of the valley you can boost your constitution at Habsburg-looking spa towns like **Krynica**.

Travelling into the Beskid Sądecki by public transport, there are regular **trains** plying the route from Nowy Sącz through the Poprad valley to Krynica, stopping at numerous village halts en route. Most Nowy Sącz–Krynica **buses**, however, bypass the Poprad valley entirely, taking the more direct Kamienica valley route to the north.

Stary Sącz

Sitting between the Dunajec and Poprad rivers 10km south of Nowy Sącz, **STARY SĄCZ** (reached via Krynica-bound trains or on buses #10, #11 or #43 from Nowy Sącz train station) is the oldest urban centre of the region. It grew

around the convent founded by St Kinga, thirteenth-century daughter of King
Bela IV of Hungary and wife of Bolesław the Chaste of Poland – Bolesław got his
nickname from the fact he vowed never to have sex with his spiritually minded
spouse. Entering the convent herself after Bolesław's death, Kinga soon became the
centre of a local cult, and was finally declared a saint by John Paul II in 1999.

Lined by one- and two-storey houses, mostly from the eighteenth century,
Stary Sącz's ancient cobbled **Rynek** is one of the best-preserved market squares
in southern Poland. A particularly fine seventeenth-century mansion at Rynek
6 houses the **town museum** (Tues–Sat 10am–4pm, Sun 10am–1pm; 3zł), a
low-key but pleasant diversion into local history. It's also worth looking into
the courtyard of the building at Rynek 21, where the walls and ceilings have
been covered with murals by artists working in the characteristic local naive
style, notably former owner Józef Racek, who died a few years ago. The
tiny town also has two noteworthy thirteenth-century churches: an imposing
fortified Gothic **parish church** south of the square, subjected to the full Baroque
treatment and with lovely pews and a fine organ from 1679; and the convent
Church of the Poor Clares, to the east, its nave decorated by sixteenth-century
murals depicting the life of St Kinga, its founder.

To **stay** overnight, try the *Motel Miś*, Rynek 2 (entrance behind the square;
☎018/446 2451, ⊛www.motelmis.com.pl; ❷), a friendly little pension that
also has an order-at-the-counter buffet serving *pierogi*, *bigos* and other staples.
Otherwise the best **place to eat** is the *Marysieńka* on the west side of the Rynek,
a first-floor restaurant with moderately priced Polish dishes and good views onto
the square from the window-side tables.

The Poprad valley

By local train or bus it's a scenic two-hour ride along the deep, winding **Poprad
valley** from Stary Sącz to Krynica, and if you're not in too much of a hurry there
are a few places worth breaking your journey at before you reach the terminus.

At **RYTRO**, 16km down the line, there are ruins of a thirteenth-century
castle, and lots of hiking trails up through the woods into the mountains; there's
also a very good PTTK hotel-cum-hostel, the *Pod Roztoką* (☎018/446 9151,
⊛www.rytro.com.pl; ❷), which offers en-suite doubles, triples and quads, and
a fine restaurant. The summit of **Radziejowa** (1262m), which is reached by
following a ridge path to the southwest, is one of the more popular destinations,
about two hours' walk from the village. Ten kilometres beyond the village is
PIWNICZNA-ZDRÓJ, with a cluster of old spa buildings on the banks of the
river, from where paths lead up onto the wooded, pudding-shaped hills. The
eastern end of Piwnicza-Zdrój is the main departure point for **raft trips** down
the Poprad River (April–Oct daily 9am–6pm; 35zł per person), which involve
being punted downstream to Rytro in shallow-hulled twelve-person boats.
Although not quite as spectacular as the Dunajec gorge raft trip (see p.455), it's a
great way to take in the scenery.

From here road and rail lines twist their way through an ever-narrowing valley for
26km before arriving at **MUSZYNA**, a village with a long history of low-key spa
tourism but little to recommend it as a place to stop off – save for the chance to stroll
up to the ruins of a thirteenth-century castle, perched on a knoll to the north.

Krynica and around

If you only ever make it to one spa town in Poland, it should be **KRYNICA**.
Redolent of *fin de siècle* central Europe, its combination of woodland setting,

traditional timber architecture and health-restoring waters have made it a popular resort for over two centuries. In winter the hills (and a large skating rink) keep the holiday trade coming in.

Arrival, information and accommodation

From the **train and bus stations** at the southern end of town, ulica Nowotarskiego heads towards the flowerbed-filled centre of the resort. The **tourist information centre** is at the northern end of the centre, inside the Jaworzyna cinema at Piłsudskiego 8 (Mon–Fri 9am–5pm, Sat 10am–2pm, longer hours in summer; ☎018/471 6105); the staff can help you find **private rooms** (❶) and book rafting trips on the Poprad (see p.337) and Dunajec (p.455) rivers.

Hotels and pensions

Małopolanka ul. Bulwary Dietla 13 ☎018/471 5896, ⊛www.malopolanka.com.pl. A lovely olde worlde pension with antique furnishings in the lobby, wi-fi internet access, and an on-site spa centre offering a full range of massages, mud baths and the like. ❹–❺

Willa Janka ul. Pułaskiego 28 ☎018/471 2057. A family-run pension with en suites and rooms

with shared facilities surrounded by a well-tended garden. ❶–❷

Wisła ul. Bulwary Dietla 1 ☎018/471 5512. Another homely, family-run place but more central, with an excellent restaurant and English-speaking staff. ❷

Witoldówka ul. Bulwary Dietla 10 ☎081/471 5577, ⊛www.witoldowka-krynica.pl. A grand old wooden building offering comfortable en suites with TV and internet access. ❺

The Town

Next to the flower-bedded pedestrianized strip that forms the resort's centre you'll find the relaxing main **Pump Room** (Pijalnia Wód Mineralnych; daily 6am–6pm), a modern pavilion with trickling fountains and huge indoor plants. Hand over a few groszy at the desk before heading for the taps, where the purply-brown Zuber is reckoned to be the most concentrated mineral water in Europe – it's certainly one of the worst-smelling. Upstairs there's a concert hall that sees plenty of action during the summer season.

The Nikifor Museum

Diagonally opposite the pump room on Bulwary Dietla is a row of handsome-looking wooden houses and pensions. One of them, the bright-blue Romanówka, houses the **Nikifor Museum** (Muzeum Nikifora; Tues–Sun 10am–1pm & 2–5pm; 6zł), devoted to the life and work of the Lemko artist Nikifor (1895–1968), a legend in Polish folk art whose style and spidery handwriting will be familiar if you've visited the *Loch Camelot* café in Kraków (see p.402). In a style reminiscent of Lowry's scenes of industrial northern England, Nikifor painted Beskid landscapes and *cerkwie* but is perhaps best known for imagining extravagant, Habsburg-style train stations in paintings of villages that were actually far from the railway line. Also look for the *Fabryka Dolarów* ("Dollar Factory") from 1930, perhaps a wry suggestion of what was needed following the 1929 stock market crash.

The Krynica funicular and the Jaworzyna gondola

At the northern end of the promenade, past a statue of Mickiewicz and a late nineteenth-century wooden church, a **funicular train** (kolej linowa; daily every 20–30min: May & June 10am–7pm; July & Aug 10am–8pm; Sept 10am–6pm; Oct–April 10am–5pm; 5zł one way, 8zł return) ascends the nearby **Góra Parkowa** (741m) and drops you at the top for an enjoyable overview of town. Alternatively, a number of paths lead up the hill.

Three kilometres northwest of Krynica (accessible via the green-marked path or on bus #2 from the centre) lies the nascent ski resort of **Carny Potok**, where the **Jaworzyna gondola** (daily May–Sept & Dec–March; 20zł return; ⓦwww.jaworzynakrynicka.pl) whisks you up to the 1114-metre-summit of Jaworzyna. Here you can soak up the views or try out the network of paths on its wooded slopes.

Eating and drinking

Lilianka, Piłsudskiego 9, is a simple **café** that serves up the best pastries and cakes in town, while the **restaurant** in the *Wisła* pension serves Polish staples with aplomb. Nearby, the slightly smarter *Pizzeria-Kaviarnia Węgierska Korona*, ul. Bulwary Dietla 18, offers so-so pizzas, good pasta and risotto dishes, and excellent ice cream in its café section. *Pod Zieloną Górką* is a lively pizzeria and pub-style **bar** at the northern end of Nowotarskiego. Local specialities such as *oscypek* (smoked cheese) are available in the **market** that runs along Bulwary Dietla.

East from Krynica: Tylicz, Wojkowa and Muszynka

The hill region east from Krynica towards the Slovak border is particularly rich in attractive villages and **cerkwie**, including some of the oldest in the country. Six kilometres east of Krynica and accessible by occasional bus (otherwise you could hire a taxi or walk, starting from ul. K. Puławskiego in Krynica), the *cerkiew* in **Tylicz** is adjacent to a wooden Roman Catholic church from the seventeenth century; the latter has an especially rich interior. Tylicz figures in Polish history as base camp of the Confederates of the Bar (1768–72), a failed aristocrat-led revolt against growing tsarist control of the country (see p.615). The *cerkiew* in **Wojkowa**, which boasts a fine Rococo iconostasis, and **Muszynka** are also worth a visit.

North from Krynica: Berest, Polany and around

Twenty kilometres northwest of Krynica on an attractive backroads route to Grybów (see p.332), the village of **BEREST** is a real treat. Set back from the road in pastoral surroundings, its nineteenth-century *cerkiew* (mass 11am) is an archetype of the harmonious beauty of this region's wooden churches, with a rich iconostasis composed of seventeenth- and eighteenth-century icons. Just a couple of kilometres up the road is **POLANY**, where the village *cerkiew* (mass 9.30am) has a Baroque pulpit and iconostasis and nineteenth-century polychromy. From here to Grybów the valley is a gorgeous riverside route; if you have a car, a brief detour south to **Brunary Wyżne**, then on to the border villages of **Banica** and **Izby**, is worthwhile, as all three have magnificent wooden *cerkwie*.

Travel details

Trains

Kraków to: Nowy Sącz (9 daily; 2hr 30min–4hr); Przemyśl (8 daily; 3–4hr); Rzeszów (15 daily; 2hr–2hr 30min).
Krynica to: Nowy Sącz (12 daily; 2hr).
Nowy Sącz to: Kraków (9 daily; 2hr 30min–4hr); Krynica (12 daily; 2hr); Muszyna (13 daily; 1hr 30min); Tarnów (13 daily; 2hr).

Przemyśl to: Jarosław (20 daily; 40min–1hr); Kraków (8 daily; 3–4hr); Lublin (2 daily; 4hr 30min); Rzeszów (20 daily; 1hr 15min–1hr 45min); Tarnów (10 daily; 2hr–3hr 15min); Warsaw (2 daily; 6–7hr).
Rzeszów to: Jarosław (20 daily; 45min); Łancut (20 daily; 20min); Lezajsk (4 daily; 1hr 30min; change at Przeworsk); Kraków (15 daily; 2hr–2hr 30min); Krosno (2 daily; 3hr); Przemyśl (19 daily;

1hr 15min–1hr 45min); Tarnów (24 daily; 1hr–1hr 30min); Warsaw (4 daily; 5–7hr); Zamość (1 daily; 4hr 30min).

Sanok to: Krosno (5 daily; 1hr 20min).

Buses

Gorlice to: Biecz (8 daily; 20min); Bobowa (3 daily; 40min); Kraków (9 daily; 3hr); Nowy Sącz (8 daily; 1hr 10min).

Kraków to: Biecz (3 daily; 3hr); Gorlice (9 daily; 2hr 40min–3hr); Nowy Sącz (10 daily; 2hr 20min); Sanok (5 daily; 4hr 20min); Ustrzyki Górne (July & Aug only; 1 daily; 6hr).

Krosno to: Bóbrka (Mon–Fri 10 daily; 20min); Dukla (minibuses; Mon–Fri 10 daily, Sat 6 daily; 40min); Haczów (Mon–Fri 8 daily, Sat 4, Sun 2; 20min); Rzeszów (every 40–50min; 1hr 30min); Sanok (12 daily; 1hr); Ustrzyki Dolne (2 daily; 2hr); Ustrzyki Górne (July & Aug 2 daily; 3hr).

Krynica to: Nowy Sącz (every 30min; 1hr); Tylicz (Mon–Fri 3 daily; 20min).

Nowy Sącz to: Gorlice (8 daily; 1hr 10min); Kraków (10 daily; 2hr 10min); Krynica (every 30min; 1hr); Muszyna (5 daily; 1hr 30min); Rzeszów (1 daily; 3hr 30min); Sanok (1 daily; 3hr 15min); Warsaw (2 daily; 7hr); Zakopane (8 daily; 2hr 30min).

Przemyśl to: Jarosław (10 daily; 40min); Krosno (6 daily; 3hr); Łańcut (6 daily; 1hr 10min); Lublin (1 daily; 5hr); Rzeszów (12 daily; 1hr 40min); Sanok (5 daily; 2hr); Ustrzyki Dolne (4 daily; 3hr).

Rzeszów to: Cisna (1 daily; 3hr 15min); Krosno (every 40–50min; 1hr 30min); Łańcut (Mon–Fri 24 daily, Sat 6 daily, Sun 4 daily; 30min); Krosno (every 40–50min; 1hr 30min); Lublin (2 daily; 4hr);

Przemyśl (12 daily; 1hr 40min); Sanok (10 daily; 2hr); Ustrzyki Dolne (4 daily; 3hr 20min); Ustrzyki Górne (Mon–Fri 2 daily; Sat & Sun 1 daily; 4hr 30min); Wetlina (1 daily; 3hr 30min); Zamość (2 daily; 4hr 15min).

Sanok to: Cisna (July & Aug 8 daily, rest of year 3 daily; 2hr); Kraków (5 daily; 4hr 20min); Krosno (12 daily; 1hr); Lesko (12 daily; 25min); Przemyśl (5 daily; 2hr); Rzeszów (10 daily; 2hr); Ustrzyki Dolne (4 daily; 1hr 10min); Ustrzyki Górne (July & Aug 8 daily, Sept–June 3 daily; 2hr 30min); Wetlina (July & Aug 8 daily; Sept–June 3 daily; 2hr).

Ustrzynski Dolne to: Ustrzyki Górne (July & Aug 8 daily; Sept–June 3 daily; 1hr 20min)

Ustrzyki Górne to: Cisna (July & Aug 8 daily, Sept–June 3 daily; 45min); Kraków (July & Aug 1 daily; 6hr); Rzeszów (Mon–Fri 2 daily, Sat & Sun 1 daily; 4hr 30min); Sanok (July & Aug 8 daily, Sept–June 3 daily; 2hr 30min); Wetlina (July & Aug 8 daily; Sept–June 3 daily; 30min).

Wetlina to: Cisna (July & Aug 8 daily, Sept–June 3 daily; 15min); Sanok (July & Aug 8 daily, Sept–June 3 daily; 2hr); Ustrzyki Gorne (July & Aug 8 daily; Sept–June 3 daily; 30min).

International trains

Nowy Sącz to: Budapest (1 daily; 6hr 30min); Košice (1 daily; 3hr 30min).

Przemyśl to: Kiev (Tues, Thurs & Sat 2 daily; other days 1 daily; 12hr); L'viv (Tues, Thurs & Sat 2 daily; other days 1 daily; 4hr 30min); Odessa (1 daily; 17hr).

International buses

Przemyśl to: L'viv (6 daily; 3hr 20min).

7

Kraków and Małopolska

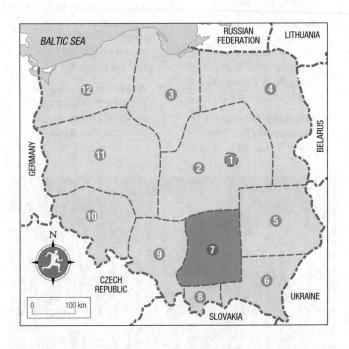

CHAPTER 7 # Highlights

* **Kraków's Old Town** One of the most wonderfully preserved old-town complexes in Europe. See p.354

* **The Wawel** Kraków's hilltop castle and cathedral was for centuries the political heart of the nation. See p.369

* **Kazimierz** The old Jewish quarter of Kraków, now the centre of a burgeoning bar scene, buzzes with visitors day and night. See p.376

* **Auschwitz-Birkenau** The infamous Nazi death camp, on the outskirts of Oświęcim, is a compelling memorial to man's inhumanity. See p.411

* **Lanckorona** Well-preserved village that demonstrates how pretty rural Poland must have been a century ago. See p.416

* **Ojców National Park** This beautiful valley of limestone crags and medieval castles makes for a great day out from Kraków. See p.417

* **Zalipie** Unique village in which traditional house-painting customs are still practiced. See p.433

▲ Wawel Castle

7

Kraków and Małopolska

The Kraków region attracts more visitors – Polish and foreign – than any other in the country. The main attraction is of course **Kraków** itself, a city that ranks with Prague and Vienna as one of the architectural gems of Central Europe. A longtime university centre, its streets are a cavalcade of churches and aristocratic palaces, while at its heart is one of the grandest of European squares, the Rynek Główny. The city's significance for Poles goes well beyond the aesthetic though, for this was the country's ancient royal capital, and has been home to many of the nation's greatest writers and artists, a tradition retained in its thriving cultural life. The Catholic Church in Poland has often looked to Kraków for guidance, and its influence in this sphere has never been greater – Pope John Paul II was archbishop of Kraków until his election in 1978. Equally important are the city's Jewish roots. Until the last war, this was one of the great Jewish centres in Europe, a past whose fabric remains clear in the old ghetto area of Kazimierz, and whose culmination is starkly enshrined at the Nazi death camps of **Auschwitz-Birkenau**, west of Kraków.

As a major transport hub Kraków serves as an ideal base from which to visit the towns and villages of **Małopolska** ("Little Poland"), an area of gently rolling lowlands which historically served as one of the heartlands of the Polish state – especially after the decline of the Piast kingdoms of Wielkopolska ("Greater Poland"; see p.533) in the west. Among the places that can be treated as easy day-trips from Kraków are the pilgrimage site of **Kalwaria Zebrzydowska**; the rustic village architecture of **Lanckorona**; and the birthplace of Pope John Paul II at **Wadowice**. The region's most handsome historic town after Kraków itself is **Tarnów**, a centuries-old market centre that stands in close proximity to two of Małopolska's most renowned folkloric sights – the village of **Zalipie** with its painted houses, and the wooden church at **Lipnica Murowana**. Further afield, the mellow main town of northern Małopolska is **Kielce**, springboard for trips to the **Paradise Cave** as well as hikes in the **Świętokrzyskie mountains**.

Kraków is also within day-trip range of several places that fall beyond the boundaries of this chapter. To the east, destinations as diverse as the palace at **Łańcut** (p.301) and the historical town of **Biecz** (p.329) are accessible by train and bus respectively; while to the south, the Tatra-mountain capital of **Zakopane** is only two hours away by road.

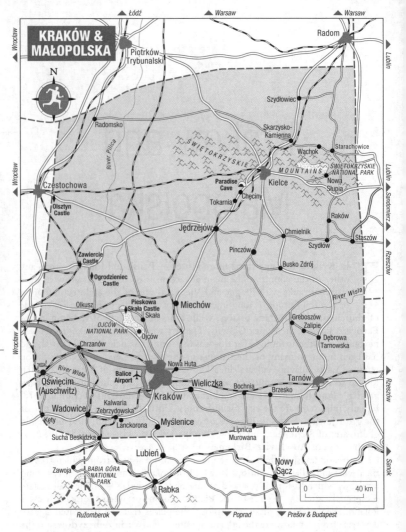

KRAKÓW & MAŁOPOLSKA

N

Łódź

Warsaw

Warsaw

Radom

Wrocław

Piotrków Trybunalski

Lublin

Szydłowiec

Radomsko

Skarżysko-Kamienna

ŚWIĘTOKRZYSKIE

Wąchok

Starachowice

MOUNTAINS

ŚWIĘTOKRZYSKIE NATIONAL PARK

River Pilica

Wrocław

Częstochowa

Paradise Cave

Kielce

Nowa Słupia

Olsztyn Castle

Tokarnia

Chęciny

Lublin

Sandomierz

Jędrzejów

Chmielnik

Raków

Staszów

Zawiercie Castle

Pinczów

Szydłów

Rzeszów

Ogrodzieniec Castle

Busko Zdrój

Olkusz

Pieskowa Skała Castle

Skała

Miechów

River Wisła

Wrocław

OJCÓW NATIONAL PARK

Ojców

Grzeboszów

Zalipie

Chrzanów

Nowa Huta

Dębrowa Tarnowska

River Wisła

Balice Airport

Wieliczka

Tarnów

Rzeszów

Oświęcim (Auschwitz)

Bochnia

Brzesko

Kalwaria Zebrzydowska

Kraków

Wadowice

Lipnica Murowana

Czchów

Kęty

Lanckorona

Myślenice

Sanok

Sucha Beskidzka

Lubień

Nowy Sącz

Zawoja

BABIA GÓRA NATIONAL PARK

Rabka

0   40 km

Ružomberok

Poprad

Prešov & Budapest

Kraków

KRAKÓW, the ancient capital of Poland and the residence of its kings for centuries, was the only major city in the country to come through World War II undamaged. The city is indeed a visual treat, with the **Wawel** one of the most striking royal residences in Europe, and the Old Town a mass of flamboyant monuments. It's a surprisingly Italianate city for this part of Europe, thanks largely to the Renaissance tastes of Poland's sixteenth-century rulers, who repeatedly lured top Italian architects north of the Alps with promises of huge bags of cash.

As a year-round city-break destination, Kraków doesn't really have a tourist season, although the place is at its prettiest in spring, summer and the depths of winter. You'll need a good two to three days to do justice to the historical centre and the Wawel; much longer if you're keen to explore the city in depth – a rich and varied urban patchwork that takes in the Jewish heritage areas of **Kazimierz** and **Podgórze**, the monasteries and parklands of the western suburbs, and the gritty Stalinist-era housing projects of **Nowa Huta**.

Some history

According to the *Polish Chronicle* penned by Wincenty Kadłubek in 1202, Kraków was founded by local strongman **Krak,** who killed the dragon of Wawel Hill by offering it animal skins stuffed with sulphur – which it duly and fatally devoured. In reality, **Slavic peoples** are known to have settled along the banks of the Wisła as early as the eighth century. Kraków's position at the junction of several east–west trade routes, including the lucrative haul to Kiev and the Black Sea, facilitated commercial development. By the end of the tenth century, it was a major market centre and had been incorporated into the emerging **Polish state**, whose early **Piast** rulers made Wawel Hill the seat of a new bishopric and eventually, in 1038, the capital of the country. Sacked by the Tatars in 1241, Kraków was rebuilt by **Prince Bolesław the Shy**, and the geometric street plan he bequeathed to the city has remained pretty much unchanged to this day.

The next great period of urban expansion occurred under **Kazimierz the Great** (1333–70), who founded a **university** here in 1364 – the oldest in Central Europe after Prague – and removed restrictions on Jewish settlement, paving the way for the growth of a thriving **Jewish community**. The advent of the Renaissance heralded Kraków's emergence as an important European centre of learning, its most famous student (at least, according to local claims) being the young **Nicolaus Copernicus**.

King Sigismund III Waza's decision to move the capital to Warsaw in 1596, following the Union of Poland and Lithuania, was a major blow. The fact that royal coronations (and burials) continued to take place on Wawel for some time after was little compensation for a significant loss of status. Kraków went into decline, a process accelerated by plague in 1652 and Swedish occupation in 1655–57.

Following the **Partitions**, and a brief period as an independent city state, Kraków was eventually incorporated into the **Austrian** province of Galicia. Habsburg rule was comparatively liberal – especially after Galicia gained a measure of autonomy in 1868 – and Kraków (in contrast to Russian-dominated Warsaw) enjoyed more or less untrammelled intellectual freedom. The city became a hotbed of underground political activity: **Józef Piłsudski** began recruiting the avowedly nationalist Polish Legion here prior to World War I, and from 1912 to 1914 Kraków was **Lenin**'s base for directing the international communist movement. Kraków also became a major centre of the arts. Painter **Jan Matejko** produced many of his stirring paeans to Polishness during his residency as art professor at the Jagiellonian University, and the city was centre of **Młoda Polska** (Young Poland; see box, p.364) – an Art Nouveau-inspired movement which drew in virtually every creative spirit who happened to be around town at the time.

The brief interlude of independence following World War I ended for Kraków in September 1939 when the **Nazis** designated it the city capital of the so-called General Government, which covered all those Polish territories not directly annexed to the Reich. Governor Hans Frank moved into the royal castle on Wawel Hill, from where he exercised a reign of unbridled terror, presaged by the arrest and deportation of professors from the Jagiellonian University in November 1939. The elimination of Kraków's Jewish community, most of whom perished in the death camps, soon followed.

The main event of the immediate postwar years was the construction of the vast **Nowa Huta steelworks** a few miles to the east of the city, a daunting symbol

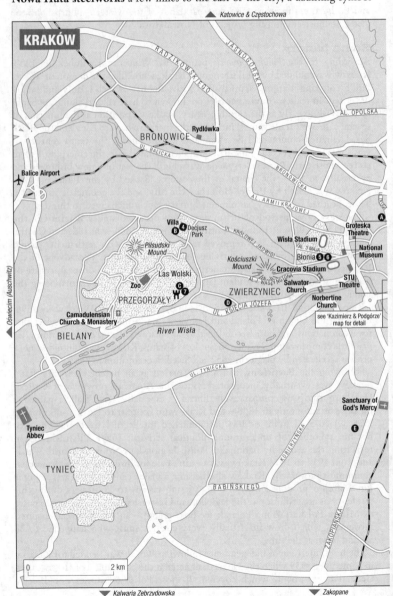

of the communist determination to replace Kraków's Catholic, intellectually oriented past with a bright new industrial future. The plan did not succeed: the peasant population pulled in to construct and then work in the steel mills never became the loyal, anti-religious proletariat that the communist party hoped for. Non-communist intellectual life continued to thrive in any case, thanks in large part to the publication of *Tygodnik Powszechny*, a Kraków Catholic weekly which was then the only independent newspaper in Eastern Europe. Kraków's

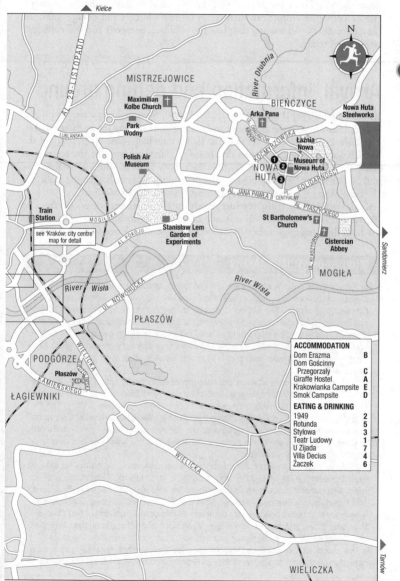

reputation as a centre of conservative Catholicism was enhanced by the election of **Pope John Paul II** in 1978, who until then had been archbishop of Kraków.

Nowa Huta also had an unforseen environmental impact on the city, with atmospheric **pollution** wreaking havoc on the fine old facades of the centre – prompting the Polish government to declare Kraków an "ecological disaster area" in the 1970s. A thorough clean-up operation in the 1990s gave the city's historic buildings a new sheen and reduced air pollution to negligible levels. Since the fall of communism in 1989, the city has been transformed by the rapid rise of consumer culture, an increase in tourist numbers and a huge influx of foreign students – all lending the place the youthful, energetic and self-confident air one sees today.

Arrival, information and getting around

Kraków's John Paul II **airport** (☎012/295 5800, ⓦ www.krakowairport.pl) is at Balice, 15km west of the city, and handles both domestic and international flights. Catch the courtesy bus (or walk) to the Balice train halt, some 600m south of the arrivals hall, from where trains depart every thirty minutes for the main train station, Kraków Główny (6zł; pay the conductor). Taxis are always available, too, and cost anything between 60 and 90zł depending on your bargaining skills and the time of day – fares rise by fifty percent between 11pm and 5am.

Kraków Główny train station stands on the northern fringes of the Old Town and is within walking distance of central sights and hotels. There is a 24-hour **left-luggage** office (*przechowalnia bagażu*; 5zł per item) outside the

MOVING ON FROM KRAKÓW

Kraków's John Paul II **airport** (☎012/295 5800, ⓦ www.krakowairport.pl) enjoys direct connections with numerous cities in the UK and Western Europe, as well as Chicago in the USA. The airport is served by regular trains from Kraków Główny station (6zł). The international terminal has a self-service restaurant and a handful of cafes, but shopping opportunities are limited so stock up on souvenirs before you get there. The domestic terminal (currently only serving Warsaw) is 400m east of the international terminal, and is a much smaller affair with correspondingly fewer facilities.

Kraków Główny **train station** provides services to pretty much all of Poland's cities. There are also daily trains to Berlin (1 daily; 10hr), Budapest (2 daily; 9–10hr), Kiev (1 daily; 20hr; sleeping-car reservations compulsory), Prague (2 daily; 7hr–8hr 30min) and Vienna (2 daily; 6hr 30min-7hr 30min). International tickets have to be purchased from the special counters at the far end of the ticket hall – there are frequently long queues here in summer. Be aware that the ticket hall is a long walk from the platforms themselves.

The **bus station** (dworzec autobusowy; ⓦ www.rda.krakow.pl), on the far side of the tracks from Kraków Główny and accessible by pedestrian underpass, covers most destinations in southern Poland. There are also services to Lwów, Bratislava, and most western European capitals. Note that long queues for tickets, especially at weekends and public holidays, are common. Buses depart from one of two storeys – the upper storey (marked as "G" or "górny" on signs and tickets) is on the same level as the ticket hall; the lower storey (marked as "D" or "dolny") is down the stairs.

The much smaller **minibus station** on ulica Pawia offers express routes to a selection of destinations in the vicinity of Kraków, notably Kielce and Lanckorona.

main ticket hall, and lockers in the subway leading to the platforms (4–8zł depending on size).

The main **bus station** (Regionalny Dworzec Autobusowy or RDA; Ⓦwww .rda.krakow.pl) is just east of the train station – to which it is connected by underground walkway. There is an ATM in the ticket hall and luggage lockers (4–16zł depending on size).

Arriving by car, major roads from all directions are well signposted, though once in the centre you'll need to cope with heavily enforced zonal **parking restrictions**, with the risk of wheel clamps on illegally parked vehicles. There's a conveniently placed **guarded car park** just behind Staro-wiślna 13, a five-minute walk southeast of the centre, but it soon fills up.

Information

The **municipal tourist office** (Mon–Fri 8am–8pm, Sat & Sun 9am–5pm; ℡012/430 2646, Ⓦwww.krakow.pl) operates information booths at three central locations: the circular pavilion in the Planty near the train station underpass; the Town Hall Tower on Rynek Główny; and the Wyspiański 2000 Pavilion on plac Wszystkich Świętych. Each has a stock of brochures listing accommodation and attractions or covering historical themes. The **Cultural Information Centre**, ul. św. Jana 2 (Centrum Informacji Kulturalnej: Mon–Fri 10am–7pm, Sat 11am–7pm; ℡012/421 1787), handles information and tickets for cultural events.

The monthly Karnet Kraków booklet (6zł; available in most city-centre bookshops; Ⓦwww.karnet.krakow.pl) is a good source of cinema, concert and theatre **listings** in English. Those who can read Polish, will find the listings in the Friday *Co jest Grane* supplement of daily newspaper *Gazeta Wyborcza* more up-to-the-minute.

Getting around

Central Kraków is compact enough to get around **on foot**, although the efficient municipal transport network (MPK), consisting of trams and buses, comes in handy if you're visiting attractions in the suburbs. Regular routes operate from about 5am until 11pm, after which night buses operate selected routes at one-hour intervals.

Tickets valid for daytime tram and bus services are purchased at kiosks and shops displaying the MPK symbol, or from the driver for a 0.50zł surcharge. You can buy single tickets valid for one journey (2.40zł); 24-hour tickets (10zł); 48-hour tickets (18zł); or 72-hour tickets (24zł). Unless you have one of the one-, two- or three-day tickets, you'll need a separate ticket to travel on night buses (5zł). Bear in mind that public transport is subject to regular price hikes, so expect changes. Remember to punch your ticket at both ends on entering the bus or tram – if you're caught without a valid ticket, you'll be fined 40zł on the spot. Annoyingly, large pieces of luggage (including backpacks) require their own individual ticket (holders of one-, two- or three-day tickets are exempt from this); failure to follow this arcane regulation will incur another fine.

Taxis cost around 6zł initial charge, followed by 3zł per kilometre. Remember to make sure that the driver turns on the meter, and note that from 11pm to 5am rates go up by half. There are ranks around the centre of town at plac św. Ducha, Mały Rynek, plac Dominikański, plac Szczepański, plac Wszystkich Świętych, ulica Sienna (roughly opposite the main post office) and at the main train station. Calling a radio taxi, such as Wawel Taxi (℡0800 666 666) or ExpresTaxi (℡0800 111 111), can work out significantly cheaper. There's a special subsidized taxi service for people with disabilities, using a small fleet of **minibuses** adapted for **wheelchair access** (6am–10pm; ☎9633 or 644 5555).

A fleet of four- to six-seater **golf carts** is permanently lined up on the north-eastern side of the main square, ready to take visitors on tours of the city (usually incorporating the Old Town, Kazimierz and Podgórze; expect to pay 120zł for 30min; 200zł for 60min). They will also ferry passengers taxi-like to destinations around the city centre although you will need to agree on a price beforehand.

Several outlets around town rent out **bikes** – a useful way of getting around the Old Town where heavy traffic is scarce. Expect to pay 6–8zł per hr, and anything from 40–70zł per day; weekend rates can be more expensive.

Accommodation

There's an impressive choice of **hotels** in Kraków, with many establishments occupying characterful old buildings in and around the Old Town. However **prices** are more expensive here than in most other Polish cities, with the majority of city-centre hotels of three-star-status and above charging 400zł a night and upwards. Cheaper rates are frequently available if you search the internet for special offers.

Decent mid-range accommodation is provided by a growing number of guest-houses offering **B&B** services in central locations (with doubles costing in the region of 180–300zł), and there is a plethora of downtown **hostels** offering self-contained double rooms for 160–180zł as well as bunk-bed dorm accom-modation for around 50–70zł per person. There is also a growing number of self-catering **apartments** in the city, sleeping anything from two to six people – an ideal solution for those travelling as a family or small group of friends.

All the accommodation prices listed below are for the high season (May–Sept); in many cases rates drop by fifteen to thirty percent outside this period.

Apartments

There's an increasing number of **apartments**, equipped with modern furnish-ings and kitchenette, being offered to both short- and long-term visitors in and around the Old Town. Agencies offering a wide choice of accommodation in good locations include Affinity Flats, ul. Karmelicka 7 (☎012/428 7200, Ⓦwww.affinityflats.com); Sodispar, ul. Lubelska 12 (☎012/631 2631, Ⓦwww.sodispar.pl) and Old Town Apartments, ul. Gołębia 2/3b (☎012/421 4201, Ⓦwww.warsawshotel.com). Prices range from about 180–250zł per night for a one- or two-person studio to 300–700zł for a three- or four-person flat – rates drop dramatically the longer you stay.

Campsites

There's a modest handful of suburban **campsites** in Kraków and, although they're several kilometres from the centre, all are well-served by public transport.

Krakowianka ul. Żywiecka Boczna 2 ☎012/268 1133, Ⓦwww.krakowianka.com.pl. Tranquil suburban site next to the wooded Solvay park, just off the Zakopane road 6km south of town. The Solvay shopping mall is a 5min walk away, but there's nothing else of sightseeing or recreational interest in this part of town. 15zł per person, 10zł per vehicle, 15–20zł per tent or caravan. Tram #8 from pl. Wszystkich Świętych. May–Sept.

Smok ul. Kamedulska 18 ☎012/429 7266. Privately run site 4km west of town on the main Oświęcim road, well-signed in both direc-tions. In a pleasant suburban setting with plenty of greenery round about, and within walking distance of both Las Wolski and Zwierzyniec. Buses #109, #209, #229, #239 and #249 from

Salwator stop off 100m east of the campsite access road. Open all year.

Hostels

There's a dense concentration of hostels in both the Old Town and the Kazimerz district, and you shouldn't have to stray beyond these central areas in order to find a bed.

Old Town and around

Hostels in this section are marked on the "Kraków: City Centre" map on p.356.

City Hostel ul. św Krzyża 21 ☎012/426 1815, ⓦwww.cityhostel.pl. Handily located on the train-station side of the Old Town, *City* consists of a couple of large functional dorms and a high proportion of self-contained doubles – most of which have en-suite shower (although WCs are in the hallway). Free computer terminals in the common room, and simple breakfast in the wooden-beamed attic. Doubles ⑤; dorm beds from 50zł.

Flamingo ul. Szewska 4 ☎012/422 0000, ⓦwww.flamingo-hostel.com. Right on top of the bar-hopping district but still reasonably relaxing and quiet, *Flamingo* offers the usual mixture of big-size dorms plus a couple of self-contained quads and doubles. There's a spacious kitchen and sitting room, free internet terminals, wi-fi access and a washing machine. Doubles ⑤; dorm beds from 50–75zł depending on room size.

Gardenhouse ul. Floriańska 5 ☎012/431 2824, ⓦwww.gardenhousehostel.com. Plain but comfortable hostel within flowerpot-throwing distance of the main square, offering bunk-bed accommodation in 4- to 6-bed dorms with a couple of self-contained doubles. There's a fully-equipped kitchen-cum-common room, although the plant-stocked patio is where you will probably want to do most of your hanging out. Free use of washing machine. Doubles ⑤; dorm beds from 60zł.

Giraffe ul. Krowoderska 31 ☎012/ , ⓦwww.hostelgiraffe.com. A short stroll from the northern limits of the Old Town, *Giraffe* is perfect for social animals, with a huge all-day bar and a separate kitchen-lounge. A brace of self-contained doubles apart, accommodation comes in the form of 6- to 8-person dorms, each with high ceilings and bright colour schemes. Wi-fi coverage throughout. Doubles ⑤; dorm beds from 45zł.

🏃 **Greg & Tom Hostel** ul. Pawia 12/7 ☎012/422 4100, ⓦwww.gregtomhostel.com. Bright and cheerful apartment block opposite the train station offering backpacker accommodation without the rough edges. Expect modern 6-bed dorms and parquet-floored doubles decked out in snazzy textiles. There's a gleaming communal kitchen, and as well as buffet breakfast there's a free buffet "supper" in the early evening. Wi-fi access throughout and a few computer terminals for guests to use. Doubles ⑤; dorm beds 50–60zł.

🏃 **Mundo** ul. Sarego 10 ⓦ012/422 6113, ⓦwww.mundohostel.eu. Tucked away in a calm courtyard midway between the Old Town and Kazimierz, this is another classy and comfortable hostel with a good mix of doubles and dorms decked out in ethnic textiles, hardwood floors and bathroom facilities that look as if they've jumped straight out of a design magazine. Relaxing kitchen-cum-lounge features a free internet terminal, and there's a decent-sized breakfast. Doubles ⑤; dorm beds 60–65zł.

Kazimierz and around

Hostels in this section are marked on the "Kazimierz & Podgórze" map on p.378.

Good Bye Lenin ul. Berka Joselewicza ☎012/421 2030, ⓦwww.goodbyelenin.pl. Hidden in a quiet corner of Kazimierz, this hostel is much more of a heavyweight than its jokey name might suggest. The spacious high-ceilinged townhouse accommodates a good mixture of rooms, with four doubles, two quads, and a range of dorms sleeping from 6 to 10. With the odd bit of socialist-influenced fresco on the walls, a guests-only bar full of sofas, and a small garden, it's a comfortable but fun place to stay. Guests can use kitchen facilities and washing machine. Doubles ⑤; dorm beds from 45zł.

Honey Miodowa 2/10 ☎012/431 2834, ⓦwww.honeyhostel.com. Simple but welcoming hostel on the first floor of a nineteenth-century apartment block, with a couple of 6- to 8-bed dorms, two triples, and a pair of double rooms which – while being somewhat on the small side – do come with the relative luxuries of a sink and a small TV. Bright happy colours, a relaxing common room, wi-fi access and free use of a washing machine are *Honey's* other main attributes. Doubles ④; dorm beds 45–55zł.

Momotown ul. Miodowa 28 ☎012/429 6929 and 509/429 648, 🌐www.momotownhostel.com. Two-storey building in a central Kazimerz location, offering fairly plain dorms (ranging in size from 10-bed to 4-bed) and plenty of doubles in a separate building round the corner on ul. Szeroka. Stairwells are wallpapered with back issues of the New Yorker – once you've stopped reading these, head for the upstairs kitchen-common room with TV and a small bar, or play table football in the downstairs sitting room. Doubles ❺; dorm beds 50–60zł.

Nathan's Villa ul. św Agnieszki 1 ☎012/422 3545, 🌐www.nathansvilla.com. Big, busy, buzzing hostel with over one hundred beds in two neighbouring buildings. There's a handful of doubles, and dorms ranging in size from 4- to

10-bed. Selling points are the cellar bar (complete with snooker, hookah pipes and small cinema), and back-garden barbeques in the early evening. Wi-fi coverage throughout. Doubles ❺; dorm beds from 60zł.

Secret Garden ul. Skawińska 7 ☎012/430 5445 and 0515/198 538, 🌐www.thesecretgarden.pl. Spacious, bright and cheerful hostel on a quiet street which aims to provide hotel-like standards at hostel prices – there's a high proportion of double and triple rooms, although none of them are en-suite. There's a roomy kitchen, a swish first-floor TV lounge, and a front yard brightened up by pot plants. Bikes can be rented for 25zł/day. Doubles ❹, triples 180zł, beds in 5-bunk dorms 45zł per person.

Hotels and B&Bs

There are hotels of every shape and size in the Old Town, and a clutch of charac-terful establishments in the Kazimierz district. You shouldn't need to look much further afield than this, unless you have a burning desire to stay in the wooded western suburbs.

Old Town

Hotels in this section are marked on the "Kraków: City Centre" map on p.356.

Amadeus ul. Mikołajska 20 ☎012/429 6070, 🌐www.hotel-amadeus.pl. Highly rated four-star in a fine old mansion, with orangey-pink colour schemes, classy furniture and impeccable standards of service. ❽

Andel's ul. Pawia 3 ☎012/660 0250, 🌐www.andelscracow.com. Facing the Old Town from the plaza outside the train station, this large concrete wedge is certainly an eye-pleaser on the inside, offering rooms with tasty chocolate, cream and purple colour schemes, flat-screen TVs and big windows – although the regular doubles are not particularly spacious and most feature showers rather than bathtubs. There are plenty of lounge-style bar and restaurant areas to hang around in, plus sauna and gym in the basement. Wi-fi access costs a few złoty extra. ❽

Campanile ul. św. Tomasza 34 ☎012/424 2600, 🌐www.campanile.com.pl. Modern building belonging to the French-run chain, offering smallish but tidy en suites, each with tea/coffee-making facilities. Good location on the northeastern edge of the Old Town beside the Planty. ❼

Copernicus ul. Kanonicza 16 ☎012/424 3400, 🌐www.hotel.com.pl. Medium-sized luxury hotel occupying a carefully renovated historic building on a quaint, cobbled street. Spacious rooms

and high standards of service – plus a small swimming pool in the basement. Not all rooms have bathtubs, so do ask if you're particular about such things. ❾

Elektor ul. Szpitalna 28 ☎012/423 2317, 🌐www.hotelelektor.com.pl. Atmospheric old town house in a fine central location, offering swish apartment-style rooms with retro furnishings, wi-fi access and all mod cons. Studio apartments in the hotel annexe (round the corner on św Marka; ❻) are more simply furnished but do come with kitchenette. ❼

Floryan ul. Floriańska 38 ☎012/431 1418, 🌐www.floryan.com.pl. Small hotel offering very stylish downtown rooms with modern furnishings. Recommended if you want a change from the faded glories on offer elsewhere. ❼–❽

Francuski ul. Pijarska 13 ☎012/627 3777, 🌐www.orbisonline.pl. Elegant, comfortable old hotel, recently renovated though still retaining some of its retro feel. A well-established favourite with upmarket travellers. ❽

Gródek ul. Na Gródku 4 ☎012/431 9030, 🌐www.donimirski.com. Intimate luxury hotel in a medieval town house, offering rooms with warm colours, smart bathrooms and characterful furniture – you're more likely to get an old-style bureau in your room than a plain desk. Apartments (from 1030zł) come with plush sitting rooms and wide-screen TVs – reserve the "Chinese room" if you want oriental-style décor and an en-suite sauna.

La Fontaine ul. Sławkowska 1 ☎012/422 6564, ⓦwww.bblafontaine.com. Located on the attic floor of an apartment block, with cute en-suites, bright red colour schemes, small TVs and electric kettles, and a handful of family-sized apartments (420–660zł). There's a small communal kitchen, and a washing machine you can use for a few extra złotys. Breakfast is served five flights of steps below, in the cellar-bound *La Fontaine* restaurant. ⑥

Maltański ul. Straszewskiego 14 ☎012/431 0010, ⓦwww.donimirski.com. Top-quality hotel with an intimate, pension-like feel. Rooms have a nice blend of modern and traditional furnishings and come with TV, video and minibar – and most of the bathrooms have tubs. ⑨

Monopol ul. św. Gertrudy 6 ☎012/422 7666, ⓦwww.rthotels.pl. A good, well-maintained mid-range choice. Even if the corridors are a little gloomy, the rooms come with warm colours. ⑧

Pałac Bonerowski ul. Św. Jana 1 ☎012/374 1300, ⓦwww.palacbonerowski.pl. Much-restored fifteenth-century town house that once belonged to the Boner family (Swiss merchants favoured by King Sigismund the Old) and now containing spacious rooms with swanky bathrooms, flat-screen TVs and all other creature comforts. Some of the smarter doubles and suites overlook the main square. Otherwise the multi-tiered chandelier in the spiral staircase is a major feature – go to the top and look down for the full effect. ⑨

Pod Różą ul. Floriańska 14 ☎012/424 3300, ⓦwww.hotel.com.pl. A hotel since the seventeenth century (and with a guest list that includes Balzac and Liszt), the much-renovated Pod Różą lives up to its pedigree with four floors of spacious rooms, each featuring swish bathrooms and important-looking leather furniture. There are several apartments (800–1600zł), including several swanky open-plan affairs with bathtubs a hop away from the double beds. ⑨

Pollera ul. Szpitalna 30 ☎012/422 1044, ⓦwww.pollera.com.pl. Charming, increasingly popular hotel with good central location and Art Nouveau decor – notably the original Wyspiański stained-glass window in the foyer. Mixed bag of old-fashioned, parquet-floored rooms and modern, carpeted ones. ⑧

PTTK Wyspiański ul. Westerplatte 15 ☎012/422 9566, ⓦwww.hotel-wyspianski.pl. Grim-looking grey high rise which is much nicer inside than out, with thoroughly modern, en-suite rooms decorated in warm colours. ⑦

Orient Ekspres ul. Stolarska 13 ☎012/422 6672, ⓦwww.rooms.krakow.pl. Neat, pine-furnished rooms overlooking a courtyard behind the *Orient*

Ekspres restaurant (see p.400). All rooms are en suite with small TV; some studio-sized doubles feature kitchenettes. ⑤–⑥

Saski ul. Sławkowska 3 ☎012/421 4222, ⓦwww.hotelsaski.com.pl. Art Nouveau-era building (and featuring an old cage-lift still in working order) in a central location with comfy rooms furnished with a mixture of old and new. En suites with TV, as well as rooms with shared facilities. ⑦–⑧

🎿 **Stary** ul. Szczepańska 5 ☎012/384 0808, ⓦwww.hotel.com.pl. Fifteenth-century merchant's house just off the main square melding original bare-stone features with resolutely modern furnishings. High-ceilinged rooms come with flat-screen TVs, sleek black armchairs and slinky designer bathrooms. As well as saunas, salt inhalation room and gym, there's a small but spectacular swimming pool located in the brick-arched cellar. ⑨

🎿 **Tango House** ul. Szpitalna 4 ☎012/429 3114, ⓦwww.tangohouse.pl. Hidden in a secluded courtyard just round the corner from the main square, *Tango* is a B&B of two halves: the old part has a spectacular nineteenth-century staircase and parquet-floored en suites in soothing citrus colours; while the new part houses smart studios (⑦) with kitchenettes. All rooms come with flat-screen TV and electric kettle. Wi-fi coverage on the ground floor. ⑥

Wentzl Rynek Główny 19 ☎012/430 2665, ⓦwww.wentzl.pl. Intimate, twelve-room hotel above a well-known restaurant, offering spacious rooms with parquet floors, classy rugs and – in some cases – direct views onto the main square. ⑨

Wit Stwosz ul. Mikołajska 28 ☎012/429 6026, ⓦwww.wit-stwosz.com.pl. Bright, comfortable rooms in a historic house, just off the Mały Rynek. Good price for the quality and location. ⑦

Kazimierz and Podgórze

Hostels in this section are marked on the "Kazimierz & Podgórze" map on p.378.

Alef ul. św Agnieszki 5 ☎012/424 3131, ⓦwww.alef.pl. With corridors and stairwells packed with paintings, this is something of a temple to twentieth-century Polish art. Rooms themselves are more prosaic, featuring a strange mix of careworn furniture, adequate bathrooms and small TVs – although there are a couple of "high standard" doubles that mix antique furnishings with flat-screen TVs, a/c and modern bathrooms. Wi-fi access on the lower floors. ⑥–⑦

Eden ul. Ciemna 15 ☎012/430 6565, ⓦwww.hoteleden.pl. Cosy late medieval building with plush, tastefully decorated rooms, staff that pay good attention to detail, and authentic Judaica scattered around the place. ❼

Karmel ul. Kupa 15 ☎012/430 6697, ⓦwww .karmel.com.pl. Medium-sized hotel with high-ceilinged rooms with hardwood floors, soothing fabrics, TV, and a/c. Cable internet connection for your laptop. Breakfast in the Mediterranean-themed ground-floor restaurant. ❼

🏃 **Klezmer-Hois** ul. Szeroka 6 ☎012/411 1245 & 411 1622, ⓦwww.klezmer .pl. Characterful 10-room hotel in a rambling old house, furnished with some choice retro pieces from various past epochs. Rooms on the top floor feature sloping attic ceilings and the kind of stripy wallpaper you last saw in a costume drama. Some rooms have WC & shower in the hallway, but don't let that put you off. ❻–❼

🏃 **Kolory** ul. Estery 10 ☎012/421 0465, ⓦwww.kolory.com.pl. Bright en-suite rooms above the *Kolory* café (see p.403), all with TV and folk-style design details and wi-fi coverage. Some rooms overlook the lively plac Nowy; marginally quieter rooms are at the back. ❺

Qubus ul. Nadwiślańska 6 ☎012/374 5100, ⓦwww.qubushotel.com. Right by the riverside and a short walk across the bridge from Kazimierz, this large, modern, business-oriented hotel is slightly lacking in atmosphere, but does offer high-quality service and a wealth of on-site facilities including wi-fi access, gym and small top-floor pool. ❽

The suburbs

Hotels in this section are marked on the "Kraków" map on p.346

Dom Erazma ul. 28 lipca 7A ☎012/625 4142, ⓦwww.erazm.pl. Soothing, 12-room hotel decked out in pastel shades, 5km out of the centre in leafy suburban streets on the northeastern fringes of Las Wolski forest. Cosy attic rooms with half-moon windows are worth reserving in advance. Bus #152 from ul. Basztowa. ❼

Dom Gościnny Przegorzały ul. Jodłowa 13 ☎012/429 7115, ⓦwww.adm.uj.edu .pl/dg/przegorz. Eighties' vintage student accommodation now open to all comers. Rooms come with parquet floors and bright colour schemes; most also have TV and bathtubs. Idyllically located on the edge of Las Wolski forest, but a 15min bus ride out of town – #209, #229, #239 and #249 from Salwator go past the access road. ❺

The City

The heart of the city centre is the Old Town (Stare Miasto), bordered by the lush, tree-shaded city park known as the **Planty**. The **Rynek Główny** is the focal point, with almost everything within half an hour's walk of it. A broad network of streets stretches south from here to the edge of **Wawel Hill**, with its royal residence, and beyond to the Jewish quarter of **Kazimierz**. Across the river, the suburb of **Podgórze** was the site of the wartime ghetto, and is within striking distance of the concentration camp at **Płaszów**. Further out to the west, the green cone of the **Kościuszko Mound** (Kopiec Kościuszki) and the attractive woodland of **Las Wolski** provide the targets for strollers and cyclists. Connoisseurs of megalomaniac urban planning will not want to miss **Nowa Huta**, the Stalinist model suburb 7km to the northeast.

The Old Town

The compact grid of medieval streets that makes up Kraków's **Old Town** is centred on the set-piece square of **Rynek Główny**, a huge expanse of flagstones, ringed by magnificent houses and towering spires. Long the marketplace and commercial hub of the city, it's an immediate introduction to Kraków's grandeur and stateliness. By day the square hums with crowds and commercial bustle, its size such that no matter how much is going on, you're never left feeling cramped for space. Architecturally the square is pretty much unchanged since its *fin-de-siècle* heyday, boasting as fine a collection of period buildings as any in Central Europe and beyond. This, combined with echoes of the events played out here, such as the Prussian Prince Albrecht of Hohenzollern's act of homage

▲ Rynek Główny

to Sigismund the Old in 1525 (see p.358) or Kościuszko's impassioned rallying call to the defence of national independence in 1794 (see box, pp.390–391), provides an endlessly renewable source of interest and inspiration. Once hooked, you'll find yourself constantly gravitating back towards the place. It's also worth exploring the stately network of passageways and Italianate courtyards leading off the square, many of them enlivened by shops, cafés and bars.

The Sukiennice

Dominating the Rynek from its central position, the medieval **Sukiennice** is one of the most distinctive sights in the country – a vast cloth hall built in the fourteenth century and remodelled in the 1550s, when an undulating facade topped with gargoyles was added to the upper storey by Florentine stonemason Santi Gucci (c.1530–1600). Its commercial traditions are perpetuated by a **covered market**, which bustles with tourists and street sellers at almost any time of year. Inside, the stalls of the darkened central arcade display a hotch-potch collection of tourist tat and genuine craft items from the Podhale region. Popular buys include amber jewellery, painted boxes in every shape and size and thick woollen sweaters from the mountains. The colonnades on either side of the Sukiennice were added in the late nineteenth century in an attempt to smarten

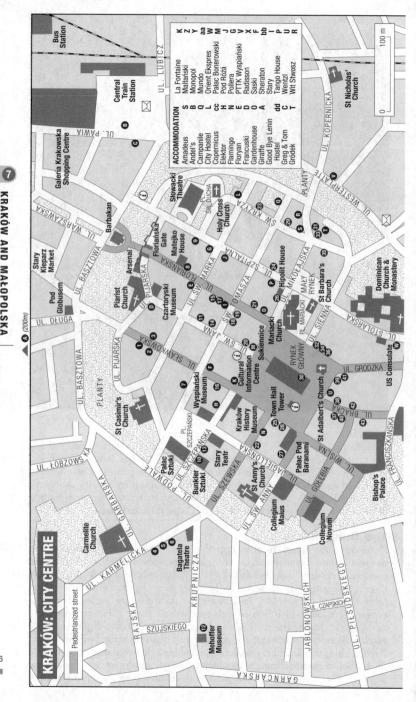

KRAKÓW: CITY CENTRE

Pedestrianized street

ACCOMMODATION			
Amadeus	S	La Fontaine	K
Andel's	B	Maltański	Z
Campanile	Q	Monopol	Y
City Hostel	L	Mundo	aa
Copernicus	cc	Orient Ekspres	W
Elektor	H	Pałac Bonerowski	M
Flamingo	E	Pod Różą	J
Floryan	D	Pollera	G
Francuski	O	PTTK Wyspiański	X
Gardenhouse	A	Radisson	F
Giraffe		Saski	bb
Good Bye Lenin		Sheraton	I
Hostel	dd	Stary	P
Greg & Tom		Tango House	U
Hostel	C	Wentzl	
Gródek	T	Wit Stwosz	R

Bus Station

Central Train Station

Galeria Krakowska Shopping Centre

Stary Kleparz Market

Barbakan

Słowacki Theatre

Holy Cross Church

Florianska Gate

Matejko House

Arsenal

Piarist Church

Czartoryski Museum

Pod Globusem

St Casimir's Church

Wyspiański Museum

Kraków History Museum

Cultural Information Centre

Sukiennice

Mariacki Church

Hipolit House

Mały Rynek

St Barbara's Church

Dominican Church & Monastery

St Nicholas' Church

Town Hall Tower

RYNEK GŁÓWNY

St Adalbert's Church

US Consulate

Palac Sztuki

Bunkier Sztuki

Stary Teatr

St Anny's Church

Pałac Pod Baranami

Collegium Maius

Collegium Novum

Bishop's Palace

Carmelite Church

Bagatela Theatre

Mehoffer Museum

ST WESTERPLATTE

ST KOPERNICKA

0   100 m

UL. LUBICZ
UL. PAWIA
UL. WARSZAWSKA
UL. BASZTOWA
UL. DŁUGA
UL. PIJARSKA
UL. ŚW. MARKA
UL. ŚW. JANA
UL. ŚW. TOMASZA
UL. SZPITALNA
UL. ŚW. KRZYŻA
UL. MIKOŁAJSKA
UL. SIENNA
UL. STOLARSKA
UL. GRODZKA
UL. BRACKA
UL. WIŚLNA
UL. GOŁĘBIA
UL. ŚW. ANNY
UL. JAGIELLOŃSKA
UL. SZEWSKA
UL. SZCZEPAŃSKA
PL. SZCZEPAŃSKI
UL. ŁOBZOWSKA
UL. PODWALE
UL. GARBARSKA
UL. KARMELICKA
RAJSKA
SZUJSKIEGO
KRUPNICZA
UL. FRANCISZKAŃSKA
JABŁONOWSKICH
UL. CZAPSKICH
UL. PIŁSUDSKIEGO
GARNCARSKA
PLANTY
UL. FLORIAŃSKA
UL. SŁAWKOWSKA
UL. ŚW. MARKA
RYNEK MARIACKI
MAŁY RYNEK

(200m)

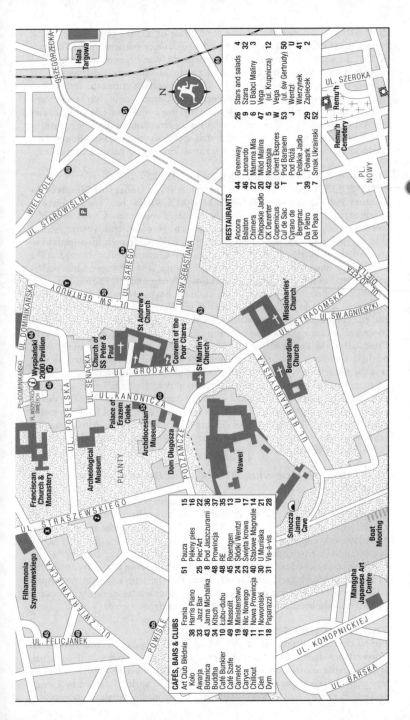

RESTAURANTS

Ancora	44	Greenway	26	Stars and salads	4
Balaton	46	Leonardo	9	Szara	32
Chimera	27	Mamma Mia	6	U Babci Maliny	3
Chłopskie Jadło	20	Miód Malina	47	Vega	12
CK Dezerter	42	Nostalgia	5	(ul. Krupnicza)	
Copernicus	T	Orient Ekspres	W	Vega	50
Cul de Sac	53	Pod Baranem	cc	(ul. św Gertrudy)	
Cyrano de	1	Pod Różą	J	Wentzl	41
Bergerac		Polskie Jadło	39	Wierzynek	2
Da Pietro		Folwark	29	Zapiecek	52
Del Papa	7	Smak Ukrainski			

CAFÉS, BARS & CLUBS

Art Club Błędne		Frania	15	Pauza	51
Koło		Harris Piano	16	Piękny pies	38
Awaria		Jazz Bar	22	Piec' Art	33
Botanica		Jama Michalika	36	Pod Jaszczurami	43
Buddha		Kitsch	37	Prowincja	8
Café Bunkier		Łubu-dubu	35	RE	48
Café Szafe		Massolit	45	Roentgen	48
Camelot		Ministerstwo	13	Słódki Wentzl	U
Caryca		Nic Nowego	24	Święta krowa	19
Chillout		Nowa Prowincja	23	Stalowe Magnolie	17
Cień		Noworolski	11	U Muniaka	14
Dym		Paparazzi	11	Vis-à-vis	21
			18		28

Filharmonia
Szymanowskiego

Franciscan
Church &
Monastery

Wyspiański
2000 Pavilion

Church of
SS Peter &
Paul

St Andrew's
Church

Convent of the
Poor Clares

St Martin's
Church

Missionaries'
Church

Archeological
Museum

Palace of
Erazem
Ciołek

Archidiocesan
Museum

Dom Długosza

Wawel

Bernardine
Church

Smocza
Jama
Cave

Boat
Mooring

Manggha
Japanese Art
Centre

Hala
Targowa

Remu'h
Cemetery

Remu'h

PL.
NOWY

PLANTY

PODZAMCZE

up the Rynek and provide a home for a brace of elegant terrace cafés, most famous of which is the **Noworolski** on the Sukiennice's eastern side. The centre of Kraków social life in the years before World War I (Lenin was one of the more famous regulars), the café boasted a series of sumptuously decorated Art Nouveau salons, of which one – with a separate entrance from the rest – was a ladies'-only tearoom. The café was turned into a German-only club by the Nazis in 1939, but resumed its status as Kraków's prime coffee-and-cakes venue after the war. Many of the *belle époque* interiors were renovated in the 1990s, making it well worth a visit (see p.402) – although the locals who used to idle away the afternoon over tea and *sernik* have been almost entirely replaced by tourists.

The Gallery of Nineteenth-Century Polish Art

Occupying the upper floors of the Sukiennice is the **Gallery of Nineteenth-Century Polish Art** (Galeria Sztuki Polskiej XIX Wieku: daily 10am–6pm; 8zł; entrance from the eastern side), a no-holds-barred collection of national heavyweights which carries a strong patriotic punch. Nowhere is this more evident than in *Torches of Nero*, the canvas donated by painter **Henryk Siemiradzki** to start off the collection in 1879. Showing early Christians being burned at the stake for the entertainment of the Roman Emperor, it was always understood by contemporaries to be a metaphor for Polish suffering under foreign rulers.

National themes are even more explicit in the huge canvases of **Jan Matejko**: occupying a whole wall of the gallery is his *Homage of Prussia*, recording the real-life (and highly symbolic) oath of fealty made by Albrecht of Hohenzollern to sixteenth-century Polish King Sigismund the Old in Kraków's main square. Presented to the Polish nation by Matejko in 1882, the painting features many of the artist's contemporaries in the guise of historical figures – Matejko's wife was the model for Queen Bona Sforza (Sigismund's Italian-born wife), while Matejko himself makes an appearance as Stanczyk, the court jester. Elsewhere in the gallery, Józef Chełmoński's *Foursome*, depicting a team of horses racing across the eastern steppe, is one of the most energy-charged (and oft-reproduced) images in the history of Polish art; although the flame-haired nude on horse-back that forms the subject matter of Władysław Podkowiński's *Ecstasy* (1895) has her fair share of admirers.

The Adam Mickiewicz Statue and St Adalbert's Church

Immediately east of the Sukiennice is a statue of national poet **Adam Mickiewicz** (see box, p.78), a facsimile of an earlier work destroyed by the Nazis, and a favourite meeting point. To its south, the copper-domed **St Adalbert's Church** (Kościół św. Wojciecha) is the oldest building in the square and the first church to be founded in Kraków. The saint was a Slav bishop who preached here around 995 AD before heading north to convert the Prussians, at whose hands he was martyred. Popular with city-centre shoppers who pop in to whisper a quick prayer, the church's intimate, snug interior is filled with exhuberant frescoes illustrating scenes from the saint's life.

The Town Hall Tower

Just off the southwestern corner of the Sukiennice, the onion-domed **Town Hall Tower** (Wieźa Ratuszowa: May–Oct only: daily 10am–1.30pm & 2.30–6pm; 6zł) is all that remains of a fourteenth-century town hall, pulled down in the 1820s by a city government eager to free up more space in the square. Reached by a steep, twisting staircase, the 70-metre-high viewing platform provides an excellent panorama of the city centre – and a close-up look at the gargoyles adorning the parapet of the Sukiennice immediately opposite.

Kraków History Museum

Occupying the Krzysztofory Palace (Pałac pod Krzysztofory) on the corner of the Rynek and ulica Szczepańska, the **Kraków History Museum** (Muzeum Historyczne Krakowa: temporary exhibitions Wed–Sun 10am–5.30pm; 8zł), is currently undergoing long-term renovation and the permanent collection won't open again until 2012, although temporary art-themed exhibitions are held in a couple of upstairs rooms and in the stone-clad basement. During Advent, the museum hosts a stupendous exhibition of *szopki*, the amazingly colourful and detailed Christmas cribs which are indigenous to Kraków and serve as one of the city's visual trademarks.

The Mariacki Church

Presiding haughtily over the northeastern corner of the square, the twin-towered **St Mary's Church** (Kościół Mariacki; 6zł) is one of the finest medieval structures in the country, and easily qualifies as Kraków's most instantly identifiable building. Dating from the 1220s, the Mariacki was for centuries the church of the merchants who lived around the Rynek, and it was they who endowed the place with altars and chapels, and stumped up the cash for numerous bouts of renovation and rebuilding. It was a late thirteenth-century spurt of reconstruction that resulted in the two Romanesque **towers**, the northern one growing taller than the other because it was adapted to serve as the lookout post of the town watchman. The northern tower's prong-like spire, encircled by eight bauble-capped turrets, was finally finished off in 1478.

Legend has it that during one of the early Tatar raids the watchman positioned at the top of the northern tower saw the invaders approaching and took up his trumpet to raise the alarm; his warning was cut short by a Tatar arrow through the throat. The legend lives on, and every hour, on the hour, a lone **trumpeter** plays the sombre *hejnał* (bugle call) melody four times (from four different windows in the southernmost of the towers), on each occasion halting abruptly at the precise point the watchman was supposed to have been hit. The national radio station broadcasts the *hejnał* live at noon every day and Polish writers are still apt to wax lyrical on the symbolism of the trumpet's warning.

The tourist entrance to the church is through the south door – the square-side west door having been set aside for the local faithful. Iluminated by light streaming in through stained-glass windows, the walls of the **nave** are decorated with neo-Gothic friezes by nineteenth-century artist Jan Matejko, rich in brightly coloured chevrons and vegetal shapes. Otherwise the main focal point is the huge stone **crucifix** attributed to the Nuremberg master craftsman Veit Stoss (see p.360), hanging in the archway to the presbytery.

The biggest crowds are drawn by the majestic **high altar** at the far east end. Carved by **Veit Stoss** between 1477 and 1489, this huge winged polyptych is one of the finest examples of late Gothic art in Europe. The outer sides of the altar feature illustrations from the life of the Holy Family executed in gilded polychromy. At 11.50am (Sundays and saints' days excluded) the altar is opened by a nun wielding a huge pole to reveal the inner panels, with their reliefs of the Annunciation, Nativity, Adoration of the Magi, Resurrection, Ascension and Pentecost; for a good view, arrive a good ten minutes before the opening. These six superb scenes are a fitting backdrop to the central panel – an exquisite **Dormition of the Virgin** in which the graceful figure of Mary is shown

Veit Stoss

Although his early career remains something of a mystery, Veit Stoss was born around 1440 in southwestern Germany, settling later at Nuremberg, where a few early works by him have been identified. He came to **Kraków** in 1477 at the behest of the German merchant community, who worshipped in St Mary's Church and paid for its new altar.

The **Mariacki altarpiece** is undoubtedly Stoss's masterpiece. It triumphantly displays every facet of late Gothic sculpture, from the huge figures in the central shrine to the tiny figurines and decoration in the borders. Subtle use is made of a whole gamut of technical devices, from three different depths of relief to a graded degree of gilding according to the importance of the scene.

While engaged on the altarpiece, Stoss carved the sandstone relief of Christ in the Garden of Gethsemane, now in the Palace of Bishop Ciołek (see p.368). His versatility with materials was further demonstrated in the tomb of King Kazimierz the Jagiellonian in the Wawel cathedral (see p.370), which was created from Salzburg marble. All of these sculptures made Stoss a great Polish celebrity, and his monuments were widely imitated for the next half-century.

It therefore seems all the more curious that he left for **Nuremberg** in 1496, remaining there until his death in 1533. Nuremberg was over-endowed with specialist craftsmen, and Stoss was reduced to churning out single, unpainted wooden figures to earn money. Attempts to maintain his well-to-do lifestyle led him into forging financial documents, in punishment for which he was branded on both cheeks and forbidden to venture beyond the city. Stoss never repeated the success of his Kraków years, although he continued to produce highly memorable sculptures, above all the spectacular garlanded Annunciation in Nuremberg's church of St Lorenz.

reclining into her final sleep in the arms of the watchful Apostles. Like most of the figures, the Apostles, several of them well over lifesize, are thought to be based on Stoss's contemporaries in Kraków. Certainly there's an uncanny mastery of human detail that leaves you feeling you'd recognize their human counterparts if you met them in the street.

Walking down towards the west end of the church, you'll have to pick your way past devotees kneeling in front of the fifteenth-century **Chapel of Our Lady of Częstochowa**, with its copy of the venerated image of the Black Madonna. Locals claim that this is actually older than the original displayed in the monastery of Jasna Góra, Częstochowa (see p.474).

St Barbara's Church and the Mały Rynek

The side door on the south side of the chancel brings you into **St Mary's Square** (plac Mariacki), a small courtyard replacing the old church cemetery closed down by the Austrians in the nineteenth century. On the far side of the courtyard stands the fourteenth-century **St Barbara's Church** (Kościół św. Barbary) which is rarely open except during services. Among its contents is a remarkable late Gothic pietà, sculpted in stone and attributed to the anonymous local artist known as "Master of the Beautiful Madonnas". During the Partitions, the ruling Austrians took over the Mariacki, so the locals were forced to use this tiny place for services in Polish.

The back of the church looks onto the tranquil **Small Rynek** (Mały Rynek), whose terrace cafés make an enjoyable venue in which to write postcards or a quiet beer. Occupying the top floor of a nineteenth-century apartment building at the south end of the square, the **Atelier of Tadeusz Kantor** at ul. Sienna 7/5 (Pracownia Tadeusza Kantora: Tues–Sat 10am–3pm; free) honours the painter and playwright who dominated the Kraków avant-garde in the sixties and seventies. A small and intimate attic space housing personal effects and photographs documenting Kantor's *Cricot 2* theatre group, it's a fascinating slice of cultural history.

The Hipolit House

Standing opposite the north side of St Mary's Church at pl. Mariacki 3, the **Hipolit House** (Kamienica Hipolitów: Wed–Sun 10am–5.30pm; 6zł) is a beautifully restored example of a late medieval merchant's house, named after an Italian family of cloth traders who lived here in the seventeenth century. The richly stuccoed rooms now provide the perfect home for a collection of domestic interiors through the ages: highlights include an over-the-top Rococo bedroom, and a nineteenth-century bourgeois parlour which, scattered with magazines and domestic knick-knacks, looks as if the owners have just popped out and will be back any minute.

Ulica Floriańska and around

Of the three streets leading north off the Rynek, the easternmost, **ulica Floriańska** is the busiest and most striking. Part of the so-called "Royal Route" (Droga Krolewska), it was via Floriańska that the Kings of Poland would enter town before continuing towards their residence on Wawel Hill (see p.369).

The Matejko House

Halfway up Floriańska, at no. 41, is the sixteenth-century **Matejko House** (Dom Matejki: Tues–Thurs, Sat & Sun 10am–3.30pm, Fri 11am–6pm; 5zł, free on Sun), home of painter Jan Matejko until his death in 1893. Famous for his colour-charged depictions of key events in Polish history, Matejko was out of step with an art establishment that saw him as a hysterical romantic, but was venerated as a patriotic visionary by the wider, gallery-going public. The painter's house was opened as a museum within three years of his death, and has been a national shrine ever since. Some of the rooms are like a sourcebook of nineteenth-century interior design, retaining the fireplaces, Italian furniture, and mother-of-pearl Middle Eastern chairs that Matejko chose himself. A suite of more modern rooms houses paintings collected by Matejko and examples of his own work, including the sketches of the windows he designed for the Mariacki Church. There's also a rousing collection of old costumes and armour that he used as inspiration for several of his more famous pictures, notably *Sobieski at Vienna*.

The Floriańska Gate and the Barbican

Presiding over the northern end of the street, the **Floriańska Gate** (Brama Floriańska), originally served as the main northern entrance to Kraków and is still busy with the constant flow of tourists and townsfolk. A stocky fourteenth-century structure, it is decorated on its south side with an animated relief of a water-pouring St Florian, patron saint of firefighters. In summer you can walk the short stretch of surviving **city wall** either side of the gate (May–Oct daily 10am–6pm; 6zł, same ticket valid for Barbican), where there's a small display illustrating what Kraków's defences looked like before they were demolished in the nineteenth century. Comprising three kilometres of wall nearly three kilometres thick, interspersed with 47 towers and bastions, they must have been an impressive sight.

Just outside the Floriańska Gate, the **Barbican** (Barbakan: May–Oct daily 10am–6pm; 6zł, same ticket valid for city wall) looks from a distance like the kind of castle that children should be bouncing around in, but is on closer inspection a formidable addition to Kraków's medieval defences. Boasting seven spiky turrets, it was built in 1498 as an extension of the city's northern defensive wall, although the covered passage linking the Barbakan to the Brama Floriańska has long since disappeared.

The Słowacki Theatre
Heading east from the Brama Floriańska will bring you to the northern end of **ulica Szpitalna**, another mansion-lined thoroughfare dominated by the suave, creamy form of the **Słowacki Theatre** (Teatr im. J. Słowackiego). Built in 1897 in imitation of the Opéra Nationale in Paris, the theatre nevertheless contains several locally inspired details – the monstrous heads lining the pediment are a clear reference to the gargoyles adorning the Sukiennice. In front of the theatre stands a statue of playwright **Aleksander Fredro** (1793–1876), whose comedies were an affectionate – if mercilessly satirical – portrayal of the nineteenth-century Polish gentry.

The Church of the Holy Cross
Round the back of the theatre, across plac św. Ducha, is the **Church of the Holy Cross** (Kościół św. Krzyża) a fabulous building whose beautifully decorated Gothic vaulting is supported by a single exquisite palm-like central pillar. The graceful fifteenth- and sixteenth-century murals decorating the nave and choir were restored at the turn of the twentieth century by artist Starisław Wyspiański among others, who was passionately devoted to the building, regarding it as one of the city's finest.

The Czartoryski Museum
Heading west from ulica Floriańska, ulica Pijarska runs past craft and souvenir stalls towards Kraków's finest art collection, the **Czartoryski Museum**, ul. św Jana 19 (Muzeum Czartoryskich; Tues & Thurs 9am–3.30pm, Wed & Fri 11am–6pm, Sat & Sun 10am–3.30pm; 7zł, free on Sun). The museum was founded by Izabela Czartoryska (1746–1835), a public-minded aristocrat who considered the establishment of a Polish national art collection to be her personal duty. Originally based at the family's estate in Puławy, the collection came to Kraków in 1876 having spent over four decades in the Hotel Lambert in Paris, where the Czartoryskis – as leading Polish nationalists – had been living in exile.

The museum starts off with a motley collection of ceramics, weaponry and jewels, all charmingly displayed in antique cabinets that date from the museum's foundation. Oriental carpets, suits of armour and scimitars captured during King Jan Sobieski's victory over the Ottoman Turks at Vienna in 1683 highlight the patriotic intent that lay behind the Czartoryskis family's mania for collecting. A passageway leads to the small but beautifully presented **ancient art** collection, centred on a group of Etruscan coffins that feature terracotta effigies of the deceased, lounging on the lids of their tombs as if participating in a country picnic. Equally attention-grabbing are the richly decorated Egyptian sarcophagi, one of which bears the vivacious features of ninth-century-BC temple dancer Asetamakhbit.

A floor above, the **picture galleries** contain a rich display of art and sculpture, beginning with Gothic and early Renaissance works. Highlights include Paolo Veneziano's fourteenth-century Crucifixion, in which blood spurts from the Saviour's chest; an early sixteenth-century Annunciation by Master George of Kraków showing a wasp-waisted Madonna in lush burgundy dress; and a wooden sculpture of a swooning, Catherine of Alexandria made in Antwerp circa 1500. However the collection's star turn is Leonardo da Vinci's *Lady with an Ermine*, in which a serene Renaissance beauty pets a twisting rodent. The sitter is believed to be Cecilia Gallerani, the mistress of Leonardo's patron and Duke of Milan, Lodovico Sforza: the Greek word for this animal is *galé* – a play on the woman's name – and one of Lodovico's nicknames was "Ermelino", meaning ermine. Opposite Leonardo's *Lady* is an empty space reserved for Raphael's famous *Portrait of a Young Man*, looted by the Nazis during World War II and never recovered. A roomful of Flemish pictures follows, with Rembrandt's brooding *Landscape with the Good Samaritan* occupying centre stage.

Just round the corner from the Czartoryski Museum on ulica Pijarska, the huge barrel-vaulted space of the former **Arsenal** (Tues–Sat 10am–6pm, Sun 10am–4pm; 8zł) provides the atmospheric backdrop to changing exhibitions of contemporary art and photography.

The Wyspiański Museum and around

Heading south from the Muzeum Czartoryskich and turning right into ulica Szczepańska will bring you to one of Kraków's newest and best-designed museums, the **Wyspiański Museum** (Muzeum Wyspiańskiego: Wed & Fri–Sun 10am–3.30pm, Thurs 10am–6pm; 5zł, free on Sun), at no. 11. Devoted to Stanisław Wyspiański (1869–1907), the writer and artist who played a crucial role in the cultural upsurge subsequently known as Młoda Polska or "Young Poland" (see box, p.364), it's stuffed with an eye-pleasing array of artworks, graphics and interior design ideas.

Most memorable items on display are Wyspiański's touching pastel portraits of friends and family – his wife is shown wearing traditional peasant costume in a clear reference to Młoda Polska's reverence for authentic folk traditions. Other notable exhibits include sketches of costumes and set designs intended for use in Wyspiański's plays, and designs for the floral-patterned frescoes he produced for the Franciscan church (see p.366). Evidence of Wyspiański's endless inventiveness is provided by the display of wacky furniture he made for leading literary figure Tadeusz Boy Żeleński – chunky, jagged-edged stools which look like props from the set of a Gothic horror film.

There's also a room recreating the apartment of Wyspiański's friend Feliks Manggha Jasieński (1861–1929), the art collector and critic whose home became Kraków's leading cultural salon. Jasieński donated his whole collection to the National Museum (see p.388), only to find that the latter had no room in which to display it – so he unilaterally declared his flat to be a branch of the National Museum and invited people to view the works there instead.

Plac Szczepański

Immediately beyond the museum the street opens out onto plac Szczepański, a broad square embellished by an impressive pair of *belle époque* buildings in the Viennese Secessionist style: the decorative **Stary Teatr** to the south (see p.406), the city's best known theatre, which was used by Oscar-winning cinema director Andrzej Wajda for his exemplary theatrical productions of Polish classics during the seventies and eighties, and the **Palace of Arts** (Pałac Sztuki: daily 8am–8pm; price depends on what's on) to the west, a stately structure with reliefs by Malczewski and niches filled with busts of Matejko, Witkiewicz and other local artists. The latter, adorned with a mosaic frieze, features high-profile art exhibitions, often featuring major international works on loan from abroad. Hugging the corner of plac Szczepański and the Planty is the **Art Bunker** (Bunkier Sztuki: Tues–Sun Mon 11am–6pm; ⓦwww.bunkier.com.pl; price

Młoda Polska

Like Art Nouveau in France and Jugendstil in Germany, **Młoda Polska** ("Young Poland") administered an invigorating dose of modernity and style to Polish culture in the decades prior to World War I. Młoda Polska was much wider in scope than its French and German counterparts, however, revitalizing painting, poetry and music as well as architecture and design. It was also unique in that most of its protagonists shared a sense of cultural mission: Poland was a country under foreign occupation at the time, and it was only natural that artists saw creative activity as a patriotic as well as a personal duty.

Młoda Polska was never an organized movement; the term was first coined in 1899 to describe a new generation of culturally active Poles who were united by their rejection of mainstream bourgeois taste. The cultural scene in Kraków contained plenty that was worth rebelling against, dominated as it was by the so-called Positivists, who advocated a sober realistic approach to the arts, or by romantic souls like Jan Matejko, the backward-looking painter of epic historical events. Matejko's former students at Kraków's art academy – Józef Mehoffer and Stanisław Wyspiański among them – were far more interested in exploring an alternative world of the unconscious, spiritual and symbolic. The new mood of rebellion also meant the cultivation of decadent, bohemian behaviour at the expense of good manners, and the replacement of cheery optimism with dreamy melancholia. It was a mind-set eloquently summed up by Młoda Polska poet **Kazimierz Tetmajer** in his most famous piece of verse *Nie wierzę w nic* ("I believe in nothing"), the kind of poem that finds a receptive audience among stroppy students to this day.

Kraków's position in the Austrian Empire made it an incubator of new ideas: news of cultural innovations arrived here quickly from Vienna, and the Austrian authorities were in any case fairly liberal when it came to cultural politics. Considerations like these certainly persuaded publicist Stanisław Przybyszewski to launch the periodical *Życie* ("Life") here in 1898, harnessing the young creative talent of the city and providing a focus for the anti-establishment scene. Przybyszewski held court in the (no longer standing) *Turliński* café on ul. Szczepańska, which soon became the unofficial headquarters of the south Polish arts world. When the landlord of the *Turliński* moved to Lwów, everyone decamped to the newly opened *Jama Michalika* on Floriańska. It was here that the Młoda Polska set initiated the Zielony Balonik cabaret in 1905 – many of Kraków's brightest talents were either performing on stage or being satirized in the sketches. The *Jama Michalika* (see p.402) still exists, although it's nowadays the territory of tourists rather than trendsetters.

Młoda Polska's key players also included **Tadeusz Boy Żeleński**, one of the main sketch-writers for Zielony Balonik, and **Feliks "Manngha" Jasieński**, the authority on Japanese art who introduced the younger generation of painters to Oriental styles. An even bigger creative impulse came from a rediscovery of Poland's indigenous folk traditions. Many Młoda Polska luminaries – notably Tetmajer, fellow poet **Jan Kasprowicz**, and architect **Stanisław Witkiewicz** – lived for much of the year in the mountain village of Zakopane (see p.441), drawing inspiration from both the natural beauty of the scenery and the age-old styles of music, dress and handicrafts cultivated by the local inhabitants. Central to the spirit of the age was the belief that Polish culture could be regenerated through renewed contact with its village roots.

After 1914 the effects of war and social upheaval opened the door to a more extreme set of aesthetics, and surviving members of the Młoda Polska generation went their separate ways. However, the era left Poland with a huge cultural legacy, exemplified more than anything by the all-embracing oeuvre of painter, dramatist and designer **Stanisław Wyspiański**. His plays, rich in national symbolism and collective soul-searching, are considered classics of Polish literature, while his work in the visual arts – above all the stained-glass windows in the Franciscan church – has helped form the visual identity of both Kraków and the country at large.

depends on what's on), a brutally modernist concrete building which is the city's main venue for large-scale contemporary art shows.

The University Quarter

Ulica Jagiellońska leads south from plac Szczepański into Kraków's main **university district**, an assemblage of academic buildings grouped around the Gothic **Collegium Maius** ("Grand College") on the corner of Jagiellońska and ul. św. Anny. The university was initially established on the Wawel by King Kazimierz in 1364, but it failed to outlive his death six years later and had to be re-founded by King Władysław Jagiełło's wife Queen Jadwiga in the early fifteenth century.

Entered from ulica Jagiellońska, the Collegium Maius's arcaded **courtyard** is one of the most magical spots in Kraków, a tranquil cloister whose walls are studded with stone staircases and overhanging oriel windows. One recent addition (dating from 1999) is the mechanical clock on the south wall, from which carved figures of Władysław Jagiełło, Queen Jadwiga and university rectors emerge five times a day (9am, 11am, 1pm, 3pm and 5pm).

The University Museum

Several first-floor rooms of the Collegium Maius play host to the **University Museum** (Muzeum Uniwerzytecki: Mon–Fri 11am–2.20pm, Sat 11am–1.20pm; 16zł; entrance is by guided tour only – the museum office will sign you up for the next English-language tour, which depart at regular intervals throughout the day). The trip begins with a series of elaborately decorated assembly halls and lecture rooms, several of which retain the mathematical and geographical murals once used for teaching, as well as an impressive library of old books. The professors' common room boasts an ornate Baroque spiral staircase guarded by wooden halberdiers, and a Gothic bay window with a replica statuette of King Kazimierz. Among the trinkets in the so-called **Treasury** (actually a glass cabinet behind a locked iron grille), the most valued possession is a tiny copper globe, constructed around 1520 as the centrepiece of a clock mechanism and featuring the earliest known illustration of America – labelled "a newly discovered land" but placed in the wrong hemisphere. The **Aula**, the grand principal assembly hall, has a Renaissance ceiling adorned with carved rosettes and portraits of Polish royalty, benefactors and professors; its Renaissance portal carries the Latin inscription *Plus Ratio Quam Vis* – "Wisdom rather than Strength".

St Anne's Church and around

Several other old buildings are dotted round this area. The university **St Anne's Church** (Kościół św. Anny), was designed by the ubiquitous Tylman van Gameren. A monumental Baroque extravaganza, built on a Latin cross plan with a high central dome, it's widely regarded as Gameren's most mature work, the classicism of his design neatly counterpoised by rich stucco decoration added by the Italian sculptor Baldassare Fontana.

The **Collegium Minus**, just round the corner on ulica Gołębia, is the fifteenth-century arts faculty, rebuilt two centuries later; Jan Matejko studied and later taught here. On the corner of the same street stands the outsize **Collegium Novum**, the neo-Gothic university administrative headquarters, with an interior modelled on the Collegium Maius. The **Copernicus statue**, in front of the Collegium Novum on the edge of the Planty, commemorates the university's most famous supposed student – although the only evidence that he ever studied in Kraków is a payment-book entry referring to one "Mikołaj son of Mikołaj from Toruń".

Mehoffer House

A short walk west of the University area on the far side of the Planty, the **Mehoffer House** (Dom Mehoffera: Tues & Thurs–Sun 10am–3.30pm, Wed 11am–6pm; 5zł, free on Sun) is an essential stop on any Młoda Polska tour of Kraków. Occupying the house where Stanisław Wyspiański's friend and colleague Józef Mehoffer (1869–1946) lived and worked, it's stuffed with *belle époque* furnishings, pictures of old Kraków and Mehoffer's own artworks. Like Wyspiański, Mehoffer was heavily involved in renovating and re-styling Kraków's historic churches, and many of his fresco designs – such as the heavenly children's faces of *Angels with Stars*, produced for Wawel Cathedral in 1901 – are given full exposure here. It was as a stained-glass artist that Mehoffer was most in demand, fashioning pieces that were intended to serve as windows or room-partitions in bourgeois homes. Positioned at the top of the main staircase here is an outstanding example of the genre in the shape of *Vita somnium breve* (1904) – an allegory of the immortality of art in which smiling muses hover fairy-like above a dying maiden. Mehoffer was also a keen horticulturalist, and his carefully designed **garden** at the back of the house has recently been returned to its original, splendid state – with restorers using Mehoffer's own watercolours as a guide.

The Dominican church and monastery

Ulica Grodzka stretches south of the Rynek, crossing the tram lines circling the city centre at plac Dominikański. East across the square stands the large brickwork basilica of the thirteenth-century **Dominican church and monastery**. The original Gothic building was seriously devastated by fire in 1850, but much of the sumptuous interior decoration survives. Today it's one of Kraków's most popular churches, with a continual stream of services held here every day of the week.

Inside, the nave is lined with a succession of chapels. Reached via a flight of steps at the end of the north aisle, **St Hyacinth's chapel** has some rich stuccowork by Baldassare Fontana on the dome above the freestanding tomb, and paintings portraying the life of the saint by Thomas Dolabella. The Baroque **Myszkowski family chapel**, in the southern aisle, is a fine creation from the workshop of Florentine mason Santi Gucci, the exuberantly ornamented exterior contrasting with the austere, marble-faced interior, with busts of the Myszkowski family lining the chapel dome. Similarly noteworthy is the **Rosary chapel**, built as a thanks-offering for Sobieski's victory over the Turks at Vienna in 1683, and housing a supposedly miracle-producing image of Our Lady of the Rosary. A fine series of **tombstones** survives in the chancel, notably those of the early thirteenth-century prince of Kraków, Leszek Czarny (the Black), and an impressive bronze tablet of the Italian Renaissance scholar Filippo Buonaccorsi, built to a design by Veit Stoss and cast at the Nuremberg Vischer works.

Through the Renaissance doorway, underneath the stairs leading up to St Hyacinth's chapel, are the tranquil Gothic **cloisters**, whose walls are lined with memorials to the great and good of Kraków, leading in the north wing to a fine Romanesque refectory with a vaulted crypt.

Franciscan church and monastery

West of plac Dominikański, on the adjacent plac Wszystkich Świętych, is the **Franciscan church and monastery**, home to the Dominicans' long-standing rivals in the tussle for the city's religious affections. As one of Kraków's major churches, it has witnessed some important events in the nation's history, notably the baptism in 1385 of the pagan Grand Duke Jogaila of Lithuania (who adopted the Polonized name Władysław Jagiełło for the occasion), prior to his assumption of the Polish throne. A plain, high, brick building, the church's most striking feature is its celebrated series of Art Nouveau **murals** and **stained-glass windows**, designed by Stanisław Wyspiański in 1895–1905 following the gutting of the church by fire fifty years earlier (see opposite). An exuberant outburst of floral and geometric mural motifs extol the naturalist creed of St Francis, culminating in the magnificent stained-glass depiction of God the Creator in the large west window, the elements of the scene seemingly merging into each other in a hazy, abstract swirl of colour. The **north chapel** contains a flowing set of Stations of the Cross by another Młoda Polska adherent, Józef Mehoffer; while the **south chapel** contains a fine early fifteenth-century image of the Madonna of Mercy, a popular local figure. The Gothic **cloisters**, reached from the southern side of the church, contain a memorable set of portraits of Kraków bishops dating back to the fifteenth century and continuing up to the present day.

Across the road from the church is the **Theology Academy** (Akademia Teologiczna), where Karol Wojtyła lived during World War II. It was here that he used to stay during his visits to Kraków as pope, greeting crowds of wellwishers from the balcony above the main portal – an event commemorated by a huge photograph of the pontiff that hangs on the façade of the building.

The Wyspiański 2000 Pavilion

Those who can't get enough of Wyspiański should head next for the **Wyspiański 2000 Pavilion** (Pawilon Wyspiański 2000: daily 9am–7pm; free), immediately east of the Franciscan Church on plac Wsystkich Świętych. A slab-like structure erected (despite the name) in 2007, the pavilion contains contemporary stained-glass windows made from Wyspiański designs originally intended for the Franciscan church but never completed at the time. It's clear to see why the Franciscans thought twice before putting these particular Wyspiański sketches into effect: the windows depict three great figures from Polish history – St Stanisław, King Henry the Pious and King Kazimierz the Great – but portray them in unabashedly modern and unsettling style. Kazimierz in particular appears as a skeletal spectre, symbolizing (for Wyspiański at least) the ghost of Poland's past glory.

The Archeological Museum

Heading south through the Planty from the Franciscan church brings you swiftly to the **Archeological Museum** (Muzeum Archeologiczne: Mon, Wed & Fri 9am–2pm, Tues & Thurs 2–6pm, Sun 10am–2pm; 7zł), housed in a former medieval monastery and subsequently Habsburg-era prison at ul. Poselska 3. The well-presented collection is particularly strong on local Neolithic finds, with a wealth of geometric-patterned ceramics and mysterious-looking fertility figures. Ancient Egypt is represented by effigies of animal-headed gods and a brace of brightly painted sarcophagi. One exhibit the locals are extremely proud of is a carved pillar bearing the head of **Światowit**, chief god in the pagan Slav pantheon. Thought to date from the ninth century, the pillar has three layers of decoration, with Światowit at the top representing the heavens, human forms in the middle symbolizing the earth, and ugly faces at the bottom to signify the underworld. Światowit himself sports what looks like a top hat, and has a face on each side of the pillar – one for each of the winds, it is thought.

Along ulica Grodzka

Heading south from plac Wszystkich Świętych towards Wawel Hill, ulica Grodzka is one of Kraków's most handsome streets. Many of its houses bear quirky decorative details, most notably the gilded stone lion above the **Kamienica Podelwie** ("House Under the Lion") at no. 32, the oldest such stone emblem in the city. Halfway down the street, the austere twin-domed **Church of Sts Peter and Paul** (Kościół św. Piotra i Pawła) is fronted by imposing statues of the twelve apostles, actually copies of the pollution-scarred originals, now kept elsewhere for preservation's sake. Modelled on the Gesù in Rome, the church is the earliest Baroque building in the city, commissioned by the Jesuit preacher **Piotr Skarga** when he came to Kraków in the 1590s to quell Protestant agitation. Nestling under a broad dome, the interior is relatively bare – clearly intended to invoke spiritual awe rather than delight the congregation with decorative detail. Skarga himself is buried in the **crypt**, accessed by steps in front of the main altar. He remains a much revered figure among the devout, who write prayers on slips of paper before pushing them into a box beside his tomb.

Immediately in front of the church stands one of Kraków's more controversial cultural monuments, a **statue of Skarga** erected in 2001 to provide a focal point for the recently tidied-up plaza that leads from here through to ulica Kanonicza (see below). A clumsy piece of work which makes the highly respected preacher look more like a comic-book superhero than a spiritual leader, the sculpture is totally out of keeping with the Baroque splendours that surround it, and has proved profoundly unpopular with Cracovians as a consequence.

Sporting an eye-catching pair of octagonal towers, the next-door **St Andrew's Church** (Kościół św. Andrzeja) is the only Romanesque structure in Kraków to have survived in anything like its original form, having withstood the Tatar raids of 1241 thanks to its partially fortified exterior. The interior was given a thorough Baroque makeover in the eighteenth century, with master of swirling stuccowork Baldassare Fontana doing his best to turn nave and choir into the ecclesiastical equivalent of an extravagantly iced cake. Positioned beside the organ is a Rococo pulpit in the shape of a sailing boat, agile cherubs swinging playfully from its rigging.

Along ulica Kanonicza

Running roughly parallel to ulica Grodzka is the atmospheric **ulica Kanonicza**, a quiet, cobbled alley lined with Gothic town houses. It was here that the Kraków catholic hierarchy lived during the middle ages, hence the place's name – "canons' street". Restoration work on the street's string of fine mansions is now almost complete, lending the ensemble a meditative aura that takes ready hold on the imagination.

The Palace of Erazem Ciołek

Kraków's most rewarding museum of religious art through the ages is housed in the wonderfully restored former **Palace of Erazem Ciołek** (Pałac Erazma Ciołka; Tues–Sat 10am–6pm, Sun 10am–4pm; 8zł; free on Sun), the fifteenth-century pied-à-terre of a Kraków-born commoner who rose to become royal confidant, diplomat and ultimately Bishop of the town of Płock (see p.123). The main part of the collection, up the stairs from the ticket office, kicks off with a stream of show-stopping highlights. First is the famous Virgin and Child of Kruźlowka, a sensuous fourteenth-century statue of a swooning Madonna holding a jauntily mischievous toddler. This is followed by several spectacular Gothic altarpieces: Nicolaus Haberschrack's Augustinian Church Altar of 1460 features wonderfully animated New Testament crowd scenes alongside an anguished and bloody *Mocking of Christ*. The late medieval taste for gore is apparent in the winged Domoradz Altar of 1520, in which heathen archers shoot arrows at pious Christian girls standing on the deck of a ship. A roomful of Renaissance marble follows, including heavenly bas-reliefs of angels executed by Gianmaria Mosca Padovano, one of the Italian masters invited to Kraków by Poland's style-hungry sixteenth-century monarchs. No less compelling is the room labelled the "Hall of Death", which commemorates Polish funerary practices of the past with a row of so-called "coffin portraits" – images of the deceased which were stuck on the end of the sarcophagus.

On the opposite side of the courtyard from the ticket office, a section devoted to **Orthodox religious art** (*sztuka cerkiewna*) contains a rich hoard of icons recovered from the decaying village churches of eastern Poland. A beautifully carved eighteenth-century iconostasis from the village of Lipowec displays the ordered hierarchy of saintly images displayed in Orthodox churches the world over from the Byzantine era onwards, with a calm-faced Jesus on the right, an aura-emanating Madonna on the left, and the patron of the church (in this case the white-bearded St Nicholas) at her side.

The Archdiocesan Museum and the Długosz House

Almost at the bottom of the street, housed in an impressive pair of recently renovated late fourteenth-century mansions belonging to the archbishop of Kraków (nos. 19/21), is the **Karol Wojtyła Archdiocesan Museum** (Muzeum Archdiecezjalne im. Karola Wojtyły: Tues–Fri 10am–4pm, Sat & Sun 10am–3pm; 5zł), with a wealth of religious art plucked from the churches of the surrounding Małopolska region. The highlight of the collection in the first gallery is a set of Gothic sculptures, including a wonderful sequence of Madonnas and female saints, and an exquisite relief of the Adoration of the Magi dating from the 1460s. Subsequent halls feature a charming fifteenth-century altarpiece from Paczółtowice bearing touching scenes of the Annunciation and the Nativity, and a delightful sixteenth-century triptych from Racławice Olkuskie in which the Virgin Mary and St Anne appear to be bouncing the Christ Child from lap to lap. Rounding off the exhibitions are several rooms filled with photos, vestments and other memorabilia relating to Karol Wojtyła, who lived in this building when a humble priest in Kraków.

Back out on the street, the fifteenth-century **Długosz House** (Dom Długosza) at no. 25, named after an early resident, the historian Jan Długosz, originally served as the royal bathhouse. Local legend has it that in preparation for her marriage to Grand Duke Jogaila of Lithuania (the future King Władysław Jagiełło of Poland), Princess Jadwiga sent one of her most trusted servants to attend the duke during his ablutions and report back over rumours of the grotesque genital proportions of the pagan Lithuanians. Exactly what the servant told her is not revealed, but at any rate the queen went ahead and married the man.

Wawel Hill

For over five hundred years, Poland was ruled from **Wawel Hill**, site of both the royal palace where kings resided, and the cathedral where they were crowned and buried. Even after the capital moved to Warsaw, Polish monarchs continued to be buried in the cathedral, as were many of the nation's venerated poets and heroes. Today, both cathedral and palace serve as a virtual textbook of Polish history, architecture and art, making Wawel a near-obligatory pilgrimage for locals and tourists alike. In more recent times Wawel has acquired an additional reputation that draws in visitors – the belief that one of the walls in the inner castle courtyard stands upon one of the world's main centres of spiritual energy. It's common for cultists and followers of the chakra to come here and lean against the wall for a few minutes in order to recharge their spiritual batteries. Distaste for New Age tourism prompted the Wawel authorities to rope the area off for a while in 2001, but it seems to be accessible again – although not marked by any sign.

The Brama Wazowska and the outer courtyard

Entrance to the Wawel is via a cobbled path that leaves Podzamcze just opposite the junction with Kanonicza. At the top of the path, a typically dramatic statue of Tadeusz Kościuszko – a copy of one destroyed by the Nazis – stands before the sixteenth-century **Waza Gate** (Brama Wazowska), protected by two huge red-brick bastions. As you emerge into the Wawel precinct the cathedral rears up to the left, with the castle and its outbuildings and courtyards beyond. Directly ahead is a huge, open **square**, once the site of a Wawel township, but cleared by the Austrians in the early nineteenth century to create a parade ground. In the middle of the square, alongside a well-tended garden, lie the remains of two Gothic churches, St Michael's (Kościół św. Michala) and St George's (Kościół św. Jerzego), both raised in the fourteenth century only to be demolished by the Austrians. Beyond the ruins, it's worth taking in the view over the river from the terrace at the western edge of the hill.

The Cathedral

"The sanctuary of the nation ... cannot be entered without an inner trembling, without an awe, for here – as in few cathedrals of the world – is contained a vast greatness which speaks to us of the history of Poland, of all our past." So was the **cathedral** (Mon–Sat 9am–5pm; 8zł) evoked by former Archbishop Karol Wojtyła of Kraków. As with Westminster Abbey in London or St Peter's

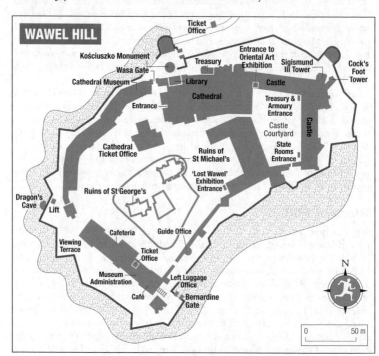

Visiting the Wawel

"Doing" the Wawel can take all day, but with the judicious use of coffee breaks it's a hugely rewarding way of spending your time, and by no means as tiring as you might expect. The outer courtyard is open to all-comers (May–Sept 8am–8pm; Oct–April 9am–5pm; free), but all other attractions require a separate ticket. Tickets for the museum attractions in the royal palace – the State Rooms, the Private Royal Apartments, the Treasury and Armoury, the Oriental Art Exhibition and the Lost Wawel – can be purchased either from the ticket office at the top of the approach path to the Wawel, or from the ticket office towards the back of the outer courtyard (both Mon–Fri 9am–3.45pm, Sat & Sun 10am–4.45pm). Entry to the State Rooms, Private Apartments and Treasury is staggered to prevent overcrowding, and your ticket will be valid for a particular time slot – on summer weekends all the available tickets for these attractions sell out quickly, so it's a good idea to arrive early. Tickets to the cathedral are sold from an office opposite the main portal. English-speaking **guides** for small groups and individuals are available for hire from the Guide Office (Biuro Przewodnickie: ☏012/429 3336, ⓦwww.przewodnicy.krakow.pl) on the south side of the main courtyard. If there's one place where it would be worth coughing up for your own guide, this is it.

in Rome, the moment you enter Wawel, you know you're in a place resonant with national history.

The first cathedral was built here around 1020 when King Bolesław the Brave established the Kraków bishopric. However the present brick and sandstone basilica is essentially Gothic, dating from the reigns of Władysław the Short (1306–33) and Kazimierz the Great (1333–70), and adorned with a mass of side chapels, endowed by just about every subsequent Polish monarch and a fair number of aristocratic families too. All bar four of Poland's 45 monarchs are buried in the cathedral, and the royal tombs and chapels are a directory of six centuries of Central European architecture, art and sculpture.

As you enter the cathedral, look out for the bizarre collection of **prehistoric animal bones** in a passage near the main entrance, supposedly the remains of the Krak dragon (see p.345), but actually a mammoth's shinbone, a whale's rib and the skull of a hairy rhinoceros. As long as they remain, so legend maintains, the cathedral will too.

The view down the nave of the cathedral, with its arched Gothic vaulting, is blocked by the **Mausoleum of St Stanisław** (Mauzoleum św. Stanisława), an overwrought seventeenth-century silver sarcophagus by the Gdańsk smith Peter van der Rennen. It commemorates the bishop who is supposed to have been murdered by King Bolesław at Skałka in Kazimierz (see p.376) in 1079 for his opposition to royal ambitions. The remains of the bishop-saint, who was canonized in 1253, were moved to Wawel the following year, and his shrine quickly became a place of pilgrimage.

Below the shrine, on the right, is the tomb of **King Władysław Jagiełło**, a beautiful marble creation from the mid-1400s with a fine Renaissance canopy added on by the king's grandson, Sigismund the Old, a century later. Beyond stands the Baroque **high altar** and choir stalls. However, most people are drawn immediately to the outstanding array of side chapels that punctuate the entire length of the building.

To the right of the entrance, the Gothic **Holy Cross Chapel** (Kaplica Świętokrzyska) is the burial chamber of King Kazimierz IV Jagiełło (1447–92), his marble effigy the characteristic expressive work of Veit Stoss, of Mariacki fame (see box, p.372). The boldly coloured, Byzantine-style paintings on the walls and ceiling were completed by Orthodox artists from the eastern fringes of the Polish-Lithuanian Commonwealth – a pointed reference to the multi-faith communities over which the Jagiellonian monarchs ruled.

The most celebrated of the Wawel chapels is the **Sigismund Chapel** (Kaplica Zygmuntowska) on the south side of the nave, a masterpiece of Renaissance sculpture and ornamentation designed for King Sigismund the Old (1506–48) by the Italian architect Bartolomeo Berrecci. The work was overseen by Sigismund's wife Bona, who as a member of the Milanese Sforza family clearly knew a thing or two about Italian style. Under a dome studded with stucco rosettes lie a series of niches containing effigies of King Sigismund the Old and his nearest family (spouse Queen Bona, daughter Anna Jagiellońka, and fork-bearded son King Sigismund August), all depicted in reclining pose as if lounging around in the wake of some regal banquet. The richly detailed walls of the chapel include reliefs of saints alongside distinctly non-Christian subject matter taken from classical myth – nymphs, griffons and sphinxes among them. The chapel's gilded cupola, originally donated by Anna Jagiellońka in honour of her father, is best viewed from the courtyard outside. Opposite the chapel is the modern **tomb of Queen Jadwiga**, wife of King Władysław Jagiełło and one of the country's most loved monarchs – in reality, her remains are buried nearby beneath her own favourite crucifix.

Venerable fourteenth-century bishops occupy several subsequent chapels, while the Gothic red Hungarian marble **tomb of King Kazimierz the Great**, immediately to the right of the high altar, is a dignified tribute in marble and sandstone to the revered monarch, during whose reign the cathedral was actually consecrated. The fourteenth-century **St Mary's Chapel** (Kaplica Mariacka), directly behind the altar and connected to the castle by a passage, was remodelled in the 1590s by Santi Gucci to accommodate the austere black marble and sandstone tomb of King Stefan Batory (1576–86). The **tomb of King Władysław the Short** (1306–33), on the left-hand side of the altar, is the oldest in the cathedral, completed soon after his death; the reclining, coronation-robed figure lies on a white sandstone tomb edged with expressive mourning figures.

Accessed from the left aisle, the **crypt** houses the remains of numerous Polish kings and queens, many encased in pewter sarcophagi, notably the Sigismunds and Stefan Batory. Also buried here are the poets Adam Mickiewicz and Juliusz Słowacki, and national heroes Prince Józef Poniatowski and Tadeusz Kościuszko. The equally sanctified prewar independence leader Józef Piłsudski lies in a separate vault nearby. Standing with the crowds filing past this pantheon, you catch the passionate intensity of Polish attachment to everything connected with past resistance and independent nationhood.

The Sigismund Tower

An ascent of the fourteenth-century **Sigismund Tower** (Wieża Zygmuntowska: same hours as the cathedral; 5zł), accessed through the cathedral sacristy, gives a far-reaching panorama over the city and close-up views of the five medieval bells. The largest, an eight-tonne monster known as "Zygmunt", cast in 1520 from melted-down Russian cannon captured at the Battle of Orsza, is two and a half metres in diameter, eight in circumference, and famed for its deep, sonorous tone, which according to local legend scatters rain clouds and brings out the sun. These days it doesn't get too many chances to perform, as it's only rung on Easter Sunday, Christmas Eve and New Year's Eve.

The Cathedral Museum

Located in a separate building opposite the main entrance, the **Cathedral Museum** (Muzeum Katedralne: Mon–Sat 9am–4pm; 5zł) displays the lavish collection of chalices, monstrances and other devotional objects amassed by the cathedral over the centuries. Several of the exhibits radiate a powerful sense of historical significance, notably the Spear of St Maurice, presented to King Bolesław the Brave by Emperor Otto III when they met at Gniezno in 1000 AD, and a delicately embroidered mitre believed to have been worn by St Stanisław.

The castle courtyard

Entering the tiered courtyard of the **royal castle**, which occupies the eastern half of the Wawel complex, you might imagine that you'd stumbled on an opulent Italian palazzo. This is exactly the effect Sigismund the Old intended when he entrusted the conversion of King Kazimierz's Gothic castle to Florentine architect Bartolomeo Berrecci (c.1480–1537) in the early 1500s. The major difference from its Italian models lies in the response to climate: the window openings are enlarged to maximize the available light, while the overhanging wooden roof – held up by an unusually sensual set of bulbous columns – is sturdier to withstand snow.

The State Rooms

Entered from the southeastern corner of the castle courtyard, the **State Rooms** (Reprezantacyjne Komnaty Królewskie: April–Oct Tues, Thurs & Fri 9.30am–4pm, Wed & Sat 9.30am–3pm, Sun 10am–3pm; Nov–March Tues–Sat 9.30am–3pm, Sun 10am–3pm; 15zł) begin with the ground-floor apartments of the castle governor, liberally scattered with furnishings through the ages – not all of which are directly associated with Wawel castle. An ensemble of large royal reception rooms await upstairs, beginning with the **Tournament Room** where people would wait before being admitted to the king's presence – it gets its name from the frieze of jousting knights painted by Hans Dürer, brother of the more famous Albrecht. The next-door **Military Room** contains another animated Dürer frieze, this time showing King Sigismund the Old reviewing his armies. A glance upwards at the carved ceiling of the **Audience Hall** at the southern end of the wing will tell you why it's nicknamed the "Heads Room". Created for Sigismund the Old in the 1530s by Sebastian Tauerbach of Wrocław and Jan Snycerz, only thirty of its original 194 heads remain, but they are all remarkably detailed and lifelike artworks in their own right – most are believed to be portraits of Kraków locals. Running around the walls, another frieze by Hans Dürer illustrates *The Life of Man* with a procession of richly costumed figures symbolizing the progression from youth to old age. Hanging on the walls both here and in the adjoining corridors are some of King Sigismund August's splendid assembly of **Flanders tapestries**, many of which came from the Brussels workshop of the "Flemish Raphael", Michiel von Coxie. The tapestries were evacuated to Britain, then Canada on the outbreak of World War II – they didn't return to Kraków until 1961.

Next come a suite of rooms furnished by the seventeenth-century Waza dynasty, most of them featuring lavish Cordoba wall-coverings fashioned from tooled leather. Highlights include the **Bird Room** (named after the wooden birds that used to hang from the ceiling), dominated by a Rubens portrait of Prince Władysław Waza; the large, tapestry-adorned **Senators' Hall,** used for formal meetings of the Senate in the days when Kraków was still the capital; and numerous connecting vestibules filled with imposing portraits of the Polish royal family.

The Private Royal Apartments

The lavish interior design tastes of Poland's monarchs are given further exposure in the **Private Royal Apartments** (Prywatne Apartamenty Królewskie: Tues–Sun 9.30am–5pm, Sat & Sun 11am–6pm; 20zł), which basically consist of the reconstructed living quarters of Renaissance monarch Sigismund the Old – the last Polish King to regard the Wawel as his full-time home. Much of the period furniture on display has been collected from various sources by curators keen to convey a sense of how a sixteenth-century monarch might have lived, the King's own possessions having long since disappeared. One surviving item of original décor is the *Story of the Swan Knight*, a mid-fifteenth-century French tapestry adorning one wall of Sigismund's bedchamber.

The Treasury and Armoury

The combined **Treasury and Armoury** (Skarbiec i Zbrojownia: same times as the State Rooms; 15zł) is located in the Gothic vaults of the Łokietek tower, one of the oldest parts of the castle. Although the Treasury's collection is short on crown jewels (most of these were plundered by the Prussians in 1795), there's a wealth of fascinating historical detail here – notably the dainty coronation slippers of Sigismund August (he was ten years old at the time), and a fifth-century ring inscribed with the name "MARTINVS", found near Kraków.

Prize exhibits are the solemnly displayed Szczerbiec, a thirteenth-century copy of the weapon used by Bolesław the Brave during his triumphal capture of Kiev in 1018, used from then on in the coronation of Polish monarchs; and the early sixteenth-century Sword of Justice, belonging to Sigismund the Old. There are also items connected with **Jan Sobieski**, most notably the regalia of the Knights of the Order of the Holy Ghost sent to him by the pope as thanks for defeating the Turks at Vienna in 1683.

The adjacent Armoury has spiky medieval halberds, primitive artillery pieces, and the exquisitely engraved suits of ceremonial armour made by the master metalworkers of Nuremberg. There are several examples of the eagle-feather wings which were strapped to the backs of seventeenth-century Polish hussars, a characteristically Polish piece of fancy dress which lent the wearer a fearsome, angel-of-death appearance. Dominating one barrel-vaulted chamber are copies of the banners captured from the Teutonic Knights during the epic Battle of Grunwald (1410) – the originals were confiscated by the Nazis during World War II.

The Oriental Art Exhibition

Housed in the west wing of the castle, the **Oriental Art Exhibition** (Sztuka Wschodu: April–Oct Tues, Thurs & Fri 9.30am–4pm, Wed & Sat 9.30am–3pm, Sun 10am–3pm; Nov–March Tues–Sat 9.30am–3pm; 7zł) was founded in 1920 to display the war loot collected by King Jan Sobieski in the wake of his victory over the Ottoman Turks outside Vienna in 1683. Pride of place goes to the tents of the Ottoman commanders, each vivaciously patterned with intertwined tulip, thistle and leaf-and-branch forms. Exposure to such examples of eastern design had a profound impact on the Polish aristocracy, who remained addicted to Oriental-styled textiles and clothes for the best part of a century. The visual feast continues with Turkish and Iranian carpets, illuminated manuscripts, and a recently added collection of Chinese and Japanese porcelain.

The Lost Wawel

Entered from the outer courtyard, the **Lost Wawel** exhibition (Wawel Zaginiony: April–Oct Mon 9.30am–noon, Tues, Thurs & Fri 9.30am–4pm, Wed & Sat 9.30am–3pm, Sun 10am–3pm; Nov–March Tues–Sat 9.30am–3pm; 7zł) consists of a subterranean walking route that takes in many of the medieval remains found underneath the current castle, most notably the well-preserved walls and towers of the tenth-century **Rotunda of Sts Felix and Adauctus** (Rotunda św. Feliksa i Adaukta), the oldest known church in Poland. A diverse collection of medieval archeological finds rounds off the display.

The Dragon's Cave and the riverfront

Accessible by lift from the western end of the Wawel courtyard, or on foot from the riverside walkway which runs below the Wawel hill, the **Dragon's Cave** (Smocza Jama: daily 10am–6pm; 3zł) is the legendary haunt of a fire-breathing beast who terrorized the local population until killed by a certain Krakus – who tricked the dragon into eating an animal skin stuffed with sulphur. There's not a great deal to see inside, but kids may well enjoy the story.

Outside the mouth of the cave, on the riverfront promenade, an effete-looking **bronze dragon** (the work of local sculptor Bronisław Chromy) entertains tourists by belching a brief blast of fire every couple of minutes. It's very popular with the school parties that descend here in droves from the castle, snapping up trinkets from the massed ranks of souvenir sellers on either side.

From the Dragon's Cave, a walk west along the bend of the river towards the **Dębnicki bridge** is rewarded by an excellent view back over the castle.

The Manggha Japanese Art Centre

Crossing either the Dębnicki bridge to the west or the Grunwaldzki bridge to the south will place you within five minutes' walking distance of the **Manggha Japanese Art Centre** at Konopnickiej 26 (Centrum Sztuki i Techniki Japońskiej Manggha: Tues–Sun 10am–6pm; Ⓦ www.manggha.krakow.pl; 8zł), a cool slab of modernist architecture designed by Arata Isozaki, whose other notable buildings include the Museum of Contemporary Art in Los Angeles and the Palau Sant Jordi sports hall in Barcelona. The centre displays the extensive collection of Japanese art amassed by Feliks "Manggha" Jasieński, a leading nineteenth-century Japanologist who wrote a much admired book about Eastern aesthetics entitled *Manggha* (his transliteration of the Japanese term "manga", or sketch), and subsequently adopted the term as his own literary pseudonym. Among the exhibits are ceramics, silks, samurai armour and one of the finest collections of late eighteenth- to early nineteenth-century woodcuts you're likely to see in Europe. The centre's terrace café, a popular meeting place, offers a good view onto the river and Wawel Hill.

The Bernardine Church

Leaving the Wawel area and heading southeast towards Kazimierz will take you past the **Bernardine Church** (Kościół Bernardynów) on the corner of Bernardyńska and Stradomska, a twin-towered Baroque basilica containing a wealth of lavish period furnishings. There is a fine sculpture of St Anne with the Virgin and Child, attributed to the workshop of Veit Stoss, in one of the side chapels; and a gripping depiction of the Dance of Death in the main aisle, a typical Baroque expression of life's transience.

Kazimierz

(The) Jews are gone. One can only try to preserve, maintain and fix the memory of them – not only of their struggle and death (as in Warsaw and Auschwitz), but of their life, of the values that guided their yearnings, of the international life and their unique culture. Cracow was one of the places where that life was most rich, most beautiful, most varied, and the most evidence of it has survived here.

Henryk Halkowski, a surviving Kraków Jew. Extracted from *Upon the Doorposts of Thy House*
by Ruth Ellen Gruber (Wiley)

South from Wawel Hill lies the suburb of **Kazimierz**, originally a distinct town named in honour of King Kazimierz, who founded the settlement in 1335. The king's intention was to break the power of Kraków's German-dominated

The Jews of Kraków

One of the major Jewish communities in Poland for much of the last six centuries, the Jews of Kraków occupy a significant place in the history of the city. The first Jews settled in Kraków in the second half of the **thirteenth century**, a small community establishing itself on ulica św. Anny, then known as ulica Żydowska (Jewish Street), in today's university district, with a synagogue, baths and cemetery beyond the city walls. By the **fourteenth century**, the community still numbered no more than a couple of hundred people, but in the **fifteenth century** it was enlarged by an influx of Jews from all over Europe – notably Bohemia, Germany, Italy and Spain – fleeing growing persecution and discrimination in their homelands. Significant numbers of Jews were by now setting up home south of the Old Town in Kazimierz, where they built their own ritual baths, a marketplace and a synagogue (the predecessor of the Stara Synagoga that you can still see standing today), thereby shifting the focus of community life away from the traditional areas of settlement around ulica św. Anny. It was a process completed in 1495, when a serious fire in the city was blamed on the Jews, provoking their expulsion from the Old Town – thus swelling the ranks of those in Kazimierz.

Economically, the Reformation era was a time of significant growth for the city, a development in which Jews participated actively as goldsmiths, publishers, furriers and, especially, butchers. Culturally the **sixteenth century** was also something of a golden age for Jewish culture in Kraków, with local Talmudic scholars and the books they produced on the printing presses of Menachim Meisler and others enjoying high international prestige. As a mark of their growing authority, rabbis and elders of the Kraków community were chosen to represent Małopolska on the Council of the Four Lands (see box, p.263) when it met for the first time in Lublin in 1581. The ghetto area was expanded in 1583, and again in 1603, with a fence and stone wall along ulica Józefa separating it from the rest of Kazimierz.

Under the terms of a **nineteenth-century** statute promulgated in the wake of the establishment of the Free City of Kraków (1815–46), the ghetto was officially liquidated and the walls separating it torn down, with a direct view to encouraging assimilation among the Jewish population. Jews were now permitted to live anywhere in Kazimierz, and, with special permits duly granted to merchants and craftsmen, to reside throughout the city area.

The period following the end of **World War I** and the regaining of Polish independence was one of intense population growth in Jewish Kraków, the community rising from 45,000 people in 1921 to nearly 57,000 a decade later, and more than 64,000 on the eve of the Nazi invasion of Poland. Most, but by no means all, of Kraków's Jews lived in Kazimierz. The inward-looking and mostly poor Hassidim dominated the synagogues, prayer houses and Talmudic schools of the quarter, while the more integrated, upwardly mobile sections of the community moved out into other city districts, and increasingly adopted the manners and educational habits of merchant class by establishing a rival market centre, and the granting of royal privileges to the new settlement led to its rapid development – as attested to by its huge Rynek and impressive collection of churches. Initially settled by Poles, the ethnic make-up of Kazimierz began to change with King Jan Olbracht's decision to move Kraków's significant **Jewish population** into the area from the Old Town in 1495.

In tandem with Warsaw, where a **ghetto** was created around the same time, Kazimierz grew to become one of the main cultural centres of Polish Jewry. Jews were initially limited to an area around modern-day ulica Szeroka and ulica Miodowa, and it was only in the nineteenth century that they began to spread into other parts of Kazimierz. By this time there were ghettoes all over

their Gentile neighbours. This was a period of rich cultural activity, notably in the Jewish Theatre, established in 1926 in southern Kazimierz, the biggest star being the legendary Ida Kamińska, still remembered today as one of the great prewar Polish actresses. Contemporary accounts make it clear that Kazimierz possessed a memorable and unique atmosphere, the predominantly poor but intensely vibrant Jewish community carrying on unchanged the traditions of its forebears, seemingly oblivious to the increasingly menacing world outside it.

Following the **Nazi invasion** of Poland in September 1939, Jews were increasingly subjected to discriminatory legislation. In March 1941, an official **ghetto** area was established in the **Podgórze** district, surrounded by two-metre-high walls. As the year progressed, Jews from the area surrounding Kraków were herded into the cramped ghetto, and from June 1942 onwards, mass deportations from the ghetto to Bełżec concentration camp began. Compounding the torture and destruction, a new forced labour camp was set up in November 1942 at Płaszów, just south of the ghetto (see p.386).

A major SS operation on March 14, 1943 removed or murdered the remains of the ghetto population. Those not killed in cold blood on the streets were either marched out to Płaszów or transported to the gas chambers of Auschwitz. Thus were nearly seven hundred years of Jewish presence in Kraków uprooted and effectively destroyed. Under the ruthless rule of its notorious commander **Amon Goeth**, Płaszów was transformed into a murderous work camp where those who didn't die from hunger, disease and exhaustion were regularly finished off at whim by the twisted Goeth himself, who was later caught, tried and executed in Kraków in September 1946. In January 1945, with Soviet forces rapidly advancing west, many of the surviving camp inmates were moved to Auschwitz (the workers at Oskar Schindler's factory excepted), and the site dynamited by the camp guards.

In many ways, the **postwar history** of Kraków's Jews parallels that of other Polish cities with notable prewar Jewish communities. By the end of 1945, roughly six thousand survivors had returned to the city, about a third of whom had lived there before the war. Subsequent waves of emigration to Israel and the USA went in step with the ups and downs of domestic and international politics, the largest occurring in the wake of the post-Stalinist "thaw" (1957), the Six Day War and the semi-official anti-Semitic campaigns subsequently unleashed in Poland in 1968–69, leaving an increasingly introverted and elderly community hanging on by the 1980s. Developments since the communist demise in 1989 have been marked by a notable upsurge in interest in the city's Jewish past, symbolized by the increasingly popular annual summer **Jewish Festival** (see "Festivals and events"; p.407) held in Kazimierz, and a determined drive to renovate and rebuild the fading architectural glories of the quarter. The city's Jewish population can never be fully reconstituted, but the effort to ensure that their culture and memory receive due recognition continues today.

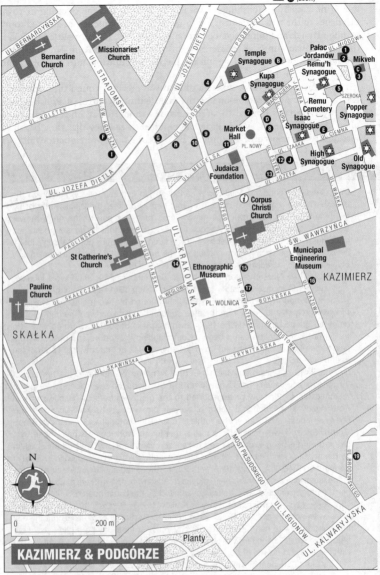

KAZIMIERZ & PODGÓRZE

the country, but descriptions of Kazimierz in Polish art and literature make it clear that there was something special about the headily Oriental atmosphere of this place.

The prewar soul of the area was to perish in the gas chambers of Bełżec, but many of the buildings, synagogues included, have survived. The past decade have seen a marked **revival** of life and activity in Kazimierz. Long-neglected

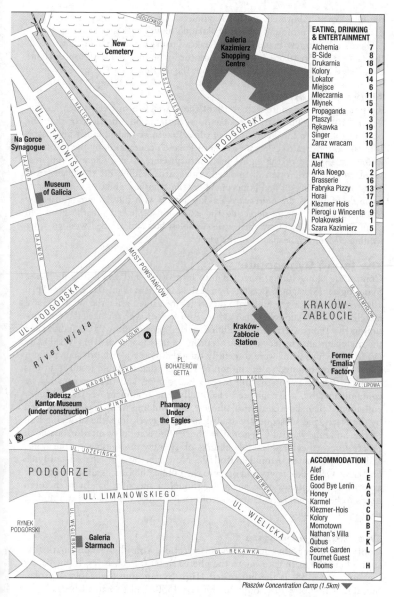

EATING, DRINKING & ENTERTAINMENT

Alchemia	7
B-Side	8
Drukarnia	18
Kolory	D
Lokator	14
Miejsce	6
Mleczarnia	11
Młynek	15
Propaganda	4
Ptaszyl	3
Rękawka	19
Singer	12
Zaraz wracam	10

EATING

Alef	1
Arka Noego	2
Brasserie	16
Fabryka Pizzy	13
Horai	17
Klezmer Hois	C
Pierogi u Wincenta	9
Polakowski	1
Szara Kazimierz	5

ACCOMMODATION

Alef	I
Eden	E
Good Bye Lenin	A
Honey	G
Karmel	J
Klezmer-Hois	C
Kolory	D
Momotown	B
Nathan's Villa	F
Qubus	K
Secret Garden	L
Tournet Guest Rooms	H

Płaszów Concentration Camp (1.5km) ▼

buildings have been renovated, and the area has seen a marked increase in visitors – in part due to Steven Spielberg's film *Schindler's List*, much of which was filmed in and around Kazimierz. Modern Kazimierz is an invigorating mixture of gentrified tourist suburb and bohemian inner-city area: cafés, bars and clubs patronized by sassy young Cracovians have successfully colonized Kazimierz's old tenement houses, making it Kraków's number one area for nightlife outside the Old Town. Above all, today's Kazimierz is a place to enjoy, as well as to ponder the more profound aspects of Poland's Jewish heritage.

There's a Kazimierz branch of the Kraków **tourist information** office at ul. Jozefa 7 (Mon–Fri 10am–4pm), and signboard-maps marked with tourist sights are planted at regular intervals throughout the district.

Along Ulica Józefa

Kazimierz is a ten-minute walk south of the Wawel (alternatively take tram #6, #8 or #10) along ulica Stradomska and its continuation, ulica Krakowska. The obvious route into the ghetto is along **ulica Józefa**, so named following Joseph II's visit to the area to celebrate southern Poland's annexation by the Habsburg Empire at the end of the eighteenth century. Here, as elsewhere in the area, wandering into the often dilapidated **courtyards** leading off the main street gives you a feeling of the atmosphere of the vanished ghetto. A memorable example of this is the **courtyard** linking Józefa with ulica Meiselsa, used by Spielberg for the scenes depicting the expulsion of Jews from the ghetto in *Schindler's List*, the whitewashed walls, cobblestones and arcaded wooden attics lending a Mediterranean aura to the place.

The Isaac Synagogue

Continuing along Józefa, turn left into ulica Kupa and you'll find the **Isaac Synagogue** (Synagoga Izaaka; Sun–Fri: May–Sept 9am–7pm; Oct–April 10am–4pm; 6zł), a graceful Baroque structure named after the wealthy local merchant, Isaac Jakubowicz (in Yiddish, Reb Ajzyk), who financed its construction in the 1630s. Getting the building started proved more of a handful than the merchant anticipated: despite securing permission from King Władysław IV, Jakubowicz's plans were forcefully opposed by the parish priest of Corpus Christi, who protested to the bishop of Kraków that it would result in priests carrying the sacraments having to pass in front of, and thus presumably be contaminated by, a synagogue. Thankfully, the bishop proved rather more enlightened than his ecclesiastical inferior, and building went ahead. Ransacked by the Nazis, and subsequently used as an artist's workshop, the surviving hull of the building was fully restored in the 1990s. The lofty interior boasts an ornate stuccoed ceiling, sizeable chunks of Hebrew inscriptions on the walls, and a reconstructed Aron Ha Kodesh. Now run by the Chabad-Lubavich branch of Orthodox Jewry and open to the public, the Isaac is all set to become a working synagogue once again – although a specially handwritten torah needs to be ceremonially delivered from Israel before the building can resume its former function.

The High Synagogue

Continuing along ulica Józefa, the intersection with ulica Jakuba marks the spot where the main gateway to the ghetto stood for centuries. Immediately beyond, at no. 38, is the buttressed **High Synagogue** (Synagoga Wysoka: Sun–Fri 9am–6pm; 8zł), built in the late 1550s and so named because the prayer hall was located on the first floor of the building, the ground floor being occupied by shops. Devastated by the Nazis, the building was renovated in the 1960s and turned into a conservation workshop. Nowadays it hosts themed exhibitions on Jewish history in the restored prayer hall, where the fragmentary remains of Hebrew inscriptions can still be seen on the walls. The Judaica-oriented Austeria bookshop (see p.409) occupies the ground floor.

▲ The Isaac Synagogue

The Old Synagogue

Further east along ulica Józefa brings you out onto **ulica Szeroka** ("Wide Street"), a broad open space whose numerous synagogues constituted the focus of religious life in Jewish Kraków. On the southern side of this truncated square stands the **Old Synagogue** (Stara Synagoga: April–Oct Mon 10am–2pm, Tues–Sun 9am–5pm; Nov–March Wed, Thurs, Sat & Sun 9am–3.30pm, Fri 10am–6pm; 8zł), the grandest of all the Kazimierz synagogues and the earliest surviving Jewish religious building in Poland. Modelled on the great European synagogues of Worms, Prague and Regensburg, the present Renaissance building was completed by Mateo Gucci in the 1570s, replacing an earlier brick building destroyed, like much of the surrounding area, by a fire in 1557.

The synagogue's story is closely entwined with the country's history. It was here that Kościuszko came to rally Kraków Jews in 1794 in support of armed resistance to the Partitions, a precedent followed by the Kazimierz rabbi Ber Meissels during the uprisings of 1831 and 1863. President Ignacy Mościcki made a symbolically important state visit to the synagogue in 1931, a move designed to demonstrate official amity with the country's Jewish population. Predictably, the Nazis did a thorough job of destroying the place. Following the war, the painstakingly rebuilt synagogue was converted into a **museum** of the history and culture of Kraków Jewry. Nazi destruction was thorough, so the museum's collection of art, books, manuscripts and religious objects has a slightly cobbled-together feel to it, though there's a powerfully evocative set of photos illustrating life in the ghetto before World War II. The superb wrought-iron bimah (pulpit) in the centre of the main prayer hall is original, the masterful product of a sixteenth-century Kraków workshop.

The Na Górce and Popper synagogues
On the east side of Szeroka, no. 22 formerly housed the **Na Górce Synagogue**, associated with Rabbi Nathan Spira, a celebrated seventeenth-century cabbalist scholar, the tercentenary of whose death was the occasion for a major commemoration in Kazimierz in 1933.

Set back from the square behind a gated yard at no. 16, the former **Popper or Stork's Synagogue** (Synagoga Poppera) is a typical brick structure raised in the 1620s by Wolf "the Stork' Popper, a wealthy merchant with trading contacts across Central Europe. These days it houses a youth cultural centre and visitors are usually welcome to look around inside, although there's little to indicate its former role as a house of prayer.

The Remu'h Synagogue and cemetery
Moving across to the western side of ulica Szeroka, the tiny **Remu'h Synagogue**, at no. 40 (Synagoga Remu: Mon–Fri: May–Sept 9am–6pm; Oct–April 9am–4pm; 6zł), is very much a functioning prayer house and a popular place of pilgrimage. It was founded in 1557 by King Sigismund August's banker, Izrael Isserlis Auerbach, probably in memory of family members felled by the plague of 1552. However, it gets its name from the founder's son Rabbi Moses Isserlis (1525–72; "Remu'h" is a shortened form of "Rabbi Moses"), whose Talmudic school was renowned throughout Europe as a leading centre of theological study. The cramped, intimate interior includes an impressive cast-iron grille surrounding the central bimah, and an ancient-looking armchair (said to have belonged to Remu'h) to the right of the Aron Ha Kodesh.

Behind the synagogue is the Remu'h **cemetery**, established twenty or so years earlier, and in use until the end of the eighteenth century, after which it was supplanted by the New Cemetery (see opposite). Many of the gravestones were unearthed in the 1950s having been covered with a layer of earth in the interwar years – a saving grace, as the rest of the cemetery was smashed up by the Nazis during the occupation. One of the finest stones is that of Rabbi Remu'h, its stele luxuriously ornamented with plant motifs. Just inside the entrance, tombstones torn up by the Nazis have been collaged together to form a high, powerful Wailing Wall.

The Museum of Galicia

Lodged in a wonderfully restored brick warehouse immediately east of ulica Szeroka, the **Museum of Galicia** (Museum of Galicia: daily 9.30am–7pm; ⓦwww.galiciajewishmuseum.org; 7zł), ul. Dajwór 18, was founded by photographer Chris Schwartz (1948–2007) to commemorate the now-disappeared Jewish communities of the former Habsburg Province of Galicia – a multi-ethic patchwork of territories which once stretched from Kraków in the west to L'viv (nowadays part of Ukraine) in the east. Centrepiece of the display is *Traces of Memory*, an evocative series of photographs by Schwarz himself illustrating the (frequently abandoned and derelict) synagogues and graveyards of southeastern Poland. The museum also hosts themed exhibitions relating to Jewish heritage, and there is a media room where you can watch 1930s documentary films illustrating Jewish life in Kraków, Vilnius and elsewhere.

The New Cemetery

A ten-minute stroll east of ulica Szeroka, on the far side of a tunnel underneath the railway tracks, the **New Cemetery** (Nowy Cmentarz) succeeded the Remu'h as the main Jewish burial site in the early 1800s. A quiet, meditative place of overgrown walkways and ivy-covered tombstones, the cemetery is among the most evocative testaments to Jewish life in the district. The New Cemetery was full by the early twentieth century and a new burial ground was established in Plaszów to the south. With the latter location destroyed by the Nazis, however, attention was re-focused on the New Cemetery as a place for post-Holocaust remembrance – and it's here that you'll find modern family memorials scattered in between the nineteenth-century gravestones.

The Tempel Synagogue

West of Szeroka along ulica Miodowa, on the corner of ulica Podbrzezie, is the **Tempel Synagogue** (Synagoga Templu: Mon–Fri 9am–5pm; 5zł), a magnificent, neo-Renaissance construction founded in 1862 by the local Association of Progressive Jews, with whose modernist, reforming theology it was long identified. This is the second of the two synagogues in Kazimierz still used for worship today. The stunning interior presents an intoxicating blend of Moorish and Gothic influences, the large central hall surrounded by the women's gallery, erected on decorated iron supports, and graced by ornate wall decorations and lavish stuccowork on the ceiling. In the centre sits the bimah, and beyond it the white marble altar, separated from the main body of the interior by a decorated screen wall. Illuminating the whole building is a glowing set of 36 stained-glass windows, featuring geometrical motifs alongside characteristic floral and plant designs.

The Kupa Synagogue

Southeast of the Tempel, ulica Warszauera leads to the **Kupa Synagogue** (Synagoga Kupa), built in the 1640s with funds collected from the local community. Extensively restored in the 2000s, it is occasionally used for religious services and also serves as a concert venue and gallery space during the annual Jewish Cultural Festival (see p.408). Few of its original interior decorations survive, save for the zodiacal paintings covering the ceiling and beams of the gallery.

Plac Nowy

At the western end of ulica Warszauera, Plac Nowy was the main market-place of nineteenth-century Kazimierz and nowadays the focus of its frenetic nightlife. Focus of the square is the centrally placed **Okrąglak** ("log"), a dodecahedron-shaped red-brick building, which served as kosher slaughterhouse and butcher's stall before World War II. It still contains a covered market, although there are talks of redeveloping it as a bar-cum-restaurant – as if Kazimierz didn't have enough of these already. The stately ochre building on the corner of plac Nowy and ulica Meiselsa was the nineteenth-century site of the Bet-ha midrash, a theological study centre which also served as a prayer house. Fully restored in the 1990s, the midrash is now home to the **Judaica Foundation** (ul. Meiselsa 17. ⓦ www.judaica.pl. Mon–Fri 10am–6pm, Sat & Sun 10am–2pm), a Jewish cultural centre that hosts regular concerts and exhibitions – it's always worth looking in to see what's going on.

The Municipal Engineering Museum

Two blocks south of plac Nowy, a former tram depot at ul. Wawryńcza 15 provide a suitably post-industrial setting for the **Municipal Engineering Museum** (Muzeum Inżynerii Miejskiej: Tues–Sun 10am–4pm; 5zł), a small but enjoyably hands-on science museum. The focus is on energy and how to generate it: you can power up a flickering light display by riding an exercise bike, plug an electric clock into a slice of fruit, or create your own hydroelectric power station by damming up a simulated mountain stream. An adjacent hall contains a small but fascinating collection of vehicles, starting with the swanky saloon cars made by the Warsaw Automobile Works in the 1950s. Unfortunately, the same models were still being churned out in the 1970s, which helps explain why Polish consumers turned their backs on domestic-designed cars and went instead for automobiles like the Polski Fiat (popularly known as the Malucha or "tiddler"), made under license in Poland until 2000. One Polish model which somehow never made it as an icon of mass-consumerism was the Smyk mini-car (made in Szczecin in 1957), which did away with the need for doors – both driver and passengers climbed in through the bonnet.

The Corpus Christi Church

As the presence of several churches indicates, the western part of Kazimierz represents the heart of the original Christian settlement. Despite its Baroque overlay, which includes some ornately carved choir stalls and a boat-shaped pulpit complete with rigging, the interior of the **Corpus Christi Church** (Kościół Bożego Ciała), on the corner of ulica Bożego Ciała, retains a high Gothic nave complete with stained-glass windows installed around 1420. Tomasso Dolabella's high-altar painting of *The Descent from the Cross* looks down on a choir lined with ornate seventeenth-century choir stalls, backed by a row of paintings illustrating scenes from the Passion. Hidden away in St Anne's chapel is the grave plaque of Italian architect Bartolomeo Berrecci, creator of the castle courtyard on Wawel Hill, who liked Kraków so much he settled down here – until killed in a drunken brawl in 1537. The Swedish king Carl Gustaf is supposed to have used the building as his operational base during the mid-seventeenth-century siege of the city.

The Ethnographic Museum

Immediately southwest of Corpus Christi is **plac Wolnica**, the old market square of Kazimierz and home to its much-rebuilt fourteenth-century **town hall**, which now houses the **Ethnographic Museum** (Muzeum Etnograficzny: Mon 10am–6pm, Wed–Fri 10am–3pm, Sat & Sun 10am–2pm; 4zł; free on Sun). This highly enjoyable treasure-trove of ethnic artefacts begins with a series of re-created peasant interiors from around Kraków. Icons painted on glass occupy corners and niches in almost every room, testifying to the richness of rural craft traditions, and the exquisitely painted furniture in the Lower Silesian room will probably have you jotting down ideas for your dream cottage. Particularly stunning is the combined kitchen, living and sleeping room from Małopolska, flamboyantly decorated with floral motifs – houses like this can nowadays only be seen in the village of Zalipie in the east of the province (see p.433). A stunningly colourful collection of costumes awaits upstairs, alongside some intriguing insights into the often bizarre world of Polish folk culture – note the goat, stork and death's-head masks worn by Christmas carollers, and the alarming straw effigies burned at Shrovetide to mark the departure of winter.

St Catherine's Church

Heading north from the Ethnographic Museum up ulica Krakowska and turning left into ulica Skałeczna brings you to **St Catherine's Church** (Kościół św. Katarzyny: Mon–Fri 10am–3pm, Sat 10am–2pm, Sun 1.30–5pm), founded by fourteenth-century monarch Kazimierz the Great for Augustine monks brought from Prague. The large basilican structure, covered by an expansive roof, is a typical and structurally well-preserved example of Kraków Gothic, though the bare interior has suffered everything from earthquakes to the installation of an Austrian arsenal. The Gothic vestibule on the southern side of the church features some delicate carved stonework, while the adjoining cloisters contain some notable surviving fragments of the original Gothic murals.

The Pauline Church at Skałka

Looming over the western end of ulica Skaleczna are the twin Baroque towers of the **Pauline Church**, traditionally known as **Skałka** (the Rock) due to the raised riverbank site it occupies. It is believed to be the place where St Stanisław, patron saint of Poland, was killed by agents of King Bolesław the Bold in 1079, and the church is very much his shrine. Main focus for pilgrims is the St Stanisław altar in the left aisle, where a piece of rock encased in glass is supposedly part of the block on which he was beheaded. Beside the Stanisław altar is a fine bust of Jan Długosz, fifteenth-century chronicler and priest on whose initiative the church was founded.

Długosz is buried in the **Vault of the Meritorious** (Grób Zaslużonych: 3zł) in the church's crypt, a patriotic shrine containing the remains of many who have made a major contribution to Polish culture. Among the artistic heavyweights laid to rest here are painters Stanisław Wyspiański and Jacek Małczewski, poet Juliusz Słowacki and composer Karol Szymanowski. The most recent inductee to the Skałka hall of fame was Nobel Prize-winning poet Czesław Milosz (1911–2004) – his stark, unadorned casket provides something of a modern counterpoint to the more ornate affairs belonging to his nineteenth-century neighbours.

Centrepiece of the church's forecourt is the **Spring of St Stanisław** (Sadzawka św Stanisława), a balustraded pool fed by natural springs. The healing qualities of the waters here are traditionally attributed to the miraculous powers of St Stanisław himself – a Baroque statue of the saint healing a sick man rises on a pillar from the centre of the pool.

Looming up behind the pool is the ungainly clump of pillars and statues that makes up the **Altar of the Third Millennium** (Altarz Trzeciego Tysiąclecia), a sculptural ensemble erected in 2007 to honour many of the spiritual figures associated with Kraków (St Stanisław and Pope John Paul II among them). An unhappy mix of modern styles, the altar seems oddly out of place in surroundings as elegant as these.

Podgórze and Płaszów

Immediately south of Kazimierz, road and rail bridges reach across the Wisła to the suburb of **Podgórze**, another part of town with strong Jewish associations. It's a gritty, workaday place that lacks the fine buildings you'll come across elsewhere in Kraków, and you'll find a corresponding shortage of cafés, restaurants or other tourist facilities.

Long an area of mixed Polish and Jewish settlement, Podgórze owes its notoriety to the creation in March 1941 of a **ghetto** (centred on the suburb's main market square, today's pl. Bohaterów Getta), into which the entire Jewish population of the city was forcibly resettled. The area was sealed off by high walls and anyone caught entering or leaving unofficially was summarily executed. In December 1942 the ghetto was divided into ghetto A for those physically fit for work, and ghetto B for the rest. In March 1943 ghetto A was relocated to the forced labour camp at Płaszów, while the inhabitants of ghetto B were either murdered on the spot or sent to the extermination camps.

The story of the wartime ghetto shot to prominence in 1994 due to Steven Spielberg's film *Schindler's List*, based on Thomas Keneally's prize-winning book recounting the wartime exploits of Oskar Schindler (1908–74), a German industrialist who saved the lives of hundreds of ghetto inhabitants. In search of authenticity, Spielberg shot the majority of the film in and around the area, sometimes using the original surviving buildings, as in the case of Schindler's Emalia factory, and in other cases, building locations from scratch – a prime example being the Płaszów concentration camp, re-created in an old quarry not far from the original site. The film has generated great interest in Podgórze's Jewish heritage, although the number of visitors who make their way down here is minuscule compared to the crowds descending on Kazimierz.

Nowadays Podgórze is the scene of major urban development. The industrial buildngs of eastern Podgórze are being demolished to make way for modern apartment blocks, while a couple of new museums – including a Museum of Contemporary Art (incorporating Schindler's former Emalia factory) and a riverfront museum devoted to theatre pioneer Tadeusz Kantor – will lend the suburb a new cultural profile.

You can get to Podgórze by heading down either Krakowska or Starowiślna from Kazimierz and crossing over the river – the cast-iron **Piłsudski Bridge** (Most Piłsudskiego) at the southern end of Krakowska provides as fine a means of approach as any. Otherwise, trams #3 and #24 trundle from the Stare Miasto via Starowiślna to Podgórze's central plac Bohaterów Getta.

Pl. Bohaterów Getta and around

Centre of the wartime ghetto, the broad expanse of plac Bohaterów Getta is home to one of the more unusual memorials to Kraków's Jewish community. Conceived by local architects Piotr Lewicki and Kazimierz Łatak in 2005, it comprises metal chairs of various heights scattered across the square. Inspiration for the memorial came from the memoirs of ghetto pharmacist Tadeusz Pankiewicz (see p.387), who witnessed the ransacking of Jewish homes during the final clearing of the ghetto in March 1943. Furniture was deliberately thrown around and smashed by the German guards, as if to symbolize the final destruction of the Jewish community in Kraków.

Sited on the southwest corner of the square is the **Pharmacy under the Eagles** (Apteka Pod Orłem: Tues–Fri 10am–4pm, Sat 10am–2pm; 5zł), the former ghetto pharmacy whose recent renovation was in part financed by Kraków ghetto survivor Roman Polański. Inside lies a well-presented photographic and documentary record of life and death in the ghetto, alongside artefacts relating to the pharmacy's wartime proprietor Dr Tadeusz Pankiewicz (1908–1993) and his three assistants – the only Gentiles permitted to live in the ghetto, and the prime point of contact between Jews and the world outside. The building at no. 6, on the other side of the square, was the headquarters of the Jewish Combat Organization (ŻOB), which helped able-bodied young Jews escape the ghetto so they could join anti-Nazi resistance groups on the outside

Podgórze's main shopping street is **ulica Limanowskiego**, just south and west of plac Bohaterów Getta. There are some fine examples of nineteenth-century red-brick architecture in the surrounding streets, one of which accommodates the **Galeria Starmach** at Węgierska 5 (Mon–Fri 11am–6pm; Ⓦ www.starmach .com.pl), Kraków's most adventurous contemporary art gallery.

The Schindler Factory

Ten minutes' walk east of the square, Oskar Schindler's **Emalia enamel factory** still stands at ul. Lipowa 4, just east of the railway tracks. It was here that the German industrialist employed over a thousand Kraków Jews in order to keep them off the Nazi deportation lists, thereby saving them from almost certain death. The building served as an electronics factory from 1945 until 2004, and is currently being redeveloped as a major cultural heritage site: a new Museum of Contemporary Art will be based here, alongside a historical exhibition devoted to wartime Kraków and the fates of the peoples who lived there – with special reference to Schindler and others who risked their lives to protect Jews.

Płaszów concentration camp

As well as imprisoning people in the ghetto, the Nazis also relocated many Jews to the **labour camp at Płaszów**, built on the far side of an old Austrian hill fort 1.5km south of Podgórze in autumn 1942. Many of the inmates succumbed to over-work, malnourishment and the arbitrary cruelty of the guards, and the site was also used for mass executions of Jews from the Podgórze ghetto. Converted into a full-blown concentration camp in January 1944, Płaszów was wound down by January the following year when its remaining prisoners were transported to Auschwitz.

Levelled after the war, the Plaszów site is now an empty heath bordered by concrete residential blocks. To get there, walk southeast from Podgórze along ulica Wielicka or take trams #3, #6, #9, #13, #23 or #24 (trams #3 and #24 come direct from the Old Town, passing through Kazimierz on the way) to the Cmentarz Podgorski stop. Head down ulica Jerozolimska (marked by a sign reading "Podgórze: dawny obóz Płaszów") to find the camp entrance, which is identified by an unassuming signboard and a bland-looking detached house – formerly the villa occupied by camp commander Amon Goeth, it's now divided up into council flats. From here a path leads southeast through the heart of the camp. Overrun by wild grasses and shrubs, this gently rolling landscape, punctuated by limestone outcrops, has the tranquil and untended feel of an inner-city nature reserve. After ten minutes a left fork leads up onto a verdant hill and to a monolithic concrete **monument** to the victims of the camp, erected in the 1960s. In true communist style, the inscription on its side refers simply to the "martyrs" of Hitlerism without mentioning their ethnicity. A smaller plaque placed nearby by the city's Jewish community states unequivocally who the victims of Płaszów actually were.

The Sanctuary of God's Mercy in Łagiewniki

Trams #11 and #23 head southwest from Podgórze's ulica Limanowskiego towards **Łagiewniki**, an area of housing projects, shopping centres and used car lots that wouldn't normally be worth a visit were it not for the strange, soaring form of the so-called **Sanctuary of God's Mercy** (Sanktuarium Bożego Miłosierdzia), a brand-new church located just uphill from the Łagiewniki tram stop. It was built to accommodate the growing number of pilgrims drawn to the next-door Convent of the Sisters of Mercy by its place in the cult of Sister Faustyna Kowalska (1905–38), a Catholic mystic who famously experienced visions of light emanating from the heart of Jesus Christ. Sister Faustyna's vision became a popular subject for spiritually inspired painters, one of whom donated a canvas to the Łagiewniki convent in 1940. Followers of Sister Faustyna – who call themselves the Apostles of Divine Mercy – have been flocking to this spot ever since. The new sanctuary, completed to coincide with the canonization of Sister Faustyna in 2000, is another example of the Polish Catholic Church's enthusiasm for boldly contemporary artistic statements. With a sky-piercing central spire and a curving, white exterior, it looks more like a beached ocean liner than a church. There's a remarkable sense of light and space inside, providing the perfect ambience for the seemingly continuous Masses which take place here throughout the day.

West of the Old Town

West of the Old Town lies a sequence of bustling residential quarters that gradually give way to several unspoilt tracts of greenery. The largest of these is **Błonia**, a large triangular meadow that hosted huge open-air masses during Pope John Paul II's visits to Poland in 1979, 1983, 1987 and 2002. This last occasion attracted an estimated 2.2 million people, and is thought to be the biggest public gathering in Polish history.

On the eastern fringes of Błonia is the National Museum, a hugely rewarding assemblage of arts and crafts that leaves few corners of Polish culture uncovered. To the west, the riverside quarter of Zwierzyniec is home to a trio of historic churches, and is also the starting point of the walk to the Kościuszko Mound, a strangely alluring man-made hill raised in tribute to a quintessentially Polish hero.

The National Museum

Ten minutes west of the Old Town along ulica Piłsudskiego, a tawny-coloured lump of interwar architecture provides a suitably imperious-looking home for the **National Museum** (Muzeum Narodowe; Tues, Thurs, Sat & Sun 10am–3pm, Wed & Fri 11am–6pm; 8zł), an impressive hoard of objects and artworks that fully merits an hour or two of your sightseeing time. The first-floor history section starts off with a **weapons gallery** packed with the shining breastplates and eagle-feather wings that made the Polish hussars such a fearsome sight on the seventeenth-century battlefields of Europe. A sizeable collection of **military uniforms** takes the story up to the twentieth century – the sober grey tunic of interwar leader Marshal Piłsudski standing in contrast to the flamboyant traditional uniforms of the Polish uhlans serving with the Austro-Hungarian cavalry.

Highlights of the first-floor **Gallery of Decorative Art** include brightly enamelled Romanesque crosses from Limoges and stunning stained glass from Kraków's medieval churches. Look out too for the display of silky robes and sashes worn by local noblemen in the seventeenth and eighteenth centuries, when the quixotic belief that the Polish aristocracy was descended from an ancient eastern tribe known as the Sarmatians sparked a craze for all things Oriental.

On the second floor, the **Gallery of Twentieth-Century Polish Art** begins with major works from artists involved in the Młoda Polska movement, including several stained-glass window designs sketched out by Józef Mehoffer, and Włodzimierz Tetmayer's canvas *Blessings of Easter Food* – a village festival scene highlighting the fascination with folk costume that fired much of the art of the period. The big names of the post-World War II era are strongly featured too: look out for Maria Jarema's jazzy abstract paintings of the 1950s, the colour-charged canvases of the subtly primitivist Jerzy Nowosielski, and a recreation of the stage-set for Tadeusz Kantor's disturbing 1975 play *The Dead Class*, pointing to the complex relationship between drama, sculpture and performance that characterized the Kraków arts scene of the time.

The Silesian House

A fifteen-minute walk north of the National Museum but well worth the detour, the **Silesian House**, ul. Pomorska 2 (Dom Śląski: May–Oct Tues–Sat 10am–5.30pm, Nov–April Tues, Thurs–Sat 9am–4pm, Wed 11am–6pm; free), is the kind of place whose mention still sends a shudder down Cracovian spines. Built in the 1930s to provide hostel accommodation for Silesian students (hence the name), it was turned into an interrogation centre by the Gestapo during the Nazi occupation, and today hosts a small museum devoted to World War II and its aftermath. The cells where Polish prisoners were tortured are preserved pretty much as they were, together with the graffiti scratched by the inmates. An adjacent hall tells the history of Kraków from 1939 to 1956, with a fascinating collection of documentary photographs drawing together the horrors of the Nazi period and the grim years of Stalinism that followed. One picture shows Plaszów concentration camp chief Amon Goeth parading for the photographer on his white horse – an image that may be familiar to those who have seen the film *Schindler's List*.

Zwierzyniec

Southwest of the National Museum lies the river-hugging Zwierzyniec district, one of the city's oldest suburbs. Perched at the edge of the river opposite the Salwator tram stop (terminus of lines #1, #2 and #6 from the Old Town), the **Norbertine church and monastery** is a fortified thirteenth-century structure with a fine Romanesque portal (all that remains of the original building) and a restful Neoclassical interior. Used by the nuns living in the complex, it's a good spot for a quiet moment away from the city bustle. The church isn't often open, though, so it's best to visit around the time of services – 5pm is generally a good bet. The Lajkonik pageant (see p.407), believed to have been initiated by the nuns, starts from outside the complex in June.

Just up the hill from here is the **Church of the Saviour** (Kościół Salwatora), one of the oldest in the city. Built on the site of a pagan Slav temple, excavations have revealed three earlier Romanesque churches, the oldest dating back to around 1000 AD. The church squats in the middle of an attractive walled graveyard, although it's rarely open except on Sundays. Diagonally opposite the church is the curious octagonal **Chapel of St Margaret** (Kaplica św. Małgorzaty), an eighteenth-century wooden structure that rises out of the earth like a big brown breast. It's rarely open however, hosting Masses on the first and third Sundays each month only.

The Kościuszko Mound

From the Salwator church, the tree-lined aleja J. Waszyngtona heads west towards the **Kościuszko Mound** (Kopiec Kościuszki: daily 9am–dusk; 5zł), a hundred-metre-high cone of soil erected in the 1820s in honour of Poland's greatest revolutionary hero, **Tadeusz Kościuszko** (see box below). A veteran of the American War of Independence, Kościuszko returned to Poland to lead the 1794 resistance against the Partitions, and has served as a personification of Poland's resistance tradition ever since. The Kościuszko's Mound is the best-known example of a uniquely Cracovian phenomenon which dates back as far as the seventh century – when man-made mounds were raised to honour chieftains or provide a platform for sky-worship. The tradition was continued with the construction of the Piłsudski Mound in the 1930s (see p.391), and current talk suggests that the next recipient of such a tribute will be Pope John Paul II.

The final approaches to the mound are dominated by a huge red-brick fort built by the city's Austrian rulers in the 1850s, and currently housing the **RMF radio station** – which explains why the fort's central courtyard bears the name of plac Paul McCartney. Work your way round to the back of the fort to gain access to the mound itself, which from this perspective looks like an enormous green pudding. An easily scaled spiral path winds its way to the top, where you can savour panoramic views back towards central Kraków, with the Wawel clearly visible in the foreground and the smokestacks of Nowa Huta further away to the northeast, even reaching as far as the Tatra mountains on really clear days.

If you're not in the mood for walking, you can catch bus #100, which runs to the mound and back from the Dębnicki stop near Rondo Grunwaldzkie, just across the river from the Wawel.

Tadeusz Kościuszko (1746–1817)

What Adam Mickiewicz (see p.78) is to the Polish literary Romantic tradition, **Tadeusz Kościuszko** is to its heroic military counterpart. The swashbuckling leader of armed resistance in the early Partition years, Kościuszko was also a noted radical whose espousal of republican ideals did little to endear him to fellow aristocrats, but did everything to win over the hearts and minds of the oppressed Polish peasantry. Kościuszko is also almost as well known in the USA as within Poland itself on account of his major role in the **American War of Independence**, in thanks for which he was made both an honorary American citizen and brigadier general in the US Army.

The bare bones of Kościuszko's life story revolve round a fabulously contorted series of battles, insurrections, revolutions and impossible love affairs. An outstanding student, he fled to Paris in 1776 to escape from a general with whose daughter he had tried to elope, continuing on to America, where he joined up with the independence forces fighting the British. In the following five years he was right in the thick of things, helping to bring about the capitulation of the British forces under General Burgoyne at Saratoga (Oct 1778), and involved in both the important **Battle of the Ninety-Six** and the lengthy **blockade of Charleston** (1781).

Returning to Poland in 1784, he faced a long period out in the political cold before finally gaining military office in 1789 – simultaneously failing (again) to win the consent of a general with whose eighteen-year-old daughter he had fallen in love. Kościuszko's finest hour came in 1792 when the tsarist armies invaded Poland to depose an anti-Russian government. After the bloody **Battle of Dubienka** (July 1792), Kościuszko was promoted to general by King Stanisław Poniatowski, also receiving honorary French citizenship from the newly established revolutionary government in Paris. Initially exiled to Saxony, Kościuszko returned to Poland at

Las Wolski and the western suburbs

Blessed with extensive patches of greenery and liberally sprinkled with low hills, Kraków's **western suburbs** offer an experience very different from the tourist-trodden streets of the city centre. Central to the area's appeal is **Las Wolski**, a huge wedge of forest which gives Cracovians a genuine piece of wild countryside right on their doorstep. A **zoo**, various historical villas and the little-visited **Camadulensian Hermitage** provide ample focus for your wanderings. Further afield, both the **Benedictine abbey** at **Tyniec** and the Art Nouveau-flavoured **Rydlówka** museum in **Bronowice Małe** offer intriguing encounters with Kraków history in an out-of-town setting.

The Las Wolski area presents several good opportunities for **cycling**: potential itineraries include the trip from Zwierzyniec past the Kościuszko Mound and into Las Wolski forest; or along the south bank of the Wisła towards Tyniec. The gravelly tracks of the Las Wolski itself are perfect for a moderate burst of **mountain biking**.

Las Wolski and the Piłsudski Mound

A rippling succession of densely wooded hill, **Las Wolski** (Wolski Forest) lies 4km west of city's Old Town. Crisscrossed by marked paths, it's a popular area for picnics, hiking and mountain biking. The ideal starting point for exploration of the area is **Kraków Zoo** (daily: May–Sept 9am–7pm; March, April Oct & Nov 9am–5pm; Dec–Feb 9am–3pm; 12zł; Ⓦwww .zoo-krakow.pl), right in the centre of the forest. The zoo can be reached on bus #134 (every 20–30min) from the *Hotel Cracovia* stop near the National Museum. The zoo itself, with cages and enclosures set out among well-tended shrubs and

the request of patriotic insurgents, swearing his famous **Oath of National Uprising** before a huge crowd assembled on the Rynek Główny in Kraków in March 1794.

Kościuszko's disciplined army, largely comprising scythe-bearing peasants, won a famous victory over Russian forces at the **Battle of Racławice** (April 1794). In a bid to gain more volunteers, Kościuszko issued the **Połaniec Manifesto** (May 1794), offering among other things to abolish serfdom, a radical move resisted by aristocratic supporters. Withdrawing to Warsaw, Polish forces held out for two months against the combined might of the Prussian and Russian armies, Kościuszko himself leading the bayonet charges at a couple of critical junctures. Kościuszko was finally defeated and captured by the Russians at Maciejowice, an event that led to the collapse of the national uprising.

Imprisoned in St Petersburg and by now seriously ill, Kościuszko was freed in 1796 and returned to the USA to an enthusiastic reception in Philadelphia, soon striking up what proved to be a lasting friendship with Thomas Jefferson. The last decades of Kościuszko's life were marked by a series of further disappointments. He revisited France in 1798 and tried, unsuccessfully, to persuade Napoleon of the need to re-establish an independent Poland. After Bonaparte's fall in 1814 Kościuszko was approached by Russian emperor Alexander I, who attempted to gain his approval for the new Russian-ruled **Congress Kingdom** established at the Congress of Vienna (1815). Uncompromising republican to the last, the radical conditions he put forward met with no response. An embittered Kościuszko retired to Switzerland, where he died in 1817. Two years later the legendary warrior's remains were brought to Kraków and buried among the monarchs in the vaults of Wawel. Reviving a pagan Polish burial custom, the people of the city raised the **memorial mound** to him that you can still visit today.

flower beds, is a pleasantly park-like space that's very popular with local families. The **café** outside the zoo gates makes for a convenient refreshment stop before moving on.

An easy ten-minute stroll northwest of the zoo stands the **Piłsudski Mound** (Kopiec Piłsudski), raised in 1934 to mark the twentieth anniversary of the Polish Legion – a military outfit formed to fight for Polish independence under the auspices of the Habsburg Empire. When the Legion's founder Marshal Józef Piłsudski died a year later, the mound was re-dedicated to him. Built by ten thousand patriotic volunteers, the mound has had something of a chequered history: during World War II the German occupiers planted it with trees in an attempt to cover it up, while serious rains in 1997 eroded the mound to the point of obliteration. Subsequent renovation (with bags of soil ceremonially delivered from historically important sites all over Poland) has produced the lush green cone visible today. Paths spiral upwards to the 38-metre-high summit, where visitors can enjoy a sumptuous panorama of Las Wolski's forest canopy, with the church spires of central Kraków further over to the east.

Decjusz Park

Some 2km north of the Pilsudski Mound, the tree-shaded lawns of the **Decjusz Park** mark the northern boundary of the Las Wolski area. Presiding over the park is the **Decjusz Villa** (Willa Decjusza), a Renaissance chateau built by Bartolomeo Berrecci for Jost Ludvik Decjusz (1485–1545), secretary to King Sigismund the Old and an enthusiastic patron of the arts. It's now occupied by the Decjusz Foundation, which organizes exchanges and get-togethers for artists and writers from all over central and eastern Europe. The Villa is not open to visitors but the arcaded, partly tiled exterior is worth a glimpse. The northern edge of Decjusza Park is marked by one of Kraków's more curious galleries, the **Bronisław Chromy Gallery** (Galeria Autorska Prof B. Chromego: April–Oct daily noon–8pm; free), a much-altered concert bowl leased to the eponymous modern sculptor to provide an exhibition space for his works. A silvery dome rising out of a grassy hollow, it looks rather like a Byzantine cathedral designed by hobbits. There's an exhibition space and café inside, and a selection of sculptures scattered across the lawn outside.

Przegorzały

Marking the southeastern edge of Las Wolski is **Przegorzały**, a wooded hilltop overlooking the river Wisła. It was here that the architect Adolf Szyszk Bohusz, chief restorer of Kraków's historical monuments during the 1920s, decided to build his family home – a mock-medieval castle that looks rather as if a fragment of Wawel Hill had been dropped unceremoniously in the forest. The building was requisitioned by Nazi governor of the Kraków district Otto Wachter during World War II, and a fancy neo-Gothic tower was added to serve as a luxury holiday home for vacationing Luftwaffe pilots. Subsequently used by Kraków University as a conference centre, and currently home to the *U Ziyada* bar-restaurant, it's popular with city folk as an out-of-town dining and drinking spot, especially during the summer. And understandably so: the main balcony offers a superb vantage point from which to take in the tranquil rural surroundings, with the Tatra mountains visible in the distance on a really clear summer's day. A few minutes' uphill from the castle lies the modern campus of the **Institute of Polish and Ethnic Studies** (Instytut Studiów Polonijnych i Etnicznych: also home to the *Dom Gościnny Przegorzały* **hotel**; see p.354), behind which you can pick up trails back into the heart of Las

Wolski. Buses #109, #209, #229, #239 and #249 from Salwator run past the access road to the centre.

The Camadulensian Hermitage at Bielany

Over on the southwestern edge of the Las Wolski, the domes and towers of the **Camadulensian Hermitage** (Pustenia Kamedułów: gates opened at half-hour intervals between 9–11am and 3–4.30pm) poke up invitingly from a tree-covered hill. It was founded in 1620 by Mikołaj Wolski Crown Marshal of Poland, a lifetime dabbler in alchemy who decided to renounce the black arts, inviting the famously ascetic Camadulensian order to Kraków by way of repentance. It's an easy walk or cycle ride from either Las Wolski Zoo or Przegorzały; otherwise take bus #109, #209, #229 or #239 from Salwator, alighting at the Srebrna Góra stop, from where it's a fifteen-minute walk up the hill. Bear in mind before you visit that **women** are not admitted in the complex except on certain religious holidays (Easter, Assumption and a smattering of other prominent Sundays throughout the year).

Hidden behind a high wall, only the hermitage's church and immediate forecourt are open to visitors: the monks themselves devote their days to gardening, prayer and long hours of silence (hence the rather restricted opening hours). Once inside the gate, the monumental facade of the **monastery church** makes an immediate impression, with bands of different-coloured limestone framed by a stout pair of square towers. Inside, a barrel-vaulted nave is lined by a series of ornate chapels, the most notable of which honours the Camadulensian order's founder **St Romuald** with a lavish series of paintings by the artist Tommaso Dolabella depicting the life of the saint. Steps lead down to the **crypt**, where the bodies of deceased hermits are stored in sealed niches for eighty years or so, after which they're taken out and buried in order to make room for the next generation of the dead.

Tyniec

Three kilometres southwest of Bielany on the opposite bank of the river, the village suburb of **Tyniec** is a popular excursion spot on summer weekends on account of its **abbey**, an eleventh-century foundation that was the Benedictines' first base in Poland. It's easy to get to from central Kraków, with bus #112 making its way here from the Dębnicki stop just across the river from the Wawel.

Perched on a white limestone cliff on the edge of the village, the abbey makes an impressive sight from the riverbank paths. The original Romanesque abbey was rebuilt after the Tatars destroyed it during the 1240 invasion, and then completely remodelled in Gothic style in the fifteenth century, when the defensive walls were also added. Most of the church's interior furnishings date from the Baroque era; particularly charming are the pulpit in the form of a ship's prow, and choir stalls individually painted with scenes from the life of St Benedict. From June to August the church holds a series of high-quality **organ concerts** during which the cloisters are opened.

Bronowice Małe

Straddling the main westbound highway 4km northwest of the centre, **Bronowice Małe** is nowadays an anonymous suburban district no different to hundreds of others around the country. However, to pre-World War I artistic folk, it was one of the most captivating places the Kraków region had to offer: an unspoiled village full of rustic buildings whose inhabitants still wore traditional costume. Many of the figures associated with the **Młoda Polska** period (see box, p.364) came here to sketch, scribble poems or meditate, among them the painter Włodzimierz Tetmayer (brother of the poet Kazimierz), who scandalized Kraków society by falling in love with – and marrying – local Bronowice girl Anna Mikołajczykówna in 1890. Not to be outdone, essayist and playwright Lucjan Rydel tied the knot with Anna's sister Jadwiga ten years later. To their Młoda Polska contemporaries both Tetmayer and Rydel were living embodiments of the effort to rejuvenate Polish culture through contact with its peasant roots. Stanisław Wyspiański (himself married to peasant girl Teofila Pytko) used the weddings as real-life source material in his epoch-defining play *Wesele* ("The Wedding") – a haunting, hypnotic piece premiered in 1901 and still an unavoidable fixture in the Polish theatrical repertoire.

Built by Tetmayer in 1894, the delightful manor house known as the **Rydlówka** at ul. Tetmajera 28 (Tues, Wed, Fri & Sat 9am–3pm, Thurs 1–5pm; 6zł) was the site of Rydel's wedding party. Rydel went on to buy the house from Tetmayer in 1908 (hence its name), and his descendants still live here. Inside lies a treasure-trove of Młoda Polska memorabilia, with cupboards and chests painted with folk motifs revealing the respect in which traditional Polish crafts were held. There are numerous photographs of the main protagonists in the Bronowice story, alongside pictures of the early productions of Wyspiański's play – with Rydel, appropriately enough, playing the groom. A display of traditional Polish wedding costumes rounds off the exhibition with a vivacious dash of colour. There's no labelling of any kind, but the English-language leaflet (3zł) is an excellent guide to the house – and one of the curators may well take time off to show you around.

Bronowice Małe can be reached by taking trams #4, #13 and #24 from Basztowa to the Bronowice terminus and walking north up Zielony Most – after passing under the railway, ulica Tetmajer is on your left. There's little else worth visiting in this part of Kraków, and precious few cafés or restaurants.

Nowa Huta and around

Raised from scratch in the late 1940s on the site of an old village, the vast industrial and residential complex of **Nowa Huta** ("New Forge") now has a population of more than 200,000, making it by far Kraków's biggest suburb. Intended by the communists to function as a working-class counterweight to Catholic, conservative Kraków, Nowa Huta confounded its creators by becoming one of the epicentres of Solidarity-era opposition activity and all-round resistance to communist rule. The locals campaigned hard for the right to build churches in what was originally intended as an atheist proletarian paradise, and it is these churches – often featuring ground-breaking modern architecture – that constitute the main reason to visit Nowa Huta today.

Much of Nowa Huta's population worked in the massive steelworks at the suburb's eastern end, its smoke-billowing chimneys creating serious environmental problems until stiff controls on emissions were introduced in the 1990s. Originally named after Vladimir Ilich Lenin, the steelworks are now owned by Arcelor Mittal and continue to produce a million tones of steel per year.

From Kraków city centre, it's a forty-minute tram journey (#4, #9, #15 or #22) to Nowa Huta's **plac Centralny**, a huge hexagonal space ringed by typically grey slabs of Socialist Realist architecture. From here, seemingly endless streets of residential blocks stretch out in all directions – a bigger contrast with Kraków's Old Town would be hard to imagine.

Plac Centralny and aleja Róż

Made up of broad avenues laid out on a geometric plan, Nowa Huta is a Stalinist-era re-working of Renaissance ideals – although the jury is still out on whether the settlement deserves to be studied as an important example of urban planning or simply consigned to the dustbin of architectural history. At its centre is **plac Centralny**, which incorporates the arcading typical of a sixteenth-century market square into a monumental series of grim residential blocks. Originally named after Josef Stalin, the square was re-dedicated to Ronald Reagan after 1990 – although plac Centralny is the moniker that has stuck in the popular consciousness.

Leading north from the square is the largely pedestrianized **Rose Alley** (aleja Róż), where a less impressive ensemble of grey Sixties-era apartments look down on the vivacious reds and pinks of well-tended rose beds. A statue of Lenin, erected here in 1973, was a long-serving focus of popular ridicule – local steelworker Andrzej Szewczuwaniec unsuccessfully tried to blow it up on the night of 19 April 1979. Ten years later it was dismantled and sold to controversial Swedish businessman "Big" Bengt Erlandsson, who re-erected it (somewhat incongruously) in a wild-west theme park just outside Stockholm.

A short distance up aleja Róż, the **Historical Museum of Nowa Huta**, os. Słonecznie 16 (Dzieje Nowej Huty: May–Oct Tues–Sat 9.30am–5pm, Nov–April Tues, Thurs–Sat 9am–4pm, Wed 10am–5pm; 4zł) doesn't have a permanent collection, but does host frequently fascinating exhibitions about the settlement's history. It also functions as a **tourist information centre**, distributing free brochures and maps.

A short walk northwest of the museum is the small and unassuming **Sacred Heart Church** (Kościół Najświętszego Serca Jezusowego) on the corner of Obrońców Krzyża and Ludźmierska, built in 2001 to mark the spot on which the settlement's inhabitants erected a wooden cross in 1960 to protest against the anti-church posture of their communist rulers. Opposite the church, ulica Ignacego Maścickiego is the site of an altogether different kind of memorial (and one of the few surviving socialist-era monuments in Nowa Huta), the **Josif Stalin 2 tank**. Basically a late version of the Soviet-built T-34, tanks such as these were used by the Polish armies who fought under Soviet command towards the end of World War II, and although this particular model may never have seen actual combat, it nevertheless serves as a fitting tribute to former combatants.

The Ark of the Lord

The best-known symbol of Nowa Huta's rejection of state-sponsored atheism is the **Ark of the Lord** (Arka Pana), a boldly innovative church whose appearance on the settlement's skyline was greeted with grim resignation by the communist authorities. Designed by Wojciech Petrzyk in the late sixties, the church's curvy Le Corbusier-influenced exterior was a clear demonstration of the Polish church's superiority to the communist party in the style stakes as well as the spiritual field. The Ark bears added significance for locals because of its close association with Karol Wojtyła. He was the bishop who lobbied for its construction, celebrated Mass at the site before building started, personally laid the foundation stone in 1969, and (by now a cardinal) consecrated the church on May 15 1977.

Although officially dedicated to the Virgin Mary, the church got its name from its ark-like shape, with a concrete cross emerging mast-like from what looks like the prow of some huge ocean-going craft. Dark and smooth when seen from a distance, the outer walls are encrusted with mountain pebbles, giving them an organic sensuous texture when close up. The interior is no less revolutionary – everything you would expect to see in a Catholic church is here, but seems to have been pulled out of place: instead of a high altar, Bronisław Chromy's bronze statue of Christ on the Cross is positioned halfway down the aisle, the Saviour seemingly poised to leap out Icarus-like over the congregation; while secondary chapels are placed at mezzanine level instead of to the right and left of the nave.

To get to the Ark, take tram #5 (from Basztowa in the Old Town or from plac Centralny in Nowa Huta) to aleja Kocmyrzowska, then walk north up ulica Obrońców Krzyża.

The Maximilian Kolbe church

The area's other main church, the large **Maximilian Kolbe Church** (Kościół św. Maximiliana Kolbego) in the Mistrzejowice district, was built on the site of a wooden shed where, for many years, people from Nowa Huta held religious services in the absence of a proper church. Priest Karol Wojtyła celebrated Midnight Mass here on Christmas Eve 1971, and returned as Pope John Paul II in 1983 to consecrate this new church dedicated to one of Catholic Poland's most important martyrs. Kolbe, canonized in 1982, was a priest sent to Auschwitz for giving refuge to Jews; in the camp, he took the place of a Jewish inmate in the gas chambers. Although not as striking as the Arka, the Kolbe church is another fine example of how the contemporary arts have been put to good use by the ecclesiastical authorities, with angular concrete ribbing adorning the ceiling, and an impressively anguished Crucifixion above the main altar. Trams #1, #16 and #20 from plac Centralny all pass by the building.

The Cistercian abbey of Mogiła

In total contrast to these recent constructions is the **Cistercian Abbey** (Opactwo Cystersów) in the semi-rural suburb of Mogiła, 2km east of plac Centralny, just off aleja Ptaszyckiego. To get there, take tram #15 or #20 from plac Centralny (the #15 runs direct from Basztowa in the Old Town) and get off at ulica Klasztorna – the monastery is five minutes' walk south. Built around 1260 on the regular Cistercian plan of a triple-aisled basilica with a series of chapels in the transepts, the Abbey Church, one of the finest examples of early Gothic in the region, is a tranquil, meditative spot, the airy interior graced with a fine series of Renaissance murals. There's a serene Gothic statue of the Madonna and Child on the main altar, and some exuberant stained glass.

Across the road from the monastery is the **Church of St Bartholomew** (Kościół św. Bartolomieja), one of the oldest wooden churches in the country, with an elaborately carved doorway from 1466 and a Baroque belfry. The interior is filled with zestful seventeenth-century paintings illustrating the life of the saint.

The Polish Air Museum

On the western side of Nowa Huta, just north of aleja Jana Pawła II, the **Polish Air Museum** (Muzeum Lotnictwa Polskiego: May–Oct: Tues–Fri 9am–5pm, Sat & Sun 10am–4pm; Nov–April: Mon–Fri 9am–4pm; ⓦwww.muzeumlotnictwa .pl; 7zł) celebrates the country's contribution to aviation with several hangars full of aircraft, including many of the Polish-made machines of the interwar years, a period when the local plane-building industry really looked as if it was going somewhere. Particularly eye-catching is the PZP PIIc, an innovative gull-wing aircraft produced in 1935 whose design was much copied by rival manufacturers. Although Poland's fledgling air force made little impact in World War II, many of its pilots escaped to Britain to serve with the Polish Air Wing of the

RAF – celebrated here with the inclusion of a Spitfire fighter aircraft. There's a row of Russian-built Cold War-era aircraft parked outside, with tube-shaped MIGs being upstaged by the sleek, silver-bodied Illyushin bombers.

Trams #4 and #15 run along aleja Jana Pawła II, just south of the museum – get off at the Park Lotników Polskich stop and walk up through the park.

The Stanisław Lem Garden of Experiments

Named after the popular science fiction writer and long-time Kraków resident Staniśaw Lem (1921–2006), the **Garden of Experiments** (Ogród Doswiadczeń im. Stanisława Lema: daily: May–Sept 9am–7pm, April & Oct 10am–6pm; 6zł, children 4zł, family ticket 18zł) occupies a large open-air site in the southeastern corner of Park Lotników Polskich – an attractively leafy area that's well worth a stroll in its own right. The main purpose of the garden is to encourage children of all ages to engage with the laws of physics by playing around with various pieces of apparatus. Visitors can swing around on the end of a huge pendulum, bang away on an outlandish xylophone to test the resonance of different materials, or try balancing on wobbly boards to learn a thing or two about the nature of equilibrium. Each of the attractions is accompanied by English-language instruction plaques, and adults will wish that science lessons had been this much fun at school.

To get to the garden, either take trams #4 or #15 to the Park Lotników Polskich stop and walk south (15min), or ride tram #22 to the M1 shopping centre, which is right opposite the garden's gate.

Wieliczka

Fifteen kilometres southeast of Kraków is the **salt mine** at **WIELICZKA** (Kopalnia Soli Wieliczka), a unique phenomenon described by one eighteenth-century visitor as being "as remarkable as the Pyramids and more useful". Today it's listed among UNESCO's World Cultural Heritage monuments. Salt deposits were discovered here as far back as the eleventh century, and from King Kazimierz's time onwards local mining rights, and hence income, were strictly controlled by the Crown. During World War II, the Germans manufactured aircraft parts in Wieliczka's subterranean chambers, using Poles and Jews as slave labour. Active mining ceased in 1997, although salt is still extracted from water seepages and much of the salt sold in Poland still comes from here. Profitability as a tourist attraction ensures that the mine remains a major employer: indeed its popularity is such that you should be prepared for big crowds in summer.

Regular **trains** run from Kraków Główny to Wieliczka-Rynek, a short distance downhill from the mine. You can also get to Wieliczka by **minibus**, from the stop on ulica Starowiślna near Kraków's main post office.

The mine

Entrance to the mine (mid-April to mid-Oct daily 7.30am–7.30pm; mid-Oct to mid-April Tues–Sun 8am–5pm; 65zł; ⓦwww.kopalnia.pl) is by guided **tour** only. Polish-language tours depart as soon as thirty people have assembled, while English-language tours are more strictly timetabled (May–Sept: 10am, 11.30am, 12.30pm, 1.45pm, 3pm and 5pm; Oct–April: 10am & 12.30pm). Ticket-office queues are long, especially in summer and at weekends. Be prepared for a bit of a walk – the tour takes two hours, through nearly two miles of tunnels. The temperature inside the mine is a constant 14°C, so remember to take a sweater or jacket.

The result of almost ten centuries of continuous excavation, the salt mine covers a much bigger area than the town itself. It consists of an estimated three hundred kilometres of passageways on nine levels, the deepest of which is nearly 330m below ground. The 3.5km-long tourist route only takes in a fraction of this, descending through three levels to a depth of 125m – still sufficient to give you an impression of the mine's staggering scale.

The journey starts by walking down a long wooden staircase, escorted by guides wearing the smart green-and-black uniforms traditionally worn by salt miners on ceremonial occasions. Down below, visitors pass through a succession of chambers carved from the dark grey salt. For much of its history the mine was a virtual underground city where people worked, ate, kept horses and stored business archives. The only thing they didn't do here was sleep.

The undoubted highlight of the tour is the **St Kinga's chapel** (Kaplica św Kingi), with stairs, banisters and chandeliers carved out of the salt by several generations of miners. Józef Markowski began decorating the chapel in 1895, fashioning a pulpit in the form of Kraków's Wawel hill, and a statue of St Kinga on the high altar. Daughter of King Bela IV of Hungary and wife of Bolesław the Chaste of Poland, Kinga allegedly lost her engagement ring somewhere south of Kraków, only to retrieve it some time later encased in a lump of Wieliczka salt – Kinga has been patron of Wieliczka's miners ever since. Work on the chapel is still going on, one of the most recent sculptural additions being a statue of Pope John Paul II.

Down at the lowest level, the cavernous Warsaw Hall (Komora Warszawa) serves as a concert venue and can hold a full symphony orchestra on its salt-carved stage. Also on the same level, a small **museum** reveals what a back-breaking job mining must have been – until the advent of mechanization, rock salt was laboriously crushed with hand-operated wooden machines. Pictures and manuscripts bear testimony to famous visitors such as Balzac, Emperor Franz Josef and Goethe who, as an official attached to the mining department in Weimar, found Wieliczka more impressive than the historical splendours of nearby Kraków.

The tour over, you can shop for salt-related souvenirs in the subterranean gift store, eat in the cafeteria, or send a card from the mine's post office, before returning to the surface via the noisily clanking lift.

Eating

Kraków's burgeoning tourist status has given rise to an ever-increasing selection of good **restaurants**, with new places springing up every week. There's still a number of traditional, order-at-the-counter **canteens** (*jadłodajnia* or *bar mleczny*, literally "milk bar") serving up filling and cheap portion of Polish standards such as *pierogi*, *barszcz* and *placki*.

Mainstream restaurants concentrate on the pork, veal and poultry dishes traditional to Polish cuisine, usually with the addition of a few steaks and other international dishes. Mediterranean cuisine is common in the more style-conscious establishments, and Asian restaurants – some Arabic and Indian, but mostly Chinese and Vietnamese – are making their presence felt in and around the centre. Several eateries in the Kazimierz district concentrate on the Jewish culinary tradition, with dishes like jellied carp and *czulent* (meat-and-barley stew) appearing on menus. Wherever you eat you'll find **prices** somewhat cheaper than in Western Europe, even in the smart places on and around the Rynek. Places can get crowded on busy summer weekends, when it's well worth reserving a table in advance if you've set your heart on a particular place.

You'll have no trouble picking up kebabs or similarly international **snack food** in the city centre. There are also numerous hole-in-the-wall joints doling out *zapiekanki*, baguette-sized slices of Polish bread topped with toasted cheese, tomato, mushrooms and a variety of other ingredients.

Canteen restaurants

The Old Town

Restaurants below are marked on the "Kraków: City Centre" map on p.356.

Chimera ul. św. Anny 3. Expansive buffet selection in a soothing courtyard, with attractively priced main courses, a salad bar, and plenty of vegetarian choices. Daily 11am–10pm.

Greenway ul. Mikołajska 12. Cheerful order-at-the-counter restaurant offering a veggie spin on traditional Polish fare – such as cabbage leaves (*gołąbki*) stuffed with *kasha* (buckwheat) – as well as a few international dishes. Mon–Fri 10am–10pm, Fri & Sat 11am–8pm.

Stars and salads ul. Karmelicka 14. Canteen food in a modern, lounge-bar environment, with a good choice of main meals (including some pasta and vegetarian choices) and a salad bar strong on traditional Polish ingredients – red cabbage, grated carrot and other crunchy vegetables. Daily 7am–10pm.

U Babci Maliny ul. Sławkowska. The grand old duchess of order-at-the-counter canteens, hidden away in the basement of the Polish Academy of Sciences (PAN) building and decked out like a nineteenth-century Polish peasant's hut. Inexpensive Polish staples (including succulent *pierogi* served in a wooden trough), as well as fancier options such as wild boar and duck. Mon–Fri 9am–7pm, Sat & Sun 10am–5pm.

Vega ul. Krupnicza 22. Comfy vegetarian café-restaurant offering an excellent choice of cheap and healthy stews and savoury pancakes, along with a good salad selection. Also at ul. św Gertrudy 7. Daily 9am–10pm.

Zapiecek ul. Sławkowska 32. Simple wooden-bench eatery that serves excellent *pierogi* made on the premises. Own-recipe specials include vegetarian *pierogi* with broccoli, and *pierogi kresowie* (*pierogi* stuffed with buckwheat and chopped liver). Daily 10am–9pm.

Kazimierz and around

Restaurants below are marked on the "Kazimierz & Podgórze" map on p.378.

Pierogi u Wincenta ul. Bożego Ciała 12. Lemon walls and a weird-shaped chandelier make this quite an arty place in which to wolf down a broad selection of own-recipe *pierogi*. Wincent's trademark minced-meat-and-lentil *pierogi* are well worth trying, and there are plenty of fruit-filled sweet *pierogi* if you're angling for a dessert. Mon–Wed & Sun noon–10pm, Thurs noon–11pm, Fri & Sat noon–midnight.

Polakowski ul. Miodowa 39. Tasty Polish food served up in a country-kitchen interior. Very popular, so be prepared to share a table. Daily 9am–10pm.

Restaurants

The Old Town and around

Restaurants below are marked on the "Kraków: City Centre" map; p.356.

Ancora ul. Dominikańska 3 ☏012/357 3355. Mediterranean-Polish fusion food in a creamy-brown contemporary space that seems squarely aimed at the young and upwardly mobile. The menu embraces everything from cold *barszcz* soup to exquisitely grilled fillets of meat and top-quality shellfish. Main courses are in the 50–60zł range; the six-course set gourmet menu (150zł) is well worth considering if you want to push the boat out. The wine list is exemplary but it does come with a price tag. Daily noon–11pm.

Balaton ul. Grodzka 37. ☏012/422 4269. Cheap, unpretentious Hungarian-themed restaurant serving up a smooth and creamy paprika-rich goulash, freshwater fish, and some robust red wines. Mains shouldn't exceed the 20zł mark. Daily noon–10pm.

CK Dezerter ul. Bracka 6. ☏012/422 7931, ⓦwww.ck-dezerter.pl. Named after a popular TV series about Polish soldiers serving the Habsburg Empire, this restaurant uses sepia photographs and antique-style knick-knacks to create a cosy nineteenth-century sense of atmosphere. The menu concentrates on tried-and-tested Polish favourites, from *pierogi*, *bigos* and the like to more substantial meat and fish dishes. Daily 10am–11pm.

Chłopskie Jadło ul. św. Jana 3 ☏012/429 5157, ⓦwww.chlopskiejadlo.pl. Rootsy re-creation of an old-time Polish country inn with rooms decorated in a variety of traditional peasant styles. A fine range of calorific traditional specialities on offer, from staples like pork chop with sauerkraut to pricier items like duck, which comes with any number of sauces. A bit of a tourist trap, but the food is always reliable. Daily noon–11pm.

Copernicus ul. Kanonicza 16 ☏012/424 3421. Plush hotel restaurant offering an imaginative European-Polish mix and a wider range of meat dishes than elsewhere – hare, pheasant and venison are usually on the menu. On the formal side, and expensive with it. Daily noon–11pm.

Cul de Sac *Hotel Gródek*, ul. Na Gródku 4 ☏012/431 2041, ⓦwww.cul-de-sac.pl. Modern European cuisine in a semi-informal, secluded setting, popular with in-the-know diners as a result. Glass-covered conservatory-type feel, and display cabinets that hold medieval finds unearthed when the building was renovated. Mains 80–90zł. Daily noon–11pm.

Cyrano de Bergerac ul. Sławkowska 26 ☏012/411 7288, ⓦwww.cyranodebergerac. pl. Upscale brick cellar restaurant popular with local gastronomes, serving classic French cuisine backed up by an extensive list of wines. Main courses clock in at a reasonable 60–80zł; while the inexpensive set-lunch menus (30–40zł) represent a great opportunity to sample some of the best cuisine in Kraków without rushing for the cashpoint. Daily 1–11pm.

Da Pietro Rynek Główny 17. ☏012/422 3279 ⓦwww.dapietro.com.pl. Best place on the Rynek Główny to tuck into a bowl of flavoursome pasta, with a brick-lined cellar down below and a sizeable terrace on the square itself. Reasonably priced salads too. Daily 11am–11pm.

🏃 **Del Papa** ul. św. Tomasza 6 ☏012/421 8343, ⓦwww.delpapa.pl. Cosy, atmospheric restaurant with a restful garden patio, serving up some of the best fresh pasta in the city. The range of Adriatic seafood is impressive, too, and there's a good list of Italian wines. Mains in the 35zł-50zł range; salads, soups and pastas come a good deal cheaper. Daily 11.30am–10.30pm.

Leonardo ul. Szpitalna 22 ☏012/429 6850, ⓦwww.leonardo.com.pl. High-quality Polish-Italian fusion food in a snug suite of underground rooms. The salads and pastas make perfect lunchtime choices, with veal, poultry and venison filling out the main-course menu. Most mains hover around the 40zł mark, although you should expect to pay double that for the game dishes. Daily 11am–11pm.

Mamma Mia ul. Karmelicka 14. ☏012/430 0492. Popular pizzeria that is smart enough to serve as an evening wining-and-dining venue, serving up thin-crust pies in the 20-25zł range with reasonably authentic Italianate toppings, plus plenty of

pasta and salad choices by way of alternative. Daily noon–11pm.

🏃 **Miód Malina** ul. Grodzka 40 ☏012/430 0411, ⓦwww.miodmalina.pl. Candlelight, rustic furniture and a colour scheme based on the restaurant's name ("Honey Raspberry") make this one of the most popular places in the centre to enjoy good food in a warm, informal atmosphere. The Polish-international menu ploughs through the usual pork, chicken, fish and steak territory – although dishes are prepared with a bit more pizzazz than elsewhere. And it always makes sense to leave room for the sweets. Mains in the 40–70zł range. Daily noon–midnight.

Orient Ekspres ul. Stolarska 13 ☏012/422 6672, ⓦwww.orient-ekspres.krakow.pl. For once here's a theme restaurant where the food actually lives up to the concept: train-travel posters, station signs and railway-compartment decor set the scene, while the menu presents a transcontinental mixture of the familiar and the exotic. Polish staples like *żurek* (sour rye soup) and *pierogi* rub shoulders with grilled steaks and distinctly middle-eastern dishes like *imam bayaldi* (vegetarian-friendly stuffed aubergine). Main courses 35–45zł. Daily noon–11pm.

Pod Baranem ul. św. Gertrudy 21. Plain, unpretentious and reliable source of moderately priced Polish food. The small menu includes the inevitable porkchop fare but also a couple of fish choices, as well as venison (35zł) and boar (40zł). Daily 11am–11pm.

Pod Różą ul. Floriańska 34 ☏012/424 3381. Perfectly prepared Polish-European cuisine in the glass-covered courtyard of the Pod Różą hotel. The menu limits itself to a handful of classic main courses, with game and fish well represented. Mains 70–80zl. Daily noon–11pm.

Polskie Jadło Folwark ul. św. Krzyża 13 ☏012/433 9785, ⓦwww.polskiejadlo.com.pl. Opting for the same formula as *Chłopskie Jadło* (see p.399), *Polskie Jadło* is an enjoyable place to feast on calorific meat-heavy Polish favourites while admiring the rather theatrical down-on-the-farm decor. Standards are always reasonable, as are the prices. Daily noon–11pm.

Smak Ukraiński ul. Kanonicza 15 ☏012/421 9294, ⓦwww.ukrainska.pl. Reasonably priced Ukrainian restaurant on the way to the Wawel, with tables squeezed into a folksy cellar – although there's courtyard seating up top. Filling meaty favourites from Poland's eastern neighbour include *tarnopolskie zrazy* (flattened dumplings stuffed with mincemeat), *zakarpatski delikates* (a pork and bacon roll in sweet and sour sauce), and various grills – washed down with *kvass* (a traditional malt drink) or Obołoń lager. Daily noon–9.30pm.

Szara Rynek Główny 6. ☎012/421 6669, ⓦwww
.szara.pl. Modern European cuisine in an upscale
but not over-formal environment, with lamb, veal
and fish dishes featuring heavily – be aware that
portions are on the moderate side. Mains hover
around the 50–60zł range but cheaper daily
specials are usually on offer as well. Too much of a
tourist-oriented machine to be a truly great restaurant, but still one of the better culinary addresses
in town. Daily 11am–11pm.

Wentzl Rynek Główny 19 ☎012/429 5712,
ⓦwww.wentzl.pl. Top-quality international cuisine
with a French accent, square-side seating and
attentive service. Deservedly expensive, with main
courses weighing in at around 60–80zł. Daily
noon–midnight.

Wierzynek Rynek Główny 15 ☎012/424 9600,
ⓦwww.wierzynek.pl. Historic restaurant on several
floors, with a refined interior and centuries of
tradition, serving up the best in Polish pork, duck
and trout dishes. Prices remain very reasonable at
around 75–100zł a head for main course and drink.
Booking is essential if you want a table inside in the
evening: the outside terrace has a faster turnover
and you may well be lucky. Daily noon–midnight.

Kazimierz, Podgórze and around

Restaurants below are marked on
the "Kazimierz & Podgórze" map on
p.378.

Alef ul. św Agnieszki 5 ☎012/424 3131. A cosy
café-restaurant done up to look like a traditional
mid-nineteenth-century Kazimierz parlour, offering
Jewish-themed fish, duck and goose dishes, and a
tasty *czulent* (meat and barley stew). Mains in the
25–30zł region. Daily noon–10pm.

Arka Noego ul. Szeroka 2 ☎012/429 1528. One
of the better-value Jewish-themed restaurants in
Kazimierz, with occasional Klezmer music and a
well-balanced menu taking in everything from fish
soup to leg of lamb. Its backyard terrace makes a
nice place to sit out in summer. Daily 10am–11pm.

Brasserie ul. Gazowa 4 ☎012/292 1998. Set in
a brick and timber building that used to form part
of Kraków tram depot, this French-flavoured place
serves up a decent *moules marinieres*, some good
fish dishes, and some tasty crêpes for afters. Main
courses weigh in at about 40zł. Daily noon–11pm.

Fabryka Pizzy ul. Józefa 34. ☎012/433 8080.
Stylish, smoke-free and good-value pizzeria, with
a tasty range of pasta dishes and salads. Very
popular, so be prepared to wait. Daily 11am–11pm.

Horai Plac Wolnica 9 ☎012/430 0358. Popular
oriental eatery that goes for restrained modern
decor rather than Far Eastern kitsch. There's a

broad range of pan-Asian cuisine on the menu,
although it's the Thai dishes that stand out. Mains
in the 20–25zł bracket. Daily noon–11pm.

Klezmer Hois ul. Szeroka 6 ☎012/411 1245.
Well-regarded Polish-Jewish restaurant with yet
more of the nostalgic nineteenth-century decor
that seems de rigueur for Kazimierz eateries,
and a reliable range of well-prepared soups and
poultry dishes. The frequent live Klezmer music is
worth reserving a table for. Main courses nudging
towards the 35zł mark. Daily 9am–11pm.

Szara Kazimierz ul. Szeroka 39 ☎012/429
1219, ⓦwww.szrakazimierz.pl. Pretty much the
same menu (and similarly good standards of
presentation and service) as the Old Town branch
of *Szara* on Rynek Główny (see opposite), but in a
wonderful Kazimierz location. In summer choose
between pavement seating on the picturesque ul.
Szeroka, or back-patio seating in a walled garden
behind the Remu'h synagogue. Daily 11am–11pm.

Las Wolski and around

Restaurants below are marked on the
"Kraków" map on p.347

U Zijada Zamek w Przegorzałach ☎012/429
7105. Occupying a cod-medieval "castle" on the
southeastern edge of the Las Wolski forest, this is a
moderately formal place with a good line in Polish
pork and poultry dishes and a few Middle Eastern
dishes thrown in for good measure. Expensive,
but you do get great views from the terrace. Daily
10am–10pm.

Villa Decjusza ul. 28 Lipca 17a ☎012/425
3521, ⓦwww.vd-restauracja.pl. Ultra-smart and
correspondingly pricey cellar restaurant favoured
by local and visiting politicians, in the cellar of the
recently renovated Villa Decjusza – hence the cod
Renaissance decor. Well out of town in the Wola
Justowska district. Booking essential. Mains 50zł.
Daily 1–10pm.

Nowa Huta

The restaurant below is marked on the
"Kraków" map on p.347

Stylowa os. Centrum bl. 3. ☎012/644 2619.
Opened in 1956 and long considered Nowa Huta's
only upmarket address, *Stylowa* is nowadays
a rather charming and old-fashioned place
that offers an insight into what top restaurants
were like in communist-era Poland. The menu
is a standard *barszcz*-to-pork-chop journey
through Polish cuisine, with the occasional racy
foreign dish like Chicken Kiev thrown in for good
measure. Mains rarely exceed the 20zł mark. Daily
10am–10pm.

Drinking and nightlife

For relaxing over coffee and cake in between bouts of sightseeing, there's a profusion of **cafés** in and around the city centre, many of which have outdoor terraces in summer. Those ringing the Rynek Główny make nice places in which to soak up the atmosphere, with the additional distraction of the assortment of roving buskers vying for the tourist złoty. Many cafés remain open well into the night and provide comfortable venues in which to indulge in more serious drinking, although the bulk of Kraków's drinking culture takes place in the innumerable **bars** of the Old Town and Kazimierz. Many bars have DJs and dancing in the evening, and there isn't always a clear distinction between drinking venues and nightspots – we've listed dedicated **clubs** with a regular line-up of DJs or live bands under a separate heading. As far as live music is concerned, **jazz** has a long tradition in Kraków and is generally easier to find than rock – although it's worth checking listings or looking out for posters on the off chance that there's something going on.

Cafés

The Old Town and around

Cafés below are marked on the "Kraków: City Centre" map on p.356.

Botanica ul. Bracka 9. ☎012/422 8980. Classy café with a good choice of light meals, including sandwiches, salads and several excellent varieties of quiche. Metallic plant-like sculptures in the front room and real-life potted specimens in the glass-roofed courtyard just about justify the name. Daily 10am–11pm.

Café Bunkier pl. Szczepański 3a. Attached to the *Art Bunker* (see p.365), this park-side terrace under a huge wrought-iron awning is a hugely popular meeting-point and people-watching spot. A good place for a pot of tea and a cake during the daytime, *Bunkier* remains popular well into the evening. Daily 9am–1am.

Camelot ul. św Tomasza 17. Atmospheric café with rustic-looking wooden tables, original watercolours by self-taught naive artist Nikifor, and wooden folk sculptures strewn around the place. English-language newspapers, and delicious *szarlotka* (apple pie). The *Loch Camelot* cellar club frequently hosts concerts and cabaret. Daily 9am–midnight.

Frania ul. Wrzesińska 6. Curious little café-cum-launderette named after the Frania washing tub, a forgotten icon of sixties' consumer culture once coveted by every self-respecting Polish housewife. Retro furnishings, pop-art pictures on the wall and free wi-fi access complete the picture. Mon–Fri 10am–8pm, Sat & Sun 10am–6pm.

Jama Michalika ul. Floriańska 45. Atmospheric old café, opened in 1895 and much patronized by artists of the Młoda Polska generation. It's worth dropping into at least once to admire the lovingly preserved Art Nouveau interior, but the atmosphere of cultural ferment has long since departed. Sun–Mon 9am–10pm, Fri & Sat 9am–11pm.

Massolit ul. Felicjanek 4 ⊛www.massolit.com. Bookshop-cum-café owned by Canadians with a Mikhail Bulgakov fixation, with a huge selection of new and used English-language books spread throughout several rooms of a nineteenth-century apartment. With café tables plonked here and there between the shelves, it's a superbly soothing place in which to wind down over coffee – and the carrot cake is well worth a try too. Daily 10am–8pm.

Nowa Prowincja ul. Bracka 5. Informal order-at-the-counter café with super-strong coffee, a good choice of snacks and salads, and a charming array of distressed-looking benches and chairs to sprawl over. Daily 9am–11pm.

Noworolski Rynek Główny 1/3. Elegant, ultra-traditional café occupying the arcaded eastern side of the Sukiennice, opened in 1910 and still boasting its original Art Nouveau interior. Once the favoured haunt of the Kraków cultural and political elite, it's nowadays patronized by older-generation Cracovians and tourists entranced by the historic setting. Daily 9am–midnight.

Prowincja ul. Bracka 3. Cosy split-level café just off the Rynek with excellent coffee and a small but irresistible choice of sweets, including a fine *tart cytrynowy* (lemon meringue pie). Daily 9am–11pm.

Słódki Wenzl Rynek Główny 19. Square-side cafe combining bright modern decor with traditional standards with regard to cakes and pastries department. Definitely the place to linger over an extravagant ice cream while observing the flow of human traffic on the square. Daily 10am–11pm.

Kazimierz and Podgórze

Cafés below are marked on the "Kazimierz & Podgórze" map on p.378.

Kolory ul. Estery 10, Kazimierz ☎012/429 4270, ⊛www.kolorycafe.pl. Parisian-themed café with reproduction French posters plastering the walls and something of a shrine to wayward songwriting genius Serge Gainsbourg above the bar. Reassuringly strong coffee makes this a popular daytime hang-out, although it's just as popular in the evening when many Kazimierz bar-crawlers kick off their nocturnal journey with a drink or two here. Sun–Thurs 8am–midnight; Fri & Sat 8am–2am.

Młynek pl. Wolnica 7, Kazimierz. Cosy, intimate and relaxing café opposite the Ethnographic Museum, offering decent coffee, a mouth-watering selection of cakes, and jazzy background music. Daily 9am–11pm.

Rękawka ul. Brodzińskiego 4, Podgórze. A supremely mellow spot featuring mildly distressed furniture and a sprinkling of houseplants, *Rękawka* serves up seriously strong coffee as well as sandwiches, fancy Mediterranean salads, and an exemplary *szarlotka* (apple pie). The perfect place to recharge your batteries if you've been looking round the Podgórze and Płaszów districts. Daily 9am–9pm.

Bars

The Old Town and around

Bars below are marked on the "Kraków: City Centre" map on p.356.

Awarja ul. Mikołajska 7. Congenial bar squeezed into a cellar so tunnel-like that you can't really drink here without bumping into all kinds of inter-esting people. Hidden away at the back is a live music room hosting an erratic programme of blues, jazz and rock. Daily noon–1am.

Buddha Rynek Główny 6. A predictable exercise in Oriental kitsch, Kraków's *Buddha* takes on a new lease of life as soon as summer arrives: the lounge furniture moves out into two adjacent courtyards, and a cocktail-swilling party groove sets in. Noon–1am.

Café-Szafe ul. Felicjanek 10 ⊛www.cafeszafe .com. With its orange walls, old settees, and rickety cupboards painted blue, *Café-Szafe* is a bit like a psychedelic strip cartoon that you can walk in and out of whenever you please – it comes as no surprise to discover that one of the owners makes quirky animated films. Coffee and cakes during the day; stronger stuff and the possibility of live music in the evenings. Daily 10am–midnight.

Caryca ul. Wielopole 12/1. Looking like a cross between a student squat and an art gallery, this three-room bar is located in a building that has become a warren of weird drinking holes (see *Kitsch* p.404, and *Łubu dubu* p.405). There's not really enough room for a stage or a sound system but alternative DJs and arty bands somehow succeed in playing here all the same. Daily noon–2am.

Chillout ul. św Jana 15. An admirably straightfor-ward Old Town bar which doesn't try too hard to be hip. Lives up to its name in summer when tables move outdoors into a large but relatively secluded courtyard. Daily 11am–midnight.

Dym ul. św Tomasza 11. Narrow coffee-bar-cum-drinking den with artfully distressed walls and similar-looking clientele. Outdoor seating in the alleyway provides a Mediterranean vibe in summer. Daily 10am–midnight.

Nic Nowego ul. św. Krzyża 15. Irish-owned bar that goes for the modern-European look rather than cliché-ridden pub nostalgia. Both Irish and Polish beers on tap, and a range of food (including pastas, salads and baguette sandwiches) that is head-and-shoulders above the usual pub-grub fare. Mon–Fri 8am–3am, Sat & Sun 10am–3am.

Paparazzi ul. Mikołajska 9. Smart pub with big cocktail menu and pictures of celebrities on the wall – and trendily dressed wannabes crowding round the bar. Mon–Fri noon–1am, Sat & Sun 4pm–1am.

Pauza ul. Floriańska 18/3, ⊛www.pauza.pl. Roomy first-floor hang-out with crowded bar area and loungey spaces on either side. The recently added basement extension is worth checking out for its minimalist interior alone. In summer, a third bar area opens up in the yard out the back. Daily noon–midnight.

Piękny Pies ul. Sławkowska 6a. Something of a late-night haven for committed drinkers, decadent intellectuals and die-hard eccentrics, the "Beautiful Dog" gets the mixture of student scruffiness and Central European chic just right. Join the throng around the semi-circular bar in the front room, slump into a dark sofa in the lounge area, or descend to the basement to check out what the weekend DJs are playing. Sun–Thurs 11am–2am, Fri & Sat 11am–4am.

Pod Jaszczurami Rynek Główny 8, ⊛www .podjaszczurami.pl. Large student pub under vaulted gothic ceilings, constantly busy as much for its cheap beer and laid-back atmosphere as for its packed programme of public events – anything from rock gigs to literary readings and political debates. Sun–Thurs 11am–1am, Fri & Sat 11am–4am.

RE ul. Mikołajska 5. One of the nicest barrel-vaulted cellars in Kraków, enduringly popular with students and young professionals. Occasional alternative rock or jazz gigs in the adjoining function room, and a sizeable outdoor beer garden in summer. Daily noon–2am.

Święta Krowa ul. Floriańska 16. Set somewhere between trendy lounge and goblin's cavern, this Hindu-themed cellar bar (the name means "sacred cow") is another Kraków one-off. Daily noon–2am.

Vis-à-vis Rynek Główny 29. Functional, matt-black café-bar on the main square, long favoured by Polish artists and still something of a cult destination among older Cracovian drinkers. Outdoor seating in spring and summer. Daily 9am–11pm.

Kazimierz and around

Bars below are marked on the "Kazimierz & Podgórze" map on p.378.

Alchemia ul. Estery 5. ⓦ www.alchemia.com .pl. Darkly atmospheric, candle-lit café-pub in the heart of Kazimierz. You'll see bohemians, fashionably arty types, local drunks and bemused tourists lolling around in its suite of four rooms. Top-quality live music (mostly jazz or alternative rock) in the basement. Daily 9am–4am.

B-Side ul. Estery 16. A cosy warren of subterranean rooms including a frequently sweaty dancefloor, B-side is the bar of choice for music buffs who take their genres seriously. DJs play alternative rock, cutting-edge dance music or retro styles on different nights of the week, and Polish indie bands occasionally squeeze onto the tiny stage. Daily noon–1pm or later.

Drukarnia Nadwiślańska 1 ⓦ www.drukarnia-podgorze. pl. Roomy bar just over the river from Kazimierz, with several rooms decked out in different styles, from arty Parisian café to brash party pub. There's also a basement-level gig venue hosting regular rock and jazz.

Lokator ul. Krakowska 10. ⓦ www.lokator .pointblue.com.pl. Less frenetic than some of the other Kazimierz pubs but still offering plenty in the way of atmosphere, Lokator is more than just an arty place to lounge around and drink. It's also a mini cultural centre in its own right, with contemporary art on the walls and regular gigs and literary readings in the back room. There's a bookshop, art gallery and small cinema in the basement. Daily 10am–midnight.

Miejsce ul. Estery 1 ⓦ www.miejsce.com.pl. Miejsce attracts the same melange of arty-bohemian Cracovians as Kazimierz's other bars, but with a slightly different recipe. Instead of distressed furniture and candlelight, expect wacky sixties design details in a white-walled art gallery-style space. Daily 10am–2am.

Mleczarnia ul. Meiselsa 20 ⓦ www.mle.pl. Small, dark and smoky, *Mleczarnia* offers the archetypal lets-get-drunk-in-grandma's-living-room Kazimierz experience. Daily 10am–2am.

Propaganda ul. Miodowa 12. Relaxing corner crammed with memorabilia from the communist period and other eras – although it has the feel of a comfortable local bar rather than an over-stylized theme pub. There's a (sadly, electric) dartboard opposite the bar should you fall prey to the competitive urge. Daily 11am–3am.

Singer ul. Estery 22. Classic Kazimierz café-bar whose retro style – nineteenth-century parlour furniture, lacy tablecloths and an old piano in the corner – has been mercilessly copied by its rivals. With a mixed clientele of laid-back locals and foreign interlopers, *Singer* comes into its own in the early hours when the bar area turns into an impromptu dancefloor. The name refers to the old tailors' sewing machines that serve as tables. Daily 9am–3am or later.

Zaraz Wracam ul. Bożega Ciała ⓦ www .zarazwracam.pl. Although it's as artfully shabby as you would expect from a Kazimierz bar, *Zaraz Wracam* is relatively low on interior-design gimmicks and attracts a broad-based mix of laid-back drinkers as a result. A good choice for a relaxing pint or two. Sun–Thurs 3pm–midnight, Fri & Sat 3pm–2am.

Clubs

The Old Town and around

Clubs below are marked on the "Kraków: City Centre" map on p.356.

Art Klub Błędnie Koło ul. Bracka 4. ⓦ www .blednie-kolo.krakow.pl. First-floor club with plush seating in one half, DJ bar in the other, and a musical policy that takes in reggae, jungle and other not-quite-mainstream genres. Daily 7pm–4am or later.

Cień ul św Jana 15. ⓦ www.cienklub.com. Funk, house and retro DJs entertain a young and glamorous crowd in a subterranean dance palace. At weekends you'll need to queue up and fork out an entrance fee of 20–25zł. Tues–Sun 8pm–5am.

Harris Piano Jazz Bar Rynek Główny 28 ⓦ www .harris.krakow.pl. Basement space right on the main square offering a regular programme of blues, funk and jazz. Jam sessions are usually free; gigs cost 10–30zł depending on who is playing. Performances usually start around 9.30pm. Daily noon–2am.

Kitsch ul. Wielpole 12. Garishly decorated former apartment on the top floor of the bar-filled

▲ Miejsce, Kazimierz

building at Wielopole 12. With an eclectic DJ policy attracting a gay-straight, teen-to-thirty-someting crowd, this is a bit like attending a packed and slightly unpredictable house party. Daily 6pm–4am.

Łubu Dubu ul. Wielopole 12 ⓦ www.lubu-dubu .prv.pl. A floor down from *Kitsch* (see above), this is an anything-goes-as-long-as-its-retro club pumping out 80s hits to a hedonistic crowd far too young to have experienced any of it the first time around. Daily 6pm–3am or later.

Ministerstwo ul. św Jana 3. Bowels-of-the-earth cellar club located at the bottom of a seemingly never-ending staircase, consisting of several rooms of kitschy decor (including bar stools that look like buttock-squeezing human hands), and an ear-splitting sound system pumping out mainstream disco and hip-hop. Daily 8pm–3am or later.

Piec'Art ul. Szewska 12 ⓣ 012/429 6425, ⓦ www.piecart.pl. Two barrel-vaulted cellars, one with a small stage at the end, with jazz gigs and jam sessions a couple of times a week (and an entrance charge depending on who's playing). There's a full menu of nibbles and main meals if you want to make an evening of it. Daily 2pm–3am.

Roentgen pl. Szczepański 3. ⓦ www .roentgenklub.pl. Deep, smoky cellar hang-out favoured by local alternative types, improbably located in the basement of a fertility clinic. Acid jazz, drum'n'bass and other non-mainstream styles on the sound system, and DJs at the

weekends. Daily 8pm–4am.

Stalowe Magnolie ul. św Jana 15. ⓦ www .stalowemagnolie.com. Upmarket club with plush furnishings, expensive drinks, and quality live music of a jazzy, funky or bluesy nature. One for the upwardly mobile rather than the disco kids. Sun–Thurs 6pm–2am, Fri & Sat 6pm–4am.

U Muniaka ul. Floriańska 3 ⓣ 012/423 1205, ⓦ www.umuniaka.krakow.pl. A tunnel-like live-music space and a cute cubby-hole of a bar area packed with antique-style clutter. Live music every night, with saxophonist-cum-host Janusz Muniak parping his horn most weekends. Daily 7pm–2am.

West of the Old Town

Clubs below are marked on the "Kraków" map on p.347.

Rotunda ul. Oleandry 3 ⓦ www.rotunda.pl. Large student club and cultural centre just west of the National Museum, offering occasional live gigs, jazz and theatre in a circular auditorium upstairs, and club nights in the basement bar.

Żaczek al. 3 Maja 5 ⓦ www.klubzaczek.pl. Student bar-cum-club in a roomy glass-fronted pavilion on the ground floor of the Żaczek hall of residence – which ensures a regular supply of party-happy customers. During term time (roughly Oct–June) the bar is open for coffee and beers during the daytime, while gigs, DJ-driven events and karaoke nights kick in during the evenings. Closed July–Sept.

Entertainment and culture

There is a good deal happening on the cultural front, with a regular diet of **classical music** and **opera**, an outstanding range of challenging **theatre** and a long-established **cabaret** tradition. For mainstream music and theatre **listings**, the monthly *Kraków Karnet* (see p.349) is invaluable, although Polish-language sources like *Gazeta Wyborcza* and *Aktivist* (see p.65) are much better sources of information on cutting-edge culture.

The **Cultural Information Centre**, ul. św. Jana 2 (Centrum Informacji Kulturalnej: Mon–Fri 10am–7pm, Sat 11am–7pm; ☎012/421 1787), handles information and tickets for cultural events.

Theatre, cabaret and cinema

Ever since Stanisław Wyspiański and friends made Kraków the centre of the **Młoda Polska** movement (see box, p.364) at the beginning of the twentieth century, many of Poland's greatest actors and directors have been closely identified with the city.

Theatre

Performances are naturally, in the Polish language, although the traditionally strong emphasis placed on the visual aspects of the performance should still make a visit to the theatre worthwhile.

Bagatela ul. Karmelicka 6 ☎012/424 5210, ⓦwww.bagatela.krakow.pl. Mainstream repertoire of popular theatre, where you might encounter anything from Ray Cooney to Anton Chekhov.
Groteska ul. Skarbowa 2 ☎012/633 3762, ⓦwww.groteska.pl. Innovative puppet theatre whose shows frequently feature a mixture of live actors and marionettes. Childrens' shows take place in the daytime, grown-up material in the evening. Also puts on fringe comedy and cabaret.
Stary Teatr ul. Jagiellońska 1 ☎012/422 4040, ⓦwww.stary-teatr.krakow.pl. The city's premium drama venue, with the main stage at ul. Jagiellońska 1 and a studio space at Starowiślna 21. Polish and international classics from a company with a strong international reputation. Box office open Tues–Sat 10am–1pm & 5–7pm.
STU al. Krasińskiego 16 ☎012/422 2744, ⓦwww.scenastu.com.pl. Company founded in 1966 by director Krzysztof Jasiński, specializing in groundbreaking contemporary drama.
Teatr im J. Słowackiego pl. św. Ducha ☎012/424 4525, ⓦwww.slowacki.krakow.pl. Biggest and best known of Kraków's theatres, in a splendid building modelled on the Paris Opéra. Regular diet of classical Polish drama, as well as ballet and opera.
Teatr Nowy ul. Gazowa 21, ⓦwww.teatrnowy.com.pl. Young guns of the Polish theatre world, performing contemporary pieces in an old warehouse in Kazimierz.

Cabaret

Cabaret in Kraków dates back to the pre-World War I period, when artists and writers associated with the Młoda Polska movement established the Zielony Balonik (Green Balloon) cabaret in order to provide a showcase for political satire, comedy sketches and song. The tradition was revived in communist times with the creation of the Piwnica Pod Baranami in 1956, initially a student-run affair that endured to become Kraków's longest running and best-loved cabaret. The *Pod Baranami*, at Rynek Główny 27 (☎012/421 2500), is still going strong today; its main rival is *Loch Camelot*, ul. św. Tomasza 17 (☎012/423 0638) – the latter established in 1992 in order to revive the traditions of the original Zielony Balonik. Check with the Cultural Information Centre (see above) for current details: when they are performing – usually at the weekend – tickets sell out fast, so it's best to book in advance.

Cinema

Films arrive in Kraków at around the same time as their release in Western Europe, and are usually shown in the original language with Polish subtitles. A rash of modern multiplexes has appeared over the last few years, although most of these tend to be miles away from the centre.

Ars ul. św. Jana 6 ☎012/421 4199, ⓦwww.ars .pl. Five screens (the Aneks, Kiniarnia, Reduta, Salon and Sztuka) grouped together in one building on the corner of ul. św. Tomasza and św. Jana, bang in the heart of the Old Town. Everything from commercial blockbusters to art films and cinema classics.

Cinema City Kazimierz ul. Podgórska 34, ☎012/254 5454, ⓦwww.cinema-city.pl. Ten-screen multiplex in the Galeria Kazimierz shopping mall, with popcorn- and snack-buying opportunities aplenty.

Kijów al. Krasińskiego 34 ☎012/433 0033, ⓦwww.kijow.pl. Current box-office hits in a big auditorium just west of the Old Town.

Kino pod Baranami Rynek Główny 27 ☎012/423 0768, ⓦwww.kinopodbaranami.pl. Current films from outside the Hollywood mainstream, and seasons concentrating on different aspects of world cinema.

Mikro ul. Juliusza Lea 5 ☎012/634 2897, ⓦwww .kinomikro.com.pl. Wonderfully small and intimate studio cinema showing art-house movies, west of the Old Town.

Classical music and opera

For classical concerts, the **Filharmonia Szymanowskiego**, ul. Zwierzyniecka 1 (box office Mon–Fri 2–7pm, Sat from 1hr before concerts; ☎012/422 9477, ⓦwww.filharmonia.krakow.pl), is home of the Kraków Philharmonic, one of Poland's most highly regarded orchestras. The **Capella Cracoviensis**, the city's best-known choir, based at the Filharmonia, gives fairly regular concert performances at churches and other venues around the city – check the local listings for details. Large-scale **opera** performances – mostly, but not always, in Polish – are put on fairly regularly at the **Teatr im J. Słowackiego** (see opposite).

Festivals and events

Hardly a week goes by without some festival or other taking over the Rynek Główny, although a large proportion of these are ephemeral affairs which simply provide an excuse to stage an open-air concert or two. However there is still much in the way of heavyweight cultural events and traditional folkloric happenings, some of which are well worth planning your holiday around.

KRT (Krakowskie reminiscencje teatralne) March ⓦwww.reminiscencje.pl. International theatre festival with a strong alternative edge, with performances in the Rotunda cultural centre (see p.405) and elsewhere around town.

Misteria Paschalia Easter week ⓦwww .misteriapaschalia.pl. Festival of religious music through the ages, with performances in historic churches or in Kraków Filharmonia.

Kraków Film Festival (Krakowski festiwal filmowy) Late May–early June ⓦwww.kff .com.pl. Highly-regarded gathering of documentaries, animated films and shorts, with the coveted Złoty Smok ("Golden Dragon") awards going to the winners.

Dragon Parade (Parada smoków) First or second Sat in June ⓦwww.groteska.pl.

A fantastic, fun-for-all-the-family occasion organized by the Groteska puppet theatre, involving a parade of dragons (made by community groups and schools) around Kraków's main square. In the evening there's a son et lumière show with dragons battling each other below Wawel hill.

Lajkonik Mid-June. A man dressed in oriental fancy dress and riding a hobby horse proceeds from the Norbertine church in Zwierzyniec to the main square, striking people with a ceremonial mace (for good luck) as he goes. It's an age-old pageant celebrating the story of a Zwierzyniec raftsman who defeated Tatar invaders and made off with the khan's clothes.

Midsummer's Eve (Wianki) June 23 or nearest weekend ⓦwww.biurofestiwalowe.pl. Traditionally celebrated by virgins throwing wreaths in the river

Wisła while bonfires are lit on the water's edge, Wianki is nowadays the excuse for a huge outdoor pop concert and firework display – held on the riverside below Wawel Hill.

Festival of Jewish Culture (Festiwal kultury żydowskiej) Late June to early July Ⓦwww .jewishfestival.pl. Ten days of music, theatre, film and discussion, with events held in the synagogues and squares of the Kazimierz district. The festival closes with a huge open-air Klezmer concert on ul. Szeroka.

Crossroads (Rozstaje) Late July Ⓦwww .biurofestiwalowe.pl. World music from Poland and abroad, usually with a strong central European flavour. Open-air gigs on the Rynek Główny, and smaller chamber-style concerts in various venues around town.

March of the Dachshunds (Marsz Jamników) First or second Sun in Sept. Sausage dogs wearing fancy dress are paraded through town to the main square, where prizes are awarded for the best outfits.

Sacrum Profanum Mid- to late Sept Ⓦwww .sacrumprofanum.pl. Open-ended festival of modern music featuring anything from Kraftwerk to Karlheinz Stockhausen. A high-quality event featuring top international performers.

Szopki competition (Konkurs szopek) Dec. Kraków craftsmen display their Szopki (ornate Christmas cribs featuring model buildings and scenery as well as nativity figures) on the main square. The best examples are chosen for a special display in the Kraków History Museum.

Advent market (Targi Bożonarodzeniowe) Dec. Craft stalls selling jewellery, accessories, woodcarving, speciality foodstuffs and mulled wine fill the main square.

Football

Wisła Kraków (Ⓦwww.wisla.krakow.pl) is one of the oldest and most successful **soccer** clubs in the country, and have been the dominant force in Polish football over the last ten years – they were champions in 1999, 2001, 2003, 2004, 2005 and 2008. They play at the relatively modern and well-equipped Wisła Stadium, ulica Reymonta, in the western Czarna Wieś district (a 25min walk from the Rynek; otherwise bus #144 passes close by). Their bitter rivals, Cracovia (Ⓦwww.cracovia.org.pl), were the first soccer team ever to be formed in Poland (in 1906) and were the favourite boyhood club of Pope John Paul II. Cracovia won the championship five times between 1921 and 1948, but have only just returned to the top flight after several seasons spent languishing in lower divisions. Their old-style stadium, complete with grassy terraces and wooden bench seating, is just beyond the *Cracovia* hotel on aleja Focha.

Shopping

Most of Kraków's mainstream fashion and household shops are concentrated in big shopping malls such as Galeria Krakowska (see below), leaving the Old Town to be colonized by an interesting mix of luxury-label clothes stores, craft shops and souvenir outlets. As you would expect from a university city, there are more second-hand **bookshops** (*antykwarjaty*) than you can shake a stick at, many of which are well worth a browse for vintage guidebooks, art albums and English-language novels.

Shopping malls

Galeria Krakowska ul. Pawia 5. Modern mall next door to the train station with more than 200 shops on 3 floors, including a well-stocked Carrefour supermarket and a plethora of clothes and accessories stores. Mon–Sat 9am–10pm, Sun 10am–9pm.

Galeria Kazimierz ul. Podgórska 34. Two floors of global brands, a multiscreen cinema, and an Alma supermarket boasting a good choice of international deli products – all just a few steps east of the Kazimierz quarter. Mon–Sat 10am–10pm, Sun 10am–8pm.

Religious architecture

If you want to get to grips with the depth and diversity of Polish culture then the country's religious buildings are as good a place as any to start. Not only do they constitute an extraordinarily fine parade of architectural styles from medieval Romanesque to twentieth-century modernism, they also reveal the varied imprint of different ethnicities and faiths. Monuments bearing witness to this diversity include the half-timbered Churches of Peace built by the Protestants of Silesia, the extraordinary wooden churches of Poland's Orthodox minorities, and a significant handful of beautifully restored small-town synagogues.

Polish synagogue ▲

Kruszyniamy mosque ▼

A church of peace, Jawor ▼

Synagogues

Up until World War II there were few parts of Poland that didn't have a Jewish presence of some sort or another, and most towns and villages in the country had at least one synagogue. Many of these were looted or destroyed during World War II and only a handful remain in anything like their former state. The Kraków suburb of Kazimierz (see p.376) boasts a handful of lovingly preserved examples, several of which still function as houses of prayer. In eastern Poland, the beautifully renovated synagogues of Tykocin (see p.240) and Włodawa (see p.269) provide a wonderful insight into the lost world of the Jewish market town.

Tatar Mosques

The rustic villages of eastern Poland harbour a wealth of surviving wooden buildings, of which the mosques of Kruszyniamy (see p.244) and Bohoniki (see p.243) are the most famous. Built by local Tatar communities who originally came to the area in the seventeenth century, the mosques are wonderful examples of the timber building techniques once used across northeastern Europe, with the addition of some delightful oriental details – notably the minarets poking modestly from the roofs, and the luxuriant collection of oriental carpets inside.

Churches of Peace

One of the consequences of the Peace of Westphalia in 1648 was that the Lutherans of Catholic-dominated Silesia were allowed their own places of worship, provided that neither brick nor stone were used in their construction. The resulting "Churches of Peace" in Świdnica (see p.510) and

Jawor (see p.508) are unique in Europe, employing clay-and-timber building techniques on a hitherto unimaginably monumental scale.

Wooden churches

Wooden village churches are scattered across the whole of southern Poland, but are particularly concentrated in the densely forested mountain valleys of the southeast. The area was traditionally home to the Boyko and Lemko minorities, most of whom belonged to either the Orthodox or the Greek Catholic Church. Local builders took their inspiration from Muscovite and Byzantine models as well as the Catholic west, producing delightful buildings with clustered onion domes. The sixteenth-century churches at Ulucz (see p.315) and Chotyniec (see p.311) are among the earliest examples.

▲ Greek Orthodox church, Nowy Sacz

▼ Mariacki Church, Kraków

Four medieval masterpieces

▸▸ **Mariacki Church, Kraków** With its asymmetrical twin towers and personably spiked turret, this Romanesque Gothic creation has to be Poland's most picturesque church. See p.359

▸▸ **St Mary's Church, Gdańsk** This outstanding example of the Baltic Gothic style is said to be the largest brick-built basilica in the world and towers above the city centre like a sentinel. See p.152

▸▸ **Holy Trinity Church, Lublin** Unassuming from the outside, this modest Gothic chapel contains fabulous fifteenth-century frescoes. See p.261

▸▸ **Cathedral, Gniezno** For centuries the seat of archbishops, this cathedral is famous for its twelfth century bronze doors with reliefs illustrating the life and martyrdom of Saint Adalbert. See p.568

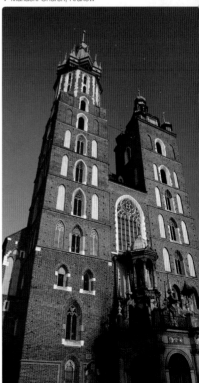

Polish Baroque

Many of Poland's churches boast lavish Baroque interiors, a trend that arrived from Italy in the late sixteenth century and quickly became the Catholic Church's defining style. It was brought to Poland by the Jesuits, whose Church of Sts Peter and Paul in Kraków (see p.368) was closely modelled on the order's Gesù Church in Rome.

However the Baroque era didn't just bring about a change of architecture, but also a change in church-going style. The cult of miracle-working saints was promoted, and popular devotion was boosted through the encouragement of pilgrimages. The shrine of Święta Lipka in Mazuria (see p.212) received a beautiful new church and abbey complex in order to meet the needs of this new culture of mass devotion. The most complete expression of Polish Baroque, however, has to be the Bernardine monastery of Kalwaria Zebrzydowska southwest of Kraków (see p.415), where a calvary route five kilometres long is sprinkled with exquisite chapels, turning the entire landscape into an outdoor theatre of spiritual renewal.

Veit Stoss altar, Kraków ▲

Church of Sts Peter and Paul, Kraków ▼

Contemporary architecture

Throughout the communist period, the struggle between church and state frequently expressed itself through architecture. The Catholic hierarchy's enthusiasm for modern styles found its most eloquent expression in Wojciech Pietrzyk's Ark of the Lord, a boldly contemporary church built in the Kraków suburb of Nowa Huta (see p.395). The Ark rises above the surrounding apartment blocks like a huge ocean-going vessel, a soaring cross recalling the mast of a tall ship.

Arka Pana (Ark of the Lord), Kraków ▼

Books and multimedia

Antykwarjat Kamiński ul. św. Jana 2. Quirkily old-fashioned second-hand bookshop with shelf after shelf of temptingly collectable tomes in all languages. Mon–Fri 10am–5pm, Sat 10am–2pm.

Antykwariat na Kazimierzu ul. Meiselsa 17. antiquarian bookstore in the basement of the Judaica Foundation, with a good selection of Judaica and history-related titles and a pile of almost-antique bric-a-brac to rummage through too. Mon–Fri 10am–6pm, Sat & Sun 10am–2pm.

Antykwarjat Wójtowicz ul. św. Marka 23. Good place for old maps and prints, as well as affordable second-hand books. Mon–Fri 10am–6pm, Sat 10am–2pm.

Austeria ul. Józefa 38 (Kazimierz) Occupying the ground floor of the High Synagogue (see p.380), Austeria carries a large selection of books about Jewish Poland in most major languages, plus a selection of world-music CDs with Klezmer artists particularly well represented. Daily 9am–7pm.

EMPiK Rynek Główny 5. Four-floor multimedia store with plenty in the way of maps, tourist-oriented books, glossy international magazines and English-language literature. Head for the basement to find a big selection of pop, jazz and classical CDs, as well as classic Polish films on DVD. Daily 10am–10pm.

Księżarnia Hetmańska Rynek Główny 17. Bookshop occupying two sides of the souvenir stall-packed Hetmańska passage, just off the Rynek. An excellent selection of English-language books about Polish history and culture, as well as Polish literature in English translation. Mon–Sat 9am–9pm, Sun 11am–9pm.

Massolit ul. Felicjanek 4. Engagingly eccentric English-language bookstore, with a warren of stuffed shelf-lined rooms. Impressive collection of Polish literature in English translation, and titles concerning every aspect of Central European history and culture. Serves tea and cakes, too. Mon–Fri 8am–8pm, Sat 10am–8pm, Sun noon–8pm.

Nestor ul. Kanoniczna 5. Specialist bookstore devoted to the Ukraine, including some beautiful coffee-table titles on old churches and icons, and a wide choice of regional maps and city plans, useful if you're heading that way. Small selection of handicrafts, too. Mon–Fri 10am–6pm, Sat 11am–4pm.

Rara Avis ul. Szpitalna 7. First-floor antiquarian bookshop with a good mixture of affordable curiosities and rare collectors' items. Also deals in old posters, maps and stamps. Mon–Fri 10am–6pm, Sat 10am–2pm.

Food and drink

Ciasteczka z Krakowa ul. św Tomasza. With a name that means "little cakes from Kraków", this back-street sweet shop is stocked to the gills with locally made cakes, chocolates and biscuits – sold by weight or in presentation packs that make good souvenirs. Mon–Fri 10am–6pm, Sat 10am–4pm.

Krakowsi kredens ul. Grodzka 7. Delicatessen serving quality local products from fresh sausage and smoked hams to jars of horseradish sauce, preserved fruit and jams. Mon–Fri 10am–8pm, Sat 11am–8pm, Sun 11am–6pm.

Produkty Benedyktyńskie ul. Krakowska 29. Preserves, honeys, cheeses, marinated mushrooms and a host of other traditional delicatessen products, bearing the brand of the Benedictine Monastery of Tyniec (see p.393). It's all high quality and mostly locally made – although none of it is produced by the Benedictines themselves (it's actually a clever franchising operation conceived by the business-savvy monks). Mon–Fri 9am–5pm, Sat 9am–2pm.

Stary Kleparz market Bustling warren of stalls 5min north of the Old Town, with the best in fresh fruit and veg. Mon–Sat till dusk.

Souvenirs, gifts and collectables

Archetyp ul. Estery 10 ☎012/421 0465, ⓦwww.archetyp.art.pl. Brightly painted wooden angels, animals and other folksy figures, echoing the age-old hand-carving traditions of rural Poland (but probably made in a garage round the corner). Daily 11am–6pm.

Maruna ul. Miodowa 2. Charming little shop selling quirky hand made accessories from belts to bags, hats, jewellery and some truly bizarre soft toys (three-legged marsupials, Siamese-twin pigs and so on). Mon–Sat 11am–7pm, Sun 11am–3pm.

Gala ul. św Getrudy 26. An impressive selection of the folksy, spotty-blue porcelain unique to the town of Bolesławiec in Lower Silesia, available here at reasonable prices. Mon–Fri 10am–6pm, Sat 9am–3pm.

Hala Targowa Grzegórzecka. Sizeable collectors' and bric-a-brac market held on Sun mornings, an easy 5min trot east of the Old Town. Stamps, coins, badges, crafts, genuine antiques and pure junk. Sun 7am–2pm.

Jan Fejkiel ul. Grodzka 25 ⓦwww.fejkielgallery .com. Big collection of graphics and prints from contemporary Polish artists. Mon–Fri 11am–7pm, Sat 11am–3pm.

Made in Poland ul. Gołębia 2. Handmade crafts and souvenirs ranging from dainty pieces of stained glass to wood-carved angels and kooky ceramics. Mon–Fri 10am–6pm, Sat 10am–3pm.

Poster Gallery/Galeria plakatu ul. Stolarska 8 ⓦ www.postergallery.art.pl. Dedicated to the best of Polish poster art, with a rich collection of originals, reproductions and graphic art postcards. Mon–Fri 11am–6pm, Sat 11am–2pm.

Sukiennice Rynek Główny. Stalls running the length of the medieval cloth hall, selling amber jewellery, woollens, embroidery and a host of other souvenirs. A bit of a tourist trap, with prices to match. Daily 8am–dusk.

Listings

Airlines BA, at the airport ☎ 012/285 5033; LOT, ul. Basztowa 15 ☎ 012/422 8989.

Banks, money and exchange ATMs are found in innumerable locations around town. For changing cash, private *kantors*, usually open during regular business hours, offer better rates than the banks, although it pays to shop around – the ones around the Rynek and on ul. Floriańska will give you fewer złotys for your money than those in the side streets.

Bike rental Bike Rental, ul. św. Anny 4 (Mon–Sat 9am–dusk); Bike Trip, ul. Tarłowska 12 (☎ 667/712 054), Kraków Bike Tours Grodzka 2 (☎ 663/731 515 ⓦ www.krakowbiketour.com). In Nova Huta: *1949 Café*, os. Urocze 12 (☎ 012/644 1162).

Bus station Information is available on ☎ 0300/300 150 from a landline, or ☎* (press star) 720 8050 from a mobile phone.

Car rental Avis ul. Lubicz 23 (☎ 601/200 702, ⓦ www.avis.pl); Budget, Balice Airport (012/285 5025, ⓦ www.budget.com); Europcar, ul. Szlak 2 (☎ 012/633 7773, ⓦ www.europcar.pl) and Balice Airport (☎ 012/257 7900); Hertz, Hotel Cracovia, ul. Focha 1 (☎ 012/285 5084, ⓦ www.hertz.com.pl) and Balice Airport (same number); Joka, ul. Starowiślna 13 (☎ 601/545 368, ⓦ www.joka.com.pl).

Consulates UK ul. św Anny 9 (☎ 012/421 7030, ⓦ ukinpoland.fco.gov.uk); USA ul. Stolarska 9 (☎ 012/424 5100, ⓦ krakow.usconsulate.gov).

Dry cleaning Betty Clean, ul. Długa 17 (Mon–Fri 8am–7pm, Sat 8am–2pm).

Emergencies Ambulance ☎ 999; police ☎ 997; fire ☎ 998. Don't expect to get an English-speaker on any of these numbers.

Hospitals The most centrally located emergency ward is at the Gabriel Narutowicz Hospital (Szpital im. Gabriela Narutowicza) north of the Old Town at ul. Prądniczka 35 (☎ 012/416 2436). In an emergency call an ambulance on ☎ 999 and you will be taken to the nearest hospital.

Internet access Garinet, ul. Floriańska 18 (daily 9am–midnight). Many of the cafés and bars in the Old Town offer wi-fi access for laptop users.

Laundry Frania Café ul. Wrzesińska 6 ☎ 783/945 021 ⓦ www.laundromat.pl. Mon–Fri 10am–7pm, Sat 10am–6pm.

Left luggage There is a 24hr left luggage office at the main train station and lockers at both the train and bus stations.

Pharmacies Useful central pharmacies include Grodzka, ul. Grodzka 26 (Mon–Fri 8am–9pm, Sat 9am–6pm, Sun 10am–5pm) and Pod Złotą Głową, Rynek Główny 13 (Mon–Fri 9am–9pm, Sat 9am–4pm). Pharmacies take it in turns to stay open 24hr according to a rota; check the information posted in their windows, or call ☎ 012/422 0511, to find out which one is on duty.

Photographic supplies Digital Photo Express, ul. Grodzka 38 (Mon–Fri 10am–8pm, Sat 11am–8pm, Sun 11am–5pm), will print your holiday snaps as well as offering the whole range of professional processing services. Sells all kinds of film.

Post offices and mail The main post office is at ul. Westerplatte 20; it has a poste restante and offers phone and fax services (Mon–Fri 7.30am–8.30pm, Sat 8am–2pm, Sun 9–11am). The branch just outside the train station has one counter open 24hr.

Swimming Park Wodny, ul. Dobrego Pasterza 126 (☎ 012/413 7399) is the city's main aquatic indoor playground, 5km northeast of the centre. Take bus #129 from the train station. Daily 7am–11pm.

Taxis There are plenty of companies to choose from. Dependable options include Wawel Taxi ☎ 9666 and ☎ 0800/666 666; Radio Taxi ☎ 919 and ☎ 0800/500 919; Euro Taxi ☎ 9664; or Metro Taxi ☎ 9667.

Train station For train enquiries, call ☎ 9436 or ☎ 012/624 1436. International tickets can be bought in advance from the Orbis agency (see Travel agents, below).

Travel agents Orbis, Rynek Główny 41 (☎ 012/422 4035), is good for train tickets, sightseeing tours and hotel bookings; Almatur, ul. Grodzka 2 (☎ 012/422 4668), specializes in youth travel and sells ISIC cards; Fregata, ul. Szpitalna 32 (☎ 012/422 4144), deals in plane tickets and hotel reservations; and Jordan, ul. Długa 9 (☎ 012/421 2125), handles international bus tickets and accommodation bookings.

Małopolska

The area around Kraków presents an attractive landscape of rolling fields, quiet villages and market towns. It traditionally goes by the name of **Małopolska** (literally "Little Poland"), a territory which – together with Wielkopolska ("Great Poland"; see p.535), formed the heartland of the medieval Polish state. It's a region marked by the progress of Polish history, from the medieval castles of the **Ojców National Park** to the Renaissance shrines of **Kalwaria Zeberzydowska** and the birthplace of the Polish pope, Karol Wotyła, at **Wadowice**. Most attractive of the Małopolska towns is **Tarnów**, a historic market centre whose dainty Rynek looks like a miniaturized version of the more famous main square in Kraków. Further north towards Warsaw, **Kielce** is an absorbing regional centre that provides a good stepping-off point for forays into the invigorating walking territory of the **Gory Świętokrzyskie**. The most visited destination in this part of Poland is also its most notorious, the **Auschwitz-Birkenau** concentration camp – preserved more or less as the Nazis left it – at Oświęcim, due west of Kraków.

All of the destinations covered in this section can be treated as day-trips from Kraków, with the possible exception of the Kielce-Gory Świętokrzyskie region, where an overnight stay will help you get the best out of the area. Most places in Małopolska can be reached by **bus** from Kraków in a couple of hours, and there are express **trains** to Tarnów and Kielce.

Oświęcim: Auschwitz-Birkenau

Seventy kilometres west of Kraków, **OŚWIĘCIM** would in normal circumstances be a nondescript provincial town – a place to send visitors on their way without a moment's thought. The circumstances, however, are anything but normal here. Despite the best efforts of the local authorities to cultivate and develop a new identity, the town is indissolubly linked with the name the Nazi occupiers of Poland gave it – Auschwitz.

Some history
Following the Nazi invasion of Poland in September 1939, Oświęcim and its surrounding region were incorporated into the domains of the Third Reich and the town's name changed to **Auschwitz**. The establishment of concentration camps in the newly conquered territory was a German priority right from the start – camps in Germany proper were already overcrowded with political prisoners, and the occupation of Poland dramatically increased the number of potential undesirables who would need to be interned. The unassuming town of Oświęcim made the perfect site – it already had a Polish-built camp for migrant workers, and the red-brick dormitory buildings could be easily converted into prison blocks. The inmates would, it was hoped, make an ideal source of slave labour for Oświęcim's burgeoning chemical industry.

Work on the camp began in April 1940, and obedient Nazi functionary **Rudolf Höss** was appointed its commander. In June of that year the Gestapo delivered the first contingent of prisoners, mostly Polish students and schoolchildren arbitrarily rounded up to serve as a deterrent to others.

Overworked, undernourished and subjected to beatings, the prisoners suffered from high mortality rates right from the beginning. Following Hitler's attack on the Soviet Union in 1941, Soviet POWs flooded into the camp necessitating the construction of a huge subsidiary camp at nearby Birkenau and conditions deteriorated further – deaths from starvation or arbitrary violence set standards of cruelty that were to worsen as the war progressed.

Auschwitz's role as an extermination camp for Jews grew out of the Wannsee Conference of January 1942, when the Nazis decided on the so-called **Final Solution** and began looking for locations where mass-murder could be conducted on an industrial scale. The technology of mass killing had already been perfected after experiments in the use of poison gas at Auschwitz and other locations, and Auschwitz-Birkenau was now chosen as one of the principal venues for the forthcoming genocide.

By the end of 1942, **Jews** were beginning to be transported to Auschwitz from all over Europe, many fully believing Nazi propaganda that they were on their way to a new life of work in German factories or farms. After a train journey of anything up to ten days in sealed goods wagons and cattle trucks, the dazed survivors were herded up the station ramp, lined up for inspection and divided into two categories by the SS: those deemed "fit" or "unfit" for work. People placed in the latter category, up to 75 percent of all new arrivals, were then ordered to undress, marched into the "shower room" and gassed with **Zyklon B** cyanide gas sprinkled through special ceiling attachments. In this way, up to two thousand people were killed at a time (the process took 15–30min), a murderously efficient method of dispatching people, which continued relentlessly throughout the rest of the war. The greatest massacres occurred from 1944 onwards, after the special railway terminal had been installed at Birkenau to permit speedier "processing" of the victims to the gas chambers. Gold fillings, earrings, rings and even hair – subsequently used, amongst other things, for mattresses – were removed from the bodies before incinerating them. Cloth from their clothes was recycled into army uniforms, their watches given to troops in recognition of special achievements or bravery.

The precise numbers of people murdered in Auschwitz-Birkenau may never be known. According to most estimates, between one and a half and two million people died in the camp, the vast majority (85–90 percent) of whom were Jews, along with sizeable contingents of Romanies (Gypsies), Poles, Soviet POWs and a host of other European nationalities.

Auschwitz and Birkenau were declared a **museum** and memorial site in 1947, although Poland's postwar leaders initially appeared ambiguous in their attitude to the true nature of the Holocaust. Central to communist thinking was the idea that Marxism-Leninism in general, and the Soviet Union in particular, were the true objects of Nazi hatred – focusing on the sufferings of a particular ethnic group, such as the Jews, was deemed politically incorrect. It was only after the fall of communism in 1989 that official guidebooks to the Auschwitz site began giving due prominence to the specifically Jewish aspects of the genocide practised here. Auschwitz's status as a place of both Polish and Jewish suffering has frequently led to arguments between both groups about how the site as a whole ought to be commemorated, leading to much suspicion and mistrust. Celebrations marking the sixtieth anniversary of the camp's liberation in January 2005 – attended by Poland's President Kwaśniewski and heads of state from around the world – suggested a symbolic laying to rest of many of these arguments.

Getting there and visiting the camps

Buses from Kraków (every 20–30min; journey time 1hr 30min) pick up and drop off at the Auschwitz site: some of these services pass through central Oświęcim before heading for Auschwitz, others go to Auschwitz first before continuing to Oświęcim – either way, the "Auschwitz Museum" sign is pretty difficult to miss. Arriving by train is less convenient: Oświęcim train station lies 2km north of central Oświęcim, and 2km northeast of the Auschwitz site. The town's **tourist information centre** (Mon–Fri 8am–6pm, Sat & Sun 8am–4pm; Ⓦwww .cit-oswiecim.neostrada.pl), in the shopping mall/restaurant complex opposite the entrance to Auschwitz camp, can help with transport information.

It makes sense to visit the Auschwitz camp first, as it is here that you can make your donation (entrance is officially free although visitors are encouraged to donate between 5 and 10zł), pick up a map of both sites, and get to grips with the history of the camps by visiting the main museum displays. From here you can walk to Birkenau (30min) or take the free shuttle bus (April–Sept only) which departs from the Auschwitz site every hour.

To get the most from your visit consider joining a **guided group** (40zł per person; apply at the clearly signed desk at the Auschwitz camp), which visits both sites and takes around three hours. English-language tours depart roughly hourly.

Auschwitz

Approaching the site from the visitors' car park where buses from Kraków terminate, the Auschwitz camp (daily 8am–dusk; donation requested) looks at first like an innocuous collection of warehouses or a semi-abandoned military barracks. It's only when you pass through the entrance gate bearing the notorious cast-iron inscription *Arbeit Macht Frei* ("Work brings freedom") that you begin to realize you are in a place of imprisonment, torture and death.

The site itself consists of the sturdy **cell blocks** built by the Poles in the 1930s and taken over by the Germans in 1939. Declared a museum in 1947, the site was reorganized in 1978 when many of the nations whose citizens suffered at Auschwitz were given a block each and invited to arrange their own memorial display. Some of these displays have been modernized since then, others have remained much as they were (most notably Block 17, which triumphantly celebrates the anti-fascist traditions of a state called "Yugoslavia"). Block 18, dedicated to Hungary, is a good example of those that have been thoroughly overhauled, employing well-chosen photos and a human-heartbeat soundtrack to commemorate Hungarian Jewry in an extraordinarily moving way. Block 13 contains a touching account of Europe's Roma communities, together with Germany's Sinti – a Roma-related people who also fell victim to Nazi race policies. Another, larger, block (no. 27), is labelled simply "Jews": there's a long, labyrinthine display of photographs inside, although they're left, unlabelled, to speak for themselves. On the second floor, there's a section devoted to Jewish resistance both inside and outside the camp, some of which was organized in tandem with the Polish AK (Armia Krajowa), or Home Army, some entirely autonomously. Further over to the southwest, Block 5 contains rooms full of spectacles, prosthetic limbs, pots and pans, all confiscated from inmates of the camp and abandoned here when the Germans retreated.

Between blocks 11 and 10 stands the flower-strewn **Death Wall**, where thousands of prisoners were summarily executed with a bullet in the back of the head. **Block 11** itself is where the first experiments with Zyklon B gas were carried out on Soviet POWs and other inmates in September 1941.

The prison blocks finish by a **gas chamber** and a pair of ovens where the bodies were incinerated. "No more poetry after Auschwitz", in the words of the German philosopher Theodor Adorno.

Birkenau

Roughly three kilometers northwest of Auschwitz, the subsidiary camp of **Birkenau** (same times as Auschwitz) was begun in autumn 1941 to accommodate Soviet POWs earmarked for use as slave labour. Most of the Soviet prisoners died of starvation that same winter, and Birkenau was adapted to suit a new and even more sinister purpose: the mass murder of Europe's Jews. Transports got under way by late 1942, with victims delivered to a railway platform right inside the camp before being marched to the gas chambers. Disposing of the murdered – and sorting through their stolen belongings – was a labour-intensive task requiring a huge population of (mostly) Jewish slave workers, who lived in appalling conditions in Birkenau's barracks.

It is along the former railway tracks that you enter the camp, passing through a red-brick archway before emerging into the numbingly huge, 170-hectare site. Most of the barrack blocks were razed in 1945 but a handful remain, empty but for examples of the wooden cots and meagre mattresses on which inmates slept.

At the northern end of the camp is a stark grey monument to the dead, rising above the twisted ruins of gas chambers dynamited by the Germans as they retreated. The monument was unveiled in April 1967, when up to 200,000 people (including many former inmates) converged on the camp to take part in what the authorities termed a "grand anti-fascist meeting". To the right of the monument, beyond a group of cylindrical sewage-treatment towers, is an area dubbed **"Canada"** by the inmates (due to its far-away position in the extreme north of the camp) where gas chambers and crematoria stood beside warehouses where the belongings of victims were processed. One of the few buildings still standing here is the so-called **Sauna**, where newly arrived prisoners were undressed, shaved and assigned camp clothes – a grim museum display takes you methodically through the process. Just beyond lie the remains of Crematorium IV, burned down in a desperate revolt by 450 Sonderkommando (the inmates who were forced to carry out body-disposal tasks) in October 1944. A few steps further on is the so-called Grey Lake, where human ashes were once deposited.

Oświęcim

The centre of Oświęcim itself lies 2km east of the Auschwitz camp on the opposite bank of the River Soła. Aside from an unassuming Rynek, ringed by cafés, and a red-brick Gothic church overlooking the river, the main focus of interest is the **Oświęcim Jewish Centre** (Centrum Żydowskie w Oświęcimiu: Mon–Fri & Sun: March–Oct 8.30am–8pm; Nov–Feb 8.30am–6pm; Ⓦwww .ajcf.pl; donation requested), which occupies a former synagogue on pl. ks. Jana Skarbka 3. The beautifully restored prayer hall centres on a handsomely balustraded bimah (pulpit), while several upstairs rooms are filled with photographs of life in prewar Oświęcim – where Christians and Jews had lived perfectly harmoniously for five centuries. Ordinary early twentieth-century snapshots of football matches, school fetes and bathing trips to the river Soła assume a hugely poignant importance in the light of what happened to the community after 1941.

Kalwaria Zebrzydowska, Lanckorona and Wadowice

Southwest of Kraków lies an enchanting landscape of rolling hills and sleepy country towns, two of which are of great religious significance to Poles: **Kalwaria Zebrzydowska**, a centre of pilgrimage second only to Częstochowa (see p.472), and **Wadowice**, birthplace of Karol Wojtyła, better known as Pope John Paul II. **Lanckorona**, a charming village of traditional wooden houses, is within walking distance of Kalwaria and can be covered in the same trip. Numerous local buses work the Kraków–Kalwaria–Wadowice route, ensuring that you can see all three places in the space of a long day.

Kalwaria Zebrzydowska

Nestled among hills some 30km southwest of Kraków, the town of **KALWARIA ZEBRZYDOWSKA** looks and feels like a footnote to its main attraction: a Baroque hilltop monastery whose miracle-working image of the Virgin has long been a focus for pilgrims. The charm of the place is considerably enhanced by the presence of a walkable Calvary route, linking various chapels, which winds its way from the monastery across the neighbouring hills. Whether you're spiritually inclined or simply want a nature hike, Kalwaria is a deeply rewarding place.

The Calvary came into being in the early seventeenth century, when Mikołaj Zebrzydowski, lord of nearby Lanckorona (see p.416), became convinced that the local countryside's similarity to the landscape outside Jerusalem gave it a special spiritual significance. Having decided to mark his discovery with the construction of a series of Calvary chapels, he sent an envoy to Jerusalem for drawings of the holy places – and many of his resulting buildings are modelled on those in the holy city – an engaging three-kilometre-long architectural tour is the result.

The area around the monastery is particularly busy during the **Festival of the Assumption** (Aug 15) and at **Easter**, when the Passion Plays are performed here on Maundy Thursday and Good Friday, with the vast accompanying crowds processing solemnly around the sequence of chapels in which the events of Holy Week are fervently re-enacted. With local volunteers tied on crosses and onlookers dressed as Romans, it's a powerful, cathartic spectacle.

Kalwaria is easy to get to, with buses running every thirty minutes or so from Kraków (journey time 45min) to the local **bus station**, a twenty-minute walk east of the monastery. The Kalwaria Zebrzydowska–Lanckorona **train station** (served less frequently by trains from Kraków to Bielsko-Biała, Sucha Beskidzka and Zakopane) is a further ten minutes' walk out in the same direction. For **eating**, the *jadłodajnia* in the monastery courtyard offers cheap, filling food and has a terrace with outstanding views.

The monastery and the Calvary chapels

Dominating the landscape from its perch, the Benedictine Monastery is reached via ulica Bernardyńska, a steep street which darts up from Kalwaria's undistinguished town centre. The towering main **Basilica of the Virgin** (Bazylika Matki Bożej) is a familiar Baroque effusion, with a silver-plated Italian figure of the Virgin standing over the high altar. The object that inspires the greatest devotion, however, is the **painting** of the Virgin and Child in the Zebrzydowski chapel, said to have been shedding tears at regular intervals since the 1640s. A corridor connects the church to a small cloister, where you'll find seventeenth-century portraits of the Zebrzydowski family.

The starting point for the **Calvary** begins immediately outside the monastery. It's really made up of two interlocking routes, the main Via Dolorosa (marked as "Dróżki pana Jesusa" on signboards), and a sequence of Marian Stations ("Dróżki Matki Bożej"), each of which wends its way up and down hillocks, along tree-lined avenues, through forest and in and out of rustic villages. Every few hundred metres or so you'll come across a cluster of chapels – some of which resemble insignificant huts, others magnificent domed structures which have the appearance of bonsai cathedrals. There are regular processions of schoolkids and coach parties "doing" the chapels nearest the monastery, but the further reaches of the Calvary routes are relatively crowd-free, contemplative places.

Lanckorona

Five kilometres east of Kalwaria Zebrzydowska, and reached by a minor road off the Kraków–Bielsko-Biała highway, the hillside village of **LANCKORONA** has long been noted for its traditional folk architecture and unhurried rustic feel. It served genteel Kraków folk as a health retreat in the years before World War I, though there are few relics of its time as a spa resort today. The village is served by regular **minibus** from Kraków, although it makes sense to combine Lanckorona with a visit to Kalwaria – the easternmost point of the Calvary route (the Bernardine Church in Brody) is only 45 minutes' walk over the hill. The Kalwaria Zebrzydowska–Lanckorona train station is about sixty minutes away on foot.

At the centre of the village lies a spacious, sloping **Rynek**, lined with low, pastel-coloured houses, their broad shingle roofs hanging over wooden-pillared porches. An old granary at the bottom of the square now accommodates a small **museum** (Tues–Sat 10am–4pm; 4zł), displaying a diverting jumble of nineteenth-century agricultural implements and craft tools. Paths leave the upper end of the square towards Lanckorona's medieval **castle**, an evocative ruin shrouded in forest. As so often with such places, there doesn't seem to be much inside save for the broken glass left by partying teenagers.

The *Pensionat* **café-restaurant** on the main square serves up Polish staples in a rustic interior decked out with semi-antique knick-knacks. Well worth considering for an overnight **stay** is *Willa Tadeusz*, just east of the centre at Lanckorona 46 (☎033/876 3592, ⊛pentadeu.republika.pl; bed and breakfast ❷), a lovely part-timbered building set in its own grassy grounds, offering simply furnished rooms with facilities in the hallway, and delicious home-cooked food if you sign up for full board (❹).

Wadowice

Fourteen kilometres west of Kalwaria Zebrzydowska is the little town of **WADOWICE**, whose rural obscurity was shattered by the election of local boy **Karol Wojtyła** to the papacy in October 1978. Almost instantly the town became a place of pilgrimage, with the souvenir industry quick to seize the opportunities. Again, buses from Kraków (roughly every 30min; 1hr 20min) are more frequent than trains. The train and bus stations are on the eastern side of the town, from where it's a ten-minute walk to the elegantly paved and flower-bedded market square. Main point of reference here is the onion-domed **parish church**, where Karol Wojtyła was baptized in 1920. Most visitors gravitate towards the Chapel of the Virgin Mary on the left-hand side of the entrance, site of a nineteenth-century image of the Virgin to which Karol Wojtyła prayed regularly as a schoolboy. Behind the church, the old **town hall** now houses a museum (Mon–Thurs 9am–3pm, Fri 9am–4.30pm, Sat 10am–2pm, Sun 11am–3pm; 2zł) with changing exhibitions on local history. A few steps away from the museum at ul. Kościelna 7 is the **pope's birthplace**, a simple two-room apartment where he spent the first eighteen years of his life. It has now been turned into a rather tasteful and restrained **museum** (daily: May–Sept 9am–1pm & 2–6pm; Oct–April 9am–noon & 2–5pm; free), packed with photographs illustrating all stages of his life. It certainly succeeds in portraying the late pontiff as a rounded personality, with pictures of him skiing, hiking, playing in goal for the school team and taking part in student drama productions. The museum is far too small to cope with the coach parties that regularly descend on the place, so be prepared for a bit of a crush.

There's a **tourist information office** in the town hall (same times as town museum; Ⓦ www.wadowice.pl). Wadowice has one culinary claim to fame in the shape of the *Kremówka Wadowicka*, a deliciously wobbly slice of creamy custard that is sold at all the town's cafés – *Kawiarna Galicja*, right next to the pope's birthplace on Kościelna, is a good place to try it. For more substantial eating, the *Piwnica* **restaurant**, just off the square on Jagiellońska, serves up good, inexpensive pork and fish dishes in an attractive cellar.

Ojców National Park

Immediately northwest of Kraków, the limestone gorge of the **Ojców valley** has a unique microclimate and an astonishingly rich variety of plants and wildlife. Most of it is protected by the **Ojców National Park** (Ojcówski Park Narodowy; Ⓦ www.opn.most.org.pl), one of the country's smallest and most memorable protected regions. With an attractive and varied landscape of scenic

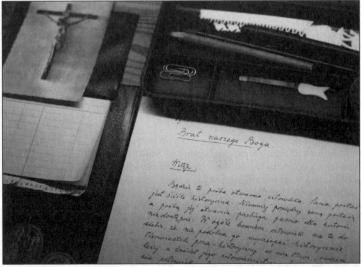

▲ Pope John Paul II's birthplace

river valley, twisted rock formations, and peaceful forests, the park is perfect for a day's trekking or cycling. The *Ojcówski Park Narodowy* map (1:22,500), widely available both in Kraków and on arrival in Ojców, is a useful aid to exploration.

The valley also gives access to the most southerly of the **castles** built by King Kazimierz to defend the southwestern reaches – and, most importantly, the trade routes – of the country from the Bohemian rulers of Silesia. Known as the **Eagles' Nest Trail** (Szlak Orlich Gniazd), these fortresses are strung along the hilly ridge extending westwards from Ojców as far as Olsztyn (see p.475).

Ojców and into the valley

The principal point of access to the river gorge is **OJCÓW**, 25km from Kraków (and served by most, but not all, Kraków–Olkusz buses), the national park's only village and in season filled to bursting with local school groups. Developed as a low-key health resort in the mid-nineteenth century, it's a delightful village, with wooden houses straggling along a valley floor framed by deciduous forest and craggy limestone cliffs. Just beyond the car park where buses stop is a small **natural history museum** (mid-May to mid-Nov Tues–Sun 9am–noon & 1–4.30pm, mid-Nov to mid-May Tues–Fri 8am–2pm; 3zł), where you'll find mammoth tusks, the jaws of prehistoric cave bears, and a modest collection of stuffed local fauna. Immediately beyond is the PTTK **regional museum** (Mon–Fri 9am–3pm; 2zł), located above the Ojców post office, which contains prints of the village as it looked in the nineteenth century, and a corner stacked with local folk costumes, notable for the extravagantly embroidered and beaded women's jackets. Overlooking the village to the north is a fine, ruined **castle** (April–Oct Tues–Sun 10am–4.45pm, stays open later at the height of summer; 3zł), the southern extremity of the Szlak Orlich Gniazd and an evocative place in the twilight hours when it is circled by squadrons of bats. There's not much of the castle left, apart from two of the original fourteenth-century towers, the main gate entrance and the walls of the castle chapel. There are excellent views over the winding valley, and a path through the woods that leads up to the Złota Góra campsite and restaurant (see opposite). A few hundred metres north up the valley from Ojców castle is the curious spectacle of the **Chapel on the Water** (Kaplica na Wodzie), straddling the river on brick piles. This odd site neatly circumvented a nineteenth-century tsarist edict forbidding religious structures to be built "on solid ground", part of a strategy to subdue the intransigently nationalist Catholic Church. These days, it's only open for visits between Masses on Sundays.

Heading south from the village takes you through a small gorge lined with strange rock formations, most famous of which, about fifteen minutes out from the village, is the **Kraków Gate** (Krakowska Brama), a pair of rocks which seem to form a huge portal leading to a side valley. Before reaching the Krakowska Brama you may well be enticed uphill to the right by a (black-waymarked) path to the **Shorty's Cave** (Jaskinia Łokietka: late April to late Oct daily 10am–5pm; 7zł), some thirty minutes' distant, the largest of a sequence of chambers burrowing into the cliffs outside Ojców. According to legend it was here that King Władysław the Short was hidden and protected by local peasants following King Wenceslas of Bohemia's invasion in the early fourteenth century. Around 250m long, the rather featureless illuminated cave is a bit of a letdown if you've come expecting spectacular stone and ice formations. Individual travellers will have to wait to join a guided group before being allowed inside.

Ojców practicalities

There's a PTTK **information office** (Mon–Fri 9am–3pm; ℡012/389 2010) next to the car park which can help you find a place to stay, and a souvenir shop in the same building which sells maps. The Ojcowianin travel agency, in the same building as the PTTK museum (℡012/389 2089), also has information on rooms. Alternatively, it's usually fairly easy to rent a room in someone's house in the village by asking around, though things get pretty full up in the summer season. There's a **campsite** in Złota Góra (℡012/389 2014), a kilometre northwest of the castle up the hill road through the forest. Back down in Ojców, the *Pod Kazimierza* **café-restaurant** mops up many of the day-trippers.

Pieskowa Skała

If the weather's fine and you're up for walking the 9km road and footpath from Ojców, **PIESKOWA SKAŁA**, home to the region's best-known and best-preserved castle, is an enjoyable and trouble-free piece of hiking. Direct buses also run from Kraków (1hr 15min) via Ojców. If you're on foot, watch out for a trail marked with red waymarkers which heads left into the woods roughly parallel with the Kaplica na Wodzie (see opposite). After 3km or so it rejoins the main road and darts uphill to the village of **Grodzisko** just to the north, site of a tiny late seventeenth-century **chapel**.

Roughly 4km further north, the castle approach is signalled by an eighteen-metre limestone pillar known locally as **Hercules' Club** (Maczuga Herkulesa), beyond which you can see the castle. Long the possession of the Szafraniec family, the **castle** (courtyard 8am–8pm; free) is an elegant Renaissance rebuilding of a fourteenth-century original. As at Wawel, the most impressive period feature is the delicately arcaded courtyard, a photogenic construction that's a regular feature in travel brochures.

The castle **museum** (Tues–Thurs & Sat 10am–3pm, Fri 10am–noon, Sun 10am–5pm; 10zł) offers a breathtaking sweep through several centuries of art, beginning with some fine Gothic wood-carved Madonnas, St Barbaras and St Catherines, and an exquisitely rendered sculpture of St Mary of Egypt, her entire body covered by the long tresses of her hair. A spectacular bevy of altarpieces includes a grippingly gruesome *Martyrdom of St Stanisław* with his tormentor King Bolesław looking impassively on; another panel bears a bizarre scene of punishment in which the unfaithful wives of Kraków are forced to suckle puppies while their own children are put to the teat of a bitch. A sequence of Baroque rooms feature sumptuously decorated Flemish and Dutch tapestries, the most notable among them depicting a series of heroic scenes from the life of Alexander the Great, culminating in his triumphant entry into Babylon in a chariot.

One of the fortified towers houses a **café-restaurant** with canteen food, a groovy interior arranged around a spiral staircase, and a roof terrace offering fine views over the valley.

Ogrodzieniec

The remaining castles of the Szlak Orlich Gniazd are very ruined, but dramatic, seeming to spring straight out of the Jurassic rock formations. The most impressive example is **OGRODZIENIEC**, 35km north of Pieskowa Skała on the main road to Olkusz. The ruin you see today was built during Kazimierz the Great's reign and remodelled into a magnificent Renaissance residence reputedly the equal of Wawel, before being ravaged by the Swedes in 1655. The castle is easy to get to by public transport, with several daily Kraków–Częstochowa **buses** passing by.

Kielce and northern Małopolska

Most people see nothing more of the northern reaches of Małopolska than the glimpses snatched from the window of a Warsaw–Kraków express train – a pity, because the gentle hills, lush valleys, strip-farmed fields and tatty villages that characterize the region are quintessential rural Poland. The main settlement is **Kielce**, a pleasant, park-filled city with a handful of good museums, but the real attraction for visitors lies in rambling about in the **Góry Świętokrzyskie** – an attractive ridge of wooded, walkable hills just to the east of the city. South of Kielce, the **Jaskinia Raj** (Raj Cave), the medieval fortress of **Chęciny** and the open-air ethnographic museum at **Tokarnia** make enjoyable excursions.

Kielce

Situated midway between Kraków and Warsaw, **KIELCE** became part of the Russian Empire as a result of Poland's eighteenth-century Partitions, and to this day looks very different to the Habsburg-influenced cities of southern Małopolska. Like most tsarist garrison towns, Kielce was laid out along a single main street, creating a 2km-long central boulevard with no real focal point – never mind a main Rynek. The town is nevertheless a pleasant and laid-back place in which to stroll, especially in spring and summer when the main strip fills up with café tables and promenaders. With a trio of absorbing museums and an ensemble of relaxing parks, it's as fine a place as any to break your journey.

Arrival and information

The **train station** is on the west side of town: the main street, ulica Sienkiewicza, is right opposite the station forecourt. Express minibuses from Kraków arrive at a small bus terminal on the northern side of the train station, although most other bus services use the **bus station** – a marvellously frivolous circular building resembling the kind of flying saucers imagined by 1950s sci-fi comic-book writers – just opposite. There's a 24-hour **left-luggage** office (*przechowalnia bagażu*) in the train station for those passing through.

   The **tourist information centre**, on the first floor of the train station's main ticket hall (Mon–Fri 9am–5pm, Sat 10am–3pm; ☎041/345 8681, ⓦwww.um.kielce.pl/turystyka), can help you to find accommodation and provides brochures. They may also have maps of Kielce and outlying regions; otherwise the bookshop on the corner of Sienkiewicza and Paderewskiego stocks a good choice.

Accommodation

There's a smallish selection of **accommodation** from which to choose, most of it directed towards commercial travellers, with prices to match.

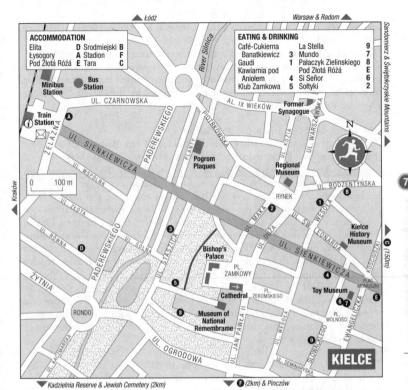

ACCOMMODATION

Elita	D	Srodmiejski	B
Łysogory	A	Stadion	F
Pod Złotą Różą	E	Tara	C

EATING & DRINKING

Café-Cukierna		La Stella	9
Banatkiewicz	3	Mundo	7
Gaudi	1	Pałaczyk Zielinskiego	8
Kawiarnia pod		Pod Złotą Różą	E
Aniolem	4	Si Señor	6
Klub Zamkowa	5	Sołtyki	2

Łódź   *Warsaw & Radom*

Sandomierz & Świębokrzyskie Mountains

Kraków

0   100 m

Kadzielnia Reserve & Jewish Cemetery (2km)   *(2km) & Pinczów*

KIELCE

Elita ul. Równa 4b ☎041/344 2230. Small, privately run hotel in a residential street within walking distance south of the stations, with comfortable, well-kept rooms. Perfectly placed for ambling in Kielce's parks. ❻

Łysogóry ul. Sienkiewicza 78 ☎041/365 5000, ⓦwww.lysogory.com.pl. Uninspiring block opposite the train station, thoroughly modernized to business standards inside. ❼

Pod Złotą Różą pl. Moniuszki 7 ☎041/341 5002, ⓦwww.hotel-pod-zlota-roza.pl. Elegant nineteenth-century town house at the eastern end of the main strip, offering plush rooms with Second Empire-style furniture and rich warm fabrics. ❼

Stadion ul. Ściegiennego 8 ☎&ⓕ041/368 7715. Utilitarian hotel aimed at visiting sports teams, 2km south of the centre but handy for the Kadzielnia reserve and the parks. Sparsely furnished rooms with shower. ❹

Śródmiejski ul. Wesoła 5 ☎041/344 1517 ⓦwww.hotelsrodmiejski.pl. Smallish place just off the main strip, offering functional en suites with small TVs. ❹

Tara Kościuszki 24 ☎041/344 2510, ⓦwww .tara.kielce.pl. Medium-sized, privately run place just east of the centre. Rooms are a little prone to over-the-top decor and colour-clash furnishings but otherwise everything is new, squeaky clean and comfortable. ❻

The City

All the monuments worth seeing are concentrated around a relatively small central area, bisected by the city's main artery, the pedestrianized **ulica Sienkiewicza**, which runs from the train station in the west to plac Moniuszki almost 2km to the east. A short way north off ulica Sienkiewicza at Planty 7/8, an anonymous-looking house at no. 7 displays two small commemorative **plaques** in Polish, Hebrew and English "to the 42 Jews murdered … during anti-Semitic riots", a reference to the notorious Kielce Pogrom of 1946 (see box opposite).

Returning to Sienkiewicza and continuing east brings you to the **cathedral**, slightly uphill on plac Zamkowy. A Baroque reconstruction of a Romanesque original, it contains a fine Renaissance monument in red marble to a female member of the local Zebrzydowski family, sculpted by Il Padovano, and some elaborate Rococo carvings in the choir stalls.

The Palace of the Bishops of Kraków

A short way west of the cathedral is the **Palace of the Bishops of Kraków** (Pałac Biskupów Krakowskich: Wed–Sun 9am–4pm, plus May–June & Sept–Oct Tues 10am–6pm; 7zł), an impressive early Baroque complex, constructed in the late 1630s as a summer residence for the bishops of Kraków, who owned Kielce at the time. Most rooms of the **upper floor** comprise the sumptuously furnished former bishop's apartments, decorated with intricately painted ceiling beams and elaborate friezes running around the tops of the walls. The finest example of this effect is in the **Great Dining Hall**, the frieze here consisting of a mammoth twin-level series of portraits of Kraków bishops and Polish monarchs. A number of rooms display striking ceiling paintings from the workshop of Thomas Dolabella, notably the **Senatorial Hall** in the west wing, featuring the ominous *Judgement of the Polish Brethren* (the Brethren in question being a sixteenth-century Protestant sect based in nearby Raków); and, in the adjoining room a grand, sweeping depiction of scenes from the Polish–Swedish and Polish–Muscovite wars of the seventeenth century.

The History Museum and the Toy Museum

Returning to ulica Sienkiewicza and continuing east soon brings you within range of the **Kielce History Museum** at ul. św Leonarda 4 (Muzeum Historii Kielc: Tues, Thurs, Sat & Sun 9am–4pm; Thurs & Fri 10am–6pm; 6zł), an attractively laid out collection of weaponry, domestic knick knacks, and photographs of Kielce during both world wars. Artfully strewn throughout the display are several references to the Kielce-born globetrotting criminal Józef Lis (aka Joseph Silver) who – according to Charles van Onselen's less than convincing book *The Fox and the Flies* – was the man responsible for London's Jack the Ripper murders in 1888.

Back across ulica Sienkiewicza to the south, the gently sloping plac Wolności is home to a highly entertaining **Toy Museum** (Muzeum Zabawek: Tues–Sun 10am–6pm; 6zł), packed with dolls throughout the ages alongside all manner of trains, planes and automobiles. There's a section devoted to traditional wooden toys made by central European craftsmen, some of which you can play with yourself.

Through the parks to the Geological Reserve

Southwest of the Bishop's Palace area is a spectacular swathe of parkland featuring a boating lake, ornamental flower beds and elegant stands of trees – all crisscrossed by paths which are thronged with locals on summer afternoons. Further south still, on the far side of Krakowska, is the **Kadzielnia Geological Reserve** (Rezerwat Geologiczny Kadzielnia) a partially submerged former limestone quarry now laid out as a park, albeit a scruffy one. With its central lake surrounded by bleak crags and scrub, it's a surprise to find such a seemingly wild landscape so close to a city centre. At the far end of the reserve

The Kielce pogrom

Despite losing most of its Jewish population in World War II, Poland was the scene of several bizarre and disturbing outbreaks of anti-semitism in the years that followed. Most notorious of these incidents was the Kielce Pogrom of July 1946, in which 46 local Jewish Holocaust survivors were murdered in a sudden outbreak of mob violence. Twelve people were sentenced to death for the killings and the whole affair was hushed up until the 1990s, when the fiftieth anniversary of the massacre was marked by the unveiling of commemorative plaques. The pogrom became topical again in 2008, when historian Jan Tomas Gross's book *Strach* ("Fear") attempted to address the issue of postwar anti-semitism head on – shocking many Poles who had previously been unaware of this episode in their history.

is an open-air concert venue, the "amphitheatre", put to good use in summer when various cultural events take place here.

Eating and drinking

There's an expanding range of good restaurants and bars in Kielce, all within striking range of the main ulica Sienkiewicza. For **snacks**, the cafés and bakeries grouped around plac Wolności, just off Sienkiewicza to the south, are the best places to grab a quick bite.

Restaurants

La Stella ul. Słowackiego 4. Relaxing Italian restaurant with reasonable thin-crust pizzas and a small selection of meat and fish dishes, few of which are likely to break the 20zł mark. Daily noon–10pm.

Pałaczyk Zielińskiego ul. Zamkowa 5. Café-restaurant in a cultural centre with a huge summer garden that sees regular concerts in summer. A full menu of Polish favourites with a few European dishes thrown in, and modest prices. Daily 11am–11pm.

Pod Złotą Różą pl. Moniuszki 7. Polish-international cuisine delivered with style, serving fish, goose and lamb dishes at around 50zł. Pleasant patio seating out the back. Daily 11am–11pm.

Si Señor pl. Wolności 1. Spanish-themed place with a good choice of Mediterranean seafood and a well-stocked wine list. Mains in the 30–40zł range. Mon–Sat noon–10pm, Sun noon–7pm.

Sołtyki Rynek 19. Moderately priced Polish meat and poultry dishes in informal surroundings. Daily 10am–9pm.

Cafes and bars

Café-Cukierna Banatkiewicz ul. Staszica 10. Midway between ul. Sienkiewicza and the parks, this is the best place for cakes and ice creams.

Gaudi ul. Wesoła 10. The only part of Kielce that could be said to look like Barcelona, this extravagantly decorated, Gaudí-themed café offers pulsating music, draft beers and cocktails around the clock. Open 24hr.

Kawiarnia pod Aniołem ul. Sienkiewicza 9. Relaxing and cosy café decorated with old sideboards and bookcases, this is a popular place for an intimate evening drink and is good for a daytime coffee-and-ice cream stop, too. Mon–Sat 10am–midnight, Sun noon–11pm.

Klub Zamkowa ul. Zamkowa 2. Daily 11am–2am or later. Relaxing café during the daytime, highly enjoyable disco at night, located in atmospheric barrel-vaulted rooms round the corner from the Bishop's Palace.

Mundo plac Wolności 1 ⓦ www.mundocafe.pl. Funky first-floor café featuring art exhibitions, a regular menu of weekend DJ events, live local bands, and jazz. Daily 4pm–1am or later.

The Raj Cave

Ten kilometres southwest of Kielce, and roughly 1km west of the main Kraków road, is the **Raj Cave** (Jaskinia Raj: mid-March to Nov Tues–Sun 9am–5pm; compulsory guided tours in Polish only; 12zł), one of the most popular cave networks in Poland and frequently busy with coach parties, especially in summer, when you're advised to get there early. The **bus** (#31 from Kielce; every 30–40min) drops you on the main road, from where you walk to the main car park and on along a wooded path to the ticket office-cum-café/museum at the cave entrance.

Only a stretch of 180m inside the caves is open to visitors, but it's a spectacular experience nonetheless, comprising a series of **chambers** filled with a seemingly endless array of stalagmites, stalactites and other dreamlike dripstone formations. Neanderthals inhabited the cave as long as fifty thousand years ago and it remained a popular refuge for Homo sapiens well into the stone age – archeologists have recently discovered a stockade constructed from reindeer antlers. Some of the finds are on display in the small museum attached to the ticket office at the cave entrance.

Chęciny

Five kilometres further south along the Kraków road (at the end of the #31 bus route from Kielce), the little town of **CHĘCINY** nestles beneath a hugely impressive set of **castle ruins** (Tues–Sun 9am–6pm; 3zł), which dominate the surrounding landscape from their hilltop perch, providing the town with an instantly recognizable visual trademark. The castle is easily reached from Chęciny's Rynek, either via a path that darts straight up the hillside or by an asphalt road which curls its way more leisurely around the side. Completed in the 1310s for King Władysław I, and remodelled three centuries later following major destruction by the Swedes, the castle is now largely a ruin. All that remains is the polygonal plan of the outer wall, the main gate and a trio of soaring towers, two of which – from a distance at least – look like the sombre chimneys of some giant hilltop factory. One of the towers – climbed via a steep spiral staircase – offers expansive views over the surrounding countryside, with Kielce, and on a clear day the Świętokrzyskie hills, visible in the distance.

For centuries the town of Chęciny was a typical Polish *shtetl*, with Jews making up more than half the population. The Jews are gone now, but their houses still line the Rynek – in silent testimony to their age-long presence. The former **synagogue** lies a short walk east of the Rynek along ulica Długa, a characteristically solid brick structure with a two-tiered roof built in the early seventeenth century. The building currently provides a home to various social and cultural organizations, and there's a good chance someone will allow you to take a peek inside if you arrive during normal office hours (roughly Mon–Fri 8am–3pm). A few decorative details apart, there's been little attempt to preserve any of the original features of the building, with the main prayer hall now a characterless space occupied – at the last visit – by a table tennis table.

If you need a bite to **eat** before heading back to town try *Restauracja Pod Zamkiem* at ul. Armii Krajowej 1, which runs the whole gamut of pork- and chicken-based Polish standards, but often closes on Mondays and Tuesdays.

Tokarnia

A further 7km south from Chęciny on the main Kraków road, the otherwise unremarkable village of **TOKARNIA** is the site of one of Poland's best outdoor ethnographic collections, the **Museum of Kielce Village Life** (Muzeum Wsi Kieleckiej; April–Oct Tues–Sun 10am–5pm; Nov–March Mon–Fri 9am–2pm; 10zł). It's right beside the main road and well signposted; if you're travelling by **bus** (from Kielce, take buses heading for Jędrzejów or Kraków) ask the driver for the *skansen* and you'll be dropped close by. In summer a basic café operates in the house at the entrance to the area.

With a well-laid-out collection of traditional buildings rescued from various locations in the Kielce region, the museum provides an enjoyable survey of local architectural traditions. The thatched and shingle-roofed buildings assembled here encompass the full range of rural life, with an emphasis on traditional farmsteads, from relatively prosperous setups – the more religious pictures on display, the wealthier the family – to the dwellings of the poorest subsistence farmers. Many houses contain an amazing array of old wooden farm implements, kitchen utensils and tools used in traditional crafts such as ostlery, shingling, brewing, woodcarving, herbal medicinal preparations and candle-making. Look out too for a wonderful old windmill, a pharmacy and a fine mid-nineteenth-century *dwór* (manor house) of the kind inhabited by the minor gentry.

The Góry Świętokrzyskie

In this low-lying region, the **Góry Świętokrzyskie**, only 600m at maximum, appear surprisingly tall. Running for almost 70km east from Kielce, the mountains' long ridges and valleys are interspersed with isolated villages. The range gets its name from the **Holy Cross** (Abbey of Święty Krzyż) right in the heart of the hills, a foundation once thought to possess a fragment of the Cross and which became a renowned pilgrimage venue as a result. It still exerts a powerful spiritual pull, and commands access to several rugged hiking trails to boot. During World War II, the area was a centre of armed resistance to the Nazis: a grim, essentially factual account of life in the resistance here is given in Primo Levi's book *If Not Now, When*. With abundant forest interspersed with twisted outcrops of broken quartzite, the whole range is encompassed within the limits of the **Świętokrzyskie National Park** (Świętokrzyski Park Narodowy), helping preserve the habitat of a range of birds and animals, including a colony of eagles.

The part of the range that most people aim for is the so-called **Łysogóry**, a scenic stretch of hilltop forest 30km east of Kielce, where the abbey, on the eastern shoulder of the ridge, provides the main focus for hikers and sightseers alike. A meagre handful of buses from Kielce head directly to the monastery, although Kielce-Ostrowiec services (16 daily, fewer at weekends) do pass through

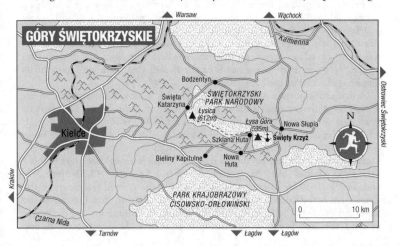

the small town of Nowa Słupia, a kilometre or two downhill, and are more frequent, making this your most likely entry- and exit-point to the region.

Nowa Słupia

Just over 30km east of Kielce, **NOWA SŁUPIA** is a dusty crossroads town whose centre consists of a bus stop, a couple of cafés, and precious little else. From the town centre, ulica Świętokrzyska heads east then veers north towards the boundary of the national park. About ten minutes' out of town it passes the **Museum of Ancient Metallurgy** (Muzeum Starożytnego Hutnictwa: Tues–Sun 9am–4pm; 5zł), a concrete pavilion built to protect a second-century smelting site – when the land around Nowa Słupia made up one of Europe's biggest ironworks. The sober, Polish-language display does little to bring the site to life – although piles of ancient cinders do have a certain mystique if you stare at them for long enough.

The **tourist office** in the local government building (Urząd Gminy) at Świętokrzyska 18 (Tues–Fri 8am–3pm, Sat & Sun noon–4pm; ☏041/317 7626) can provide information on B&B **accommodation** in local houses; while the *Pod Skalką* **campsite**, near the museum at Świętokrzyska 57 (May–Sept; ☏041/317 7085), has dorm beds in wooden huts (❷), a grassy field for tents, and a restaurant.

On to Święty Krzyż

A short way beyond Nowa Słupia's metallurgy museum, a small car park girdled by souvenir stalls marks the end of the road and the beginning of the walking trail up onto the Łysogóry ridge. The trail starts with a small national park office charging an entrance fee (5zł) and selling maps. After a thirty-minute ascent through trees, a path marked "Miejsce pamięci narodowej" (literally "place of popular remembrance") leads off to the right, arriving after five minutes at an overgrown **Soviet war cemetery**, last resting place of POWs imprisoned by the Germans in Święty Krzyż abbey.

Back on the main track it's only a few more minutes to **ŚWIĘTY KRZYŻ** itself, an abbey established by Italian Benedictines in the early twelfth century. Legend has it that Bolesław the Wrymouth ordered the construction of the monastery in order to house a fragment of the True Cross, brought to Kraków by Prince (later Saint) Emeric, son of King Stephen of Hungary. The abbey soon established itself as a pilgrimage centre much patronized by Polish royals – Władysław Jagiełło liked it so much he came here seven times. The Benedictine Order left Święty Krzyż after a change in diocesan boundaries in 1818 and the abbey served as a priests' retirement home before being turned into a prison in 1882. It's now back in the hands of the Benedictines, although some of its buildings are used by the national park.

Romanesque doorway apart, the abbey **church** is mostly Baroque in appearance. Lining the interior walls is a fine clutch of paintings by Neoclassicist Franciszek Smugliewicz, most impressive of which is *The Vision of St Emeric* – in which the eponymous hero is accosted by an angel while out with his hunting dogs. Working your way round the cloister from here soon brings you to the **sacristy**, beautifully decorated with Baroque ceiling paintings, and the adjoining **Oleśnicki Chapel** (Mon–Sat 9am–12.30pm & 1–5pm, Sun 12.30–5pm; 3zł), endowed in 1620 by Mikołaj Oleśnicki to hold the revered fragments of the Cross – hence the Rococo reliquaries either side of the main altar. Frescoes to the right and left depict St Helena, mother of Emperor Constantine and discoverer of the Cross, and St Emeric presenting fragments of the Cross to the Bishop of Kraków. Mikołaj Oleśnicki and wife Sofia are treated to a splendid pair of funerary effigies. From the middle of the chapel, steps lead down into a small **crypt**, where a collection of open-lidded sarcophagi display the mummified remains of Mikołaj Oleśnicki and children, a nameless participant in the 1863 uprising (still wearing his black leather boots) and, most famously of all, Jeremi Wiśniowiecki (1612–51), who as Grand Hetman of the Ukraine during the Cossack revolts features strongly in the historical novels of Henryk Sienkiewicz. Wiśniowiecki left his widow with funds insufficient to finance the extravagant funerary spectacle a man of his standing was thought to deserve, and his corpse was entrusted to the monks of Święty Krzyż pending the family's financial recovery. His withered leathery form has been here ever since, wrapped in a fancy green shroud that in other circumstances would have made a fantastic pair of curtains.

The west wing of the abbey harbours the **Museum of the Świętokrzyskie National Park** (Muzeum Świętokrzyskiego Parku Narodowego: April–Oct daily 10am–5pm; Nov–March Tues–Sun 10am–3pm; 5zł), one of the country's best natural history collections, covering every aspect of the area's wildlife, with exhibits ranging from butterflies and snakes to huge deer and elk. There's a good view down into the valley below the edge of the abbey, and you can also see some of the large tracts of broken stones that are a distinctive glaciated feature of the hilltops.

Round the back of the abbey building steps lead down to a basement exhibition devoted to the abbey's period as a **prison**, particularly the 1941–45 period when, as Stalag XII C, it was used by the Germans to incarcerate Soviet POWs. Just how appalling the conditions were is indicated by photographs of camp signs (in Russian and German) forbidding cannibalism on pain of death.

Back in the cloisters, the *Jadłodajnia Benedyktyńska* **snack bar** (daily 10am–5pm) doles out delicious – and ridiculously cheap – portions of *bigos* (meat and cabbage stew) and *żurek* (rye soup) in an attractive cellar space. A few doors away, the *Stara Aptieka* sells natural remedies based on traditional Benedictine recipes, and herbal teas.

From the abbey it's a twenty-minute walk westwards through the woods followed by a sharp southbound descent to the tiny settlement of **SZKLANA HUTA**, where there's another national park hut for the benefit of those entering the park from this direction, and a trio of enormous iron crosses erected in memory of Poles massacred by the Soviet authorities in 1939–40. Off to one side is the *Jodłowy Dwór* **hotel** (☏041/302 5028, ⓦ www.jodlowydwor .com.pl; ❹), a modern concrete building with small but comfy en-suite rooms and its own restaurant.

From Święty Krzyż to Święta Katarzyna

Continuing due west from Szklana Huta will take you towards the highest point of the Łysogóry, the 611-metre-high **Łysica**, 10km away at the western end of the range, a legendary witches' meeting place with an excellent viewpoint. From here the path continues for a further 2km through the woodland, past memorials to resistance fighters hunted down by the Nazis, to the village of **ŚWIĘTA KATARZYNA** – where you can catch a bus back to Kielce. In Święta Katarzyna itself, there's a **convent** that's been home to an enclosed order of Bernardine nuns since the fifteenth century. If you turn up during daylight hours you can usually peer in at the church. The *Jodelka* **hotel**, ul. Kielecka 3 (☏041/311 2111, ⓦ www.hoteljodelka.pl; ❸), will sort you out with a sparsely furnished room with shared bathroom or a more comfortable en suite (**④**).

Tarnów and around

Although somewhat in the shadow of its larger neighbour to the west, the regional centre of **TARNÓW**, 80km east of Kraków, is nonetheless a fascinating town in its own right, with a fine medieval Old Town, excellent museums, and a haunting Jewish cemetery. Founded in the 1330s, Tarnów rapidly grew fat on the lucrative trade routes running east to Ukraine and south to Hungary. Long the seat of the wealthy local Tarnowski family, Tarnów grew under their patronage to become an important Renaissance-era centre of learning, a branch of the Jagiellonian University in Kraków being set up here in the mid-1500s. Later, wars and partition brought the inevitable decline, and in the twentieth century Tarnów's long-standing Jewish population was a particular target for the Nazis. Frequent and fast rail connections make it an easy and attractive day-trip from Kraków, but Tarnów can also serve as a base for trips around the region, including north to the folk art centre of **Zalipie**.

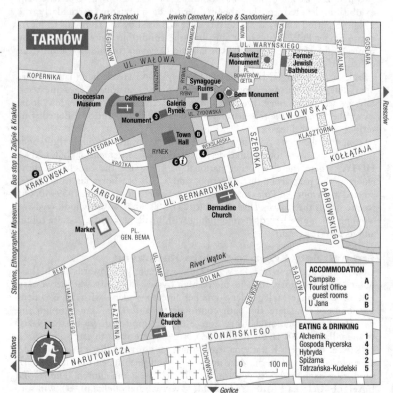

▲ Tarnów town hall

Arrival, information and accommodation

The main **bus and train stations** are situated next to each other on the southwest side of town, a ten-minute walk from the centre – buses #2, #9 or #41 will drop you on the edge of plac Gen Bema at the southern side of the Stare Miasto. There's an **internet** café in the old Jewish bathhouse off plac Bohaterów Getta.

The helpful **tourist information centre** at Rynek 7 (Mon–Fri 8am–6pm, Sat & Sun 9am–5pm; ☎014/688 9090, ⓦwww.it.tarnow.pl) has a wealth of information on the region and also offers **accommodation** in the form of four guest rooms (❷) above the office; clean and good-value modern en suites that should be booked ahead. Occupying a historic mansion at Rynek 14, *U Jana* is a well-run and intimate hotel consisting of two-person apartments (☎014/626 0564, ⓦwww.hotelujana.pl; ❻–❽). The *Pod Jabłoniami* **campsite**, fifteen minutes' walk north of the centre at Piłsudskiego 28A (or bus #30 from the train station; ☎014/621 5124, ⓦwww.camping.tarnow.pl), offers four-person cabins (❶), and tent and caravan pitches in an attractive apple orchard.

The Old Town

The well-preserved Old Town retains all the essentials of its original medieval layout. Oval in shape, the chequerboard network of angular streets, cobbled alleyways and open squares is ringed by the roads built over the ruins of the sturdy defensive walls that were pulled down by the Austrians in the late nineteenth century.

The Rynek

Centrepiece of Tarnów's arcaded Rynek is the fifteenth-century **town hall**, a chunky, two-storey building whose parapet is topped by grotesque heads reminiscent of those adorning Kraków's Sukiennice. Inside, the town **museum** (Tues & Thurs 9am–5pm, Wed & Fri–Sun 9am–3pm; 4zł or 8zł *karnet* for town hall, Galeria Rynek and Muzeum Etnograficzne; ⓦwww.muzeum.tarnow.pl) displays armour and weapons, including some beautiful Persian and Turkish

The collection of seventeenth-century aristocratic portraits in Tarnów town hall is the most comprehensive pictorial record we have of the phenomenon known as **Sarmatism**, a loose system of fashions, beliefs and values that defined Polish society in the seventeenth and early eighteenth centuries. Based on the erroneous belief that the Polish nobility was directly descended from the ancient **Sarmatians** – a tribe of Iranian origin who swarmed across eastern Europe between the first and fifth centuries AD – Sarmatism engendered a fascination with all things eastern that manifested itself in the craze for caftans, sashes, topknots and moustaches so evident in the Tarnów portraits.

The idea that Poles could be descended from Sarmatians seems to have sprung from a cartographical misunderstanding. Many Renaissance map-makers were unsure of what geographical label to apply to Eastern Europe, and scoured their classical history books in search of a suitable name: "Sarmatia" was what they came up with. Learned minds in Poland seized upon the beguiling idea that the Sarmatians had resided in Polish territory during antiquity, and were increasingly happy to adopt these mysterious horse-riding nomads as their ancestors.

The idea that a Slav race like the Poles could claim descent from the Sarmatians was clearly absurd; however, intellectuals got round the obvious objections by arguing that it was merely the Polish aristocracy, not the common people, who were descended from the Sarmatians, and it was precisely this unique lineage that gave them the right to rule.

Polish high society knew very little about the Sarmatians, but assumed that they were similar in appearance to other eastern races with whom they'd had more recent contact – especially the Turks and **Tatars**, who were a constant presence on Poland's southeastern borders. It was under the influence of these neighbours that wealthy Poles developed a taste for luxuriant gowns and silken sashes, and this style of dress became universally adopted by a nobility eager to demonstrate its Sarmatian credentials. Armenian merchants did a roaring trade in caravanning exotic textiles into Poland from the East, and set up wholesale depots in Zamość and Kraków to deal with the demand.

Adherence to the Sarmatian ideal was not just a matter of fine clothes. The idea that the original Sarmatians were warlike conquerors was enthusiastically taken up by Polish aristocrats who were themselves expected to spend long months in the saddle campaigning on Poland's eastern borderlands. Sarmatism became a **moral code** which placed a higher value on action and bravery than on domestic pursuits, and which cultivated a brash disregard for social niceties in preference to the courtly manners of Western Europe. Hunting, feasting and drinking were extolled as the only activities worthy of a true Sarmatian lord.

By the middle of the eighteenth century, however, Poles in Kraków and Warsaw were increasingly adopting Western – particularly French – modes of dress and behaviour, and Sarmatism was left to the more conservative-minded aristocrats of rural Poland, especially in the east. Indeed Sarmatism reached its apogee in the person of Polish-Lithuanian aristocrat **Karol Radziwiłł**, a man who deliberately played the hooligan in order to rile an increasingly etiquette-obsessed Warsaw court. He habitually subjected his peers to humiliating drinking marathons, once blew up one of his own castles in order to amuse party guests, and famously entered the royal palace in Warsaw in a carriage drawn by bears.

The Polish-Lithuanian state had ceased to exist by 1795, and what was left of Sarmatism quietly shuffled off with it. However the Sarmatist mindset has exerted a subtle influence over Polish society ever since. Whether in the extravagant exhibitionism of today's nouveau riche, the boorish behaviour of provincial politicians, or even in the shape and size of Lech Wałęsa's moustache, one has the feeling that the Sarmatians are yet to breathe their last.

pieces. The spacious upstairs meeting hall houses a show-stopping gallery of Sarmatian portraits (see box opposite) from the seventeenth-century onwards, remnants of a collection which once hung in Podhorce Castle, east of L'viv. At the fore are members of the wealthy Rzewuski and Sanguszko families, in Eastern-influenced period dress.

The attractively decorated Renaissance mansion at Rynek 21 now houses the **Galeria Rynek** (Tues & Thurs 10am–5pm, Wed & Fri 9am–3pm, Sat & Sun 10am–2pm; 4zł or 8zł *karnet*), where high-quality temporary exhibitions are held in impressive wood-beamed rooms and an ancient cellar.

The cathedral, diocesan museum and around

Immediately west of the Rynek stands the **cathedral**, ostensibly dating from the fourteenth century but rebuilt in the nineteenth. A relatively uneventful interior is redeemed by a fine collection of Renaissance tombs near the altar, beginning with the grand sixteenth-century memorial to **Jan Tarnowski**, designed by Giovanni Maria Mosca and surrounded with friezes representing his military triumphs. Nearby is the Ostrogski family monument, a sumptuous mannerist ensemble featuring marble representations of family members kneeling beneath a crucifix.

Behind the cathedral, a series of sixteenth-century tenements on a quiet, atmospheric side street house the **Diocesan Museum** (Muzeum Diecezjalne: Tues–Sat 10am–noon & 1–3pm, Sun 9am–noon & 1–2pm; free; ⓦwww.wsd.tarnow .pl/muzeum), one of the best collections of Gothic art in the country. The setting itself is splendid, with artworks hung gracefully in ancient rooms with original ceiling beams. Highlights include three large, fifteenth-century triptychs from St Leonard's Church in Lipnica Murowana (see p.434); a lovely painting of a white-robed St Catherine of Alexandria, from Biecz; and an elegant set of fourteenth-and fifteenth-century wooden pietà. There's also a rich collection of nineteenth-century religious folk art. Out behind the museum, as at several points around the Old Town area, you can see surviving sections of the Old Town walls.

South of the Old Town, ulica NMP leads towards **St Mary's Church** (Kościół Mariacki), a charming wooden structure topped with a steep shingle roof. Built in the village of Przedmieście Większe in 1621 and moved to Tarnów two centuries later, it contains original floral designs on the ceiling, and a Baroque statue of the Madonna on the main altar. The church is normally locked, but opens for daily Mass at 6.30pm, and on Sundays also at 10.30am. The free-standing bell tower dates from 1910.

The Ethnographic Museum

A ten-minute walk west of the Old Town along busy ulica Krakowska brings you to the outstanding **Ethnographic Museum** (Muzeum Etnograficzne: Tues & Thurs 10am–5pm, Wed & Fri 9am–3pm, Sat & Sun 10am–2pm; 6zł), devoted in large part to the customs and culture of Poland's **Roma** (gypsy) community. An estimated twenty thousand Roma live in the country, the majority concentrated in eastern Małopolska and the Carpathians. Along with the general historical sections, there's a good collection of costumes, folk art and archival photographs, a sombre account of their treatment at the hands of the Nazis and, bravely, a section detailing contemporary ill-treatment of and prejudice against Roma in Polish society. There's also memorabilia relating to **Papusza**, a Roma poetess whose work was "discovered" and translated into Polish in the 1970s. To round off, there are a group of four traditional painted Roma caravans displayed in the yard at the back of the museum. Each May a traditional Roma camp is re-created in the yard as part of the **Gypsy Summer Festival**.

Park Strzelecki

Five minutes' walk north of the centre along ulica Piłsudskiego, **Park Strzelecki** (literally "Shooters' Park", a reference to the rifle associations that used to practise here in the nineteenth century) is the town's main strolling ground, a tranquil kilometre-long stretch of flower beds and landscaped woodland. At its northern end stands the **mausoleum** of General Bem, an arresting Neoclassical structure built to house the relics of the hero, brough back to Poland from Aleppo in 1929 (see box below). The general's casket, bearing inscriptions in Hungarian and Ottoman Turkish as well as Polish, is held aloft by six Corinthian columns, the whole ensemble occupying an island in the middle of a lily pond patrolled by fat grey fish.

Jewish Tarnów

East of the Rynek takes you into what used to be the **Jewish quarter** of the town, a fact recalled in the names of streets such as ulica Żydowska and Wekslarska ("moneylenders"). The first Jewish settlers arrived here in the mid-fifteenth century, and on the eve of World War II they constituted forty percent of Tarnów's population. In 1939 the Nazis established a ghetto to the east of the Old Town, filling it with local Jews as well as many transported in from elsewhere, and the population of the massively overcrowded area rose to forty thousand. Between June 1942 and September 1943, virtually all the ghetto's residents were shot or deported to death camps, principally Auschwitz, and most of the area was destroyed. A few Jewish monuments, however, remain.

Architecturally the narrow streets around ulica Żydowska, all of which escaped wartime destruction, are essentially as they were before the war. The battered bimah, covered by a brick-pillared canopy that stands forlornly in the middle of a small square, is all that remains of the magnificent sixteenth-century **synagogue** that stood here until the Nazis gutted it in November 1939. Just northeast of here on the opposite side of plac Bohaterów Getta, the Moorish-looking **Jewish bathhouse** is now a shabby shopping arcade-cum-office block; it was from here that a group of 728 local people were transported to Auschwitz in June 1940 to become the first inmates of the camp, a fact commemorated by the monument just across the street.

Some way north of plac Bohaterów Getta is the **Jewish cemetery**, a fifteen-minute walk along ulica Nowodąbrowska. One of the largest and oldest in Poland, the cemetery was established as early as the 1580s, though the oldest surviving gravestone dates from considerably later. Surprisingly untouched by the Nazis, and still in pretty good shape, the overgrown cemetery contains a large number of tombstones, the emphasis being on the traditional type of tablet in

Józef Bem 1784-1850

The Tarnów-born patriot and adventurer **Józef Bem** was a leading figure in the failed 1830–31 uprising against central Poland's tsarist rulers, a role for which he was widely celebrated. A prototype of the dashing military figures beloved of the Polish Romantic tradition, the swashbuckling general is almost equally celebrated in Hungary for his part in the 1848 uprising in Vienna. Following the failure of the Hungarian revolt, Bem travelled east to join Turkish forces in their struggle with Russia, assuming the name Murat following a rapid (and tactically appropriate) conversion to Islam. Before having the chance to do much for the Turks, however, he died in Aleppo, Syria, his cult status among Poles already safely assured.

which biblical and other illustrative reliefs are used only sparingly. Although the cemetery is usually locked, the Tarnów tourist information centre (see p.429) will gladly tell you who is the current holder of the key (*klucz*).

Eating and drinking

Given Tarnów's small size, the selection of **places to eat** around the centre is impressive. *Spiżarnia*, ul. Żydowska 12 (closed Sun), is a bright little spot offering salads and pitta sandwiches, with some vegetarian options. *Tatrzańska-Kudelski*, ul. Krakowska 1, offers an international menu and well-priced lunch specials – this is also the local favourite for ice cream and cakes. *Gospoda Rycerska*, just off the Rynek at Wekslarska 1, has pizza as well as grill food and Polish standards, served up in a cosy wooden interior. For a **drink**, *Hybryda* at Rynek 22 is the best of the outdoor cafés around the main square. *Alchemik*, nearby at ul. Żydowska 20, is a cosy subterranean café-bar with a bohemian clientele.

Zalipie

The sprawling village of **ZALIPIE**, 30km north of Tarnów, is a charming diversion into the folk traditions of rural Poland. Before the late nineteenth century, cottages here lacked chimneys, and village women used lime to whiten the soot-blackened outer walls of their houses. When chimneys were introduced the practice survived as a novel form of decoration, with women painting **geometric and floral motifs**, first inside their houses and later on outer walls. Word of the tradition spread, and Zalipie's best painters, including Felicja Curyło (1904–74), were feted at Kraków ethnographic fairs in the 1930s. A first house-painting competition was organized in 1948, and since 1965 the event has been held annually on the weekend following Corpus Christi (May/June), with around twenty of Zalipie's houses receiving a fresh array of colourful flowers and patterns each year.

Approaching Zalipie from the main Dąbrowa Tarnowska-Gręboszów road, signs point the way to the **Felicja Curyło Museum** (Muzeum Felicji Curyłowej: Tues–Sun 10am–4pm; 3zł), a century-old building which is today cared for by the granddaughter of Zalipie's most famous artisan. Inside, the "black" room, where the family actually lived, contains a massive stove, black-and-white photographs, costumes, painted ceramics and heirlooms; while the "white" room, which was only used on Sundays and special occasions, holds the better furniture and embroideries. In the yard you'll find a painted barn, well and outhouse. The loop road that runs around the village (roughly 3km in all) leads past more painted houses before reaching the **Painter's House** (Dom Malarek: Mon–Fri 8am–4pm, Sat & Sun 11am–6pm; free), the local cultural centre, where there is a display of photographs from past competitions as well as a gallery of oil paintings by local artists and a small souvenir shop. Continuing past the Dom Malarek, turn right at the village church to get back to the main road.

Practicalities

Private **minibuses** operating the Tarnów–Gręboszów route (roughly hourly Mon to Fri, 5 daily Sat & Sun; catch them from the stop on ul. Krakowska near Tarnow's bus station) pick up and drop off on the main road 1km south of Zalipie. The last minibus back to Tarnów passes through Zalipie around 6pm. Driving from Kraków, you'll cross the Wisła on an old-fashioned river barge (5zł) at Nowy Korczyn. Once in Zalipie, you can buy snacks and supplies from the general store five hundred metres east of the village church.

Lipnica Murowana

Some fifty kilometres southeast of Kraków, on a branch road running out of Wieliczka, the ancient village of **LIPNICA MUROWANA** is home to one of the region's finest wooden churches. **Buses** from Kraków (the town is an intermediate destination on several routes; ask at Kraków's bus station information desk) drop you off at the pretty, cobblestone Rynek, lined with one-storey wooden houses from the nineteenth century.

The wooden **St Leonard's Church** (Kościół św. Leonarda: June–Aug Sat 10am–1pm & 2pm–6pm, Sun 9am–1pm & 2pm–3.30pm; donations welcome), down the hill behind the main stone church and picturesquely set between a creek and the village cemetery, was built late in the fifteenth century on the site of an older church. The arcades date from the seventeenth century, but otherwise the building retains its original form. The most outstanding feature is the fifteenth- to eighteenth-century interior polychromy. Oldest are the floral patterns decorating the ceiling, while the biblical scenes on the nave walls are mostly Baroque. The original Gothic altars are now on display in the diocesan museum in Tarnów (see p.431), but the eighteenth-century pulpit remains, as does an attractive set of Baroque candlesticks. St Leonard's is open at weekends during the summer and there's a 4pm Sunday Mass in August, but otherwise you'll have to look for the priest, who lives next to the main church and is usually available from 2 to 5pm. If he's not around, try the Dom Kultury (Cultural Centre) just north of the Rynek. The one town **restaurant**, *Łokietek*, isn't especially appealing, but there's the country-style *Gospoda Pod Kamieniem* serving tradional Polish cuisine five kilometres west. To return to Kraków, take one of the frequent buses to Bochnia and change there.

Travel Details

Trains

Kielce to: Częstochowa (4 daily; 2hr 20min); Katowice (3 daily; 2hr 20min–3hr 30min); Kraków (7 daily; 2–3hr); Lublin (3 daily; 3–4hr); Warsaw (7 daily; 3hr).

Kraków to: Białystok (1 daily; 10hr); Gdańsk (5 daily; 8–11hr); Katowice (15 daily; 1hr 30min–2hr); Kielce (7 daily; 2–3hr); Krynica (3 daily; 4hr 30min–5hr); Lublin (2 daily; 5hr 30min); Nowy Sącz (5 daily; 3hr–3hr 20min); Oświęcim (10 daily, 1hr 40min); Poznań (6 daily; 7–8hr); Przemyśl (10 daily; 3hr 20min–4hr); Rzeszów (10 daily; 2–3hr); Szczecin (3 daily; 10–11hr 30min); Tarnów (10 daily; 50min–1hr 20min)); Warsaw (12 daily; 3hr–6hr); Wrocław (10 daily; 4–5hr); Zakopane (6 daily; 3hr 40min).

Tarnów to: Kraków (10 daily; 50min–1hr 20min); Krynica (4 daily; 3hr 30min); Nowy Sącz (10 daily; 1hr 40min–2hr).

Buses

Kielce to: Chęciny (every 30min; 35min); Kraków (7 daily; 2hr 30min); Łódź (7 daily; 3hr);

Nowa Słupia (Mon–Fri 16 daily; Sat 8 daily; Sun 6 daily; 50min); Sandomierz (4 daily; 3hr); Starachowice (hourly; 2hr); Staszów (4 daily; 2hr); Święty Krzyż (Mon–Fri 4 daily, Sat 2 daily, Sun 3 daily; 1hr).

Kraków bus station to: Kalwaria Zebrzydowska (every 30min; 40min); Kielce (7 daily; 2hr 30min); Oświęcim-Auschwitz (9 daily; 1hr 30min); Tarnów (15 daily; 1hr 30min); Wadowice (every 30min; 1hr 20min).

Kraków minibus station to: Kielce (hourly; 1hr 40min); Lanckorona (Mon–Fri 8 daily; Sat & Sun 4 daily; 1hr 20min).

Tarnów to: Kielce (4 daily; 2hr 45min); Kraków (15 daily; 1hr 30min); Krynica (5 daily; 2hr 45min); Nowy Sącz (16 daily; 1hr 45min); Zakopane (3 daily; 4hr); Zalipie (Mon–Fri hourly, Sat & Sun 5 daily; 40min).

Wadowice to: Bielsko-Biała (hourly; 1hr 15min); Kraków (every 30min; 1hr 20min); Kalwaria Zebrzydowska (every 30min; 40min).

Podhale, the Tatras and the Pieniny

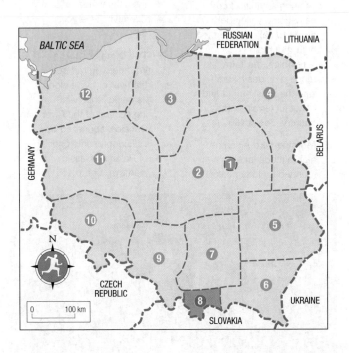

BALTIC SEA

RUSSIAN
FEDERATION

LITHUANIA

GERMANY

BELARUS

N

CZECH
REPUBLIC

0   100 km

UKRAINE

8

SLOVAKIA

CHAPTER 8

Highlights

* **Zakopane architecture**
The highland town of
Zakopane has long been
celebrated for its pointy-
gabled, timber-built
houses, a rustic style
which is still practised in
local building. See p.446

* **Hiking in the Tatras**
Offering anything from
easy-going valley-bottom
strolls to calf-straining
high-mountain
scrambles, the Tatra
range provides hikers
with the most varied and
beautiful terrain in the
country. See p.450

* **Morskie Oko** A serene
high-altitude lake sur-
rounded by lofty peaks,
the Morskie Oko ("Eye
of the Sea") is one of
the most popular targets
for trippers in the Tatra
Mountains. See p.451

* **Niedzica Castle** This
medieval cluster of
towers and bastions
rears dramatically above
the calm waters of the
Czorstyn Reservoir.
See p.454

* **The Dunajec Gorge**
Whether you raft down
the river or cycle along
its banks, this twist-
ing section of the River
Dunajec, squeezed by
cliffs, represents one
of Poland's classic
journeys. See p.455

▲ Niedzica Castle

8

Podhale, the Tatras and the Pieniny

T he Tatra Mountains, which form the border with Slovakia, are Poland's grandest and most beautiful, snowcapped for much of the year and markedly alpine in feel. Along with their foothills, the Podhale, and the neighbouring, more modest peaks of the Pieniny, they have been an established centre for hikers for the best part of a century. The region as a whole is perfect for low-key rambling, and there are few areas in Europe where you can get so authentic a mountain experience without having to be a committed climber. Other outdoor activities are well catered for, too, with raft rides down the Dunajec Gorge in summer and some fine winter skiing on the higher Tatra slopes.

Eighty kilometres long, with peaks rising to over 2500m, the Polish **Tatras** are actually a relatively small part of the range, most of which rises across the border in Slovakia. A two-hour bus ride south of Kraków, the bustling resort of **Zakopane** is the main holiday centre, conveniently placed for access to the highest Tatra peaks and with plenty of attractive folk architecture in the immediate surroundings. The mountain valleys running south from Zakopane provide easy-going hiking through spectacular scenery, while the peak-fringed **Morskie Oko** lake just to the southeast is one of Poland's most celebrated beauty spots.

The route to Zakopane runs through the **Podhale** region, a sparsely populated region of lush meadows, winding valleys and old wooden villages that starts to the south of **Nowy Targ**. To the east, the **Pieniny** range are lower than the Tatras but no less dramatic, steep slopes crowding above the **Dunajec River** to create a spectacular gorge. The best place from which to explore the Pieniny is the former spa resort of **Szczawnica**, a quaint little place currently enjoying a growing reputation as a summertime centre for walking and biking.

Both Zakopane and Szczawnica are easily reached by bus from Kraków. Once there, minibuses shuttle from the resort centres to the outlying attractions, depositing hikers at trail heads and ferrying them back to town before nightfall.

The Podhale

From Kraków, the main road to Zakopane runs south through the **Podhale**, the hilly farming terrain that forms the approach to the Tatra Mountains. The road runs through a memorable landscape of gentle valleys, undulating slopes and

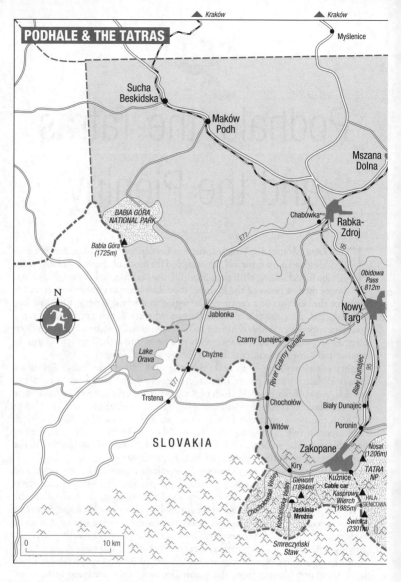

PODHALE & THE TATRAS

▲ Kraków   ▲ Kraków

Myślenice

Sucha
Beskidska

Maków
Podh

Mszana
Dolna

*BABIA GÓRA
NATIONAL PARK*

Chabówka

Rabka-
Zdroj

E77

*Babia Góra
(1725m)*

*Obidowa
Pass
812m*

N

Nowy
Targ

Jablonka

River Czarny Dunajec

Czarny Dunajec

*Lake
Orava*

Chyżne

Biały Dunajec

95

E77

Trstena

Chocholów

Biały Dunajec

Witów

Poronin

SLOVAKIA

Zakopane

*Nosal
(1206m)*

Kiry

*Giewont
(1894m)*

Kuźnice

*TATRA
NP*

Chochołowska Valley

Kościeliska Valley

Cable car

*Kasprowy
Wierch
(1985m)*

*HALA
GĄSIENICOWA*

**Jaskinia
Mroźna**

*Świnica
(2301m)*

*Smreczyński
Staw*

0   10 km

strip-farmed fields, many of which are still worked by stocky horses attached
to a variety of carts and ploughs. Few Podhale towns merit an overnight stay in
their own right but there are plenty of enticing mid-journey stop-offs if you're
passing through.

Rabka-Zdrój and Chabówka

Sixty kilometres south of Kraków, **RABKA-ZDRÓJ** is a pleasant if rather
unexciting spa resort dunked between the rolling hills of the northern Podhale.

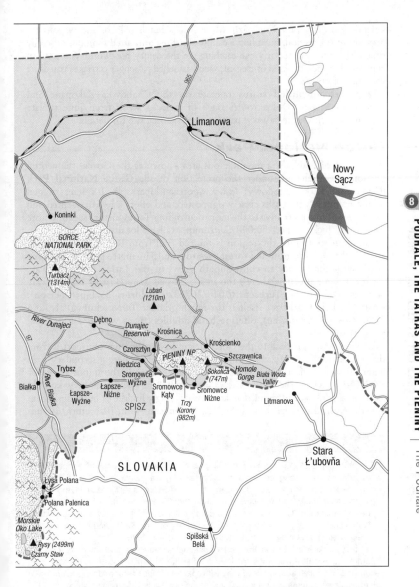

At its centre is a beautiful seventeenth-century wooden **church**, now housing the **Władysław Orkan Ethnographic Museum** (Muzeum im. Władysława Orkana: daily 9am–4pm; Oct–May closed Tues; 6zł). There's a wonderful display of local woodcraft and pottery inside, together with a room devoted to Władysław Orkan (1875–1930), the local writer who did much to popularize Podhale folk culture.

Three kilometres west of Rabka, the nondescript village of **CHABÓWKA** grew around an important nineteenth-century railway junction, and appropriately enough is now the site of a fascinating open-air **Railway Museum** (Skansen taboru kolejowego; daily 7am–7pm; 5zł). More than a hundred locos and wagons are lined up for inspection, including a cannon-bristling armoured train once used by the Polish army. Particularly eye-catching are the dainty pre-World War I steam engines, alongside the kind of elegant, wood-panelled passenger carriages you don't see much of nowadays.

Special **steam-pulled trains** operate on the Chabówka–Zakopane and Chabowka–Mszana Dolna routes once or twice a week from June to late September – check the ⓦwww.parowozy.pl/skansen site for details.

Gorce National Park

Rising east of Rabka is a mountainous area known as the **Gorce**, the central portion of which falls under the protection of the **Gorce National Park** (Gorczański Park Narodowy: ⓦwww.gorczanskipark.pl). It's fine, rugged hiking country, with paths clearly signposted, and offers a less frequented and more easy-going alternative to the more demanding Tatras further south. Before setting out, pick up the 1:50,000 *Gorce* **map**, available locally.

The main route into the region is the red trail from Rabka-Zdrój, which ascends through meadow and forest towards the 1314-metre peak of **Turbacz** (7hr), with the chance to enjoy superb views of the Tatras along the way. To break your journey, there's the small, 25-bed *Stare Wierchy* **hut** halfway between Rabka and Turbacz (☎018/267 5297; dorms 25zł per person); while just below Turbacz itself is the much grander *Turbacz* hut (☎018/266 7780, ⓦwww.turbacz.eu), offering basic doubles (❷) as well as dorms (30zł per person).

An alternative approach to the Gorce if you have your own transport is from the market town of Mszana Dolna to the north. From here a secondary road branches south, via the village of Niedźwiadź, towards the minor resort of **KONINKI**, where the *Ostoja Górska hotel* (☎018/331 7580, ⓦwww.koninki .com.pl; ❸) offers prim en suites in an outwardly ugly huddle of buildings. From here the **Koninki chairlift** (May–Sept Sat & Sun 9am–4pm; 10zł return) ascends

The górale

The inhabitants of the Tatra region, the **górale**, are fiercely independent mountain farmers, known throughout Poland for preserving traditions that have died out elsewhere. The region was "discovered" by the Polish intelligentsia in the late nineteenth century and the *górale* tradition rapidly emerged as a symbol of an age-old, authentic Polish culture unsullied by outside influence. However, this was also an economically backward region, the poverty of rural life leading thousands of *górale* to emigrate to the United States in the 1920s and 1930s.

Many *górale* still dress in traditional costume on Sundays and for other major community events – weddings, festivals and the like. The men's costume consists of tight-fitting woollen trousers decorated with coloured strips of embroidery (*parzenice*), high, leather cummerbund-type bands round the waist, decorated jackets and waistcoats and a feather-topped hat. The women wear thin woollen blouses, thickly pleated skirts festooned with flowers and brightly coloured headscarves.

The *górale* are also the guardians of one of Poland's most vibrant folk-music traditions, retaining an appetite for the kind of rootsy, fiddle-driven dance music that has all but died out in the lowlands. Traditional bands regularly appear at local festivities and weddings (which are usually a high-profile component of any given Sat), and also appear regularly in the bars and restaurants of Zakopane – which is also a good place to seek out CDs.

Nowy Targ marks the starting point of an unofficial **Lenin Trail**: the old prison just beyond the southeast corner of the main square is where he was briefly interned on suspicion of spying in 1914. The Bolshevik leader had already been a full-time resident of the Podhale region for over a year, renting a room in the village of Biały Dunajec, just north of Zakopane. The locality had several advantages for Lenin: it was near enough to the Russian border for him to retain contact with his revolutionary colleagues, and the area's reputation as a rural retreat for all manner of eccentric intellectuals ensured that his presence here was unlikely to attract the unwelcome curiosity of the locals. He drank coffee and read the papers in Zakopane's main society hangout of the time, *Café Trzaski* on ulica Krupówki – an establishment that is, sadly, no more. The arty Polish types who divided their time between Kraków and Zakopane tended to regard Lenin as a kindred spirit, and the revolutionary's arrest prompted novelist Stefan Żeromski and poet Jan Kasprowicz to intercede on his behalf, thereby speeding his release. Lenin subsequently relocated to Switzerland, from where he returned to Russia in 1917 to take command of the Revolution.

to Polanie Tobolow, a highland meadow which offers an expansive panorama of the Podhale hills. From here the ridge-top green trail leads south towards the minor peaks of Suchora (1000m) and Obidowac (1106m), before joining the red trail (see opposite) for the ascent of Turbacz.

Nowy Targ

From Rabka the Zakopane road continues over the **Obidowa Pass** (812m), then down onto a plain crossed by the Czarny Dunajec River and towards Podhale's capital, **NOWY TARG** (New Market). The oldest town in the region, established in the thirteenth century, Nowy Targ was redeveloped as an administrative and industrial centre after World War II, and is now a dispiriting grey sprawl. The only real attraction is the animated **market** (Nowotarsky jarmark), held each Thursday and Saturday on a patch of ground just east of the centre. Once an authentic farmers' event, with horse-drawn carts lining the streets, it's now a much more mainstream affair, with agricultural produce sold alongside sack-loads of cheap clothes and shoes. There are also a few Polish craft items on display – for the most part wooden kitchen utensils, and locally made *pantofle* (leather slippers).

Zakopane and around

South of Nowy Targ, the road continues another 20km along the course of the Biały Dunajec before reaching the edges of **ZAKOPANE**, a major mountain resort, deluged with visitors throughout its summer **hiking** and winter **skiing** seasons. It has been an established attraction for Poles since the 1870s, when the purity of the mountain air began to attract the attention of doctors and their consumptive city patients. Within a few years, this inaccessible mountain village of sheep farmers was transformed, as the medics were followed by Kraków artists and intellectuals, many of whom lived here for several months in the year. In the years before World War I, Zakopane experienced more in the way of *belle époque* hedonism than Kraków itself, with all manner of poets, painters and composers descending on the place to get drunk, behave outrageously and steal each other's girlfriends. As well as personal liberty, Zakopane symbolized a free Poland: as

Młoda Polska writer Wojciech Kossak notoriously remarked, "Austrian rule doesn't reach beyond Nowy Targ." After World War I more mainstream forms of tourism took over, Zakopane becoming Poland's premier skiing centre – a status it retains today. Nowadays its central thoroughfares have the hollow, overdeveloped feel of a major European tourist trap, although the Zakopane of old, with charming timber houses lining leafy streets, still lives on in the suburbs. Above all, the town remains the best possible place from which to access the most stunning scenery anywhere in Poland.

Arrival and information

The **bus** and **train stations** are both a ten-minute walk east of the main street, ulica Krupówki. Some **private buses** to Kraków pick up and drop from a stop on ulica Kościuszki, just west of the stations. If you have your own transport, note that **parking** can be a problem in the centre; your best bet is the big car park at the southern end of town near the ski jump.

The **tourist office**, housed in a wooden chalet a few steps west of the stations at ul. Kościuszki 17 (daily 9am–5pm; ☎018/201 2211, ⓦwww.zakopane .pl), is a helpful source of information on the whole area. The Tatrzański Park Narodowy, or Tatra **national park office**, at Chałubińskiego 44 (daily 8am–4pm; ☎018/206 3799, ⓔkozica@tpn.zakopane.pl), is an essential source of expert information if you're planning a serious mountain trek.

Accommodation

Zakopane is increasingly well served with a wide range of accommodation, although it's still worth **booking** rooms well in advance in midsummer or during the skiing season. **Private rooms** (❷) and pensions (❹) can be booked through the tourist office (see above), and a number of private travel agents in town – the most helpful being Teresa at Kościuszki 7 (Mon–Fri 9am–5pm, Sat 9am–3pm; ☎018/201 3660, ⓦwww.teresa.zakopane.pl).

For **campers** there are two sites: *Camping Pod Krokwią* (☎018/201 2256), ulica Żeromskiego, across from the bottom of the ski jump at the south end of town; and *Za Strugiem*, ul. Za Strugiem 39 (☎018/201 4566), a thirty-minute walk west of the centre. The **hotels** listed below can be subject to considerable price hikes during high season.

Hostels

Dom Turysty ul. Zaruskiego 5 ☎018/206 3281, ⓦwww.domturysty.z-ne.pl. Cheap, central hostel-cum-hotel in a characterful interwar building sheltering under a massive wooden-shingle roof. Gets a lot of students in season. En suites, rooms with shared facilites and some dorms (30zł per person). Breakfast costs a few złoty extra. En-suite doubles ❹; with shared facilities. ❷

Goodbye Lenin ul. Chłabówka 44 ☎018/200 1330, ⓦwww.goodbyelenin.pl. Traditional-style timber building with snug dorm rooms (from 50zł per person) and one self-contained double (❸). Located in calm semi-rural suburbs some 3km east of the centre, it's initially difficult to find under your own steam so call in advance for directions.

Stara Polana ul. Nowotarska 59 ☎018/206 8902, ⓦwww.starapolana.pl. Traditional-style villa dating from 1905 just north of the train and bus stations, offering wood-panelled rooms. The doubles (en suites ❺; with shared facilities ❹) are more expensive than those offered by local pensions, and don't make economic sense unless you're specifically looking for a backpacker atmosphere. Dorm beds from 50zł.

Hotels and pensions

Antałówka ul. Wierchowa 3 ☎018/201 3271, ⓦwww.antalowka.zakopane.pl. Biggish concrete hotel with servicable en suites, ideally located a short uphill walk away from the bus station and town centre. Excellent views over the town and mountains. ❻

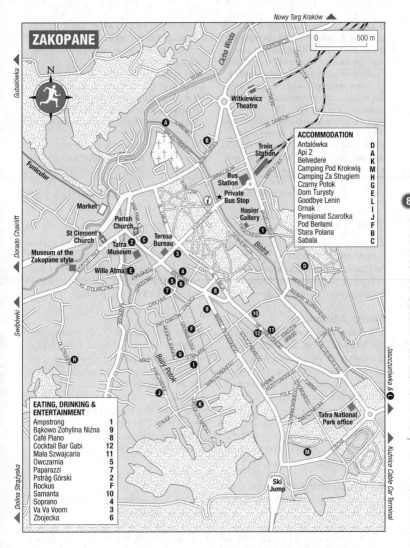

Api 2 Kamieniec 13a ☎018/206 2931, ⓦwww
.api2.pl. Cosy pension north of the stations
with smallish en suites with TV and a decent
breakfast. ④

Belvedere Droga do Białego 3 ☎018/202 1200,
ⓦwww.belvederehotel.pl. Top-drawer hotel 1.5km
from town, with high standards of service and
smart, comfortable rooms – not all have bathtubs
though so ask when you book. Attic ceilings in the
top-floor rooms add a bit of extra atmosphere. On-
site swimming pool, gym and beauty centre make
this the perfect place for a spa-style break. ⑨

Czarny Potok ul. Tetmajera 20 ☎018/202 0204,
ⓦwww.czarnypotok.pl. Medium-sized hotel on a
quiet street 1km south of town, offering simple
doubles decked out in warm colours, each with
TV, fridge and a neat bathroom. Local rugs and
tapestries in the hallways add a homely touch, and
there's a sauna and pool in the basement. ⑦

Ornak ul. Grunwaldzka 20 ☎018/201 5679
& ☎604 985 025, ⓦwww.ornak.net.pl.
This wooden villa of 1902 vintage is decked out in
period furniture, complete with grandfather clocks
and the kind of big wooden beds that seem prefect

for sinking into. The one concession to modernity is the sleek flat-screen TV in the communal lounge. The rooms don't have en-suite facilities (it's a listed building and the law wouldn't allow their installation) but there's a row of WC/showers in the modern basement – where you'll also find a fully equipped kitchen-diner. Breakfast prepared on request for a few extra złotys. ❹

🎿 **Pensjonat Szarotka** Małe Żywczańskie 16a ☎018/201 4802, ⓦwww.szarotka .pl. Charming pointy-gabled suburban house in a quiet neighbourhood 1km from the centre, with a range of different shaped en-suite rooms with TV, many with quirky semi-antique furnishings. The olde-worlde theme extends to the interwar

tourist posters and sepia photographs of skiing champions that decorate the hallways. Buffet breakfast available for an extra 20zł. Apartments ❻, doubles ❷–❺.

Pod Berłami ul. Grunwaldzka 9 ☎018/201 3221, ⓦwww.podberlami.zakopane.pl. Secluded and peaceful pension owned by Kraków's Jagiellionian University and popular with studious professorial types. Small but snug en-suite rooms with TV and desk space. ❺

Sabała ul. Krupówki 11 ☎018/201 5092, ⓦwww.sabala.zakopane.pl. Ultra-modern place occupying the building, dating from 1894, of one of Zakopane's first ever hotels, the *Staszeczkówka*. Lovely, wood-furnished en suites with TV. ❼

The Town

Zakopane's main street, **ulica Krupówki**, is a bustling pedestrian precinct given over to an assortment of restaurants, cafés and souvenir stalls. Uphill, the street merges into **ulica Zamoyskiego**, which runs on out of town past the fashionable *fin de siècle* **wooden villas** of the outskirts, while in the other direction, it follows a rushing stream down towards **Gubałówka Hill** (see p.448).

Tatra Museum

The **Tatra Museum** (Muzeum Tatrzanskie: Tues–Sun 9am–3.30pm; 3zł), just off Krupówki on ulica Zaruskiego, extolls the virtues of local folk culture through a beautiful sequence of recreated peasant house interiors and some stunning costumes – note the colourfully embroidered, strutting-peacock jackets traditionally worn by *górale* menfolk. Zakopane's emergence as a society resort is remembered with pictures of Titus Chałubinski, the doctor who did more than anyone to promote the health-giving properties of the mountain air; Stanisław Witkiewicz (see below), whose book *Na Przełęczy* ("At the Pass"; 1891) was a landmark in the propagation of Podhale culture; and the wealthy Dembowski family, who collected Podhale folk crafts and held high-society salons in their Zakopane villa.

St Clement's Church

Towards the northern end of Krupówki, ulica Kościeliska veers off towards an area liberally sprinkled with traditional buildings, kicking off with the wooden **St Clement's Church** (Kosciół św. Klemensa). The low-ceilinged interior gives off an attractive piney smell, and holds several examples of a popular local form of folk art: devotional paintings on glass, in this case depicting the Stations of the Cross. Outside in the graveyard lie the tombs of many of the town's best-known writers and artists, among them that of **Stanisław Witkiewicz** (1851–1915), who developed the distinctive Zakopane architectural style based on traditional wooden building forms. The houses he built – all steep pointy roofs and jutting attic windows – went down a storm with a pre-World War I middle class who were crazy for all things rustic. Witkiewicz's grave is marked by a canopied shrine-pole from Samogitia, the rustic area of Lithuania where the artist spent his youth. There's also a commemorative tablet to Witkiewicz's equally famous son, **Witkacy** (see box opposite), whose body was returned to Zakopane in 1988 from its previous resting place (Jeziory in the Ukraine) by a communist regime

Witkacy

Painter, dramatist and hallucinogenic drug enthusiast Stanisław Ignacy Witkiewicz (1885–1939) – **Witkacy** as he's commonly known – was born the son of Stanisław Witkiewicz, the eminent artist and art critic who created the so-called Zakopane Style of primitivist wooden architecture (see p.446). Educated at home by a father who distrusted schools, Witkacy was surrounded from an early age by the artists, poets and performers who made up the Kraków cultural elite.

As a resort town attracting all kinds of free-thinking and glamorous personalities, Zakopane functioned as a kind of artistic and personal playground for Witkacy, and his private life was rather complicated as a result. After a long affair with actress Irena Solska, ten years his senior, Witkacy got engaged to one of his mother's boarding house guests, Jadwiga Jaczewska, in 1914 – she shot herself in dramatic style (at the foot of a cliff, next to a bouquet of flowers) after learning that her fiancé was still seeing both Solska and one other lover. Eager to leave this behind Witkacy set off on a long expedition to New Guinea and Australia with family friend and celebrated anthropologist Bronisław Malinowski (with whom he also had an intimate relationship), returning home when World War I broke out. He signed up for the Russian army with enthusiasm (an act of rebellion against his proudly Polish, anti-Russian father), and after qualifying as an officer fought with distinction on the Austrian front. Wounded near Voronezh he was sent for rehabilitation in St Petersburg, then a wildly decadent city full of opportunities for a good party. It was here that Witkacy first began to experiment with hallucinogenic drugs. In 1918 Witkacy re-established himself in Zakopane and joined the Formists, a group of painters influenced by Cubism and Futurism, abandoning them in 1924 to set up a commercial **portrait-painting** studio: intended as an ironic statement on the position of the artist in capitalist society, it turned out to be extraordinarily successful with the interwar middle classes. Witkacy's portraits of well-heeled society figures were relatively sober and realistic, while those of his friends were wild and deranged in comparison; you'll see examples of both these styles hanging on the walls of Poland's museums and galleries. In the corner of the canvas on the wackier portraits, Witkacy habitually noted which narcotic he had been taking when painting. The portrait company provided Witkacy with the funds he needed to finance other artistic interests. During the interwar years Witkacy produced over twenty **plays**, many of which were premiered in Zakopane by his own theatre company, formed in 1925, with several productions being staged in the epic surroundings of Morskie Oko Lake. An exponent of an avant-gardist theory of drama that extolled the virtues of "pure form" over content, Witkacy wrote dramas that are generally bizarre, almost surrealist pieces spiced up with large dollops of sex and murder. Cold-shouldered by uncomprehending 1920s Polish audiences, the Witkacy dramatic *oeuvre* was rediscovered in the 1950s, when Tadeusz Kantor opened the legendary Cricot 2 Theatre with a performance of Witkacy's absurdist *Cuttlefish*. Witkacy's prose works offered similarly fantastic excursions to the far shores of the writer's consciousness. His first **novel**, *622 Downfalls of Bungo*, begun before 1914, was a surrealistic take on his own life story, with central characters based on Solska, Malinowski and himself. Later works were more doom-laden, most notably the brilliant but untranslatable *Nienasycenie* ("Insatiability"; 1930), which revolves around an epic futuristic struggle between a Poland ruled by the dictator Kocmołuchowicz ("Slovenly") and communist hordes from China hell-bent on invading Europe from the east. In a sense, reality fulfilled Witkacy's worst apocalyptic nightmares. Following the Nazi invasion of Poland in 1939, the artist fled east. On learning that the Soviets were also advancing into Poland in the pincer movement agreed under the terms of the notorious Molotov–Ribbentrop Pact, a devastated Witkacy committed suicide, a legendary act that ensured his place in the pantheon of noble patriots, as well as that of great artists, in the eyes of the nation.

desperate to curry favour with Poland's intelligentsia. Fifty thousand mourners turned up to pay their respects, and only later was it revealed that the authorities had delivered the wrong body – the genuine corpse having proved impossible to locate.

Museum of the Zakopane Style

Some 200m west of the cemetery stands the **Willa Koliba**, Stanisław Witkiewicz's first architectural experiment, and now the **Museum of the Zakopane Style** (Muzeum Stylu Zakopańskiego: Wed–Sat 9am–5pm, Sun 9am–3pm; 7zł). A must for anyone interested in Polish architecture or design, the museum starts off with a ground-floor display of the folk crafts from which Witkiewicz got his inspiration, before moving on to the kind of furniture that he set about designing – chunky chairs adorned with squiggly details in an engaging mixture of Art Nouveau and folkloric forms. There's also a scale model of Witkiewicz's greatest architectural creation, the Willa Pod Jedłami, an extraordinarily intricate wooden house which brings to mind a Scandinavian timber church redesigned as a country mansion – enjoy the model while you're here, because it's difficult to get close up to the real thing (see opposite). A biographical words-and-pictures display reveals what a rogue Witkiewicz was, using his poor health as an excuse to conduct a series of love affairs in the spas of Europe. Accompanied by long-time mistress Maria Dembowska, Witkiewicz eventually went to live full time in the Croatian resort of Lovran in 1907, leaving his wife in Zakopane to eke a living renting out rooms to the very tourists attracted here by her husband's books. Finally, there's a marvellous collection of deranged portraits by Witkiewicz's son, Witkacy, including a lot of distorted, angular depictions of the people he painted while high on one substance or another, believing that his intake of drugs would reveal the true personality of the sitter. Most of his subjects are female, members of what he called his "metaphysical harem".

The Willa Atma

Moving back towards ulica Krupówki and turning south down ulica Kasprusie soon leads to the **Willa Atma**, a traditional-style villa and long-time home of composer **Karol Szymanowski** (see box opposite), to whom as a museum it is now dedicated (Tues–Sun 10am–4pm; 4zł). The display is labelled in Polish only, but many of the exhibits speak for themselves: look out for photographs of the *górale* folk musicians Szymanowski was inspired by and the fantastic folk-inspired costumes featured in his ballet *Harnasie*.

The Hasior Gallery

East of the main drag, near the bus and train stations, a wooden building at ul. Jagiellońska 18b – it's just off the road in a side alley – houses the **Hasior Gallery** (Wed–Sat 11am–6pm, Sun 9am–3pm), presenting the work of one of the country's key postwar artists, **Władysław Hasior** (1928–99). Whether building installations from piles of junk or constructing pseudo-religious banners from pieces of metal, Hasior was typical of many Polish artists of the 1960s and 1970s in developing a quirky and often subversive form of sculpture that had little to do with the ideological dictates of either church or state – although both institutions sponsored his work at different stages. Ranging from massive landscape installations to jokey throwaway pieces, Hasior's *oeuvre* will leave you uncertain as to whether he was a visionary or a charlatan, but the gallery is entertaining enough to make such confusion worthwhile.

Karol Szymanowski

After Chopin, **Karol Szymanowski** (1882–1937) is Poland's greatest composer, forging his own distinctive style in an exotic and highly charged mix of orientalism, opulence and native folk music. From the 1920s onwards he spent much time in Zakopane and became a key member of a group of intellectuals who were enthused by the folklore of the Tatras and dubbed themselves "the emergency rescue service of Tatra culture". Among Szymanowski's works directly influenced by Tatra music are the song cycle *Słopiewnie* (1921), the *Mazurkas for piano* (1924–25) and, above all, the ballet *Harnasie* (1931), which is stuffed full of outlaws, features a spectacular highland wedding and includes authentic *górale* melodies in orchestral garb. Alongside two violin concertos and his *Symphony Song of the Night*, Szymanowski's greatest work is the **Stabat Mater** (1926), a stunning choral piece of austere beauty which draws on the traditions of old Polish church music.

Szymanowski died in 1937, receiving an illustrious state funeral. The Obrochta family, one of the leading *górale* bands, played around his tomb in the Skałka Church in Kraków.

Bystre, Jaszczurówka and Swibówki

The southeastern fringes of town contain a couple of Witkiewicz's best-known creations. The **Willa Pod Jedłami** in the suburb of **Bystre**, 2km from the centre, is now in private hands and is hard to get a good look at, so you'd be well advised to press on 1.5km further east to the **wooden chapel** at **Jaszczurówka** (hourly buses to Brzeziny pass by), a fairy-tale structure encrusted with folksy ornamentation. The traditional *górale* woodcraft from which Witkiewicz took his inspiration is still very much alive, featuring most notably in the **Sanctuary of Our Lady of Fatima** (Sanktuarium Matki Bożej Fatimskiej) at **Swibówki**, a thirty-minute walk west of central Zakopane along ulica Kościeliska, which also has a remarkable chapel at the rear of the main church complex.

Eating and drinking

Central Zakopane offers a surfeit of **restaurants** – many offering local food in faux-rustic surroundings to the accompaniment of live folk music. One local product well worth trying is *oscypek*, the bun-shaped **sheep's milk cheeses** offered by street vendors all over town; the smoked variety (easily identifiable by its tawny brown rind) is particularly delicious.

There are innumerable **drinking** dens along ulica Krupówki, although the more characterful places are usually found a step or two away from the main street.

Cafés

Cocktail Bar Gabi ul. Zamoyskiego 10. It's not a bar and it doesn't sell cocktails, but does qualify as probably the best café in town. The long glass cabinet filled with how-can-you-possibly-refuse cakes often includes a mouth-watering pear-and-meringue pie, and there's a big choice of ice cream to boot. Reliably good coffee also. Daily 10am–10pm.

Samanta ul. Witkiewicza 2. Not quite as heavenly as *Gabi*, but still an ideal place in which to sink your spoon into a succulent slice of *szarlotka* (apple pie), accompanied by a reassuringly strong cup of coffee. The bakery counter is a good place to stock up on fresh bread and rolls. Daily 8.30am–8pm.

Restaurants

Bąkowo Zohylina Niźna ul. Piłsudskiego 6. One of the better folk-style restaurants in the centre, offering well-presented Polish meat and fowl dishes in a huge log-built variation on the mountain-hut theme. Live folk music most nights. Daily noon–11pm.

Mała Szwajcaria ("Little Switzerland") ul. Zamoyskiego 11. If the Tatras and the

Alps ever met, then this is what people would eat on the border – an imaginative fusion of Polish and Swiss cuisine – *pierogi* and fondue – that brings out the best in both. Prices are very reasonable, and the set-lunch menu's a steal. Daily 11am–11pm.

Owczarnia ul. Generała Galicy. Restaurant on two floors that looks like a cross between a nineteenth-century barn and a Scandinavian furniture showroom. Food (mostly pork and mutton) from an open grill, live music in the evenings, and wait-staff wearing folksy floral skirts. Daily 10am–midnight.

Pstrąg Górski ul. Krupówki 50. Simple fish-fry place on the main drag, with al fresco seating beside a babbling brook. Grilled local trout is the order of the day. Daily 9am–10pm.

Soprano ul. Krupówki 60. Decent quality pasta and pizza, plus some good Mediterranean salads for those who are missing their greens. In a main-street location with an outdoor terrace in summer. Daily 10am–11pm.

Zbojecka ul. Krupówki 30. Cellar bar-restaurant on the main strip with large wooden benches draped with sheepskins, grilled meat dishes, and live folk music (or loud pop on the sound system, depending on your luck). Daily 10am–midnight.

Bars and clubs

Ampstrong Jagiellońska 18, ⓦwww.ampstrong .org.pl. Hard-to-find basement club just off Jagiellońska near the Hasior Gallery, hosting occasional live gigs and alternative DJ nights – look out for street posters. From 5pm onwards.

🏃 **Café Piano** ul. Krupówki 63, in a secluded alleyway behind the *Bacówka* tavern. Contemporary design meets rustic chic here, with swings instead of bar stools and a garden patio thick with shrubs and ferns. Daily noon–midnight.

Paparazzi ul. Generała Galicy 8a. Smartish cellar pub just off the main street, which caters for the dedicated late-night beer drinkers as well as the cocktail crowd. There's also outdoor seating beside the Młyniska stream. Mon–Fri 4pm–1am, Sat & Sun noon–1am.

Rockus ul. Zaruskiego 5, underneath the *Dom Turysty*. Rock-pop disco bar popular with a teen crowd, and decorated with reproduction album covers. Busy at weekends; at other times a low-key place in which to sink into the eighties-era upholstery. From 8pm.

Va Va Voom ul. Kościuszki 10, ⓦwww.vavavoom .pl. Chic lounge bar-cum-dance club at the top of a spiral staircase, with a DJ repetoire which extends beyond top-forty pap. Ring the bell for admission. From 8pm onwards.

Entertainment

Entertainment in Zakopane varies according to season. Founded in memory of the man who staged many of his own plays here, the **Witkiewicz Theatre** (Teatr im. Stanisława Witkiewicza: box office in the PTTK travel agency, open Mon–Fri 10am–4pm, Sat 10am–2pm; ⓣ018/206 3281, ⓦwww .witkacy.zakopane.pl), at ul. Chramcówki 15, north of the train station, stages a regular variety of performances (a lot of Witkacy pieces, but also featuring twentieth-century greats like Miller and Camus) throughout the year – check with the tourist offices for current details.

Biggest annual event is the **International Festival of Mountain Folklore** (Festiwal zespołów regionalnych ziem gorskich: mid- to late Aug), a week-long celebration of traditional music which attracts groups from highland regions around the world as well as the top local acts – and you're unlikely to get a better chance to sample the tub-thumping exuberance of a *górale* choir dressed to the nines, whooping their way through a string of joyous mountain melodies. Other events of note include the **Karol Szymanowski Music Days** held every July, featuring classical recitals by Polish and foreign artists in and around the town.

Gubałówka Hill and beyond

There's an excellent view of the Tatras from the top of **Gubałówka Hill** (1120m) just northwest of the centre and best reached by taking the **funicular** from the northern end of ulica Krupówki (July & Aug 7am–9pm; Sept–June 8am–5pm; 16zł return). The Dorado chairlift (daily 9am–5pm; 13zł return)

PODHALE, THE TATRAS AND THE PIENINY | Zakopane and around

448

Poles have been enjoying the winter **ski slopes** in Zakopane for as long as there's been a resort, and in the case of the *górale*, for a good deal longer. The winter season traditionally runs from December to March, though the snow has been very unpredictable in recent years. Slopes in the area vary greatly in difficulty and quality. In accordance with international standards, they are graded black, red, blue and green in order of difficulty, with the cross-country routes marked in orange. Many otherwise closed areas of the national park are open to skiers once the snows have set in, but you must remember to avoid the avalanche (*lawina*) areas marked on signs and maps, and check conditions before leaving the marked routes.

The most popular runs are on **Nosal** and **Kasprowy Wierch**, as these are the ones with ski lifts. From the village of Kuźnice (a few minutes by bus from the centre of Zakopane) you can travel by cable car (see p.450) to the top of Kasprowy Wierch (1985m) and ski either back down to the village (5–7km, depending which trails you use) or to one of the surrounding valleys, Goryczkowa or Gąsienicowa, from where you can take the lift back up again. The Nosal slope is short and steep (650m with a 233m height difference), while on the other side of town Gubałówka offers a much gentler slope reached by funicular (see below). It's south-facing, so you can rent beach chairs (even in winter) and sunbathe on its slopes. You can also get **skiing lessons** – the instructors at the Nosal ski school speak English and charge 60–70zł per hour. **Ski rental** costs about 35zł per day. **Mountain biking** is a popular summertime pursuit, with legions of enthusiastic bikers heading for the slopes. Designated cycle routes within the national park area include: around Morskie Oko; up to Dolina Suchej Wody; to Hala Gąsienicowa; to Kałatówki; and along the Kościeliska and Chochołowska valleys. In addition, there are a number of cycle routes in the hills north of Zakopane – some 650km of them in total. You can **rent mountain bikes** at a number of places around town, including: Wypożyczalnia, ul. Piłsudskiego 4; Rent a Bike, ul. Sienkiewicza 37 (☏018/206 4266); and the *Pod Krokwią* campsite. Bike rental costs around 50zł a day. **Paragliding** is also popular, though it's confined to areas outside the national park, including the Nosal slope, Gubałówka and Wałowa Góra. There are several instructors in town who also rent all the necessary gear. Try Air Sport, ul. Strążyska 13 (☏018/201 3311, ⓦ www.air-sport.pl).

provides a slightly out-of-the-way alternative, beginning its ascent from bul. Powsańców śląskich, 1.5km west of the centre of town. Failing that you can always walk (1hr). At the summit you'll find a string of souvenir stalls no less tacky than the ones clogging up the centre of Zakopane, but the panorama of jagged peaks to the south is splendid enough to more than justify the trip. Just below the summit, the dry **toboggan run** (June–Sept daily 10am–5pm; 5zł) is well worth a circuit or two, while walking along the ridge-top road to the west will bring you to the **Trollandia high-wire park** (park linowy; 30zł) where – suitably clad in protective gear – you can slide along wires and negotiate wobbly walkways high up in the trees.

Gubałówka is also the starting point of several excellent **hikes**, taking you through a characteristic Podhale landscape of rolling meadows edged by dark pines. Heading west from the summit, the **black route** gradually descends to the Czarny Dunajec valley ending up at the village of **WITÓW**, around two hours' walking in all; buses back to Zakopane take fifteen minutes. Alternatively, the **red route** (which forks off to the north some 2km west of the summit) takes you on a four-hour hike through rolling terrain to the village of **CHOCHOŁÓW**, with its fine wooden houses and church.

The Tatra National Park

The **Tatra National Park** (Tatrzański park narodowy) begins right outside Zakopane's southern outskirts, where the wooded flanks of the Tatra Mountains rise dramatically above rustic suburban houses. They are as beautiful as any mountain landscape in northern Europe, the ascents taking you on boulder-strewn paths alongside woods and streams up to the ridges where grand, windswept peaks rise in the brilliant alpine sunshine. With their highest peaks sporting snow for much of the year, the Tatras support a good skiing season from mid-December through to March (see box, p.449). Wildlife thrives here: the whole area was turned into a national park in the 1950s and supports rare species such as lynx, golden eagles and brown bear, and there's a good chance of glimpsing them.

Though many of the peak and ridge climbs are for experienced climbers only, much is accessible to regular walkers, with waymarked paths which give you the top-of-the-world exhilaration of bagging a peak. The national park charges a small fee (currently 2zł) to all visitors entering the park area, collected at booths at the main access points to the mountains.

Hiking in the Tatras: practicalities

It is as well to remember that the Tatras are an alpine range and as such demand some respect and preparation. The most important rule is to stick to the marked paths, and to arm yourself in advance with a decent **map**. The best is the *Tatrzański Park Narodowy/Tatra National Park* (1:30,000), which has all the paths accurately marked and is colour-coded. Remember never to leave the tree line (about 2000m) unless visibility is good, and when the clouds close in, start descending immediately.

Overnighting is possible in the seven PTTK-run **huts** dotted across the mountains and clearly marked on the *Tatra National Park* map (for up-to-date information on openings, check at the national park office in Zakopane). The huts provide dorm beds (25–30zł per person), mattress space on the floor in busy periods, and basic canteen food. Even if you don't want to lug large weights around the mountain-tops, it's sensible to have to supply of basic rations as well as water. **Camping** isn't allowed in the national park area, and **rock-climbing** only with a permit – ask at the park offices (see p.442) for details. For anyone attempting more than a quick saunter, the right **footwear and clothing** are, of course, essential. Lastly, take a **whistle** – blow six times every minute if you need help.

The **weather** is always changeable, and you should not venture out without waterproofs and sturdy boots; most rain falls in the summer, when there may also be thunderstorms and even hail- and snow-showers. Even on a warm summer's day in the valleys, it can be below freezing at the peaks. Set out early (the weather is always better in the morning), and tell someone when and where you're going – a **weather information** service is available on ☎018/206 3019. The number of the **mountain rescue service** (Tatrzańskie Ochotnicze Pogotowie Ratunkowe or TOPR) is ☎018/206 3444, though don't expect much English to be spoken.

In addition, respect the **national park rules**: don't leave any rubbish, keep to the marked paths and don't pick flowers or disturb the wild animals.

Kasprowy Wierch and Orła Perć

The easiest way up to the highest Tatra peaks is by **cable car** (March & April 7.30am–5.30pm, May, June & Sept 7.30am–6pm, July & Aug 7am–9pm; Oct 7.30am–5pm, Nov–Feb 8am–4pm; 40zł return) from the hamlet of

KUŹNICE, a three-kilometre walk (or 3min minibus journey) south from Zakopane along the Dolina Bystrego. Queues can be enormous in both summer and winter peak seasons and tickets can't be bought in advance – expect an average wait of two hours unless you turn up at the crack of dawn. For the journey down, priority is always given to people who've already got return tickets.

The cable car ends near the summit of **Kasprowy Wierch** (1985m), where weather-beaten signs indicate the border with Slovakia. From here, many day-trippers simply walk back down to Kuźnice through the Hala Gąsienicowa (2hr). An equally popular option is to walk up and return by cable car (2hr 30min). A rather longer alternative is to strike west to the summit of **Giewont** (1894m), the "Sleeping Knight" that overlooks Zakopane (allow 3hr for this). Watch out if it's been raining, however, as the paths here get pretty slippery and are very worn in places. The final bit of the ascent is rocky: secured chains aid your scramble to the top. From the summit, topped with a tall cross, the views can be spectacular on a good day. For the return, head down to Kuźnice through the Dolina Kondratowa past the *Hala Kondratowa* hut (☎018/201 9114; dorm beds from 30zł per person); allow forty minutes to get to the hostel, then a further hour to get to the village. This downward journey is fairly easy going and the whole trip is quite feasible in a day if you start out early.

East of Kasprowy Wierch, the walking gets tougher. From **Świnica** (2301m), a strenuous ninety-minute walk, experienced hikers continue along the **Orla Perć** (Eagles' Path), a challenging, exposed ridge with spectacular views. The *Pięc Stawów* hostel (☎018/207 7607), occupying a lovely lakeside position in the high valley of the same name, provides overnight shelter at the end (4hr).

From the hostel you can hike back down Dolina Roztoki to **Łysa Polana**, a border-crossing point with Slovakia in the valley (2hr). Here you can either catch a bus back to Zakopane, or head southwards towards Morskie Oko (see below).

Morskie Oko

Encircled by spectacular sheer cliff faces and alpine forest, the large glacial lake of **Morskie Oko** (Eye of the Sea; 1399m) is one of the Tatras' big attractions, and one of the most popular day-trip destinations for tourists staying in Zakopane. It's particularly busy in April and May, when the area is deluged by Polish school-trip outings. Most people begin the journey by car or bus rather than on foot, following the road that loops east then south from Zakopane, passing through Poronin before climbing up into the Tatra foothills. It's a spectacular journey at times, with a road following a mountain ridge whose forest cover occasionally parts to reveal superb views of the Tatras. After descending towards the border crossing at Łysa Polana, the road continues a few more kilometres to its final destination, a large car park surrounded by snack stalls at **Polana Palenica**. From the car park, a fairly obvious track leads past a national park booth (charging the 2zł entrance fee to the park) and climbs slowly through the trees towards Morskie Oko, which is some 9km (1hr 45min) uphill. Horse-drawn carts (35zł per person) are on hand to ferry those tourists who can't face the walk.

The *Przy Morskim Oku* hostel, situated by the side of the lake, serves up decent grilled-sausage-type fare, and provides a convenient base for the ascent of **Rysy** (2499m), the highest peak in the Polish Tatras. Closer to hand, on the same red-marked route is **Czarny Staw** (1580m), a lake that, if anything, appears even chillier than Morskie Oko.

Dolina Białego and Dolina Strążyska

For some easy and accessible valley hiking, Dolina Białego and Dolina Strążyska each provide a relaxed long afternoon's walk from Zakopane; taken together they make an enjoyable and not overly strenuous day's outing. Leaving Zakopane to the south, along ulica Strążyska, you reach **Dolina Strążyska** after around an hour's walk. At the end of the valley (3hr) you can climb to the **Hala Strążyska**, a beautiful high mountain pasture (1303m); the **Siklawica waterfall** on the way makes an enjoyable rest point, a stream coursing down from the direction of Giewont. The views are excellent, too, with **Mount Giewont** (1894m) rearing up to the south, and to the north a wonderful panorama of Zakopane and the surrounding countryside. Walk east along the meadow to the top of **Dolina Białego** and you can descend the deep, stream-crossed valley, one of the gentlest and most beautiful in the region, continuing back to the outskirts of Zakopane (6–7hr in total).

Dolina Kościeliska

Six kilometres west from Zakopane on the Czarny Dunajec road, the hamlet of **KIRY** marks the entrance to the **Dolina Kościeliska**, a deep verdant valley much in evidence on postcards of the region. **Buses** from Zakopane to Chochołów and Czarny Dunajec pass the entrances to the valley; there's also a shuttle service operated by private **minibuses** from Zakopane bus station in summer.

For around 120zł a horse-drawn cart will run you down the first section of the valley to a point known as **Polana Pisana**, but from here on it's walkers only. A distinctive feature of Kościeliska is the caves in its limestone cliffs – once the haunts of robbers and bandits, legend has it. Take a detour off to the left from Polana Pisana – marked *jaskinia* (caves) – and you can visit various examples, including **Jaskinia Mroźna**, where the walls are permanently encased in ice.

Beyond Polana Pisana, the narrow upper valley is a beautiful stretch of crags, gushing water, caves and greenery reminiscent of the English Lake District. The awe-inducing scenery so inspired Witkacy's fiancée Jadwiga Jaczewska (see box, p.445) that she chose this as the venue for her suicide. About 45 minutes beyond

▲ Giewont

the Polana is the *Hala Ornak* **hostel** (☎018/207 0520, ⊛www.ornak.tatrynet
.pl; dorm beds from 22zł per person, simple doubles ❷), a popular overnight
stop with a **restaurant**. Day walkers return back down the valley to take the
bus back to Zakopane, but there are two marked paths leading beyond the hostel
for those who want to continue. The eastern route takes you the short distance
to **Smreczyński Staw** (1226m), a tiny mountain lake surrounded by forest; the
western route follows a high ridge over to Dolina Chochołowska (see below) – a
demanding walk and only for the fit.

Dolina Chochołowska

Two kilometres northwest of Kiry lies the entrance to the **Dolina Chochołowska**,
a 10km-long defile following the course of a stream deep into the hills. From
the car park at the head of the valley, it's a good hour's walk to the *Chochołowska*
hut (☎018/207 0510, ⊛www.chocholowska.zakopane.pl; dorms from 30zł per
person, doubles ❷), beautifully situated overlooking the meadows, with the high
western Tatras and the Czech border behind. A clandestine meeting between the
pope and Lech Wałęsa took place here in 1983 and is commemorated by a tableau
on the wall. The steep paths up the eastern side lead to ridges that separate the
valley from Dolina Kościeliska – one path, from a little way beyond the car park,
connects the two valleys, making the cross trip possible.

East of the Tatras

East of the Tatras, the mountains scale down to a succession of lower ranges
stretching along the Slovak border. The walking here is less dramatic than in the
Tatras, but excellent nonetheless. The highlights of the region are the **Pieniny**,
mountains hard by the Slovak border, and a raft run through the **Dunajec Gorge**
far below. Routes towards the Pieniny pass through the rolling hills of the **Spisz**
region, site of the postcard-pretty **Niedzica Castle**. The best base from which
to explore the region is the spa town of **Szczawnica**, from where local buses
provide access to the surrounding towns and villages.

The Spisz region

The road east from Nowy Targ to Szczawnica follows the broad valley of the
Dunajec through the **Spisz**, a backwoods region whose villages are renowned for
their wooden houses, churches and folk art. Annexed by Poland from the newly
created Czechoslovak state in 1920, it had for centuries been a frontier province
alternating frequently between Hungarian and Polish control. The old aura of a
quiet rural backwater remains, the region's Slovak minority bearing testimony to
its historic borderland position. Nowy Targ–Szczawnica **buses** cover the route
ten to twelve times a day.

Dębno

Fourteen kilometres from Nowy Targ, **DĘBNO** has one of the best-known
wooden churches in the country, a shingled, steep-roofed larch building, put
together without using nails and surrounded by a charming wicket fence, with a
profile vaguely reminiscent of a snail. Inside, the full length of walls and ceiling
is covered with exuberant, brilliantly preserved fifteenth-century polychromy
and **woodcarving**. The subjects are an enchanting mix of folk, national and

religious motifs, including some fine hunting scenes and curiously Islamic-looking geometric patterns. In the centre of the building, fragments survive of the original rood screen, supporting a tree-like cross, while the original fifteenth-century altarpiece triptych features an unusually militant-looking St Catherine. In addition, there's a fine carved statue of St Nicholas, a medieval wooden tabernacle and some banners reputedly left by Jan Sobieski on his return from defeating the Turks in Vienna in 1683. The church is usually open during daylight hours; if not, local enquiries may reveal the whereabouts of the priest (he lives just over the road), who will probably open things up.

Czorsztyn

Immediately east of Dębno lies the **Czorsztyn Reservoir**, a controversial hydroelectric project which was opposed by many environmentalists before the valley – and a couple of its villages – were finally subsumed by water in 1997. A minor road branches off to follow the southern banks of the river before arriving at Niedzica (see below), although most traffic staying on to the high ground north of the water. Staying on this latter route, it's about 12km from Dębno to the hamlet of Krośnica, at the eastern end of which is a right turn to the village of **CZORSZTYN**, 2km south. The village sits on a south-facing slope overlooking the reservoir, on the banks of which sits a memorable **castle**. It's largely a ruin – struck by a thunderbolt in the 1790s, it was abandoned after the resulting fire – although a couple of towers and battlements have been made safe for visitors. From its heights you get sweeping **views** south to the castle of Niedzica across the mouth of the Dunajec Gorge.

There are about six daily **buses** from Nowy Targ to Czorsztyn; otherwise catch one of the more frequent Nowy Targ–Szczawnica buses, get off in Krośnica and walk. In summer, **taxi boats** (3zł) cross the water between Czorsztyn and Niedzica every hour or so, making it possible to visit both fortresses in the space of an afternoon.

Niedzica Castle

Built in the fourteenth century to guard a strategic position on the Polish-Hungarian border, **Niedzica Castle** is one of the most dramatically situated strongholds in the country, perched precariously above the waters of the Czorsztyn Reservoir. The sweeping concrete crescent of the reservoir's **dam**, immediately east of the castle, only adds to the setting.

Niedzica's castle **museum** (May–Sept daily 9am–7pm; Oct–April Tues–Sun 9am–5pm; 10zł) is a limited affair consisting of a scale model of the castle, a few old prints, and the odd suit of chain-mail armour. It is the building itself that is the real star turn, offering a wonderfully evocative succession of stone chambers clad with animal skins and sweeping views from its towers. According to local folk wisdom, documents revealing the location of the lost treasure of the Incas are concealed somewhere in the castle – local magnate and adventurer Sebastian Berzeviczy married a descendent of the Inca royal house in the eighteenth century, reportedly acquiring sacred texts which were passed down to subsequent generations.

Just downhill from the castle gates, a footpath leads along the top of the **dam** (*zapora*), providing excellent views back across the reservoir, with the battlements of Czorstyn visible on the far side of the water.

Practicalities

Despite being just across the water from Czorsztyn (and served in summer by regular taxi boat; see p.454), Niedzica is a fairly roundabout trip by road, involving heading back to Dębno, or southeast towards Sromowce Niżne. By **public transport**, it is served by bus from Nowy Targ, or summer-only minibus from Szczawnica. Best of the local **accommodation** possibilities are at **POLANA SOSNY**, 1km east of the main dam, where the *Pensjonat Chata Spiska* (☎018/262 9403, ⓔpolana.sosny@niedzica.pl; ❹) occupies a traditional farmhouse building, moved here from the village of Łapszy Niżny and transformed into a comfortable B&B with original wooden fittings. There's a well-appointed **campsite** next door (same contact details). A good budget option is the outwardly graceless *Pod Taborem*, a concrete building 500m below the castle (☎018/262 9322), offering rooms with shared facilities (❷) or en suite (❸).

The Pieniny

A short range of Jurassic limestone peaks, rearing above the spectacular Dunajec Gorge, the **Pieniny** offer some stiff hillwalking but require no serious climbing to reach the 1000-metre summits. Jagged outcrops are set off by abundant greenery, the often humid mountain microclimate supporting a rich and varied flora. Like the Tatras, the Pieniny are an officially designated national park and have a network of controlled paths. The detailed *Pieniński Park Narodowy* (1:22,500) **map** is useful and is available in most tourist offices and bookshops.

The main range, a ten-kilometre stretch between Czorsztyn and Szczawnica, is the most popular hiking territory, with the peaks of **Trzy Korony** (Three Crowns; 982m) the big target. The principal point of access to the park is the small town of **Krościenko**, although Szczawnica, 4km east, offers better accommodation possibilities. Both are served by regular buses from Nowy Targ and Kraków.

Krościenko and the Trzy Korony

The town of **KROŚCIENKO**, a one-hour bus ride east of Nowy Targ, is a dusty, unexciting little place which would hardly merit a stopoff were it not the main starting point for **hikes** to the Trzy Korony. The **PTTK office**, in the centre at ul. Jagiellońska 65 (☎018/262 3081), provides private rooms (❷), and there's a large riverside **campsite**, the *Cypel* (☎018/262 3368), just across the bridge from the town centre.

From the bus stop in the middle of Krościenko you can follow the signs – and in summer the packs of hikers – south on the yellow route. The path soon begins to climb through the mountainside woods, with plenty of meadows and lush clearings on the way. Around two hours from Krościenko, you'll reach **Okrąglica**, the highest peak of the **Trzy Korony**, via some chain-bannistered steps. On a clear day there's an excellent view over the whole area: the high Tatras off to the west, the slopes of Slovakia to the south, and the Dunajec Gorge far below.

Many hikers take the same route back, but two alternatives are worth considering. One is to walk to Szczawnica (p.456), a two- or three-hour trip. Head back along the route you came as far as Bajków Groń (679m), about three-quarters of the way down, and from there follow the blue path across the mountains south to Sokolica (747m). The other, if you want to combine the walk with the Dunajec Gorge, is to descend the mountain southwest to Sromowce Kąty (3hr), starting point for the raft trip downriver (see below).

The Dunajec Gorge

Below the heights of the Pieniny, the fast-moving Dunajec twists its way between a succession of craggy peaks. The river is a magnet for **canoeists**, who shoot fearlessly through the often powerful rapids; for the less intrepid, the two- to three-hour **raft trip** provides a gentler though thoroughly enjoyable version of the experience. Tourists have been rafting down these waters since the 1830s, a tradition derived in turn from the ancient practice of floating logs downriver to the mills and ports.

Run by the Polskie Stowarzyszenie Flisaków Pienińskich (Association of Pieniny Raftsmen: daily: April & Sept 9am–4pm; May–Aug 8.30am–5pm; Oct 9am–3pm; 40zł; ☎018/262 9721, ⊛www.flisacy.com.pl), the trips begin at **SROMOWCE KĄTY**; regular buses run to Kąty from Nowy Targ, and in season there are minibuses from Szczawnica and Niedzica. Most of the travel agents in Zakopane and Szczawnica offer trips, which usually include a stopoff at Niedzica Castle as well – excursions cost anything from 80–180zł depending on whether food is laid on. Rafts seat 10–12 and leave as soon as they're full – although note that on summer weekends you might have to queue. The trip runs to Szczawnica at the eastern end of the gorge, where a bus (8zł) will bring you back to Kąty if you so desire.

The rafts are sturdy log constructions, made of four pontoons held together with rope, and are punted downstream by two navigators (wearing traditional embroidered jackets), who usually commentate on the trip in impenetrable Pieniny dialect. Although the river has some fast-flowing stretches, the raft journey is for the most part a leisurely downstream drift, allowing plenty of time to enjoy the scenery – especially the sheer limestone crags that hover above the sharp turns of the river. The Dunajec here forms the border with Slovakia, and at several points Slovak villages face their Polish counterparts across the banks, with their own rafters and canoeists hugging the southern side of the river.

Szczawnica and around

Set back from the confluence of the Dunajec and Grajcarek rivers, **SZCZAWNICA** is a quaint nineteenth-century spa resort which has outgrown its original purpose to become the main holiday base for the Pieniny region. There's plenty of private accommodation in town, and – in summer at least – frequent minibus services to the regions main tourist draws, most notably the castle at Niedzica and the rafting embarkation point at Sromowce-Kąty.

From the bus drop-off point, it's a short walk east to what passes for a main square, followed by a short uphill hike to the old centre of the village, where you'll find a nineteenth-century **tap room** (*pijalnia*) serving up cups of Szczawnica's waters. Opposite the *pijalnia* there's a **museum** (Tues–Sun 10am–1pm & 2–4pm; 5zł), with a small but engaging collection of Pieniny costumes, including the embroidered waistcoats for which the region is famous.

You can get up onto an eastern spur of the Pieniny by taking the **chairlift** (June–Aug & Dec–April; 12zł return), just below the main street, to the 722-metre-high Góra Palenica, which provides excellent views of the valley. There's a short downhill run and a modest snowboard park here in winter, although it's nothing for the serious winter-sports enthusiast to get excited about.

The chairlift terminal is also the starting point for the Dunajec Gorge **foot-** and **cycle-path**, which runs westwards along the south bank of first the Grajcarek and then the Dunajec, crossing over into Slovakia after 3km, and continuing for another 9km along the banks of the gorge as far as Cerveny Klǎstor, the main Slovakian starting point for rafting trips. You should at least follow the path for the 2km it takes you to reach the west end of Szczawnica village; here you get excellent **views** of the sheer cliffs marking the eastern end of the Dunajec Gorge, from which the bobbing forms of rafts emerge at regular intervals.

Practicalities

Buses run to Szczawnica from both Nowy Targ (40km) and, on a slightly roundabout route, from Zakopane (50km), dropping you in the centre of town, just above the Grajcarek. **Tourist information** duties are carried out by the PTTK office, ul. Główna 1 (Mon–Fri 8am–3pm; ☎018/262 2332, ⓦwww.pttk.szczawnica.pl), which sells hiking maps and books tours to beauty spots both in Poland and on the Slovakian side of the border. Both the PTTK and Szewczyk Travel, just across the road at Zdrojowa 2 (☎018/262 1895, ⓦwww.szewczyktravel.pl), handle private rooms (❶–❷). **Bikes** can be hired (15–20zł per day) from numerous outlets throughout town, notably at the Palenica chairlift terminal.

Best of the **hotels** is the *Batory*, uphill from the centre at Park Górny 13 (☎018/262 0207, ⓦwww.batory-hotel.pl; ❺), offering smart en suites in a thoroughly renovated nineteenth-century building where novelist Henryk Sienkiewicz (see p.544) was once a guest. *Willa Marta*, ul. Główna 30 (☎018/262 2270, ⓦwww.pensjonatmarta.pl; ❸), is another historical pension once patronized by Poland's cultural elite, and still popular with artists and journalists – the en-suite rooms are smallish, simply decorated but comfortable. Smart en suites with TV, plus a kitchen that guests can use, are on offer at *Willa Dutka*, a large B&B 1km west of the centre at ul. Skotnicka 3 (☎018/262 2391, ⓔmdutka@poczta.onet.pl; ❸). A more down-to-earth alternative is the *Orlica* PTTK **hostel** at ul. Pienińska 12 (☎018/262 2245, ⓦwww.orlica.com), which has dorm rooms (25zł per person) and some en-suite doubles (❸) right on the edge of the gorge, a kilometre south of the raft disembarkation point. You can **camp** at the *Orlica*, or at the more central *Pole Namiotowe U Ewy*, downhill from the bus station at Nad Grajcarkiem 51 (☎018/262 2665).

The *Willa Marta* (see above) has a good **restaurant** offering well-presented local and international dishes, while the *Restaurant-Pub Alt*, on the opposite side of the park, produces better-than-average traditional Polish stodge. There's not a great deal of **nightlife** in Szczawnica, although if you like the idea of couples dancing to seventies' hits under a mirrorball, then you're in the right place.

Jaworki and around

Six kilometres east of Szczawnica and served by regular bus, the pleasantly rustic village of **JAWORKI** is the starting point for several low-intensity hikes in the pasture-covered uplands that make up the eastern Pieniny. Sitting above the centre of the village is a bulb-domed eighteenth-century **church**, built for the Uniate Lemko community before their resettlement in other parts of Poland during Operation Vistula (see p.314) in 1947. Although now belonging to the Catholic Church, the structure retains a beautiful, Orthodox-influenced altar-piece studded with saintly icons. High in the eaves nests Poland's biggest colony of horseshoe **bats**.

A well-signed path at the western end of the village heads south into the **Homole Gorge** (Wąwoz Homole: 1.50zł), where a fast-flowing stream gurgles its way beneath jagged rock formations. Featuring steel bridges and staircases, the path zig-zags through the gorge for about 30 minutes before leading up onto the surrounding pastures. A sign to the left leads to the *Szałas Bukowinki* **hut**, where you can enjoy basic refreshments in a meadow munched by cows and the odd horse. Alternatively, follow the sign to the right that leads up to the surrounding hilltops and the 1050-metre peak of **Wysokie Skałki** (1hr 30min), right on the Polish–Slovak border. There's a basic PTTK **campsite** below the summit.

Following the road east out of Jaworki provides access to a longer but gentler walking route through the narrow **Biała Woda valley**, again bordered by rugged, rocky terrain. Carry on past the Slovak border (no passport control but keep identity documents handy) and you'll eventually reach the village of **Litmanova** (2–3hr out from Jaworki), famous for its collection of traditional timber farmhouses.

Back in Jaworki, the *Lowisko pstrąga* **grill-bar** in the centre of the village serves pan-fried trout in a grassy stream-side garden, while close by the *Bacówki* **restaurant** offers a stomach-filling selection of traditional pork-and-potato dishes in traditional-style wooden-beamed surroundings.

Travel details

Trains

Kraków to: Zakopane (8 daily; 3hr 30min–4hr).
Zakopane to: Częstochowa (2 daily; 6–7hr); Gdańsk (1 daily; 15hr; sleeper); Katowice (1 daily; 5hr 30min); Kraków (8 daily; 3hr 30min–4hr); Nowy Targ (10 daily; 20min); Warsaw (1 daily; 6hr).

Buses

Kraków to: Zakopane (every 30min; 2hr–2hr 30min); Szczawnica (8 daily; 2hr 30min–3hr).
Nowy Targ to Czorsztyn (Mon–Sat 6 daily, Sun 4 daily; 40min); Dębno (10–12 daily; 20min); Kraków (every 30min; 1hr 40min); Krościenko (10–12 daily; 40min); Niedzica (Mon–Sat 8 daily; Sun 4 daily; 40min); Sromowce Kąty (5 daily; 1hr);

Szczawnica (10–12 daily; 1hr); Zakopane (every 30min; 30–50min).
Szczawnica to: Jaworki (regular buses 7 daily; 15min; summer-season minibuses hourly; 10min); Kraków (4 daily; 3hr); Niedzica (summer-season minibuses hourly; 35min); Nowy Sącz (6 daily; 1hr); Sromowce Kąty (summer-season minibuses hourly; 25min).
Zakopane to: Bielsko-Biała (3 daily; 2hr 30min–4hr); Katowice (2 daily; 4hr); Kraków (12 daily; 2hr 30min–3hr); Lublin (1 daily; 8hr); Nowy Sącz (3 daily; 1–2hr); Nowy Targ (every 30min; 40min); Polana Palenica (June & Sept 12 daily, July & Aug 20 daily, Oct–May 6 daily; 45min); Rzeszów (1 daily; 3–4hr); Szczawnica (5 daily; 1hr 20min); Tarnów (3 daily; 4hr); Warsaw (1 daily; 8–9hr).

9

Upper Silesia

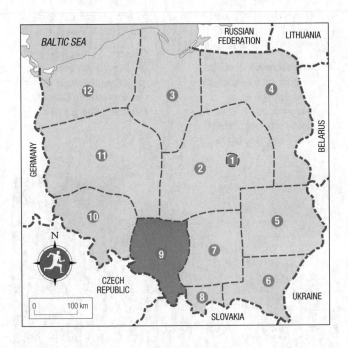

CHAPTER 9

Highlights

* **Park of Culture and Rest, Katowice** This mammoth-sized city park boasts fairground rides, rose gardens, a folk museum and more. See p.464

* **Góra świętej Anny** Both a pilgrimage site and a former battlefield, "St Anne's Hill" is of great symbolic significance to Silesian Poles. See p.467

* **Częstochowa** Home to the enigmatic holy image known as the Black Madonna, this is Poland's most important place of pilgrimage. See p.472

* **Pszczyna** One of the finest palaces in the country, surrounded by bison-grazed parkland. See p.476

* **The Silesian Beskids** Rippling pine-covered hills criss-crossed by hiking trails, accessed from the mountain resorts of Ustroń, Wisła and Szczyrk. See p.476

* **Cieszyn** A charming historic market town straddling Poland's frontier with the Czech Republic. See p.479

▲ Ducal palace, Pszczyna

9

Upper Silesia

L
ong thought of as the heartland of Polish heavy industry, Upper Silesia remains an area of stark contrasts. At its centre stands a huge conurbation of towns which rejoices in the collective name of **GOP** (Górnośląski Okręg Przemysłowy, or Upper Silesian Industrial District). With two million inhabitants, this is the most densely populated part of the country. To the south, however lies some of the most bewitching countryside in Poland, in the form of the fir-clad Silesian Beskid Mountains that make up the province's border with the Czech Republic.

The once-mighty coal and steel industries of the GOP went into steep decline after 1989 (see box, p.463), but with factories becoming art galleries and mines being redeveloped as tourist attractions, there's plenty in the way of **industrial heritage** to enjoy. Having both an international airport and a major international railway junction, the GOP's main city, **Katowice**, is your most likely entry point to the region, although it's a gritty place best treated as a gateway to the more appetizing areas beyond. A train ride away lie two of the most important spiritual sites in Poland: to the north, **Częstochowa** is the site of mass pilgrimages inspired by the miracle-working icon known as the Black Madonna; while to the west the hilltop village of **Góra świętej Anny** is an altogether more rustic, restful spot associated with the cult of St Anne. Northwest of Góra św. Anny, the riverside town of **Opole** makes a relaxing stopoff on the main route to Wrocław, while south of Katowice, rolling farmland rises gently to meet the pine-cloaked **Beskids**, providing a surfeit of attractive hiking territory. Ranged around the foothills, the Baroque palace at **Pszczyna**, the delightful town of **Cieszyn** and the up-and-coming ski resort of **Szczyrk** are the main targets for travellers.

Katowice is Upper Silesia's main **transport** hub, with rail lines radiating outwards to most of the places mentioned in this chapter. The smaller towns and resorts of the Beskids are served by plentiful local buses, with regional centre **Bielsko-Biała** serving as the fulcrum of the network.

Katowice and around

Standing at the heart of the upper Silesian conurbation, 400,000-strong **KATOWICE** is very much the ugly duckling of Polish cities. Despite a few surviving pockets of nineteenth-century grandeur, it's a predominantly grey place grouped around a distinctly unengaging twentieth-century centre. However, thanks to its international airport and rail links, Katowice represents many peoples' first taste of southwestern Poland, and you may well find yourself here en route to somewhere else. Central Katowice is low on sightseeing attractions, but with the odd museum and a spectacular park, the city's outlying areas do possess some very interesting places to visit.

Arrival, information and accommodation

Katowice's **airport** is at Pyrzowice, 25km northeast of the centre. Some flights are met by direct minibuses to Kraków and other cities (contact your airline for details), meaning that you might not have to pass through Katowice at all. Otherwise, city buses (pay the driver) run from the airport roughly hourly to the **train station**, bang in the centre on plac Szewczyka, a ten-minute walk southwest of the drab road junction that passes for a Rynek. The **bus station** is ten minutes' north of the train station on ulica Piotra Skargi. The City Information Centre at Młyńska

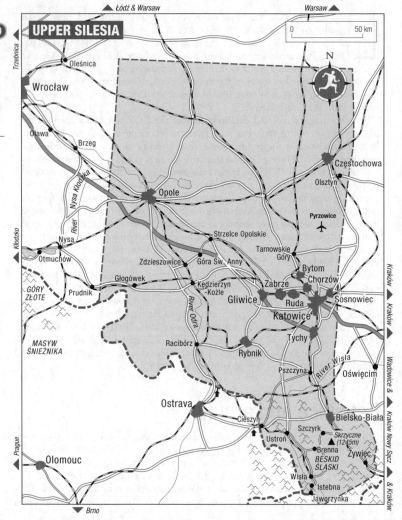

A short history of Upper Silesia

Upper Silesia's rich mineral seams have been extensively mined since the Middle Ages – nearly a tenth of the world's known coal exists here – but it wasn't until the nineteenth-century **Industrial Revolution** that the area became heavily urbanized. With a population composed almost equally of Germans and Poles (and with many of mixed blood), the fate of the area became a hot political issue after **World War I**, with both Poland and Germany laying claim to the territory. The Western powers at first favoured Poland, which would otherwise have been a poor agricultural country with no industrial base. Strong support for the Polish claim came from the French, who wished to weaken Germany and establish a strong ally to its east. This unnerved the British, who argued that Upper Silesia's industrial economy would suffer as a consequence: Prime Minister Lloyd George went so far as to suggest that allocating Upper Silesia to Poland was like giving a clock to a monkey. Pending a final decision on the issue Upper Silesia remained under German administration, with the international community playing for time by suggesting that the future of the province be settled by means of a **plebiscite**. Fearful that any vote would be manipulated by the German authorities, the Silesian Poles mounted **insurrections** in 1919 and 1920. Finally held in March 1921, the plebiscite was won by the Germans – a result discredited by the fact that a large number of former citizens were shipped back into Silesia from elsewhere in Germany in time for the vote.The Poles responded by launching a third insurrection in May 1921, this time wresting control of many urban areas from the Germans. The League of Nations was called upon to arbitrate, and decided that **partition** of Upper Silesia was the only fair solution. line was drawn roughly down the middle of the province, leaving the Germans with the agriculturally rich western half while the Poles were granted Katowice and the majority of the coal mines.

The borders were re-drawn once again in **1945**, when the whole of Silesia was awarded to Poland. Most of the German population either fled or was encouraged to leave, and Polish settlers arrived from the east to take their place. Throughout the **communist period**, Upper Silesia's industrial workers enjoyed a privileged position; mining wages, for example, were three times the national average income. One obvious side effect of industrial development was a catastrophically high level of atmospheric **pollution** and a correspondingly high incidence of breathing complaints among the local population. Many of the less profitable factories closed in the 1990s, reducing environmental problems but adding to the ranks of local unemployed. However, Upper Silesia's skilled workforce and excellent communications have made it an obvious target for foreign investment, and those travellers who stop off in Upper Silesia's coal and steel heartland will find that the aura of post-industrial decay is increasingly overlaid with a palpable sense of big-city bustle.

---

2 (Centrum Informacju o Mieście; Mon–Fri: May–Oct 10am–6pm, Nov–April 9am–5pm; ☎032/259 3808) is your most likely source of **information**.

Should you wish to stay, there are a handful of affordable **hotels** in the centre. **Camping** in an industrial city like Katowice might sound paradoxical, but there's a tranquil, lakeside site south of the city at ul. Murckowska 6 (mid-May to late Sept; ☎032/256 5939) and reached by bus #4 from aleja Korfantego.

Hotels

Campanile ul. Sowińskiego 48 ☎032/205 5050, ⓦwww.campanile.com.pl. Neat, tidy, cube-shaped business hotel 2km southeast of the centre, offering en suites with TV, neutral colour schemes and tea-making facilities. Handily placed for the A4 Wrocław–Kraków highway if you're touring by car; otherwise bus #910 from the train station passes by. ⓺

Diament ul. Dworcowa 9 ☎032/253 9041, ⓦwww.hoteldiament.pl. Dependable three-star right by the station, offering pastel-coloured en suites with desk space and cable internet connection. ⓻
Etap al. Rozdzieńskiego 18 ☎032/350 5040, ⓦwww.orbis.pl. Functional en suites in nondescript office-block surroundings, but clean and well placed, within walking distance of the centre. ⓸

Katowice al. Korfantego 9 ☎032/258 8281. Sixties-era grey block offering plain but habitable en suites with TV. The upper floors would offer great views if downtown Katowice was actually worth looking at. ❻

Olimpijski al. Korfantego 35 ☎032/258 2282, Ⓦwww.hotelspodek.katowice.pl. Worth staying in simply for the novelty of sleeping in an annexe of the Spodek, Katowice's futuristic sports hall and concert venue (see below), the *Olimpijski* offers threadbare en suites with tiny TVs but they're good value for the location. ❺

Skaut al. Harcerska 3 ☎032/241 3291, Ⓦwww.hotel-chorzow.pl. Plain but nicely situated low-rise block at the northern end of the huge Park of Culture and Rest (see below), with functional en-suite doubles, plus a few triples and quads. Trams #6, #11, #23 or #41 run from the Rynek to Stadion Śląski, from where it's a 5min walk north. ❹

The town and around

Despite a handsome ensemble of nineteenth-century buildings, central Katowice is notoriously low on tourist attractions, and many of the more enticing sights are in outlying areas. Happily, the huge park on the northwestern borders of town, and the former coal-mining suburb of Nikiszowiec, are only a short tram or bus ride away.

Central Katowice

Those who do have time to kill in central Katowice could do worse than peep into the **Museum of Silesia** (Muzeum Śląskie: Tues–Fri 10am–5pm, Sat & Sun 11am–4pm; 6zł) at ul. Korfantego 3, just north of the Rynek. Inside lies a reasonable collection of Polish art, with some touching pastel portraits of the artist's family by Stanisław Wyspiański (see p.364), and a couple of canvases by Olga Boznańska (1865–1940), one of the few female painters active in pre-World War I Poland. North of the Rynek you can't miss Katowice's most alluring structure, the futuristic sports hall known as the **Spodek** ("flying saucer"), a smooth, dark doughnut of a building that looks like the kind of battleship that Darth Vader might cruise around the universe in. Rock fans from all over southern Poland flock here to attend major gigs – numerous big names have appeared in recent years. Rising above the Rondo Jerzego Ziętka tram stop immediately in front of the Spodek is the **Rondo Sztuki** (Art Roundabout: Tues–Fri 11am–7pm, Sat & Sun 10am–6pm; Ⓦwww.rondosztuki.pl), a crescent-shaped glass pavilion housing ambitious contemporary art shows. With a super-sleek café-bar on the first floor (see p.467), it's probably the coolest public transport interchange you'll ever encounter.

The Park of Culture and Rest

Three kilometres northwest of the centre, on the administrative boundary between Katowice and the neighbouring city of Chorzów, the **Regional Park of Culture and Rest** (Wojewódzki Park Kultury i Wypoczynku, or "WPKiW" for short) is very much the pride of the Upper Silesian conurbation – an enormous expanse of greenery conceived by socialist planners in the 1950s as an area of leisure, relaxation and escape for the proletarian hordes of the GOP. Combining ornamental gardens, areas of woodland wilderness and a worthwhile ethnographic museum, the park arguably deserves more of your sightseeing time than anything else in the Katowice area. It's easy to get to from the city centre, with trams #6, #11, #23 and #41 from the Rynek (destination Chorzów) all passing along the park's southern edge. A novel way of getting round the park is provided by a horizontal chairlift, which floats above the lawns and flower beds on a triangular route (you can get on and off at each point of the triangle; tickets cost 3zł for one stretch, 6zł for all three).

Marking the southeastern entrance to the park is **Wesołe Miasteczko** (Happy Town: Mon–Fri 10am–7pm, Sat & Sun 10am–9pm; 25zł), a garish amusement

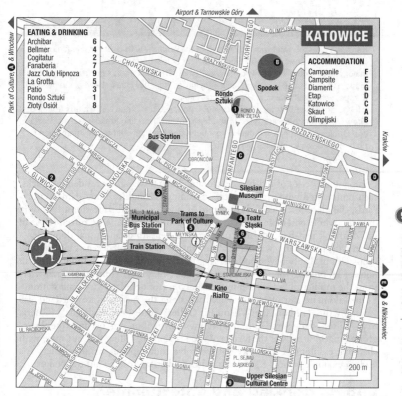

EATING & DRINKING

Archibar	6
Bellmer	4
Cogitatur	2
Fanaberia	7
Jazz Club Hipnoza	9
La Grotta	5
Patio	3
Rondo Sztuki	1
Złoty Osioł	8

KATOWICE

ACCOMMODATION

Campanile	F
Campsite	E
Diament	G
Etap	D
Katowice	C
Skaut	A
Olimpijski	B

park offering a variety of rides. From here a central avenue leads northwest through the heart of the park, passing a boating lake, seven hectares of rose garden and a sizeable **zoo** (daily: summer 10am–7pm; winter 10am–4pm). At the northwestern end of the avenue looms the huge bowl of the **Silesia Stadium** (Stadion Śląski: ⓦ www.stadionslaski.pl), one of the principal venues for the European Football Championships of 2012. English fans may wish to forget that Katowice was the scene of a famous 2–0 defeat in June 1973 that helped to confirm England's decline as a footballing power. The Poles, meanwhile, went on to enjoy a golden decade of international success. A kilometre beyond the stadium, the **Upper Silesian Ethnographic Park** (Górnośląski Park Etnograficzny: May–Sept Tues–Fri 9am–5pm, Sat & Sun 11am–7pm; Oct Tues–Sun 9am–5pm; Nov–April Mon–Fri 9am–2pm; 6zł) presents a fascinating array of rural buildings ranged across an area of gently rolling meadowland. Jostling for attention are timber cottages from the Beskid mountains, straw-thatched farmhouses from the Pszczyna region, and – most arrestingly of all – an eighteenth-century wooden church from the village of Nieboczowy, with a wonderfully wavy shingle roof and a rash of pimply onion domes.

Nikiszowiec

Arguably the most alluring part of Katowice's industrial heritage is **Nikiszowiec** (colloquially known as "Nikisz"), a model suburb 6km southeast of the centre, built in 1908–15 to house workers employed in the nearby Wieczorek coal mine.

Comprising a series of red-brick quadrangular and triangular residential blocks, each punctuated with arched gateways leading through to inner garden courtyards, the place resembles a vast system of interlocking fortifications. Presiding over the whole ensemble is the similarly red-brick **St Anne's Church** (Kościół św. Anny), a neo-Baroque structure basking beneath a fat sensual dome. It's a fascinating place for a wander – although the absence of decent cafés or food shops will probably have you scurrying back towards central Katowice after an hour or so. Nikiszowiec can be reached on bus #12 or #13 (direction Giszowiec) from the municipal bus station immediately in front of Katowice train station.

One kilometre east of Nikiszowiec back along the road to Katowice (and also served by the #12 bus), the **Wilson Pit Gallery** at ul. Oswobodzenia 1 (Galeria Szyb Wilson: daily 9am–7pm; free; Ⓦwww.szybwilson.org) occupies the above-ground machine halls of the former Wilson coal mine. Filling this vast space with changing exhibitions of quirky but accessible contemporary art, the gallery is a leading example of how Katowice's industrial heritage can be put to good use.

Eating, drinking and entertainment

Sit-down **eating** venues are not Katowice's strong point, although there are plenty of cafés, snack outlets and pizzerias in the pedestrianized streets near the station: ulica Stawowa, ulica Dyrekcyjna and ulica Staromiejska. There's an increasing number of rewardingly characterful **drinking** dens in Katowice, although they're spread throughout the city rather than concentrated in an easily crawlable area.

Restaurants

Fanaberia ul. Dyrekcyjna 1. Basement-level restaurant specializing in Russian cuisine – from simple lunchtime meals like *pelmeni* (meat-filled blobs of boiled pastry; 15zł) to more elaborate pork and duck dishes in the 30–40zł bracket. Tables creep out onto the pedestrianized street in summer. Daily noon–midnight.

Jazz Club Hipnoza pl. Sejmu śląskiego 2 Ⓦwww.jazzclub.pl. South of the train station on the second floor of the Upper Silesian Cultural Centre (Górnośląski Centrum Kultury), this is primarily a laid-back drinking venue which offers a solid food menu too – with pizzas (15–20zł) and grilled steaks (30–35zł) predominating. Live jazz or blues about once a week. Daily noon–1am.

La Grotta ul. Wawelska 3. Good-quality and inexpensive pasta, pizza and salads in a cosy taverna-style interior or (in summer) the street-side beer garden. Daily 9am–midnight.

Patio ul. Stawowa 3. Serviceable grill bar serving up moderately priced chop-and-chips fare on a central street. Daily 10am–11pm.

Złoty Osioł ul. Mariacka 1. Cult café-restaurant that looks like a cross between a student bedsit and an oriental textile market, offering an inexpensive range of vegetarian stews, lasagnes and quiches. Daily 10am–10pm.

Bars and clubs

Archibar ul. Dyrekcyjna 9 Ⓦwww.archibar .pl. Located in the local branch of the Union of Architects and oozing with contemporary style, this is a minimalist white space with loungey furniture, cool cocktails and DJs spinning discs at weekends. Mon–Sat 10am–1am or later; Sun 4pm–midnight. **Bellmer** Rynek 2. Mildly bohemian hide a way in the basement of Katowice's main theatre – head through the side entrance on ul. Warszawska to find it. Named after Katowice-born artist Hans Bellmer, famous for his obsession with life-size female dolls, it's full of appropriately weird *objets d'art* and wall-paintings. Daily noon–midnight. **Cogitatur** ul. Gliwicka 9 ⓦwww.cogitatur.pl. Large café-bar-cum-club which nevertheless retains an intimate feel, thanks to antique-shop furnishings

and candles on the tables. Occasional gigs, and a DJ-driven repertoire of alternative rock and hip-hop. You'll find it off the street at the back of the courtyard. Sun–Thurs 3pm–midnight, Fri & Sat 3pm–4am. **Rondo Sztuki** Rondo Jerzego Ziętka ⓦwww .kawiarnia.rondosztuki.pl. Ultra-contemporary, glass-enclosed café-bar with plenty in the way of loungey couches to sink into. A great place for coffee and ice cream during the day, or cocktails at night. A regular schedule of gigs and club nights provides added inducement to visit. Daily 11am–11pm or later, depending what's on.

Gliwice

Only twenty minutes west of Katowice by train, **GLIWICE** was one of the original powerhouses of Upper Silesian industry, thanks in large part to the coke-fired blast furnaces established here by trailblazing Scottish engineer John Baildon in 1796. Evidence of Gliwice's erstwhile prosperity can be seen in the parade of fine nineteenth-century apartment blocks lining the main street, ulica Zwycięstwa. However the city's star turn is the **Villa Caro**, just off the main drag at ul. Dolnych Wałów 8a (Tues & Thurs 11am–6pm, Wed & Fri 9am–2.30pm, Sat & Sun 10am–3pm; 6zł; ⓦwww.muzeum.gliwice.pl), which has the best-preserved nineteenth-century interiors in southern Poland. Built by German-Jewish magnate Oscar Caro in 1885, the villa is richly decorated with stucco ceilings, intricate wall panelling and all manner of fine furniture. Caro himself was an enthusiastic collector, with Renaissance paintings, seventeenth-century Samurai armour and Chinese opium pipes adding up to an eclectic personal museum.

Two kilometres northeast of the centre, Gliwice's vintage 1930s **radio mast** (Radiostacja Gliwicka) is one of Upper Silesia's most emblematic sights. Standing 111m tall, this gauntly elegant structure is reckoned to be the highest surviving wooden structure in the world. Locals remember it as the scene of a notorious provocation on the night of August 31, 1939, when the Germans – eager to start a war with Poland for which the Poles would be blamed – arranged for their agents to attack the station in the guise of Polish "insurgents": World War II kicked off the following day. The former transmission station at the base of the mast, filled with archaic pre-World War II control panels, now serves as a modest **museum** (Tues–Sat 9am–5pm; July & Aug also Sun; 4zł). Visitors are treated to an enthusiastic lecture about the station's history (English spoken on request), before filing out to admire the iconic mast at close quarters.

Gliwice's **train station** is at the northern end of ulica Zwycięstwa; the centre of town (with the main Rynek and the Villa Caro) is twenty minutes' walk south from here, while the radio station is twenty minutes walk north along ulica Tarnogorska. There are several unexciting restaurants and pizzerias on Gliwice's Rynek, but northing worth making a special trip for.

Góra świętej Anny

Seventy kilometres west of Katowice, the hilltop village of **GÓRA ŚWIĘTEJ ANNY** (St Anne's Hill) is of enormous symbolic significance to Silesian Poles. A popular pilgrimage site since the seventeenth century, it was also the scene of bitter fighting between Poles and Germans during the Silesian Uprising of May

Some of Upper Silesia's most spectacular industrial heritage sites are to be found in the former coal- and silver-mining regions, where a handful of disused pits have been opened to the public as show mines. As well as offering insights into mining history, each of the sites below involves visitors in a memorable underground journey, and is well worth a day-trip from Katowice to see.

Visits to all the mines below are by **guided tour**, which usually depart every 30 minutes or on the hour. Individual tourists can turn up and hope to join one of these, although it's advisable to book in advance on the telephone numbers provided below. Regular tours are in Polish, but this shouldn't detract too much from the experience. If you want an English-language guide ring a couple of days in advance and expect to stump up an extra 50–60zł.

Tarnowskie Góry

Twenty kilometres north of Katowice and accessible by regular train, **Tarnowskie Góry** has been a major silver- and lead-mining centre ever since the thirteenth century. Some idea of its underground wealth is given in a document dated 1632 listing twenty thousand places where minerals could be exploited.

There are two heritage sites here, beginning with the **Museum of Silver Mining**, 2.5km south of town at ul. Szczęść Boże 52 (Kopalnia Zabytkowa Rud Srebronosnych: daily 9am–3pm; 20zł; ☎032/285 4996, ⓦwww.kopalniasrebra.pl). Dating back to medieval times, the mine was formerly worked for silver, lead and copper, and in the small museum you'll see the old equipment, plus models of how the mine was operated and water levels controlled. The highlight, though, is a motorboat trip along the flooded drainage tunnels that were excavated as needs arose; dozens of kilometres of passageways undermine the entire area. From Tarnowskie Góry train station, catch bus #151, #734 or #735 to the Kopalnia Zabytkowa stop.

Situated in the wooded Park Repecki 4km southwest of the centre, the **Black Trout Gallery** (Sztolnia Czarnego Pstrąga: May, June, Sept & Oct Sat & Sun 10am–4pm; July & Aug daily 11am–4pm; Nov–April Sat & Sun 11am–3pm; 15zł; same website and phone numbers) is a 600-metre-long drainage tunnel linking two mine shafts, Szyb Ewa and Szyb Sylwester. It takes its name from the eponymous fish which occasionally found their way into the tunnels from the rivers into which they drain. Entering via Szyb Ewa, the tour consists of a spooky journey by boat along the narrow rock-hewn gallery, during which associated legends are recounted; at one point any woman wanting to find a husband within the year is invited to rap on the wall. From Tarnowskie Góry train station, catch bus #1, #134, #614 or #780 to the end of the line.

Zabrze

Just east of Gliwice and served by regular Katowice–Gliwice trains, **Zabrze** was one of Upper Silesia's most prolific coal-producing cities, and the local skyline is still studded with the skeletal pithead structures of the mines.

Located in the southern suburbs of Zabrze, the **Guido Mine** (Kopalnia Guido: Wed–Fri 9am–2.30pm, Sat & Sun 9am–5pm; 22zł; ☎032/271 4077 extn 5183; ⓦwww.kopalniaguido.pl) was founded by Count Guido von Donnersmarck in 1855, and more or less exhausted by the 1940s. It was reopened for tourists in 2007. Once you've descended in rattling cage-lifts to a depth of 170m, the 90-minute tour takes in displays of mining machinery through the ages, and a re-creation of the underground stables where pit ponies spent their working lives. The mine is a twenty-minute walk south of Zabrze train station or brief trip on tram #3.

1921, and has been shrouded in patriotic mystique ever since. Focus of religious veneration is the sanctuary **church** (sanktuarium) at the summit of the hill, where a tiny statue of St Anne (mother of Mary) perches high above the main altar. It's a delightful piece of folksy Gothic carving, with the saint cradling Virgin and Child, both of whom are portrayed as chubby-faced infants. Below the monastery buildings is the mid-eighteenth century **calvary**, an elaborate processional way with 33 chapels and shrines telling the story of the Passion.

Góra św. Anny fell under German control after the partition of Upper Silesia in 1921, a fact celebrated by the Nazis just over a decade later with the construction of a huge hillside **amphitheatre** ten minutes' walk west of the church. Now crumbling and covered in weeds, this overblown venue for torch-lit parades and bombastic ritual still makes a mind-boggling impression. A mausoleum commemorating the German fallen of 1921 was demolished by the Poles after 1945, and replaced by an equally monumental cenotaph in honour of the other side. Further memories of the 1921 fighting are preserved in the **Museum of the Silesian Uprising** (Muzeum Czynu Powstańczego: Tues–Sun 9am–3pm; 6zł), 2km east of the village on the road to Leśnica, using blown-up photographs and colourful tableaux to conjure up a stirring sense of patriotic endeavour.

Góra świętej Anny is easy to visit under your own steam, lying just off the main Katowice–Wrocław highway. By **public transport**, take the train to the nondescript town of Strzelce Opolskie, 14km to the north (accessible by regular train from either Gliwice or Opole (from Katowice, change at Gliwice), and pick up one of seven buses a day to the village. The pleasantly rustic *Alba* **restaurant** on the village square serves inexpensive local food; while the next-door *Anna* offers pastas and salads, a gallery of graphic art, and comfortable **B&B accommodation** (☏077/461 5412, ⓦwww.pensjonatanna.pl; ❹) to boot.

Opole

Straddling the River Odra midway between Katowice and Wrocław, the medium-sized city of **OPOLE** has a brace of rewarding churches and an attractive riverside setting. The centre presents a well-balanced spread of old and new, ringed by a green belt and with the unsightly industrial installations banished to the outskirts. Originally settled by the Slavonic Opolane tribe in the ninth century, Opole was conquered by and fortified by the Polish Piast dynasty in the eleventh. As Oppeln, it was one of the cities that voted to remain part of Germany in the plebiscite of 1921, subsequently becoming the capital of the German province of Upper Silesia. In contrast to most other places ceded to Poland after World War II, the Opole region has retained a sizeable German minority, an asset that can be admitted now that Germany and Poland are partners in the European Union.

Arrival, information and accommodation

Opole's main **train and bus stations** are at the southern end of town close to the centre, just a few minutes along ulica Wojciecha Korfantego from the Wyspa Piaseka. The **tourist office** at ul. Krakowska 15 (Mon–Fri 10am–6pm, Sat 10am–1pm; ☏077/451 1987, ⓔpromocja@um.opole.pl) will give you the low-down on local **accommodation** possibilities. Best located of the city's four-stars is the comfortable *Piast*, ul. Piastowska 1 (☏077/454 9710, ⓦwww .hotel-piast.com; ❼), which has deep-carpeted en suites and a pleasant terrace overlooking the river. The *Weneda*, one kilometre east of the train and bus stations at ul. 1 Maja 77 (☏077/456 4499, ⓦwww.hotel-weneda.opole.pl; ❻), offers comfortable en suites with TV, although rooms are on the small side and come in odd colour combinations. Of the inexpensive places, the frumpy but tolerable *Zacisze*, in a residential area a short walk east of the centre at Grunwaldzka 28 (℡077/453 9553, Ⓦwww.hotel-zacisze.opole.pl; ❸–❹), offers a mixture of simply decorated, smallish rooms with en-suite or shared facilities.

The City

Opole's historical heart is the **Wyspa Piaseka**, an island in the middle of the Odra, but the city's hub has long moved to the river's right bank, where the central area is laid out on a gridiron pattern. Nonetheless, the island in many ways makes a historically appropriate place to begin an exploration.

The island

Of the four bridges crossing the arm of the river, look out for the second as you move northwards from the train station, one of several structures in Opole built around 1910 in Art Nouveau style. Arched like a bridge in a Japanese garden, this steel construction is known as the **Groschen Bridge** (Most Groszowy) after the fee that was initially charged for crossing it, the *Groschen* being the smallest coin then in circulation. Halfway across the bridge, take a glance in either direction: the thick lining of willow trees along the bank give an uncannily rural impression light years away from its urban location.

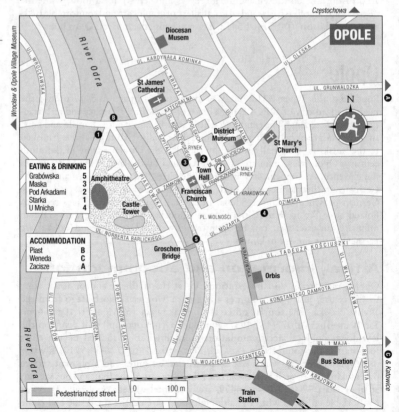

Originally occupying the middle of the island 400m north of the bridge, the medieval Piast **castle** hasn't been done any favours by the city planners, its surviving **round tower** now partly hidden behind the ugly 1930s council offices that were built over the ruins. The castle's grounds have been converted into a park with a large artificial lake and an open-air amphitheatre, the setting for the **Festival of Polish Song** – the Polish pop industry's most important annual showcase – held each June. Continuing north along ulica Piastowska, you get a good view of the Old Town on the opposite bank, lined with a jumble of riverside buildings.

The city centre

Returning across the Odra by ulica Zamkowa, you soon arrive at the Franciscan **church**, a much-altered Gothic construction chiefly remarkable for the richly decorated Chapel of St Anne, erected in 1309, off the southern side of the nave. Endowed by the local Piasts to serve as their **mausoleum**, it has an exquisite star vault painted with floral and heraldic motifs. The two magnificent double tombs were carved around 1380 by a member of the celebrated Parler family. Although he was still alive, an effigy of Duke Bolko III was made to accompany that of his recently deceased wife, with a similar monument created in belated memory of his two ancestral namesakes.

Immediately beyond the Franciscan monastery is the buzzing **Rynek**, some of whose cheerful mansions were badly damaged in World War II, but which have been deftly restored. A **town hall** has stood on the square since 1308, but the fine tower you see today – a wonderful pastiche of the Palazzo Vecchio in Florence – originates from a nineteenth-century neo-Renaissance design; it was rebuilt in the mid-1930s when it unexpectedly collapsed during repairs.

Housed in the former Jesuit college at ul. św. Wojciecha 13, just off the Rynek, is the **Regional Museum** (Muzeum Śląska Opolskiego: Tues–Fri 9am–3.30pm, Sat 10am–3pm, Sun noon–5pm; 3zł), whose main strength is its archeology section, with exhibits from prehistoric to early medieval times. Also worth looking out for are some tinted photographs from the early twentieth century showing the castle making way for the council offices, the town hall's tower reduced to a pile of rubble, and a chilling monochrome shot of Opole's synagogue ablaze on the Kristallnacht of 1938.

The cathedral quarter

From the Rynek, ulica Książąt Opolskich leads to **St James's Cathedral** (Katedra św. Jakuba), mixing fourteenth-century Gothic and nineteenth-century imitation with the usual Baroque excesses. Raised to the status of a cathedral only a couple of decades ago, the church, which soars with Gothic verticality, is chiefly famous for the allegedly miraculous, jewel-encrusted icon to the right of the main altar – the *Opole Madonna* crowned by a gaggle of gaily cavorting cherubs.

Occupying a block of modern buildings on ulica Książąt Opolskich (entrance round the corner on ul. Kardynała Kominka) is the **Diocesan Museum** (Muzeum Diecezjalne: Tues & Thurs 10am–noon & 2–5pm, first Sun of the month 2–5pm; 3zł). The ground floor features several outstanding Gothic sculptures, including an *Enthroned Madonna*, while upstairs pride of place is taken by a fourteenth-century reliquary made to house a fragment of the True Cross; there's also a lovely *Virgin and Child* attributed to Fra Filippo Lippi.

The Opole Village Museum

By the side of the main road to Wrocław, 8km west of the city centre at ul. Wrocławska 174, is the excellent **Opole Village Museum** (Muzeum Wsi

Opolskiej: mid-April to mid-Oct Tues–Sun 10am–6pm; mid-Oct to mid-April Mon–Fri 8am–2pm; 8zł). Some sixty examples of the wooden rural architecture of the region have been erected here, many grouped in simulation of their original environment. Particularly notable is the wooden church from Gręboszów built in 1613, a typical example of what is still the main place of worship in a few Silesian villages. Other highlights are a windmill and an eighteenth-century water mill in full working order, as well as an orchard full of beehives built in the same rustic idiom. The museum can be reached by bus #5 from Opole's main bus station.

Eating and drinking

Eating out in Opole is unspectacular, save for a handful of highly regarded establishments. Pick of the **restaurants** is the *Starka* at ul. Ostrówek 19, which offers an excellent range of central European pork chops and schnitzels on a riverside terrace. *U Mnicha*, Ozimska 10, serves up a mixture of domestic and Middle Eastern grill dishes in a rough-hewn cellar done up with hi-tech fittings. The order-at-the-counter *Grabówska* creperie, next to the Groschen Bridge at ul. Mozarta 2, serves the best pancakes in Silesia.

In summer the Rynek is alive with people **drinking** into the early hours: try the excellent *Maska*, a lively pub-style venue at Rynek 4 which also does restaurant-quality food. *Pod Arkadami*, on the corner of the Rynek and Krakowska, is a comfy wicker-chair-furnished **café** with decent coffee and excellent cakes.

Częstochowa and around

To get an understanding of the central role that Catholicism still holds in contemporary Poland, a visit to **CZĘSTOCHOWA**, 70km north of Katowice, is essential. Home to the famous icon know as the **Black Madonna**, the city-centre monastery of **Jasna Góra** (Clear Mountain) is one of the world's greatest places of pilgrimage. It's not a place you can react to dispassionately; indeed it's hard not to be moved as you overhear the faithful breaking into hymn as they shuffle between the Stations of the Cross, or watch pilgrims praying mutely before the icon they've waited a lifetime to see. Crowds are at their largest during the major Marian **festivals** – May 3, August 26, September 8, December 8 and most of all **August 15** (Assumption), when up to a million pilgrims converge. Many come on foot, with tens of thousands making the nine-day walk from Warsaw to celebrate the occasion.

Once you've seen Jasna Góra there's not a lot else to detain you in Częstochowa save for an out-of-town jaunt to the ruined fortress at **Olsztyn** (see p.475), and you'd do best to treat the city as a day-trip from Katowice, Kraków or Łódź rather than an overnight stay in its own right.

Some history

The modern city of Częstochowa grew up around the hilltop monastery of Jasna Góra, founded in 1382 by Duke Ladislaus II of Opole. Ladislaus donated the miraculous icon known as the Black Madonna a couple of years later, turning the monastery into a major focus for pilgrims. According to legend the Black Madonna was painted from life by Saint Luke on a beam from the Holy Family's house in Nazareth, although it is more likely to be of early medieval Italian origin. The black refers to the heavy shading used by the artist, subsequently darkened by age and exposure to incense. The image on show today may indeed

▲ Festival Mass at the Jasna Góra Monastery, Częstochowa

be a copy made in the 1430s following the icon's first great "miracle", when thieves attempted to steal the painting only to find that it increased in weight and could not be carried. In frustration the thieves slashed the Virgin's face, which immediately started shedding blood.

The monastery was fortified in the early **seventeenth century**, enabling Jasna Góra and its defenders to hold out against a numerically superior army of Swedes in 1655 – inspiring a national fightback against a foe who had all but extinguished Polish independence. This dramatic turn of fortune was attributed to the miracle-working powers of the Black Madonna, although the image wasn't actually here at the time – it had been removed to southern Silesia for safekeeping. The monastery was the scene of another heroic defence in 1770, when it was held by the Confederates of Bar against Russian forces.

After **World War II** Jasna Góra became a major focus of opposition to the communist regime. The Church skilfully promoted the pilgrimage as a display of patriotism and passive resistance, a campaign that received a huge boost in 1978 with the election of Karol Wojtyła, archbishop of Kraków and a central figure in its conception, as **Pope John Paul II**. His devotion to Jasna Góra ensured worldwide media attention for Częstochowa in particular and Poland in general, cementing the site's status as a national shrine.

Arrival, information and accommodation

The main exit of Częstochowa's Lego-like **train station** brings you out onto a neat plaza bordered by the **bus station** to the south. Turn right onto aleja Wolności to reach the town's main artery, a dead straight three-kilometre-long boulevard, aleja Najświętszej Marii Panny (usually abbreviated to NMP). The well-stocked and well-organized **tourist information centre** is at al. NMP 65 (Mon–Fri 9am–5pm, Sat 9am–2pm; ℡034/368 2250, ⓦwww .czestochowa.pl).

As you'd expect, there's a fair choice of **hostel** accommodation geared to pilgrims, best of which is offered by the large and well-organized *Dom Pielgrzyma* at ul. Wyszyńskiego 1 (☏034/377 7564), north of the car park on the west side of the monastery, where you can stay in four-person dorms (25zł per person) or prim en-suite doubles (❸). Of the **hotels**, try the *Sekwana*, ul. Wieluńska 24 (☏034/324 6367, ⓦsekwana.pl; ❹), a small, intimate place in a good location immediately north of the monastery complex. There's a **campsite**, *Camping Oleńka*, with a few bungalows (❶) in an ideal spot on the west side of the monastery's car park at ul. Oleńki 22/30 (☏034/360 6066, ⓦwww.mosir.pl).

The monastery

Aleja NMP cuts through the modern commercial heart of Częstochowa, terminating at the foot of **Jasna Góra** (ⓦwww.jasnagora.pl). A green swathe of public park girdles the lower reaches of the hill, above which protrude the monastery's seventeenth-century battlements and a rather more modern podium for open-air Masses. Visitors enter the complex via the south gate, beyond which lies a visitor **information centre** (daily: May–Sept 7.30am–7pm; Oct–April 8am–5pm), run by nuns and, usefully, complete with an ATM.

The tower and the church

The best way to begin an exploration is to ascend the hundred-metre-high **tower** (May–Sept daily 8am–4pm), a pastiche of its eighteenth-century predecessor, which was destroyed in one of the many fires which have plagued the monastery. An earlier victim was the monastic **church**, which has been transformed from a Gothic hall into a restrained Baroque basilica, now without pews, to make room for more pilgrims – not that it's without its exuberant features, notably the colossal high altar in honour of the Virgin and the two sumptuous family chapels off the southern aisle.

The Chapel of the Miraculous Image

Understandably, the **Chapel of the Miraculous Image** (Kaplica Cudownego Obrazu), a separate church in its own right, is the focal point of the monastery. It's also the only part to retain much of the original Gothic architecture, though its walls are so encrusted with votive offerings and discarded crutches and leg-braces that this is no longer obvious. Masses are said here almost constantly but you'll have to time it right if you want a view of the **Black Madonna**, a sight that should not be missed. Part of the time the icon is shrouded by a screen, each raising and lowering of which presumably exists to add a certain dramatic tension and is accompanied by a solemn trumpet fanfare. When it's on view (Mon–Fri 6am–noon & 1.30–9pm, Sat & Sun 6am–1pm & 2–9pm), only the faces and hands of the actual painting are visible (the Virgin's countenance being famously dour) as the figures of the Madonna and Child are always "dressed" in varying sets of jewel-encrusted robes that glitter all the more impressively against the black walls.

The museums

Jasna Góra's treasures are kept in three separate buildings, each of which is open daily from 9am to 5pm. At the southwestern end of the monastery is the **Arsenał**, devoted to the military history of the fortress and containing a superb array of weapons, including Turkish war loot donated by King Jan Sobieski. Nearby, the **Treasury of National Memory** (Skarbiec Pamięci Narodu) contains a fascinating collection of Solidarity banners from the 1980s, and a diorama (complete with model soldiers) illustrating the Swedish siege of 1655.

A few doors up is the **Six Hundredth Anniversary Museum** (Muzeum Sześćsetlecia), which tells the monastery's story from a religious standpoint. Exhibits include the seventeenth-century backing of the Black Madonna, with panels illustrating the history of the picture, and votive offerings from famous Poles, prominent among which is Lech Wałęsa's 1983 Nobel Peace Prize certificate, along with the oversized pen he used to sign the landmark August 1980 Gdańsk Agreements (see p.625). Finally, it's worth strolling around the ramparts to the eastern end of the complex, which is where the big festival Masses are celebrated before the crowds of pilgrims assembled in the park below, as evidenced by the large rock stadium-style platform in place during the spring and summer.

Eating and drinking

The *Dom Pielgrzyma* hostel, just outside the Jasna Góra complex, has a sizeable self-service café-restaurant catering for the needs of most day-trippers. There's a large choice of places along aleja NMP, including *Baraonda*, at no. 55, which serves pasta, pizza and fish dishes in a quirky interior that mixes folksy wooden sculpture with wall-mounted drum kits and other bric-a-brac, and *Blikle*, at no. 49, the place to treat yourself to top-quality pastries and cake. Nearby, *Café Skrzynka*, at ul. Dąbrowskiego 1, is the place to go for sweet and savoury pancakes. For drinking, *Szafa Gra*, al. NMP 37, in a courtyard off the main street, is a cosy café-bar popular with a local student crowd.

Olsztyn

Thirteen kilometres southeast of Częstochowa, the village of **OLSZTYN** (bus #58 or #67 from ul. Piłsudskiego) is dominated by the grizzled remains of a fourteenth-century **castle** – the northernmost link in the chain of fortifications built by King Kazimierz III and nowadays known as the Eagles' Nest Trail (see p.418). Laid to waste during the Swedish "Deluge" of the 1650s, it sits atop a limestone ridge scaled easily via a path from the village Rynek. Unusually, the castle was laid out in two parts, with a round watchtower crowning one outcrop of rock, and a keep on top of another; from the ruins of each there's a superb view over the whole region, the effect heightened by the winds buffeting the place most of the time. Back down in the village, a brightly painted private house just off the Rynek hosts the **Mobile Crib** (Ruchoma Szopka), a variation on the Christmas-Crib theme which features hundreds of wooden figures in motion – folk dancers dancing, ironmongers hammering, and so on – made by local artisan Jan Wewiór.

The best **place to eat** is the *Spichlerz*, located in a meadow 500m east of the castle (it's a long way round by road from the village), a nineteenth-century thatched-roof granary moved timber by timber from a nearby village and pressed into service as a top-notch and none-too-expensive traditional Polish restaurant.

The Silesian Beskids

Running along Silesia's border with the Czech Republic, the **Silesian Beskids** (Beskid Śląski) present an archetypal central European mountain landscape characterized by fir-clad slopes reaching up towards bald summits. It is a region of wooden churches, folk costumes, occasional castles and manageable hikes. The industrial city of **Bielsko-Biała** is the main entry point to the region, although this is a place in which to change buses to more enticing destinations rather than a resort in its own right. To its south is **Szczyrk**, the main hiking and skiing resort, though nearby **Ustroń** and **Wisła** provide equally rewarding base camps for highland hikes. Perhaps the best base from which to tour the region is **Cieszyn**, a historic market town which commands onward routes into the Czech Republic. If you're travelling towards the Beskid region from Katowice, the outstanding palace museum in **Pszczyna** makes an unmissable stopover on the way.

Pszczyna

About forty minutes from Katowice by train, and the same number of kilometres by road, the small town of **PSZCZYNA** is dominated by the eight-eenth-century **ducal palace** that stands in the town centre, a kilometre west of the train and bus stations. Occupying the western side of a handsome Rynek lined with fine mansions, the palace originated as a Piast hunting lodge in the twelfth century. Sold to the Promnitz family in the sixteenth century, it was transformed into an aristocratic residence in the Renaissance style before under-going a thorough Baroque rebuild following a fire. The palace was subsequently taken over by the Hochbergs, one of Germany's richest families, who expanded it and added the English-style park that extends behind. Stunningly refurbished, it now houses the **Palace Museum** (Muzeum Zamkowe: April–June, Sept & Oct Mon 11am–3pm, Tues 10am–3pm, Wed 9am–5pm, Thurs & Fri 9am–4pm, Sat 10am–4pm, Sun 10am–5pm; July & Aug Mon 11am–3pm, Tues 10am–3pm, Wed–Fri 9am–5pm, Sat 10am–5pm, Sun 10am–6pm; Nov–March Tues 11am–3pm, Wed 9am–4pm, Thurs & Fri 9am–3pm, Sat 10am–3pm, Sun 10am–4pm; 12zł; ⓦwww.zamek-pszczyna.pl), which features furniture and historic artefacts rescued from stately homes all over Silesia.

Much of the ground floor is taken up with the so-called **Royal Apartments** (Apartamenty Cezarskie), where Kaiser Wilhelm of Germany – together with much of his general staff – took up residence during World War I. His bedroom, dressing room and office have been faithfully re-created, with photographs of the likes of Ludendorff and Hindenburg recalling the strategic brainstorming sessions that took place here.

Ascending the aptly named Grand Staircase bordered by its stone balustrade, past a green serpentine vase used to hold wine at feasts, tapestries with stucco borders and marble sculptures, you reach the apartments designed for Princess Daisy von Pless, an English lady from the Cornwallis-West family who married head Hochberg, Prince Hans Heinrich XV, in 1891. There are some lovely portraits of Princess Daisy, and a room full of the antlers formerly belonging to beasts butchered by Heinrich himself, a keen hunter. The highlight, however, comes when you have passed through the prince's apartments and library and reach the stunning **Chamber of Mirrors**. At each end of the hall, huge mirrors in gilded brass frames create an impression of a much larger room, embellished by crystal chandeliers hung from a ceiling depicting a swirling sky. Splendidly ornate balconies look down onto the chamber from the second-floor gallery, while murals depicting the four seasons and the signs of the zodiac are squeezed in between the gilded stucco decoration. Subsequent rooms include an Art Nouveau dining room, a mirror gallery, and a charming billiard-room, while the final point of interest inside is the **Hunting Gallery** (Galeria Myśliwska), hung with still more antlers and half a wild boar leaping out of the wall.

Behind the castle lies the extensive landscaped **park**, with small lakes spanned by a sequence of gracefully arching bridges. A special enclosure in the west of the park is grazed by a herd of bison, raised at the reserve of Jankowice 7km southeast of town. Heading east through the park will bring you onto ulica Dworcowa and (eventually) back to the train and bus stations, but not before first passing a small **skansen** of reassembled rural buildings brought here from locations throughout the Beskids (Tues–Sun 10am–3pm; 5zł). There's a farmhouse filled with hand-painted furniture and a granary containing carriages, a sleigh and an Art Nouveau hearse.

Practicalities

From the **train** and **bus stations** it's a ten-minute walk to the town's Rynek. The helpful **tourist office**, just off the Rynek in the palace gateway (Mon–Fri 8am–4pm, Sat & Sun 10am–3pm; ☏032/210 1155, ⓦwww.pszczyna .pl), advises on accommodation as well as selling local maps and souvenirs. Best **places to stay** are the *Zamkowy*, Rynek 20 (☏032/449 1720, ⓦwww .hotelzamkowy.eu; ⑥), with fully equipped rooms in warm colours, and the *Michalik*, midway between the stations and the palace at ul. Dworcowa 11 (☏032/210 1355, ⓦwww.umichalika.com.pl; ④), offering small but bright rooms with contemporary furnishings, shower and TV.

Best of the **restaurants** is the *Stara Piekarnia* on the ground floor of the *Zamkowy* hotel, serving good-quality Polish classics, with goose a speciality. *Café u Telemanna*, in the palace gateway, is as cosy a place as any for a quick **drink** and cake; its name is a reminder that Baroque composer Georg Philipp Telemann was once kapellmeister at Pszczyna.

Bielsko-Biała

A further 25km south of Pszczyna, at the foot of the Beskids, lies **BIELSKO-BIAŁA**, formerly two separate towns divided by the River Biała which were united in 1951 and now form one seamless whole. Both towns were major centres of textile production in the nineteenth century and remain overwhelmingly industrial. Bielsko-Biała's appeal lies chiefly in its proximity to the Beskid Mountains, which rise suddenly from the city's southern outskirts; the town has easy bus connections to both the mountain resort of

Szczyrk and market town of Cieszyn, either of which makes a more attractive place to stay than Bielsko-Biała itself.

The city centre

The modern city's bustling shopping and commercial districts are in **Biała**, just east of plac Bolesława Chrobrego, although it's in **Bielsko** immediately uphill to the west that most of the historic sights are concentrated. Perched on a knoll is the grey bulk of Bielsko's **castle**, formerly occupied by the Dukes of Cieszyn and rebuilt as a nineteenth-century office block before being taken over by the **Regional Museum** (Muzeum Okręgowe; Tues & Wed 9am–3pm, Thurs 10am–5pm, Fri 9am–5pm, Sat 10am–3pm, Sun 10am–4pm; 7zł). A varied display embraces weaponry through the ages, models of the castle as it looked in various past epochs, and a picture gallery strong on pre-World War I Polish work, including Piotr Stachiewicz's dreamy *Pocałunek* ("The Kiss"; 1910), one of the most frequently reproduced paintings of the era. Beyond the museum lies a small **Rynek** overlooked by the unusual **St Nicholas's Cathedral** (Katedra św. Mikołaja), its eccentric twentieth-century belfry providing the city with its most visually striking landmark.

Practicalities

The main **bus and train stations** are in the northern part of Bielsko, from which it's a fifteen-minute walk down ul. 3 Maja to the busy and central plac Bolesława Chrobrego. A left turn here will bring you in five minutes to the centre of Biała, where the **tourist office**, opposite the town hall at pl. Ratuszowy 2 (Mon–Fri 8am–6pm, Sat 8am–4pm; ☎033/819 0050, ⊛www.it.bielsko.pl), is well supplied with accommodation listings and other local information.

There's a wide range of places to **eat and drink**, most of them in Biała. The Sfera shopping centre, on ulica Mostowa, is full of coffee bars and snack-stops, while *Nirvana*, Cechowa 18, is a laid-back café specializing in tasty inexpensive vegetarian food. The *Pod Jemiołami* restaurant, at ul. Cechowa 6, serves up everything from *pierogi* to wild boar in a wood-beamed interior with traditional fireplaces and herbs hanging from the rafters. Equally pleasant is *Nowy Świat*, ul. 11 Listopada 25, offering a mixture of traditional Polish and modern European cuisine in a sequence of plant-filled, glass-fronted rooms.

Szczyrk

Fifteen kilometres southwest of Bielsko-Biała, the long, straggling village of **SZCZYRK** is the main resort of the Beskids, popular with hikers in summer and offering some pretty demanding **downhill skiing** in winter. If you're heading for the hills, the locally available *Beskid Śląski i Żywiecki* (1:75,000) **map** will come in very handy.

Fifteen minutes' walk southwest of the bus station, an all-year-round two-stage **chairlift** (8.30am–5.30pm; return 16zł) runs to the summit of **Skrzyczne** (1245m), the highest peak in the range, where there's the usual refuge and restaurant; opposite is the 1117-metre peak of Klinczok, with the conurbation of Bielsko-Biała beyond. The energetic alternative to the chairlift is to slog up either the blue or the green trail for a couple of hours from Szczyrk; the latter trail continues south to Barania Góra (1220m), the source of the **River Wisła**, Poland's greatest waterway, which winds a serpentine 1090-kilometres course through Kraków, Warsaw and Toruń before disgorging itself into the Baltic near Gdańsk.

Szczyrk's **bus station** is roughly at the midpoint of its single street. Get off the bus here – otherwise you'll end up several kilometres away at the final stop, in the town's westernmost reaches. The **tourist information office**, just up from the bus station at ul. Beskidzka 41 (☎033/815 8388, ⓦwww.szczyrk.pl), will direct you towards private rooms (❶) and pensions (❸) and sells local hiking maps. *Pensjonat Koliba*, right by the Skrzyczne chairlift at ul. Skośna 17 (☎033/817 9930, ⓦkoliba.szczyrk.com.pl; ❹), is a good-value source of simple en suites with TV and breakfast; while the *Willa Bianka*, ul. Górska 10 (☎033/817 8455, ⓦwww.willabianka.pl; ❺), offers bright pine-furnished rooms in a traditional half-timbered villa. Plusher still is the *Klimczok*, 3km west of the centre at Poziomkowa 20 (☎033/826 0100, ⓦwww.klimczok.pl; ❽), which looks like a cross between an alpine chalet and a corporate headquarters; it's very much the winter resort hotel of choice, featuring a restaurant, pub, swimming pool and disco. The *Skalite* **campsite** at ul. Kempingowa 4 (☎033/817 8760) is clearly visible from the roadside when entering the village from the Bielsko-Biała direction.

Plenty of **snack bars** line Szczyrk's main road, and there are several good **restaurants** specializing in filling Polish cuisine: *Stara Karczma*, ul. Myśliwska 2, offers filling meat-and-potato dishes in a wooden-hut environment, complete with antlers, boar skins and wait-staff in traditional costume. Another timber-cabin restaurant, the *Silveretta* at ul. Myśliwska 8, offers a something-for-everybody mix of kebabs, traditional Polish dishes and pizzas.

Cieszyn

Straddling the Czech frontier 35km west of Bielsko-Biała, **CIESZYN** has the kind of attractive market squares, cobbled streets and well-preserved buildings that most other towns of Upper Silesia conspicuously lack. It's also fairly unusual in being a town that's shared between two countries: with both Czechoslovakia and Poland laying claim to Cieszyn in the wake of World War I, the town was split in two, with the river Olza forming the frontier. The medieval centre, complete with Rynek and castle, fell to the Poles, while the Czechs had to make do with the suburb (now known as Český Těšín) on the opposite side of the river. The division cut across family boundaries and left estranged nationals on either side of the frontier. Nowadays, with both Poland and the Czech Republic belonging to the borderless Schengen zone of the EU, people are free to wander where they wish: in Cieszyn you can sightsee on one side of the border, and eat and drink on the other. It's also an excellent base for onward travel, with three daily trains running from the Czech side of town to Prague.

Arrival, information and accommodation

Cieszyn's **bus** and **train stations** are on the eastern side of town. It's about ten minutes' walk uphill to the Rynek, where the well-organized **tourist office** (Miejskie Centrum Informacji: Mon 10am–6pm, Tues–Sat 8am–6pm; ☎033/479 4249, ⓦwww.cieszyn.pl) will provide you with pretty much everything you need to know about the town.

There's a reasonable range of **hotel** accommodation in town, as well as the *Olza* **campsite**, attractively situated beside the river, a 25-minute walk south of the centre at al. Łyska 13 (☎033/852 0833), with plenty of woodland walks on its doorstep.

Akademikus ul. Paderewskiego 6 ☎033/854 6139, ✉zajazd@admc.us.edu.pl. Student hostel-cum-hotel attached to the Silesian University campus 1km east of the bus and train stations. Simply decorated rooms with shower and TV. ❸

Central Nádražní 16, on the Czech side of town opposite Český Těšín train station ☎+420 558 713 113, ⓦwww.hotel-central.cz. Unexciting but adequate en suites with TV and wi-fi internet, plus a ground-floor Mexican restaurant that gets lively at weekends. Polish złotys aren't accepted, but

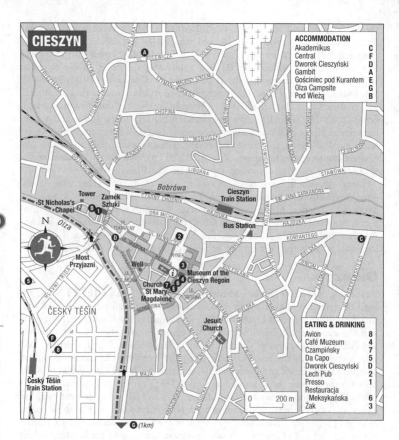

CIESZYN

ACCOMMODATION

Akademikus	C
Central	F
Dworek Cieszyński	D
Gambit	A
Gościniec pod Kurantem	E
Olza Campsite	G
Pod Wieżą	B

EATING & DRINKING

Avion	8
Café Muzeum	4
Czampiński	7
Da Capo	5
Dworek Cieszyński	D
Lech Pub	2
Presso	1
Restauracja Meksykańska	6
Żak	3

credit cards will do fine. 650–950 Kč, depending on size.

Dworek Cieszyński ul. Przykopa 14 ☏033/858 1178, ⓦwww.dworekcieszynski.pl. A handful of cosy rooms above the restaurant of the same name, just below the town centre and near the riverbank. ❹

Gambit ul. Bucewicza 18 ☏033/852 0651, ⓦwww.hotelgambit.com.pl. Concrete lump a 15min walk north of the stations which is actually quite nice once you get inside. Simply furnished en suites, some with ravishing views of the surrounding hills. ❸

Gościniec pod Kurantem ul. Srebrna 7 ☏033/851 8522, ⓦpodkurantem.com. Cosy pension in an alleyway off the Rynek with a handful of doubles and one triple. ❹

Pod Wieżą ul. Zamkowa 3B ☏600/591 241 and 695/946 807, ⓔbakochan@neostrada.pl. Simply decorated guest rooms in the administrative building opposite Cieszyn's castle tower. No breakfast, but there is a communal kitchen. ❸

The Town

Cieszyn's central **Rynek**, with the eighteenth-century town hall, stands at the highest point of the central area. Just off its southwest corner is the Gothic **Church of St Mary Magdalene** (Kościół św. Marii Magdaleny), containing a mausoleum of (yet more) Piast dukes who established an independent principality here in 1290. Heading east from the Rynek along Regera brings you to a handsome eighteenth-century mansion, former residence of the princes of Cieszyn and now home to the **Museum of the Cieszyn Region** (Muzeum Śląska Cieszyńskiego:

Tues–Sun 10am–2.30pm; 6zł). Inside lies an attractively laid out assemblage of art and furniture through the ages, and one room devoted to the museum's nineteenth-century founder, Jesuit priest Jan Leopold Szersznik, whose collection – including everything from Japanese clogs to mammoth's teeth – is displayed in the cabinet-of-curiosities style in which he left it. Among the lovingly restored period interiors are a ballroom decorated with Arcadian landscape paintings and plaster cherubs riding on goat-back, and a richly decorated stable built by horse-mad aristocrat Filip Saint-Genois d'Anneaucourt (who bought the mansion in 1831), which now serves as the museum café (see below).

Running west from the Rynek, Cieszyn's main street, **ulica Głęboka**, sweeps downhill from the Rynek towards the river, passing a sequence of imposing mansions on the way. If you take ulica Sejmowa to the left and then the first turning right, you'll find yourself on ulica Trzech Braci ("Street of the Three Brothers"). Here stands the **well** associated with the legend of the town's foundation. In the year 810, the three sons of King Leszko III met at this spring after a long spell wandering the country. They were so delighted to see each other again that they founded a town and named it "I'm happy" (*cieszym się*). From the foot of ulica Głęboka, it's only a few paces along ulica Zamkowa to the **Most Przyjazni** (Friendship Bridge), which leads across the river to the Czech part of town.

A little further up ulica Zamkowa and to the west rises a hill crowned by a fourteenth-century Gothic **tower** (daily: April 9am–5pm; May & Sept 9am–6pm; June–Aug 9am–7pm; Nov–March 9am–4pm), the only surviving part of the Piast palace. From the top, there's a superb view over both sides of the town and the Beskidy beyond. Alongside stands one of the oldest surviving buildings in Silesia, the **Chapel of St Nicholas** (Kaplica św. Mikołaja), a handsome Romanesque rotunda dating back to the eleventh century, with the vestiges of a well from the same period in front of it. The administrative buildings opposite the rotunda (formerly a Habsburg hunting lodge) now house the **Zamek Sztuki** (Art Castle: daily 10am–5pm), an attractive gallery space hosting some of the best art exhibitions in Silesia, with the emphasis on contemporary design.

Eating and drinking

There are plenty of places to drink coffee and eat cakes on and around Cieszyn's main square. With Český Těšín only ten minutes' walk away, it's likely that you'll want to sample the eating and drinking possibilities there too – although be warned that you won't be able to spend Polish złotys on the Czech side of the river.

Cieszyn

Café Muzeum Museum of the Cieszyn Region. Refined spot in the ornate nineteenth-century stable building of the Cieszyn Museum – it's entered from the courtyard. Pots of tea, top-notch coffee and hot chocolate, and a good choice of cakes. Daily 10am–8pm.

Czampińsky ul. Srebrna 14. Despite calling itself a "kebab beer lounge" (whatever that may be), this is essentially a youth-oriented pub which serves grilled meats on the side. Good choice of bottled beers. Daily 10am–11pm.

Dworek Cieszyński ul. Przykopa 14. A good place to tuck into traditional meat and fish dishes in a suite of comfortable dining rooms. With mains in the 25–35zł range, it's not too pricey. Daily 11am–10pm.

Lech Pub Rynek 12. Main-square drinking venue, with cast-iron partitions and curving banquettes providing a snug and intimate feel. Daily 9am–midnight.

Presso ul. Zamkowa. Arty café next to the Zamek Sztuki gallery, with designer couches, tea, coffee and the odd cake. Wi-fi access. Daily 9am–9pm, till 10pm Fri & Sat.

Restauracja Meksykańska ul. Srebrna 3. Comfortable place offering a familiar-looking menu of Mexican-themed food, alongside a few Polish dishes. Daily noon–midnight.

Żak Rynek 20. Cosy main-square dining venue decked out to look like granny's parlour, offering a classy pork- and chicken-based repertoire at moderate prices, and some good pasta dishes. Daily 11am–11pm.

Český Těšín

Avion corner of Nádražní and Czapkova. Bright and friendly coffee-and-cake venue just across the road from Český Těšín train station. Mon–Sat 10am–10pm, Sun 11am–7pm.

Da Capo Sokola tumny. Italian restaurant with rustic interior offering steaks, grilled fish and pasta dishes as well as satisfying pizzas. A cut above similar places on the Polish side of the border, and the beer is better too. Daily 11am–11pm.

Along the Wisła valley: Ustroń, Wisła and around

Due west from Szczyrk the valley of the Wisła River provides the perfect niche for a string of highland resorts. They can be reached by car direct from Szczyrk via a scenic road that heads west from the village and zigzags its way over the hills before dropping down into Wisła. Otherwise they're best accessed by bus from Cieszyn.

Ustroń

Roughly parallel with Szczyrk and 5km south of the main road from Bielso-Biała to Cieszyn, the spa resort of **USTROŃ** is at first sight a futuristic-looking place, with a cluster of glass-fronted, pyramid-shaped hotels sprouting from the forested hillside on the eastern side of town. The town centre doesn't amount to much save for a single street, although there's an attractive riverside park and an engaging **Museum of Metallurgy** (Muzeum Hutnictwa i Kuźnictwa; Tues 9am–5pm, Wed–Fri 9am–2pm, Sat 9am–1pm, Sun 9.30am–1pm; 4zł), where ancient steam-hammers and various water-powered machines provide mute testimony to Ustroń's erstwhile role as a major iron-working centre.

Hikers are drawn to Ustroń by its proximity to one of the most popular peaks in the Beskids, **Równica** (884m), just to the east. It can be reached by the red trail, well signposted from the car park-cum-bus stop in the middle of the resort, or you can try to negotiate a vehicle up the tortuous mountain road. A second recommended hike in the area is southwest from Ustroń by the blue route, which follows the main street south before darting uphill towards **Czantoria** (995m), right on the Czech frontier.

Practicalities

Buses from Cieszyn pick up and drop off on the main street, a few steps away from the **tourist office** (Mon–Fri 8.30am–5pm, Sat 8.30am–1pm; ☏033/854 2653, ⊛www.ustron.pl) at Rynek 2, which will sort you out with a **private room** in the centre of Ustroń (❶), or send you up to one of the pyramid-shaped **hotels**, spread across forest-fringed meadows. Both the *Jaskółka*, ul. Zdrojowa 10 (☏033/854 4840, ⊛www.jaskolka.com.pl; ❻), and the *Wilga*, ul. Zdrojowa 7 (☏033/854 3311, ⊛www.wilga.beskidy.pl; ❻), offer comfortable, modernized en suites with great views of the hills, providing you insist on a south- or east-facing room. *Café Chopin*, on the opposite side of the road to the tourist office, is the place to tuck into cakes and ice cream, and there are several fried-fish **restaurants** grouped near the river just to the east.

Wisła

Six kilometres upriver from Ustroń, **WISŁA** is another long, thin village clinging to either side of the valley-bottom road. An unpretentious socialist-era health resort favoured by holiday-makers from the Katowice conurbation, its main appeal to the independent traveller is as a staging-post en route to the mountain villages further south rather than as a destination in its own right. Wisła's principal modern-day claim to fame is that it's the home town of ski jumper Adam Małysz, three-times individual world champion (most recently in 2007) and now national folk hero – the village's shops are full of Małysz-related souvenirs.

The only sight of interest in town is the **Beskid Museum** (Muzeum Beskidzkie; Tues, Thurs & Fri 9am–3pm, Wed 9am–5pm, Sat & Sun 10am–2pm; 3zł), just off the main square, plac B. Hoffa, which displays agricultural implements, folk costumes and examples of the goatskin bagpipes on which the local herders used to tootle away. The best **hike** from Wisła is along the yellow trail that strikes southeast from the southern end of the resort to **Stożek** (978m), a fine vantage point which forms part of the border with the Czech Republic, and which has a pleasant chalet-type **hostel** near the summit, the *Schronisko na Stożku*.

Practicalities

Wisła's **bus station** is at the northern end of the village, just short of the long pedestrianized strip that leads to plac B. Hoffa. The **tourist office**, pl. B. Hoffa 3 (Mon–Fri 9am–4pm, Sat & Sun 9am–1pm; ☎033/816 6566), is a good place to pick up information on the region and buy maps. Wistour (Mon–Fri 10am–6pm, Sat 10am–8pm, Sun 10am–2pm; ☎033/855 2167, ⓦwww .rezerwacja-wisla.pl), near the bus station at ulica Wodna can find **accommodation** in private rooms (❶) and pensions (❸) in Wisła and in villages further south towards Istebna (see below). The *Inna Epocha* **café-restaurant**, in a beautifully restored nineteenth-century hunting lodge next to the bus station, is a good place for a bite to eat before moving on.

South of Wisła: Istebna and Jaworzynka

The road south from Wisła heads up into some attractive highland terrain, with the traditional village architecture of settlements like **Istebna** and **Jaworzynka** offering an agreeable antidote to the comparative greyness of Wisła. Both villages are served by about twelve buses a day from Wisła, fewer at weekends.

The Kubalonka Pass

Once beyond Wisła's southern outskirts the road winds steeply through the forested spurs of the Beskid Mountains, after about 8km reaching the **Kubalonka Pass** (Przełęcz Kubalonka), a popular starting point for ridge-top walks. The most popular itineraries for hikers are the well-signposted red-marked route heading east to the peak of **Przysłop** (1021m), with the Barania Góra (1220m) just beyond and, in the other direction, the hike to Stożek (see above). The *Zajazd u Mihola*, just beyond the pass's summit, is a popular **food and drink** stop with a panoramic terrace out the back. On the south side of the pass, the roadside **Church of the Holy Cross** (Kościół św. Krzyża) is a wonderful example of local building techniques, with heavy pine logs supporting a delicately shingled roof and cluster of plump domes.

Istebna

Three kilometres beyond the Church of the Holy Cross lies **ISTEBNA** (ⓦwww .ug.istebna.pl), a sleepy village spread over a sequence of pasture-filled bowls. Just east of the village centre on the Koniaków road, the timber-built **Izba Regionalna** (Regional Dwelling; enquire at the house opposite to gain admission) at Istebna 824 contains original nineteenth-century interiors and a fascinating collection of flutes, bagpipes and other instruments made by local craftsmen. Back on the main road, the *Szarotka* **hotel**, Istebna 467 (☎033/855 6018, ⓦwww .hotelszarotka.pl; ❺–❻), is a convenient touring base for this part of the Beskids, with comfy en-suite doubles, studio apartments and bike hire for guests.

Jaworzynka

Five kilometres south of Istebna the ridge-top village of **JAWORZYNKA** has a shop, a couple of cafés and wonderful views of pine-clad hills on either side. Lurking beside the main road, the **Na Grapie Museum** (Muzeum na Grapie: allegedly Mon–Sat 10am–4pm, although you might have to wait around for the curator) contains an absorbing display of local lace, embroidery and carved wooden toys. If Jaworzynka's end-of-the road location appeals, then consider staying at the *Hotel Jano*, just southeast of the village in the hamlet of Kręźelka (☎033/855 6320, ⓦwww.hoteljano.pl; ⑤), which offers chintzy rooms, an on-site gym and children's play area – all in mixed meadow and woodland surrounds. Three kilometres beyond Jaworzynka is the Czech border, although the nearest road crossing is 10km east at Mito/Zwardoń.

⑨ Travel details

Trains

Bielsko-Biała to: Cieszyn (8 daily; 1hr); Katowice (every 30min; 1hr 30min–2hr 30min); Pszczyna (every 30min; 30–50min).

Cieszyn to: Bielsko-Biała (8 daily; 1hr).

Częstochowa to: Katowice (hourly; 1hr 30min–2hr); Kielce (8 daily; 2hr); Kraków (2 daily; 2–3hr); Łódź (4 daily; 2–3hr); Warsaw (8 daily; 3–4hr).

Gliwice to: Katowice (every 30min; 20min); Strzelce Opolskie (hourly; 40min).

Katowice to: Bielsko-Biała (every 30min; 1hr 30min–2hr 30min); Częstochowa (hourly; 1hr 30min–2hr); Gliwice (every 30min; 20min); Jelenia Góra (3 daily; 7hr); Kielce (8 daily; 2hr 30min–3hr 30min); Kraków (hourly daily; 1hr 30min–2hr); Łódź (4 daily; 3hr 30min–5hr); Nysa (4 daily; 4hr); Opole (every 30min–1hr; 2hr); Poznań (12 daily; 5–7hr); Przemyśl (7 daily; 5hr 30min); Pszczyna (every 30min; 1hr–1hr 30min); Rzeszów (8 daily; 4–5hr); Szczecin (3 daily; 9–10hr); Wałbrzych (3 daily; 6hr); Warsaw (17 daily; 3hr 30min–5hr); Wrocław (21 daily; 2–3hr).

Opole to: Gliwice (every 30min–1hr; 1hr 30min); Katowice (every 30min–1hr; 2hr); Strzelce Opolskie (hourly; 50min); Wrocław (hourly; 2hr).

Buses

Bielsko-Biała to: Cieszyn (hourly; 1hr 10min); Kraków (12 daily; 3hr); Szczyrk (every 30min; 40min); Wisła (3 daily; 1hr 10min); Zakopane (3 daily; 3hr 30min).

Cieszyn to Bielsko-Biała (hourly; 1hr 10min); Katowice (Mon–Sat 15 daily, Sun 10 daily; 1hr 30min); Kraków (6 daily; 4hr); Ustroń (every 30min; 30min); Wisła (every 30min; 45min).

Katowice to: Bielsko-Biała (12 daily; 1hr 45min); Cieszyn (Mon–Sat 15 daily, Sun 10 daily; 1hr 30min); Kłodzko (3 daily; 5hr); Kudowa-Zdrój (2 daily; 5hr 50min)

Opole to: Kłodzko (3 daily; 3hr 40min); Nysa (12 daily; 2hr 20min).

Wisła to: Istebna (Mon–Fri 12 daily; Sat & Sun 5 daily; 25min); Jaworzynka (Mon–Fri 12 daily; Sat & Sun 5 daily; 35min).

International trains

Katowice to: Berlin (1 daily; 8hr); Ostrava (3 daily; 2hr 30min); Prague (3 daily; 4hr 30min); Vienna (1 daily; 9hr).

Lower Silesia

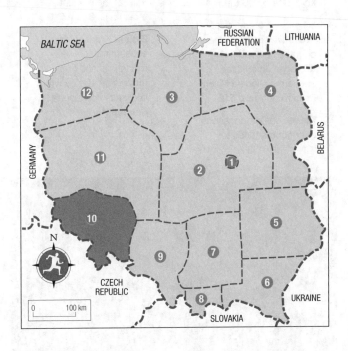

CHAPTER 10

Highlights

* **Wrocław** The main square of this boisterous, burgeoning city ranks with any in Poland. **See p.487**

* **Churches of Peace** The beautiful Unesco-listed timber-framed churches in Jawor and Świdnica are the largest of their kind. **See p.508 & p.511**

* **Książ** One of the most evocative castles in the country, perched fairy-tale-style on a hilltop above the winding River Pełcznica. **See p.512**

* **Riese** Tens of thousands of prisoners toiled to build this massive and mysterious underground complex for the Nazis. **See p.513**

* **Karpacz** Snugly situated in a narrow wooded valley, this popular holiday village is the gateway to the hiking trails of the Karkonosze mountains. **See p.518**

* **Ziemia Kłodzka** An enchanting area of rolling hills and fir-clad mountains, dotted with laid-back spa resorts. **See p.521**

▲ Wrocław main square

10

Lower Silesia

C hanging ownership several times between Poland, Bohemia and Prussia after first being conquered in 990 by Polish king Mieszko I, Lower Silesia was only definitely assigned to Poland in 1945, 24 years after the region around Katowice had joined. Mainly Germanic up till that point, most original inhabitants were expelled after the war, with the towns and villages repopulated by refugees originating from all corners of Poland, but especially from what is now western Ukraine. Although the original mix of cultures has been replaced by the Polish monoculture now, the region is **economically vibrant**, very beautiful in its southern reaches and delightfully **easy to get around** due to the Prussians' penchant for building railways everywhere.

The best place to begin exploring Lower Silesia is **Wrocław**, one of Poland's most attractive cities and an enticing cosmopolitan centre which combines modern commercial bustle with the attractions of a medieval Old Town. The landscape around Wrocław is largely made up of level, undramatic arable terrain, although old ducal capitals like **Legnica**, **Świdnica**, and **Brzeg** offer plenty in the way of historical interest.

For natural beauty, it's best to make a beeline for the mountains to the south and west – where the Sudety chain contains some of the most popular recreation areas in the country. Of these, the **Karkonosze national park** is the easiest to reach from Wrocław, with the regional centre of **Jelenia Góra** providing access to the skiing and hiking resorts of **Karpacz** and **Szklarska Poreba**. Slightly further east, the **Kłodzko region**'s outlying massifs provide some of Poland's best walking country, with refined old health resorts like **Kudowa-Zdrój**, **Lądek-Zdrój** and **Międzygórze** offering everything from spa treatments to winter sports.

Wrocław

Lower Silesia's historic capital, **WROCŁAW** is the fourth-largest city in Poland, with an exhilarating big city feel to it. However, behind this animated appearance lies an extraordinary story of ruin and regeneration. Its special nature comes from the fact that it contains the souls of two great cities. One of these is the city that has long stood on this spot, Slav by origin but for centuries German (who knew it as Breslau). The other is Lwów (now **L'viv**), capital of Polish Ukraine, which was annexed by the Soviets in 1939 and retained by them in 1945. After the war, its displaced population was encouraged to take over the

10

LOWER SILESIA | Wrocław

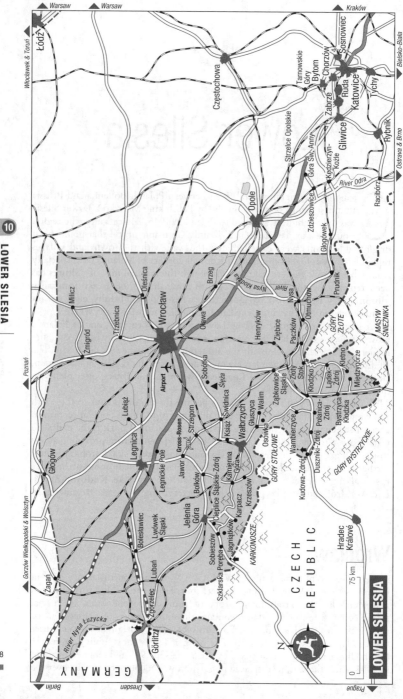

LOWER SILESIA

GERMANY

CZECH

REPUBLIC

N

0   75 km

Warsaw   Warsaw   Kraków

Łódź   Sosnowiec

Wrocławek & Toruń   Bielsko-Biała

Częstochowa

Tarnowskie
Góry   Chorzów   Bytom
Zabrze   Ruda   Katowice
Tychy
Gliwice
Strzelce Opolskie   Rybnik
Góra Św. Anny
Kętrzyn-
Koźle   Ostrava & Brno

River Odra

Zdzieszowice   Racibórz

Opole

Głogówek

Poznań

Brzeg

Oleśnica

Milicz

Żmigród

Trzebnica

Wrocław

Oława

Henryków

Ziębice

Paczków

Nysa River Kłodzka

Otmuchów

Prudnik

GÓRY
ZŁOTE

MASYW
ŚNIEŻNIKA

Złoty
Stok   Kletno
Kłodzko   Lądek-
Ząbkowice   Zdrój   Międzygórze
Śląskie   Polanica-   Bystrzyca
Świdnica   Ślęża   Zdrój   Kłodzka
Sobótka   Walim   Głuszyca   Duszniki-Zdrój   GÓRY BYSTRZYCKIE
Airport   Książ   Wałbrzych   Wambierzyce
Strzegom   Osówka   Kudowa-Zdrój
Gross-Rosen   GÓRY STOŁOWE

Lubiąż

Głogów

Legnica

Legnickie Pole   Jawor   Bolków   Kamienna
Lwówek   Góra   Krzeszów
Śląski   Jelenia   Cieplice Śląskie-Zdrój   Karpacz
Bolesławiec   Góra   Sobieszów   Jagniątków
Lubań   Szklarska Poręba   KARKONOSZE

Żagań

Zgorzelec   Hradec
Zgorzelec   Králové
Görlitz
River Nysa Łużycka

Gorzów Wielkopolski & Wolsztyn

Berlin   Dresden   Prague

severely depopulated Breslau, which had been confiscated from Germany and offered them a ready-made home.

Part re-creation of Lwów, part continuation of the tradition of Breslau, postwar Wrocław has a predominantly industrial character. However, there's ample compensation for this in the old city's core. The multinational influences which shaped it are graphically reflected in its architecture: the huge Germanic brick **Gothic churches** that dominate the Old Town are intermingled with Flemish-style Renaissance mansions, palaces and chapels of Viennese Baroque, and boldly utilitarian public buildings from the early years of the twentieth century. The tranquillity of the parks, gardens and rivers – which are crossed by more than one hundred **bridges** – offers a ready escape from the urban bustle, while the city has a vibrant cultural scene, its **theatre** tradition enjoying worldwide renown.

Some history

The earliest documentary evidence of Wrocław is a ninth-century record of a Slav market town called **Wratislavia** situated on a large island at the point where the sand-banked shallows of the River Odra were easily crossed. Subsequently, this became known as **Cathedral Island** (Ostrów Tumski) in honour of the bishopric founded here in 1000 AD by Bolesław the Brave.

German designs on Wratislavia came to the fore in 1109, when the army of Emperor Henry V was seen off by Bolesław the Wrymouth. This proved to be only a temporary setback to German ambitions. German settlers were soon encouraged to develop a new town on the southern bank of the river. Destroyed by the Tatars in 1241, this was soon rebuilt on the grid pattern that survives today. In 1259 the city, by now known as **Breslau**, became the capital of an independent duchy. It joined the Hanseatic League, and its bishop became a prince of the Holy Roman Empire of Germany.

The duchy lasted only until 1335, when Breslau was annexed by the **Bohemian kings**. During the two centuries of Bohemian rule the mixed population of Germans, Poles and Czechs lived in apparent harmony, and the city carried out the construction of its huge brick churches. Most of these were transferred to Protestant use at the Reformation, despite the Bohemian crown passing to the staunchly Catholic **Austrian Habsburgs** in 1526. Breslau's economy was devastated and its population halved during the Thirty Years' War.

The years of Austrian rule saw Breslau become increasingly Germanized, a process accelerated when it finally fell to Frederick the Great's **Prussia** in 1763, in time becaming Prussia's most important city after Berlin.

After World War I, Breslau's **Polish community** held a series of strikes in protest at their exclusion from the plebiscite held elsewhere in Silesia to determine the boundaries of Poland. Being only twenty thousand strong and outnumbered by thirty to one, their actions made little impact. Nor did Breslau figure among the targets of Polish leaders when looking for possible gains at the expense of a defeated Nazi Germany. In the event, they gained it by default. The Nazis made the suicidal decision, on retreating from the Eastern Front, to turn the entire city into a fortress. It managed to hold out for four months against the Red Army, only capitulating on May 6, 1945, the day before the unconditional surrender. However, street fighting had left seventy percent of the city in ruins, with three-quarters of the civilian population having fled west.

Rechristened with the modern Polish version of its original name, the city was subsequently returned to Poland. Most of the remaining German citizens were shunted westward, while the inhabitants of Lwów were transferred here across Poland, bringing many of their institutions with them.

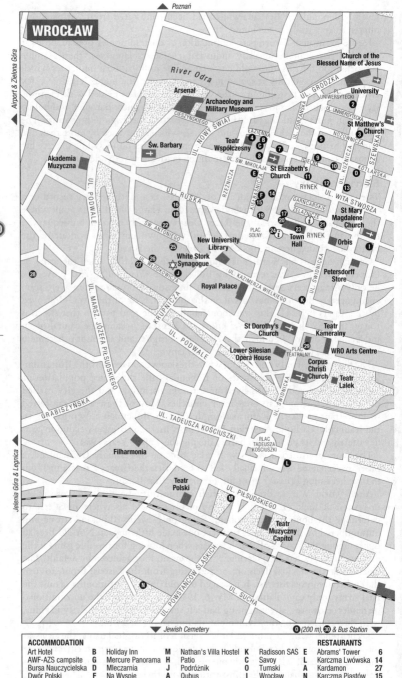

WROCŁAW

Poznań

River Odra

Airport & Zielona Góra

Jelenia Góra & Legnica

Church of the Blessed Name of Jesus

Arsenał

Archaeology and Military Museum

University

UL. GRÓDZKA

PL. UNIWERSYTECKI

UL. GARNCARSKA

UL. UNIWERSYTECKA

St Matthew's Church

Św. Barbary

Teatr Współczesny

Akademia Muzyczna

UL. PODWALE

UL. NOWY ŚWIAT

UL. ŚW. MIKOŁAJA

UL. RUSKA

RZEŹNICZA

KIEŁBAŚNICZA

UL. KUŹNICZA

NOZOWNICZA

KOTLARSKA

SZEWSKA

St Elizabeth's Church

RYNEK

UL. WITA STWOSZA

GARNCARSKIE

ŻELAZNICZE

St Mary Magdalene Church

Orbis

RYNEK

Town Hall

PLAC SOLNY

ŚW. ANTONIEGO

New University Library

White Stork Synagogue

UL. KAZIMIERZA WIELKIEGO

Royal Palace

UL. ŚWIDNICKA

Petersdorff Store

UL. MARSZ. JÓZEFA PIŁSUDSKIEGO

KRUPNICZA

UL. PODWALE

UL. WŁODKOWICA

St Dorothy's Church

Teatr Kameralny

PLAC TEATRALNY

Lower Silesian Opera House

Corpus Christi Church

WRO Arts Centre

Teatr Lalek

GRABISZYŃSKA

UL. TADEUSZA KOŚCIUSZKI

UL. ŚWIDNICKA

Filharmonia

PLAC TADEUSZA KOŚCIUSZKI

Teatr Polski

UL. PIŁSUDSKIEGO

Teatr Muzyczny Capitol

UL. POWSTAŃCÓW ŚLĄSKICH

UL. SUCHA

Jewish Cemetery

(200 m), 30 & Bus Station

ACCOMMODATION							RESTAURANTS	
Art Hotel	B	Holiday Inn	M	Nathan's Villa Hostel	K	Radisson SAS	E	Abrams' Tower	6
AWF-AZS campsite	G	Mercure Panorama	H	Patio	C	Savoy	L	Karczma Lwówska	14
Bursa Nauczycielska	D	Mleczarnia	J	Podróżnik	O	Tumski	A	Kardamon	27
Dwór Polski	F	Na Wyspie	A	Qubus	I	Wrocław	N	Karczma Piastów	15

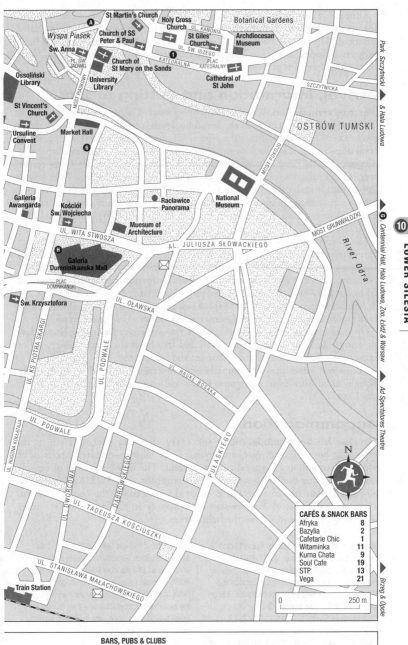

Although a relatively modest amount of government aid was made available for its **restoration**, a distinctive and thoroughly Polish city has gradually emerged. The local economy has boomed recently, with many infrastructural projects including the renovation of the city centre streets making Wrocław an increasingly pleasant place to visit.

Arrival, information and getting around

The main **train station**, Wrocław Główny – a mock-Tudor structure that is itself one of the city's sights – faces the broad boulevard of ulica Piłsudskiego, about twenty minutes' walk south of the centre. The main **bus station** (Dworzec PKS) is on ulica Sucha, at the back of the train station. Wrocław's Mikołaja Kopernika **airport** (⑦071/358 1381, ⑩www.airport.wroclaw.pl) which lies 10km to the west in the suburb of Strachowice, is linked to the centre by bus #406 (every 20–40min), which drops passengers off on ulica Podwale, near the Stare Miasto, before terminating on ulica Dworcowa just north of the train station. A central **taxi** rank is on ulica Wita Stwosza; otherwise try MPT ⑦9191 or Taxi Plus ⑦0601/700 753.

The helpful **tourist information** office at Rynek 14 (daily: April–Oct 9am–9pm; Nov–March 9am–8pm; ⑦071/344 3111, ⑩www.wroclaw-info.pl) has many maps and leaflets, and can book accommodation. Directly opposite at Sukiennice 12, the new **Tourist and Cultural Information Centre** (April–Oct Mon–Fri 8am–8pm, Sat & Sun 9am–9pm; Nov–March Mon–Fri 8am–7pm, Sat & Sun 8am–8pm; ⑦071/342 0185) has cultural information and sells tickets to concerts and events, offers free internet access and even has coffee to go.

Updated four times a year, the *Wrocław in Your Pocket* city guide (5zł; ⑩wroclaw .inyourpocket.com), available at hotels and free from the tourist office, is the most up-to-date source for the restaurant and bar scene.

Trams and **buses** provide comprehensive coverage for Wrocław. **Tickets** are bought in advance from newspaper kiosks and cost 2.40zł each; night services are 2.80zł.

Accommodation

Wrocław has **accommodation** to suit every taste and pocket. There is no especially busy time of year, and most of the business-oriented hotels offer weekend reductions of around twenty percent. The new generation of hostels offer good-value double rooms as well as dorm beds. The AWF-AZS **campsite** also has chalets (❷) to rent and is situated northeast of the centre near the Olympic Stadium at ul. Paderewskiego 35 (May–Sept; ⑦071/348 4651) – tram #17 (direction Sępolno) from the train station.

Around the train station

Holiday Inn ul. Piłsudskiego 49/57 ⑦071/787 0000, ⑩www.holiday-inn.com. The first Western hotel in town, with the standards of comfort and service that you would expect at this price. A short walk west of the train station. ❽

Podróżnik ul. Sucha 1-11 ⑦071/373 2845, ⑩www.podroznik.emeteor.pl. Simple no-frills place situated above the bus station's ticket hall, offering neat, if smallish, en suites. ❹

Savoy pl. Tadeusza Kościuszki 19 ⑦071/340 3219, ⑩www.savoy.wroc.pl. Simple, good-value en-suite rooms located midway between the train station and the Old Town. Reductions at weekends. ❹

Wrocław ul. Powstańców Śląskich 7 ⑦071/361 4651, ⑩www.orbisonline.pl. A prestigious Orbis hotel, located a short distance west of the main train station. Rooms are up to international business standard, and there's an indoor swimming pool. ❼

The Old Town

Art Hotel ul. Kiełbaśnicza 20 ⑦071/378 7100, ⑩www.arthotel.pl. Comfortable hotel with modern interiors and not a lot of art, but it's superbly situated just off the main square. Doubles are spacious and modern. **❼**–**❽**

Bursa Nauczycielska ul. Kotlarska 42 ☎071/344 3781, ⓦ www.dodn.wroclaw.pl/bursa. Plain but cheap rooms with 1970s furniture and shared bathrooms, right in the centre of town. No breakfast. **❸**

Dwór Polski ul. Kiełbaśnicza 2 ☎071/372 3415, ⓦ www.dworpolski.wroclaw.pl. Small and classy establishment offering quality service and well-equipped, atmospherically old-fashioned double rooms or suites. The house is said to be the place where King Zygmunta Waza of Poland had romantic trysts with future wife Anna von Habsburg. **❼**

Mercure Panorama pl. Dominikański 1 ☎071/323 2700, ⓦ www.orbisonline.pl. Flashy glass-and-steel four-star, conveniently attached to the Galeria Dominikańska mall on the eastern side of the centre. A reasonable business-standard choice. **❼**–**❽**

Patio ul. Kiełbaśnicza 24/25 ☎071/375 0400, ⓦ www.hotelpatio.pl. Bright, fully equipped rooms in a modern building, not too far from the main square. **❻**

Qubus ul. św. Marii Magdaleny 2 ☎071/797 9800, ⓦ www.qubushotel.com. New and rather plush hotel with attentive service, swimming pool and all creature comforts, a stone's throw from the main square. **❾**

Radisson SAS ul. św. Mikołaja 67 ☎071/358 8300, ⓦ www.sofitel.com. Classy modern hotel immediately west of the main square, offering fully equipped rooms decked out in calming colours. Sauna and gym on site. **❹**–**❻**

Tumski Wyspa Słodowa 10 ☎071/322 6088, ⓦ www.hotel-tumski.com.pl. Hotel just north of the town centre enjoying a quiet riverside location on Wyspa Piasek. Pastel-coloured rooms with shower and TV. **❼**

Hostels

Mleczarnia ul. Włodkowica 5 ☎071/787 7570, ⓦ www.mleczarniahostel.pl. Poland's most charming hostel, with lovely antique-furnished dorms (from 40zł) and doubles (**❺**), bike rental and a covered courtyard with rocking chairs.

Na Wyspie Wyspa Słodowa 10 ☎071/322 6099, ⓦ www.hotel-tumski.com.pl. Hostel in the *Tumski* hotel building with cramped but modern rooms sleeping up to 10 people. Dorm beds from 40zł; 25 percent off for HI members; 10pm curfew.

Nathan's Villa Hostel ul. Świdnicka 13 ☎071/344 1095, ⓦ www.nathansvilla.com.pl. Large and central hostel along a noisy road, with free laundry service, breakfast and more included in the price. Doubles **❺**, dorm beds from 45zł.

The City

Wrocław's **central area**, laid out in the usual grid pattern, is delineated by the **River Odra** to the north and by the bow-shaped **ulica Podwale** to the south – the latter following the former fortifications whose defensive moat, now bordered by a shady park, still largely survives. The main concentration of shops and places of entertainment is found at the southern end of the centre and in the streets leading south to the train station. Immediately bordering the Odra at the northern fringe of the centre is the **university quarter**. Beyond are a number of peaceful islets, formerly sandbanks where the shallow river was once forded, and now linked to each other and to the mainland by graceful little bridges that add a great deal to the city's appeal. The southern part of the much larger island of **Ostrów Tumski**, further east, is the city's ecclesiastical heart, with half a dozen churches and its own distinctive hubbub. Further north is an area of solidly nineteenth-century tenements, while the city's main green belt lies off the eastern side of the island.

The main square

Fittingly, the core of the Old Town's grid is occupied by the vast space of the **main square** (**Rynek**), surrounded by grandly renovated town houses. Its centre is taken up by the superb edifice of the **town hall**, and an accompanying ensemble of municipal buildings divided up by lateral passageways. No longer a place of commerce, the square is now a leisure-oriented zone, given over mainly to restaurants, al fresco cafés and bookshops.

Of the mansions lining the main sides of the Rynek, those on the south and western sides are the most distinguished and colourful. Among several built in the self-confident style of the Flemish Renaissance, no. 2, the **Griffin House** (Pod Gryfami), is particularly notable. Number 5, with a reserved Mannerist facade, is known as the **Waza Court** (Dwór Wazów), rumoured to be the place where King Zygmunt Waza stayed during secret negotiations for his marriage to Anna von Habsburg. Next door, at no. 6, is the Baroque **House of the Golden Sun** (Pod Złotym Słońcem). The last striking house in the block is no. 8, again Baroque but preserving parts of its thirteenth-century predecessor; it's known as the **House of the Seven Elektors** (Pod Siedmioma Elektorami), a reference to the seven grandees superbly depicted on the facade who elected the Holy Roman emperor, Leopold I. A black Habsburg eagle cowers menacingly over the building's doorway.

The town hall

The magnificent **town hall**, symbol of the city for the last seven centuries, was originally a modest one-storey structure erected in the wake of the ruinous Tatar sacking and progressively expanded down the years. Its present appearance dates largely from the fifteenth-century high point of local prosperity, when the south aisle was added and the whole decorated in an elaborate late Gothic style. The international mix of stylistic influences reflects the city's status as a major European trading centre, creating one of the city's finest and most venerable buildings.

The **east facade** is the one that catches the eye and figures in all Wrocław's promotion material. It features an astronomical clock from 1580 and an elaborate central gable decorated with intricate terracotta patterns and exquisite pinnacles. In contrast, the west facade (the main entrance) is relatively plain, save for the octagonal Gothic belfry with its tapering Renaissance lantern. The intricate carvings embellishing the **south facade** are worthy of more protracted scrutiny, lined up between the huge Renaissance windows crowned with their spire-like roofs. Along its length are filigree friezes of animals and foliage as well as effigies of saints and knights, mostly nineteenth-century pastiches, overshadowed by an old crone and a yokel.

Relieved of its municipal duties by the adjoining nineteenth-century offices, the town hall now serves as the **City Museum**, (Muzeum Miejskie: Wed–Sat 11am–5pm, Sun 10am–6pm; 10zł; Ⓦwww.mmw.pl). It's largely given over to changing exhibitions, such as photo series, rather than a permanent display, although the chance to see the largely unaltered interior provides sufficient reason to visit.

The kernel of the town hall, dating back to the 1270s, is the twin-aisled **Burghers' Hall** (Hala Mieszczańska) on the ground floor. Not only the venue for important public meetings and receptions, the hall doubled as a covered market, functioning as such for 450 years. Upstairs is the resplendent three-aisled **Great Hall** (Sala Wielka), its vaulted ceiling studded with bosses depicting all kinds of real and imaginary creatures. Even more richly decorated is the coffer-ceilinged oriel window, which gives a Renaissance flourish to the otherwise Gothic character.

At the far end of the hall are two stone portals, the one on the right adorned with hairy wild men and giving access to the elegantly panelled 15th-century **Chamber of Council** (Izba Rady). Behind the left doorway lies the **Duke's Hall** (Sala Książęca), a pure example of fourteenth-century Gothic with a vault resting on a single central pillar. It was originally built as a chapel, but takes its name from its later use as a meeting place for the rulers of Silesia's principalities.

West of the main square

The southwest corner of the main square leads to a second, smaller square, **plac Solny**. Its traditional function as a market has been revived, with the salt from which the market takes its name now replaced by flowers. The square itself is a minor sensory delight, girdled by restored nineteenth-century town houses painted in a range of vivacious colours.

Just off the northwest corner of the main square are two curious Baroque houses known as **Hänsel and Gretel** (Jaś i Małgosia), linked by a gateway giving access to **St Elizabeth's Church** (Kościół św. Elżbiety). Proving that brick need not be an inherently dull material, this is the most impressive of Wrocław's churches. Since the mid-fifteenth century its huge ninety-metre **tower** (5zł), under construction for 150 years, has been the city's most prominent landmark. Originally, a lead-sheeted spire added another 36m to the steeple's height, but this overambitious pinnacle was blown down by storms a year after completion and never rebuilt. Ill fortune has continued to dog the church, which having been destroyed by a hailstorm in 1529 was burnt out under suspicious circumstances in 1976. The lofty, bright interior is well worth a peek.

Facing the inner ring road just west of here is the only other block of old **burghers' houses** surviving in the city. Across the road and down ulica Antoniego Cieszynskiego is the impressive red-brick **arsenal** at no. 9, originally sixteenth-century but considerably altered by the Prussians a couple of hundred years later. It now provides a rather splendid home to both the **Military Museum** (Muzeum Militariów: Wed–Sat 11am–5pm, Sun 10am–6pm; 7zł, Wed free; ⓦ www.mmw .pl), which displays a bristling selection of medieval swords and pikes as well as uniforms throughout the ages, and the **Archeology Museum** (Muzeum Archeologiczne: same times and price), with a relatively undramatic, though well-presented, collection of finds from the stone age to medieval times. Highlights include a scale model of Ostrów Tumski as it looked in the twelfth century, and the weathered tombstone of a certain Kantor David – dating from 1203, it's thought to be the oldest Jewish tombstone in Poland.

Wrocław's **Jewish quarter** was located around ulica Włodkowica, a ten-minute walk south of the arsenal. The partly restored Neoclassical **White Stork Synagogue** (Synagoga pod Białym Bocianem: Mon–Thurs 9am–5pm, Fri 9am–3pm), tucked away on a tiny square off the southern side of ulica Włodkowica, has a small exhibition about Breslau's Jewish population; after renovations are completed, the Wroclaw Center for Jewish Culture and Education plans to open a Jewish museum here. Another poignant reminder of the Judaic heritage is the **Jewish cemetery** (Cmentarz Żydowski; daily 8am–6pm), 3km south of the city centre at ulica Ślężna, where many of the imposing family memorials have been restored. To get there take tram #9 or #16 (direction Park Południowy) from the train station.

South of the main square

Immediately to the east of the Jewish quarter – and southwest to the Rynek – lies a part of the city built in obvious imitation of the chilly classical grandeur of the Prussian capital, Berlin. Indeed it was Carl Gotthard Langhans, designer of the Brandenburg Gate, who built the Neoclassical palace on the northern side of ulica Kazimierza Wielkiego, now the **New University Library** (Nowa Biblioteka Uniwersytecka). He also had a hand in the monumental **Royal Palace** (Pałac Królewski) on the opposite side of the street, which at time of writing was being renovated to hold several collections of the City Museum. Further east, along ulica Świdnicka, the royal flavour of this quarter continues in a different vein with the lofty Gothic **St Dorothy's Church** (Kościół św. Doroty), also known as the "Church of Reconciliation". This was founded in 1351 by Charles IV, king of Bohemia and the future Holy Roman emperor, in thanks for the conclusion of his negotiations with Kazimierz the Great, which secured Bohemia's rule over Silesia in return for a renunciation of its claim to Poland. Unlike most of Wrocław's other brick churches, it stayed in Catholic hands following the Reformation, becoming a Franciscan monastery. Its interior was whitewashed and littered with gigantic altars in the Baroque period, giving it a relatively opulent appearance in comparison to its neighbours, which still bear the hallmarks of four centuries of Protestant sobriety.

Behind St Dorothy's stands the **Lower Silesian Opera House** (Opera Dolnośląska), built by Carl Ferdinand Langhans in a faithful continuation of his father's Neoclassical style. Facing it is another example of fourteenth-century Gothic, the **Corpus Christi Church** (Kościół Bożego Ciała), distinguished by the delicate brickwork of its facade, porch and gable, and by the elaborate interior vaulting. Just to the east, the new **WRO Art Center** at ul. Widok 7 (Tues 2pm–6pm, Wed–Sat 10am–6pm, Sun 12.30pm–4pm; free; ⓦ www.wrocenter.pl) has exhibition rooms and PCs for viewing multi-media art including videos and computer animation.

A short ride east on trams #3 or #5 brings you to the **Ethnographic Museum** at ul. Traugutta 111/113 (Muzeum Etnograficzne: Tues, Wed & Fri–Sun 10am–4pm, Thurs 9am–4pm; 5zł), which has a good collection of Silesian traditional clothes.

East of the Rynek

The first building of note moving east of the Rynek is the former **Petersdorff store**, now an office building, at the junction of ulica Oławska and ulica Szewska, which is a classic of twentieth-century design built by German Expressionist architect Erich Mendelssohn in 1927. The concrete and glass building relies for its effect on the interplay between the bold horizontals of the main street fronts and the dramatically projecting cylinder on the corner.

The twin-towered **St Mary Magdalene's Church** (Kościół św. Marii Magdaleny), a block north of here, is another illustration of the seemingly inexhaustible diversity of Wrocław's brick churches: this fourteenth-century example is unusual in having flying buttresses, giving it a French feel. It survived the war, only to be destroyed just three days after liberation, when the munition that the Soviet army had stored inside accidentally exploded. Rebuilt in the 1970s, the exterior has a bevy of funeral plaques and epitaphs from the fifteenth to eighteenth centuries, though the most striking adornment is the twelfth-century Romanesque sandstone **portal** on the south side. The Büsserinnen bridge between the two church towers was only rebuilt in 2001 and can be visited (4zł) for excellent views. In medieval times unfaithful wives were punished by carrying two buckets of water up to this bridge to clean it – adulterous men were chained and mocked in the main square.

Moving due east from here along ulica Wita Stwosza soon leads to the **Galeria Awangarda** (Avant-garde Gallery) at no. 32 (Tues–Sun 11am–6pm; 8zł; ⓦ www.bwa.wroc.pl), Wrocław's leading contemporary art gallery, and a good place to catch high-profile exhibitions of Polish and international art. The building itself is worth a look, incorporating the surviving Neoclassical remnants of a bombed-out nineteenth-century town house into a modern, glass-and-steel pavilion. Three hundred metres to the east, the gargantuan former **Bernardine monastery** is the last important example of Gothic brickwork in the city. The monastery was begun in the mid-fifteenth century and finished only a few years before the Reformation, whereupon it was dissolved and the church used as a Protestant parish church. Inside, the somewhat misleadingly named **Museum of Architecture** (Muzeum Architektury: Tues, Wed, Fri & Sat 10am–4pm, Thurs noon–6pm, Sun 11am–5pm; 7zł; ⓦwww.ma.wroc.pl) is a fascinating documentary record, using sculptural fragments and old photos, of the many historic buildings in the city that perished in the war.

The Racławice Panorama

Wrocław's best-loved sight, the **Racławice Panorama** (Panorama Racławicka; mid-April to Sept daily 9am–5pm; Sept & Oct Tues–Sun 9am–5pm; Nov to mid-April Tues–Sun 9am–4pm; 20zł, also valid for the National Museum) is housed in a specially designed rotunda in the park by the Museum of Architecture. The building contains a truly enormous painting, 120m long and 15m high, commissioned in 1894 to celebrate the centenary of the defeat of the Russian army by the people's militia of Tadeusz Kościuszko near the village of Racławice, between Kraków and Kielce. Ultimately this triumph was in vain: the third and final Partition of Poland, which wiped it off the map altogether, occurred the following year. Nonetheless, it was viewed a century later by patriots of the still subdued nation as a supreme example of national will and self-sacrifice which deserved a fitting memorial.

The **history of the painting** is a remarkable saga which mirrors the fate of Poland itself. Despite an attempt by Polish-Americans to buy it and have it shipped across the Atlantic, it was placed on public view in Lwów, which was then part of Austria – the only one of the Partitioning powers that would have tolerated such nationalist propaganda. It remained there until 1944, when it was substantially damaged by a bomb. Although allocated to Wrocław, it was then put into storage – officially because there were no specialists to restore it and no money to build the structure the painting would need. The truth was that it was politically unacceptable to allow Poles to glory in their ancestors' slaughter of Russians.

That all changed with the events of 1980, when the rise of Solidarity forced the Polish authorities to place more emphasis on Polish patriotic traditions. Within five years the painting had been immaculately restored and was on display in a snazzy new building, with much attention being paid to a natural foreground of soil, stones and shrubs, which greatly adds to the uncanny appearance of depth. Visitors are admitted at thirty-minute intervals, and are supplied with headphones with English-language commentary and appropriate sound effects. Afterwards you can study the scale model of the battlefield downstairs at leisure.

The National Museum

At the opposite end of the park is the ponderous neo-Renaissance home of the **National Museum** (Muzeum Narodowe: Wed, Fri & Sun 10am–4pm, Thurs 9am–4pm, Sat 10am–6pm; 15zł, free on Sat; ⓦwww.mnwr.art.pl), which unites the collections of Breslau and Lwów. An important collection of medieval stone **sculpture**, housed on the ground floor, includes the delicately linear carving *The Dormition of the Virgin*, which formed the tympanum of the portal of Kościół św. Marii Magdaleny. The other major highlight is the poignant early fourteenth-century **tomb** of Henryk IV, the armour-clad effigy of the prince surrounded by a floor-level frieze of weeping mourners.

Upstairs lies an impressive display of medieval Silesian art, with a colossal set of late fourteenth-century saintly statues, several rooms of fifteenth-century altarpieces and a comprehensive collection of **Polish paintings** on the top floor.

A leading exhibit here is an unfinished blockbuster by Matejko, *Vows of King Jan Kazimierz Waza*. Set in Lwów Cathedral, it illustrates the monarch's pledge to improve the lot of the peasants at the end of the war against his invading Swedish kinsmen. A number of galleries are devoted to contemporary **arts and crafts**, much of it surprisingly daring for work executed under communist rule. There's an impressive contingent of larger-than-life male figures, looking something like a Chinese emperor's terracotta army, courtesy of Magdalena Abakanowicz, Poland's best-known living sculptor.

The university quarter

Wrocław's academic quarter can be reached in just a few minutes from the main square by way of ulica Kuźnicza, but the most atmospheric approach is to walk there from the National Museum along the south bank of the Odra, for a series of delightful **views** of the ecclesiastical quarter opposite.

Overlooking the Piaskowski Bridge is the **Market Hall** (Hala Targowa), a preformed concrete update of the brick church idiom built in 1908, it is piled high most days with irresistible food and other commodities. From this point, the triangular-shaped university quarter, jam-packed with historic buildings, is clearly defined by two streets, ulica Uniwersytecka to the south and ulica Grodzka, which follows the Odra.

Along the northern side of ulica Uniwersytecka stands **St Vincent's Church** (Kościół św. Wincentego), founded as a Franciscan monastery by Henryk the Pious, badly damaged in the war, rebuilt in 1991 and now used by the Ukrainian Greco-Catholic community. Inside, several altarpieces by the renowned Silesian artist Michael Willmann (see p.506) have been returned to their former glory. Beside an Ursuline Convent is the fourteenth-century **St Matthew's Church** (Kościół św. Macieja), currently used as a student's church and worth entering for the artful stained glass and altar decorations; it also contains the tomb and memorial portrait of the city's most famous literary figure, the seventeenth-century mystic poet Johann Scheffler – better known as **Angelus Silesius** ("the Silesian Angel").

Behind St Matthew's, and best viewed from the newly restored walled Baroque garden, stands one of Wrocław's most distinguished buildings, the **Ossoliński** library. The library collections are another legacy from Lwów, where they were assembled by the family whose name they still bear, but they can only be viewed during special exhibitions. West along plac Uniwersytecki is one of the most obviously Austrian features of the city, the **Church of the Blessed Name of Jesus** (Kościół Najświętszego Imienia Jezus), built in the Jesuit style at the end of the seventeenth century, one of the rash of Counter-Reformation religious buildings in the Habsburg lands. Its most arresting feature is the huge allegorical ceiling fresco by the most celebrated Austrian decorative painter of the day, Johann Michael Rottmayr.

Adjoining the church is the 171-metre-long facade of the Collegium Maximum of the **university** (daily except Wed 10am–3.30pm; 10zł), founded in 1702 by Emperor Leopold I. The wide entrance portal bears a balcony adorned with statues symbolizing various academic disciplines and attributes; more can be seen high above on the graceful little tower. A frescoed staircase leads up to the **main assembly hall** (Aula Leopoldina). It's one of the greatest secular interiors of the Baroque age, fusing the elements of architecture, painting, sculpture and ornament into one bravura whole. The huge illusionistic **ceiling frescoes** show the Apotheosis of Divine and Worldly Wisdom above the gallery and auditorium. Continue upstairs to reach the **Mathematicians' Tower** (Wieża Matematyczna), where there is an exhibition on the astronomical and meteorological research that was done here, and a terrace offering fine views over the Old Town.

Wyspa Piasek and Ostrów Tumski

From the Market Hall, the Piaskowy Bridge leads you out to **Wyspa Piasek island**, with a cluster of historic buildings crammed together. The first you come to on the right-hand side is the **university library**, installed in an Augustinian monastery which was used as the Nazi military headquarters. Beside it is the fourteenth-century **Church of St Mary on the Sands** (Kościół NMP na Piasku), dull on the outside but majestically vaulted inside. The aisles have an asymmetrical tripartite rib design known as the Piast vault, which is peculiar to this region. Operated by an attending nun, the kitschy mechanical manger in the side chapel (ruchowa szopka: daily 10am–6pm) is well worth a glance.

The two elegant little bridges of Most Młynski and Most Tumski connect Wyspa Piasek with **Ostrów Tumski**. For those not already sated by medieval churches, there's a concentration of five more here. With its massive bulk, giant buttresses and pair of dissimilar towers, the imperious **Holy Cross Church** (Kościół św. Krzyźa) is particularly interesting, as it's really two churches, one on top of the other; the lower one originally dedicated to St Bartholomew.

Ulica Katedralna leads past several Baroque palaces to the slender twin-towered **Cathedral of St John** (Katedra św. Jana). Grievously damaged in 1945, the cathedral has been restored to its thirteenth-century form – it was Poland's first cathedral built in the Gothic style, completed in 1272. The one exterior feature of note is the elaborate porch. Inside, three chapels behind the high altar make a visit to the gloomy interior worthwhile. On the southern side, **St Elizabeth's chapel** dates from the seventeenth century, its integrated architecture, frescoes and sculptures created by Italian followers of Bernini. Next comes the Gothic **Lady chapel**, with the masterly Renaissance funerary plaque of Bishop Jan Roth. Last in line is the **Corpus Christi chapel**, a perfectly proportioned and subtly decorated Baroque gem.

Opposite the northern side of the cathedral is the tiny thirteenth-century **St Giles's Church** (Kościół św. Idziego), the only one in the city to have escaped destruction by the Tatars, and preserving some finely patterned brickwork. Next door at pl. Katedralny 16, the **Archdiocesan Museum** (Muzeum Archidiecezjalne: Tues–Sun 9am–3pm; 4zł) is a treasure trove of religious art, with late medieval wooden sculptures from all over Silesia, and a wonderful array of altarpieces. For some respite, follow ulica Kanonia to the **botanical gardens** at ul. Sienkiewicza 6 (April–Oct: daily 8am–6pm; 7zł), established in the Odra's former riverbed at the beginning of the twentieth century when a municipal ornamentation programme of the city was undertaken.

Ulica Szczytnicka leads east to the elongated avenue of plac Grunwaldzki, which gained notoriety in 1945 when it was flattened into an airstrip to allow the defeated Nazi leaders to escape. At its southern end is the most famous of the city's bridges, **Most Grunwaldzki**, built in 1910.

East of Ostrów Tumski

Wrocław's most enticing stretch of greenery is the **Szczytnicki Park**, east of Ostrów Tumski, which can be reached on trams #2 and #10 from ulica Szczytnicka or #4 and #10 from ulica Kazimierza Wielkiego in the Old Town. Its focal point is the **Centennial Hall** (Hala Stulecia), a huge hall built in 1913 to celebrate the centenary of the liberation of the city from Napoleon.

Designed by the innovative Max Berg, it combines traditional Prussian solidity with a modernistic dash – the unsupported 130-metre-wide dome is an audacious piece of engineering even by present-day standards, used for trade fairs and sporting events, with the occasional exhibition. Around the hall are a number of striking colonnaded pavilions; these were built a few years earlier by Berg's teacher Hans Poelzig, who was responsible for making the city a leading centre of the *Deutscher Werkbund*, the German equivalent of the English Arts and Crafts Movement.

In the same park is a work by a yet more famous architect: the box-like **Kindergarten** is eastern Europe's only building by Le Corbusier. Along with the huge steel needle beside the hall, this is a legacy of the Exhibition of the Regained Territories, held here in 1948. Other delights in the park include an amphitheatre, a Japanese garden and pagoda, an artificial lake and a sixteenth-century **wooden church**, brought here from Upper Silesia. Across the road lies the attractive **Zoo** (Ogród Zoologiczny: summer 9am–6pm; winter 9am–5pm; 8zł), with Poland's largest collection of wild animals and a huge terrarium with reptiles and butterflies.

Eating, drinking and entertainment

Wrocław has a good selection of **places to eat**, most of which are within the Old Town area. Wrocław's **drinking and nightlife** scene is as vibrant as you would expect from a large university city. The area between the main square and the university is packed with bars, while the Pasaż Niepolda passageway between ulica Ruska and ulica św. Antoniego is a key pub-crawling zone, with several quirky restaurants in the streets just beyond.

Restaurants

Abrams' Tower ul. Kraińskiego 14 ⓦ www .abramstower.pl. Excellent authentic Tex-Mex and fusion dishes and good wines served in a medieval city wall tower by a Californian artist. Try the excellent chipotle shrimp tacos with avocado (24zł). Find the tower hidden in the park just south of the market hall. Open Sun–Wed 4pm–midnight, Thurs–Sat till later.

Karczma Lwówska Rynek 4. No-nonsense meat-and-potatoes mains, well-priced at around 25zł, in an interior decked out with Ukrainian folk motifs and sepia photographs of old Lwów. The stuffed cabbage leaves (*gołąbki*, 22zł) are excellent. Open 11am–midnight.

Karczma Piastów ul. Kiełbaśnicza 6. A good place for typical Polish cooking at reasonable prices, in the cellars of the *Dwór Polski* hotel. Open 11am–11pm.

Kardamon ul. Włodkowica 8. Extravagantly decorated old villa with dining in several rooms and a large garden; the food is fusion and varied. Skip the sandwiches but do try the steaks or fish dishes (mains cost 25–45zł). Open 11.30am–10pm, Thurs–Sat till 11pm.

Od Nova ul. Włodkowica 9 ⓦ www.odnova .pl. Popular bar/restaurant attracting a trendy, mixed crowd enjoying cocktails, pasta and Asian dishes; the Siamese papardelle (24zł) and duck brochettes (38zł) are worth a try. Open 11am–11pm, Fri & Sat till midnight.

Oregano ul. Kuźnica 57/58 ⓦ www.oregano .com.pl. Cosy basement restaurant decorated with antique-shop bric-a-brac, and offering reliably tasty pizzas and salads. Entered from ul. Igielna. Open noon–11pm.

Piwnica Świdnicka Rynek-Ratusz 1 ⓦ www .piwnicaswidnicka.com. This famous old restaurant under the town hall is a city institution, serving up a filling range of meat-heavy Polish favourites and some international dishes too. It's on the formal side, meals costing 50–80zł. Open noon–11pm.

Pod Złotym Jeleniem Rynek 44. Cosy square-side restaurant with open-plan grill and dining area, herbs hanging from the ceiling and rustic-looking paintings on the walls. Grilled slabs of pork and beef mains (25–60zł) form the mainstay of the menu. Open noon to midnight.

Cafés and snack bars

Afryka ul. Kiełbaśnicza 24. Dozens of types of freshly ground coffee and tea to take out or drink in on low stools. Tasty home-baked cakes, too. Open 9.30am–10pm, Fri & Sat till midnight.

Bazylia ul. Kuźnicza 42. Modern, minimalist, order-at-the-counter place, offering a big but functional choice of canteen food from *pierogi* to pork chops. Huge windows offer nice views to the main university building, and it's correspondingly full with snacking students. Daily 8am–8pm.

Cafetarie Chic ul. Katedralna 6. Lovely, classic café that makes a good stop for coffee and cakes when exploring the cathedral area. Open daily 10am–9pm.

Kurna Chata ul. Odrzańska 17 ⓦ www.kurnachata .pl. Folksy decor, wooden tables and a choice selection of Polish staples, from *bigos* and *placki* to more substantial chicken fillets and steaks. Cheap, filling, and often busy. Open Tues–Fri 10am–11.30pm, Mon, Sat & Sun from 10am.

Soul Cafe pl. Solny 4. Relaxing, upmarket place serving decent coffee, dainty canapés and fancy cakes. Open Mon–Thurs 7.30am–10pm, Fri & Sat till 11pm, Sun 10am–10pm.

STP ul. Kuźnicza 10. The *Szybko Tanio Pysznie* ('Fast Cheap Delicious') self-service canteen has tasty Polish nosh paid by weight (29zł per kilo); half price from 9pm. Open daily 10am–10pm.

Vega Rynek-Ratusz 27a. Good, inexpensive vegetarian haunt with plant-filled interior just to the right of the town hall's famous facade. Open Mon–Sat 8am–7pm, Sun 9am–5pm.

Witaminka Rynek 50. Not particularly rich in vitamins, this is an enjoyably old-fashioned cake and ice cream emporium right on the main square. Open Mon–Sat 9am–9pm, Sun 11am–9pm.

Nightlife

Many of Wrocław's bars and pubs feature DJs and dancing as the night wears on. Additionally, there's a handful of dedicated music clubs with a regular programme of disc-spinning events and/or gigs by local bands. To find out what's on, ask at the tourism office, look out for posters or trawl through *Co Jest Grane* – the **listings** supplement of Friday's *Gazeta Wyborcza* newspaper.

Bars and pubs

Klub na Jatkach ul. św. Elżbiety 3, on the Jatki alley. Popular drinking den with a classy pub-like space with dark wooden tables in one half, and a minimally furnished room with DJ podium and dance floor in the other. Open noon–1am, Fri & Sat till 4am.

Mleczarnia ul. Włodkowica 5 ⓦ www.mle .pl. The most atmospheric bar in town is a dark, candlelit place characterized by antique furniture, nineteenth-century knick-knacks, and sepia family photographs, where a bohemian crowd sips coffee and cocktails. There's a lovely summer terrace overlooking the synagogue at the back. Open 8am–4am.

Niebo ul. Ruska 51, Pasaż Niepolda ⓦ www .niebocafe.pl. Big pub-like venue with distressed furniture, grungy vibe, occasional rock concerts and a healthy mix of oblivion-seeking students crowding round the bar till very very late. Open 1pm–4am, Mon from 5pm.

Novocaina Rynek 13. Buzzing bar/restaurant in glamorous classic design. There's Italian food on the menu, but come for the cocktails or the Fri and Sat club nights downstairs. Open 10am–midnight, Thurs–Sat till 3am.

Pod Kalamburem ul. Kuźnicza 29a, ⓦ www .kalambur.org. Bar located between the square and the university quarter, with beautiful Art Nouveau decor, some lethal cocktails and occasional concerts and exhibitions. Open Mon–Thurs noon–2am, Fri–Sun till 4am.

Pod Papugami Sukiennice 9a ⓦ www .podpapugami.com.pl. Brash bar for yuppies and stick-thin platinum blondes, decorated in mixture of industrial and Gothic styles. Live music and dancing some nights. Open noon–1am, Fri & Sat till 2am.

Pod Zielonym Kogutem pl. Teatralny 8. Inviting bar with wooden panelling, all kinds of pub junk on the walls, and a line of cast iron street lamps running down the middle of the room. Open 4pm–2am, Fri & Sat till 4am.

Pracoffnia ul. Więzennia 6. A mysterious under-ground bar imaginatively decorated with various old projectors, machines and second-hand clutter. Entered via a courtyard that makes a great summer terrace. Open noon–2am, Fri & Sat till 5am.

Rura Łazienna 4 ⓦ www.jazzklubrura.art.pl. Music club with a long bar for boozing and chatting upstairs, and a table-strewn cellar with a stage often occupied by blues or jazz bands. Open 1pm–2am, Sun 4pm–1am.

Spiż Rynek-Ratusz 2 ⓦ www.spiz.pl. Superior cellar pub incorporating Poland's first boutique brewery, with several beers brewed on the premises. Bread and dripping (*chleb ze smalcem*) is the traditional side order. A wider range of Polish nosh is available in the rather more formal *Spiż* restaurant next door. Open 10am–midnight, Fri & Sat till 2am.

Clubs

🏃 **Bezsenność** ul. Ruska 51, Pasaż Niepolda ⓦ www.bezsennosc.wroclaw.pl.

The high-ceilinged rooms of an old apartment are home to the coolest alternative club in town, hosting parties, plays and other events.
Droga do Mekki ul. Ruska 51, Pasaż Niepolda Ⓦ www.mekka.pl. Innovative house club with occasional concerts and a non-smoking chill-out room. Open 4pm–2am, Fri & Sat till 4am.
Kamfora ul. św. Antoniego 24c Ⓦ www.kamfora.pl. Atmospheric basement club hidden in a courtyard, where you can dance the tango on Mondays, or to funk, nu jazz and bossa nova and other styles on Friday and Saturday. Open Mon–Fri 5pm–2am, Sat 6pm–4am, Sun closed.

Madness ul. Hubska 6 Ⓦ www.madnes.website .pl. Ska, punk and reggae club in a red-brick warehouse decorated in the style of an alternative tropical island. Frequent DJ sessions and live gigs but check what's on first – it's located in between factories ten minutes' east of the train and bus stations. Open 6pm–2am, Fri & Sat till 4am.
Wagon Club pl. Orląt Lwowskich 20 Ⓦ www .wagonclub.com. Agenda-setting house club located in the former Dworzec Swiebodzki train station on the western fringes of the Old Town, attracting international DJs and an enthusiastic crowd. Open 2pm–3am, Fri & Sat till 5am.

Entertainment and festivals

There's a good deal of high-quality **classical music** in Wrocław – the best place to find out about concerts and buy tickets is the Tourist and Cultural Information Centre (see p.492). The city has been at the forefront of contemporary European **drama** ever since the early 1960s, when experimental director Jerzy Grotowski established the groundbreaking **Laboratory Theatre** (Teatr Laboratorium) on Wrocław's Rynek. Although the Laboratory was dissolved following Grotowski's emigration to Italy in 1982, avant-garde traditions still live on – not least in the productions organized by the Grotowski Centre (see below).

Wrocław hosts several prestigious annual **festivals**: the renowned Jazz on the Odra (Jazz nad Odrą; Ⓦ www.jnofestival.pl) in March brings together several international performers; while Wratislavia Cantans (Ⓦ www.wratislavia .art.pl), in September, is devoted to oratorios and cantatas and features choral groups from all over the world. There's also a festival of early music at the beginning of December. The city's annual **drama festivals** include one devoted to monologues in January, and a contemporary Polish play season in May and June.

The tourist office (see p.492) can provide details of most events – otherwise *Gazeta Wyborcza*'s *Co jest grane* supplement (on Fri) is the place to look for listings.

Music venues
Akademia Muzyczna (Academy of Music) pl. Jana Pawła II 2 ☎ 071/355 7276, Ⓦ www.amuz.wroc.pl. Frequent chamber concerts, usually performed by students and very often free of charge.
Filharmonia Wrocławska ul. Piłsudskiego 19 ☎ 071/342 2459, Ⓦ www.filharmonia.wroclaw.pl. Orchestral concerts and recitals, usually Fridays and Saturdays.
Opera Dolnośląska (Lower Silesian Opera) ul. Świdnicka 35 ☎ 071/344 5779, Ⓦ www.opera .wroclaw.pl). Top-notch warbling and superb stagecraft from one of Poland's top companies.
Teatr Muzyczny Capitol ul. Piłsudskiego 72 ☎ 071/789 0451, Ⓦ www.teatr-capitol.pl. Operetta, musicals and cabaret.

Theatres
Ad Spectatores ul. Powstańców Śląskich 82/58 ☎ 071/792 0677, Ⓦ www.adspectatores.art.pl.

Imaginative, spectacular contemporary works, performed in a nineteenth-century water tower, the train station or in other venues around town.
Ośródek Grotowskiego (Grotowski Centre) Rynek-Ratusz 27 ☎ 071/343 4267, Ⓦ www .grotcenter.art.pl. Keeping the traditions of Jerzy Grotowski's famous studio theatre alive in the shape of workshops, performances, and occasional concerts.
Teatr Lalek (Puppet Theatre) pl. Teatralny 4 ☎ 071/344 1216, Ⓦ www.teatrlalek.wroclaw.pl. Grandiose nineteenth-century building with two auditoria, each staging superbly designed shows – some of which start at 11am or earlier. Very popular, so book early.
Teatr Polski ul. G. Zapolskiej 3 ☎ 071/316 0780, Ⓦ www.teatrpolski.wroc.pl. Main venue for classical drama, with performances in the main hall or in the Kameralny subsidiary at ul. Świdnicka 28 (☎ 071/316 0752).

Wrocław's Mikołaja Kopernika airport (☎071/358 1381, ✆www.airport.wroclaw .pl) can be reached by bus #406, which departs every twenty to forty minutes from ulica Dworcowa, north of the train station before skirting the Old Town along ulica Podwale. Travel time is about thirty minutes, but can be up to an hour depending on traffic. Snacks, sandwiches and drinks can be bought at the airport.

Wrocław Główny main train station is well-connected to the rest of Poland, with express services to all major cities and some useful night train connections (to Warsaw, Gdańsk and Kraków). There are also daily international trains to Berlin-Lichtenberg (6–8hr), Prague (6hr 30min) and L'viv (14hr).

The bus station (dworzec autobusowy; ☎071/361 6135☐ ✆www.polbus.pl) serves destinations throughout Poland and abroad. Buy train and bus tickets in advance at Orbis offices to avoid queues at the stations.

Teatr Współczesny ul. Rzeźnicza 12 ☎071/358 8922, ✆www.wteatrw.pl. Best place to go for contemporary Polish work as well as modern international plays in Polish translation.

Listings

Airlines LOT, ul. Piłsudskiego 36 ☎071/341 5151, ✆www.lot.com.

Bicycle rental W Sercu Miasta, Przejście Żelazniczne 4, centre of the main square (Mon–Sat 9am–midnight, Sun noon–midnight; 8zł/hr or 40zł/ day; bring ID and 100zł deposit).

Books and maps EMPiK, with stores on the north side of the main square and on pl. Kościuszki, has the best all-round selection of foreign magazines, maps and English-language paperbacks.

Car rental Avis, at the airport and at ul. Piłsudskiego 49 ☎071/372 3567, ✆www.avis.pl;

Budget, at the airport ☎071/353 7750, ✆www .budget.pl; Hertz, at the airport ☎071/353 7743, ✆www.hertz.com.pl; and Joka, ul. Kościuszki 34 ☎071/781 8188, ✆www.joka.com.pl.

Internet access Free access at the tourism office (see p.492) and for 6zł/hr at W Sercu Miasta (see bicycle rental, above).

Left luggage At bus station (daily 6am–10pm). Lockers at the train station.

Pharmacy Apteka Herbowa, just off the main square at Wita Stwosza 3, is the most convenient for the centre. Details of 24hr duty pharmacies will be posted in the window.

Post office Rynek 28 (24hr) and outside the train station at Piłsudskiego 12 (Mon–Fri 8am–8pm).

Travel Agents Orbis, Rynek 29 ☎071/344 4109, ✆www.orbis.wroclaw.pl, sells bus, train and plane tickets, as well as handling car rental.

Around Wrocław

Once outside Wrocław, the northern swath of Lower Silesia is not an area of outstanding interest to tourists, and you'd be best advised to move quickly towards the mountains of the south and east if time in this part of Poland is limited. Despite the lack of a focus for visitors, a number of settlements here make worthwhile stopoffs if you're passing through the region – either because of their historical significance or due to their possession of an architectural monument of note. With its extensive **public transport** network, Wrocław itself makes a perfectly adequate touring base, though there's plenty of **accommodation** elsewhere should you prefer to stay in a more tranquil location.

Trzebnica

TRZEBNICA, 24km north of Wrocław, has a long and distinguished history. It's on the nearby Winna Góra hill that the oldest traces of human habitation in Poland were found – 500,000 year-old flintstones and bones. In 1250, the town was granted a charter by Duke Henryk III, so making it one of Silesia's oldest recorded towns. Henryk's marriage to the German princess Hedwig was largely responsible for shifting Silesia towards a predominantly German culture, setting the trend for the next six centuries.

The couple established a **Cistercian convent** in the town in 1202, the sole monument of note. Built in the plain style favoured by this order – still Romanesque in shape and feel, but already with the Gothic pointed arch and ribbed vault – it was progressively remodelled and now has a predominantly Baroque appearance evident in its main feature, the **Basilica of St Hedwig** (Bazylika św. Jadwigi). A survival from the original building is the **portal**, which was found during excavation work and re-erected, half-hidden, to the left of the porch. Its sculptures, showing King David playing the harp to Bathsheba attended by a maidservant, are notably refined thirteenth-century carvings.

Inside the church, every column features a sumptuous Baroque altarpiece, while, to the right of the choir, the **St Hedwig's chapel**'s resplendent gilt and silver altar almost outshines the main item. The princess, who spent her widowhood in the convent, was canonized in 1267, just 24 years after her death, whereupon this chapel was immediately built in her memory. In 1680, her simple marble and alabaster sepulchral slab was incorporated into a grandiose tomb, whose sides are lined with sacred statuary while Hedwig clutches a model of the basilica. At the same time, a considerably less ostentatious memorial to her husband was placed in the choir, its entrance guarded by statues of St Hedwig and her even more celebrated niece, St Elizabeth of Hungary.

Served by half-hourly services from Wrocław, Trzebnica's bus station is 250m northwest of the convent, just below the largely modern and uninteresting town centre. On the way back, make sure you board a bus for Wrocław-Dworzec PKS (the main bus station) rather than Wrocław-Nadodrze – the latter terminates a good 2km north of the centre. The *Ratuszowa* **restaurant**, uphill from the bus station at Rynek 4, is a conveniently central place to eat.

Brzeg

Half an hour east of Wrocław by train, the old ducal seat of **BRZEG** is an easily manageable market town grouped around a worthwhile castle museum. Originally a fishing village on the bank (*brzeg*) of the Odra, Brzeg became a regional capital in 1311, when it ousted Legnica as the main residence of the local branch of the Piast family. The Piasts remained here until 1675 when the male line of the family finally died out.

The Town

Starting from the adjacent bus and train stations on the south side of town, it's a short walk up ulica Piastowska to get to the centre, which focuses on a drab main square arranged around a much rebuilt **town hall**. Just off the eastern side of the square is the arresting red-brick bulk of the fourteenth-century **St Nicholas's Church** (Kościół św. Mikołaja), its twin towers rebuilt last century and linked by an unusual arched bridge. The interior is startlingly spacious and has a varied collection of finely carved memorial plaques of prominent families.

A five-minute walk west of the main square, Brzeg's sixteenth-century **Castle of the Piasts** (Zamek Piastowski) is fondly referred to locally as the "Silesian Wawel" (Wawel being the famous castle in Kraków; see p.373), although the results of war and reconstruction have left it looking something of a hotch-potch. The extravagantly rich **gateway** is perhaps the finest Renaissance feature, modelled on Dürer's woodcut of a triumphal arch in honour of Emperor Maximilian.

Through the gate lies a beautifully proportioned **courtyard** with three storeys of arcades, and the entrance to the **Museum of the Silesian Piasts** (Muzeum Piastów Śląskich: Tues & Thurs–Sun 10am–4pm, Wed 10am–6pm; 8zł, Sat free; Ⓦzamek.brzeg.pl). Centrepiece of the display is the burial vault of the Brzeg Piasts, which lies beneath the north wing of the castle and contains several ranks of dukes and duchesses in pewter coffins – most eye-catching of which is the casket of Duke George III (1611–64), richly decorated with scenes of fabulous animals, and a grim-faced Death hunting his victims through the Silesian countryside. Elsewhere there's a wonderful scale model of Brzeg in the eighteenth century, a suite of period function rooms, and a collection of religious art.

Next to the **castle** is the superbly renovated **Jesuit Church of the Holy Cross** (Kościół św. Krzyża), which dates back to the turn of the eighteenth century. Sober enough from the outside, its single interior space is encrusted with Rococo decorations with an illusionist altar replacing the usual epic construction.

Practicalities

With regular trains to Wrocław and Opole you shouldn't need to stay in Brzeg. If you do get stuck, the comfortable, family-run **pensjonat** Zofia *Demska* east of the centre at ul. Rzemieślnicza 7 (Ⓣ077/416 4688, Ⓔpensjonat_brzeg @op.pl; ❺) is preferable to the tacky *Piast* **hotel**, situated near the station on the way to the town centre at ul. Piastowska 14 (Ⓣ077/416 2028, Ⓦwww.piast .strefa.pl; ❷–❹). The classiest **restaurant** remains the *Ratuszowa* in the town hall cellars, which is an excellent source of good, medium-price Polish food.

In late May, Brzeg's castle, town hall and churches are put to impressive use for a four-day-long international **festival** of classical music.

Ślęża and Sobótka

The flatness of the plain southwest of Wrocław is abruptly broken some 30km out of town by an isolated outcrop of rocks with two peaks, the higher of which is known as **Ślęża** (718m). One of the most enigmatic sites in Poland, Ślęża was used for pagan worship in Celtic times, and was later settled by the Slav tribe after whom the mountain – and Silesia itself – are named.

Ślęża is normally approached from **SOBÓTKA**, a dormitory town served by half-hourly buses from Wrocław. Between the bus terminal and the train station is the Gothic parish church, outside which stands the first of several curious ancient **sculptures** to be seen in the area – consisting of one stone placed across another, it's nicknamed *The Mushroom*. On the slopes of Ślęża, there's a large and voluptuous statue of a woman with a fish, while the summit has a carved lion on it. Exactly what these carvings symbolize is not known: some certainly postdate the Christianization of the area, but that hasn't prevented their association with pagan rites. It's not exactly a place to look for quiet mystery, however, being enormously popular with day-trippers and often teeming with busloads of schoolkids.

Five separate **hiking trails** traverse the hillsides, some of them stony, so it's wise to wear sturdy shoes. More than an hour is necessary for the busiest stretch, the direct ascent from Sobótka's main street to the top of Ślęża by the route indicated by yellow signs. The summit is spoiled by a number of ugly buildings including the inevitable television tower, while the neo-Gothic chapel is a poor substitute for the castle and Augustinian monastery which once stood here. Recompense is provided in the form of an extensive panoramic view including, on a clear day, the Karkonosze and Kłodzko highlands to the south and west.

The *Pod Misiem* **hotel** in Sobótka (ul. Mickiewicza 7/9 ⓣ071/316 2035; doubles ❷, dorm-style triples 30zł per person) has a decent **restaurant**, and you'll find a couple of **snack bars** on the main square.

Lubiąż

Set close to the north bank of the Odra, 51km west of Wrocław and signposted off the Wrocław–Legnica road, the quiet village of **LUBIĄŻ** stands in the shadow of a **Cistercian abbey** that ranks as one of the largest and most impressive former monastic complexes in central Europe. It's an easy day-trip destination if you have your own transport, but is more difficult to get to by bus, with only one or two services a day from Wrocław and one from Legnica.

Although resting on medieval foundations, the appearance of the complex – laid out in the ground plan of a squared-off figure six – is one of sober Baroque: the community flourished in the aftermath of the disastrous Thirty Years' War, and was able to build itself palatial new headquarters, with more than three hundred halls and chambers. Silesia's greatest painter, **Michael Willmann** (see p.498), lived here for over four decades, carrying out a multiplicity of commissions for the province's religious houses, and was interred in the church's crypt. However, prosperity was short-lived: decline began in 1740, when Silesia came under the uncompromisingly Protestant rule of Frederick the Great's Prussia, and continued until the monastery was dissolved in 1810. Since then, the complex has served as a mental hospital, stud farm, munitions factory, labour camp and storehouse, in the process drifting into a state of semi-dereliction. After the fall of communism, the Lubiąż Fund was established to attract foreign capital to renovate the site.

Most impressive, and readily accessible by walking through the gatehouse, is the 223-metre-long **facade**, whose austere economy of ornament is interrupted only by the twin towers of the church. Only parts of the rest of the abbey are open and can be visited on hourly tours in Polish (daily: April–Sept 9am–5pm; Oct–March 10am–3pm; 10zł), but you should be able to see a number of beautifully restored rooms decorated in the Baroque style, including the refectory and the showpiece **Knights' Hall** (Hala Książęca).

Located in former stables next to the abbey gateway, the *Karczma Cysterska* **restaurant** offers simple meat-and-potatoes meals in rustic surroundings.

Legnica and around

Although often ravaged by fires and badly damaged in World War II, **LEGNICA**, 70km west of Wrocław, has maintained its role as one of Silesia's most important cities, and is nowadays a busy regional centre of 110,000 inhabitants. Despite a lively town centre and a pair of rewarding churches, it's never going to be a major tourist destination, and is important primarily as a transport hub offering onward connections to prettier places to the south – notably Legnickie Pole and Jawor.

The Town

If you're arriving by train or bus, the main sights can be covered by a circular walk in a clockwise direction from the stations, which are just over the road from each other at the northeastern end of town. Crossing the pedestrian bridge next to the bus station and heading straight down ulica Skarbowa will bring you after ten minutes to the huge twin-towered **Cathedral of Sts Peter and Paul** (Katedra św. Piotra i Pawła), with its rich red-brick neo-Gothic exterior, stylistically matched by the arcaded turn-of-the-twentieth-century buildings facing it on the corner of the main square. The lovely fourteenth-century northern portal features a tympanum of the Adoration of the Magi flanked by statues of the church's two patrons. Immediately northwest lies the elongated **Rynek** (main square), which has lost much of its character save for eight arcaded Renaissance houses which still survive next to a much rebuilt town hall.

Leaving the northwestern corner of the Rynek by ulica św Jana will take you past a former Cistercian monastery building which now houses the **Copper Museum** (Muzeum Miedzi: Tues–Sat 11am–5pm, April–Oct also Sun; 7zł, free on Sat), a small but rewarding collection devoted to the history of copper mining and smelting in the region. Standing behind the museum on ulica Ojców Zbigniewa Michała is the massive Baroque facade of the twin-towered **St John's Church** (Kościól św. Jana). Protruding from the eastern side of the church, its orientation and brick Gothic architecture looking wholly out of place, is the presbytery of the thirteenth-century Franciscan Monastery which formerly occupied the spot. It owes its survival to its function as the **Mausoleum of the Legnica Piasts** (Mauzoleum Piastów Legnickich: Tues–Sat 9.30am–6.30pm; tickets from the Muzeum Miedzi; 3zł). Inside you'll see several sarcophagi, plus Baroque frescoes illustrating the history of Poland and Silesia under the dynasty.

Heading back towards the stations along ulica Partyzantów you'll pass the **castle** (zamek), a grim red-brick structure rebuilt in the nineteenth century and preserving few original features save for the foundations of a **Romanesque chapel** (May–Sept Tues–Sun 9am–5pm), protectively housed in a purpose-built modern pavilion inside the castle courtyard.

Practicalities

The tourist office on ul. NMP 1 (Mon–Fri 9am–5pm, March–Oct also Sat 10am–2pm; ☏076/722 3100, ✉elzbieta@elzbieta.beep.pl) has brochures, maps and can point you to the city's **hotels**, best of which is the business-oriented *Qubus*, opposite the train and bus stations at Skarbowa 2 (☏076/866 2100, ⊛www .qubushotel.com; ❻). The *Kamieniczka* at ul. Młynarska 15-16 (☏076/723 7392, ⊛www.hotel-kamieniczka.pl; ❺) is a nicely modernized town house just east of the Rynek with a mixture of en suites and rooms with shared facilities.

There are several moderately priced **restaurants** in town: the *Kamieniczka* hotel restaurant serves excellent Polish cuisine, while the popular *Don Giovanni*, next to the tourist information office at ul. NMP 3, has good Italian dishes. For drinks, head to the lively *Cubana Bar* at Rynek 33.

Legnickie Pole

On April 4, 1241 the Tatar hordes – having ridden six thousand kilometres from their Mongolian homelands and ravaged everything in their path – won a titanic battle 60km west of Wrocław against a combined army of Poles and Silesians, killing its commander, Duke Henryk the Pious. Silesia's subsequent division among Henryk's descendants into three separate duchies began a process of dismemberment which was thereafter to dog its history. Standing on the site of the battlefield today is the village of **LEGNICKIE POLE**, 11km southeast of Legnica and served by municipal bus services #9, #16, #17 and #20.

A church was erected on the spot where Henryk the Pious' body was found (according to tradition, his mother, later St. Hedwig of Trzebnica, was only able to identify the headless corpse from his six-toed foot), and in time this became the centre of a Benedictine monastery. The church was deconsecrated after World War II, and now houses the **Museum of the Battle of Legnica** (Muzeum Bitwy Legnickiej: Wed–Sun 11am–5pm; 4.50zł, free on Wed), which includes diagrams and mock-ups of the conflict and a copy of Henryk's tomb (the original is in Wrocław's National Museum; see p.497).

The Benedictines, who were evicted during the Reformation, returned to Legnickie Pole in the early eighteenth century and had **Kilian Ignaz Dientzen-hofer**, the creator of much of Prague's magnificent Baroque architecture, construct the large **St Hedwig's Church** (Kościół św. Jadwigi), opposite the museum. The interior of the church (usually closed outside Mass times; ask at the museum and they may unlock it) features an oval nave plus an elongated apse and is exceptionally bright, an effect achieved by the combination of white walls and very large windows. Complementing the architecture are the bravura **frescoes** covering the vault; look out for the scene over the organ gallery, which shows the Tatars hoisting Henryk's head on a stake and celebrating their victory, while the duke's mother and wife mourn over his body.

Jawor

Some 20km south of Legnica, on the main road to Jelenia Góra, the small town of **JAWOR** was formerly the capital of one of the independent Silesian duchies. Severely bashed up in World War II, the central square is now fairly modern and colourless, although it has retained its arcaded style. Off to one side, is **St Martin's Church** (Kościół św. Marcina), a fine Gothic building, with varied furnishings including Renaissance choir stalls and a Baroque high altar.

From the Rynek, ulica Grundwalska heads northwest through plac Wolności towards the town's most intriguing monument, the barn-like, timber-framed **Church of Peace** (Kościół Pokoju: April–Oct Mon–Sat 10am–5pm, Sun noon–5pm, Nov–March by appointment; 6zł; ℡076/870 3273, ✆jawor@luteranie.pl). Its name derives from the Peace of Westphalia of 1648, which brought to an end the morass of religious and dynastic conflicts known as the Thirty Years' War. The church was one of three (two of which survive) that Silesia's Protestant minority were allowed to build following the cessation of hostilities, and the ruling Habsburg emperor demanded that it be built without stone or brick, without stone foundations or a church tower, to a different design than existing churches and outside the town walls – but within range of the cannons. Designed by an engineer, the church was cleverly laid out with four tiers of balconies in such a way that an enormous congregation could be packed into a relatively modest space, an effect illustrated even more clearly in its equally charismatic counterpart in Świdnica (see p.510).

Hourly **buses** from Legnica terminate in the marketplace below Jawor's main square, passing the Church of Peace on the way. You can grab a bite to eat at the *Ratuszowa* **restaurant** at Rynek 4: and there's a rather nice small **hotel**, the *Jawor*, just off the Rynek at Staszica 10 (℡076/871 0624, ✆www.hoteljawor.com.pl; ❺), offering a handful of fully equipped, pastel-coloured doubles.

Gross-Rosen

Just south of the village of **Rogoźnica**, 10km southeast from Jawor, lies the site of the **Gross-Rosen** concentration camp, established by the Nazis as a forced-labour camp beside a stone quarry in August 1940 and subsequently used as an extermination site. An estimated forty thousand Jews, Poles and others died here, either from exhaustion or by injections of cyanide into the heart. The reconstructed brick gateway, inscribed with *Arbeit macht frei* ("Work makes you free"), as at Auschwitz, leads to a large field with the remains of the barracks, at the end of which stands a memorial and the remains of the ovens. Gross-Rosen was the centre of a network of dozens of sub-camps, providing slave labour for projects such as the underground Riese complex (see p.513). The museum in the former officer's casino near the entrance (daily 8am–7pm) has a good exhibition, with English texts available and screenings of a thirty-minute English-language film on request (2zł). There's a cafeteria with drinks and snacks on the lower level. Regular buses between Jawor and Strzegom stop at the village, from where it's a four-kilometre walk to the site; there's also one bus a day from Strzegom that stops at the site gates.

Bolesławiec and Lwowek Śląski

Forty-five kilometres west of Legnica, on the main train line from Wrocław to Jelenia Gora, the charming old town of **BOLESŁAWIEC** sits near the edge of the great Lower Silesian forest, stretching for miles to the west. Founded in 1190 by Bolesław the Tall after the discovery of gold in the area, the town later became especially well-known for its blue-glazed **ceramics**, and the dainty blue-painted pottery made here can be seen all over Poland. Despite several large fires that burnt down parts of the town, the newly renovated centre has a fine collection of medieval buildings and a stretch of town wall.

From the train and bus stations it's a short walk south along ulica Tamka and ulica Daszyńskiego to the main square, (Rynek), with its lovely town hall, which retains its fifteenth-century tower, surrounded by some fine town houses. Overlooking the square from a raised position behind a Baroque portal, the Gothic thirteenth-century **Church of the Holy Assumption** (Wniebowzięcia Najświętszej Marii Panny) has a lavish Baroque interior, added after this part of town burnt down in 1652. Just up the hill from the church are the last remains of the once mighty town walls, the area around them now turned into a pleasant park. It's near here that in the mid-sixteenth century water from a spring was diverted along an aquaduct to bring fresh water into houses and to transport sewage through tunnels out into the city moats – only the second such system in medieval Europe. About 200m north of the church at ul. Mickiewicza 13 is the **Museum of Ceramics** (Muzeum Ceramiki: April–Sept Tues & Wed 10am–5pm, Thurs–Sat 10am–4pm, Sun 11am–4pm. Oct–March Tues–Sat 10am–4pm, Sun 11am–4pm; 3zł; Ⓦ www.muzeum.boleslawiec.net), with a varied collection of pottery from the town and beyond, as well as a small shop. To learn about the craft, it's worth visiting one of the ceramics workshops around town, most of which can be found along ulica Kościuszki, north of the train station; Ceramika Artystyczna at number 23 (Mon–Fri 9am–5pm, Sat 8am–2pm; Ⓦ www.ceraart .com.pl) has tours and a good gift shop. On the second weekend of August, the Ceramic Feast is celebrated in Bolesławiec, with stalls, events, and even a "clay love parade", with participants smeared in white clay.

The **tourism office** at ul. Sierpnia 80 nr. 12/13 (Mon–Fri 9am–5pm, Sat 9am–2pm; ℡075/732 0212, Ⓔ boleslawiec.it@data.pl) hands out the excellent *Bolesławiec Passport* booklet and can help book **accommodation**. The best place to stay is the lovely *Blue Beetroot* (℡075/736 4420, Ⓦ www.bluebeetroot.com; ⑤), set in a converted 18th century barn at Łaziska 50, 2.5km east of the centre. In town, the *Piast* hotel at ul. Asnyka 1 (℡075/732 3291 Ⓦ www.hotel-piast .pl; ⑤) is a functional 1950s building with slightly old-fashioned but comfortable en-suite rooms; the shared-facility rooms at *Pensjonat Maria*, just south of the main square at ul. 1-Maja 5 (℡075/735 1174; ❸) make a great budget option. The spacious old *Pod Złotym Aniołem* restaurant at Rynek 29 serves delicious Polish food, while *Savanna* in the town hall cellar is a very decent pizzeria with a pleasant summer terrace.

Twenty kilometres south of Bolesławiec, the run-down town of **LWÓWEK ŚLĄSKI** is worth a short stop if you're passing by. It suffered badly during the Thirty Years', War and again in the last months of World War II, when nearly half the town was destroyed. As a result, the impressively restored town hall on the main square is now surrounded by uninspired 1950s apartment buildings. The impressive medieval town walls which completely encircle the old town can be visited at the **Lubańska Tower** (Baszta Lubańska; Thurs 4–5pm; 2zł) on the western side of town. The adjacent **Church of the Holy Assumption** (Wniebowzięcia Najświętszej Marii Panny) is worth seeing for its fifteenth-century Romanesque facade with statues in the portal depicting the coronation of Mary. The **bus and train stations** are 500m east of the main square. The *Pod Czarnym Krukiem* restaurant and bar, on the main square opposite the town hall entrance, serves cheap and good Polish meals.

Świdnica and around

In the stretch of land between Wrocław and the Karkonosze mountains to the southwest lie several historic sites, most of them connected with the former **Duchy of Świdnica**, which lasted only from 1290 to 1392 but exerted a profound influence on Silesian culture. With the exception of the sprawling industrial city of Wałbrzych, it's a delightfully rustic corner of Silesia to travel through, consisting largely of rolling arable land fringed by sizeable patches of forest. Wałbrzych is an important transport hub lying on the Wrocław–Jelenia Góra rail line, although road travellers can avoid it altogether by following the main roads to Świdnica (easily accessible by bus from Jelenia Góra, Wrocław and Kłodzko) just to the north.

Świdnica

ŚWIDNICA, 50km southwest of Wrocław, and for centuries Silesia's second most important city, is blessed by the fact that it suffered little damage in World War II. Today the town still manages to preserve some of the grandeur of a former princely capital, resulting in an attractive Silesian town with a tangible self-confidence.

Although Świdnica's period of independent glory – coming soon after its twelfth-century foundation – was short-lived, the town continued to flourish under Bohemian rule. Not only was it an important centre of trade and commerce, it ranked as one of Europe's most renowned brewing centres, with its famous *Schwarze Schöps* forming the staple fare of Wrocław's best-known tavern and exported as far afield as Italy and Russia.

Arrival, information and accommodation

From the **train** and **bus stations** it's a couple of minutes' walk east to the main square. The **tourist information centre**, right on the square at ul. Wewnętrzna 2 (May–Sept Mon–Fri 9am–5pm, Sat 8am–4pm, first Sun in month 9am–4pm; Oct–April Mon–Fri 9am–5pm, first and second Sat in month 8am–4pm;

⊤074/852 0290, ⓦwww.it.swidnica.pl), can advise on **accommodation** possibilities, which include the swish and comfortable *Park*, a short walk south of the bus and train stations at ul. Pionierów 20 (⊤074/853 7722, ⓦwww .park-hotel.com.pl; ❺). The *Piast Roman*, situated just west of the Rynek at ul. Kotlarska 11 (⊤074/852 1393; ⓦwww.hotel-piast-roman.pl; ❺), also offers cosy if slightly basic en suites; while a cheaper option is the *Sportowy*, 1km south of the centre at ul. Śląska 31 (⊤074/852 2532; ❷–❸), which has functional en suites and rooms with shared facilities.

The Town

The lively main square is predominantly Baroque, though the core of many of known as the houses is often much older. Two particularly notable facades are at no. 7, **Under the Crown**, and no. 8, **The Gilded Man**. In the central area of the square are two fine fountains and the handsome early eighteenth-century **town hall**, which preserves the tower and an elegant star-vaulted chamber from its Gothic predecessor. Round the back of the town hall, the **Museum of Shopkeeping** at Rynek 37 (Muzeum Dawnego Kupiectwa: Tues–Fri 10am–3pm, Sat & Sun 11am–5pm; 3zł) sheds light on Świdnica's mercantile past, with re-creations of traditional shop interiors, their counters bearing the cumbersome but decorous weights and measures used by the town's traders.

Church of Sts Stanislaw and Wenceslas

Off the southeastern corner of the square, the main street, ulica Długa, curves gently downhill. The view ahead stretches past a number of Baroque mansions to the majestic **belfry** – at 103 metres the third highest in Poland – of the Gothic parish **Church of Sts Stanislaw and Wenceslas** (Kościół św. Stanisława i Wacława). Intended as one of a pair, the tower was so long under construction that its final stages were finished in 1613, long after the Reformation. Nevertheless, the facade, in front of which stands a Baroque statue of St Jan Nepomuk, is impressive, featuring a sublime late Gothic relief of St Anne, the Virgin and Child.

After the Thirty Years' War the church was given to the Jesuits, who carried out a Baroque transformation of the **interior**. A massive high altar with statues of the order's favourite saints dominates the east end; the organ with its carvings of the heavenly choir provides a similar focus to the west, while the lofty walls were embellished with huge Counter-Reformation altarpieces.

The Church of Peace

Set in a quiet walled close ten minutes' walk north of the main square (leave the northeastern corner of the square along ulica Pułaskiego, turn left into ul. Bohaterów Getta and keep going), the **Church of Peace** (Kościół Pokoju: April–Oct Mon–Sat 9am–1pm & 3–5pm, Sun 3–5pm; Nov–March by appoint-ment; 6zł; ⊤074/852 2814, ⓦwww.kosciolpokoju.pl) was built in the 1650s for the displaced Protestant congregation of SS Stanislaw and Wenceslas, according to the same strict conditions on construction applied at Jawor (see p.508) a few years before and to plans drawn up by the same engineer. Although the smaller of the two, it is the more accomplished: indeed, it's considered by some to be the greatest timber-framed church ever built. Thanks to the double two-tiered galleries, more than 3500 worshippers can be seated inside.

The whole appearance of the church was sharply modified in the eighteenth century, as the Protestant community increased in size and influence after Silesia came under the rule of Prussia. A domed vestibule using the hitherto banned

materials was added to the west end, a baptistery to the east, while a picturesque group of **chapels and porches** was tagged on to the two long sides of
the building. The latter, recognizable today by their red doorways, served as
the entrances to the private boxes of the most eminent citizens whose funerary
monuments are slowly crumbling away on the exterior walls. At the same time,
the church was beautified inside by the addition of a rich set of furnishings
– pulpit, font, reredos and the large and small organs.

Eating and drinking

The *Ziemiańska*, on the ground floor of the town hall building at Rynek 43, serves
up superbly prepared traditional Polish **food** in a soothing ambience; while the
Stylowa, a couple of blocks northwest of the main square at ul. Księcia Bolka
Świdnickiego 4, does food with a Hungarian slant. A good daytime **drinking**
option is the *Café 7*, a cosy split-level place with wooden furnishings and art
hanging on the walls, occupying the gatehouse of the Church of Peace on ulica
Kościelna. For evening drinks, head for the pub inside the *Ziemiańska* restaurant.

Książ

One of the best-preserved castles in Silesia – and the largest hilltop fortress in
the country – is to be found at **KSIĄŻ**, 12km west of Świdnica just off the road
to Wałbrzych. Despite its rural location the castle is easy to get to by public
transport; the bus from Świdnica to Wałbrzych will drop you off along the main
road, from where it's a ten-minute walk. Coming from Wrocław, your best
bet is to take a Wrocław–Jelenia Góra train as far as Wałbrzych-Miasto station,
where you can catch municipal bus #8 (every 30min–1hr) right to the gates of
the castle. If you miss the #8, you can ride bus #12 northwards to the end of the
line and walk the remaining distance (20min).

The **castle** (April–Sept Mon–Fri 10am–5pm, Sat & Sun 10am–6pm; Oct–
March Tues–Sun 10am–3pm, Sat & Sun 10am–4pm; 12zł; Ⓦ www.ksiaz
.walbrzych.pl) is well worth visiting for its setting alone, perched on a rocky

▲ Castle in Książ

promontory surrounded on three sides by the Pełcznica river, and tightly girdled by a belt of ornamental gardens. Despite a disparity of styles taking in practically everything from the thirteenth-century Romanesque of Duke Bolko I's original fortress to idealized twentieth-century extensions (Książ served as an HQ for both the German Wehrmacht and the Soviet Red Army), it's an impressive sight.

The most striking function rooms like the **Maximilian Hall**, a piece of palatial Baroque, can be visited individually, though the castle's main **tower** (6zł) and World War II air-raid tunnels (6zł) can only be visited as part of a Polish-language tour, for which a minimum of six people are required – hang around at the ticket office to team up with other visitors.

Occupying an outbuilding close to the entrance gate, the *Książ* **hotel** (☎074/664 3890, same website; ❹–❻) is one of three similarly- priced hotels in the complex, and makes an unusual place to spend the night. **Several cafés** and the atmospheric Polish/Italian *Brama* restaurant can be found in the complex; otherwise consider a coffee and cake in the **Palmarnia** (Palm House: daily till 6pm) 3km downhill on the northern outskirts of Wałbrzych, an extensive green-house complex stuffed with exotic plants and with a charming café at its heart.

The Riese underground complex

Between November 1943 and the end of the World War II, the German Wehrmacht built a huge underground complex in the remote Sowie mountains near the town of Głuszyca, 30km south of Świdnica and 15km southwest of Wałbrzych. Using prisoner labour supplied by the Gross-Rosen concentration camp and its sub-camps (see p.508), 213,000 cubic metres of bomb-proof tunnels and halls were carved out of the rocks under the code-name Riese ("giant"), at a cost of 150 million German marks, using 257,000 cubic metres of reinforced concrete. The removal of all machines and documents by the retreating Germans and invading Soviets means that even today the exact purpose of the underground facilities is unclear; underground factories manufacturing V1 and V2 rockets and planes could have been built here, or it could have been the headquarters for Hitler and his army and air force command. The project was certainly very important, as it had a top-priority status, required 28,000 prisoners to work on it, and in 1944 was allocated more concrete than were all civilian air-raid shelters constructed in Germany that year. Documentation suggests that much more concrete was used than is currently visible – indicating that there may be many more tunnels that remain uncovered.

In 1997, three of the six sections of the complex were opened to tourists, of which **OSÓWKA**, near Sierpnice village, four kilometres east of Głuszyca and best accessed via that town, is the most impressive. The Osówka **visitor centre** (daily: April–Sept 10am–6pm, Oct–March 10am–4pm; ☎074/845 6220, ⓦwww.osowka.pl) organizes various guided tours of the complex, most popular of which is the forty-minute general tour (8 per day in summer, 4 per day in winter; 10zł). There's also a one-hour historical tour, a two-hour "underground trail" tour and an adventurous three-hour "expedition" tour; book ahead for all. Depending on the group size and guide, translations in English can be given; otherwise you need to book an English-language tour guide (an additional 120zł) in advance.

On the other side of the mountain near **WALIM**, the smaller **Rzeczka complex** (Muzeum Sztolni Walimskich: May–Sept Mon–Fri 9am–6pm, Sat & Sun 9am–7pm, Oct–April Mon–Fri 9am–5pm, Sat & Sun 9am–6pm; 10zł;

☎074/845 7300, ⓦ www.sztolnie.pl) has several tunnels and halls that can be visited on guided tours; hiring an English-language guide costs 100zł extra. Walim is best reached directly from Wałbrzych.

The Głuszyca **tourist office** at ul. Grunwaldzka 20 (Mon–Fri 9am–4pm, Oct–April also Sat 9am–2pm; ☎074/845 6220) can help with accommodation and transport information to both complexes and. From Monday to Saturday, three buses (the first at 10.20am) link Wałbrzych with Głuszyca and Sierpnica; ask the driver and you'll be dropped off at the Osówka visitor centre and picked up later. Up to eight daily buses connect Wałbrzych to Walim.

Krzeszów

The village of **KRZESZÓW** lies in the shade of a huge **abbey** complex which ranks, historically and certainly artistically, among the most exceptional monuments in Silesia. Situated 25km west of Wałbrzych it's some way off the main rail and road routes, but you won't regret making the effort to visit the place – to get there by public transport, catch a bus to the grubby textile town of Kamienna Góra (hourly services from Wałbrzych, less frequently from Jelenia Góra and Wrocław) and change there.

The abbey was originally founded in 1242 by Benedictines at the instigation of Anne, widow of Henryk the Pious. However, they stayed for less than half a century; the land was bought back by Anne's grandson, Bolko I of Świdnica, who granted it to the Cistercians and made their church his family's mausoleum. Despite being devastated by the Hussites and again in the Thirty Years' War, the abbey flourished, eventually owning nearly three hundred square kilometres of land, including two towns and forty villages. This economic base funded the complete rebuilding in the Baroque period, but not long afterwards the community went into irreversible decline as the result of the confiscation of its lands during the Silesian Wars. For over a century the buildings lay abandoned, but in a nicely symmetrical turn of events they were reoccupied by Benedictine monks from Prague in 1919, with a contingent of nuns joining them after World War II.

There are two churches here, both very different in size and feel. The smaller and relatively plainer exterior of the two, **St Joseph's Church** (Kościół św. Józefa), was built in the 1690s for parish use. In replacing the medieval church, its dedication was changed to reflect the Counter-Reformation cult of the Virgin Mary's husband, designed to stress a family image that was overlooked in earlier Catholic theology. Inside, the **fresco** cycle in which Joseph – previously depicted by artists as a shambling old man – appears to be little older than his wife and is similarly transported to heaven, is a prime artistic expression of this short-lived cult.

Built in the grand Baroque style, the monastic **church** was begun in 1728 and finished in just seven years. Its most striking feature is undoubtedly its imposing **facade**, with two domed towers. Inside, the most notable painting is a Byzantine icon which has been at Krzeszów since the fourteenth century. The Piast **mausoleum** behind the high altar is kept open when tourist groups are around (which is quite frequently in summer); at other times you'll have to persuade a monk or nun to open it up. Focal point of the chapel is the grandiose coloured marble monument to Bernard of Świdnica, to each side of which are more modest Gothic sarcophagi of Bolko I and II.

For an **overnight stay**, the *Willmanowa Pokusa* hotel right outside the abbey complex (☎075/742 3150; ❹) offers comfortable en suites in an atmospheric old building. Alternatively the charming *Betlejem* pension (☎075/742 3324, ⓦ www .betlejem.com; ❷), signposted 2km west of town in the forest, makes an idyllic retreat; do book ahead. Adjacent to the building is the Krzeszów bishops' Water Pavilion (Pawilion na Wodzie), which the pension owners can open up for you for a small fee. The *Willmanowa Pokusa* has a good **restaurant** serving traditional Polish nosh; and there are a couple of other places to eat and drink around the car park in front of the abbey.

Jelenia Góra and around

Some 110km southwest of Wrocław, **JELENIA GÓRA** is the gateway to one of Poland's most popular holiday and recreation areas, the **Karkonosze national park**. Its name means "Deer Mountain", but the rusticity this implies is scarcely reflected in the town itself, which has been a manufacturing centre for the past five centuries. Founded as a fortress in 1108 by King Bolesław the Wrymouth, Jelenia Góra came to prominence in the Middle Ages through glass and iron production, with high-quality textiles taking over as the cornerstone of its economy in the seventeenth century. With this solid base, it was hardly surprising that, after it came under Prussian control, the town was at the forefront of the German Industrial Revolution. Jelenia Góra is best reached by the regular buses from Wrocław as the train connections are very slow.

Arrival, information and accommodation

The main **train station** is about fifteen minutes' walk from the centre, at the east end of ulica 1 Maja. Local buses plus a few services to nearby towns (notably Karpacz) leave from the bays in front, but the **bus station** for all intercity departures is at the opposite end of town, just west of the Rynek on the far side of ulica Obrońców Pokoju. The **tourist office** at ul. Bankowa 27 (Mon–Fri 9am–6pm, Sat 10am–2pm, July–Sept also Sun 10am–2pm; ☏075/767 6925, ⓦcitik.jeleniagora.pl/en) offers a wealth of brochures and advice on tourism throughout the Karkonosze region.

Given the existence of plentiful buses to the nearby mountain resorts of Karpacz and Szklarska Poręba, it's unlikely that you'll want to stay in Jelenia Góra, although the tourist office can help find a **hotel** in town – or in the spa suburb of Cieplice (see p.516). The central *Jelonek*, ul. 1 Maja 5 (☏075/764 6541, ⓦwww.hotel-jelonek.com.pl; ❸), is a welcoming, intimate place in a Baroque town house; while the *Park* at ul. Sudecka 42 (☏075/752 4525, ⓦwww.camping.karkonosz.pl; ❸), has clean en suites as well as year-round **camping** facilities.

The Town

Thankfully Jelenia Góra's present-day factories have been confined to the peripheries, leaving the traffic-free historic centre remarkably well preserved. Even in a country with plenty of prepossessing central squares, the **plac Ratuszowy** is an impressive sight. Not the least of its attractions is that it's neither a museum piece nor the main commercial centre: most of the businesses are restaurants and cafés, while the tall mansions are now subdivided into flats. Although their architectural styles range from the late Renaissance via Baroque to Neoclassical, the houses form an unusually coherent group, all having pastel-toned facades reaching down to arcaded fronts at street level. Occupying the familiar central position is the large mid-eighteenth-century **town hall**, its unpainted stonework providing an apposite foil to the colourful houses.

To the east of plac Ratuszowy rises the slender belfry of the Gothic parish **church**. Epitaphs to leading local families adorn the outer walls, while the inside is chock-full of Renaissance and Baroque furnishings. Yet another eye-catching tower can be seen just to the east, at the point where the main shopping thoroughfare, ulica Marii Konopnickiej, changes its name to ulica 1 Maja. Originally part of the sixteenth-century fortifications, it was taken over a couple of centuries later to serve as the belfry of **St Anne's Chapel** (Kaplica św. Anny).

A few hundred metres down ulica 1 Maja and enclosed in a walled park-like cemetery is the **Holy Cross Church** (Kościół św. Krzyża), built in the early eighteenth century by a Swedish architect, Martin Franze, on the model of St Catherine's in Stockholm. Though sober from the outside, the double-galleried interior, which can fit four thousand worshippers, is richly decorated with trompe l'oeil frescoes.

From the bustling ulica Bankowa which skirts the Old Town to the south, ulica Jana Matejki leads to the **Karkonosze Museum** at no. 28 (Muzeum Karkonoskie: Tues, Thurs & Fri 9am–3.30pm, Wed, Sat & Sun 9am–4.30pm; 3zł, free on Wed) at its far end, just below the wooded Kościuszki Hill. Apart from temporary exhibitions, the display space here is given over to the history of **glass** from antiquity to the present day, with due emphasis on local examples and a particularly impressive twentieth-century section.

Eating and drinking

There are numerous cafés and **restaurants** grouped around the main square, most offering outdoor seating and cheap, reasonable food. Underneath the arcades at no. 22, the elegant *Sorrento* is the best place for Polish and Italian specialities; *4 Pory Roku*, at no. 39, is a simpler venue for Polish dishes and pizza. *Azteka*, pl. Ratuszowy 6/7, is a fun place to tuck into the blander side of Mexican cooking, or simply have a drink; while *Kaligrafia Klub* is an atmospheric cellar bar below the town hall with regular live music and dancing.

Cieplice Śląskie-Zdrój

The municipal boundaries of Jelenia Góra incorporate a number of communities to the south, nearest of which is the old spa town of **CIEPLICE ŚLĄSKIE-ZDRÓJ**, 8km away. Although it has a number of modern sanatoria, Cieplice still manages to bask in the aura of an altogether less pressurized age. To catch this atmosphere at its most potent, attend one of the regular concerts of **Viennese music** in the spa park's delightful Neoclassical **theatre**; Jelenia Góra's tourist information centre (see p.515) has up-to-date events listings.

The broad main street of Cieplice is designated as a square – plac Piastowski. Its main building is the large eighteenth-century **Schaffgotsch palace**, named after the German grandees who formerly owned much of the town. There are also a couple of Baroque **parish churches** – the Catholic one stands in a close at the western end of the street and is generally open, whereas its Protestant counterpart to the east of the palace is locked except on Sunday mornings.

A walk south through the Park Norweski, which continues the spa park on the southern side of the River Podgórna, brings you to the small **Natural History Museum** at ul. Wolności 268 (Muzeum Przyrodnicze: May–Sept Tues–Fri 9am–6pm, Sat & Sun 9am–5pm; Oct–April Tues–Sun 9am–4pm; 4zł; Ⓦwww.muzeum-cieplice.com) housed in a Norwegian-style wooden building from the 1909, you'll find cases of butterflies as well as the stuffed avians in which the museum specializes.

Local **bus** #9 from Jelenia Góra passes through the centre of Cieplice; #7 and #15 stop on the western side of town, while #4, #13 and #14 stop on the eastern side. The local **tourist office**, pl. Piastowski 36 (Mon–Fri 9am–5pm, Sat 10am–2pm; ☎075/755 8844), can help find **private rooms** (❶) or a **hotel**, should you want to stay here. The *Cukierna Weronika* **café** on plac Piastowski offers some hard-to-resist home-made cakes; while the *Pod Złotym Łukiem* **restaurant**, just off plac Piastowski at ul. Leśnica 2, serves up superb Polish cuisine in elegant surroundings.

The Karkonosze

The mountains of the **Karkonosze** are the highest and best-known part of the chain known as the Sudety, which stretches 300km northwest from the smaller Beskid range, forming a natural border between Silesia and Bohemia. Known for its raw climate, the predominantly granite Karkonosze range rises abruptly on the Polish side, and its lower slopes are heavily forested with fir, beech, birch and pine. At around 1100m, these trees give way to dwarf mountain pines and alpine plants, some of them endemic to the region.

Primarily renowned as **hiking** country, these moody, mist-shrouded mountains strongly stirred the German Romantic imagination and were hauntingly depicted by the greatest artist of the movement, Caspar David Friedrich. From the amount of German you hear spoken in the resorts, it's clear that the region offers a popular and inexpensive vacation for its former occupants – and the Polish tourist authorities certainly aren't complaining.

Lying just outside the park's boundaries, the two sprawling resorts of **Szklarska Poręba** and **Karpacz** have expanded over recent years to meet this need, and constitute well-equipped bases from which to embark on summer hiking and winter skiing expeditions. As the area is relatively compact – the total length of the Karkonosze is no more than 37km – and the public transport system good (if circuitous), there's no need to use more than one base. The upper reaches of the Karkonosze have been designated a **national park** (entry 3zł per day; ⓦ www.kpnmab.pl), but, as elsewhere, this label does not guarantee an unequivocal vision of natural splendour. If you're not into extended walking or off-road biking, a **chairlift** ascent up to the summits will make an enjoyable day's excursion.

The 1:25,000 **map** of the park, available from kiosks and tourism offices, shows all the paths and viewpoints and is a must if you intend doing any serious walking. Like all mountain areas, the range has changeable weather; take warm clothing and water even on a sunny summer's day. **Mist** and clouds hang around on about three hundred days in the year; in such circumstances stick to the **marked paths** and don't expect to see much.

Szklarska Poręba

SZKLARSKA PORĘBA lies 18km southwest of Jelenia Góra and just to the west of a major international road crossing into the Czech Republic. It can be reached from Jelenia Góra either by train, depositing you at the station on the northern heights of the town, or by bus, whose terminus is at the eastern entrance to the resort. On the way into town the main road passes through the Kamienna river gorge, and you can stop off to see the **Szklarka waterfall**, situated a short walk from the road in a beautiful canyon setting.

The Kamienna river slices Szklarska Poręba in two, with the main streets in the valley and the rest of the town rising high into the hills on each side. It's well worth following the stream all the way through the built-up part of the resort, as there's a picturesque stretch on the far side of the centre, with some striking **rock formations** (the Kruce Skalny) towering above the southern bank.

From the busy town the quickest way up to the summits is on the Szrenica **chairlift** (late April to mid-Oct & Dec to early April daily 8am–4pm; 28zł return), which goes up in two stages and terminates a short walk from the summit of **Szrenica** (1362m). Its departure point is at the southern end of town: from the bus station, follow ulica 1 Maja, then turn right into ulica Turystyczna, continuing along all the way to the end. From the top of the lift, you can walk back down following the red trail to the tourist information office or the green and then blue trails to the eastern end of town. More ambitiously, follow the ridge east to the sister peak of Śnieżka and the resort of Karpacz beneath it (see p.518), a good day's walking.

Over on the northern side of town, the **Hauptmann House** at ul. 11 Listopada 23 (Dom Hauptmannów: Tues, Thurs & Fri 9am–3.30pm, Wed, Sat & Sun 9am–4.30pm; 2zł) has photographs and manuscripts of the German novelist and playwright Gerhard Hauptmann, one of the many artists and writers who spent their holidays in Szklarska at the close of the nineteenth century. It was here that Hauptmann wrote much of *The Weavers*, a drama of Silesian industrial life that helped bag the Nobel Prize for Literature in 1912.

Practicalities

As you'd expect, Szklarska Poręba has a great variety of accommodation. Online information is available at Ⓦwww.szklarskaporeba.pl, while at the top end of town, the **tourist information centre** at ul. Jedności Narodowej 1a (Mon–Fri 8am–4pm, Sat & Sun 10am–5pm; Ⓣ075/754 7743, Ⓦwww.sklarskaporeba.pl) has access to over thirty **pensions** (❷–❸) offering good-value accommodation, often involving worthwhile half-board deals. They also have a team of **guides** (around 500zł per day) if you want assistance getting up and down the mountains.

Good-value **hotels** include the *Eden*, ul. Okrzei 13 (Ⓣ075/717 2181; ❸) a big modern house offering en suites just south of the centre; and the *Bornit*, ul. Mickiewicza 21 (Ⓣ075/647 2503, Ⓦwww.bornit.interferie.pl; ❻), a glass-fronted monolith overlooking the town centre from a hillside perch just to the west. *Carmen*, near the Szrenice lift at ul. Broniewskiego 8 (Ⓣ075/717 2558, Ⓦwww.carmen.info.pl; ❹–❺), is a largish pension with well-appointed en suites. The main **youth hostel** (Ⓣ075/717 2141) is open all year but is a long way northeast of the centre at ul. Piastowska 1, on the wrong side of town for the best walks. The most convenient **campsite** is the *Pod Mostem* at ul. Gimnazi-jalna 5 (Ⓣ075/717 3062), just west of the bus station.

There's a cluster of inexpensive snack huts at the foot of the Szrenica chairlift; otherwise the central ulica Jedności Narodowej and ulica 1 Maja offer the main concentration of **places to eat**. *Fantazja*, at ul. Jedności Narodowej 14, is good for meat and fish dishes, and has a separate café section with coffee and ice cream. The weird hobbit home interior of ⅔ *Metafora*, just off ulica 1 Maja at ul. Objazdowa 1, is the quirkiest place to eat good Polish food, perhaps followed by drinks and a jazz or blues concert at the stylish *Klub Jazgot* in the basement.

Karpacz and around

KARPACZ, 15km south of Jelenia Góra and linked to it by hourly buses, is an even more scattered community than Szklarska Poręba, occupying an enormous area for a place with only a few thousand permanent inhabitants. It's a fairly characterless place if the centre of town is all you see, but the sheer range of easily accessible hikes in the neighbouring mountains make this the most versatile of Silesia's highland resorts.

Karpacz is a long, thin settlement built along the main road, ulica 3 Maja (ul. Karkonoska in its upper reaches), which stretches and curves uphill for some five kilometres. Most tourist facilities are located in **Karpacz Dolny** (Lower Karpacz), at the lower, eastern end of the resort, although **Karpacz Górny** (Upper Karpacz), up the valley to the west, has its fair share of hotels and pensions. In between lies the **Biały Jar** roundabout, which is the main starting point for most of the hiking trails.

Arrival, information and accommodation

Most **buses** from Jelenia Góra terminate at Biały Jar (picking up and dropping off at numerous stops along ul. 3 Maja on the way), although some continue all the way to Karpacz Górny. Bearing in mind that it can take an hour to walk from one end of the resort to the other, these buses represent a useful way of shuttling up and down the resort once you get established.

The **tourist information centre** at ul. Konstytucji 3 Maja 25 (Mon–Sat 9am–5pm; ☎075/761 9716, ⓦwww.karpacz.pl) in Karpacz Dolny sells hiking maps, and will help you find a bed in one of Karpacz's innumerable **private rooms** (❷–❸) and **pensions** (❸–❹).

Hotels

Bacówki ul. Obrońców Pokoju 6a ☎075/761 9615, ⓦwww.bacowki.wczasy.net.pl. Cluster of wooden huts spread over a meadow just east of Karpacz Dolny, with bathrooms shared between every two or three rooms. ❷–❸

Dom Parafialny Wang ul. Na Śnieżkę 8 ☎075/761 9228, ⓦwww.wang.com.pl. Cheap, simple rooms in the church buildings right beside the Wang Chapel and mountain trails. ❷–❸

Dziki Potok ul. Mysliwska 22 ☎075/761 6478, ⓦwww.dzikipotok.pl. Elegant new spa hotel in a quiet setting one kilometre northwest of the centre. The modern en-suite rooms and apartments are very comfortable, and there's a good

restaurant serving Polish, Mediterranean and Indonesian food. ❼

Karkonosze ul. Wolna 4 ☎075/761 8277, ⓦwww.hotel-karkonosze.com.pl. Attractive alpine chalet-style building in a quiet residential street, and right next to a nursery skiing slope. Small bright rooms with shower and TV. ❺

Rezydencja ul. Parkowa 6 ☎075/761 8020, ⓦwww.hotelrezydencja.pl. Elegant, upmarket place in Karpacz Dolny whose understated plushness makes it the cosiest place to stay in town. ❺

Skalny ul. Obrońców Pokoju 3 ☎075/752 7000, ⓦwww.orbis.pl. A 300-bed block that lacks the character and intimacy of the other places in town, but has reliable standards of comfort and the added bonus of a swimming pool. ❻

The Town

Located in the upper reaches of Karpacz Górny is the most famous, not to say curious, building in the Karkonosze – the **Wang Chapel** (Świątynia Wang: mid-April to Oct Mon–Sat 9am–6pm, Sun 11.30am–6pm; Nov to mid-April Mon–Sat 9am–5pm, Sun 11.30am–5pm; 5zł; ⓦwww.wang.com.pl). Girdled at a discreet distance by souvenir stalls and snack bars, this twelfth-century wooden church with Romanesque touches boasts some wonderfully refined carving on its portals and capitals, as well as an exterior of tiny wooden tiles. It stood for nearly six hundred years in Vang village in southern Norway, but by 1840 it had fallen into such a state of disrepair that the parishioners sought a buyer for it. Having failed to interest any Norwegians, they sold it to one of the most enthusiastic architectural conservationists of the day, King Friedrich Wilhelm IV of Prussia. He had the church dismantled and shipped to this isolated spot, where

▲ Wang Chapel

it was reassembled. The chapel is still used on Sunday mornings for Protestant worship; there are also organ recitals on alternate Sundays in summer.

A couple of kilometres downhill from the chapel, above Biały Jar, the **Toy Museum** at ul. Karkonoska 5 (Muzeum Zabawek: Tues 9am–5.30pm, Wed–Fri 9am–3.30pm, Sat 10am–3.30pm, Sun 10am–4.30pm; 6zł) is as much a tribute to local crafts as to the history of playthings, with a host of wood-carved animals, carriages and sleds. Down in Karpacz Dolny, just east of the main strip at ul. Kopernika 2, the **Museum of Sport and Tourism** (Muzeum Sportu i Turystyki: Tues–Sun 9am–5pm; 4zł), has an enjoyable selection of archaic bobsleighs and crampons and, upstairs, a room full of lace, carved furniture and traditional dress.

Eating and drinking

Karpacz is full of places where you can refuel after a hard day in the hills, with the stretch of ul. Konstitucji 3 Maja just west of the tourist office offering a particularly generous selection of **eating** and **drinking** venues. *Bar Mieszko*, at the top end of Karpacz Dolny in what passes for a village square, is the place to go for cheap *pierogi*, *bigos* and other filling Polish staples; *Pizzeria Verde*, a little way further down the main ul. Konstitucji 3. Maja, offers a good range of thin-crust pies in stylish surroundings; and the nearby *Zagroda Goralska*, ul. Konstitucji 3 Maja 46, serves up cheap and filling cuts of roast meat in a timber hut. Ducha Gór at ul. Olimpijska 6 is another rustic place with good quality Polish and international dishes. *Country Grill*, ul. Obrońców Pokoju 6a, is a ranch-like place where you can eat traditional Polish food and sink numerous beers in a large wooden stable.

Hiking in the park

Before undertaking any day-walks in this area it's worth getting yourself a copy of the 1:30,000 Karpacz i Okolice **map**, if you haven't already got the national park map mentioned on p.517.

Booths next to the Wang Chapel and the Biały Jar roundabout sell entrance **tickets** to the national park (4zł). Biały Jar is the more popular entrance point to the park, not least because it's twenty minutes' walk from the lower station of the **chairlift** (April–Nov 8.30am–5pm; Dec–March 8.30am–4pm; return 25zł) which leads up towards Kopa (1377m), just twenty minutes from the Karkonosz's high point of Śnieźka (see below).

A short detour west from the lift station takes you to the upper of two **waterfalls** on the River Łomnica, which rises high in the mountains and flows all the way through Karpacz, defining much of the northern boundary of the town, as well as the course of ulica Konstytucji 3 Maja, which follows a largely parallel line. The second waterfall, below Biały Jar on a path waymarked in red, is less idyllic, having been altered to form a dam.

The most popular goal for most walks is the summit of **Śnieźka**, at 1602m the highest peak in the range and sometimes covered with snow for up to six months of the year. Lying almost due south of Karpacz, it can be reached by the **black trail** in about three hours from the *Biały Jar*, or in about forty minutes if you pick up the trail at the top of the Kopa chairlift. From the chairlift you pass through the Kocioł Łomniczki, whose abundant vegetation includes Carpathian birch, cloves, alpine roses and monk's hood. Access to the actual summit is by either the steep and stony "Zigzag Way" (the red trail) which ascends by the most direct method, or the easier "Jubilee Way" (the blue route), which goes round the northern and eastern sides of the summit. At the top is a large modern weather station-cum-snack bar, where you can get cheap hot **meals**; refreshments are also available in the refuges on Kopa and *Pod Śnieźką*, and at the junction of the two trails.

The **red trail** also serves the summit. From Biały Jar it follows the stream to the chairlift terminal and then forks right near the Orlinek hotel onto an unmade track which climbs steadily for forty minutes to a junction with a yellow path and a refuge. The path continues above the tree line and after some steeper zigzags reaches the *Pod Śnieźką* refuge, another forty minutes later: the refuge is less than fifteen minutes above the Kopa chairlift terminal, following the black waymarkers. From here the side-trip east to the summit of Śnieźka takes twenty minutes by the "Zigzag Way". On a clear day, the **view** from Śnieźka stretches for eighty kilometres, embracing not only other parts of the Sudety chain in Poland and the Czech Republic, but also the Lausitz mountains in Germany.

Once at the summit, it's worth following the red trail immediately to the west above two glacial **lakes**, Mały Staw and Wielki Staw just above the tree line. Assuming you don't want to continue on to Szklarska Poręba, you can then descend by the blue trail, which brings you out at Karpacz Górny. If you're feeling energetic you might like to go a bit further along the red trail and check out the Słonecznik and the Pielgrzymy **rock formations** thereafter descending by the yellow and later blue trails back to Karpacz Górny. If the above routes seem too strenuous, a satisfyingly easy alternative is to take the blue trail from the Karpacz Górny to the *Samotnia* refuge on the shore of Mały Staw, a round trip taking about three hours.

The Ziemia Kłodzka

Due south of Wrocław is a rural area of wooded hills, gentle valleys and curative springs that provides a welcome antidote to the heavy industry that blights much of lowland Silesia. Known as the **Kłodzko Region** (Ziemia Kłodzka) after its largest town, it's surrounded on three sides by the Czech Republic with which the Sudety mountains form a natural frontier.

A popular holiday area for Silesians looking for a break from the industrial conurbations, the five **spa resorts** (identified by the suffix -*zdrój*) have suffered from decades of neglect, although in recent years they've received a boost from increasing health tourism with busloads of Germans and Austrians arriving to "take the waters". A sense of faded grandeur still prevails in some resorts.

In the hills above the towns, are some fine hiking routes passing through landscapes dotted with sometimes bizarre rock outcrops. A network of marked paths covers the entire region, in which there are several separate ranges; the best are found in the southeast of the area, taken up by the Śnieżnik Massif. This specific area is as yet little touched by the more rapacious tourist development elsewhere and is a worthwhile destination for spending a few quiet days in the hills. The red and yellow 1:90,000 Ziemia Kłodzka map, easily available from local bookshops, is an essential companion.

Accommodation throughout the Kłodzko region is plentiful, although the bigger resorts tend to fill up with partying youngsters in high summer. Nevertheless it's possible to stay here very cheaply, with the **pensions** offering particularly good value. For **getting around**, buses, which eventually get to even the smallest villages, are your best bet as train stations are often on the outskirts of the towns.

Kłodzko

Spread out beneath the ramparts of a stolid Prussian fortress, the thousand-year-old town of **KŁODZKO** was for centuries a place of strategic importance and today its old town still retains some of the charm of its medieval origins – a rarity in Silesia, which makes a stopover here rewarding. Situated on the main trade route between Bohemia and Poland, until the eighteenth-century Prussian takeover Kłodzko's ownership fluctuated between the adjacent nations. A devastating flood hit the lower part of town in July 2007, drowning seven people and destroying property; however, most of the damage has now been repaired.

Kłodzko's bus station is the main public transport hub for the whole region. There's not a great choice of accommodation in town, so you're best advised to head for one of the spa resorts, like Kudowa-Zdrój, if you're going to be staying in this part of Silesia for any length of time.

Arrival, information and accommodation

Kłodzko Miasto **train station**, beside the **bus station**, is only a few minutes' walk east from the centre; this station is also the best place to catch trains heading south, and to the two spa valleys to the east and west. The main station, Kłodzko Główny, is over 2km north and only worth using if you're heading to Wrocław or Jelenia Góra. The **tourist office**, inside the town hall at pl. Chrobrego 1 (daily 10am–6pm; ☎074/865 4689, ⓦwww.powiat.klodzko.pl), can fill you in on accommodation possibilities throughout the region. PTTK at ul. Wita Stwosza 1 is the place to buy local hiking **maps**.

The best of the hotels is the *Casa D'Oro* at ul. Grottgera 7 between the station and the Old Town (☎074/867 0216, ⓦwww.casadoro.pl; ❺) which offers decent-sized en-suite rooms. Just south of the centre the *Marhaba* at ul. Daszyńskiego 16 (☎074/865 9933, ⓦwww.marhaba.ng.pl; ❸) offers small but tolerable rooms, some of which are en suites, others just with a sink. The *Korona*, northwest of the town centre at Noworudzka 1 (☎074/867 3737; ⓦwww.hotel-korona.pl; ❸), may look dour on the outside but has cheerful little en-suite rooms inside. There's a basic **youth hostel** (☎074/867 2524) 1km north of the centre at ul. Nadrzeczna 5, which will put you up for under 20zł a head – to get there, follow ulica Łukasińskiego from the main square.

The Town

From the main train and bus stations situated side by side in the centre of town, the best way to enjoy an exploration of the attractive **Old Town** is to cross the steel-girder bridge onto ulica Grottgera. At the end of this street you'll find the main survivor of the town's medieval fortifications, the Gothic **bridge**, the oldest of its kind in Poland, adorned in the Baroque period by a collection of sacred statues who still manage to look pleadingly heavenward despite centuries of weathering.

On the opposite bank, grand nineteenth-century mansions rise high above the river. Passing them, you ascend to the sloping main square, **plac Bolesława Chrobrego,** which has a number of fine old houses from various periods, a grand nineteenth-century town hall and an ornate Baroque fountain which looks up to the fortress's walls. Greatly extended by the Prussians in the eighteenth century from earlier defensive structures built on the rocky knoll, the squat **Kłodzko Fortress** (Twierdza Kłodzka: daily 9am–6pm; 13zł) lost its reputation for impregnability when captured by the all-conquering army of Napoleon in 1807. As with other historical monuments which have suffered the vagaries of several disparate owners, the fortress nowadays has become a repository for a variety of objects from old fire engines to contemporary local glassware, and you can even learn to abseil in one of the courtyards. However, most visitors come here for the stronghold's **dungeons** and extensive **tunnels** (Polish-speaking guided tours daily May–Oct 9am–6pm, Nov–April 10am–4pm; 6zł), which were excavated by prisoners of war during the Prussian era.

By the entrance of the fortress is the northern aperture of the 600m **underground passageway** (podziemna trasa; daily May–Oct 10am–6pm, Nov–April 10am–4pm; 7zł), passing under the Old Town. There are various instruments of torture to see along the way, including miniature French guillotines and even more barbaric Prussian methods of execution. The exit brings you out on plac Koscielny beside the parish **Church of Our Lady** (Kościół NMP: daily 9.30am–4pm) with its fine Baroque interior. Look out for the fourteenth-century tomb of the founder, Bishop Ernst of Pordolice, which managed to survive the desecrations of the Hussites five centuries ago.

Heading due west brings you to the **Kłodzko Regional Museum** at ul. Łukasiewicza 4 (Muzeum Ziemi Kłodzkiej; Wed–Fri 10am–4pm, Sat & Sun 11am–5pm; 5zł, free on Sun), which has a large collection of local glassware, and an exhaustive assembly of more than four hundred **clocks** from the Świedbodzia and Srebrna Góra clock factories. The display features everything from ancient astronomical devices, working grandfather and irritating cuckoo clocks, to porcelain-backed kitchen clocks.

Eating and drinking

U Ratusza, inside the town hall at pl. Chrobrego 3, is the place to go for a slap-up Polish meal. *Oregano,* opposite the Franciscan church at ul. Daszyńskiego 8, is a stylish place with a wide range of both Italian and Polish food. The one-room ⚥ *Cynamonowa* café on the corner of ulica Wojska Polskiego and ulica Kościuszki has a lovely 1950s atmosphere, great coffee and cakes and regular cultural events including film screenings and alternative music concerts. For **drinking**, there's a handful of beer gardens on and around the main square in fine weather; otherwise try *AK*, ul. Armii Krajowej 2, an atmospheric cellar bar that's popular with the local goths.

Wambierzyce

Heading west from Kłodzko on the main road to Prague are a string of **spa towns**. The first of these, **Polanica-Zdrój**, is not in itself worth the detour, but a right turn at the west end of town leads 9km to the village of **WAMBIERZYCE** (Kłodzko–Polanica–Radków buses pass through several times per day), a tiny rural settlement which is the site of huge religious institution.

The Baroque **basilica**, perched above a broad flight of steps above the village square has been the site of pilgrimages since 1218, when a blind man allegedly regained his sight by praying at a statue of the Virgin Mary enshrined in a lime tree. The impressive monumental facade of the basilica is all that remains of the third shrine built here at the end of the seventeenth century, the main body of the building collapsing soon after completion, at which point it was rebuilt with the interior you see today. The basilica is circumvented by a broad ambulatory with a variety of chapels and grottoes representing the Stations of the Cross and biblical scenes. The small nave of the basilica is a fairly reserved octagon, while the all-important pulpit gets the usual excess of ornamentation. On the ceiling is a fresco depicting an angel passing the design for the basilica to the local people, its anticipated form appearing as a ghostly image on the hill behind them. The oval chancel has a cupola illustrating the fifteen Mysteries of the Rosary with a magnificent silver tabernacle from Venice bearing the miraculous image, accompanied by a profusion of votive offerings encased at its side.

Found all around the town are nearly one hundred **shrines** depicting further scenes from the passion, culminating at **Calvary**, the wooded hill facing the basilica which is reached by a long series of steps also lined by shrines. At the foot of the hill is the wonderful **Moving Crib** (Ruchoma Szopka; Tues–Sun: May–Sept 9am–6pm, Oct–April 10am–1pm & 2pm–4pm; 5zł), a room with eight clockwork mechanical contraptions from the nineteenth century with hundreds of moving figures in miniature theatre sets that present biblical scenes, some of them rather gruesome, as well as local themes such as coal mining.

There's a comfortable **hotel**, the *Wambierzyce*, on the main square at pl. NMP 1 (℡074/871 9186, ⓦwww.hotel-wambierzyce.pl; ❻), which also has a good **restaurant**.

Duszniki-Zdrój

Back on the main Prague road, continuing 10km west of Polanica-Zdrój brings you to the much older spa resort of **DUSZNIKI-ZDRÓJ**. The town is best known for its **Chopin Musical Festival** (ⓦwww.chopin.festival.pl) held here in early August each year, an event which commemorates the concerts given by the sixteen-year-old composer during a convalescence in 1826.

Duszniki's **train station** is just to the north of the main road, with the Old Town and spa area to the south. On the **main square**, a few Renaissance and Baroque facades remain, one of them bearing a plaque recording Chopin's stay. Leaving the market square to the east down ulica Kłodzko, you pass the parish **Church of Sts Peter and Paul** (Kościół św. Piotra i Pawła), an externally bland example of early eighteenth-century Baroque with an unusually ornate pulpit shaped like a whale, with the creature's gaping maw forming a preaching platform.

At the bottom of the same street the **Museum of Papermaking** (Muzeum Papiernictwa; May–Oct daily 9am–5pm, Nov–April Tues-Sun 9am–3pm; 8zł; ⓦwww.muzpap.pl), which occupies a large paper mill dating from the early seventeenth century, constitutes the town's chief curiosity. One of Poland's most precious industrial buildings, its fine half-timbering, sweeping mansard roof, novel domed entrance turret and crude gable end form an eye-catching example of Baroque architecture. Inside lies a worthy history lesson on paper-making through the ages, and for a few extra złoty you get the chance to press your own carpet-thick sheets of paper.

The town's spa park lies over to the southwestern side of the main square, a long stretch of tree-shaded walkways that culminates after about one kilometre with an ensemble of nineteenth-century buildings including the **Dworek Chopina** (Chopin Palace), a dinky Neo-classical pavilion that holds recitals throughout the summer season, including those connected with the Chopin Festival.

Practicalities

Buses pick up and drop off on the Wrocław–Prague road, while the **train station** is just off the road to the north. Dusznik-Zdrój is easily visited from the surrounding towns, but if you want to stay here the **tourist office**, Rynek 9 (Mon–Fri 9am–5pm, Sat 10am–2pm; ☎074/866 9413, ⓦwww.duszniki.pl), will direct you towards the town's private rooms (❶) and pensions (❸). The best hotel is the *Frederyk* in the spa park at ul. Wojska Polskiego 10 (☎074/866 0488 ⓦwww.fryderyk.com.pl; ❺). There's a rash of **bars** and **pizzerias** in the park.

Kudowa-Zdrój and the Table Mountains

Nestling at the foot of the Góry Stołowe some 16km west of Duszniki, the border town of **KUDOWA-ZDRÓJ** is one of the most popular health resorts anywhere in Poland. Patronized by the internationally rich and famous in the nineteenth century, it's nowadays an appealing under-commercialized place which has preserved plentiful helpings of charm. A decent choice of accommodation and proximity to the mountains help to make Kudowa-Zdrój the best place to base yourself in the region.

Arrival, information and accommodation

Buses deliver you to ulica 1 Maja on the eastern side of the town centre, from where it's a short walk back the way you came to the centrally placed **tourist office**, ul. Zdrojowa 44 (May–Sept Mon–Fri 9am–6pm, Sat 9am–5pm, Sun 10am–3pm; Oct–April Mon–Fri 9am–5pm, Sat 9am–3pm; ☎074/866 1387, ⓦwww.kudowa.pl), which has lists of private rooms (❷) and pensions (❸) in town. The *OSiR* complex at ul. Łąkowa 12 (☎074/866 1627; ❷) is in a scruffy area 1km west of town just off the main road, but it does have a **hostel** (30–40zł per person) and a **campsite** in the grounds.

Accommodation

Alga ul. 1. Maja 20 ☎074/866 1460, ⓦwww .alga2.republika.pl. Modern pension diagonally opposite the bus terminal, offering comfortable rooms with shower and TV. ❹

Kaprys ul. Sikorskiego 2 ☎074/866 1663, ⓦwww .kudowa.zdroj.pl/kaprys. Medium-sized place in a residential street near the bus stop, with simple en-suite doubles, triples and quads. ❸–❹

Kudowa ul. Buczka 16 ☎074/866 5000, ⓦwww .hotelkudowa.pl. The best place to stay in town; a brand new large hotel with elegant en-suite rooms and an excellent spa centre just west of the centre. ❼

Villa Fonte ul. Słowackiego 4 ☎074/866 2412, ⓦwww.villafonte.pl. A small boutique hotel nicely done up in Art Deco style and equipped with a mini-spa. Just south of the centre. ❺

Willa Diament ul. Buczka 7 ☏ 074/866 4156, ⓦ.willadiament.w.interia.pl. A hundred-year-old pension in a characterful old building complete with half-timbering and turrets, offering modernized en-suite rooms with laminate floors, and a big garden out the back. ❸

The Town

Grand old villas set in their own grounds give Kudowa its aristocratic air, yet it has no obvious centre other than the **spa park**. Here the huge domed pump room (pijalnia) houses the venerated marble fountain from which issue hot and cold springs. Nearby stalls cash in on visitors' health worries, selling the pipe-like *kóbki*, small flattened jugs with swan-necked spouts, from which the surprisingly refreshing water – slightly sweet and carbonated and allegedly good against obesity, fatigue and general weakness – is traditionally drunk. Adjacent to the pump room is a concert hall where a festival celebrating the music of composer Stanisław Moniuszko takes place each July. The spacious spa park's appeal continues with well-kept flower beds and more than three hundred different species of tree and shrub. Occupying a building on the south side of the park, the **Toy Museum** (Muzeum Zabawek: daily May–Sept 9am–6pm, Oct–April 9am–5pm; 6zł) is a hands-off though enjoyable history of playthings through the ages with soft toys, train sets and costumed dolls among the exhibits.

Eating and drinking

The *Zdrojowa* restaurant at ul. Słoneczka 1 near the central bus stop is the best place for sampling Polish staples as well as some Czech dishes from across the border. Similar fare can be had at the nearby *Piekełko*, ul. Moniuszki 2, featuring dining and dancing to easy listening tunes. *Ania*, beside the tourist office at ul. Zdrojowa 42, serves up cheap Polish snacks. The sunny terrace of *Café Sissi* inside the pump room is a great place for a coffee with views of the park; the nearby *Pod Palmami* café-bar is a stylish place for drinks later on in the day.

The Kaplica Czaszek and the Muzeum Kultury Ludowej

Twenty minutes' walk north of town (follow ulica Moniuszki through the park and keep going), the outlying hamlet of **CZERMNA** is host to the macabre **Chapel of Skulls** (Kaplica Czaszek: Tues–Sun 9.30am–1pm & 2–5.30pm; 4zł). Its walls and ceiling are decorated with more than three thousand skulls and crossed bones from the dead of various wars and epidemics. The chapel's priest, with the help of his devoted grave-digger, amassed the collection during the last decades of the eighteenth century. Their own remains are set in a glass case by the altar and thousands more skulls are stashed in the crypt. Ossuaries are common in central Europe, often based on the belief that having one's bones stored in a suitably holy site will increase the chances of enjoying a favourable afterlife.

A walkable 3km north of Czermna, the village of **Pstrążna** plays host to an enjoyable open-air ethnographic collection, the **Museum of the Sudeten Foothills** (Muzeum Kultury Ludowej Pogórza Sudeckiego: May–Oct: daily 10am–6pm), with a wide-ranging collection of vernacular buildings from local villages. Among the more curious of these are the wooden, bell-topped watchtowers that used to be a feature of many a village, warning the local inhabitants of fire or avalanche danger.

Into the Table Mountains

Rising above 900 metres and almost as flat as their name suggests, the **Table Mountains** (Góry Stołowe) are not the most enticing range in the Kłodzko region, but do have some extraordinary rock formations which can be appreciated in a full day's walk from Kudowa.

The easiest way to access the area is to continue northeastwards from Pstrążna (see opposite), picking up the well-signed green trail before that leads to the first of several fantastic rock formations in the range, the **Erratic Rocks** (Błędne Skały: daily 9am–6pm; 5zł), where it twists and turns, squirming through narrow gaps between gigantic rocks. It then continues via Pasterka to the village of **Karłów**, from where a climb of nearly seven hundred steps leads to the **Szczeliniec Wielki**, the highest point in the range at 919 metres. Here the rocks have been weathered into a series of irregular shapes and are named after camels, elephants, and so on. There's a small entrance fee once you get to the top where a café offers refreshments, then you follow the trail that goes down through a deep chasm, on to a viewpoint and back by a different route.

From Błędne Skały the **red trail** leads directly to Karłów continuing east 5km to the largest and most scattered group of rocks in the area, the **Petrified Mushrooms** (Skalne Grzyby), rocks whose bases were worn away by uneven erosion producing the top-heavy appearance their name suggests.

If you want to tackle Szczeliniec Wielki or the Skalne Grzyby without walking all the way from Kudowa, consider catching a shared taxi or a bus as far as Karłów (May–Sept 3 daily), and starting from there.

South of Kłodzko: Międzygórze and the Śnieżnik Massif

At the southeastern corner of the Kłodzko region is the enticing **Śnieżnik Massif** (Masyw Śnieżnika), the best of whose scenery can be seen in a good day's walk and which, unlike the overrun Karkonosze to the west, seems to be gratifyingly ignored by the crowds. The main jumping-off point is the charming hill resort of **Międzygórze** ("among the hills"), a dead end 30km southeast of Kłodzko and served by six buses a day.

Miedzygórze

Lying at the head of a wooded valley east of the unremarkable town of Bystrzyca Kłodzka, **MIĘDZYGÓRZE** is one of the quieter, more pleasant corners of the Kłodzko region – well worth a couple of days' stay if rustic peace and hiking opportunities are what you need. The village is characterized by the **wooden villas** (drzewnianki) built to serve as rest homes at the beginning of the nineteenth century. Ramshackle affairs with carved balustrades, neo-Gothic turrets and creaky interiors, they're still in use as tourist accommodation today.

Built around a central T-junction, the village is easy to find your way around. Five minutes' walk west of the junction, steps descend from the dour *Nad Wodospadem* hotel to a 27-metre-high **waterfall**, surrounded by deep forest. On the far side of the waterfall paths ascend towards the **Fantasy Garden** (Ogród Bajek) about twenty minutes away, a hilltop garden designed by local forester Izydor Kriesten before World War II. It's an attractive spot consisting of huts constructed from roots, branches and cones, each of which is inhabited by an assemblage of gnomes and model animals. Overlooking the village centre, the charming **St Jozef's Church** (św. Jozefa), a Baroque-style wooden building from 1742, has a lovely balconied interior which can be visited on Sundays after morning Mass.

Accommodation in three of Międzygórze's largest *drzewnianki* (❶) is handled by the FWP agency (daily 7am–11pm; ☎074/813 5109, ⓦwww.fwp.pl) just uphill from the T-junction at ul. Sanatoryjna 2, though rooms can be rather run-down.

The *Willa Millennium* guesthouse (☎074/813 5287, ⓦwww.millennium.ta.pl; ❸) in the village centre at ul. Wojska Polskiego 9 has modern en suites. Hikers and peace-seekers should try the quiet *Słoneczna Willa* at the very top of the village at ul. Śnieżna 27 (☎074/813 5270, ⓦwww.slonecznawilla.tp2.pl; ❹) with its well-appointed en suite rooms and popular restaurant; or the small *Larix* pension (☎605 841 142, ⓦwww.oranska.com; ❸) set in a meadow high above the entrance to the village at ul. Wojska Polskiego 25a. The *Millennium* has a good **restaurant**; while the 🍴 *Orańska* café overlooking the junction at ul. Wojska Polskiego 2/10 is the best place for coffee and snacks. A few steps uphill is the laid-back *Wilczy Dol* café, with graffiti-style decor, simple snacks and alternative music – outdoor gigs are sometimes organized in summer.

Walking in the Śnieżnik Massif

A signpost at Międzygórze's main junction indicates the many marked hiking routes in the area. One particularly good walk follows the **red trail**, which rises steeply through lovely wooded countryside for about two hours, leading to the *Na Śnieżniku* **refuge** (☎074/813 5130), an isolated PTTK hostel which offers dorm beds for 15zł per person and also serves inexpensive homely meals. From here it's then a much gentler ascent to the flat summit of **Śnieżnik** (1425m), the highest point in the Kłodzko region, set right on the Czech border.

From the summit it's worth descending north by the **yellow trail** towards Kletno, which will bring you in about an hour to the **Bear's Cave** (Jaskinia Niedźwiedzia: Tues, Wed & Fri–Sun: Feb–April & Sept–Nov 10am–4.40pm; May–Aug 9am–4.40pm). Discovered in 1966 during quarrying, the cave takes its name from the bear fossils discovered there. Bats still inhabit the cave, which has the usual wondrous stalactites and stalagmites. Visits are by Polish-language guided tour only, with group numbers limited to fifteen people, exploring 600 metres of cave in about forty minutes. You can also get to the cave directly from Międzygórze in about two hours by following the red trail (see above) and then branching off northwards after a couple of kilometres when you see signs to the Bear's Cave and Kletno.

From the cave, another kilometre's walk brings you to the village of **KLETNO**, which has a couple of snack bars, a bus service to Kłodzko via Stronie Śląskie (see below) and Lądek-Zdrój (see below), and a rather basic **youth hostel** at Kletno 8 (☎074/814 1358; 15zł per person).

Lądek-Zdrój and beyond

Returning to Bystrzyca Kłodzka, a scenic drive winds back up into the hills directly east of town. Climbing up through forested slopes and emerging from the trees, the narrow road reaches a **pass** where it's worth stopping to appreciate the superb panorama; in winter this is the main area for skiing. Descending down the other side, the valley unfolds revealing an isolated Lutheran chapel near the village of Sienna, and brings you to the small town of **Stronie Śląskie** (terminus of the rail line from Kłodzko).

Eight kilometres further north is the spa resort of **LĄDEK-ZDRÓJ**, where, according to tradition, the waters were known for their healing properties as early as the thirteenth century, when the bathing installations were allegedly destroyed by the Tatars. They've certainly been exploited since the late fifteenth century, and in later years attracted visitors as august as Goethe and Turgenev. Today the town, strung out along the Biała Lądecka river, retains a charm that other spa resorts in the area cannot match, though many buildings are still rather run-down.

Centrepiece of the grandiose Neoclassical **spa complex** at the east end of town is the recently restored main sanatorium, a handsome domed building evoking the heyday of the spa (Tues–Sun 8am–5pm; a 30min soak costs 18zł; ⓦwww .uzdrowisko-ladek.pl) and hereabouts you'll find villas still surviving from that era. In the older part of town, about a kilometre to the west, a mid-sixteenth-century stone **bridge** can still be seen, decorated with statues of religious figures. The town's spacious main square, currently undergoing much-needed EU-sponsored renovation works, features several handsome Baroque-fronted houses facing the octagonal tower of the town hall.

For those dependent on public transport, the hourly **bus** from Kłodzko represents the only route in and out of town. Tourist information duties are handled by the **PTTK**, near the spa quarter at ul. Kościuszki 44 (Mon–Fri 9.30am–4pm, Sat 9.30am–12.30pm; ⓣ074/814 6255, ⓦwww.ladek.pl). As for **accommodation**, the spacious rooms in the grand *Arabeska* at ul. Paderewskiego 4 (ⓣ074/814 7922, ⓦwww.almabus.com.pl/arabeska; ❹) constitute the best option; the *Mir-Jan*, 1km south of the centre at ul. Kościuszki 78 (ⓣ074/814 6339; ❸), has reasonable en suites; and there's a **youth hostel** (ⓣ074/814 6645; 22zł per person) in the outlying hamlet of Stojków, 3km to the south – although you'll have to walk there if you don't have your own transport.

For **eating**, standard and inexpensive Polish food is on offer at the *Polska Chata*, ul. Kościuszki 5 and at *Karczma Lądecka*, ul. Kościuszki 25.

Immediately to the east of the town, the **Golden Mountains** (Góry Złote) offer some good hiking routes. Check out the blue trail which leads southeast of the town, ascending within an hour to a ruined medieval castle near the summit of **Karpień** (776m), via a series of oddly weathered rocks of the type so often found throughout the region.

For those with their own transport it's well worth exploring the scenic road north out of Lądek, which winds its way through forested highlands. Soon the road desends swiftly to the town of **Złoty Stok**, on the edge of the interminable plain which stretches, with only modest variations in elevation, all the way to the Baltic.

Paczków and Nysa

Heading east from the Kłodzko region, you traverse an undulating plateau peppered with small fortified towns that were associated for most of their history with the bishops of Wrocław, who ruled an independent principality here from 1195 until its dissolution by Prussia in 1810. Like much of southern Silesia, it's an entrancing landscape of rolling farmland broken up by forest, largely unaffected by significant industrial development. The terrain levels out a bit towards Nysa, where most of the surrounding fields are given over to the cultivation of rapeseed, producing a blaze of bright yellow ground cover in the early summer.

Buses operating the Kłodzko–Paczków–Nysa route present your best way of **getting around**, and placing the region within easy day-trip range of Kłodzko or one of the spa resorts. Should you be approaching from the north, Nysa is well connected by bus to Wrocław and Opole. Trains trundle through the region on their way from Kłodzko to Katowice, but they're both slow and infrequent.

Paczków

In contrast to its neighbours, the quiet little market town of **PACZKÓW**, 30km east of Kłodzko, has managed to preserve its medieval fortifications almost intact

– hence its designation as "Poland's Carcassonne". In reality, Paczków is hardly in that league, it does have it does have the advantage of being untouched by the hands of romantically inclined nineteenth-century restorers, as well as being generally overlooked by crowds of tourists.

Nowadays, the mid-fourteenth-century **ramparts** form a shady promenade around the centre of the Old Town. Their visual impact is diminished by the enveloping later buildings, though it's a wonder that the town managed to grow so much without their demolition. Nineteen of the twenty-four towers survive, as does nearly all of the original 1350 metres of wall, pierced by three barbicans: the square Wrocław Gate of 1462 and the cylindrical Zabkow and Kłodzko gates from around 1550.

The area within the walls, spread across a gentle slope, consists of just a handful of streets, but is centred on a large **main square** with a much-rebuilt **town hall**. Rearing up behind the main square stands the strongly fortified **St John's Church** (Kościół św. Jana), a part of the town's defences. Inside, the box-like geometry of the design is particularly evident, with the chancel the same length as the main nave.

Practicalities

There's no need to spend the night, but if you're stuck note that the best hotel is the *Korona*, ul. Wojska Polskiego 31 (☏077/431 6177; ❷), outside the ramparts on a street leading directly off the southeastern side of the main square. As far as **places to eat** are concerned, the *Carcassonne* at Rynek 33 has simple Polish food.

Nysa

In spite of the devastation of 1945, the town of **NYSA**, 26km east of Paczków, still preserves memories of the days when it basked in the fanciful title of "the Silesian Rome", a reference to its numerous religious houses and reputation as a centre of Catholic education. It came to the fore when the adoption of the Reformation in Wrocław forced the bishops to make Nysa, the capital of their principality for the previous couple of centuries, their new power base. With its sprinkling of architectural monuments left stranded in a sea of postwar concrete, Nysa is a place for a brief wander rather than a protracted stay.

The Town

From both the bus and train stations, bear right along the edge of the park, then turn left into ulica Kolejowa which leads to the centre. On the way, you pass the fourteenth-century **Wrocław Gate** (Brama Wrocławska), an unusually graceful piece of military architecture with wrought-iron dragons' heads acting as gutter flues, left stranded by the demolition of the ramparts.

Having lost its town hall and all but four of its old houses during the war, Nysa's vast main square is currently being brought back to its original proportions as the missing houses are rebuilt in a respectful contemporary style. The town hall tower was nearly completed at time of writing; it will house restaurants and shops when it opens. Of the old buildings, the seventeenth-century **Weigh House** (Waga Miejska), which looks as if it belongs somewhere in the Low Countries, is particularly attractive.

Off the northeastern side of the main square is the **Cathedral of Sts James and Agnes** (Katedra św. Jakuba i Agnieszki), which long served the exiled bishops. Put up in just six years in the 1420s and sporting Europe's steepest church roof, it was badly damaged during World War II, and faithfully restored soon afterwards. It's a fine example of the hall church style, with nave and aisles of equal height. Entering through the graceful double portal, it's the spareness of the lofty thirty-metre interior which makes the strongest impression; the slender brick pillars visibly bow under the strain of the vault. One chapel has photos of the incredible wartime destruction. Outside, the church's detached stone **belfry** was abandoned after fifty years' work and further damaged during the war.

South of St James's lies the well-preserved if generally deserted Baroque episcopal quarter. **The Bishops' Palace** (Pałac Biskupi), at ul. Jarosławka 11 is now fitted out as the surprisingly good **Nisa Museum** (Muzeum Nyskie: Tues 9am–5.30pm, Wed–Fri 9am–3pm, Sat & Sun 10am–3pm; 5zł, free on Sat), with displays of sixteenth- to eighteenth-century engravings, several pictures of Nysa's postwar ruin, a shrapnel-damaged 1574 weather vane as well as fragments from irreparable buildings. There's also a model of the town as it was three hundred years ago, various secular and religious treasures, and some wonderfully chunky Baroque furniture.

Immediately south of here lies the complex of Jesuit buildings on Rynek Solny, which includes the white-walled **Church of the Ascension** (Kościół NMP), its austerity softened by some ceiling frescoes and a beautiful eighteenth-century silver tabernacle at the high altar. Adjoining it is the famous **Carolinum College**, whose luminaries included the Polish kings Michał Korybut Wiśniowiecki and Jan Sobieski.

South of the main square, the only other reminder of the "Silesian Rome" is the **Monastery of the Hospitallers of the Holy Sepulchre** (Klasztor Bożogrobców). This order moved to Nysa from the Holy Land at the end of the twelfth century, but the huge complex you see today dates from the early eighteenth century. The magnificent Baroque **Church of Sts Peter and Paul** (Kościół św. Piotra i Pawła) on ulica Bracka is part of the complex, and has a resplendent interior featuring gilt capitals, a multicoloured marble altar and a reproduction of the Holy Sepulchre in Jerusalem.

Heading northwest from the Rynek along ulica Krzywoustego brings you to the **Ziębicka Gate** (Brama Ziębicka), a plain brick tower standing in the middle of a roundabout. You can climb up its 150 steps for a few złoty.

Practicalities

The **bus** and **train stations** are 1km east of the main square at the end of ulica Kolejowa. The helpful **tourist office** at Rynek 32 (May–Oct Mon–Sat 8am–6pm, Sun 10am–2pm; Nov–April Tues–Fri 8am–6pm, Sat 8am–4pm, Sun 10am–2pm; ☏077/433 5927, ⊛www.nor.nysa.pl) can help book accommodation and also rents out bicycles (5zł/hr or 20zł/day) to explore the parks and lakes in the surroundings. Nysa's one central **hotel**, the *Piast*, right by the Ziębicka Gate at ul. Krzywoustego 14 (☏077/433 4084, ⊛www.hotel-piast .com.pl; ❸), offers comfortable en suites. Otherwise, there's the *Villa Navigator* (☏077/433 4170, ⊛www.villanavigator.pl; ❸), a friendly, upscale B&B 300m west of the main square at ul. Wyspiańskiego 11.

For **eating**, *Restauracja*, Rynek 26, is the best place to refuel on solid meat-and-potatoes fare; while *Lucia*, set in a quirky fortress-like building at ul. Sobieskiego 3 south of the the **Carolinum College**, serves excellent pizza and Italian dishes.

Travel details

Trains

Jelenia Góra to: Gdańsk (1 daily, overnight; 12hr 30min); Szklarska Poręba (6 daily; 1hr 10min); Wałbrzych (9 daily; 1hr 30min); Warsaw (1 daily, overnight; 10hr); Wrocław (10 daily; 3hr 30min).
Wrocław to: Białystok (2 daily of which one overnight; 9hr); Bolesławiec (9 daily; 2hr); Brzeg (twice per hour; 30–40min); Bydgoszcz (3 daily; 5hr); Gdańsk (3 daily of which one overnight; 8hr); Jelenia Góra (10 daily; 3hr 30min); Kalisz (4 daily; 2hr 30min); Katowice (16 daily; 2hr 30min–3hr); Kłodzko (hourly; 2hr); Kraków (11 daily; 5hr); Legnica (hourly; 1hr 15min); Leszno (hourly; 1hr 30min); Łódź (4 daily; 4hr 15min); Lublin (1 daily; 8hr 30min); Opole (twice per hour; 1hr–1hr 30min); Poznań (hourly; 2hr 30min); Przemyśl (7 daily of which one overnight; 9hr); Rzeszów (9 daily of which one overnight; 7hr); Szczecin (7 daily of which one overnight; 6–7hr); Wałbrzych (12 daily; 2hr); Warsaw (13 daily of which one overnight; 5hr–6hr 30min); Zielona Góra (6 daily; 3hr 30min).

Buses

Brzeg to: Nysa (2 daily; 2hr).
Jelenia Góra to: Kamienna Góra (6 daily; 55min); Karpacz (every 30min; 40min); Legnica (10 daily; 2hr); Świdnica (5 daily; 1hr 50min); Szklarska Poręba (hourly; 45min); Wrocław (hourly; 2hr 30min).
Kamienna Góra to: Krzeszów (hourly; 30min).
Kłodzko to: Duszniki Zdrój (hourly; 50min); Kudowa-Zdrój (hourly; 1hr 10min); Lądek-Zdrój (hourly; 50min); Międzygórze (5 daily; 1hr 20min); Nysa (7 daily; 1hr 20min); Opole (3 daily; 3hr 40min); Świdnica (6 daily; 1hr 50min); Wambierzyce (1 daily; 1hr).
Kudowa-Zdrój to: Duszniki Zdrój (hourly; 20min); Karłów (May–Sept: 5 daily; 20min); Katowice (1 daily; 6hr); Kłodzko (hourly; 1hr 10min).
Legnica to: Jawor (hourly; 40min); Lubiąż (1 daily; 40min).
Świdnica to: Wałbrzych (every 30min; 40min); Wrocław (buses 6 daily; 1hr 30min; minibuses hourly; 1hr 15min).
Wałbrzych to: Głuszyca/Sierpnica (3 daily; 45min); Kamienna Góra (hourly; 1hr 20min), Walim (5–8 daily; 45min).
Wrocław to: Karpacz (2–3 daily; 3hr 30min); Nysa (hourly; 2hr 45min); Świdnica (hourly; 1hr 30min); Trzebnica (every 30min; 50min).

International trains

Wrocław to: Berlin (2 daily of which one overnight; 6–8hr); Prague (2 daily; 6hr 30min).

Wielkopolska

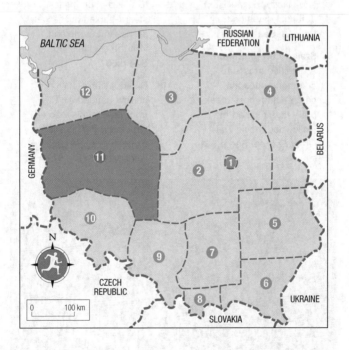

CHAPTER 11

Highlights

* **Poznań** Wielkopolska's bustling commercial and cultural capital is also home to the leafy cathedral district of Ostrów Tumski. **See p.535**

* **Wielkopolska National Park** This wonderfully tranquil area of forests and lakes tops the list of potential day-trips from Poznań. **See p.554**

* **Stalag Luft III, Żagań** A dignified museum commemorates the camp – and mass breakout – that inspired the Hollywood movie *The Great Escape*. **See p.561**

* **Gniezno** An easy-going provincial town which was for centuries the seat of Poland's archbishops, and is still the site of a truly wonderful cathedral. **See p.565**

* **Wolsztyn steam train shed** Travel from Poznań to Wosztyn on the last steam–hauled passenger service in Europe and visit the engine shed. **See p.567**

* **Biskupin** Take the narrow-gauge train from Żnin to this reconstructed Iron Age village, situated in a rolling rural landscape. **See p.572**

▲ Marketplace, Poznań

Wielkopolska

alfway between Warsaw and Berlin, the gently undulating landscape of **Wielkopolska** may not offer much drama, but its human story is an altogether different matter, as its name – "Greater Poland" – implies. This area has been inhabited continuously since prehistoric times, and it was here that the Polish nation first took shape. The name of the province, and of Poland itself, derives from a Slav tribe called the **Polonians**, whose leaders – the Piast family – were to rule the country for five centuries. Their embryonic state emerged under Mieszko I in the mid-tenth century, but the significant breakthrough was achieved under his son, Boleslaw the Brave, who gained control over an area similar to that of present-day Poland, and made it independent from the German-dominated Holy Roman Empire. Though relegated to the status of a border province by the mid-eleventh century, Wielkopolska remained one of the indisputably Polish parts of Poland, resisting the **Germanization** which swamped the nation's other western territories.

The relics of the early Piast period can be seen at **Lake Lednica**, located just west of **Gniezno**, the first city to achieve dominance before decline brought about the consolation role of Poland's ecclesiastical capital. It was quickly supplanted as the regional centre by nearby **Poznań**, a burgeoning business centre.

Even older than either of these cities is **Kalisz**, which dates back at least as far as Roman times, while the region's prehistoric past is vividly represented at the Iron Age village of **Biskupin**, a halfway point on the **narrow-gauge rail line** that rattles along between the town of **Żnin** and the village of **Gąsawa**. Another town in the province which has played an important part in Polish culture, albeit at a later date, is **Leszno**, once a major Protestant centre. Yet this is predominantly a rural province, and perhaps its most typical natural attraction is the **Wielkopolska national park**, epitomizing the region's glaciated landscape.

As elsewhere in Poland, there are plentiful trains and buses, even to the smallest outpost, with the former usually having the edge in terms of speed and convenience.

Poznań

Thanks to its position on the Berlin–Warsaw–Moscow rail line, **POZNAŃ** is many visitors' first taste of Poland. In many ways it's the ideal introduction, as no other city is more closely identified with Polish nationhood. *Posnania elegans Poloniae civitas* ("Poznań, a beautiful city in Poland"), the inscription on the oldest surviving

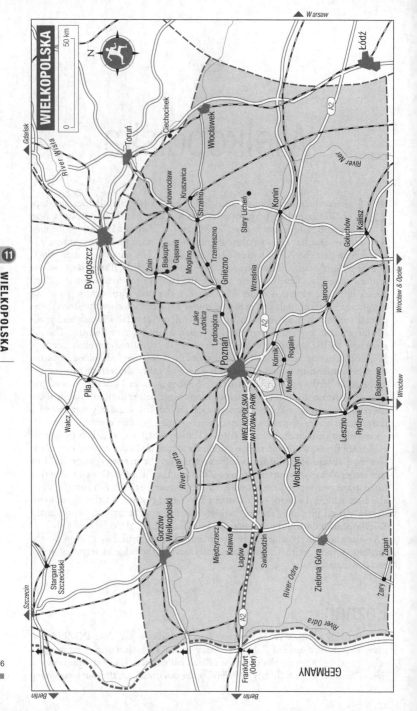

WIELKOPOLSKA

0   50 km

N

▲ Warsaw

Łódź

Gdańsk

River Wisła

Toruń

Ciechocinek

Włocławek

River Ner

A2

Inowrocław

Kruszwica

Strzelno

Konin

Stary Licheń

Gołuchów

Kalisz

Bydgoszcz

Żnin

Biskupin

Gąsawa

Mogilno

Trzemeszno

Gniezno

Września

Jarocin

Lake Lednica

Lednogóra

A2

Poznań

Kórnik

Rogalin

Wrocław & Opole ▶

Piła

Wałcz

Mosina

Leszno

Rydzyna

Bojanowo

Wrocław ▶

WIELKOPOLSKA NATIONAL PARK

River Warta

Wolsztyn

Gorzów Wielkopolski

Stargard Szczeciński

Szczecin ◀

Międzyrzecz

Kalawa

Łagów

Świebodzin

Zielona Góra

Żagań

Żary

River Odra

A2

River Odra

GERMANY

Frankfurt (Oder)

Berlin ◀

Berlin ▼

depiction of the town, has been adopted as a local catchphrase to highlight its unswerving loyalty to the national cause over the centuries. Nowadays, it's a city of great **diversity**, encompassing a tranquil cathedral quarter, an animated centre focused on one of Europe's finest squares and a dynamic business district whose trade fairs are the most important in the country and western Poland's main urban tourist draw. A number of fine museums and a wealth of nightlife opportunities ensure that a couple of days are well spent here.

Poznań may be a big city, but most of its primary attractions are grouped in a central core. Outside the central area the rattle of trams and tyres on cobbled streets makes it a noisy but invigorating place. It's also a good base from which to explore the region's other key attractions, with regular trains running to the Wielkopolska national park, Gniezno and beyond.

Pride of place in the Poznań **festival** calendar goes to the St John's Fair (Jarmark Świętojański), a traditional knees-up of medieval origins, with handicraft stalls and folk-music performers taking over the main square in the days leading up to St John's Day (June 24). St Martin's Day (Nov 11) is marked by the mass-consumption of *rogale świętomarcińskie*; locally produced croissant-like pastries which can be bought in bakeries and food shops.

Some history

In the ninth century the Polonians founded a castle on a strategically significant island in the River Warta, and in 968 Mieszko I made this one of the two main centres of his duchy, and the seat of its first bishop. The settlement that developed here was given the name **Ostrów Tumski** (Cathedral Island), which it still retains.

Although initially overshadowed by Gniezno, Poznań did not follow the latter's decline after the court moved to Kraków in the mid-thirteenth century. Instead, it became the undisputed capital of Wielkopolska and the main bastion of Poland's western border. The economic life of the city shifted to the west bank of the river, adopting the familiar grid pattern around a market square. Poznań's prosperity soared as it profited from the fifteenth-century decline of both the Teutonic Order and the Hanseatic League, and the city became a key junction of European trade routes as well as a leading centre of learning.

Regression inevitably set in with the ruinous Swedish Wars of the seventeenth and eighteenth centuries. Revival of sorts came during the Partitions period, when Poznań became the Prussian city of Posen, and shared in the wealth of the Industrial Revolution. It also consolidated its reputation as a rallying point for **Polish nationalism**, resisting Bismarck's Germanization policy and playing an active role in the independence movements. An uprising in December 1918 finally forced out the German occupiers, ensuring that Poznań would become part of the resurrected Polish state.

Poznań's rapid expansion during the interwar period has been followed by accelerated growth, doubling in population to its present level of 580,000, and spreading onto the right bank of the Warta. The city's association with the struggle against foreign hegemony – this time Russian – was again demonstrated by the **food riots** of 1956, which were crushed at a cost of 74 lives.

Nowadays, as well as being a vibrant **university town**, Poznań is a brash, self-confident commercial centre revelling in its key position on the Berlin–Warsaw road and rail routes. Above all it is known for the international **trade fairs** held on the exhibition grounds just west of the train station – a tradition begun when the Great East German Exhibition was held here in 1908, restarted by the Poles in 1921, and now symbolic of the city's post-communist economic dynamism.

Map labels:
- **A** (1km)
- **B** (1km)
- UL. KILIŃ
- UL. WIELKOPOLSKA
- UL. K. PUŁASKIEGO
- UL. PRZEPADEK
- UL. GRUDZIENIEC
- UL. CICHA
- UL. NOWOWIEJSKIEGO
- AL. NIEPODLEGŁOŚCI
- **C**
- UL. KOŚCIUSZKI
- UL. SPORNA
- UL. POZNAŃSKA
- UL. F. CHOPINA
- **D**
- UL. SOLNA
- **Carmelite Monastery**
- UL. KAROLA LIBELTA
- **E**
- UL. NOWOWIEJSKIEGO
- UL. GEN. J. H. DĄBROWSKIEGO
- **Teatr Nowy**
- MOST TEATRALNY
- UL. SŁOWACKIEGO
- **Teatr Wielki**
- UL. DZIAŁYŃSKICH
- UL. KAROLA LIBELTA
- AL. K. MARCINKOWSKIEGO
- UL. 23 LUTEGO
- @
- **National Museum**
- PLAC CYRYLA RATAJSKIEGO
- **Park Adama Mickiewicza**
- **1**
- **Raczyński Library**
- UL. ALEKSANDRA FREDRY
- **University Aula**
- **Zamek**
- **Okrąglak**
- **Teatr Polski**
- *i*
- PLAC WOLNOŚCI
- **H**
- RONDO KAPONIERA
- **3**
- UL. 27 GRUDNIA
- **Academy of Music**
- **I**
- UL. ŚW. MARCIN
- **Orbis**
- UL. BUKOWSKA
- **L**
- **K** **J**
- UL. GWARNA
- UL. KANTAKA
- UL. ŚW. MARCIN
- UL. WYSOKA
- **Trade Fair Grounds**
- UL. TAYLORA
- **M**
- UL. GARNCARSKA
- UL. FRANCISZKA RATAJCZAKA
- UL. PIEKARY
- UL. SKŁADOWA
- UL. TACZAKA
- **5**
- UL. OGRODOWA
- MOST DWORCOWY
- **Park Karola Marcinkowskiego**
- UL. NIEZŁOMNYCH
- AL. NIEPODLEGŁOŚCI
- **Park Henryka Dąbrowskiego**
- **N**
- **Biuro Zakwaterowania Przemysław**
- **Teatr Muzyczny**
- UL. TOWAROWA
- **Poznań Główny Train Station**
- **P**
- PLAC WL. ANDERSA
- **Stary Browar**
- **6**
- UL. KRÓL. JADWIGI
- **Bus Station**
- UL. WIERZBIĘCICE
- UL. PRZEMYSŁA
- UL. KOŚCIUSZKI
- Wilson Park
- **(1.5km) & Airport (6 km)**
- UL. FRANKLINA ROOSEVELTA
- UL. GŁOGOWSKA
- UL. DWORCOWA
- **Q** (400m)

Arrival, information and city transport

The main **train station**, Poznań Główny, is 2km southwest of the old town; the front entrance, not immediately apparent, is situated between platforms one and four, but the nearest **tram stop** is reached from the western exit beyond platform seven (if in doubt, follow the *McDonald's* signs) which leads out onto ulica Głogowska. Tram #5 heads from here to aleja Marcinkowskiego, 300m short of the

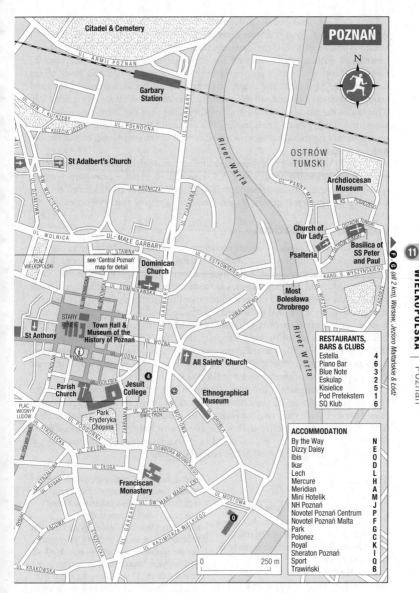

POZNAŃ

N

Citadel & Cemetery

UL. ARMII POZNAN

Garbary Station

UL. GEN. T. KUTRZEBY

UL. KSIĘCIA JÓZEFA

UL. PÓŁNOCNA

UL. GARBARY

River Warta

OSTRÓW TUMSKI

UL. ŚW. WOJCIECH

UL. DZIAŁOWA

St Adalbert's Church

UL. BOŹNICZA

UL. PANNY MARII

Archdiocesan Museum

UL. KS. T. POSADZEGO

UL. WOLNICA

UL. MAŁE GARBARY

UL. PIASKOWA

Church of Our Lady

UL. OSTRÓW TUMSKI

Basilica of SS Peter and Paul

PLAC WIELKOPOLSKI

see 'Central Poznań' map for detail

UL. STAWNA

Dominican Church

UL. E. ESTKOWSKIEGO

Psalteria

UL. OSTRÓW TUMSKI

UL. WIEŻOWA

G (all 2 km), Warsaw, Jezioro Maltańskie & Łódź

UL. DOMINIKAŃSKA

GARBARY

UL. CHWALISZEWO

KARD. S. WYSZYŃSKIEGO

Most Bolesława Chrobrego

UL. WIEŻOWA

River Warta

STARY RYNEK

St Anthony

UL. WIELKA

Town Hall & Museum of the History of Poznań

UL. WOŹNA

UL. WODNA

All Saints' Church

RESTAURANTS, BARS & CLUBS

Estella	4
Piano Bar	6
Blue Note	3
Eskulap	2
Kisielice	5
Pod Pretekstem	1
SQ Klub	6

UL. KOZIA

UL. GOŁĘBIA

Parish Church

Jesuit College

@

Ethnographical Museum

UL. GRÓBLA

UL. KOSTIWA

PLAC WIOSNY LUDÓW

Park Fryderyka Chopina

UL. WSZYSTKICH ŚWIĘTYCH

UL. ZABRANKA

UL. PODGÓRNA

UL. STRZELECKA

UL. ZIELONA

UL. DOWBORA MUŚNICKIEGO

UL. PÓŁWIEJSKA

UL. DŁUGA

ACCOMMODATION

By the Way	N
Dizzy Daisy	E
Ibis	O
Ikar	D
Lech	L
Mercure	H
Meridian	A
Mini Hotelik	M
NH Poznań	J
Novotel Poznań Centrum	P
Novotel Poznań Malta	F
Park	G
Polonez	C
Royal	K
Sheraton Poznań	I
Sport	Q
Trawiński	B

UL. STRZAŁOWA

UL. RYBAKI

BRAMA

UL. ŁĄCOWA

Franciscan Monastery

UL. ŚW. MARII MAGDALENY

UL. MOSTOWA

UL. STRZELECKA

UL. KAZIMIERZA WIELKIEGO

UL. KRAKÓWSKA

0   250 m

main square; while tram #8 delivers you to plac Ratajskiego in the western part of the downtown area. The **bus station** is five minutes' walk to the east of the train station along ulica Towarowa. Poznań's **airport** is 7km west of the city in the suburb of Ławica – express bus #L (tickets 7.50zł) runs to the main train station every hour, taking twenty minutes. Alternatively city bus #59 (tickets 3.60zł) departs twice an hour, taking thirty minutes to get to the Bałtyk stop just north of the station.

There's an excellent **tourist information centre at** Stary Rynek 59/60 (mid-April to mid-Oct: Mon–Fri 9am–8pm, Sat 10am–8pm, Sun 10am–6pm; mid-Oct to mid-April: Mon–Fri 10am–7pm, Sat 10am–5pm; ☎061/852 6156, ⓦwww.cim .poznan.pl) with another outlet on the corner of ulica Ratajczaka and ulica 27 Grudnia (Mon–Fri 10am–7pm, Sat 10am–5pm; ☎061/851 9645). Both offices hand out free pamphlets and maps, give out information on accommodation and transport connections, and sell the excellent *Poznań In Your Pocket* city guide (5zł). This is also the place to buy the Poznań City Card (one day 30zł; two days 40zł; three days 45zł), which provides free use of public transport and free access to museums and sights in and around town, as well as offering reductions at various hotels and restaurants.

The city is well served by a dense and efficient network of **tram** and **bus** routes, with services running from about 5.30am until 10.45pm – after which infrequent night buses run on selected routes. Tickets (bought from kiosks) cost 2zł for a trip of fifteen minutes or under, 3.60zł for a trip of thirty minutes.

Accommodation

Poznań has a good range of accommodation, but **hotels** tend to be overpriced for what they offer – and rates can rise by an additional fifty percent or more during trade fairs. Poznań gets booked full during the four biggest fairs, in late January, early April, late May and mid-September. On the plus side, most hotels offer considerable discounts on weekends and in the summer months. Inexpensive hotel accommodation is scarce, however, and those on a tight budget will be dependent on the city's **hostels**, or on **private rooms** (❷), which are available from the 24-hour Glob-Tour office in the main hall of the train station (☎061/866 0667; private rooms available until 10pm) or from the Biuro Zakwaterowania Przemysław (Mon–Fri 8am–6pm, Sat 9am–2pm; ☎061/866 3560, ⓦwww.przemyslaw.com.pl), just across the road from the train station's western exit at Głogowska 16.

The nearest **campsite** is the *Malta* (☎061/876 6203, ⓦcampingmalta.poznan .pl), situated 3km east of the centre at the northeastern end of the eponymous lake, although its luxury two- to four-person bungalows, complete with satellite TV (❺), are more expensive than some downtown hotel rooms. Trams #6 and #8 from the train station pass along ulica Warszawska (get off after passing the *Novotel* on your right), a good 600m north of the site.

Hotels

Central

Brovaria Stary Rynek 73/74 ☎061/858 6868, ⓦwww.brovaria.pl. Popular boutique hotel right on the main square offering cream-coloured rooms with all the creature comforts. ❻
Domina ul. św. Marcin 2 ☎061/859 0590, ⓦwww.dominahotels.com. Swish, fully equipped apartments in a downtown location. ❽–❾
Ibis ul. Kazimierza Wielkiego 23 ☎061/858 4400, ⓦwww.ibishotel.com. Reliable source of blandly functional but comfortable accommodation, a walkable 800m southeast of the main square. ❻
Ikar ul. Kościuszki 118 ☎061/658 7105, ⓦwww .hotelikar.com.pl. A rather soulless-looking concrete building, but the rooms are comfortable and come with fridge and TV. ❼

Lech ul. św. Marcin 74 ☎061/853 0151, ⓦwww .hotel-lech.poznan.pl. A long-established mid-range hotel in the heart of town with standard, bland rooms and modern bathrooms. ❻
Mercure ul. Franklina D. Roosevelta 20 ☎061/855 8000, ⓦwww.orbisonline.pl. Comfortable corporate four-star right next to the trade fair grounds. ❽–❾
Mini Hotelik al. Niepodległości 8a (entrance on ul. Taylora) ☎061/633 1416, ⓦwww.trans-tor.poznan .pl. One of the best budget options in the city centre; simple double rooms (some with shared facilities) and an apartment with a fireplace (160zł). ❹
NH Poznań ul. św. Marcin 67 ☎061/624 8800. New and centrally located business hotel offering more luxury than similarly priced hotels. Stylishly furnished in dark brown, it has spacious and quiet doubles and suites. ❽

Novotel Poznań Centrum pl. Andersa 1 ☎061/858 7000, ⓦwww.orbisonline.pl. Located just 1km south of the city centre, but still well within walking distance, this high-rise business hotel is the flagship of Orbis's concrete fleet. ❻

Royal ul. św. Marcin 71 ☎061/858 2300, ⓦwww.hotel-royal.com.pl. Characterful, renovated place with bags of charm, tucked into a quiet courtyard just off the main downtown street. The en-suite rooms are on the small side but are cosily furnished in warm colours. ❽

Rzymski al. K. Marcinkowskiego 22 ☎061/852 8121, ⓦwww.rzymskihotel.com.pl. Spruced-up hotel with a good restaurant, just a couple of minutes' walk from the main square. Uninspiring but adequate doubles with shower, and some plushed-up business-class rooms. ❻

Sheraton Poznań ul. Bukowska 3/9 ☎061/655 2000, ⓦwww.sheraton.com. The best hotel in town; top-notch rooms, staff, services and restaurants. Opposite the trade fair, a short taxi or tram ride to the Old Town. ❾

Out of the centre

Meridian ul. Litewska 22 ☎061/656 5353, ⓦwww.hotelmeridian.com.pl. Intimate, medium-sized hotel in a tranquil setting by a lake in Park Sołacki, 2km northwest of the centre. Rooms are en suite with minibar. Tram #11 from the train station passes nearby. ❺

Novotel Poznań Malta ul. Warszawska 64/66 ☎061/654 3100, ⓦwww.orbisonline.pl. Plush motel situated in parkland 2km east of the centre, a short walk from the northern shores of Lake Maltańskie. ❻–❽

Park ul. Baraniaka 77 ☎061/874 1100, ⓦwww.hotelepark.pl. Comfortable business hotel on the southern bank of Lake Maltańskie, 2km east of the city centre. Rooms with lakeside views are more expensive than those on the landward side. ❻

Polonez al. Niepodległości 36 ☎061/864 7100, ⓦwww.orbisonline.pl. A concrete Orbis monster like all the others, with boxy rooms of good standard and a wide range of boutiques and services on offer. ❻

Sport ul. Chwiałkowskiego 34 ☎061/833 0591, ⓦwww.sporthotel.poznan.pl. Simple, clean budget hotel, a 20min walk south of the centre, with en-suite rooms. Tram #6 or #12 from Most Dworcowy (two stops) to al. Królowej Jadwigi, then walk south past the stadium. ❺

Trawiński ul. Żniwna 2 ☎061/827 5800, ⓦwww.hoteltrawinski.com.pl. Modern business-oriented four-star offering pastel coloured en suites in the pleasant environs of the Cytadela park, 2km northwest of the main square. ❼

Hostels

By the Way ul. Półwiejska 19/10 ☎698 380 473. Friendly small hostel with dorm beds (from 45zł) and doubles (❹) along the bustling shopping street; unfortunately there's only one toilet and shower for all rooms.

Dizzy Daisy al. Niepodległości 26 ☎061/622 2810, ⓦwww.hostel.pl. Summer-only hostel in a student dorm within easy walking distance of the centre. Beds in triples or doubles for 40–50zł per person. It's the cheapest hostel in the centre but lacks the atmosphere of other hostels. Free pickups from the station before 10pm.

🏃 **Frolic Goats** ul. Wrocławska 16/6 (entrance on ul. Jaskółcza) ☎061/852 4411, ⓦwww.frolicgoatshostel.com. The best and most central hostel in town is a friendly, rambling place with dorm beds (from 50zł) and double rooms (❺); prices include breakfast and internet, and there's a laundry service too.

⓫

The main square

For seven centuries the distinguished **main square** (Stary Rynek) has been the hub of life in Poznań, even if these days it has lost its position as the centre of political and economic power. Archetypically Polish, with the most important public buildings sited in the middle, it was badly damaged during the last war, subsequently gaining the sometimes overenthusiastic attentions of the restorers. However, it's now among the most attractive of Poland's rejuvenated old city centres. Lined with a characterful mixture of facades it is at its best in the spring and summer months, when **pavement cafés** and beer bars crowd the cobblestones.

Outside the **town hall** (Ratusz, see p.543) stands a fine Rococo **fountain**, alongside a copy of the **pillory** in its traditional location. Still in the centre of the main square, running southwards from the town hall, is a colourful line of buildings, once home to the market traders, many of whom sold their wares

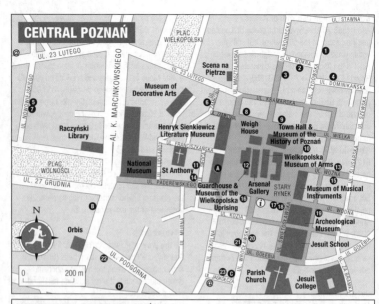

CENTRAL POZNAŃ

ACCOMMODATION		RESTAURANTS & CAFÉS				BARS & CLUBS			
Brovaria	A	Bar Przysmak	22	Herbaciarnia Chimera	4	Buddha Bar	14	Pod Minogą	7
Domina	D	Brovaria	A	Kawka	3	Czarna Owca	23	W Starym Kinie	5
Frolic Goats	C	Cacao Republika	6	Kresowa	12	Czerwony Fortepian	2	Za Kulisami	19
Rzymski	B	Cymes	13	Ratuszowa	17	Déjà Vu	15		
		Czekolada Cafe	1	Sarp Jazz Café	18	Habana	11		
		Dom Wikingów	16	Sioux	9	Lizard King	8		
		Dramat	10	Valpolicella	20	Pod Aniołem	21		

in the arcaded passageways on either side. The present structures date from the sixteenth century and are the oldest in the square.

Immediately behind the western side of the town hall is the **Weigh House** (Waga Miejska), once the most important public building in this great trading centre; what you see today is a reproduction of the original, the work of architect Giovanni Battista Quadro of Lugano. Adjoining it to the south is the sternly Neoclassical **Guardhouse** (Odwach), a single-storey pavilion built for the "defence and decoration" of the city in the 1780s, and surmounted by a pair of distinctly unmilitary-looking female figures blowing trumpets. It houses the recently overhauled **Museum of the Wielkopolska Uprising** (Muzeum Powstania Wielkopolskiego 1918–1919: Tues, Thurs & Fri 10am–5pm, Wed 10am–6pm, Sat & Sun 10am–3pm; 4zł, Sat free; Ⓦwww.muzeumniepodleglosci.poznan.pl), commemorating the fight against the Germans with photos and documents.

On the southern side of the central ensemble, the two low concrete pavilions erected during the communist period add the only discordant notes to the square. In one pavilion, the **Wielkopolska Museum of Arms** (Wielkopolskie Muzeum Wojskowe: Tues–Sat 10am–4pm, Sun 10am–3pm; 3.50zł, Sat free; Ⓦwww.mnp.art.pl) vividly documents the arms development in Poland with uniforms, weapons and shining armour. The other pavilion is home to the **Arsenał Gallery** (Galeria Arsenał: Tues–Sat 11am–6pm, Sun 10am–3pm; 3zł; Ⓦwww.arsenal.art.pl), the prime venue in the city for changing exhibitions of contemporary art.

Many a medieval and Renaissance interior lurks behind the Baroque facades of the **gabled houses** lining the outer sides of the main square, most of them shops, restaurants, cafés or antique shops. On the eastern side, at no. 45, is the **Museum of Musical Instruments** (Muzeum Instrumentów Muzycznych: Tues–Sat 11am–5pm, Sun 10am–3pm; 5.50zł, Sat free), the only collection of its kind in Poland. Its exhibits range from folk instruments from all over the world, through Chopin memorabilia to a vast array of violins. The last is a reminder that every five years the city hosts the Wieniawski International Violin Competition, one of the most prestigious events for young virtuosi (next due in 2011).

The western side of the square is almost equally imposing, above all because of the massive green and white **Działyński Palace** at no. 78, its facade topped by a monumental swan which cranes its neck down towards the square. Cultural soirées took place here in the nineteenth century, helping to keep Polish-language culture alive in what was a Prussian-governed city. Also on this side of the square, the house at no. 84 was once home to Giovanni Battista Quadro – a statue of the architect, sketchbook in hand, occupies a niche in the facade.

Its interior houses the **Henryk Sienkiewicz Literature Museum** (Muzeum Literackie im. Henryka Sienkiewicza: Mon–Fri 10am–5pm; 3zł). Although Poland's most celebrated novelist (see box, p.544) had only a rather tenuous connection with Poznań – he penned a few short stories here – this is the most important museum dedicated to his life and works. Inside lies a straightforward words-and-pictures account of the author's life, accompanied by first editions of his works in innumerable languages.

The town hall

The **town hall** (Ratusz) is in every way predominant. Originally a two-storey Gothic brick structure, it was radically rebuilt in the 1550s. The arcaded eastern facade presents the building at its most vivacious, its lime-green pilasters framing a frieze of Polish monarchs, who are accompanied here by **portraits** of statesmen and poets from ancient Greece and Rome – a propagandist attempt to present Poland's rulers as the guardians of classical wisdom. Every day at noon, the effigies of two goats emerge onto the platform of the **clock** above the facade and butt their heads twelve times. This commemorates the local legend in which the two animals locked horns on the steps of the town hall, and thereby drew attention to a **fire** which had just begun there, so saving the city from a potentially disastrous conflagration. Other sides of the building are inscribed with the words of Polish Renaissance sages, to which post-World War II restorers were forced to add extracts from the communist constitution.

The interior is now the **Museum of the History of Poznań** (Muzeum Historii Miasta Poznania: Tues, Thurs & Fri 9am–4pm, Wed 11am–6pm, Sun 10am–4pm; 5.50zł, free Sun), though the main reason for entering is to see the building itself. Surviving from the Gothic period, the vaulted **cellars** were transformed into a prison in the sixteenth century; they now contain the earliest objects in the display, notably items excavated on Ostrów Tumski and the medieval pillory. However, the most impressive room is the Renaissance **great hall** (*wielka sień*) on the first floor, dating from 1555. Its coffered vault bears polychrome bas-reliefs which embody the exemplary civic duties and virtues through scenes from the lives of Samson, King David and Hercules. The southern section by the staircase depicts astrological and bestial figures, while the marble busts of Roman emperors around the walls are reminders of the weighty tradition of municipal leadership.

Henryk Sienkiewicz (1846–1916)

Outside Poland, **Henryk Sienkiewicz**'s reputation has rested largely on *Quo Vadis?* an epic on the early Christians in the decadent days of the Roman Empire, which won him the 1905 **Nobel Prize for Literature** and quickly became a favourite subject with movie moguls. Yet the huge popular success of this led, after the author's death, to the almost total international neglect of the remainder of his colossal oeuvre, which, even in hopelessly inadequate translations, had marked him out as Poland's answer to Charles Dickens.

Born in the Podlasie region to a minor aristocratic family, Sienkiewicz began his career as a **journalist** and **short story writer**, the culmination of which was a trip to the United States in 1876–77, where he worked in a short-lived Polish agricultural commune in California. Here he wrote *Letters from America* (containing vivid descriptions of such diverse subjects as New York City and the Indian campaigns), and the burlesque novella *Charcoal Sketches*, a satire on rural life in Russian Poland. On his return home, he drew on his experiences of émigré life in *American Stories*, which includes his one work in this genre which frequently turns up in literary **anthologies**, *The Lighthouse Keeper*. These were followed by the despairing novella *Bartek the Conqueror*, the finest of a number of works set in the Poznań region – which, being under Prussian control, made a safer medium for the nationalist message of an author subject to **Russian censors**.

Thereafter, Sienkiewicz changed tack, reviving what was then regarded as the outmoded form of the **historical epic**. His vast trilogy *With Fire and Sword*, *The Deluge* and *Fire in the Steppe* is set against the heroic backdrop of Poland's seventeenth-century wars with the Cossacks, Swedes and Turks. It is remarkable for its sure sense of structure, employing a permanent set of characters – whose language is skilfully differentiated according to their class and culture – with plentiful genealogical digressions and romantic interludes to break the unfolding of the main plot. Historical **realism**, however, was sacrificed in favour of Sienkiewicz's own Catholic, nationalist, chivalrous and anti-intellectual outlook. Despite its non-Polish setting, *Quo Vadis?*, which followed the trilogy, was always regarded as a fable about the country's oppression under the Partitions. Ironically, it is really one of Sienkiewicz's weaker works. He showed a greater concern for historical accuracy in his final epic, *The Teutonic Knights*.

Sienkiewicz also produced a couple of novels with **contemporary** settings, *Without Dogma* and *The Połaniecki Family*. These helped to increase his cult status in nationalist circles, and political activity became increasingly important to him after the turn of the twentieth century. On the outbreak of World War I Sienkiewicz moved to Switzerland where he was instrumental in setting up the **Polish National Committee**, which in due course came to be recognized by the Western allies as a provisional government.

Always an important part of the curriculum in Polish schools, Sienkiewicz has made something of a comeback in the last decade, with the Polish film industry turning his oeuvre into a cinematic gold mine. Veteran director Jerzy Hoffman, who had already filmed creditable adaptations of *The Deluge* and *Fire in the Steppe* in the 1960s and 1970s, set the ball rolling with a lavish big-screen version of *With Fire and Sword* in 1999. It was the most expensive Polish film ever made at the time, and soon became the most successful, garnering an incredible seven million paying viewers. A celluloid version of Sienkiewicz's *In Desert and Wilderness*, a children's adventure story set in Africa, was one of the big box office hits of 2001, while a new Polish TV version of *Quo Vadis?* was unleashed the following year.

West of the main square

Just to the west of the main square stands a hill with remnants of the inner circle of the **medieval walls**. This particular section guarded what was once Zamek Przemysława, the castle and seat of the rulers of Wielkopolska. Modified down the centuries and almost completely destroyed in 1945, a part has been restored to house the **Museum of Decorative Arts** (Muzeum Sztuk Użytkowych: Tues, Wed, Fri & Sat 10am–4pm, Sun 10am–3pm; 5.50zł, free Sat; ⓦwww .mnp.art.pl). This features an enjoyable collection from medieval times to the present day, while the Gothic cellars are used for exhibitions of the work of contemporary Polish artists.

Below the hill is the Baroque **Church of St Anthony** (Kościół św. Antoniego), its interior decorated by the Franciscan brothers Adam and Antonin Swach, the former a painter, the latter a sculptor and stuccoist. The church's most eye-catching corner is the sumptuous Chapel of the Virgin Mary on the left-hand side of the main altar.

The National Museum

Immediately west of St Anthony's church, Poznań's **National Museum** (Muzeum Narodowe: Tues 10am–6pm, Wed, Fri & Sat 9am–5pm, Thurs 10am–4pm, Sun 10am–4pm; 10zł, Sat free; ⓦwww.mnp.art.pl) contains one of the best collections of Polish and international art outside Warsaw. From the entrance in the contemporary north wing on aleja K. Marcinkowskiego, steps ascend through an extensive display of Polish art, featuring examples of virtually every **art movement** to have impacted on the country. Nineteenth-century symbolist Jaczek Malcewski features prominently, with his distinctive spade-bearded countenance peering from numerous large-format canvases, in each of which his self-portrait is joined by a host of mystical and metaphorical characters. The Art Nouveau-esque **Młoda Polska movement** (see p.364) is represented by monumental Mehoffer pastels and touching family portraits by Stanisław Wyspiański. Further up, look out for some explosive 1950s abstract art from Maria Jarema as well as cartloads of stuff by Jerzy Nowosielski, whose enigmatic daubs have made him postwar Poland's most highly priced artist. **International art** is housed in the older, south wing of the museum, where an impressive Italian section includes panels from Gothic and Renaissance altarpieces, and the extensive display of Flemish art includes works by Massys and Joos van Cleve.

Plac Wolności and beyond

Spreading west from the museum is the elongated space of **plac Wolności**. Here stands another seminal centre of the fight to preserve Polish culture, the **Raczyński Library** (Biblioteka Raczyńskich), founded in the early nineteenth century to promote Polish-language learning and literature, and still functioning as a library. Architecturally, it's one of the most distinguished buildings in the city, erected in the 1820s in cool Neoclassical style.

Moving into the business and shopping thoroughfares that branch out west from plac Wolności, you shortly come to the **Teatr Polski**, (see p.551) a charming wedding-cake of a building at ulica 27 Grudnia, erected in the 1870s by voluntary contributions. Overlooking the busy junction at the end of the street is the **Okrąglak** or "Big Log" – an imposing ten-storey cylinder built in the mid-1950s to house the city's main **department store**.

The large buildings standing further to the west reflect the self-confidence of the German occupiers in the first decade of the twentieth century. The most imposing of the group, the huge neo-Romanesque **Kaiserhaus** was intended to accommodate the Kaiser whenever he happened to be in town. Renamed the **Zamek** (castle) and recently renovated, it's now a vibrant cultural centre with exhibitions, theatre, film screenings and concerts. In front of the building stands a monument covered in numbers, commemorating the three Poznań University graduates who cracked the **Enigma encryption codes** in World War II and thereby probably did more than anyone else to bring an end to the war. In the park beyond the Zamek are two huge crucifixes bound together with heavy rope, forming a **monument** to the victims of the Poznań food riots of June 1956. The riots – and their brutal suppression by the security forces – sent shockwaves through Polish society, resulting in the return to power of the reform-minded communist Władysław Gomułka. The lesson that workers' protests could make and break regimes was not lost on future generations, helping to precipitate the rise of **Solidarity** in 1980. It was during Solidarity's extraordinary period of power and influence in communist Poland – before the declaration of martial law in December 1981 – that the monument was unveiled, in June 1981, marking the twenty-fifth anniversary of the riots.

West of the Zamek, ulica św. Marcin crosses the railway tracks and arrives at Rondo Kaponiera roundabout, just south of which lies the main entrance to the trade-fair grounds. A good reason to venture this far is provided by **Wilson Park** (Park Wilsona; named after the American president) 800m further south along ulica Głogowska, whose **Palm House** (Palmiarnia: March & April: Tues–Sun 9am–5pm; May–Oct: Tues–Sat 9am–5pm, Sun 9am–6pm; Nov–Feb: Thurs–Sat 9am–4pm, Sun 9am–5pm; 5.50zł; ⊛www.palmiarnia.poznan.pl) is one of the horticultural wonders of Poland.

South and east of the main square

Heading east from the main square along ulica Wodna brings you to the **Górka Palace** (Pałac Górków) at no. 27, which still preserves its intricate Renaissance portico and sober inner courtyard. The mansion now houses the **Archeology Museum** (Muzeum Archeologiczne: Tues–Fri 10am–4pm, Sat 10am–6pm, Sun 10am–3pm; 6zł; ⊛www.muzarp.poznan.pl), which traces the history of the region in entertaining fashion, with a sequence of dioramas illustrating the daily life of Wielkopolska inhabitants from the time of the nomadic hunters all the way to the early feudal society of the seventh century AD. Poznań University's **archeological expeditions** abroad – notably to Egypt and Sudan – are documented with an absorbing display of artefacts.

Ulica Świętosławska ends in a cluster of gloriously salmon-coloured former Jesuit buildings, the finest examples of Baroque architecture in the city. The end of this street is closed by the facade of the **Parish Church of St Mary Magdalene** (Kościół Farny św. Marii Magdaleny), completed just forty years before the expulsion of the Jesuits in 1773. Its magnificently sombre interior has a painting over the high alter illustrating a legendary episode from the life of **St Stanisław**. Then a bishop, Stanisław was accused by King Bolesław the Generous of not having paid for a village he had incorporated into his territories. In order to prove his innocence, the saint resurrected the deceased former owner of the land to testify on his behalf.

Across the road is the **Jesuit school**, now one of Poland's main ballet academies, and to the east of the church is the front section of the former **Jesuit college**. The Jesuits have returned to Poznań, now occupying the oldest left-bank building, the **Dominican church** to the northeast of the main square. Despite a Baroque recasing, this still preserves original Romanesque and Gothic features, as well as a stellar-vaulted Rosary chapel. The late Baroque **All Saints' Church** (Kościół Wszystkich Świętych), almost due east of the main square, is the epitome of a Lutheran church, with its democratic central plan layout and overall plainness.

At no. 25 on the adjacent ulica Grobla is the former lodge of the freemasons, now the **Ethnographical Museum** (Muzeum Etnograficzne: Tues–Thurs 10am–3pm, Fri noon–9pm, Sat & Sun 11am–6pm; 5.50zł, Sat free; ⓦwww .mnp.art.pl), with some interesting carvings, ceramics and musical instruments. Further south you'll see the twin-towered Baroque church of the **Franciscan monastery**. Built in 1473, it has been gleamingly restored by the monks who repossessed it following its wartime use as a warehouse.

From here a brief walk west along ulica Długa brings you to the pedestrianized ulica Półwiejska, the most animated of Poznań's **shopping streets**. It's worth following it southwards all the way to the end in order to take a look at the **Stary Browar** shopping mall (Mon–Sat 9am–9pm, Sun 9am–8pm; ⓦwww .starybrowar.pl), which combines a nineteenth-century brewery building with modern architecture to create an eye-pleasing palace of red brick and steel. The top floor of the complex, curiously at the same level as the adjacent park, houses several bars and restaurants, and the Japanese-designed **Art Stations gallery**, (daily noon–7pm; ⓦwww.artstations.pl).

North of the main square

The northern quarters are best approached from plac Wielkopolski, a large square now used for markets. From here, ulica Działowa passes two churches facing each other on the brow of the hill. To the right is the Gothic **St Adalbert's Church** (Kościół św. Wojciecha), chiefly remarkable for its little seventeenth-century wooden belfry which somehow got left on the ground in front of the brick facade. Opposite, the handsome Baroque **Carmelite monastery** reflects a more complete image.

Beyond, aleja Niepodległości heads northeast towards the **Citadel** (Cytadela), a vast earthwork fortress built by the Prussians in the nineteenth century and subsequently pressed into service by the interwar Polish state as the linchpin of their western defenses. The scene of bitter fighting in both 1939 and 1945, it is now an extensive, partly wooded park, the southern slopes of which are occupied by a **memorial garden** in honour of the six thousand Russians and Poles who lost their lives here. A stairway just off the northern end of Niepodległości leads uphill through the graves towards a huge **memorial** to the Red Army. A couple of hundred metres east of the stairway lies a small British and Commonwealth cemetery – interred here are POWs from both World Wars, including those shot after the "Great Escape" (see p. 000), as well as airmen shot down over Poland between 1939–45. Beyond the Red Army memorial, a crumbling red-brick bastion harbours the **Museum of Arms** (Muzeum Uzbrojenia: Tues–Sat 9am–4pm, Sun 10am–4pm; 4zł, Fri free ; ⓦwww.muzeumniepodleglosci.poznan.pl), with a small but absorbing collection of tanks and armoured cars. Further north, the midpoint of the park is marked by **Nierozpoznani** ("The Undiagnosed"), a cast-iron army of 112 larger-than-life headless figures by contemporary artist Magdalena Abakanowicz.

Ostrów Tumski

The Most Bolesława Chrobrego bridge crosses to the island of **Ostrów Tumski**, a world away in spirit, if not in distance, from the hustle of the city (trams #1, #4 and #8 go over the bridge.) Only a small portion of the island is built on, and a few priests and monks comprise its entire population. Lack of parishioners means that there's not the usual need for evening Masses, and after 5pm the island is a ghost town.

The first building you see is the late Gothic **Psalteria**, characterized by its elaborate stepped gable. It was erected in the early sixteenth century as a residence for the cathedral choir. Immediately behind is an earlier brick structure, the small **Church of Our Lady** (Kościół Panny Marii), while a couple of minutes' walk north of the cathedral is the **Archdiocesan Museum** (Muzeum Archidiecezjalne: Mon–Fri 10am–5pm, Sat 9am–3pm; 6zł; ⓦwww .muzeum.poznan.pl), located at ul. Lubrańskiego 1, with a spread of sculptures, treasures and some rather fine religious art.

The Basilica of Sts Peter and Paul

The streets of the island are lined with handsome eighteenth-century houses, all very much in the shadow of the **Basilica of Sts Peter and Paul** (Basylika św. Piotra i Pawła), one of Poland's most venerated cathedrals. Over the centuries the brickwork exterior succumbed to Baroque and Neoclassical remodellings, but when much of this was stripped by wartime devastation it was decided to restore as much of the Gothic original as possible. The Baroque spires on the two facade towers and the three lanterns around the ambulatory were also reconstructed.

Inside, the basilica is impressive, but not outstanding. The **crypt**, entered from below the northern tower, has been extensively excavated, uncovering the thousand-year-old foundations of the pre-Romanesque and Romanesque cathedrals which stood on the site – two models depict their probable appearance. Parts of the sarcophagi of the first two Polish kings, Mieszko I and Bolesław the Brave, currently rest in the **Golden Chapel** behind the altar. Miraculously unscathed during the war, this hyper-ornate creation, representing the tastes of the 1830s, is the antithesis of the plain architecture around it.

Of the many other **funerary monuments** which form one of the key features of the cathedral, that of Bishop Benedykt Izdbieński, just to the left of the Golden chapel, is notable. This was carved by Jan Michałowicz, the one native Polish artist of the Renaissance period who was the equal of the many Italians who settled here. The other outstanding **tomb** is that of the Górka family, in the Holy Sacrament chapel at the northern end of the nave, sculpted just a few years later by one of these itinerant craftsmen, Hieronimo Canavesi. Other **works of art** to look out for are the late Gothic carved and gilded high altar triptych from Silesia, the choir stalls from the same period and fragments of sixteenth-century frescoes, notably a cycle of the Apostles on the south side of the ambulatory.

Jezioro Maltańskie

Crossing Most Mieska I bridge and heading southeast of Rondo Śródka, follow paths leading down to the western end of **Lake Malta** (Jezioro Maltańskie), the city's most popular summertime playground. This two-kilometre-long stretch of water was built to accommodate rowing regattas and is surrounded by pleasant footpaths. At the eastern end of the lake a couple of grassy strands are equipped with bathing piers, alongside children's play areas, a dry-ski slope, and an all-weather toboggan run. Just beyond the lake's eastern shore is the sizeable, open-plan **Zoo** (Zoo Nowy: daily 9am–7pm; 7zł). A **narrow-gauge rail line** especially designed for children (mid-April to mid-Oct 10am–7pm; Mon–Fri every hour, Sat & Sun every 30min; 4.50zł) runs from Rondo Śródka to the zoo, passing alongside the northern shore of the lake on the way.

Eating, drinking and nightlife

There's a constantly expanding range of restaurants, cafés and bars in this fast-changing city. Most **eating and drinking** takes place around the main square or in neighbouring alleys such as Wrocławska, Wodna and Woźna; and you'll rarely have to travel outside the walkable confines of the town centre in search of an evening out. Many of Poznań's central bars feature DJs and dancing at the weekend. In addition there's a growing number of **clubbing** venues to choose from – look out for street posters, or read the events listings in Friday's *Gazeta Wyborcza* newspaper.

Restaurants

Brovaria Stary Rynek 73–74. Boutique brewery with huge restaurant attached, decked out in cool post-industrial style and serving some of the best meat and fish dishes in the city. Prices are very reasonable for the quality offered; grilled salmon for 38zł, lamb cutlets for 52zł. Open 7am–midnight.

Cymes ul. Woźna 2/3. Hearty Jewish food (though not kosher) served in a charming restaurant decorated like someone's living room. There's trout with almonds for 22zł, or duck with orange for 34zł. Open 1pm–midnight; Mon 4pm–midnight.

Dom Wikingów Stary Rynek 62. Bringing together café, restaurant and a couple of bars all in one place, it's likely that you'll find at least one corner of this establishment that you'll like. Danish meat and fish dishes are the house speciality, but just about everything else in the international pub-grub line crops up on the menu too. Open 10am–midnight.

Estella ul. Garbary 41. Probably the best pizza place in town, with a broad choice of authentic pies (13–25zł), plenty of pasta dishes, and comfortable slow-food surroundings. Open noon–midnight.

Kresowa Rynek 3. Formal service and high standards, yet reasonable prices, in a traditional Polish restaurant, hidden away in one of the alleys running through the main square's central ensemble of buildings. Open 1–11pm.

Piano Bar ul. Półwiejska 42 (Stary Browar mall) Ⓦ www.pianobar.poznan.pl. A very elegant, upmarket Italian restaurant and bar on the top floor of the mall; try the roe-stuffed ravioli (38zł) or an Argentinian steak (115zł). Open noon–midnight.

Ratuszowa Stary Rynek 55 ☎061/851 0513. Imaginative and delicious variations of traditional Polish meals served below artfully decorated cellar vaults. Open noon–11pm.

Sioux Stary Rynek 93. The best of the chain restaurants; a quirky and roomy faux Wild West saloon in an ideal location. Get seated on a wagon and tuck into steaks (from 36zł), pizzas, kebabs, and even fajitas for around 29zł. Sun–Thurs noon–11pm, Fri & Sat till 1am.

Valpolicella ul. Wrocławska 7. Cosy, intimate venue for a good-quality Italian meal washed down with decent wine. A good place for scampi or calamari. Open noon–11pm.

Cafés and snack bars

Bar Przysmak ul. Podgórna 2. Functional canteen serving up cheap stodge to young and old. Mon–Fri 9am–9pm; Sat & Sun 11am–7pm.

Cacao Republika ul. Zamkowa 6. Cosy bolt-hole a stone's throw from the main square offering an intriguingly large menu of hot chocolate-based drinks, alongside exceedingly palatable teas and coffees. Open 10am–midnight.

Czekolada Cafe ul. Żydowska 29 ☎061/851 9291, Ⓦ www.czekoladacafe .pl. A quirky chocolate-themed café with drinks and snacks (many made with chocolate) and in summer an excellent picnic service including a rental bike, blanket and filled hamper for two (50–58zł). Open 11am–midnight.

Dramat Stary Rynek 41. Uncomplicated menu of breakfasts, pancakes and *pierogi* in an atmospheric brick-lined dining room. Featuring table service and well-presented food, it's a cut above the canteen-style places. Open 10am–midnight.

Herbaciarnia Chimera ul. Dominikańska 7. Refined tea-shop-cum-restaurant with a wide range of brews, some fancy salads and snacks such as deep-fried camembert (14zł) and a full menu of main courses. Open 10am–midnight.

Kawka ul. Wroniecka 18. Old furniture and mismatching chairs create an intimate atmosphere for the students sipping coffee and eating freshly made cakes in this friendly café. Open 10am–midnight, Sun 11am–midnight.

Sarp Jazz Café Stary Rynek 56. Pretty much what you'd expect from a café run by the Polish Architects' Association: a chic orange-lit lounge bar serving good coffee, various snacks and dainty desserts, both inside and on the sunny terrace. Daily 11am–2am, Fri & Sat 11am–4am.

Bars and pubs

Buddha Bar ul. Sieroca 10 Ⓦ www .buddhabar-poznan.pl. Poland's largest Buddha statues can be found in this fun, over-the-top Asian restaurant and bar. There's good Indian food (mains from 20–40zł) and regular "Oriental shows" and DJ parties at night. Open noon–midnight, Wed–Sat till 3am.

Déjà Vu ul. Woźna 21. Several simply decorated, dimly lit rooms, each of which is perpetually full of amiable students sipping cheap beer. Open 10am–3am, Sun from 1pm.

🏃 **Habana** ul. Paderewskiego 10 ⓦwww .habanarestaurant.pl. Glamorous-looking new Cuban-themed bar and restaurant that's packed with an equally glamorous cocktail-sipping crowd at night. Open noon–midnight.

Kisielice ul. Taczaka 20. Eccentric lounge bar beloved by art-academy students and their mildly bohemian hangers-on. There's a DJ playing strange music most nights of the week. Open Mon–Thurs 10am–2am, Fri 10am–4am, Sat 2pm-4am, Sun 2pm–2am.

Lizard King Stary Rynek 86. Enjoyable main-square pub decked out with pictures of Doors frontman Jim Morrison and sundry other psycho-rockers. Packed out at weekends with hedonistically inclined locals jigging to live cover bands. Open 11am–midnight.

Pod Aniołem ul. Wrocławska 8. Stylish, comfortable café-bar in an atmospheric old building. Good place for an intimate evening drink or a simple meal. Mon–Sat 11am–midnight, Sun 1pm–midnight.

Pod Minogą ul. Nowowiejskiego 8. Perennial student favourite, featuring a club-like back room and upstairs section where DJs play alternative music. Open noon–5am.

Pod Pretekstem ul. św. Marcin 80/82, entrance from ul. Fredry ⓦwww.podpretekstem.pl. Refined café-pub at the rear of the Zamek in the courtyard. Regular programme of live jazz, blues and cabaret. Open Mon–Fri 10am–midnight, Sat & Sun noon–midnight.

🏃 **W Starym Kinie** ul. Nowowiejskiego 8. Dimly lit, comfy and relaxing place with a cinema theme, moderately bohemian clientele, soothing soul/jazz/reggae mix on the sound system and DJ parties in the club section. Open 10am–3am, Thurs–Sat 10am–5am.

Za Kulisami ul. Wodna 24. Cosy two-room place not far from the main square, so stuffed with bric-a-brac that it looks like a library, stable and country cottage all rolled into one. Equally good for a daytime drink or an evening boozing session. Open Mon–Thurs 4pm–1am, Fri & Sat 4pm–2am, Sun 6pm–1am.

Nightlife

🏃 **Blue Note** ul. Kościuszki 76/78 ⓦwww .bluenote.poznan.pl. Renowned jazz club underneath the Zamek with two tiers of seating. Frequent gigs (rock as well as jazz) and club nights, for which tickets (15–80zł) can also be bought at the tourist information centre. Open Sun-Wed 7pm-midnight, Thurs–Sat 7pm–3am.

Czarna Owca ul. Jaskółcza 13. Welcoming warren of subterranean rooms just round the corner from the main square, with mainstream music and a friendly fun-seeking crowd. Open Sun–Wed 6pm-1am, Thurs–Sat 6pm–3am.

Czerwony Fortepian ul. Wroniecka 18 (entrance on ul. Mokra) ⓦwww.czerwony-fortepian.pl. Upmarket restaurant and bar with jazzy music and frequent live gigs. Open noon–midnight.

Eskulap ul. Przybyszewskiego 39 ⓦwww .eskulapklub.pl. Agenda-setting club hosting big DJ nights, and concentrating on the cutting edge of dance music. A bit of a hike, located about 2km west of the centre near the university's medical faculty. Open Thurs–Sat 9pm–4am.

SQ Klub ul. Półwiejska 42 (Stary Browar mall) ⓦwww.sqklub.pl. The main party venue for big-name local and foreign DJs playing house, electro and other styles, attracting an enthusiastic crowd. Dress up to get in. Open Wed–Sat 10pm–4am.

Entertainment

There's always a great deal going on in Poznań when it comes to highbrow culture. **Tickets** to performances are reasonably priced and easy to come by, and are sold at the tourist information centre. There are a dozen **cinemas** in town, showing international releases with Polish subtitles. For details of what's on, get a copy of *IKS* (3.90zł), a monthly **listings** booklet with an English-language calendar of events. A more up-to-the-minute (albeit Polish-language) source of information is the Friday edition of the *Gazeta Wyborcza* newspaper.

Music and dance

Akademia Muzyczna ul. św. Marcin 87 ☎061/856 8900, ⓦwww.amuz.poznan.pl. Regular programme of vocal and instrumental concerts, featuring students at the Poznań Musical Academy – entrance is often free.

Centrum Kultury Zamek ul. św. Marcin 80/82 ☎061/646 5200, ⓦwww.zamek.poznan.pl. Concerts featuring all kinds of music from classical recitals to pop.

Filharmonia Poznańska Box office (daily 1–6pm) at ul. św. Marcin 81 ☎061/852 4708,

@ www.filharmonia.poznan.pl. Regular performances by the Poznań Philharmonic (usually on Fri
or Sat), interspersed with chamber concerts and
solo recitals. The concerts take place at
the University Aula (Aula Uniwerzytecka), ul.
Wienawskiego 1.
Polski Teatr Tańca ul. Kozia 4 ☎ 061/852 4242,
@ www.ptt.poznan.pl. Rich diet of classical ballet and
contemporary dance. Box office Tues–Sun 1–6pm.
Teatr Muzyczny ul. Niezłomnych 1e ☎ 061/852
1786, @ www.teatr-muzyczny.poznan.pl. Main
venue for musicals and operetta. Box office Mon
9am–2pm, Tues–Fri 9am–7pm, Sat 3–6pm & Sun
2hr before performance.
Teatr Wielki ul. Fredry 9 ☎ 061/659 0200,
@ www.opera.poznan.pl. Home of the Poznań
opera. There are usually several operas running
concurrently throughout the season, with
performances several nights a week. Box office
Mon–Sat 1–7pm, Sun 4–7pm.

Theatre
Scena na Piętrze ul. Masztalarska 8 ☎ 061/852
8833, @ www.estrada.poznan.pl. Contemporary
drama from visiting companies.
Teatr Animacji al. Niepodległości 14 ☎ 061/853
7220, @ www.teatranimacji.pl. Enjoyable and
inventive productions from one of Poland's best-
known theatres for children, located in the Zamek.
Sometimes starring live actors; sometimes featuring
puppets. Performances often start at 10 or 11am.
Box office Tues–Sun 10am–noon & 3–5pm.

Teatr Nowy ul. Dąbrowskiego 5 ☎ 061/847 2440,
@ www.teatrnowy.pl. Contemporary drama from
Poland and further afield, with performances taking
place in either the main auditorium or the studio-
sized Scena Nowa. Box office Tues–Sat 1–7pm,
Sun 4–7pm.
Teatr Ósmego Dnia ul. Ratajczaka 44. ☎ 061/855
2086, @ www.osmego.art.pl. Experimental drama
from one of Poland's leading companies. Box
office Mon–Fri 11am–2pm or 30min prior to the
performance.
Teatr Polski ul. 27 Grudnia 8/10 ☎ 061/852 5628,
@ www.teatr-polski.pl. Drama from classical to
contemporary, with a strong accent on the Polish
theatrical canon. Box office Tues–Sat 10am–7pm,
Sun 4–7pm.

Cinema
Apollo ul. Ratajczaka 18 @ www.apollo.poznan
.pl. Mainstream movies and comfy atmosphere in
a traditional two-screen cinema, nicely renovated
in 2005.
Malta ul. Filipińska 5 @ www.kinomalta.pl. A
student cinema across the river, a good twenty
minutes east of the main square, this has the
widest range of art movies and cinema classics.
Multikino ul. Półwiejska 42 (Stary Browar mall)
@ www.multikino.pl. Handiest of the multiplexes,
inside the Stary Browar mall.
Muza ul. św. Marcin 30 @ www.kinomuza.pl.
Mainstream films and special film series in a
central location.

Listings

Airlines LOT, at the airport ☎ 080/170 3703,
@ www.lot.com.
Airport information ☎ 061/849 2343,
@ www.airport-poznan.com.pl.
Books and maps The Empik store at ul. Ratajczaka 44 (Mon–Sat 9am–9pm, Sun 10am–8pm) has
the best overall selection of maps, English-language
magazines and books. Globetrotter, just off the
northern side of the main square at ul. Żydowska 1,
is a specialist store for maps and guidebooks.
Car rental Avis, at the airport ☎ 061/849 2335,
@ www.avis.com; Budget, near the station at
Globus, ul. Roosevelta 18 ☎ 061/845 1489 and at
the airport ☎ 061/849 2361, @ www.budget.pl;
Europcar, at the airport ☎ 061/849 2357, @ www
.europcar.pl; Hertz, at the airport ☎ 061/868 4177,
@ www.hertz.com.
Hospital ul. Chełmońskiego 20 ☎ 061/866 0066.
Internet access Café Pralnia, ul. Mostowa 3a and
Strong, ul. 23 Lutego nr.7. There's free wi-fi on the
main square and pl. Wolności.

Laundry Café Pralnia, ul. Mostowa 3a.
Left luggage At the train station (24hr) and the
bus station (8am–10pm).
Libraries The British Council-supported
English-language library at ul.
Ratajczaka 39 (Mon–Fri 10am–6pm, Sat
10am–2pm) has a generous stock of books
and periodicals.
Pharmacies There's a 24hr pharmacy
just northwest of the main square at ul. 23
Lutego 18 and south of the square at ul.
Strzelecka 2.
Post office Main office at ul. Kościuszki 77
(Mon–Fri 7am–8pm, Sat 8am–3pm).
The train station branch, just outside the
western entrance at Głogowska 17, is
open 24hr.
Taxis ☎ 061/9191 or ☎ 061/9622.
Travel agents Orbis, al. Marcinkowskiego 21
☎ 061/853 2052, deals with international bus, train
and air tickets.

Around Poznań

It's simple to escape from the big-city feel of Poznań as its outskirts soon give way to peaceful agricultural villages set in a lake-strewn landscape. Within a 25-kilometre radius of the city is some of the finest scenery in Wielkopolska, along with two of Poland's most famous **castles**, which, if you have a car, combine to make a full day's excursion. If you're dependent on public transport, you'll probably have to devote a day to each of them.

Kórnik

Twenty-two kilometres southeast of Poznań on the main road to Katowice, the lakeside village of **KÓRNIK** is the site of one of the great castles of Wielkopolska. There's an hourly bus service (Kombus #501) from Poznań's suburban Rondo Rataje bus station, 1.5 kilometres east of the centre along ul. Królowej Jadwigi; don't go by **train**, as the station is 4km from the village.

Buses pick up and drop off on the main square, a well-signed five-minute walk from the **castle** (Tues–Sun May–Sept 10am–6pm; Oct–March 10am–4pm; closed mid-Dec to mid-Jan; 11zł), which stands amid extensive parkland at the southern edge of the village. Originally built for the Górka family in the fourteenth century, the castle was rebuilt in neo-Gothic style in the nineteenth century by Italian and German craftsmen including Karl Friedrich Schinkel, best known for his Neoclassical public buildings in Berlin. However, his designs were considerably modified, and credit for the final shape of the castle is due to the owner, Tytus Działyński, whose aim was as much to show off his collection of arms and armour, books and *objets d'art* as to provide a luxurious home for himself.

In contrast to the affected grandeur of the exterior, with its mock defensive towers and Moorish battlements, the interior is rather more intimate. On the ground floor, the **drawing room** with its superb gilded ceiling and huge carved wooden portal bears Działyński's coat of arms, and none other than Chopin once ran his fingers across the keyboard of the nearby grand piano. On the first floor the **Moorish Hall** attempts to mimic Granada's Alhambra.

Stretching away behind the castle is Działyński's **arboretum** (May–Oct daily 9am–5pm; 4zł; in winter usually accessible during restricted hours for free) a landscaped collection of more than three thousand types of tree. Originally in the formal French style, this was transformed in the seemingly arbitrary manner of a *jardin anglais*. The lakeside offers an even more pleasant stroll, particularly the western bank with its fine distant views.

▲ Kórnik castle

Rogalin

With your own transport, it's easy to combine a visit to Kórnik with a look round the palace at **ROGALIN**, a hamlet 10km to the west on the road to Mosina. With only a few buses a day from Poznań, those dependent on public transport will have to check times carefully in advance, or try hitchhiking.

The **palace** (May–Sept Tues–Sat 10am–4pm, Sun 10am–6pm; Oct–April Tues–Sun 10am–4pm; 10zł, free on Thurs Ⓦwww.rogalin.eu) was the seat of many Polish nobles from the eminent Poznań family, the Raczyńskis. It's one of Poland's finest mansions, a truly palatial residence forming the axis of a careful layout of buildings and gardens. Begun in 1768 and only finished 47 years later, the palace represents a remarkable and rather tasteful fusion of the Baroque and Neoclassical styles. Two bowed palace **wings** feature some fine furniture and house the **art gallery**, a well-laid-out collection of nineteenth-century Polish and German works. Jacek Malczewski was a frequent guest at Rogalin and his works are well represented here, as are those of **Jan Matejko**, his epic *Virgin of Orleans* taking up an entire wall.

Fronting the palace courtyard is a long forecourt, to the sides of which are the stables and **coach house**, the latter now a repository of carriages once used by owners of this estate, along with the last horse-drawn cab to operate in Poznań. Passing outside the gates, a five-minute walk brings you to the unusual **chapel** which undertakes the duties of a parish church and mausoleum of the now defunct Raczyńskis.

At the back of the main palace is an enclosed *jardin français;* more enticing is the English-style park beyond, laid out on the site of a primeval forest. This is chiefly remarkable for its **oak trees**, three of the most ancient of which have been fenced off for protection and are known as the **Rogalin Oaks**. They are at least one thousand years old – and thus of a similar vintage to the Polish nation itself. Following World War II they became popularly known as Lech, Czech and Rus, after the three mythical brothers who founded the Polish, Czech and Russian nations.

There's a **restaurant** and bar by the road, opposite the entrance to the palace, and a comfortable **hotel** (℡061/813 8480; ❹) in one of the palace outbuildings.

Wielkopolska national park

The only area of protected landscape in the province, the **Wielkopolska national park** occupies an area of some 100 square kilometres to the south of Poznań. Unspoiled by development, it's a popular day-trip destination from the regional capital. Formed in geologically recent times, it's a post-glacial landscape of low moraines, gentle ridges and lakes. Half the park is taken up by forest, predominantly pine and birch planted as replacements for the original hardwoods.

Access to the park from Poznań is fairly easy, with a dozen daily **trains** (the slow *osobowy* services from Poznań to Leszno or Wrocław) passing through a sequence of settlements on the eastern fringes of the park – **Puszczykowo**, **Puszczykówko** and **Mosina** – from where you can pick up hiking trails into the park itself. The western border of the park is served by the Poznań–Wolsztyn rail line (some of the services are still pulled by steam engines from the Wolsztyn depot; see p.558), which passes through the trail-head town of Stęszew. Catching a train to the eastern side of the park, walking across it, and returning to Poznań from Stęszew (or vice versa), makes for a perfectly feasible **day-trip**; Poznań's tourist office can help plan the trip so that you're sure to catch the steam train. It's also popular to cross the park by **bike** (trails open to cyclists have orange-red waymarks); you can rent good bikes at Puszczykowo's train station (Sat & Sun 9am–7pm, Mon–Fri by appointment; 8zł per hr or 40zł per day; ℡600/040 581, ⓦwww.rowerowo.com.pl) though make sure to book in advance.

Fifteen kilometres south of Poznań, the twin villages of **PUSZCZYKOWO** and **PUSZCZYKÓWKO** lie on the west bank of the snaking River Warta, both serving as the starting points for trails heading into the northern section of the park. Puszczykówko is marginally the more appealing of the two, if only because it's the site of the **Arkady Fiedler Museum** (Muzeum Arkadego Fiedlera: Tues–Sun: May–Oct 9am–6pm, Nov–April 10am–3pm; 7zł; ⓦwww.fiedler.pl), located just east of the station in the former house of the prolific Polish travel writer. Fiedler was one of the most popular travel writers in the Eastern Bloc, churning out books on his experiences in Africa, South America and the East. The museum is full of the personal knick-knacks brought back from his sojourns abroad, while the delightful **garden** has an impressive array of replica Aztec, Easter Island and other sculptures as well as a scale replica of Columbus's Santa Maria boat.

Another 2km south of Puszczykówko is **MOSINA**, the best starting point for exploring the eastern reaches of the park (see below).

Walking in the park

Exploring the park, it's best to stick to the three official **hiking paths**, which are generally well marked and unstrenuous. Each takes several hours if you cover the entire length, though it's easy enough to switch from one to the other – the best idea if you're restricted for time.

Walking from Mosina gets you into the best of the terrain quickly. Heading out of town on the road to Stęszew, turning right at the *Morena Hotel*, turning

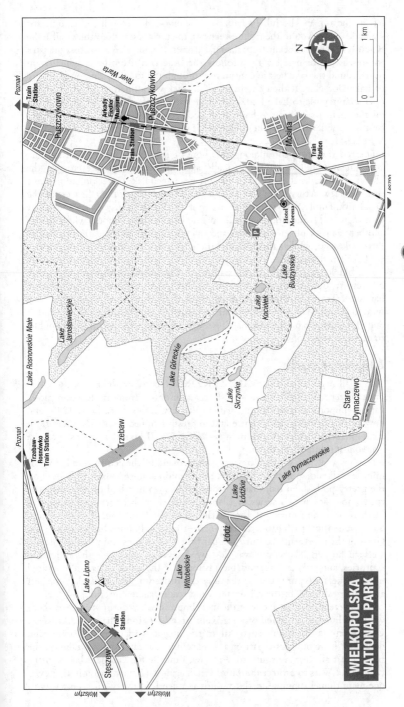

WIELKOPOLSKA NATIONAL PARK

Poznań

River Warta

Train Station

Puszczykowo

Arkady Fiedler Museum

Train Station

Puszczykówko

Mosina

Train Station

Lezno

P

Hotel Morena

Lake Budzyńskie

Lake Kocioɫek

Lake Rosnowskie Małe

Lake Jarosławieckie

Lake Góreckie

Lake Skrzynka

Stare Dymaczewo

Lake Dymaczewskie

Poznań

Trzebaw-Rosnówko Train Station

Trzebaw

Lake Łódźkie

Lake Łódźkie

Łódź

Lake Witobelskie

Lake Lipno

Train Station

Stęszew

Wolsztyn

Wolsztyn

N

1 km

0

left at the top of the hill (waymarks – orange-red for cyclists and blue for walkers – point you in the right direction), the path descends to the small **Lake Kociołek,** which is beautifully shaded by trees. If your plan is to cross the park to Stęszew, your best bet is to follow the **blue trail** from here, which leads north round the lake before continuing through the forest to the southern end of Lake Góreckie. It then climbs through thick woods before passing through open countryside to Lake Łódźkie, on the far side of which – off the trail but on the main road – is the hamlet of Łódź, clustered around a seventeenth-century wooden church. The route then leads along the northern shore of Lake Witobelskie to Stęszew.

The **red trail** runs south along the shore of Lake Kociołek before travelling circuitously uphill, skirting the small Lake Skrzynke just before crossing the blue trail. It arrives at the bend in the sausage-shaped Lake Góreckie, from where there's a view across to an islet with a ruined castle – a former fortress of the Działyński family, and a meeting point for the Polish insurgents of 1863. The path then leads round the perimeter of the lake as far as Jeziory, where there's another car park plus a restaurant and café. Two separate red paths proceed to Puszczykówko, while a third follows the long northerly route to Puszczykowo via Lake Jarosławieckie.

The **black trail** begins at the station of **Trzebaw-Rosnówko** (just north of Stęszew, on the Poznań–Wolsztyn rail line), then traverses the fields to the hamlet of Trzebaw, before continuing through the woods to Lake Łódźkie. It's wise to skip the last part of this trail, as it passes Lake Dymaczewskie to end at Stare Dymaczewo on the Mosina–Stęszew road, which has no convenient public transport connections.

Międzyrzecz

The small market town of **MIĘDZYRZECZ** ("between the rivers"; ⓦwww .miedzyrzecz.pl), 100km west of Poznań, profited from its location along various important trade routes, gaining its city rights as early as 1248, and now retains a pretty town centre and impressive ruined castle. Defences from a completely different era – a massive World War II bunker complex – can be visited just south of the town.

The bus and train stations are at the eastern end of the centre, and it's a ten-minute walk along ulica 30 Stycznia to the **main square**, which is focused on the pretty pink town hall, dating from 1581. Two hundred metres west, the road slopes down to a series of islands in the river that form the protective earthen walls and moats of the **castle** (Tues–Sat 9am–4pm, Fri 9am–6pm, Sun 10am–4pm; park grounds daily 6am–10pm; 4zł), built by Kazimierz the Great in the fourteenth century to guard the trade routes and protect Poland's western border. The castle was destroyed several times over the following centuries, and only two formidable bastions and the outer walls can be visited now. Tickets are purchased at the adjacent **museum**, which displays various archeological finds, historical artefacts and reconstructed interiors.

Międzyrzecz lies near to one of the most impressive – yet least visible – defence works in Europe, the **Międzyrzecz Reinforced Region** (Międzyrzecki Rejon Umocniony); an incredible thirty-kilometre-long network of tunnels connecting dozens of huge bunkers – part of a defence line that ran from Koszalin on the Baltic coast all the way south to Wrocław. Built by the Germans between the two World Wars to protect the Third Reich against a Soviet invasion, there was one main tunnel running north to south at a depth of thirty-fifty metres, with various side tunnels leading to staircases to the bunkers, which had steel domes and 25cm-thick concrete walls. This underground complex had all the power, water, sewage and communication systems necessary to operate independently, and even an underground narrow-gauge railway, but was never used as the Soviets captured it without much resistance in 1945.

Parts of the complex are now protected as an **underground nature reserve** as the tunnels houses tens of thousands of bats every winter. Guided **tours** of the complex (mid-April to Sept daily 10am–6pm; Oct to mid-April Tues–Fri 10am–4pm; 14–17zł; ☎095/741 9999, ⓦwww.bunkry.pl) are possible at **Pniewo**, fifteen minutes walk west of Kaława, which is 10km south of Międzyrzecz on the main road and bus route to Świebodzin. There's a short (1hr 30min) and long (2hr 30min) tour, and an extra long (4–8hr) tour on demand in the summer season. The 12.15pm tours on Sat and Sun are in German and English, otherwise call ahead to book an English guide for 75–85zł extra. Keep in mind that it's 8°C year round in the tunnels, so dress warmly. Above ground, there's a small **museum** and **restaurant**.

Practicalities

Międzyrzecz can be reached in under two hours by **train** (with a change at Zbąszynek) or **bus** from Poznań. There's a small tourist information centre inside Międzyrzecz's castle gate (daily 10am–5pm; ☎095/742 6964) with brochures and maps. Halfway between the stations and the castle, the concrete *Tequila* hotel at ul. Stoczniowców Gdańskich-1970 nr. 1 (☎095/741 2031; ⓦwww.tequila.prv.pl; ❷) is the only decent central option, though best avoided on weekend nights when the restaurant is used by wedding parties. The *Costa Café*, opposite the *Tequila* at ul. 30 Stycznia 47, is a good place for pasta, snacks and sandwiches.

Łagów

Tiny **ŁAGÓW** village (ⓦwww.lagow.pl) lies 26km southwest of Międzyrzecz. It attracts large numbers of visitors due to its picturesque position amid deep beech **forests** and between two beautiful **lakes** – Jezioro Trześniowskie to the north and Jezioro Łagówskie to the south – and the surrounding **Łagów Landscape Park** (Łagowski Park Krajobrazowy) is perfect for gentle walks. Łagów can be reached several times per day by bus from Świebodzin, which is on the main Berlin–Poznan rail line.

The main sight is the small brick-towered **Joannite Castle** (Zamek Joannitów) built on a hill overlooking the village and the lakes, and home to the Joannite order in medieval times. The castle now houses a restaurant and a rather charming hotel (☎068/341 2010, ⓦwww.zamek-lagow.pl; ❺), where you can sleep in the deluxe Commanders room or in a real torture room complete with some pretty hardcore SM gear.

Southern Wielkopolska

Those with a nostalgia for the days of steam should make tracks for the little lakeside town of **WOLSZTYN**, 75km southwest of Poznań, the only remaining rail depot in Europe that still proudly uses **steam locomotives** to haul passenger services. Pride of the fleet is the green-liveried *Piękna Helena* (Beautiful Helena), built for the Polish state railways in 1937 and still going strong. Just one of several locomotives shuttling passengers between Wolsztyn and Poznań (currently departing Wolsztyn at 5.40am and 11.40am; returning from Poznań at 8.25am and 3.55pm; confirm with the Poznań tourism office), the train is also a much-valued showpiece, periodically trundling around Europe to represent Poland at various railway nostalgia events. In addition to the daily services, various special trips are made throughout the year and a **parade** of steam locomotives (*parada parowozów*) is staged at Wolsztyn station on the first Saturday of May every year. Railway enthusiasts can follow train-driving courses organized by the UK-based Wolsztyn Experience (℡01628/524876, Ⓦwww.thewolsztynexperience.org) – it's thanks to these activities that the steam trains keep running.

Wolsztyn's main attraction is the **engine shed** (*parowozownia*; daily 8am–3pm; Ⓦwww.parowozowniawolsztyn.pl; 3zł) 1km southeast of the train and bus stations at ul. Fabryczna 1, where there's a small museum (Mon–Fri only) and several working locomotives on display. An impressive row of old steam engines stretches along the tracks between here and the station. The rest of Wolsztyn, spread out to the northwest, is a drab place but does include a couple of time-killing attractions (Ⓦwww.muzea-wolsztyn .com.pl): the **Marcin Rożek Museum** (Museum Marcin Rożka: Tues–Sat 9am–4pm, Sun 10am–3pm; 3zł), on the main street at ul. 5 Stycznia 34, has a collection honouring leading interwar sculptor Marcin Rożek, sent to his death in Auschwitz after refusing to design a monument to Adolf Hitler; while the small **Robert Koch Museum**, round the corner at ul. Roberta Kocha 12 (Tues–Sat 9am–4pm, first and third Sun of the month 10am–3pm; 3zł), remembers the local doctor who recived the Nobel Prize in 1905 for his discovery of the tuberculosis bacillus.

On the northwestern side of the town centre lies **Lake Wolsztyn**, where there's a small sandy beach and secluded lakeside paths. Walking westwards and following the shore through wooded parkland brings you after fifteen minutes to a **skansen** (mid-April to mid-Oct: Tues–Sat 9am–5pm, Sun noon–5pm; mid-Oct to Nov & Feb to mid-April: Tues–Fri 10am–2pm; closed Dec & Jan; 4zł), which has a small but impressive collection of sturdy traditional farm buildings, each topped by a thick thatch of reeds taken from the lake.

Practicalities

Wolsztyn is best treated as a day-trip from either Poznań or Zielona Góra (see below). Should you need **to stay**, the *OSiR* sports **hotel** opposite the skansen at ul. Bohaterów Bielnika 30 is an option (℡068/384 3320, Ⓦwww.osir.wolsztyn.pl), a utilitarian block with simple doubles with sink (❶) and some en suites (❷). Moving up in price, the *Kaukaska*, just west of the train station at ul. Poniatowskiego 19 (℡068/347 1284, Ⓦwww.kaukaska.pl; ❹), offers smart, modern en suites with TV. There's a **campsite** next to the *OSiR* hotel.

The al fresco **cafés** by the beach offer the best places to grab a quick meal and a drink in summer; otherwise the **restaurant** of the *Kaukaska* has the best range of food.

Zielona Góra

Sixty kilometres southwest of Wolsztyn, and served by regular buses from both Wolsztyn and Poznań, the medium-sized city of **ZIELONA GÓRA** straddles the border between Wielkopolska and Lower Silesia. Little damaged in World War II, it's one of Poland's more handsome provincial centres,

▲ Steam train at Wolsztyn

preserving an eclectic mixture of nineteenth-century buildings. There are good public transport connections and a reasonable choice of places to stay and eat.

The Town

Central Zielona Góra presents an engaging patchwork of turn-of-the-twentieth-century architectural styles, with quirky neo-Gothic turrets poking from the corners of some town houses, Art Nouveau decoration dripping from the facades of others. Few of the buildings around the eighteenth-century town hall on the main square are of any great vintage, but their pastel colour schemes give the city a cheerful air. Most imposing of the monuments is the **Church of Our Lady of Częstochowa** (Kościół Matki Boskiej Częstochowskiej), just north of the main square, an eighteenth-century half-timbered building. The beautiful interior has two levels of galleries and a pulpit standing on a carved palm tree. The nearby **Lubuskie Land Museum** (Muzeum Ziemi Lubuskiej: Wed–Fri 11am–5pm, Sat 10am–3pm, Sun 10am–4pm; 6zł, Sat free; Ⓦwww.zgora.pl/muzeum), northeast of the main square at al. Niepodległości 15, has an exhibition on torture as well as an overview of the local winemaking industry – Zielona Góra being one of the few places in Poland where this tipple was ever produced. The **Wine Park** (Park Winny) southeast of the old town is planted with vines and is crowned by the newly built **Palmiarnia greenhouse** (daily 10am–11pm; free), housing a café and restaurant and offering fine views over town.

Practicalities

Zielona Góra's adjacent **train** and **bus stations** are on the northeastern edge of the centre, a fifteen-minute walk from the main square. The helpful **tourist information office** (mid-June to mid-Sept Mon–Fri 9am–5pm, Sat & Sun 10am–2pm; mid-Sept to mid-June Mon–Fri only; ☏068/323 2222, Ⓦwww .zielona-gora.pl), just east of the main square at ul. Kupiecka 15, has information on the whole region and will direct you towards accommodation options; there's a branch inside the town hall on the main square (same times).

Best of the **hotels** is the *Ruben*, just south of the centre at al. Konstytucji 3 Maja 1 (☏068/456 7070, Ⓦwww.rubenhotel.pl; ❻), a modern glass-fronted building with spacious and stylish en suites. Cheaper alternatives include the *Śródmiejski*, in the pedestrian area just northeast of the main square at ul. Żeromskiego 23 (☏068/325 4471, Ⓦwww.srodmiejski.emeteor.pl) with neat en suites (❹) and simple rooms with just a sink (❷); and the small *Pod Lwem*, a functional B&B near the stations at ul. Dworcowa 14 (☏068/324 1055, Ⓦwww.hotelpodlwem.emeteor.pl; ❸–❺). More space and personal service can be found at *Betti*, a recently renovated town house at ul. Drzewna 1 (☏509 246 205, Ⓦwww.apartamenty.zgora.pl), which has colourful en-suite rooms (❺–❻) and fully equipped apartments (❼–❾).

Three good **restaurants** can be found on plac Pocztowy, one block south of the main square: *Winnica* serves up skilfully prepared Polish-Ukrainian standards and some inventive and delicious grape-themed dishes and desserts; *Ermitaż* offers snacks in the ground floor *grand café* and full Polish and international meals in the downstairs dining room; and ⚲ *Haust* is a cheerful microbrewery with traditional Polish food, beer snacks and six types of beer. *La Gioconda*, just off the main square at ul. Mariacka 5, is the place to go for pizzas, pancakes and ice cream.

Żagań

Some 50km southwest of Zielona Góra, and reachable from there by hourly bus, the melancholy-looking town of **ŻAGAŃ** has two major assets in the form of a Baroque ducal **palace** set in an attractive park, and the captivating museum commemorating the archipelago of German POW camps that once stretched southwest of town. One of these camps, **Stalag Luft III** was the scene of the break-out that provided the inspiration for the film *The Great Escape*.

The Town

Standing near the run-down main square, the most impressive of Żagań's town-centre buildings is the fourteenth-century **Ascension Church** (Kościół Wniebowzięcia NMP), a high-gabled lump of bricks surrounded by former monastery buildings. Its interior, with a beautiful Renaissance altar, was completely remodelled during the Baroque period. A five-minute walk southeast of the main square lies the **Wallenstein Palace** (Pałac Wallensteina), begun in the Renaissance period by order of Albrecht von Waldstein (aka Wallenstein), the military genius who commanded Austrian forces during the Thirty Years' War and was awarded the Duchy of Żagań (then part of Austrian-ruled Silesia). Completed in Italianate Baroque style after Waldstein's death, it was badly damaged during World War II and is now used by the municipal authorities. The monumental winged facade, facing south across parkland towards the swan-patrolled waters of the Bóbr River, is an impressive sight.

Stalag Luft III and the Great Escape

The area of pine forest and heath immediately southwest of town was used by the Nazis as the site of several **POW camps** during World War II. The first, Stalag VIIIC, was established in 1939 to incarcerate captured Poles; other camps were added as the war progressed and the volume of prisoners increased. Most famous of the Żagań camps was **Stalag Luft III**, built by the Luftwaffe in 1942 to house allied air officers – who were considered a high-risk category due to their propensity to infect rank-and-file prisoners with ideas of escape. Concentrating officers together, however, turned the camp into a veritable academy of escapology, with numerous tunnelling operations underway at any given time. One group used a wooden vaulting horse to hide their digging activities, making a successful getaway in October 1943 – an exploit subsequently immortalized in escapee Eric Williams' best-selling account *The Wooden Horse*, which also became a hit film. A far more ambitious operation, masterminded by Squadron Leader Roger Bushell, aimed to get hundreds of prisoners out of the camp via a trio of **tunnels** nicknamed "Tom", "Dick" and "Harry". The first two were discovered by the Germans, but on the night of March 24, 1944, a total of 76 prisoners made their way out of Harry and into the surrounding woods. Three eventually made it to freedom; the rest were rounded up by the enraged German authorities, who decided to shoot fifty of the escapees as an example to the others. The whole extraordinary episode was first dubbed **the Great Escape** in the big-selling book of that name written by Australian ex-POW Paul Brickhill in 1950; although it's probably thanks to John Sturges' 1963 Hollywood film of the same name that the escape occupies such a memorable and unique niche in Western popular culture.

Żagań's POW camps are remembered in the **Museum of the Martydom of Allied Prisoners of War** (Muzeum Martyrologii Alianckich Jeńców Wojennych: Tues–Fri 10am–4pm, Sat & Sun 10am–5pm; Ⓦ www.muzeum .zagan.pl; donation requested), beside the Żagań–Lubań road, 3km southwest of the town centre – a taxi from Żagań bus station (see p.562) will cost about 10zł. Inside, there's a **scale model** of Stalag Luft III, a mock-up of the ingenious tunnelling techniques employed by the escapees, and a display devoted to the other camps established here – some 200,000 prisoners from all over the world were housed outside Żagań at one time or another, most of whom had to endure conditions far more squalid and brutal than those enjoyed by the relatively privileged air officers held at Stalag Luft III.

Outside the museum building there's a newly built wooden **barracks** displaying the living conditions of the POWs and a reconstruction of a short stretch of tunnel Harry, complete with a wooden trolley. You're free to explore the network of marked paths covering the site of the camps, although little remains save for a few scraps of brickwork poking up between the pine trees; all sites of interest now have English-language **information panels**. The most evocative spot is thirty minutes' walk northeast of the museum (and also signposted next to the industrial area on the main road), where a symbolical path indicates the exact length of tunnel Harry, with an engraved boulder (placed here on the sixieth anniversary of the Great Escape) marking the spot where it emerged. From here it's possible to walk through the forest to the train station at the southern end of town in about twenty minutes.

Practicalities

Żagań is a feasible **day-trip** from Zielona Góra, and is just about possible from Wrocław too. Żagań's **bus station** is on the west bank of the River Bóbr, five minutes' walk from the main square. The **train station** is midway between the town centre and the site of the POW camps. The **tourist information centre** at ul. Jana Pawła II 15 (Mon–Fri 9am–5pm; May to mid-Sept: also Sat & Sun 10am–2pm; ℡068/477 1090, ⊛www.um.zagan.pl) hands out a city walk brochure and a useful map of the town and surroundings.

Best value of Żagań's **hotels** is the half-timbered *Młynówka*, ul. Żelazna 2 (℡068/377 3074, ⊛www.mlynowka.pl; ❸), which offers reasonable standards of comfort at an acceptable price and enjoys a restful riverside location just east of the palace. The best **place to eat** is the *Kepler*, Rynek 27, serving up traditional Polish fare in a nicely restored town house. *Tropik*, on the opposite side of the square at no.8, is a good source of cheap and filling Polish staples.

Leszno

Roughly midway between Poznań and Wrocław, and served by regular trains from both cities, **LESZNO** is a pleasantly low-key market town with a charming and colourful central square whose history is inextricably bound up with one of Poland's most remarkable dynasties, the Leszczyński family, who founded Leszno in the late fourteenth century. The last of the male line, **Stanisław Leszczyński**, deposed the hated Augustus the Strong of Saxony to become king of Poland in 1704, only to be overthrown by the same rival six years later. He briefly regained the throne in 1733, but met with far more success in exile in France, marrying his daughter to Louis XV, and himself becoming duke of Lorraine and gaining a reputation as a patron of the arts.

The Town

The handsome cobbled **main square** is ringed by predominantly Neoclassical buildings with the odd Baroque facade surviving the Swedish Wars that left Leszno in ruins. The colourist approach favoured by the architects – prominent among whom was the Italian Pompeo Ferrari – is shown to best effect in the salmon pink tones of the **town hall**.

Just south of the main square, the exterior of the twin-towered **St Nicholas's Church** (Kościół św. Mikołaja) strikes a more typically sombre note. Its interior, on the other hand, displays a good example of florid Rococo ornamentation. The clean, sober lines of the **Church of Holy Cross** (Kościół św. Krzyża) are a couple of minutes' walk to the southwest on plac Metziga. Inside the vestibule a life-size angel bears a huge shell, an unusual vessel for holy water.

On the same square, shaded by a huge oak tree, is the **regional museum** (Muzeum Okręgowe: Tues noon–5pm, Wed–Fri 9am–2pm, Sat & Sun 10am–2pm; 3zł), a miscellaneous local collection, featuring several coffins bearing sculpted reliefs of the deceased, and a room devoted to Comenius of the Bohemian Brethren (see box below).

Practicalities

The **train** and **bus stations** lie just west of Leszno's main street, ulica Słowiańska, which runs east to meet the main square, and once you've pottered around Leszno's town centre you'd be wise to move on. There's a **tourist office at** ul. Słowiańska 24 (Mon–Fri 9am–5pm, Sat 9am–3pm; ☎065/529 8191, ⓦwww .leszno.pl) and several accommodation possibilities should you want to stay.

The *Wieniawa*, Rynek 29 (☎065/529 5058, ⓦwww.wieniawa.pl; ❺), is a handily placed source of cosy rooms above a restaurant; although it can't compare in the comfort stakes with the *Akwawit* at the far end of the flyover (visible from the train and bus stations) on the west side of town, ul. św. Jozefa 5 (☎065/529 3781, ⓦwww.akwawit.pl; ❼) which exudes an aura of plush modernity and has an adventure swimming pool next door. For a taste of the high life, try the *Zamek w Rydzynie* hotel in Rydzyna Castle (☎065/529 5040, ⓦwww.zamek-rydzyna.com.pl; ❻), a seventeenth-century stately home 10km southeast of town – the en-suite doubles are quite bland but the function rooms and surrounding parks are splendid.

Back in Leszno, the *Wienawa* **restaurant** offers well-presented Polish food at reasonable prices, and a cosy ground-floor pub; while *Culinaria* at ul. Słowiańska 35 is one of the most stylish and satisfying order-at-the-counter canteens you're likely to find in this part of Poland. Occupying the ground floor of the town hall, the *Kawiarnia w Ratuszu* is a chic place to linger over coffee and cakes.

Kalisz

At the extreme southeastern corner of Wielkopolska, midway between Poznań and Łódź, lies the industrial town of **KALISZ**. Almost universally held to be Poland's oldest recorded city, it was referred to as *Calissia* by Pliny in the first century and was described in the second century as a trading settlement on the "amber route" between the Baltic and Adriatic. Though apparently inhabited without interruption ever since, it failed to develop into a major city. Built

---

The Bohemian Brethren

Along with many other Polish grandees, the Leszczyńskis enthusiastically adopted the Reformation, though Stanisław Leszczyński, like Augustus the Strong, was forced to convert to Catholicism in order to launch his bid for the crown. In the first half of the seventeenth century Leszno became a refuge for the **Bohemian Brethren**, Czech Protestants who were forced to flee their homeland by the religious intolerance of the Thirty Years' War. The Academy these exiles founded in Leszno developed into one of Europe's great centres of learning, thanks to the leadership of Jan Amos Komenski, known as **Comenius**. Creator of the first illustrated textbook, he was called to put his educational theories into practice in England, Sweden, Hungary and The Netherlands, and even received invitations from the Protestant-loathing Cardinal Richelieu in France and from Harvard University, which wanted him as its president. Though Comenius and his colleagues were eventually forced to leave Leszno by the Swedish Wars of the 1650s, the town remained a major educational centre into the nineteenth century. The Brethren were later transformed into the **Moravian Church**, a body which continues to have an influence out of all proportion to its size, particularly in the USA.

around an attractive main square and its surrounding grid of cobbled alleys, Kalisz makes for a convenient stopover if you're passing through, especially if you're on the way to the **palace** at Gołuchów (see opposite).

The Town

Kalisz's pleasant if unspectacular main square centres on a large Neoclassical **town hall**. Down ul. Kanonicka at the northern end of the square is the brick Gothic **St Nicholas's Cathedral** (Katedra św. Mikołaja) with its attention-grabbing flying-buttressed spire. Inside, the principal attraction is *The Descent from the Cross* on the high altar, a copy of the seventeenth-century original, brought here from Rubens' workshop in Antwerp and lost in a fire in 1973. Located just off the southeastern corner of the main square is a smaller square which lies in front of the **Franciscan Church** (Kościół Franciszkanów), an older and simpler example of Gothic brickwork, but with generous Baroque interior decorations.

From here, it's just a short walk north to ulica Kolegialna, which defines the eastern perimeter of the Stare Miasto. Along it you'll pass the long facade of the **Jesuit College,** a severe Neoclassical composition incorporating a finely carved Renaissance portal. The only part of the building that visitors are allowed to enter is the church, which follows the plain Mannerist style of the Jesuits' most important church, the Gesu in Rome. Immediately beyond the college, standing beside the surviving fragment of the city's ramparts, is the single-towered **Church of the Assumption** (Bazylika Wniebowzięcia NMP), a more adventurous example of late eighteenth-century Baroque which includes parts of its Gothic predecessor. The interior bristles with works of art, including a sixteenth-century Silesian polyptych in the left-hand aisle. The chapel of St Joseph in the right-hand aisle is a popular place of pilgrimage, thanks to an allegedly miracle-working late medieval painting of the Holy Family. Ten minutes' walk southwest of the centre, across the River Prosna, the **Kalisz Land Regional Museum** (Muzeum Okręgowe Ziemi Kaliskiej: Tues & Thurs 10am–3pm, Wed & Fri 11am–5.30pm, Sat & Sun 10.30am–2.30pm; 4zł, Sun free; ⓦwww.muzeum.kalisz.pl), at ul. Kościuszki 12, accommodates a small but riveting collection of locally excavated Neolithic, Celtic and Roman pottery.

Practicalities

Both the **train** and **bus** stations are to be found 3km from the centre at the southwestern end of the city. To reach the centre, take bus #2, #11, #12, #15 or #19 from the stop on the main road outside the bus station – all these end up on plac św. Jozefa just east of the main square.

There's a **tourist office** one block north of the main square at ul. Zamkowa 11 (Mon–Fri 10am–5pm, Sat 10am–2pm; ☎062/598 2731, ⓦwww.osir.kalisz.pl). Accommodation options include *U Bogdana*, ul. Legionów 15–17 (☎062/753 0823, ⓦwww.hotel.ig.pl; ❷), which offers simple rooms with shared bathrooms in a residential block about 100m north of the train and bus stations. Moving upmarket, *Europa*, just south of the main square at al. Wolności 5 (☎062/767 2032, ⓦwww.hotel-europa.pl), is the best city-centre option, with neat simple en suites (❺) and plusher rooms with Jacuzzi (❻).

For a quick bite to **eat** or **drink**, there are plenty of places around the main square. *Bar Delicije*, on the southeast corner of the square, is a simple place, good for *pierogi*; *Baja Mexico*, just off the main square on ulica Piskorzewska, has a good range of Mex-type fare; *Piwnica Ratuszowa*, in the town hall cellars, serves

Polish staples in elegant surroundings; and Złoty Róg, next to the *Europa* hotel at al. Wolności 3 is a lively microbrewery with solid Polish dishes and four excellent types of beer brewed on the premises.

Gołuchów

Twenty kilometres from Kalisz on the main road to Poznań, and reached by frequent Poznań-bound buses, **GOŁUCHÓW** village is worth a stopover for its **palace**, the one outstanding monument in the Kalisz area.

It began as a small defensive **castle**, built in 1560 for Rafał Leszczyński, but within a century was transformed into a palatial residence. After falling into ruin it was bought by Tytus Działyński, the owner of Kórnik (see p.552) in 1853, as a present for his son Jan. His wife Izabella Czartoryska devoted herself to recreating the glory of the castle, eventually opening it as one of Poland's first museums. Rather than revert to the Italianate form of the original, she opted for a distinctively French touch, with steeply pitched roofs, prominent chimneys, pointed towers and a graceful arcaded terrace. The small **apartments** (Tues–Fri 10am–4pm, Sat & Sun 10am–5pm; 8zł) are crammed with paintings and *objets d'art*. The highlights of the display are some magnificent antique vases.

The landscaped **park** surrounding the palace contains a **café** and the uninspiring **Museum of Forestry** (Muzeum Leśnictwa: Tues–Sun 10am–4pm; 6zł). Near here you'll also come across Izabella's neo-Baroque funerary chapel.

For a **place to stay**, there's the *Dom Pracy Twórcej* **hotel** just east of the palace at ul. Borowskiego 2 (☎062/761 5044; ⊛www.dpt.prv.pl; ❸), which offers plainish but adequate en-suite rooms with TV, and has a restaurant.

Gniezno and around

Despite the competing claims of Poznań, Kruszwica and Lednica, **GNIEZNO**, 50km east of Poznań, is generally credited as the first capital of Poland, a title based on the dense web of myth and chronicled fact that constitutes the story of the nation's earliest years. Nowadays Poland's ecclesiastical capital has the feel of a quiet but charming small town, but there are sufficient historical attractions here to make Gniezno well worth a couple of days' stay. It's also an excellent base from which to visit places featured on the **Piast Route** (Szlak Piastowski), a tourist trail between Poznań and Inowrocław, which highlights salient locations associated with the Piast dynasty. Most important of these is the medieval archeological site at **Lake Lednica** (also the site of a large ethnographic museum), which is a short journey from town by bus.

Some history

Lech, the legendary founder of Poland, supposedly came across the nest (*gniazdo*) of a white eagle here; he founded a town on the spot, and made the bird the emblem of his people, a role it still maintains. Less fancifully, it's known for sure that Mieszko I had established a court here in the late tenth century, and that in the year 1000 it was the scene of a turning point in the country's history. The catalyst for this, ironically enough, was a Czech, św. Wojciech (**St Adalbert**), the first bishop of Prague. In 997 he set out from Gniezno to evangelize the Prussians, a fierce Baltic tribe who lived on Poland's eastern borders – and who quickly dispatched him to a martyr's death. In order

GNIEZNO

RESTAURANTS AND BARS
Królewska	B
Pizzeria Pod Piątką	2
Pub	B
Za Drzwiami	1
Złoty Smok	3

ACCOMMODATION
Adalbertus	A
AWO	D
Nest	C
Orzeł	F
Pietrak	B
Youth hostel	E

Archdiocesian Museum
St John's Church
Św. Jerzego Cathedral
Franciscan Church
Museum of the Origins of the Polish State
Lake Jelonek
Church of the Holy Trinity
Park Piastowski
Stadium
Park Miejski
Park Kościuszki
Bus Station
Train Station

0 — 400 m

F (1km)

to recover the body, Mieszko I's son, **Bolesław the Brave**, was forced to pay Wojciech's weight in gold, an astute investment as it turned out. At the pope's instigation, Emperor Otto III made a pilgrimage to Gniezno, bringing relics with him which would add to the site's holiness. Received in great splendour, he crowned Bolesław with his own crown, confirming Poland as a fully-fledged **kingdom** and one which was independent of the German-dominated Holy Roman Empire. Furthermore, Gniezno was made the seat of Poland's first archbishopric and Wojciech's brother Radim was the first to be appointed to the post.

Gniezno was soon replaced as **capital** by the more secure town of Kraków, and although it made a partial recovery in the Middle Ages, it never grew very big. Nevertheless, it has always been important as the official seat of the primate of Poland. Throughout the period of elected kings, the holder of this office functioned as **head of state** during each interregnum, and it is still one of the most prestigious positions in the land. In recent times, the Gniezno archbishopric has been coupled to that of Warsaw, with the primate tending to spend far more time in the capital.

Arrival, information and accommodation

The **train** and **bus** stations are side by side about 500m south of the centre – walk straight down ulica Lecha to ulica Bolesława Chrobrego to reach the main square. The **tourist information office** at Rynek 14 (May–Sept Mon–Fri 8am–6pm, Sat 9am–3pm, Sun 10am–2pm; Oct–April Mon–Fri 8am–4pm; ☏061/428 4100, ⓦturystyka.powiat-gniezno.pl, ⓦwww.szlakpiastowski.com.pl), can sort you out with **B&B accommodation** with local families (❶–❷), though these are spread out around the area and you'll need your own transport to reach most of them. The **youth hostel**, close to the stations at ul. Pocztowa 11 (on the top floor; ☎061/426 2780), is a basic but welcoming place with beds from 12-25zł and bike rental.

Hotels

Adalbertus ul. Tumska 7a ☎061/426 1360, ⓦwww.pietrak.pl. Small but comfy modern en-suite rooms in a charming palace-like archdiocese building on Lech Hill, right opposite the cathedral. ❺

AWO ul. Warszawska 32 ☎061/426 1197, ⓦwww.hotel-awo.pl. Mid-sized hotel located in a courtyard on a lively shopping street. Comfortable en suites with TV and warm colour schemes make this a welcoming pied-à-terre. ❺

Nest ul. Sobieskiego 20 ☎061/423 8000, ⓦwww .hotelnest.pl. A new business hotel located between the station and the centre. Features neat rooms and helpful staff. Discounts at weekends. ❹–❺

Orzeł ul. Wrzesińska 25 ☎61/426 4925, ⓔhro @op.pl. Sports hotel situated right next to a speedway oval, offering simple but clean rooms. Twenty minutes' walk south of the centre, or take bus #3 or #11. Cheaper doubles come with shared facilities. ❷–❸

Pietrak ul. Chrobrego 3 ☎061/426 1497, ⓦwww .pietrak.pl. Friendly place in the middle of the pedestrianized area, providing comfortable en-suite rooms and a big buffet breakfast. There's a lively restaurant on site too. ❺

The City

The compactness of Gniezno is immediately evident: from either the **train** or **bus station** it's only a few minutes' walk straight down ulica Lecha to ulica Bolesława Chrobrego, the quiet end of a main thoroughfare that has several brightly colourwashed buildings. In ten minutes you pass into the pedestrianized section of this street, which ends up at the quiet, cobbled **main square**.

There are three Gothic churches worth a quick look. Just off the southern side of the main square is the **Church of the Holy Trinity** (Kościół św. Trójcy), partly rebuilt in the Baroque style following a fire, beside which stand the only surviving remains of the city walls. Off the opposite side of the main square towers the **Franciscan Church** (Kościół Franciszkanów), while further to the

▲ Gniezno Cathedral

north is **St John's Church** (Kościół św. Jana). The latter, a foundation of the Knights Templar, preserves fourteenth-century frescoes in its chancel and has carved bosses and corbels depicting virtues and vices.

The Cathedral

Northwest from the main square along ulica Tumska lies Gniezno's episcopal quarter, and protruding fittingly above it is the **cathedral** (Katedra), in front of which stands a statue of Bolesław the Brave. Reminiscent of Poznań Cathedral, the basic brick structure was built in the fourteenth century in the severest Gothic style, but was enlivened in the Baroque period by a ring of stone chapels and by the addition of steeples to the twin facade towers. Entering the cathedral by the south door and following the ambulatory takes you past a sequence of richly decorated chapels, in which many of Poland's primates are buried. Behind the high altar lies the silver **shrine of St Adalbert** (św. Wojciech), the martyr seen here reclining on his sarcophagus. The work of Gdańsk craftsman Peter van Rennen, the shrine is surrounded by figures representing the different social classes, along with depictions of the chief events of the saint's life. Other monuments to prominent local clerics and laymen can be seen throughout the cathedral. One which may catch your attention is that to Primate Stefan Wyszyński, in the north side of the ambulatory (see box below).

Cardinal Stefan Wyszyński (1901–81)

In the history of communist Europe, there is nothing remotely comparable to the career of **Stefan Wyszyński**, who adapted the traditional powers of the primate of Poland to act as spokesman and regent of his people.

Wyszyński's early ministry was centred in Włocławek, where he was ordained in 1924, quickly establishing a reputation in the social field. He spent the war years in the **underground resistance movement**, having been saved from the German concentration camps through the prompt action of his bishop, who had ordered him to leave the town. He returned as head of the Włocławek Seminary in 1945 before enjoying a meteoric rise through the church hierarchy, being appointed bishop of Lublin the following year, and elevated to the archdiocese of Gniezno and the title of **Primate of Poland** in 1948.

The elimination of Poland's formerly substantial Jewish, Orthodox and Protestant minorities as a result of World War II and its aftermath meant that nearly 98 percent of the population professed **Catholicism**, as opposed to the prewar figure of 75 percent. At the same time, however, organized religion came under threat from increased state-imposed atheism. Matters came to a head with the Vatican's worldwide **decree** of 1949, which ordered the withholding of sacraments to all communist functionaries and sympathizers: this caused particular tensions in Poland, where the new administration, particularly in rural areas, was dependent on practicing Catholics. Wyszyński reached a compromise agreement with the government the following year whereby the affairs of Church and State were clearly demarcated.

This cosy relationship did not last long: a wave of Stalinist **repression** in 1952–53 led to the end of religious instruction in schools, the usurpation of most of the Church's charitable activities, and to the imprisonment and harassment of thousands of priests. As a culmination, the bishop of Kielce was sentenced to twelve years' imprisonment on charges of espionage. Wyszyński's protests led to his own **arrest**, and he was confined to the Monastery of Komańcza in the remote Bieszczady Mountains. The detention of a man widely regarded as possessing

The cathedral's highlight is the magnificent pair of **bronze doors** located at the entrance to the southern aisle. Hung around 1175, and an inevitable influence on Van Rennen, these are among the finest surviving examples of Romanesque decorative art, and are unique in Poland. Wojciech's life from the cradle to beyond the grave is illustrated in eighteen scenes, going up the right-hand door and then down the left, all set within a rich decorative border. Quite apart from their artistic quality, the doors are remarkable as a documentary record: even the faces of the villainous Prussians are based on accurate observation. The doors are sometimes locked away out of sight, but you can view a replica in the Archdiocesan Museum (see below). Beyond the doorway is an intricate **portal;** though its tympanum of Christ in Majesty is orthodox enough, the carvings of griffins and the prominent mask heads give it a highly idiosyncratic flavour.

Just north of the cathedral, the **Archdiocesan Museum** (Muzeum Archidiecezjalne: daily: May–Sept 9am–5.30pm; Oct–April 9am–4pm; 4zł; Ⓦ www.muzeumag.pl) houses a sumptuous collection of silverware, ecclesiastical sculpture and art; the star items being a copy of the Cathedral doors and a tenth-century Byzantine chalice said to have belonged to St Adalbert.

Lake Jelonek

Just west of the cathedral is **Lake Jelonek**, a peaceful spot with a wonderful view of the town. Overlooking its far bank is a large modern building containing the

⑪

Museum of the Origins of the Polish State (Muzeum Pociątków Państwa Polskiego: Tues–Sun 10am–5pm; 6zł; ⓦwww.muzeumgniezno.pl). It's a disappointing collection, relying on copies of medieval sculptures rather than original exhibits, although there are some skillfully made models of Gniezno through the centuries. A thirty-minute audiovisual presentation (English commentary available) elaborates on medieval life in Wielkopolska and the significance of the Piast dynasty.

Eating and drinking

There are several pleasant **restaurants** with outdoor seating in the pedestrianized streets around the main square. The welcoming ℀ *Za Drzwiami* at ul. Tumska 11 has good Polish and international dishes served in a cosy, rustic setting – the terrace is good for coffee and cakes with views of the cathedral. The *Pietrak* hotel at ul. Bolesława Chrobrego 3 (see p.567) houses a cheap and cheerful grill bar on the ground floor, and the more formal, starched-tablecloth *Królewska* with an international menu, in the cellar. *Pizzeria Pod Piątką*, ul. Tumska 5, is a cheap place for a quick bite; while *Złoty Smok*, a few steps off the west side of the main square at ul. Kaszarska 1a, offers good, inexpensive Chinese and Vietnamese food in unpretentious surroundings.

For **drinking**, there's a brace of outdoor bars in the main square in summer, although *Pub* inside the *Pietrak* is the most comfortable of the central bars. *Basement* on the corner of Rynek and ulica Farna is the place to check your **emails**.

Lake Lednica

One of the most worthwhile excursions you're likely to make in this corner of Poland is to the slender **Lake Lednica**, 18km west of Gniezno and easily reached from there by taking any Poznań- or Pobiediska-bound bus. Site of a tenth-century courtly residence equal in importance to Gniezno, the lake is now the site of both an absorbing **archeological site** and one of the largest *skansens* in the country. The bus stop is by the access road to Dziekanowice and the museums (ⓦwww.lednicamuzeum.pl). If you're visiting more than one of the sights buy the 12zł combined ticket.

From the main road it's a ten-minute walk north to the **Wielkopolska Ethnographic Park** (Wielkopolski Park Etnograficzny: mid–Feb to mid–April: Tues–Sat 9am–3pm, Sun 10am–3pm; mid-April to end April & July–Oct: Tues–Sat 9am–5pm, Sun 10am–5pm; May–June: Tues–Sat 9am–6pm, Sun 10am–6pm; Nov–Feb closed; 8zł), an open-air museum consisting of about fifty traditional rural buildings including windmills, a Baroque cemetery chapel and several farmsteads. Some of the more eye-catching of the latter belonged to the Wielkopolska Dutch – **immigrants** from the Low Countries who were encouraged to settle here in the seventeenth and eighteenth centuries because of their superior knowledge of land irrigation techniques. They built solid, prosperous-looking farmhouses with red-tiled roofs, unlike their Polish neighbours, who preferred thatch.

From the *skansen*, continue north through the village of Dziekanowice and turn left at the T-junction to reach the disparate tourist complex known as the **Museum of the First Piasts** at Lednica (Muzeum Pierwszych Piastów na Lednicy: same times; 8zł). Just beyond the village you'll come across a small exhibition hall filled with replica tenth-century arms and armour. From here it's another ten-minute walk to the impressive wooden gateway that marks the entrance to the core of the site. Take the **ferry** (mid-April to Oct) to **Ostrów Lednicki**, the largest of the three tiny islands in Lake Lednica, where it's believed that Mieszko I once held court.

This unlikely site, uninhabited for the last six centuries, was once a royal seat equal to Poznań and Gniezno in importance – **Bolesław the Brave** was born here, and it may also have been where his coronation by Emperor Otto III took place, rather than in Gniezno. It began life in the ninth century as a fortified town and, in the following century, a modest **palace** was constructed, along with a church: the excavated remains only hint at its former grandeur, but the presence of stairways prove it was probably at least two storeys high. By the landing jetty a model of the former settlement gives an idea of how it may have looked, surrounded by the extant **earth ramparts**. The buildings were destroyed in 1038 by the Czech Prince Brzetysław and for centuries the island served as a cemetery, until it was lulled out of its sleep by tourism.

Żnin, Biskupin and around

Forty kilometres north of Gniezno on the Bydgoszcz road (and reached by hourly buses) the small town of **Żnin** would be unremarkable were it not for two major attributes – the ageing **narrow-gauge rail line** that meanders for 12km through the pastures south of town to the village of **Gąsawa**, and the reconstructed Iron Age settlement of **Biskupin** which lies along the route. In between Żnin and Biskupin, a small railway museum in the village of **Wenecja** adds to the list of attractions. The narrow-gauge line still operates a limited tourist-oriented service, and presents the most enjoyable way of reaching Venecja and Biskupin in summer – otherwise, a combination of local buses and walking will enable you to see the sites and still get back to Gniezno by nightfall.

Żnin

The train, bus and narrow-gauge stations in the plain town of **ŻNIN**, 40km northeast of Gniezno, are all within 100m of each other on the northeastern side of the centre. It's a good idea to head for the narrow-gauge station first in order to check the timetable: if there are no convenient services running that day, then consider catching a bus to Gąsawa, from where you can walk to Biskupin in about thirty minutes. If you need to spend the night or eat, you can't go wrong with the comfortable *Basztowy hotel and restaurant* near the main square at ul. 700-lecia 1 (☏ 052/302 0006, ⓦ www.hotel-basztowy .com.pl; ❹).

The Żnin–Gąsawa narrow-gauge rail line

The **Żnin–Gąsawa narrow-gauge rail line** (ⓦ www.paluki.pl/ciuchcia) has been running for over a century, and now functions almost exclusively as a tourist attraction. The railway has retained a steam engine, although it only sees action on selected summer weekends, and all other services are hauled by diesel locomotives. There are five daily Żnin–Gąsawa services in July and August and two or three daily from May to June and September to November – though it's worth checking timetables in advance. Additional departures are often laid on for tour groups, and individual travellers are allowed to tag along if space allows – so it always pays to ask. The journey to

Biskupin takes forty minutes, with trains barely exceeding walking pace, but the trip – through gently rolling countryside dotted with silver-blue lakes – is definitely worthwhile.

The train rattles noisily through hay fields and vegetable patches, its second stop, **Wenecja** (optimistically named after Venice), being the halfway point. To the left of the station are the ruined remains of the fourteenth-century **castle** of Mikołaj Nałięz, a notoriously cruel figure known as the "Devil of Wenecja". On the opposite side of the tracks is the quirky open-air **Narrow-Gauge Railway Museum** (Muzeum Kolei Wąskotorowej: daily May to Oct 9am–6pm; Nov to April 10am–2pm; 6zł), exhibiting Europe's largest collection of undersized trains.

From Wenecja the train continues along the edge of Lake Biskupin and stops right outside the entrance to the settlement a few minutes later. You can also walk from Wenecja to Biskupin in about thirty minutes.

Biskupin

The Iron Age village of **BISKUPIN**, 10km south of Żnin, is one of the most evocative archeological sites in Europe. Discovered in 1933 when a schoolmaster noticed some hand-worked stakes standing in the reeds at the lakeside, excavations uncovered the remains of a **fortified village** of the Lusatian culture, founded around 550 BC and destroyed in tribal warfare some 150 years later.

The site

In contrast to the overcautious approach that makes so many famous archeological sites disappointing to non-specialists, it was decided to take a guess and reconstruct the palisade, ramparts and part of the village. The price to be paid for this approach is evident at the entrance to the **archeological park** (daily: April to mid-Nov 8am–7pm; mid-Nov to March 8am till dusk; 8zł; call ahead in winter at ☏052/302 0702, ⓦwww.biskupin.pl), with souvenir and snack bars lining the car park on the other side of the tracks.

The museum has English-language captions and provides a pretty good introduction to the site, displaying all manner of objects dug up here – tools, household utensils, weapons, jewellery, ornaments and objects for worship, some thought to be ten thousand years old. Piecing together the evidence, archeologists have been able to draw a picture of a society in which hunting had been largely superseded by arable farming and livestock breeding. Their **trade patterns** were surprisingly extensive – their iron came from Transylvania, and there's an intriguing group of exhibits imported from even further afield, the most exotic being some Egyptian beads. Most remarkable of all was the tribe's prowess in building, as can be seen in the model reconstruction of the entire village.

It's only a couple of minutes' walk from the museum to the **reconstructed site**. The foreground consists of the uncovered foundations of various buildings, some from as late as the thirteenth century; of more interest are recreations of the Iron Age buildings. The **palisade** was particularly ingenious: it originally consisted of 35,000 stakes grouped in rows up to nine deep and driven into the bed of the lake at an angle of 45 degrees. It acted both as a breakwater and as the first line of the fortifications. Immediately behind was a circular **wall** of oak logs guarded by a tall watchtower. Inside the defences were a ring road plus eleven symmetrical streets; the **houses** were grouped in thirteen terraces ranged from east to west to catch the sun. An entire extended family would live in each house, so the population of the settlement probably numbered more than a thousand. As you can see from the example open for inspection, each house had two chambers: pigs and cattle were kept in the lobby, while the main room, where the family slept in a single bed, was also equipped with a loft for the storage of food and fuel. The *Diabeł Wenecki* pleasure boat offers thirty-minute **cruises** on the lake (Tues–Sun 9am–5pm; 6zł), allowing you to view the site from the water.

A clutch of **snack huts** can be found at the entrance. If you've missed the last **train**, note that some Żnin–Gąsawa **buses** pass the site entrance, although perhaps the easiest thing to do is walk uphill to Gąsawa (30min), from where you can catch regular buses plying the Gniezno–Bydgoszcz route.

Trzemeszno to Inowrocław

Once you've seen Gniezno, Lednica and Biskupin, the rest of eastern Wielkopolska is a bit of a letdown, characterized by a string of unassuming, semi-industrialized towns which have little in the way of attention-grabbing appeal. However, with spare time and using Gniezno as a base, the reminders of the **Piast** dynasty are enough to structure an itinerary around. Trzemeszno, Mogilno, Strzelno and Inowrocław are easily reached by bus and train from Gniezno; you may need to change at Inowrocław for the bus to Kruszwica.

Trzemeszno

Fifteen kilometres east of Gniezno, **TRZEMESZNO** is a lightly industrialized town that was founded, according to tradition, by St Adalbert (św. Wojciech). It's best reached by bus from Gniezno, as the train station is fifteen minutes' walk north of town.

The ancient church that St Adalbert is said to have established was succeeded by a Romanesque structure, parts of which are incorporated in the town's main sight, the Baroque **Assumption Basilica** (Basylika Wniebowzięcia NMP). From the outside it appears merely pleasingly rotund, but the Baroque interior is a revelation of light and colour with superb **paintings** in the dome and along the transept that for once take the attention away from the central altar, under which an effigy of Adalbert reposes. The ceiling frescoes vividly depict three crucial scenes from the saint's life and death: his vicious slaying by the Prussian pagans (provoked, as Adalbert had chopped down all their sacred trees); the retrieval of his remains for their weight in gold, with Adalbert just a few body parts on a scale; and his eventual entombment in the basilica.

Strzelno

More artistic treasures are to be found 16km east of Mogilno in the sleepy town of **STRZELNO**. Both the **bus** and **train stations** lie at the southwestern fringe of town; from there, walk straight ahead, turning left up ulica Ducha to reach the rather unprepossessing main square. Continuing down to the right brings you to two outstanding Romanesque buildings.

The **Monastery of the Holy Trinity** (Klasztor św. Trójcy) is a typically Polish accretion: brick Gothic gables and a monumental Baroque facade sprout from a late twelfth-century Romanesque shell. Two of the original nave **pillars** are adorned with figurative carvings, crafted with a delicacy found in few other European sculptures of the period. Another slimmer column of almost equal quality forms the sole support of the vault of the somewhat neglected chapel of St Barbara, to the right of the altar.

Beside the monastery stands the slightly older little red sandstone **Chapel of St Procopius** (Kaplica św. Prokopa). In contrast to its neighbour, this has preserved the purity of its original form. It's often locked, but you can ask for the key in the buildings alongside.

Kruszwica

Of the many sites associated with the Piast dynasty perhaps the oddest is in **KRUSZWICA**, a frumpy town straddling the pencil-slim **Lake Gopło**, 15km northeast of Strzelno. Dominating a shady tree-lined peninsula just east of Kruszwica's main square is a 32-metre-high brick octagon known as the **Mice Tower** (Mysia Wieża: May–Sept daily 9am–6pm; 5zł). Legend tells that it's the place where evil King Popiel met his doom before being replaced by the first of the Piast rulers (see box above), but in fact the tower was built by the last of the Piast dynasty, Kazimierz the Great, although this hasn't prevented it from becoming one of the most popular places of historical pilgrimage in this part of Poland. Nevertheless, the sweeping views down the length of Lake Gopło make a trip to the top worthwhile.

Kruszwica's only other historic monument is the early twelfth-century **Collegiate Church** (Kolegiata), reached by heading east from the tower, crossing the road bridge, and turning left to follow the far bank of the lake. A grim granite basilica with three apses, it has been stripped of most of its later accretions, except for the brick Gothic tower, and gives a good impression of what an early Christian church may have once looked like.

Kruszwica is served by frequent **buses** from Inowrocław and less frequently from Bydgoszcz (see below), with services picking up and dropping off on the main square. There's a gaggle of snack stalls at the foot of the tower.

Inowrocław

Approaching Kruszwica by public transport from Gniezno to the west or Bydgoszcz and Toruń to the east, chances are you'll need to hop from train to bus at **INOWROCŁAW** 16km north; a nineteenth-century spa town blighted by industrialization. The town's **train station** is at the northern end of town, about fifteen minutes' walk from the centre; the **bus station** is five minutes' further in. If you've got time to kill, it's best to head straight for the **Spa Park** (Park Uzdrowiskowy) at the western end of town (a 15min walk from the stations), a grassy expanse ringed by grand turn-of-the-twentieth-century buildings. Dominating its western extremity is the **Tężnia**, a fortress-like construction raised in the 1990s from vast piles of compacted twigs. Rather like the more famous one in Ciechocinek (see p.195), the edifice acts as a huge filter through which the local spa water is pumped, creating an allegedly recuperative salt-rich atmosphere for those who come to stroll around it.

The only rewarding monument in town is the **Church of Our Lady** (Kościół NMP), a contemporary of the Romanesque basilica in Kruszwica, and boasting a similarly impressive, bare-stone interior. It's located behind the much bigger, neo-Gothic **Church of the Annunciation** (Kościół Zwiastowania NMP), a few minutes' walk beyond the big roundabout south of the bus and train stations.

Licheń Stary

Newly built Catholic churches may be a rarity in Europe, but Poland has plenty of them, and the lakeside village of **LICHEŃ STARY**, 67km south of Inowrocław and 16km north of Konin (an intercity train stop on the main Poznań–Warsaw line), is dominated by one of the most impressive – and kitsch – modern churches of all, devoted to the worship of the Virgin Mary. On approach to the town, the gleaming tower and dome of the **Sanctuary of Our Lady of Licheń** (Sanktuarium Maryjnye w Licheń: ⓦ www.lichen.pl), a few minutes' walk east of the village centre and bus stop, are visible for miles. The multitude of restaurants, hotels, guesthouses and car parks around the compound's various entrances are an indication of the huge number of pilgrims the site attracts; in 2008 alone it had more than a million visitors.

The story goes that Tomasz Kłossowski, a **soldier** from Licheń fighting in Napoleon's army during the 1813 battle of Leipzig, was wounded and had a vision of Mary hugging a white eagle, promising he would survive and instructing him to revere a picture of her on his return. He found such a miraculous picture on a later pilgrimage, a small **painting** of sixteen by twenty-five centimetre, and hung it in a forest near the village, where in 1850 a shepherd had another vision of Mary, urging people to be more pious. The image is said to have performed thousands of miraculous recoveries since then.

A sanctuary, monastery and reconstruction of Golgotha Hill were soon built, and pilgrims' donations helped fund the construction of the modern **Basilica**, built between 1994 and 2004 with Mary's image crowning the altar. With a capacity of 7000, it's the largest church in Poland and the eighth largest in Europe, with five aisles as high as a fifteen-storey building, a massive dome that's just twenty metres lower than that of St Peter's in Rome, and a separate **tower** (with a top floor viewpoint reached by elevator; Mon–Sat 9am–6.30pm, Sun 9am–5pm) and Poland's largest bell. The excessive use of gold and marble, the jumble of architectural styles and the sheer opulence on show may not be to everyone's taste, but the devotion of the pilgrims is certainly impressive.

Buses from Konin to Licheń Stary run every half hour. Regular trains to Konin make it possible to visit on a day-trip from Poznań and even Warsaw, but there's plenty of accommodation should you need to stay the night; the *Arka* hotel inside the compound (☎063/270 8162, ⓦwww.arka.lichen.pl; ➍) has basic en-suite rooms and a restaurant. The Pilgrimage Office on the first floor of the Basilica tower (☎063/270 8163) can recommend other options and also arranges guided tours.

Travel details

Trains

Gniezno to: Bydgoszcz (8 daily; 1hr 40min); Inowrocław (hourly; 50min); Mogilno (hourly; 25min); Poznań (hourly; 50min); Toruń (6 daily; 1hr 30min).
Kalisz to: Łódź (10 daily; 2hr); Poznań (5 daily; 3hr); Wrocław (4 daily; 2hr 20min).
Leszno to: Poznań (every 30min; 1hr); Wrocław (hourly; 1hr 40min).
Poznań to: Bydgoszcz (9 daily; 2hr 20min–3hr); Gdańsk (6 daily; 5hr 30min); Gniezno (hourly; 50min); Inowrocław (hourly; 1hr 30min–2hr); Kalisz (5 daily; 3hr); Konin (hourly; 50min–1hr 20min); Kraków (9 daily; 7hr 15min); Leszno (every 30min; 1hr); Łódź (5 daily; 4hr–4hr 30min); Międzyrzecz (5 daily, via Zbąszynek; 2hr–3hr 30min); Mosina (every 30min; 25min); Szczecin (16 daily; 2–3hr); Świebodzin (3 daily; 50min–1hr 30min); Toruń (6 daily; 2hr 30min); Warsaw (16 daily; 3hr–3hr 30min); Wrocław (hourly; 2hr 30min); Zielona Góra (6 daily; 2hr 30min); Wolsztyn (7 daily; 1hr 40min).

Żnin to: Biskupin (July & Aug 5 daily; May–June & Sept–Nov 2–3 daily; 40min).
Zielona Góra to: Poznań (6 daily; 2hr 30min); Żagań (4 daily, via Żary; 1hr 30min–2hr 30min); Wrocław (7 daily; 3hr 30min–4hr 30min).

Buses

Gniezno to: Gąsawa (3 daily; 50min); Trzemeszno (2 daily; 20min); Żnin (6 daily; 45min–1hr).
Inowrocław to: Kruszwica (every 30min; 35min); Żnin (Mon–Fri 7 daily, Sat & Sun 4 daily; 1hr 20min).
Kalisz to: Gołuchów (7 daily; 20min); Poznań (10 daily; 1hr 45min–2hr 30min).
Konin to: Licheń Stary (every 30min; 30min).
Poznań to: Kórnik (hourly; 30min); Rogalin (8 daily; 30–50min).
Żnin to: Gąsawa (every 30min; 20min); Gniezno (8 daily; 1hr 5min); Inowrocław (Mon–Fri 8 daily; Sat & Sun 6 daily; 1hr 20min).

International trains

Poznań to: Amsterdam (1 overnight; 13hr 30min); Berlin (6 daily; 2hr 30min–5hr).

12

Pomerania

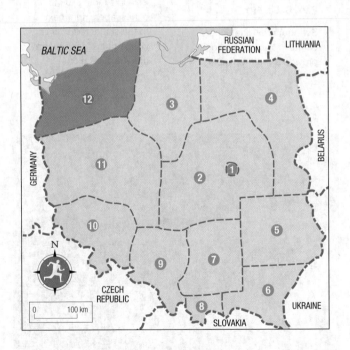

CHAPTER 12

Highlights

* **Szczecin** Brash, bustling port city with varied nightlife. See p.579

* **Międzyzdroje** A charming, old-fashioned seaside town, conveniently located at the edge of the thickly forested Woliński National Park. See p.591

* **Świnoujście** Nineteenth-century Prussian era forts provide a gruff reminder

of Świnoujście's former strategic importance. See p.595

* **Mielno** Peaceful seaside village sitting on a wonderful stretch of beach. See p.599

* **Słowiński National Park** Poland's most alluring dunescapes, right next to the characterful fishing village-cum-beach resort of Łeba. See p.604

▲ Słowiński National Park

Pomerania

Edged by gloriously long stretches of white-sand beach, **Pomerania** (*Pomorze*) attracts hundreds of thousands of Polish tourists every year. Due to the Pomeranian coast's northerly latitude the holiday season is rather short; but in July and August hordes of visitors arrive to soak up what sun there is, with fish-and-chip stalls and beer tents springing up to service basic gastronomic needs. Although relatively quiet, spring and early autumn can be rewarding times to visit, especially if beach strolling – rather than sunbathing – is your thing.

The fishing village of **Łeba**, gateway to the famed sand dunes of the **Słowiński National Park**, is the place to aim for in eastern Pomerania, although any number of other charming beachside settlements await exploration nearby. Over to the west, the island of **Wolin** offers yet more in the way of fine sands, as well as a much-visited bison reserve in the forested **Woliński National Park**. Inland, Pomerania is peppered with grey, rather downbeat towns, which serve as useful nodal points for transport connections, but offer little else. However, several architectural nuggets stand out: **Stargard Szczeciński** harbours some fine examples of the brick Gothic buildings so typical of the Baltic lands, and **Kamień Pomorski** is an old lagoon settlement with a wonderful cathedral.

Pomerania's administrative and industrial capital, **Szczecin** is never likely to make it into Polish tourism's top ten, but shouldn't be overlooked entirely, possessing an appealing urban vigour and a wealth of cultural diversions. Szczecin is also the region's main **transport hub**, with rail and bus services fanning out to serve the western half of the province. The **beach resorts** of central and eastern Pomerania are connected by bus to inland towns such as Koszalin, Słupsk and Lębork – all of which lie on the main Szczecin–Gdańsk rail line.

Szczecin

The largest city in northwestern Poland, with 400,000 inhabitants, **SZCZECIN** (pronounced "Shchechin") sprawls around the banks of the Odra in a tangle of bridges, cranes and dockside machinery, a city with a long maritime and shipbuilding heritage. It's a gruff, workaday place that bares few of its charms to the passing visitor. However, it's also a fast-paced, fast-changing city with a clutch of cultural diversions, not to mention an impressive collection of **bars**.

The Slav stronghold established here in the eighth century was taken by the first Piast monarch, Mieszko I, in 967 and Szczecin became the residence of a local branch of Piast princes. German colonists were present from the earliest times, and came to dominate local life once the city joined the Hanseatic League in the mid-thirteenth century. The Swedes captured Szczecin in 1630 but sold it to the Prussians ninety years later. The city remained under Prussian rule until 1945, when it became an outpost on Poland's newly established western frontier. With the border just west of the city limits and Berlin only a couple of hours away by car or train, the German presence is palpable.

Wartime pummelling destroyed most of the **old centre**, which never received quite the same restorative attention as some less controversially "Polish" cities. Despite Szczecin's size and importance, there isn't that much to take in – a full day is enough to cover all the main sights.

As well as being the main transport hub for western Pomerania, Szczecin is a good base-camp for **side trips to Berlin** (170km distant), which is reached by two direct daily trains.

Arrival and information

Szczecin **airport** is located at Goleniów (℡091/481 7400, ⓦwww.airport .szczecin.pl), 45km north of the city, with bus services to and from the LOT office at al. Wyzwolenia 17 (journey time 1hr; buses timed to coincide with arrivals and departures; 15zł).

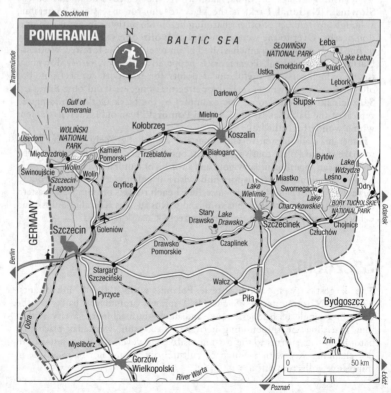

In prehistoric times the southern Baltic coast was inhabited by the Celts, who were later displaced by a succession of Germanic tribes. By the end of the fifth century they too had been ousted by Slav people known as the **Pomorzanie**. The lands of the Pomorzanie were in turn conquered by the Piast **King Mieszko I**, who took Szczecin in 979 – a campaign that is cited by the Poles in support of their claim to ownership of this often disputed territory.

Throughout the medieval era, Pomerania evolved as an essentially independent dukedom ruled by a local Slav dynasty commonly called the **Pomeranian dukes**. Eastern Pomerania, meanwhile; was conquered by the Teutonic Knights in 1308, and was later known as Royal Prussia; this part of the region returned to the Polish sphere of influence under the terms of the 1466 Treaty of Toruń (see p.189 & p.201).

The ethnic mix of the region played a dominant part in governing its allegiances. While a Slav majority retained its hold on the countryside, heavy **German colonization** of the towns inexorably tilted the balance of power, with the Pomeranian dukes transferring allegiance to the Holy Roman Empire in 1521. The inroads of the Reformation further weakened the region's ties with Catholic Poland. In 1532, the ruling Gryfit dynasty divided into two lines, and their territory was partitioned along a line west of the Odra delta: the larger eastern duchy was henceforth known as Hinter Pomerania; the small one to the west as Lower or Hither Pomerania. None of the latter's territory has ever subsequently formed part of Poland.

Control of the region was fiercely disputed during the **Thirty Years' War**, with the Swedes taking over all of Lower Pomerania, plus some of the coastline of Hinter Pomerania. Some seventy-five years later, following the departure of the Swedes in the 1720s, the **Prussians** reunited Lower and Hinter Pomerania into a single administrative province. No further boundary changes occurred until 1919, when a strip of eastern Pomerania was awarded to Poland by the Versailles Treaty. The rest of Hinter Pomerania remained German until 1945, when it was ceded to Poland in compensation for the loss of territories further east. Mass emigration of the area's German population, which started during the final months of the war, gathered apace after the transfer of sovereignty; in their place came displaced Polish settlers, mostly from the east.

The central **train station** and the nearby **bus terminal** are a fifteen-minute walk (or a quick tram ride) downhill from the town centre, near the Odra river. There are **left-luggage** facilities (daily 6am–midnight) in the pedestrian underpass beneath the train station's ticket hall. **City maps**, available from the tourist office, bookstores and kiosks, give details of the comprehensive bus and tram **city transport** routes. Bus and tram tickets cost 2.20zł for twenty minutes of travel, 3.50zł for one hour. Buy them at newspaper kiosks near stops.

The municipal **tourist office**, which occupies a squat circular pavilion at al. Niepodległości 1 (Mon–Fri 9am–5pm; ☎091/434 0440, ⓦ www.szczecin.pl), gives advice on accommodation, as well as selling town maps.

Accommodation

There's a fair spread of **accommodation** in town, ranging from the most luxurious international-class hotels to a couple of post-communist fleapits, and even in high summer you shouldn't have too much trouble finding a bed for the night.

Hotels

Arkona ul. Panieńska 10 ☎091/488 0261, ⓦ www.zlotehotele.pl. Orbis-owned concrete block with not-quite-groovy 1970s furnishings.

Nice location below the castle, just behind the old town hall. ⑥

Elka-Sen ul. 3 Maja 1A ☎091/433 5604, ⓦ www .elkasen.szczecin.pl. Charming little place in the

SZCZECIN

ACCOMMODATION
Arkona	F
PTTK Camping Marina	K
Elka-Sen	H
Focus	E
Ibis	I
HI Hostel	A
Łagoda	D
Park	C
Radisson	B
Rycerski	G
Victoria	J

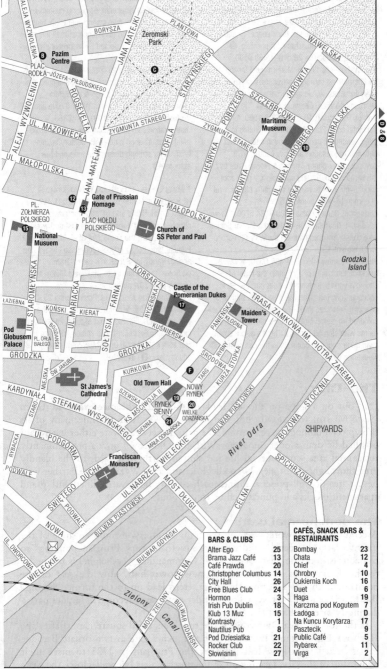

BARS & CLUBS

Alter Ego	25
Brama Jazz Café	13
Café Prawda	20
Christopher Columbus	14
City Hall	26
Free Blues Club	24
Hormon	3
Irish Pub Dublin	18
Klub 13 Muz	15
Kontrasty	1
Nautilus Pub	8
Pod Dziesiatka	21
Rocker Club	22
Słowianin	27

CAFÉS, SNACK BARS & RESTAURANTS

Bombay	23
Chata	12
Chief	4
Chrobry	10
Cukiernia Koch	16
Duet	6
Haga	19
Karczma pod Kogutem	7
Ładoga	D
Na Kuncu Korytarza	17
Pasztecik	9
Public Café	5
Rybarex	11
Virga	2

K, Airport, Świnoujście & Kołobrzeg

basement of a hotel-and-catering school, handy for both the city centre and the stations. The en-suite rooms are on the careworn side but come with colourful furnishings, desk space, TV and wi-fi coverage. Reserve in advance if possible. ⑤

Focus ul. Małopolska 23 ☎091/433 0500, ⓦwww.hotelsporting.pl. Modern hotel for the middle-ranking business travellers, with spick-and-span en suites, wireless internet and a marvellous riverbank position. ❼; weekends ⑥

Ibis ul. Dworcowa 16 ☎091/480 1800, ⓦwww.ibishotel.com. Plain, functional en suites in a plain, functional building, conveniently placed between train station and city centre. Wi-fi coverage throughout. There's a *Novotel* (run by the same company; ⑧) immediately next door should you wish to sample a slightly higher level of corporate-hotel comfort. ⑥.

Ładoga ul. Jana z Kolna ☎091/434 5700, ⓦwww.ladoga.pl. Neat en suite cabins in a former Soviet lake cruiser, moored beneath the Wały Chrobrego embankment. ⑥

Park ul. Plantowa 1 ☎094/434 0050, ⓦwww.parkhotel.szczecin.pl. Definitely the hotel of choice if you're pushing the boat out, the *Park* occupies a historic interwar villa in the middle of peaceful Żeromski Park. The fully equipped pastel-coloured en suites include some nice attic-level rooms with sloping ceilings. There's also a small swimming pool and Jacuzzis in the spa centre. ⑧; weekends ❼.

Radisson pl. Rodła 10 ☎091/359 5595, ⓦwww.szczecin.radissonsas.com. Gleaming custom-built luxury hotel with its own casino, nightclub, fitness centre and swimming pool, along with all the other upmarket facilities expected by its largely expense-account clientele. ⑧

Rycerski ul. Potulicka 2a ☎091/488 8164, ⓦwww.hotelrycerski.pl. Smart, central place in a handsome-looking nineteenth-century red-brick building, offering tasteful en suites with TV. Wi-fi coverage. ⑥

Victoria pl. Batorego 2 ☎091/434 3855, ⓦwww.hotelvictoria.com.pl. Comfortable medium-sized hotel in refurbished nineteenth-century building within easy striking distance of train and bus stations. ⑤

Hostels and campsites

HI Hostel ul. Monte Cassino 19a ☎091/422 4761. Comfortable and friendly hostel with simply-furnished dorms situated just northwest of the centre, past the south end of ul. M. Kopernika. Popular with Polish school groups, so always ring ahead. Handy for Szczecin's parks. Tram #3 to pl. Rodła, then tram #1 to the Piotra Skargi stop. Dorms from 20zł per person.

PTTK Camping Marina ul. Przestrzenna 23 ☎091/460 1165, ⓦcampingmarina.pl. By the waterside in Dąbie, 5km east of town – take the local train to Szczecin-Dąbie station, followed by bus #56, #62 or #79. Open May–Sept; tent space and chalets (❷) available.

The City

Laid out on a slope on the left bank of the Odra, the medieval **Old Town** (Stare Miasto) was heavily bombed in World War II and, while many of its showpiece buildings were restored, the gaps in-between were either left vacant or filled by drab modern housing. With the Old Town now a predominantly residential area, **commercial** life has shifted north-westwards to the blandly grey thoroughfares of aleja Niepodległości and aleja Wyzwolenia. Further west lies an area of well-preserved nineteenth-century boulevards, lined with grand apartment blocks and punctuated by roundabouts.

The commercial centre

Ascending ulica Dworcowa from the train station, you soon see some of the massive late nineteenth- and early twentieth-century Prussian buildings so characteristic of the heart of the city. Commanding the heights is the bulky red-brick frame of the neo-Gothic **new town hall**, now the seat of the maritime authorities. Across the street, steps lead up to the former **Savings Bank**, a Jugendstil fantasy, whose slender tower and decorative facades have a distinctly oriental flavour.

At the top of ulica Dworcowa is the traffic-engulfed square named after the **Harbour Gate** (Brama Portowa); not so much a gate as two ornate Baroque gables linked by a long hall, built by the Prussians in 1725 to mark their ownership of the city. Leading off to the north is aleja Niepodległości, the city's main thoroughfare, on whose western side stand two more Prussian public buildings: the **post office**, still fulfilling its original function, and the administration building of the Pomeranian district, which has been taken over by the displaced Savings Bank.

St James's Cathedral and around

Heading east from the Harbour Gate to the river, ulica Kardynała Wyszyńskiego brings you to **St James's Cathedral** (Katedra św. Jakuba), a massive Gothic church which was grievously damaged in 1945 and subsequently suffered over-restoration (including some concrete windows). The oldest parts of the church date back to the fourteenth century and are the work of Hinrich Brunsberg, the finest of the specialist brickwork architects of the Baltic lands. In the middle of the following century, the single **tower** was constructed to replace the previous pair; this is now only half of its prewar height of 120m, having been rebuilt minus the spire and further trivialized with the addition of a clock. Its five-and-a-half-tonne bell now hangs in a frame outside.

On plac Orła Białego, the square on the north side of the cathedral, is the Baroque **Pod Globusem Palace**, originally built for the ruler of the Prussian province of Pomerania and now used as the medical academy. Across from it, part obscured by a willow tree, stands the intriguing **White Eagle Fountain** (Fontanna Orła Białego) adorned with the eponymous bird overlooking a group of satyrs who gurgle stoically into an enormous clam. Hidden among the trees at the cathedral end of the square is another piece of Baroque frippery, a statue of the goddess Flora.

The lower town

Down ulica Wyszyńskiego towards the river, you come, on the right-hand side, to the oldest surviving building in Szczecin, the **Franciscan Monastery of St John** (Klasztor św. Jana), part of which dates back to the thirteenth century. Its distinctive feature is its geometric inconsistency, showing that medieval builders could (and did) get their calculations wrong. The chancel is an irregular decagon, yet has a seven-part vault, while the later nave adjoins at an oblique angle, its off-centre vaulting a vain attempt to align the bays with the aisle windows. It's a rare example of a building that was never rebuilt properly but never quite collapsed; looking inside you can see the alarmingly warped columns braced by a network of steel girders.

Immediately east of here lies the **Stary Rynek**, where concrete blocks and vacant lots rub shoulders with several reconstructed burghers' houses gaudily decked out in bright blue and orange colour schemes. By far the most personable of Szczecin's buildings is the gabled **old town hall** in the Rynek's centre, an artful reconstruction of the fourteenth-century original, probably designed by Hinrich Brunsberg, which was flattened in the war. The restorers opted to return it to something like its original appearance, right down to the bulging lopsided walls. These days the building serves as a small **Museum of the History of Szczecin** (Muzeum Historii Miasta Szczecina: Tues–Fri 10am–6pm, Sat & Sun 10am–4pm; 6zł), with a worthy but unengaging display of porcelain and metalwork through the ages.

The Castle of the Pomeranian Dukes

By now you'll have spotted the **Castle of the Pomeranian Dukes** (Zamek Książąt Pomorskich) commanding views of the river from its hillside perch. A Slav fortified settlement on this spot was replaced in the mid-fourteenth century by a stone structure, the oldest section of the current building. The whole thing was given a Renaissance enlargement in the late sixteenth century, and again remodelled in the 1720s. Dukes aside, the building has been used as a brewery, office block, barracks and anti-aircraft emplacement – the last function being the direct cause of its flattening in an air raid in 1944.

Reconstruction continued into the 1980s, since when it's been turned into a museum and cultural centre. The **Castle Museum** (Muzeum Zamkowe: Tues–Sun: July–Aug 10am–6pm; Sept–June 10am–4pm; 10zł) occupies a few vaults, displaying the sarcophagi of several dukes as well as photographs of the castle's restoration from postwar ruin. If you're here in summer, you might get to hear an open-air concert in the castle courtyard.

It's worth climbing the two hundred or so steps up the **bell tower** (*wieża*; same hours as museum; 5zł) for the view over the city, port and surroundings, with church spires and dockside cranes piercing the skyline.

Beyond the castle, little of Szczecin's formidable fifteenth-century fortification system survives – save for the appropriately graceful **Maiden's Tower**, now stranded between the castle and a network of interchanges funnelling the city's traffic over the river.

North of the castle

Immediately to the west of the castle is ulica Farna, where the residence of the commandant formerly stood. This was the birthplace of Sophie von Anhalt-Zerbst (1729–96), a princess of a very minor German aristocratic line who has gone down in history as **Empress Catherine the Great of Russia**. A character of extreme ruthlessness – she deposed her own husband, and was probably behind his subsequent murder – she presided over an extraordinary period of Russian expansion, and played a leading role in the Partitions that wiped Poland off the map. That her native city is now Polish is truly ironic.

A couple of blocks further west is ulica Staromłyńska, at the corner of which rises an elegant Baroque palace, formerly the Pomeranian parliament, and now home to a section of the **National Museum** at no. 27 (Muzeum Narodowe: Tues–Sun 10am–4pm; 10zł). The ground floor features an impressive display of medieval Pomeranian **sculpture**. Highlights include the thirteenth-century columns topped with delicately carved capitals, from the monastery of Kołbacz, and several fifteenth-century triptychs from throughout Pomerania. Upstairs, later sections emphasize Polish painters, alongside the occasional token German work. On the other side of the street, a branch of the National Museum at Staromłyńska 1 holds the **Contemporary Art Museum** (Muzeum Sztuki Współczesnej; same times and price), hosting changing exhibitions of modern art and photography.

Across the broad open space of plac Żołnierza Polskiego is the Baroque **Gate of Prussian Homage** (Brama Hołdu Pruskiego), whose design, with reliefs of military trophies, echoes those of the Harbour Gate (see p.584). Its barrel-vaulted interior now provides an atmospheric home to the *Brama Jazz Café* (see p.588). Facing it to the east is the beguiling fourteenth-century **Church of Sts Peter and Paul** (Kościół św. Piotra i Pawła), a Gothic church containing a fine assemblage of seventeenth-century memorial tablets honouring local burghers, and some unusual wooden vaulting.

Wały Chrobrego and the Maritime Museum

On the north side of the church, ulica Małopolska leads to **Wały Chrobrego**, a leafy promenade commanding an expansive panorama of the Odra River and the suburbs on the far shore. The promenade – conceived as a showpiece of muscular civic architecture by Szczecin's pre-World War I German masters – is lined with an imposing sequence of prestigious public buildings.

The central sandstone edifice, fronted by a grandiose staircase leading down to the river, now houses the **Maritime Museum** (Muzeum Morskie: Tues–Fri 10am–6pm, Sat & Sun 10am–4pm; 10zł). Inside lies a wealth of material on seafaring Slavs and Celts, with graphic displays from the Stone, Iron and Bronze ages. Huge arrow-covered maps delineate bygone migrations, while upstairs a gallery is devoted to objects from classical antiquity. Most impressive and unexpected, however, is an inspired ethnographic exhibition with detailed dioramas of villages in Mali and the Ivory Coast, along with West African statues, fetishes and carved masks, displayed with highly dramatic lighting.

Kasprowicza Park and Głębokie Park

Despite the patchily built-up character of its centre, Szczecin has plenty of stretches of greenery, which are ideal for a quick break from the urban bustle, particularly on summer evenings.

Just to the north of the centre is the **Kasprowicz Park** which can be reached on trams #1 or #9 or by walking for ten minutes up aleja Jedności Narodowej from the centre. After negotiating the ornamental flower beds at the park's southern end, you soon reach the huge triple-eagle monument made to commemorate the fortieth anniversary of the outbreak of World War II, symbolizing the three generations of Poles who lost their lives. Proceeding northwest through the park, the **Dendrological Garden** (Ogród Dendrologiczny) on the east bank of the narrow Lake Rusałka contains more than two hundred species of trees and shrubs, including a host of exotic varieties, such as Californian redwoods. Beyond the lake, tree-lined paths continue towards **Głębokie Park**, a full 5km out of the centre (and also reached by taking tram #1 or #9 to the **Głębokie** terminus), the park is arranged around the sausage-shaped lake of the same name. This is a much wilder, less developed area, perfect for tranquil woodland walks.

Eating, drinking and nightlife

The gastronomic situation in Szczecin is as varied as in any other big Polish city, with a reasonable number of places offering good-quality Polish food, alongside a growing number of ethnic alternatives.

There are plenty of good **pubs** and **bars**, although they tend to be spread out through the city centre rather than concentrated in easily strollable areas. One place where you will find several drinking venues clustered within easy reach of each other is the tangle of streets around the **Stary Rynek**.

Cafés and snack bars

Cukiernia Koch al. Wojska Polskiego 4. Prime downtown venue for relaxing over a cup of coffee or pigging out on the decadent range of pastries and cakes. Mon–Sat 9am–8pm, Sun 11am–8pm.

Duet ul. Bogusława 1/2. Relaxing café with a wide choice of teas, cakes and ice creams. Daily 10am–1pm.

Pasztecik al. Wojska Polskiego 46. Minimally decorated stand-up buffet that sells *pasztecik*i (tube-shaped pies filled with meat, mushroom or cheese) and nothing else. Pay at the till before collecting your *pasztecik* from a hole in the wall. Mon–Fri 10am–9pm, Sat 10am–4pm.

Rybarex ul. Obrońców Stalingradu 5a. Inexpensive order-at-the-counter fish bar with a wide selection of dishes: ideal for fast lunchtime service. Mon–Fri 9am–7pm, Sat 10am–5pm.

Restaurants

Bombay ul. Partyzantów 1. Upmarket Indian restaurant a few steps south of the Brama Portowa, with exemplary service and a reasonably authentic menu, including some vegetarian dishes and naan breads – although you'll need to ask for extra spice if you like your food hot. Mains in the region of 25–35zł. Daily 1–11pm.

Chata pl. Hołdu Pruskiego 8. One of the best places in town for traditional Polish food, offering roast duck, wild boar and pheasant alongside traditional porky standards, with mains hovering around the 35zł mark Lots of homely wooden furniture, and folksy paintings on the wall. Turns into a retro disco late Fri and Sat nights. Sun–Thurs noon–10pm, Fri & Sat noon–3am.

Chief ul. Rayskiego 16. Seafood specialist offering up succulent fillets of pan-fried and grilled fish with a 40–60zł price tag. Worth a visit for the decor alone – one wall is covered in shells, another in stuffed fish heads and the window is filled by an enormous sturgeon. Daily 11am–midnight.

Chrobry Wały Chrobrego 18. Pub-restaurant with a great position on the embankment above the river, serving steaks, *golonka* (pork knuckle) and other meat-heavy meals, with mains in the 30–40zł range. Daily noon–midnight.

Haga ul. Sienna 10. Cosy Dutch-style pancake restaurant decorated with an attention-grabbing collection of old clocks. Good location opposite the old town hall, with thick, filling pancakes for around 25zł, alongside Mediterranean salads and tasty soups. Mon–Thurs 11am–10pm, Fri & Sat 11am–11pm, Sun noon–10pm.

Karczma pod Kogutem pl. Lotników 3 ⓦwww .karczmapodkogutem.pl. Folk-themed restaurant with wooden benches and farmhouse furnishings, focused squarely on classic Polish cuisine. Lamb, rabbit and game dishes fill out a varied menu. Mains 40–60zł. Sun–Thurs 11am–midnight; Fri & Sat 11am–1am.

Ładoga ul. Jana z Kolna. Stately cruise ship parked permanently on the riverbank, providing fine dining with a strong Russian slant. Excellent beef stroganoff, although the steaks, fish and game are good too. Expect to shell out 50–60zł for a main course. Daily noon–midnight.

Public Café al. Jedności Narodowej. Café-restaurant decked out in lounge-bar style with cushion-strewn sofas set on bare floorboards. Pizzas, pasta dishes and salads dominate the menu, with main courses averaging around 25–30zł. Mon–Sat 10am–midnight, Sun 11am–11pm.

Na Kuncu Korytarza Inside the castle (see p.585). A mildly bohemian spot decked out with mirrors, chandeliers and old furnishings, traditionally popular with opera-goers and performers. An imaginative mix of traditional Polish and modern European cuisine, with mains carrying a 40–60zł price tag. Daily 10am–10pm.

Virga Park Głębokie. Five kilometres northwest of the centre, just behind the terminus of trams #1 and #9, this is an ideal stopoff after an afternoon walking in the nearby woods of Głębokie Park. Solid and not-too-expensive veal-and-pork repertoire, in a cosy room decorated with kooky ceramics and glassware.

Bars

Brama Jazz Café Inside the Gate of Prussian Homage (Brama Hołdu Pruskiego), pl. Hołdu Pruskiego 1. Chic, barrel-vaulted space, usually with art exhibits on the walls. Good choice of baguettes and salads. Frequent live jazz. Outdoor terrace in summer.

Café Prawda Wielka Odrzańska 20. Cool bar for cool people on the riverfront, just behind the old town hall. Minimalist decor, cutting-edge dance music in the background, and a basement bar where DJs play at weekends.

Christopher Columbus Wały Chrobrego. Curving timber-and-glass pavilion on a leafy promenade, enjoying good views of the riverfront down below. Plenty of outdoor seating; a good place to spend a summer afternoon.

Hormon ul. Monte Cassino 6 (entrance round the corner on al. Piłsudskiego) ⓦwww.hormon .pl. Spacious bare-brick cellar welcoming a trendy cross-section of teens and twentysomethings. DJs or live bands provide entertainment at the weekends, when there's an entrance fee (10–15zł).

Irish Pub Dublin ul. Kaszubska 57. Prime place for a relaxing drink immediately north of the Brama Portowa, with dark wood furnishings, minimal lighting and unobtrusive music. Hearty meat dishes, and a good choice of salads on the menu.

Pod Dziesiątką ul. Osiek 10. Relaxing drinking venue with burgundy walls and candlelight, just round the corner from the old town hall.

Rocker Club ul. Partyzantów 2 ⓦwww.rockerclub .pl. Large, pub-style basement bar a block south of the Brama Portowa, with middle-of-the-road rock music either on tape or performed by local cover bands, and karaoke twice a week. Entrance fee on gig nights.

Clubs and live music venues

Alter Ego pl. Batorego 4 ⓦwww.alterego.art .pl. Lively alternative bar and clubbing venue that calls itself the "club of unpopular culture" – which basically means that you'll hear DJs spinning indie rock, reggae, cutting-edge house and techno and other not-quite-top-of-the-charts styles. Opposite the bus station. Entrance fee ranges from zero to 15zł depending on who's spinning the discs. Wed–Sun.

City Hall 3 Maja 18 ⓦ www.cityhall.pl. Mainstream clubbing venue with plenty of students in attendance. 15-20zł. Thurs–Sat.

Free Blues Club ul. Powstanców Wielkopolskich 20 ⓦ www.freebluesclub.pl. Top quality live blues once or twice a week with a 15–45zł entrance fee depending on who is playing. A 20min walk southwest of the centre so check the schedule before setting out.

Kontrasty ul. Wawrzyniaka 7a ⓦ www.kontrasty .szczecin.pl. Student cultural centre with a packed

programme of indie gigs, latin nights and DJ events. Weeknights free, weekends 10–15zł.

Klub 13 Muz pl. Żołnierza Polskiego 2 ⓦ www .klub13muz.pl. Live music and culture venue that encompasses everything from art rock through jazz to theatre and literary readings. Price depends on who is playing.

Słowianin ul. Korzenowskiego 2 ⓦ www .slowianin.org. Grungy alternative cultural centre which serves as the city's best medium-sized rock venue. The best place to catch touring bands. Prices from 15–50zł depending on who is playing.

Entertainment

The Filharmonia Szczecińska at pl. Armii Krajowej 1 (☎091/422 1252) has a regular programme of **classical music** concerts, while operas and operettas are performed in the opera house at ul. Korsarzy 34 (☎091/480 0340).

Szczecin's main **theatre** is the Teatr Polski, at ul. Swarożyca 3 (☎091/433 0075), although the Teatr Wspólczesny at ul. Wały Chrobrego 3 (☎091/489 2323, ⓦ www.wspolczesny.szczecin.pl) offers a wider range of contemporary drama. **Puppet shows** are held at the Teatr Lalek Pleciuga at ul. Kaszubska 9 (☎091/433 2821). Biggest of the central **cinemas** is the Multikino, al. Wyzwolenia 18-20 (☎091/485 5101, ⓦ www.multikino.pl). For art films and retro seasons head for Pionier 1909, al. Wojska Polskiego 2 (☎091/434 7702, ⓦ www.kino-pionier.com.pl), which was founded in the year of its title and claims to be the oldest continuously operating cinema in the world.

Listings

Airlines LOT, ul. Wyzwolenia 17 ☎080/170 3703 from a landline, ☎22 9572 from a mobile.

Books and newspapers English-language press, guidebooks and maps at EMPiK, on the corner of al. Wojska Polskiego and pl. Zwycięstwa.

Ferries Polska Żegluga Bałtycka, ul. Wyszyńskiego 28 (☎091/488 0238, ⓦ www.polferries.com), and Unity Line, pl. Rodła 8 (☎091/359 5600, ⓦ www.unityline.pl) sell tickets for services from Świnoujście to Denmark and Sweden.

Hospital Pomorski Akademii Medycznej, al. Unii Lubelskiej 1. Tram #1 or #9.

Internet access Portal, ul. Kaszubska 52, south off pl. Zwycięstwa, entrance in the yard round the back of the building (daily 24hr).

Left luggage At the train station (see p.581).

Pharmacy There's a 24hr *Apteka* at ul. Więckowskiego 12, off the north side of pl. Zwycięstwa.

Post office Main office at ul. Bogurodzicy 1 (Mon–Fri 8am–8pm, Sat 9am–2pm).

Travel agents Orbis, pl. Zwycięstwa 1 (☎091/434 7563), handles international plane and bus tickets. Interglobus, at the train station (☎091/485 0422), sells bus tickets to Germany, Britain and other European destinations.

Stargard Szczeciński

Some 35km southeast of Szczecin on the River Ina, **STARGARD SZCZECIŃSKI** was once an important trading town, and, in the seventeenth century, served briefly as Pomerania's capital when the Swedes occupied Szczecin. Stargard suffered severe damage in World War II, but a handful of spectacular medieval buildings survives and is definitely worth a brief look.

With trains (every 30min) and buses (roughly hourly) running to Stargard from Szczecin, it's an easy half-day trip. From the train or bus station, it's just a few minutes' walk down ulica Kardynała Wyszyńskiego to the **Old Town** (Stare Miasto) girded by substantial remains of the fifteenth-century city walls. **Park Chrobrego** stretches along the outer side of the wall and contains the longest-surviving portion of the ramparts. Following ulica Chrobrego downhill from here brings you to the river. To your left stands the most impressive survivor of the fortification system, the **Mill Gate** (Brama Młyńska), protected by a mighty pair of spire-topped octagonal towers. The gate bridges the river and was big enough for boats to pass beneath.

The **Rynek**, five minutes' walk from the Mill Gate, is a mixture of the old – handsome burghers' houses – and the new – unprepossessing 1970s concrete. At the corner stands the renovated **town hall**, a plain Renaissance structure featuring a superbly curvaceous gable adorned with colourful terracotta tracery. Next to it is the **guard house**, whose open arcades and loggia suggest the Mediterranean rather than the Baltic, and the **Weigh House** (Waga Miejska). Here you'll find the local **museum** (Tues–Sun 10am–4pm; 5zł, free Sat) along with a small **tourist information** office (Mon–Fri 10am–4pm, Sat 10am–1pm).

Beside the town hall stands the magnificent **Church of Our Lady** (Kościół Mariacki), one of the most original and decorative examples of the brickwork Gothic style found in the Baltic lands, probably the work of Hinrich Brunsberg and commissioned around 1400. The two towers, with their glazed green and white ceramics, can be seen from all over the town. The southern one, flanked by a luscious coat of ivy, resembles a great tower house, while its higher northern counterpart is a truly bravura creation, topped by four turrets and a great central octagon, itself crowned with a two-storey copper lantern. The east end of the church and the protruding octagonal chapel are decorated with carved brick.

If you need a **place to eat**, try the *Ratuszowa* on the Rynek for straightforward Polish food, or the café in the tourist information building.

Wolin

WOLIN, is the first of two large, heavily indented **islands** that separate the Szczecin Lagoon from the Gulf of Pomerania. The gap dividing it from the mainland is at times so narrow that Wolin is often described as a peninsula rather than an island; indeed, roads are built directly over the River Dziwna in two places – near its mouth at Dzwinów, some 12km from Kamień Panarski, and at **Wolin Town** towards the island's southern extremity, where it is also forded by the rail line from Szczecin. You can choose to approach by either of these two roads, the only ones of significance on the island. They converge at the seaside town and hiking centre of **Międzyzdroje**, before continuing onwards to **Świnoujście,** which straddles the channel dividing Wolin from the neighbouring island of Uznam, and constitutes an engaging mixture of bustling port, health spa and beach resort.

The island, which is 35km long and between 8km and 20km across, offers a wonderfully varied landscape of sand dunes, lakes, forest, meadows and moors. The dramatic **coastline** has attracted crowds of holidaymakers since the nineteenth century but remains relatively unspoilt. A sizeable portion of the island is under the protection of the **Wolin National Park**, and you really need to take time to hike if you want to appreciate it to the full.

Getting to Wolin is easy enough, with six **trains** a day heading from Szczecin to Świnoujście, calling at Wolin and Międzyzdroje on the way.

Minibuses from Szczecin are slightly faster: if you're heading for Świnoujście there are direct Szczecin–Świnoujście minibuses which depart from a stop on aleja 3 Maja; while Szczecin-Wolin–Międzyzdroje–Świnoujście minibuses operate from stand eleven of Szczecin bus station. In summer there is a hydrofoil (*wodolot*) service from Szczecin to Świnoujście (April–Sept; two daily; journey time 75min; 70zł).

Wolin Town

Squatting beside the Dzwina River on the island's southeastern tip, the town of **WOLIN** occupies the site of one of the oldest Slav settlements in the country. Pagan Slavs established themselves here in the eighth century, developing one of the most important early Baltic **ports**, and carrying on a healthy trade with the Vikings (who called the place Jomsborg). A temple to Światowid and to Trzygłów, a triple-headed Slav deity, existed here until the early twelfth century, when Bishop Otto of Bamberg arrived to persuade the locals that acceptance of Christianity would be good for business (most of the region's other mercantile communities having already converted).

Echoes of the town's pagan past are present in the totem-like reconstructed wooden figures dotted around close to the water, all depicting Slav gods. The ruins of the medieval **Church of St Nicholas** (Kościół św Mikołaja), just up from the main square, provide echoes of a Christian past, too. Excavations have uncovered plentiful evidence of the original Slav settlement: you can see their discoveries in the local **museum** (July & Aug daily 9am–5pm; Sept–June Tues–Sun 9am–4pm; 5zł) on the main road at the eastern end of town. A bridge just east of the museum leads to the Ostrów Recławski island, site of a **skansen** (daily: July & Aug 10am–6pm; April–June, Sept & Oct 10am–4pm; 6zł) dedicated to the hybrid Slav-Viking culture that existed here a millennium ago. The imaginatively recreated pre-Christian settlement features twelve houses (built from logs filled in with cow dung), each containing replica furnishings and kitchen utensils of the kind that would have been in use at the time. In summer, staff in period costume are frequently on hand to demonstrate iron-age crafts.

Trains and minibuses plying the Szczecin–Świnoujście route stop on the northeastern side of town, a five-minute walk from Wolin's main street. Wolin is well worth a night or two if you're **camping**, with an attractive, partly wooded waterside site located 1.5km south of the centre at ul. Slowiańska 27a (☎725 147 260, ⓦwww.camp-wolin.eu).

Międzyzdroje

By far the best base for exploring the island is **MIĘDZYZDROJE**, which offers easy access to a long sandy beach and the best hiking trails in the area. A favourite Baltic resort with the prewar German middle class, it is now one of the west Baltic's busiest resorts. New **hotels** are springing up in the beachside areas, and the number of German and Scandinavian visitors is on the increase. However the centre of town remains a laid-back, far-from-overdeveloped place, its streets filled with trade-union-owned sanatoria and holiday homes. It may not look all that snazzy to the outsider, but Międzyzdroje was traditionally one of the places where Polish TV and film stars spent their holidays. A modicum of showbiz glitter still exists in the shape of the **Festiwal Gwiazd** (Star Festival) held at the beginning of July, when a horde of minor celebrities and their hangers-on descend on the town to attend public film screenings and concerts and generally hang out.

Arrival, information and accommodation

The **train station** is at the southeastern fringe of town, five minutes' walk uphill from the centre, while **buses** and **minibuses** pick up and drop off closer to the centre, on ulica Niepodległości.

Międzyzdroje's **tourist information office** spends the summer in a pavilion next to the Dom Kultury at ul. Bohaterów Warszawy 20, and moves inside the Dom Kultury during the off-season (Mon–Sat 9am–5pm; ☎091/328 2778, ✉informacja@mdkmiedzyzdroje.com). They have free maps of town and can help with accommodation. There's a good choice of pensions and hotels in town. Best of the **campsites** is the *Gromada* on ul. Bohaterów Warszawy 1 (☎091/328 0779) at the western end of the seafront.

Hotels and B&Bs

Amber Baltic ul. Bohaterów Warszawy 26a ☎091/322 8500, ✆www.hotel-amber-baltic.pl. Outwardly ugly piece of seafront concrete, with well-equipped, balconied rooms and a host of on-site extras: spa facilities, indoor and outdoor swimming pools included. ❽

Marina Gryfa Pomorskiego 1 ☎091/328 0449, ✆www.marinahotel.az.pl. Smart new building on the main road through town providing smallish but extremely cosy en-suite rooms with TV. ❻

Perła Pomorska 7 ☎091/328 2513, ✆www .perla.ta.pl. Bright, modern hotel just off the main promenade, a little to the east of the pier. Plush-carpeted en suites with TV and a bit of desk space. ❻

Pingwin ul. Promenada Gwiazd 10 ☎501/125 105, ✆pingwin.ta.pl. Comfortable family-run B&B right opposite the beachfront-hogging Amber Baltic (see opposite). Neat en suites with TV. ❺

Willa 777 ul. Krasickiego 8 ☎091/328 1644, ✆www.willa777.maxmedia.pl. Plain but comfortable en suites in a large, centrally located house. ❺

The Town

The centre of town, 1km inland from the sea, revolves around **plac Neptuna**, a modern, pedestrianized, café-filled square which brings to mind the mall-like plazas of Mediterranean holiday resorts. Immediately to the south is the main traffic thoroughfare, ulica Niepodległości, which is overlooked by the **National Park Museum** (Muzeum Przyrodnice Wolińskie o Parku Narodowego; Tues–Sat 9am–5pm; 5zł) – a well-presented display of the island's flora and fauna which is worth visiting before heading into the park itself.

It's a ten-minute walk northwards from plac Neptuna to ulica Bohaterów Warszawy, the **promenade** which stretches for some 4km along the shore. Its focal point is the nineteenth-century **pier**, the entrance to which is framed by an imposing pair of domed pavilions now occupied by ice-cream kiosks. The first one hundred metres or so of the pier is covered by a canopy, forming an arcade-like space filled with cafés and boutiques selling beach gear.

Set back from the pier, Międzyzdroje's **Wax Museum** (Muzeum Figur Woskowych: April–Sept daily 9am–6pm; Oct–March Mon–Sat 10am–4pm; 7zł) contains an entertainingly random muddle of celebrity likenesses – there can't be many spots in the world where you can meet Danny de Vito and Lech Wałęsa in the same place.

The bison reserve

Wolin's densely wooded National Park starts right on the outskirts of Międzyzdroje, and the **bison reserve** (Tues–Sun 10am–6pm; 5zł) lies a twenty-minute walk through the park from the town centre. Head uphill from the PTTK office on ulica Niepodległości and follow the signs. You'll pass through a park gate after about five minutes, beyond which a trail leads through deep forest to the reserve itself. Bison died out here in the 1300s and the animals on show are descended from those brought from Białowieża in eastern Poland (see p.246). The aim of the reserve is to breed the shaggy beasts in captivity to save them from extinction. You'll also see deer, eagles and a clutch of wild boar who loll about in the mud, twitching their prodigious snouts.

▲ Pier In Międzyzdroje

Eating and drinking

You'll find numerous fish-and-chip stalls along the seafront promenade, and a modest selection of bars and restaurants on the streets inland.

Cukiernia Marczello pl. Neptuna 3. A small square-side bakery with not many tables, this is still your best bet for pastries, cakes and strong coffee.
Kuchnia u Marii ul. Krasickiego 8. Simple but smart canteen restaurant with a wide choice of *pierogi*, Polish-style cabbage-heavy salads, and pork-based main courses, all at low prices.
Rio ul. Światowida 8. Businesslike pizzeria that also has a good choice of pastas and Mediterranean salads, with mains around 20–25zł.

Roza Wiatrów pl. Neptuna 7. A smart, cosy pub-restaurant with nautical prints and model boats stashed around the place. The menu concentrates on the tried-and-tested repertoire of pork, chicken and fish dishes, with mains around 30zł.
Scena ul. Bohaterów Warszawy 20. Large and comfortable pub in the basement of the Dom Kultury, with a regular programme of DJ-led events in season.

Wolin National Park

Wolin National Park (Woliński Park Narodowy: Ⓦ www.wolinpn.pl) is an area of outstanding natural interest. Apart from its richly varied landscapes, it is also the habitat of more than two hundred different types of bird – the sea eagle is its emblem – and numerous animals such as red and fallow deer, wild boar, badgers, foxes and squirrels. It would take several days to cover all its many delights, but a reasonable cross-section can be seen without venturing too far from Międzyzdroje. A good aid to walking in this region is the 1:75,000 *Zalew Szczeciński* **map** which has all the paths clearly marked; it's readily available in Międzyzdroje, notably from the National Park Museum (see p.593).

The trails

Some of the most impressive scenery in the park can be seen by following the **red trail** along its eastward stretch from Międzyzdroje, which passes for a while directly along the beach. You soon come to some awesome-looking tree-crowned **dunes**, where the sand has been swept up into cliff-like formations up to 95 metres in height – the highest to be seen anywhere on the Baltic. Quite apart from its visual impact, much of this secluded stretch is ideal for a spot of **swimming** or sunbathing away from the crowds. After a few kilometres, the markers point the way upwards into the forest, and you follow a path which skirts the tiny Lake Gardno before arriving at the village of **WISEŁKA**, whose setting has the best of both worlds, being by its eponymous lake, and above a popular stretch of beach. Here there's a **restaurant**, snack bars, and several shops. The trail continues east through the woods and past more small lakes to its terminus at **KOŁCZEWO**, set at the head of its own lake, and the only other place along the entire route with **refreshment facilities**. From either here or Wisełka you can pick up a bus back to Międzyzdroje.

Also terminating at Kołczewo is the **green trail**: if you're prepared to devote a very long day to it, you could combine this with the red trail in one circular trip. The trail begins in Międzyzdroje and passes by the bison reserve (see p.593) before continuing its forest course, emerging at a group of glacial **lakes** around the village of Warnowo (which can also be reached directly by train), where there's another reserve, this time for mute swans. Five lakeshores are then skirted en route to Kołczewo.

The third route, the **blue trail**, follows a southerly course from Międzyzdroje's train station, again passing through wooded countryside before arriving at the northern shore of the Szczecin Lagoon. Following this to the east, you traverse the heights of the Mokrzyckie Góry, then descend to the town of Wolin.

Finally, the western section of the **red trail** (see opposite) follows the coast for a couple of kilometres, then cuts straight down the narrow peninsula at the end of the island to the shore of the islet-strewn Lake Wicko Wielkie, before cutting inland to Świnoujście.

Świnoujście

Occupying both sides of the channel that divides Wolin from the island of Uznam, the bustling fishing port, naval base and beach resort of **ŚWINOUJŚCIE** is a popular entry point into Poland, thanks to the passenger ships which sail here from Sweden and Denmark. It's also 3km away from the land border with Germany, to whom the vast bulk of the island of Uznam belongs.

Świnoujście's gruff semi-industrialized appearance makes it slightly less attractive as a base than nearby Międzyzdroje, but it does demand at least a day-trip thanks to the well-preserved Prussian-era fortifications on both banks of the River Świna.

Arrival, information and accommodation

Świnoujście's international **ferry terminal**, together with both the **bus** and **train stations**, is stranded on the eastern bank of the Świna estuary – which separates Uznam from Wolin. A half-hourly car ferry (on which pedestrians travel free) runs over to the centre of town, which lies on the western bank.

The **tourist office**, right by the ferry landing at pl. Słowiański 15 (Mon–Fri 9am–5pm, Sat 9am–3pm; ☏091/322 4999, ✉cit@um.swinoujscie.pl) can direct you towards private rooms (❷) and pensions (❸–❹). Among the hotels, *Pod Kasztanami*, in the town centre at ul. Paderewskiego 14/1 (☏091/321 3947, ⓦwww.pod-kasztanami.pl; ❻) provides elegant en suites in a nicely restored nineteenth-century villa. Dating from a similar era is the *Cis*, midway between town centre and beach at ul. Piłsudskiego 26 (☏091/321 2114; ⓦwww.hotel-cis.pl; ❻) with bright en suites in pastle tones, a small garden, and breakfast delivered to your room on a tray.

There's an HI **youth hostel** 1km west of the town centre at Gdyńska 26 (☏091/327 0613, ⓦwww.schronisko.e-swinoujscie.pl) which has a few double rooms (❶) as well as dorms from 20zł per person, although it's frequently booked solid by groups. The *Relax* **campsite** is more handily located at ul. Słowackiego 1 (☏091/321 3912, ⓦwww.camping-relax.com.pl), between the spa park and the beach, and has chalets (❷).

The town and the forts

The centre is fairly nondescript, and it's best to head directly to the town's superb white-sand **beach** – twenty minutes north on the far side of the spacious **spa park**. Once you reach the shore, you'll probably be drawn into the endless stream of strollers passing along the pedestrianized ulica Żeromskiego, which runs from east to west along the seafront, passing neat flower beds and stately seaside villas on the way.

East of the park lies the mouth of the Świna river, guarded by a trio of brick-built **forts** erected by the Prussians in the mid-nineteenth century. Set in the northeastern corner of the park, nearest the sea, **Western Fort** (Fort Zachodni: daily: May–Sept 9am–dusk; April & Oct 10am–6pm; 5zł) contains a small history museum and an open-air display of artillery pieces. A ten-minute walk south, **Angel Fort** (Fort Anioła: daily: May–Sept 10am–dusk; Oct–April 10am–3pm; 5zł), so named because of its alleged resemblance to Castel Sant'Angelo in Rome, doesn't have as much to see inside but is worth visiting for its attractive, cylindrical form. Over on the other bank of the river, **Fort Gerhard** (daily 9am–dusk; 6zł) is harder to get to than the other two, lying a 3km walk north of the bus and train stations on the far side of Świnoujście's container port. It's worth contacting the tourist office (see p.595) to see what's going on at Gerhard, though: from May to September staff don nineteenth-century Prussian uniforms (complete with *Pickelhaube* spiked helmet) and perform a show several times a day, barking parade-ground instructions at tourists. Next door to Fort Gerhard, the 68m **lighthouse** (*latarnia*: daily 10am–6pm; 6zł), offers excellent views of the surrounding coast from the top of its steep 300-step staircase.

Eating and drinking

For a substantial meal try, *Restauracja Centrala*, just west of the tourist office at ul. Armii Krajowej 3, which serves up pork chops, fish and an excellent wild-boar goulash in an arty, café-like environment. The restaurant of the *Pod Kasztanami* hotel (see p.595) is another good source of straightforward meat, poultry and fish dishes; while further afield, the chic *Konstelacja*, near Fort Zachodni at Jachtowa 2, offers steaks and seafood in a superbly restored red-brick arms depot. The *Jazz Club* underneath the restaurant is the coolest place in town to **drink**.

Kamień Pomorski

Immediately east of Wolin island, the quiet waterside town of **KAMIEŃ POMORSKI** squats on the opposite bank of the River Dziwna, which here widens to form the Kamień Lagoon (Zalew Kamieński). An atmospheric former trading centre with a fine cathedral and some attractive burghers' mansions, Kamień enjoys good bus connections with Międzyzdroje, Świnoujście and Szczecin, and makes for a rewarding side-trip.

All Kamień's sights are on and around the **Rynek**, whose northern edge opens onto the lagoon. Parts of the walls ringing the Old Town have survived, notably the **Wolin Gate** (Brama Wolińska) west of the square, an imposing Gothic gateway, surrounded by apartment buildings.

East of the square stands the brick and granite **Cathedral of St John the Baptist** (Katedra św Jana Chrziciela), begun in the 1170s but much added to over the centuries. Inside, you're enveloped by majestic Gothic vaulted arches; the presbytery is older, and covered with flowing early thirteenth-century decoration. Other

Moving on from Świnoujście

Świnoujście provides plenty of onward travel opportunities to Scandinavia and Germany. From the passenger port just south of the train and bus stations, Unity Line (℡091/359 5600, ⓦwww.unityline.pl) operates a daily car ferry to Ystad in Sweden; while Polferries (℡091/488 0238, ⓦwww.polferries.com) runs ferries daily to the Danish capital Copenhagen and weekly to Rønne on the Swedish island of Bornholm (Sat from mid–June to late Aug only). Passenger-only boats (intended for day-trippers) head to the German beach resorts of Ahlbeck, Bansin and Heringsdorf.

sections of early polychromy are tucked away in corners around the transept, including a stern *Christ Pantocrator* and a fine *Crucifixion* that was uncovered in the 1940s. The focus of attention, though, is the superb fifteenth-century triptych gracing the altar, with a central scene of St Mary flanked by John the Baptist and St Faustyna undergoing various tortures.

At the back of the cathedral stands the famous Baroque **organ**, its forest of silver pipes crowned by a procession of dreamy gilded saints. As you approach from the nave, a portrait of the instrument's creator, a local bishop by the name of Bogusław de Croy i Archot, stares down on the congregation from a cherub-encircled frame. In July the cathedral hosts an **International Organ and Chamber Music Festival**, with concerts every Friday – details from the Biuro Katedralny opposite. To complete the ensemble, across plac Katedralny is the **Bishop's Palace** (Pałac Biskupski), a stately, late Gothic structure with a finely carved attic.

Downhill from the cathedral lie the grassy banks of the **lagoon**. There's no real beach here, but it's a relaxing place to stretch your legs, and there's a footbridge leading over to a tranquil, reedy area on the opposite bank.

Practicalities

All Kamień's sights are a straightforward ten-minute walk north of the **bus** and **train stations**. The *Pod Muzami* **hotel**, Gryfitów 1 (℡091/382 2240; ⓦwww .podmuzami.pl ➍), offers bright, cosy en suites in an old half-timbered building, and there's a **campsite** by the lagoon at al. Wyzwolenia 2 (℡091/382 0076).

You'll find the customary gaggle of **snack bars** and **fish-fry huts** down by the water's edge, although it's the restaurant of the *Pod Muzami* that offers the best in the way of pan-fried fish, alongside traditional Polish meat and fowl dishes.

Kołobrzeg

Some 140km northeast of Szczecin, **KOŁOBRZEG** is Poland's most popular beach resort and health spa, but is also the one that foreign visitors are least likely to want to stay at. Most of its hotels look as if they've escaped from a big-city housing project, and the line of greying sanatoria along the seafront convey little sense of Riviera panache. **Tourism** here is organized on an industrial scale, and there's a corresponding lack of the informal, pension-style lodgings you'll find in smaller coastal places. Several communist-era sanatoria still offer the curative salt-water baths for which Kołobrzeg was once famous, but if you're eager for the spa-resort experience you should really head for **Krynica** (see p.337) or **Kudowa-Zdrój** (p.525) instead. Points in the town's favour include the beach, which is as good as any in the region, and the kind of year-round facilities (such as **shops**, **restaurants** and **bars**) that are often lacking in its sleepier Pomeranian neighbours.

Arrival, information and accommodation

Kołobrzeg's **train** and **bus** stations are next to each other on ulica Kolejowa. The town centre lies ten minutes' walk south along ulica Dworcowa, while the seafront is an equal distance to the north.

The **tourist information** office is directly opposite the station entrance at ul. Dworcowa 1 (July & Aug daily 7am–1pm and 3–7pm; Sept–June Mon–Fri 8am–4pm; ℡094/352 7939, ⓦwww.kolobrzeg.turystyka.pl). You can pick up town maps and book private **rooms** (❷) here. The *Relaks*, at ul. Kościuszki 24 (☎094/352 7735, ⓦwww.wypoczynek-rodzinny.pl; ❻) is one of the few pleasant pensions in town, offering en-suite rooms with balconies near the eastern end of the beach, and a nice garden with children's swings. Located well inland just west of the centre, the modern *Pensjonat Sanit*, ul. Żurawia 10 (☎094/351 7939, ⓦwww.nadmorze.pl/sanit; ❺) offers small but neat en suites in an attractive white sugar-lump of a building. Midway between the train station and the beach, the all-new *Sand Hotel*, ul. Zdrojowa 3 (☎094/353 4100, ⓦwww.sandhotel.pl; ❼) goes for plush en suites with designer furnishings and wi-fi coverage, with gym, spa treatments and indoor pool on site. The *Baltic* **campsite**, 1500m east of the stations at ul. IV Dywizji Wojska Polskiego 1 (☎094/352 4569, ⓦwww.campingkolobrzeg.pl), is beside a wooded park ten minutes' walk from the sea.

The Old Town and the beach

Much of the town centre is modern; an area of pedestrianized streets and squares, lined with brightly painted apartments and office blocks built in imitation of the Hanseatic town houses of old. Dominating the skyline, however, is the collegiate **St Mary's Church** (Kościół Mariacki), originally built as a simple Gothic hall, but extended in the fifteenth century with the addition of star-vaulted aisles, adding to the impression of depth and spaciousness. A particularly striking effect was achieved with the facade, whose twin towers were moulded together into one imposing mass of **brick**. Many of the furnishings perished in the war, but some significant items remain, notably several Gothic triptychs and a fourteenth-century bronze font.

To the north stands the other key public building, the **town hall**. A castellated Romantic creation incorporating some of its fifteenth-century predecessor, it was built from designs by the great Berlin architect Karl Friedrich Schinkel.

However, it's the **beach** that the visitors come for, and throughout the summer you'll find throngs of Polish holidaymakers soaking up the sun on the main strand. There's 1.6km of beach to lie on, complete with deck chairs, wicker cots, parasols and rowing boats for rent. There's plenty of scope for a decent stroll, with a **promenade** running the length of the beach and a pier towards the western end. Beyond the pier stands a tall brick **lighthouse** (*latarnia*; daily: July & Aug 10am–sunset; Sept & Feb–June 10am–5pm; Oct–Jan 10am–4pm; 4zł) offering good views of the surroundings, and a stone monument commemorating "Poland's Reunion with the Sea", a highly symbolic event which took place here in 1945. With the German withdrawal from Kołobrzeg in March, a band of **Polish patriots** gathered on the beach to hurl a wedding ring into the sea, thereby marking Poland's re-marriage to a stretch of coast that had for so long been in German hands.

Eating and drinking

There are numerous excellent **fish-and-chip bars** along the seafront, some of which – notably *J. Rewinski* near the lighthouse – are quite swish-looking places sited in stylish plate-glass pavilions. For a more leisurely sit-down meal, the *Pod Winogronami*, two blocks south of the lighthouse at Towarowa 16, is a good place to tuck into a familiar repertoire of steak, pork, poultry and fish; while *Pergola*, on the seafront east of the lighthouse at Szymanskiego 14, offers excellent **seafood**, good pasta and a superb duck with dumplings; and is well worth the slightly higher prices.

Kołobrzeg is not short of venues for **drinking** and evening entertainment. The hotel cafés along the seafront offer "proper" dancing to evergreen tunes. **Bars** tend to be located in the modern centre: *Café Mariacka*, Mariacka 27, functions as both daytime café and night-time drinking den, and has the feel of a cosy living room; *Fiddlers Green*, Dubois 16, is a smart little pub with Irish brews on tap and a worthwhile menu of main meals; and *Underground Pub*, in the basement of the *New Skanpol* hotel at Dworcowa 10, has extended opening hours and DJs at weekends.

The central Pomeranian coast

East of Kołobrzeg lies a string of comparatively relaxing and laid-back resorts, with **Darłowo** and **Mielno** offering the kind of small-town charm and unspoiled surroundings that Kołobrzeg itself largely lacks. Lying just inland are the regional administrative centres of **Koszalin** and **Słupsk** – important transport hubs, which you'll pass through en route to the coastal settlements, but hardly worthy of an overnight stop in their own right.

Koszalin

As even the determinedly upbeat tourist brochures tacitly admit, **KOSZALIN**, the bustling provincial capital 40km east of Kołobrzeg, isn't the sort of place that gets the crowds shouting. The **Old Town** was badly damaged during 1945, and much of the centre was rebuilt in utilitarian style in the years that followed. Set back some 10km from the sea, Koszalin is certainly not a holiday resort – but you're likely to pass through its bus and train stations if you're heading for the beaches at nearby Mielno and Unieście.

There's the customary scattering of sights here if you have time to kill between connections. Ten minutes' walk east of the **train** and **bus stations**, the modern flagstoned **Rynek** contains one of the strangest examples of Polish 1960s architecture – an orange-and-blue town hall that was considered the epitome of cool modernity when it was first built. Just south of the square is **St Mary's Cathedral** (Katedra Mariacka), an imposing, oft-remodelled Gothic structure with a few pieces of original decoration, notably a large fourteenth-century crucifix and a scattering of Gothic statuary which was originally from the main altarpiece and is now incorporated into the stalls, pulpit and organ loft. The nineteenth-century water mill facing the Old Town walls from the corner of ulica Młyńska houses the **Regional Museum** (Muzeum Okręgowie: Tues–Sun 10am–4pm; 6zł) at no. 38, with a varied collection of folk art, archaeological finds and other regional bits and pieces.

It's on ulica Młynska that you'll find the best spots for a bite to **eat**: the folksy *Gospoda Jamnenska* at no. 37 does a great line in grilled and roast meats, while the more formal *Zielony Młyn* at no. 33 features modern European cuisine and slightly higher prices.

Mielno and Unieście

Bus #1 from Koszalin train station departs every thirty minutes or so for the resort of **MIELNO** some 12km northwest of town, a long, straggling beachside settlement that bleeds into **UNIEŚCIE** (where most buses terminate), the next village to the east. Formerly the main port for Koszalin, Mielno is now one of the quieter, more laid-back resorts on the coast; although the presence of a large saltwater lake just inland from the beach ensures a steady influx of **sailing** enthusiasts in summer.

It's best to get off the bus at the western entrance to the resort, from where ulica 1 Maja leads down to a seaside promenade overlooked by a smattering of *belleépoque* holiday villas – including some attractively rickety timber constructions. It's roughly a half-hour's walk from here to Unieście, which has a comparatively sleepy, village-like feel, with wooden fishing boats parked up on the dune-fringed beach. The beach gets more unspoilt (and more deserted) the further east you go – once you've cleared Unieście, it's 10km to the next settlement.

The **tourist office**, just by Mielno's bus stop at ul. Lechitów 23 (Mon–Fri 8am–4pm; ☎094/316 6152) has details of private rooms (❷) and pensions (❸) throughout the two villages. The *Eden* at Morska 20 in Unieście (☎094/318 9800, ⓦwww.eden.mielno.pl; ❺) looks as though the builders followed the plans for a modern French ski hotel, but is well-placed for the quiet, eastern end of the beach and has gym and spa facilities on site. Midway between Mielno and Unieście, the smallish *Czarny Staw*, ul. Chrobrego 11 (☎094/318 9835, ⓦwww.czarnystaw.mielno.pl; ❺) is a welcoming pension with cosy en suites. Close to the beach in the centre of Mielno, the *Willa Milenium*, at ul. 1 Maja 10 (☎094/318 9674; ❻) is a modern place aping the half-timbered style of the nearby villas, and comes with all the creature comforts.

Campsite *Bulaj*, at the western end of Unieście, occupies a grassy site right by the lake. For **eating**, there's *Café Floryn*, at the point where ulica 1 Maja meets the sea, a bright pavilion filled with leafy houseplants and boasting a terrace both front and back – a great place for a fishy fry-up or just a drink.

Darłowo and beyond

Thirty kilometres northeast of Mielno and reached by a handful of buses from either Koszalin or Słupsk (see opposite), **DARŁOWO** is the one town along the coast that preserves its medieval **Rynek** and street plan more or less intact. The beaches just north of the town, around the coastal suburb of **Darłówko**, are as popular as any.

The Rynek here is the site of a gracefully reconstructed **town hall**, complete with its Renaissance doorway and an unusual fountain. On one side of the Rynek sits the Gothic **St Mary's Church** (Kościół NMP) an attractive brick building with a relatively restrained Baroque interior. Inside there's an eighteenth-century wooden pulpit decorated with scenes from the Last Judgement; while in among a clutch of royal tombs located beneath the tower is that of the notorious **King Erik VII** (1397–1459), a local-born aristocrat who acceded to the thrones of Denmark, Sweden and Norway, and married Henry V of England's daughter Phillipina – whom he later tired of and banished to a nunnery. Deposed in 1439 he returned to Darłowo and lived out the last years of his life here as the Duke of Słupsk, living off piracy in the Baltic Sea.

South of the Rynek lies the well-preserved fourteenth-century **castle** of the Pomeranian dukes, now home to the **Regional Museum** (Muzeum Regionalne: daily: May–Sept 10am–4pm; Oct–April 10am–1.30pm; 8zł) which contains exhibits on local folklore as well as furnishings from the castle itself – notably the ornate seventeenth-century limewood pulpit which once graced the castle chapel.

About 400m northeast of the Rynek along ulica Ojca Damiana Tyneckiego is the extraordinary white-walled **St Gertrude's Chapel** (Kaplica św. Gertrudy), a twelve-sided seventeenth-century structure which squats beneath a tapering, inverted ice-cream cone of a roof covered in slender wooden shingles. The galleried interior is decorated with pictures of shoes and boots donated by pious tradesmen – St Gertrude being, among other things, the patron saint of cobblers.

Darłówko

On the coast 3km west of Darłowo (and reached by regular shuttle service from the bus station) lies Darłówko, a low-rise, **leafy resort** straddling the mouth of the Wieprza. Clogged by fishing boats, the river is spanned by a pedestrian **drawbridge**, whose control tower – a mushroom-shaped affair resembling something out of a 1960s sci-fi movie – is very much a local attraction. There are the usual expanses of sand backed by woods, making this as restful a place as any if you're in need of a seaside breather.

Practicalities

Darłowo's **bus station** is just west of the town centre: walk down Boguslawa X-ego and cross the river to reach the **Rynek**. The local **tourist office** in Darłowo's castle (see opposite; same hours; ℡094/314 3051) can help out with private rooms and pensions in Darłowo and Darłówko.

Of Darłowo's **accommodation** options, the *Irena*, midway between the bus station and the Rynek, at ul. Wojska Polskiego 64 (℡094/314 3692, ⓦwww .irena.darlowo.info; ❺), and the *Hotel nad Wieprza*, just west of the centre at ul. Traugutta 6 (℡094/314 3657; ❹), are both medium-sized places that provide reasonable en-suite rooms. There's more variety in Darłówko – and you're closer to the **sea**. The *Albatros*, ul. Wilków Morskich 2 (℡094/314 3220, ⓦwww .dwalbatros.afr.pl; ❹) is a cosy pension, while the *Apollo*, ul. Kapielowa 11 (℡094/314 2453, ⓦwww.hotelapollo.pl; ❻) is in a different league altogether – a historic beachside establishment with plush en suites. There's a **campsite** midway between Darłowo and Darłówko at ul. Conrada 20 (℡094/314 2872).

Erik, in the centre of town at ul. Rynkowa 2d, is one of only a few **places to eat** in Darłowo. Darłówko bristles with fish bars in season – for respite from the fish, try *Pizza Papperino* on Wladyslawa IV.

Słupsk

Travelling onwards from the central Pomeranian coast probably necessi-tates passing through **SŁUPSK**, an inland administrative town 40km east of Darłowo. What little there is worth seeing in town can be covered in an hour or two. By the banks of the River Słupia on the southeastern fringe of the centre, the Renaissance castle on Zamkowa houses the **Museum of Central Pomerania** (Muzeum Pomorza Środkowego: Tues–Sun: July–Aug 10am–5pm; Sept–June 10am–3pm; 7zł). Alongside displays of local ethnography, there's a large collection of modern Polish art, most notably the distorted caricatures and self-portraits of Stanisław Ignacy Witkiewicz – the avant-garde artist and playwright who committed suicide soon after the start of World War II (see box, p.445). The old castle **mill** opposite is one of the earliest specimens of its kind in the country, packed with more folksy exhibits (same times, same ticket), while the reconstructed Gothic **Dominican church** has a fine Renaissance altarpiece and the tombs of the last Pomeranian dukes.

Słupsk's **train station**, with the **bus station** just opposite, is at the west end of aleja Wojska Polskiego, the kilometre-long boulevard leading to the centre. There's a useful **tourist information centre** at ul. Sienkiewicza 19 (Mon–Fri

POMERANIA | The central Pomeranian coast

9am–5pm; ☏059/842 0791, ⊛www.slupsk.pl). Best **place to eat** in town is the *Karczma Słupska* at ul. Wojska Polskiego 11, where you can enjoy moderately priced Polish fare in traditional surroundings.

Łeba and around

Of all the Pomeranian seaside resorts, **ŁEBA** is the most celebrated; an attractive old fishing settlement presiding over kilometre upon kilometre of irresistible dune-backed beaches. Small enough to preserve a village-like feel, it nevertheless receives enough visitors in summer to generate an invigorating holiday bustle. The bigger of the local **dunes** (*wydmy*), just west of town in the **Slowinski National Park**, forms one of Poland's prime natural attractions, and draws hordes of sightseers as a result. There are plenty of unspoiled Baltic pine forests and silvery sands nearby if you want to escape the crowds.

Arrival, information and accommodation

Regular **buses** run to Łeba from the provincial town of Lębork just to the south, which stands on the main east-west road and rail routes connecting Szczecin to Gdańsk. There are also direct buses to Łeba from **Gdynia** (see p.166). Other than checking out ⊛www.leba.pl, you can get information just round the corner from the train and bus stations, where the public library on ulica 11 Listopada houses the local **tourist office** (summer: Mon–Fri 8am–4pm, Sat & Sun 10am–1pm; winter: closed Sat & Sun; ☏059/866 2565) which will help you find a **place to stay** in one of the innumerable private rooms (❸) and pensions (❸–❺). If it's closed, note that many of the houses along Nadmorska and the surrounding streets display "*pokoje*" signs, indicating vacancies.

For **campers** – and there are plenty of them in summer – there are several sites along ulica Turystyczna and ulica Nadmorska, all close to the beaches, and a number of them let chalets, too. Best of the bunch are *Ambre* on Nadmorska (☏059/866 2472, ⊛www.ambre.leba.info), a large, well-organized place

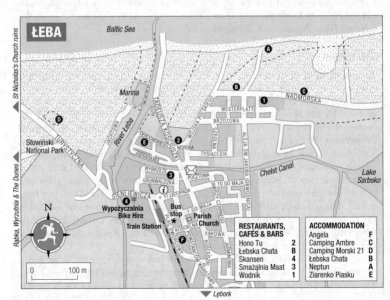

stretched out beneath birch trees which also has four-person bungalows (from 300zł); and *Morski 21* on ulica Turystyczna, which offers four-person self-catering maisonettes (300zł).

Bikes can be hired from the Wypożyczalnia on ulica Sienkiewicza.

Hotels and pensions

Angela ul. Dworcowa ☎059/866 2647. A largish place right by the station with balconied rooms and a neat garden at the front. ❹

Łebska Chata Nadmorska 7 ⓦwww.lebskachata .eu. Charming timber structure with cosy en-suite rooms set in the attic above the Łebska Chata pub-restaurant (see below). ❸

Neptun ul. Sosnowa 1 ☎059/866 1432, ⓦwww .neptunhotel.pl. Right on the beach among the pine trees in a hundred-year-old villa with a mock castle turret. Plush en suites, and tennis court and swimming pool on site. ❼

Ziarenko Piasku ul. Dzerdowskiego 13 ☎059/866 1555, ⓦwww.ziarenkopiasku .pl. Family-oriented B&B offering en-suite rooms with small wooden balconies, TV and electric kettle. Plenty of kids' toys in the social areas. ❹

The village

The **village** is set a kilometre back from the sea: dunes and beaches cover the original site of the settlement, which was forced to move inland in the late sixteenth century because of shifting sands. Buses and trains drop you two blocks west of ulica Kościuszki, the main street running down the middle of the resort, which is still lined with several of the one-storey, brick-built fishermen's houses once common to the region. A little further north, Kościuszki bridges a canalized branch of the River Łeba, where **trawlers** and **pleasure boats** moor, before veering eastwards and becoming Nadmorska, a shore-side avenue which leads to the bigger hotels and campsites. In summer the area is busy with cheerful holidaymakers heading for the unbroken sandy **beaches** that are widely regarded as among the cleanest on the Baltic coast.

Another stretch of beach, to the west of town, can be reached by walking down ulica Turystyczna, which heads west from the train and bus stations and passes a swanky new yachting marina and the turn-off to **Rąbka** (see p.604), before arriving at another clutch of beachside campsites. Round the back of the *Chemik* campsite, just before the access to the beach, a path leads off into the forest towards the meagre ruins of **St Nicholas's Church** (Kościół św. Mikołaja), a lone reminder of the village's former location.

Eating and drinking

There's a surfeit of **fish-fry stalls** (*smażalnia ryb*) selling fresh cod or halibut with chips; they are particularly concentrated by the Chełst canal where local boats unload their catch. In addition, there's a string of pizzerias and pubs along ulica Nadmorska and ulica Turystyczna, and a modest handful of mainstream restaurants scattered throughout the town centre. For outdoor **drinking**, the *Skansen*, overlooking the bridge at the western end of ulica Sienkiewicza is the place where most of the visiting Varsovians hang out, and it generates a seductive party vibe on summer weekends.

Opening hours fluctuate widely according to how many visitors are in town, and many places close their doors altogether outside the tourist season (roughly May–Sept). The establishments listed below are open year-round.

Hono Tu ul. Wojska Polskiego. Lively central pub-restaurant with a generous range of thin-crust pizzas, meat dishes and grilled fish, with mains hovering in the 20–30zł range.

Łebska Chata Nadmorska 7 ⓦwww.lebskachata .eu. Enjoyable cross between fisherman's cottage and Tatra mountain hut, with sheepskins on the chairs and hearty Polish staples in the 25–35zł range.

Smażalnia Maat Wybrzeże. Order-at-the-counter fish-fry establishment in a modern glass-and-timber pavilion right by the canal bridge. Good for a succulent fillet of halibut or turbot, priced by weight.

Wodnik ul. Nadmorska 10. Smart but bland hotel restaurant worth visiting for its fish dishes, with pan-fried Baltic eel (*węgorz*) the stand-out. Mains 20–30zł.

Słowiński National Park

West of Łeba is **Lake Łebsko** (Jezioro Łebsko), the largest of several lagoons separated from the sea by a belt of mobile **sand dunes** that form the centre of **Słowiński National Park** (Słowinski Park Narodowy: Ⓦwww.slowinskipn.pl), one of the country's most memorable natural attractions, special enough to be included in UNESCO's list of world Biosphere Reserves. The park gets its name from the **Slovincians**, a small ethnic group of Slav origin who, like their neighbours the Kashubians, have retained a distinctive identity despite centuries of German influence.

This area is an ornithologist's paradise, with more than 250 **bird** species either permanently inhabiting the park or using it as a migratory habitat. The six hundred scenic lakes attract **fishing**, while the postglacial lakes incorporated into the river systems have created excellent **canoe trails**. Both activities are very popular here.

Geomorphically this is an unusual region: the shallow **lagoons** covering the central part of the park once formed a gulf, which the deposition of sand eventually isolated from the sea. Between them a narrow spit of land emerged roughly two thousand years ago, whose dense original covering of oak and beech forests was gradually eroded by intensive animal grazing and tree felling, the forests disappearing under the **dunes** that overran the thirty-kilometre spit. Abandoned to the elements by its few original human inhabitants, during World War II the expanse of shifting, undulating sand provided an ideal training ground for units of the Afrika Korps, who drilled here in preparation for the rigours of Rommel's North African campaigns. In the latter stages of the war the spit west of Łeba was turned into a **rocket research station**; the missiles tested here were close cousins of the fearsome V1 and V2 rockets that later bombarded London.

Park access

The eastern entrance to the park is at **RĄBKA**, a small cluster of houses and snack bars on the shores of Lake Łebsko, one and a half kilometres west of Łeba. The shores of the lake are covered with thick reeds that provide ideal cover for **birds**: sanctuaries at several points protect the main breeding sites. To get to Rąbka on foot or by car, go down ulica Turystyczna and take the signed left turn about 500m beyond the canal. Alternatively you can take one of the boats or tourist "trains" (electric buses, really) that leave from beside the bridge.

Fauna in Słowiński National Park

Birds in the park are classified into three main groups: nesting, migratory and wintering. Nesters include such rare species as the white-tailed eagle, crane, eagle owl and black stork. This is also a popular area for the more common white stork. During the late autumn migration period you'll see large flocks of wild geese winging over the lakes, and in winter you'll find ducks and other fowl from the far north of Europe sheltering – velvet scoters, mergansers, auks and whooper swans included.

Mammals are numerous too, the shores of the lakes harbouring deer and boar, with elks, racoons and badgers in the surrounding woods. Shy red squirrels are a common sight in among the trees surrounding Łeba.

The **pathway to the dunes** begins on Rąbka's western edge, where a kiosk sells **tickets** to the park (8am–dusk; 4zł) as well as local maps. Though walking is a very pleasant option, a multitude of alternative forms of **transport** is on offer at the park entrance: horses and carts (25zł per person), tourist trains (5zł) and chauffeured golf carts (15zł), as well as boats from Rąbka's landing stage in season. By far the most popular option is to rent a **bike** in Łeba or Rąbka (4–6zł per hour). While boat passengers glide across Lake Łebsko, those going by land proceed through the birch trees down a narrow road built by the German military in World War II to serve the rocket research station – you'll see a couple of cone-headed concrete pillboxes standing guard beside the route.

Wyrzutnia

Three kilometres west of Rabka lies a small clearing known as **Wyrzutnia** (Launchpad), the site of the World War II base where the German military experimented with various forms of rocket between 1943 and 1945 – part of Hitler's strategy of producing terror **weapons** that would give Germany a psychological advantage over its adversaries. A museum (April–Oct daily 9am–5pm; 8zł) built inside one of the observation bunkers contains sepia photographs of prewar Łeba, alongside diagrams of the **rockets** developed here by Hitler's scientists. The first of these was the stumpy, five-and-a-half-metre-long *Rheintochter* (Rhine Daughter), although this was soon superseded by the much larger *Rheinbote* (Rhine Messenger), a sleek eleven-metre affair that resembles the ground-to-air missiles in use today. Despite more than eighty test launches, the *Rheinbote* never saw active service, the Germans instead opting for the V2 rockets that were developed by a separate team at Peenemünde in eastern Germany.

Outside the bunker is one of the launchpads – a concrete pit topped by rails onto which a rocket gantry was wheeled. Nearby are replicas of the *Rheintocter* and the *Rheinbote*, together with a pair of postwar Soviet rockets that look very similar to the German-designed missiles – an eloquent demonstration of how **Nazi technology** was eagerly adopted by the Cold War superpowers after 1945.

The dunes

Passengers on boats and tourist trains (but not those in traps, golf carts or on pushbikes) disembark at Wyrzutnia and proceed to the dunes on foot, following a path which forges westwards through deep forest for a further 2km before emerging at the base of the **Biała Góra** (White Mountain), the first – and, with an altitude of 40m, the highest – of the **dunes**, which stretch westwards for about 5km.

Even a brief hike will give you the flavour of the terrain. Dried by the sun and propelled by the wind, the dunes migrate over ten metres per year on average, leaving behind the broken tree stumps you see along the path. Out in the middle of the dune area, there's a desert-like feeling of desolation with the sands rippling in the wind giving an eerie sense of fluidity.

Crossing the dunes northwards will bring you down onto the **seashore** within a few minutes: from here you can walk back to Łeba along the beach (8km) if you don't fancy returning the way you came.

Kluki and Smołdzino

Twenty kilometres southwest of Łeba, on the southern edge of Lake Łebsko and at the end of a minor road, is the little Slovincian village of **KLUKI**, which is accessible by occasional bus from Słupsk, or by lake cruiser from Łeba in the summer months. Entirely surrounded by woods, Kluki has a charming *skansen* of Slovincian timber-framed architecture (mid-May to mid-Sept: Mon 9am–3pm, Tues–Sun 9am–6pm; mid-Sept to mid-May: daily 9am–3pm; 5zł); you'll see similar, if more dilapidated, buildings still in use in several villages all over the region.

The road to Kluki passes through **SMOŁDZINO**, home to the park headquarters and Słowninski National Park Museum (Muzeum Przyrodnicze Słowińskiego Parku Narodowego; daily 9am–5pm; 5zł), which contains an extensive display on the park's flora and fauna. The park offices can provide you with detailed information about the area, including advice on birdwatching around the lake. Just to the west of the village is the 115-metre-high **Rowokół Hill**, whose observation tower affords a panoramic view over the entire park area.

Smołdzino has one of the nicer **pensions** in the area: *U Bernackich* (℡059/811 7364, ⓦwww.ubernackich.pl; ❹) is in a comfortable red-brick villa set in a large garden just off the main road, and has a great **restaurant** with rustic interior and excellent Polish food. There's a wealth of **private rooms** – although there's no accommodation office, so you'll have to try your luck by looking for *pokoje* signs.

Travel details

Trains

Kamień Pomorski to: Szczecin (3 daily; 1hr 30min).
Kołobrzeg to: Gdańsk (2 daily; 3hr 30min); Koszalin (6 daily; 50min); Szczecin (2 daily; 2hr 40min); Warsaw (2 daily; 9hr).
Międzyzdroje to: Szczecin (6 daily; 1hr 45min); Świnoujście (6 daily; 20min); Wolin (8 daily; 15min).
Słupsk to: Gdańsk (10 daily; 2hr–2hr 30min); Kołobrzeg (2 daily; 2hr); Koszalin (hourly; 50min); Szczecin (7 daily; 3hr 10min–4hr).
Szczecin to: Gdańsk (3 daily; 5hr 15min); Kamień Pomorski (3 daily; 1hr 30min); Kołobrzeg (2 daily; 2hr 40min); Koszalin (8 daily; 2hr 30min–3hr 30min); Kraków (5 daily; 9hr 30min–11hr); Lębork (4 daily; 3hr 40min–4hr); Poznań (12 daily; 2hr 20min); Słupsk (7 daily; 3hr 10min–4hr); Świnoujście (8 daily; 2hr 5min); Warsaw (6 daily; 5hr 30min–6hr 20min); Wolin (8 daily; 1hr 30min).
Świnoujście to: Międzyzdroje (8 daily 20min); Szczecin (8 daily; 2hr 5min); Wolin (8 daily; 35min).

Buses

Darłowo to: Koszalin (3 daily; 1hr); Słupsk (4 daily; 1hr 20min).
Kamień Pomorski to: Kołobrzeg (4 daily; 1hr 45min); Międzyzdroje (hourly; 1hr); Szczecin (9 daily; 1hr 45min); Świnoujście (hourly; 1hr 15min); Wolin (12 daily; 1hr).
Kołobrzeg to: Kamień Pomorski (4 daily; 1hr 45min); Koszalin (7 daily; 1hr 10min); Szczecin (3 daily; 3hr).

Koszalin to: Darłowo (3 daily; 1hr); Kołobrzeg (7 daily; 1hr 10min); Mielno (5 daily; 20min); Unieście (5 daily; 25min).
Łeba to: Gdynia (July–Aug 3 daily; Sept–June 1 daily; 2hr 10min); Lębork (hourly; 30min); Słupsk (3 daily; 1hr 45min).
Międzyzdroje to: Kamień Pomorski (hourly; 1hr); Szczecin (minibuses; hourly; 1hr 30min); Świnoujście (every 20min; 20min); Wolin (minibuses; hourly; 20min).
Słupsk to: Darłowo (4 daily; 1hr 20min); Łeba (3 daily; 1hr 45min).
Szczecin to: Międzyzdroje (minibuses; hourly; 1hr 30min); Stargard Szczeciński (hourly; 50min); Świnoujście (minibuses; every 30min; 1hr 40min); Wolin (minibuses; hourly; 1hr 10min).
Świnoujście to: Kamień Pomorski (hourly; 1hr 20min); Międzyzdroje (every 20min; 20min); Szczecin (minibuses; every 30min; 1hr 40min).

International trains

Szczecin to: Berlin (direct: 2 daily; 2hr; changing at Angermünde: 12 daily; 2hr 40min).

International ferries

Świnoujście to: Ahlbeck (June–Sept; 8 daily; 15min); Bansin (June–Sept; 3 daily; 25min); Bornholm (1 weekly; 6hr); Copenhagen (daily; 10hr); Heringsdorf (June–Sept 3 daily; 20min); Ystad (1 daily; 9hr).

Contexts

Contexts

History

F ew other European countries have had so chequered a history as Poland. At its mightiest, it has been a huge commonwealth stretching deep into the Baltics, Russia and the Ukraine; at its nadir, it has been a nation that existed only as an ideal, its neighbours having on two occasions conspired to wipe it off the map. Yet, for all this, a distinctive Polish culture has survived and developed without interruption for more than a millennium.

The beginnings

The great plain that is present-day Poland, stretching from the River Odra (or Oder) in the west all the way to the Russian steppes in the east, has been inhabited since the **Stone Age**. For thousands of years it was home to numerous tribes – some nomadic, others settlers – whose traces have made Poland a particularly fruitful land for archeologists.

Lying beyond the frontiers of the Roman Empire, it did not sustain anything more socially advanced than a tribal culture until a relatively late date. The exact period when this plain was first settled by **Slav tribes** is uncertain, but it may have been as late as the eighth century. Although diffuse, the various Slav groups shared a common culture – certainly to a far greater extent than is true of the Germanic tribes to the west – and the Polish language can be said to have existed before the Polish state.

It was the Polonians (the "people of the open fields"), based on the banks of the River Warta between Poznań and Gniezno, who were responsible for forging a recognizable nation, which thereafter bore their name. From the early ninth century, they were ruled by the Piast dynasty, whose early history is shrouded in legend but emerges into something more substantial with the beginnings of recorded history in the second half of the tenth century.

In 965, the Piast **Mieszko I** married the sister of the Duke of Bohemia and underwent public baptism, thus placing himself under the protection of the papacy. Mieszko's motives appear to have been political: Otto the Great, the Holy Roman Emperor, had extended Germany's border to the Odra and would have had little difficulty in justifying a push east against a pagan state. By 990, Mieszko had succeeded in uniting his tribal area, henceforth known as Wielkopolska (Great Poland), with that of the Vistulanian tribe, which took the name of Małopolska (Little Poland). Silesia, settled by yet another Slav tribe, became the third component of this embryonic Polish state.

Mieszko's policies were carried to their conclusion by his warrior son **Bolesław the Brave**. In 1000, the Emperor Otto III was dispatched by the pope to pay tribute to the relics of the Czech saint, Adalbert, which Bolesław had acquired. During his stay, the emperor crowned Bolesław with his own crown, thus renouncing German designs on Polish territory. Subsequently, Bolesław established control over Pomerania, Kujawy and Mazovia; he also gained and lost Bohemia and began Poland's own easterly drive, pushing as far as Kiev. The name "Poland" came into general use, and its status as a fully fledged kingdom was underlined by Bolesław's decision to undergo a second coronation in 1022.

Piast Poland

By the middle of the eleventh century, Małopolska had become the centre of the nation's affairs and Kraków had replaced Gniezno as capital, owing to Wielkopolska's vulnerability to the expansionist Czechs and Germans. Political authority was in any case overshadowed by the power of the Church: when **Bishop Stanisław** of Kraków was murdered in 1079 on the orders of **Bolesław the Generous**, the clergy not only gained a national saint whose cult quickly spread, but also succeeded in dethroning the king.

In the early twelfth century, centralized monarchical power made a comeback under **Bolesław the Wrymouth**, who regained Pomerania – which had become an independent duchy – and repulsed German designs on Silesia. However, he undid his life's work with a decision to divide his kingdom among his sons; for the rest of the century and beyond, Poland lacked central authority and was riven by feuds as successive members of the Piast dynasty jostled for control over the key provinces. Pomerania fell to Denmark, while Silesia began a long process of fragmentation, becoming increasingly Germanic.

In 1225 Duke Konrad of Mazovia, under threat from the heathen Prussians, Jacwingians and Lithuanians on his eastern border, invited the **Teutonic Knights**, a quasi-monastic German military order, to help him secure his frontiers. The knights duly based themselves in Chełmno, and by 1283 they had effectively eradicated the Prussians. Emerging as the principal military power in northern Europe, the knights built up a theocratic state defended by some of the most awesome castles ever built, ruthlessly turning on their former hosts in the process. They captured the great port of Gdańsk in 1308, renaming it Danzig and developing it into one of Europe's richest mercantile cities. At the same time, German peasants were encouraged to settle on the fertile agricultural land all along the Baltic. Poland was left cut off from the sea, with its trading routes severely weakened as a result.

If the Teutonic Knights brought nothing but disaster to the Polish nation, the effects of the **Tatar invasions** of 1241–42 were more mixed. Although the Poles were decisively defeated at the Battle of Legnica, the Tatars' crushing of the Kiev-based Russian empire paved the way for Polish expansion east into White and Red Ruthenia (the forerunners of Belarus and Ukraine), whose principalities were often linked to Poland by dynastic marriages. On the down side, the defeat spelt the beginning of the end for Silesia as part of Poland. It gradually split into eighteen tiny duchies under the control of Bohemia, then the most powerful part of the Holy Roman Empire.

It was only under the last Piast king, **Kazimierz the Great** (1333–70), that central political authority was firmly re-established in Poland. Kraków took on some aspects of its present appearance during his reign, being embellished with a series of magnificent buildings to substantiate its claim to be a great European capital. It was also made the seat of a university, the first in the country and before long one of the most prestigious on the continent. Kazimierz's achievements in domestic policy went far beyond the symbolic: he codified Poland's laws, created a unified administrative structure with a governor responsible for each province, and introduced a new silver currency.

With regard to Poland's frontiers, Kazimierz was a supreme pragmatist. He secured his borders with a line of castles and formally recognized Bohemia's control over Silesia in return for a renunciation of its claim to the Polish crown. More reluctantly, he accepted the existence of the independent state of the Teutonic Knights, even though this meant Poland was now landlocked. To compensate, he extended his territories east into Red Ruthenia and Podolia, which meant that, although the Catholic Church retained its prominent role, the country now had sizeable Eastern Orthodox and Armenian minorities.

Even more significant was Kazimierz's encouragement of **Jews**, who had been the victims of pogroms all over Europe, often being held responsible for the Black Death. A law of 1346 specifically protected them against persecution in Poland and was a major factor in Poland's centuries-long position as the home of the largest community of world Jewry.

The Jagiellonians

On Kazimierz's death, the crown passed to his nephew Louis of Anjou, king of Hungary, but this royal union was short-lived, as the Poles chose Louis' younger daughter **Jadwiga** to succeed him in 1384, while her sister ascended the Hungarian throne. This event was important for two reasons. First, it was an assertion of power on the part of the aristocracy and the beginnings of the move towards an elected monarchy. Second, it led soon afterwards to the most important and enduring alliance in Polish history – with **Lithuania**, whose grand duke, Jogaila (henceforth known to history by his Polish name, Władysław Jagiełło), married Jadwiga in 1386. Europe's last pagan nation, Lithuania had resisted the Teutonic Knights and developed into an expansionist state that now stretched from its Baltic homeland all the way to the Crimea.

After Jadwiga's death in 1399, Jagiełło reigned over the two nations alone for the next 45 years, founding the Jagiellonian dynasty – which was to remain in power until 1572 – with the offspring of his subsequent marriage. One of the first benefits of the alliance between Poland and Lithuania was a military strength capable of taking the offensive against the Teutonic Knights, and at the **Battle of Grunwald** in 1410, the order was defeated, beginning its long and slow decline. A more decisive breakthrough came as a result of the **Thirteen Years' War** of 1454–66. By the Treaty of Toruń, the knights' territory was partitioned: Danzig became an independent city-state, run by a merchant class of predominantly German, Dutch and Flemish origins, but accepting the Polish king as its nominal overlord; the remainder of the knights' heartlands around the Lower Wisła (Vistula) became subject to Poland under the name of Royal Prussia; and the order was left only with the eastern territory thereafter known as Ducal Prussia or East Prussia.

Towards the end of the fifteenth century, Poland and Lithuania began to face new dangers from the east. First to threaten were the Crimean Tatars, whose menace prompted the creation of the first Polish standing army. A far more serious threat – one which endured for several hundred years – came from the **Muscovite tsars**, the self-styled protectors of the Orthodox faith who aimed to "liberate" the Ruthenian principalities and rebuild the Russian empire. The Jagiellonians countered by building up their power in the west. The Bohemian crown was acquired by clever politicking in 1479 after the religious struggles of the Hussite Wars; that of Hungary followed in 1491. However, neither of these unions were able to last.

The Renaissance and Reformation

The spread of **Renaissance** ideas in Poland – greatly facilitated by the country's Church connections with Italy – was most visibly manifested in the number of Italianate buildings constructed throughout the country. Science and learning also prospered under native Polish practitioners such as Nicolaus Copernicus.

This period saw a collective muscle-flexing exercise by the Polish nobility (*szlachta*). In 1493, the parliament, or **Sejm**, was established, gaining the sole right to enact legislation in 1505 and gradually making itself an important check on monarchical power.

The **Reformation** had a far greater impact on Poland than is often admitted by Catholic patriots. Its most telling manifestation came in 1525 with the final collapse of the Teutonic Order when the grand master, Albrecht von Hohenzollern, decided to accept the new Lutheran doctrines. Their state was converted into a secular duchy under the Polish crown but with full internal autonomy – an arrangement which removed any lingering military strength from the order. Lutheranism also took a strong hold in Danzig and the German-dominated cities of Royal Prussia, while the more radical Calvinism won many converts among the Lithuanian nobility. Poland also became home to a number of refugee sects: along with the acceptance already extended to the Jewish and Orthodox faiths, this added up to a degree of **religious tolerance** unparalleled elsewhere in Europe.

The Republic of Nobles

Lacking an heir, the last of the Jagiellonians, **Sigismund August**, spent his final years trying to forge an alliance strong enough to withstand the ever-growing might of Moscow. The result of his negotiations was the 1569 **Union of Lublin**, whereby Poland and Lithuania were formally merged into the Commonwealth of the Two Nations. Lithuania, whose aristocracy was by now almost wholly Polish-speaking, lost many of its autonomous privileges, and its huge territories in the east were integrated more closely into the Polish state. In the same year the Sejm moved to **Warsaw**, a more central location for the capital of this new agglomeration; its capital status became official in 1596.

On the death of Sigismund August in 1572, the royal chancellor, Jan Zamoyski, presided over negotiations which led to the creation of the so-called **Republic of Nobles** – thenceforth kings were to be elected by an assembly of the entire nobility, from the great magnates down to the holders of tiny impoverished estates. On the one hand this was a major democratic advance, in that it enfranchised about ten percent of the population, by far the largest proportion of voters in any European country; but on the other hand it marked a strengthening of a feudalistic social system. **Capitalism**, then developing in other European countries, evolved only in those cities with a strong German or Jewish burgher class (predominantly in Royal Prussia), which remained isolated from the main power structures of Polish society.

In 1573, the Frenchman **Henri Valois** was chosen as the first elected monarch and, as was the case with all his successors, was forced to sign a document that reduced him to a managerial servant of the nobility. The nobles also insisted on their Right of Resistance, a licence to overthrow a king who had fallen from favour. The Sejm had to be convened at two-yearly intervals, and all royal taxes, declarations of war and foreign treaties were subject to ratification by the nobles.

Although candidates for the monarchy had to subscribe to Catholicism, the religious freedom that already existed was underpinned by the **Compact of Warsaw** of 1573, guaranteeing the constitutional equality of all religions. However, the Counter-Reformation left only a few Protestant strongholds in Poland: a large section of the aristocracy was reconverted, while others who had recently switched from Orthodoxy to Calvinism were persuaded to change allegiance once more. The Orthodox Church was further weakened by the schism of 1596, leading to the creation of the Uniate Church, which recognized the authority of Rome. Thus Poland gradually became a fervently Catholic nation once more.

The Republic of Nobles achieved some of its most spectacular successes early on, particularly under the second elected king, the Transylvanian prince Stefan Bathory who, having carried out a thorough reform of the army, waged a brilliant campaign against the Russians between 1579 and 1582, neutralizing this particular threat to Poland's eastern borders for some time to come.

The Waza dynasty and its aftermath

The foreign policy of the next three elected monarchs, all members of the Swedish Waza dynasty, was less fortunate. **Sigismund August Waza**, the first of the trio, was a Catholic bigot who soon came into conflict with the almost exclusively Protestant population of his native land and was deposed from the Swedish throne in 1604. Though his ham-fistedness meant that Poland now had a new (and increasingly powerful) enemy, he continued as the Polish king for the next 28 years, having fought off a three-year-long internal rebellion.

In 1618, Ducal Prussia was inherited by the elector of Brandenburg, **John Sigismund von Hohenzollern**, who set about weakening Poland's hold on the Baltic seaboard. A couple of decades later, the Hohenzollerns inherited much of Pomerania as well, with another section being acquired by Sweden. Poland managed to remain neutral in the calamitous series of religious and dynastic conflicts known as the **Thirty Years' War**, from which Sweden emerged as Europe's leading military power.

The reign of the third of the Wazas, **Jan Kazimierz**, saw Poland's fortunes plummet. In 1648, the year of his election, the Cossacks revolted in the Ukraine, eventually allying themselves with the Russian army, which conquered eastern Poland as far as Lwów. This diversion inspired the Swedes to launch an invasion of their own, known in Polish history as the **Swedish Deluge** ("Potop"), and they soon took control of the remainder of the country. A heroic fightback was mounted, ending in stalemate in 1660 with the Treaty of Oliwa, in which Poland recovered all its former territories except for Livonia. Three years earlier, the Hohenzollerns had wrested Ducal Prussia from the last vestiges of Polish control, merging it with their other territories to form the state of Brandenburg-Prussia (later shortened to **Prussia**).

As well as the territorial losses suffered, these wars had seen Poland's population reduced to four million, less than half its previous total. A further crucial development of this period had been the first use in 1652 of the liberum veto, whereby a single vote in the Sejm was enough to stall any piece of legislation. Once established, the practice soon became widespread in the protection of petty interests, and Poland found itself on the slippery slope towards **ungovernability**. This process was hastened when it was discovered that one dissenter was constitutionally empowered to object not only to any particular measure, but to dissolve the Sejm itself – and in the process repeal all the legislation it had passed. Meanwhile, the minor aristocracy gradually found themselves squeezed out of power, as a group of a hundred or so great magnates gradually established a stranglehold.

Jan Sobieski

Before repeated use of the liberum veto led to the final collapse of political authority, Poland had what was arguably its greatest moment of glory in international power politics – a consequence of the Ottoman Turks' attempt to advance from the Balkans into central Europe. They were eventually beaten back by the Poles, under the command of **Jan Sobieski**, at the **Battle of Chocim** (in southwestern Ukraine) in 1673 – as a reward for which Sobieski was elected king the following year. In 1683 he was responsible for the successful defence of Vienna, which marked the final repulse of the Turks from western Europe.

However, Poland was to pay a heavy price for the heroism of Sobieski, who had concentrated on the **Turkish campaign** to the exclusion of all other issues. His relief of Vienna exhausted Poland's military capacity while enabling Austria to recover as an imperial power; it also greatly helped the rise of the predatory state of Prussia, which he had intended to keep firmly in check. His neglect of domestic policy led to the liberum veto being used with impunity, while Poland and Lithuania grew apart as the nobility of the latter engaged in a civil war.

The decline of Poland

Known as "Augustus the Strong", owing to his fathering of more than three hundred children, Sobieski's successor, **Augustus Wettin**, was in fact a weak ruler, unable to shake off his debts to the Russians who had secured his election. In 1701, Friedrich III of Brandenburg-Prussia openly defied him by declaring Ducal Prussia's right to be regarded as a kingdom, having himself crowned in Königsberg. From then on, the Hohenzollerns plotted to link their territories by ousting Poland from the Baltic; in this they were aided by the acquisition of most of the rest of Pomerania in 1720. Augustus's lack of talent for power politics was even more evident in his dealings with Sweden, against whom he launched a war for control of Livonia. The conflict showed the calamitous decline of Poland's military standing, and the victorious Swedes deposed Augustus in 1704, securing the election of their own favoured candidate, **Stanisław Leszczyński**, in his place.

Augustus was reinstated in 1710, courtesy of the Russians, who reduced Poland to the role of a client state in the process. The **Silent Sejm** of 1717, which guaranteed the existing constitution, marked the end of effective parliamentary life. The Russians never hesitated to impose their authority, cynically upholding the Republic of Nobles as a means of ensuring that the liberal ideals of the Age of Reason could never take root in Poland and that the country remained a buffer against the great powers of western Europe. When Leszczyński won the election to succeed Augustus the Strong in 1733, they intervened immediately to have him replaced by the deceased king's son, who proved to be an even more inept custodian of Polish interests than his father.

In 1740, Frederick the Great launched the **Silesian Wars**, which ended in 1763 with Prussia in control of all but a small part of the province. As a result, Prussia gained control over such parts of Poland's foreign trade as were not subject to Russia. The long-cherished ambition to acquire Royal Prussia and thus achieve uninterrupted control over the southern coast of the Baltic was Frederick's next objective.

When the younger Augustus Wettin died in 1763, the Russians again intervened to ensure the election of **Stanisław-August Poniatowski**, the former lover of their empress, Catherine the Great. However, Poniatowski proved an unwilling stooge, even espousing the cause of reform. Russian support of the Orthodox minority in Poland led to a growth of Catholic-inspired nationalism, and by obstructing the most moderately liberal measures, Russian policy led to an outbreak of revolts. By sending armies to crush these, they endangered the delicate balance of power in Eastern Europe.

The Partitions

Russia's Polish policy was finally rendered impotent by the revolt of the **Confederacy of Bar** between 1768 and 1772. A heavy-handed crackdown on these reformers would certainly have led to war with Prussia, probably in alliance with Austria; doing nothing would have allowed the Poles to reassert their national independence. As a compromise, the Russians decided to support a Prussian plan for the **Partition of Poland**. By a treaty of 1772, Poland lost almost thirty percent of its territory. White Ruthenia's eastern sectors were ceded to Russia, while Austria received Red Ruthenia plus Małopolska south of the Wisła – a province subsequently rechristened Galicia. The Prussians gained the smallest share of the carve-up in the form of most of Royal Prussia, but this was strategically and economically the most significant.

Stung by this, the Poles embarked on a radical programme of reform, including the partial emancipation of serfs and the encouragement of immigration from the three empires which had undertaken the Partition. In 1791, Poland was given the first codified **constitution** in Europe since classical antiquity and the second in the modern world, after the United States. It introduced the concept of a people's sovereignty, this time including the bourgeoisie, and adopted a separation of powers between executive, legislature and judiciary, with government by a cabinet responsible to the Sejm.

This was all too much for the Russians, who, buying off the Prussians with the promise of Danzig, invaded Poland. Despite a tenacious resistance under **Tadeusz Kościuszko**, erstwhile hero of the American War of Independence, the Poles were defeated the following year. By the **Second Partition** of 1793, the constitution was annulled; the Russians annexed the remaining parts of White and Red Ruthenia, with the Prussians gaining Wielkopolska, and parts of Mazuria and Toruń in addition to the star prize of Danzig.

In 1794, Kościuszko launched a national insurrection, achieving a stunning victory over the Russians at the **Battle of Racławice** with a militia largely composed of peasants armed with scythes. However, the rebellion was put down, Poniatowski forced to abdicate, and Poland wiped off the map by the **Third Partition** of 1795. This gave all lands east of the Bug and Niemen rivers to Russia, the remainder of Małopolska to Austria, and the rest of the country, including Warsaw, to Prussia. By an additional treaty of 1797, the partitioning powers agreed to abolish the very name of Poland.

Napoleon and the Congress of Vienna

Revolutionary France was naturally the country that Polish patriots looked to in their struggle to regain national independence, and Paris became the headquarters for a series of exiles and conspiratorial groups. Hopes eventually crystallized around **Napoleon Bonaparte**, who assumed power in 1799, but when three Polish legions were raised as part of the French army, Kościuszko declined to command them, regarding Napoleon as a megalomaniac who would use the Poles for his own ends.

Initially, these fears seemed unfounded: French victories over Prussia led to the creation of the **Duchy of Warsaw** in 1807 out of Polish territory annexed by the Prussians. Although no more than a buffer state, this seemed an important first step in the recreation of Poland and encouraged the hitherto uncommitted **Józef Poniatowski**, nephew of the last king and one of the most brilliant military commanders of the day, to throw in his lot with the French dictator. As a result of his successes in Napoleon's Austrian campaign of 1809, part of Galicia was ceded to the Duchy of Warsaw.

Poniatowski again played a key role in the events of 1812, which Napoleon dubbed his **"Polish War"** and which restored the historic border of Poland-Lithuania with Russia. The failure of the advance on Moscow, leading to a humiliating retreat, was thus as disastrous for Poland as for France. Cornered by the Prussians and Russians near Leipzig, Poniatowski refused to surrender, preferring to lead his troops to a heroic, suicidal defeat. The choice faced by Poniatowski encapsulated the nation's hopeless plight, and his act of self-sacrifice was to serve as a symbol to Polish patriots for the rest of the century.

The **Congress of Vienna** of 1814–15, set up to organize post-Napoleonic Europe, decided against the re-establishment of an independent Poland, mainly because this was opposed by the Russians. Instead, the main part of the Duchy of Warsaw was renamed the **Congress Kingdom** and placed under the dominion of the Russian tsar. The Poznań area was detached to form the Grand Duchy of Posen, in reality no more than a dependency of Prussia. Austria was allowed to keep most of Galicia, which was governed from Lwów (renamed Lemberg). After much deliberation, it was decided to make Kraków a city-state and "symbolic capital" of the vanished nation.

The struggle against the Partitions

The most liberal part of the Russian Empire, the Congress Kingdom, enjoyed a period of relative prosperity under the governorship of **Adam Czartoryski**, preserving its own parliament, administration, educational system and army. However, this cosy arrangement was disrupted by the arch-autocrat **Nicholas I**, who became tsar in 1825 and quickly imposed his policies on Poland. An attempted **insurrection** in November 1830, centred on a botched assassination of the tsar's brother, provoked a Russian invasion. Initially, the Polish army fared well, but it was handicapped by political divisions (notably over whether the serfs should be emancipated) and lack of foreign support, despite the supposed guarantees provided by the Vienna settlement. By the end of the following year, the Poles had been defeated; their constitution was suspended and a reign of repression began. These events led many to abandon all nationalist hopes; the first great wave of Polish **emigration**, principally to America, began.

An attempted insurrection against the Austrians in 1846 also backfired, leading to the end of Kraków's independence with its reincorporation into Galicia. This setback was a factor in Poland's failure to play an active role in the European-wide **revolutions** of 1848–49, though by this time the country's plight had attracted the sympathy of the emergent socialist movements. Karl Marx and Friedrich Engels went so far as to declare that Polish liberation should be the single most important immediate objective of the workers' movement. The last major uprising, against the Russians in 1863–64, attracted the support of Lithuanians and Galicians but was hopelessly limited by Poland's lack of a regular army. Its failure led to the abolition of the Congress Kingdom and its formal incorporation into Russia as the province of "Vistulaland". However, it was immediately followed by the **emancipation of the serfs**, granted on more favourable terms than in any other part of the tsarist empire – in order to cause maximum ill-feeling between the Polish nobility and peasantry.

Following the crushing of the 1863–64 rebellion, the **Russian sector** of Poland entered a period of quiet stability, with the abolition of internal tariffs opening up the vast Russian market to Polish goods. For the next half-century, Polish patriots, wherever they lived, were concerned less with trying to win independence than with keeping a distinctive culture alive. In this they were handicapped by the fact that this was an era of great empires, each with many subjugated minorities whose interests often conflicted: Poles found themselves variously up against the aspirations of Lithuanians, Ukrainians and Czechs. They had the greatest success in Galicia, because they were the second largest ethnic group in the **Habsburg Empire**, and because the Habsburgs had a more lax attitude towards the diversity of their subjects. The province was given powers of self-government and, although economically backward and ruled by a reactionary upper class, flourished once more as a centre of learning and the arts.

Altogether different was the situation in **Prussia**, the most efficiently repressive of the three partitioning powers. It had closely followed the British lead in forging a modern industrial society, and Poles made up a large percentage of the workforce in some of its technologically most advanced areas, notably the rich minefields of Upper Silesia. The Prussians, having ousted the Austrians from their centuries-long domination of German affairs, proceeded to exclude their rivals altogether from the **united Germany** they created by 1871, which they attempted to mould in their own Protestant and militaristic tradition.

For the Poles living under the Prussian yoke, the price to be paid for their relative prosperity was a severe clampdown on their culture, seen at its most extreme in the **Kulturkampf**, whose main aim was to crush the power of the Catholic Church, with a secondary intention of establishing the unchallenged supremacy of the German language in the new nation's education system. It misfired badly in Poland, giving the clergy the opportunity to whip up support for their own fervently nationalistic brand of Catholicism.

Meanwhile, an upturn in political life came with the establishment, in response to internal pressure, of representative assemblies in Berlin, Vienna and St Petersburg. Towards the end of the century, this led to the formation of various new Polish **political parties** and movements, the most important of which were the Polish Socialist Party (PPS), active mainly in the cities of Russian Poland; the Nationalist League, whose power base was in the peripheral provinces; the Peasant Movement of Galicia; and the Christian Democrats, a dominant force among the Silesian Catholics.

The resurrection of Poland

World War I smashed the might of the Russian, German and Austrian empires and allowed Poland to rise from the dead. Desperate to rally Poles to their cause, both alliances in the conflict made increasingly tempting offers: as early as August 1914 the Russians proposed a Poland with full rights of self-government, including language, religion and government, albeit one still ultimately subject to the tsar.

When the German and Austrian armies overran Russian-occupied Poland in 1916, they felt obliged to trump this offer, promising to set up a Polish kingdom once the war was over. The foundations of this were laid immediately, with the institution of an interim administration – known as the **Regency Council** – and the official restoration of the Polish language. Even though carried out for cynical reasons, these initial steps were of crucial importance to the relaunch of a fully independent Poland, a notion which had soon gained the support of the US President Woodrow Wilson and of the new Bolshevik government in Moscow.

Meanwhile, two bitter rivals emerged as the leading contenders for leadership of the Polish nation. **Józef Piłsudski**, an impoverished noble from Lithuania and founding member of the PPS, had long championed a military solution to Poland's problems. During the war, his legions fought for the Germans, assuming that the defeat of the Russians would allow him to create the new Polish state on his own terms. In this, he favoured a return to the great tradition of ethnic and religious diversity of centuries past. **Roman Dmowski**, leader of the Nationalist League, represented the ambitions of the new middle class and had a vision of a purely Polish and staunchly Catholic future, in which the Jews would, as far as possible, be excluded. He opted to work for independence by exclusively political means, in the hope that victory over Germany would lead the Western allies to set up a Polish state under his leadership.

In the event, Piłsudski came out on top: the Germans, having held him in internment for well over a year, released him the day before the armistice of November 11, 1918, allowing him to take command of the Regency Council. He was sworn in as head of state three days later. Dmowski had to accept the consolation prize of head delegate to the Paris Peace Conference, though his associate, the concert pianist **Ignacy Jan Paderewski**, became the country's first prime minister.

Poland redefined

The new Poland lacked a defined territory. Initially, it consisted of the German and Austrian zones of occupation, centred on Warsaw and Lublin, plus Western Galicia. Wielkopolska was added a month later, following a revolt against the German garrison in Poznań, but the precise frontiers were only established during the following three years on an ad hoc basis. Yet, though the Paris Conference played only a minor role in all this, it did take the key decision to give the country access to the sea by means of the **Polish Corridor**, a strip of land cut through the old Royal Prussia, which meant that East Prussia was left cut off from the rest of Germany. Despite intense lobbying, it was decided to exclude **Danzig** from the corridor, on the grounds that its population was overwhelmingly German; instead, it reverted to its former tradition as a city-state – an unsatisfactory compromise that was later to have tragic consequences.

The **Polish–Soviet War** of 1919–20 was the most significant of the conflicts that crucially determined the country's borders. Realizing that the Bolsheviks would want to spread their revolution to Poland and then to the industrialized West, Piłsudski aimed to create a grouping of independent nation-states stretching from Finland to Georgia to halt this new expansionist Russian empire. Taking advantage of the civil war between the Soviet "Reds" and the counter-revolutionary "Whites", his army marched deep into Belarus and the Ukraine. He was subsequently beaten back to Warsaw, but skillfully regrouped his forces to pull off a crushing victory and pursue the Russians eastwards, regaining a sizeable chunk of the old Polish-Lithuanian commonwealth's eastern territories, an acquisition confirmed by the **Treaty of Riga** in 1921.

At the very end of the war, Piłsudski seized his home city of **Wilno** (Vilnius), which had a mixed Polish and Jewish population, but was claimed by the Lithuanians on the grounds that it had been their medieval capital. Other border issues were settled by plebiscites organized by the **League of Nations**, the new international body set up to resolve such matters. In the most significant of these, Germany and Poland competed for Upper Silesia. The Germans won, but the margin was so narrow that the League felt that the distribution of votes justified the partition of the province. Poland gained most of the Katowice conurbation, thus ensuring that the country gained a solid industrial base.

The interwar years

The fragility of the new state's political institutions became obvious when Piłsudski refused to stand in the 1922 presidential elections on the grounds that the office was insufficiently powerful. Worse, the victor, **Gabriel Narutowicz**, was hounded by the Nationalists for having won as a result of votes cast by "non-Poles", and assassinated soon afterwards. For the next few years, Poland was governed by a series of weak governments presiding over hyperinflation, feeble attempts at agrarian reform and a contemptuous army officer class.

In May 1926, Piłsudski staged a military coup, ushering in the so-called **Sanacja** regime, named after a slogan proposing a return to political "health". Piłsudski functioned as the state's commander-in-chief until his death in 1935, though he held no formal office after an initial two-year stint as prime minister. Parliamentary life continued, but opposition was emasculated by the creation of the so-called **Non-Party Bloc for Co-operation with the Government**, and disaffected groups were brought to heel by force if necessary.

Having a country led by **Stalin** on one frontier was bad enough; but when **Hitler** seized power in Germany in 1933, Poland became a sitting target for two ruthless dictators. Hitler had always been open about his ambition of wiping Poland off the map again, regarding the Slavs as a race who were fit for no higher role than to be slaves of the Aryans. He also wanted to unite all ethnic Germans under his rule: a foreign policy objective that was quickly put into effect by his annexation of Austria in March 1938 and of parts of Czechoslovakia – with British and French connivance – in September of the same year. As Hitler's attentions turned towards Poland, his foreign minister Joachim von Ribbentrop and his Soviet counterpart Vyacheslav Molotov concluded the notorious **Nazi–Soviet Pact** in August 1939, which allowed either side to pursue any aggressive designs without the interference of the other. It also included a secret clause which agreed on a full partition of Poland along the lines of the Narew, Wisła and San rivers.

World War II

On September 1, 1939, Hitler invaded Poland, beginning by annexing the free city of Danzig, thereby precipitating **World War II**. The Poles fought with great courage, inflicting heavy casualties, but were numerically and technologically in a hopeless position. On September 17, the Soviets invaded the eastern part of the country, claiming the share-out agreed by the Nazi–Soviet Pact. The Allies, who had guaranteed to come to Poland's defence, initially failed to do so, and by the end of the first week in October the country had capitulated. A government-in-exile was established in London under **Władysław Sikorski**.

Millions of civilians – including virtually every Jew in Poland – were to be slaughtered in the **Nazi concentration camps** that were soon being set up in the occupied territory. As this was going on, Soviet prisoners were being transported east to the Gulag, while wholesale murders of the potentially troublesome elements in Polish society were being carried out, such as the **massacre of Katyń**, where 4500 officers were shot.

Nazi control of western Poland entailed further territorial dismemberment. Some parts of the country were simply swallowed up by the Reich, with north-western districts forming part of the newly created Reichgau of Danzig-West Prussia, and west-central territories around Poznań being absorbed into the Warthegau. Everything else – Warsaw and Kraków included – was placed under a German-controlled administration known as the **Gouvernement Generale**, an ad hoc structure designed to exploit the economic and labour potential of Poland while the war lasted. Poles everywhere were subjected to dislocation and hardship. Those living in the Warthegau were forced to emigrate to the Gouvernement Generale in an attempt to Germanize the province; while those in Danzig-West Prussia fared a bit better, being allowed to stay where they were providing they adopted German names and passports.

The Nazi invasion of the Soviet Union in June 1941 prompted Stalin to make an alliance with Sikorski, ushering in a period of uneasy cooperation between Soviet forces and the Polish resistance, which was led by the **Home Army** (AK). The Red Army's victory at Stalingrad in 1943 marked the beginning of the end for the Nazis, but it enabled Stalin to backtrack on promises made to the Polish government-in-exile. At the **Tehran Conference** in November he came to an arrangement with Britain and America with regard to future spheres of influence in Europe, making it almost inevitable that postwar Poland would be forced into the Soviet camp. He also insisted that the Soviet Union would retain the territories it had annexed in 1939. Allied support for this was obtained by reference to the current border's virtual coincidence with the so-called Curzon Line, which had been drawn up by a former British Foreign Secretary in 1920 in an unsuccessful attempt at mediation in the Polish–Soviet War.

During the **liberation of Poland** in 1944, any possibility of reasserting genuine Polish control depended on the outcome of the uprising in Warsaw against the Nazi occupiers. On July 31, with the Soviets poised on the outskirts of the city, the Home Army was forced to act. The Red Army lay in wait during

POLAND 1938

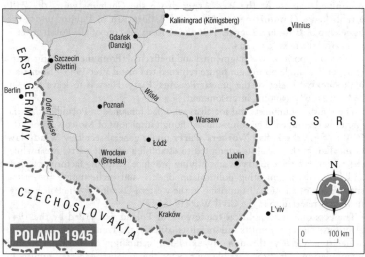

POLAND 1945

the ensuing bloodbath. When the insurgents were finally defeated at the beginning of October, Hitler ordered that the city be razed before leaving the ruins to the Red Army. In early 1945, as the Soviets pushed on through Poland, the Nazis set up last-ditch strongholds in Silesia, but these were overrun by the time of the final armistice in April.

No country suffered so much from World War II as Poland. In all, around 25 percent of the population died, and the whole country lay devastated. Moreover, although the Allies had originally gone to war on its behalf, it found itself reduced in size and **shifted west** across the map of Europe by some 200 kilometres, with its western frontier fixed at the lines of the Odra and Nysa rivers. Stalin had in effect achieved his twin aims of moving his frontiers and his sphere of influence well to the west.

The losses in the east – including Lwów and Wilno, both great centres of Polish culture – were painful, and involved the transfer of millions of people across the country in the following two years. There were compensations, however: Pomerania and the industrially valuable Silesia were restored after a gap of some seven centuries; and the much-coveted city of Danzig, which had been detached since its seizure by the Teutonic Knights, was also returned – and, as Gdańsk, was later to play a major role in postwar Polish history.

The rise of Polish communism

The Polish communists took power, not through popular revolution, as their Soviet counterparts had – nor even with significant public support, as the Czech communists had – but through the military and political dictate of an occupying force. Control was seized by the **ZPP** (Union of Polish Patriots), an organization formed by Stalin in 1943 from Polish exiles and Russian placemen with polonized names. As the Red Army drove the Germans west, the ZPP established a **Committee for National Liberation** in Lublin, under the leadership of **Bolesław Bierut**. This was to form the core of the Polish government over the next few years.

Political opposition was fragmented and ineffectual. From the government-in-exile, only a single prominent figure returned to Poland after 1945 – **Stanisław Mikołajczyk**, leader of the prewar Peasants' Party. He was to leave again in 1947, narrowly avoiding imprisonment.

The Polish communists and socialists who had remained in Poland during the war now regrouped. The communists, though suspicious of Moscow, joined the ZPP to form the **Polish Workers' Party** under general secretary **Władysław Gomułka**, as the socialists attempted to establish a separate party. Meanwhile, the Soviets ran the country as an outlying province, stripping factories of plant and materials, intimidating political opponents, and orchestrating the brutal suppression of a nationalist uprising in the western Ukraine by the Polish army, in what is referred to as the **Civil War** (1945–47).

The economic and political framework of Poland was sealed by the 1947 elections. The communists and socialists, allied as the **Democratic Bloc**, won a decisive victory through an extended campaign of harassment and manipulation. After the forcible merger of the socialists and communists in 1948 as the **PZPR** (Polish United Workers' Party), it only remained for the external pressures of the emerging **Cold War** to lock Poland completely into the Soviet sphere of influence and model of economic and political development. In the authoritarian climate of the era, even Polish communists were considered suspect if they failed to display unswerving loyalty to Stalin, and in 1951 Gomułka was deposed and arrested for showing too much independence of thought.

The birth of the PRL

In 1952 a new Constitution enshrined the leading role of the **PZPR** in every aspect of Polish society, designating the country as the Polish People's Republic or Polska Rzeczpospolita Ludowa – nowadays remembered by its acronym, **PRL**. Further, while the trappings of elections and a two-house parliament were retained, the other parties – the Democratic Party (SD) and the reconstituted Peasants' Party (ZSL) – were under the effective political control of the PZPR. Real power lay with the Politburo, Central Committee and the newly formed economic and administrative bureaucracies. Only the **Catholic Church**, although harassed and extensively monitored by the authorities, retained a degree of independence as a political and cultural organization – its defiance characterized by the primate, **Cardinal Wyszyński**, arrested in 1953 for "anti-state" activities and imprisoned for three years.

Nationalization continued throughout this period, accelerated through the **Three Year Plan** (1947–50) and the **Six Year Plan** (1950–56). Although the former retained some emphasis on the role of private ownership, the thrust of both was towards the collectivization of agriculture and the creation of a heavy industrial base. Collectivization proved impossible in the absence of the sort of force used by Stalin against the Kulaks: the programme slowed in the mid-1950s and was tacitly abandoned thereafter. Industrially the plans proved more successful: major iron and steel industries were established, mining extensively exploited in Silesia and an entire **shipbuilding** industry developed along the Baltic coast – most notably in Gdańsk. There were, inevitably, costs: standards of living remained almost static, food was scarce, work was long, hard and often dangerous, and unrestrained industrialization resulted in terrible pollution and despoilation of the land. Perhaps the most significant achievement of the period was the creation of an urban industrial working class for the first time in Polish history. Paradoxically, these very people proved to be the backbone of almost every political struggle against the Party in the following decades.

1956 – the Polish October

In Poland, as in Hungary, 1956 saw the first major political crisis of the communist era. Faction and dissension were already rife, with intellectuals calling for fundamental changes, splits within the Party leadership and increasing popular disenchantment with the excesses of Stalinism. In February 1956 **Khrushchev** made his famous "secret" speech to the Twentieth Congress of the Soviet Communist Party, denouncing Stalin and his crimes; for **Bolesław Bierut**, president and first secretary of the PZPR, as for other Eastern European leaders, the speech was a bombshell, unmasking the lie of the absolute correctness of Stalin's every act. Reform-minded members of the Party in Poland were the first to make copies available in the West, but for Bierut and the hardline leadership it was the end: Bierut died directly after the Congress, many suspecting that he had committed suicide.

In June, workers in Poznań took to the streets over working conditions and wages. The **protest** rapidly developed into a major confrontation with the authorities, and in the ensuing street battles with the army and security police up to eighty people were killed and many hundreds of others wounded. Initial government insistence that "imperialist agents" had instigated the troubles gave way to an admission that some of the workers' grievances were justified and that the Party would try to remedy them.

The **Poznań riots** further divided an alarmed and weakened Party. Hardliners pushed for Defence Minister General Rokossowski to take over the leadership, but it was **Gomułka**, with his earnest promises of reform, who carried the day. In October, the Party plenum elected Gomułka as the new leader, without consulting Moscow. An enraged Khrushchev flew to Warsaw to demand an explanation of this unprecedented flouting of the Kremlin's authority. East German, Czech and Soviet troops were mobilized along Poland's borders, in response to which Polish security forces prepared to defend the capital. Poland held its breath as Gomułka and Khrushchev engaged in heated debate over the crisis. In the end, Gomułka assured Khrushchev that Poland would remain a loyal ally and maintain the essentials of communist rule. Khrushchev returned to Moscow, Soviet troops withdrew, and four days later Gomułka addressed a huge crowd in Warsaw as a national hero. The **Soviet invasion of Hungary** to crush the national uprising there in early November 1956 provided a clear reminder to Poles of how close they had come to disaster.

The **Polish October**, as it came to be known, raised high hopes of a new order, which initially seemed justified. Censorship was relaxed, Cardinal Wyszyński was released and state harassment of the Church and control over the economy eased. A cultural thaw encouraged an explosion of creativity in art and theatre – much of it wildly experimental – and opened the doors to "decadent" Western preoccupations such as jazz and rock and roll. But the impetus for political reform quickly faded, and the 1960s saw a progressive return to centralized planning, a stagnant economy and sporadic attempts to reassert some measure of control over an increasingly disaffected populace.

1970–79: from Gomułka to Gierek

The final days of the Gomułka years were marked by a contrast between triumph in foreign policy and the harsh imposition of economic constraint. Pursuing his policy of Ostpolitik, West German chancellor **Willy Brandt** visited Poland in December 1970 to sign the **Warsaw Treaty**, recognizing Poland's current borders and opening full diplomatic relations. In an emphatic symbolic gesture, Brandt knelt in penance at the monument to those killed in the Warsaw Ghetto Uprising.

A few days later, on December 12, huge **food price rises** were announced, provoking a simmering discontent that was to break out in strikes and demonstrations along the Baltic coast, centring on Gdańsk. When troops fired on demonstrators, killing many, the protests spread like wildfire, to the point of open insurrection (Gomułka's defence minister, **Wojciech Jaruzelski**, was to be put on trial for the killings some twenty years later). A traumatized Central Committee met five days before Christmas, hurriedly bundling Gomułka into retirement and replacing him as first secretary with **Edward Gierek**, a member of the Party's reformist faction in the 1960s. Price rises were frozen and wage increases promised, but despite a Christmas calm, strikes broke out throughout January 1971, with demands for free trade unions and a free press accompanying the more usual economic demands. Peace was only restored when Gierek and Jaruzelski went to the Gdańsk shipyards by taxi to argue their case and admit their errors to the strikers.

The Gierek period marked out an alternative route to social stability. Given access to Western financial markets by Brandt's reconciliation, the Gierek government borrowed heavily throughout the early 1970s. Food became cheaper and more plentiful as internal subsidies were matched by purchases from the West and the Soviet Union. Standards of living rose and a wider range of **consumer goods** became available. However, the international economic recession and oil crises of the mid-Seventies destroyed the Polish boom at a stroke. Debts became impossible to service, new loans harder to obtain, and it became apparent that earlier borrowing had been squandered in unsustainable rises in consumption or wasted in large-scale projects of limited economic value.

By 1976 the wheel had turned full circle. The government announced food price rises of almost treble the magnitude of those proposed in the early Seventies. This time the ensuing **strikes** were firmly repressed and many activists imprisoned. In response to the imprisonment of strikers, the **KOR** (Committee for the Defence of Workers) was formed. Comprising dissident intellectuals, it was to provide not only valuable publicity and support for the opposition through Western contacts, but also new channels of **political communication** through underground samizdat publications, plus a degree of strategic sophistication that the spontaneous uprisings had so far lacked.

Perhaps even more decisive was the election of Karol Wojtyła, archbishop of Kraków, as **Pope John Paul II** in 1978. A fierce opponent of the communist regime, he visited Poland in 1979 and was met by the greatest public gatherings that Poland had ever seen. For the Polish people he became a symbol of Polish cultural identity and international influence, and his visit provided a public demonstration of their potential power.

1980–89: Solidarity

Gierek's announcement of one hundred percent price rises on foodstuffs in July 1980 led to more strikes, centring on the **Gdańsk shipyards**. Attempts by the authorities to have a crane operator, Anna Walentynowicz, dismissed for political agitation intensified the unrest. Led by a shipyard electrician, **Lech Wałęsa**, the strikers occupied the yards and were joined by a hastily convened group of opposition intellectuals and activists, including future prime minister **Tadeusz Mazowiecki**. Together they formulated a series of demands – the **Twenty-one Points** – that were to serve not only as the principal political concerns of the Polish opposition, but also as an intellectual template for every other oppositional movement in Eastern Europe.

Demands for consultation over the economic crisis, the freeing of political prisoners, freedom of the press, the right to strike, free trade unions and televised Catholic Mass were drawn up, along with demands for higher wages and an end to Party privileges. Yet the lessons of Hungary in 1956 and Czechoslovakia in 1968 had been learnt, and the opposition was careful to reiterate that they "intended neither to threaten the foundations of the Socialist Republic in our country, nor its position in international relations".

The Party caved in, after protracted negotiations, signing the historic **Gdańsk Agreements** in August 1980, after which free trade unions, covering over 75 percent of Poland's 12.5 million workforce, were formed across the country, under the name Solidarność – **Solidarity**. Gierek and his supporters were swept from office by the Party in September 1980, but the limits of Solidarity's power were signalled by an unscheduled Warsaw Pact meeting later in the year. Other Eastern European communist leaders perceptively argued that Solidarity's success would threaten not only their Polish counterparts' political futures, but their own as well. Accordingly, Soviet and Warsaw Pact units were mobilized along Poland's borders. The Poles closed ranks: the Party reaffirmed its Leninist purity, while Solidarity and the Church publicly emphasized their moderation.

Throughout 1981 deadlock ensued while the economic crisis gathered pace. Solidarity, lacking any positive control over the economy, was only capable of bringing it to a halt, and repeatedly showed itself able to do so. **General Jaruzelski** took control of the Party in July 1981 and, in the face of threats of a general strike, continued to negotiate with Solidarity leaders, but refused to relinquish any power. A wave of strikes in late October 1981 were met by the imposition of **martial law** on December 12: occupations and strikes were broken up by troops, Solidarity banned, civil liberties suspended and union leaders arrested. However, these measures solved nothing fundamental, and in the face of creative and determined resistance from the now underground Solidarity movement, still actively supported by large segments of the populace, martial law was lifted in the wake of Pope John Paul II's second visit to his home country in 1983.

The period 1984 to 1988 was marked by a final attempt by the Jaruzelski government to dig Poland out of its **economic crisis**. The country's debt had risen to an astronomical $39 billion, wages had slumped, and production was hampered by endemic labour unrest, the cutting edge of what throughout the 1980s remained Eastern Europe's most organized and broadly based opposition movement. In 1987, Jaruzelski submitted the government's programme of price rises and promised democratization to a referendum. The government lost, the real message of the vote being a rejection not merely of the programme but of the notion that the Party could lead Poland out of its crisis.

Jaruzelski finally acknowledged defeat after a devastating wave of strikes in 1988 and called for a "courageous turnaround" by the Party, accepting the need for talks with Solidarity and the prospect of real **power sharing** – an option of political capitulation only made possible by the election of Mikhail Gorbachev as secretary general in the Kremlin.

1989–90: the new Poland

The **round-table talks** ran from February to April 1989, government representatives ultimately agreeing to the opposition's demands for the legalization of Solidarity, the establishment of an independent press and the promise of what were termed "semi-free" elections. All hundred seats of a reconstituted upper chamber, the Senate, were to be freely contested; while 65 percent of seats in the lower house, the Sejm, were to be reserved for the PZPR and its allied parties, with the rest openly contested.

The communists suffered a humiliating defeat in the elections of 1989, with Solidarity winning almost every seat it contested. Thus, while the numerical balance of the lower chamber remained with the PZPR, the unthinkable became possible: a Solidarity-led government. The parties that had been allied to the

PZPR broke with their communist overlords and voted to establish journalist **Tadeusz Mazowiecki** as prime minister in August 1989, installing the first non-communist government in Eastern Europe since World War II. Subsequently the PZPR disintegrated, voting to dissolve itself in January 1990.

President Wałęsa and the first free elections

After a long period away from the political limelight, Lech Wałęsa re-emerged to win the presidential elections of 1990, promising a faster pace of reform and the removal of the privileges of the communist elite. In January 1991 he appointed business-oriented liberal **Jan Krzysztof Bielecki** as prime minister. Bielecki's hard-headed finance minister Leszek Balcerowicz embarked on a tough austerity programme, with steadily rising prices, rocketing unemployment and continued government spending cuts. These policies won the confidence of Western financial institutions, resulting in a landmark agreement with the International Monetary Fund (IMF) about the reduction of Poland's $33 billion debt.

Elections – the first fully free ones since World War II – were held in October 1991. A spectacular array of parties (nearly seventy in total) took part, including everyone from national minorities like the Silesian Germans to the joke Beer Lovers' Party. As a result a total of 29 parties entered the new Sejm, with the highest scorer, the Democratic Union (UD), gaining a meagre 14 percent of the alarmingly low (43 percent) turnout. Bielecki resigned, and Wałęsa called on **Jan Olszewski**, a lawyer and prominent former dissident, to form a new coalition.

The new centre-right coalition government put together by Olszewski adopted an increasingly aggressive stance on the subject of "decommunization", pushing for the unmasking of public figures suspected of having collaborated with the security services during the communist era. The question of lustration – the exclusion from public life of those who had compromised themselves under the previous regime – has been a controversial issue in Poland ever since, and, in June 1992, cost Olszewski his job.

His successor, **Halina Suchocka** of the Democratic Union, proved surprisingly successful in knitting together a functioning coalition from an unruly bundle of fractious right-of-centre parties. On the darker side, the increasingly powerful role of **the Church** in Poland's political and social life came to the fore, above all in the heated debate sparked by government moves to criminalize abortion, supported strongly by the Catholic Church but opposed by many within the country.

President Wałęsa called for fresh elections in September 1993, which resulted in victory for a coalition between the former-communist Democratic Left Alliance (SLD) and the Peasants' Party (PSL).

1993–97: the SLD in power

Led by PSL leader **Waldemar Pawlak**, the new government affirmed its commitment to continued market reforms, but at the same time pledged to do more to address its negative social effects. However, serious outbreaks of SLD-PSL infighting weakened Pawlak's authority, and a new wave of public-sector strikes, initiated by a revived Solidarity in the early spring of 1994, damaged the government's standing still further.

Ultimately, however, the conflict that most undermined Pawlak's government was a prolonged tussle with President Lech Wałęsa. The showdown came in February 1995, when Wałęsa demanded Pawlak's resignation and threatened to dissolve parliament if he was not replaced immediately. Incensed by this blatant display of presidential arrogance, the Sejm voted to initiate **impeachment proceedings** against Wałęsa. A full-scale crisis was prevented by Pawlak's decision to quit, to be replaced in March by the SLD's Józef Oleksy, who proceeded to form a new government based on the same coalition.

The 1995 presidential elections

The focus of political attention now shifted towards the November presidential elections, with opinion polls suggesting the public were weary of Wałęsa's unquenchable appetite for political intrigue. This time his main rival was the SLD's **Aleksander Kwaśniewski**, a polished, smooth-talking character who knew how to win over audiences by talking of Poland's future as a speedily modernizing country.

Following a final campaign marked by some pretty gruesome mudslinging, Kwaśniewski carried the day by a slim margin. A chastened Wałęsa made little effort to hide his anger at the result, and the final weeks of his presidency were marked by further characteristically intemperate outbursts, notably his refusal to attend Kwaśniewski's swearing-in ceremony just before Christmas.

In December 1995 Oleksy had to step down amid allegations that he was a former agent of the KGB, but things continued pretty much as they were under his successor **Włodzimierz Cimoszewicz**. Needing to regroup to stand any chance of winning back power, the centre-right came together to form the **Solidarity Election Action** (AWS) coalition in June 1996. This was a makeshift alliance of some 25 parties, comprising heavyweights Solidarity, the Centre Agreement (PC) and the Christian National Union (ZChN), alongside a string of minor rightist groupings. The AWS succeeded in making rapid political headway, not least due to the astute leadership of Solidarity chairman **Marian Krzaklewski**, who soon emerged as the coalition's leading figure.

The focus of national attention swung firmly away from politics following severe **floods** in July 1997. At least 55 people died, more than 140,000 were evacuated from their homes, and cities such as Wrocław suffered extensive damage, prompting an influx of aid from international sources. The government came in for severe criticism of what was perceived as a failure to act decisively, and in August it barely survived a PSL-sponsored vote of no confidence.

The return of the centre-right

The September 1997 **elections** handed victory to the Solidarity-led AWS, but with just 34 percent of the vote they had to forge a **coalition** with Leszek Balcerowicz's neo-liberal Freedom Union (UW). The new prime minister was Jerzy Buzek, a veteran Solidarity activist from Silesia who owed his elevation to Krzaklewski's decision to forgo the premiership and concentrate instead on the presidential elections scheduled for 2000.

The main planks of the government's programme were little different from those of its predecessor, emphasizing integration into NATO and the EU, continuing privatization and economic retrenchment. Other components, notably Buzek's pledge to promote Christian beliefs and "family values" indicated real differences in ideological background and approach, characterized by the new Sejm's acceptance of a **Constitutional Tribunal** ruling overturning the liberalized abortion law passed the previous year.

Despite the conciliatory, confidence-building style of Buzek himself, his government was ultimately hamstrung by the split between the Balcerowicz faction, which was committed to free market reforms and public spending cuts, and those closer to Solidarity, who favoured a less radical style. The economic growth of the mid-1990s was beginning to slow down by the end of the decade, unemployment was rising, and those in work were frustrated by having to put up with negligible pay rises from one year to the next. In these conditions, the SLD – guided by affable former Politburo member **Leszek Miller** – bounced back into popular affections.

Kwaśniewski wins again

The first test of the SLD's resurgent popularity came with the **presidential elections** of October 2000. The incumbent, SLD-supported **Aleksander Kwaśniewski** had represented the interests of his country with much more dignity than his crotchety predecessor Lech Wałęsa, and possessed an accessible blokeishness that appealed strongly to the average Pole. Most importantly, he was seen as a consensus-building national figurehead who resisted the temptation to interfere too much in day-to-day politics.

Kwaśniewski's subsequent **landslide victory** over AWS candidate Marian Krzaklewski left the government in disarray, its death warrant ultimately delivered by the very organization whose interests it had been formed to promote. In May 2001, Solidarity finally faced up to the dilemma that had been dogging its leaders throughout the previous decade: how could a movement formed to defend **workers' rights** continue to participate in right-of-centre governments whose policies repeatedly conflicted with workers' interests? Desperate to retain the confidence of its core membership, Solidarity decided to withdraw from the AWS in order to concentrate on its role as a trade union.

The volatile nature of party politics throughout this period had little impact on the main goals of Polish **foreign policy**: membership of **NATO** and the **European Union**. Initially, membership of NATO appeared to be the least likely of the two ambitions to be realized, but throughout the 1990s the weak international position of Russia – the country most threatened by NATO enlargement – allowed Poland unexpected freedom of manoeuvre. In January 1994, Poland signed up to the organization's newly formed **Partnership for Peace Agreement**, and, together with the Czech Republic and Hungary, was invited to join the organization three years later, despite considerable Russian grumbling. All three were formally accepted into the alliance in March 1999.

The political present

Profiting from government mistakes rather than presenting a radically different programme of its own, the SLD won the **parliamentary elections** of September 2001, although with 200 of the Sejm's 460 seats it still needed the support of the PSL to form a government. Both the AWS and the Freedom Union were wiped out entirely and replaced by the Civic Platform.

The new administration of **Leszek Miller** proved just as ineffectual as its predecessors' in fulfilling the huge public expectations invested in it. Despite clear evidence that the Polish economy was becoming more efficient and attracting increasing levels of foreign investment, unemployment remained high and average wages low. In foreign policy the SLD remained true to the pro-Western line and supported the American-led invasion of **Iraq** in spring 2003 by sending several thousand troops. Poland assumed command of one of the three military zones into which Iraq was subsequently divided, although Poland's participation in the venture was increasingly questioned by the public.

However, it was domestic policy that led to serious strains in the ruling coalition, with the PSL withdrawing its support in 2003 and a group of SDL MPs leaving to form a separate Social Democratic Party a year later. Government prestige was further tarnished by a wave of corruption scandals, culminating in the case of **Lew Rywin**, the movie producer who told newspaper *Gazeta Wyborcza* he could ease their entry into the satellite TV market if they paid $17.5 million to his associates in the ruling party. Rywin got two years in prison; support for the SLD went into freefall. Miller resigned as prime minister in March 2004, to be replaced by economist Marek Belka.

Ironically, Miller resigned on the eve of what should have been his greatest triumph, Poland's entry into the **European Union** in May 2004. Poland's drive to gain membership of the EU had been far from straightforward – not least because of the existence of an anti-EU lobby in Poland itself. A referendum on EU membership held in June 2003 produced a huge majority in favour however, the result symbolizing for many Poland's extraordinary voyage from Soviet satellite to equal member of the wider European family.

The main beneficiary of the SLD's declining support was the right-of-centre **Citizens' Platform** (PO). However, the lack of ideological differences between Poland's main political groupings encouraged the emergence of new populist parties eager to exploit those discontents which the mainstream, pro-market and pro-European politicians seem unable to face head-on. Winning their first-ever seats in the parliamentary elections of 2001 were **Samoobrona** (Self-Defence), a peasants' rights party led by Andrzej Lepper, a maverick populist notorious for his controversial and often anti-democratic outbursts, and the **League of Polish Families** (LPR) headed by Roman Giertych, a much more openly anti-European, anti-liberal party combining a left-wing social programme with a right-wing mix of nationalism and reactionary moral values.

The terrible twins

The rightward shift in the balance of political forces culminated in elections held in September 2005. The traditionalist-conservative **Law and Justice** (PiS) party, led by Jaroslaw Kaczynski, scored a narrow victory over the Civic Platform (PO), with the SLD suffering near electoral wipeout. Completing the political turnaround, one month later **Lech Kaczynski**, twin brother of the PiS leader, triumphed over the PO's Donald Tusk in the second round of presidential elections. Despite significant policy differences between the two parties their successful previous parliamentary cooperation led many to expect them to form a coalition. In the event, however, such expectations proved unfounded. The prolonged election campaign had been a fraught, bitter affair, the fallout of which was soured relations between the two parties. Post-election coalition negotiations between them foundered, and a PiS minority government was formed. Responding to concerns that his brother's prospects of winning the presidential elections might be damaged by placing himself in pole governmental position, PiS leader Jaroslaw Kaczynski nominated **Kazimierz Marcinkiewicz**, regarded as a member of the party's "liberal" faction, as prime minister.

Since the PiS' tally of deputies in the Sejm (155) fell well short of the number needed to muster a parliamentary majority, it was forced to look to support from other smaller parties. A makeshift cooperation agreement – dubbed a "**stabilisation pact**" - was initially cemented with Samoobrona and the LPR in January 2006. The habitually quarrelsome style of all parties involved made for a highly unstable political alliance, however, and in a bid to shore up support for the government a formal coalition agreement was hammered out in May.

Any illusions that calmer political waters lay ahead were rudely shattered by the resignation of Marcinkiewicz in July 2006, after which the president seized the opportunity to bring his brother into the political limelight by appointing him as the new prime minister. Kaczynski focused on a staunchly **anti-communist programme** of national renewal aimed at sweeping away what he and many in his party see as the moral and political corruption of the post-1989 era. Viewed from this avowedly conspiratorial perspective, the facade of democratic institutions that has developed in Poland is seen as nothing more than a smokescreen for a corrupt and powerful network – popularly referred to as the uklad ("system") - linking organized crime with politicians, businesss people and former security service personnel whose control of the country has (supposedly) remained substantially untouched since the communist era.

Earlier initiatives to further processes of **lustration** were revived with a vengeance, notably via a powerful new Anti-Corruption Bureau (CBA), which was furnished with wide-ranging powers to investigate and prosecute public officials, in particular within the intelligence services, which were suspected of being dominated by communist-era functionaries. In tandem with widespread questioning of what, to some, appeared tantamount to a crude campaign of political witch-hunting, in May 2007 the government suffered a major setback to its plans when a Constitutional Tribunal struck down crucial aspects of a new lustration law intended to broaden the scope of the authorities' power to vet public officials for suspected links to the communist-era security services.

Internationally the Kaczynski brothers demonstrated a similar talent for putting people's backs up. Previous administration's efforts to promote cooperation, particularly with neighbours Germany and the broader community of EU member states, was replaced by an unabashed emphasis on "defending national interests". An early casualty of the new approach were relations with EU institutions. After initially opposing the new **EU Constitutional Treaty**, the government eventually signed up to the reform treaty package tabled at the June 2007 EU Summit – but only after it managed to secure an agreement on a ten-year transition period before the new voting arrangements came into effect.

Relations with **Russia** also took something of a nosedive. In retaliation for a Russian ban on Polish meat exports, the government vetoed the Commission's efforts to initiate talks with Moscow over a new bilateral EU-Russia cooperation agreement. And the unabashedly **pro-American stance** of the Kaczynski administration – evidenced in the decision to extend the presence of Polish troops in Iraq until the end of 2007 – served to heighten tensions with EU member states, France and Germany included, that adopted a more critical approach to the post-9/11 "war on terror".

A new coalition

Less than two years into its period of office things took a decided turn for the worse for the PiS when continued infighting with its smaller radical allies culminated in the collapse of the government coalition in July 2007. The Sejm voted to dissolve itself, thereby paving the way for early general elections in October 2007. The elections resulted in an emphatic victory for **Donald Tusk**'s PO. The resounding success of the election campaign was based on effectively persuading the electorate – notably younger and centrist voters – that the PO offered a genuine alternative to the PiS-led administration's combative approach. A new coalition government between the PO and the Polish Peasant's Party (PSL) with Donald Tusk at the helm, was formed. To date the PO-led administration has proved stable and, as of early 2009, continues to enjoy high popularity ratings. Predictably, however, tensions between the coalition partners have begun to surface, and there is increasing criticism of the government for showing excessive caution over, for example, the introduction of critical economic reforms – the product, it is suggested, of a preoccupation with doing nothing that might risk undermining the Prime Minister's goal of winning the next presidential elections, scheduled for 2010.

On the **foreign policy** front the Tusk administration has engineered a significant improvement in Poland's relations with the EU, in particular setting about mending fences with **Germany** after the bitter clashes that were a marked feature of the previous government's term of office. With **Russia**, however, the picture remains more complex. While Tusk initially made improving relations with Moscow a priority, significant differences in approach remain palpable. Polish fears over the potential impact of a joint Russian-German project to build a natural gas pipeline under the Baltic Sea continue to be voiced loudly, not least in Brussels. In addition, the Polish government's vocal support for **Georgia** during its conflict with Russia in August 2008 and a standing agreement to host a new base for US missile shields mean that the Warsaw-Moscow relationship looks set fair to remain as problematic – and as vital to broader European security issues – as ever.

Books

A vast amount of writing both from and about Poland is available in English, and the quantity increased at an accelerated pace with the advent of the post-communist regime. Most of the books listed below are in print, and those that aren't (listed as "o.p.") should be easy enough to track down in second-hand bookshops or online at specialist websites.

Travel writing and guidebooks

Anne Applebaum *Between East and West*. Well-informed, vividly written account of a British-based US journalist's travels through the eastern Polish borderlands. Starting from Kaliningrad and moving down through Lithuania, Belarus, Ukraine and Moldova, Applebaum's broad-ranging cultural-historical frame of reference means the book suffers less than others from being too close to immediate events.

Tim Burford *Hiking Guide to Poland and Ukraine* (o.p.). Thoroughly researched guide to hiking in the region.

Ruth E. Gruber *Jewish Heritage Travel: A Guide to East-Central Europe*; and *Upon the Doorposts of Thy House: Jewish Life in East-Central Europe Yesterday and Today* (both o.p.). The first title is a useful country-by-country guide to Jewish culture and monuments of the region. The practical information tends to be basic, verging on the hieroglyphic, so will need supplementing for the serious searcher. The more discursive *Upon the Doorposts of Thy House* gives Gruber the space she needs to stretch out and really get into her subject. The sections on Auschwitz and Kraków's Kazimierz district are masterly, thought-provoking essays.

Eva Hoffman *Exit into History: A Journey through the New Eastern Europe*. US journalist of Polish-Jewish origin returns to her roots on a journey through the early Nineties post-communist landscape. Inevitably already dated, but the sections on Poland stand out for their combination of shrewd political insight and human warmth.

Philip Marsden *The Bronski House: A Return to the Borderlands*. Sensitively written account of the author's journey to the Polish–Belarusian borderlands in the company of Zofia Ilińska, an aristocratic former resident returning for the first time in fifty years.

Rory McLean *Stalin's Nose*. One of the best of the flurry of accounts of "epic" journeys across post-communist east-central Europe. The author's quirky brand of surrealist humour enlivens the trip, which takes in obvious Polish stopoffs, Auschwitz and Kraków, en route for Moscow.

Agata Passent *Long Live the Palace!* Sharply written history of Warsaw's Palace of Culture (see p.91), the Stalinist-era building which serves as a melancholy metaphor for communist-era Poland. Written by a young Polish journalist and published by Spis Treści in Poland, it comes in a bilingual edition available from Warsaw bookstores.

Colin Saunders and **Renata Narozna** *The High Tatras*. Detailed and comprehensive recent guide to the ins and outs of scaling the Tatras. For dedicated hikers and climbers.

Miriam Weiner *Jewish Roots in Poland: Pages from the Past and Archival Inventories*.

Monumental coffee-table-sized guide to all aspects of Polish Jewry, the fruit of years of meticulous and painstaking

trailing through archival sources – and the country itself – by its US-based author.

History

David Crowley *Warsaw*. Up-to-date history of the Polish capital written with enthusiasm and attitude by a leading cultural historian.

Norman Davies *The Heart of Europe: A Short History of Poland*. A brilliantly original treatment of modern Polish history, beginning with the events of 1945 but looking backwards over the past millennium to illustrate the author's ideas. Scrupulously gives all points of view in disentangling the complex web of Polish history.

Norman Davies *God's Playground*. A bigger, more detailed alternative to the above, this is a masterpiece of erudition, entertainingly written and pretty much definitive for the pre-Solidarity period.

Norman Davies and **Roger Moorhouse** *Microcosm*. The story of the city of Wrocław, from medieval beginnings as the Slavonic settlement of Wrotizla, through life as the German-language mercantile centre of Breslau, to its current

status as go-ahead capital of Poland's southwest. An exemplary exercise in urban history, and a good introduction to the history of Silesia in general.

Iwo Pogonowski *Jews in Poland: A Documentary History*. Thorough if idiosyncratically presented account of Polish Jewry from the earliest times up until the present day – not too many axes to grind, either. Contains an intriguing selection of old prints from everyday life in the ghettos, *shtetls* and synagogues.

Carl Tighe *Gdańsk: National Identity in the German–Polish Border Lands*. Alternatively titled *Gdańsk: the Unauthorised Biography*, an apt description of the fascinating history of a city that Poles and Germans have tussled over for centuries. Studiously avoiding Polish or German favouritism, the author sets out to capture the unique story of the Gdańsk/Danzig citizenry, arguing that claims of real Polish or German identity tell us more about the needs of latter-day nationalists than the cultural complexities of the past.

World War II and the Holocaust

Norman Davies *Rising '44*. Impeccably researched and eminently readable piece of narrative history, published simultaneously in the UK and in Poland to coincide with the sixtieth anniversary of the ill-starred Warsaw Uprising. The question of whether the insurgents were the victims of allied betrayal is treated in balanced, meticulous fashion.

Martin Gilbert *The Holocaust*. The standard work, providing a

trustworthy overview on the slaughter of European Jewry – and the crucial role of Poland, where most Nazi concentration camps were sited.

Martin Gilbert *Holocaust Journey*. Account of a study trip undertaken by Gilbert and his students in the 1990s, taking in the towns and cities where Polish Jews once lived in large numbers, as well as the key memorial sites associated with Nazi crimes. A moving and ultimately uplifting read.

Rudolf Höss *Death Dealer: Memoirs of the SS Kommandant at Auschwitz*. Perhaps the most chilling record of the barbarity: a remorseless autobiography of the Auschwitz camp commandant, written in the days between his death sentence and execution at Nürnberg.

Stefan Korbonski *The Polish Underground State*. Detailed account of the history and inner workings of the many-faceted Polish wartime resistance by a leading figure of the time. Korbonski has produced a number of other books on related themes, notably *Fighting Warsaw*, an account of the 1944 Warsaw Uprising drawing on his own experience.

Primo Levi *If This Is a Man*; *The Truce*; *Moments of Reprieve*; *The Drowned and the Saved*; *The Periodic Table*; *If Not Now, When?* An Italian Jew, Levi survived Auschwitz because the Nazis made use of his training as a chemist in the death-camp factories. Most of his books, which became ever bleaker towards the end of his life, concentrate on his experiences during and soon after his incarceration in Auschwitz, analyzing the psychology of survivor and torturer with extraordinary clarity. *If Not Now, When?* is the story of a group of Jewish partisans in occupied Russia and Poland; giving plenty of insights into eastern European anti-Semitism, it's a good corrective to the mythology of Jews as passive victims.

Betty Jean Lifton *Janusz Korczak: The King of the Children*. Biography of the Jewish doctor who died in Treblinka with the orphans for whom he cared. He was the eponymous subject of an Andrzej Wajda film.

Milton Nieuwsma (ed.) *Kindertransport*. Oral accounts of wartime survival from Jews who were deported to the death camps as children, collected and presented without mawkishness by a skilled and sensitive compiler.

Gunnar S. Paulsson *Secret City: The Hidden Jews of Warsaw 1940–1945*. More than 11,000 Jews survived World War II in Warsaw, and this study helps explain how they did it: establishing safehouses, hunkering down in underground hideouts, disguising themselves as Gentiles and relying on the help of a significant number of Poles who were prepared to help fugitives escape. Meticulously researched, gripping stuff.

Laurence Rees *Auschwitz*. Grave, unflinching history of the Final Solution focusing on the most notorious death-camp of all. Published to accompany a BBC TV series of the same name, it contains much new research, and makes full and revealing use of interviews conducted with camp survivors, civilian witnesses and former guards.

Emmanuel Ringelblum *Polish–Jewish Relations during the Second World War*. Penetrating history of the Warsaw Ghetto focusing on the vexed issue of Polish–Jewish wartime relations. Written from the inside by the prominent prewar Jewish historian – history recorded as it was occurring. Tragically, only a portion of Ringelblum's own writings and the extensive Ghetto archives he put together were recovered after 1945.

Saul Rubinek *So Many Miracles* (o.p.). Actor and director Rubinek's interviews with his parents about their early life in Poland and survival under Nazi occupation make a compelling piece of oral history, and one that paints a blacker than usual picture of Polish–Jewish relations.

Art Spiegelman *Maus*. Spiegelman, editor of the cartoon magazine *Raw*, is the son of Auschwitz survivors. *Maus* is a brilliant comic-strip exploration of the ghetto and concentration camp experiences of his father, recounted in flashbacks.

The story runs through to Art's father's imprisonment at Auschwitz; subsequent chapters of the sequel – covering Auschwitz itself – have been printed in recent editions of *Raw*, now available as a separate book, *Maus II*. In 2001, *Maus* was published in Poland to great acclaim – despite the fact that the Polish characters in the book are depicted as pigs.

Władysław Szpilman *The Pianist*. Wartime memoirs of concert pianist and composer Szpilman (1911–2000), who miraculously survived the Warsaw Ghetto. Originally published as *Smierc Miasta* (*Death of a City*) in 1945, Szpilman's book was initially buried by a postwar Polish regime unwilling to recognize the full extent of Jewish suffering during World War II. Now available again in both Polish and English versions, *The Pianist* has already made it onto celluloid courtesy of Kraków Ghetto survivor Roman Polański.

Nechama Tec *Defiance*. Inspiring tale of Polish-Jewish partisans who fought the Nazis in the forests of Belarus, impeccably researched through interviews with participants and their descendants. Filmed for Hollywood by Ed Zwick in 2008.

Harold Werner *Fighting Back: A Memoir of Jewish Resistance in World War II*. Gripping, straightforwardly written account of the author's experiences as a member of a Jewish partisan unit fighting against the Nazis in wartime Poland.

Politics and society

Timothy Garton Ash *The Polish Revolution: Solidarity 1980–82* (o.p.); *The Uses of Adversity* (o.p.); *We The People: The Revolution of 89* (o.p.). Garton Ash was the most consistent and involved Western reporter on Poland during the Solidarity era, displaying an intuitive grasp of the Polish mentality. His *Polish Revolution* is a vivid record of events from the birth of Solidarity – a story extended in the climactic events of 1989, documented as an eyewitness in Warsaw, Budapest, Berlin and Prague.

Radek Sikorski *The Polish House: An Intimate History Of Poland* (o.p.). Highly personalized and passionately penned account of modern Polish history by former Solidarity activist, UK exile and journalist who became Poland's Foreign Minister in 2007. The author's trenchantly anti-communist views begin to grate after a while, but overall you'd be hard put to find a better insider's introduction to contemporary realities.

Essays and memoirs

Kazimierz Brandys *Warsaw Diary 1977–81* (o.p.); and *Paris, New York: 1982–84* (o.p.). The *Warsaw Diary*, by this major Polish journalist and novelist, brilliantly captures the atmosphere of the time, and especially the effect of John Paul II's first papal visit in 1979. During martial law, possession of this book carried an automatic ten-year prison sentence. *Paris, New York* powerfully traces his early life in imposed exile while continually reflecting on developments at home.

Eva Hoffman *Lost in Translation* (o.p.). Wise, sparklingly written autobiography of a Polish Jew centring, as the title suggests, around her experience of emigration from Kraków to North America in the 1960s. Plenty of insights into the postwar Jewish/Eastern European émigré experience.

Eva Hoffman *Shtetl: The Life And Death Of A Small Town and The World Of Polish Jews* (o.p.). Imaginative, well-researched reconstruction of life in a typical prewar Polish *shtetl*. Good on broader issues of Polish–Jewish relations, although her carefully balanced conclusions have come in for predictable criticism from those who say it paints too rosy a picture of the prewar period.

Ryszard Kapuściński *Another Day of Life*. For many years Kapuściński was Poland's only full-time foreign correspondent, his elegant, essayistic reportage setting a standard for all other journalists of his generation. This, his first book, covers the Angolan wars of the mid-1970s, and is full of impressionistic description and insightful comment. Of his subsequent works, *Emperor* is a gripping behind-the-scenes take on Haile Selasse's doomed regime in the Ethopia of the 1970s; while *Imperium* traces his travels in the former Soviet Union and

contains revealing reflections on Poland's historically fraught relationship with near-neighbour Russia.

Czesław Miłosz *The Captive Mind*; *Native Realm*; *Beginning with My Streets*. The first is a penetrating analysis of the reasons so many Polish artists and intellectuals sold out to communism after 1945, with four case studies supplementing a confession of personal guilt. *Native Realm*, the unorthodox autobiography of the years before Miłosz defected to the West, is especially illuminating on the Polish–Lithuanian relationship. The last is a wide-ranging collection of essays by this Nobel Prize-winning author, including an invigorating set of pieces revolving around Wilno (Vilnius), the author's boyhood home and spiritual mentor in later life.

Adam Zagajewski *Two Cities*. Born in Lwów, raised in the Silesian city of Gliwice and now based in Paris, contemporary poet Zagajewski's collection of essays and prose pieces roves across the themes of exile and displacement.

Culture, art and architecture

Tadeusz Budziński *In the Borderland of Cultures*. Well-presented photo album of wooden churches in southeastern Poland, published by Libra (wwww.libra.pl) in Rzeszów. Available in both coffee-table and pocket editions, and found in bookshops and museums throughout the southeast.

Czesław Miłosz *The History of Polish Literature*. Written in the mid-1960s, this is, however, still the standard English-language work on the subject, informed by the author's consummate grasp of the furthest nooks and crannies of Polish literature.

Roman Vishniac *Polish Jews – A Pictorial Record*. Haunting selection of pictures by the legendary

photographer, evoking Jewish life in the *shtetls* and ghettos of Poland immediately before the outbreak of World War II. A good introduction to the great man's work if you can't get hold of *A Vanished World* (o.p.), the acclaimed album that brings together most of the two thousand or so photos from Vishniac's travels through Jewish Poland.

Tomasz Wiśniewski *Jewish Bialystok and Surroundings in Eastern Europe*. Encyclopedic survey of the wealth of prewar Jewish architecture in the eastern borderlands, much of it destroyed but with a significant number of buildings still surviving. Great for exploring the Białystok-Tykocin region.

Polish fiction

Shmuel Yozef Agnon *A Simple Story*; and *Dwelling Place of My People* (o.p.). Agnon, Polish-born Nobel Prize-winner and father-figure of modern Hebrew literature, sets *A Simple Story* in the Jewish communities of the Polish Ukraine, belying its title by weaving an unexpected variation on the traditional Romeo-and-Juliet-type tale of crossed lovers. In *Dwelling Place* he recalls his childhood in Poland, in a series of highly refined stories and prose poems.

Jerzy Andrzejewski *Ashes and Diamonds*. Spring 1945: resistance fighters, communist ideologues and black marketeers battle it out in small-town Poland. A gripping account of the tensions and forces that shaped postwar Poland, and the basis for Andrzej Wajda's film of the same title.

Asher Barash *Pictures from a Brewery* (o.p.). Depiction of Jewish life in Galicia, told in a style very different from the mythic, romantic approach favoured by Agnon.

Tadeusz Borowski *This Way for the Gas, Ladies and Gentlemen*. These short stories based on his Auschwitz experiences marked Borowski out as the great literary hope of communist Poland, but he committed suicide soon after their publication, at the age of 29.

Joseph Conrad *A Personal Record*. An entertaining, ironic piece of "faction" about Conrad's family and his early life in the Russian part of Partition Poland, addressing the painful subjects of his loss of his own country and language.

Ida Fink *A Scrap of Time*. Haunting vignettes of Jews striving to escape the concentration camps – and of the unsung Polish Gentiles who sheltered them.

Witold Gombrowicz *Ferdydurke*; *Pornografia*; and *The Possessed*. The first two experimentalist novels concentrate on humanity's infantile and juvenile obsessions, and on the tensions between urban life and the traditional ways of the countryside. *The Possessed* explores the same themes within the more easily digestible format of a Gothic thriller.

Marek Hłasko *The Eighth Day of the Week*; *Killing the Second Dog* (o.p.); and *Next Stop – Paradise & the Graveyard*. Once considered Poland's "Angry Young Man", Hłasko articulated the general disaffection of those who grew up after World War II, his bleak themes mirrored in a spare, taut prose style.

Pawel Huelle *Who Was David Weiser?*; *Moving House*; and *Mercedes-Benz*. The first novel from the award-winning Gdańsk-based writer centres on an enigmatic young Jewish boy idolized by his youthful contemporaries. The author's themes and style show an obvious debt to fellow Danziger Günter Grass. Huelle's magic-realist propensities are further developed in *Moving House*, a marvellous collection of short stories, with the intersecting worlds of Polish and German/Prussian culture again providing the primary frame of reference. *Mercedes-Benz* is a hugely entertaining four-wheeled meditation on Polish history, the much-loved metal crate of the title having been requisitioned from the narrator's grandfather by the Soviets outside Lwów in 1939.

Tadeusz Konwicki *A Minor Apocalypse*; *A Dreambook for our Time*; *The Polish Complex* (o.p.); and *Bohin Manor*. A convinced Party member in the 1950s, Konwicki eventually made the break with

Stalinism. Since then a series of highly respected novels, films and screenplays have established him as one of Poland's foremost writers. Describing a single day's events, *A Minor Apocalypse* is narrated by a character who constantly vacillates over his promise to set fire to himself in front of the Party headquarters. *Dreambook* is a hard-hitting wartime tale, while *The Polish Complex* is a fascinating, often elusive exploration of contemporary life in Poland. Finally, *Bohin Manor* is an elegiac novel set among the Polish-Lithuanian gentry in the wake of the 1863 anti-tsarist uprising: like Miłosz (see opposite) and many others who grew up in Lithuania, Konwicki betrays a yearning for a mystic homeland.

Janusz Korczak *King Matty the First.* Written by the famous Jewish doctor who died, along with his orphans, at Treblinka, this long children's novel, regarded as the Polish counterpart of *Alice in Wonderland*, appeals also to adults through its underlying sense of tragedy and gravitas.

Marek Krajewski *Death in Breslau.* Compellingly noir crime thriller set in 1930s Wrocław (then part of Germany and known as Breslau), bringing the interwar city to life with a thrilling mixture of grime, seediness and political extremism.

Stanisław Lem *Solaris*; *The Futurological Congress: From the Memoirs of Ijon Tichy*; *Tales of Pirx the Pilot*; *His Master's Voice.* The only recent Polish writing to have achieved a worldwide mass-market readership, Lem's science fiction focuses on the human and social predicament in the light of technological change. An author of considerable range and invention, Lem's best-known work, *Solaris*, is a disturbing and meditative account of a spiritual quest, while *The Futurological Congress* is a sophisticated satire on the absurdity of our times.

Czesław Miłosz *The Issa Valley.* Wonderfully lyrical, semi-autobiographical account of growing up in the Lithuanian countryside.

Jan Potocki *The Manuscript Found at Saragossa: Ten Days in the Life of Alphonse von Worden.* A self-contained section of a huge unfinished Gothic novel written at the beginning of the nineteenth century by a Polish nobleman: a rich brew of picaresque adventures, dreams, hallucinations, eroticism, philosophical discourses and exotic tales.

Bolesław Prus *Pharaoh* and *The Doll.* The first, a late nineteenth-century epic, set in ancient Egypt, offers a trenchant examination of the nature of power in a society that was of more than passing relevance to Partition-era Poland. *The Doll* is probably the most famous of the "Polish Tolstoy's" lengthier works: widely regarded as one of the great nineteenth-century social novels, this is a brilliantly observed story of obsessive love against the backdrop of a crisis-ridden *fin de siècle* Warsaw.

Władysław Reymont *The Peasants* and *The Promised Land* (both o.p.). Reymont won the Nobel Prize for *The Peasants*, a tetralogy about village life (one for each season of the year), but its vast length has led to its neglect outside Poland. *The Promised Land*, which was filmed by Wajda, offers a comparably unromanticized view of industrial life in Łódź.

Bruno Schulz *Street of Crocodiles* and *Sanatorium under the Sign of the Hourglass.* These kaleidoscopic, dream-like fictions, vividly evoking life in the small town of Drohobycz in the Polish Ukraine, constitute the entire literary output of their hugely influential author, who was murdered by the SS. For more on Schulz, get hold of *Regions of the Great Heresy*, a recent biography written by renowned Polish scholar Jerzy Ficowski.

Henryk Sienkiewicz *Quo Vadis?*; *Charcoal Sketches and Other Tales*; *With Fire and Sword*; *The Deluge*; and *Fire in the Steppe*. Sienkiewicz's reputation outside Poland largely rests on *Quo Vadis?* (which won him the Nobel Prize), treating the early Christians in Nero's Rome as an allegory of Poland's plight under the Partitions. Until recently, Sienkiewicz's other blockbusters existed only in inadequate and long out-of-print translations, but the Polish-American novelist W.S. Kuniczak has recently rendered the great trilogy about Poland's seventeenth-century wars with the Swedes, Prussians, Germans and Turks into English in a manner that at last does justice to the richly crafted prose of the originals.

Isaac Bashevis Singer *The Magician of Lublin* (o.p.); *The Family Moskat* (o.p.); *Collected Stories*; *The Slave*; *Satan in Goray*; *The King of the Fields* (o.p.). Singer, who emigrated from Poland to the US in the 1930s, wrote in Yiddish, so his reputation rests largely on the translations of his novels and short stories. Only a selection of his vast output is mentioned here. *The Magician of Lublin* and *The Family Moskat*, both novels set in the ghettos of early twentieth-century Poland, are masterly evocations of life in vanished Jewish communities. *The Slave* is a gentle yet tragic love story set in the seventeenth century, while *Satan in Goray* is a blazing evocation of religious hysteria in the same period. His penultimate work, *The King of the Fields*, recreates the early life of the Polish state, and is his only novel without a Jewish emphasis.

Andrzej Stasiuk *Tales of Galicia* and *9*. Edgy prose from a leading contemporary novelist and travel writer. The first contains surreal and melancholic snatches of life from the southeastern corner of Poland; while the second is a grimly poetic novel set in post-communist Warsaw.

Andrzej Szczypiorski *The Beautiful Mrs Seidemann*. Bestselling novel by prominent contemporary Polish writer who survived both the Warsaw Uprising and subsequently the concentration camps. The story centres around a Jewish woman who uses her wits – and beauty – to survive the Nazis. Stirringly written, though the fatalistic historical musings (he's obviously got a foreign audience in mind) become increasingly oppressive as the book progresses.

Olga Tokarczuk *House of Day, House of Night*. Award-winning novel from one of the most distinctive new voices in Polish fiction, evoking the small-town world of Nowa Ruda (a real-life mining settlement in the Polish–Czech–German borderlands) through a dream-like mixture of narrative fragments, extracts from the life of a medieval saint, and recipes for forest mushrooms.

Stanisław Ignacy Witkiewicz *Insatiability*. Explicit depiction of artistic, intellectual, religious and sexual decadence against the background of a Chinese invasion of Europe. The enormous vocabulary, complicated syntax and philosophical diversions don't make for an easy read, but this is unquestionably one of the most distinctive works of twentieth-century literature.

Various authors *The Eagle and the Crow*. Superb short-story compilation featuring almost all the big names of Polish twentieth-century fiction. If you're new to Polish literature, you won't find a better place to start.

Polish poetry

S. Barańczak and **C. Cavanagh** (eds.) *Spoiling Cannibal's Fun: Polish Poetry of the Last Two Decades of Communist Rule.* Representative anthology of recent Polish poetry with informative introductory essay by co-editor and translator Stanisław Barańczak, one of the country's pre-eminent émigré literary figures whose poems are also featured in this volume.

Adam Czerniawski (ed.) *The Burning Forest.* Selected by one of Poland's leading contemporary poets, this anthology covers Polish poetry from the laconic nineteenth-century verses of Cyprian Norwid, through examples of Herbert, Różewicz and the editor, up to young writers of the present day.

Zbigniew Herbert *Selected Poems.* Arguably the greatest contemporary Polish poet, with a strong line in poignant observation; intensely political but never dogmatic. The widespread international mourning occasioned by Herbert's death in 1998 confirmed the man's special place in contemporary literary affections.

Adam Mickiewicz *Pan Tadeusz; Konrad Wallenrod* and *Grażyna.* The first is Poland's national epic, set among the gentry of Lithuania at the time of the Napoleonic invasion – the most readable translation, that by George Rapall Noyes, has long been out of print but is available in some libraries. In contrast to the self-delusion about Polish independence shown by the characters in *Pan Tadeusz, Konrad Wallenrod* demonstrates how that end can be achieved by stealth and cunning; like *Grażyna,* its setting is Poland-Lithuania's struggle with the Teutonic Knights.

Czesław Miłosz *New and Collected Poems.* A writer of massive integrity, Miłosz in all his works wrestles with the issues of spiritual and political commitment; this collection encompasses all his poetic phases, from the Surrealist of the 1930s to the émigré sage of San Francisco.

Czesław Miłosz (ed.) *Polish Postwar Poetry.* Useful anthology selected and mostly translated by Miłosz, with an emphasis on poetry written after the thaw of 1956. The closer you get to the 1980s the grittier and more acerbic they become, as befits the politics of the era.

Wisława Szymborska *People on the Bridge.* For some time this was virtually the only volume of poems by the 1996 Nobel Prize-winning Polish author available in English. Szymborska remains one of the most distinctive modern (female) voices, translated here by fellow poet, Adam Czerniawski. Of the volumes to appear in the wake of the Nobel award, *View With a Grain of Sand* is an excellent introduction to the Szymborska oeuvre; *Poems New and Collected 1957–1997* is a large, well-translated selection of her poems spanning the last four decades; *Sounds, Feelings, Thoughts: Seventy Poems,* a reissue, covers similar territory, albeit less comprehensively.

Adam Zagajewski *Without End.* Highly regarded verse from a writer following in the footsteps of Herbert and Miłosz. Drawing on Zagajewski's best-known collection *Mysticism for Beginners,* as well as other volumes, this is the best possible introduction to his work.

Isaac Babel *Red Cavalry*, from *Collected Stories*. A collection of interrelated short stories about the 1919–20 invasion of Poland, narrated by the bizarrely contradictory figure of a Jewish Cossack communist, who naturally finds himself torn by conflicting emotions.

Günter Grass *The Tin Drum*; *Dog Years*; and *Cat and Mouse*. These three novels, also available in one volume as the *Danzig Trilogy*, are one of the high points of modern German literature. Set in Danzig/Gdańsk, where the author grew up, they hold up a mirror to the changing German character this century. The later *The Call of the Toad*, provides a satirical commentary on post-communist Polish and German attitudes towards the same city's past.

James Hopkin *Winter Under Water*. Poetic, sophisticated and powerful piece of writing with an east-west love affair at its heart and the city of Kraków as its setting.

Unusually for novels written about eastern Europe since 1990, modern Poland is not reduced to a collection of post-communist clichés.

Thomas Keneally *Schindler's List*. Originally entitled *Schindler's Ark* before becoming the subject of Spielberg's film, this powerful, 1982 Booker Prize-winning novel is based on the life of Oskar Schindler, a German industrialist who used his business operations to shelter thousands of Jews.

Joseph Roth *Hotel Savoy*. Austrian-Jewish writer Roth's nightmarish look at Europe in the wake of World War I is set in an unnamed industrial city that is clearly based on Łódź. The hotel of the title still stands (see p.132), although is no longer the nest of paranoia described by Roth.

Leon Uris *Mila 18*. Stirring tale of the Warsaw Ghetto Uprising – Mila 18 was the address of the Jewish resistance militia's HQ.

Music

T
raditional music in Poland isn't exactly a widespread living tradition. The country has Westernized rapidly and the memory of communist fakelore has tainted people's interest in the genuine article. However, in certain pockets, Poland boasts some of the most distinctive sounds in Europe. The events calendar (see p.46) contains details of some of Poland's best **folk festivals**.

Roots and development

In Poland, as elsewhere in Eastern Europe, an interest in folklore emerged in the nineteenth century, allied to aspirations for national independence – folk music and politics in the region often have symbiotic links. The pioneering collector of songs and dances from all over the country was **Oskar Kolberg** (1814–90), who painstakingly transcribed folk tunes region by region and published them in a series of ground-breaking volumes. From the early years of this century gramophone recordings were made, although archives were destroyed during **World War II** and scholarly collecting had to begin anew in 1945. Postwar communist regimes throughout Eastern Europe endorsed folk culture as a cheerful espousal of healthy peasant labour, ensuring the preservation of folk culture (albeit in somewhat sanitized form).

The official face of Polish folk music was presented by professional folk troupes – most famously the **Mazowsze** and **Śląsk ensembles** – who gave (and still give) highly arranged and polished virtuoso performances: middle-of-the-road massed strings and highly choreographed foot-stamping. The repertoire was basically core Polish with a slight regional emphasis (the Mazowsze territory is around Warsaw, the Śląsk around Wrocław), but the overall effect was homogenization rather than local identity. Smaller, more specialized groups, like Słowianki in Kraków, were also supported and kept closer to the roots, but for the most part the real stuff withered away as the image of folk music became tarnished by the bland official ensembles.

Classical music

The nation's wealth of folk tunes have found their way into some of the best of the country's classical music, of which Poles are justifiably proud, the roster of Polish **composers** containing a number of world-ranking figures, including Chopin, Moniuszko, Szymanowski, Penderecki, Panufnik, Lutoslawski and Henryk Górecki, composer of the 1990s runaway bestseller *Symphony no.3*. The country has also produced a wealth of classical musicians, mostly in the first half of the twentieth century when pianists Artur Rubinstein and musician-premier Ignacy Paderewski gained worldwide prominence. A cluster of Polish orchestras, notably the **Polish Chamber Orchestra**, the **Warsaw** and **Kraków Philharmonics**, and the Katowice-based **Radio and TV Symphony Orchestra**, have made it into the world league and are regularly in demand on the international touring circuit.

All the big cities have music festivals of one sort or another, which generally give plenty of space to national composers, the international **Chopin Piano Competition** in Warsaw (held every five years) being the best known and most prestigious of the events. Throughout the year it's easy to catch works by Polish composers since the repertoires of many regional companies tend to be oriented towards national music.

Polish dances

Thanks to Chopin, the **mazurka** and **polonaise** (*polonez*) of central Poland are probably the best-known dance forms and are at the core of the folk repertoire. Both are in triple time, with the polonaise generally slower and more stately than the mazurka. In fact there are really three types of mazurka, the slower *kujawiak*, medium tempo *mazur* and faster *oberek*.

The polonaise is particularly associated with the more ceremonial and solemn moments of a wedding party. It was taken up by the aristocracy from a slow walking dance (*chodzony*), given a French name to identify it as a dance of Polish origin and then filtered back down to the lower classes. In addition to the triple-time dances of central Poland, there are also some characteristic five-beat dances in the northeastern areas of Mazury, Kurpie and Podlasie.

As you move south, somewhere between Warsaw and Kraków there is a transitional area where the triple-time dances of central Poland give way to the duple-time dances of the south like the **krakowiak** and **polka**. Generally speaking the music of central Poland is more restrained and sentimental than that of the south, which is wilder and more full-blooded. The *krakowiak* is named after the city of Kraków and the polka is claimed by both the Poles and the Bohemians as their own, although it was in Bohemia that it became most widely known. Of course, all these dances are not confined to their native areas, and many have become staples across the country and abroad.

Folk music today

Today, with the notable exception of the Tatra region and a few other pockets, traditional music has virtually ceased to function as a living tradition and has been banished to regional **folk festivals**. Several of these are very good indeed, with the Kazimierz Festival at the end of June foremost among them (see box p.277). But the best way to hear this music is at the sort of occasion it was designed for – for instance a **wedding** (*wesele*), where lively tunes are punched out by ad hoc groups comprising (nowadays) clarinet, saxophone, accordion, keyboard and drums. The areas where traditional wedding music has survived most tend to be on the fringes of the country – notably Podlasie in the northeast and the highland regions along the southern border.

Górale music

The district around Zakopane is home to the **górale** (highland) people and has the most vibrant musical tradition in the country. It has been one of Poland's most popular resort areas for years and is in no way remote or isolated. *Górale* musicians are familiar with music from all over the country and beyond, but choose to play in their own way. This sophisticated approach is part of a pride in Podhale identity which probably dates from the late nineteenth century, when several notable artists and intellectuals (including the composer **Karol Szymanowski**, see p.647) settled in Zakopane and enthused about the music and culture. Music, fiddlers and dancing brigands are as essential to the image of górale life as the traditional costumes of tight felt trousers, embroidered jackets and black hats. This music has more in common with the peasant cultures along the Carpathians in Ukraine and Transylvania than the rest of Poland.

The typical **górale ensemble** is a string band (the clarinets, saxophones, accordions and drums that have crept in elsewhere in Poland are much rarer here) comprising a lead violin (*prym*), a couple of second violins (*sekund*) playing accompanying chords, and a three-stringed cello (*bazy*). The tunes tend to be short-winded, angular melodies in an unusual scale with a sharpened fourth. This is known to musicians as the "Lydian mode" and gives rise to the Polish word **lidyzowanie** to describe the manner of singing this augmented interval. The fiddlers typically play these melodies with a "straight" bowing technique – giving the music a stiff, angular character as opposed to the swing and flexibility of the more usual "double" bowing technique common in Eastern Europe and typified by gypsy fiddlers. The straining high male vocals which kick off a dance tune are also typical. At the heart of the repertoire are the **ozwodna** and **krzesany** couple dances, both in duple time. The first has an unusual five-bar melodic structure and the second is faster and more energetic. Then there are the showy **zbójnicki** (Brigand's Dances), performed in a circle by men wielding small metal axes, celebrating the outlaw traditions of a region that produced more than its fair share of bandits – many of whom ended up swinging for their crimes. "To hang on the gibbet is an honourable thing!", said the nineteenth-century *górale* musician Sabała. "They don't hang just anybody, but real men!"

Ethnic minorities

Since the political changes of the 1980s, there's been something of a revival in the music of some of the national minorities living in Poland. There is now a more liberal climate in which to express national differences and travel is easier across the borders between related groups in Lithuania, Belarus and Ukraine. Poland's **Boyks** and **Lemkos** are ethnically and culturally linked to Ukrainians and the Rusyns of Slovakia, and their music betrays its eastern Slavonic leanings in its choral and polyphonic songs.

World War II saw the effective extermination of Jewish life and culture in Poland along with the exuberant and melancholy **klezmer** music for weddings and festivals that was part of it. The music had its distinctive Jewish elements, but drew heavily on local Polish and Ukrainian styles. The music now flourishes principally in the US and is barely heard in Poland except at the annual Festival of Jewish Culture in Kraków. The city is, though, home to a brace of highly regarded klezmer bands. **Kroke**, a trio led by violinist **Tamasz Kukurba**, started off playing schmaltzy standards, but has evolved into an inventive and exciting band who've proven their ability on tour (at the Womad festivals held worldwide, for example). The **Cracow Klezmer Band**, founded in 1997 by accordionist Jarosław Bester (and renamed **The Bester Quartet** in 2007), has made similarly genre-bending journeys into the borderlands of klezmer, recording for John Zorn's New York-based Tzadik label.

Revival and new folk music

The last two decades have seen a modest revival in Polish roots music. Not surprisingly, some of the most interesting developments have come out of the górale region and in particular the **Trebunia** family band of Poronin. Here the fiddler Władysław Trebunia and his son Krzysztof are both preservers of and experimenters with the tradition, as well as being leaders of one of the very best wedding bands around. In 1991 they joined up with reggae musician Norman "Twinkle" Grant to produce two albums of **Podhale reggae**, or perhaps more accurately, reggae in a Polish style. Surprising as it might seem, once you get used to the rigid beat imposed on the more flexible Polish material, the marriage works rather well and there are interesting parallels between Rasta and Podhale concerns. In 1994, the Trebunias teamed up on another project with one of Poland's leading **jazz** musicians, saxophonist Zbigniew Namysłowski. Here the usual *górale* ensemble meets saxophone, piano, bass and drums in an inventive romp through classic Tatra-mountain hits.

Also making a name for themselves in the nineties were Poznań-based **Kwartet Jorgi**, who take their music from all round Poland and beyond, with many of the tunes coming from the nineteenth-century collections of **Oskar Kolberg**. The group's leader, Maciej Rychły, plays an amazing range of ancient Polish bagpipes, whistles and flutes, which are sensitively combined with guitars, cello and drums. The music isn't purist, but is inventive and fun and shows how contemporary Polish folk music can escape a legacy of sanitized communist fakelore.

Among the most prominent of the currently active folk bands is Lublin-based **Orkiestra św. Mikołaja**, back-to-basics traditionalists whose upbeat danceable repertoire loses nothing in terms of authenticity. Working in a similar direction but with more counter-cultural attitude, the ironically named **Kapela ze wsi**

Discography

Cracow Klezmer Band *Sanatorium under the Sign of the Hourglass* (Tzadik). Outstanding album of klezmer-jazz-contemporary fusion inspired by the works of Polish-Jewish writer Bruno Schulz. Joyous, lyrical and strange in equal measure.

Nigel Kennedy and Kroke *East Meets East* (EMI Classical). Classical violinist and Kraków resident Kennedy teams up with one of the city's leading klezmer outfits to produce a cornucopia of cross-genre delights, with ex-Killing Joke frontman Jaz Coleman handling production duties. Kennedy/Kroke's highly individual readings of Polish, central European and Balkan tunes (Macedonian melodies looming largest) are full of surprises.

Kroke *Ten Pieces to Save the World* (Oriente). Using klezmer as a basis for further exploration rather than an end in itself, this virtuoso Kraków outfit present a shimmering instrumental set which ranges from the energizing to the contemplative, and draws on a variety of central and southern European styles for inspiration. Investigate this first, then move on to their earlier studio albums *Time*, *Sounds of the Vanishing World*, *Eden* and *Trio* (all on Oriente).

Kwartet Jorgi *Jam* (Jam, Poland). This is the quartet's first release from 1990, featuring lots of old tunes collected by Kolberg. The Jewish-sounding *Ubinie* tune seems to tie in with the Chagall picture on the cover. Their second, eponymously titled CD, (Polskie Nagrania, Poland) is a release of older material recorded in 1988. It ventures more widely into repertoire with Irish and Balkan tunes as well as excursions into what sounds like medieval jazz.

Sowa Family Band *Songs and Music from Rzeszów Region* (Polskie Nagrania, Poland). A wonderful disc of authentic village dances from a family band with over 150 years of recorded history. The 1970s recordings are rather harsh, but splendid all the same. Sadly, the band is no longer playing.

Trebunia Family Band *Music of the Tatra Mountains* (Nimbus, UK). A great sample of *górale* music recorded not in a cold studio session, but at an informal party to bring that special sense of spontaneity and fun. Fiddler Władysław Trebunia is the father-figure and the band includes his son Krzysztof (who often leads in his own right), daughter Hania and several other family members. Wild playing from one of the region's best bands and well recorded.

Trebunie-Tutki & The Twinkle Brothers *Songs of Glory/Pieśni Chwały* (Agora, Poland). The latest in a series of *górale*-reggae crossover records, fruit of collaboration

Warszawa (renamed **Warsaw Village Band** for the benefit of Western consumers) combines reverence for traditional roots and field research in Mazovian villages with a contemporary urban taste for large-scale noise. With a conventional fiddle-and-cello string section enlivened by the addition of an archaic *suka* (a scratchy-sounding violin-like instrument of sixteenth-century origin) and a muscular rhythm section, the Warsaw Village Band is one of the most vital and original sounds to come out of Poland for a long time.

Jazz

Jazz has had a well-established pedigree in Poland ever since the 1950s, when **bebop** broke through in a country hungry for Western forms of free expression. This explosion of interest in jazz brought forth a wealth of local talent, most notably **Krzysztof Komeda**, who wrote edgy, experimental scores for Roman Polański's early movies, including the satanic lullaby theme tune of *Rosemary's Baby* (1968). Other home-grown musicians who made it into the international big league include alto saxophonist Zbigniew Namysłowski, violinist Michał

between the Trebunia family and the Twinkle Brothers going back to the early 1990s. Works better than you might imagine.

Warsaw Village Band *Uprooting* (Jaro). This 2004 release sees the traditional music of central Poland brought thrillingly up to date, with an authentic love of ancient tunes and instruments blending nicely with anarcho-punkish attitude and energy. Their previous album *Spring of Nations* (Jaro) is equally accomplished.

Gienek Wilczek's Bukowina Band *Music of the Tatra Mountains* (Nimbus, UK). Gienek is an eccentric peasant genius taught by Dziadonka, a notorious female brigand of Podhale who had learnt from Bartus Obrochta, the favoured *górale* fiddler of Szymanowski. His playing is eccentric, with a richly ornamented, raw but inspirational sound.

Various *Polish Folk Music: Songs and Music from Various Regions* (Polskie Nagrania, Poland). An excellent cross-section of music from eight different regions, from Kashubia in the north to Podhale in the south. Recordings from Polish radio give the perfect overview.

Various *Polish Village Music: Historic Polish-American Recordings 1927–1933* (Arhoolie, US). Recordings from old 78s of Polish bands now in the US. Most still have a great down-home style. *Górale* fiddler Karol Stoch "Last Evening in Podhale" was the most highly regarded of his day and the first to record commercially. His music sounds astonishingly similar to that heard in the region today: not true for the bands from elsewhere in Poland. Very good notes and translations.

Various *Pologne: Instruments Populaires* (Ocora, France). Predominantly instrumental music ranging from shepherds' horns and flutes, fiddles and bagpipes to small and medium-sized ensembles. A compilation, by Maria Baliszewska, of field recordings of the real thing in the best Ocora tradition. Good notes.

Various *Sources of Polish Folk Music* (Polish Radio Folk Collection, Poland). An excellent ten-volume series issued by Polish Radio, documenting Polish folk music with recordings from the 1960s to the mid-90s, many of them recorded at the Kazimierz Festival. Each disc focuses on a different area and comes with good notes in Polish and English on the characteristics of the region, the vocal and instrumental music and biographies of the musicians. Vol 1: Mazovia; Vol 2: Tatra Foothills; Vol 3: Lubelskie; Vol 4: Małopolska Północna; Vol 5: Wielkopolska; Vol 6: Kurpie; Vol 7: Beskidy; Vol 8: Krakowskie Tarnowskie; Vol 9: Suwalskie Podlasie; Vol 10: Rzeszowskie Pogórze. Available in the bigger Polish record shops.

Urbaniak, trumpeter Tomasz Stańko and singer Urszula Dudziak – the latter responsible for ultra-catchy 1976 jazz-disco hit *Papaya*. The late Krzystof Komeda excepted, all of the above are still very much around on the gig circuit, and CD reissues of their oeuvre can be picked up in most Polish record shops. Poland's considerable **jazz heritage** is increasingly attracting the attention of sample-hungry hip-hop producers – most notably Polish DJ duo Skalpel, who record for hip UK label Ninja Tune.

As far as major jazz events are concerned, the annual Warsaw Jazz Jamboree in October always attracts a roster of big names from abroad. There's a reasonably healthy jazz club scene in the major cities – especially Kraków, which regards itself as the spiritual home of Polish jazz.

Rock and pop

There was a time when Poland was the Liverpool of Eastern Europe, producing a stream of guitar-wielding mop-tops and warbling starlets whose music was exported all over the Soviet bloc. It started in the early 1960s, when a whole raft of groups emerged to cover the skiffle, rock-and-roll and rhythm-and-blues hits that had entered the country via the long-wave radio transmissions of Radio Luxembourg. Aided by the emergence of a **nightclub scene** in Gdańsk and Sopot, and the inauguration of the **Festival of Polish Song** in Opole (see p.469), Poland developed a home-grown version of Western pop which went under the name of **Bigbeat** – with groups like Czerwone Gitary and Skaldowie providing the local answer to the Beatles and the Rolling Stones. However the biggest name to emerge from the Sixties was **Czesław Niemen** (1939–2004), a national institution who began with earthy rhythm-and-blues and moved on through psychedelia, then prog-rock. Niemen introduced a new breadth of vision to Polish pop, although his voice – a cross between Otis Redding and a castrated wildebeest – is very much an acquired taste.

Poland's strong cabaret tradition also fed into the pop mainstream, with bards like **Marek Grechuta** (a stalwart of the Pod Baranami club in Kraków) producing intelligent, wistful, well-constructed songs that bear comparison with the likes of Jacques Brel, Serge Gainsbourg and Leonard Cohen. By the late 1970s and early 1980s punk and reggae came to the fore, the popularity of both due in part to their latent espousal of political protest – anything gobbing at authority or chanting down Babylon went down particularly well in post-martial-law Poland. Nowadays the Polish pop scene resembles that of any other European country, with hardcore, rap, reggae and death-metal subcultures coexisting with a mainstream diet of techno. There are plenty of intelligent rock-pop outfits around, however, with the melodic indie sound of Myslowitz and the unclassifiably eclectic rock-folk-chanson style of Lao Che providing most in the way of album-listening pleasure.

With thanks to Simon Broughton and Songlines magazine.

Polish film

Polish cinema has over the years been as important as Chopin piano concertos and bison-grass vodka in shaping the country's cultural profile in the eyes of outsiders. Much of this is due to the work of director **Andrzej Wajda**, who has addressed many of the key moments in Polish history in the course of a fifty-year film-making career. In addition, the oblique personal dramas of **Jerzy Skolimowski**, **Krzysztof Zanussi** and **Krzysztof Kieślowski** have given rise to an ethically complex school of cinema that remains hugely influential today. Many Polish films are available on DVD with English subtitles, so there's no reason not to stock up on local celluloid history while you're in the country.

Poland's reputation for producing a sophisticated, morally complex and frequently edgy cinema owes a lot to the political events of the 1950s, when a moderate party leadership relaxed political controls over the arts, but stopped short of removing censorship altogether. This created an ill-defined no-mans-land of cultural liberty in which film-makers could tackle difficult subjects – providing they did so with subtlety and restraint.

Andrej Wajda's wartime trilogy

The main exponent of this new spirit in Polish cinema was Andrzej Wajda (born 1926), a graduate of the **Łódź film school** whose first three films, *A Generation* (Pokolenie; 1954), *Kanal* (1956) and *Ashes and Diamonds* (Popiół i Diament; 1958) dealt with Poland's World War II experience in a way that departed from the official party line and presented Polish patriotism as a much more complex affair. Set during the **Warsaw Uprising** of 1944, *Kanal* had a particularly electrifying effect on Polish cinema-goers, focusing on non-communist insurgents rather than Soviet tanks – although the hellish voyage of the film's characters through the Warsaw sewer system served as a grim metaphor that disturbed everyone. Wajda's follow-up *Ashes and Diamonds* entered even more controversial territory, dealing with the anti-communist resistance fighters of the immediate postwar years – and it's the young assassin (iconically portrayed by Zbigniew Cybulski) who emerges as the existential hero of the film.

The sixties

Both *Kanal* and *Ashes and Diamonds* were well received abroad, ensuring an appreciative **international audience** for the blossoming of Polish talent that was to come in the sixties, another product of Łódź film school. The early works of **Roman Polański** seemed to grow out of the absurdist traditions of Polish theatre and the discordant modernism of Polish jazz. His comic but unsettling debut *Knife in the Water* (Nóż w wodzie; 1962) received an Oscar nomination for best foreign film, allowing Polański to pursue a career abroad. *Knife* was co-written by **Jerzy Skolimowski**, another Łódź graduate who stitched his student showreels together to form his first full-length feature film *Identification Marks* (Rysopis; 1964), the opening part of a six-film series of semi-autobiographical works which enhanced Poland's reputation as a heartland of philosophical art-cinema. Skolimowski was another director who spent most of his subsequent career abroad – the US production *Lightship* (an adaptation of a Siegfried Lenz story starring Klaus Maria Brandauer and Robert Duvall) was his most successful international film, winning a Golden Lion in Venice in 1984.

Man of Marble, Man of Iron

With the industrial unrest of 1970–71 and the subsequent failure of Edward Gierek's consumer-oriented socialism, the social anxieties of the 1970s soon found their way into film. Once again it was Andrzej Wajda who best expressed the spirit of the times with his *Man of Marble* (Człowiek z marmura; 1977), in which an investigative journalist tries to track down a working-class hero of the 1950s who disappeared from public view after challenging the party line. By revealing the extent to which **Polish communism** had betrayed the working class while claiming to govern in its name, *Man of Marble* seemed to lay the intellectual foundations for the Solidarity-led strikes of the 1980s. The other Polish film-maker who made a major artistic breakthrough in this period was Wajda's long-time script collaborator **Agnieszka Holland** (born 1948), whose *Provincial Actors* (Aktorzy Prowincjonalni; 1978) uses goings-on in a small-town theatre to mount a critique of Polish society under communism.

Wajda went on to make a sequel to *Man of Marble* in the shape of *Man of Iron* (Człowiek z żelaza; 1981), a political thriller which was in large part filmed inside the Gdańsk shipyards during the Solidarity strike of 1980. Wajda improvised the script as the strike went on, capturing real events. Widely hailed as a **masterpiece of political film-making**, *Man of Iron* won the Palme d'Or at Cannes in 1981 and did much to popularize the cause of Solidarity abroad.

Martial Law and after

The imposition of martial law in December 1981 closed the door on overtly political film, and directors such as Wajda and Holland chose to make movies abroad in preference to compromising with the Jaruzelski regime. The limited cultural freedoms of **the eighties** did, however, encourage the growth of a new cinema keen to explore the moral choices made by people living in circumstances where total freedom of choice is not always possible. The outside world took notice too: Krzysztof Zanussi won a Golden Lion at Venice in 1985 for his Polish-American love story *Year of the Quiet Sun* (Rok Spokojnego Słońca; 1985), a subtle meditation on fate and freedom. However the big discovery of the 1980s was **Krzystof Kieślowski** (1941–96), another product of the Łódź film school, who was commissioned by Polish TV to film a series of hour-long dramas loosely based on the Ten Commandments. Using a bleak modern housing estate as a metaphor for Polish society under socialism, the resulting *Decalogue* (Dekalog; 1988) explored ten contemporary dilemmas that were only obliquely related to the Commandments themselves. Two of the episodes (*A Short Film About Killing* and *A Short Film About Love*) were released as full-length features; and the series itself has remained a classic of thoughtful and often disturbing, social drama ever since.

Poland and the Oscars

Although Roman Polański has received awards for films he made outside Poland (picking up the Best Director Oscar for *The Pianist* in 2003), the only Oscar which can be described as genuinely Polish is the honorary award received by Andrzej Wajda for lifetime achievement in 2000. The statuette itself is currently on show in Kraków's University Museum (see p.365). Wajda also has an outstanding record in Oscar nominations, having been in contention for the Best Foreign-Language Film award for *Promised Land* (1974); the *Maids of Wilko* (1979); *Man of Iron* (1981); and most recently *Katyń* (2008).

Cult comedies

Although it's the serious face of Polish cinema that is most familiar to outsiders, comedy has played an equally important role in exposing the absurdities of socialism. In many cases the humour only served to make the **political satire** more effective, and a handful of communist-era comedies have earned cult status among successive generations of Poles as a result. Something of a pioneer in the genre was **Marek Piwowski's** *Rejs* (Cruise; 1970), a largely plotless portrait of a cross-section of Poles going on a river excursion. In a series of sketch-like dialogues, working families, party bosses and pompous intellectuals all receive their comeuppance. A more straightforward form of situation comedy came in the shape of **Stanisław Bareja's** *Miś* (Teddy Bear; 1981), in which a minor sports-club official tries to obtain a passport in order to collect savings deposited in a London bank. As well as outrageously lampooning every aspect of life under socialism, *Miś* is also a satire on the Polish film industry itself – much of the film's budget having been spent on dangling a huge straw bear from a helicopter and flying it pointlessly over the centre of Warsaw.

Historical epics and literary adaptations

One of the mainstays of Polish film has been the historical epic, a tradition going back to **Aleksander Ford's** monumental *Crusaders* (Krzyżacy; 1960), in which the defeat of the Teutonic Knights at the Battle of Grunwald (1412) is recreated in a stirring display of patriotic pomp. This and subsequent films played an important role in providing Poles with visions of a past greatness that often stood in stark contrast to Soviet-dominated reality. The works of nineteenth-century novelist Henryk Sienkiewicz (see p.544) provided much of the source material, with director **Jerzy Hoffman** turning epic tales of seventeenth-century struggle and chivalry, such as *Pan Wolodyowski* (1968) and *The Deluge* (Potop; 1974) into box office gold. *Pan Wolodjowski* was watched by an estimated three million Polish cinema-goers; both were Oscar-nominated as best foreign film.

Many of the literary adaptations filmed by Polish directors in the sixties and seventies were extraordinarily lavish, and even today present a fantastic opportunity for outsiders to get to grips with the classic books that many Poles were force-fed at school. **Kawalerowicz's** *Pharoah* (Faraon; 1966), shot on location with a cast of thousands, is a sumptuous evocation of the ancient Egypt described in Bolesław Prus's novel of the same name. Andrzej Wajda's Oscar-nominated version of Własysław Reymont's *Promised Land* (Ziemia Obiecana; 1974) was a fabulously rich recreation of life in nineteenth-century Łódź which, industrial grime and greed notwithstanding, still functions as a uniquely seductive advertisement for the city it is set in.

Into the present

In 1988 the inaugural awards ceremony of the European Film Academy declared Kieślowski's *Short Film About Killing* to be the year's **best film**. Kieślowski himself went on to become one of the great art-film directors of the 1990s, producing a series of internationally-funded features with his scriptwriter Krzysztof Piesiewicz and favourite soundtrack composer Zbigniew Preisner still in tow. His *Double Life of Veronique* (1990) and the subsequent *Three Colours* trilogy (1993–4) were met with almost universal critical acclaim, picking up **awards** at the Venice and Berlin film festivals in the process.

Within Poland the film industry turned in on itself, producing **dramas** that were relevant to Polish audiences but lacked the kind of universal appeal that would make them popular abroad. Most importantly, the home-grown historical blockbuster made a major comeback. Jerzy Hoffman's swashbuckling 1999 adaptation of Henryk Sienkiewicz's patriotic novel *With Fire and Sword* (Ogniem i Mieczem) became the most successful box- office Polish film of all time. Even more money was spent on a new screen version of Sienkiewicz's *Quo Vadis*, directed by veteran **Jerzy Kawalerowicz** in 2001. Andrzej Wajda carried off a seemingly impossible feat by filming Adam Mickiewicz's epic nineteenth-century poem *Pan Tadeusz* (1998), using a screenplay that stuck to the rhyming verse of the original. Wajda's *Katyń* (2008) revisited the tragedy of World War II by dramatizing the mass murder of Polish officers by Stalin's secret police in 1939. The film's release was seen as an event of national importance in Poland itself, but it has rarely been screened outside the country.

Poland continues to have a thriving film industry. The Łódź film school, incubator of so much Polish talent in the past, still produces highly qualified scriptwriters, directors and camera operators, and is increasingly recognized internationally as a centre of excellence.

Language

Language

Polish

P olish is one of the more difficult European languages for English-speakers
to learn. Even so, it is well worth acquiring the basics: not only is Polish
beautiful and melodious, but a few words will go a long way. This is
especially true away from the major cities where you won't find a lot of
English spoken. Knowledge of German, however, is quite widespread.

The following features provide an indication of the problems of Polish
grammar. There are three genders (masculine, feminine and neuter) and no word
for "the". Prepositions (words like "to", "with", "in" and so on) take different
cases, and the case changes the form of the noun. Thus, *miasto* is the Polish for
"town", but "to the town" is *do miasta* and "in the town" is *w miescie*. You don't
have to learn this sort of thing off by heart, but it can be useful to be able to
recognize it.

Finally, a brief word on how to address people. The familiar form used among
friends, relations and young people is *ty*, like French *tu* or German *du*. However,
the polite form which you will usually require is *Pan* when addressing a man and
Pani for a woman ("Sir" and "Madam"). Always use this form with people
obviously older than yourself, and with officials.

The *Rough Guide to Polish* **phrasebook** provides more detailed advice on using
the language.

Pronunciation

While Polish may look daunting at first, with its apparently unrelieved rows of
consonants, the good news is that it's a phonetic language – that is, it's
pronounced exactly as spelt. So once you've learnt the rules and have a little
experience you'll always know how to pronounce a word correctly.

Stress

Usually on the penultimate syllable, eg *Warszawa, przyjaciel, matka*.

Vowels

a: as "a" in "cat".

e: "e" in "neck".

i: "i" in "Mick", never as in "I".

o: "o" in "lot", never as in "no" or "move".

u: "oo" in "look".

y: unknown in Standard English; cross
between "e" and Polish "i", eg the "y" in the
Yorkshire pronunciation of "Billy".

There are three specifically Polish
vowels:

ą: nasalized – like "ong" in "long" or French
"on".

ę: nasalized – like French "un" (eg Lech
Wałęsa).

ó: same sound as Polish "u".

Vowel combinations include:

ie: pronounced y-e, eg *nie wiem* (I don't know): ny-e vy-em (not nee-veem).

eu: each letter pronounced separately, eg "E-u-ropa" (Europe).

ia: rather like "yah", eg *historia* (history): his-tor-i-yah.

Consonants

Those which look the same as English but are different:

w: as "v" in "vine", eg "wino" pronounced "vino" (wine).

r: trilled (as in Scottish pronunciation of English "r").

h: like the "ch" in Scottish "loch".

Some consonants are pronounced differently at the end of a word or syllable: "b" sounds like "p", "d" like "t", "g" like "k", "w" like "f".

Polish-specific consonants include:

ć and **ci**: "ch" as in "church".

ł: "dark l" sounding rather like a "w".

ń and **ni**: soft "n", sounding like "n-ye", eg koń (horse): kon-ye.

ś and **si**: "sh" as in "ship".

ź and **zi**: like the "j" of French *journal*.

ż and **rz**: as in French "g" in *gendarme*. (Note that the dot over the "z" is sometimes replaced by a bar through the letter's diagonal.)

Consonantal pairs

cz: "ch" (slightly harder than "ć" and "ci").

sz: "sh" (ditto "ś" and "si").

dz: "d" as in "day" rapidly followed by "z" as in "zoo", eg *dzwon* (bell): d-zvon. At the end of a word is pronounced like "ts" as in "cats".

dź: "d-sh", eg *dźungla* (jungle): d-shun-gla.

dż: sharper than the above; at the end of a word is pronounced like "ć" (ch).

szcz: this fearsome-looking cluster is easy to pronounce – "sh-ch" as in "pushchair", eg *szczur* (rat): sh-choor.

Useful words and phrases

Words

Yes	Tak	Later	Później
No/not	Nie	Open	Otwarty
Please/you're welcome	Proszę	Closed/shut	Zamknięty
		Earlier	Wcześniej
More emphatic than proszę	Proszę bardzo Dziekuję/dziekuję	Enough	Dosyć
Thank you	bardzo	Over there	Tam
Where	Gdzie	This one (masc/ fem/ neuter)	Ten/ta/to
When	Kiedy	That one (masc/ fem/ neuter)	Tamten/tamta/tamto
Why	Dlaczego		
How much	Ile	Large	Wielki
Here, there	Tu/tam	Small	Mały
Now	Teraz	More	Więcej

Less	Mniej		Hot	Gorący
A little	Mało		Cold	Zimny
A lot	Dużo		With	Z
Cheap	Tani		Without	Bez
Expensive	Drogi		In	W
Good	Dobry		For	Dla
Bad	Zły/niedobry			

Phrases

Good day/hello	Dzień dobry		I'm British (male /female)	Jestem Brytyjc zykiem/ Brytyjką
Good evening	Dobry wieczór			
Good night	Dobra noc		Irish	Irlandczykiem/ Irlandką
"Hi!" or "'Bye" (like Italian *ciao*)	Cześć!			
			American	Amerikaniem/ Amerikanką
Goodbye	Do widzenia			
Excuse me (apology)	Przepraszam		Canadian	Kanadyjczykiem/ Kanadyjką
Excuse me (requesting information)	Proszę Pana/Pani			
			Australian	Australyjczykiem/ Australyjką
How are you? (informal)	Jak się masz?			
			I live in . . .	Mieszkam w . . .
How are you? (formal)	Jak się Pan/Pani ma?		Today	Dzisiaj
Fine	Dobrze		Tomorrow	Jutro
Do you speak English?	Czy Pan/Pani mówi po angielsku?		Day after tomorrow	Pojutrze
			Yesterday	Wczoraj
I understand	Rozumiem		Moment!/ Wait a moment	Chwileczkę
I don't understand	Nie rozumiem			
I don't know	Nie wiem		In the morning	Rano
Please speak a bit more slowly	Proszę mówić trochę wolniej		In the afternoon	Po południu
			In the evening	Wieczorem
I don't speak Polish very well	Nie mówię dobrze po polsku		Where is . . . ?	Gdzie jest . . .?
			How do I get to . . . ?	Jak dojechać do . . . ?
What's the Polish for that?	Co to znaczy po polsku?		What time is it?	Która (jest) godzina?
			How far is it to . . . ?	Jak daleko jest do . . . ?
I'm here on holiday	Jestem tu na urlopie			

Accommodation

Hotel	Hotel		Two nights	Dwie noce
Lodgings	Noclegi		Three nights	Trzy noce
Is there a hotel nearby?	Czy jest gdzieś tutaj hotel?		A week	Tydzień
			Two weeks	Dwa tygodnie
Do you have a room?	Czy Pan/Pani ma pokój?		With a bath	Pokój z łazienką
			With a shower	Z prysznicem
Single room	Pojedynczy pokój		With a balcony	Z balkonem
Double room	Podwójny pokój		Hot water	Z ciepłą wodą
For one night (*doba*: 24hr)	Będziemy jedną dobę		Running water	Z bieżącą wodą
			How much is it?	Ile kosztuje?

That's expensive	To drogo	Is there a campsite nearby?	Czy jest gdzieś tutaj camping?
That's too expensive	To za drogo	Tent	Namiot
Does that include breakfast?	Czy to obejmuje śniadanie?	Cabin	Schronisko
Do you have anything cheaper?	Czy nie ma tańszego?	Youth hostel	Schronisko młodziezowe
Can I see the room?	Czy mogę zobaczyć pokój?	The menu, please	Proszę o jadłospis
		The bill, please	Proszę o rachunek
Good, I'll take it	Dobrze, wezmę		
I have a booking	Mam rezerwację		
Can we camp here?	Czy możemy tu rozbić namiot?		

Travelling

Car	Auto	When does the Warsaw train leave?	Kiedy odjeżdża pociąg do Warszawy?
Aircraft	Samolot	Do I have to change?	Czy muszę się przesiadać?
Bicycle	Rower		
Bus	Autobus	Which platform does the train leave from?	Z jakiego peronu odjedzie pociąg?
Ferry	Prom		
Train	Pociąg		
Train station	Dworzec, samochód, stacja	How many kilometres is it?	Ile to jest kilometrów?
Bus station	Autobusowy	How long does the journey last?	Ile czasu trwa podróż?
Taxi	Taksówka		
Hitchhiking	Autostop	Which bus is it to . . . ?	Jakim autobusem do . . . ?
On foot	Piechotą		
A ticket to . . ., please	Proszę bilet do . . .	Where is the road to . . . ?	Gdzie jest droga do . . . ?
Return	Bilet powrotny		
Single	W jedną stronę	Next stop, please	Następny przystanek, proszę
I'd like a seat reservation	Proszę z miejscówką		

Signs

Entrance; exit/way out	Wejście; wyjucie	Pull; push	Ciągnąć; pchać
No entrance	Wstęp wzbroniony	Out of order; closed (ticket counters etc)	Nieczynny
Toilet	Toaleta	Platform	Peron
Men	Dla panów; męski	Cash desk	Kasa
Women	Dla pan; damski	Stop	Stop
Occupied	Zajęty	Polish state frontier	Granica międzynarodowa
Free, vacant	Wolny		
Arrival; departure (train, bus)	Przyjazd; odjazd	Republic of Poland	Rzeczpospolita Polska
		Beware, caution	Uwaga; baczność
Arrival; departure (aircraft)	Przylot; odlot	Danger	Uwaga; niebezpieczeństwo
Closed for renovation /stocktaking	Remont	Police	Policja

LANGUAGE | Useful words and phrases

| Information | Informacja | Do not touch | Nie dotykać |
| No smoking | Nie palić; palenie wzbronione | | |

Driving

Car	Samochód, auto	Petrol/gas	Benzyna
Left	Na lewo	Petrol/gas station	Stacja benzynowa
Right	Na prawo	Oil	Olej
Straight ahead	Prosto	Water	Woda
Parking	Parking	To repair	Naprawić
Detour	Objazd	Accident	Wypadek
End (showing when a previous sign ceases to be valid)	Koniec	Breakdown	Awaria
		Speed limit	Ograniczenie prędkości
No overtaking	Zakaz wyprzedzania		

Days, months and dates

Monday	Poniedziałek	July	Lipiec
Tuesday	Wtorek	August	Sierpień
Wednesday	Środa	September	Wrzesień
Thursday	Czwartek	October	Październik
Friday	Piątek	November	Listopad
Saturday	Sobota	December	Grudzień
Sunday	Niedziela	Spring	Wiosna
January	Styczeń	Summer	Lato
February	Luty	Autumn	Jesień
March	Marzec	Winter	Zima
April	Kwiecień	Holidays	Wakacje
May	Maj	Bank holiday	Święto
June	Czerwiec		

Numbers

1	Jeden	14	Czternaście
2	Dwa	15	Piętnaście
3	Trzy	16	Szesnaście
4	Cztery	17	Siedemnaście
5	Pięć	18	Osiemnaście
6	Sześć	19	Dziewiętnaście
7	Siedem	20	Dwadzieścia
8	Osiem	30	Trzydzieści
9	ziewięć	40	Czterdzieści
10	Dziesięć	50	Pięćdziesiąt
11	Jedenaście	60	Sześćdziesiąt
12	Dwanaście	70	Siedemdziesiąt
13	Trzynaście	80	Osiemdziesiąt

90	Dziewięćdziesiąt	600	Sześćset
100	Sto	700	Siedemset
200	Dwieście	800	Osiemset
300	Trzysta	900	Dziewięćset
400	Czterysta	1000	Tysiąc
500	Pięćset	1,000,000	Milion

Food and drink

Common terms

Filiżanka	Cup	Obiad	Lunch
Gotowany	Boiled	Śniadanie	Breakfast
Grill/z rusztu	Grilled	Święzy	Fresh
Jadłospis	Menu	Słodki	Sweet
Kolacja	Dinner	Smacznego!	Bon appetit!
Kwaśny	Sour	Surowy	Raw
Łyżka	Spoon	Szklanka	Glass
Marynowany	Pickled	Sznycel	Escalope/schnitzel
Mielone	Minced	Talerz	Plate
Na zdrowie!	Cheers!	Wegetariański	Vegetarian
Nadziewany	Stuffed	Widelec	Fork
Nóż	Knife		

Basic foods

Bułka	Bread rolls	Masło	Butter
Chleb	Bread	Mięso	Meat
Chrzan	Horseradish	Ocet	Vinegar
Cukier	Sugar	Olej	Oil
Drób	Poultry	Owoce	Fruit
Frytki	Chips/French fries	Pieczeń	Roast meat
Jajko	Egg	Pieprz	Pepper
Jarzyny/warzywa	Vegetables	Potrawy jarskie	Vegetarian dishes
Kanapka	Sandwich	Ryby	Fish
Kołduny	Lithuanian ravioli-like parcels stuffed with meat	Ryż	Rice
		Śmietana	Cream
		Sól	Salt
Kotlet	Cutlet	Surówka	Salad
Makaron	Macaroni	Zupa	Soup

Soups

Barszcz czerwony (z pasztecikem)	Beetroot soup (with pastry)	Żurek	Soup made from fermented rye flour and potatoes
Barszcz ukraiński	White borsch	(zupa) Cebulowa	Onion soup
Bulion/rosół	Bouillon	(zupa) Fasolowa	Bean soup
Chłodnik	Sour milk and vegetable cold soup	(zupa) Grochowa	Pea soup
		(zupa) Grzybowa	Mushroom soup
Fasólka po bretońsku	Spicy bean soup with bacon bits	(zupa) Jarzynowa	Vegetable soup
Kapuśniak	Cabbage soup	(zupa) Ogórkowa	Cucumber soup
Krupnik	Barley soup	(zupa) Owocowa	Cold fruit soup
		(zupa) Pomidorowa	Tomato soup

Meat, fish and poultry

Baranina	Mutton	Kurczak	Chicken
Bażant	Pheasant	Łosoś	Salmon
Befsztyk	Steak	Makrela	Mackerel
Bekon/boczek	Bacon	Pstrąg	Trout
Cielęcina	Veal	Śledź	Herring
Dziczyzna	Game	Salami	Salami
Dzik	Wild boar	Sardynka	Sardine
Gęś	Geese	Sarnina	Elk
Golonka	Leg of pork	Szaszłyk	Shish kebab
Indyk	Turkey	Wątróbka	Liver with onion
Kaczka	Duck	Węgorz	Eel
Karp	Carp	Wierprzowe	Pork
Kiełbasa	Sausage	Wołowe	Beef
Kotlet schabowy	Pork cutlet		

Fruit and vegetables

Ananas	Pineapple	Kalafior	Cauliflower
Banan	Banana	Kapusta	Cabbage
Ćwikła/buraczki	Beetroot	Kapusta kiszona	Sauerkraut
Cebula	Onion	Kasza	Buckwheat
Cytryna	Lemon	Kompot	Stewed fruit
Czarne jagody/ borówki	Blackberries	Maliny	Raspberries
		Marchewka	Carrots
Czarne porzeczki	Blackcurrant	Migdały	Almonds
Czereśnie	Cherries	Morele	Apricots
Czosnek	Garlic	Ogórek	Cucumber
Fasola	Beans	Ogórki	Gherkins
Groch	Peas	Orzechy włoskie	Walnuts
Gruszka	Pears	Papryka	Paprika
Grzyby/pieczarki	Mushrooms	Pomarańcze	Orange
Jabłko	Apple	Pomidor	Tomato

Śliwka	Plum	Truskawki	Strawberries
Szparagi	Asparagus	Winogrona	Grapes
Szpinak	Spinach	Ziemniaki	Potatoes

Cheese

Bryndza	Sheep's cheese	(ser) Myśliwski	Smoked cheese
Oscypek	Smoked goats' cheese	(ser) Tylżycki	Hard yellow cheese
Twaróg	Cottage cheese		

Cakes and desserts

Ciastko	Cake	Makowiec	Poppyseed cake
Ciasto drożdżowe	Yeast cake with fruit	Mazurek	Shortcake
Czekolada	Chocolate	Pączki	Doughnuts
Galaretka	Jellied fruits	Sernik	Cheesecake
Lody	Ice cream	Tort	Tart

Drinks

Cocktail mleczny	Milk shake	Sok	Juice
Gorąca czekolada	Drinking chocolate	Sok pomarańczowy	Orange juice
Herbata	Tea	Sok pomidorowy	Tomato juice
Kawa	Coffee	Winiak	Polish brandy
Koniak	Cognac/brandy (imported)	Wino	Wine
Miód pitny	Mead	Wino słodkie	Sweet wine
Mleko	Milk	Wino wytrawne	Dry wine
Napój	Bottled fruit drink	Woda	Water
Piwo	Beer	Woda mineralna	Mineral water
		Wódka	Vodka

Glossary

General terms

Aleja – Avenue (abb. *al.*)

Biuro Zakwaterowania – Accommodation office

Brama – Gate

Cerkiew – (pl. *cerkwie*) Orthodox church, or a church belonging to the Uniates (Greek Catholics), a tradition loyal to Rome but following Orthodox rites that date back to the 1595 Act of Union (see box on p.230)

Cmentarz – Cemetery

Dolina – Valley

Dom – House

Dom Kultury – Cultural House, a community arts and social centre

Dom Wycieczkowy – Cheap, basic type of hotel

Droga – Road

Dwór – Country house traditionally owned by member of the *szlachta* class

Dworzec – Station

Główny – Main – as in Rynek Główny, main square

Góra – (pl. *góry*) Mountain

Granica – Border

Jezioro – Lake

Kantor – Exchange office

Kaplica – Chapel

Kawiarnia – Café

Katedra – Cathedral

Klasztor – Monastery

Kościół – Church

Ksiądz – Priest

Ksiażę – Prince, duke

Księgarnia – Bookshop

Kraj – Country

Las – Wood, forest

Masyw – Massif

Miasto – Town (Stare Miasto – Old Town; Nowe Miasto – New Town)

Most – Bridge

Naród – Nation, people

Nysa – River Neisse

Odra – River Oder

Ogród – Gardens

Pałac – Palace

Piwnica – Pub

Plac – Square (abb. *pl.*)

Plaża – Beach

Poczta – Post office

Pogotowie – Emergency

Pokój – (pl. *pokóje*) Room

Pole – Field

Prom – Ferry

Przedmieście – Suburb

Przystanek – Bus stop

Puszcza – Ancient forest

Ratusz – Town hall

Restauracja – Restaurant

Ruch – Chain of newpaper kiosks also selling public transport tickets

Rynek – Marketplace, commonly the main square in a town

Rzeka – River

Sejm – Parliament

Shtetl – Yiddish name for a rural town, usually with a significant Jewish population

Skała – Rock, cliff

Skansen – Open-air museum with reconstructed folk architecture and art

Stocznia – Shipyards

Święty – Saint (abb. *św.*)

Starowiercy – (Old Believers) Traditionalist Russian Orthodox sect, small communities of which survive in east Poland

Stary – Old

Szlachta – Term for the traditional gentry class, inheritors of status and land

Ulica – Street (abb. *ul.*)

Województwo – Administrative district

Wieś – (pl. *Wsie*) Village

Wieża – Tower

Winiarnia – Wine cellar

Wisła – River Vistula

Wodospad – Waterfall

Wzgórze – Hill

Zamek – Castle

Zdrój – Spa

Ziemia – Region

Street names

Polish streets and squares are frequently named after events or personalities crucial to the nation's history, and as such represent a fascinating lexicon of national culture. Listed below are some of the most common examples.

Generał Władysław Anders (1892–1970) – Renowned military figure who led the Polish troops, was exiled to Siberia at the start of World War II and later returned to fight on the Allied side in the Middle East, then in Europe.

Armii Krajowej (AK) – The Home Army, forces of the wartime Polish resistance.

Józef Bem (1794–1850) – Swashbuckling military figure who participated in the 1848 "Springtime of the Nations" in both Austria and Hungary.

Generał Zygmunt Berling (1896–1980) – First commander-in-chief of communist-sponsored Polish forces in the Soviet Union.

Bohaterów Getta – Heroes of the Ghetto, in memory of the April 1943 Warsaw Ghetto Uprising against the Nazis.

Tadeusz Bór-Komorowski (1895–1966) – Commander of AK (Home Army) forces during the 1944 Warsaw Uprising.

Władysław Broniewski (1897–1962) – Early socialist adherent of Piłsudski's World War I Legions, revolutionary poet and famously unreformed drunkard.

Fryderyk Chopin (1810–49) (also sometimes spelt "Szopen" in Polish) – Celebrated Romantic-era composer and pianist, long a national icon (see box, p.120).

Chrobrego – Refers to Bolesław Chrobry (Bolesław the Brave), first king of Poland and the man who established the country as a definite independent state.

Maria Dąbrowska (1889–1965) – Fine modern Polish writer best known for her epic novels.

Aleksander Fredro (1793–1876) – Popular dramatist, especially of comedies.

Grunwald – Landmark medieval battle (1410) where combined Polish-Lithuanian forces thrashed the Teutonic Knights.

Berek Joselewicz (1764–1809) – Polish-Lithuanian Jew who led a Jewish unit in the patriotic Kościuszko rebellion of 1794, and subsequently fought with Polish volunteers under Napoleon.

Jan Kasprowicz (1860–1926) – Popular peasant-born neo-Romantic poet and voluminous translator of Western classics into Polish.

Jan Kochanowski (1530–84) – Renaissance-era poet, the father of the modern Polish literary canon.

Maksymilian Kolbe (1894–1941) – Catholic priest martyred in Auschwitz, canonized by Pope John Paul II.

Maria Konopnicka (1842–1910) – Children's story writer of the nineteenth century, adherent of the "Positivist" School which developed in reaction to the traditional national preference for Romanticism.

Mikołaj Kopernik (1473–1543) – Indigenous name of the great astronomer known elsewhere as Copernicus, who spent much of his life in the Baltic town of Frombork.

Tadeusz Kościuszko (1746–1817) – Dashing veteran of the American War of Independence and leader of the 1794 insurrection in Poland (see box, p.390–391).

Józef Ignacy Krasicki (1735–1801) – Enlightenment-era poet-bishop of Warmia, dubbed the "Polish Lafontaine".

Zygmunt Krasiński (1812–59) – Author of Nieboska Komedia, one of the trio of Polish Romantic messianic greats.

Józef Kraszewski (1812–87) – Hugely popular historical novelist. His novels (more than two hundred of them) cover everything from the early Piasts to the Partition era.

6 Kwietnia (April 6) – Date of the Battle of Racławice, where Kościuszko's largely peasant army defeated the tsarist forces in 1794.

11 Listopada (Nov 11) – Symbolically important post-World War I Polish Independence Day.

29 Listopada (Nov 29) – Start of (failed) November 1830 uprising against the Russians.

1 Maja (May 1) – Labour Day.

3 Maja (May 3) – Famous democratic Constitution of 1791.

9 Maja (May 9) – Polish "V" Day – the Russian-declared end of World War II – one day after Britain and other Western European countries.

Jan Matejko (1838–93) – Patriotic *fin de siècle* painter closely associated with Kraków, where he lived most of his life.

Adam Mickiewicz (1798–1855) – The Romantic Polish poet, a national figure considered kosher by just about everyone, former communist leaders included (see p.78).

Stanisław Moniuszko (1819–72) – Romantic composer of patriotic operas, popular in Poland but little known elsewhere.

Gabriel Narutowicz (1865–1922) – First president of the Second Polish Republic, assassinated a few days after his nomination.

Ignacy Paderewski (1860–1941) – Noted pianist and composer who became the country's first prime minister post-World War I and the country's regaining of independence.

Jan Paweł II (1920–2005) – Catholic pontiff and Polish national hero. Many streets are now renamed after Pope John Paul II.

Józef Piłsudski (1867–1935) – One of the country's most venerated military-political figures, key architect of the regaining of independence after World War I, and national leader in the late 1920s and early 1930s.

Emilia Plater (1806–31) – Spirited daughter of Polish-Lithuanian landowners, who volunteered to fight in the 1831 November Uprising and died of a fever soon afterwards.

Józef Poniatowski (1767–1813) – Nephew of the last Polish king who fought in numerous Polish and Napoleonic campaigns: an archetypal Polish military-Romantic hero.

Jerzy Popiełuszko – Radical Solidarity-supporting priest murdered by the Security Forces in 1984, and since elevated to the ranks of national martyrs.

Bolesław Prus (1847–1912) – Positivist writer, best known for quasi-historical novels such as *Pharaoh* and *Lalka* ("The Doll").

Kazimierz Pułaski (1747–79) – Polish-American hero of the US War of Independence.

Mikołaj Rej (1505–69) – So-called "Father of Polish Literature", one of the first to write in the language.

Władysław Reymont (1867–1925) – Nobel Prize-winning author of *The Peasants* and *The Promised Land*.

Henryk Sienkiewicz (1846–1916) – Stirring historical novelist who won the Nobel Prize for his epic *Quo Vadis?*

15 Sierpnia – Date of the Battle of Warsaw (August 1920) that halted the Soviet offensive against Poland, popularly known as the "miracle on the Vistula".

Władysław Sikorski (1881–1943) – Prewar Polish prime minister and wartime commander-in-chief of Polish forces in the West.

Marie Skłodowska-Curie (1867–1934) – Nobel Prize-winning scientist and discoverer of the radioactive elements radium and polonium.

Juliusz Słowacki (1809–49) – Noted playwright and poet, one of the three Polish Romantic greats.

Jan Sobieski (1635–96) – Quintessentially Polish king famous for his celebrated rescue of Vienna (1683) from the Ottoman Turks.

Bohaterów Stalingradu – "Heroes of Stalingrad", a reference to the turning point in the defeat of Nazi Germany; less common than it was, but one of the few communist names to survive.

22 Stycznia – Date of the start of January Uprising of 1863 against the Russians.

Świętego Ducha – Holy Spirit, generally used in square names.

Świętej Trójcy – Holy Trinity

Karol Szymanowski (1882–1937) – Noted modern Polish classical composer, a long-time Zakopane resident.

Kazimierz (Przerwa) Tetmajer (1865–1940) – Turn-of-the-twentieth-century neo-Romantic poet, part of the Kraków-based Młoda Polska school.

Westerplatte – The Polish garrison the attack on whom by the Nazis in September 1939 signalled the start of World War II.

Wilsona – After US President Woodrow Wilson, who supported the cause of Polish independence at the Versailles Conference (1919).

Stanisław Ignacy Witkiewicz (1885–1939) – Maverick modernist artist and writer whose plays anticipated postwar Theatre of the Absurd.

1 Września (Sept 1) – Start of World War II – the September 1939 Nazi invasion of Poland.

Stanisław Wyspiański (1867–1907) – Renowned Młoda Polska era poet, playwright and painter best known for his plays *Wesele* (The Wedding) and *Wyzwolenie* ("Liberation").

Kardynał Stefan Wyszyński (1901–81) – Tenacious postwar Catholic primate of Poland, figurehead of popular resistance to communism.

Wszystkich Świętych – All Saints – a popular Catholic festival.

Stefan Żeromski (1864–1925) – One of the most renowned Polish novelists, a neo-Romantic writer best known for his historical novel *Popioly* ("Ashes").

Small print and
Index

A Rough Guide to Rough Guides

Published in 1982, the first Rough Guide – to Greece – was a student scheme that became a publishing phenomenon. Mark Ellingham, a recent graduate in English from Bristol University, had been travelling in Greece the previous summer and couldn't find the right guidebook. With a small group of friends he wrote his own guide, combining a highly contemporary, journalistic style with a thoroughly practical approach to travellers' needs.

The immediate success of the book spawned a series that rapidly covered dozens of destinations. And, in addition to impecunious backpackers, Rough Guides soon acquired a much broader and older readership that relished the guides' wit and inquisitiveness as much as their enthusiastic, critical approach and value-for-money ethos.

These days, Rough Guides include recommendations from shoestring to luxury and cover more than 200 destinations around the globe, including almost every country in the Americas and Europe, more than half of Africa and most of Asia and Australasia. Our ever-growing team of authors and photographers is spread all over the world, particularly in Europe, the USA and Australia.

In the early 1990s, Rough Guides branched out of travel, with the publication of Rough Guides to World Music, Classical Music and the Internet. All three have become benchmark titles in their fields, spearheading the publication of a wide range of books under the Rough Guide name.

Including the travel series, Rough Guides now number more than 350 titles, covering: phrasebooks, waterproof maps, music guides from Opera to Heavy Metal, reference works as diverse as Conspiracy Theories and Shakespeare, and popular culture books from iPods to Poker. Rough Guides also produce a series of more than 120 World Music CDs in partnership with World Music Network.

Visit www.roughguides.com to see our latest publications.

Rough Guide travel images are available for commercial licensing at www.roughguidespictures.com

SMALL PRINT

Rough Guide credits

Text editor: Edward Aves, Emma Gibbs, Helen Ochyra
Layout: Ankur Guha
Cartography: Rajesh Mishra
Picture editor: Mark Thomas
Production: Rebecca Short
Proofreader: Susanne Hillen
Cover design: Chloë Roberts
Photographer: Chris Christoforou
Editorial: Ruth Blackmore, Andy Turner, Keith Drew, Alice Park, Lucy White, Jo Kirby, James Smart, Natasha Foges, Róisín Cameron, Emma Traynor, Kathryn Lane, Christina Valhouli, Monica Woods, Mani Ramaswamy, Harry Wilson, Lucy Cowie, Amanda Howard, Alison Roberts, Joe Staines, Peter Buckley, Matthew Milton, Tracy Hopkins, Ruth Tidball; **Delhi** Madhavi Singh, Karen D'Souza, Lubna Shaheen
Design & Pictures: **London** Scott Stickland, Dan May, Diana Jarvis, Chloë Roberts, Nicole Newman, Sarah Cummins, Emily Taylor; **Delhi** Umesh Aggarwal, Ajay Verma, Jessica Subramanian, Pradeep Thapliyal, Sachin Tanwar, Anita Singh, Nikhil Agarwal
Production: Vicky Baldwin

Cartography: **London** Maxine Repath, Ed Wright, Katie Lloyd-Jones; **Delhi** Rajesh Chhibber, Ashutosh Bharti, Animesh Pathak, Jasbir Sandhu, Karobi Gogoi, Alakananda Bhattacharya, Swati Handoo, Deshpal Dabas
Online: **London** Georgina Atwell, Faye Hellon, Jeanette Angell, Fergus Day, Justine Bright, Clare Bryson, Aine Fearon, Adrian Low, Ezgi Celebi, Amber Bloomfield; **Delhi** Amit Verma, Rahul Kumar, Narender Kumar, Ravi Yadav, Debojit Borah, Rakesh Kumar, Ganesh Sharma, Shisir Basumatari
Marketing & Publicity: **London** Liz Statham, Niki Hanmer, Louise Maher, Jess Carter, Vanessa Godden, Vivienne Watton, Anna Paynton, Rachel Sprackett, Libby Jellie, Laura Vipond, Vanessa McDonald; **New York** Katy Ball, Judi Powers, Nancy Lambert; **Delhi** Ragini Govind
Manager India: Punita Singh
Reference Director: Andrew Lockett
Operations Manager: Helen Phillips
PA to Publishing Director: Nicola Henderson
Publishing Director: Martin Dunford
Commercial Manager: Gino Magnotta
Managing Director: John Duhigg

Publishing information

This seventh edition published July 2009 by **Rough Guides Ltd**,
80 Strand, London WC2R 0RL
14 Local Shopping Centre, Panchsheel Park, New Delhi 110017, India
Distributed by the Penguin Group
Penguin Books Ltd,
80 Strand, London WC2R 0RL
Penguin Group (USA)
375 Hudson Street, NY 10014, USA
Penguin Group (Australia)
250 Camberwell Road, Camberwell,
Victoria 3124, Australia
Penguin Group (Canada)
195 Harry Walker Parkway N, Newmarket, ON, L3Y 7B3 Canada
Penguin Group (NZ)
67 Apollo Drive, Mairangi Bay, Auckland 1310, New Zealand
Cover concept by Peter Dyer.

Typeset in Bembo and Helvetica to an original design by Henry Iles.

Printed and bound in Singapore by SNP Security Printing Pte Ltd

© Jonathan Bousfield and Mark Salter

No part of this book may be reproduced in any form without permission from the publisher except for the quotation of brief passages in reviews.

680pp includes index

A catalogue record for this book is available from the British Library

ISBN: 978-1-84836-064-8

1 3 5 7 9 8 6 4 2

Help us update

We've gone to a lot of effort to ensure that the seventh edition of **The Rough Guide to Poland** is accurate and up-to-date. However, things change – places get "discovered", opening hours are notoriously fickle, restaurants and rooms raise prices or lower standards. If you feel we've got it wrong or left something out, we'd like to know, and if you can remember the address, the price, the hours, the phone number, so much the better.

Please send your comments with the subject line "**Rough Guide Poland Update**" to Ⓔmail@roughguides.com. We'll credit all contributions and send a copy of the next edition (or any other Rough Guide if you prefer) for the very best emails.

Have your questions answered and tell others about your trip at
Ⓦcommunity.roughguides.com

Acknowledgements

Jonathan Bousfield would like to thank Iwona Parzynska at the Muzeum Narodowe in Kraków; Marcin Drobisz at Bureau of Promotion and Marketing, Kraków City Council; Ewa Wojciechowska at the Instytut Książki, Kraków; Zofia Dworzak at Wawel Castle, Kraków; and the staff of the Jagiellonian University Library in Kraków, the Małopolska County Library in Kraków, and the Polish Institute in Vilnius. Double vodkas all round to Stuart Wadsworth, Fergus Mahon and Jamie Howard for sharing research trips and insights.

Thanks are also due to Edward Aves, Emma Gibbs and Helen Ochyra for ensuring the author reached the finishing line; cartographer Rajesh Mishra for labouring heroically to prepare new maps, Susanne Hillen for proofreading and Mark Thomas for picture research.

Jeroen van Marle would like to say dzięki to Jon, Edward, Emma and Helen in London, Przemek Ślązak, the Kitson family, Goska Drząszcz, Poland's many patient tourism information office employees, all Wrocław car vandals, the Karwat family and Marta.

Readers' letters

Many thanks to all the readers who took the time and trouble to write in with comments and updates on the sixth edition. Apologies for any omissions or misspellings:

Paul Burton, Brian Davis, Gary Elflett, Philip Garrison, Steve Gillon & Colin Hood, David Halford, Paul Hansford, Bartosz Nabrdalik, Nick Nicolaides, Dale C Rielage, James Tartaglia & Zoe Hoida, John Wright

SMALL PRINT

Photo credits

All photos © Rough Guides except the following:

Title page
Tatra Mountains © Peter Adams/Getty Images

Full page
Gdansk © Peter Adams/Getty Images

Introduction
Golka cheese © Gallo Images/Getty Images
Buildings in Warsaw © Peter Adams/Alamy
Girls in traditional costume © Jonathan Bousfield
Gasienicowa Valley © Jan Wlodarczyk/Alamy
Jewish cemetery © Bart Nedobre/Alamy
Rural landscape © PCl/Alamy

Things not to miss
01 Zamość © John Norman/Alamy
02 Slowiński National Park © Jan Wlodarczyk/ Alamy
03 The Tatras © tompiodesign/Alamy
05 Traditional wooden church © Bartek Wrzesniowski/Alamy
07 Baltic beach © PCL/Alamy
08 Zalipie © Michel Setboun/Corbis
09 Mazurian Lakes © PCL/Alamy
10 Hiking in the Bieszcady © PCl/Alamy
11 Lublin © David Sutherland/Alamy
12 Kazimierz Dolny © Caro/Alamy
14 Ulica Dluga, Gdańsk © Robert Clare/Getty Images
16 Poznań © Peter Forsberg/Alamy
17 Rafting on the Dunajec © Robert Clare/Alamy
18 Toruń © Gregory Wrona/Alamy
19 Stalag Luft and the *Great Escape* featuring Steve McQueen © Corbis
20 Wroclaw © Peter Brown/Alamy
21 Palace of culture © Photo's Poland/Alamy
22 Łodź © Les Polders/Alamy
23 Malbork Castle © PCL/Alamy
25 European Bison © Ryszard Laskowski/Alamy
26 Warsaw Old Town © Edward Aves

Religious architecture colour section
Seventeenth-century Polish church © Stan Kujawa/Alamy
Synagogue in Krakow © Ed Wright
Podlasie Lruszyniany Mosque © Witold Skrypczak
Peace church © JTB/Alamy
Orthodox church © Danita Delimont/Alamy

Food and drink colour section
Bortsch © Bon Appetit/Corbis
Polish mushroom soup © Tim Hill/Alamy
Pierogi © Simon Reddy/Alamy
Food market © Crispin Rodwell/Alamy

Black and whites
p.060 Royal Palace, Wilanow © Photo's Poland/ Alamy
p.073 Warsaw Old Town © Edward Aves
p.091 The Palace of culture © Edward Aves
p.105 Bar in Warsaw © Caro/Alamy
p.114 Manufaktura © Stan Kujawa/Alamy
p.127 Folk coctumes © Maria Aridgides/Alamy
p.140 Gdańsk © Edward Aves
p.155 Gdańsk ship yeard © Edward Aves
p.165 Sopot pier © Gregory Wrona/Alamy
p.192 Monastery Gate, Toruń © Peter Forsberg/ Alamy
p.198 Mamry Lake © PCL/Alamy
p.206 St John's Church © Marek Zuk/Alamy
p.226 Czańa Hańcza River © A&P/Alamy
p.254 Holy Trinity chapel © David Sutherland/ Alamy
p.276 Rynek, Kazimierz Dolny © Photo's Poland/ Alamy
p.294 Forest train © PCL/Alamy
p.303 Lancut Palace © Jan Wlodarczyk/Alamy
p.324 Church in Turzansk © David Sutherland/ Alamy
p.429 Tarrow Town Hall © Phil Robinson/Alamy
p.436 Niedizca Castle © Jan Wlodarczyk/Alamy
p.452 Glewont © Robert Harding/Alamy
p.460 Ducal Palace © Marek Zuk/Alamy
p.473 Festival Mass © Photo's Poland/Alamy
p.486 Wrocław main square © Imagestate/Alamy
p.512 Castle in Ksiaz © Jan Wlodarczyk/Alamy
p.520 Wang Chapel © Imagestate/Alamy
p.534 Poznań © Gregory Wrona/Alamy
p.553 Kornik Castle © Jan Wlodarczyk/Alamy
p.559 Wolsztyn steam train © Sherab/Alamy
p.567 Gniezno Cathedral © Photo's Poland/ Alamy
p.578 Slowiński National Park © David Sutherland/Alamy
p.593 Pier in Miedzyzdroje © Caro/Alamy

SMALL PRINT

Index

Map entries are in colour.

E

F

G

H

I

J

INDEX

INDEX

O

INDEX

675

Map symbols

maps are listed in the full index using coloured text

══════	Motorway	@	Internet access
═══	Paved road	⊠	Post office
⊞⊞⊞⊞	Steps	★	Bus stop
- - - - -	Path	P	Parking
═══	Pedestrianized street	⊞	Hospital
━━━	Railway	Ⓜ	Metro station
— —	Ferry route	⊠	Gate
———	River	♜	Castle
━━·━	National boundary	⚊	Lighthouse
— — —	Chapter division boundary	⚊	Church (regional)
⧫	Point of interest	✡	Synagogue
▲	Mountain peak	⚐	Museum
🏔	Mountain range	—	Wall or fortifications
⌂	Cave	⚰	Concentration camp
✈	Airport	⬭	Stadium
⚐	Border crossing	▬	Building
⚠	Campsite	⊞	Church (town)
◉	Accommodation	⊡	Christian cemetery
▣	Restaurant	⌣	Jewish cemetery
ⓘ	Information office	▨	Park/forest